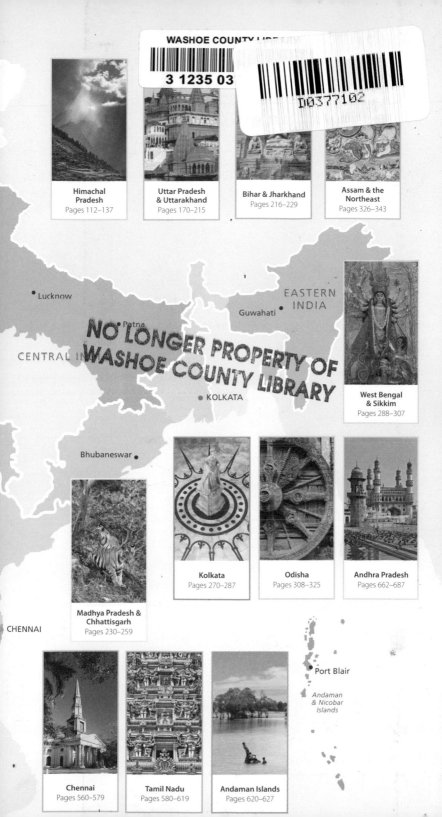

Lucknow

EASTERN INDIA

Guwahati

Patna

CENTRAL IN

KOLKATA

Bhubaneswar

CHENNAI

Port Blair

Andaman & Nicobar Islands

EYEWITNESS TRAVEL

INDIA

EYEWITNESS TRAVEL

INDIA

DK

LONDON, NEW YORK,
MELBOURNE, MUNICH AND DELHI
www.dk.com

Managing Editor Aruna Ghose
Managing Art Editor Bindia Thapar
Project Editor Nandini Mehta
Editors Madhulita Mohapatra, Vandana Mohindra,
Ranjana Saklani, Alissa Sheth
Designers Benu Joshi, Mugdha Sethi, Priyanka Thakur
Cartographers Uma Bhattacharya, Kishorchand Naorem
Photo Editor Radhika Singh
Picture Researcher Kiran K Mohan
Dtp Coordinator Shailesh Sharma
Dtp Designer Jessica Subramanian

Main Contributors
Roshen Dalal, Partho Datta, Divya Gandhi, Premola Ghose,
Ashok Koshy, Abha Narain Lambah, Annabel Lopez, Sumita Mehta, George Michell,
Rudrangshu Mukherji, Meenu Nageshwaran, Rushad R Nanavatty, Ira Pande, Usha Raman,
Janet Rizvi, Ranee Sahaney, Deepak Sanan, Darsana Selvakumar,
Sankarshan Thakur, Shikha Trivedi, Lakshmi Vishwanathan

Consultant George Michell

Photographers
Clare Arni, Fredrik & Laurence Arvidsson, M Balan, Dinesh Khanna, Amit Pasricha,
Bharath Ramamrutham, Toby Sinclair, BPS Walia

Illustrators
Avinash Ramsurrun, Dipankar Bhattacharya, Danny Cherian, R Kamalahasan, Surat Kumar
Mantoo, Arun P, Suman Saha, Ajay Sethi, Ashok Sukumaran, Gautam Trivedi, Mark Warner

Printed by Vivar Printing Sdn Bhd, Malaysia

Reprinted with revisions 2005, 2008, 2011, 2014

Copyright 2002, 2014 © Dorling Kindersley Limited, London
A Penguin Random House Company

First American Edition, 2002
14 15 16 17 10 9 8 7 6 5 4 3 2 1

Published in the United States by:
Dorling Kindersley Limited,
80 Strand, London WC2R 0RL, UK

A CIP catalogue record is available from the Library of Congress.

ISSN 1542-1554
ISBN 978-1-46541-184-6

MIX
Paper from
responsible sources
FSC
www.fsc.org
FSC™ C018179

**The information in this
DK Eyewitness Travel Guide is checked regularly.**

Every effort has been made to ensure that this book is as up-to-date as possible
at the time of going to press. Some details, however, such as telephone numbers,
opening hours, prices, gallery hanging arrangements and travel information are
liable to change. The publishers cannot accept responsibility for any consequences
arising from the use of this book, nor for any material on third party websites, and
cannot guarantee that any website address in this book will be a suitable source of
travel information. We value the views and suggestions of our readers very highly.
Please write to: Publisher, DK Eyewitness Travel Guides, Dorling Kindersley,
80 Strand, London, WC2R 0RL, UK, or email: travelguides@dk.com.

Front cover main image: The Taj Mahal at sunset, Agra

◀ Pretty interiors of the historic City Palace in Udaipur, Rajasthan

Ashokan Capital, Sarnath

Contents

Introducing India

Delhi & The North

Central India

The Gateway of India with the red-domed Taj Mahal Hotel behind it

An array of tangy savouries, very popular
among Rajasthanis

Kandariya Mahadev Temple
(see pp240–41) at
Khajuraho, Madhya Pradesh

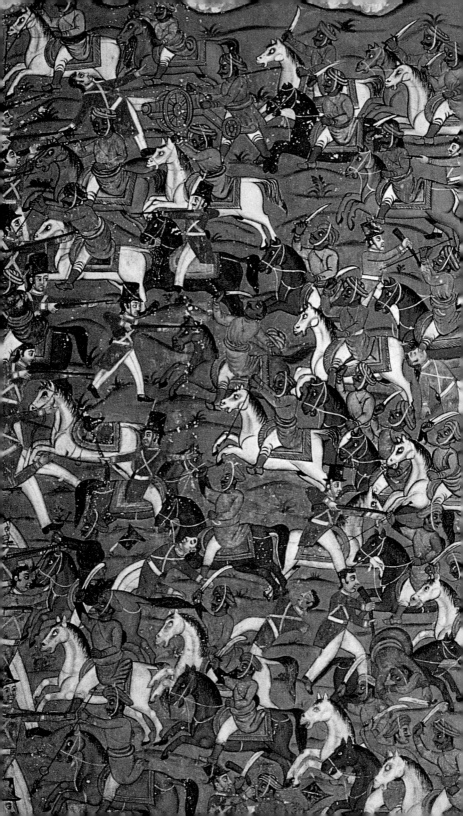

INTRODUCING INDIA

DISCOVERING INDIA

The following tours have been designed to take in as many of this vast country's highlights as possible, separated into regions to keep long-distance travel within reason. First comes a 3-day tour of India's grand capital Delhi, which can be combined with the Golden Triangle to make a ten-day tour. Next, comes a more extensive two-week itinerary, covering the majestic Himalayan region of the far north. The first of the four subsequent week-long itineraries covers Mumbai & Maharashtra in central India, followed by three exotic southern routes, featuring the highlights of Goa & Karnataka, Kerala and Tamil Nadu. Pick, combine and follow your favourite tours, or simply dip in and out and be inspired.

10 Days in the Golden Triangle

- Rub shoulders with devout Muslims at the **Jama Masjid** in Old Delhi.

- Stroll along the wide, avenues of **New Delhi,** admiring its grand colonial architecture.

- Savour superb views of the **Taj Mahal** across the Yamuna River from the ramparts of **Agra Fort**.

- Gaze at the sculpted domes crowning the stunning buildings of the former Mughal capital of **Fatehpur Sikri**.

- Admire the pink façade of Jaipur's **Hawa Mahal**.

- Sit comfortably atop an elephant as it ambles up the cobbled pathway to **Amber Fort**.

Key

--- 10 Days in the Golden Triangle
--- 2 Weeks in the Himalaya
--- 1 Week in Mumbai & Maharashtra
--- 1 Week in Goa & Karnataka
--- 1 Week in Kerala
--- 1 Week in Tamil Nadu

RAJASTHAN

GUJARAT

Tapti

0 kilometres   300
0 miles   300

Arabian Sea

Mumbai
Pune

A decorated elephant at the Hawa Mahal in Jaipur, Rajasthan

1 Week in Goa & Karnataka

- Walk around and admire the Portuguese colonial architecture and the churches of Goa's capital, **Panaji**.

- Relax on the beach and sip a drink beneath the palms at **Palolem** or even more laid back **Agonda**.

- Meander through the sprawling ruins of **Hampi**.

- Stand agog at the pure opulence and magnificence of Mysore's **Amba Vilas Palace**.

- Stock up on tropical fruit at Mysore's colourful market for the walk downhill from the temple atop **Chamundi Hill**.

Panaji
Palolem

1 Week in Mumbai & Maharashtra

- Take a boat ride from the imposing **Gateway of India** to **Elephanta Island** and explore its Hindu cave temples.

- Be amazed at the wealth of sculptures at the stately **Prince of Wales Museum**.

- Gain an insight into the life of Mahatma Gandhi at the **Aga Khan Palace** in Pune, where he was imprisoned.

- Admire the details of the extraordinary murals at the Buddhist rock-cut caves of **Ajanta**.

◀ Painting of the Battle of Pollilur in Tipu Sultan's summer palace

2 Weeks in the Himalaya

- Wind your way up through the Himalayan foothills from Kalka to the hill station of **Shimla** on the famous toy train.

- Sample the delights of Tibetan hospitality and food at **McLeodganj**, home of the Dalai Lama.

- Admire the panoramic mountain vistas of the high ranges that surround Ladakh's charming capital, **Leh**.

- Visit the ancient monasteries of **Ladakh** and marvel at the exquisite murals at **Alchi.**

Palolem beach in Goa, perfect for relaxing

1 Week in Kerala

- Admire the architecture of **Padmanabhapuram Palace**.

- Go for a dip at **Varkala** beach, then enjoy some fresh, grilled fish at a clifftop restaurant.

- Enjoy a cruise along Kerala's serene backwaters.

- Savour the cool, fresh air at **Munnar** and drink tea, freshly picked from a nearby plantation.

- Take a stroll through the narrow streets and spice markets of **Fort Kochi**.

1 Week in Tamil Nadu

- Learn all about South Indian culture, history and art at the vast **Government Museum Complex** in Chennai.

- Be part of a puja ceremony at one of the magnificent temples in **Kanchipuram**.

- Visit the monument-strewn hill behind the ornately carved Arjuna's Penance and the stunning Panch Rathas complex in **Mamallapuram**.

- Stroll along the beach from **Tiger Cave** to the **Shore Temple**.

3 Days in Delhi

India's capital is full of contrasts, from the Muslim flavour of its Moghul heritage, through the colonial echoes of the Raj, to the buzzing modernity of a constantly developing metropolis.

- **Arriving** IG International airport is around 20 km (12 miles) from the city centre. The main train station is New Delhi, in the centre of town. The ISBT bus station is a short way north of Old Delhi.

The colourful Kinari Bazaar in Old Delhi

Day 1

Morning A good way to spend the first day is by soaking up the atmosphere of predominantly Islamic Old Delhi. Start at the magnificent **Red Fort** (pp90–91, closed Mon), named after its distinctive rust-coloured ramparts. Among its highlights, arranged around pristine lawns, are the sixty-pillared Diwan-i-Aam, the royal apartments of the Khas Mahal and the elegant hamams. Afterwards, dive into the bustling streets of the old city, whose narrow alleys contain a kaleidoscope of bazaars, selling anything from sparkling jewellery to less glamorous auto parts.

Afternoon Pay your respects at **Jama Masjid** (p90), one of the world's largest mosques, whose

three domes are visible from miles around. Don't miss the panoramic view from the south minaret. Walk north from here to **Chandni Chowk** (pp88–9), the frenetically busy main thoroughfare of Old Delhi, lined with shrines of various religions, including the fascinating Digambar Jain Temple. Finish off with a tasty tandoori snack from one of the many hole-in-the-wall restaurants lining the side streets.

Day 2

Morning Attend a puja ceremony at the lively **Lakshmi Narayan Mandir** (p82), which offers a fine introduction to modern Hindu practice. From here walk east to circular **Connaught Place** (p79), still the hub of New Delhi, whose landscaped central park provides respite and the underground mall shopping opportunities. Follow

Janpath south to the **National Museum** (pp80–81, closed Mon), whose rich collection chronicles millennia of Indian history and includes priceless gems such as Aurangzeb's sword and Chola bronzes.

Afternoon Enjoy a stroll along the wide open spaces of Lutyens-designed **Rajpath** (p78), admiring the grand buildings of the British Raj, which now house Indian government ministries, galleries and museums. Pass by the gigantic sandstone arch of **India Gate** (p78) en route east to the **Crafts Museum** (pp84–5, closed Mon). Don't miss the artisans displaying their skills in the Crafts Demonstration Area. End the afternoon in the tranquil surroundings of the **Purana Qila** (p83), the sixth city of Delhi, just to the south. The ornate Qila-i-Kuhna Mosque and octagonal Sher Mandal tower are its most noteworthy structures.

Day 3

Morning Begin exploring south Delhi with a ramble through **Lodi Gardens** (p83), a picturesque park landscaped around some imposing 15th-century tombs. Then head east towards the stunning edifice of **Humayun's Tomb** (p87), a prototype for the Taj Mahal, via the absorbing **Nizamuddin Complex** (p86), a historic necropolis dedicated to the memory of various Sufi saints.

Afternoon Further southwest, another venerable monument

One of Delhi's most popular landmark's ,India Gate, Rajpath

not to be missed is the tapered 12th-century **Qutb Minar** (p98), which stands proudly amidst the verdant **Mehrauli Archaeological Park** (pp96–7). This extensive compound also contains a variety of important tombs, mosques and the beautiful **Dargah Qutb Sahid** (p96). Having absorbed some of the world's great faiths, an appropriate place to end the Delhi tour is at the delightful lotus-shaped **Baha'i House of Worship** (p99), a modern shrine that honours all religions.

10 Days in the Golden Triangle

- **Airports** Arrive and depart from Delhi's IG International.
- **Transport** The best way to travel between the three main hubs of Delhi, Agra and Jaipur is by train: Delhi to Agra takes 2–3 hours, Agra to Jaipur 4–5 hours and Jaipur to Delhi around 6 hours. The local day trips are best done by bus or taxi and most involve only an hour or two of travelling time.

Day 1, 2 & 3: Delhi
See the city itinerary on p10.

Day 4: Agra
Leave for **Agra** (pp172–3), the seat of the Mughal Court in the 16th and 17th centuries, and home to the magnificent **Taj Mahal** (pp176–7, closed Fri). The majesty of the world's most famous testament to love is best appreciated over an entire day, from sunrise to sunset, which allows visitors to witness the changing light play on the marble mausoleum. Look out for the elaborate designs and calligraphy of the main Tomb Chamber and exquisite Pishtaq. End the day by enjoying a snack beside the reflecting Lotus Pool.

Day 5: Mathura & Brindavan
Spend the morning admiring the rambling complex of courtly buildings that constitute **Agra Fort** (pp174–5). The precipitous walls of the main harem, known as the Jahangiri Mahal, and the

The Taj Mahal in Agra, one of the most famous monuments in the world

marble hall of the Khas Mahal both afford splendid views across the Yamuna river towards the Taj Mahal. After a lunch of local Mughlai cuisine, embark on a tour of two riverside towns north of Agra with strong Krishna associations. **Mathura** (pp182–3), which is reputed to be Krishna's birthplace, is best known for the busy **Sri Krishna Jamabhoomi Temple** (p182), while his childhood hometown of **Brindavan** (pp183) is brimming with shrines.

Day 6: Around Agra
A great day-trip from Agra, or stop-over en route to Jaipur, is another former Mughal capital, **Fatehpur Sikri** (pp184–6). Among its highlights are the Diwan-i-Khas hall and sandstone pavilions of the Panch Mahal and Turkish Sultana's House.

Day 7: Jaipur
The central area of interest in the "pink city" of Jaipur is **Badi**

Chaupur (pp358–9), which houses the unusual shapes of the Jantar Mantar observatory, the lovely **Hawa Mahal** (pp356–7) and the exotic **Johari Bazaar** (p359). Another unmissable nearby attraction is the **City Palace Museum** (pp360–61), full of dazzling costumes, weaponry and royal relics.

Day 8: Around Jaipur
Rise early and head north to **Gaitor** (p367), which boasts a set of marble cenotaphs from various historical periods, and on to nearby **Jal Mahal** (p367). This 18th-century palace is especially impressive during the monsoon, when the surrounding lake is full. A few kilometres further north lies the superb late 16th-century **Amber Fort** (pp368–70), which vistors can head to on the back of a regally festooned elephant.

Day 9: Ajmer
Take a longer day trip further west to Ajmer, renowned for its important Sufi shrine, **Dargah Sharif** (p380). Take time to visit the ruined mosque complex of **Adhai-Din-ka-Jhonpra** (p380), situated on a nearby hillside. Push on to **Pushkar** (pp378–9), a holy pilgrim town where you can while away some time on the ghats beside the lake.

Day 10: South of Jaipur
The Golden Triangle tour would be incomplete without a visit to the sights to the south of Jaipur. These include the turreted **Moti Doongri Palace** (p364) and the far more contemporary **Jawahar Kala Kendra** (p364). End the tour by returning to Delhi

The spectacular Jal Mahal seen at sunset

2 Weeks in the Himalaya

- **Airports** Arrive at Delhi's IG International (unless flights have resumed to Shimla airport). Return to Delhi from Leh's domestic airport.

- **Transport** Travel from Delhi to Shimla takes 10 hours by bus or longer via the toy train from Kalka. The rest of the mountain journeys described below have to be done by taxi, minibus or shared jeep and vary in length from a few hours to two days.

Entrance to the Jakhu Hill Temple, dedicated to Hanuman, Shimla

Day 1: Shimla

Begin the tour in **Shimla** (pp114–16), the state capital of Himachal Pradesh, draped across thickly forested hills. It was the summer capital of the British Raj and still retains much character from that period, most evident in the Mock Tudor and other colonial architectural styles of **The Ridge** (p114), and epitomised by Gothic **Christ Church** (p114). This is a great place to sit and enjoy the cool air and rolling clouds that regularly envelop the town. Just below The Ridge runs **The Mall** (p114), packed with places to eat. Stop here to enjoy some refreshments. Next, visit the **State Museum** (pp114–15, closed Mon), which has a vast array of artifacts from all over Himachal Pradesh.

Day 2: In and around Shimla

For amazing panoramic views, rise early for the fairly strenuous hike up to the town's highest point at **Jakhu Hill** (p115), where there is a **Hanuman Temple** (p115) and enormous orange concrete statue of the monkey god. Head back downhill to the thriving stalls and small shops of the much more local **Lower Bazaar** (p114), a great spot for spicy snacks. In the afternoon, take the 15 minute stroll up **Observatory Hill** (p115) to the **Viceregal Lodge** (p115), the grandest edifice of all and former summer administrative headquarters of British India.

Day 3: Dharamsala & Kangra Valley

The long trip to **Dharamsala** (p126), seat of the Tibetan Government-in-Exile and the Dalai Lama, takes visitors through the impressively green **Kangra Valley** (pp124–5), which carves its way through the lower ranges of the Himalaya. Stop and explore the market town of **Mandi** (p124) and the nearby **Rewalsar Lake** (p124), which is hemmed in by several Buddhist monasteries and a vibrant Sikh gurudwara.

Day 4: McLeodganj

Spend an hour or so at the **Museum of Kangra Art** (p126, closed Mon) in Dharamsala, most noted for its fine collection of Pahari miniature paintings. **Dharamsala** (p126) is a fairly busy Indian hill town, so it is better to spend most of your time in the upper town of **McLeodganj** (p126), accessible by bus or by walking the more direct but steep route that passes the Tibetan administrative centre of **Gangchen Kyishong** (p126). The centre is home to the excellent **Library of Tibetan Works and Archives** (p126). Be sure to stop at the nearby **Nechung Monastery** (p126), seat of the Tibetan State Oracle.

Day 5: Around McLeodganj

While away most of the day taking in the laid back atmosphere of McLeodganj, sampling traditional Tibetan *momos* or *thukpa*, buying souvenirs such as *thangkas*, and admiring the views. Don't miss the colourful **Tsuglagkhang Complex** (p126), just south of town. Next, take a walk along the gaily painted **Norbulingka Institute** (p126) to the lovely neighbouring village of **Dharamkot** (p126).

Picturesque view of the pretty hill station of Dharamsala

Street sellers with their wares in Leh bazaar

the views more spectacular and the terrain more arid as you cross the Bara Lacha pass at nearly 5,000 m (16,404 ft) and descend into Ladakh. The irrigated farmlands around the Indus river provide relief amid the high altitude desert.

Day 6: Kullu
En route back east through the Kangra Valley stop to clamber around the crumbling ruins of **Kangra Fort**. Take time out for lunch at **Mandi** *(p124)*, before moving on towards Kullu Valley. On arrival in the main town of **Kullu** *(p130)*, walk up through the bazaar to the spacious **Dhalpur Maidan** *(p130)*, which is surrounded by some of the best restaurants.

Day 7: In and around Kullu
Go for a morning puja service at Kullu's 17th-century **Ragunath Temple** *(p130)*, which houses colourful images of Rama and Sita. Other notable Hindu pilgrimage spots within a few kilometres of the town are the **Vaishno Devi Cave Shrine** *(p130)*, and the **Jagannathi Devi Temple** *(p130)*. Later, travel up to **Naggar** *(p132)*, which affords splendid valley views from its perch above the east bank of the fast-flowing Beas river. The peaceful village also boasts a castle-cum-hotel and the **Roerich Art Gallery** *(p132)*.

Day 8: Manali
After the short journey north, settle into the peaceful atmosphere of Old **Manali** *(p132)*. This village is blessed with a plethora of friendly cafés and restaurants amid the traditional Himachal houses and their farming folk. Take an afternoon stroll back across the Beas and up to the wooden pagoda-style **Hadimba Temple** *(p132)*, set among tall deodar trees.

Day 9: Around Manali
Walk back down into the modern town of Manali, where the busy market largely caters to the Indian honeymoon crowd but also has a range of decent eateries. From Manali, head back across the rushing Beas and about 3 km (2 miles) up above the east bank to Vaishist, where visitors can take a dip in the sulphur springs of the temple tank.

Day 10 & 11: Manali–Leh
Travel the legendary Manali–Leh Highway, not so much a road as an unforgettable destination in itself, as it climbs over the first main range of the Himalaya via a series of precipitous passes, beginning with the **Rohtang Pass** *(p132)*. Stop at the villages of **Keylong** *(p133)* or **Darcha** *(p133)*. In the northernmost **Lahaul** *(p133)* region. The road becomes rougher,

Day 12: Leh
After the rigours of the journey relax and acclimatize, if feeling up to it explore the travellers' cafés and bazaars of **Leh** *(p133)* Choose between heading up to the imposing **Leh Palace** *(p140)* or the white Buddhist landmark of **Shanti Stupa** *(p140)* in the Changspa area.

Day 13: South of Leh
Spend the day touring the most impressive monuments an hour or two south of Leh, starting with the Namgyal residence of **Stok Palace** *(p143)* then across the Indus to **Shey Palace** *(p143)*, below which are some fine rock carvings. Later move on to the monasteries of **Thikse** *(p142)* and **Hemis** *(p144)*, both with spectacular lofty locations.

Day 14: West of Leh
Devote an entire day to reach and explore the venerable complex of **Alchi Monastery** *(pp148–50)*, three hours west of Leh, to be rewarded by some of the best preserved Buddhist mural artwork in the world. The best examples are to be found in the **Dukhang** *(p150)* and **Sumstek** *(p150)* temples.

Typical colourful truck on the Manali-Leh Highway

1 Week in Mumbai & Maharashtra

- **Airports** Arrive at Mumbai's Chhatrapati Shivaji International Airport and return to Mumbai from Aurangabad's domestic Chikal Thana Airport.

- **Transport** Travel from Mumbai to Pune takes three to four hours by train or road From Pune to Aurangabad, it is around five hours by bus and from there to Ellora and Ajanta only buses and taxis are available.

The caves at Ajanta, a World Heritage Site

Day 1: Mumbai

Mumbai *(pp446–67)* is India's modern business and entertainment capital, simultaneously the most wealthy and squalid city in the country. Start by admiring another great monument of the British Raj, the massive waterfront **Gateway of India** *(p450)*, built for George V's visit in 1911. Not far from it stands the equally grand **Taj Mahal Hotel** *(p450)*, where you must treat yourself to tea. From beside the Gateway, take a boat to **Elephanta Island** *(p465)*, whose chiselled Hindu rock caves hide some stunning sculpture.

Day 2: In and around Mumbai

Visit the huge **Prince of Wales Museum** *(pp454–5)*, which houses priceless art such as Mughal miniatures and Buddhist sculpture. Stop to wonder at the architectural

Bollywood film poster of the popular hindi movie, *Barfi*

splendor of nearby **Victoria Terminus** *(pp458–9)* station before heading up **Marine Drive** *(p462)* and mingling with the crowds and chaat wallahs on **Chowpatty Beach** *(p462)*. After climbing **Malabar Hill** *(p462)*, end the day with a vibrant ritual at **Mahalaxmi Temple** *(p463)*. Mumbai is also home to the Hindi film industry, better known as Bollywood. Look out for the huge colourful hoardings promoting the latest films across the city.

Day 3: Pune

Travel to **Pune** *(p474)* to see the **Aga Khan Palace** *(p474)*, where Mahatma Gandhi was once imprisoned, now dedicated to his memory. For those with interest in New Age phenomena, Pune is where the **Osho International Commune** *(p474)*, founded by the guru Bhagwan Rajneesh, is located. For a more conventional cultural experience, take a look at the household objects on display at **Raja Dinkar Kelkar Museum** *(p474)*.

Day 4: Aurangabad

The first half of the day will be spent getting to **Aurangabad** *(pp478–9)*, capital of the last great Mughal Emperor Aurangzeb. After orientating yourself, cross the Khan river and join the lively throng of pilgrims at the **Dargah of Baba Shah Musafir** *(p478)*, the Sufi saint who inspired Aurangzeb. At the **Himroo Factory** *(p478)*

nearby, select from the variety of shawls and saris on sale.

Day 5: Ellora

Take a trip out to the magnificent rock cave compound at **Ellora** *(p482)*, which requires an entire day to explore. Pride of place goes to the vast 8th-century **Kailasanatha Temple** *(pp480–82)*, hewn from a solid cliff face. Note the carved elephants supporting the structure around its base and the exquisite panel of Ravana Shaking Mount Kailasa.

Day 6: Ajanta

Another day trip is required to visit the region's other extraordinary cave complex at **Ajanta** *(pp483–5)*. The naturally horseshoe-shaped set of caves that date from two distinct periods make up this Buddhist complex. Their main features are some intricately carved friezes and numerous beautiful murals – the large mandala in Cave 2 is a prime example.

Day 7: Around Aurangabad

Back in Aurangabad, visit the town's main attraction, the splendid **Bibi Ka Maqbara** *(p478)*, a 17th-century imitation of the Taj Mahal with multiple freestanding minarets, built by Aurangzeb's son. Two other noteworthy monuments within the walled city are the ruined **Naukonda Palace** *(p478)*, and the solid **Jama Masjid** *(p478)*.

1 Week in Goa & Karnataka

- **Airports** Arrive at Goa's Dabolim International Airport and depart from Bengaluru International Airport.

- **Transport** Travel within Goa is mainly by local bus, while the overnight tourist bus to Hampi saves time, as does the overnight Hampi Express train to Bengaluru, which has frequent bus and train connections to Mysore, which is three hours away.

Serene waters at Anjuna beach, Goa

Day 1: Goa

A good place to get a feel for the Portuguese ambience of **Goa** (pp488–513) is by spending half a day in the capital **Panaji** (pp490–93), ideally located on the Mandovi river, and nearby Old Goa. Marvel at the colonial grandeur of the early 17th-century **Old Secretariat** (p490) on the riverfront and a number of splendid old churches, such as **Basilica de Bom Jesus** (pp502–503). In the afternoon, go for a swim at either **Anjuna** (p494) or one of the beaches on the bay of **Vagator** (p496), the largest of which is lorded over by ruddy **Chapora Fort** (p496).

Day 2: Palolem & Agonda

Decamp to the southern end of the small state for a relaxing day by the warm waters of the Arabian Sea. The beaches down here are generally quieter and more relaxed, two fine candidates

being **Palolem** (p511) and even more secluded **Agonda** (p511). Both offer numerous restaurants specializing in fresh fish.

Day 3: Hampi

Wake up to find yourself in the magical surroundings of **Hampi** (pp534–5) in Karnataka, the deserted capital of the Vijayanagar Kingdom, on the banks of the Tungabhadra. Set amid sugarcane fields and rice paddies, the backdrop of peculiar rock formations adds a surreal aspect to the extensive archaeological remains. Follow the slightly cooler route along the river to the splendid **Vitthala Temple** (pp536–7), with its famous musical pillars. I lead back to Hampi's **Bazaar Street** (p536), sadly being ruined by a government project, but it still houses some wonderful rooftop restaurants.

Day 4: In and around Hampi

Join the early morning puja at the village's living **Virupaksha Temple** (p536) and accept a blessing by the resident elephant

Laskhmi. Spend the rest of the morning visiting the extensive remains of the **Royal Centre** (p537), replete with the **Hazara Rama Temple** (p537) and **Elephant Stables** (p537). Finally, clamber around **Hemakuta Hill** (p536) and the marvellous bug-eyed Narasimha Monolith in time to watch a superb sunset.

Day 5: Bengaluru

On arrival in Karnataka's busy capital **Bengaluru** (pp516–17), these days a hi-tech and business hub, spend the morning visiting the ornate 18th-century **Tipu Sultan's Palace** (p518) and rest during the midday heat in the leafy botanical gardens of **Lalbagh** (p518). In the afternoon, tour **Cubbon Park** (p516) and the huge **Government Museum** (p516, closed Mon), paying special attention to the **Venkatappa Art Gallery** (p517). Later sample the busting nightlife around Mahatma Gandhi Road.

Day 6: Mysore

Classy and unhurried **Mysore** (pp522–3) exudes a far more old-fashioned vibe and is a fine city just to explore on foot. Its one unmissable sight is the incredibly ostentatious **Amba Vilas Palace** (pp522–3), lit up like a Christmas tree in the evening. A number of rooftop restaurants afford views of this spectacle.

Day 7: In and around Mysore

Check out the Neo-Classical **Chamarajendra Art Gallery** (p522). Next, buy fresh fruit at the Devaraja Market. Enjoy them in the afternoon on the way up to the temple atop **Chamundi Hill** (p523), then walk back down via the massive Nandi monolith.

Lakshmi, the temple elephant at Hampi

1 Week in Kerala

- **Airports** Arrive at Thiruvananthapuram International Airport and depart from Kochi International Airport.

- **Transport** Travel is most easily accomplished by road, with trains available for some sectors such as Thiruvananthapuram to Varkala and Kollam. Kerala also offers the unique travel artery of its backwaters.

Day 1: Thiruvananthapuram

Palm lined Thiruvananthapuram, better known as Trivandrum, is one of India's most laid-back state capitals. The **Napier Museum** (p630, closed Mon & Wed am) is worth a visit for its collection of arts and crafts. Make an afternoon trip to the **Padmanabhapuram Palace** (pp634–5), in its lush rural setting, and admire this prime example of Keralan wooden architecture.

Day 2: Around Thiruvananthapuram

Enjoy a relaxing dip in the Arabian Sea at **Varkala** (pp632–3) beach, nestled below a dramatic clifftop, choc-a-bloc with enticing eateries offering delights such as fish in local coconut-flavoured curries and magnificent sunsets. In the centre of the village, the ancient **Janardhana Swamy Temple** (p632) is worth a look from the walls but is unfortunately, not open to non-Hindus.

Day 3: Kollam to Alappuzha

Take the day-long cruise from **Kollam** to **Alappuzha** (pp638–9) through idyllic backwaters, fringed by millions of swaying palms. The verdant green harbours rich birdlife, while on the banks, the daily lives of the people reveals itself. It is possible to take a more expensive but less crowded overnight houseboat tour instead.

Day 4: Kottayam & Munnar

Travel up into the Western Ghats via **Kottayam** (p642), beautifully located at the foot of the range and also accessible by local ferry. **Munnar** (p652) is a relaxing hill station surrounded by a green carpet of tea plantations, which make for ideal rambling territory. Relax at a tea house here.

Day 5: Around Munnar

Hike to **Mattupetty Lake** (p652), surrounded by semi-Alpine forest, where visitors can opt to go boating or ride an elephant. Much longer treks are available for those with time and energy. In the afternoon, enjoy the drive back down to **Kochi** (pp646–7), the jewel of the Keralan coast.

Day 6: Kochi

Amble at your own pace around the picturesque narrow backstreets and seafront promenade of **Fort Kochi** (pp648–9). Highlights are the photogenic **Chinese Fishing Nets** (p648), imposing **Santa**

The scenic Mattupetty Lake in Munnar, perfect for boating

Cruz Cathedral (p648) and a number of grand colonial buildings now converted into hotels. Take an afternoon boat ride across the bay to **Bolghatty Island** (p647), where the palace has been converted into a state-run hotel, a great place for tea. Return to Fort Kochi in the evening to attend a mesmeric Kathakali dance performance.

Day 7: Around Kochi

Towards the southern reaches of Fort Kochi, visit the 16th-century **Mattancherry Palace** (p646). Originally built by the Portuguese, it is now a museum, which houses a wonderful array of murals and regal paraphenalia. To the south, lies the uniquely-decorated **Pardesi Synagogue** (pp646–7), India's oldest and one of the few still active.

Pretty view of the Varkala beach, Thiruvananthapuram

For practical information on travelling around India, see pp750–59

1 Week in Tamil Nadu

- **Airports** Arrive and depart from Chennai's Aringar Anna International.

- **Transport** Trains are available between Chennai and Kanchipuram, while the other towns are connected only by road. All journeys take between two and three hours.

Day 1: Chennai

Tamil Nadu's capital **Chennai** (p561), formerly Madras, is a rather hot, noisy and polluted city, with some relief provided by the sea breezes that can be enjoyed anywhere along its extended seafront. The oldest and most attractive parts of the metropolis are both at the north end of the centre: **Fort St George** (pp564–5) is Britain's original foothold in the subcontinent, nearby **George Town** (p565) boasts a collection of colonial edifices. For a good introduction into the ancient architectural and religious art of South India, visit the **Government Museum Complex** (pp568–9, closed Fri).

Day 2: Kanchipuram

Kanchipuram (p586) is one of India's most renowned temple towns, dominated by the soaring *gopuras* so distinctive of southern temple architecture. First visit the delightful **Kamakshi Temple** (p586), which sports a dazzling gold-plated roof. After a delicious vegetarian lunch at one of the many small restaurants, move on to the majestic 8th-century **Kailasanatha Temple** (p586), adorned with fine frescoes. The town is also a fantastic place to buy quality silk products.

Day 3: Mamallapuram

Before leaving Kanchipuram, don't miss two more Pallava dynasty sanctuaries, the magnificent **Ekambareshvara Temple** (p586), whose compound contains an ancient and sacred mango tree, and the **Vaikuntha Perumal Temple** (p586), dedicated to Vishnu. Spend the afternoon

Typical French restaurant serving Gallic cuisine in Pondicherry

on the beach at the stone-carving centre of **Mamallapuram**, (pp582–3) swimming and watching the fishermen from one of the beachside restaurants. Visit the famous **Shore Temple** (p582), which juts out into the Bay of Bengal on a rocky promontary.

Day 4: In and around Mamallapuram

In the centre of the village stands the elaborately carved bas relief best known as **Arjuna's Penance** (p582). Above this clamber along with the local goats across a hilltop strewn with various monuments and a huge natural boulder called **Krishna's Butterball** (p582). A short walk to the south of the village stand the **Panch Rathas** (pp584–5), an impressive set of five rock-cut shrines and other monolithic structures such as a life-sized elephant. Relax in the travellers' hangouts in the village.

Day 5: North of Mamallapuram

Spend the morning counting the myriad reptiles that lounge languidly in the many compounds of the **Crocodile Bank** (p582, closed Tue) north of the village, where visitors can also watch Irula tribesmen extracting snake venom. Then relax by the quieter stretch of beach in front of the skillfully carved **Tiger Cave** (p583) before a seaside stroll back to the village.

Day 6: Puducherry

Get a feel of the colonial French influence on **Puducherry** (pp590–91) in the quiet and leafy boulevards and streets of the elegant French Quarter, which occupies the grid of blocks between the canal and the seafront Goubert Salai. Towards the north end of the quarter visit the **Aurobindo Ashram** (p593), which contains the mausoleum of the rebel-turned-guru and his wife, "The Mother".

Day 7: In and around Puducherry

In the morning visit the French-themed **Puducherry Museum** (p592), the startling white **Church of the Sacred Heart of Jesus** (p589) and the peaceful **Botanical Gardens** (p592). After lunch head for **Auroville** (p593) to see a New Age spiritual community and visit the **Matri Mandir** (p593) meditation centre. Round it all off with the rare treat of quality Gallic cuisine and palatable local wine.

Tiger Cave, Mamallapuram

Putting Northern India on the Map

Encompassing an area stretching from the Greater Himalayan Range in the north to the upper part of the Deccan Plateau, northern India covers 2,331,318 sq km (900,127 sq miles). It is watered by three rivers – the Indus, the Ganges and the Brahmaputra – all of which originate in the Himalayas. The vast, densely-populated Indo-Gangetic Plains form its heartland. Some 705 million people, who speak 10 major languages, live here. The two largest cities are Delhi, the capital, and Kolkata (formerly Calcutta), both well-connected internationally by air.

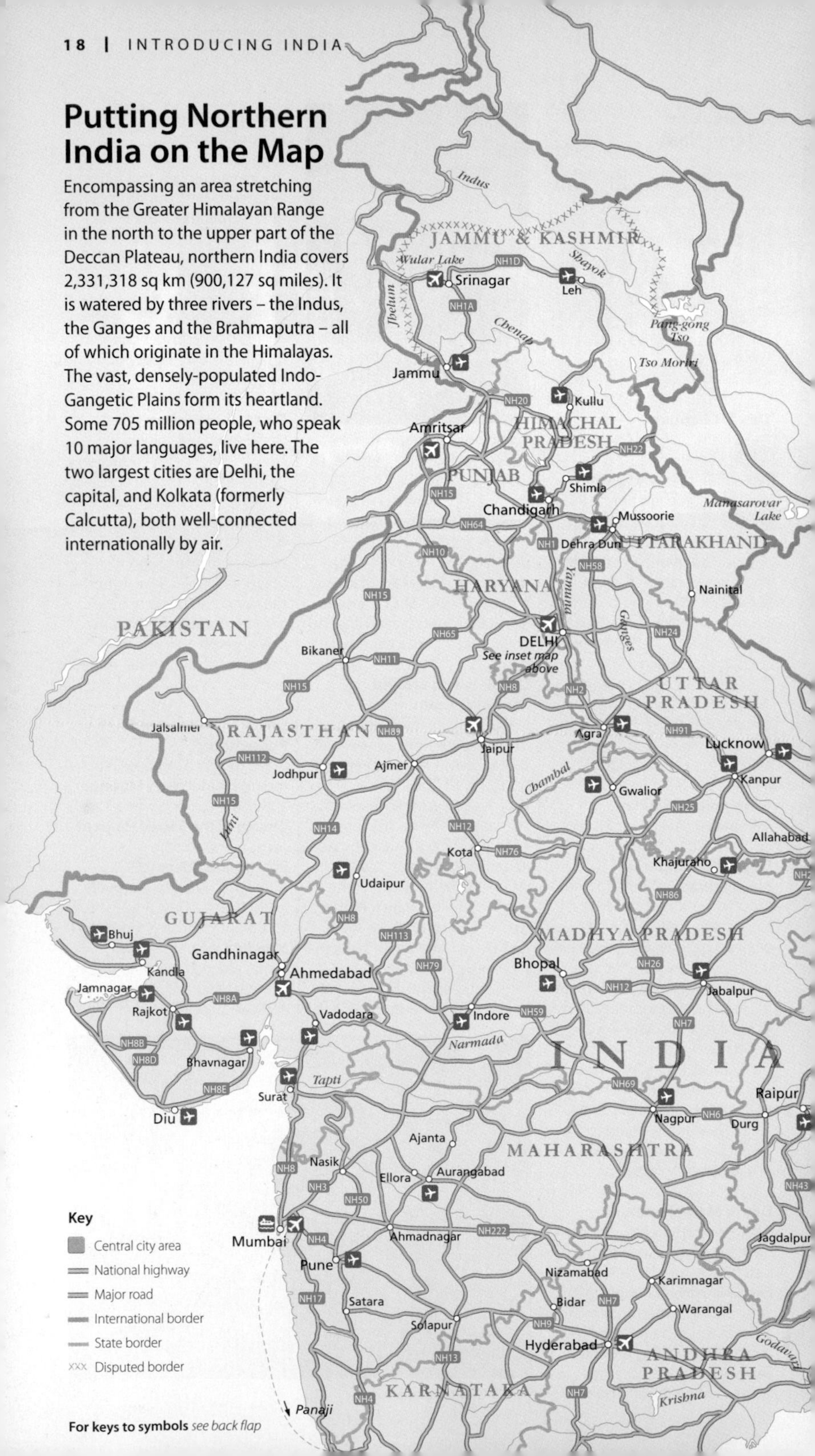

Indus

JAMMU & KASHMIR

Wular Lake   NH1D
Srinagar   Shyok
Leh   Pangong Tso

Jhelum   NH1A
Chenab   Tso Morari

Jammu

NH20   Kullu
HIMACHAL PRADESH   NH22

Amritsar
Manasarovar Lake
PUNJAB   Shimla
NH15   Chandigarh   Mussoorie
NH64   NH1 Dehra Dun   UTTARAKHAND
NH10   NH58   Nainital

HARYANA   Yamuna   Ganges   NH24

PAKISTAN   NH65   DELHI   NH2
See inset map above

Bikaner   NH11   NH8   UTTAR PRADESH
NH15   NH91   Lucknow
Jaisalmer   RAJASTHAN   NH89   Jaipur   Agra   Kanpur
NH112   Jodhpur   Ajmer   Gwalior   NH25   Allahabad
NH15   NH14   NH12   Chambal   Khajuraho
Kota   NH76   NH86
Udaipur   NH8

GUJARAT   NH113   MADHYA PRADESH
NH79   Bhopal   NH26   Jabalpur
Bhuj   Gandhinagar   NH12
Kandla   Ahmedabad   NH7
Jamnagar   NH8A   Vadodara   Indore   NH59   I N D I A
Rajkot   Narmada   NH69   Raipur
NH8B   NH8   Nagpur   NH6   Durg
NH8D   Bhavnagar   Tapti
NH8E   Surat   Ajanta   MAHARASHTRA   Jagdalpur
Diu   Nasik   Ellora   Aurangabad   NH7
NH8   NH3
NH50   NH222
Mumbai   NH4   Ahmadnagar   Nizamabad   Karimnagar
Pune   Bidar   NH7   Warangal
NH17   Satara   NH9
Solapur   Hyderabad   ANDHRA PRADESH
NH13
KARNATAKA   NH7   Godavari
NH4   Panaji   Krishna

Key

■ Central city area
═ National highway
═ Major road
─ International border
─ State border
✕✕✕ Disputed border

For keys to symbols *see back flap*

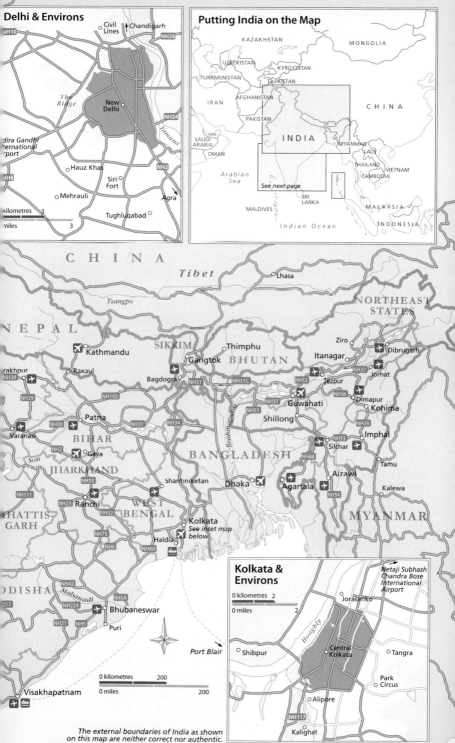

Delhi & Environs

NH10
Civil Lines
Chandigarh
NH24
New Delhi
The Ridge
NH24
Yamuna
NH2
Hauz Khas
Siri Fort
Agra
NH8
Mehrauli
Tughluqabad
ndira Gandhi
ternational
rport
kilometres 3
miles 3

Putting India on the Map

KAZAKHSTAN
MONGOLIA
UZBEKISTAN
KYRGYZSTAN
TURKMENISTAN
TAJIKISTAN
CHINA
IRAN
AFGHANISTAN
PAKISTAN
SAUDI ARABIA
UAE
OMAN
INDIA
MYANMAR
LAOS
THAILAND
VIETNAM
CAMBODIA
Arabian Sea
SRI LANKA
MALDIVES
MALAYSIA
INDONESIA
See next page
Indian Ocean

CHINA
Tibet
Lhasa
Tsangpo
NORTHEAST STATES
NEPAL
SIKKIM
Kathmandu
Thimphu
BHUTAN
Ziro
Itanagar
Dibrugarh
akhpur
Gangtok
Jorhat
NH28
Raxaul
Bagdogra
NH31
NH31C
NH52
Tezpur
NH37
NH36
Dimapur
Kohima
NH29
NH102
Guwahati
NH51
NH39
Patna
NH31
NH34
Shillong
Imphal
NH30
Varanasi
NH2
Gaya
BIHAR
Son
BANGLADESH
NH53
Silchar
Tamu
JHARKHAND
Shantiniketan
NH44
Aizawl
Kalewa
NH111
Dhaka
Agartala
HATTIS-
GARH
NH33
WEST BENGAL
NH54
MYANMAR
NH23
Ranchi
NH32
Kolkata
See inset map below
NH75
NH6
Haldia
NH60
ODISHA
Mahanadi
NH42
NH5A
NH224
Bhubaneswar
217
NH21
NH5
Puri
Port Blair
0 kilometres 200
0 miles 200
Visakhapatnam

Kolkata & Environs

0 kilometres 2
0 miles 2
Netaji Subhash Chandra Bose International Airport
Jorasanko
Hooghly
Central Kolkata
Tangra
Shibpur
Park Circus
Alipore
NH117
Kalighat

The external boundaries of India as shown on this map are neither correct nor authentic.

Putting Southern India on the Map

The six states of Southern India lie within the triangular peninsula that forms the lower part of the Indian subcontinent. With a population of 322 million, speaking six major languages, they cover an area of 955,945 sq km (369,092 sq miles) – larger than France and Germany combined. The western coast is flanked by the Arabian Sea, and the eastern coast by the Bay of Bengal, while the southern tip juts into the Indian Ocean. The rocky Deccan Plateau forms southern India's heartland, bordered on either side by the wooded hills of the Western and Eastern Ghats. The two largest cities are Mumbai (formerly Bombay) and Chennai (formerly Madras).

Key

- Central city area
- National highway
- Major road
- International border
- State border

Chennai & Environs

For keys to symbols see back flap

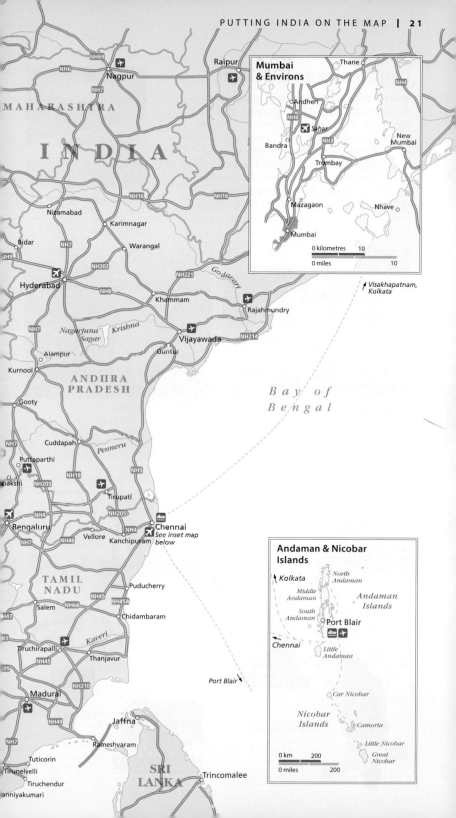

MAHARASHTRA

I N D I A

NH69
NH6
NH7
Nagpur
Raipur

Mumbai & Environs

Thane
Andheri
NH8
Sahar
NH3
Bandra
New Mumbai
Trombay
Mazagaon
Nhave
Mumbai

0 kilometres 10
0 miles 10

↗ *Visakhapatnam, Kolkata*

Nizamabad
Karimnagar
Bidar
NH9
NH7
Warangal
NH202
NH221
Godavari
Hyderabad
Khammam
Rajahmundry
NH7
Nagarjuna Sagar
Krishna
Alampur
Vijayawada
Guntur
NH214
Kurnool
ANDHRA PRADESH

B a y   o f
B e n g a l

Gooty
NH7
Cuddapah
Penneru
Puttaparthi
NH5
NH18
pakshi
NH205
Tirupati
Bengaluru
NH4
NH205
Chennai
See inset map below
NH7
NH46
Vellore
Kanchipuram
NH4

TAMIL NADU

Puducherry
NH45
NH45A
Salem
NH68
Chidambaram
H47
Kaveri
65
Tiruchirapalli
NH45
Thanjavur
.09
Madurai
NH210
NH49
Jaffna
NH7
Rameshvaram
Tuticorin
Tirunelveli
Tiruchendur
anniyakumari

SRI LANKA

Trincomalee

Andaman & Nicobar Islands

↖ *Kolkata*
North Andaman
Middle Andaman
Andaman Islands
South Andaman
Port Blair
← *Chennai*
Little Andaman

Port Blair ↘

Car Nicobar

Nicobar Islands
Camorta
Little Nicobar
Great Nicobar

0 km 200
0 miles 200

Landscape and Wildlife

India has an extraordinary diversity of landscapes and vegetation, supporting a rich variety of wildlife. The country is bounded on the north by the majestic Himalayas. Along their foothills, sweeping the breadth of Central India, are the fertile, densely populated Indo-Gangetic Plains, while the arid Thar Desert covers much of Western India. South of the Gangetic Plains is the Deccan Plateau, flanked by the hills of the Eastern and Western Ghats. India's 7,516-km (4,670-mile) long coastline borders on the Arabian Sea, the Indian Ocean and the Bay of Bengal.

The Himalayan landscape features snowcapped peaks, glacial streams and pine-covered slopes *(see pp68–9)*.

The Arid West

The Thar Desert and the semi-arid scrublands adjoining it support a surprising variety of flora and fauna. The sand dunes of Rajasthan give way further west to the barren salt-flats and marshes of the Rann of Kutch.

The Gangetic Plains

The rich alluvial soil of these vast plains, which stretch across India from the northwest to the east, has been cultivated for thousands of years. Today rice, as well as wheat, sugarcane and pulses are grown here.

Blackbucks are among the swiftest animals, covering up to 80 km (50 miles) per hour.

Asian elephants number only 32,000 in comparison to a quarter of a million African elephants, making this smaller species the more endangered one.

Asiatic lions, once found all over northern India, are now seen only in the Gir Sanctuary in Gujarat *(see p427)*.

Painted storks migrate to lakes and swamps during their breeding season, between July and October.

Crested serpent eagles are large raptors with a distinctive pattern of black and white bands on their underwings.

Wild boars are common in most deciduous forests in India. The males have tusks and can be very aggressive.

Avocets migrate to the coasts and marshes of Gujarat and Maharashtra in November.

The Coasts

The diverse landscapes of the coasts include sandy beaches in Goa and Kerala, fringed by coconut palms, coral reefs in the Andamans, and mangrove forests in West Bengal and Odisha. The east coast is often hit by cyclones.

Starfish, which cling tenaciously to rocks, can be seen in tidal pools all along the Indian coastline.

The Deccan Plateau

Separated from the Gangetic Plains by the scattered ranges of the Vindhyas, the Deccan Plateau is covered with black volcanic soil and ancient crystalline rocks. The plateau's mineral wealth includes gold and diamonds.

The Ghats

The hills of the Western and Eastern Ghats are covered with forests of teak, rosewood, *sal (Shorea robusta)* and sandalwood *(Santalam album)*, prized for its fragrant wood. Many orchid species also grow here.

Tigers, an endangered species and numbering only 1,700 in the country, are found across peninsular India.

Nilgiri tahrs live in the higher elevations of the Western Ghats *(see p653)*.

Daniel butterflies are common in the region.

Bullfrogs display their large vocal sacs during their mating season in the monsoon.

Langurs or Hanuman monkeys *(Semnopithecus entellus)*, live in large groups, led by an adult male.

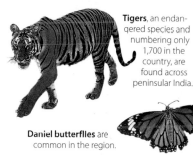

Spectacled cobras have characteristic spectacle-shaped markings on their hoods. Another reptile is the king cobra, the world's largest venomous snake.

Peacocks, India's national bird, perform a spectacular dance when rain clouds appear.

Sacred Architecture

India's 2,000-year-old architectural heritage is intrinsically linked to the country's major religions. Indigenous forms include Buddhist stupas and monasteries and Hindu and Jain temples *(see pp400–401)* in diverse styles. Many Indian temples, however, share common structural characteristics, being mostly built of stone columns and horizontal blocks, often richly carved with sacred imagery and decorative motifs. The true arch and the dome, as well as the use of mortar, were introduced in the 12th century by the Muslim conquerors.

Detail on a sculpted column, Narayana Temple, Melkote

Buddhist Architecture

India's earliest religious monuments are stupas, hemispherical funerary mounds, and rock-cut shrines *(chaityas)* and monasteries *(viharas)*. While *chaityas* were places of worship, *viharas* were dwelling places for Buddhist monks and consisted of small residential cells arranged around four sides of an open court

Entrance · Vaulted ceiling · Model stupa

Chaityas served as halls *(grihas)* for congregational worship and enshrined a model stupa at one end.

Circumambulatory path · Hemispherical mound · Torana *(gateway)* · Railing

Stupas were monumental reliquaries in which the ashes of Buddhist teachers, including the Buddha, were interred. The Sanchi Stupa *(see pp248–9)* is faced in stone, and surrounded by a high railing with gateways *(toranas)*.

Rock-cut *chaityas* have distinctive barrel-vaulted ceilings, expressed on the exterior as a horseshoe-shaped arch.

Hindu Temples

In North India, the soaring tower above the inner sanctum takes the form of a curving *shikhara* (spire) topped with a circular ribbed motif, the *amalaka*. South Indian temples, however, have multi-staged, pyramidal spires *(vimana)* crowned with a hemispherical or barrel-vaulted roof. Worship in both types takes place in a small dark sanctuary known as the *garbhagriha* (womb chamber).

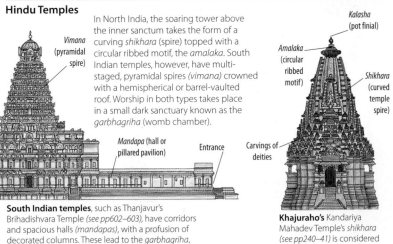

Vimana (pyramidal spire) · *Mandapa* (hall or pillared pavilion) · Entrance

Kalasha (pot finial) · Amalaka (circular ribbed motif) · Shikhara (curved temple spire) · Carvings of deities

South Indian temples, such as Thanjavur's Brihadishvara Temple *(see pp602–603)*, have corridors and spacious halls *(mandapas)*, with a profusion of decorated columns. These lead to the *garbhagriha*, above which rises the multi-staged spire.

Khajuraho's Kandariya Mahadev Temple's *shikhara* *(see pp240–41)* is considered the finest in North India.

Islamic Architecture

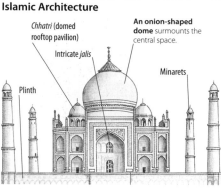

Chhatri (domed rooftop pavilion)

An onion-shaped dome surmounts the central space.

Intricate *jalis*

Minarets

Plinth

Taj Mahal *(see pp176–7)*, the zenith of Islamic architecture

Mihrab, Bidar mosque *(see p549)*

Mosques and tombs represent an imported tradition that was absorbed into Indian architecture. Mosques have domed prayer halls at one end of an open courtyard. The *mihrab* (arched niche) faces west, towards Mecca. The Mughals introduced the garden tomb, raised on a high plinth in the centre of a *charbagh*, an enclosed garden divided into four quarters. Decorative elements include Persian and Arabic calligraphy, geometric patterns and floral motifs, typical of Islamic art.

Gurdwaras

The Sikh gurdwara, a prayer chamber where the *Granth Sahib*, or Holy Book, is housed, is often roofed with a dome flanked by arcades. Based on the late-Mughal style prevailing in North India in the 18th century, gurdwaras blend Islamic and Hindu architectural styles.

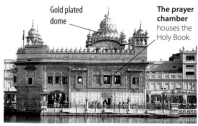

Gold plated dome

The prayer chamber houses the Holy Book.

The Golden Temple in Amritsar *(see pp110–11)*

Churches

Though church architecture in Kerala predates the arrival of Europeans, most Christian places of worship, such as those in Goa *(see pp500–501)*, are built in European styles. A common design has a Neo-Classical portico topped with a tapering steeple. Many Indian churches are also built in a Neo-Gothic style, such as the Afghan Memorial Church of St John the Evangelist *(see p451)*.

Tower with thin tapering steeple

Pointed arched windows

Entrance

Afghan Memorial Church, Mumbai

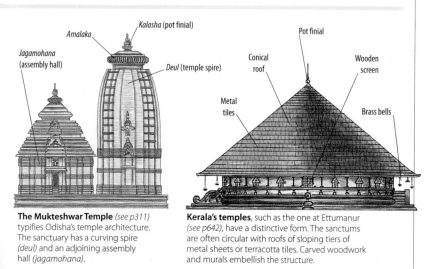

Amalaka

Kalasha (pot finial)

Jagamohana (assembly hall)

Deul (temple spire)

Pot finial

Conical roof

Wooden screen

Metal tiles

Brass bells

The Mukteshwar Temple *(see p311)* typifies Odisha's temple architecture. The sanctuary has a curving spire *(deul)* and an adjoining assembly hall *(jagamohana)*.

Kerala's temples, such as the one at Ettumanur *(see p642)*, have a distinctive form. The sanctums are often circular with roofs of sloping tiers of metal sheets or terracotta tiles. Carved woodwork and murals embellish the structure.

Secular Architecture

Magnificent secular buildings, such as forts, palaces and mansions *(havelis)* were built by powerful ruling and aristocratic families. Many of these, especially in Rajasthan and Gujarat *(see pp350–51)*, harmoniously combine monumental scale with superb decorative elements. The British imposed their own architectural stamp, a fusion of East and West. A variety of indigenous domestic forms that have remained unchanged through the ages can be seen throughout rural India.

Mughal dome

Windows are inspired by Rajput palaces.

Laxmi Vilas in Vadodara *(see p423)*, built in the late 19th century

Civic Architecture

In the mid-19th century, the British began to incorporate elements from Indian Islamic architecture into European Neo-Classical or Gothic Revivalist styles. Known as Indo-Saracenic, this style reflected imperial and civic pride. Indo-Saracenic public buildings include Victoria Terminus *(see pp458–9)* and Mumbai University, and the High Court and Egmore station in Chennai. This culminated in the building of the new capital at New Delhi *(see pp76–7)*, where Sir Edwin Lutyens and his associates evolved a grand architectural style which was a more elegant synthesis of Indian and European traditions.

Sculpture, Churchgate Station, Mumbai

Typical Gothic window, Mumbai University

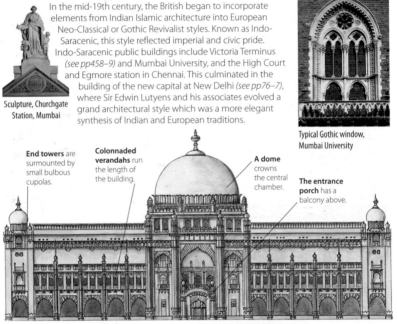

End towers are surmounted by small bulbous cupolas.

Colonnaded verandahs run the length of the building.

A dome crowns the central chamber.

The entrance porch has a balcony above.

Prince of Wales Museum, Mumbai *(see pp454–5)*, inspired by Bijapur's Gol Gumbad *(see p547)*

The Courtyard

Domestic architecture in India is governed by public and private spaces. The front portion of the house was open to visitors and guests, but just beyond that was the courtyard, the heart of the house, restricted to the family. Larger mansions, such as those at Shekhawati *(see p376)*, Jaisalmer *(see p391)* and Chettinad *(see p616)*, had several courtyards surrounded by elaborate colonnades. The separation of private and public spaces within the home grew out of social conventions that secluded women from the public gaze.

Courtyard with wooden pillars and carved doors

Vernacular Architecture

A painted niche

Rural houses in India reflect the country's varied climate and the range of available materials. In spite of the diversity, certain overall principles prevail. A typical dwelling is approached from the street through a formal doorway, often sheltered by a verandah, flanked by raised seating. The first room is usually used for both living and sleeping, and is thus larger. Cooking and eating take place to the rear, on the other side of an inner courtyard, near the well, or water supply. Hindu homes have a small masonry stand (*vrindavan*), in the courtyard, where the sacred *tulsi* (basil) plant is grown for daily worship.

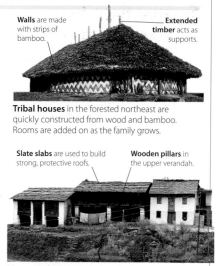

Walls are made with strips of bamboo.

Extended timber acts as supports.

Tribal houses in the forested northeast are quickly constructed from wood and bamboo. Rooms are added on as the family grows.

Slate slabs are used to build strong, protective roofs.

Wooden pillars in the upper verandah.

Mountain homes are built on high ground, and are double storeyed, with the ground floor serving as a stable for livestock in winter.

Central Indian villages are tightly packed with houses that are either one-roomed tiled structures or larger ones. Some have flat-roofs where the family sleep at night in summer.

Mud walls are reinforced with straw and cowdung.

Thatch roofs, made of local elephant grass, are replaced every year.

Coastal houses have sloping tiled roofs as protection from sun and rain. The *tulsi* plant indicates that this is a Hindu home.

Desert dwellings are built with mud and consist of a single thatched room, enclosed by a wall. The circular *kothi* is used to store grain. Designs in white lime embellish the outer walls.

Materials for Construction

Circular thatch ceiling

Traditionally, most houses were built of locally available material. Bamboo and thatch were employed in house construction in Bengal, Odisha and the northeast, while stone and terracotta tiles were preferred in Madhya Pradesh, Maharashtra and South India. Sadly, such materials are now rapidly being replaced by steel and concrete. However, mud is still the most common material and is either applied directly or mixed with cowdung and straw.

Woven bamboo panel for walls

Coconut palm leaf roof

Thatched roof made of grass

Typical half-cylinder tiles

Terracotta sun-dried bricks

Stone slabs, ideal for walls

Hindu Mythology

The vast pantheon of Hindu gods, goddesses and their divine exploits is best explored through sculpture. The principles of temple architecture were defined and established under the imperial Guptas (4th–6th centuries AD). Indian temples are adorned by a profusion of sculptures that are not merely decorative but also provide a visual interpretation of Hindu mythology. The numerous manifestations of deities, such as Shiva, Vishnu and Devi (the goddess also known as Parvati, Durga, Kali) are depicted in great detail. Semi-divine beings, such as devotees, nymphs and musicians complete the picture.

Dvarapala is the armed guardian who stands outside the entrance of the temple or by the door of the inner sanctum. These forbidding figures carry weapons to protect the deity from intruders.

Vedic gods, such as Surya the Sun God, were manifestations of nature and the elements. They were absorbed into the Hindu pantheon of deities almost 2,000 years ago.

Karttikeya is mounted on his peacock vehicle (vahana).

Indra, the Vedic God of the Heavens, sits on Airavata, the four-trunked white elephant representing the rain-cloud.

Female attendant

Lakshmi, the consort of Vishnu

Garuda, the vehicle (vahana) of Vishnu, is half man and half eagle.

Lakshmi, the Goddess of Wealth, appears as Gajalakshmi in this panel from Mamallapuram (see p583). She is seen with two elephants (gaja) who bathe her with their upturned trunks.

Vishnu Anantasayana

This 5th-century panel from Deogarh (see p237) depicts Vishnu asleep on the serpent Ananta, whose hood shelters him. Brahma on a lotus rises from behind, while Shiva sits with Parvati on his vahana, the bull Nandi. Attendants and celestial beings surround the figure. The mace, discus, shield and sword, Vishnu's attributes, are personified below to ward off demons.

Vishnu's dwarf incarnation, Vamana (see p683) transforms himself into a giant to measure out the universe in three steps. This panel from Badami (see pp540–41) shows him with one leg raised skywards.

Mohini, the female form of Vishnu, is described as an enchantress, the most alluring maiden imaginable. Courtesans and nymphs are also carved as bracket figures.

Brahma, the Creator, is part of the holy Trinity (Trimurti) of gods that also include Vishnu and Shiva. He is depicted with four heads, of which only three are usually visible, and holds a sceptre, a spoon, a string of beads and the Vedas. He is seen here with his consort, Saraswati, the Goddess of Learning.

Shiva, the God of Destruction, is seated with his wife, Parvati, who represents his peaceful and domestic aspect. Shiva holds an elephant goad and drum (dumroo), while Parvati has a lotus (kamal) in her hand.

Shiva and Parvati

Flying celestial figure

Ananta, the Many Headed Serpent, is also known as Adishesha.

Vishnu, the Preserver

Durga, the fierce form of gentle Parvati, slaying the buffalo-demon, Mahishasura. This panel from Mamallapuram, known as Mahishasuramardini, shows Durga riding a lion with a deadly weapon in each of her eight arms, given to her by the gods to annihilate the demon.

Karttikeya, Shiva's warrior son, has a peacock as his vahana. He is also known as Skanda, Subramanya and Murugan in South India. The other son of Shiva is Ganesha (see p471).

Attendants, the personifications of Vishnu's four attributes, protect the god from demons.

Devotees are often elevated to the status of saints and are honoured for their devotion to either Shiva or Vishnu. This 11th-century bronze is of a Shaivite boy-saint holding cymbals in his hands.

Dancers, musicians and other performers are usually carved on the lower plinths of temples

The Great Epics

The two great epic poems, the *Ramayana* and the *Mahabharata*, have had an abiding impact on Indian culture and philosophy. Over the centuries, their stories have inspired a great deal of art, music, dance, theatre and, more recently, popular TV serials. Containing a fund of wisdom about human behaviour, emotions and moral dilemmas, the epics continue to guide the daily lives of millions of Indians. Though known in their oral form since at least 500 BC, they were only put into writing around the 4th century AD.

Arjuna shot the eye of a fish reflected in water, and won the hand of Draupadi, who then married all five brothers.

In a game of dice with the Kauravas, the Pandavas lost their kingdom and Draupadi. She was saved from the shame of being disrobed by the Kauravas when her sari kept growing magically to cover her.

The Mahabharata

This epic recounts the rivalry between the five heroic Pandava brothers – Yudishthira, Bhima, Arjuna, Nakul and Sahdeva – and 100 members of the Kaurava clan, headed by Duryodhana, and culminates in a great battle. Several other fables, legends and discourses are woven into the main story, making the Mahabharata eight times longer than the Iliad and the Odyssey put together.

Forced into exile after the game of dice, the Pandavas wandered all over India for 13 years. In the final year, Arjuna lived in disguise as a eunuch, giving dance lessons.

The Bhagavad Gita is a sermon given to Arjuna by Lord Krishna, who acted as Arjuna's charioteer, on the battlefield of Kurukshetra. It is a famous discourse on ethics and morality, that contains the essence of Hindu religion and philosophy.

In the final battle the Kauravas created a cobweb-shaped defensive formation called the *chakravyuha*, inside which Arjuna's son was trapped and killed. However, on the 18th day of this fierce battle, the Pandavas, with Krishna's divine guidance, finally emerged victorious, and regained their kingdom, which they ruled with Draupadi as their queen.

The Ramayana

Rama, the ideal hero, was prevented from becoming king of Ayodhya by the intrigues of his stepmother, and sent into exile with his wife Sita and brother Lakshman. The demon-king, Ravana, abducted Sita, who was then rescued by the two brothers with the help of the monkey god, Hanuman. Rama is worshipped as an incarnation of Vishnu (see p683).

The wedding of Rama and Sita took place after Rama succeeded in breaking the great bow of Shiva, which other suitors for her hand could not even manage to lift off the ground.

Exiled to the forest for 14 years, Rama, Sita and Lakshman lived simply and visited the hermitages of many holy sages.

Sita was abducted from her forest hut by Ravana, the demon-king of Lanka, who came disguised as a mendicant. The brave vulture Jatayu tried to save her, but his wings were slashed by Ravana. However, Jatayu was able to tell Rama what had happened before he died.

Ravana's ten heads and 20 arms signify his great intellectual and physical strength.

Hanuman, the Monkey God, is a much-loved figure in the pantheon of Hindu gods, worshipped for his miraculous powers, his courage and physical prowess.

Ravana's palace at Lanka was attacked by Rama and Lakshman who, with the help of Hanuman and his army of monkeys, rescued Sita and killed Ravana. Lakshman was gravely wounded in the battle, but saved by the magical mountain herb, Sanjivini, brought by Hanuman.

Rama's triumphant return to Ayodhya is celebrated in the festival of lights, Diwali *(see p41)*, which symbolizes the victory of good over evil.

Classical Music and Dance

Indian music and dance are simultaneously modes of worship and a joyous celebration of life. Based on ancient codified texts, they originated as a form of worship in the temples, and gradually acquired a more secular character with royal patronage. Different regions of India have their own classical dance forms, while classical music is distinguished by two main styles – Hindustani and Carnatic *(see p599)*, the latter specific to South India.

Kuchipudi is a highly dramatic dance form from Andhra Pradesh, which often enacts scenes from the great epics.

Frieze of a dancer from an 11th-century South Indian temple

The tiara is shaped like a temple spire.

Sensuous and spiritual at the same time, Odissi has sinuous movements and highly sculptural poses.

Complex footwork and rhythms, and multiple pirouettes characterize this dance form.

Fan pleats decorate the front of the sari.

Classical Dance

A wide range of hand gestures, facial expressions and body postures, codified in the Natya Shastra, *a 4th-century treatise, constitute the "language" of Indian classical dance forms. Their themes are mostly based on religious mythology, and percussion and music play an important role.*

A swirling skirt is worn over tight pyjamas.

Ghungroos (bells) help mark the rhythmic beat.

Kathak was a favourite dance at the royal courts of northern India.

Odissi developed in the temples of Odisha as an offering to the deities.

Hindustani Music

The origins of Hindustani classical music date to about 3000 BC. The raga (melodic line) and the *tala* (rhythmic cycle) are its foundation, and there is no formal written score. This gives artistes great latitude to improvise within the melodic framework of a raga. There are more than a 100 ragas, each assigned to a particular time of day or season, according to the mood or images its melody evokes. Royal patrons founded different *gharanas* or schools of music, which have preserved their individuality by passing knowledge down orally from guru (teacher) to *shishya* (disciple).

Pt Ravi Shankar (1920–2012), one of India's foremost sitar players, introduced Indian classical music to the West.

Amjad Ali Khan plays the *sarod*, an instrument developed by his grandfather from the *rabab*, a medieval Central Asian lute.

Nine rasas (moods) are mentioned in the 4th-century treatise *Natya Shastra*. From the erotic, comic and pathetic to the odious, marvellous and quiescent, the *rasas* cover every mood and expression, whether in music, dance or painting. This 17th-century miniature painting depicts the serene mood of the morning *Raga Todi*.

Kerala's Kathakali dance featuring spectacular masks *(see p661)*

Fresh flowers adorn the hair.

Elaborate jewellery

Red colour on the hands and feet draw attention to intricate movements.

Diaphanous veil

Crinoline-like skirts and gentle swaying movements are typical of Manipuri dance.

Chiselled movements and symmetrical stances are typical of this dance form.

Beautiful silk sari

Bharat Natyam, from Tamil Nadu, has eloquent eye and hand movements *(mudras)*.

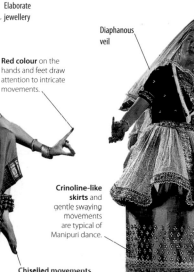

Manipuri, from the northeast, enacts the legend of Radha and Krishna *(see p183)*.

Bismillah Khan (1913–2006) played the *shehnai*, a ceremonial reed pipe, which the late maestro popularized into a concert instrument.

Zakir Hussain plays the tabla, a pair of drums that provide percussion at most music and dance performances.

Kishori Amonkar is a leading singer. A concert usually begins with a slow evocation of the raga, followed by an elaboration of the melodic line, and culminating in a fast-paced climax.

Costumes of India

One of the most remarkable features of Indian apparel is the ingenious way in which a simple length of unstitched cloth is used. Gracefully draped as a sari, or wrapped around the head as a turban, the length of fabric is versatile, and is worn by both men and women. Stitched garments include the *kurta*, pyjama, sherwani, the voluminous skirt *(ghaghara* or *lehenga)*, and of course, the trouser, shirt and ubiquitous blue jeans. Today, despite the growing influence of contemporary Western fashion trends, most Indians continue to dress traditionally. The sari, particularly, is still worn all over India, even though the style of draping differs from region to region.

The Veil *(odhni* or *dupatta)* is an essential part of dress in conservative societies.

The sari, usually 5.5 m (6 yd) long, is tied around the waist, with the pleats tucked into an under-skirt. The *pallav* (end-piece) is either drawn over the left shoulder or draped over the head.

Safa (turban)

Angavastram is the unstitched mantle draped over the shoulder.

Sari blouse

Sari

Salwar-kameez, consisting of a baggy pyjama *(salwar)*, a loose tunic *(kameez)* and *dupatta*, are worn by women in Punjab. This outfit is now worn all over India.

The Indian Wedding

Festivals and weddings are glittering events that showcase the range and variety of clothes worn by both men and women in India. Such occasions are what keep traditional customs and attire alive today.

Bracelet-like folds of the *churidar*.

Maharashtrian women wear 8-m (9-yd) saris in a style very similar to a dhoti. The extra fabric is pleated in front, drawn between the legs and tucked in at the back, to allow freedom of movement.

In Kerala, women wear a two-piece sari *(mundu-veshti)*, of which the *mundu* forms the lower garment, while the *veshti* is tucked into the waist to form the *pallav*. Men just wear the lower garment, with an *angavastram*.

Headdresses

For Indian men, the most important accessory is the turban, *(pagri* or *safa)*, an unstitched length of cloth that is deftly tied around the head. More than just a fashion statement, the turban's style and colour also indicates the wearer's social, religious, caste and regional status. Rajasthani turbans are intrinsic to the cultural ethos of the land, whereas in Punjab, the Sikh turban is characteristic of their identity as a martial community *(see p107)*. From the mid-19th century onwards, *topis* (caps) became popular, especially among courtiers in the Muslim courts. Even today, men wear plain or ornamental caps in mosques or during festivals.

Topi, worn by a young Muslim boy

A turbaned patriarch from Jodhpur, Rajasthan

Choli (tight-fitting blouse)

Odhni (veil)

Kurta

The dhoti-kurta is the traditional male attire and comprises a dhoti (loincloth) or *lungi,* either tied around the waist or tucked between the legs. The upper garment Is the stitched, long-sleeved *kurta.*

Sherwani, a long coat with a high collar, is worn above the *churidar* pyjama, so-called because of the bracelet- *(churi-)* like folds near the ankles.

The bridegroom wears a formal sherwani-*churidar* in ivory silk.

The bride's lehenga is red silk, heavily encrusted with gold embroidery.

Ghaghara, the ankle-length, gathered skirt worn in Rajasthan and Gujarat, is tied with a drawstring. A *choli* (tight-fitting blouse) is worn on top, while the *odhni* has one end tucked into the waistband and the other taken over the right shoulder to cover the head.

In Manipur, women wear the sarong-like *phanek*, while men wear a garment known as the *khudei*. Each tribe, however, is identified by its distinctive colours and stripes. This couple is from the Paite tribe.

Bollywood's Magic Formula

Hindi films from Bollywood (Bombay or Mumbai) are a fascinating mix of romance, violence, comedy, and tragedy, interspersed with song and dance sequences, and with a clear social or moral message. Ever since its inception in 1899, fashions in Bollywood have swung from mytho-logical epics to action thrillers to family dramas. But the basic masala (spicy mix) formula, which appeals to a large and diverse audience, remains unchanged.

Romance trickles down into almost every plot that a film explores. The hero wooing the heroine always forms a very popular sequence.

Heroines add an essential touch of glamour to Bollywood films. Slim, fashionable and gorgeously dressed stars, such as Kareena Kapoor, set the standard for feminine beauty and grace.

Star-studded, high-budget films usually ensure a box-office hit.

The hero cult and Shah Rukh Khan are synonymous. Affectionately called King Khan, he is popular both in India and abroad, even boasting a wax statue at Madame Tussaud's in London. Aishwarya Rai and superstar Amitabh Bachchan share the honour with him.

The Hindi Film Industry

It costs anywhere between US$1.75 million and $30 million to produce a Bollywood film. The budget is spent on massive fees for the stars, exotic locations, special effects, and on huge promotional campaigns. Of the more than 100 films produced every year, some are dubbed into regional Indian languages, or subtitled in English for international audiences.

Song and dance sequences range from duets between the hero and heroine to spectacular set pieces with lots of male and female dancers. These are released before the film as music videos for TV, and often become hits, even if the film flops at the box office.

Family values form the core of most films. The home can be the scene of great happiness or discord, and in the end everyone comes together.

Villains are portrayed as evil incarnate. In *Omkara* (2006), which was based on Shakespeare's *Othello*, the villain is a loyalist turned traitor who seeks to avenge himself at the cost of many innocent lives.

Violence can often be of the comic book variety. Dramatic fights are staged between the hero and villain at the climax, and invariably end with the triumph of good over evil.

Fashion statements made by Bollywood stars inspire youngsters to follow suit.

The hero usually anchors the film, with the plot and other characters revolving around him. Aamir Khan is one of Bollywood's most sought-after stars. His powerhouse performances have earned him a huge fan following.

Katrina Kaif as the heroine represents the fun-loving, urban, Westernized youth.

New Wave Cinema

In the 1950s and 60s parallel or "art" cinema was dominated by Satyajit Ray *(see p264)*, whose thought-provoking films portrayed everyday life in Indian villages and small towns. By focusing on realism and social issues rather than fantasy and entertainment, he paved the way for internationally acclaimed directors such as Deepa Mehta and Mira Nair to make films that made an impact on society.

Deepa Mehta with the star cast of her Oscar-nominated film *Water*

Youth, the prime focus of Bollywood films, saw a paradigm shift with *Rang De Basanti* (2006), a commercial film that didn't just set fashion trends but made a case for a better society with the participation of the younger generation.

INDIA THROUGH THE YEAR

Indians love celebrations and the year is filled with innumerable fairs and festivals. Almost every day marks a religious or social event celebrated by the diverse religious or local communities, where ritual fasting and feasting go hand in hand. Some festivals are linked to the pantheon of gods and goddesses, others follow the changing seasons and mark pastoral occasions. Some commemorate anniversaries and events of national importance such as the Republic Day *(see p79)*. Hindu festivals usually follow the lunar calendar and both the full moon *(purnima)* and the new moon *(pradosh)* are considered auspicious. Muslim festivals, too, are determined by the new moon. This means that the dates of most religious festivals vary from year to year. See also special festival columns in each chapter.

Holi celebrations in the area around Mathura

Spring (Feb–Mar)

From mid-February to the end of March, spring (Basant) is India's most glorious season with flowers in full bloom and pleasant, not-too-hot temperatures. It is also the main season for weddings, parades, cricket matches, horse racing, flower shows and other events.

Vasantahabba *(Feb)*, Nrityagram. One of Bengaluru's most awaited dance festivals. Acclaimed artistes from all over India perform from dusk till dawn.

Kala Ghoda Festival *(Feb)*, Mumbai. A two-week extravaganza of the visual and performing arts is held in Mumbai's main cultural district of Kala Ghoda. The National Gallery of Modern Art and the Jehangir Art Gallery, as well as the area's sidewalks, become venues for sitar and tabla performances, dance recitals and exhibitions of paintings, prints, photographs and installation art.

Nishagandhi Dance Festival *(Feb)*, Thiruvananthapuram. Artistes of almost all classical dance forms perform at the open-air Nishagandhi Auditorium.

Milad-ul-Nabi *(Feb)*. Prophet Mohammed's birthday is observed with prayers and readings from the holy Koran.

Shivratri *(Feb/Mar)*. Devotees of Shiva observe the night of his celestial wedding to Parvati.

Shankarlal Sangeet Sammelan *(Feb/Mar)*, Delhi. This is the capital's oldest Hindustani classical vocal and instrumental music festival.

The aim of this extravaganza is to preserve the country's cultural heritage and promote the performing arts. It is today a forum for talented youth to interact and perform with eminent music maestros.

Delhi Dhrupad Samaroh *(Mar)*, Delhi. Leading exponents of Dhrupad, a classical musical tradition, present a series of recitals.

Holi *(Mar)*. One of the most important Hindu festivals, Holi is celebrated in the morning after a full moon night and marks the end of winter. On the eve of Holi, bonfires are lit, and an effigy of the demon Holika is burnt to signify the triumph of good over evil. The next day, people swarm the streets, sprinkling coloured water and powder *(gulal)* on each other. This exuberant festival is especially dear to Lord Krishna, and around Mathura, his birthplace *(see p182)*, it is celebrated with great abandon.

Jahan-e-Khusrau *(Mar)*, Delhi. Held at Humayun's Tomb *(see p87)*, this festival commemorates the death of the Sufi poet Amir Khusrau and attracts composers and

Show jumping at the Delhi Horse Show

Namaaz (prayers) being offered during Id-ul-Zuha

performers of Sufi music from all over the world.

Nauchandi Mela *(Mar, 2nd Sun after Holi),* Meerut. Held around the shrine of a Muslim saint and a temple, this fair has come to symbolize Hindu-Muslim unity. Its origins date to the late 17th century when local leaders decided to merge festivities held concurrently at both shrines. Today, this is more a fun-filled carnival than a religious event.

Jamshed-e-Navroz *(Mar).* Celebrated by the Parsi community as their New Year's Day, the festival is named after the Persian king Jamshed, who is believed to have first introduced the solar calendar. Parsis celebrate this day with family gatherings and feasts. They also visit fire-temples and make offerings of sandalwood.

Ramnavami *(Mar/Apr).* Nine days of fasting *(navaratris)* precede the birth of the hero-god Rama *(see p31)* on Ramnavami (the ninth day). During this period, many Hindu households maintain a strict vegetarian diet, and prepare special food cooked in ghee (clarified butter) without garlic or onions.

Delhi Horse Show *(Mar/Apr),* Delhi. A two-day sporting event, where thoroughbred horses from all over the country take part in show-jumping, tent-pegging and dressage events.

Four Square White-Water Rafting Challenge *(Mar/Apr),* Rishikesh. The premier white-water rafting event in India, this is also one of the richest competitions in the world with a cash prize of US$25,000.

Mahavir Jayanti *(Mar/Apr).* Jains celebrate the birth of the founder of Jainism, Mahavira *(see p400).* This is celebrated on a large scale in Rajasthan and Gujarat. Devotees offer prayers to the 24 *tirthankaras* (saints).

Summer (Apr–Jun)

From early April until June, the northern plains, and much of the south, have a hot and dry summer. By May and June, the heat in the north builds up to a scorching 40° C (104° F) and above – a signal for those who can afford it to move up to the hill stations in the Himalayas. Meanwhile, temperatures in the Deccan Plateau and the south rise to about 38° C (100° F). Most festivities come to a halt.

Baisakhi *(13 Apr).* This festival heralds the harvest season in the north.

International Flower Festival *(Apr/May),* Gangtok. A show of rare and exotic flowering plants found in Sikkim,

Symbol of National School of Drama

including almost 500 varieties of orchids.

Himachal Hang Gliding Rally *(May),* Kangra. An international competition that draws professionals from all around the world.

Buddha Jayanti *(May).* The Buddha was born, attained enlightenment and died on the full moon of the fourth lunar month. Buddhists gather in *viharas* (refuges) for prayers.

NSD Repertory Festival *(May/Jun),* Delhi. This all-India festival is organized by the National School of Drama.

National Holidays

Republic Day (26 Jan)
Independence Day (15 Aug)
Gandhi Jayanti (2 Oct)

Public Holidays

Milad-ul-Nabi (Feb)
Shivratri (Feb/Mar)
Holi (Mar)
Good Friday (Mar/Apr)
Ramnavami (Mar/Apr)
Mahavir Jayanti (Mar/Apr)
Baisakhi (13 April)
Buddha Jayanti (May)
Janmashtami (Aug/Sep)
Dussehra (Sep/Oct)
Id-ul-Zuha (Oct)
Diwali (Oct/Nov)
Guru Purab (Nov)
Christmas (25 Dec)

Procession of Buddhist lamas on Buddha Jayanti

Women teams participating in the Nehru Trophy Boat Race, Kerala

Monsoon (Jul–Sep)

The monsoon season is celebrated for the magical transformation of the earth. The south, especially the coastal areas, and the northeast experience very heavy rains. Rainfall is fairly good in the northern plains.

International Mango Festival *(Jul)*, Delhi. Over 1,000 varieties of mangoes grown in North India are exhibited and sold at the Talkatora Stadium.

Kanwar Mela *(Jul/Aug)*, Haridwar. Thousands of Kanwarias (Shiva devotees) journey to the Ganges barefoot and saffron-clad, to carry gaily decorated *kanwars* (vessels hung on bamboo poles) filled with water from the sacred river back to their local Shiva temple.

Independence Day *(15 Aug)*. A national holiday commemorating India's freedom from British rule in 1947. The Prime Minister addresses the nation from the ramparts of the historic Red Fort in Delhi.

Raksha Bandhan *(Aug)*. Women tie sacred threads *(rakhis)* on their brothers' wrists as a token of love, and receive in exchange gifts and a promise of everlasting protection.

Id-ul-Fitr *(Aug)*. This festival is celebrated when the sighting of the new moon signals the end of Ramadan, the 40-day long period of fasting for Muslims that marks the revelation of the Koran to the Prophet by Allah. It is also called Mithi (sweet) Id, as *sewian*, a delicacy made with sweetened vermicelli, is prepared on the occasion.

Lalbagh Flower Show *(Aug)*, Bengaluru. This pretty flower show is held in the Glass House of the Lalbagh Gardens.

Nehru Trophy Boat Race *(Aug)*, Kerala. Lavishly decorated snake boats *(see p637)* take part in a thrilling race at Alappuzha.

Janmashtami *(Aug/Sep)*. The day is given to fasting and festivities reach their peak at midnight which is when Lord Krishna was born. The merrymaking in Mathura *(see p182)* and Brindavan *(see p183)* is especially grand.

A gaudy modern day *rakhi*

Winter (Oct–Feb)

This is the best season in India. The monsoon is over, and the days now begin to grow cooler. It is also the most auspicious period in the Indian calendar and ushers in a number of festivals. Winter also marks the sowing of crops such as mustard and wheat. The chill is at its worst in the northern plains between mid-December and mid-January, and though temperatures often fall below 3° C (37° F), the days are sunny. The southern region does not experience very low winter temperatures, the minimum being around 19° C (66° F).

Dussehra *(Sep/Oct)*. For nine days, episodes from the *Ramayana (see p31)* depicting Rama's adventures against Ravana are enacted. The tenth day, Vijaya Dashami, celebrates Rama's defeat of Ravana, and huge effigies of the demon-king, his brother and son are burnt. In Delhi, the Shriram Bharatiya Kala Kendra's month-long dance-drama encapsulates the epic. Bengalis celebrate Durga Puja *(see p285)* at this time.

Gandhi Jayanti *(2 Oct)*. Mahatma Gandhi's birthday is widely celebrated as a national holiday.

Id-ul-Zuha *(Oct)*. The Muslim feast of sacrifice popularly known as Bakr Id, commemorates Abraham's willingness to sacrifice his own son, Ismail. Since then, a goat is sacrificed to Allah on this day, prayers are offered in mosques and special delicacies are served.

Pushkar Fair *(Oct/Nov)*, Pushkar. Asia's largest camel, horse and cattle fair takes place in this pilgrim town.

Diwali *(Nov)*. Oil lamps illuminate homes to

Huge effigies of Ravana and his son during Dussehra, Delhi

commemorate Rama's return to Ayodhya after 14 years of exile. Firecrackers are lit and sweets exchanged. Every locality holds Diwali *melas*.

Guru Purab *(Nov)*. On the first full moon night after Diwali, Sikhs celebrate the birthday of Guru Nanak, the founder of Sikhism.

Prithvi International Theatre Festival *(Nov)*, Mumbai. Prithvi Theatre is one of Mumbai's best known theatres. This week-long festival brings to the city international theatre groups, who perform a variety of contemporary plays, along with a handful of Indian theatre groups.

International Trade Fair *(14–21 Nov)*, Delhi. In this major event for Indian industry, goods manufactured in India and abroad are exhibited at Pragati Maldan. Cultural events are also held in the fair grounds.

International Film Festival of India *(Nov/Dec)*, Goa. India's premier film event, showcasing state-of-the-art films by Indian as well as international directors.

International Film Festival of Kerala *(Dec)*, Kerala. This event invites films from around the world, in categories such as world cinema, short films, documentary and Malayalam cinema.

Madras Music Festival *(Dec/Jan)*, Chennai. The city celebrates its rich heritage of Carnatic music and dance with recitals by numerous well-known artistes.

Island Tourism Festival *(Dec/Jan)*, Port Blair. A ten-day festival of dance, theatre and music reflects the multi-cultural population of the Andaman Islands. There are also exhibitions of local crafts, flora and marine life.

Lohri *(13 Jan)*, Punjab. Bonfires and merriment mark what is believed to be the coldest day in winter.

Makar Sankranti *(14 Jan)*, Jaipur. Kites are flown to celebrate the return of the

Immaculate vintage cars at the Kolkata rally

sun from the Equator to the Tropic of Capricorn. This day coincides with the Tamil festival of Pongal *(see p593)*.

Republic Day *(26 Jan)*. Pomp and pageantry mark India's birth as an independent republic. In Delhi, a colourful military parade is held at Rajpath.

Beating of the Retreat *(29 Jan)*, Delhi. This ceremony recalls the end of the day's battle when armies retreated to their camps. A grand display of regimental bands perform against the spectacular backdrop of North and South Blocks. As the sun sets, a bugle sounds the retreat, fireworks are lit and the buildings are framed with fairylights.

Decorative paper kite

Vintage and Classic Car Rally *(Jan)*, Kolkata. *The Statesman* group of newspapers organizes this event when vintage cars, or the "grand old ladies", are flagged off on a short race. Their owners often dress up

in period costumes. A similar rally is held in Delhi in March.

Mamallapuram Dance Festival *(Jan/Feb)*, Mamallapuram. Leading Indian classical dancers, perform Bharat Natyam, Kuchipudi, Kathakali and Odissi against a backdrop of the famous Pallava rock-cut sculptures.

Thyagaraja Aradhana Festival *(Jan/Feb)*, Thiruvaiyaru. An eight-day music festival is held in honour of the saint composer Thyagaraja, attracting eminent musicians from all over the country.

Basant Panchami *(Jan/Feb)*. Considered to be the first day of spring, Basant is celebrated all over North India. People dress in shades of yellow, echoing the yellow mustard blossoms that are in bloom. In Eastern India, the same day is celebrated as Saraswati *puja*, honouring the Goddess of Learning and Wisdom.

Desert Festival *(Jan/Feb)*, Jaisalmer. A cultural festival, held on the sand dunes over three days, with camel races, camel polo, folk dances and music performances.

Bagpipers of an army regiment at the Beating of the Retreat ceremony

The Climate of India

Summer, monsoon and winter, with a brief but glorious spring and autumn, span the seasons in India. The climate changes with latitude and geographical location. In the north, temperatures soar in the vast Gangetic Plains, though the Himalayan belt remains pleasantly cool in summer. In winter, the high mountain passes remain snowbound. The central Deccan and deep south, however, have a tropical monsoon climate, with high temperatures and virtually no winter. India's coastal belts, on the other hand, remain humid and warm, with torrential rain. The semi-arid regions of Rajasthan and Kutch, as well as the rain shadow areas east of the Western Ghats, are among the country's worst drought hit areas, while the coasts and the northeast states, face the full onslaught of the monsoon, and are devastated by cyclones and floods each year.

Giant cacti growing in the arid Thar Desert, Jaisalmer

Key

- Tropical rainy region: consistently high temperatures and heavy summer rainfall.
- Humid subtropical region: hot summer followed by heavy rainfall. Dry winter.
- Tropical savannah region: long, dry season with high summer temperatures. Mild winter.
- Tropical and subtropical steppe region: semi-arid. Low and erratic rainfall leading to drought.
- Tropical desert region: high summer and very low winter temperatures. Scanty rainfall.
- Mountain region: cold and dry climate. Short summer.
- Mountain region: cold, humid winter. Short summer.

JAIPUR

°C/°F	Apr	Jul	Oct	Jan
	37/99	34/93	33/91	
	21/70	26/79		22/72
			18/64	
				8/46
☀ hrs	9.3	4.4	9.6	8.6
☂ mm	4.2	193	19.3	14
month	Apr	Jul	Oct	Jan

MUMBAI

°C/°F	Apr	Jul	Oct	Jan
	32/90	30/86	32/90	
	25/77	25/77	25/77	29/84
				19/66
☀ hrs	9.6	2	8.3	9.1
☂ mm	2.8	710	88	2
month	Apr	Jul	Oct	Jan

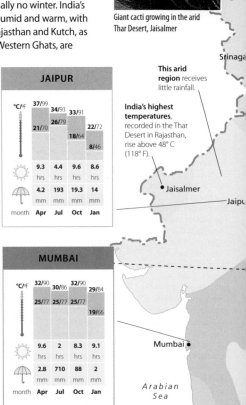

This arid **region** receives little rainfall.

Srinaga

India's highest temperatures, recorded in the Thar Desert in Rajasthan, rise above 48° C (118° F).

Jaisalmer

Jaipu

Mumbai

Arabian Sea

Lakshadweep Islands

Thiruvananthapur

The Monsoon

Torrential showers typify Kerala's monsoon

The word monsoon, from the Arabic *mawsim* (season), refers to South Asia's seasonal moisture-laden winds. In India, the Southwest Monsoon hits Kerala in end May. Simultaneously, one branch sweeps across the Bay of Bengal towards the Eastern Himalayas and the northeast, while the other, deflected westwards by the vast Himalayan barrier, moves towards the Gangetic Plains and gradually spreads across the mainland. At the end of September, the monsoon reverses direction and, as the Northeast Monsoon, brings heavy rain to southern Andhra Pradesh and the eastern coast of Tamil Nadu in October and November. Nothing in India is awaited more eagerly than these annual rains; and songs and poems celebrate the months of Sawan and Bhadon (July and August), as a time of renewal and hope.

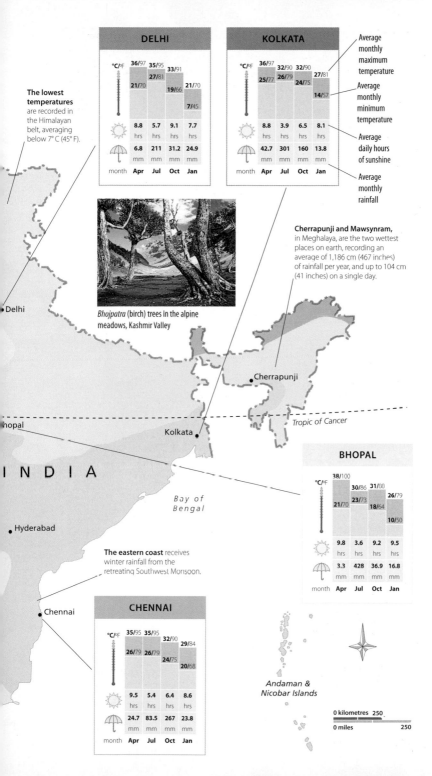

DELHI

°C/°F			
36/97	35/95	33/91	
21/70	27/81	19/66	21/70
			7/45

8.8 hrs	5.7 hrs	9.1 hrs	7.7 hrs
6.8 mm	211 mm	31.2 mm	24.9 mm

| month | **Apr** | **Jul** | **Oct** | **Jan** |

KOLKATA

°C/°F			
36/97	32/90	32/90	
25/77	26/79	24/75	27/81
			14/57

8.8 hrs	3.9 hrs	6.5 hrs	8.1 hrs
42.7 mm	301 mm	160 mm	13.8 mm

| month | **Apr** | **Jul** | **Oct** | **Jan** |

Average monthly maximum temperature

Average monthly minimum temperature

Average daily hours of sunshine

Average monthly rainfall

The lowest temperatures are recorded in the Himalayan belt, averaging below 7° C (45° F).

Bhojpatra (birch) trees in the alpine meadows, Kashmir Valley

Cherrapunji and Mawsynram, in Meghalaya, are the two wettest places on earth, recording an average of 1,186 cm (467 inches) of rainfall per year, and up to 104 cm (41 inches) on a single day.

• Delhi

hopal

• Hyderabad

Cherrapunji •

Kolkata •

Bay of Bengal

Tropic of Cancer

I N D I A

BHOPAL

°C/°F			
38/100			
	30/86	31/00	
21/70	23/73	18/64	26/79
			10/50

9.8 hrs	3.6 hrs	9.2 hrs	9.5 hrs
3.3 mm	428 mm	36.9 mm	16.8 mm

| month | **Apr** | **Jul** | **Oct** | **Jan** |

The eastern coast receives winter rainfall from the retreating Southwest Monsoon.

• Chennai

CHENNAI

°C/°F			
35/95	35/95	32/90	29/84
26/79	26/79	24/75	20/68

9.5 hrs	5.4 hrs	6.4 hrs	8.6 hrs
24.7 mm	83.5 mm	267 mm	23.8 mm

| month | **Apr** | **Jul** | **Oct** | **Jan** |

Andaman & Nicobar Islands

0 kilometres 250
0 miles 250

THE HISTORY OF INDIA

The name India comes from "Indoi", a Greek word for the people who lived beyond the Indus river. The roots of Indian civilization lie in the country's precise and awesome natural boundaries, formed by the Himalayas in the north, and seas to the east, south and west. These have fostered a remarkable physical and cultural unity, despite the size and diversity of the area they enclose.

Indus Valley Civilization

Prehistoric sites in India date back to at least 250,000 BC, with agricultural settlements appearing around 7000 BC. By 2500 BC, a sophisticated urban civilization emerged, stretching across the Indus Valley and northwest India, all the way down to Gujarat. Its main cities were marked by solid brick structures, roads in a grid pattern, and elaborate drainage systems. Stone seals with an as yet undeciphered script, and standardized weights and measures were among the artifacts found in this culture (also known as Harappan Civilization), which had a thriving trade with Mesopotamia. Remains of two of these cities can be seen at Lothal and Dholavira in Gujarat. By 1800 BC, these cities declined, perhaps because of tectonic or ecological changes.

The Vedic Age

Around 1500 BC, a people commonly known as the Aryans, who were probably migrants from Central Asia, settled in the Indus region. Described in the *Rig Veda*, a Sanskrit text of that period, they had a mixed pastoral and agrarian economy. Three later Vedas, written between 1000–600 BC, and associated Sanskrit texts, record the extension of their settlements across the Gangetic Valley. This was also the time of the *Mahabharata* epic *(see p30)*, which describes a great war between two clans.

While the Rig Vedic religion worshipped nature gods, the deities of the later Vedic period were more complex. Later Vedic literature included a remarkable set of Sanskrit treatises called the *Upanishads*, which advocated a philosophical quest for truth, through enquiry. By this period, a social structure based on the caste system had developed. It was earlier occupational, but was now becoming hereditary and increasingly rigid. At the apex were the Brahmins or priests, followed by the *kshatriyas* (rulers and warriors). Below them were *vaishyas* (farmers and traders), and *shudras* (servants and labourers). Sacrifices and rituals to appease the gods were prescribed by the Vedas, and became a part of daily life.

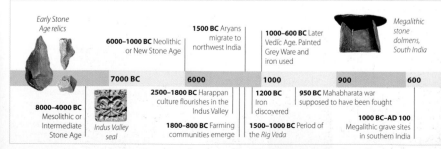

Early Stone Age relics	**6000–1000 BC** Neolithic or New Stone Age	**1500 BC** Aryans migrate to northwest India	**1000–600 BC** Later Vedic Age. Painted Grey Ware and iron used		*Megalithic stone dolmens, South India*
8000–4000 BC Mesolithic or Intermediate Stone Age	**7000 BC** *Indus Valley seal*	**6000** **2500–1800 BC** Harappan culture flourishes in the Indus Valley **1800–800 BC** Farming communities emerge	**1000** **1200 BC** Iron discovered **1500–1000 BC** Period of the *Rig Veda*	**900 BC** Mahabharata war supposed to have been fought	**600** **1000 BC–AD 100** Megalithic grave sites in southern India

◀ Miniature painting of the Battle of Panipat, 1526, which established the Mughal dynasty in India

The Age of Mahavira and Buddha

The 6th century BC saw the rise of several urban centres in the north, accompanied by widespread trade. Urbanization led to changes in social stratification, and encouraged the emergence of new religious sects which challenged Brahmin dominance. Chief among these were Buddhism and Jainism, founded respectively by Gautama Siddhartha (566–486 BC) who became the Buddha, and Vardhamana Mahavira (540–467 BC). These religions gained popularity as they had neither caste nor sacrifice, and were open to everyone, including women. The Buddha's simple yet profound teachings *(see p225)* had particularly wide appeal. Mahavira believed in an ascetic life accompanied by truth and non-acquisitiveness *(see p400)*. Both religions disregarded god, discussed the laws of the universe, and advocated ahimsa – not harming any living being. Merchants, traders and others who adopted these religions gained new social status.

Detail on an Ajanta painting showing Lord Buddha with a monk

The Mauryan Empire

The first empire in India was founded in 321 BC when Chandragupta Maurya, an unknown adventurer, defeated the ruling Nanda dynasty of Magadha (in Bihar) and established an empire extending down to the Narmada river in the Deccan. Chandragupta's grandson, Ashoka (269–232 BC) became one of India's greatest rulers, extending the Mauryan Empire to reach from Afghanistan to Karnataka. But after his bloody conquest of Kalinga *(see p313)*, Ashoka gave up violence and became a great patron of

Lion capital of
Ashokan pillar

Buddhism. He recorded his ethical code on rocks and pillars all over his vast empire, enjoining his subjects to respect others' religions, give liberally to charity and avoid the killing of animals. These edicts were written in the Brahmi script, from which most Indian scripts have evolved. Ashoka also built many stupas enshrining Buddhist relics, including the one at Sanchi *(see pp248–9)*.

Central Asian Invaders

After Ashoka, the Mauryan Empire soon declined. Local kingdoms arose across North India, while from the northwest a series of invaders, all from Central Asia, established successive dynasties. These

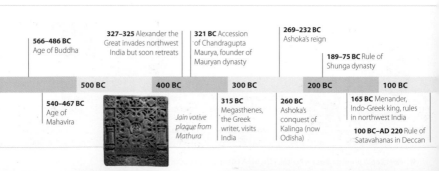

566–486 BC
Age of Buddha

327–325 Alexander the Great invades northwest India but soon retreats

321 BC Accession of Chandragupta Maurya, founder of Mauryan dynasty

269–232 BC
Ashoka's reign

189–75 BC Rule of Shunga dynasty

500 BC	400 BC	300 BC	200 BC	100 BC

540–467 BC
Age of Mahavira

Jain votive plaque from Mathura

315 BC
Megasthenes, the Greek writer, visits India

260 BC
Ashoka's conquest of Kalinga (now Odisha)

165 BC Menander, Indo-Greek king, rules in northwest India

100 BC–AD 220 Rule of Satavahanas in Deccan

included the Indo-Greeks from Bactria (200–80 BC), the Scythians or Shakas with many branches (from 80 BC), the Parthians (1st century AD), and the Kushanas (AD 50–300). The territory of Kanishka, the greatest Kushana king, covered the northwest, Kashmir, and most of the Gangetic Valley. He too was a patron of Buddhism. Mahayana Buddhism developed at this time, reflected in two great schools of art, with Buddha sculptures in the Graeco-Roman Gandhara style in the northwest, and in a more indigenous style at Mathura.

As the Kushanas declined, the Gupta dynasty emerged in northern India to establish another great empire (AD 320–500). The Gupta period saw a great cultural flowering, with fine sculptures, classical Sanskrit poetry and drama, and learned treatises on mathematics and astronomy produced at this time. In religion, the two Hindu sects of Vaishnavism and Shaivism (followers of Vishnu and Shiva) became prominent, and the Buddhist university of Nalanda was established (see pp222–3). But inroads by the Huns, marauding tribes from Central Asia, contributed to the decline of the Guptas after AD 450.

The next major empire was established by Harsha (AD 606–647) at Kanauj. His long and enlightened rule is described by the Chinese traveller Hiuen Tsang (see p223).

Buddha head,
Gupta period

Rulers in the South

Meanwhile, in the Deccan region, numerous dynasties arose after the decline of the

Mauryas. They included the Satavahanas (100 BC–AD 220), and the Ikshvakus (AD 225–310) in the eastern Deccan, under whom Buddhist stupas were constructed at Amravati (see p679) and Nagarjunakonda (see p680). Another Deccan dynasty were the Vakatakas (AD 250–550), during whose reign many of the superb sculptures and paintings at Ajanta (see pp483–5) were made. In the western Deccan, the Chalukyas came to power and built great temples at Badami (see pp540–41), Pattadakal (see pp542–3) and Aihole (see pp544–5). Their most powerful ruler, Pulakeshin II (AD 608–642), defeated Harsha, and stopped his southward advance.

In the far south, the three kingdoms of the Cheras (now Kerala), Cholas and Pandyas ruled between 400 BC and AD 400. The people of this region were of non-Aryan origin and were known as Dravids. Another major dynasty in the south were the early Pallavas, who ruled from AD 275–550, with their capital at Kanchipuram. During these centuries, cities, craft guilds, and inland and foreign trade flourished across India. The South Indian kingdoms grew rich on trade with Rome till AD 300, exporting luxury goods such as spices, fine silks, precious gems, and exotic creatures such as monkeys and peacocks.

The Drunken Courtesan, 2nd-century Kushana panel

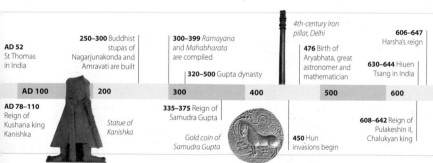

AD 52
St Thomas
in India

250–300 Buddhist
stupas of
Nagarjunakonda and
Amravati are built

300–399 Ramayana
and Mahabharata
are compiled

320–500 Gupta dynasty

4th-century Iron
pillar, Delhi

476 Birth of
Aryabhata, great
astronomer and
mathematician

606–647
Harsha's reign

630–644 Hiuen
Tsang in India

| AD 100 | 200 | 300 | 400 | 500 | 600 |

AD 78–110
Reign of
Kushana king
Kanishka

Statue of
Kanishka

335–375 Reign of
Samudra Gupta

Gold coin of
Samudra Gupta

450 Hun
invasions begin

608–642 Reign of
Pulakeshin II,
Chalukyan king

The elaborate traditional ceremonial procession of a Rajput prince

Northern Kingdoms (AD 750–1200)

Kanauj, once the capital of Harsha's empire, centrally located in the Gangetic Plains, had by 750 become the focus of conflict between three major dynasties – the Pratiharas, the Rashtrakutas and the Palas. The Pratiharas were a Rajput clan who ruled in Rajasthan and Malwa, while the Rashtrakutas (740–973) ruled in the northern Deccan. The Palas (750–1150), who were a Buddhist dynasty, ruled Bengal. Each captured Kanauj for a short while, but finally around 836, the Pratiharas gained control and held it for nearly two centuries. Soon other Rajput clans began to establish independent kingdoms.

The origins of the Rajputs are shrouded in mystery, but they are known from the 7th century AD in Western India. Some of them may have been descended from Central Asian tribes who settled in India in the wake of the Hun invasions (see p47). They called themselves *rajaputra* or "sons of kings", and their 36 clans claimed descent from the sun and moon, from fire, or from mythical

Woman writing a letter, Khajuraho

ancestors, in order to enhance their political and social status. Early Rajput dynasties included the Paramaras in Malwa, the Solankis in Gujarat, the Tomars in Delhi, the Chandelas in Central India, and the Chauhans in Rajasthan, whose best known king, Prithviraj, is still extolled in Rajasthani ballads for his legendary valour and chivalry. During this period, independent kingdoms also existed in Kashmir, the northwest, the northeast, and in Odisha, where the Eastern Ganga dynasty, builders of the great temples at Konark and Puri (see pp314–16) ruled.

All these Rajput and non-Rajput dynasties fought frequent wars with each other to gain control of strategic areas, setting the stage for their downfall – they would be unable to form a united front to defend themselves against outside attack. In between wars, however, the rulers and princes lived in great luxury, in grand forts and richly ornamented palaces. Agriculture was well-developed, with over 100 types of cereals cultivated. Trade with the Arab lands flourished, bringing new prosperity to cities, merchants and craftsmen, and leading to the emergence of many new towns. This period also saw a flowering of literature, as well as sculpture and temple architecture. Outstanding examples, apart from those in Odisha, are the Khajuraho temples of the Chandelas (see pp240–41), the Modhera Sun Temple (see pp422–3) and the Dilwara marble temples (see p398), which were built under the Solankis of Gujarat.

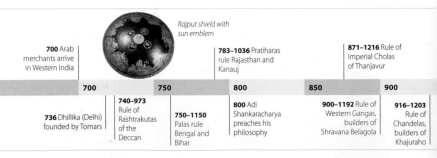

Rajput shield with sun emblem

700 Arab merchants arrive in Western India		**783–1036** Pratiharas rule Rajasthan and Kanauj	**871–1216** Rule of Imperial Cholas of Thanjavur

700	750	800	850	900

736 Dhillika (Delhi) founded by Tomars	**740–973** Rule of Rashtrakutas of the Deccan	**750–1150** Palas rule Bengal and Bihar	**800** Adi Shankaracharya preaches his philosophy	**900–1192** Rule of Western Gangas, builders of Shravana Belagola	**916–1203** Rule of Chandelas, builders of Khajuraho

Southern Dynasties (AD 600–1200)

In the Deccan and South India too several dynasties existed between 600 and 1200 AD. A new Pallava dynasty had risen to power in the 6th century, at Kanchipuram. In 642, the Pallava ruler Narasimha Varman I defeated and killed the Chalukya king Pulakeshin II, after which the great Chalukya kingdom declined.

In the late 9th century, the Cholas (see pp50–51), who had gone into decline in the 4th century, reasserted their power. They defeated the Pallavas, the Western Ganga dynasty which ruled near Mysore, and the Pandyas of Madurai, and established their supremacy in the south. They would later be challenged by the Hoysalas of Karnataka (see p527) who came to power in the 12th century.

As in northern India in this period, trade flourished in the south, despite constant wars. The Pallavas' maritime trade extended as far as Cambodia, Annam, Java, Sumatra, Malaysia and China.

In religion, this was a period of questioning and ferment. From the 7th century, itinerant Tamil poet-saints known as Alvaras and Nayannars, devotees of Vishnu and Shiva respectively, preached against caste divisions and orthodox Brahmanical practices, and emphasized a personal union with god through love and devotion (bhakti). Their teachings had great popular appeal. Other influential sages were Adi Shankaracharya (see p652) who travelled across the country, elaborating on the ideas contained in the Upanishads (see p15) and challenging Buddhism, Jainism and the bhakti cult; and the 11th-century philosopher Ramanuja, who expanded on Shankaracharya's teachings. By the 12th century, with the reforms and revival that had taken place in Hinduism, Buddhism went into decline, except in Eastern India.

Great monuments were built in the Deccan and South India in this period, among them the magnificent temples of the Pallavas at Mamallapuram (see pp582–5) and Kanchipuram (see p586), and the monolithic image of the Jain saint Bahubali at Shravana Belagola (see p526) erected by the Western Ganga kings. In the southwest, the superb rock-cut Kailasanatha Temple (see pp480–81) was built at Ellora by the Rashtrakutas.

Impressive exterior of the Shore Temple of the Pallavas in Mamallapuram

Bronze image of a Nayannar saint, 13th century

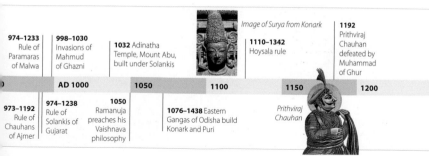

Image of Surya from Konark

| 974–1233 Rule of Paramaras of Malwa | 998–1030 Invasions of Mahmud of Ghazni | 1032 Adinatha Temple, Mount Abu, built under Solankis | | 1110–1342 Hoysala rule | 1192 Prithviraj Chauhan defeated by Muhammad of Ghur |

| | AD 1000 | 1050 | 1100 | 1150 | 1200 |

| 973–1192 Rule of Chauhans of Ajmer | 974–1238 Rule of Solankis of Gujarat | 1050 Ramanuja preaches his Vaishnava philosophy | 1076–1438 Eastern Gangas of Odisha build Konark and Puri | Prithviraj Chauhan | |

The Chola Dynasty

Between the 9th and 13th centuries, South India was dominated by the Chola dynasty, whose extensive empire covered much of peninsular India. Their two greatest kings were Rajaraja I (985–1014) and Rajendra I (1014–1044), under whom literature, architecture and sculpture reached new heights. They built magnificent temples, endowed with land and enormous wealth, and these became the focal point of their economy, as well as their social and cultural life. In 1216, the Cholas were defeated by the Pandyas, who then became the dominant power in South India.

King Rajaraja I
The first great Chola king, Rajaraja I (above) subdued other southern kingdoms and conquered Sri Lanka.

Infrastructure
The Cholas' irrigation dams on the Kaveri river (see p605) ensured the fertility of their lands. Civil and military officials, provincial chieftains, and elected village committees formed part of their efficient administration.

Wrestlers formed part of the Chola army.

Chola Warriors
This panel from the temple at Darasuram (see p597) celebrates the martial skills of the Cholas. Rajaraja I had a huge army of 31 regiments, which included elephant and horse cavalry, as well as foot soldiers.

Two faces of a copper coin of Rajaraja I

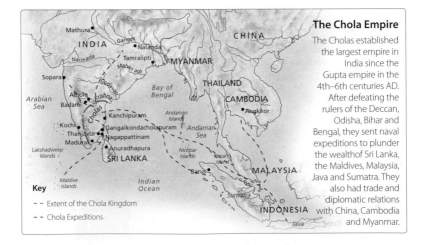

The Chola Empire
The Cholas established the largest empire in India since the Gupta empire in the 4th–6th centuries AD. After defeating the rulers of the Deccan, Odisha, Bihar and Bengal, they sent naval expeditions to plunder the wealth of Sri Lanka, the Maldives, Malaysia, Java and Sumatra. They also had trade and diplomatic relations with China, Cambodia and Myanmar.

Key

-- Extent of the Chola Kingdom

-- Chola Expeditions

Architecture
The Brihadishvara Temple *(see pp602–603)* at Thanjavur, King Rajaraja I's capital, represents the zenith of Chola temple architecture, which is distinguished by its monumental scale and towering sculpted spires and gateways.

Sculpture
This *Ardhanarishvara* (half man, half woman) image of Shiva, symbolizing the union of male and female aspects, exemplifies the superb grace of Chola bronze sculpture *(see p562)*. Other famous sculptures portray queens, princely warriors, scenes from Shaivite texts, and Shiva as Nataraja, the God of Dance.

Soldiers used swords and shields with great skill.

Religion
The Chola kings, who spent lavishly on religion, worshipped Shiva, but Vishnu worship was also popular in South India. This stone sculpture of Harihara, a composite of Shiva and Vishnu, symbolizes a bridge between the two sects.

Seat of Power
Gangaikondacholapuram *(see p596)* was built in 1035 by King Rajendra I as his new capital, after his successful military expedition to the Gangetic Valley in northern India. The temple here, watched over by Shiva's bull Nandi, also served as a treasury, and a cultural and educational centre.

Dance and Music
Hundreds of musicians and dancers performed at the Chola temples every evening, under royal patronage.

The Coming of Islam (1206–1555)

Constant internal warfare between the different kingdoms, in the north as well as the south, had left them vulnerable to outside attack. From the 11th century, a volatile political situation in Central Asia, coupled with tales of India's fabulous wealth, fuelled a new wave of invasions by Muslim Turkic rulers from the northwest. Many of them stayed on in India to found dynasties, and with them came soldiers, scholars and merchants, artists and Sufi preachers, who brought new ideas in art, architecture, theology and warfare from the Islamic world. These were to have a lasting impact on religion, art, culture and history in the Indian subcontinent.

Ceramic tile detail, Lodi period

The first major invader was Mahmud of Ghazni who raided India repeatedly between 998–1030, and took back vast wealth from its temples. He was followed by Muhammad of Ghur, who conquered Punjab and Delhi, and established his control over areas earlier dominated by Rajputs, after defeating Prithviraj Chauhan in 1192. He was succeeded by his slave, Qutbuddin Aibak (1206–1210), who founded the first of many Muslim dynasties, collectively known as the Delhi Sultanate. Qutbuddin built the towering Qutb Minar in Delhi. His successors

included Iltutmish and Balban (see p97). Next came the Khiljis (1290–1320), whose ruler Alauddin conquered Gujarat, Rajasthan and Bengal, and made the kings of the Deccan and South India his tributaries. After the Khiljis came the Tughluqs (1320–1414), whose second ruler, Muhammad bin Tughluq, completed the conquest of the Deccan (see p479) and South India, and annexed them. But he was unable to maintain control over these distant areas, which soon began to reassert their independence. This process was accelerated by the devastating invasion of northern India by Timur of Samarkand in 1398, which further weakened the power of the Delhi Sultans. The last two Sultanate dynasties, the Sayyids (1413–1451) and the Lodis (1451–1526), were riven by infighting among their nobles, and had only a tenuous hold over their territories.

Independent Kingdoms

During the early years of the Delhi Sultans, a number of independent kingdoms, such as the Solankis in Gujarat, the Eastern Gangas in Odisha, and the Kakatiyas, Pandyas and Hoysalas of the Deccan and South India had been absorbed into the Sultanate. However, as the Tughluqs began to decline, many new independent states emerged. The Hindu Vijayanagar Empire (see pp534–5) in southern India established its

The 13th-century Qutb Minar in Delhi

independence in 1336, while the Muslim kingdom of the Bahmani sultans was founded in 1347 in the Deccan, by a Tughluq noble. By the early 16th century, the Bahmani kingdom had broken up into the five smaller Muslim kingdoms of Bijapur, Ahmadnagar, Golconda, Berar and Bidar. In 1565, the combined forces of three of these kingdoms defeated the Vijayanagar forces, after which this powerful Hindu empire declined.

The 14th-century Sufi saint Nizamuddin

Meanwhile, as the Delhi Sultanate declined, its nobles and governors rebelled and founded their own kingdoms in Bengal (1388), Gujarat (1407), Mandu (1401) and Jaunpur (1408). In northeast India, the Ahoms who had migrated from Myanmar in 1228, established a kingdom in Assam (see p336). In Rajasthan too, several Rajput kingdoms, such as Mewar (see p102) and Marwar (see p384), reasserted their independence.

New Cultural Influences

Despite the turbulence throughout India between the 13th and 15th centuries, several new methods and technologies in agriculture, irrigation, administration, arts and crafts were introduced, many of them by the Muslim rulers. Trade flourished with Iran, the Arab countries, Southeast Asia, China and Europe, and a 14th-century historian records that Delhi was the largest city in the eastern Islamic world. The mosques, tombs and forts built by the Delhi Sultans ushered in new trends in architecture; and distinct regional styles, fusing Islamic and Hindu elements,

developed at places such as Ahmedabad, Mandu, and the Muslim kingdoms of the Deccan.

In religion, mystical Sufi sects of Islam and saint-poets of the bhakti movement, such as Meerabai and Kabir, popularized the practice of religion as devotion to god, rejecting caste hierarchies. Guru Nanak (1494–1530) founded the Sikh religion (see p107), taking elements from the bhakti movement and Islam.

The Coming of the Mughals

In 1526 Babur, a Central Asian prince descended from Timur, and a brilliant military campaigner, marched into India, overthrew the Lodis at the historic battle of Panipat, and laid the foundations of the Mughal Empire. Mughal rule was briefly interrupted when Babur's son Humayun was overthrown in 1540 by an Afghan chieftain, Sher Shah Suri. But Humayun regained his throne in 1555, and it was left to his son Akbar to consolidate and expand the Mughal Empire. The next two emperors, Jahangir and Shah Jahan, left a legacy of magnificent art and architecture. Aurangzeb, the last great Mughal, expanded the empire by adding new territories in the south.

Frieze of an elephant hunt from Hampi, Vijayanagar

Bara Gumbad, a 15th-century Lodi tomb

1451–1526 Reign of Lodi sultans of Delhi		**1555** Reconquest of Delhi by Humayun	**1643** Shah Jahan begins Taj Mahal	**1674** Shivaji crowned Chhatrapati
1469–1539 Guru Nanak, founder of Sikhism		**1571–85** Akbar builds Fatehpur Sikri		**1690** Calcutta founded by Job Charnock
1500	**1550**	**1600**	**1650**	**1700**
1498 Portuguese Vasco da Gama reaches Calicut	**1540** Sher Shah Suri defeats Humayun and takes Delhi	**1600** Queen Elizabeth I grants charter to East India Company		**1661** Bombay transferred from the Portuguese to the English
1526 Babur defeats Ibrahim Lodi at Panipat	**1530** Humayun succeeds Babur	**1556** Akbar becomes Mughal emperor		

The Great Mughals

The Mughals, like their contemporaries the Ottomans of Turkey, the Safavids of Iran and the Tudors of England, were a powerful and influential dynasty. They ruled India for over 300 years, their empire extending at its height from Kandahar in the northwest to Bengal in the east, and from Kashmir in the north to the Deccan in the south. Great patrons of literature, architecture, and arts and crafts, which reached new heights under their patronage, the Mughals established a rich pluralistic culture, blending the best of Islamic and Hindu traditions.

Decorative Arts
Sumptuous objects, such as this blue glass and gold enamelled hookah base, were made in the royal Mughal workshops.

Emperor Akbar
The greatest Mughal, Akbar (r.1556–1605) was a brilliant administrator and enlightened ruler. He built the city of Fatehpur Sikri (see pp184–7).

A nobleman presents a gift to the emperor.

Weaponry
War elephants formed an important part of the Mughal army. They were controlled and commanded with sharp but beautifully crafted goads.

Mughal Coins
Gold *mohurs* struck during the reigns of Akbar and his son Jahangir are renowned for their fine calligraphy.

Court robes and turbans indicated status and religion.

Rajput princes were loyal allies.

Diwan-i-Khas was the special audience hall.

The Nine Jewels
Akbar gathered at his court brilliant men from different professions, whom he called his "nine jewels". They included the musician Tansen (centre) who, it is said, could light a lamp with the power of his voice.

Political Alliances
Raja Man Singh I of Amber gave his daughter in marriage to Akbar, beginning a tradition of Mughal-Rajput alliances that would bring peace and prosperity to the Mughal Empire.

Nur Jahan
A formidable combination of brains and beauty, Jahangir's Persian-born queen (b.1577) was the real power behind the throne.

Architecture
A monument of ethereal beauty, built by Shah Jahan for his wife, the Taj Mahal *(see pp176–9)* represents the zenith of Mughal architecture.

Jewellery
The legendary wealth of the Mughals included fabulous jewellery, such as this pendant encrusted with large, flawless diamonds.

Illuminated Manuscripts
Works of literature, history and biography were produced on gilded paper with beautiful calligraphy and illustrations.

Shah Jahan on his splendid throne.

Shah Jahan's Court
The splendour of the Mughal court is illustrated in this 17th-century painting of Emperor Shah Jahan, with his nobles grouped in strict hierarchical order around the throne. Mughal emperors, whose capitals were at Agra and later Delhi, used glittering court rituals and pageantry to display their supreme authority, as they took stock of the state of affairs in their empire.

Wars of Succession
Aurangzeb, the last great Mughal, came to power after imprisoning his father Shah Jahan, and killing his brothers. Ruthless and bigoted, he alienated many of his Hindu subjects, but expanded the Mughal Empire.

The Mughal Dynasty
The Mughal Empire flourished from 1526 until Aurangzeb's death in 1707. After that, the dynasty gradually declined under weak rulers, and finally ended in 1857. Its first six rulers were:
Babur (r.1526–30)
Humayun (r.1530–56)
Akbar (r.1556–1605)
Jahangir (r.1605–27)
Shah Jahan (r.1627–58)
Aurangzeb (r.1658–1707)

The Decline of the Mughals

The death of Emperor Aurangzeb, the last great Mughal, in 1707, heralded the decline of the Mughal Empire. He left a ruined economy and weak successors, and independent states now began to be established by the Rajputs in Rajasthan, the nawabs of Avadh and Bengal, the nizams of Hyderabad, and the Wodeyars of Mysore. Two new powers were the Marathas in the Deccan and the Sikhs in the north. The Marathas under their leader Shivaji (*see p475*) expanded their territories after 1647. The Sikhs, originally a religious group, began to acquire territory in the hill states of the north, Jammu and Punjab. Under Ranjit Singh (*see p108*), they became a powerful state in the early 19th century.

The Europeans

But India would no longer remain a battleground for indigenous groups and dynasties – European traders, who had begun to arrive in the 16th century, were to change the course of its history. To set up trading factories in areas where their agents had settled, the Europeans began to acquire land, and fought numerous wars, both against one another and against Indian rulers. The trading groups were organized into companies, and included the Portuguese, French, Dutch and English. The Portuguese, who were the first to arrive, lost most of their territories to the Dutch and English by the end of the 17th century, retaining only Goa and a few

Sahib and mahout on elephant

adjacent enclaves. The Dutch, in turn, lost out to the English. The 18th century saw major conflicts between the French and English, with three Carnatic Wars fought between 1740 and 1763, in South India and involving Indian powers on both sides. Ultimately, the English were the victors, the French retaining only Puducherry and a few small settlements.

The Rise of the British

Meanwhile, the English East India Company was acquiring territory in the north by gaining trade concessions from the Mughal emperors from the early 17th century onwards. They defeated the nawabs of Bengal in the Battles of Plassey (Palasi) in 1757 and Buxar in 1764. By this time, the invasions of Nadir Shah of Persia in 1739, and Ahmad Shah Abdali of Afghanistan in 1761, had further weakened the Mughals. In the battle with Abdali the Marathas, who had gained control of Delhi, suffered a crushing defeat. From these beginnings, the British began to expand their power. Robert Clive (*see p565*), responsible for many of their successes, became Governor of Bengal in 1757. From 1773, the

Rachol Church in Portuguese Goa

1707 Death of Mughal emperor Aurangzeb

Nadir Shah's battle axe

1727 The city of Jaipur founded by Sawai Jai Singh II

1739 Nadir Shah of Persia invades Delhi

1750

1757 Battle of Plassey, British defeat Siraj-ud-daulah, Nawab of Bengal

1761 Ahmed Shah Abdali of Afghanistan defeats Marathas in the Third Battle of Panipat

1764 Battle of Buxar, British granted Diwani of Bengal

1774–85 Warren Hastings, first Governor General

1775

1789 Marathas occupy Delhi

1799 Tipu Sultan defeated

A Maratha soldier

Sepoys (Indian foot soldiers of the East India Company) rebelling at Fatehpur during the Mutiny of 1857

Parliament in England started to exercise some control over the Company. Warren Hastings, appointed Governor in 1772, was soon given the title of Governor General of Bengal (1774–1785), with supervisory powers over all the Company's territories. Under him and his successors (who from 1833 onwards were known as governors general of India), expansion continued, with major wars being fought against the Marathas, the Punjab, and Haider Ali and Tipu Sultan in Mysore. Other states too were conquered or brought under British control by various policies, such as the Subsidiary Alliance, under which Indian states had to maintain British troops and allow a British official to reside in the state and advise them. Another policy was the Doctrine of Lapse, under which states "lapsed" to the Company if a ruler died without a direct male heir. Thus by 1857, the Company's control extended over much of

India, and obtained them vast profits. After the Industrial Revolution, raw materials from India were exported to Britain, and machine-made British goods, particularly textiles, flooded the country. Artisans were impoverished, and crafts, towns and cities declined. Discontent with the alien rulers was growing. Unlike earlier conquerors of India, the British maintained their separateness, and their base in another country. In 1857, a combination of factors led to a major revolt, which began as a soldiers' mutiny, but soon had widespread civilian participation. Thousands of rebels marched towards Delhi in May and proclaimed the titular Mughal ruler, Bahadur Shah Zafar, emperor of India. By September the British had regained control over Delhi. Bahadur Shah was exiled to Rangoon (Yangon), and his young sons executed. Other rebel areas were also brutally taken over, ending the first major challenge to British rule.

Toy showing Tipu's tiger mauling a British soldier

1803 British capture Delhi from the Marathas	*Queen Victoria's head on a Company coin*	**1853** First railway from Bombay to Thana	**1857** The Indian Mutiny
			1863 Simla becomes summer capital of the Raj
1800	**1825**	**1850**	
1799–1839 Reign of Ranjit Singh	**1818** Rajasthani kingdoms accept British control	**1829** Governor General Bentinck bans *sati*, the Hindu practice of widow burning	**1856** Annexation of Avadh
		Nawab Wajid Ali Shah of Avadh	**1858** Crown takes over the East India Company, Lord Canning becomes the first Viceroy

Pax Britannica

The foundations of British rule, or the Raj, were laid after the Indian Mutiny of 1857, which revealed the unpopularity of the East India Company's rule. By an Act of Parliament in 1858, the Company's rule ended, and its Indian territories became part of the British Empire, to be ruled through a viceroy. Though the *raison d'être* of the Raj was economic profit and political control, its abiding legacy was the political unification of the subcontinent, together with the introduction of Western education, a centralized administrative system, and a network of railways.

British India

☐ British territory, 1858

Caparisoned elephants carry Raj officials.

Indian attendants in viceregal livery re-enact a Mughal procession.

Administration
Some 2,000 British officers, members of the prestigious Indian Civil Service, ruled over 300 million Indians. Dubbed the "Steel Frame of India", they brought British-style law and order to the remotest corners of the country.

Lord Curzon
Viceroy from 1899 to 1905, Curzon believed British rule was necessary to civilize "backward" India. Paradoxically, the Western-style educational institutions set up by the Raj helped make Indians more aware of the injustices of colonial rule.

A Sahib Travelling
A vast rail network was set up to facilitate commerce and travel. This 19th-century print shows first-class travel, a privilege of "whites only". The sahibs travelled in style, with several servants in attendance.

Raj Cuisine

The British soon developed a taste for Indian curries, toned down to make them a bit less spicy. Restaurants such as London's *Chutney Mary* have been popular in Britain ever since.

Memsahib and Tailor

Despite the climate, the British clung to their own dress and lifestyle. Children were sent "home" to study, and a large Indian staff enabled a leisurely lifestyle.

The Viceroy, Lord Curzon, and his wife lead the procession.

Crowds line the streets to see the grand spectacle.

Cemeteries of the Raj

The harsh Indian climate took a heavy toll on British women and children. Their tombs fill the Raj's graveyards.

The Imperial Durbar, 1903

This painting of Curzon's Delhi Durbar (1903), held to celebrate the coronation of Edward VII in London, shows a procession winding through the historic streets of Delhi. Held periodically, such assemblies announced the grandeur and the political might of British Rule in India.

The Company School

Paintings by Indian artists, such as this fanciful portrait of King Edward VII and Queen Alexandra in Indian royal attire, were specially commissioned for the British market.

Colonial Architecture

The most imposing edifice in New Delhi, built as the imperial capital between 1911 and 1931, was the viceroy's sprawling residence.

Crowds of supporters around Mahatma Gandhi

The National Movement

After 1857, nationalist aspirations began to grow, and the founding of the Indian National Congress in 1885 gave Indians a platform from which to demand self-goverment. A turning point came in 1919, when General Reginald Dyer's troops fired on an unarmed crowd protesting against the suppression of civil liberties in Jallianwala Bagh in Amritsar. More than 300 people died, and Indians of every caste, class and religion united in their outrage at British brutality. By 1920, the leadership of the National Movement was taken over by Mohandas Karamchand Gandhi, a Gujarati lawyer who had recently returned from South Africa. Popularly known as Mahatma or "great soul", Gandhi's charismatic appeal and identification with the poor of India converted the freedom struggle into a mass movement. His strategy was to launch a moral crusade of non-violent resistance (satyagraha) to British laws and institutions, interspersed with construction

A popular poster of political heroes, past and present

work at the grassroot level in villages Working alongside Gandhi were several outstanding Indians, including Pandit Jawaharlal Nehru.

At first, the movement for freedom was ruthlessly suppressed, but after World War II, Britain no longer had the strength or the will to enforce its rule. Meanwhile, from 1940 onwards, the Muslim League, led by Mohammad Ali Jinnah, had been demanding an independent state of Pakistan for Muslims.

Finally, at midnight on 14/15 August, 1947, the era of British rule ended, and the new nations of India and Pakistan were born. Casting a dark shadow over the celebrations was the Partition of the Indian subcontinent into two countries, accompanied by mass migrations of millions of Hindus and Muslims across the borders, and communal riots in which thousands were killed.

Independent India

After Independence, the new government integrated more than 550 princely states, which had been semi-independent in British days, into the Indian Union. In late 1947, a war between India and Pakistan took place over the accession to India of the princely state of Kashmir, and this continues to be a major point of dispute between the two countries. In 1948, Mahatma Gandhi was assassinated by a Hindu fanatic who felt he favoured

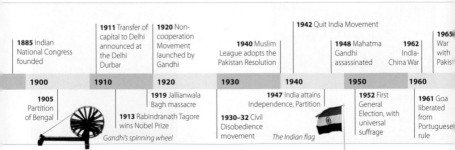

1885 Indian National Congress founded
1905 Partition of Bengal
1911 Transfer of capital to Delhi announced at the Delhi Durbar
1919 Jallianwala Bagh massacre
1913 Rabindranath Tagore wins Nobel Prize
Gandhi's spinning wheel
1920 Non-cooperation Movement launched by Gandhi
1930–32 Civil Disobedience movement
1940 Muslim League adopts the Pakistan Resolution
1947 India attains Independence, Partition
The Indian flag
1942 Quit India Movement
1948 Mahatma Gandhi assassinated
1952 First General Election, with universal suffrage
1962 India-China War
1961 Goa liberated from Portuguese rule
1965 War with Pakis

| 1900 | 1910 | 1920 | 1930 | 1940 | 1950 | 1960 |

Nehru, with his daughter
Indira and grandson Rajiv

Muslims. This so shocked and grieved both communities that peace was finally restored. As India's first prime minister, Jawaharlal Nehru laid the foundations of a modern nation state, with a democratic, secular polity, a strong industrial base and a planned economy, with Non-alignment as the keystone of its foreign policy. In 1962, China invaded northeast India and then withdrew after inflicting a humiliating defeat on the Indian army. This brought about much-needed modernization of India's military machine. Nehru died in May 1964, and in 1966 his daughter Indira Gandhi became prime minister. She continued his pro-poor and socialist policies, and in 1971, she stripped the Indian princes of their titles and abolished their privy purses. Later in the same year, she aided East Pakistan in its struggle against West Pakistan, leading to the formation of Bangladesh. But in 1975, perceiving a threat to her power and popularity, she declared a state of Emergency, under which the press was censored and dissidents imprisoned. When the general elections

took place, in 1977, she was defeated, and the Congress party lost power for the first time since Independence. By 1980, Indira and the Congress were back in power, but a military action against Sikh terrorists holed up in the sacred Golden Temple led to her assassination by her Sikh guards in 1984. Her son, Rajiv Gandhi, took over in a sympathy wave, and began liberalizing the economy. He was assassinated by a Sri Lankan Tamil separatist during the 1991 election campaign, but economic reforms encouraging private enterprise and foreign investment continued. Since 1996, a series of coalition governments have been in power, with the Hindu nationalist Bharatiya Janata Party (BJP) emerging as a major force to challenge the Congress

Significant progress has been made in the years since Independence, though unemployment and poverty continue to exist. The literacy rate has risen from 18 per cent in 1951 to 74 per cent in 2011. In urban areas, women can be seen working in all professions. From frequent food shortages in the 1950s, India now has a food surplus, and its industrial base has expanded to produce a wide range of goods, from toys to aircraft.

Rural women learning to read
during a literacy campaign

Economic reforms have flooded the market with consumer goods, and helped the rise of a prosperous middle class. In the field of information technology, there has been a veritable revolution, with India now established as a world leader in software development.

1998 BJP comes to power. AB Vajpayee becomes Prime Minister	**1999** India-Pakistan conflict in Kargil	**2004** Tsunami hits coastal Tamil Nadu and the Andamans	
1982 India sends scientific team to Antarctica		**2010** India hosts the 19th Commonwealth Games in Delhi	

'71 Birth of Bangladesh

0	**1980**	**1990**	**2000**	**2010**	**2020**

1975 Indira Gandhi declares Emergency
'71 Princes lose titles and privy purses

1991 Rajiv Gandhi assassinated
1992 Destruction of Babri Masjid leads to communal riots

2001 Gujarat earthquake
2000 Population reaches 1 billion
1998 Amartya Sen wins the Nobel Prize for Economics

2007 Pratibha Patil becomes the first woman President of India

DELHI & THE NORTH

Introducing Delhi & the North

As rich in natural beauty as in historic sites, North India is a much visited region. A wide variety of landscapes can be enjoyed here, from the snowcapped peaks, alpine valleys and pine forests of Ladakh and Himachal Pradesh, to the flat plains of Haryana and Punjab, dappled with fields of golden mustard and wheat. In sharp contrast is the urban sprawl of Delhi, a bustling metropolis and the nation's capital. Ladakh's dramatically sited cliff top monasteries and pristine trekking trails are major attractions for visitors, as are Shimla's Raj-era ambience and Dharamsala's distinctive Tibetan flavour. Amritsar's great Sikh shrine, the Golden Temple, and Delhi's magnificent Mughal monuments are other popular destinations.

The lush green landscape of Srinagar, in the Kashmir Valley

Punjabi farmers enjoying a ride in a tractor-trailer

Getting Around

Delhi has good air, rail and road links to the rest of the region. There are daily flights to Leh, Srinagar, Amritsar and Chandigarh. Amritsar and Chandigarh are also connected to Delhi by fast trains and a National Highway. From Chandigarh, there are air services to Shimla and Manali, as well as road links with frequent bus services. A particularly charming journey is on any of the five deluxe rail motor cars run by Kalka–Shimla Railways *(see p753)*. Other great journeys, with spectacular mountain scenery en route, include the trip by road from Manali to Leh, and the journey along the old Hindustan-Tibet Road (National Highway 22), which runs from Shimla to the India-China border near Shipkila.

◄ View of the snow-capped mountains at Sonamarg, Kashmir

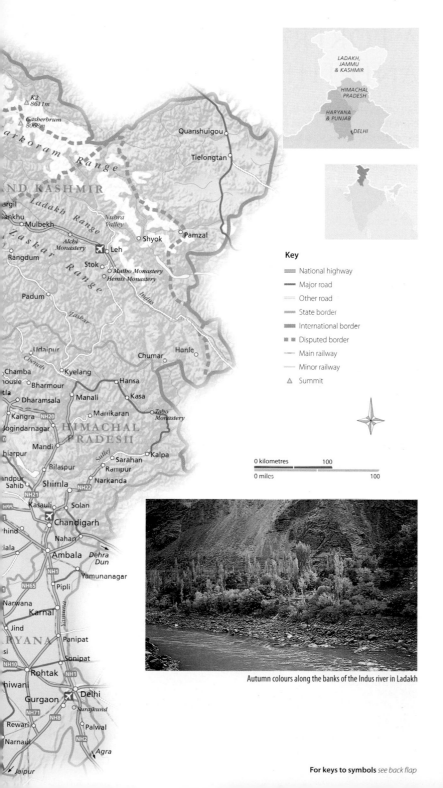

Key

━━ National highway
━━ Major road
══ Other road
━ State border
▬▬ International border
▪ ▪ Disputed border
— Main railway
— Minor railway
△ Summit

0 kilometres   100
0 miles   100

Autumn colours along the banks of the Indus river in Ladakh

For keys to symbols *see back flap*

A PORTRAIT OF DELHI AND THE NORTH

The peaks of the Himalayas, the most spectacular natural barrier in the world, mark the boundaries of the area that extends northwards from Delhi. A variety of cultures and landscapes lies within this region. Delhi's bustling urban sprawl gradually gives way to the lush, flat farmlands of Punjab and Haryana, north of which are the serene mountainous lands of Himachal Pradesh and Ladakh.

In geological terms, the Himalayas are very young (see pp68–9), but for humans, they evoke a feeling of timeless eternity, and have been a source of spiritual inspiration for Indians for thousands of years. The monasteries and temples situated on their slopes perfectly complement the profound beauty of these mountains.

Saffron flowers

Most visitors to the region start out from Delhi, the country's capital, a city that is a blend of several historical eras. Its grand Mughal past is evident in its many superb monuments and tombs. The elegant tree-lined avenues and bungalows of New Delhi evoke the period of the British rule. Yet both coexist alongside the modern world of Internet cafés, shopping arcades and posh multiplex cinemas.

Delhi's population swelled massively to accommodate the millions of people displaced by the Partition of India in 1947, when the western portion of Punjab became part of Pakistan. Homeless refugees from west Punjab have since prospered in Delhi, and now dominate the city's commercial life. As the nation's capital, Delhi continues to attract people from all over India, giving this vibrant city a resolutely cosmopolitan air.

The hardworking, resilient Punjabis have also transformed their home state with modern farming techniques, introduced in the 1960s. As a result of this "Green Revolution", Punjab and Haryana today produce much of India's wheat and rice, and one-third of its dairy products. Punjabis are also among the most successful immigrant communities in the world, and today, many families have at least one member living abroad, whether in London, New

A deep blue glacial lake near Thamsar Pass in Himachal Pradesh

Mustard fields in the fertile plains of Punjab

York, Vancouver or Hong Kong, as portrayed in Mira Nair's film, *Monsoon Wedding* (2001).

The name "Punjab" refers to the five *(panch)* rivers *(ab)* which traverse this green land. The sixth "river", if one can call it that, is the legendary Grand Trunk Road *(see p183)*. Travelling almost anywhere north of Delhi, one is bound to use this route. The kind of traffic may have changed since Rudyard Kipling's *(see p259)* day, and it is now rather prosaically rechristened National Highway 1, but it still lives up to the author's description: "Such a river of life exists nowhere in the world".

A Delhi wedding procession

During the Raj-era, the British would escape from the summer heat of the plains and head for the hills. Today's visitors follow in their footsteps all year round. Himachal Pradesh has a number of delightful hill stations, such as Shimla, Kasauli and Dalhousie. The hillsides are covered with orchards, and apple farming is an important part of the state's economy. Himachal Pradesh also offers spectacular treks, some of which start from Dharamsala, a town with a distinct Tibetan flavour as the home of the Dalai Lama *(see p126)*.

Jammu and Kashmir, which includes Ladakh, is India's northernmost state. Tragically, the militant separatist movement in the beautiful Kashmir Valley has effectively had a negative impact on tourism there. But Ladakh remains an oasis of peace. Often perceived as having a purely Buddhist culture, its population is, in fact, almost equally divided between Buddhists and Muslims, who coexist here in harmony. Ladakh's uniquely syncretic culture, together with its astonishing natural beauty and the dramatic architecture of its monasteries, make it one of India's most fascinating areas.

A Kashmiri family gathered around their *samovar*

The Great Himalayas

The highest and youngest mountains in the world, the Himalayan Range stretches for 2,500 km (1,553 miles) along the Indian subcontinent's northern borders, separating it from Central Asia and the Tibetan Plateau. The Himalayas were formed about 30 million years ago, when the Indian plate broke away from Gondwanaland, drifted northwards and collided with the Eurasian landmass, driving the earth's crust up to form three parallel ranges, which include 30 of the world's highest peaks.

Locator Map
- The Himalayas
- Area illustrated below

High altitude desert, where little grows except lichen, is found above the tree line. One such area is between Diskit and Hundar in Ladakh's Nubra Valley *(see p147)*, which has sand dunes and camels.

Glaciers are especially abundant in the Western Himalayas. They are the source of three great Indian rivers – the Indus, the Ganges and the Brahmaputra.

The Himalayas

Fourteen peaks in the Himalayas tower above 8,000 m (26,247 ft), including Mount Everest, the world's highest peak at 8,848 m (29,029 ft). The two highest peaks in India are Kanchendzonga (see p306) at 8,598 m (28,209 ft), and Nanda Devi (seen above) at 7,817 m (25,646 ft).

Bandar Punch ("Monkey Tail"), 6,316 m (20,722 ft), attracts many mountaineers. This peak is visible from Dodital *(see p192)*.

Jaonli Peak, 6,633 m (21,762 ft)

Phating Pithwar Peak, 6,904 m (22,651 ft)

Kedarnath, 6,940 m (22,769 ft), is regarded as Shiva's sacred mountain. Below it is the famous Kedarnath Temple.

A traditional Himalayan dwelling is generally built of stone and wood, or sun-dried mud bricks. Typically it has two or three storeys, the lowest level filled with stone to provide stability during earthquakes, the next level housing livestock, and the top floor where the family rooms are laid out.

Flora and Fauna

Subtropical jungles, temperate coniferous forests and alpine meadows are among the varied vegetation zones in the Himalayas. They support a rich and abundant variety of plant and animal life.

Brahma Kamal (*Saussurea obvallata*) is a popular offering at most hill temples.

Deodar (*Cedrus deodara*) is a towering conifer found in temperate forests in the Western Himalayas.

Bar-headed geese (*Anser indicus*) are attractive water birds that breed in high altitude lakes in Ladakh.

Bharal (*Pseudois nayaur*) are called blue sheep because of the blue sheen on their grey coats. They inhabit the harsh, stony slopes above the snow line.

Marine fossils and rocks that have been found in high altitudes in the Himalayas, and even on peaks such as Mount Everest, testify that these mountains were once a part of the Tethys seabed.

Nanda Devi, 7,817 m (25,646 ft)

Trishul ("Trident"), 7,120 m (23,360 ft)

The snow leopard (*Uncia uncia*), now endangered, lives above 4,000 m (13,123 ft). It preys on wild sheep and hares.

The Flavours of Delhi & the North

Several culinary strands cross the region of Delhi and the Punjab, which, despite national boundaries, begins at the Khyber Pass, now in Pakistan. Wheat is the staple food and a variety of breads (rotis) are baked in a *tandoor*, the domed clay oven, also used to barbecue marinated meats and vegetables. Rich curries, legacies of the imperial kitchen, are still prepared as is the post-Partition cuisine of butter chicken, *tikkas* and *dal makhani*. Kashmiri flavours are a delicate blend of yoghurt, spices, aniseed, dried ginger powder, red chillies and a pinch of asafetida or garlic. Rice and mutton are the standard fare of both communities.

Strands of saffron

Mangoes and other fruit on sale in a Delhi fresh produce market

Delhi

Centuries of Muslim rule have given Delhi its succulent *shami* and *burra* kebabs, as well as creamy *kormas* and *salans*, rich *biryanis* and *pulaos*, all delicately spiced main dishes. Once served at the courts of kings, emperors and sultans, this imperial cuisine is still eaten by most people.

Today, Delhi is a city of immigrants and each community has brought its own food. By far the most dominant is Punjabi and "Frontier" cuisine. The ubiquitous *tandoori* chicken, served with pickled onions and mint chutney was "invented" in Daryaganj's Moti Mahal restaurant in 1947. Other popular foods are the *dosa*

and *idli* from South India (see pp558–9).

Delhi has an abundance of street foods. *Bhutta* (corn-on-the-cob) roasting on makeshift stoves, fruit juices and cooling sherbets sold from handcarts and the range of *chaat* (savoury snacks) are legendary. Equally famous are *jelabis* (crisply fried batter in syrup), *phirni* (rice

Tandoori murg | Murg zafrani (spiced chicken) | Reshmi kebab (chicken kebab) | Seekh kebab (lamb kebab) | Burra kebab (char-grilled lamb)

A tandoori platter with a selection of barbecued meats

Local Dishes and Specialities

From the old city of Delhi comes the *nahari*, the delectable mutton (which can mean goat meat too in India) dish that is cooked through the night and served at breakfast with *naans*. Snacks include the popular *chhole-bhatura* and vegetable *pakora* (Indian tempura). Specialities of the Punjab include *dal makhani*, *baigan ka bharta* (smoked and puréed aubergines/eggplant) and various stuffed breads. Vegetarian dishes in Kashmir are few, the most famous being *haaq* (a special spinach), *aloo dum* (potatoes in yoghurt) and *chaman* (cottage cheese in gravy). Lamb or mutton dishes include *rishta* (meatballs) cooked in a sauce and *tabak maz* (fried ribs cooked in milk).

Mint and chillies

Aloo puri is a spicy potato dish eaten with puffy deep-fried bread and a mint and coriander chutney.

Shikras (skiffs) carrying fresh vegetables, Dal Lake, Srinagar, Kashmir

Punjab

Punjabi food is robust and linked to the lifestyle of the largely farming communities. It is dominated by milk and its products, such as yoghurt and *paneer* (cottage cheese), prepared in innumerable ways. Popular drinks are *lassi* (buttermilk) and a variant, *chhach*, made with ginger, coriander and powdered cumin. Wheat is the staple cereal and dishes include *aloo parathas* (fried bread stuffed with potatoes and other vegetables and eaten with yoghurt) and the seasonal *sarson ka saag* (mustard greens) and *makke* (corn) *ki roti*.

Although vegetarian food is the main fare, the non vegetarian dishes from this state are a mixture of Northwest Frontier and Mughlai cuisines. The hub of Punjabi cuisine is Amritsar, famous for its batter-fried fish. The *dhabas* (eateries) that dot the main highways offer the best local food as truck drivers demand a hot and tasty meal.

Winnowing wheat, a common sight in the Punjab

Kashmir

Food here ranges from a simple family meal to a 36-course wedding banquet, the *wazawan*, where guests are seated on cushioned rugs in groups of four, in front of large silver platters. Rice, grown in the Kashmir Valley, mutton, chicken or fish are of prime importance. The generous use of yoghurt in the sauces gives the dishes a creamy consistency, while the locally-grown saffron adds flavour and colour. Walnuts and almonds are also added for texture and flavour. A meal ends with *kahva*, a green tea flavoured with cardamom and cinnamon.

ON THE MENU

Aloo tikki Potato cutlets.

Chhole-bhatura Spiced chickpeas and puffy bread.

Dal makhani Lentils flavoured with ginger, garlic, spices and a dollop of cream.

Gushtaba Large meatballs flavoured with fresh mint.

Phirni A sweet rice pudding, garnished with nuts.

Shami kebab Mincemeat patties flavoured with spices.

Tandoori murg Barbecued spring chicken.

Yakhni A yoghurt and mutton or lotus root curry with a delicate hint of fennel.

pudding) and crushed almond or pistachio *kulfi* (ice cream), garnished with noodle ribbons.

Rogan josh has pieces of mutton simmered in yoghurt which is then thickened with *khoya* (solidified milk).

Dal combines lentils with a heady mix of onions, garlic and spices. It is considered India's "soul food".

Gulab jamuns are deep-fried milk and flour balls in a sweet syrup flavoured with rosewater and cardamom.

DELHI

Delhi, the capital of India, is also its third largest city, with a population of about 17 million. Its strategic location along the north-south, east-west route has given it a focal position in Indian history, and many great empires have been ruled from here. The monuments and ruins of these are scattered throughout the city, often cheek by jowl with modern structures and highrise towers.

The vast urban sprawl of contemporary Delhi is, in fact, a conglomeration of several distinct enclaves, chief among which are Old Delhi, with its 16th- and 17th-century Mughal-built monuments and congested souk-like bazaars; and New Delhi with its wide avenues, grand vistas and Colonial mansions, built by the British in the 1930s as their imperial capital. New Delhi has government buildings and also houses the Diplomatic Enclave where all the embassies are located. The picturesque 12th-century ruins of citadels built by the first Islamic rulers can be seen in the Qutb-Mehrauli area, and the affluent new middle class suburbs of South Delhi lie close by. Slums and shanty towns dot the outer fringes of the city.

All the contradictions and contrasts of India are particularly visible in the capital: denim-clad youngsters rubbing shoulders with robed sadhus (holy men), and bullock carts travelling alongside the latest luxury cars. Adding to Delhi's fascinating diversity is the fact that it is largely a city of migrants. After the violent Partition of India and Pakistan in 1947, millions of refugees, mainly from West Punjab, flocked here in search of a new life. Since then there has been a steady influx of people from all over India. Yet each regional community has retained its distinct cultural identity, making Delhi less a melting pot than a *thali* (platter) whose offerings may be savoured singly or in various interesting combinations.

People leaving the Jama Masjid after the Friday prayers

◀ Detailing on a wall in the Qutub complex, Delhi

Exploring Delhi

Some of Delhi's most impressive buildings can be seen in the area shown in this map. Vijay Chowk is the vantage point for the grand sweep of Raj buildings grouped on Raisina Hill. To the north, the magnificent Jama Masjid with its busy hive of lanes, is the focus of Old Delhi. To the southeast, the medieval quarter around the tomb of the Sufi saint Nizamuddin Auliya leads along Mathura Road to the ruined fort, Purana Qila. And to the south, the Mehrauli area (shown on the Greater Delhi map), has a fascinating cluster of monuments built in the 12th and 13th centuries.

Vijay Chowk (see pp76–7), at the base of Raisina Hill, surrounded by government offices

Sights at a Glance

Historic Buildings, Streets & Neighbourhoods

1 Around Vijay Chowk pp76–7
2 Rashtrapati Bhavan
3 Raisina Hill
4 Rajpath
9 Jantar Mantar
13 Purana Qila
15 Nizamuddin Complex
16 Humayun's Tomb p87
17 Chandni Chowk pp88–9
19 Red Fort
20 Rajghat
21 Feroze Shah Kotla
22 Around Kashmiri Gate
23 Coronation Memorial
26 Safdarjung's Tomb
28 Hauz Khas
29 Khirkee
30 Jahanpanah
31 Mehrauli Archaeological Park pp96–8
33 Tughluqabad

Churches, Temples & Mosques

10 Lakshmi Narayan Mandir
18 Jama Masjid
34 Baha'i House of Worship

Museums

5 National Museum pp80–81
6 National Gallery of Modern Art
11 Nehru Memorial Museum and Library
14 Crafts Museum pp84–5

25 National Rail Museum
32 Sanskriti Museum

Shops & Markets

8 Connaught Place
27 INA Market

Parks & Gardens

12 Lodi Gardens
24 The Ridge

Theatres & Art Galleries

7 Mandi House Complex

Key

- Sight
- Railroad
- National Highway (Inset map)
- Major road (Inset map)

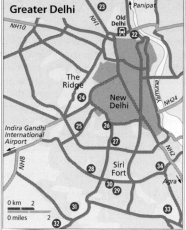

Greater Delhi

- 23 (near Panipat, Old Delhi)
- NH10
- NH1
- 22
- The Ridge
- 24
- New Delhi
- Yamuna
- NH24
- Indira Gandhi International Airport
- 25
- 26
- 27
- NH8
- 28
- Siri Fort
- 34
- Agra
- 30
- 29
- 31
- 33
- NH2
- 32

0 km   2

0 miles   2

Map labels (left map):

- UKHERJI MARG
- RING ROAD
- H C SEN RD
- NETAJI
- Moti Masjid
- Diwan-i-Khas
- CHOWK
- 17
- ndni owk
- DNI
- 19
- Diwan-i-Aam
- Rang Mahal
- MAHATMA GANDHI MARG
- ri Bazaar
- 18
- Karim's
- SUBHASH MARG
- ANSARI ROAD
- HURI WALI GALI
- BAZAAR CHITLI QABAR
- RING ROAD
- AF ALI ROAD
- A RD
- JAWAHARLAL NEHRU MARG
- RANJEET SINGH MG
- Gandhi Memorial Museum
- 20
- MIRDARD MARG
- BAHADUR SHAH ZAFAR MG
- KOTLA MARG
- 21
- DEEN DAYAL UPADHYAYA MG
- RING ROAD
- hamba Rd
- Shri Ram Centre
- Mandi House
- Tilak Bridge
- AD
- indra avan
- SIKANDRA RD
- NSD
- 7
- mani rium
- Pragati Maidan
- MATHURA ROAD
- COPERNICUS MARG
- TILAK MARG
- Indraprastha
- Pragati Maidan
- India Gate
- PURANA QILA RD
- 14
- BHAIRON MARG
- RING ROAD
- SHERSHAH RD
- 6
- 13
- DR ZAKIR HUSSAIN MG
- MATHURA ROAD
- PANDARA ROAD
- an ept
- NATIONAL ZOOLOGICAL PARK
- MAHATMA GANDHI MARG
- MANIAM
- ARCHBISHOP MAKARIOS MG
- BHARTI MARG
- DELHI GOLF COURSE
- MATHURA ROAD
- 16
- ROAD
- ARAB KI SARAI RD
- 15
- HARSHA RD
- RAHIM KHAN ROAD
- KHAN RD
- Nizamuddin Station
- ISBT Sarai Kale Khan
- BARAPULLAH
- FLYOVER

Getting Around

The areas shown here are best covered by the metro, taxi, auto-rickshaw or a hired car and driver. Guided coach tours run by Delhi Tourism (see p737) also cover many sights. Avoid buses!

Boating near one of Delhi's oldest historical sites, the Purana Qila

0 metres   800

0 yards   800

For keys to symbols see back flap

❶ Street-by-Street: Around Vijay Chowk

Vijay Chowk or "Victory Square", a large piazza at the base of Raisina Hill, was planned as a commanding approach to the Viceroy's House, now the Indian President's residence. This is where the "Beating of the Retreat" ceremony takes place each year on 29 January *(see p41)*. Vijay Chowk is flanked by two long, classical Secretariat buildings (the North and South Blocks), which house several ministries as well as the Prime Minister's Office. Ministers and government officials live in spacious bungalows on the tree-shaded avenues nearby. From Vijay Chowk, Lutyens's grand Central Vista lies ahead – large trees and fountains line the lawns of Rajpath up to India Gate, the Statue Canopy and the National Stadium at the far end.

★ **Vijay Chowk**
This piazza, flanked by red sandstone obelisk-shaped fountains, faces a grand vista.

North Block, designed by Herbert Baker, has an imposing Central Hall.

Sansad Bhavan, formerly known as Parliament House.

The Iron Gates
Copied from a pair Lutyens saw in Chiswick, England, these are set into ornamental sandstone gateposts. They lead to Rashtrapati Bhavan *(see p78)*.

Key

━ Suggested route

Sir Edwin Landseer Lutyens

Architect Sir Edwin Landseer Lutyens (1869–1944), President of the Royal Academy from 1938 to 1944, was commissioned to design India's new capital in 1911. With Herbert Baker, his colleague, it took him 20 years to build the city in a unique style that combined Western Classicism with Indian decorative motifs. The result is an impressive and harmonious synthesis, with Neo-Mughal gardens and grand vistas meeting at verdant roundabouts. Delayed by World War I and quarrels between Baker and Lutyens, spiralling costs met by Indian revenues led Mahatma Gandhi to term it a "white elephant". Ironically, the British lived here for only 16 years.

The red sandstone National Archives, designed by Lutyens

★ **South Block**
The Prime Minister's Office and the Defence Ministry are located within this section of the Secretariat.

Sunehri Bagh Mosque
This simple 18th-century mosque, built by a
saint called Sayyid Sahib, makes for a picturesque
roundabout. The adjoining Sunehri Bagh Road is lined
with shady trees – a feature of all Lutyens's avenues.

Locator Map
See Delhi Map pp74–5

Roundabout
Beautifully
landscaped road
intersections are a
haven for workers
during lunch.

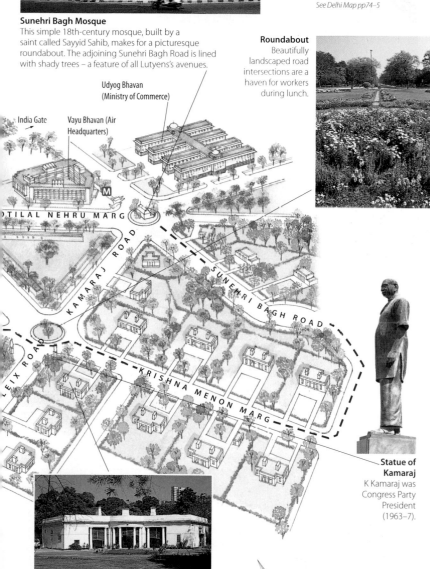

Udyog Bhavan
(Ministry of Commerce)

India Gate

Vayu Bhavan (Air Headquarters)

OTILAL NEHRU MARG

KAMARAJ ROAD

SUNEHRI BAGH ROAD

EIX ROAD

KRISHNA MENON MARG

Statue of Kamaraj
K Kamaraj was
Congress Party
President
(1963–7).

★ **Bungalow-lined Avenues**
Strict building bylaws preserve the original
architecture of the colonial bungalows in the
tree-lined avenues of this area.

| 0 metres | 25 |
| 0 yards | 25 |

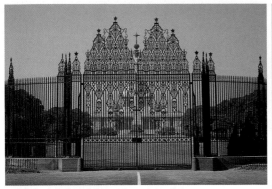

Ornate iron gates leading to Rashtrapati Bhavan, designed by Lutyens

❷ Rashtrapati Bhavan

Tel (011) 2301 5321. Ⓜ Central Secretariat. ⏰ 9am–4pm Fri–Sun. Change of Guard Ceremony: Apr–Oct: 8am; Nov–Mar: 10am Sat only. Mughal Gardens: **Open** Feb–Mar. Ⓦ **presidentofindia.nic.in**

Designed by Sir Edwin Lutyens (see p76) as the British Viceroy's Palace, Rashtrapati Bhavan, situated at the crest of Raisina Hill, is now the official residence of the President of India. A vast, copper-clad cupola soars over this elegant beige and red sandstone building which covers an area of 2 ha (5 acres). The *pièce de résistance* is the circular Durbar Hall, situated directly beneath the dome, where all important state ceremonies and functions are held.

To the west, the beautifully landscaped grounds include Rashtrapati Bhavan's **Mughal Gardens**. These terraced gardens with watercourses and fountains built on three levels, are open to visitors in the spring months.

❸ Raisina Hill

Cathedral Church of the Redemption: **Tel** (011) 2309 4229. Ⓜ Central Secretariat. **Open** 8am–noon; 4–6pm daily. Galleries: Official pass & letter from MP). Ⓦ **theredemptionchurch.org**

The barren, treeless grounds around Raisina Hill were selected by the British as the site of the new capital. Now a heavily guarded, verdant

area, it is dominated by stately buildings such as the twin North and South Blocks (see p76) of the **Secretariat**. The two virtually identical buildings that rise from the top of Raisina Hill, were designed by Sir Herbert Baker, who also designed the grand circular **Sansad Bhavan** (Parliament House) to the north of Vijay Chowk. Both the Rajya Sabha (Upper House) and the Lok Sabha (House of the People) convene here when Parliament is in session. After the December 2001 terrorist attack, access is limited and visitors can only visit the galleries of Sansad Bhavan.

Behind Sansad Bhavan is the Anglican **Cathedral Church of the Redemption**, inspired by Palladio's Church of Il Redentore in Venice. Originally built for senior British officials in 1931, it is now the diocese of the Bishop of the Church of North India.

❹ Rajpath

National Archives: Janpath. **Tel** (011) 2338 3436. Ⓜ Central Secretariat. **Open** 10am–5:30pm Mon–Fri. **Closed** public hols & Sun. Indira Gandhi National Centre for the Arts: Janpath. **Tel** (011) 2338 8155. **Open** 9am–5:30pm Mon–Fri.

Running east of Vijay Chowk is Rajpath, a two-mile-long avenue used for parades, with ornamental fountains, canals and lawns on either side. The **National Archives**, situated at the intersection with Janpath, houses a major collection of state records and private papers. Opposite is the **Indira Gandhi National Centre for the Arts** with an archive of rare manuscripts. It holds many national and international exhibitions and symposia.

At Rajpath's eastern end is **India Gate**, a massive red sandstone arch, built to commemorate the Indian and British soldiers who died in World War I, and those who fell in battle in the North-West Frontier Province and the Third Afghan War. An eternal flame burns in memory of the soldiers who died in the 1971 India-Pakistan War. Facing India Gate is the sandstone canopy where a statue of King George V was installed in 1936. The statue is now at Coronation Park (see p92) and the canopy stands empty.

India Gate

❺ National Museum

See pp72–3.

Sansad Bhavan, where the Constitution of India was drafted

❻ National Gallery of Modern Art

Jaipur House, near India Gate. **Tel** (011) 2338 6208. **Open** 10am–5pm Tue–Sun. **Closed** Mon & public hols. 📷 🎫 **W** ngmaindia.gov.in

Jaipur House, the former residence of the maharajas of Jaipur, is one of India's largest museums of modern art, covering the period from the mid-19th century to the present day. Its excellent collections include works by modern Indian painters such as Jamini Roy, Rabindranath Tagore, Raja Ravi Varma and Amrita Shergill, as well as contemporary artists such as Ram Kumar and Anjolie Ela Menon. Also on display are works by British artists such as Thomas Daniell and his nephew William Daniell, and an interesting group of "Company Paintings" – 18th- and 19th-century works by Indian artists commissioned specially for the British market.

❼ Mandi House Complex

Ⓜ Mandi House. Triveni Kala Sangam: Tansen Marg. **Tel** (011) 2371 8833. **Open** 10am–6pm Mon–Sat. **Closed** public hols. 📷 🖥 Rabindra Bhavan: Ferozeshah Rd. **Tel** (011) 2338 1833 (Sahitya Akademi). 📷 Kamani Auditorium: Copernicus Marg. **Tel** (011) 4350 3351. Shri Ram Centre: Safdar Hashmi Marg. **Tel** (011) 2371 4307. 🖥 National School of Drama: Bhagwan Das Rd. **Tel** (011) 2338 9402. For Tickets: see Entertainment: p100.

Mandi House, today the offices of the state-owned television centre, lends its name to this cultural complex encircling the roundabout. **Triveni Kala Sangam** has contemporary art galleries, an open-air amphi-theatre for concerts and plays, a popular café and a bookshop specializing in Indian arts publications. The state-sponsored **Rabindra Bhavan** arts complex houses the national academies of literature (Sahitya Akademi), fine arts and sculpture (Lalit Kala Akademi), and the performing arts (Sangeet Natak Akademi) in separate wings. All three have

Connaught Place, the British-built shopping complex in New Delhi

libraries and display galleries that sell reproductions. Regular exhibitions of photography and ceramics are also held here. **Kamani Auditorium**, the **Shri Ram Centre** and the **National School of Drama** are vibrant centres for theatre, music and dance performances.

Mirrorwork skirts on sale at Janpath

❽ Connaught Place

Ⓜ Rajiv Chowk. Shops: **Open** 10:30am–8pm Mon–Sat. **Closed** public hols.

Opened in 1931 and named after the Duke of Connaught, this shopping complex, with its Palladian archways and stuccoed colonnades, was designed by Robert Tor Russell as a deliberate contrast to the noises and chaos of an Indian bazaar. The central circle of Connaught Place (CP) has now been renamed Rajiv Chowk, and the outer circle Indira Chowk. Its arcades and pave-ments spill over with paan kiosks, book stalls and shoe shine boys, while the eclectic mix of shops is interspersed with eateries and cinema halls. Efforts to give CP a facelift for the 2010 Commonwealth Games only ended in 2013. Though no longer Delhi's premier shopping area, its shaded arcades are pleasant to stroll through. The nearby Central Park features an amphitheatre, 21 fountains and plush lawns. Nearby popular shopping centres include the state emporia at **Baba Kharak Singh Marg** and the stalls along **Janpath. Cottage Industries** (see p101) is also located on Janpath.

Republic Day Parade

Ever since 1950, when India became a republic, this parade on 26 January has attracted large crowds despite the often chilly weather. Soldiers and sailors, war veterans and school children, and even elephants and camels, march smartly down

The annual Republic Day Parade

Rajpath. Especially popular are the folk dancers and the inventive floats representing each state of the country. A ceremonial flypast by the Indian Air Force signals the end of the always colourful parade.

❺ The National Museum

Five millennia of Indian history can be explored at the National Museum, with a collection of more than 200,000 pieces of Indian art. The nucleus collection of about 1,000 artifacts was sent to London in the winter of 1948–9 for an exhibition at the Royal Academy's Burlington House. After its return, it was housed in the Durbar Hall of Rashtrapati Bhavan until the present building, built of the same beige and pink stone as the imposing new capital, was complete in 1960. The museum's collection of Indus Valley relics and Central Asian treasures from the Silk Route is considered among the finest in the world.

★ **Dara Shikoh's Marriage Procession**
An 18th-century Mughal miniature painting in gold and natural pigments.

★ **Nataraja**
This 12th-century Chola statue of the cosmic dance of Lord Shiva is the centrepiece of the museum's South Indian bronzes.

Maritime Heritage Gallery

The Coins Gallery
displays an impressive collection of coins.

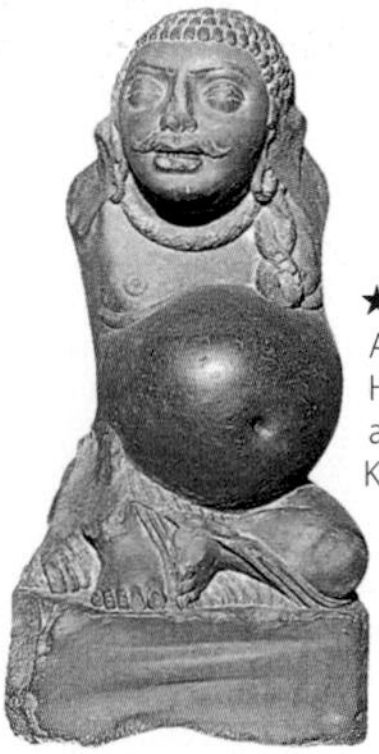

Ground floor

★ **Kubera**
A rare example of a Hindu god shown as a 2nd-century Kushana (see pp50–51) grandee with marked Central Asian features is among a large collection of Mathura Art.

Library

Harappan Civilization Gallery

Entrance

Audio-visual room

The Serindian Collection

Silk painting, 7th–8th century

Almost 700 years after the Silk Route fell into disuse, Sir Aurel Stein, a British archaeologist, led a series of expeditions (1900–16) to uncover its treasures. On view at the National Museum, Stein's Central Asian collection of the artifacts he found in the Taklamakan Desert has silk paintings, Buddhist manuscripts and valuable records of life along this ancient trade route.

Terracotta Mask
This unusual human mask made of terracotta dates back to 2700 BC, and was unearthed in Mohenjodaro in the early 20th century.

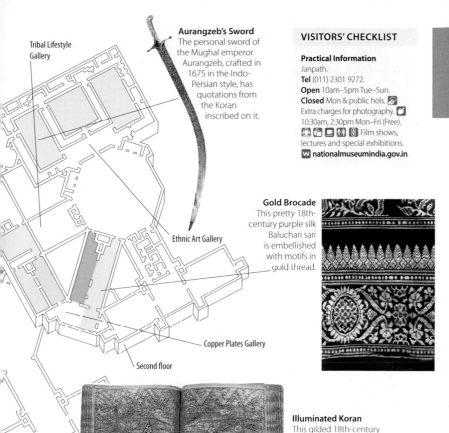

Tribal Lifestyle Gallery

Aurangzeb's Sword
The personal sword of the Mughal emperor Aurangzeb, crafted in 1675 in the Indo-Persian style, has quotations from the Koran inscribed on it.

Gold Brocade
This pretty 18th-century purple silk Baluchari sari is embellished with motifs in gold thread.

Ethnic Art Gallery

Copper Plates Gallery

Second floor

Illuminated Koran
This gilded 18th-century Koran, a superb example of the elegant Islamic art of calligraphy, is not on display but preserved in the archives. The museum's collection also includes an 8th-century Koran in the ancient Kufic script, among the oldest of its kind in the world.

First floor

Key to Floorplan

- 🟦 Ancient & Medieval Sculptures
- ⬜ Chola Bronzes, Jewellery, Wood Carving
- 🟦 Buddhist Art, Decorative Art
- ⬜ Central Asian Antiquities, Indian Manuscripts and Coins, Wall Paintings
- ⬜ Early Man
- 🟦 Pre-Columbian and Western Art
- ⬜ Ajanta Paintings, Thanjavur Paintings, Indian Miniature Paintings
- ⬜ Textiles, Arms and Armour, Musical Instruments

Gallery Guide

The collection is displayed on three floors, grouped according to theme, epoch and style. The central foyer itself has a display of sculptures from various parts of the country. The museum also has a library, audio-visual room and auditorium where film shows and lectures are regularly held. Information on these is published in the newspapers. Information regarding catalogues and souvenirs can be had at the ticket office in the foyer. The display is changed from time to time for variety, and special exhibitions are also mounted.

The brick and plaster astronomical instruments in Jantar Mantar

❾ Jantar Mantar

Sansad Marg. Ⓜ Rajiv Chowk.
Open daily. ▨

Sawai Jai Singh II of Jaipur, a keen astronomer, built this observatory in 1724 because he wanted to calculate planetary positions and alignments accurately, in order to perform sacred rituals and *pujas* at propitious moments. One of the five observatories he built *(see pp362–3)*, Jantar Mantar's instruments are large and fixed, making them resistant to vibration and therefore exact. The Samrat Yantra, a right-angled triangle whose hypotenuse is parallel to the earth's axis, is a gigantic sun-dial, with two brick quadrants on either side of it to measure the sun's shadow. The Ram Yantra, reads the altitude of the sun, and the Jai Prakash Yantra (invented by Jai Singh II himself) verifies the time of the spring equinox. Now obsolete, the observatory lies in the centre of a park surrounded by high-rises. Today, the area has become synonymous with *dharnas* (protests).

❿ Lakshmi Narayan Mandir

Mandir Marg. Ⓜ R.K. Ashram Marg.
Open daily.

Built in 1938 by the industrialist BD Birla, this was one of the earliest Indian temples without caste restrictions, and Mahatma Gandhi attended its first *puja*. A fairly typical example of modern Indian temple architecture, with its marble entrance and ochre and maroon *shikharas* (spires), the Birla Mandir, as it is popularly known, has images of Vishnu and his consort Lakshmi in its main shrine. Subsidiary shrines set around the courtyard, are inscribed with verses from sacred Hindu texts and are decorated with paintings depicting scenes from the great epics, the *Mahabharata* and *Ramayana*.

⓫ Nehru Memorial Museum and Library

Teen Murti Marg. **Tel** (011) 2301 7587 (canteen & bookshop). Ⓜ Race Course. **Open** 9am–5:30pm Tue–Sun. **Closed** public hols. Nehru Planetarium: **Tel** (011) 2301 4504. **Closed** Mon & public hols. ▨ Shows: 11:30am, 3pm.

The residence of Jawaharlal Nehru, India's first prime minister, Teen Murti Bhavan was converted into a museum and library for research scholars after Nehru's death in 1964. Originally built in 1930 as the residence of the Commander in Chief of the British Indian Army, this beautiful building became the residence of India's first prime minister, Jawaharlal Nehru. Nehru's bedroom and study, still exactly as he left them, reflect his austere yet elegant personality and his eclectic taste in books.

Teen Murti Memorial

The extensive grounds are home to the **Nehru Planetarium** and the square, three-arched **Kushak Mahal**, a 14th-century hunting lodge built by Sultan Feroze Shah Tughluq *(see p91)*. On the roundabout in front of the house stands the **Teen Murti** ("Three Statues") **Memorial**. This is dedicated to the Indian soldiers who died in World War I. The house derives its name from this landmark.

Teen Murti Bhavan, Nehru's official residence, now the Nehru Memorial Museum and Library

For hotels and restaurants see p694 and pp706–707

Athpula, the 17th-century bridge near the entrance to Lodi Gardens on South End Road

⓲ Lodi Gardens

Entrance on Lodi Rd & South End Rd.
Ⓜ Race Course. **Open** daily 🚫

Lodi Gardens is one of Delhi's most picturesque parks, and a favourite haunt of joggers, yoga enthusiasts, political bigwigs accompanied by their bodyguards, and families who come to picnic on weekends. Landscaped at the behest of Lady Willingdon, the vicereine, in 1936, the park acts as a "green lung" for the people of Delhi. Its tree lined pathways and well-kept lawns and flowerbeds are laid out around the imposing 15th-century tombs of the Sayyid and Lodi dynasties, Delhi's last sultans. Many of them still have traces of the original turquoise tilework and calligraphy.

The elegantly proportioned octagonal **Tomb of Muhammad Shah** (r.1434–44), the third ruler of the Sayyid dynasty, is said to be the oldest in the garden. The largest of the structures is the **Bara Gumbad** ("Big Dome") with an attached mosque built in 1494, and a guesthouse. At the South End Road entrance to the gardens is a lovely stone bridge called **Athpula** (literally "eight piers"), said to date from the 17th century. To its west are ramparts that enclose the **Tomb of Sikander Lodi** (r.1489–1517).

⓳ Purana Qila

Mathura Rd. **Tel** (011) 2435 4260.
Ⓜ Pragati Maidan. **Open** sunrise–sunset daily. Museum: **Tel** (011) 2435 5387. **Open** 9am–5pm. **Closed** Friday. 🎫 Tickets: from site and the Delhi Tourism office.

Purana Qila, literally "Old Fort", stands on an ancient site that has been continuously occupied since 1000 BC, as archaeological excavations have revealed. The brooding ramparts of the fort now enclose the remains of the sixth city of Delhi, Dinpanah (see p95), which was begun by the second Mughal emperor, Humayun. His reign, however, was short and in 1540 he was overthrown by the Afghan chieftain Sher Shah Suri (see p53). Sher Shah added several new structures and renamed the citadel Shergarh ("Lion's Fort"). After Sher Shah's death Humayun regained his throne. Of the many palaces, barracks and other edifices built by these two rulers, only Sher Shah's mosque and a building that was probably Humayun's library remain standing today.

The **Qila-i-Kuhna Mosque**, built in 1541, is a superbly proportioned structure with fine decorative inlay work in red and white marble and slate. To the south of the mosque is Humayun's library, known as **Sher Mandal**. A double-storeyed octagonal tower of red sandstone, it is crowned by an elaborate *chhatri* (open pavilion) supported by eight pillars. This was the tragic spot where the devout emperor, hurrying to kneel on the steps for the evening prayer, missed his footing and tumbled to his death in January 1556. The ramparts of the Purana Qila have three principal gateways, of which the imposing red sandstone **Talaagi Darwaza** on the western wall is the main entrance. Humayun's Tomb (see p87) can be seen from the southern gate.

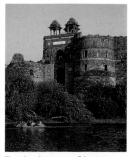

Chhatri with decorative tilework

The red sandstone gate or Talaagi Darwaza, Purana Qila

⑭ Crafts Museum

For centuries, Indian craftsmen such as potters, weavers, masons and carvers, have created a range of objects for everyday use that are both beautiful and practical. A unique project was started in 1956 to promote indigenous artisans by giving them a place to display their work, and by the early 1980s, over 20,000 objects had been collected. This was the core around which India's first Crafts Museum developed.

Wooden ritual mask of Bhima

★ **Bandhini Odhni**
This exquisite veil is the work of the Khatri community of Bhuj, Gujarat. Tie-and-dye (bandhini) is done by tying threads around grains to form a pattern, and dyeing the cloth in different colours.

Mukhalinga
This rare, late 19th-century phallic image (linga) with a human face (mukha) is made of brass and silver. The third eye and tiny snake-earrings are symbols of Shiva.

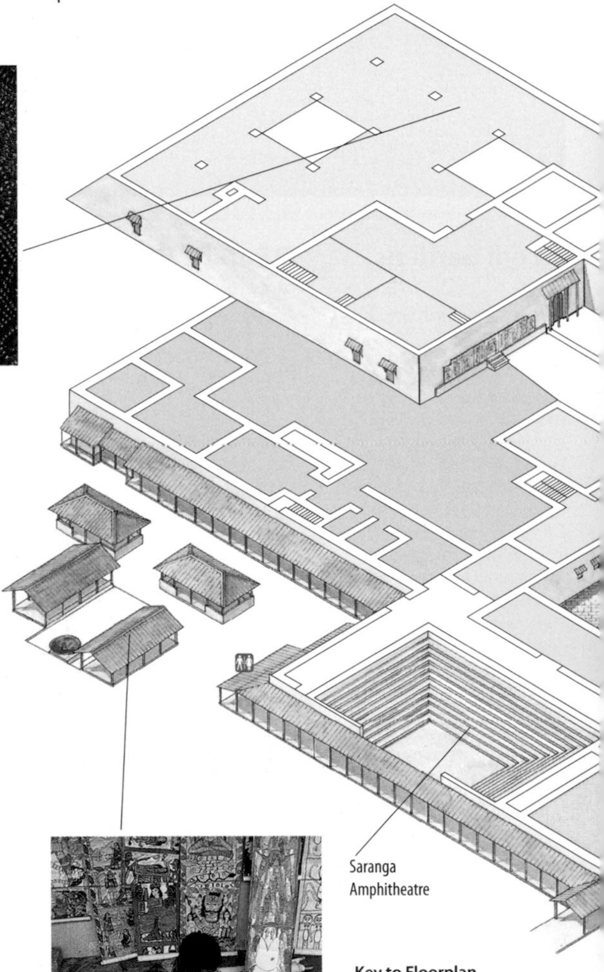

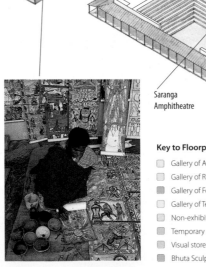

Crafts Demonstration Area
Artisans from all over India set up workshops each month (barring the monsoon) to display their skills to visitors.

Saranga Amphitheatre

Key to Floorplan

- ☐ Gallery of Aristocratic Arts
- ☐ Gallery of Ritual Arts
- ☐ Gallery of Folk and Tribal Cultures
- ☐ Gallery of Textiles
- ☐ Non-exhibition space
- ☐ Temporary exhibitions gallery
- ☐ Visual store
- ☐ Bhuta Sculpture Gallery

For hotels and restaurants see p694 and pp706–707

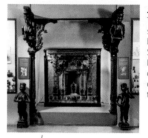

Jain shrine
This 18th-century wooden shrine from Gujarat once belonged to a wealthy Shvetambara Jain family. It features elaborate wood carvings of elephants, celestial musicians and the Goddess Laxmi.

VISITORS' CHECKLIST

Practical Information
Bhairon Marg, Pragati Maidan.
Tel (011) 2337 1641.
Open 10am–5pm Tue–Sun.
Closed public hols. Crafts demonstration:
Open 10am–6pm daily.

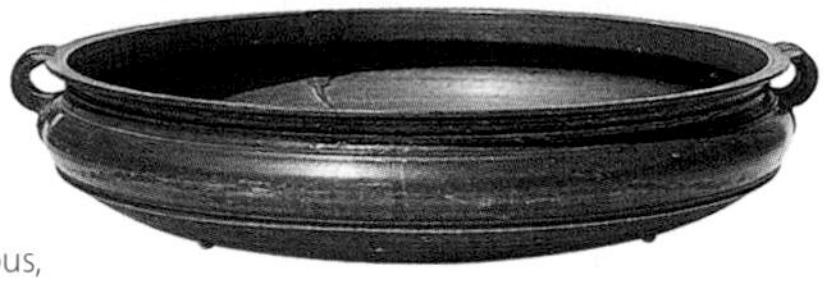

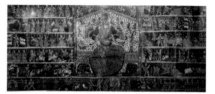

★ Charraku
These enormous, circular vessels are cast of an alloy known as bell metal. They are still used in Kerala for wedding feasts or at temples for making *payasam* (a type of rice pudding) for devotees during festivals.

Kalamkari panel
This traditional hand-painted textile from Andhra Pradesh depicts a female deity with 12 arms.

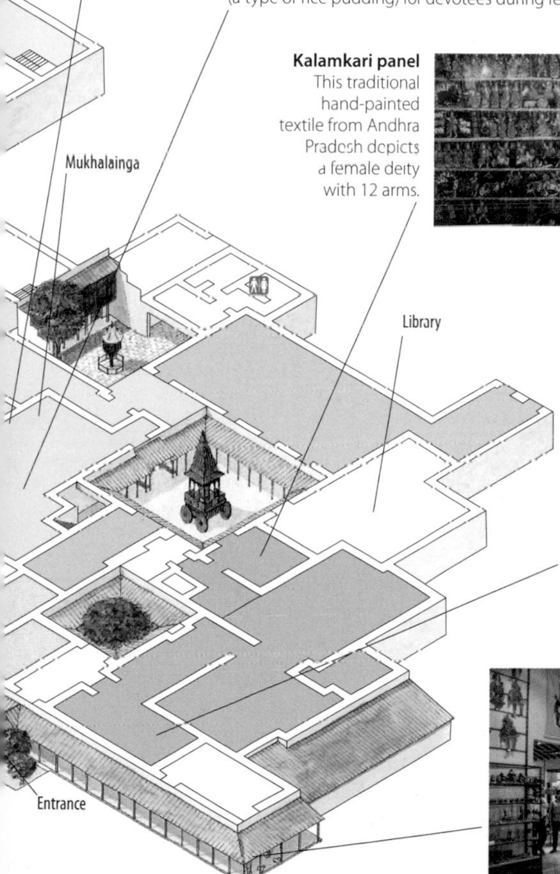

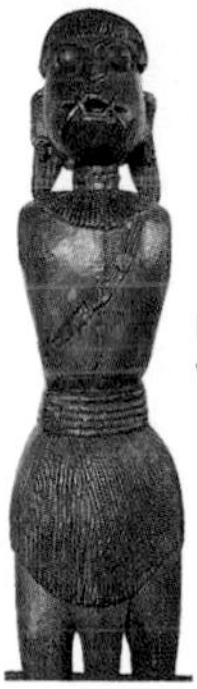

Mukhalainga
Library
Entrance

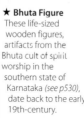

★ Bhuta Figure
These life-sized wooden figures, artifacts from the Bhuta cult of spirit worship in the southern state of Karnataka *(see p530)*, date back to the early 19th-century.

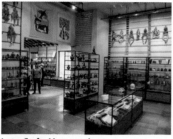

Lota, Crafts Museum shop
This shop sells a fine selection of items made by indigenous artisans, including house-hold objects, decorative pieces and textiles.

Gallery Guide

The museum's exhibits are spread over two floors of the complex, divided into separate areas by courtyards that also double up as exhibition spaces. A large open area is used for live art displays by visiting artisans each month, except during the rainy season.

⑮ Nizamuddin Complex

W of Mathura Rd. Dargah: **Open** daily. Qawwali performance: 7pm Thu. 🎵 Urs (Jul & Dec).

This medieval settlement, or *basti*, is named after Sheikh Hazrat Nizamuddin Auliya, whose grave and hospice are located here. Nizamuddin belonged to a fraternity of Sufi mystics, the Chishtis, respected for their austerity, piety and disdain for material desires, and was a spiritual descendant of Moinuddin Chishti *(see p380)*. His daily assemblies drew both the rich and the poor, who believed that he was a "friend of God" who would intercede on their behalf on Judgement Day. He died in 1325 but his disciples call him a *zinda pir* (living spirit) who continues to heed their pleas. A three-day Urs is observed, with *qawwalis* sung, on the anniversary of his death, and another on the death of his disciple Amir Khusrau.

The congregational area in the Nizamuddin Complex

A winding alley leads to the saint's grave. It is crowded with mendicants and lined with stalls selling flowers and *chadors* (ceremonial cloths), polychrome clocks and prints of Mecca. The main congregational area is a marble pavilion (rebuilt in 1562) where, every Thursday evening, followers sing devotional songs composed by the celebrated Persian poet, Amir Khusrau (1253–1325). Women are denied entry beyond the outer verandah but may peer through *jalis* into the small, dark chamber where the saint's grave lies draped with a rose petal strewn cloth, surrounded by imams who continuously recite verses from the Koran. Amir Khusrau is buried in the complex, as are other eminent disciples, such as Jahanara Begum.

Colourful stalls in the alley leading to Nizamuddin's tomb

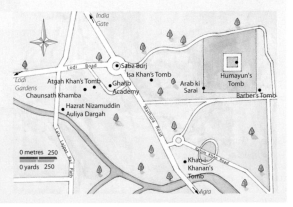

Tomb of the famous poet Mirza Ghalib

Across the western side of the open courtyard is the red sandstone Jama't Khana Mosque, built in 1325. To its north is a *baoli* (stepwell), excavated in secret while Tughluqabad *(see p99)* was being built, because Ghiyasuddin Tughluq had banned all building activities elsewhere. Legend has it that labourers worked here at night with the help of lamps lit not with oil but with water blessed by Nasiruddin, Nizamuddin's successor. The early 16th-century **Tomb of Atgah Khan** is to the north. A powerful minister in Emperor Akbar's court, he was murdered by Adham Khan, a political rival *(see p97)*. The open marble pavilion, **Chaunsath Khamba** ("64 pillars"), is close by and just outside is an enclosure containing the simple grave of Mirza Ghalib (1786–1869). One of the greatest poets of his time, Ghalib wrote in both Urdu and Persian, and his verses are still recited. Nearby is the **Ghalib Academy**, a repository of paintings and manuscripts.

Despite its crowds, the *basti* preserves with miraculous serenity the legend of Nizamuddin, described by Khusrau as "a king without throne or crown, with kings in need of the dust of his feet".

Nizamuddin Complex

One of Delhi's historic necropolises, many of the saint's disciples, such as Amir Khusrau and Jahanara Begum, Shah Jahan's favourite daughter, are buried close to their master. Jahanara's epitaph echoes her master's teachings: "Let naught cover my grave save the green grass, for grass well suffices as a covering for the grave of the lowly".

[Map labels:] India Gate • Lodi Road • Sabz Burj • Isa Khan's Tomb • Lodi Gardens • Atgah Khan's Tomb • Ghalib Academy • Arab ki Sarai • Humayun's Tomb • Chaunsath Khamba • Barber's Tomb • Hazrat Nizamuddin Auliya Dargah • Mathura Road • Lala Lajpat Rai Path • Khan-i-Khanan's Tomb • Begum Khan Road • Agra

0 metres 250
0 yards 250

⑯ Humayun's Tomb

Humayun, the second Mughal emperor *(see p83)*, is buried in this tomb, the first great example of a Mughal garden tomb, and inspiration for several later monuments, such as the incomparable Taj Mahal *(see pp176–7)*. Built in 1565 by Persian architect Mirak Mirza Ghiyas, it was commissioned by Humayun's senior widow, Haji Begum. Often called "a dormitory of the House of Timur", the graves in its chambers include Humayun's wives and Dara Shikoh, Shah Jahan's scholarly son. Also in the complex are the octagonal tomb and mosque of Isa Khan, a 16th-century nobleman, and the tomb of Humayun's favourite barber. The Arab ki Sarai was a rest house for the Persian masons who built the tomb.

VISITORS' CHECKLIST

Practical Information
Off Mathura Rd, Bharat Scout Guide Marg.
Tel (011) 2435 5275.
Open daily. 🚗 🏫 🚻 ♿

The perfectly symmetrical Humayun's Tomb as seen from the entrance

The Dome
This imposing white marble double dome is a complete half-sphere, and is surmounted by a finial with a crescent in the Persian style. Later Mughal finials, such as the one at the Taj Mahal, added a lotus base.

Geometric designs inlaid on panels

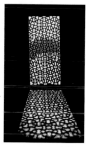

Jalis
Fine trellis work in stone later became a signature Mughal feature.

The Tomb Chamber
The plain white marble sarcophagus stands on a simple black and white marble platform. The grave itself, no longer accessible, lies in the dark basement below.

The imposing plinth is decorated with red sandstone arches and consists of multiple chambers, a departure from the single chamber of previous tombs.

⑰ Street-by-Street: Chandni Chowk

Once Shahjahanabad's *(see p95)* most elegant boulevard, Chandni Chowk ("Silvery, Moonlit Square"), laid out in 1648, had a canal running through it, and was lined with grand shops and mansions. Today, it is still the heart of Old Delhi, a bustling area where religious and commercial activity mix easily. At the entrance to Chandni Chowk is the Digambar Jain Temple. Built in 1656, it is the first of many shrines along the boulevard's length.

Sisganj Gurdwara
In 1675, Guru Tegh Bahadur, the ninth Sikh guru, was beheaded at this site.

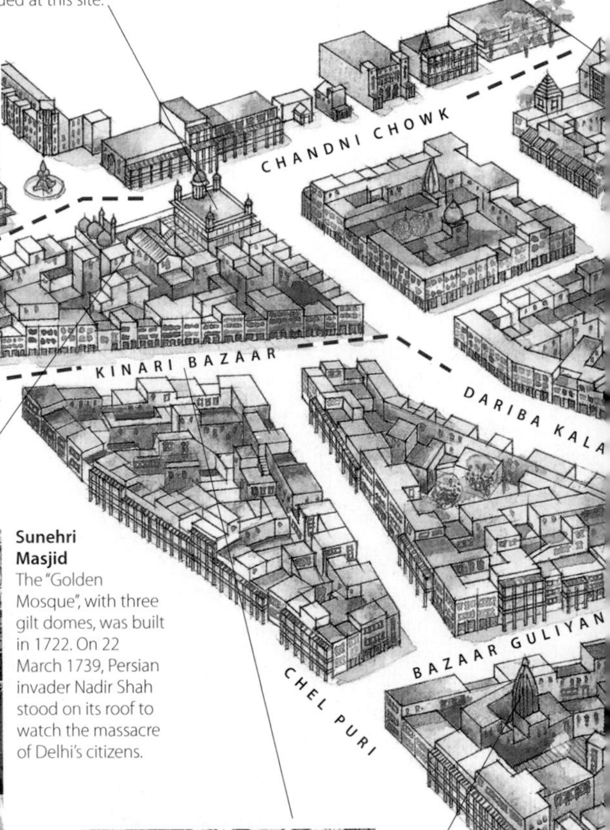

Charity box for donations at the Bird Hospital

CHANDNI CHOWK

Fatehpuri Masjid (built in 1650)

KINARI BAZAAR

Nai Sarak

DARIBA KALA

Sunehri Masjid
The "Golden Mosque", with three gilt domes, was built in 1722. On 22 March 1739, Persian invader Nadir Shah stood on its roof to watch the massacre of Delhi's citizens.

CHEL PURI

BAZAAR GULIYAN

Shiv Temple

★ **Kinari Bazaar**
Tightly packed stalls sell all manner of glittering gold and silver trimmings such as braids, tinsel garlands and turbans for weddings and festivals.

0 metres	25
0 yards	25

★ Lahore Gate
This imposing red sandstone gateway is the main entrance to the Red Fort *(see p90)*. The Prime Minister addresses the Independence Day rally here.

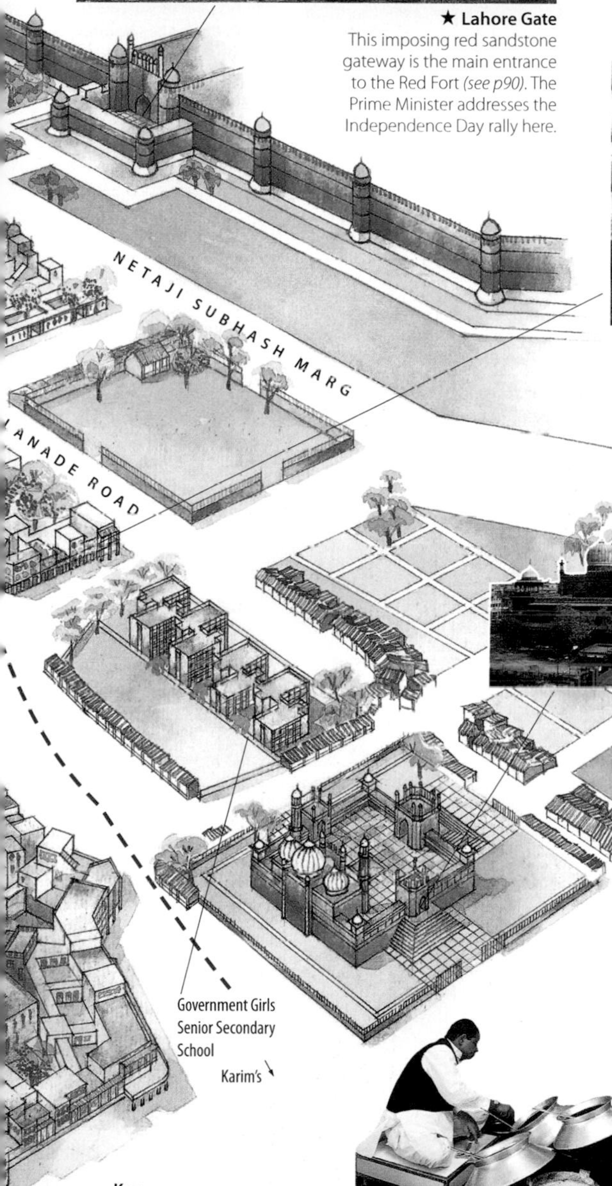

Locator Map
See Delhi Map pp74–5

★ Dariba Kalan
Gold and silver ornaments are sold along this lane. Gulab Singh's famous perfume shop *(see p100)* is located here.

NETAJI SUBHASH MARG

ANADE ROAD

★ Jama Masjid
India's largest mosque, Jama Masjid, with its soaring minarets and vast marble domes, is grandly positioned on top of a mound *(see p90)*.

Government Girls
Senior Secondary
School

Karim's

Karim's
Tucked away in a narrow lane to the south of Jama Masjid is Delhi's most authentic Mughlai eatery *(see p706)*. Named after a legendary 19th-century chef, the restaurant is now run by his descendants.

Key

— Suggested route

The sandstone and marble Jama Masjid, India's largest mosque

⑱ Jama Masjid

Off Netaji Subhash Marg. Ⓜ Chawri Bazaar. **Closed** for non-Muslims during prayer time and after 5pm. Extra charges for photography.

Built on the orders of the Emperor Shah Jahan, this grand mosque, with three imposing black and white marble domes, and twin minarets framing its great central arch, took six years and 5,000 workers to construct, at a cost of nearly a million rupees. It was completed in 1656. A magnificent flight of sandstone steps leads to the great arched entrances. In Aurangzeb's time, the area attracted horse sellers and jugglers; today, shoe minders and beggars mill around. The huge 28-m (92-ft) square courtyard can accommodate up to 20,000 people at Friday prayer sessions and at Id, when it looks like a sea of worshippers. The south minaret is an attraction for visitors as it offers unrivalled views across all of old Delhi. The 120 steps leading to the top are narrow and can get crowded, but the views are definitely worth the effort.

⑲ Red Fort

Chandni Chowk. **Tel** (011) 2327 7705. Ⓜ Chandni Chowk. **Open** 9:30am–4:30pm Tue–Sun. **Closed** pub hols. 🎭 Son et Lumière: (English) Feb–Apr, Sep & Oct: 8:30–9:30pm daily; Nov–Jan: 7:30–8:30pm daily; May–Aug: 9–10pm daily. 🏛 Museum: **Open** Tue–Sun. 📷

Red sandstone battlements give this imperial citadel its name, Lal ("Red") Qila ("Fort"). Commissioned by Shah Jahan in 1639, it took nine years to build and was the seat of Mughal power until 1857 when the last Mughal emperor, Bahadur Shah Zafar, was dethroned and exiled. Today, the Red Fort remains a powerful symbol of Indian nationhood. It was here that the national flag was hoisted for the first time when India became an independent nation on 15 August 1947.

Entry is through **Lahore Gate**. One of the fort's six gateways, this leads on to the covered bazaar of **Chatta Chowk**, where paintings and trinkets are sold. Beyond this lies the **Naqqar Khana**, a pavilion where ceremonial music was played three times a day.

A path from here leads to the **Diwan-i-Aam**, a 60-pillared, red sandstone hall where the emperor gave daily audience to the public. The emperor sat beneath the lavishly carved stone canopy, while the low bench in front of it was for his chief minister. Beyond this hall is the **Rang Mahal**.

Inside its gilded chambers, once exclusively for women, is an inlaid marble fountain shaped like an open lotus.

Nearby, is the **Khas Mahal**, the emperor's royal apartments with special rooms for private worship and for sleeping. The Robe Room ("Tosh Khana") has a superb marble *jali* screen carved with the scales of justice, a motif seen in many miniature paintings. North of the Khas Mahal is the **Diwan-i-Khas**, built completely of white marble. The legendary Peacock Throne, embedded with priceless jewels

The throne canopy at the Diwan-i-Aam

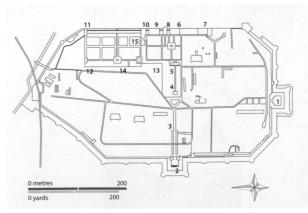

	Red Fort
1	Delhi Gate
2	Lahore Gate
3	Chatta Chowk
4	Naqqar Khana
5	Diwan-i-Aam
6	Rang Mahal
7	Mumtaz Mahal
8	Khas Mahal
9	Diwan-i-Khas
10	Hamams
11	Shah Burj
12	Sawan
13	Bhadon
14	Zafar Mahal
15	Moti Masjid

0 metres 200
0 yards 200

was kept here until it was taken away as war booty by the Persian chieftain Nadir Shah in 1739. The walls and pillars of this exclusive pavilion, where the emperor met his most trusted nobles, were once inlaid with gems. The ceiling was of silver inlaid with precious stones.

A little further away are the **Hamams** (Royal Baths) with inlaid marble floors and three enclosures. The first chamber provided hot vapour, the second scented rosewater through sculpted fountains, and the third cold water.

To the west of the baths is the elegant little **Moti Masjid** ("Pearl Mosque"), named after the pearly sheen of its marble. It was built by Emperor Aurangzeb in 1659.

Mahatma Gandhi's *samadhi* (memorial) at Rajghat

⑳ Rajghat

Mahatma Gandhi Rd. **Open** daily. Prayer meetings. 5pm Fri. Gandhi National Museum: **Tel** (011) 2331 0168. **Open** 9:30am–5:30pm Tue–Sun. **Closed** public hols. Film shows: 4–5pm Sat & Sun.

India's most potent symbol of nationhood, Rajghat is the site of Mahatma Gandhi's cremation. A sombre, black granite platform inscribed with his last words, *He Ram!* ("Oh God") now stands here. The only splash of colour comes from the garlands of orange marigolds that are draped over the platform. All visiting heads of state are taken to this *samadhi* (memorial) to lay wreaths in memory of the "Father of the Nation". On Gandhi's birthday (2 Oct) and death anniversary (30 Jan), the nation's leaders gather here for prayer meetings.

The Ashokan Pillar, rising above the ruins of Feroze Shah Kotla

Just across the road is the **Gandhi National Museum**, crammed with memorabilia, including Gandhi's letters and diaries. A framed plaque on the wall sets out his simple philosophy: "Non-violence is the pitting of one's whole soul against the will of the tyrant... it is then possible for a single individual to defy the might of an unjust empire".

㉑ Feroze Shah Kotla

Bahadur Shah Zafar Marg. Ⓜ Pragati Maidan. **Open** daily.

Only some ramparts and ruined structures remain of Feroze Shah Kotla, the palace complex of Ferozabad, Delhi's fifth city *(see p95)*, erected by that indefatigable builder Feroze Shah Tughluq. Entry is from the gate next to the Indian Express Building. At one end of the walled enclosure stand the roofless ruins of the Jama Masjid, of which only the rear wall is still extant. This was once Delhi's largest mosque and according to popular legend, Timur, the Mongol conqueror from Samarkand who sacked Delhi in 1398, came here to say his Friday prayers.

Next to the mosque are the remains of a pyramidal structure, topped by one of the Mauryan emperor Ashoka's polished stone pillars *(see p46)*. Brought from the Punjab, it was installed here in 1356 by Feroze Shah. It was from the inscriptions on this pillar that James Prinsep, the Oriental linguist, deciphered the Brahmi script, a forerunner of the modern Devanagari, in 1837.

Khuni Darwaza (the "Bloodstained Gate"), opposite the Express Building, was built by Sher Shah Sur as one of the gates to his city *(see p83)*. This was where the Emperor Bahadur Shah Zafar's sons were shot by Lieutenant Hodson after the Mutiny of 1857 was quashed *(see p57)*.

The Bazaars of Old Delhi

Old Delhi's bazaars are legendary. An English visitor over a 100 years ago, wrote in praise of the "Cashmere shawls, gold and silver embroidery, jewellery, enamels and carpets" found here. Today the great wholesale bazaars of Chandni Chowk still retain

Indian spices on sale in Khari Baoli, Asia's largest spice market

a souk-like quality. Their narrow streets are lined with shops, whose goods spill out onto the pavements. Each lane specializes in a commodity: Dariba Kalan, for instance, is the lane of jewellers and silversmiths, while Kinari Bazaar *(see p88)* sells a bewildering array of tinsel and sequins.

❷ Around Kashmiri Gate

Between Nicholson Rd, Ramlal Chandok Marg & Church Rd. **Ⓜ** Kashmiri Gate. St James's Church: Lothian Rd. **Tel** (011) 2386 0873. **Open** daily. **✝** English: 8:30am (summer), 9am Sun.

This landmark, from where the Mughals would set off to spend their summers in Kashmir, resonates with memories of the Mutiny of 1857 *(see p57)*. The short stretch between Kashmiri Gate and the Old Delhi General Post Office (GPO) witnessed bitter fighting, as the city of Delhi lay under siege by the British. A final assault led to the blasting of the Gate, and a plaque on its western side honours "the engineers and miners who died while clearing the gate for British forces on September 14, 1857". In the 1920s, this area was also a favourite haunt of the British residents living in nearby Civil Lines.

The historic **St James's Church**, Delhi's oldest, is the most striking sight in the vicinity. It was consecrated in 1836 by Colonel James Skinner. A flamboyant adventurer of mixed parentage who was rejected by the British Army, Skinner raised his own cavalry regiment which proceeded to fight with great distinction. The church was erected in fulfillment of a vow Skinner made on the battlefield. An unusual structure, the church is in the shape of a Greek cross, surmounted by an imposing eight-leafed dome. Its two stained-glass windows were installed in the 1860s. A marble tablet in front of the altar marks Skinner's simple grave.

Statues of former viceroys around the Coronation Memorial

❸ Coronation Memorial

S of NH1 Bypass. **Open** daily.

The Royal Durbar, held in 1911 to proclaim the accession of George V as King Emperor of India, was held at this site. A red sandstone obelisk commemorates the coronation. More than 100,000 people thronged to see the King Emperor and Queen Empress sit beneath a golden dome mounted on a crimson canopy. Today, it is a dusty and forlorn spot, surrounded by statues of former viceroys, including Lords Hardinge and Willingdon (distinguished for their role in the construction of New Delhi). Towering over them all is the 22-m (72-ft) high statue of the King Emperor himself, which was removed from the Statue Canopy at India Gate *(see p78)* and installed here in the 1960s.

About 3 km (2 miles) southeast is a forested park area known as the **Northern Ridge**, cut through by

Coronation Memorial

Ridge Road and Rani Jhansi Road. At its southern end lies the **Mutiny Memorial** (known locally as Ajitgarh), a Victorian Gothic tower which commemorates the soldiers "both British and native… who were killed" in 1857. Panoramic views of Old Delhi can be enjoyed from here.

Running parallel to the Northern Ridge is the sprawling **Delhi University** area. St Stephen's College, one of the most distinguished colleges dotting the campus, was designed by Walter George in 1938. The office of the Vice Chancellor, once the guesthouse for British officials, is also the spot where the young Lord Louis Mountbatten proposed to Edwina Ashley in 1922. A plaque celebrates the event. They eventually became India's last viceroy and vicereine.

❹ The Ridge

Upper Ridge Rd. **Open** daily. Buddha Jayanti Park: **Open** daily.

Delhi's ridge, the last outcrop of the Aravalli Hills extending northwards from Rajasthan, runs diagonally across the city from southwest to northeast. The area was originally developed by Feroze Shah Tughluq in the late 14th century as his hunting resort. The ruins of his many lodges can still be seen here. This green belt of undulating,

The impressive yellow and white edifice of St James's Church

rocky terrain is covered by dense scrub forest consisting mainly of laburnum (Cassia fistula), kikar (Acacia arabica) and flame of the forest (Butea monosperma), interspersed with bright splashes of bougainvillea.

A large area in the centre is now the **Buddha Jayanti Park**, a peaceful, well-manicured enclave, with paved paths. Pipal (Ficus religiosa) trees abound, and on a small ornamental island is a simple sandstone pavilion shading the large gilt-covered statue of the Buddha, installed by the 14th Dalai Lama in 1993. An inscription nearby quotes the Dalai Lama: "Human beings have the capacity to bequeathe to future generations a world that is truly human". Every year in May, Buddhist devotees celebrate Buddha Jayanti here (see p39)

㉕ National Rail Museum

Chanakyapuri. **Tel** (011) 2688 1816. **Open** Tue–Sun. **Closed** public hols 🚂 Extra for train rides. 🕐 **Open** 9.30am–5.30pm. 📷

India's railway network can boast some astonishing statistics. It has a route length of 64,460 km (40,054 miles) and tracks that cover 113,994 km (70,833 miles). There are about 7,500 stations, 12,600 passenger trains, and 1,350 goods trains that run every day. The railways employ 1.6 million people, while 25 million passengers travel by train each day, consuming 6 million meals through the course of their journey.

This museum encapsulates the history of Indian

railways. Steam locomotive enthusiasts will appreciate the collection that traces the development of the Indian railways from 1853, when the first 34 km (21 miles) of railway between Bombay (now Mumbai) and Thane was laid. The wealth of memorabilia on display inside includes the skull of an elephant that collided with a mail train at Golkara in 1894, and a realistic model of an 1868 first-class passenger coach with separate compartments for accompanying servants.

Outside, are several retired steam locomotives built in Manchester and Glasgow in the late 19th century, and the salon that carried the Prince of Wales (later King Edward VII) on his travels during the 1876 Royal Durbar. A "toy train" offers rides around the compound, and the shop sells a range of model locomotives.

㉖ Safdarjung's Tomb

Aurobindo Marg. **Open** daily. 🚂 Extra charges for video photography. 🚻

This is the last of Delhi's garden tombs and was built in 1754 for Safdarjung, the powerful prime minister of Muhammad Shah, the Mughal emperor between 1719 and 1748. Marble was allegedly stripped from the tomb of Abdur Rahim Khan-i-Khanan in Nizamuddin to construct this rather florid example of late Mughal architecture. Approached by an ornate gateway, the top storey of which houses the library of the Archaeological Survey of

India (ASI), the tomb has an exaggerated dome and stands in a charbagh, a garden cut by water channels into four parts. Its façade is extensively ornamented with well-preserved plaster carving and the central chamber has some fine stone inlay work on the floor.

A well-stocked shop selling imported foodstuffs at INA Market

㉗ INA Market

Aurobindo Marg. Ⓜ INA. Shops: **Open** Tue–Sun.

This lively bazaar retains all the trappings of a traditional Indian market but also sells imported foodstuffs such as cheese, pasta and exotic varieties of seafood. The stalls are crammed together under a ramshackle roof, mostly corrugated iron and oilcloth, and sell every manner of stainless steel utensils, spices, Punjabi pickles, readymade garments and even live chickens. Tiny restaurants in between offer Indian fast food. Diplomats, out of-town shoppers and locals all patronize this market for its reasonable prices and wide variety of products.

The name is derived from Indian National Airports, as the adjacent colony used to house employees of the nearby Safdarjung Aerodrome. Built in the 1930s, the aerodrome was the headquarters of the South Eastern Command Air Wing during World War II. It now contains the offices of the Ministry of Civil Aviation and the Delhi Gliding Club and Flying Club. Indian Airlines also has a 24-hour booking office here (see p749).

A late 19th-century steam engine at the National Rail Museum

The double-storeyed *madrasa* (school) at Hauz Khas

28 Hauz Khas

W of Aurobindo Marg. Ⓜ Hauz Khas.
Monuments: **Open** daily.

Beyond the boutiques, art galleries and restaurants that have taken over the village of Hauz Khas, are the medieval monuments from Feroze Shah Tughluq's reign. In 1352, the sultan erected a number of buildings on the banks of Hauz Khas, the large tank which was excavated by Alauddin Khilji for his city of Siri. The tank, which shares its name with the surrounding village, was revived in 2004 after being dry for many years.

Contemporary accounts claim that Feroze Shah was a prolific builder, and during his 37-year reign he constructed an astounding 40 mosques, 200 towns, 100 public baths and about 30 reservoirs.

Among the buildings around Hauz Khas are a *madrasa*, Feroze Shah's tomb and the ruins of a small mosque. The *madrasa*, close to the edge of the tank, contains plaster carvings and niches for books. The *chhatris* (open pavilions) in the entrance forecourt are said to cover the teachers' burial mounds. At one end of the *madrasa* lies the austere tomb of Feroze Shah. Wine-red painted plaster calligraphy decorates its interior.

The complex is best viewed in the afternoon, when sunlight filters through the *jalis* to cover the graves of the sultan, his sons and grandson with delicate star-shaped shadows. East of Hauz Khas, off Aurobindo Marg, is a small tapering structure called **Chor Minar** ("Tower of Thieves") dating back to the 14th- century Khilji period. Its walls, pockmarked with holes, are said to have held the severed heads of thieves, intended to deter others from crime.

Close by, to the northwest, is the **Nili Masjid** ("Blue Mosque"). Named after the blue tiles above its eaves, it was built in 1505 by a certain Kasumbhil, nurse to the governor of Delhi's son.

29 Khirkee

N of Press Enclave Marg. Ⓜ Malviya Nagar. Monuments: **Open** daily.

The unusual two-storeyed Khirkee ("Windows") Mosque, built by Feroze Shah Tughluq's prime minister, Khan-i-Jahan Junan Shah, in the mid-14th

The imposing fortress-like Khirkee Mosque

century lends its name to this little village in South Delhi. The mosque has a fortress-like appearance, broken by rows of arched windows, which give the mosque its name. Its innovative design was not repeated again as its many pillared divisions were found impractical for large congregations.

Further down is **Satpula**, the seven-arched stone weir built by Muhammad bin Tughluq in 1326. It formed part of a reservoir used for irrigation, and also made up a portion of the fortified wall enclosing Jahanpanah.

An arched window with a carved stone *jali*, Khirkee Mosque

30 Jahanpanah

S of Panchsheel Park. Monuments: **Open** daily.

In the heart of Jahanpanah, Muhammad bin Tughluq's capital, stands **Begumpuri Mosque**, also built by Khan-i-Jahan Junan Shah. (Ask specifically for the old mosque, as a new one is located nearby.) The mosque is remarkable for its 44 domes which surmount the cloisters surrounding the central courtyard. It is said that in times of need, this mosque also functioned as a treasury, a granary and a general meeting place.

To the north is the palace of **Bijay Mandal**, from where, according to the 14th-century Arab traveller Ibn Batuta, Muhammad bin Tughluq reviewed his troops. The upper platform offers a grand view of Delhi, extending from the Qutb Minar to Humayun's Tomb and beyond.

Early Capitals of Delhi

Delhi's famous "seven cities" range from the 12th-century Qila Rai Pithora, built by Prithviraj Chauhan, to the imperial Shahjahanabad, constructed by the Mughals in the 17th century. Each of these cities comprised the settlements that grew around the forts erected by powerful sultans with territorial ambitions. As the Delhi Sultans consolidated their territories, they moved their defensively situated capitals in the rocky outcrops of the Aravallis, to the northeast, towards the open plains by the banks of the Yamuna. Today, Delhi is an amalgam of the ruins of medieval citadels, palaces, tombs and mosques, and an ever-expanding, modern concrete jungle.

Shahjahanabad *was* Delhi's seventh city, built between 1638 and 1649 by Shah Jahan who shifted the Mughal capital here from Agra *(see pp172–81).*

Ferozabad *(see p91)*, stretching north from Hauz Khas to the banks of the Yamuna, is Delhi's fifth city built by Feroze Shah Tughluq (r.1351–88).

Siri, Delhi's second city can still be seen near the Siri Fort Auditorium and the adjacent village of Shahpur Jat. The once prosperous city of Siri was built by Alauddin Khilji around 1303.

Purana Qila *(see p83)*, the citadel of Delhi's sixth city, Dinpanah, was built by Humayun. It was captured and occupied by the Afghan chieftain, Sher Shah Sur (r.1540–45) who called it Shergarh.

Jahanpanah was built by Muhammad bin Tughluq (r.1325–51) as a walled enclosure to link Qila Rai Pithora and Siri. The ruined battlements of Delhi's fourth city stand near Chiragh.

Qila Rai Pithora was the first of Delhi's seven cities, built by the Chauhans in about 1180. In 1192, it was captured by Qutbuddin Aibak who established his capital here *(see pp96–7).*

Tughluqabad *(see p95)*, a dramatic fort on the foothills of the Aravallis, was Delhi's third city built during Ghiyasuddin Tughluq's four-year reign (1320–24).

③ Mehrauli Archaeological Park

Best known for the Qutb Minar, a UNESCO World Heritage Monument, Mehrauli was built over Rajput territories called Lal Kot and Qila Rai Pithora. In 1193, Qutbuddin Aibak, then a slave-general of Muhammad of Ghur *(see p52)*, made it the centre of the Delhi Sultanate. By the 13th century the small village, Mehrauli, had grown around the shrine of the Sufi saint, Qutb Sahib. Later, Mughal princes came here to hunt and some 19th-century British officials built weekend houses, attracted by the area's orchards, ponds and game. Many of Delhi's rich and famous now own sprawling retreats in the area.

Dargah Qutb Sahib
The 13th-century *dargah* of Sufi saint Qutbuddin Bakhtiyar and the nearby Moti Masjid ("Pearl Mosque") attract many pilgrims.

0 metres 250
0 yards 250

★ Jahaz Mahal
Venue of the Phoolwalon ki Sair (a colourful flower procession), this square pleasure pavilion, built during the Lodi era (1451–1526), seems to float on the Hauz-i-Shamsi tank.

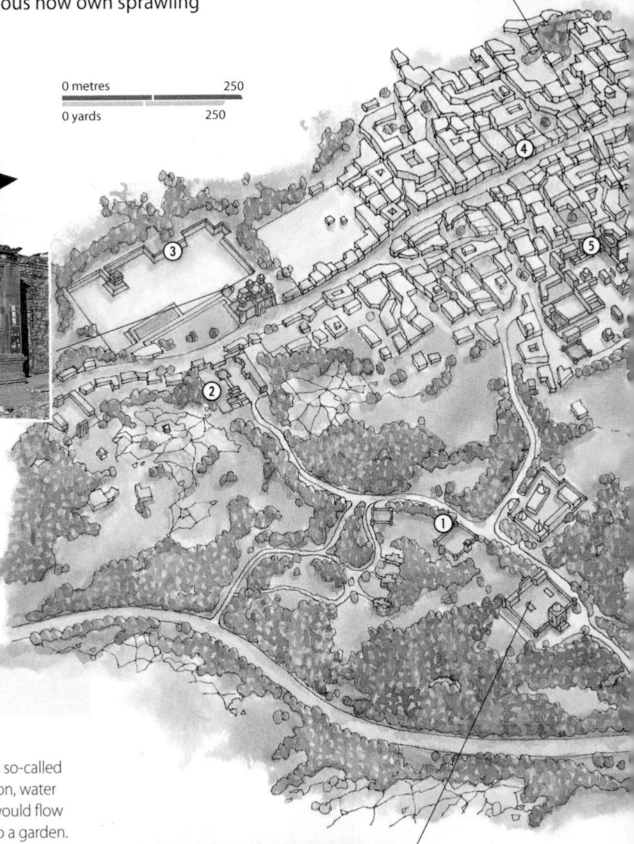

KEY

① **Bagichi Mosque**

② **Jharna** (waterfall) was so-called because after the monsoon, water from the Hauz-i-Shamsi would flow over an embankment into a garden.

③ **Hauz-i-Shamsi** reservoir was built in 1230 by Sultan Iltutmish *(see p52)*, who is supposed to have been guided to this site by the Prophet in a dream.

④ **Mehrauli village**

⑤ **Zafar Mahal** is a palace named after the last Mughal emperor, Bahadur Shah Zafar.

⑥ **Dilkusha Gardens**

Madhi Masjid
Surrounded by bastions and a high wall, this fortress-like mosque, dating back to 1200, has a large open courtyard and a three-arched, heavily ornamented prayer hall.

Adham Khan's Tomb
The son of Emperor Akbar's wet nurse, Adham Khan murdered a political rival and was executed by the emperor for his crime. Akbar later built this large tomb for mother and son.

VISITORS' CHECKLIST

Practical Information
Delhi-Gurgaon Rd.
Open daily. 🛈 Conservation Assistant's Office, (011) 2664 3856.
🌳 📷 🚻 🏍 🛍 Phoolwalon ki Sair (early Oct).

★ Qutb Minar
India's highest single tower, Qutb Minar (Arabic for pole or axis), marked the site of the first Muslim kingdom in North India, established in 1193 (see p98).

← New Delhi

Rajon ki Baoli
This dramatic three-storeyed stepwell was also called Sukhi Baoli (dry well). Nearby is the five-storeyed Gandhak ki Baoli, named after its strong sulphur (gandhak) smell. These *baolis* once supplied fresh water to the area.

Balban's Tomb
The 13th-century tomb of Balban, Qutbuddin's successor, lies in a square rubble-built chamber.

★ Jamali-Kamali Mosque and Tomb
The tomb of Jamali (the court poet during the late Lodi and early Mughal age) is inscribed with some of his verses. Its well-preserved interior has coloured tiles and richly decorated painted plasterwork. The second grave is unidentified but is widely believed to be that of his brother, Kamali.

Mehrauli: The Qutb Complex

The Qutb Minar towers over this historic area where Qutbuddin Aibak laid the foundation of the Delhi Sultanate *(see p52)*. In 1192, he built the Quwwat-ul-Islam ("Might of Islam") Mosque and the Qutb Minar to announce the advent of the Muslim sultans. The mosque is a patchwork fusion of decorative Hindu panels, salvaged from razed temples around the site, and Islamic domes and arches. Later, Iltutmish, Alauddin Khilji and Feroze Shah Tughluq added more structures, heralding a new architectural style.

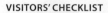

Iron Pillar
This 4th-century pillar, originally made as a flagstaff in Vishnu's honour, is a tribute to ancient Indian metallurgy.

Qutb Minar
The five-storeyed Victory Tower started by Qutbuddin Aibak was completed by his successor, Iltutmish.

Carved Panels
Panels carved with inscriptions from the Koran embellish the gateway.

Entrance

Alai Darwaza
This gateway to the complex, erected in 1311 by Alauddin Khilji, is one of the earliest buildings in India to employ the Islamic principles of arched construction.

Quwwat-ul-Islam Mosque
Hindu motifs, such as bells and garlands, are clearly visible on the pillars of this mosque.

Pots displayed at the unique Sanskriti Museum

❷ Sanskriti Museum

Anandgram, Mehrauli-Gurgaon Rd.
Tel (011) 2650 1796. **Open** 10am–5pm Tue–Sun. **Closed** public hols.
W sanskritifoundation.org

This unusual museum is set amid beautifully landscaped, spacious grounds. Exhibits are displayed both in the garden and in specially constructed rural huts. The collection itself is equally unusual in its devotion to objects of everyday use, that have been exquisitely crafted by unknown, rural artisans. OP Jain, whose personal collections gave birth to this museum, has donated combs, nutcrackers, lamps, toys, foot-scrubbers and kitchenware, to demonstrate how even the most utilitarian objects can possess an innate beauty. Terracotta objects from all over India, in every shape and size, are also on display. They include pots made in traditional techniques unchanged for centuries, and figures of South Indian village deities.

❸ Tughluqabad

Off Mehrauli-Badarpur Rd.
Monuments: **Open** daily.

The third of Delhi's early capitals (see p95), Tughluqabad is dominated by its spectacular fort, built by Ghiyasuddin Tughluq early in the 14th century. The fort was so sturdily constructed that its rubble-built walls, following the contours of the hill, survive intact all along the 7-km (4-mile) perimeter. Rising from the citadel to the right of the main entrance are the ruins of the Vijay Mandal ("Tower of Victory"). To the left is a rectangular area where arches are all that remain of a complex of palaces, houses and halls. Legend has it that when Ghiyasuddin tried to prevent the building of the *baoli* at Hazrat Nizamuddin Auliya's *dargah* (see p86), the saint cursed him, saying that one day only jackals and the Gujjar tribe would inhabit his capital.

A good view of the fort and of the smaller, adjoining Adilabad Fort, is possible from the walls. Adilabad was built by Muhammad bin Tughluq, who is believed to have killed his father Ghiyasuddin by

Ghiyasuddin Tughluq's Tomb

contriving to have a gateway collapse on him. Both are buried in **Ghiyasuddin's Tomb**, attached to the Tughluqabad Fort by a causeway that crossed the dammed waters of a lake. Constructed in red sandstone and inlaid with white marble, the tomb's sloping walls pioneered a style that was used in all subsequent Tughluq architecture.

❹ Baha'i House of Worship

Bahapur, Kalkaji. **Tel** (011) 2644 4029.
M Kalkaji Mandir. **Open** 9am–5:30pm Tue–Sun. **Closed** public hols. Prayer services: 10am, noon, 3pm & 5pm.

Delhi's most innovative modern structure, the Baha'i House of Worship is a world where silence and order prevail. Designed by the Iranian architect Fariburz Sahba, it was completed in 1986. The arresting shape of its unfurling, 27-petalled, white marble lotus has given it its more popular name, the Lotus Temple. The edifice is circled by nine pools and 92 ha (227 acres) of green lawns.

The Baha'i sect originated in Persia and is based on a view of humanity as one single race. Followers of all faiths are invited to meditate and attend the daily 15-minute services in the lofty auditorium, which can seat up to 1,300 people.

The lotus-domed Baha'i House of Worship, one of Delhi's most spectacular sights

Shopping & Entertainment in Delhi

The hallmark of shopping in Delhi is the bewildering variety of merchandise, markets and styles. Besides Connaught Place, almost every residential colony boasts a market. Old, established shops, bazaars and markets co-exist happily with glitzy, high-end boutiques and department stores and one can buy anything from seasonal fruits and traditional handicrafts to designer clothes and the latest imported electronic items. Delhi also has a rich and varied cultural life. The city's cultural calendar livens up between October and March when the season is in full swing. The number of events multiply as all major festivals of music, dance, theatre and cinema are held at this time of the year.

Shops and Markets

New Delhi's main shopping centres are in and around Connaught Place and Janpath where the state emporiums and Cottage Industries offer an exciting and varied range of textiles, jewellery and souvenirs at fixed and reasonable prices. In the north is Chandni Chowk (see pp88–9), the traditional market, while to the south are Khan Market, Sundar Nagar and Santushti, the old urban villages of Hauz Khas, Shahpur Jat and Mehrauli, and Dilli Haat, a crafts bazaar on Aurobindo Marg. The five-star hotels also have convenient shopping arcades selling carefully selected goods.

Antiques, Jewellery and Silver

Genuine antiques are rare to come by and, in any case, cannot be taken out of the country unless certified by the ASI (see p735). However, **Lota**, the Crafts Museum shop, hotel boutiques and Sundar Nagar market stock excellent reproductions of miniature paintings, woodcarvings and bronzes made by artisans today. Superb pieces of traditional jewellery, including kundan and meenakari, are available at Sundar Nagar market, especially at **Bharany's**. Silver jewellery, both traditional and modern, can be found in the gullies of Dariba Kalan, in Chandni Chowk and Sundar Nagar. **Ravissant** and **Cooke &**

Kelvy are the best places for contemporary silverware.

Textiles, Shawls and Carpets

Traditional textiles are available in most of the better shops and emporiums, particularly **Cottage Industries** on Janpath. A wide and exclusive selection of personal care products are on offer at **Forest Essentials** in Khan Market. **The Shop**, **Anokhi** and **FabIndia** are the best places for good quality ready-made garments, linen and light cotton quilts. Lodi Colony market has several boutiques offering eclectic Indian designer-wear, including the stylish **Abraham & Thakore**. **Shyam Ahuja** sells linen, textiles and dhurries, while **The Carpet Cellar** is an excellent outlet for Afghan and Kashmiri carpets and pashmina shawls.

Handicrafts and Gifts

Lota, the Crafts Museum shop, **Tulsi**, **Kamala** and Dilli Haat have a wide selection of Indian handicrafts and other gift items, while **Tibet House** has woollen shawls, jackets, thangkas and carpets. For quality leather goods such as, handmade shoes and jackets, the many Chinese-owned outlets in Connaught Place, set the standards for comfort and durability. For trendier goods there is **Da Milano**.

In Chandni Chowk's Dariba Kalan is **Gulab Singh Johari Mal**,

a marvellous old-fashioned shop where one can test Indian perfume (attar) from cut-glass bottles. Their soaps are also worth buying. Herbal cosmetics, incense sticks, perfumed candles and aromatherapy oils and lotions are available in many of the larger stores, including **Good Earth**, which also stocks towels, bathrobes and massage mats. Cosmetics by Vama Ayurveda, Biotique and Shahnaz Herbal are found at most chemists.

Spices and fresh seasonal fruit are found at INA Market (see p93) and Indian tea is sold in Kaka Nagar Market (near the Oberoi Hotel on Zakir Hussain Marg), Khan Market and at **Mittal Tea House** in Lodi Colony market.

Entertainment Guides, Tickets and Venues

All newspapers list the day's entertainment on their engagements page. Other useful sources of information on events, restaurants, sports and related activities are the fortnightly TimeOut Delhi and the monthly First City.

At several venues in the city, such as the **India International Centre**, entry is free. At others, such as the **Indian Council for Cultural Relations** (ICCR), it is by invitation only. Tickets for selected music and dance festivals and theatre, however, are advertised and sold at certain bookshops or at the box office.

Most of Delhi's cultural activities are clustered around Mandi House (see p79). The largest auditorium, **Kamani** on Copernicus Marg, hosts concerts, plays and classical music and dance performances throughout the year. During the season, music and dance events are also held at FICCI Auditorium, on the roundabout, **Triveni Kala Sangam**, on Tansen Marg, and at Azad Bhavan, the main venue for performances organized by the state-run ICCR. Excellent plays, in both Hindi and English, are held at the open air auditorium of the **National School of Drama**, the main repertory company at Bhawalpur House, and at the **Shri Ram Centre** nearby. Colourful folk dances from all over India, organized by the **Trade Fair Authority of India**, are held during the annual Trade India Fair in November, at Pragati Maidan, the huge exhibition grounds on Mathura Road.

Both the **India Habitat Centre** and the India International Centre, on Lodi Road, organize a variety of events that include films, plays, concerts, exhibitions, lectures and discussions. The mega **Siri Fort Complex**, in South Delhi, is the venue for most prestigious events.

Popular Indian and foreign films are screened at the many cinema halls dotted all over the city. Among the better equipped halls are **PVR Select Citywalk** and **DT Cinemas** in Saket.

Performing Arts

Delhi is the best place to experience the range and richness of classical dance and music. Performances by the best exponents of the major styles of Odissi, Kathak, Bharat Natyam and Kathakali take place during the high season, between October and March. The same is true of concerts of Hindustani and Carnatic classical music. India's vibrant folk dance and music traditions, such as the devotional music of the Sufis, dance-dramas from Kerala, puppet shows from Rajasthan and Karnataka, can also be seen at various venues. Check newspapers for details on location and tickets.

Exhibitions

Major exhibitions are held at the **National Museum**, **National Gallery of Modern Art**, **Art Heritage** and the **Crafts Museum**. These include special collections of rare sculpture and paintings from museums all over India, as well as from abroad. Recent years have seen exhibitions of Picasso's paintings, the Nizam of Hyderabad's fabulous jewels and Mughal paintings from Queen Elizabeth II's private collection.

Regular exhibitions of contemporary art and craft, photography and graphics are also held in the many art galleries around Mandi House.

DIRECTORY

Antiques, Jewellery and Silver

Bharany's
14, Sundar Nagar Market.
Tel (011) 2435 8528.

Cooke & Kelvy
Janpath.
Tel (011) 2331 3712.

Lota (Crafts Museum)
Pragati Maidan.
Tel (011) 2337 1269.

Ravissant
New Friends Colony Market.
Tel (011) 2683 7278.

Textiles, Shawls and Carpets

Abraham & Thakore
D-16, 2nd Floor, Moonriver, Defence Colony.
Tel 9871774436.

Anokhi
Khan Market.
Tel (011) 2460 3423.

The Carpet Cellar
1 Anand Lok.
Tel (011) 2626 1777.

Cottage Industries
Janpath.
Tel (011) 2332 0439.

FabIndia
Greater Kailash I, N-Block Market.
Tel (011) 4669 3724.

Forest Essentials
45-B, Khan Market.
Tel (011) 4175 7057.

The Shop
Connaught Place.
Tel (011) 2334 0971.

Shyam Ahuja
Santushti.
Tel (011) 2467 0112.

Handicrafts and Gifts

Da Milano
Connaught Place.
Tel (011) 2341 5490.

Good Earth
9ABC, Khan Market.
Tel (011) 2464 7175.

Gulab Singh Johri Mal
Dariba Kalan, Chandni Chowk.
Tel (011) 2328 1345.

Kamala
Rajiv Gandhi Handicrafts Bhavan, Baba Kharak Singh Marg.
Tel (011) 2374 3322.

Mittal Tea House
8-A, Lodi Colony Mkt.

Tel (011) 2461 5709.

Tibet House
Lodi Rd.
Tel (011) 2461 1515.

Tulsi
Santushti.
Tel (011) 2687 0339.

Entertainment Venues

DT Cinemas
Saket.
Tel (011) 6147 5555.

India Habitat Centre
Lodi Rd.
Tel (011) 2468 2222.

India International Centre
40, Lodi Estate, Max Mueller Marg.
Tel (011) 2461 9431.

Indian Council for Cultural Relations
Azad Bhavan, IP Estate.
Tel (011) 2337 9309.

Kamani Auditorium
Copernicus Marg.
Tel (011) 4350 3351.

National School of Drama
Bhawalpur House, Bhagwan Das Rd.
Tel (011) 2338 9402.

PVR Select Citywalk
Saket.
Tel (011) 4060 1700.

Shri Ram Centre
Safdar Hashmi Marg.
Tel (011) 2371 4307.

Siri Fort Complex
Asian Village Complex.
Tel (011) 2649 3370.

Trade Fair Authority of India
Pragati Maidan.
Tel (011) 2337 1540.

Triveni Kala Sangam
205, Tansen Marg.
Tel (011) 2371 8833.

Exhibitions

Art Heritage
205, Tansen Marg, Triveni Kala Sangam.
Tel (011) 2371 9470.

Crafts Museum
Bhairon Marg, Pragati Maidan.
Tel (011) 2337 1641.

National Gallery of Modern Art
Jaipur House, India Gate.
Tel (011) 2338 2835.

National Museum
Janpath.
Tel (011) 2301 9272.

HARYANA & PUNJAB

Haryana and Punjab cover the vast plains that stretch between the River Indus and the Gangetic belt. Fertile soil and the improved agricultural techniques of the 1960s Green Revolution *(see p66)*, have made this region the granary of India, producing more than half the wheat, rice and millet grown in the country. Industrial development followed the success of the Green Revolution, and the two states now also have flourishing dairy and wool-based industries. Most visitors pass only briefly through Haryana and Punjab, usually on their way to Himachal Pradesh, taking in en route the states' two best known attractions: Chandigarh, the planned city built by the famous architect Le Corbusier, which is the shared capital of Haryana and Punjab, and the Golden Temple at Amritsar, the holiest shrine of the Sikhs. For those who care to explore further, there are the former princely states of Patiala and Kapurthala, with their distinctive architecture, and the holy *dargahs* at Panipat and Sirhind. Above all, the warmth and hospitality of the people is this area's special attraction.

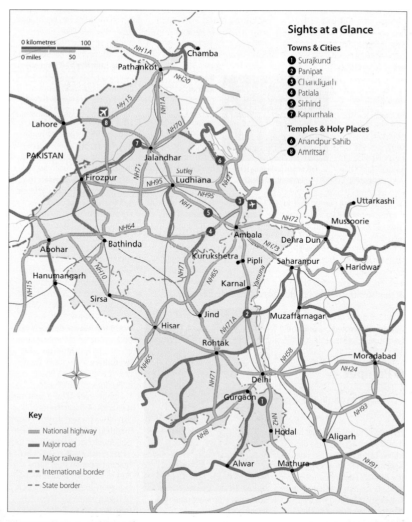

Sights at a Glance

Towns & Cities
1 Surajkund
2 Panipat
3 Chandigarh
4 Patiala
5 Sirhind
7 Kapurthala

Temples & Holy Places
6 Anandpur Sahib
8 Amritsar

Key
▬ National highway
▬ Major road
— Major railway
- - International border
- - State border

◀ The Golden Temple at sunset, Amritsar

For keys to symbols *see back flap*

Sufi saint Qalandar Shah's *dargah* at Panipat, built in the 14th century

① Surajkund

Faridabad district. 21 km (13 miles) S of Delhi. ⊞ ⅰ Haryana Tourism, Chanderlok Building, 36, Janpath, New Delhi, (011) 2332 4910. 🖼 Surajkund Crafts Mela (Feb).

This historic reservoir, built between the 10th and 11th centuries by King Surajpal of the Rajput Tomar dynasty, is today a popular picnic spot. Also known as the Lake of the sun, the original embankment of stone terraces surrounding the tank, specially built to trap rainwater, still exists. Nearby, an artificial lake is well-equipped with boating

Folk singers performing at the Surajkund Crafts Mela

facilities. The area comes alive in the first two weeks of February, when an excellent crafts *mela* is held here, with artisans from all over India selling their wares in a specially created village. Puppets from Rajasthan, bell metal beasts from Odisha, and mirrorwork from Gujarat are displayed alongside a variety of food stalls, while musicians and folk dancers weave through the crowds, giving the fair a joyous, carnival air.

② Panipat

Panipat district. 89 km (55 miles) N of Delhi. 🚉 ⊞ 🖼 Urs of Qalandar Shah (Jul/Aug).

The site of three decisive battles that changed the course of Indian history, including one which led to the founding of the Mughal Empire *(see pp54–5)* in 1526, Panipat is situated on a flat, dusty plain and traces its history to the epic age. The

older part of the town has some interesting *havelis*, and a 14th-century tomb-shrine dedicated to the Sufi saint Qalandar Shah. The new town is a busy, bustling settlement, strung along National Highway 1, which follows the route of the historic Grand Trunk Road *(see p183)*. Today, Panipat is well-known for its furnishing fabrics and carpets.

Environs
Karnal, 34 km (21 miles) north of Panipat, lies at the heart of a rich pastoral region and is an important agricultural and cattle breeding centre. The National Dairy Research Institute is situated here. Some 90 km (56 miles) north of Panipat, the pilgrim town of **Kurukshetra** is dotted with temples and marks the mythical site of the epic battle between the Pandavas and Kauravas, the heroes of the *Mahabharata (see p30)*.

Ritual prayers at the sacred temple tank at Kurukshetra

③ Chandigarh

Chandigarh district. 248 km (154 miles) N of Delhi. 🚊 900,500. ✈ 8 km (5 miles) S of city centre. 🚌 🖼 ⅰ Interstate Bus Terminal, SCO 1064–65, Sector 22-B, (0172) 278 1138. 🖼 Rose Festival (Feb).

The state capital of both Haryana and Punjab, Chandigarh was built in the early 1950s by the internationally renowned architect Le Corbusier. It is considered the first modern city of post-Independent India and is laid out on a grid, divided evenly into 57 blocks or sectors.

Le Corbusier conceived the city along the lines of a modular man, with the **Capitol Complex**, which includes the Secretariat, Assembly and High Court buildings, as its "head". The main shopping area, **Sector 17**, is the "heart" of Le Corbusier's plan, and is set around a central plaza and fountain, lined with shops indicating that Chandigarh's affluent citizens are extremely fond of good food and clothes. Adjoining this sector is a gently undulating stretch of green, the city's "lungs", with an enormous **Rose Garden** that is at its best in February. Over 1,000 varieties of colourful roses bloom amidst winding paths, fountains and sprawling, beautifully tended lawns.

The city's extensive residential sectors make up its "torso", with neat houses and gardens showing impressive evidence of the residents' green fingers. Each road is lined with a different species of flowering tree – laburnum, jacaranda, *gulmohar* – adding colour to the cityscape.

Chandigarh's **Museum and Art Gallery** in Sector 10 houses one of the country's finest collections of Gandharan sculpture *(see p47)* and miniature paintings. Among the best exhibits are a serene 6th-century Standing Bodhisattva in the Gandharan style, and a rare 11th-century statue of Vishnu holding a conch shell from Kashmir. The miniatures section has a comprehensive selection of Pahari paintings *(see p125)* from the Kangra, Basohli and

Chandigarh's Capitol Complex, typical of Le Corbusier's functional style

Guler schools, while modern art includes mountainscapes by the Russian painter Nicholas Roerich *(see p132)*.

Lying opposite the Capitol Complex, the **Rock Garden** is one of the city's most popular tourist spots. Spread over 1.6 ha (4 acres) in Sector 1, it was created in the 1970s by an ex-road inspector, Nek Chand, and is a refreshing contrast to Le Corbusier's severely symmetrical cityscape. The area encloses a unique "kingdom", a labyrinth with hills, waterfalls and caves, and serried ranks of sculptures crafted from such unlikely material as discarded neon lights, fuse switches, broken crockery and glass.

A short distance away is the man-made **Sukhna Lake**, where a pleasant promenade attracts joggers and walkers. This is one of Chandigarh's prettiest areas, especially in the evenings, when visitors can enjoy dramatic sunsets and views of the twinkling lights of the nearby hill station, Kasauli *(see p117)*.

Ceramic figures at Nek Chand's Rock Garden

🏛 **Museum and Art Gallery**
Tel (0172) 274 2501/0261. **Open** 10am–4:30pm Tue–Sun. 📷

Environs
The **Pinjore Gardens**, lying 22 km (14 miles) north of Chandigarh, were designed in the 17th century by Fidai Khan, foster brother of the Mughal emperor Aurangzeb. They are terraced in the Mughal style and dotted with domed pavilions, fountains and water chutes. **Sanghol**, 40 km (25 miles) west of Chandigarh, has an excavated site of a 2nd-century Buddhist stupa with an interesting museum of Kushana sculpture.

Festivals of Haryana & Punjab

Surajkund Crafts Mela *(1–15 Feb)*, Surajkund. Craftsmen from all over the country gather with a selection of their wares, from fabrics to folk toys.

Rose Festival *(Feb)*, Chandigarh. The city's vast Rose Garden hosts flower shows and a weekend of dance and music.

Hola Mohalla *(Mar/Apr)*, Anandpur Sahib. The highlight of this fair, held the day after Holi, is a spectacular display of fencing and tent-pegging, as the Nihang Sikhs show off their legendary martial and equestrian skills.

Skilled swordsmanship at the Hola Mohalla festivities

Baisakhi *(13 Apr)*. Several gala processions, dancing and feasting take place all over Punjab to mark the spring equinox and the beginning of the harvest. Lively *melas* are held at all the major gurdwaras.

Qalandar Shah's Urs *(Jul/Aug)*, Panipat. This festival honours the Sufi saint Qalandar Shah with qawwali singing and a colourful fair at his shrine.

Guru Purab *(Nov)*. Celebrated across Punjab on the first full moon night after Diwali *(see p41)*, the birthday of Guru Nanak, the founder of Sikhism, is particularly spectacular at the Golden Temple at Amritsar. Thousands of lamps illuminate the temple every night from Diwali onwards.

Le Corbusier's City

The "open hand", Chandigarh's emblem

In 1950, India's first prime minister, Jawaharlal Nehru, commissioned the French-Swiss architect Charles Edouard Jeanneret ("Le Corbusier") to create a new capital for Punjab, as the old capital, Lahore, had become a part of Pakistan after Independence in 1947. The result was a city of concrete blocks and straight arterial roads, projecting Le Corbusier's philosophy of functional efficiency, free of unnecessary ornamentation such as domes and arches. Without any crowded bazaars, Chandigarh lacks the typical bustle and vitality of older Indian towns, and some of Le Corbusier's buildings now look weather-beaten. Yet it remains the country's cleanest and most orderly city and this, perhaps, is Le Corbusier's lasting legacy.

The splendid Durbar Hall at the Qila Mubarak, Patiala

❹ Patiala

Patiala district. 63 km (39 miles) SW of Chandigarh. 🚗 303,000. 🚉 🚌 🎏 Basant (Feb). 🛍 Mon–Sat.

Patiala, situated between the Satluj and Ghaggar rivers, was formerly a princely state, ruled by a string of flamboyant rulers in the 19th century, who made its name a byword for everything larger than life. Thus, the "Patiala Peg" is a whopping measure of whisky, the Patiala *salwar* three times the width of an ordinary one, and the gargantuan palace, to quote an overawed English visitor, "makes Versailles look like a cottage". Its rulers were also enthusiastic patrons of the arts, architecture and sports, and the city's gracious ambience and its rich folk crafts owe a great deal to their generous encouragement.

The present city has grown around the **Qila Mubarak**, a fort built in 1763. Its oldest part, Qila Androon, though derelict, has traces of fine wall paintings. The **Durbar Hall**, added later, stands to the right of the entrance gates and is now a museum with a beautifully ornamented ceiling and well-preserved murals. Inside it, is a spectacular display of cannons and arms, including the sword of the Persian ruler Nadir Shah *(see p56)* who invaded India in 1739. The lively bazaar around the fort offers the city's famous

A typical *phulkari* motif

hand-crafted leather shoes *(jutties)*, tasselled silken braids *(pirandis)* and brightly embroidered *phulkari* fabric.

The enormous **Old Moti Bagh Palace**, completed in the early years of the 20th century in the Indo-Saracenic style, has as many as 15 dining halls. Counted as one of the largest residences in Asia, it is set amidst terraced gardens and water channels, inspired by Mughal gardens. The terraces lead to the Sheesh Mahal, where the **Art Gallery** displays miniature paintings, rare manuscripts, objets d'art, and hunting trophies from the former royal collection. Pride of place is given to a collection of medals, some awarded to, and some collected by, the former rulers. The Art Gallery overlooks a large tank flanked by two towers, with a rope suspension bridge to connect them. The main palace has now been given

Hand-embroidered *jutties* on sale in Patiala's bazaar

over to the National Institute of Sports and the large pleasure pool where the maharaja once watched dancing girls cavorting has been converted into a wrestling pit.

In the north of the city are the **Baradari Gardens**, laid out in the late 19th century by Prince Rajinder Singh, an avid horticulturist, who also created a rock garden and fern house here. The splendid **Kali Temple**, which is located within the walled city, has a large marble image of Kali, brought here all the way from Makrana in Rajasthan.

🏛 **Durbar Hall Museum**
Open Tue–Sun. 📷 without permission. ♿

🏛 **Old Moti Bagh Palace**
Open Tue–Sun. ♿

❺ Sirhind

Fatehgarh Sahib district. 55 km (34 miles) W of Chandigarh. 🚗 31,000. 🚉 🚌 ℹ️ Punjab Tourism, (01763) 22 9170. 🎏 Urs at Rauza Sharif (Aug), Shaheedi Jor Mela (Dec).

The town of Sirhind was one of the most important settlements in North India between the 16th and 18th centuries. Once the capital of the Pathan Sur sultans, the ruins of whose massive fort can still be seen, Sirhind was also a favourite halting place for the Mughal emperors on their annual journeys to Kashmir. In the 11th century, Mahmud of Ghazni *(see p52)* expanded his empire up to this area, thus giving the town its name, which in Persian means "Frontier of India".

The Mughals constructed several beautiful buildings here, in the area now called **Aam Khas Bagh**, which today is a tourist complex run by the government. Especially interesting is the **Royal Hamam**, a complex structure for hot and cold baths, that uses water drawn from wells nearby through an intricate system of hand pulleys. Close to the baths are the ruins of Shah Jahan's double-storeyed palace, the **Daulat Mahal**, and the better preserved **Sheesh**

Rauza Sharif, Sahaikh Ahmad Faruqi Sirhindi's *dargah* in Sirhind

Mahal, whose walls still have traces of the original tilework and decorative plaster.

To the north of Aam Khas Bagh is the white **Fatehgarh Sahib Gurdwara**, standing in the midst of bright yellow mustard fields, which bloom in January. It was built to honour the memory of the martyred sons of the tenth Sikh guru, Gobind Singh, who were walled in alive at this spot by the Mughal emperor Aurangzeb in 1705, for refusing to convert to Islam.

Adjacent to the gurdwara is an important pilgrimage site for Muslims, the tomb-shrine of the Sufi saint and theologian, Shaikh Ahmad Faruqi Sirhindi, who is also known as Mujaddad-al-Saini ("The Reformer of the Millennium"). This magnificent octagonal structure, with its dome covered in glazed blue tiles, was built in the 16th century. Known as the **Rauza Sharif**, it is considered as holy as the Dargah Sharif in Ajmer *(see p380)*. Standing close to it is a striking tomb from the same period, the **Mausoleum of Mir Miran**, son-in-law of one of the Lodi kings. Also of interest is the **Salavat Beg Haveli**, a fascinating and exceptionally well preserved example of a large Mughal-era house.

🏠 **Aam Khas Bagh**
Open Tue–Sun.

⊙ Anandpur Sahib

Roopnagar district. 73 km (45 miles) N of Chandigarh. 🚉 31,000. 🚗 🚌 🛺 Hola Mohalla (Mar/Apr).

Guarded by the Shivalik Hills and a ring of imposing forts, Anandpur Sahib is a complex of historic Sikh gurdwaras. It was here that the severed head of the ninth guru, Tegh Bahadur, was brought to be cremated, at a site now marked by the **Sisganj Sahib Gurdwara**. The gurdwara also marks the place where the tenth and last guru, Gobind Singh, founded the Khalsa or "Army of the Pure" in 1699, along with five volunteers to help him defend the faith. The **Kesgarh Sahib Gurdwara**, which was built to commemorate this event, is regarded as one of the four *takhts* or principal seats of the Sikh religion – the others are at Amritsar *(see p108)*, Nanded in Maharashtra, and Patna *(see p218)* in Bihar. A week-long celebration was held here in April 1999, to mark the 300th anniversary of the Khalsa.

A series of forts surround Anandpur Sahib on all sides – **Lohagarh Fort** was used as the armoury of the Khalsa army, **Fatehgarh Fort** guarded the route between Delhi and Lahore, and **Taragarh Fort** protected it from attacks by the hill states lying to the north.

Anandpur Sahib comes to life every year during the Hola Mohalla festival *(see p105)* when thousands of devotees congregate here to watch the blue-robed Nihang Sikhs, descendants of the gurus' personal guards, display heir formidable martial and equestrian skills.

A Nihang Sikh in full regalia

Sikhism

A mid-19th-century painting of Guru Nanak with his disciples

With their characteristic turbans and full beards, the Sikhs are easy to identify. The Sikh religion is a reformist faith, founded by Guru Nanak in the 15th century. Strongly opposed to idol worship, rituals and the caste system, it believes in a formless God. Sikhism is also called the Gurmat, meaning "the Guru's Doctrine" and Sikh temples are known as gurdwaras, literally "doors to the guru". Nanak, the first of a series of ten gurus, chose his successor from among his most devout disciples. Gobind Singh (1666–1708), the tenth and last guru, reorganized the community in 1699 as a military order, the Khalsa, to combat religious persecution by the Mughals. He gave the Sikh community a distinctive religious identity, and from then onwards they were meant to wear the Khalsa's five symbols: *kesh* (long hair), *kachha* (underwear), *kirpan* (small sword), *kangha* (comb) and *kara* (bracelet). Their holy book, the *Guru Granth Sahib*, is kept in the Golden Temple *(see pp110–11)*.

Detail of a marble sculpture, Elysée Palace, Kapurthala

❼ Kapurthala

Kapurthala district. 165 km (103 miles) NW of Chandigarh. 🚉 🚌

This former princely state owes its extraordinary architectural heritage to the eccentric Maharaja Jagatjit Singh, who created amidst the rich agricultural fields of Punjab, a corner that will be forever France. In 1906, this passionate Francophile, commissioned a French architect to build him a palace modelled on Versailles, with elements of Fontainebleu and the Louvre added on. This amazing structure, which he grandly named the Elysée Palace (now the **Jagatjit Palace**), sits amidst gardens embellished with stone statuary and fountains, and is surrounded by villas built for his officials, modelled on those that were in vogue in the suburbs of Paris in the late 19th century. The palace is now a school, but the building with its ornate interiors and Renaissance-style painted ceilings, is open to public. After this palace was built,

the maharaja went through a Spanish phase. This found expression in the **Buena Vista Hunting Lodge**. Located on the outskirts of the town, it is occupied by his descendants. Another impressive sight is the town's **Moorish Mosque**. Inspired by the grand Qutubiya Mosque in Marrakesh, this was designed by yet another French architect employed by Jagatjit Singh. Its inner dome has been beautifully painted by Punjabi artists.

🏛 **Jagatjit Palace**
Open Tue–Sun. 📷

The Jagatjit Palace at Kapurthala, modelled on Versailles in France

Maharaja Ranjit Singh

Maharaja Ranjit Singh was one of North India's most remarkable rulers. By persuading rival Sikh chieftains to unite, he established the first Sikh kingdom of the Punjab. A military genius, his strong army kept both the British and ambitious Afghan invaders at bay, making Punjab a prosperous centre of trade and industry. A devout

Maharaja Ranjit Singh (r.1790–1839)

Sikh who did much to embellish the Golden Temple, the one-eyed Ranjit Singh was an enlightened ruler who liked to say "God intended me to look at all religions with one eye". A decade after his death, the British annexed the Punjab and seized his fabulous treasures, including the famous Kohinoor diamond.

❽ Amritsar

Amritsar district. 227 km (141 miles) NW of Chandigarh. 🚊 1,500,000. ✈ 12 km (8 miles) NW of city centre. 🚉 🚌 ℹ Palace Hotel opp railway station, (0183) 240 2452. 🎉 Guru Purab (Nov).

Founded in 1577 by the fourth Sikh guru, Ram Das, Amritsar was built on a site donated by the Mughal emperor Akbar. Located in the heart of the city is the **Golden Temple** *(see pp110–11)*, the Sikh community's holiest shrine, surrounded by a maze of lanes and 18 fortified gateways. In 1984, parts of the Golden Temple were badly damaged during an army operation to flush out extremists holed up inside, who were demanding a separate Sikh homeland. It has now been repaired and carefully restored to its original glory.

The temple complex is actually a city within a city, and the main entrance is through its northern gateway, known as the **Darshani Deorhi**, which also houses the **Central Sikh Museum**. On display are paintings, coins, manuscripts and arms, that combine to create a vivid picture of Sikh history. Steps lead down to the **Parikrama** (marble pathway) which encircles the **Amrit Sarovar** ("Pool of Nectar", after which the town is named), and the main shrine, the golden-domed **Harmandir Sahib** ("Temple of God"). Several holy and historic sites line the Parikrama, among them a tree shrine called the **Gurudwara Dukh Bhanjani Ber**, said to have miraculous powers for healing diseases, and the **Ath-Sath Tirath**, which represents 68 of the holiest Hindu pilgrim shrines.

The Parikrama continues on to the **Sri Akal Takhat Sahib**, the seat of the Sikh religious order. Its construction began in 1589 and was completed in 1601 by the sixth guru, Guru Hargobind, when he began organizing the Sikh community into a political entity. The upper floors were built by Maharaja Ranjit Singh. As part of the daily

View of the Golden Temple complex, with the central shrine and main entrance

ritual, the Holy Book of the Sikhs, the *Guru Granth Sahib*, is carried out of the Sri Akal Takhat Sahib to the Harmandir Sahib at daybreak. The head priest then opens it for the *vaq*, the message for the day. From dawn till late at night the temple echoes with the music of *ragis*, musicians employed by the temple trust to sing verses from the Holy Book. Every visitor entering the Harmandir Sahib (including non-Sikhs) is given a dollop of sweet *prasad* (holy offering), and no visit is considered truly complete without a meal at the **Guru ka Langar**, a free kitchen where all visitors are fed a simple meal of *dal-roti* (lentil curry and bread). Run by volunteers, this kitchen can feed 10,000 people a day. Its vast hall, which can seat 3,000 people at a time, serves as a symbol of the caste-free, egalitarian society that the Sikh gurus strove to create. The notion of *kar-seva* (voluntary manual labour for a cause) is an important part of the Sikh order. Tasks such as sweeping the temple precincts, cooking at the *langar* or looking after the pilgrims' shoes, are enthusiastically performed by volunteers. The final evening prayers are over by 9:45pm, when the Holy Book is reverently closed and carried in a silver

Memorial, Jallianwala Bagh

palanquin back to the Sri Akal Takhat Sahib. The floors of the temple are then washed with milk and water before the doors of the Darshani Deorhi are closed.

A few other shrines are found just outside the Temple complex. These include a shrine dedicated to Guru Hargobind Singh, as well as the nine-storeyed **Baba Atal Tower** which marks the spot where Atal Rai, the son of Hargobind attained martyrdom. The 16th-century **Durgiana Temple**, visited by Hindus, is dedicated to Durga. It lies 2 km (1.3 miles) northeast of the Golden Temple.

Jallianwala Bagh, also a short distance from the Golden Temple, is the site of an infamous massacre that took place in 1919. Hundreds of unarmed demonstrators were gunned down in this enclosed garden on the orders of General Reginald Dyer, who arrived heading a platoon of infantry from Jalandhar. It was an event which helped hasten the end of British rule in India. A memorial to those killed stands at the east end.

Environs

The last checkpost on the Indian border with Pakistan is at **Wagah**, 29 km (18 miles) from Amritsar. Each evening, as buglers sound the last post, two splendidly uniformed guards on either side of the border goose step across to the flagpoles to lower their respective national flags. Their steps are matched so perfectly that it is like watching a mirror image of the same exercise. The ceremony, which attracts crowds of spectators on both sides, is a poignant reminder of the Partition of 1947 *(see p60)*, when Punjab was divided between two nations.

Ceremonial guards outside the Sri Akal Takhat Sahib

Amritsar: The Golden Temple

The spiritual centre of the Sikh religion, the Golden Temple was built between 1589 and 1601, and is a superb synthesis of Islamic and Hindu styles of architecture. In keeping with the syncretic tradition of those times, its foundation stone was laid by a Muslim saint, Mian Mir. It was virtually destroyed in 1761 by an Afghan invader, Ahmed Shah Abdali, but was rebuilt some years later by Maharaja Ranjit Singh, ruler of Punjab, who covered the dome in gold and embellished its interiors with lavish decoration.

First Floor
The marble walls have *pietra dura* inlay and decorative plasterwork, bearing animal and flower motifs covered in gold leaf.

Harmandir Sahib
The holiest site for Sikhs, the three-storeyed temple, decorated with superb *pietra dura*, is where the Holy Book is kept during the day.

★ **Sheesh Mahal**
The Hall of Mirrors on the top floor has a curved *bangaldar* roof, and its floors are swept with a special broom made of peacock feathers.

★ **Guru Granth Sahib**
Covered by a jewelled canopy, the Holy Book lies in the Durbar Sahib ("Court of the Lord").

Sri Akal Takhat Sahib
The seat of the supreme governing body of the Sikhs, it houses the gurus' swords and flagstaffs, as well as the Holy Book at night.

VISITORS' CHECKLIST

Practical Information
Circular Rd. ℹ Information Bureau, (0183) 255 3954.
Open daily. Photography allowed outside shrines. Visitors must remove their shoes, wash their feet & cover their heads with a scarf at the entrance. Alcohol & tobacco are forbidden within the complex.

4
3
5

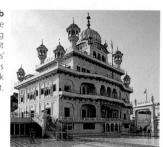

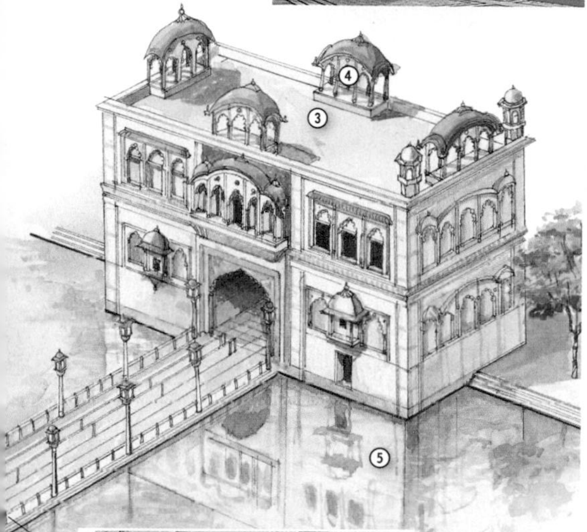

KEY

① **The lower wall** of the temple is made of white marble.

② **The dome**, shaped like an inverted lotus, is covered in 100 kg (220 lbs) of gold donated by Ranjit Singh in 1830.

③ **Darshani Deorhi** is a gateway, which provides the first glimpse of the temple's inner sanctum. It has two splendid silver doors and sacred verses carved on its walls.

④ **Sri Akal Takhat Sahib**

⑤ **Amrit Sarovar**, the pool where Sikhs are baptized, was built in 1577 by Ram Das, the fourth guru.

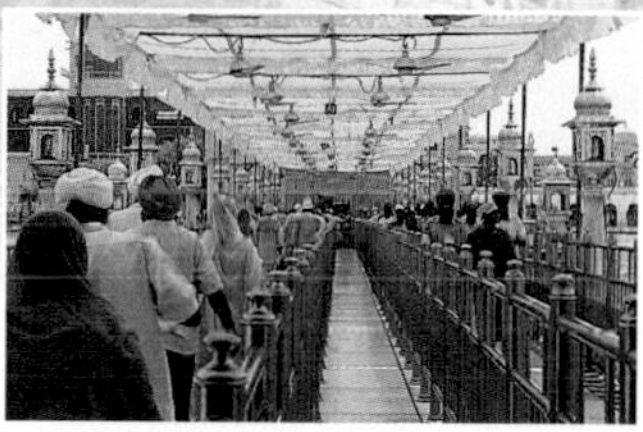

The Causeway
The 60-m (197-ft) long marble causeway is flanked by nine gilded lamps on each side, and leads to the temple across the Amrit Sarovar.

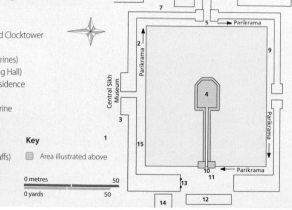

Golden Temple Complex

1 Temple Office
2 Cloakrooms
3 Darshani Darwaza and Clocktower
4 Harmandir Sahib
5 Ath-Sath Tirath (68 Shrines)
6 Guru ka Langar (Dining Hall)
7 Baba Karak Singh's Residence
8 Assembly Hall
9 Baba Deep Singh's Shrine
10 Darshani Deorhi
11 Arjun Dev's Tree
12 Sri Akal Takhat Sahib
13 Nishan Sahibs (Flagstaffs)
14 Gobind Singh's Shrine
15 Beri Baba Buddhaji (Tree Shrine)

Key
Area illustrated above
0 metres 50
0 yards 50
Parikrama
Central Sikh Museum
1
2
3
4
5
6
7
8
9
10
11
12
13
14
15

HIMACHAL PRADESH

Himachal, the "Abode of Snow", covers over 56,000 sq km (21,622 sq miles) of the Western Himalayas. The state's terrain rises from the foothills of the Shivaliks bordering the plains of Punjab, and extends to the trans-Himalayan heights of the Zanskar Range, bordering Ladakh and Tibet. Himachal's capital Shimla, famous as the summer capital of the British Raj, remains a popular destination for visitors. Manali, the state's other big hill station, is in the heart of the idyllic Kullu Valley. Watered by the Beas river, it is an excellent base for treks and excursions. West of Kullu, with the magnificent Dhauladhar Range as its backdrop, is the Kangra Valley, dotted with apple orchards. Its main town is Dharamsala, home to the Dalai Lama and a vibrant Tibetan community, and the seat of the Tibetan Government-in-Exile. In the eastern part of the state is Kinnaur with its green pastures and enchanting villages, while Lahaul and Spiti to the north are lands of rugged grandeur, with Buddhist monasteries clinging to steep, rocky cliffs.

Sights at a Glance

Towns & Cities
- **5** Nahan
- **6** Rampur
- **7** Sarahan
- **10** Mandi

Hill Stations & Areas of Natural Beauty
- **1** Shimla
- **2** Chail
- **3** Narkanda
- **4** Kasauli
- **12** Dharamsala

- **13** Dalhousie
- **14** Chamba
- **15** Bharmour
- **19** Manali

Monasteries
- **21** Tabo Monastery

Valleys & Districts
- **9** Kinnaur
- **11** Kangra Valley

- **16** Kullu Valley
- **17** Parvati Valley
- **20** Lahaul and Spiti

National Parks
- **18** Great Himalayan National Park

Tours
- **8** Sangla Valley Tour

0 kilometres 50
0 miles 50

Pir Panjal Range
Chenab
Pattan Valley
Udaipur
Trilokinath
Darcha
Keylong
Tandi
20
Hansa
Rohtang Pass
13
Khajjiar
14
15
Manimahesh Lake
Dhauladhar Range
Kaza
Pathankot
Kotla
12
17
Gaggal
19
Naggar
21
Masroor
11
Palampur
Beas
NH 20
Jogindernagar
16
Manikaran
17
Jwalamukhi
NH1A
18
9
NH70
10
Rewalsar
Rekong Peo
Jalandhar
Govind Sagar
Sutlej
7 NH 22
8 Chitkul
NH 70
Bilaspur
6
NH 21
Naldera
3
Yamunotri
NH 88
1 Kufri
Gangotri
2
4
Solan
Uttarkashi
Chandigarh
5 NH 72
Mussoorie
Ambala
Dehra Dun

Key

- ═══ National highway
- ━━━ Major road
- ═══ Minor road
- ──── Railway
- ─ ─ International border
- ─ ─ State border

◄ The Lahaul Valley with the Himalayas in the background

For keys to symbols *see back flap*

❶ Shimla

A popular hill station in North India, Shimla's spectacular location, thickly forested slopes and invigorating climate have attracted countless visitors since the small village was discovered by Captain Charles Kennedy in the early 19th century. In 1864, it became the summer headquarters of the British government in India. Today it is the fast-growing capital of Himachal Pradesh. Though many of the surrounding spurs and forests are now covered with concrete buildings, Shimla still retains much of its colonial charm.

Christ Church and the Library on the Ridge

🚋 The Ridge
N of The Mall.

A popular promenade and the centre of Shimla's busy social and cultural scene, the Ridge, situated at a height of 2,230 m (7,316 ft), is an open stretch of land on the western shoulder of Jakhu Hill. From here, the snowcapped peaks of the Himalayan Range stretch in an arc across the northern horizon. Ceremonial parades and official state functions are also held here.

🏛 Christ Church
Open daily. 🕐 8am, 11am Sun. Contact caretaker if church is closed.

Dominating the eastern end of the Ridge is the Gothic Christ Church, a prominent landmark. Constructed in 1846, it was one of the first churches built in North India. Its fine stained-glass windows and impressive organ were acquired in the 19th century. The now absent fresco around the chancel window was designed by Lockwood Kipling, Rudyard Kipling's father. Shimla's mock-Tudor **Library** is nearby.

🏛 The Mall
Shops: **Open** Mon–Sat. Restricted vehicular movement.

This 7-km (4-mile) long thoroughfare, running from Boileauganj in the west to Chhota Shimla in the southeast, demarcates the original limits of the town. The central section of The Mall, flanked by rows of half-timbered buildings, has always been, and still remains, its most fashionable area with a profusion of restaurants, bars and upmarket shops. The Mall's highest spot, Scandal Point, is marked by a statue of Lala Lajpat Rai, the famous freedom fighter. The so-called "scandal" refers to the reputed abduction of an English

lady in the late 19th century from this spot by a Maharaja of Patiala (see p106). Nearby are the timber-framed Post Office, the Town Hall and the jewel-like Gaiety Theatre, opened in 1887, and still a popular venue for amateur dramatics; the theatre has recently been restored to its Victorian glory. A favoured pastime for both local residents and visitors, is to stroll along The Mall, from Scandal Point to Combermere Bridge. Further ahead on this stretch lies the mock-Tudor Clarkes Hotel.

🏛 Lower Bazaar
Shops: **Open** Mon–Sat.

Below the central section of The Mall is the Lower Bazaar, which Kipling once referred to as "that crowded rabbit warren catering to the native population of Shimla". Offering the option of cheaper wares and less fashionable hostelries and eating places, it remains the poor man's Mall. Lower still is the **Ganj**, a congested bazaar where the town's wholesale trade in groceries takes place. This, more than any other part of town, retains a flavour of times gone by. Customers and coolies mingle in crowded lanes redolent with the aroma of the many spices on display.

🏛 State Museum
Chaura Maidan. **Tel** (0177) 280 5044. **Open** Tue–Sun. **Closed** public hols. 📷 ♿

The State Museum, housed in a restored and expanded Raj building called Inverarm, was opened to the public in 1974. It has, since then, built up a fairly good collection of almost 10,000 artifacts from various parts of Himachal Pradesh. The exhibits, displayed in 15 galleries, include stone sculptures dating

The interior of the Gaiety Theatre, a focal point of Shimla's cultural life

from the 6th to 11th centuries, belonging to the Gupta and Pratihara periods, and a collection of Kangra miniatures *(see p125)* representing various themes, based on the seasons *(Baramasa)*, musical modes *(Ragamala)* and episodes from the *Gita Govinda*, a devotional poem. Most impressive, however, is a spectacular series of mid-19th-century wall paintings from Chamba.

🏛 Jakhu Hill Temple

Jakhu Hill. **Open** daily.

The forested dome of Jakhu Hill, at 2,450 m (8,038 ft) is the highest point in Shimla. At its peak stands a temple dedicated to the monkey god, Hanuman. A 33 m (108 ft) high statue of Hanuman towers over the temple. According to the epic *Ramayana* *(see p31)*, Hanuman rested here during his journey to fetch the Sanjivini herb from the Himalayas to save the wounded Lakshman's life. A steep 2 km (1.3 miles) climb from the Ridge to the summit through deodar and oak forests offers panoramic views of Shimla and its suburbs. Monkeys are a common sight all over Shimla but Jakhu is their kingdom. Visitors should watch out for

simian hands rifling through their pockets and belongings.

🚌 Viceregal Lodge

The Mall. **Tel** (0177) 283 1375. **Open** daily. 🎫 🚻

The most imposing British-built building in Shimla is the former Viceregal Lodge. Situated atop Observatory Hill, this grey stone structure in the English Renaissance style was built under the guidance of Lord Dufferin in 1888, as a suitable summer residence for the viceroys of India. Well-maintained gardens surround the stately mansion on three sides. The interior is as impressive, with two rows of balconies overlooking the magnificent teak-panelled entrance hall. A bronze plaque behind the building lists the peaks visible at

a distance. It is now called Rashtrapati Niwas and houses the Indian Institute of Advanced Study. Only the entrance hall, a couple of rooms on the ground floor, a picture gallery and the gardens are open to the public.

The stately Viceregal Lodge, set amid manicured lawns

Shimla City Centre

① The Ridge
② Christ Church
③ The Mall
④ Lower Bazaar

0 metres   200
0 yards   200

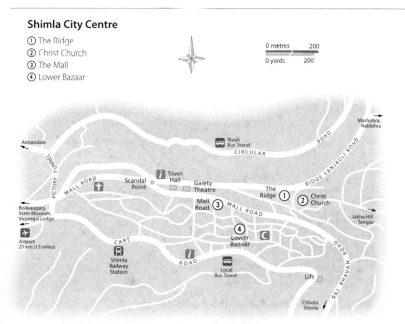

View from Kufri, under a heavy blanket of snow in winter

Exploring Shimla

The best way to explore Shimla is to walk along the many meandering roads and byways. Beyond the centre *(see pp114–15)*, the glade of **Annandale** is accessed by a sharp slope and is 5 km (3 miles) northwest of the Ridge. During the Raj, several social and sporting events such as fancy fairs, races and cricket matches were held here. Today, it has a nine-hole golf course and a fine museum of army history. The **Glen**, another popular picnic spot is further west. Both can be reached by a road that branches off near the Oberoi Cecil *(see p697)*. This grand colonial structure, built on a precipice, is reminiscent of Raj-era luxury. A 4-km (2.5-mile) long forest road, starting from Christ Church on the Ridge, continues along the wooded slopes of Jakhu Hill. This road winds southeast to end near one of Shimla's oldest educational institutions, St Bede's College for Women, en route overlooking

Musk deer in the Himalayan Nature Park

the quaint bazaar of Chhota Shimla. Deeper into the hills and along the same ridge system as Shimla, are a number of places to visit. At Charabra, 13 km (8 miles) north of Shimla, **Wildflower Hall**, the former retreat of the Commander-in-Chief, Lord Kitchner, is now a plush hotel *(see p697)*. About 10 km (6 miles) north along the old Hindustan-Tibet (HT) Road, just above the diversion to the left leading to the village of **Mashobra**, a gravel road barred by a gate to the right, indicates the entrance to the **Seog Wildlife Sanctuary** and the old Seog rest house. The sanctuary is home to local species of wildlife, including deer, hill fox and monal pheasants; with permits visitors can visit the sanctuary. At Mashobra, a steep forest pathway leads to a lovely little temple dedicated to a local deity, set in a grove of deodars. The annual Sipi Fair is held here.

Continuing north from Mashobra, 3-km (2-mile) along a motor road, is the **Craignano Rest House**. Once the home of an Italian chef, the Chevalier Peliti, it commands superb views from its hilltop garden. Further north (10 km/6 miles) is **Naldehra** with a nine-hole golf course set amidst sloping meadows

and fringed by deodar and blue pine. A British legacy dating from the 19th century, the golf course was designed by the viceroy, Lord Curzon. About 16 km (10 miles) east of Shimla, is the picturesque little village of **Kufri**, which is at an altitude of 2,650 m (8,694 ft). Kufri's small zoo, the **Himalayan Nature Park**, counts the Himalayan black bear and the musk deer among its residents.

⌂ Seog Wildlife Sanctuary
For permission contact: Divisional Forest Officer, Shimla Municipal Corporation. **Tel** (0177) 265 2911. ⌂

⌂ Himalayan Nature Park
Kufri. **Open** daily. ⌂

❷ Chail

Solan district. 45 km (28 miles) SE of Shimla. 🚌 *i* Hotel Chail Palace, (01792) 248 141.

This tiny hill station is situated on a wooded ridge at a similar altitude to Shimla. Chail was developed as the summer capital of the Patiala maharajas *(see p106)* in the 1920s. **Chail Palace**, a stone mansion occupying a flattened hilltop, amid beautiful orchards and garden, is now a deluxe hotel *(see p696)*. The cricket pitch, near the top of a hill, is said to be the highest in the world. The Patiala rulers, enthusiastic cricketers themselves, invited the Marylebone Cricket Club (the MCC) to play here in 1933. Walks through the deodar forests of the Chail Wildlife Sanctuary, where Scottish red deer were introduced, are the best way to discover Chail's natural beauty.

Naldehra's scenic golf course

A temple on Hatu Peak, a day's hike from Narkanda

❸ Narkanda

Shimla district. 64 km (40 miles) N of Shimla. 🚌

Narkanda, at a height of 2,750 m (9,022 ft), stands on the HT Road as it winds along the edges of the ridge line dividing the Satluj and Yamuna catchments. From here, the Himalayan peaks are even closer, and the walks through dense temperate forests where spruce, fir and high-altitude oak take over from the deodar and blue pine, are quite spectacular. The best walk is the 6-km (4-mile) hike to Hatu Peak (3,300 m/10,827 ft), which is crowned by a temple dedicated to Hateshwari Devi. The area around Narkanda is lush with apple orchards. In winter, the slopes are ideal for skiing.

❹ Kasauli

Solan district. 77 km (48 miles) S of Shimla. 🚹 5,000. 🚌

The closest hill station to the plains, Kasauli offers the charm of quiet walks shaded by *chir* pine, oak and horse chestnut trees. It is at its best just after the monsoon, when colourful dahlias cover the hillsides. As an army cantonment, restrictions imposed by the authorities have prevented the old town from being taken over by concrete modern structures. As a result, old-fashioned buildings with gable roofs and wooden balconies remain intact on the **Upper** and **Lower Malls**, the two main streets that run right through the town. **Monkey Point**, the highest spot in the town, is 4 km (2.5 miles) from the bus station. From here there are clear views of Shimla, the meandering Satluj and Chandigarh. A 5-km (3-mile) trail from Kasauli leads to the **Lawrence School** at Sanawar, a public school founded by Sir Henry Lawrence (*see p201*) in 1847.

Postbox, Kasauli

Environs

About 60 km (37 miles) northeast of Kasauli is **Nalagarh**, the seat of the former princely state of Hindur. The palace is now a heritage hotel called the Nalagarh Fort Resort (*see p697*).

Hill Stations

By the late 19th century, when the British had consolidated their rule in India, families began to come over from Britain to join their menfolk. In the years that followed, more than 80 settlements were established in the lower hill ranges, as summer retreats for the burgeoning expatriate population, keen to escape the intense heat of the plains. Hill stations endeavoured to recreate a way of life reminiscent of the home country, complete with half-timbered houses, clubs, churches, hospitals, parks with bandstands and a main street invariably known as The Mall. Boarding schools, with excellent teaching facilities, were also set up for children who were unable to go back to study in England.

Kennedy's Cottage, by Captain J Luard, Shimla, 1822

Colourful Kinnauri shawls on sale at the Lavi Fair, Rampur

Trekking in Himachal Pradesh

This mountainous state, with its vast variety of terrains, offers a wide range of treks from easy, one-day hikes to week-long routes. At lower altitudes, trails wind through forests of oak, deodar (*Cedrus deodara*) and pine, while steeper climbs lead to flower-strewn alpine meadows above the tree line. The towns of Manali and Dharamsala are starting points for several popular treks. The best season for trekking is during the month of June, and then later between mid-September and October, after the monsoon. During the rains (June–September), the trans-Himalayan cold deserts of Spiti (*see p134*) and Upper Kinnaur are ideal destinations, completely shielded from monsoon showers.

Locator Map

☐ Area shown below

0 km   20

0 miles   20

Dharamsala to Macchetar

A challenging 75-km (47-mile) route crosses rocky terrain to the meadows at Triund. A steep ascent leads to the Indrahar Pass, with views of the Pir Panjal peaks, and ends at the small town of Macchetar, connected by road to Chamba.

Duration: 5 days
Altitude: 4,350 m (14,272 ft)
Level of difficulty: Moderate to tough

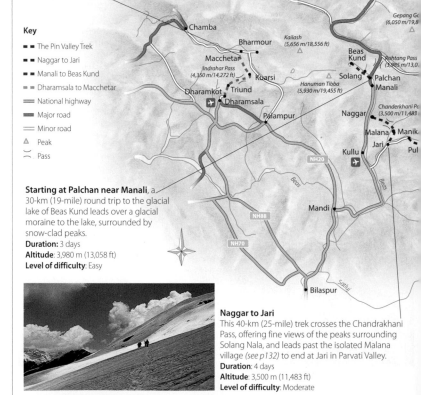

Key

- ▪ ▪ The Pin Valley Trek
- ▪ ▪ Naggar to Jari
- ▪ ▪ Manali to Beas Kund
- ▪ ▪ Dharamsala to Macchetar
- ▬ National highway
- ▬ Major road
- ═ Minor road
- △ Peak
- ⌣ Pass

Starting at Palchan near Manali, a 30-km (19-mile) round trip to the glacial lake of Beas Kund leads over a glacial moraine to the lake, surrounded by snow-clad peaks.

Duration: 3 days
Altitude: 3,980 m (13,058 ft)
Level of difficulty: Easy

Naggar to Jari

This 40-km (25-mile) trek crosses the Chandrakhani Pass, offering fine views of the peaks surrounding Solang Nala, and leads past the isolated Malana village (*see p132*) to end at Jari in Parvati Valley.

Duration: 4 days
Altitude: 3,500 m (11,483 ft)
Level of difficulty: Moderate

The Pin Valley Trek

Starting at Manikaran, famous for its hot springs, the 130-km (81-mile) path goes over the Pin-Parvati Pass to the cold desert region of the beautiful Pin Valley. It ends at Mikkim, 40 km (25 miles) from the main roadhead at Kaza.

Duration: 7 days
Altitude: 5,319 m (17,451 ft)
Level of difficulty: Tough

Practical Tips

Be prepared: Acclimatization is essential for areas over 3,000 m (9,843 ft). See p743 for tips on altitude sickness. Guides are needed as maps are insufficient for safe passage across glaciers. For details on trekking, see p727.
On the trek: Drink plenty of water. Carry a first aid kit and cooking fuel. Never burn wood, which is a scarce resource. Put out all fires properly, leaving no burning embers. Do not litter, and carry your rubbish back with you.
Permits: Foreign visitors require travel permits for parts of Spiti and Kinnaur, obtainable from the district or subdivisional magistrate's offices in Shimla (see p115), Rekong Peo (see p123), Kaza and Kullu (see p130). The offices at Kaza, (01906) 222 302 and Rekong Peo, (01789) 222 253 are the most efficient. For general details, see p734.
Equipment hire & operators: The Institute of Mountaineering and Allied Sports in Manali (01902) 252 342, and Yeti Trekking in McLeodganj (01892) 221 887, organize treks. The Regional Mountaineering Centre in McLeodganj, (01892) 221 787, offers mountaineering courses. In Manali, Himalayan Adventurers, (01902) 252 365, is a reputable rafting agency, the Himalayan Institute of Adventure Sports, (01902) 253 050, offers paragliding, and Himalayan Journeys, (01902) 252 365, offers mountain biking. See also p731.
Caution: Trekkers have gone missing in Parvati Valley. It is advisable to trek in groups and to take an experienced guide along.

Other Adventure Activities

Climbing a rock face, Tirthan Valley

Himachal Pradesh has several peaks over 3,000 m (9,843 ft), suitable for climbing. The Institute of Mountaineering and Allied Sports at Manali offers three-week courses. Skiing is possible at Narkanda and at Solang Nala near Manali. Summer is the best season for rafting and kayaking on the Beas river at Manali, and for paragliding at Solang and Billing in Kangra. Himalayan Journeys (see p728) in Manali offers mountain biking near the Rohtang Pass.

Renuka Lake, venue of the Renuka Fair held in November

❺ Nahan

Sirmaur district. 100 km (62 miles) S of Shimla. 🚌 🚗 Renuka Fair (Nov).

Lying in the lower Shivalik Hills close to the plains, Nahan nestles sleepily on a low wooded ridge at 930 m (3,051 ft). The old town retains its network of narrow cobbled streets and has an interesting bazaar dating to the 17th century. The old palace (Raja Mahal) is closed to visitors. Other attractions include the Ranzore Palace facing the Chaugan (the royal polo ground), the lively Jagannath Temple in the bazaar, and the quiet walks through the *chir* pine forests on the Villa Round. Nahan serves as a convenient stopover for visiting the popular Renuka Lake nearby.

Environs

Lying 42 km (26 miles) east of Nahan, is the sacred **Renuka Lake**, whose shoreline traces the shape of a reclining woman. According to Hindu mythology, Renuka was the wife of the sage Jamdagni and mother of Parasurama, an incarnation of Lord Vishnu (see p683). She was killed by her son at his father's command, and miraculously came back to life, only to disappear again, leaving behind an imprint in the shape of her body. At the far end of the lake is a small wildlife park housing a pride of lions, Himalayan black bear and antelope. Nearby lies a smaller lake called Parasurama Tal, and below this, an open area where the Renuka Fair (see p117) is held every year in November.

Kaza
Spiti
Dankar
Mikkim
anga *Pin Valley* *Sangam*
Mud
av *Mantalai*
e
Pin Parvati Pass (5,319 m/17,451 ft)

The pavilion in the spacious gardens of Rampur's palace

❻ Rampur

Shimla district. 130 km (81 miles) NE of Shimla. 🚌 🛥 daily. 🎪 Lavi Fair (Nov).

Once on the main trade route between India and Tibet, Rampur is today a big commercial town. It comes alive in November each year when the vibrant Lavi Fair (see p117) takes place.

The early 20th-century palace of the old kings is still their private residence, though visitors are allowed to walk around the sprawling gardens. A Hindu temple and a small pavilion are set in their midst.

❼ Sarahan

Shimla district. 198 km (123 miles) NE of Shimla. 🚌 🛥 daily. 🎪 Dussehra (Sep/Oct).

Perched high above the left bank of the Satluj, Sarahan was once the summer residence of the Bushahr kings. At 2,165 m (7,103 ft), it has a pleasant climate enhanced by the vista of the Srikhand Range across the valley, with the twin peaks of Gushu-Pishu and the holy mountain Srikhand Mahadev standing out prominently. Sarahan's most interesting sight is the spectacular tower temple, **Bhimakali**. It also has a short nature trail leading to a pheasantry. The many pheasants housed here include the monal and the near-extinct Western Himalayan tragopan.

Sarahan: Bhimakali Temple

The palace-cum-temple complex of the Bushahr kings, Bhimakali owes its origin to the tradition of housing the family deity on the top floor of the feudal chief's home. Its elaborate layout consists of a series of courtyards connected by beautiful gateways. The presiding deity, Bhimakali, one of the myriad forms of the goddess Kali, is housed in the first floor of the pagoda-style temple. Although the exact age of the temple is not known, it is associated with historical events dating to the 7th century, while parts of it are around 800 years old.

View of the Bhimakali Temple Complex
The twin towers of the Bhimakali Temple, covered in snow and framed against the backdrop of the Srikhand Range, present an awesome sight.

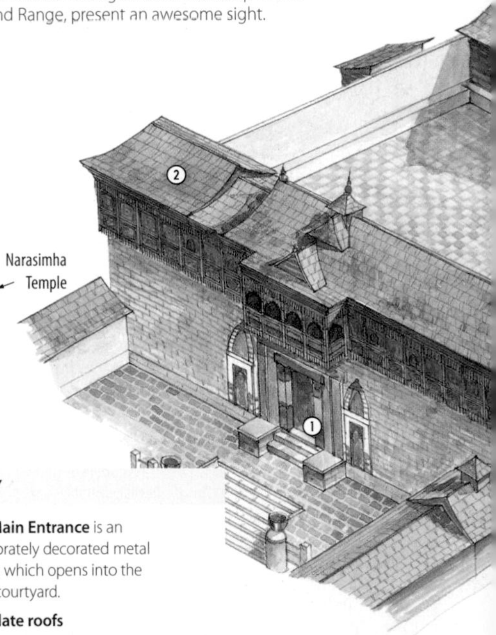

Narasimha Temple

KEY

① **Main Entrance** is an elaborately decorated metal door, which opens into the first courtyard.

② **Slate roofs**

③ **The Ram Mandir** is located in the second courtyard.

④ **Carved tiger statue**

⑤ **Alternating bands of stone and timber**

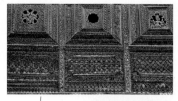

★ Carved Balconies
The uppermost storey of the renovated temple is fringed by overhanging balconies with exquisitely carved panels.

★ Tower Shrines
The Leaning Tower (on the right) was the main temple until it was damaged during an earthquake in 1905. The adjoining tower has since become the main shrine.

Golden Finials
The finials, a combination of symbols of the sun and the moon, represent the deity and the royal patrons.

Wooden Skittles
Carved wooden skittles hang from the eaves of the temple roofs.

★ Silver Doors
The silver doors that lead to the second courtyard are embellished with panels depicting various Hindu gods. They were added during the reign of Padam Singh (1914–47), a Bushahr king.

Dussehra Festival
Dussehra is the only time of the year when the original 200-year-old image of Bhimakali is actively worshipped.

❽ Sangla Valley Tour

The largest village in Kinnaur, Sangla, often lends its name to the whole Baspa Valley. A drive through this area over two to three days can encapsulate a dramatic transition in landscape, from the spectacular river gorge at the entrance to Kinnaur to alpine valley pastures. It takes in awesome mountain scenery and mixed forests of oak and rhododendron, before reaching charming slate-roofed villages that nestle amidst orchards and fields.

0 kilometres 5
0 miles 5

① Kafour
Strung out along a little spur below the road, scenic Kafour is the first inhabited village in Kinnaur. The Hirma Temple, dedicated to a local mother goddess, stands out amid the slate rooftops.

③ Maheshwar Temple at Sungra
The temple's pagoda-like roof and the fine wooden carvings on its doorways and walls make this an interesting stopover.

② The Satluj Gorge at Tranda
From the road there are striking views of sheer rock walls falling 500 m (1,640 ft) to the river. On the other side, cliffs of equal magnitude enclose the Satluj in a narrow impenetrable gorge.

❾ Kinnaur

Kinnaur district. 244 km (152 miles) NE from Shimla to Rekong Peo. ⛰ 19,250. 🚌 🚉 Sazi (Jan). Travel permits: required for parts of Kinnaur. Contact the Subdivisional Magistrate's office in Rekong Peo, (01786) 222 253. For details, see p119.

Kinnaur, the remote northeastern corner of Himachal Pradesh fringing the Tibetan Plateau, is a region of awesome grandeur. In the past, difficult terrain made Kinnaur inaccessible to all but the most intrepid of travellers, while in the 1950s, its proximity to the international border with Tibet resulted in restrictions on entry. However, these restrictions have been eased since 1992.

The variations in terrain, vegetation, climate and wildlife have broadly divided this region into Lower, Middle and Upper Kinnaur. Lower Kinnaur

View of the Kinner Kailash on a clear winter day

hugs both banks of a gorge-like Satluj river. The left bank's forested mountain slopes, contour-hugging terraced fields and tightly packed rows of houses clinging to the hillsides are picturesque in contrast to the right bank which is steeper, with higher peaks and a smaller population. Middle Kinnaur is much more rugged. Dominating its heart are the majestic

heights of the Kinner Kailash Range, while to its south is the gentler valley of the Baspa, one of the Satluj's largest tributaries. The arid sweep of the Zanskar peaks makes Upper Kinnaur a cold desert country of stark, barren mountains interspersed with occasional villages and irrigated fields.

Rekong Peo, the new district headquarters, is a bustling

④ Sapni
Sapni village has a tower temple that contains some of the finest examples of wooden sculpture in Kinnaur.

Key

■■ Tour route
══ Road
▦▦ River

Tips for Drivers

Length: 90 km (56 miles).
Getting around: The tour begins at Kafour village. The steep road is rough and winding, and is best negotiated with a 4-wheel drive. Sangla and Chitkul villages offer places to stay and eat, as well as a few shops with basic provisions.

⑥ Sangla
The largest among the villages that dot the Baspa Valley, Sangla has some beautiful walks to offer.

⑦ Chitkul
The tour ends at the village of Chitkul, just before the pastures of the Upper Baspa Valley. The valley's blue poppy was admired by the explorer Marco Pallis in 1933.

⑤ Kamroo
The tower of the Kamroo Narayan Temple commands a picturesque view of the valley. Fields and orchards slope down to the Baspa on one side of the river, while on the other side, thick forests rise up to pasturelands.

little township on the right bank of the Satluj river, with some shops and adequate transport connections. About 13 km (8 miles) higher up on the same mountain is **Kalpa**, the old headquarters. With its panoramic view of the Kinner Kailash Range, Kalpa is a must in any Kinnaur itinerary. The choice of walks include one to the upland pastures through deodar and *chilgoza* pine *(Pinus gerardiana)* forests. There are remarkably built wood and stone temples that are capped by slate roofs in the area.

About 20 km (12 miles) from Rekong Peo, the Baspa river joins the Satluj at its left bank. The beauty of the **Sangla Valley** (or Baspa Valley) has been extolled both in local legend and by visitors over the years, and the region lends itself to a lovely trip by road. Apart from a furious rush in its

last stretch of its course, the Baspa river ambles along a wooded valley past serene villages. Stupendous gneiss faces and forests of deodar, pine and birch reaching up to long swards of pasture and snow-covered peaks surround the valley. Every village in this valley, from Sangla to Chitkul, offers glorious walks and a choice of festivals to celebrate with the local people.

Buddhism holds sway throughout Upper Kinnaur. Fluttering prayer flags and mud-walled Buddhist temples with clay images and wall paintings dot the region, reflecting its proximity to Tibet. Many temples are credited to the 11th-century

scholar Rinchen Zangpo, revered in Tibetan Buddhism as the Lotsawa (Translator), who initiated the mammoth task of translating Indian texts into Tibetan. He was also the main force behind a great temple-building movement and supposedly built 108 monasteries in one night.

Nako, 100 km (62 miles) from Rekong Peo, has a small lake and is close to Reo Purgyal, the highest peak in Himachal Pradesh at 6,816 m (22,362 ft).

Young Buddhist monks in a monastery, Kinnaur

A cluster of village houses with sloping roofs in Mandi

⑩ Mandi

Mandi district. 156 km (97 miles) N of Shimla. 🚹 26,900. 🚌 Joginder Nagar, 53 km (33 miles) NW of Mandi, then taxi or bus. 🚌 🎎 Shivratri (Feb/Mar).

Often referred to as the gateway to the Kullu Valley *(see p130)*, Mandi is situated at the confluence of the Beas river with a small rain-fed tributary. The capital of the erstwhile princely state of Mandi, this small market town once functioned as a vital link between the hill communities on either side of it. The busy market located in a sunken garden in the centre of town, where all manner of merchandise is sold, is one of the more interesting sights here. Also situated in the town centre is the former residence of the Mandi kings, built in the colonial style, and now the heritage Rajmahal Palace Hotel. Several 16th- to 17th-century temples with beautiful stone carvings can be found all over the town. The most famous among these are the Madho Rai Temple, the Tarna Devi Temple and the Bhootnath Temple where the Shivratri festival is celebrated.

Environs

Rewalsar, a bustling village at a height of 360 m (1,181 ft) is 24 km (15 miles) southeast of Mandi. On the shores of the Rewalsar Lake, resting in the hollow of a mountain spur, are three Buddhist monasteries, three temples and a gurdwara commemorating the month-long stay of the tenth Sikh guru, Gobind Singh, in 1738. It is said that Padmasambhava, the 8th century Indian apostle credited with bringing Buddhism to Tibet, used his legendary powers to fly from here to Tibet. His spirit is believed to reside in the tiny floating reed islands on the lake.

Mandi district apple orchard

Mandi's hinterland contains many other places of scenic beauty. To the east, **Jhanjheli** and **Karsog**, both about 100 km (62 miles) away in apple orchard country, offer the possibility of lovely treks to the hilltop temples of Shikari Devi and Mahunag.

⑪ Kangra Valley

Kangra district. 222 km (728 miles) NW of Shimla. 🚹 9,200. ✈ Gaggal, 10 km (6 miles) N of Kangra town. 🚌 Joginder Nagar and Una. 🚌

Located in the western part of Himachal Pradesh and spread between the Shivalik foothills and the Dhauladhar Range, the Kangra Valley is a land of gentle beauty. Undulating expanses of tea gardens and terraced paddy fields are crisscrossed by sparkling snow-fed rivulets. Kangra is the most populated district of Himachal Pradesh, and is well connected with the plains as it is situated along the border with Punjab.

The valley derives its name from the ancient town of Kangra, even though Dharamsala *(see p126)* is the present district headquarters. The history of the town goes back 3,500 years when it was called Nagarkot and was the capital of the kingdom of Trigartha. In 1620, Kangra and its fort were captured by Emperor Jahangir, after which it became a Mughal province. Dominating the town today are the ruins of the once formidable Kangra Fort, perched on top of a steep cliff overlooking the Banganga and Majhi rivulets. Within the fort's compound are two Hindu temples dedicated to

The square-shaped Rewalsar Lake resting in the hollow of a mountain spur

The towering spire of Brajeshwari Devi Temple in Kangra town

Ambika Devi (a local goddess) and Lakshmi Narayan, and a Jain temple with a stone image of Adinath. Behind the crowded bazaar is the Brajeshwari Devi Temple, whose fabled riches were plundered by Mahmud of Ghazni (see p52) in 1009. The present structure was built in 1920, after the terrible earthquake of 1905 destroyed the city and original temple.

Some 40 km (25 miles) southwest of Kangra town, are the 15 monolithic rock-cut temples of **Masroor**, dating to the 10th century and carved in a style similar to those at Ellora (see pp480–82). The picturesque **Jwalamukhi Temple**, 35 km (22 miles) southwest of Kangra, is one of North India's most important pilgrimage sites.

Further east of Kangra, the beauty of the tea garden country unfolds around **Palampur**, 45 km (28 miles) away. East of Palampur, are the 9th-century stone Baijnath Temple dedicated to Shiva, Bir with its Tibetan Buddhist monastery, and Billing, well-known as a take-off point for paragliding over the valley.

About 40 km (25 miles) southeast of Palampur, is the fortress of **Sujanpur-Tira**, located on the right bank of the Beas. Built by the Kangra kings in the early 18th century, it was the favoured residence of Raja Sansar Chand, the renowned patron of Kangra miniature painting. The fortress also preserves some excellent wall paintings.

At the far end of the Kangra Valley is **Jogindernagar**, 55 km (34 miles) south of Palampur, the terminus of a narrow gauge railway line that winds up the valley from Pathankot in the west.

The **Maharana Pratap Sagar Lake**, created in 1979 by the construction of the Pong Dam across the Beas, lies to the southwest of Kangra district. This large wetland, spread over 45,000 ha (111,200 acres) when full, is a favoured stopover for migratory birds from Central Asia.

Terraced paddy fields in the Kangra Valley

Pahari Miniature Paintings

Pahari or "hill" painting refers to the various schools of miniature painting such as Kangra, Basohli, Mankot and Guler, that flourished between the mid-17th and the late 19th centuries in the Rajput kingdoms situated in the long, narrow region of the Himalayan foothills. Although there is evidence of painting in this region as early as 1552, the earliest group of distinctive Pahari style paintings appeared in about 1650 in the small state of Basohli. These miniatures, horizontal in format, use flat

planes of bold colours, mainly reds and yellows. Stylized architecture and figures with large eyes and straight profiles wearing elaborate costumes and jewellery, are typical of these miniatures, which illustrate the *Rasamanjari*, a Sanskrit poem on the behaviour of lovers. In the 18th century, the neighbouring state, Mankot, developed an equally vibrant style, remarkable for a series of portraits of grandees of the court. By the late 18th century, the vitality of local tradition had mellowed under Mughal influence and a lyrical, more tranquil palette with a naturalistic rendering of forms characterized the miniatures from Guler and Kangra. Guler's painting tradition was dominated by one family of artists of whom the most talented was Nainsukh. Painting in Kangra flourished under the reign of Raja Sansar Chand (r.1775–1823). The highly refined style that emerged during this period concentrated on the lush, idyllic landscape as the backdrop for romantic scenes. Other centres of Pahari painting included Mandi, Jammu, Nurpur, Chamba and Kullu.

Kangra miniature, 1788, depicting Krishna killing the serpent-demon, Kaliya

⑫ Dharamsala

Kangra district. 238 km (148 miles) NW of Shimla. 🚹 19,100. ✈ Gaggal, 11 km (7 miles) S of town centre. 🚂 Pathankot, 80 km (50 miles) NW of Dharamsala, then bus or taxi. 🚌 *i* HP Tourism, McLeodganj (01892) 221 205. 🗓 daily. 🎭 Summer Festival (May), Bodh Festival (Oct/Nov).

Tibetan nuns in their red robes, a common sight in Dharamsala

This hill station, established by the British in the mid-19th century, is today the home of the Dalai Lama and the Tibetan Government-in-Exile. Located on the lower spurs of the Dhauladhar Range, the town consists of two sections – the lower town with the main bus stand and bazaar, and the upper town, known as **McLeodganj**, 9 km (5 miles) to its north, which is the destination of most foreign visitors. There is little of interest in the lower town, apart from the lively **Kotwali Bazaar** and the **Museum of Kangra Art**. The museum has an excellent collection of Kangra miniatures *(see p125)*, and also houses a school which teaches the art of miniature painting.

McLeodganj, the upper town, named after Donald McLeod, the lieutenant governor of Punjab in 1848, is primarily a Tibetan settlement. Its focal point is the **Tsuglagkhang Complex**, located at the southern edge of the town, which contains the residence of the Dalai Lama (not open to visitors), the **Namgyal Monastery** where monks can be seen debating in the after-noons, and the important **Tsuglagkhang Temple**. A simple hall, painted in yellow, the

temple has a raised dais from where the Dalai Lama holds discourses, and three beautiful images from the Buddhist pantheon – Sakyamuni (the Historical Buddha), Avalokitesvara *(see p145)*, and Padmasambhava *(see p124 & p143)*. The Dalai Lama is believed to be an incarnation of Avalokitesvara. Another temple in the complex has an intricate mural of the Kalachakra ("Wheel of Time") and beautiful sand mandalas, painstakingly created by the monks over a period of time and then ritually destroyed.

Situated at the northern edge of town are the **Tibetan Institute of Performing Arts**, and the beautiful **Norbulingka Institute**, where traditional arts and crafts are promoted.

Gangchen Kyishong, the administrative centre of the Tibetan Government-in-Exile, is midway between the upper

Stained glass, St-John-in-the-Wilderness

and lower towns. This complex includes the excellent **Library of Tibetan Works and Archives**, a museum on the first floor with bronze images and *thangkas*, as well as the **Institute of Tibetan Medicine**. Nearby is the **Nechung Monastery**, the seat of the Tibetan State Oracle, whose predictions about major events in the coming year carry great weight in the Tibetan community. Also on the road to Kotwali Bazaar, close to McLeodganj, is the picturesque **Church of St-John-in-the-Wilderness**, a grey stone structure built in 1852. Brass plaques and superb Belgian stained-glass windows can be seen inside the church. The tomb of Lord Elgin, the British viceroy who died here in 1863 while on holiday, lies in the churchyard.

Environs
The pretty village of **Dharamkot**, north of McLeodganj, is reached by a 3-km (2-mile) long road, lined with deodar and oak trees. There are superb views of the Kangra Valley from the village.

🏛 **Museum of Kangra Art**
Main Rd, Dharamsala. **Tel** (01892) 224 214. **Open** Tue–Sun.

🏛 **Library of Tibetan Works and Archives**
Gangchen Kyishong, McLeodganj Rd. **Open** Mon–Fri.

⛪ **St-John-in-the-Wilderness**
Open daily. ✝ 11am Sun.

The brightly-painted façade of Namgyal Monastery, McLeodganj

Little Tibet

When the 14th Dalai Lama, Tenzin Gyatso, fled Tibet in 1959 after the Chinese occupation, Dharamsala became his new home, and the base of the Tibetan Government-in-Exile. The town is today often called Little Tibet, preserving Tibet's religious and cultural heritage, keeping the Tibetan cause alive internationally, and serving as the focal point for the 100,000 Tibetans scattered in refugee settlements all over India. Dharamsala also attracts Buddhists from across the world, such as the Hollywood actor Richard Gere.

The Tibetan flag is dominated by a snow-covered mountain representing Tibet. The six red bands symbolize the six Tibetan tribes.

Religion and Culture

Dharamsala's many monasteries and crafts centres, and its performing arts school, ensure that Tibet's distinctive religion and culture continue to flourish.

Tibetan opera, known as *lhamo*, has traditional folk tales, legends and myths as its themes.

The Dalai Lama, who won the Nobel Peace Prize in 1990, is head of the Gelugpa or Yellow Hat sect *(see p143)* and is revered as Tibet's god-king.

Thunderbolt sceptre

The altar in a Tibetan monastery includes, apart from images of the deities, seven ritual bowls of water, butter lamps, intricate butter sculptures, as well as a bell and a thunderbolt sceptre used during prayers and special rites.

Butter sculpture

Prayer bell

Sand mandalas symbolizing the universe are meticulously created and then ceremonially destroyed. They help monks to meditate.

Thangkas, or scroll paintings framed in silk depicting Buddhist divinities, are among the traditional arts kept alive by the refugees.

See also features on Buddhist Iconography *(p145)* and In the Buddha's Footsteps *(p225)*

Silverton, one of the many colonial houses in Dalhousie

⓭ Dalhousie

Chamba district. 336 km (209 miles)
NW of Shimla. 🔼 7,400. 📧
ⓘ Geetanjali Hotel, near bus
stand, (01899) 242 136. 🔺 daily.
🎭 Summer Festival (Jun).

Sprawling over five hills that
range in height from 1,525 m
to 2,378 m (5,003 ft to 7,802 ft),
Dalhousie still retains its Raj-era
ambience, with spacious, gable-
roofed bungalows and churches
flanking its leafy lanes. Originally
conceived as a sanatorium for
the expatriate population rather
than as a fashionable summer
retreat, it was founded in 1853
and named after Lord Dalhousie,
the governor-general of British
India between 1848 and 1856.
The most popular walks are the
twin rounds of **Garam Sarak**
("Warm Road") and **Thandi Sarak**
("Cold Road"), so called because
one path is sunnier than the
other. A shorter walk from the
Circuit House to Gandhi Chowk
– the central part of town where
a school, church and the post
office are situated – offers
spectacular views of the Pir
Panjal Range. From Gandhi
Chowk, another pleasant ramble,
about 3 km (2 miles) long,
leads south to the pretty
picnic spot of Panjpula or
"Five Bridges".
    For Raj aficionados, a track
leading off to the right from
the main bus stand moves past
the old British cemetery in the
woods, before reaching the
cantonment. One of the two
churches here boasts pretty
stained-glass windows and
sandstone arches.

Environs

A scenic road through dense
forests of pine, deodar, oak, horse
chestnut and rhododendron
leads to the **Kalatope Wildlife
Sanctuary**, about 8 km (5 miles)
east of Dalhousie. With prior
permission from the wildlife
authorities at Chamba it
is possible to take a
diversion at Bakrota
and drive to a rest
house deep inside the
sanctuary. About 26
km (16 miles) east of
Dalhousie is **Khajjiar**,
situated at a height of
2,000 m (6,562 ft). This
saucer-shaped expanse
of green meadow,
bordered by towering deodars,
has a picture postcard beauty,
comparable with the finest
views in Kashmir or Switzerland.
The centre has a small lake
and the glade is flanked by a
temple dedicated to the local
deity, Khajjinag.

🏛 Kalatope Wildlife Sanctuary
For permission contact: Forest Department, Chamba. **Tel** (01899) 222 639.

⓮ Chamba

Chamba district. 378 km (235 miles)
NW of Shimla. 🔼 20,300. 📧
🔺 daily. 🎭 Sui (Apr), Minjar (Jul/
Aug). Travel permits: Contact the
Deputy Commissioner, (01899) 225
371. For details, see p734.

This town was chosen as the
capital of the former princely
state of Chamba in the 10th
century, when Raja Sahil Varman
moved here from Bharmour.
He named it Chamba after his
favourite daughter, Champavati,
also called Chameshni, who
legend says, sacrificed herself to
provide water for the parched city.
During the Sui festival, women
and children sing her praises in
the town's many temples.
    A bridge over the Ravi river
leads up to the town, situated
on the ledge of a mountain,
overlooking the right bank
of the river. In the town's
centre is the **Chaugan**,
a huge expanse of
meadow, that is the
focal point of all
cultural and social
life. Clustered around
it are a number of
imposing buildings,
including the old
Akhand Chandi Palace,
part of which is now a
college. The Chaugan is also the
main marketplace with shops
that sell a variety of merchandise,
ranging from traditional silver
jewellery with enamelled clasps
to embroidered Chamba *chappals*
(sandals) that may look flimsy
but are excellent for walking
up hillsides.
    Chamba's towering stone
temples are some of the finest in
the region. The most important

Silver mask of
Parvati, Chamba

Images of deities on the walls of Lakshmi Narayan Temple, Chamba

Hillsides around Chamba ablaze with the colours of autumn

are the six North Indian *shikhara*-style temples *(see p24)* that comprise the **Lakshmi Narayan Temple** complex, to the west of the Chaugan. Of these, three are dedicated to Vishnu and three to Shiva. The white marble image of Lakshmi Narayan, in the main temple, was brought from Central India in the 10th century. The carved panels on the temple walls illustrate mythological scenes as well as animal and floral motifs.

Other temples include the **Madho Rai Temple**, near the palace, with a bronze image of Krishna, and further up, the **Chamunda Temple**.

A glimpse of Chamba's rich heritage can be seen at the **Bhuri Singh Museum**, set up in 1908 by the king of Chamba at the time. His rare collection of miniature paintings formed the nucleus of the museum. Today, it has a fine collection of Pahari paintings *(see p125)*, murals, inscribed fountain slabs, carved stone panels and other artifacts, such as Chamba *rumals*, metal masks, copper plates and silver jewellery.

🏛 **Bhuri Singh Museum**
S of Chaughan. **Tel** (01899) 222 590.
Open Tue–Sun.

⑮ Bharmour

Chamba district. 64 km (40 miles) SE of Chamba. 🚌 🎧 Manimahesh Yatra (Aug/Sep).

The Bharmour region, homeland of the semi-nomadic, sheep-herding Gaddis and the first capital of the Chamba rulers, spreads across a steep mountainside, high above Budhil, a large tributary of the Ravi river. Bharmour's main attraction is the fascinating **Chaurasi** (literally, "Eighty-Four") **Temple** complex, built in the 10th century under Raja Sahil Varman, to honour the 84 saints who visited Bharmour. The major shrines are dedicated to Narasimha, Ganesha, and the local deities Larkana Devi and Manimahesh. The intricate wooden carvings on the temple lintels and the images of the main deities are outstanding, and it is said that the sculptor's hands were cut off to prevent him from replicating such remarkable work.

Environs
Situated at a height of 3,950 m (12,959 ft), **Manimahesh Lake**, 35 km (22 miles) from Bharmour, is the area's most sacred lake, as its holy waters are believed to cleanse all sins. In August/September, thousands of pilgrims converge here to participate in the annual Manimahesh

Yatra *(see p117)*. The main motor road continues up to Hadsar, 16 km (10 miles) beyond Bharmour, and from there the *yatra* (procession) ascends in two stages via Dhanchho to the lake, nestling at the base of the Manimahesh Kailasa.

For the adventurous, Bharmour also offers a tough five-day trek over the Kugti Pass (5,040 m/16,535 ft) to Lahaul *(see p133)*. Holi, 26 km (16 miles) away in the main Ravi Valley, is the base for a number of trails over the Dhauladhar Range to the Kangra Valley. It offers the option of a longer walk to the Kullu Valley as well. Down the course of the Ravi, on the road to Chamba, the **Chatrari Temple** with its exquisite bronze image of Shakti Devi, is also worth a stop.

Well-preserved 10th-century temples at Bharmour

Chamba Rumals

Chamba *rumals*, exquisitely embroidered handkerchiefs or coverlets, generally square in shape, were used primarily to wrap gifts, either for temple offerings or for ceremonial exchanges during wedding rituals. At times, they also formed the canopies draped above deities in temples. Pale colours, silk thread, a double-sided satin stitch and an unbleached muslin base were the framework within which intricate compositions, inspired by delicate Pahari miniatures, were created. Originally the work of the ladies of the court, the themes were religious, interspersed with animal and plant motifs, and enclosed within floral borders.

Hand-embroidered Chamba *rumal*

Brightly coloured tiger guarding the Jagannathi Devi Temple, Kullu

⑯ Kullu Valley

Kullu district. 240 km (149 miles) N of Shimla. 🚶 18,300. ✈ Bhuntar, 10 km (6 miles) S of Kullu town. 🚌 ℹ HP Tourism, near Maidan, (01902) 222 349. 🎭 Dussehra (Sep/Oct). Travel permits: Contact Deputy Commisioner, (01902) 222 727. For more details, see p119.

The Kullu Valley in central Himachal Pradesh, watered by the Beas river, has long been a site of human habitation. In ancient Sanskrit texts it is referred to as Kulantpith, or "end of the habitable world" – an apt description when one compares the lush fields and apple orchards

Typical geometric pattern on the border of a Kullu shawl

of this 80-km (50-mile) long valley with the desolate expanse of Lahaul (see p133), which is separated from it by the Pir Panjal Range. The local name for Kullu is the "Valley of the Gods" – its alpine setting is the gathering place for 360 gods from different temples in the region, who congregate here for the famous Dussehra festival.

Unlike British-built hill stations in the Himalayas, Kullu remained unknown to the outside world until it was "discovered" in the 1960s by the flower children, who were enchanted as much by its hillsides covered with marijuana plants (Cannabis sativa), as by its gentle beauty, superb mountain vistas and amiable people. The men of Kullu Valley usually wear the distinctive Kullu *topi*, a snug woollen cap with a colourful upturned flap. The women weave thick shawls with striking geometric designs on their borders, and few visitors can resist acquiring these attractive products, now a flourishing local industry. Equally attractive are the village houses, their slate roofs rising above green meadows. **Kullu**, the district headquarters and the largest settlement in the valley, is located on the right bank of the Beas. The town's chief attraction is the 17th-century **Raghunath Temple**, dedicated to Rama and Sita, whose richly adorned images lead the processions at the Dussehra festival. Also worth exploring is the Akhara Bazaar, at the northern end of the town, famous for its handicrafts shops, selling shawls and traditional silver jewellery. At the southern end of town is the large green open space called **Dhalpur Maidan**, where the colourful Dussehra festivities take place.

A number of temples, all with superb stone carvings and impressive images, lie in the vicinity of Kullu town – the **Vaishno Devi Cave Shrine** is 4 km (2.5 miles) to the northeast; the **Jagannathi Devi Temple** at Bekhli, 5 km (3 miles) to the north; and the **Vishnu Temple** at Dayar, 12 km (8 miles) to the west. The pyramidal **Basheshwar Mahadev Temple** at Bajaura, 15 km (9 miles) to the south, has superb images of Vishnu, Ganesha and Durga. However, the most famous is the **Bijli Mahadev Temple**, dedicated to the "Lord of Lightning", 14 km (9 miles) to the southeast. Located on a high spur on the left bank of the river, opposite the town, this temple has an 18-m (59-ft) high staff, which periodically attracts lightning during thunderstorms especially in spring. This is regarded as a divine blessing, even though it shatters the Shivalinga in the sanctum of the temple. The stone fragments are then painstakingly put together again with a mortar of clarified butter and grain, by the head priest.

Environs

Jalori Pass, about 70 km (44 miles) south of Kullu, on the ridgeline forming the divide between the Beas and Satluj rivers, offers two beautiful walks through dense, high-altitude oak forests and meadows. The first walk goes through a path with gentle gradients to the tarn of Saryolsar, 5 km (3 miles) away. The other walk, up a neighbouring hill, leads to the picturesque ruins of a fort occupied by the Gurkhas in the 19th century.

A waterfall in Kullu Valley

Hot springs in Manikaran, a popular pilgrim spot

⑰ Parvati Valley

Kullu district. 180 km (112 miles) NE of Shimla. 🚌 ⓘ HP Tourism, near Maidan, Kullu, (01902) 222 349.

The scenic Parvati Valley, with its green, terraced rice fields and apple orchards, draws an increasing number of visitors. However, because of illegal marijuana cultivation in the surrounding country-side, the Parvati Valley has, in recent years, gained notoriety as a centre for the narcotics trade, and some foreign visitors

have gone missing from the area. It is advisable to take guides and porters available from Naggar (see p132) and **Manikaran**, for treks in this region.

The main settlement in the Parvati Valley is Manikaran, famous for its hot springs. It is also the starting point for a number of treks (see pp118–19). An interesting legend explains the origins of the hot springs. A serpent stole the earrings of Parvati, the consort of Lord Shiva, and disappeared with them into a deep burrow. On witnessing Shiva's terrible anger, the snake was too terrified to come out of its hole, but managed to snort the earrings out through the earth, thus creating vents from which the hot springs bubble out. A bath here is said to be good for the body and the soul, and local people sometimes boil rice in the geo-thermal steam.

The Rama Temple and the Shiva Temple next to a Sikh gurdwara is always thronged with sadhus.

⑱ Great Himalayan National Park

Kullu district. 205 km (127 miles) N of Shimla, (via Jalori Pass). Entry points: Sainj, Gushani. 🚌 Shamshi, 15 km (9 miles) S of Kullu, then jeep. ⓘ For bookings & permits contact Director, GHNP, Shamshi, (01902) 265 320. 🛅

The great Himalayan National Park, covering an area of 754 sq km (291 sq miles), ranges in altitude from 1,300 m (4,265 ft) to 6,100 m (20,013 ft), and abuts the cold desert region of Pin Valley National Park (see p134). The variety of flora and fauna found here represents the entire Western Himalayas. A vast range of subtropical species along with alpine grasslands are covered with edelweiss and oak forests. Mammals include the Himalayan tahr, musk deer and the elusive snow leopard. Among the 300-odd species of birds, there are at least six kinds of pheasant.

Monal pheasant

A number of trekking trails and forest huts in the buffer zone offer an opportunity to explore the park.

Gathering of the Gods

Kullu celebrates the festival of Dussehra with unique gusto. All over India, this festival commemorates the defeat of the demon-king, Ravana, by the god Rama, a story recounted in the Hindu epic, Ramayana (see p31). In Kullu, local traditions add their own piquancy to this pan-Indian myth. These traditions originated in the 17th century, when the ruler, Jagat Singh, inadvertently caused the death of a Brahmin priest. To expiate his sin, he installed the deity Raghunath (another name for Rama), on his throne and vowed that thereafter he and his descendants would rule Kullu only as regents. The image of this god was brought all the way from the holy town of Ayodhya (see p203), the birthplace of Lord Rama. From then on, every September/October, Raghunath "invites" all the local gods of the valley, to celebrate Dussehra in Kullu. These gods, 360 of them, include Hadimba, the patron deity of the Kullu rajas from Manali (see p132), and Jamlu, the reigning deity of Malana who administers justice via the village priest. The gods are carried on palanquins from their own temples and arrive at the Dhalpur Maidan in a cheerful procession accompanied by the frenzied beat of drums. Nine days of festivities follow, when a temporary market is set up, which sells everything from locally-made shawls and shoes, to brightly-hued plastic toys. The graceful natti dance, performed amidst a lot of friendly rivalry by several local groups, can also be watched.

Image of Vashishtha Devta, a local god

Preparing for the Dussehra festival celebrations

⑲ Manali

Kullu district. 281 km (175 miles) N of Shimla. 🏔 6,300. 🚌 ℹ️ The Mall, (01902) 253 531. 🗓 daily. 🎿 Winter Carnival (Jan), Dhungri Mela (May).

Picturesque Manali, situated along the west bank of the Beas river, is a prime destination for visitors, offering a variety of scenic walks and treks through dense forests. Though hotels and shops now overrun downtown Manali, its environs still retain much of the natural beauty that gives this hill station a unique flavour. Particularly charming is the original village, about 3 km (2 miles) north of the main bazaar, with its temple dedicated to Manu, the Hindu sage after whom Manali is named.

Located 1.5 km (1 mile) north of the main bazaar is the sacred **Hadimba Temple**, shaded by a grove of stately deodars. This four-tiered wooden temple with its pagoda-style roof was built in 1553 around a small natural cave enshrining the footprints of the demoness turned goddess, Hadimba, wife of Bhima, the mighty Pandava brother (see p30).

On the left bank of the Beas, about 3 km (2 miles) north of the bazaar, the hot sulphur springs in the village of **Vashisht** are piped into Turkish-style baths. Further up, the lovely **Solang Valley**, 14 km (9 miles) from downtown Manali, is the scene of most of the area's outdoor activities. Treks lead up to the pastures of Dhumti and the small snow-fed lake of Beas

The 16th-century wooden Hadimba Temple in Manali

Kund (see p118). Paragliding, a popular activity, takes place on the nearby slopes, which also attract skiers in the winter.

Environs

Rohtang Pass, the perilous pass crossing into Lahaul, at an altitude of 3,980 m (13,058 ft), is 52 km (32 miles) north of Manali. It is a day's excursion, though the pass is closed in winter, with a brief halt at the spectacular Rahalla Falls along the way.

Woodcarving on a door in Malana

The first capital of the Kullu kings, **Jagatsukh** is 6 km (4 miles) south of Manali, on the left bank of the Beas. The two shikhara-style (see p25) stone temples here possibly date back to the 6th century. **Naggar**, further south, on the same side of the river, succeeded Jagatsukh as the capital till it was moved to Kullu (see p130) in the 17th century. The Naggar Castle, built in the 15th century, is now a hotel. It is an excellent

example of traditional local architecture with walls composed of alternate layers of wooden beams and evenly hewn stone. It commands a fine view of the Beas Valley. Nearby is the **Roerich Art Gallery** displaying the work of the Russian painter Nicholas Roerich. Lying across the river from Naggar, is scenic **Katrain**, surrounded by orchards. Trout fishing is a popular pastime here.

The remote village of **Malana**, beyond Chanderkhani Pass, is 25 km (16 miles) southeast of Naggar. Malana's isolated people live by their own code of conduct and shun contact with outsiders. Their unique culture, language and system of government set them apart from the rest of the valley. Visitors should enter the village only if invited.

🏛 **Roerich Art Gallery**
Naggar. **Open** daily. 🎨

A tiny stream crisscrossing the lush landscape around Manali

Nicholas Roerich (1874–1947)

This multi-faceted Russian who painted, wrote poetry and expounded a universalist philosophy distilled from many religions, travelled extensively through Tibet and the Himalayas. He is best remembered for the colourful celebration of nature in his trans-Himalayan landscapes. Roerich lived in Naggar where he died in 1947. His old home is now the Roerich Museum. His son Svetoslav, also a painter, made India his home and established the gallery as well.

A mountainscape by Roerich

⓴ Lahaul and Spiti

Lahaul and Spiti district. 610 km (379 miles) N from Shimla to Keylong via Kunjam Pass. 🏔 33,200. 🚌 🎭 Ladarcha Festival, Spiti (Aug).

The meandering Chandra river, near Gondhla village

At an average altitude of 2,750 m (9,022 ft), Lahaul and Spiti, bordering Tibet and Ladakh's Zanskar Valley, comprise the trans-Himalayan regions of western Himachal Pradesh. Unlike the lush meadows of the Kullu Valley, this is a barren land of rocky massifs and hanging glaciers, enclosed by the Himalayas to the north and the Pir Panjal to the south. Rainfall is scarce and the region is dependent upon glacial melt for the cultivation of its main crops, barley, millet and seed potato.

While the difficult terrain inhibits many travellers from going to Spiti (see pp134–5), Lahaul is more accessible. Upper Lahaul is a stark land of high mountains enveloping the deep valleys of the Chandra and Bhaga rivers, while Lower Lahaul lies below Tandi, where the two rivers meet and become the Chandrabhaga, or Chenab.

Today, Lahaul's social structure is an interesting mix of Buddhism and Hinduism, reflecting the close ties the region had with Tibet, Ladakh and neighbouring Kullu.

Keylong, the district headquarters on the Bhaga river, is the region's principal town. With many basic facilities, it is widely used as a stopover by travellers en route to Leh (see pp140–41) or as a base for treks. Across the river, opposite Keylong, a steep tree-shaded pathway leads to **Drugpa Kardang Gompa**, the largest monastery (gompa) in Lahaul. It has a fine collection of thangkas (see p127), musical instruments and old weapons. Nearby is the 16th-century **Shashur Gompa**. This monastery is renowned for its long 4.5 m (15 ft) thangka.

On the road to Manali, about 16 km (10 miles) south of Keylong, the eight-storeyed tower of the Gondhla chiefs dominates the landscape. The

Detail of a prayer wheel at Keylong

oldest monastery in Lahaul, the 800-year-old **Guru Ghantal Gompa** at Tandi, 11 km (7 miles) southwest of Keylong, is believed to have been etablished by Guru Padmasambhava, the founder of Tibetan Buddhism. Other places worth visiting are the carved wooden Mrikula Devi Temple at **Udaipur**, in the Pattan Valley, 44 km (27 miles) west of Tandi, and **Trilokinath**, with its marble image of Avalokitesvara (see p145).

Beyond Keylong, the road to Leh passes the last Lahaul village of **Darcha** with a trekking route to Zanskar (see p156) via the Shingo-la.

Suraj Tal, the glacial lake that is the source of Bhaga river, one of the main rivers in Lahaul

Spiti: The Sacred Valley

The heart of Himachal's cold desert, Spiti is a land of fascinating contrasts. Monasteries and prayer flags are dotted along the banks of glacial streams, while blue sheep and ibex graze amidst sparse pastures sprinkled with marine fossils. Once part of a West Tibetan kingdom, Spiti submitted to Ladakhi rule in the 17th century and became a part of British India in the 19th century. Through these changes in its political history, Spiti remained a locked land, enclosed between tall mountain ranges and international borders. Though now part of Himachal Pradesh, it has retained its Tibetan character and is an important preserve of ancient Buddhist heritage.

Bare multi-hued rock faces, a typical feature of the Spiti area

Chandra Tal, or the "Moon Lake", at a height of 4,270 m (14,009 ft), lies at the entrance to Spiti when approached from Lahaul. Oval in shape with deep blue waters, it is overlooked by craggy peaks and hanging glaciers.

Key Monastery, possibly founded in the 13th century, is the largest monastery in Spiti. Perched on an escarpment, it has a fine collection of *thangkas* and is the seat of Lochen Tulku, a reincarnation of Rinchen Zangpo *(see p123)*.

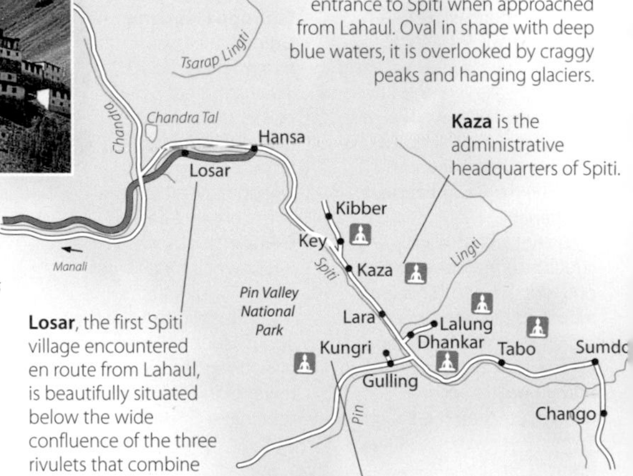

Kaza is the administrative headquarters of Spiti.

Losar, the first Spiti village encountered en route from Lahaul, is beautifully situated below the wide confluence of the three rivulets that combine to form the Spiti river.

Kungri Monastery in Pin Valley belongs to the Nyingmapa sect *(see p143)*. The uppermost hall, in the main temple, contains some ancient wall paintings and wooden sculptures.

Key

- ■ Area illustrated
- ▬ Major road
- ═ Minor road

0 km   25
0 miles   25

Tsarap Lingti
Chandra
Chandra Tal
Hansa
Losar
Manali
Kibber
Key
Kaza
Lingti
Spiti
Pin Valley National Park
Lara
Lalung
Kungri
Dhankar
Tabo
Sumdo
Gulling
Chango
Pin

The land of the ibex and the snow leopard, the Pin Valley National Park is an untrammelled pastureland in the shadow of virgin snowcapped peaks. It surrounds the upper reaches of the Pin river and its tributary, the Paraiho. Among the carnivores, the fox and the snow wolf are common, while the beautiful snow leopard is more elusive.

Chorten at a village in Pin Valley

Dhankar, the old capital of Spiti, is wedged between the pinnacles of a razor sharp spur of crumbling rock and alkaline deposits. The old monastery here is richly endowed with beautiful frescoes, and a bronze statue of Avalokitesvara.

Children in Spiti

An impressive image of Guru Padmasambhava, covered in gold leaf, is the highlight of Lalung Monastery. This monastery is one of the 108 structures credited to Rinchen Zangpo.

Vibrant mural showing a scene from Buddhist mythology, Tabo Monastery

❷ Tabo Monastery

Lahaul and Spiti district. 460 km (286 miles) NE of Shimla. 🚌 Open Apr–Sep. 🎪 Monastery Festival (Oct/Nov). Travel permits: required to travel between Tabo and Jangi (in Kinnaur). Contact Deputy Commisioner, Shimla (see p115), or SDM's office in Rekong Peo (see p122). For details, see p119.

Tabo Monastery, Spiti's pride, is linked to an important era in the growth of Buddhism in Tibet. Tibetan Buddhism suffered a major setback during the reign of King Langdarma in the 9th century, and it took a whole century for the religion to recover. The resurgence, also known as the "second diffusion of Buddhism", was spearheaded by Ye-she-od, the Lama king of Guge in Western Tibet. Under his patronage, the legendary scholar Rinchen Zangpo spread the faith by translating Buddhist texts and promoting a tremendous temple-building movement.

The *gompa* at Tabo is one of the products of this movement, established in the 11th century by Rinchen Zangpo himself. Dating from a period when monastic temples were constructed close to villages, it is one of the largest of such centres. The squat, mud structures of Tabo are enclosed within a mud wall about 84 m by 75 m (276 ft by 246 ft) and appear quite unimpressive from the outside. The exquisite wall paintings inside,

however, make Tabo one of the most significant art treasures of the Tibetan Buddhist world. The earliest paintings in the *dukhang* (assembly hall) are from the 10th and 11th centuries and depict scenes from various incidents and tales associated with the life of the Buddha. The hall also contains imposing clay sculptures of the chief deities from the Buddhist pantheon. Seven other chapels in the complex contain paintings from the 15th and 16th centuries. One of the shrines houses a huge clay idol of a sitting Maitreya (the Future Buddha). Tabo is also a favourite retreat of the Dalai Lama.

Accessing parts of the Spiti Valley that lie below Tabo remains difficult. Travel is restricted due to the proximity of the border with Tibet.

Monks praying at Tabo Monastery

A view of the dramatically-situated Key Monastery, Spiti ▶

LADAKH, JAMMU & KASHMIR

Lying across six major mountain ranges, and covering an area of 222,000 sq km (85,715 sq miles), Jammu and Kashmir is India's northernmost state, bordering Pakistan and China's Tibetan Plateau. Its three distinct regions – Ladakh, Jammu and the Kashmir Valley – offer a rich diversity of landscapes, religions, and people. The predominantly Muslim Kashmir Valley is a mosaic of forests, ricefields, lakes and waterways, its gentle beauty now shattered by armed insurgency *(see p158)*. Jammu, encompassing plains, mountains and foothills, boasts the famous hilltop shrine of Vaishno Devi, an important pilgrimage site for Hindus. Sparsely populated Ladakh, which accounts for two-thirds of the state's area, is a high altitude desert. Its harsh lines are softened by the emerald green of oasis villages, the crystal light of cloudless blue skies, and the drama- tic silhouettes of ancient Buddhist monasteries which, for many visitors, are Ladakh's main attraction.

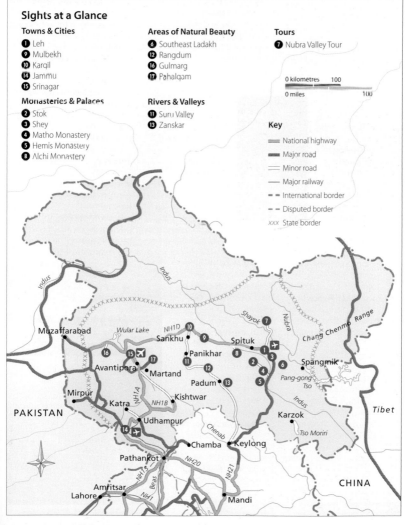

Sights at a Glance

Towns & Cities
1 Leh
9 Mulbekh
10 Kargil
14 Jammu
15 Srinagar

Monasteries & Palaces
2 Stok
3 Shey
4 Matho Monastery
5 Hemis Monastery
8 Alchi Monastery

Areas of Natural Beauty
6 Southeast Ladakh
12 Rangdum
16 Gulmarg
17 Pahalgam

Rivers & Valleys
11 Suru Valley
13 Zanskar

Tours
7 Nubra Valley Tour

0 kilometres 100
0 miles 100

Key
National highway
Major road
Minor road
Major railway
- - International border
- - Disputed border
xxx State border

◀ Spectacular view of Ladakh, also known as land of the high passes

For keys to symbols *see back flap*

The abandoned Leh Palace, once the seat of the royal family

❶ Leh

Leh district. 1,077 km (669 miles) N of Delhi. 🚶 15,000. ✈ 11 km (7 miles) S of town centre. 🚌 ℹ (01982) 252 297. 🎭 Muharram (Mar/Apr), Buddha Jayanti (May), Losar (Dec). Travel permits: required for certain restricted areas in Ladakh (see p146).

From the 17th century right until 1949, Ladakh's principal town, Leh, was the hub of the bustling caravan trade (see p146) between Punjab and Central Asia, and between Kashmir and Tibet. The large **Main Bazaar**, with its broad kerbs, was clearly designed to facilitate the passage of horses, donkeys and camels, and to provide room for the display and storage of merchandise.

The Buddha, Leh Palace

The town is dominated by the nine-storeyed **Leh Palace**, built in the 1630s by Sengge Namgyal. A prolific builder of monasteries and forts, with many conquests to his name, he was Ladakh's most famous king. The palace's massive inward-leaning walls are in the same architectural tradition as the Potala Palace in Lhasa which, in fact, the Leh Palace antedates by about 50 years. Sadly, the solidity of its exterior belies the dilapidation inside, although some repair work is now being done. Visitors can go up to the open terrace on the level above the main entrance.

Much of Leh's charm lies in the opportunities it offers for pleasant strolls and walks. In the heart of town are the Main Bazaar and **Nowshar**, with their eateries and curio shops selling precious stones and ritual religious objects such as prayer wheels. Along the Bazaar's wide kerb, women from nearby villages sit with large baskets of fresh vegetables, spinning wool on drop spindles and exchanging lively chatter in between intervals of brisk commerce. The **Jokhang**, a modern ecumenical Buddhist establishment, and the town mosque, built in the late 17th century, are close to each other in the Main Bazaar.

Between the Main Bazaar and the Polo Ground, at the eastern end of town, is the fascinating **Old Town**, with its maze of narrow alleys dotted with *chortens* and *mani* walls (see p145), and its cluster of flat-roofed houses constructed of sunbaked bricks.

On the peak above the town are the small fort and monastery complex of **Namgyal Tsemo** (mid-16th century), believed to be the earliest royal residence in Leh. Next to its now ruined fort are a *gonkhang* (Temple of the Guardian Deities) and a temple to Maitreya (the Future Buddha), both of which have vibrant murals. Those inside the *gonkhang* include a court scene with a portrait believed to be that of King Tashi Namgyal (mid-16th century), the founder of the complex.

At the western edge of Leh is the **Ecological Centre**, which runs development projects in agriculture, solar energy, health and environmental awareness in several of the surrounding villages. The centre also houses a library and a shop selling local handicrafts.

The gleaming white **Shanti Stupa** ("Peace Pagoda"), founded in the 1980s under the sponsorship of Japanese Buddhists, is situated on a hilltop west of the city.

Less than ten minutes' walk, in any direction away from the heart of town, will bring one to a green area or gold

Acclimatizing to Leh

Visitors flying into Leh, situated at an altitude of 3,500 m (11,483 ft), should allow themselves enough time to acclimatize. Any strenuous physical activity should be avoided for at least the first 24 hours. During the first few days, Leh's high altitude can often cause insomnia, headaches, breathlessness and loss of appetite.

Barley fields around Leh

An archery contest near Leh

according to the season. Down the hill in the village of **Skara**, the massive mud walls of the 19th-century **Zorawar Fort** catch the eye. Another lovely walk is up past the **Moravian Church** to the serene village of **Changspa** with its ancient *chorten*. From here a road turns towards the beautifully-maintained 19th-century **Sankar Monastery**, with its impressive images of Avalokitesvara and of Vajra-Bhairav, Guardian of the Gelugpa order *(see p143)*.

Environs

Choglamsar, 10 km (6 miles) south of Leh, is the main Tibetan refugee settlement in Ladakh. It includes the Dalai Lama's prayer ground, known as Shanti Sthal, an SOS Children's Village, the Central Institute of Buddhist Studies, a solar-heated hospital and workshops that promote colourful Tibetan handicrafts Dramatically situated on a hilltop, so close to the airport

that the wings of landing aircraft come perilously close to its walls, is the 15th-century **Spituk Monastery**, the oldest establishment of the Gelugpa sect in Ladakh. It houses the library of Tsongkapa, the sect's founder, and a shrine devoted to the goddess Tara *(see p145)* in her myriad manifestations. Situated in one of Ladakh's most charming villages, **Phiyang Monastery**, is one of only two that represent the Drigungpa sect. It was founded by Ladakh's 16th-century ruler, Tashi Namgyal, supposedly as an act of atonement for the violence and treachery by which he came to the throne. Among its many treasures is a large and interesting collection of Kashmiri bronzes of Buddhist deities, dating back to the 13th century, or possibly even earlier.

🏠 **Leh Palace**
Open daily. 📷 Book in advance. 🚫

🏛 **Namgyal Tsemo**
Open daily. 📷 Book in advance.

🏢 **Ecological Centre**
Open Mon–Fri. **Tel** (01982) 253 221.

🏛 **Jokhang**
Open daily.

🏛 **Sankar Monastery**
Open daily. 📷

🏛 **Spituk Monastery**
Open daily. 📷 Photography with permission of the lama-in-charge.

🏛 **Phiyang Monastery**
Open daily. 📷 Photography with permission of the lama-in-charge.

Festivals of Ladakh, Jammu & Kashmir

Hemis Festival *(Jun/Jul)*, Hemis. Of all Ladakh's monastery festivals *(see p144)* the one at Hemis is the most famous. This religious performance with colourful masks and costumes, offers a wonderfully authentic experience of Buddhist culture.

Masked dancers performing at the Hemis Festival

Sindhu Darshan *(11–13 Jun)*, Leh. This festival is held annually as a homage to the Indus. Held on the river banks, it includes exhibitions, polo matches and archery contests

Ladakh Festival *(20–26 Sep)*, Leh and Kargil. Subsidized by the Tourism Department, this is held for a week in the Sindhu Sanskriti Hall, as well as in Kargil and some selected villages. Apart from the traditional masked dances, the events include polo matches and archery contests – both being popular traditional sports in the region. A handicrafts exhibition is also held.

Thikse Festival *(Oct/Nov)*, Thikse. The annual festival of the Gelugpa sect takes place in a beautiful setting. The precise dates of monastery festivals are fixed according to the Tibetan lunar calendar and vary every year.

Milad-ul-Nabi *(Apr/May)*, Srinagar. The Prophet's birthday is celebrated with special fervour at the Hazratbal Mosque, when its sacred relic, a lock of the Prophet's hair, is displayed to devotees.

Spituk Monastery's labyrinth of shrines linked by narrow passages

Monasteries Along the Indus

Several of Ladakh's world-famous monasteries are situated along the Indus Valley, the region's historical and cultural heartland. Typically, a Ladakhi monastery *(gompa)* stands on a hill or ridge above the village that adjoins it. Its upper part consists of temples *(lhakhang)* and assembly halls *(dukhang)*, together with the *gonkhang*, the Temple of the Fearsome Guardian Deities. The monks' dwellings spill picturesquely down the hillside. The monasteries are still active centres of worship, so approach them respectfully.

Monks dancing in the courtyard of Lamayuru Monastery

★ **Likir**, founded in the 12th century, houses a fine collection of *thangkas* and images, the latter enclosed in beautifully carved wooden frames.

★ **Basgo** has beautiful 16th-century murals in its fort and temple dedicated to Maitreya, the Future Buddha. It was the capital of Lower Ladakh in the 14th and 15th centuries.

Ri-dzong is built on top of a ridge of glacial debris which blocks a winding gorge. Founded in the 1840s by the Gelugpa sect, its monks follow a particularly austere regime.

Kargil

Indus

Lamayuru

Ri-dzong

Likir

Basgo

Alchi *(see pp144–6)*

Leh *(see pp136–7)*

Indus

Sh

Stok

Stakr

Zanskar Valley

Hemis *(see p144)* is Ladakh's largest and richest monastery. It has superb murals and *thangkas*.

He

0 kilometres 15
0 miles 15

Lamayuru is dramatically situated on a high spur overlooking an eerily eroded landscape. Believed to date to the 11th century, its oldest temple has a famous image of Vairocana, the Central Buddha of Meditation *(see p150)*. Lamayuru also has a fine collection of *thangkas*.

Stakna, built in the early 17th century, has an exquisite silver *chorten* in its *dukhang*, surrounded by vividly-coloured murals.

★ **Thikse**, a 15th-century architectural gem crowning the crest of a hill, is a Gelugpa monastery which also has a modern Maitreya temple, consecrated by the Dalai Lama.

★ **Chemrey**, perched on a hilltop and dating from the 1640s, houses Buddhist scriptures with silver covers and gold lettering.

Thak-thok Monastery belongs to the Nyingmapa sect. It is built around a cave which Guru Padmasambhava, the 8th-century saint, is believed to have used for meditation.

Key

══ Road

Stok Palace, residence of Ladakh's erstwhile royal family

❷ Stok

Ladakh district. 14 km (9 miles) S of Leh. 🚌 *i* Leh Tourist Office, (01982) 252 094/297. 🎭 Stok Monastic Festival (Feb/Mar). Stok Palace: **Open** May–Oct. 🎫 📷

The palace at Stok has been the residence of the Namgyals, the former rulers of Ladakh, since its independence in 1843. Part of the palace has been converted into a fine museum of the dynasty and its history. Its collections include a set of 35 *thangkas (see p127)* representing the life of the Buddha, said to have been commissioned by the 16th-century king, Tashi Namgyal. Images and ritual religious objects, such as the bell and *dorje* (thunderbolt), are of unsurpassed workmanship. Secular objects include fine jade cups, the queens' jewellery, including a spectacular headdress, the kings' turban-shaped crown, and ceremonial robes. There is also a sword with its blade twisted into a knot, said to have been contorted by the enormous strength of Tashi Namgyal.

❸ Shey

Ladakh district. 15 km (9 miles) SE of Leh. 🚌 *i* Leh Tourist Office, (01982) 252 094/297. 🎭 Shey Shrubla (1st week of Sep). Shey Palace: **Open** daily. 📷

Shey was the ancient capital of Ladakh. Its abandoned palace contains a temple with a gigantic, late 17th-century Buddha image, surrounded by murals of deities, painted in rich colours and gold. Another beautiful Buddha image is housed in a nearby temple. Just below the palace, are huge 11th-century rock carvings of the Five Buddhas of Meditation *(see p150)*.

A Ladakhi couple bringing their baby to be blessed at Shey

Buddhist Sects in Ladakh

Five sects of Tibetan Buddhism are represented in Ladakh. Thak-thok monastery belongs to the Nyingmapa, which is based on the teachings of the 8th-century saint, Padmasambhava *(see p124)*, while Matho *(see p144)* with its oracle monks belongs to the Sakyapa. The Drugpa and Drigungpa sects are based on the teachings of a line of Indian masters from the 11th century. The lamas of all these sects wear red hats on ceremonial occasions. The lamas who wear yellow hats belong to the reformist Gelugpa sect, headed by the Dalai Lama *(see p127)*, which exercised political control in Tibet until 1959. Apart from Thak-thok and Matho, and the two Drigungpa monasteries of Phiyang *(see p141)* and Lama-yuru, all Ladakh's monasteries belong to either the Drugpa or Gelugpa sects.

Monks of the Gelugpa sect chanting prayers

See also features on Little Tibet *(p127)*, Buddhist Iconography *(p145)*, and In the Buddha's Footsteps *(p225)*.

Dance of the Oracle at the 16th-century Matho Monastery

❹ Matho Monastery

Leh district. 30 km (19 miles) SE of Leh.
🚌 Open daily. 📷 🎭 Annual Matho Festival (Feb/Mar).

The only monastery in Ladakh of the Sakyapa sect *(see p143)*, Matho, built in the early 16th century, is also one of the few that continues to attract many new entrants. Its main impor-tance, however, lies in its Oracles – two monks who, after months of purification by fasting and meditation, are possessed by a deity. This event takes place during Matho's annual festival, held between February and March. The drama of the occasion is tremendous as the Oracles traverse the topmost parapet of the monastery blindfolded, despite the 30-m (98-ft) drop onto the rocks below. The

Oracles answer questions put to them about public and private affairs, and great faith is reposed in their predictions. Matho also has a small museum with a rare collection of 16th-century *thangkas* and costumes.

❺ Hemis Monastery

Leh district. 43 km (27 miles) SE of Leh.
🚌 Open daily. 📷 🎭 Annual Hemis Festival (Jun).

Tucked away up a winding glen in the mountains south of the Indus, Hemis is the largest as well as the richest of the central Ladakh monasteries. It was founded in the 1630s as a Drugpa establishment by King Sengge Namgyal, and continued to be the most favoured monastery of the

Namgyal dynasty. Of its several temples, the most rewarding is the *tshog-khang*, a secondary assembly hall which contains a fine image of the Buddha in front of a huge silver *chorten* set with flawless turquoises.

Hemis is also renowned for its spectacular annual festival, dedicated to Guru Padmasambhava, the 8th-century Indian apostle who took Buddhism to Tibet. A unique feature of this festival, which is held in the summer and attracts huge crowds, is the 12-yearly unveiling of the monastery's greatest treasure – an enormous, three-storey high *thangka* of Padmasambhava, embroidered and studded with pearls and semi-precious stones. The next unveiling of the *thangka* is due in 2016.

The giant *thangka* unfurled during the festival at Hemis Monastery

The Monastic Dance-dramas of Ladakh

The dance-dramas performed at Ladakh's annual monastery festivals are immensely popular events, constituting a link between popular and esoteric Buddhism. Attended by high lamas and novice monks in their ceremonial robes and hats, as well as by local families dressed in their splendid traditional costumes, these events are a vibrant expression of age-old cultural and religious values. The dancers, representing divine or mythological figures, wear colourful brocade robes and heavy masks as they perform ceremonial dances around the monastery courtyard. The solemnity of the occasion is lightened

by comic interludes performed by dancers in skeleton costumes, who bound into the arena performing agile gymnastics, and caricaturing the solemn rites just enacted, to the delight of the assembled spectators. In the climactic scene the masked figures ritually dismember a doll moulded from barley flour dough (perhaps symbolizing the human soul) and scatter its fragments in all directions. Besides attracting large numbers of outside visitors, these monastery festivals also provide people from far-flung Ladakhi villages an eagerly awaited opportunity to meet each other, and exchange news and views.

Masked dancers at a monastery festival

Buddhist Iconography

The external manifestations of Buddhism are ubiquitous in Leh district and Zanskar – prayer flags fluttering in the breeze, prayer wheels turning in the hands of the elderly, chortens and mani walls inset with stone slabs carved with the sacred invocation Om mani padme hum ("Hail to the Jewel in the Lotus"). Inside the monasteries, the iconography is more complex. Each divinity of the Mahayana Buddhist pantheon is depicted in several different manifestations, together with a host of saints, teachers and mythical figures, mandalas and allegorical compositions. Shown below are some images that are encountered most frequently.

The Bodhisattvas

Bodhisattvas are supremely compassionate almost-Buddhas who have attained enlightenment, but are willing to forgo nirvana so that they can help others obtain liberation from the endless cycle of rebirths.

Tara is the female form of Avalokitesvara and is depicted in 21 different forms.

Avalokitesvara, the Bodhisattva of Compassion, is often shown with 11 heads and multiple arms, symbolizing his benign omnipresence.

Manjushri, the Bodhisattva of Wisdom, bears a flaming sword in his hand, to cut through the fog of ignorance.

Guardian Deities are usually represented as fierce forms, with skull headdresses, wicked fangs and flames in place of hair. Most commonly seen is Mahakala, usually above the main door of a temple.

The Wheel of Life, with animated human and animal figures on it, is mostly painted on temple verandahs. It shows the temptations and sins that make life on earth an endless misery.

The Lords of the Four Quarters guard the four cardinal directions. The Lord of the North is recognized by the banner in his right hand, and a mongoose in his left hand.

See also features on Little Tibet (p127) and In the Buddha's Footsteps (p225).

Glaciers and peaks encircling the blue-green waters of Pang-gong Tso

❻ Southeast Ladakh

Pang-gong Tso: Leh district. 150 km (93 miles) E of Leh. Tso Moriri: Leh district. 220 km (1,137 miles) SE of Leh. *i* Leh Tourist Office, (01982) 252 297. Travel permits: required. Contact Deputy Commissioner, Leh, (01982) 252 010. Permits are granted on condition that visitors travel in groups of not less than four, with the tour organized by a registered travel agent along specific tour routes. For more details, see p157.

Southeast Ladakh, on the sensitive international border with Tibet, is a region with a series of spectacularly beautiful lakes. The two major lakes, **Pang-gong Tso** and **Tso Moriri**, are accessible by road, although there are no scheduled bus services.

The biggest of the lakes is the long and narrow Pang-gong Tso. It is 130-km (81-mile) in length and lies at an altitude of 4,420 m (14,500 ft), extending far into Western Tibet. Visitors may go as far as **Spangmik**, 7 km (4 miles) along the lake's southern shore, from where there are spectacular views to the north of the Chang-chenmo Range, its reflection shimmering in the ever-changing blues and greens of the brackish water. Above Spangmik rise the glaciers and snowcapped peaks of the Pang-gong Range.

Tso Moriri, 30 km (19 miles) to the south of Pang-gong Tso is a 140-sq km (54-sq mile) expanse of intensely blue water. At an altitude of 4,600 m (15,092 ft), it is set among rolling hills behind which lie snow-covered mountains. The region's only permanent settlement is on the lake's western shore, **Karzok** – a handful of houses and a monastery, whose barley fields must be among the highest cultivated areas anywhere in the world.

The lake and its freshwater inlets are breeding areas for many species of migratory birds, such as the rare black-necked crane, bar-headed geese and the great crested grebe. Wild asses, marmots and foxes can also be seen in the region.

Among the human inhabitants of Southeast Ladakh are the nomadic herders, known as Chang-pa, who brave extreme cold (-40° C/-40° F in winter, and freezing nights even in summer) throughout the year, living in their black yak-hair tents. They raise yak and sheep, but their main wealth is the pashmina goat. The severe cold of winter stimulates the goats to grow an undercoat of soft warm fibre, which they shed at the beginning of summer. This fibre, known as *pashm*, is the raw material for Kashmir's renowned shawl industry and is, in fact, the unprocessed form of the world-famous cashmere wool. The lucrative trade in *pashm* from Ladakh's high-altitude pastures as well as from Western Tibet was the motive behind Ladakh's annexation by the Maharaja of Kashmir in 1834.

Pashmina goat

Environs

The twin lakes of **Tso Kar** and **Startsapuk Tso** are 80 km (50 miles) north of Tso Moriri, on the road to Leh. Startsapuk Tso has fresh water, but Tso Kar is so briny that the Chang-pa herders regularly collect salt from deposits near its margins.

The Caravan Trade

For centuries until 1949, Ladakh was the route for a busy trade between Punjab and Central Asia. The caravans invariably halted at Leh *(see pp140–41)*, where a lot of business was transacted, before proceeding to cross the 5,578-m (18,301-ft) high Karakoram Pass, one of the highest points on any trade route in the world. In summer the caravans traversed Nubra, while in winter they crossed the upper valley of the Shayok river. Every year, over 10,000 pack animals – horses, yaks, Bactrian camels, and an especially sturdy breed of local sheep – traversed the Nubra region, carrying Varanasi brocades, Chinese silk, pearls, spices, Indian tea, *pashm* wool, salt, indigo, opium, carpets, and gold.

A Ladakhi horseman taking a break for prayers

Tso Moriri, a breeding ground for the great crested grebe

❼ Nubra Valley Tour

The tour of the Nubra region starts from Leh and follows the old caravan trade route to Central Asia, a "feeder" of the famous Silk Route. It takes in the world's highest motorable mountain pass – the Khardung-la, pretty villages with banks of wild flowers and stands of willow and poplar, valleys covered with seabuckthorn shrubs, stretches of sand dunes and double-humped Bactrian camels, remote monasteries, and medicinal hot springs.

The Karakoram Range, visible from the top of the Khardung-la

⑥ Panamik
A major halt on the caravan trade route, Panamik also has medicinal hot springs. This Panamik lady is seen in her local traditional dress.

③ Hundar
The fascinating vista of sand dunes between Diskit and Hundar can be explored on the back of a Bactrian camel.

Lhayul Gompa

Nubra

④ Shayok-Nubra confluence
Flat sandy plains surround the confluence of these two rivers.

Shayok

⑤ Samstangling
Overlooking the green fields of Sumur village, this 19th-century monastery has impressive images.

Kargil

Shayok

Leh

Leh

② Diskit
Diskit, which has the region's only bazaar, also has a 17th-century monastery with exquisite murals.

Tips for Drivers

Length: 195 km (121 miles).
Getting around: This tour takes three days. Diskit, Hundar and Panamik have guesthouses and camps, for overnight stay.
Travel permits: Visitors must obtain an Inner Line Permit from the Deputy Commissioner, Leh, (01982) 252 010, to travel in the Nubra region. Permits are granted only to groups of four or more, and should be carried all the time.

① Khardung-la
From the top of this pass (5,578 m/18,301 ft) there are superb views, south over the Zanskar Range, and north to the towering Saser Spur of the Karakoram Range.

| 0 kilometres | 8 |
| 0 miles | 8 |

Key
▬ Tour route
═ Other road
┈ River

❽ Alchi Monastery

Founded in the early 12th century AD, the religious enclave of Alchi is the jewel among Ladakh's monasteries. Because Alchi was abandoned as a site of active worship, for reasons unknown, as early as the 16th century, the 12th- and 13th-century paintings in its temples have remained remarkably well preserved, undimmed by the soot from butter lamps and incense sticks. Of the five temples in the enclave, the finest murals are in the two oldest, the Dukhang and the Sumtsek. These have been executed with great delicacy and skill by master painters who were probably from Kashmir.

Lhakhang Soma
This painting of a Guardian Deity and his female counterpart symbolizes the union of opposites.

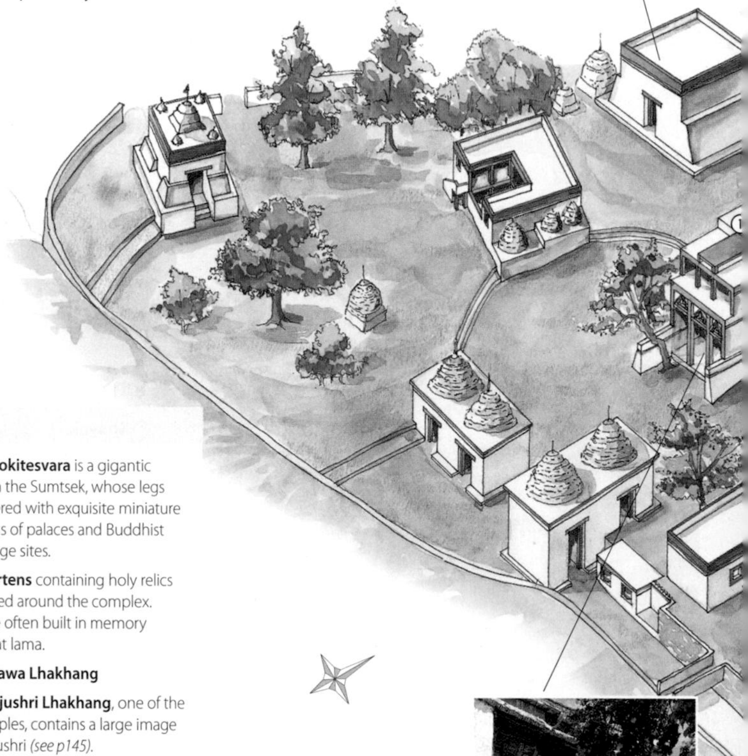

KEY

① **Avalokitesvara** is a gigantic statue in the Sumtsek, whose legs are covered with exquisite miniature paintings of palaces and Buddhist pilgrimage sites.

② **Chortens** containing holy relics are dotted around the complex. They are often built in memory of a great lama.

③ **Lotsawa Lhakhang**

④ **Manjushri Lhakhang**, one of the five temples, contains a large image of Manjushri (see p145).

Green Tara

There are several exquisite images of this goddess, variously identified as Green Tara, the Saviour, and Prajnaparamita (the Perfection of Wisdom) in the Sumtsek. Five of them are to the left of the gigantic Avalokitesvara statue, opposite his leg. The Green Tara seems to have held a special place in Alchi, since the goddess is not given such importance in other monasteries.

Green Tara or Prajnaparamita

★ **Sumtsek**
The carved wooden façade of this temple is in the style of Kashmiri temple architecture.

View of Alchi
Idyllically located on
a bend in the Indus
river, Alchi's simple
whitewashed buildings
with their band of deep
red trim, stand out against
an impressive backdrop
of barren mountains.

★ Dukhang
The serene image of the
Vairocana Buddha
(see p150) is surrounded
by elaborate woodwork,
decorative friezes and
superb mandalas.

King and Queen
This mural in the Dukhang
shows details of royal dress
and hairstyles.

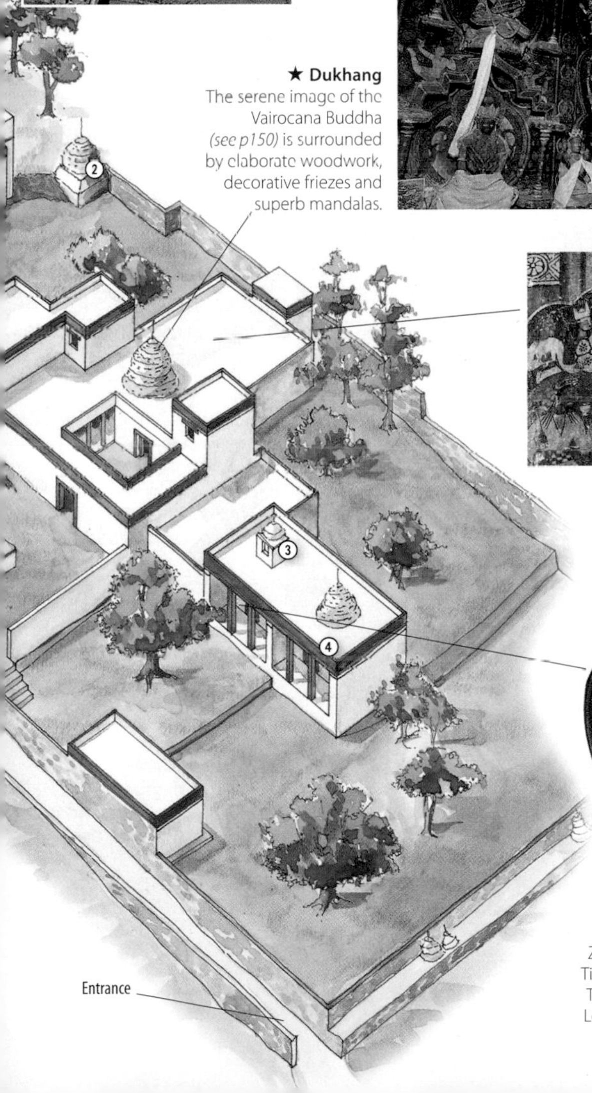

Rinchen Zangpo
This rare portrait of Rinchen
Zangpo *(see p123)*, an influential
Tibetan saint known as the Great
Translator, is in the 12th-century
Lotsawa ("Translator") Lhakhang.

Entrance

Exploring Alchi Monastery

Unknown to the outside world until 1974, when Ladakh was opened up to tourists, Alchi is now one of Ladakh's major attractions, renowned as a great centre of Buddhist art. It was built as a monument to the Second Spreading – the revival of Buddhism that took place in Tibet in the 11th century, on the basis of religious texts brought from Kashmir. The entire Mahayana Buddhist pantheon of deities is represented within its five temples, together with superb paintings of court life, battles and pilgrimages, depicting the costumes, architecture and customs of the time.

One of the many prayer rooms in Alchi Monastery

The assembly hall, known as **Dukhang**, is the oldest of the five temples and holds some of Alchi's greatest treasures. The beautiful central image of Vairocana, the main Buddha of Meditation, is surrounded by a wooden frame exuberantly carved with dancers, musicians, elephants and mythical animals. It is flanked by four other Buddhas of Meditation. Even more impressive are the six elaborate mandalas painted on the walls, together with small scenes of contemporary life. The space between the mandalas is filled with fine decorative details that have an unexpectedly Rococo look about them.

In the three-storeyed **Sumtsek**, the second-oldest temple, are spectacular images and paintings. The temple's most unique features are the gigantic images of Avalokitesvara, Manjushri (see p145) and Maitreya, that stand in alcoves in three of its walls. Only their legs and torsos are visible from the ground floor, while their heads protrude into the upper storey. From waist to knee they are draped in dhoti-like garments, covered with remarkably animated and sophisticated miniature paintings. It is advisable to take a torch to examine their incredible detail. The Avalokitesvara image is covered with shrines, palaces, and vignettes of contemporary life. The Maitreya image has scenes from the Buddha's life painted within roundels, and the Manjushri image depicts the 84 Masters of the Tantra.

The three other temples probably date from the late 12th to early 13th centuries, and though they would win acclaim in any other setting, they fade in comparison with the Dukhang and the Sumtsek. The **Manjushri Lhakhang** has murals of the Thousand Buddhas and an enormous, recently-repainted image of Manjushri. The **Lotsawa Lhakhang** has rather more austere paintings and images. It is dedicated to the saint Rinchen Zangpo, who was also closely associated with the Thikse (see p143) and Tabo (see p135) monasteries. The **Lhakhang Soma**, the last temple to be built at Alchi, has a profusion of fierce-looking deities on its walls, and scenes showing the Buddha preaching.

Riders, Central Asian in appearance, on the Avalokitesvara image

The Five Buddhas of Meditation

Mandala with the Five Dhyani Buddhas

Buddhism in the 12th century laid emphasis on the Five Dhyani Buddhas, or Buddhas of Meditation, who feature in several mandalas in Alchi. Each of these Buddhas is associated with a direction and a colour. Vairocana (the Resplendent) is associated with the centre and the colour white; Amitabha (the Boundless Light) with the west and the colour red; Akshobhya (the Imperturbable) with the east and the colour blue; Amoghasiddhi (Infallible Success) with the north and the colour green; and Ratnasambhava (the Jewel-Born) with the south and the colour yellow. The Five Buddhas of Meditation symbolize the different aspects of the Buddha, and the mandalas help devotees to meditate on them.

⑨ Mulbekh

Kargil district. 190 km (118 miles) NW of Leh. 🚌 ℹ️ Kargil Tourist Office, (01985) 232 721.

A pretty village in the Kargil district, Mulbekh, spread over the broad green valley of the Wakha river, is the point at which the proselytizing tide of Islam, spreading towards central Ladakh, lost its impetus. As a consequence, Mulbekh has a mixed population of Buddhists and Muslims, and supports a mosque as well as a monastery, perched on a crag above the village. Its main attraction, however, is a giant engraving of Maitreya, the Future Buddha, on a huge free-standing rock by the roadside. It is believed to date back to the 8th century.

The 8-m (26-ft) high Maitreya Buddha at Mulbekh

⑩ Kargil

Kargil district. 230 km (143 miles) NW of Leh and NE of Srinagar. 🚌 ℹ️ Kargil Tourist Office, (01985) 232 721. 🎭 Muharram (Mar/Apr), Ladakh Festival (Sep). Travel permits: required for the Dha-Hanu region, available at Leh (see p146).

For travellers between Leh and Srinagar, Kargil town is a good place to stop for the night. The second largest urban centre in Ladakh, Kargil was an important trading centre before the Partition of India, when the road to Skardu in Baltistan (Pakistan) was still open. The majority of Kargil's population are Shia Muslims, an Islamic sect that regards Muhammad's cousin

View of the Nun-kun massif from Suru Valley

Ali and his successors as the true imams.

Kargil apricots are famous, and its hillside orchards are an enchanting sight in May when the trees are in bloom, and in July when the fruit is ripe. The town is also the base for expeditions to the Suru Valley, Zanskar and Nun-kun. Kargil suffered shelling during the conflict between India and Pakistan in 1999, so check the situation before a visit there.

⑪ Suru Valley

Kargil district. 19 km (12 miles) S of Kargil. 🚌 to Sankhu.

The Suru Valley starts from Kargil and runs 100 km (62 miles) to the southeast. One of Ladakh's loveliest and most fertile regions, it boasts rolling alpine pastures, mud-walled villages and views of majestic snowcapped peaks. Abundant water from melting snows gives the Suru Valley rich harvests of barley and plantations of willow and poplar, especially around **Sankhu** village. Close to Sankhu are the ruins of ancient forts, together with rock engravings of Maitreya and Avalokitesvara from the valley's pre-Islamic past. The upper valley is dominated by the peaks, ridges and glaciers of the Nun-kun massif which is 7,135 m (23,409 ft) high. Expeditions to the mountain take off from the picturesque village of **Panikhar**, whose pastures are covered with alpine flowers in June and July.

Prehistoric rock paintings in the Suru Valley

The Dards

A conspicuous sight in the bazaars of Kargil and Leh are the Dards, in their colourful caps adorned with flowers. Their aquiline features and fair complexions set them apart from other Ladakhis, as do their customs and traditions. There are several theories about the origins of this small community – among others, that they are the descendants of Alexander the Great's soldiers. Anthropological research, however, indicates that their ancestors migrated from Gilgit in Pakistan before it came under the influence of Islam. There are Dard villages at Dha-Hanu, east of Kargil on the Indus, close to where the river leaves Ladakh for Baltistan (Pakistan).

A Dard in his distinctive cap

Camel caravan across the sand dunes at Nubra Valley ▶

⑫ Rangdum

Kargil district. 110 km (68 miles) SE of Kargil. 🚌 ℹ️ Kargil Tourist Office, (01985) 232 721.

The village of Rangdum serves as a night halt between Kargil (see p151) and Zanskar. Though geographically part of the Suru Valley, its largely Buddhist population and its monastery orient it culturally towards Zanskar. Situated on a wide flat plateau at 3,800 m (12,467 ft), crisscrossed by water courses, and framed by snow peaks and hills of curiously striated rock, Rangdum has a wild, desolate beauty. The fortress-like 18th-century **Gelugpa Monastery** is built on a hillock, and a small temple in the complex has a fine wall painting of a battle-scene, with warriors sporting Mongolian-looking armour and battledress.

⑬ Zanskar

Kargil district. 230 km (143 miles) SE from Kargil to Padum. 🚌 to Padum. ℹ️ Padum Tourist Office, (01983) 254 017. 🎭 Karsha Monastery Festival (Jul/Aug).

There is a certain mystique about Zanskar. This is no doubt due to its remoteness and altitude, between 3,350 m (10,991 ft) and 4,400 m (14,436 ft), and the fact that the region is difficult to access – the only motorable road into the valley is usually open from around early June to mid-October. But Zanskar's reputation as a Shangri-la also derives from

the grandeur of its landscapes, the simplicity of life in its villages, and the serene ambience in its *gompas*, often built around ancient cliff-top meditation caves.

Zanskar contains the valleys of two rivers, the Stod and the Lungnak which, flowing towards each other along the northern flank of the Greater Himalayas, join to become the Zanskar river. This continues north through a gorge in the Zanskar Range, to join the Indus.

The western arm of Zanskar, the Stod Valley, and its central plain are fertile and well-watered – villages form green pockets and the virtual absence of trees contributes to an extraordinary sense of light and space. The inhabitants of this region are mostly agricultural farmers, growing barley, wheat and peas in the lower villages, and raising livestock – yaks, sheep and *dzos* (a hybrid between cows and yaks) – in the higher villages. In winter, many of these farmers take the only route out of the area, trekking for six gruelling days across

The Zanskar river, running through a gorge

Perak, the traditional female headdress

the frozen Zanskar river, to sell their highly prized yak butter in Leh. In contrast to the fertile western arm and central plain, the eastern arm of Zanskar – the Lungnak Valley – is a forbidding and stony gorge, with few villages to be found in the vicinity.

The main gateway to Zanskar is the **Pensi-la** (4,400 m/ 14,436 ft), about 130 km (81 miles) southeast of Kargil. There are spectacular views from the top of this pass, especially of the impressive **Drang-drung Glacier**, which is the origin of the Stod river. The road then continues down to **Padum**, 230 km (143 miles) southeast of Kargil, at an altitude of 3,500 m (11,483 ft). Padum is Zanskar's main village and administrative headquarters. This is the only place in the region with basic facilities including accommodation, transport and a few rudimentary shops. It is also the starting point for a number of treks in the region (see pp156–7). Padum itself has few sites of interest, except for a rock engraving of the Five Dhyani Buddhas (see p150) in the centre of the village. A mosque serves Padum's small community of Muslims. There are a number

Stucco decoration and images in bas-relief at Sani Gompa, Zanskar

of interesting sites to explore in the vicinity. Within easy reach on foot, is the village of **Pipiting**, which has a temple and *chorten* on top of a mound of glacial debris, and a pavilion which was specially constructed for the Dalai Lama's prayer assemblies.

A short distance away is **Sani**, 8 km (5 miles) northwest of Padum, one of the oldest religious sites in the Western Himalayas. Within the monastery walls stands the Kanika Chorten, its name possibly linking it to the Kushana ruler Kanishka *(see p47)*, whose empire stretched from Afghanistan to Varanasi in the 1st and 2nd centuries AD. The monastery itself is said to have been founded by Padmasambhava *(see p124)* in the 8th century, and its main temple has some fine murals. Even more interesting is another small temple in the complex, which has unique, beautifully painted stucco bas-relief decorations, and niches in the walls for images. Sani is surrounded by a stand of poplars, conspicuous in this otherwise treeless landscape.

Visible from Padum, the buildings of the Gelugpa monastery of **Karsha**, 10 km (6 miles) northeast of Padum, seem to spill down the mountainside west of the main valley, until they merge with the houses and fields of the village. This site includes ancient rock engravings, and the murals in its Avalokitesvara temple, just outside the main complex, seem to put it in the same period

Fertile fields of barley and wheat in the Stod Valley in Zanskar

as Alchi *(see pp148–50)*. Tradition, however, attributes the monastery's foundation to the ubiquitous Padmasambhava. Karsha has a large community of resident monks, and holds its colourful annual festival between July and August.

Stongde, on the opposite side of the valley, 12 km (7 miles) from Padum, is perched on a ridge, high above the mosaic of the village's fields. Believed to have been founded in the 11th century, it houses no fewer than seven well-maintained temples, some of them containing exquisite murals.

The villages of Sani, Karsha and Stongde are connected by motor transport, though the monasteries in the **Lungnak Valley** are less accessible. The narrow footpath leading up the valley winds along unstable scree slopes high above the

Mandala, Bardhan Monastery

river, and the walk is strenuous. It takes a sharp climb on foot or on horseback to reach **Bardhan** and **Phugtal** monasteries.

Bardhan, 9 km (6 miles) southeast of Padum, is spectacularly located atop a crag jutting out from the mountain and rising some 100 m (328 ft) sheer out of the river. It has fine wall paintings dating back to the time of the monastery's foundation in the early 17th century. Of all Ladakh's many monasteries however, none, not even Bardhan or Lamayuru, can rival Phugtal, 60 km (37 miles) southeast of Padum, for the grandeur and drama of its location. Its main temples are constructed inside a huge cave on the mountainside above the Tsarap river, at a point where the drop to the water is almost sheer. Yet below the temples the monks' dwellings have somehow been built on or into the cliff-face, and the whole improbable complex is linked by a crazy system of ladders and walkways. There is no record of Phugtal monastery's foundation, but the style of its paintings, some of them quite striking, link it with the Tabo monastery in Spiti *(see p135)* and the traditions established by the Tibetan saint Rinchen Zangpo *(see p123)* in the 11th century. Its monks belong to the Gelugpa order.

Sani, Karsha, Stongde, Bardhan and Phugtal Monasteries Open daily.

Phugtal Monastery, built into a sheer cliff-face

Trekking in Ladakh and Zanskar

Trekking in the arid, extremely cold trans-Himalayan desert of Ladakh and Zanskar, very often at altitudes that exceed 5,000 m (16,404 ft), can be a uniquely exhilarating experience. The terrain, as starkly beautiful as any highland setting in the world, has a number of trails, many of which trace ancient trading routes to Central Asia. They lead past spectacularly located monasteries, remote passes, sometimes staggeringly high, deep river gorges and lush meadows scattered with *mani* walls and *chortens*. The best time to trek is between June and September, when the land is not snowbound and the terraced fields are being harvested.

Locator Map
Area shown below

Likir to Tingmosgang is an easy, two-day, 22-km (14-mile) path, past a number of villages at 4,000 m (13,123 ft).

From Lamayuru, a tough five-day, 65-km (40-mile) trek, via Konki-la at 4,905 m (16,093 ft), ends at Alchi (*see pp148–9*).

Padum to Lamayuru
This 160-km (99-mile) path follows the Zanskar river via Karsha, past the impressive Lingshet Monastery and Singe-la ("Lion Pass"), ending at Lamayuru. A slightly easier route past Zangla, joins the main trail at Yelchang village.
Duration: 10 days
Altitude: 5,000 m (16,404 ft)
Level of difficulty: Tough

Padum to Darcha
The 115-km (71-mile) path goes from Zanskar into Himachal Pradesh, along the beautiful Tsarap river, past Phugtal Monastery and Kurgiakh, Zanskar's highest village at 4,100 m (13,451 ft).
Duration: 10 days
Altitude: 5,100 m (16,732 ft)
Level of difficulty: Moderate

Other Outdoor Activities

White-water rafting on the Indus and Zanskar rivers, is a popular activity from July to mid-September. The rafting trips are organized by local agencies. There are various options to consider on the Indus river, from calm "float trips" between Hemis and Choglamsar, to longer stints between Spituk and Alchi. **Jeep safaris** to the lakes of Tso Kar and Tso Moriri and back, take three days, with tents pitched near Karzok village. The region's rich wildlife include bar-headed geese, black-necked cranes and the *kiang* (Tibetan wild ass).

Rafting down the Indus river on rubber dinghies, a popular sport

Spituk to Hemis
Ladakh's most popular trek, this 105-km (65-mile) path runs along the Indus river through Markha Valley, past Skiu village and the high pass of Kongmaru, and ends at Hemis Monastery *(see p144)*.
Duration: 8 days
Altitude: 5,274 m (17,303 ft)
Level of difficulty: Easy

Rafting trips on the Indus are organized by local agencies.

Leh to Tso Moriri is a 230-km (143-mile), ten-hour journey by jeep.

Tso Kar or "White Lake", lying northwest of Tso Moriri

Practical Tips

Be prepared: Most of the walking is hard, and it is imperative to be well acclimatized to the altitude, as even the bottoms of river gorges are 3,000 m (9,843 ft) above sea level. For tips on altitude sickness, see p743. Reliable guides and ponies are essential for all treks in the region. Maps are insufficient, so don't wander off on your own as it could prove fatal. For more details on trekking *see p727*.

On the trek: Drink plenty of water. Do not litter; carry all rubbish back with you. Plastics can be taken to the Ecology Centre (01982) 253 221 in Leh. Carry cooking fuel. Never burn wood, which is a scarce resource. Permits: Permits are required for the Nubra Valley, Pang-gong Tso, Tso Moriri and the Dha-Hanu region *(see p146)*. For general details on permits, see p734.

Equipment, jeep hire and operators: Dreamland Trek & Tours in Leh, (01982) 252 089 hires out trekking gear. Rafting agencies include Indus Himalayan Explorers (01982) 253 454 and Rimo Expeditions (01982) 253 348. Jeeps are expensive and can be hired from Leh for trips to Nubra *(see p147)* and the lakes. Check the price list at the taxi stand. For more details, see p731.

Key

━━ National highway
– – Spituk to Hemis
– – Likir to Tingmosgang
– – Lamayuru to Alchi
■ ■ Padum to Lamayuru
– – Padum to Darcha
━━ Leh to Tso Moriri
━━ Minor road
△ Peak
‿ Pass

Srinagar's 14th-century Shah Hamadan Mosque, made entirely of wood

Caution

At present, it is not advisable to visit Jammu and Kashmir, due to continued unrest. In recent years, there have been reports of terrorist activity by militant groups in the area. Foreign tourists are advised to be careful while visiting the region.

🄼 Jammu

Jammu district. 500 km (311 miles) NW of Delhi. 🄼 378,400. ✈ 8 km (5 miles) SW of city centre. 🚃 🚌 🚗 J&K Tourism, Vir Marg, (0191) 254 8172. 🎉 Lohri (13 Jan), Jammu Festival (Apr), Navratra (Sep/Oct).

The winter capital of Jammu and Kashmir state, Jammu is located on a bluff of the Shivalik Range, overlooking the northern plains. The main site of interest is the **Amar Mahal**, once the residence of the maharajas, and today a museum with artifacts relating to the region's culture and history. Jammu is also the base for the pilgrimage to the cave shrine of the goddess **Vaishno Devi** in the Trikuta mountains, 50 km (31 miles) away. The shrine attracts four million Hindus every year.

🏛 **Amar Mahal Museum**
Off Srinagar Rd. **Open** Tue–Sun. 🎫

🄼 Srinagar

Srinagar district. 700 km (435 miles) NW of Delhi. 🄼 895,000. ✈ 8 km (5 miles) S of city centre. 🚌 🅸 J&K Tourism, (0194) 245 2690. 🎉 Milad-ul-Nabi (May).

Srinagar, the summer capital of Jammu and Kashmir, is a city of lakes and waterways, gardens and picturesque wooden architecture. The old quarters of the city sprawl over both sides of the Jhelum river, crossed by seven bridges. Although the bridges have their own names (such as Amira Kadal and Zaina Kadal), they are also known by

their numbers; an Eighth Bridge, built more recently (in the 20th century) above First Bridge, is known with typical Kashmiri wit as Zero Bridge. This serves the modern part of the city, built in the late 19th century. At the city's edge are the idyllic **Dal** and **Nagin Lakes**, linked by a network of backwaters. Srinagar's mosques and shrines are among the city's most attractive features. Typically, these are built of wood intricately carved in geometric patterns, and instead of a dome they are surmounted by a pagoda-like steeple.

Chinar leaves in autumn colours

The most striking examples are the **Mosque of Shah Hamadan** in the old city, and the **Shah Makhdum Sahib Shrine** on the slopes of Hari Parbat hill. Two conventional stone mosques, the **Patthar Mosque** and the **Mosque of Akhund Mulla Shah**, both beautifully proportioned structures, date from the 17th

century. In an altogether different style is the **Hazratbal Mosque**, with its dazzling white dome and single slender minaret. Rebuilt in the Saracenic style after a fire in the 1960s, it contains Kashmir's most sacred relic, a hair from the beard of the Prophet Muhammad.

The Mughal emperors delighted in Kashmir's beauty and further enhanced it by introducing the stately *chinar* tree (*Platanous orientalis*) to the Kashmir Valley. They also created terraced hillside gardens designed around fountains and watercourses, which were formed by channeling water from natural springs or streams. Of the 777 Mughal gardens that reportedly once graced the Kashmir Valley, not many survive. There are three, however, within easy reach of Srinagar, on the eastern shore of the Dal Lake – **Chashmashahi**, **Nishat** and **Shalimar Gardens**. Above the pretty Chashmashahi Garden, and rising tier upon tier on the mountainside, are the ruins of

The impressive ruins of the 8th-century Sun Temple at Martand

A house in Gulmarg, one of India's few ski resorts

a 17th-century religious college. Built by a Mughal prince for his teacher, it is somewhat incongruously known as **Pari Mahal** or "Palace of the Fairies". From this vantage point, there are heart-stopping views of Dal Lake and the snowy ridge of the Pir Panjal Range.

Environs
Vestiges of Kashmir's pre-Islamic past can be seen in the ruins of magnificent Hindu temples at **Avantipora**, 28 km (17 miles) southeast of Srinagar, and **Martand**, 60 km (37 miles) southeast of Srinagar. The Sun Temple at Martand is believed to date from the 8th century AD, while the two Avantipora temples are probably from the 9th century AD. Built with great limestone blocks fitted together without mortar, these temples bear witness to the astonishing degree of technical expertise that prevailed in the early medieval period.

⑯ Gulmarg

Srinagar district. 58 km (36 miles) W of Srinagar. 🚌 ℹ️ J&K Tourism, Gulmarg Tourist Office, (01954) 254 439.

Gulmarg, or the "Meadow of Flowers", at an altitude of 2,730 m (8,950 ft), was developed by the British around a meadow on the northern flank of the Pir Panjal Range. The central bowl has been laid out as a golf course, one of the highest in the world. Around it are fairy-tale cottages with pine forests behind them. Gulmarg, together with **Khilanmarg**, some 300 m (984 ft) higher up in the mountains, is among India's few ski resorts. Its facilities, catering to all levels of proficiency, also include beginner courses.

🏛 **Chashmashahi Garden**
Open daily. ✉

🏛 **Nishat and Shalimar Gardens**
Open daily.

⑰ Pahalgam

Srinagar district. 96 km (60 miles) E of Srinagar. 🚌 ℹ️ J&K Tourism, Pahalgam Tourist Office, (01936) 243 224.

In the valley of the Lidder river, Pahalgam is on the southern slope of the Great Himalayas. It is the base for several treks to Kishtwar and the Suru Valley (see p151), and for the pilgrimage to the holy cave of **Amarnath**, the destination of several thousand Hindu pilgrims, every August.

Pahalgam, dotted with mustard fields, also offers trout fishing, golf and short expeditions into the nearby mountains. The road from Srinagar to Pahalgam passes by **Pampore**, famous for its fields of saffron (Crocus sativa), which has been cultivated in Kashmir since the 10th century. The saffron flower blooms in late autumn.

Mustard fields surrounding a farmhouse in Pahalgam

Houseboats and Shikaras

In the 19th century, some of Srinagar's boat-dwelling community started building luxury versions of their own homes to cater to visitors. These houseboats, which remain moored in one place, have become the favoured accommodation for most visitors. Those in the deluxe class are astonishingly elaborate, their plush living rooms and bedrooms a showcase for the celebrated Kashmiri handicrafts – exquisite woodcarving, embroidery, carpets and papier mâché. Mobility between houseboat and shore is ensured by a *shikara*, a skiff propelled by a boatman with a heart-shaped paddle. Whether luxuriating in the comfort of a houseboat, or accommodated more prosaically in a hotel on dry land, there can be no more idyllic way to spend a day in Srinagar than reclining on the cushions of a *shikara* in the shade of its awning, cruising the city's lakes and backwaters.

Houseboats and *shikaras* on Dal Lake

CENTRAL INDIA

Introducing Central India

Some of India's most visited destinations are in this vast and varied region, which covers the flat Gangetic Plains, several Himalayan ranges and the verdant forests of the Central Indian heartland. These include the Taj Mahal at Agra, the holy city of Varanasi, the exquisitely sculpted temples of Khajuraho, and the great Buddhist sites of Sanchi and Bodh Gaya. Other attractions in Central India include the game sanctuaries of Kanha and Corbett, the medieval forts and palaces of Gwalior and Orchha, and the hill stations of Mussoorie, Nainital and Ranikhet, which are the base for many treks.

Luxuriant forested hills of *chir* pine in Uttarakhand

```
0 kilometres        160
0 miles        80
```

A view of the cenotaphs of the Orchha rulers, lying along the Betwa river

◀ India's most iconic monument, the Taj Mahal, Agra

Key

═══ National highway
─── Major road
─── State border
▬▬▬ International border
-·-· Main railway
──── Minor railway

Getting Around

Major destinations and state capitals in this region, such as Agra, Lucknow, Varanasi, Dehra Dun, Khajuraho, Bhopal, Raipur and Patna are served by domestic airlines, as well as fast intercity trains. An air-conditioned special train, the Taj Express, makes a comfortable day trip from Delhi to Agra possible. An extensive road network connects most of the towns in this region. National Highway 2 connects Agra, Allahabad, Varanasi and Bodh Gaya. State highways branch off from National Highway 24 to the hills of Nainital and Mussoorie.

A rustic scene in a provincial town in Bihar

For keys to symbols see back flap

A PORTRAIT OF CENTRAL INDIA

Three of India's largest states – Uttar Pradesh, Bihar and Madhya Pradesh – lie in Central India. This vast and densely populated region is the country's Hindi-speaking belt (often called the "cow belt"), an area remarkable as much for its rich historical past and religious and cultural diversity as for its mineral wealth.

The River Ganges, which flows through Uttar Pradesh (UP) and Bihar, has shaped much of the history and culture of both states. On its fertile banks, civilizations, cities and empires have grown and flourished, from 1500 BC onwards *(see p45)*. Today, the river continues to play a crucial role in the economy, culture, religion as well as imagination of the millions of people who live in the surrounding Gangetic Plains.

Detail from the great stupa at Sanchi

UP is both the spiritual heartland of Hinduism and the cultural heartland of Indian Islam the former symbolized by Varanasi, the holiest of Indian cities *(see pp206–212)*, and the latter by the Taj Mahal, the country's greatest monument *(see pp176–9)*. With a population of 200 million, UP elects more members to the Indian parliament than any other state, and therefore plays a dominant role in national politics. Eight Indian prime ministers have been from here, including

Pandit Jawaharlal Nehru, his daughter Indira Gandhi and grandson Rajiv Gandhi and, Atal Behari Vajpayee. The tides of contemporary politics often hinge on the strength of caste and religious sentiments. One tragic result of this was the demolition of a 16th- century mosque in the town of Ayodhya in 1992, by Hindu religious extremists, because they claimed it stood at the spot where Lord Rama *(see p31)* was born. The incident led to widespread Hindu-Muslim riots and the issue continues to simmer.

In November 2000, several new states were created. In UP, the northernmost section, covering the Kumaon and Garhwal hills, became the new state of Uttarakhand. This is an area of great natural beauty, with picturesque hill stations, trekking trails, and ancient Hindu pilgrimage centres, in the shadow of towering Himalayan peaks.

Bihar, like UP, is a densely populated

The Chhota Imambara complex at Lucknow, capital of Uttar Pradesh

Pilgrims on the banks of the Ganges in Bihar

state, and its political agenda too has in recent years been dominated by caste-based issues, at the expense of social and economic development. As a result, rural poverty is still widespread and the literacy rate remains abysmally low, at around 62 per cent. Ironically, this was a state that once had one of the ancient world's greatest universities, at Nalanda *(see pp222–3)*, and was the seat of two of India's greatest empires, the Maurya and Gupta empires *(see pp46–7)*. Bihar also occupies an important place in the history of Indian civilization, as the birthplace of Buddhism – for it was here, at Bodh Gaya *(see p226)*, that the Buddha gained enlightenment. This historic legacy can be seen in the state's famous Buddhist sites. Present-day Bihar has an earthy vitality, which can be experienced at the huge annual cattle fair at Sonepur *(see p220)*, where a prime attraction is the unique elephant bazaar.

The new state of Jharkhand, in what was southern Bihar, came into being in November 2000. An area of great natural beauty, Jharkhand comprises a forested plateau, home to a large population of tribal people with distinctive cultures, who now dominate the political and economic life of their nascent state. Jharkhand is blessed with great mineral wealth, and its rich deposits of coal and iron, in particular, ensure its future prosperity.

Madhya Pradesh (MP) provides a sharp contrast to the flat, crowded plains of UP and Bihar, with its varied terrain and relatively sparse population. The countryside here is an enchanting

mosaic of cotton fields, craggy ravines, rolling hills, and vast tracts of forest and grassland, which are home to at least half of India's tiger population. A tragic industrial disaster in the state capital, Bhopal, in 1984 *(see p244)* has made the people of this state especially active in environmental issues, and many of them have been campaigning against a large dam on the Narmada river *(see p255)*. Madhya Pradesh still gets relatively few visitors, yet few other states can rival its range of attractions, which include the World Heritage monuments at Sanchi *(see pp248–9)* and Khajuraho *(see pp240–42)*, and some of India's finest wildlife sanctuaries.

At the same time as Jharkhand and Uttarakhand, Chhatisgarh came into being. This southeastern part of Madhya Pradesh is a thickly forested area, populated by different tribal communities, engaged in agriculture and a variety of beautiful crafts *(see p257)*. Facilities are still being developed to welcome visitors to this fascinating part of the country.

A poster depicting Varanasi as the home of Shiva

The River Ganges

Rising in an ice cave, 4,140 m (13,583 ft) high in the Himalayas, the Ganges flows for 2,525 km (1,569 miles) through the mountains of Uttarakhand, and the vast plains of Uttar Pradesh, Bihar and Bengal, before entering the sea in the Bay of Bengal. Through the ages, great civilizations have flourished on its banks, which are, even today, lined with teeming cities, fertile paddy fields and innumerable temples and ghats. For, above all, the Ganges is India's main spiritual and religious artery, sacred to millions of Hindus who believe that to bathe in its waters is to be absolved of all sins, and to be cremated on its banks and have one's ashes immersed in its waters ensures salvation of the soul.

Gaumukh ("Cow's Mouth") at the mouth of the Gangotri Glacier, is the source of the Ganges. Emerging as an icy torrent, the river is called the Bhagirathi here.

Rishikesh (see p188) has famous ashrams offering yoga and meditation courses where studies in Hinduism are pursued.

Devprayag (see p191), set amidst dramatic mountain gorges, is an important pilgrimage town where the rivers Bhagirathi and Alaknanda meet to become the Ganges.

Votive offering floated in the river

UTTAR PRADESH

Key

- - - International border

– – State border

Haridwar, the "Gateway to the Gods" (see p188), is where the Ganges finally descends from the Himalayas and begins its long journey through the plains that constitute India's heartland. Haridwar teems with temples, holy men and pilgrims, especially around its main ghat, Har-ki-Pauri, sanctified by the footprint of Lord Vishnu. It is one of the four sites where the mammoth Kumbh Mela is held every 12 years (see p215).

Allahabad (see p214) marks the confluence of three holy rivers, the Ganges, the Yamuna, and the mythical Saraswati. The Kumbh Mela held here in 2013 attracted some 120 million pilgrims.

The Myth of the Ganges holds that the celestial River Ganga was brought to earth by sage Bhagiratha so that he could sprinkle her holy water on the ashes of his ancestors, who were struck down by Lord Vishnu for their wickedness. The river water would ensure salvation for their souls. When the Ganga descended, Lord Shiva broke her enormous force by winding her through his hair, to save the earth from being destroyed in a deluge. This myth is often depicted in paintings and sculptures.

Varanasi *(see pp206–212)* is regarded by Hindus as the holiest spot on this holiest of rivers. Around 90 ghats line the river front, where the living come to be purified by the waters of the Ganges, and the dead are brought to attain *moksha* (release from the endless cycle of death and rebirth).

Fertile fields, enriched by alluvial soil, can be seen all along the Indo-Gangetic Plains. These fields of wheat and mustard are in Bihar.

Kanwarias are devotees of Shiva who make an arduous annual journey every August *(shravan)*, to the Ganges on foot, carrying back the river's sacred water in brightly decorated pots, to their temples at home.

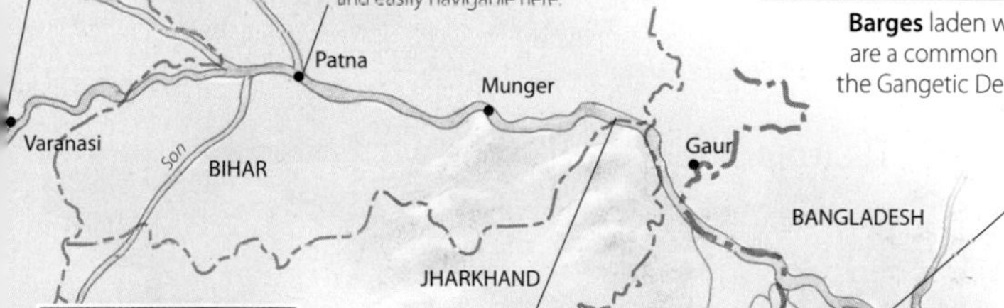

Patna *(see pp218–19)* is always busy with river traffic as the Ganges is wide and easily navigable here.

Barges laden with jute fibre are a common sight around the Gangetic Delta in Bengal.

Gandak

Ghaghara

Varanasi

Son

BIHAR

Patna

Munger

Gaur

JHARKHAND

BANGLADESH

Nabadwip

WEST BENGAL

Hooghly

Kolkata

Sagar Island

Ganges Delta

Bay of Bengal

The otter, about 70-cm (28-in) long, has a brown waterproof coat, webbed paws and stiff whiskers. This playful creature can often be seen gambolling on the banks of the river.

Ganga Sagar Mela is a colourful festival *(see p299)*, held in January at Sagar Island, close to where the river enters the sea.

The Flavours of Central India

Since a large part of the region falls within the fertile Gangetic Plain, this area is rich in agricultural produce. Stretching across the land are endless fields of rice and wheat as well as vast dark-green mango and litchi orchards. Rice and wheat are both eaten in the so-called Hindi-speaking states, although the food differs from community to community. The two main culinary influences are the sophisticated vegetarian cuisine from the holy city of Varanasi and Lucknow's refined mutton dishes and *biryanis* that evolved in the royal kitchens.

Bay leaves, cinnamon, cardamom, cumin, cloves and turmeric

Street vendor frying *samosas*, a popular snack, in a *kadahi* (wok)

Uttar Pradesh & Uttarakhand

Roughly, this region has three types of cuisine: vegetarian, Mughlai or nawabi and Uttarakhandi. The vegetarian food of the plains is very refined, cooked in pure *ghee* (clarified butter) and tempered with asafetida, *garam masala* (curry powder), cumin and chilli powder. Uttar Pradesh's street food, such as savoury *chaat*, is famous and the best can be found in the lanes of Varanasi.

The states of Awadh (now Lucknow) and Rampur produce an unsurpassable cuisine. Traditional *Dum pukht*, where food is sealed with dough in large pots and cooked on a slow fire, is the essence of Awadhi cuisine, as is the subtle use of spices. From this region come two exquisite lamb *kebabs*: *galauti* and *kakori*, while the delicately flavoured *pulaos* (rice dishes) are legendary.

In the Himalayan state of Uttarakhand the food leans heavily on lentils, soya beans and *mundua* (buckwheat).

Litchi   Melon   Watermelon   Mango   Papaya   Pomegranate   Guava

A selection of fruits grown in Central India

Local Dishes and Specialities

Subtlety and refinement are the main features of both vegetarian and non-vegetarian cooking. A regular meal comprises lentils, a vegetable dish, rice or *roti* (bread) with pickles to add piquancy. Typical of Varanasi is *sattvik* or "pure" food, which is strictly vegetarian and lightly spiced, but without onions and garlic. The Muslim courts of Bhopal, Patna and Lucknow further enriched the culinary repertoire with fragrant mutton *biryanis*, rich *kormas* and succulent *kebabs*. Some of the finest sweets from this region include *jalebis* (crisp golden spirals of fried batter), rich *badam halwa* (almond sweet) and the syrup-soaked *malpua* (type of pancake). *Paan* (betel leaf) is served at the end of a hearty meal.

Mung dal

Savouries include samosas (potato-filled turnovers) and kachoris (stuffed fried bread, with chutney).

A roadside stall in Agra selling a selection of fresh vegetables

Rice is the staple and the food is cooked in either *ghee* or mustard oil. A popular spice in this area is *bhanga* or hemp seeds.

Madhya Pradesh & Chhattishgarh

The food of Madhya Pradesh is as varied as the region. The princely states of Bhopal and Gwalior developed a distinctive cuisine that can be sampled in Gwalior's *barbat* (coriander (cilantro)-flavoured mutton curry), or Bhopal's *rizala* (chicken with yoghurt, green chillies and coriander). A gourmet maharaja from the small state of Sailana even produced his own cookbook, *The Cooking Delights of the Maharajas*, with recipes culled from royal kitchens.

The Malwa Plateau and the city of Indore have a wide array of savouries, sweets and thirst-quenchers that keep the city buzzing until midnight. Here, visitors can savour *bhutta ri kees* (grated corn cooked in *ghee*, milk and spices) or drink the cooling Malwa *kairi pana*, (fresh mango juice). Breads include *baati* and *bafla*, both made from wheat and shaped into balls. *Baati* is roasted and eaten with lentils while *bafla* is fried in *ghee*.

Paan or betel leaf, often eaten as a digestive after a meal

Bihar & Jharkhand

An abundance of fruits and vegetables and a simple style makes Bihar's cuisine special. A popular ingredient is *sattu* (roasted chickpea flour), which is energy-giving and nutritious. It can be made into drinks, breads or mixed with wheat, potatoes and mashed aubergine (eggplant).

The tribes of Jharkhand eat cereals and a curry of boiled vegetables, tubers or edible roots, lamb and chillies. A favourite ingredient is the flower of the *mahua* (Madhuca indica) tree which has hallucinogenic properties. It is used to flavour rice in *asur kichdi*.

ON THE MENU

Aloo dum Banarsi Spicy potatoes cooked with cottage cheese, nuts and raisins.

Kele ke kofta Green bananas mashed, made into balls and cooked in a lightly spiced yoghurt sauce.

Kurwai biryani Steaks are used instead of pieces of mutton in this rice dish, a speciality of Madhya Pradesh.

Mawa-bati A *gulab jamun* (deep-fried milk and flour dumpling) filled with nuts.

Musallam raan Leg of lamb roasted with various spices.

Shabdeg A classic mutton dish slow-cooked with turnips and flavoured with spices.

Mutton korma has pieces of mutton in a yoghurt and saffron sauce, flavoured with cloves and cardamom.

Okra is a favourite summer vegetable, served stuffed and fried or cooked in a yoghurt sauce.

Shahi tukra is a royal bread pudding in a rich sauce of thickened milk, garnished with sliced almonds.

UTTAR PRADESH & UTTARAKHAND

Stretching from the Himalayas to the Indo-Gangetic Plains, Uttar Pradesh (UP) and Uttarakhand cover a vast area of 294,000 sq km (113,514 sq miles), with a population of almost 210 million. Hindi is the main language. Both states offer a wide variety of landscapes and historic monuments. In UP's plains are the famous Taj Mahal and other great Islamic monuments, as well as the holy Hindu city of Varanasi and the Buddhist stupas of Sarnath. The mammoth Kumbh Mela takes place every 12 years at Allahabad as well as Haridwar. In November 2000, the hill areas of Uttar Pradesh became the separate state of Uttarakhand. Its numerous attractions include beautiful trekking trails, the picturesque hill stations of Mussoorie and Nainital, river rafting tours and yoga ashrams around Rishikesh, and Corbett National Park, famous for its tigers.

Sights at a Glance

Towns & Cities
1. Agra
9. Dehra Dun
19. Rampur
20. Aligarh
21. Jhansi
22. Kanpur
23. Lucknow
25. Jaunpur
28. Allahabad

Hill Stations & Areas of Natural Beauty
10. Mussoorie
11. The Garhwal Hills
12. Nainital
13. Almora
14. Ranikhet
15. Lansdowne
16. Kausani

Historic Sites
2. Sikandra
5. Fatehpur Sikri
24. Ayodhya
27. Sarnath
30. Kalinjar Fort

Temple Towns & Holy Places
3. Mathura
4. Brindavan
6. Haridwar
7. Rishikesh

29. Chitrakoot
26. Varanasi

National Parks
17. Corbett National Park
18. Dudhwa National Park

Tours
8. River Tour along the Ganges

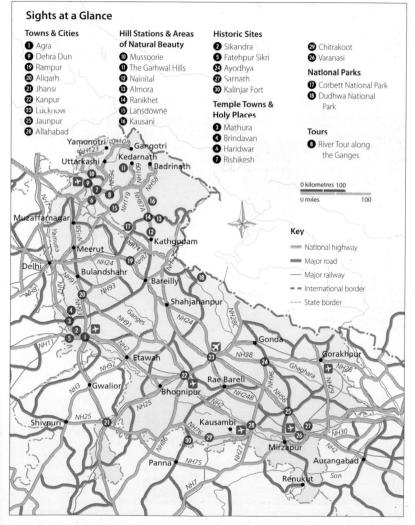

Key

─── National highway
─── Major road
─── Major railway
- - - International border
--- State border

0 kilometres 100
0 miles 100

❶ Agra

Agra was the seat of the imperial Mughal court during the 16th and 17th centuries, before the capital was shifted to Delhi. The city, strategically located on the banks of the Yamuna and along the Grand Trunk Road, flourished under the patronage of the emperors Akbar, Jahangir and Shah Jahan, attracting artisans from Persia and Central Asia, and also from other parts of India, who built luxurious forts, palaces, gardens and mausoleums. Of these, the Taj Mahal, the Agra Fort and Akbar's abandoned capital of Fatehpur Sikri have been declared World Heritage Sites by UNESCO. With the decline of the Mughals, Agra was captured by the Jats, the Marathas, and finally by the British, early in the 19th century.

St John's College, designed by Sir Samuel Swinton Jacob

🏛 Agra Fort
See pp174–5.

◖ Jama Masjid
Open daily. **Closed** to non-Muslims during prayer times.

A magnificently proportioned building in the heart of the historic town, the "Friday Mosque" was sponsored by Shah Jahan's favourite daughter, Jahanara Begum, who also commissioned a number of other buildings and gardens, including the canal that once ran down Chandni Chowk *(see pp88–9)* in Delhi. Built in 1648, the mosque's sandstone and marble domes with their distinctive zigzag chevron pattern dominate this section of the town. The eastern courtyard wing was demolished by the British in 1857 *(see p57)*. Of interest are the tank with its *shahi chirag* (royal stove) for heating water within the courtyard, and the separate

Detail of minaret, Jama Masjid

prayer chamber for ladies. The area around Jama Masjid was once a vibrant meeting place, famous for its kebab houses and lively bazaars. A stroll or rickshaw ride through the narrow alleys can be a rewarding experience, offering glimpses of an older and very different way of life, reminiscent of Mughal Agra. This is also the city's crafts and trade centre where a vast array of products such as jewellery, *zari* embroidery, inlaid marble objects, *dhurries*, dried fruit, sweets, shoes and kites are available. Some of the main bazaars are Johri Bazaar, Kinari Bazaar, Kaserat Bazaar and Kashmiri Bazaar. Quieter lanes such as Panni Gali have many fine buildings, with imposing gateways leading into secluded courtyards where the thriving workshops of master craftsmen still exist.

🏛 St John's College
Mahatma Gandhi Rd. **Tel** (0562) 324 7846. **Open** Mon–Sat. **Closed** public hols. ⓦ stjohnscollegeagra.in

The unusual architecture of St John's College has been described as "an astounding mixture of the antiquarian, the scholarly and the symbolic". It consists of a group of red sandstone buildings, including a hall and library, arranged around a quadrangle, all designed in a quasi-Fatehpur Sikri style by Sir Samuel Swinton Jacob *(see p357)*, who perfected the Indo-Saracenic style of architecture. Started by the Church Missionary Society, the college was inaugurated in 1914 by the viceroy, Lord Hardinge, and it continues to be one of Agra's most prestigious institutions.

🏛 Roman Catholic Cemetery
Opp Civil Courts. **Open** daily.

Towards the north of the town is the Roman Catholic Cemetery, the oldest European graveyard in North India, established in the 17th century by an Armenian merchant, Khoja Mortenepus.

A number of Islamic-style gravestones, with inscriptions in Armenian, survive today, and include those of the cannon expert, Shah Nazar Khan, and Khoja Mortenepus himself. The cemetery also contains tombs of European missionaries, traders and adventurers such as the 18th-century French freebooter, Walter Reinhardt. The largest

Jama Masjid, built by Shah Jahan's favourite daughter, Jahanara

John Hessing's tomb in the Roman Catholic Cemetery

tomb is that of John William Hessing, a British commander in the army of the Scindias, the rulers of Gwalior (see p232). Hessing's red sandstone tomb, built after his death in 1803, is modelled on the lines of the Taj Mahal. One of the oldest tombs belongs to the English merchant, John Mildenhall (1614), envoy of Elizabeth I, who arrived at the Mughal court in 1603 seeking permission to trade. Other interesting graves include those of the Venetian doctor, Bernardino Maffi, and Geronimo Veroneo (once wrongly regarded by some as the architect of the Taj). Near the chapel, an obelisk marks the grave of the four

children of General Perron, French commander of the Scindia forces. Another Frenchman, Jean Philippe Bourbon, a kinsman of Henry IV of France, is also buried here.

🚉 Fort Railway Station
Tel (0562) 246 4131.

This memorable Raj building was constructed in 1891 as a stopping-off point for colonial tourists visiting Agra's monuments. The octagonal bazaar *chowk* that originally connected the Delhi Gate and Agra Fort to the old city and the Jama Masjid was demolished and this station, with its French château-style slate-roofed platforms, was built in its place. It is still in

use today. Agra's two other railway stations are located in the cantonment and at Raja ki Mandi.

Auto-rickshaws parked outside the Fort Railway Station

Agra City Centre

① Agra Fort
② Jama Masjid
③ St John's College
④ Roman Catholic Cemetery
⑤ Fort Railway Station

0 metres   1000
0 yards   1000

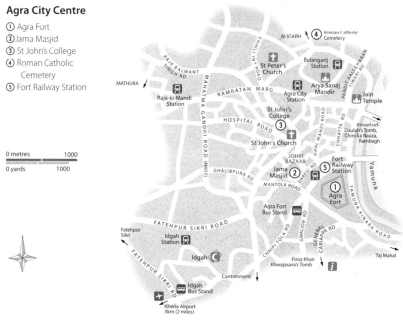

For keys to symbols *see back flap*

The colonnaded arches of the Diwan-i-Aam, the hall used for the emperor's public audiences

🏛 Agra Fort

Open daily. 🎭 Son et Lumière: 7:30pm daily. 📷 🌐 **agrafort.gov.in**

Situated on the west bank of the Yamuna, Agra Fort was built by Emperor Akbar between 1565 and 1573. Its imposing red sandstone ramparts form a crescent along the river front, and encompass an enormous complex of courtly buildings, ranging in style from the early eclecticism of Akbar to the sublime elegance of Shah Jahan. The barracks to the north are 19th-century British additions. A deep moat, once filled with water from the Yamuna, surrounds the fort.

The impressive **Amar Singh Gate**, to the south, leads into the fort. To its right is the

so-called **Jahangiri Mahal**, the only major palace in the fort that dates back to Akbar's reign. This complex arrangement of halls, courtyards and galleries, with dungeons underneath, was the zenana or main harem. In front of the Jahangiri Mahal is a large marble pool which, according to legend, used to

be filled in Nur Jahan's time with thousands of rose petals so that the empress could bathe in its scented waters.

Along the river front are the **Khas Mahal**, an elegant marble hall with a vividly painted ceiling, characteristic of Shah Jahan's style of architecture, and two golden pavilions with *bangaldar*

A riverside view of the Jahangiri Mahal, the emperor's main harem

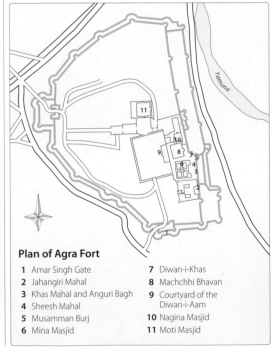

Plan of Agra Fort

1 Amar Singh Gate
2 Jahangiri Mahal
3 Khas Mahal and Anguri Bagh
4 Sheesh Mahal
5 Musamman Burj
6 Mina Masjid
7 Diwan-i-Khas
8 Machchhi Bhavan
9 Courtyard of the Diwan-i-Aam
10 Nagina Masjid
11 Moti Masjid

St George's Church in Agra Cantonment, built in 1826

roofs (curved roofs derived from Bengali huts). These pavilions were once associated with the princesses Jahanara and Roshanara, and have narrow niches which could have been used to conceal jewels. Facing them is **Anguri Bagh** ("Grape Garden") with its lily-pools and candle-niches. The **Sheesh Mahal** and royal baths are to the northeast, near the gloriously inlaid **Musamman Burj**, a double-storeyed octagonal tower with clear views of the Taj. This was where Shah Jahan, imprisoned by his son Aurangzeb, spent the last years of his life. **Mina Masjid** ("Gem Mosque"), probably the smallest in the world, the emperor's private mosque, is nearby. Next to Musamman Burj is the **Diwan-i-Khas**, a lavishly decorated open hall with fine *pietra dura* work on its columns, where the emperor would meet his court. Two thrones, in white marble and black slate, were placed on the terrace so that the emperor could watch the elephant fights below. Opposite is the **Machchhi Bhavan** ("Fish House"), once a magnificent water palace. To its west is the **Diwan-i-Aam**, an arcaded hall within a courtyard. Its throne-alcove of inlaid marble provided a sumptuous setting for the fabled Peacock Throne. To the northwest is the **Nagina Masjid** ("Jewel Mosque") built by Shah Jahan for his harem, and the **Moti Masjid** ("Pearl Mosque").

Musamman Burj

🏛 Cantonment

Enclosed by Mahatma Gandhi Rd, Grand Parade Rd & Mall Rd.

The pleasant, tree-shaded army cantonment area, with its own railway station and orderly avenues has many interesting public buildings, churches, cemeteries and bungalows in a medley of styles dating from colonial times. **St George's Church** (1826), a plastered, ochre-coloured building was designed by Colonel JT Boileau, architect of Shimla's Christ Church (*see p114*). **Havelock Memorial Church**, constructed in 1873 in a "trim Classical style", commemorates one of the British generals of the Indian Mutiny of 1857.

Other buildings in this area include **Queen Mary's Library**, the **Central Post Office** and the **Circuit House**, which used to accommodate Raj officials.

🕌 Firoz Khan Khwajasara's Tomb

S of Agra, on Gwalior Rd. **Open** daily.

A signpost on the Gwalior Road indicates the turning to this unusual 17th-century octagonal structure, standing on the edge of a lake. This marks the spot where Firoz Khan Khwajasara, a natural-born eunuch and the custodian of Shah Jahan's palace harem, is buried.

The red sandstone edifice stands on a high plinth and has a gateway attached to the main building. Steps lead to the upper storey where a central pavilion containing the grave is located. Highly stylized stone carvings embellish the surface. Interestingly, unlike other buildings of the period, there is an absence of calligraphic inscriptions. If the tomb is closed, the watchman from the village will open the gate

A view of the 17th-century tomb of Firoz Khan Khwajasara

Gold Thread and Bead Zardozi

Agra's flourishing traditional craft of elaborate gold thread (*zari*) and bead embroidery is known as *zardozi*. This technique was Central Asian in origin and came to the region with the Mughal emperors. Local craftsmen in the old city developed further refinements and complex new patterns to create garments and accessories for the imperial court. However, with the decline of court patronage, the skill languished and almost vanished. It owes its revival to encouragement from contemporary fashion designers.

Detail of an embroidered textile

Agra: Taj Mahal

One of the world's most famous buildings, the Taj Mahal was built by the Mughal emperor Shah Jahan in memory of his favourite wife, Mumtaz Mahal, who died in 1631. Its perfect proportions and exquisite craftsmanship have been described as "a vision, a dream, a poem, a wonder". This sublime garden-tomb, an image of the Islamic garden of paradise, cost nearly 41 million rupees and 500 kilos (1,102 lbs) of gold. About 20,000 workers laboured for 12 years to complete it in 1643.

The Dome
The 44-m (144-ft) double dome is capped with a finial.

★ **Marble Screen**
The filigree screen, daintily carved from a single block of marble, was meant to veil the area around the royal tombs.

Yamuna river

★ **Tomb Chamber**
Mumtaz Mahal's cenotaph, raised on a platform, is placed next to Shah Jahan's. The actual graves, in a dark crypt below, are closed to the public.

Main entrance

VISITORS' CHECKLIST

Practical Information
UPSTDC, Taj Khema.
Tel (0562) 233 0140.
Open 6am–7pm Sat–Thu.
Closed Fri. 🚭 🚽 🛗 Taj
Mahotsava (Feb). Museum: **Open**
10am–5pm Tue–Thu. **Closed** public
hols. 🚭 W tajmahal.gov.in

The Lotus Pool
Named after its lotus-shaped fountain spouts,
the pool reflects the tomb. Almost every visitor is
photographed sitting on the marble bench here.

KEY

① **Plinth**

② **Four minarets**, each 40 m (131 ft)
high and crowned by an open
octagonal pavilion or *chhatri*, frame
the tomb, highlighting the perfect
symmetry of the complex.

③ **The *charbagh*** was irrigated with
water from the Yamuna river.

④ **Pishtaq** are the recessed arches,
which provide depth while their inlaid
panels reflect the changing light to
give the tomb a mystical aura.

④ **Calligraphic Panels** The size
of the Koranic verses increases as
the arch gets higher, creating the
subtle optical illusion of a uniformly
flowing script.

★ **Pietra Dura**
Inspired by the paradise
garden, intricately carved floral
designs inlaid with precious
stones embellish the austere
white marble surface to give it
the look of a bejewelled casket.

Taj Mahal

1 Main Tomb
2 *Masjid* (mosque)
3 *Mehmankhana*
   (guesthouse)
4 *Charbagh* (quadrifid
   garden)
5 Gateway

Key

☐ Area illustrated
☐ *Charbagh*

Decorative Elements of the Taj

It is widely believed that the Taj Mahal was designed to represent an earthly replica of one of the houses of paradise. Its impeccable marble facing, embellished by a remarkable use of exquisite surface design, is a showcase for the refined aesthetic that reached its height during Shah Jahan's reign. Described as "one of the most elegant and harmonious buildings in the world", the Taj indeed manifests the wealth and luxury of Mughal art as seen in architecture and garden design, painting, jewellery, calligraphy, textiles, carpet-weaving and furniture.

Detail of the marble screen with an inlaid chrysanthemum

Pietra Dura

The Mughals were great naturalists and believed that flowers were the "symbols of the divine realm". In the Taj, pietra dura has been extensively used to translate naturalistic forms into decorative patterns that complement the majesty of its architecture.

Flowers such as the tulip, lily, iris, poppy and narcissus were depicted as sprays or in arabesque patterns. Stones of varying degrees of colour were used to create the shaded effects.

Marble inlay above the mosque's central arch

White marble, black slate and yellow, red and grey sandstone used for decoration

The Art of Pietra Dura

The Florentine technique of *pietra dura* is said to have been imported by Emperor Jahangir and developed in Agra as *pachikari*. Minute slivers of precious and semi-precious stones, such as carnelian, lapis lazuli, turquoise and malachite, were arranged in complex stylized floral designs set into a marble base. Even today, artisans in the old city maintain pattern books with the fine motifs used on the Taj to recreate 17th-century designs in contemporary pieces.

A contemporary marble inlaid platter

A single flower, often with more than 35 variations of carnelian

Carved Relief Work

Decorative panels of flowering plants, foliage and vases are realistically carved on the lower portions of the walls. While the pietra dura adds colour to the pristine white marble, these highlight the texture of the polished marble and sandstone surface.

Floral sprays, carved in relief on the marble and sandstone dado levels, are framed with *pietra dura* and stone inlay borders. The profusion of floral motifs in the Taj symbolizes the central paradise theme.

Jali patterns on the octagonal perforated screen surrounding the tombs are a complex combination of the geometric and floral. The filtered light captures the intricate designs and casts mosaic-like shadows on the tombs.

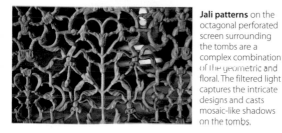

Calligraphy

Inlaid calligraphy in black marble was used as a form of ornamentation on undecorated surfaces. The exquisitely detailed panels of inscribed Koranic passages, that line the recessed arches like banners, were designed by the Persian calligrapher, Amanat Khan.

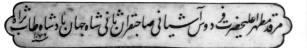

Exploring Agra: the East Bank

The picturesque east bank of the Yamuna is dotted with historic gardens, palaces, pavilions and the exquisite tomb of **Itimad-ud-Daulah**. North of Itimad-ud-Daulah is **Chini ka Rauza** (literally "China Tomb", after its tiled exterior), built by Afzal Khan, a poet-scholar from Shiraz (Persia) who was Shah Jahan's finance minister. The surface of this large, Persian-style square structure was once covered with glazed tiles from Lahore and Multan, interspersed with graceful calligraphic panels. The burial chamber within has painted stucco plaster designs that must have complemented the tiled exterior.

Lying further upriver is the quiet, tree-shaded **Rambagh** or Aram Bagh ("Garden of Rest"). This is believed to be the earliest Mughal garden, laid out by Babur, the first Mughal emperor, in 1526. The garden also served as his temporary burial place before his body was taken to Kabul to be interred. The spacious walled garden, divided by walkways that lead to a raised terrace with open pavilions overlooking the river, was further developed by the empress Nur Jahan.

🏠 **Chini ka Rauza**
1 km (0.6 miles) N of Itimad-ud-Daulah's Tomb. **Open** daily. 📷

🌳 **Rambagh**
3 km (2 miles) N of Itimad-ud-Daulah's Tomb. **Open** daily. 📷 free on Fri.

Riverside pavilion at Rambagh, a Persian-style garden

Agra: Itimad-ud-Daulah's Tomb

Lyrically described as a "jewel box in marble", the small yet elegant garden-tomb of Itimad-ud-Daulah, the "Lord Treasurer" of the Mughal empire, was built by his daughter Nur Jahan, Jahangir's favourite wife. Begun in 1622, it took six years to complete. The tomb is a combination of white marble, coloured mosaic, stone inlay and lattice work. Stylistically, this is the most innovative 17th-century Mughal building and marks the transition from the robust, red sandstone architecture of Akbar to the sensuous refinement of Shah Jahan's Taj Mahal.

Upper Pavilion
The replica tombs of Itimad-ud-Daulah and his wife are placed in the marble-screened upper pavilion.

★ **Marble Screens**
Perforated marble screens with complex ornamental patterns are carved out of a single slab of marble.

KEY

① **Mosaic Patterns** and panels of geometric designs, created by inlaid coloured stones, decorate the dado level of the tomb.

② **Tapering pinnacles** with lotus mouldings crown the minarets.

③ **The dome,** with its canopy-like shape, is different from the conventional domes of this period.

④ **Marble latticed balustrade**

VISITORS' CHECKLIST

Practical Information
E bank of Yamuna. 4 km (2 miles) upstream from the Taj Mahal.
Open sunrise–sunset daily.
[W] agra.nic.in

The Tomb
The square two-storeyed tomb stands in the centre of a *charbagh*. At the four corners of the low platform are four squat, attached minarets.

★ **Tomb Chamber**
The ceiling has incised, painted and gilded stucco and stalactite patterns. The yellow marble caskets appear as if carved out of wood.

Chhatri
Open-pillared domed pavilions top the minarets.

★ **Pietra Dura**
The polished marble surface is covered with stone inlay, the first time this technique was extensively used in Mughal architecture.

Entrance

Painted Floral Patterns
Niches with painted floral bouquets, trees, fruit and wine decanters embellish the interior of the central chamber of the main tomb.

The entrance to Akbar's mausoleum at Sikandra

❷ Sikandra

Agra district. 8 km (5 miles) NW of Agra. 🚌 Akbar's Mausoleum: **Tel** (0562) 264 1230 (contact for permission to go to the tomb terrace). **Open** daily. 🎫 free on Fri. 📷 📹 🎦 Urs at Akbar's Tomb (mid-Oct). **W** agra.nic.in/historyof_sikandra.html

The Mughal Emperor Akbar is buried in this small village on the outskirts of Agra. It is believed that Akbar designed and started the construction of his own mausoleum, which was modified and completed by his son Jahangir. The result is this impressive, perfectly symmetrical complex, with the tomb located in the centre of a vast walled garden. The main gateway, to the south, is a magnificent red sandstone structure with a colossal central arch, finished with an exuberant polychrome mosaic of inlaid white marble, black slate and coloured stone. On each corner are four graceful marble minarets, considered to be the forerunners of those

that can be seen at the Taj Mahal in Agra *(see pp176–7)*.

The large garden, where monkeys frolic, is a typical *charbagh*, an enclosed garden divided into four quarters (representing the four quarters of life) by a system of raised walkways, sunken groves and water channels.

The main tomb is a distinct departure from the conventional domed structure of the tomb of Akbar's father, Humayun, at Delhi *(see p87)*. The first three storeys of this majestic, four-tiered composition, consist of red sandstone pavilions. Above them is an exquisite marble-screened terrace enclosing the replica tomb, which is profusely carved with floral and arabesque designs, Chinese cloud patterns and the 99 names of Allah.

The upper levels, previously accessible through special permission, are now closed due to security reasons.

❸ Mathura

Mathura district. 62 km (39 miles) NW of Agra. 🚹 2,547,184. 🚉 🚌 🛈 Old Bus Stand, (0565) 240 6468 District Tourism Office, (0565) 250 5351. 🎉 Holi (Mar), Hariyali Teej (Jul), Janmashtami (Jul/Aug), Kansa Vadha (Sep), Annakut (Sep/Oct). **W** mathura.nic.in

Mathura, on the west bank of Yamuna river, is revered as the birthplace of one of India's most popular gods, Lord Krishna. A dark, cell-like room in the modern **Sri Krishna Janmabhoomi Temple**, on the periphery of the city, is reputed to be the actual site of his birth. Further away,

along the river front, Mathura's 25 ghats form a splendid network of temples, pavilions, trees and stone steps leading down to the water. The **Jama Masjid**, with its striking tilework, lies behind the river front. A charming oddity is the Roman Catholic **Church of the Sacred Heart**, built in 1860, in the army cantonment. It combines Western elements with details taken from local temple architecture.

A religious image, Mathura

The **Government Museum** has a superb collection of sculpture in the distinctive local white-flecked red sandstone. These date from about the 5th century BC until the 4th century AD, when Mathura was part of the Kushana empire *(see p47)* and flourished as a major centre of

Vishram Ghat at Mathura, where every evening at sunset oil lamps are floated on the river

Buddhism. Outstanding pieces include a Standing Buddha, and the famous headless statue of the great Kushana king, Kanishka.

🏛 **Government Museum**
Dampier Nagar. **Tel** (0565) 250 0847.
Open 10:30am–4:30pm Tue–Sun.
Closed public hols and alternate Sat.
📷 Extra charges for photography.

❹ Brindavan

Mathura district. 68 km (42 miles) N of Agra. 🚌 🚆 daily. 📷 Holi (Mar), Rath ka Mela (Mar), Hariyali Teej (Jul), Janmashtami (Jul/Aug).

Situated along the Yamuna, Brindavan ("Forest of Fragrant Basil") is an important pilgrim centre for devout Hindus who believe that the young Krishna once lived here as a humble cowherd and romanced the beautiful milkmaid Radha. Their love is widely celebrated in dance, art and literature. Brindavan's numerous temples, ashrams and ghats were mainly built by Hindu kings and rich merchants. Many Hindu widows, clad in white with their heads shaven, live in ashrams here, devoting their lives to the worship of Krishna. At the edge of the town is the historic **Govindeoji Temple** (see p356), built in 1590 by Raja Man Singh I of Amber. Across is the

Gopura of the South Indian-style Ranganathji Temple

19th-century **Sri Ranganathji Temple** with a gold-plated ritual pillar and an interesting museum of temple treasures.
Amidst the narrow streets of the old town are the sacred walled groves of **Seva Kunj**, associated with the traditional Raslila dance which narrates the life of Krishna. Other notable temples in Brindavan include the red sandstone **Madan Mohan Temple**, built in 1580, which stands on a hill next to the river, the popular **Banke Bihari Temple**, near the main bazaar, and the 16th-century **Jugal Kishore Temple**. The **ISKCON Temple**, on the outskirts of the town, is a more recent addition to Brindavan.

Festivals of Uttar Pradesh & Uttarakhand

International Yoga Week *(Feb)*, Rishikesh. Yoga is taught on the banks of the Ganges during this rejuvenating week-long festival.

Taj Mahotsava *(Feb)*, Agra. This ten-day cultural fiesta of music and dance is held in the vicinity of the Taj Mahal.

Jhansi Festival *(Feb)*, Jhansi. A five-day arts and crafts extravaganza unfolds against the backdrop of Jhansi's historic fort.

Rang Gulal *(Feb/Mar)*. The festival of colours, also known as Holi, is played with great abandon all over Uttar Pradesh.

Rang Gulal celebrations

Janmashtami *(Aug/Sep)*, Brindavan and Mathura. To mark the birth of Krishna, pilgrims perform a circum-ambulation *(parikrama)* of sacred sites. Festivities reach a peak at midnight.

Ganga Festival/Dev Deepavali *(Oct/Nov)*, Varanasi. The ancient glory of the Ganges is celebrated by devotees, who pay homage to the sacred river.

Lucknow Mahotsava *(Nov/Dec)*, Lucknow. Lucknow's historic past and continuing traditions are celebrated with food, crafts, music and dance.

Buddha Mahotsava *(Dec)*, Sarnath and Kushinagar. Religious festivities mark the Buddha's birth, attainment of enlightenment and death. These are held at Sarnath, where he preached his first sermon, and at Kushinagar, where he attained nirvana.

The Grand Trunk Road

The Grand Trunk Road, Rudyard Kipling's "stately corridor" that linked Calcutta (now Kolkata) in the east with Kabul in the

A roadside *dhaba*

northwest, was laid out by Sher Shah Suri *(see p83)* in the 16th century. In those days, it resounded with the movement of armies on campaign, and in times of peace, with the pomp and pageantry that accompanied the Mughal emperors as their court moved from Agra to Delhi. This remains one of Asia's great roads and North India's premier highway. Some ancient shade-giving trees still stand, but the old caravanserais are now in ruins. Instead, at frequent intervals along the highway, there are *dhabas* where long-distance travellers, especially lorry-drivers, can stop for a cheap and filling meal of *dal* and *roti*, washed down with hot tea or cooling *lassi*. They can also snatch a quick nap on string cots *(charpoys)* thoughtfully provided by *dhaba* owners.

❺ Fatehpur Sikri

Built by Emperor Akbar between 1571 and 1585 in honour of Salim Chishti, a famous Sufi saint of the Chishti order *(see p380)*, Fatehpur Sikri was the Mughal capital for 14 years. A fine example of a Mughal walled city with defined private and public areas and imposing gateways, its architecture, a blend of Hindu and Islamic styles, reflects Akbar's secular vision as well as his style of governance. After the city was abandoned, some say for lack of water, many of its treasures were plundered. It owes its present state of preservation to the initial efforts of the viceroy, Lord Curzon, a legendary conservationist.

Pillar in the Diwan-i-Khas
The central axis of Akbar's court, supported by carved brackets, was inspired by Gujarati buildings.

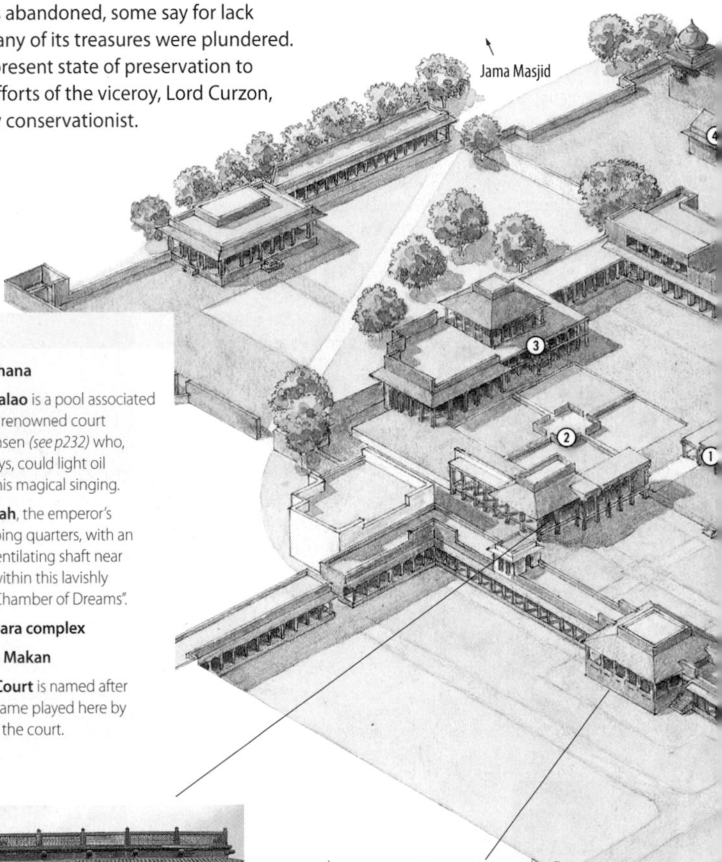

Jama Masjid

KEY

① **Abdar Khana**

② **Anoop Talao** is a pool associated with Akbar's renowned court musician Tansen *(see p232)* who, as legend says, could light oil lamps with his magical singing.

③ **Khwabgah**, the emperor's private sleeping quarters, with an ingenious ventilating shaft near his bed, lie within this lavishly decorated "Chamber of Dreams".

④ **Haram Sara complex**

⑤ **Sunehra Makan**

⑥ **Pachisi Court** is named after a ludo-like game played here by the ladies of the court.

★ Turkish Sultana's House
The fine dado panels and delicately sculpted walls of this ornate sandstone pavilion make the stone seem like wood. It is topped with an unusual stone roof of imitation clay tiles.

Entrance

Diwan-i-Aam
This large courtyard with an elaborate pavilion was originally draped with rich tapestries and was used for public hearings and celebrations.

For hotels and restaurants see p696 and pp708–709

★ Panch Mahal
This five-storeyed open sandstone pavilion, overlooking the Pachisi Court, is where Akbar's queens and their attendants savoured the cool evening breeze. Its decorative screens were probably stolen after the city was abandoned.

VISITORS' CHECKLIST

Practical Information
Agra district. 37 km (23 miles) W of Agra. 🛈 UPTDC, 64 Taj Rd, Agra, (0562) 222 6431; Gulistan Tourist Complex (UPSTDC), (05613) 282 490. **Open** daily. 🎟 📷 📹 Extra charges for video photography. 🅆 up-tourism. com/destination/ fatehpur/ fatehpur.htm

Jodha Bai's Palace

Birbal's House

★ Diwan-i-Khas
This hall for private audience and debate is a unique fusion of different architectural styles and religious motifs.

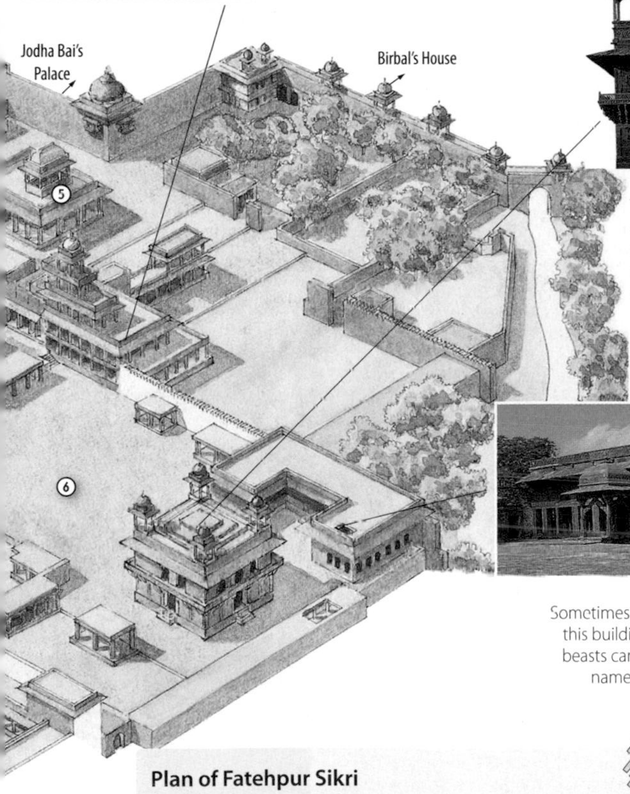

Ankh Michauli
Sometimes identified as the treasury, this building has mythical guardian beasts carved on its stone struts. Its name means "blind man's buff".

Plan of Fatehpur Sikri

Fatehpur Sikri's royal complex contains the private and public spaces of Akbar's court, which included the harem and the treasury. The adjoining sacred complex with the Jama Masjid, Salim Chishti's Tomb and the Buland Darwaza (see p187), are separated from the royal quarters by the Badshahi Darwaza, an exclusive royal gateway.

Key
☐ Area illustrated
☐ Other buildings
☐ Sacred complex (Jama Masjid)

Exploring Fatehpur Sikri

The principal buildings of the imperial palace complex, clustered on a series of terraces along the sandstone ridge, formed the core of Akbar's city. Stylistically, they marked the absorption of Gujarat into the Mughal Empire and reveal a successful synthesis of pre-Islamic, Hindu and Jain architecture (as in the carved brackets) with the elegant domes and arches of Islamic buildings. The concentric terraces clearly separate the public spaces from the private royal quarters. The buildings are mostly in Akbar's favourite red sandstone, which was quarried from the ridge on which they stand.

Stone "tusks" on the Hiran Minar or deer tower

Aerial view of Fatehpur Sikri, Emperor Akbar's grand capital

Even today, access to the city that was Akbar's capital is provided by a straight road built by the emperor, once lined with exotic bazaars. It leads visitors through the Agra Gate to the triple-arched **Naubat Khana**, where the emperor's entry used to be announced by a roll of drums. Leading off from the Naubat Khana, is the western entrance to the imperial palace complex which opens into the spacious cloistered courtyard of the **Diwan-i-Aam**, where Akbar gave public audiences. A passage behind it leads into the "inner citadel". This contains the **Diwan-i-Khas**, **Khwabgah** and **Anoop Talao**, along with the treasuries and the **Abdar Khana** where water and fruit for the royal household were stored. It also contains the curiously named **Turkish Sultana's House**. Though probably built for one of Akbar's wives, the identity of the "Turkish Sultana" remains

unclear. The great courtyard in front of the Diwan-i-Khas has the **Pachisi Court**, named after the central space that resembles the board of *pachisi*, a traditional game.

The **Haram Sara**, or harem complex, was a maze of interconnected buildings beyond Maryam's House or **Sunehra Makan** ("Golden House"), named after its rich frescoes and gilding. The massive and austere exterior of the harem leads to **Jodha Bai's Palace**, a large inner courtyard, surrounded by pavilions decorated with azure glazed tiles on the roof. A screened viaduct, presumably for privacy, connected the palace to the **Hawa Mahal** facing a small formal garden. The **Nagina Masjid**, adjoining the garden, was the royal ladies' private mosque. The two-storeyed pavilion

popularly said to be **Birbal's House**, to the east of Jodha Bai's palace, has an unusual layout and fine carvings on its exterior and interior. Beyond this lie a large colonnaded enclosure surrounded by cells, probably meant for the servants of the harem, and the royal stables.

The **Hathi Pol** and **Sangin Burj**, the original gateways to the harem, lead to the outermost periphery of the palace complex. This was laid out in concentric circles around the inner citadel and is made up of ancillary structures, such as the caravanserais, the domed *hamams* (baths) and waterworks. The **Hiran Minar**, believed to be a memorial to Akbar's favourite elephant, was probably an *akash deep* ("heavenly light") with lamps suspended from stone "tusks" to guide visitors.

Entrance to Birbal's House

Jama Masjid

This grand open mosque towers over the city of Fatehpur Sikri and was the model for several Mughal mosques. Flanked by arched cloisters, its vast congregational area has monumental gateways to the east and south. The spiritual focus of the complex is the tomb and hermitage of the Sufi mystic, Salim Chishti, as popular today as it was during the time of Akbar.

Tomb of Sheikh Salim Chishti
Exquisite marble serpentine brackets and almost transparent screens surround the inner tomb which has a sandalwood canopy inlaid with mother-of-pearl.

Hujra
Symmetrically flanking the main mosque, this pair of identical cloistered prayer rooms have flat-roofed pillared galleries that run round the complex.

Badshahi Darwaza
Akbar used the steep steps of this royal gateway to enter the complex. The view of the sacred mosque directly across, greeted his entry.

Corridors

Buland Darwaza
Erected by Akbar to mark his conquest over Gujarat in 1573, this huge 54-m (177-ft) gateway later inspired other lofty gateways.

Making a Wish in Salim Chishti's Tomb

Ever since Akbar's childlessness was ended by the remarkable prediction of Salim Chishti in 1568, the saint's tomb has attracted crowds of supplicants, particularly childless women in search of a miracle. Visitors to the *dargah*, lavishly endowed by both Akbar and his son Jahangir, make a wish, tie a small cotton thread on the screen around the tomb, and go back confident that the saint will make it come true.

A thread tied to a screen in Chishti's tomb

Pilgrims taking a dip in the holy Ganges at Haridwar

❻ Haridwar

Haridwar district. 214 km (133 miles) N of Delhi. 🚉 🚌 near railway station. ℹ️ GMVN Tourist Office, Rahi Motel, (01334) 265 304. 🎭 Kumbh Mela (every 12 years; Feb–Mar), Ardh Kumbha Mela (every 6 years; Feb–Mar), Haridwar Festival (Oct), Dussehra (Sep/Oct). 🌐 haridwar.nic.in

The Ganges, India's holiest river (see pp166–7), descends from the Himalayas and begins its journey through the plains at Haridwar. This gives the town a unique status, making a pilgrimage to Haridwar every devout Hindu's dream.

Surprisingly bare of ancient monuments, Haridwar's most famous "sight", as well as a constant point of reference, is the Ganges itself with its numerous bathing ghats, tanks and temples. These

Sign of Chotiwala, a popular restaurant

bustling sites of ritual Hindu practices, performed by pilgrims for the salvation of their ancestors and for their own expiation, demonstrate their deep faith in the power of the river. The main ghat, **Har-ki-Pauri**, is named after a supposed imprint of Vishnu's feet at the site. Hundreds attend the daily evening *aarti* at this ghat, when leaf boats are filled with flowers, lit with lamps and set adrift on the Ganges. Further south, a ropeway connects the town to the **Mansa Devi Temple** on a hill across the river, which offers panoramic views of Haridwar. Also situated south of the town is the **Gurukul Kangri University**, a renowned centre of Vedic knowledge, where students are taught by their gurus in the traditional oral style. A section here displays archaeological

finds. A good way to experience Haridwar's ambience, which has changed little since ancient times, is to stroll along the riverside bazaar, lined with small eateries and stalls full of ritual paraphernalia – small mounds of vermilion powder, coconuts wrapped in red and gold cloth, and brass idols. The most popular items with the pilgrims are the jars and canisters sold here. These are used to carry back a vital ingredient of Hindu rituals: water from the Ganges (Gangajal) which, the faithful believe, remains ever fresh.

❼ Rishikesh

Dehra Dun district. 228 km (142 miles) N of Delhi. 🚌 Yatra bus station, (0135) 242 0006. ℹ️ GMVN Office Shail Vihar, (0135) 243 1793; Uttarakhand Tourism Office, (0135) 243 0209. 🎭 International Yoga Week (Mar).

This twin city of Dehra Dun, situated at the confluence of the Chandrabhaga and the Ganges, marks the starting point of the holy Char Dham pilgrim route (see p191). Muni-ki-Reti (literally "Sand of the Sages") lies upstream from the Triveni Ghat and is said to be a blessed site since ancient sages meditated at this spot. It has several famous ashrams, including Sivanand, Shanti Kunj and Purnanand, which offer courses in India's ancient knowledge systems (see p730). North of Muni-ki Reti are two suspension bridges across the Ganges, Rama or Sivananda Jhula and Lakshman Jhula.

Yoga: the Ancient Path to Holistic Health

Over 2,000 years ago, the sage Patanjali formulated a series of physical postures called *asanas* which, along with controlled breathing and meditation (*pranayama*), were meant to set the individual on the path to self-realization. Ever since, yoga has been practised by ascetics and non-ascetics alike. Essentially, yoga calms and focuses the mind by stimulating blood circulation while relaxing nerves and muscles. This helps to combat the stress of daily life and is particularly suited to modern lifestyles as it does not require equipment or visits to the gym. Yoga entered the wider popular consciousness in the late 1960s when the Beatles paid a visit to the Maharishi Mahesh Yogi's ashram in Rishikesh, and today many schools of yoga have centres in India as well as in Europe and North America. Rishikesh, with its plethora of yoga ashrams, is touted as the yoga capital of the world. An International Yoga Week (see p183) is also held here in February.

A woman performing an *asana*

❽ River Tour Along the Ganges

From September to April, the Ganges, swollen by the monsoon rains of the upper catchment areas, becomes a torrent, gushing over rocky boulders as it hurtles out of the mountains to the plains. During this period a few stretches of rapids, where the flow is rough but safe, become a popular circuit for enthusiasts of white-water rafting. Only organized tours, run by certified experts, are allowed. For the less adventurous, a scenic driving tour meanders through this valley of the sages, whose ashrams nestle in the surrounding forests along the holy river.

The Ganges flowing serenely through a forested valley

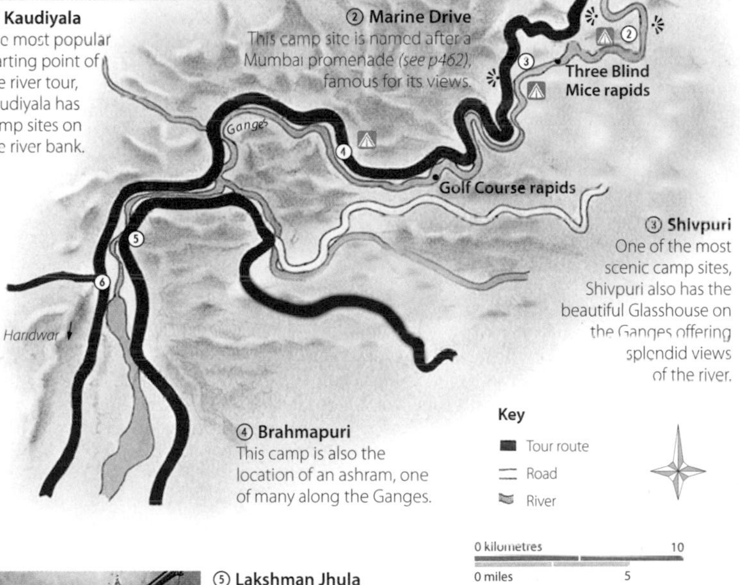

① **Kaudiyala**
The most popular starting point of the river tour, Kaudiyala has camp sites on the river bank.

② **Marine Drive**
This camp site is named after a Mumbai promenade (see p462), famous for its views.

The Wall rapids

Three Blind Mice rapids

Golf Course rapids

Gangotri

Devprayag

③ **Shivpuri**
One of the most scenic camp sites, Shivpuri also has the beautiful Glasshouse on the Ganges offering splendid views of the river.

④ **Brahmapuri**
This camp is also the location of an ashram, one of many along the Ganges.

Haridwar

Key

- ■ Tour route
- ⚌ Road
- ⚍ River

```
0 kilometres          10
0 miles          5
```

⑤ **Lakshman Jhula**
A modern suspension bridge (jhula) across the Ganges, replaced the old rope bridge in 1929. This lies at the northern end of Rishikesh, and offers fine views of the river.

⑥ **Rishikesh**
An ancient spiritual centre, Rishikesh is serenely located on the banks of the Ganges amid lush, wooded hills.

Tips for Rafters

Length: 36 km (22 miles).
Getting around: Rafting can be done over two or three days, with night halts at camps situated at Kaudiyala, Marine Drive, Shivpuri and Brahmapuri. A shorter tour of the same stretch can also be done in one day. For organized tours, tour operators and equipment hire (see p731).

For keys to symbols see back flap

The façade of the Forest Research Institute, Dehra Dun, established in 1914

❾ Dehra Dun

Dehra Dun district. 256 km (159 miles) NE of Delhi. 🏛 1,696,694. ✈ Jolly Grant, 24 km (15 miles) SE of town centre. 🚉 🚌 ISBT, (0135) 264 3838 ℹ GMVN, 74/1, Rajpur Road, (0135) 274 7898; Uttarakhand Tourism Office, Patel Nagar, (0135) 265 3217. 🌐 dehradun.nic.in

Fringed by the Shivalik Hills, Dehra Dun lies in the pretty Doon Valley, flanked by the Ganges to the west and the Yamuna to the east. The provisional capital of the newly formed state of Uttarakhand, the town is also the gateway to the Garhwal Hills. A number of prestigious institutions have their headquarters here, such as the Survey of India and the Forest Research Institute. India's very own Eton, Doon School, as well as the country's foremost training academy for army officers, the Indian Military Academy, are also situated here. Rajpur Road, the main link to the hills, is lined with bakeries and restaurants and has the old Clock Tower, the town's principal landmark, at one end. Dehra Dun's bracing climate and its proximity to Mussoorie make it a popular retirement retreat. The Doon Valley is also famous for its fragrant basmati rice, and its mango and litchi orchards.

Environs

The **Rajaji National Park**, 5 km (3 miles) southeast of Dehra Dun, is a picturesque wildlife sanctuary covering over 800 sq km (309 sq miles). It is best known for its birdlife and herds of elephants.

❿ Mussoorie

Uttarkashi district. 35 km (22 miles) N of Dehra Dun. 🏛 30,118. 🚌 ℹ Uttarakhand Tourist Bureau, The Mall, (0135) 263 2863.

One of the Raj's most popular summer retreats, Mussoorie is perched on a horseshoe-shaped ridge above the Doon Valley at a height of 1,920 m (6,299 ft), and is inundated with Indian visitors in summer. Life in Mussoorie centres around The Mall, the main thoroughfare, which is lined with shops and eating places. The old library lies at the town's western end. About 7 km (4 miles) further west, is a house known as **Everest House**. This was the home of Sir George Everest, the legendary Surveyor-General who mapped Mount Everest, and one of Mussoorie's earliest

Little blue kingfisher

residents. The town's small Tibetan community is settled in **Happy Valley**, close to Convent Hill. The **Tibetan Market**, below The Mall, sells a range of woollens. A ropeway from The Mall leads up to **Gun Hill**, which, on a clear day, has fine views of many Greater Himalayan peaks, including Nanda Devi, Kedarnath and Badrinath *(see pp68–9)*. **Camel's Back Road** named after a distinctively shaped rock, offers a pleasant walk along the upper ridge, and **Kempty Falls**, lying 12 km (8 miles) northwest of town, is a popular picnic spot.

Landour, a short distance east of Kulri bazaar, was originally a barracks and convalescence area for British soldiers. With its colonial bungalows and relative quiet, it has managed to preserve some of Mussoorie's old character and is the town's prettiest quarter.

The Pundits

Up to the mid 19th-century, Tibet and Central Asia were vast blanks on the map of the world, yet strategically important to the British in their rivalry with Imperial Russia. As foreigners were forbidden from entering these lands, between 1865 and 1885, the Survey of India trained and sent an intrepid group of Indians to survey the region. Known as the Pundits, these men went disguised as Buddhist pilgrims and traders, with compasses and survey notes concealed in their prayer wheels, and mercury thermometers hidden in their hollowed-out pilgrims staffs. The beads of a rosary helped them measure the distance they covered every day. The most remarkable of the Pundits was Nain Singh, who brought back invaluable and accurate topographical information on large tracts of Tibet.

A portrait of Nain Singh (1830–95)

⓫ The Garhwal Hills

Uttarkashi and Chamoli districts.
148 km (92 miles) N from Rishikesh
to Uttarkashi. 🚌 TGMA Bus Station,
(01374) 222 154. ℹ️ Uttarakhand
Tourist Bureau, Uttarkashi, (01374)
223 573/130. 🌐 uttarkashi.nic.in

The northern stretches of
Garhwal (Uttarakhand's western
hills) are strewn with pilgrim
towns, ancient shrines and
forbidding snowbound peaks.
Uttarkashi, the main town,
lies 148 km (92 miles) north of
Rishikesh (see p188), and is an
important starting point for
treks to the upper reaches of
Garhwal. A leading school for
aspiring climbers, the **Nehru
Institute of Mountaineering**,
is situated in this town, and
boasts of having trained
Bachendri Pal, the first Indian
woman to scale Mount
Everest in 1984.

This region also encompasses
an area traditionally known as
Dev Bhoomi ("Abode of the
Gods"). The Char Dham or four
major places of pilgrimage,
Gangotri, Yamunotri, Kedarnath
and **Badrinath**, are all situated
here at altitudes over 3,100 m
(10,171 ft), in the shadow of some
awe-inspiring Himalayan peaks.
The pilgrimage season lasts
from April to early November,
after which the snows drive
away all but the most devout.
All four sites can be reached

Badrinath, Garhwal's foremost *dham* and source of the Alaknanda river

from Uttarkashi, Haridwar
and Rishikesh.

Yamunotri, 209 km (130 miles)
north of Rishikesh, is the source
of the Yamuna, and a 13-km
(8-mile) walk from
Hanuman Chatti. Its
temple was rebuilt
in the 20th century
after the earlier one
was destroyed by
floods. The small
village of Gangotri,
named after the
Ganges which flows
through it, lies 100
km (62 miles) northeast
of Uttarkashi. Its 18th-
century temple has images of
Hindu deities. **Gaumukh**, the
source of River Ganges, lies 18 km
(11 miles) upstream, below the
soaring Bhagirathi peaks, and

A mendicant in
saffron robes

can be reached via
a path that follows
the lovely river valley.
At this point, the
river is known as the
Bhagirathi, and only
becomes the Ganges
proper after it joins
the Alaknanda river at
Devprayag (see p166).

The impressive
Kedarnath peaks
form the backdrop
for the pilgrim town
of Kedarnath, sacred
to Shiva, and 223 km
(139 miles) northeast
of Rishikesh. A
beautifully carved
stone temple, said
to be 800 years old,
lies 4 km (9 miles)
north of the road

head at Gaurikund. The most
visited of all the Char Dham
shrines, Badrinath is situated
298 km (185 miles) northeast of
Rishikesh. Its colourfully
painted temple,
dedicated to Vishnu,
is usually packed with
pilgrims. The town
has a spectacular
setting, wedged
between the Nar
and Narayan ranges.
The Neelkanth or
"Blue Throat Peak",
named after Lord
Shiva, towers over
Badrinath at a
height of 6,957 m (22,825 ft).

Joshimath, lying 250 km
(155 miles) northeast of Rishikesh
at the confluence of the Dhauli
Ganga and Alaknanda rivers
at Vishnuprayag, is one of the
four *mathas* (seats of learning)
established by the great 9th-
century sage, Adi Shankaracharya
(see p652). It is also the junction
of two ancient trans-Himalayan
trading routes. The town was a
gateway to the Nanda Devi
Sanctuary (see p193), until the
sanctuary was closed to the public
in 1983. Today, visitors head mostly
for the ski slopes of **Auli**, reached
via road or cable car from
Joshimath. The trek to the Sikh
shrine of **Hemkund Sahib** and
the **Valley of Flowers National
Park** (see p193) begins 20 km
(12 miles) north of Joshimath,
from Ghangaria. The Valley of
Flowers, best visited between the
months of June and September,
is a carpet of anemones, roses,
primulas and other alpine flora.

Gaumukh, the glacial source of the Ganges, backed
by the Bhagirathi peaks

Trekking in Garhwal and Kumaon

No Himalayan ranges are as rich in myth and legend as those of Garhwal and Kumaon (Uttarakhand's eastern hills). Known as Dev Bhoomi ("Abode of the Gods"), every peak, river and trail is either named after a Hindu god or goddess, or finds mention in holy scriptures. Relatively easy to access, Garhwal and Kumaon are a wonderful introduction to the Himalayas. A single walk can lead through forests, valleys bursting with wild flowers, and glacial moonscapes of rock and ice. The best seasons are between February and May and September and November.

Locator Map
■ Areas shown below

The Gaumukh Trail
This 26-km (16-mile) path traces the infant River Ganges along an ancient pilgrim trail, from Gangotri to its glacial source at Gaumukh (*see p166*). The route crosses the Gangotri Glacier and forks, leading to the meadows of Tapovan and Nandanvan, dominated by the imposing Bhagirathi and Shivling peaks.
Duration: 6 days
Altitude: 4,500 m (14,764 ft)
Level of Difficulty: Moderate to tough

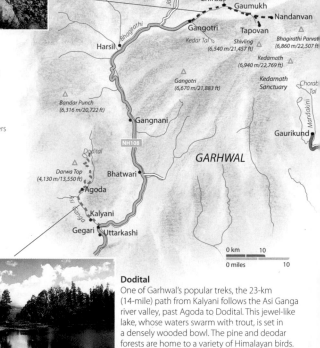

Key
- ▬ ▬ The Gaumukh Trail
- ▬ ▬ Dodital
- ‑ ‑ The Curzon Trail
- ▬ ▬ Pindari Glacier
- ▬ ▬ The Valley of Flowers
- ══ National highway
- ▬▬ Major road
- ══ Minor road
- △ Peak
- ⁀ Pass

Chirbas
Gaumukh
Nandanvan
Gangotri
Tapovan
Kedar Tal
Shivling (6,540 m/21,457 ft)
Bhagirathi Parvat (6,860 m/22,507 ft)
Harsil
Kedarnath (6,940 m/22,769 ft)
Gangotri (6,670 m/21,883 ft)
Kedarnath Sanctuary
Chorab Tal
Bandar Punch (6,316 m/20,722 ft)
Gangnani
Gaurikund
Dodital
NH108
GARHWAL
Darwa Top (4,130 m/13,550 ft)
Bhatwari
Agoda
Kalyani
Gegari
Uttarkashi

0 km 10
0 miles 10

Dodital
One of Garhwal's popular treks, the 23-km (14-mile) path from Kalyani follows the Asi Ganga river valley, past Agoda to Dodital. This jewel-like lake, whose waters swarm with trout, is set in a densely wooded bowl. The pine and deodar forests are home to a variety of Himalayan birds.
Duration: 3 days
Altitude: 3,024 m (9,921 ft)
Level of Difficulty: Easy

The Curzon Trail

The 70-km (44-mile) trail is named after the British viceroy who followed this route. From Ghat, it skirts the western edge of the Nanda Devi Sanctuary, crossing over the Kuari Pass, with clear views of Nanda Devi. It ends at Tapovan, 12 km (8 mile) northwest of Joshimath.

Duration: 6 days
Altitude: 4,268 m (14,003 ft)
Level of Difficulty: Tough

The Valley of Flowers National

Park, a 20-km (12-mile) climb from Govindghat, has a profusion of wild flowers *(see p191)*.

Duration: 3 days
Altitude: 3,352 m (10,997 ft)
Level of Difficulty: Moderate

Tips for Walkers

Be prepared: Acclimatization is essential for altitudes over 3,000 m (9,843 ft). See p743 for information on altitude sickness. For longer routes, guides are necessary. For more details on trekking, see p727.
On the trek: Drink plenty of water. Carry a first aid kit and cooking fuel. Never burn wood, which is a scarce resource. Put out all fires properly, leaving no burning embers. Do not litter, and carry your rubbish back with you.
Permits: In Garhwal, travel permits are required for border areas which can be obtained from the District Magistrate's Office in Uttarkashi, (01374) 222 280 or the GMVN, Rishikesh, (0135) 243 1793. No permits are required for Kumaon. For more information, see p734.
Equipment hire & operators: In Garhwal, contact Mount Support in Uttarkashi, GMVN (0135) 243 1793, in Rishikesh, GMVN (0135) 274 7898, for trekking assistance; in Dehra Dun *(see p190)*, contact Garhwal Trekking & Mountaineering Division, GMVN (0135) 248 0799. In Kumaon, Parbat Tours in Nainital, (05942) 235 656, and the Nainital Mountaineering Club, (05942) 235 051, organize treks. For more details, see p731.

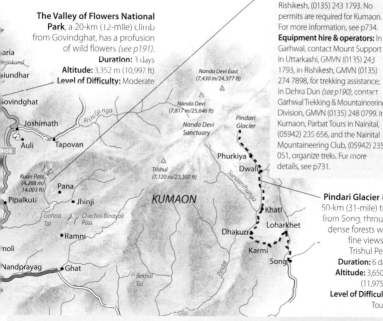

Nanda Devi East
(7,430 m/24,377 ft)

Nanda Devi
(7,817 m/25,646 ft)

Nanda Devi
Sanctuary

Pindari
Glacier

Joshimath

Govindghat

Rishi Ganga

Auli

Tapovan

aria
lemkund
iundhar

Phurkiya

Dwali

Sundardhunga

Trishul
(7,120 m/23,360 ft)

Kuari Pass
(4,268 m,
14,003 ft)

Pana

Pipalkoti

Jhinji

Gohna
Tal

Chechni Binayak
Pass

KUMAON

Khati

Loharkhet

Ramni

Dhakuri

noli

Karmi

Nandprayag

Ghat

Bekhal
Tal

Song

Pindar

Pindari Glacier is a
50-km (31-mile) trek from Song, through dense forests with fine views of Trishul Peak.

Duration: 6 days
Altitude: 3,650 m (11,975 ft)
Level of Difficulty: Tough

Nanda Devi Sanctuary

The 630-sq km (243-sq mile) Nanda Devi Sanctuary has three splendid peaks – Nanda Devi, Nanda Devi East and Nanda Kot, which form a snowy wall in the north. Nanda Devi *(see pp68–9)* is India's second highest peak at 7,817 m (25,646 ft). Believed to be the birthplace of Shiva's consort, Parvati, the mountain is revered as a goddess. The area was thought to be impenetrable till British mountaineers

Nanda Devi and Nanda Devi East

Eric Shipton and Bill Tilman discovered a route in 1936. A spate of expeditions followed, to the distress of the local people who believed this would incur the wrath of the goddess. In 1976, American mountaineer Willi Unsoeld, along with his 22-year-old daughter Nanda Devi (whom he had named after the peak), set off for the mountain, but Nanda Devi died tragically during the expedition. The core area of the sanctuary was closed in 1983 to protect its fragile ecosystem, which is the habitat of rare fauna such as the snow leopard and the monal pheasant.

⑫ Nainital

Nainital district. 322 km (200 miles) NE of Delhi. 🚉 Kathgodam, 35 km (22 miles) S of Nainital, then taxi or bus. 🚌 (05942) 235 518. 𝒊 KMVN, Om Park, (05942) 231 436. 🆆 nainital.nic.in

This pretty hill station, nestled in the Kumaon Hills, is named after the emerald green eyes (naina) of Parvati, Shiva's consort. A temple dedicated to the goddess stands on the northern shore of the large freshwater lake (tal). The old summer capital of the British Raj's United Provinces, Nainital is today part of the state of Uttarakhand. The lake is encircled by the Mall Road, and the "flats", a large field which is a popular promenade and recreation centre. The **Boat House Club**, set up in 1890 on the water's edge, is the hub of many activities and has a number of sail boats and rubber dinghies for hire. The many attractive colonial buildings include the governor's summer residence (built in 1899), St Joseph's School, the old Secretariat (now the Uttarakhand High Court) and the Municipal Library. **St-John-in-the-Wilderness** is an evocatively named Gothic church, with fine stained-glass windows and dark wooden pews. Nainital also has some beautiful walking trails, one of which leads up from the flats, through the densely wooded Ayarpata Hill, to **Tiffin**

The lake at Nainital, with facilities for boating and water sports

The 11th-century complex of stone temples at Jageshwar, near Almora

Top and **Dorothy's Seat**, lookout points offering panoramic views of the lakeside. Close by, and almost hidden by the forest, is an old public school, the appropriately named **Sherwood College**. The Upper Cheena Mall leads to Naina Peak, with breathtaking views of the mountain ranges. Less energetic visitors can take the cable car up to **Snow View** for scenic views.

Environs
Described as India's Lake District, Nainital's environs have a number of serene lakes, surrounded by thick forests. Excursions are offered to **Bhim Tal**, 22 km (14 miles) east of Nainital; **Naukuchiya Tal**, just 4 km (2.5 miles) from Bhim Tal, is a lake with nine corners, rich in birdlife; and **Sat Tal**, a conglomeration of seven lakes, located 21 km (13 miles) northeast of Nainital. **Mukteshwar**, 30 km (19 miles) northeast of Nainital, is one of the most beautiful spots in the area, along with the orchards at **Ramgarh**, close by.

⑬ Almora

Almora district. 380 km (236 miles) NE of Delhi. 🚉 Kathgodam, 90 km (56 miles) S of Almora, then taxi or bus. 🚌 (05962) 230 046. 𝒊 KMVN, Holiday Home, (05962) 230 250.

The large market town of Almora is the headquarters of the surrounding district. Its curving ridge offers

expansive views of the spectacular Greater Himalayan Range, including peaks such as Trishul and the spectacular Nanda Devi (see p193). The cobbled street of Almora's distinctive bazaar lies above The Mall, where locally crafted tamta products (hand-beaten copper and brass utensils plated with silver) are on sale. The town's trademark confectionery, the bal mithai, is available here as well.

Also of interest are the tall, narrow houses with their delicately carved wooden façades, a hallmark of local architecture. The historic **Almora Jail**, probably one of the few in the country with such picturesque surroundings, once held important political prisoners such as Mahatma Gandhi and Jawaharlal Nehru. A number of temples dot the landscape; the most popular of these are the **Chitai Temple** and the **Udyotchandeshwar Temple**. On the western edge of town, **Brighton End Corner** has fine mountain views.

Sculpture, Jageshwar

Environs
Binsar, 34 km (21 miles) northeast of Almora, at an altitude of 2,412 m (7,913 ft), is a wonderful spot from which to view the mountains. The steep drive up through tangy forests of pine is very pretty, and there is a 13th-century Shiva Temple set in the forest, just short of the summit. **Jageshwar**, located 34 km (21 miles) east of Almora, is of great religious significance.

Ranikhet's nine-hole golf course, offering fine mountain views

This is an impressive complex of over 100 splendidly carved stone temples, dating back to the 11th century.

⑭ Ranikhet

Almora district. 367 km (228 miles) NE of Delhi. 🚌 ℹ️ Tourist Reception Centre, Mall Rd, (05966) 220 893.

Primarily a cantonment town, Ranikhet is home to the Indian Army's renowned Kumaon Regiment. Not surprisingly, the army is the town's most visible presence, its many red-roofed bungalows spreading across the wide "Queen's Field", a literal translation of the town's name. **Sadar Bazaar** is the main market, while the **Upper Mall** leads away from the bazaar to the quieter part of town. **Chaubatia**, once a British sanatorium, lies further along The Mall and now houses the Government Fruit Garden, which grows 200 varieties of fruit. Ranikhet's true allure, however, lies in its untrammelled Himalayan views that offer a spectacular vista of nearly 350 km (217 miles) of the Greater Himalayan Range. The **Army Golf Course**, 6 km (4 miles) down the Almora Road at Uphat, is one of the country's highest golf courses, and was originally a racetrack. It welcomes visitors who are willing to pay green fees, so take no notice of the signboard that threatens trespassers.

A green bee-eater with its catch

⑮ Lansdowne

Almora district. 240 km (149 miles) NE of Delhi. 🚃 Kotdwar, 45 km (28 miles) SW of town centre, then taxi or bus. 🚌

The cantonment town of Lansdowne, is one of the few hill stations that has managed to remain wonderfully unchanged over the last century. Away from the main tourist circuit, the town has been spared the frenzied building and modernization that has crept into other popular destinations. A loosely spread out jumble of bungalows and shops, it is set on gentle forested slopes of pine, deodar and silver oak. The Army's Garhwal Rifles have their regimental centre here, and a visit to the beautifully maintained regimental mess is a must. A pleasant walk leads to **Tip-n-Top**, a lookout point 3 km (2 miles) from town, which offers excellent mountain views.

⑯ Kausani

Almora district. 431 km (268 miles) NE of Delhi. 🚌 ℹ️ Tourist Reception Centre, (05962) 258 006.

Kausani was Mahatma Gandhi's favourite abode in the hills. After a long stay here at the **Anashakti Yoga Ashram** in 1929, he remarked on how unnecessary it was for Indians to visit the European Alps for their health, when they had the beauty of Kausani at their doorsteps. A 400-km (249-mile) uninterrupted panorama of the Nanda Devi Range can be seen from the old **Circuit House**.

Environs
Baijnath, 20 km (12 miles) north of Kausani, is known for a cluster of temples, now in ruins, built in the 11th century. The main attraction is the **Parvati Temple**, with a 2 m (7-ft) high image of the goddess, dating from the 12th century. **Bageshwar**, 41 km (26 miles) east of Kausani, lies at the confluence of the Gomti and Saryu rivers, and was once a major trading post between Tibet and Kumaon. Although the link with Tibet no longer exists, local merchants still bring wool and animal hide to the town's annual Uttaryani Fair. With its stone temples dedicated to Shiva, Bageshwar is also an important pilgrimage centre in Kumaon. Nila Parvat (the "Blue Mountain"), stands proudly between the two rivers, and locals believe that it is home to all the 330 million deities of the Hindu pantheon. Many visitors to Bageshwar are en route to the Pindari Glacier (see p193).

Pumpkins drying on a slate roof below the peaks at Kausani

⑰ Corbett National Park

Situated along the valley of the Ramganga river and fringed by the Himalayan foothills in the north, Corbett is considered one of India's finest wildlife sanctuaries. The 1,288-sq km (497-sq mile) reserve was originally a hunter's paradise during the British Raj. In 1936, it became India's first national park, largely due to the efforts of the great British hunter-turned- conservationist Jim Corbett, after whom the park is named. The park encompasses varied terrain, from savannah grasslands to hilly ridges of deciduous forests with *chir* pine and *sal (Shorea robusta)*. Corbett is renowned for its remarkable variety of wildlife, notably tigers, elephants, *chausingha* (four-horned antelopes) and an astonishing 600 species of birds.

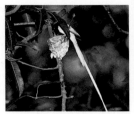

Paradise Flycatcher
The male has beautiful plumage, and measures 50 cm (20 in) in length.

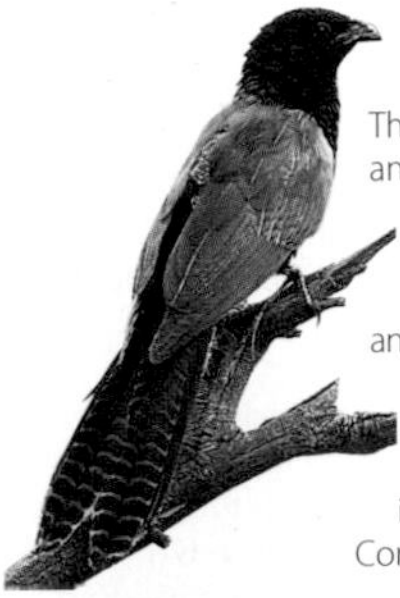

Coucal or Crow Pheasant
This striking, black and brown bird is found all over northern India. Its loud and resonant call echoes over the valleys and forests in and around Corbett.

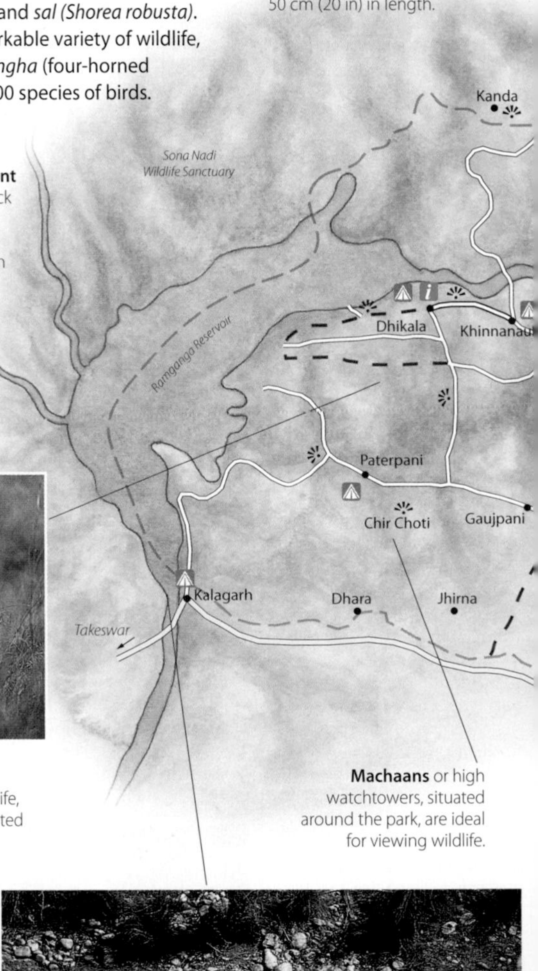

Kanda
Sona Nadi
Wildlife Sanctuary
Ramganga Reservoir
Dhikala
Khinnanau
Paterpani
Chir Choti
Gaujpani
Kalagarh
Dhara
Jhirna
Takeswar

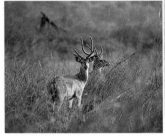

Grasslands
Vast savannah grasslands *(chaurs)*, ideal for viewing deer and other wildlife, surround Dhikala, the park's hub, located by the Ramganga Reservoir.

Machaans or high watchtowers, situated around the park, are ideal for viewing wildlife.

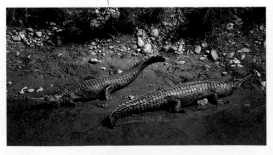

Gharial
The *gharial* (Gavialis gangeticus) is a species that can be seen on the banks of the Ramganga Reservoir (formed by a dam on the Ramganga river). The reservoir also attracts a variety of water birds such as geese, ducks, grebes and storks.

For hotels and restaurants see p696 and pp708–709

Ramganga River
The lifeline of the park's wildlife, the Ramganga river is surrounded by tall elephant grass *(nall)* and scrub.

Elephant Safari
The highlights of a trip to Corbett are the sunrise and sunset elephant safaris, available from Dhikala and Bijrani. Apart from the herds of wild elephants and deer, it is sometimes possible to encounter a lone tiger or leopard

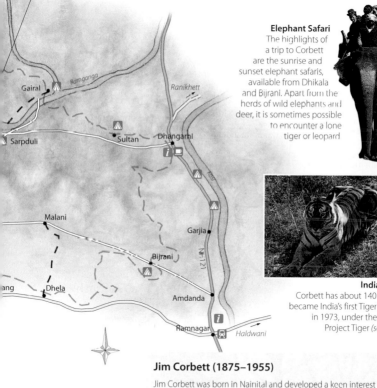

Indian Tiger
Corbett has about 140 tigers. It became India's first Tiger Reserve in 1973, under the aegis of Project Tiger *(see p293)*.

Jim Corbett (1875–1955)

Jim Corbett was born in Nainital and developed a keen interest in the jungles of Kumaon. An avid hunter in his early years (he shot his first leopard when he was eight), the turning point came when, on a duck shoot, he was appalled by the mindless slaughter of 300 birds. Corbett then decided to use his rifle solely to kill the man-eating leopards and tigers that plagued the nearby villages. Riveting accounts in his first book, *Man-eaters of Kumaon*, describe how he tracked and shot the dreaded Champawat tigress who had killed 434 people. In 1956, after Corbett's death, the park was named after him as a tribute to his pioneering efforts at conservation.

Bust of Corbett, Dhikala

0 kilometres 5
0 miles 5

Key
- – Park boundary
- – Trail
- National highway
- Major road
- Minor road

For keys to symbols *see back flap*

⑱ Dudhwa National Park

Lakhimpur-Kheri district. 220 km (137 miles) N of Lucknow. Entry point: Palia. 🚉 🚌 ℹ️ For bookings, contact Field Director, Dudhwa, (05872) 252 106. **Open** 15 Nov–15 June. 📷 Extra charges for photography. Jeeps available. 🏠 🌐 **dudhwatigerreserve.com**

Located close to the border with Nepal, Dudhwa National Park covers 680 sq km (263 sq miles) of densely wooded plains. Its forests have some of the finest specimens of *sal* trees in India. In 1977, Dudhwa was recognized as a Tiger Reserve, mainly due to the efforts of Billy Arjan Singh, a legendary environmentalist. Arjan Singh is best-known for the tigress, Tara, he hand-reared and returned to the wild in 1978.

Today, the park has more than 30 tigers. The park is also well known for its herds of swamp deer *(Cervus duvauceli)*. Better known as *barasingha* (literally, 12-antlered), these deer find their ideal habitat in the grassy wetlands in the southern reaches of the park.

Other species include leopards, sloth bears and a small herd of rhinos, brought here from Assam and Nepal, in an attempt to re-introduce the species into Dudhwa. The park is also home to nearly 400 species of birds, among them swamp partridges, lesser floricans and hornbills. The park's lakes attract waterfowl such as fishing eagles and ibis.

⑲ Rampur

Rampur district. 310 km (193 miles) NW of Lucknow. 🚉 2,335,819. 🚉 🚌 🌐 **rampur.nic.in/home4new.asp**

Earlier a stronghold of the Afghan Rohilla chieftains (highlanders from Peshawar), Rampur became a princely state under the British. It was ruled by a dynasty of Muslim nawabs who were great connoisseurs of the arts. They drew hundreds of scholars and artists to their court, whose books and paintings became part of the state collection. They also established a famous *gharana* (school) of classical music. The Hamid Manzil, built by Nawab Hamid Ali Khan Bahadur who came to the throne in 1896, now houses the renowned **Raza Library**, which has a collection of almost 5,000 Mughal miniatures, over 60,000 books, numerous rare manuscripts, and portraits dating from the 16th to 18th centuries. It is open to the public daily, except Fridays. Hamid Ali Khan was also responsible for renovating many of Rampur's palaces, including the sprawling palace and fort complex to the northwest of the town. Rampur is a maze of bazaars and was once known for its fine cotton *khes* (damask). Traces of its Rohilla warrior ancestry are visible in the famous daggers, always on sale, and in the touches of Pashto (the native tongue of

Nawab Hamid Ali of Rampur

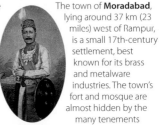

Rampur knives and daggers, a local speciality

Peshawar) which pepper the Urdu that is spoken here.

📚 **Raza Library**
Tel (0592) 232 5045/5346. **Open** 10am–5pm daily. **Closed** Fri & public hols. 🌐 **razalibrary.gov.in**

Environs
The town of **Moradabad**, lying around 37 km (23 miles) west of Rampur, is a small 17th-century settlement, best known for its brass and metalware industries. The town's fort and mosque are almost hidden by the many tenements and bazaars.

⑳ Aligarh

Aligarh district. 371 km (231 miles) NW of Lucknow. 🚉 3,673,889. 🚉 🚌 🎪 Numaish (Feb). 🌐 **amu.ac.in**

Historically important because of its location in an agriculturally rich region, Aligarh was a Rajput stronghold from the end of the 12th century onwards, until it was wrested by the Mughals. Its fort, which dates to 1524, fell to the British under Lord Lake in 1803. British presence influenced many of its foremost citizens, such as Sir Syed Ahmed Khan who founded the **Aligarh Muslim University** in 1875, for which the town is most famous today. The sprawling campus has many imposing buildings, such as a mosque that is an

Swamp deer, also known as *barasingha*, in Dudhwa's grasslands

exact replica of the Jama Masjid *(see p90)* in Delhi, only one-third its size.

㉑ Jhansi

Jhansi district. 301 km (187 miles) SW of Lucknow. 🏙 1,998,603. 🚉 🚌 *i* UP Tourism, Shivpuri Rd, (0517) 244 1267. 🛕 Jhansi Ayurveda Festival (Feb). 🌐 uptourism.com/destination/jhansi

Most famous for the role that its queen, Rani Lakshmibai, played during the Indian Mutiny of 1857, Jhansi is a key transit point for visitors travelling from Delhi to the temples of Khajuraho *(see pp240–42)*. The main site of interest is **Shankar Fort**, built in 1613 by Raja Bir Singh Deo. It has 9-m (30-ft) high walls built in concentric rings around its centre, and offers fine views from its ramparts.

The **Archaeological Museum**, located outside the fort on the road back to town, has medieval Hindu sculpture, royal artifacts, and some prehistoric tools.

🏛 **Archaeological Museum**
Tel (0510) 233 0035. **Open** Tue–Sun. **Closed** 2nd Sat. 🎥 Extra charges for video photography.

㉒ Kanpur

Kanpur district. 79 km (49 miles) SW of Lucknow. 🏙 4,581,268. 🚉 Kanpur Central, (0512) 232 8170. 🚌 Chunni Ganj, (0512) 253 0646.

One of British India's largest garrisons Kanpur, or Cawnpore

The ramparts of Shankar Fort at Jhansi, stormed by British forces in 1858

as it was then known, witnessed some of the bloodiest battles in 1857. More than 1,000 British soldiers and civilians were killed when Nana Sahib, the Maratha ruler, broke the British siege held by General Sir Hugh Wheeler in June 1857. When British reinforcements arrived, equally ferocious reprisals occurred.

Today, Kanpur is an industrial city with leather, cotton and oil as its main products. The old garrison, now an enclave of the armed forces, has some interesting relics of the Raj. Among them is the **All Souls' Memorial Church**, a grand Gothic style structure with an intricate stained-glass window over the west door. Built after 1857, it is a memorial to those killed during the siege. East of the church, the pretty **Memorial Garden** has a statue of an angel surrounded by a Gothic screen. This statue originally stood at the site of a terrible massacre, where British women and children were hacked and thrown down a well near Bibighar, in the town's

centre. Northeast of the church, **Sati Chaura Ghat** along the Ganges, is the spot where Indian forces killed 500 British soldiers and civilians. The **Military Cemetery** on the edge of the cantonment has many interesting graves, while in the town, the **King Edward VII Memorial Hall** and **Christ Church** (built in 1840) are also worth visiting.

Environs

Bithur, 25 km (16 miles) west of Kanpur, boasts a fort built by the Peshwas *(see p475)*. It is also the legendary birthplace of Lav and Kush, the twin sons of Rama and Sita *(see p31)*. About 60 km (37 miles) south of Kanpur, lies the beautiful 5th-century brick temple at **Bhitargaon**, built by the Gupta kings. The only one of its kind still surviving, most of the relief panels on the temple have vanished, but some terracotta sculptures inside remain.

Stained-glass window in the All Souls' Memorial Church, Kanpur

Rani Lakshmibai of Jhansi

India's Joan of Arc, Rani Lakshmibai single-handedly defied the British when her husband, Raja Gangadhar Rao, died in 1853 leaving no adult heir. She wished to rule as Regent but the British

Rani Lakshmibai astride her horse

invoked the infamous Doctrine of Lapse *(see p57)* and she was driven from her kingdom. While the Indian Mutiny of 1857 brewed in the north, the queen and her general, Tantia Tope, captured Gwalior Fort. She died defending it at Kotah-Sarai near Gwalior in 1858. According to the historian Christopher Hibbert, "she died dressed as a man, holding her sword two-handed and the reins of her horse in her teeth". She remains one of India's best-loved heroines.

㉓ Lucknow

As the Mughal Empire disintegrated, many independent kingdoms, such as Avadh, were established. Its capital, Lucknow, rose to prominence when Asaf-ud-Daula, the fourth nawab, shifted his court here from Faizabad *(see p203)* in 1775. The city was also a great cultural centre, and its nawabs, best remembered for their refined and extravagant lifestyles, were patrons of the arts. Under them music and dance flourished, and many buildings were erected. In 1856 the British annexed Lucknow and deposed its last nawab, Wajid Ali Shah. This incident helped instigate the Indian Mutiny of 1857, when the city witnessed one of the bloodiest episodes in colonial history.

Sikandar Bagh's stately gateway, adorned with the fish emblem

View of the Tomb of Khurshid Zadi, Qaiser Bagh

🏛 Qaiser Bagh Palace

Qaiser Bagh. **Open** daily.

Once the most magnificent palace in Lucknow, Qaiser Bagh, was built by Wajid Ali Shah (r.1847–56), the last nawab. When the British recaptured Lucknow in 1858, they demolished many of the complex's more fanciful structures, with their florid sculptures of mermaids and cherubs. However, the remaining buildings, although in ruins, hint at their former splendour. The **Lal Baradari** now houses a fine arts academy as well as the archaeological section of the State Museum; the **Bhatkhande Music Deemed University** is a school for Hindustani music; and the **Safaid Baradari**, now an office building, was where the nawab, dressed as a fakir, used to hold court. Only two wings of the residential quarters that once housed the nawab's

vast harem remain. Carvings of fish, the nawabs' royal emblem, adorn many of the structures. Nearby, lie two grand tombs, the **Tomb of Saadat Ali Khan** (the fifth nawab) and the **Tomb of Khurshid Zadi**, his wife.

Under Nawab Wajid Ali Shah, Lucknow witnessed an artistic flowering. An aesthete who was not interested in governance, he devoted himself to poetry and music and is believed to have introduced the *thumri* (a form of light classical music). Dance forms benefited as well, and the Lucknow *gharana* (school) of Kathak *(see p32)* reached new heights during his short reign, before he was deposed by the British in 1856 and exiled to Calcutta.

🏛 Sikandar Bagh

Sikandar Bagh. **Open** daily.

Named after Wajid Ali Shah's favourite queen, Sikandar Bagh was the royal pleasure garden of the nawabs. In 1857, British troops led by Sir Colin Campbell relieved the siege of the Residency at this site. The **National Botanical Gardens and Research Centre**

are now located in its grounds. To the west, the **Shah Najaf Imambara** has the tomb of Ghazi-ud-din Haidar (the sixth nawab).

🏛 Chattar Manzil

NW of Qaiser Bagh. **Open** daily.

Built during Saadat Ali Khan's reign (1798–1814), the Chattar Manzil ("Umbrella Palace"), derives its name from the umbrella-shaped gilt dome *(chattar)* crowning the structure. A basement *(tehkhana)* was built below the level of the Gomti river, so that its waters could keep the area cool in the summer. The building now houses the state's department of Archaeology.

🏛 The Residency

NW of Qaiser Bagh. **Tel** (0522) 232 8220. **Open** Sunrise–sunset daily. 🖼
W asi.nic.in

Lucknow's most haunting monuments are the desolate ruins of the Residency. This complex of buildings which grew around the large brick home of the Resident, was an exclusive British enclave, protected by fortifications. In 1857, all the city's British citizens took refuge here during the five-month siege. Sir

The British Residency before it was destroyed during the siege of 1857

Henry Lawrence, the commander of the troops, expected relief to arrive within 15 days. But, it was 87 days before a force led by Sir Henry Havelock broke through the ranks of sepoys, only to find themselves trapped inside. For the next seven weeks they faced constant bombardment, until Sir Colin Campbell finally retook the Residency on 17 November. By then, almost 2,000 people had died either from bullet wounds or from cholera and typhoid.

Today, the Residency looks just as it did in 1857. In its small museum, the gaping holes made by cannon fire. are still visible. The **Model Room** on the ground floor, has a model depicting British defences during the siege. Lying below, are the cellars where the women and children took shelter. The cemetery near the ruined church, has the forlorn graves of those who died, including that of Sir Henry Lawrence. An **Indian Martyrs' Memorial** stands opposite, on the banks of the Gomti river.

🏛 Bara Imambara

Hussainabad. **Open** Sunrise–sunset daily. **Closed** during Muharram (Mar/Apr). 🈺
Lucknow's most distinctive architectural structures are

the *imambaras*, or ceremonial halls used during Muharram *(see p673)*. The Bara ("Great") Imambara, built by Asaf-ud-Daula in 1784, was essentially a famine relief project providing much-needed employment. It is said that while one group of workers were involved with its construction during the day, another group dismantled it at night. Elaborate gates lead to this sprawling, low edifice. Its most remarkable feature is a large hall, 50-m (164-ft) long and 15-m (49-ft) high, totally unsupported by pillars.

Above it is the *bhulbhulaiya*, a labyrinth of balconies. The **Asafi Mosque** (also known as Shahi Masjid) and a stepwell also lie in the compound.

VISITORS' CHECKLIST

Practical Information
Lucknow district. 516 km (321 miles) E of Delhi. 🚆 4,589,838. 🛈 Regional Tourist Office, Paryatan Bhawan, Gomti Nagar (0522) 230 4870. 🎭 Muharram (Mar/Apr). 🌐 up-tourism.com

Transport
✈ Amausi, 15 km (9 miles) SW of Lucknow 🚆 🚌 Alambagh, (0522) 245 5477.

Asaf-ud-Daula also erected the 18-m (59-ft) high **Rumi Darwaza**, just outside. This portal, embellished with lavish decorations, was the Imambara's west facing entrance.

The Bara Imambara complex, built in the late 18th century

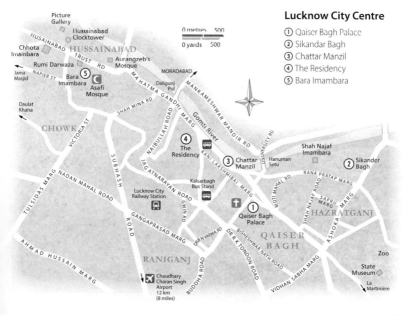

Lucknow City Centre

① Qaiser Bagh Palace
② Sikandar Bagh
③ Chattar Manzil
④ The Residency
⑤ Bara Imambara

0 metres 500
0 yards 500

Picture Gallery
Hussainabad Clocktower
HUSAINABAD
Chhota Imambara
HUSSAINABAD
TRUST RD
Rumi Darwaza
Aurangzeb's Mosque
MORADABAD
Jama Masjid
NAPIER ST
Bara Imambara ⑤
Asafi Mosque
Daliganj Pul
MAHATMA GANDHI MARG
MANKAMESHWAR MANDIR RD
Daulat Khana
SHAH MINA RD
Gomti River
CHOWK
VICTORIA ST
NAIBULLAH ROAD
④ The Residency
RANI LAKSHMIBAI MARG
③ Chattar Manzil
Hanuman Setu
UNIVERSITY RD
Shah Najaf Imambara
② Sikandar Bagh
SUBHASH
JAG ATNARAYAN ROAD
Kaisarbagh Bus Stand
RANA PRATAP MARG
NADAN MAHAL ROAD
Lucknow City Railway Station
GWIN RD
MOTI MAHAL RD
SHAH NAJAF MARG
SAPRU MARG
TULSIDAS MARG
GANGAPRASAD MARG
DR B N VARMA RD
① Qaiser Bagh Palace
BISHESHWAR NATH ROAD
HAZRATGANJ
ASHOKA MARG
AHMAD HUSSAIN MARG
ROAD
DR R K TONDON ROAD
BUDDHA ROAD
QAISER BAGH
VIDHAN SABHA MARG
Zoo
RANIGANJ
✈ Chaudhary Charan Singh Airport 12 km (8 miles)
State Museum
La Martinière

Lucknow: The Outer Sites

Some of Lucknow's best architectural sites lie beyond the city centre. The religious monuments, such as the *imambaras* and mosques, reveal a distinct Persian influence, while the secular buildings, which include the palaces of the nawabs as well as colonial structures, are more European in style. A particularly extravagant example among the latter is La Martinière. The home and mausoleum of a French adventurer, it later became a school, serving as the model for St Xavier's School which was immortalized in Rudyard Kipling's novel *Kim*.

Portrait of Nawab Wajid Ali Shah in the Picture Gallery

Close to the Rumi Darwaza *(see p201)*, **Aurangzeb's Mosque** stands on high ground known as Lakshman Tila, the location of Lucknow's original township. To the east is the **Hussainabad Clocktower**, erected in 1887. The 67-m (220-ft) high Gothic tower was built to mark the arrival of Sir George Cooper, Avadh's first lieutenant governor. To its west lies the 19th-century Baradari, built by Muhammed Ali Shah (the eighth nawab), where the **Picture Gallery** is located. Splendid life-sized portraits of the ten nawabs, painted between 1882 and 1885, are on display here.

To the west of the Picture Gallery is the Hussainabad Imambara, better known as the **Chhota Imambara**. This gem-like structure is surmounted by a delicate gold dome, and its outside walls are engraved with superb calligraphy. The interiors are adorned with gilt-edged mirrors, ornate chandeliers, silver pulpits and colourful stucco decorations. The *tazias* (replica tombs) and *alams* (standards) used during the Muharram festival between March and April, are kept here. The **Jama Masjid**, to the south-west is another striking structure, built by Muhammed Ali Shah in the early 19th century. Its walls are heavily ornamented and its arches are covered with fine stucco work.

Northwest of the Jama Masjid, the **Daulat Khana** was the palace of Asaf-ud-Daula. Constructed in the late 1780s, it includes numerous Indo-European buildings. The most

Alam, Chhota Imambara

prominent of these is the **Asafi Kothi**, its elegant façade marked by semi-circular bays.

Lucknow's main market is situated in the **Chowk**, the city's atmospheric old quarter. Stretching from Gol Darwaza to Akbari Darwaza, this maze of narrow *galis* (lanes) is lined with shops selling a range of goods from colourful kites to *paan* to Lucknow's famed *chikankari* – fine muslin delicately embroidered with thread-work. Wholesale flower markets overflow with roses and jasmine, and *attar* shops sell tiny bottles of fragrant perfume. The Chowk is also the best place to sample some authentic local cuisine (especially the many varieties of succulent kebabs), refined to an art form by chefs attached to nawabi households *(see p169)*.

At the southeastern corner of the city, situated in the Zoological Gardens, is Lucknow's **State Museum**. Its collection includes rare silver and gold coins, 16th-century paintings, and stone sculpture from the 2nd century BC.

The extraordinary **La Martinière** stands further south. It was built by Major General

Claude Martin, a French soldier of fortune and, in 1793, the richest European in Lucknow. A fanciful Gothic château, it has four enormous octagonal towers. The exterior is decorated with animals and mythological figures, including lions, gargoyles and a female sphinx. One of the two cannons on the terrace was cast by Martin, as was the bronze bell. He died in 1800 and is buried in the basement. In 1840, the building, in accordance with Martin's will, became a school for boys. The school was evacuated during the siege of Lucknow, but re-opened a year later.

🏛 **Picture Gallery**
Open Mon–Sat.

🏛 **State Museum**
Tel (0522) 223 9588. **Open** Tue–Sun.

🏫 **La Martinière College**
Prior permission required from the principal. **Tel** (0522) 223 5415.
W **lamartiniere lucknow.org**

The elaborate façade of La Martinière College for boys

The colourful Hanuman Garhi Temple in Ayodhya

㉔ Ayodhya

Faizabad district. 127 km (79 miles) E of Lucknow. ✉ (05278) 232 067.
ℹ Ayodhya Tourist Information Centre, (05278) 232 435. 🗓 Ram Navmi (Mar/Apr), Kartik Purnima (Oct/Nov), Ramayan Mela (Dec/Jan).

Located on the banks of the Sarayu river, Ayodhya is said to be the birthplace of Rama, the divine hero of the *Ramayana (see p31)*. Dozens of temples in this small pilgrim town commemorate his birth. Whether this is a historical fact or simply part of oral tradition, for devout Hindus Ayodhya remains inextricably linked with the legend of Rama. As a result, when the Mughal emperor Babur built a mosque near the supposed spot of Rama's birthplace in 1526, he left behind a bitterly contested site. Known as the **Babri Masjid** ("Mosque of Babur"), it was a long-simmering source of tension between Hindus and Muslims. In 1992, a mob of Hindus tore down the mosque, leading to rioting all over the country. Security personnel now guard the site. A makeshift temple outside the security ring still attracts pilgrims, particularly during the full moon night of Kartik Purnima. One of the more renowned temples, among the hundreds of shrines on the river bank, is the **Hanuman Garhi**. Built within the walls of an old fort, it is dedicated to the monkey god, Hanuman.

Environs

Ayodhya's twin city, lying 6 km (4 miles) to its west, **Faizabad** has a sizeable Muslim population and was Avadh's first capital before it was shifted to Lucknow in 1775. In the town's centre is the Jama Masjid, built by the later Mughals, while the 18th-century tomb of Bahu Begum, the wife of Shuja-ud-Daula (Avadh's third nawab), is an austere structure built in marble. Faizabad has a pretty rose garden.

㉕ Jaunpur

Jaunpur district. 250 km (155 miles) SE of Lucknow. 🗺 4,494,204. 🚉 🚌

Though largely bypassed by visitors, Jaunpur has a wealth of medieval Islamic architecture. Located along the Gomti river, Jaunpur was established by Feroze Shah Tughluq *(see p95)* in the late 14th century and soon grew into an important trading post. It was subsequently ruled by the independent Muslim rulers of the Sharqi dynasty who held sway for much of the 15th century, until Ibrahim Lodi conquered the city in 1479. It eventually fell to the Mughals in the early part of the 16th century.

Jaunpur's many rulers each left a distinct architectural stamp on the city. The Mughal emperor Akbar built the great **Shahi Bridge** across the river, which still stands. To its north is the **Old Shahi Fort** from the Tughluq era. It contains a mosque, built with yellow and blue enamelled bricks, and an exact replica of a traditional Turkish bath or *hamam*. The most striking mosque, the **Atala Masjid**, just outside the fort, dates to the Sharqi period. It is embellished with recessed arches and ornamental fringes, and square courts surround the central structure. Though built on a grander scale, the 15th-century **Jama Masjid** borrows its basic architectural inspiration from the Atala Masjid.

The Mango: King of Fruits

Langra mangoes, available in summer

The mango *(aam)* is considered the king of tropical fruits and is the best-loved fruit of the country. The Mughal emperor Babur called it the "finest fruit of Hindostan". The popular paisley motif is derived from the shape of the mango fruit, and mango leaves, considered auspicious, are used as buntings at festive occasions. Of the hundreds of varieties grown all over the subcontinent, few are as aromatic and juicy as the mangoes of Jaunpur. The *langra* is arguably the best among the varieties grown here. It is fleshy, juicy and sweet, and possessed of a distinct tangy flavour. It sells at a premium countrywide and is widely exported to the Middle East and Europe. The *dussehri* from Lucknow, and the *chausa* from the Rampur region, are also popular varieties. The raw *chausa* is considered ideal for spicy chutneys and pickles, without which no meal is complete.

The grand façade of the Jama Masjid in Jaunpur

26 Varanasi

Also known as Kashi ("the City of Light"), or as Benares, Varanasi is situated on the west bank of the Ganges and is India's holiest Hindu city, with a spiritual and religious legacy that goes back nearly 3,000 years. This is the city of Shiva, the foremost among the 12 places where the god burrowed and then burst into the sky in a fiery pillar of light *(jyotirlinga)*. Sanctified by Shiva's all-pervading presence and the sacred Ganges, the 90 or so ghats along the river define the life and identity of Varanasi. Stretching from the southern Assi Ghat to the northern Adi Keshava Ghat, close to the Malviya Bridge, the ghats cover more than 6 km (4 miles). Lined with temples and shrines they reverberate with the endless cycle of Hindu religious practice – from daily rituals to profound rites of passage.

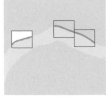

Locator Map
Assi Ghat to Shivala Ghat

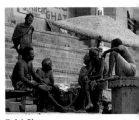

Tulsi Ghat
One of Varanasi's oldest sites, this ghat (earlier known as Lolarka Ghat), was renamed after the poet-saint Tulsidas, who lived here in the 16th century. His house and temple still stand nearby.

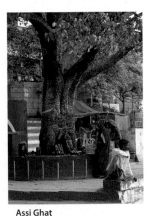

Assi Ghat
A linga stands beneath a *pipal* tree on Varanasi's southernmost ghat, which marks the confluence of the Asi and Ganges rivers.

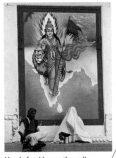

Mural of goddess on the walls at Ganga Mahal Ghat

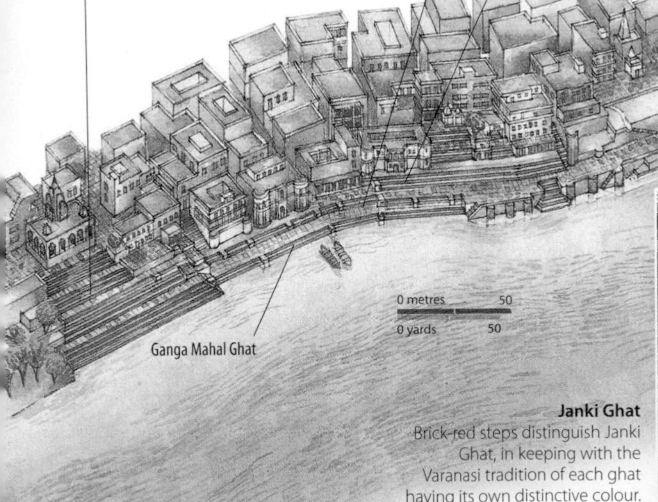

Bhadaini Ghat
Rewa Ghat
Ganga Mahal Ghat
0 metres 50
0 yards 50

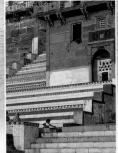

Janki Ghat
Brick-red steps distinguish Janki Ghat, in keeping with the Varanasi tradition of each ghat having its own distinctive colour.

For hotels and restaurants see p696 and pp708–709

Chet Singh Ghat
The fort on this ghat marks the spot where Maharaja Chet Singh was defeated by the British in the mid-18th century.

VISITORS' CHECKLIST

Practical Information
Varanasi district. 286 km (178 miles) SE of Lucknow. 3,676,841. Parade Kothi, (0542) 220 8162, Varanasi Junction Station, (0542) 234 6370. daily. Shivratri (Feb/Mar), Ramlila (Sep/ Oct), Ganga Festival/ (Dev Deepavali) (Oct/Nov).

Transport
22 km (14 miles) NW of the city.

Anandamayi Ghat
The ashram founded by, the Bengali female saint, Anandamayi Ma, draws thousands of devotees.

Mahanirvani Ghat

Niranjani Ghat

Prabhu Ghat

Panchkot Ghat

Jain Ghat

Vaccharaj Ghat

Shivala Ghat
This ghat, dating to 1770, was built by Balwant Singh, the maharaja of Varanasi.

Ramlila

The Ramlila is a cycle of plays which tells the story of the *Ramayana (see p31)*, in which Lord Rama is exiled from his kingdom for 14 years. The Ramlila tradition was started in Varanasi by Tulsidas, author of the *Ramcharitmanas* (a popular version of the epic). Street performances take place in the evenings at different venues, in September/October, attracting thousands of spectators. The performance at the residence of the former maharaja at Ramnagar Fort is by far the most spectacular of the Ramlilas in Varanasi.

Young boys dressed as the main characters

Boat Building
Planks lie waiting to be jointed into boats, which are an essential mode of transportation along the busy river front.

Varanasi: Digpatiya Ghat to Mir Ghat

These centrally located ghats are the city's most sacred, and many of them were built under the patronage of India's erstwhile princely states, such as Darbhanga, Jaipur and Indore. One of Varanasi's two cremation ghats, Harishchandra Ghat, lies just to the south. Behind the holy Dasashvamedha Ghat meanders a winding lane known as Vishwanath Gali, lined with a multitude of shops that sell all manner of religious objects. It leads to the city's principal shrine, the Vishwanath Temple, said to be over 1,000 years old.

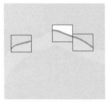

Locator Map
Digpatiya Ghat to Mir Ghat

Chausatthi Ghat
Lessons in the scriptures take place at this ghat, named after the temple of the Chausath Yoginis or 64 female divinities.

Digpatiya Ghat

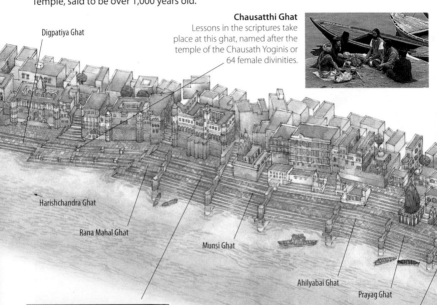

Harishchandra Ghat

Rana Mahal Ghat

Munsi Ghat

Ahilyabai Ghat

Prayag Ghat

0 metres 50
0 yards 50

Darbhanga Ghat
The towers and turrets of old *havelis*, built in the early 1900s by two princes of Bihar, dominate this ghat. Some of the massive pillars in these *havelis* are reminiscent of the Greek style.

Dasashvamedha Ghat
This centrally located ghat, Varanasi's holiest spot, is named after the ten simultaneous horse sacrifices (*dasashvamedh*) performed by Brahma the Creator. Rows of priests sit under bamboo parasols, ready to perform ritual prayers for the pilgrims that swarm here.

Vishwanath Gali
Lacquer jars, vermilion powder, bottled Ganges water, bangles and brocade, are all sold in the lane that leads to the Vishwanath Temple, the focal point of all worship in Varanasi.

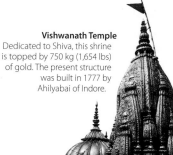

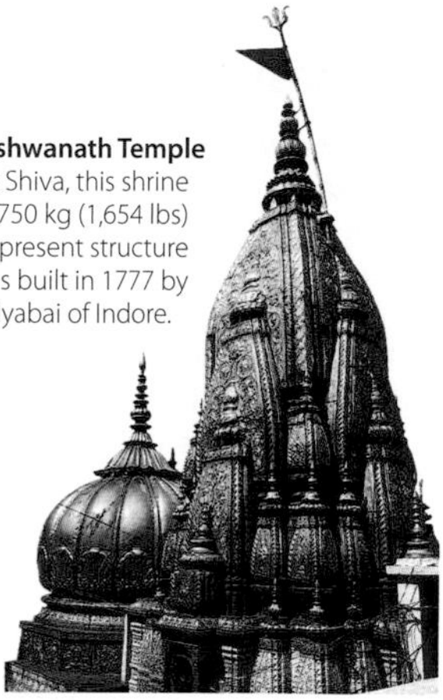

Vishwanath Temple
Dedicated to Shiva, this shrine is topped by 750 kg (1,654 lbs) of gold. The present structure was built in 1777 by Ahilyabai of Indore.

Vishwanath
↗ Temple

Man Mandir Ghat
Jai Singh II of Jaipur built one of his four Jantar Mantars (see pp362–3) above Raja Man Singh's palace in 1710. Its sundial is visible from the ghat.

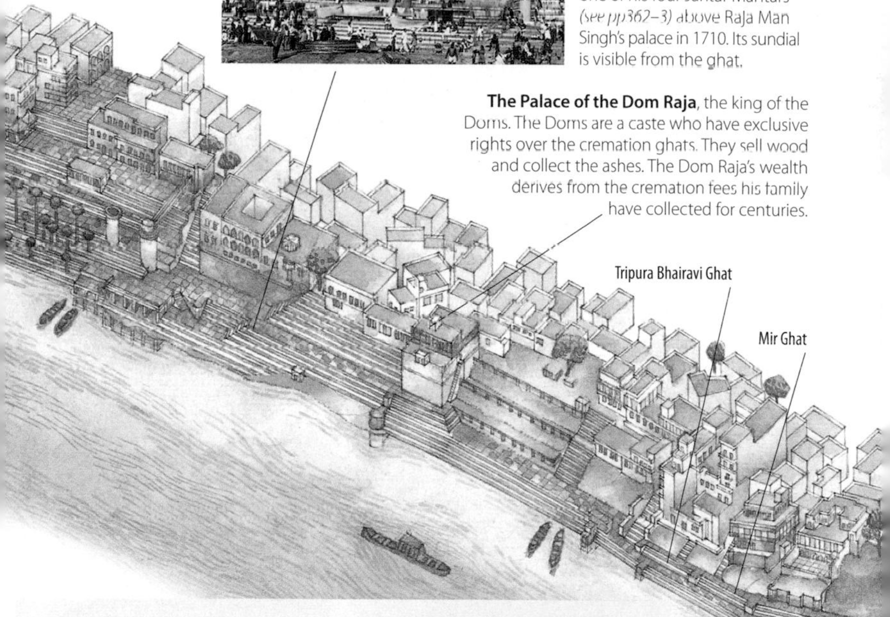

The Palace of the Dom Raja, the king of the Doms. The Doms are a caste who have exclusive rights over the cremation ghats. They sell wood and collect the ashes. The Dom Raja's wealth derives from the cremation fees his family have collected for centuries.

Tripura Bhairavi Ghat

Mir Ghat

Boat Rides

A sunrise boat ride is the highlight of a trip to Varanasi, when the temples along the river front are bathed in soft light. The people of Varanasi trickle out of the labyrinthine lanes and head for the ghats at dawn. Here, they wash clothes, perform yoga *asanas*, offer flowers and incense to the river, and take a ritual dip. The most fascinating

Dasashvamedha Ghat at sunrise

ride is from Dasashvamedha to Manikarnika Ghat *(see p210)*. Dozens of rowing boats ply up and down the river, and can be hired by the hour. Rates are negotiable, so do fix the price before hiring one.

Varanasi: Nepali Ghat to Panchaganga Ghat

Along this stretch is the famed Manikarnika Ghat, one of the city's two cremation ghats. According to legend, Shiva's *mani* (crest jewel) and his consort Parvati's *karnika* (earring), fell into the nearby well while they were bathing, hence the name. Dying in Varanasi is a cause of celebration for Hindus, as it is believed to bestow instant salvation or *moksha* (liberation from the cycle of birth and death). It is said that Shiva whispers into the ears of the dying, and the old and infirm, sages and ordinary people, come here to breathe their last.

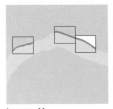

Locator Map
Nepali Ghat to Panchaganga Ghat

| 0 metres | 50 |
| 0 yards | 50 |

Jalasen Ghat

Nepali Ghat
A lion stands outside a pagoda-style, woodwork temple, built by the royal family of Nepal.

Scindia Ghat
The elaborate structures on this ghat were so top heavy that they collapsed, and were rebuilt by Daulat Rao Scindia of Gwalior in 1937. A temple stands half submerged in the river, with its sanctum knee deep in the water.

Manikarnika Ghat
Funeral pyres burn day and night at this cremation ghat, while bodies wrapped in shrouds lie on biers besides piles of wooden logs. In the middle of the ghat is the well *(kund)* that Vishnu carved out with his discus before the Ganges flowed here.

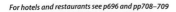

Rituals Performed in the Ganges

Although there are over 700 temples in Varanasi, none are more sacred than the river itself. The Ganges is worshipped as a living goddess, with the power to cleanse all earthly sins. Daily baths in her waters are advised by Hindu scriptures to prepare for the soul's final journey to liberation. Offerings of flowers and diyas floating down the river are a common and very pretty sight.

A Ritual Dip
Thousands come to Varanasi everyday, to bathe and pay obeisance to the Ganges.

Evening Aarti
The daily prayers *(aarti)* at dawn and dusk, serve as salutations to the river. Oil lamps are offered and bells rung while sacred mantras are chanted.

Wayside Shrine
A widow clad in white assembles flowers, incense and Ganges water in a small brass container, for paying homage at a wayside shrine.

Ganga Mahal Ghat was also built by the king of Gwalior in the early 19th century.

Akharas
The city's *akharas* or wrestling arenas are famous. Men live and train at these centres full time, as part of their tutelage under a guru.

Bhonsle Ghat

Aurangzeb's mosque, built on the site of a Hindu temple that was destroyed, is a grand structure that dominates the skyline.

Mehta Ghat

nkatha Ghat

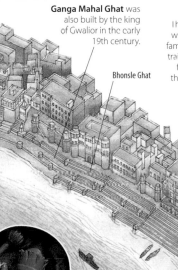

Jatar Ghat

Hanuman, the Monkey God, at Ganga Mahal Ghat

Panchaganga Ghat
This ghat marks the mythical meeting place of five sacred rivers, and has numerous images of the five river goddesses – Ganga, Yamuna, Saraswati, Dhutpapa and Kirana.

Adi Keshava Ghat

Exploring Varanasi

Varanasi, one of the oldest cities in the world and a contemporary of Babylon and Nineveh, dates to the 7th century BC. This eternal city, where religion is an integral part of daily life, has drawn saints, poets and pilgrims through the ages. Behind the riverside ghats are narrow crowded lanes and bazaars, where people jostle with sacred cows, saffron-robed sadhus and devotees making offerings at roadside shrines. Varanasi is also renowned as a centre of Sanskrit learning and Hindu philosophy, attracting scholars and students from all over India. The Benares Hindu University, established in the early 1900s, perpetuates this tradition.

Dramatic ramparts of the Ramnagar Fort rising from the river bank

The narrow, winding Vishwanath Gali leads to the **Vishwanath Temple**, dedicated to Shiva, who is known here as Vishwanath, "Lord of the Universe". Painted floral carvings adorn its exterior and interior walls, and it is nearly always crowded. Adjacent to it lies the ancient **Gyan Vapi Well** ("Well of Wisdom"), whose waters are said to bring enlightenment. According to legend, this well is believed to contain the linga from the original Vishwanath Temple which was destroyed by the Mughal emperor Aurangzeb in the 17th century. The **Gyan Vapi Mosque** is built on the ruins of the temple.

Further south lies the sprawling **Benares Hindu University**, founded by the eminent Sanskrit scholar, Madan Mohan Malviya. Within the campus is the renowned **Bharat Kala Bhavan Museum**, known for having one of the country's best collections of Indian paintings. About 12,000 in number, they cover the period from the 11th century to the 20th century. Most impressive are the Mughal miniatures, notably a depiction of the Emperor Shah

Jahan. The Indian sculpture section is equally impressive, housing around 2,000 pieces, from 300 BC to AD 1400. Among them are a fine 10th-century sculpture of the marriage of Shiva and Parvati and an 11th-century statue of Vishnu as Varaha *(see p683)*. The display of Gandhara sculpture is also noteworthy.

The 17th-century **Ramnagar Fort**, lying across the river beyond Asi Ghat, has been home to the maharajas of Varanasi for 400 years. Although now in a state of disrepair, the palace still retains its charm. Ornamented swords, photographs of tiger shoots and visits by the King and Queen of Belgium line the walls. The Durbar Hall now houses the museum, where numerous objects are on display including palanquins and elephant howdahs.

🏛 **Bharat Kala Bhavan**
Tel (0542) 231 6337 or 236 9227.
Open 10am–4:30pm Mon–Sat.

🏛 **Ramnagar Fort and Museum**
Tel (0542) 2339322. **Open** daily.

㉗ Sarnath

Varanasi district. 10 km (6 miles) NE of Varanasi. 🚌 🚉 Buddha Mahotsava (May).

To Buddhists, Sarnath is as sacred as Varanasi is to Hindus. The Buddha came to the Deer Park here in 528 BC, to preach the Dharmachakra, or the Wheel of Law, his first major sermon after gaining enlightenment *(see p225)*. Sarnath was then one of ancient India's greatest centres of learning, visited by Chinese travellers Fa-Hsien and Hiuen Tsang who wrote of its flourishing monasteries.

The central monument of the existing complex is the 5th-century AD **Dhamekh Stupa**, which is built at the site where the Buddha is believed to have delivered his sermon to five disciples. To its west, are the remains of the Dharmarajika Stupa, built by the Mauryan emperor Ashoka *(see p46)* to preserve the Buddha's relics. The complex also has several smaller monasteries and temples, as well as a Bodhi Tree, planted in 1931, and the statue of Anagarika Dharmapala, the founder of the society that maintained Sarnath and Bodh Gaya *(see pp226–7)*.

The **Archaeological Museum** exhibits a superb collection of Buddhist artifacts. The highlight is the Ashokan lion capital in polished sandstone *(see p4)*, India's national emblem.

🏛 **Archaeological Museum**
Tel (0542) 259 5095. **Open** Sat–Thu.

The Dhamekh Stupa, Sarnath's principal monument

Brocades from Varanasi

Varanasi, India's most ancient pilgrimage centre, is also famous for its textiles. Renowned for its gossamer-fine cotton weaves for over 2000 years, its weaving traditions acquired new splendour from the 16th century onwards, with the patronage of the Mughal emperors. Varanasi's weavers soon became adept at weaving silk with gold and silver thread, to create sumptuous brocades for royal costumes and court furnishings, embellished with the exquisite floral, animal and geometric motifs favoured by the Mughals. They also produced brocades for Tibetan monasteries, decorated with Buddhist motifs such as clouds, lotus flowers and flames. Today, a wide range of brocade saris, scarves, and Tibetan-style fabrics are made and sold in the city.

The pallav, the culminating end piece of a sari (see p34), is the most elaborately designed part of the sari. Its rich and complex weave requires very fine and deft craftsmanship.

Gyaser textiles were traditionally woven for trade with Tibet. This contemporary textile has taken a single element (the flame) from a ritual cloth to create a stunning pattern.

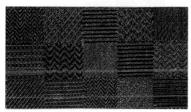

A panel of more than 600 geometric motifs has been specially created as a design directory for Varanasi's brocade weavers.

The flower motif, the classic *latifa buta*, combines gold and silver threads in a style known as Ganga-Yamuna, after the two rivers whose waters are pale and dark.

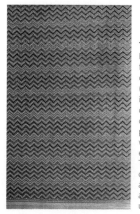

The Panch Ranga sari, or the five-colour sari, creates a *leheriya* (wave) design in alternating colours of blue, orange, purple, pink and green, with a patterned edging in gold. The sheer richness of the design and colours are its distinguishing features.

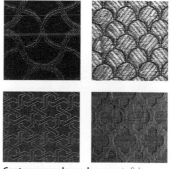

Contemporary brocades recreate fish scale patterns in gold and silver threads, inspired by *Gyaser* textiles, as well as *jali* or trellis designs used in Mughal architecture.

The creeper-covered ramparts of Allahabad Fort, built by the Mughal emperor Akbar

❷❽ Allahabad

Allahabad district. 204 km (141 miles) SE of Lucknow. 🚗 5,954,391. 🚉 🚌 Civil Lines, (0532) 240 7257. 🏛 Tourist Bungalow, 35 MG Marg, Civil Lines, (0532) 210 2784/8374. 🎫 Kumbh Mela (every 12 years), Magh Mela (every year).

Allahabad's sacred location at the confluence *(sangam)* of three rivers – the Ganges, the Yamuna and the mythical Saraswati – has given it a cultural, political and religious importance for nearly 3,000 years. Hiuen Tsang, the Buddhist monk and scholar *(see p223)*, visited the town, then known as Prayag, in AD 643, and wrote in great detail of its prosperity and fame.

In the 16th century it was captured by the Mughals who renamed it Allahabad. Later, the British maintained a large military presence in the city and established the law courts and the university. Jawaharlal Nehru *(see p61)*, India's first prime minister, was born here in 1889, and the city later became a major centre of the Independence Movement. Today Allahabad is a quietly

prosperous provincial centre, the broad, tree-lined avenues of the Civil Lines area contrasting with the congested bustle of the old city.

Allahabad Fort was built in 1583 by Akbar, who had a 3rd-century BC Ashokan pillar brought here from Kausambi. The pillar, unfortunately, is in a part of the fort that is not open to the public. On the fort's eastern side, is a temple complex with an undying banyan tree, the **Akshaivata**. Legend has it that anyone who leapt from its branches would achieve salvation from the endless cycle of rebirths. After too many such attempts, the tree was fenced off, and a special permit is required from the local tourist office to view it.

Gothic façade of the All Saints' Cathedral

Khusro Bagh, a tranquil Mughal garden on the western edge of town, is named after Emperor Jahangir's eldest son who led an unsuccessful rebellion against his father and was later murdered during the battle over succession with his brother, Shah Jahan in 1622. His tomb lies next to those of his sister and his mother. The latter, a Rajput

princess from Jaipur, distraught by the war between her husband and her son, took an overdose of opium. The *chhatris* on her tomb show Rajput influence.

Anand Bhavan, ancestral home of India's premier political dynasty, the Nehru-Gandhi family, now houses a museum of Nehru memorabilia and chronicles the high points of the Independence Movement. Close by, in the Civil Lines area, is the fantastically arched and turreted **Muir College** (now part of Allahabad University) built in 1870, and regarded a fine example of Indo-Saracenic architecture. Some glazed blue and white tiles still cling to the dome and a single tower soars to a height of 60 m (197 ft). Across the road is the **Allahabad Museum**, which has an interesting collection of terracottas from Kausambi and some 10th-to 13th-century sculpture from the Chandela era. Across Civil Lines to the west stands the **All Saints' Cathedral**. Constructed in 1877 and designed by William Emmerson, architect of the Victoria Memorial in Kolkata *(see pp278–9)*, it is lined with Jaipur marble inside.

🏛 **Allahabad Fort**
Closed to the public.

🏛 **Anand Bhavan**
Tel (0532) 246 7071/7096.
Open 10am–5pm Tue–Sun. 📷

🏛 **Allahabad Museum**
Tel (0532) 240 8690.
Open 10am–5pm Tue–Sun. 📷

The tombs of Prince Khusrau and his sister, Khusro Bagh

For hotels and restaurants see p696 and pp708–709

Environs

Kausambi, is 63 km (39 miles) and about an hour's drive from Allahabad on the eastern bank of the Yamuna. Excavated ruins of a stupa, a palace and extensive ramparts lie within a 2-km (1.3-mile) radius. While local legend holds that the city was built by the Pandavas, heroes of the *Mahabharata (see p30)*, excavations reveal that a Buddhist community flourished here between 600 BC and AD 600. The Buddha himself came here to preach. The site contains the remains of a paved brick road, small houses, each with a ceramic drain, and the stump of an Ashokan pillar dating to the 3rd century BC (a second pillar was moved to the Allahabad Fort). Some terracotta artifacts and seals from 200 BC which were found here are now in the Allahabad Museum. Surrounded by fields and villages, with the river in the background, Kausambi has an aura of great serenity.

Chitrakoot's Ramghat, with temples on the banks of the Mandakini river

The remains of mud and brick ramparts at Kausambi

㉙ Chitrakoot

Chitrakoot district. 125 km (78 miles) SW of Allahabad. 🚊 Karwi, 8 km (5 miles) NE of town centre, then taxi or bus. 🚌 *i* UPSTDC Tourism Bungalow, (05198) 224 219. 🏠 daily.

This pilgrim town on the banks of the Mandakini river, though in neighbouring Madhya Pradesh, is easier to access from Allahabad. Chitrakoot, literally "the Hill of Many Wonders" refers to the forested **Kamadgiri Hill**, where according to the *Ramayana*, Rama, Sita and Lakshman spent a portion of their 14 year exile. Below the hill lies **Hanuman Dhara**, a natural spring that flows over a delightful image of the monkey god, Hanuman, placed in a recess. Dotted with numerous temples, and full of sadhus, the town has a unique charm. Boat rides from the attractive **Ramghat**, the town's main ghat, provide an impressive view of the temples along the river bank.

㉚ Kalinjar Fort

Banda district. 205 km (127 miles) W of Allahabad. 🚊 Banda, 62 km (39 miles) N of Kalinjar Fort, then bus. 🚌 *i* UP Government Assistant Tourist office, Chitrakoot (05198) 224 219/ 222 218. 🏠 daily

One of India's oldest forts, Kalinjar was called Kanagora by Ptolemy, the 2nd-century AD Greek geographer. Its strategic location on the route between North and South India made it a coveted target for many rulers. It has thus had a very turbulent history, and was successively occupied by many medieval rulers, until it fell to the Afghan ruler Sher Shah Suri *(see p83)* in 1545.

Seven gateways, named after seven planets, and lined with sculptures and carvings lead to the fort. These include a giant Shiva with 18 arms and a dancing Ganesha. The **Neelkanth Temple** inside the fort, is dedicated to Shiva. Still in worship, the temple's inner sanctum contains an ancient linga.

The Kumbh Mela

Hindu legend has it that during a war over the urn (*kumbh*) of immortal nectar *(amrit)* between the gods and demons, Vishnu gave the urn to Garuda, his winged mount. During his flight, four drops of the nectar fell on four places, Nasik *(see p478)*, Ujjain *(see p250)*, Haridwar *(see p188)* and Allahabad. A Kumbh Mela is thus held at each spot in turn, every three years,

Pilgrims at Allahabad's Kumbh Mela in 2001

when certain planetary configurations, transform the waters of the Ganges into nectar. Pilgrims from all over India, converge at the Kumbh Mela to wash away their sins, making it the world's largest religious gathering. Specially built tent-cities and stalls spring up to cater to the influx. At Allahabad's Kumbh Mela (Jan–Mar 2013) more than 30 million devotees took a bath on Mauni Amavasya (10 Feb), the most sacred of the six main bathing days. The next Kumbh Mela will be held in Allahabad in 2025.

BIHAR & JHARKHAND

The name Bihar derives from the Sanskrit word *vihara*, or monastery –
an apt appellation for a state which was the birthplace of Buddhism.
Major sites associated with the life and teachings of the Buddha,
such as Bodh Gaya, Nalanda and Rajgir, lie in the dry plains of central
Bihar and are the main attractions for visitors to the state. Northern
Bihar is a fertile agricultural plain, watered by the River Ganges and
its tributaries, where the famous Patna rice is grown. In November
2000, the southern part of Bihar became the new state of Jharkhand, which
is dominated by a scenic and thickly forested highland called the Chhota
Nagpur Plateau. The game sanctuaries of Palamau and Hazaribagh are located here.
Jharkhand is rich in mineral resources, and is also the home of several indigenous
tribes, believed to be among the earliest settlers of the Indian subcontinent.

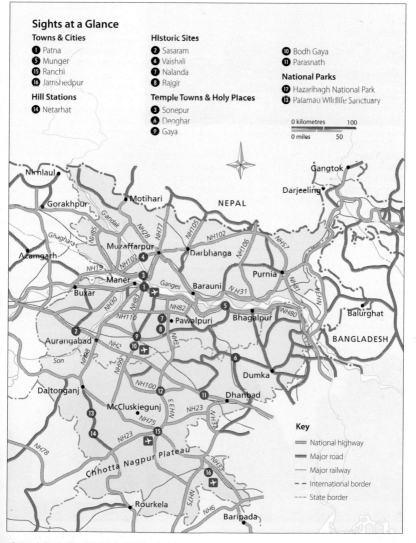

Sights at a Glance

Towns & Cities
1 Patna
5 Munger
15 Ranchi
16 Jamshedpur

Hill Stations
14 Netarhat

Historic Sites
2 Sasaram
4 Vaishali
7 Nalanda
8 Rajgir

Temple Towns & Holy Places
3 Sonepur
6 Deoghar
9 Gaya

10 Bodh Gaya
11 Parasnath

National Parks
12 Hazaribagh National Park
13 Palamau Wildlife Sanctuary

0 kilometres 100
0 miles 50

Key
— National highway
— Major road
— Major railway
-- International border
--- State border

◀ Statue of the Buddha at the Mahabodhi Temple, Bodh Gaya

For keys to symbols *see back flap*

❶ Patna

The capital of Bihar is a modern city with ancient roots going back to 600 BC. During the reign of the Maurya and Gupta empires *(see p46)* Patna, then known as Pataliputra, was renowned as one of the great cities of Asia, but today it is a congested urban sprawl, stretching along the banks of the Ganges. West Patna, laid out by the British, has gracious mansions and administrative buildings, while the eastern end comprises the old city, a warren of crowded lanes surrounding medieval monuments and bustling bazaars.

A view of Patna, lying on the south bank of the Ganges

🏛 Golghar
Open daily.

Patna's signature landmark, the Golghar (literally "round house"), is an extraordinary dome that resembles a giant beehive. Built in 1786 by Captain John Garstin as a silo to store grain during the famines that occurred frequently in those days, the Golghar was never actually put to use. The structure is 125 m (410 ft) wide at the base and gradually tapers up to a height of 29 m (95 ft). Two external staircases spiral upwards along its sides, with platforms to rest on along the way. The idea was to haul the grain up, and pour it down a hole

at the top into the dome's pit, which had a capacity of 124,285 tonnes. A remarkable echo can be heard inside the structure. During the monsoon, the dome's summit offers impressive views of the Ganges which, in this season, can swell to a width of 8 km (5 miles).

🏛 Patna Museum
Tel (0612) 223 5731. **Open** Tue–Sun.
Some remarkable treasures are displayed in the Patna Museum.

Among them is the Mauryan-era (probably 3rd century BC) polished stone image of the Didarganj Yakshi (female attendant), considered a master-piece of Indian sculpture. Other highlights include Gandharan style statues of Bodhisattvas; outstanding Buddha images in bronze and black stone, dating from the Pala period (8th–12th centuries); terracotta figurines, ancient Buddhist scriptures and a collection of Tibetan *thangkas*. The museum also boasts a 15-m (49-ft) long fossilized tree trunk, believed to be 200 million years old.

📖 Khudabaksh Library
Tel (0612) 267 0209. **Open** Sat–Thu.
🌐 **kblibrary.bih.nic.in**
Founded in 1900, this library has a renowned collection of rare Persian and Arabic manuscripts, including a group of beautiful illuminated medieval Korans, and superb Mughal miniature paintings. Its rarest exhibits are volumes salvaged from the sacking of the Moorish University in Cordoba, Spain, in the 11th century, though how they found their way to India still remains a mystery.

🚩 Harmandir Sahib
Open daily.
This historic Sikh gurdwara marks the birthplace of the firebrand tenth guru, Gobind Singh *(see p107)*, who was born here in 1666. Regarded as one of the four holiest Sikh shrines, the marble temple was built in the 19th century by Maharaja Ranjit Singh *(see p108)*.

The beehive-shaped Golghar, built as a granary in the 18th century

The eclectic private collection at the Jalan Museum

On the floor above the main sanctum is a museum with the guru's relics.

🏛 Jalan Museum

Tel (0612) 264 1121. **Open** by appt.

Also known as Qila ("Fort") House, this museum's eclectic collection, gathered by a 19th century ancestor of the Jalan family, includes Chinese paintings, Mughal jade and silverware, Napoleon's bed and Marie Antoinette's Sèvres porcelain. Qila House itself is an interesting structure, built on the ruins of a 16th-century fort constructed by the Afghan ruler, Sher Shah Sur (see p83).

🏛 Kumrahar

Open Tue–Sun. 🖾

This site contains the ruins of the ancient city of Pataliputra. Excavations have unearthed elaborately carved wooden ramparts, polished sandstone pillars and the remains of a vast Mauryan assembly hall that is said to have stood here in the 2nd century BC. A museum here displays some of these finds, which date from an era when Patna was described by Megasthenes, the Greek envoy to the Mauryan court, as "a city of light, where even wooden walls shine bright as glass".

VISITORS' CHECKLIST

Practical Information

Patna district. 1,015 km (631 miles) E of Delhi. 🅜 1,377,000. 🚹 Department of Tourism, Barrack no. 9D, Old Secretariat, (0612) 221 7163. 🗓 Mon–Sat. 🎪 Patliputra Mahotsava (Mar). 🆆 **bstdc.bih.nic.in**

Transport

✈ 6 km (4 miles) SW of the city centre. 🚆 🚌

🚇 Old Opium Warehouse

Gulzarbagh. **Open** Mon–Fri.

Located in a walled compound on the river bank, the opium warehouse of the East India Company is now the Government Printing Press. Opium was packaged in its three long, porticoed buildings and sent by boat to Kolkata.

Environs

Maner, 30 km (19 miles) west of Patna, is a major centre of Islamic learning. It has the fine 16th-century mausoleum of the Sufi saint Hazrat Makhdum Yahya Maneri. It is also famous for *laddoos*, a confection made of gramflour and molasses.

Patna City Centre

① Golghar
② Patna Museum
③ Khudabaksh Library

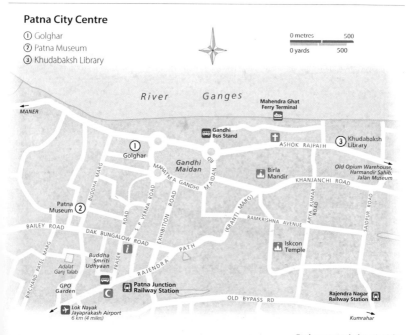

0 metres 500
0 yards 500

River Ganges

MANER

Mahendra Ghat Ferry Terminal

Gandhi Bus Stand

ASHOK RAJPATH

③ Khudabaksh Library

① Golghar

Gandhi Maidan

Birla Mandir

Old Opium Warehouse, Harmandir Sahib, Jalan Museum

KHANJANCHI ROAD

ARYA KUMAR ROAD

SAIDPUR ROAD

BUDDHA MARG

MAHATMA GANDHI MARG

S P VERMA ROAD

EXHIBITION ROAD

KRANTI MARG

RAMKRISHNA AVENUE

Patna Museum ②

BAILEY ROAD

DAK BUNGALOW ROAD

FRASER ROAD

RAJENDRA PATH

Iskcon Temple

BIRCHAND PATEL MARG

Buddha Smriti Udhyaan

Adalat Ganj Talab

GPO Garden

Patna Junction Railway Station

OLD BYPASS RD

Rajendra Nagar Railway Station

Lok Nayak Jayaprakash Airport 6 km (4 miles)

Kumrahar

The magnificent 16th-century tomb of the Afghan ruler Sher Shah Sur at Sasaram

❷ Sasaram

Rohtas district. 158 km (98 miles) SW of Patna. 🚌 🚍

The dusty town of Sasaram, a three-hour drive west of Patna on the historic Grand Trunk Road *(see p183)*, is famous for the **Mausoleum of Sher Shah Sur**, the great Afghan ruler *(see p83)*. This mid-16th-century architectural masterpiece is, to quote architectural historian Percy Brown, a testament to, "the aesthetic capacity of the Indian architect at its greatest, and his genius at its highest".

With a spectacular setting in the middle of an artificial lake, the pyramidal sandstone structure rises in five tiers to a height of 45 m (148 ft). The first two tiers comprise of a stepped basement and a high terrace that seems to emerge from the water, with a pavilion at each corner. The octagonal tomb is set on this plinth, and tapers towards the dome in three elegant layers of arches, crenellated parapets and small pillared kiosks. The broad dome is crowned by a large gilded lotus finial. All these elements combine to create a superbly proportioned structure that appears to float above the lake.

Curiously, the tomb is orientated eight degrees off its main axis – a mistake that the architect, Aliwal Khan, has skilfully disguised. The brilliant yellow and blue tiles are still seen in places. Nearby is the tomb of Sher Shah's father, Hasan Sur, built by the same architect.

❸ Sonepur

Saran district. 25 km (16 miles) N of Patna. 🚍 ℹ️ Bihar Tourism, Patna, (0612) 222 5411. 🎪 Sonepur Mela (Oct/Nov).

North of Patna, across the 7.5-km (5-mile) long Mahatma Gandhi Bridge over the Ganges, is the little town of Sonepur, known for its annual *mela*, reputedly the largest livestock fair in Asia. The month-long fair begins on the full moon of Kartik Purnima, which usually falls in October or November. The *mela* site is a sandy bank at the confluence of the

A mobile zoo at Sonepur's huge cattle fair

Ganges and Gandak rivers, and attracts millions of sadhus, pilgrims and local rural families, as well as livestock traders from all over India. On sale are elephants, camels, horses and cows, and an array of exotic birds. As a sideshow to the buying and selling of animals, grain and fodder, are several troupes of folk singers and magicians, *nautanki* (vaudeville) groups, dance bands, wrestlers and gymnasts, all exhibiting their skills on the sands. In between trading and entertainment, everyone takes a holy dip in the river during this most auspicious period in the Hindu calendar.

The state tourism department sets up a tourist village a week in advance of the fair, and cottages and tents can be booked at their office in Patna. Even if buying an elephant (prices begin at about US$200) is not on a visitor's agenda, the Sonepur Mela, with its colourful combination of religion, entertainment and commerce, is an unforgettable experience.

Elephants being bathed during the Sonepur Mela

❹ Vaishali

Vaishali district. 55 km (34 miles) N of Patna. 🚌 🛈 Tourist Information Centre, Vaishali (06225) 284 425.

Set in the lush green landscape of north Bihar, dotted with groves of banana and litchi trees, Vaishali is an important religious site. Mahavira, founder of the Jain faith *(see p400)*, is said to have been born here in 599 BC. It is also the place where the Buddha preached his last sermon *(see p225)*. In the 6th century BC, Vaishali was a flourishing city under the Lichhavi rulers who established one of the world's first city republics here. A well-preserved **Mauryan Stone Pillar**, dating from the 3rd century BC, with a life-size lion sitting atop it, is located 4 km (2.5 miles) west of the Tourist Lodge.

Close to the pillar is the **Abishek Pushkarni Tank**, also known as the Monkey Tank, which is now a stagnant pond. According to legend, it was dug by monkeys, who offered the hungry Buddha a bowl of honey here – a scene often depicted in Buddhist sculpture and painting. Also near the pillar, are the ruins of a 5th-century BC brick stupa. It is believed to have been built by the Lichhavi rulers soon after the Buddha's death to enshrine his ashes. Ongoing excavations have revealed the brick foundations of various other stupas. In 1996, Japanese Buddhists built a temple and a huge white **Vishwa Shanti Stupa** ("World Peace Stupa"), re-establishing Vaishali on the Buddhist pilgrimage circuit.

The lion atop the 3rd-century BC pillar, Vaishali

Madhubani Painting

The vibrant Madhubani folk paintings *(see p85)* of north Bihar have now gained international acclaim and popularity. Painted on the walls of village homes by women, Madhubani art features motifs and themes inspired by Hindu mythology, nature and festivals, as well as by everyday life. Especially intricate compositions are created for the *kohbar*, or bridal room, for the wedding night, usually featuring a god and goddess surrounded by a host of small birds and animals, and watched over by the sun, moon and stars. In recent years, with Madhubani women having participated in international exhibitions in foreign countries, new motifs have crept into their work, such as skyscrapers, aeroplanes and women in stiletto heels. The vibrant colours used are made of vegetable and mineral dyes, and the paintings are drawn with thin bamboo sticks. Madhubani paintings are now also being done on paper and fabric, and are widely available for sale in many Indian cities.

A Madhubani painting, with its strong lines and colours

The renowned Bihar School of Yoga, inside Munger Fort

❺ Munger

Munger district. 180 km (112 miles) E of Patna. 🚉 🛈 Tourist Information Centre, Fort Area, Munger (06344) 222 392.

Picturesquely located on the banks of the Ganges, Munger is home to the famous **Bihar School of Yoga**, established by Swami Satyanand, and now run by his disciple Swami Niranjananand. The school lies within the 15th-century Munger Fort, and welcomes visitors. The fort was successively occupied by the Mughals, various regional rulers and the British. Near the north gate of the fort is an 18th-century British cemetery with ornate pyramid-shaped tombs.

🏠 **Bihar School of Yoga**
Tel (06344) 222 430. **Open** daily
🌐 biharyoga.net

❻ Deoghar

Deoghar district. 180 km (112 miles) E of Patna. 🚉 🚌 🛈 Tourist Information Centre, (06432) 222 422. 🎊 Mela (Jul/Aug).

Deoghar's **Baidyanath Dham** is an important Shiva temple in India. It is said to mark the spot where the heart of Shiva's consort Parvati fell, as the grief-stricken Shiva carried her corpse across the earth *(see p283)*. An object of special worship is the linga inside the temple, one of Shiva's 12 *jyotirlingas* *(see p206)*, believed to have miraculously materialized out of light. The month-long annual *mela* here attracts over 100,000 pilgrims every day.

❼ Nalanda

Once the most prestigious centre of learning in Asia, the Buddhist University of Nalanda, founded in the 5th century AD, had over 5,000 international students and teachers, and a library of nine million manuscripts. Built on a hallowed site where the Buddha had often stayed, Nalanda flourished until AD 1199, when it was looted and destroyed by the Turkish raider, Bakhtiar Khalji. The evocative ruins of its monasteries and temples still convey a vivid impression of the serene and ordered life of contemplation and learning that prevailed here.

KEY

① **Monastery 1A** was probably built by a king of Sumatra in the 9th century.

② **Temple 12**, a 7th-century temple, faces the row of monasteries. The remains of a *torana* stand in front of this temple.

③ **Temple 13** has a brick-making furnace to its north.

④ **Monastery 8** has an imposing shrine in its courtyard. All the monasteries stand on terraces.

★ **Temple 3**
Nalanda's main temple, and its largest structure (31 m/102 ft high), dates to the 6th century. It has a shrine chamber at the top and small stupas at its corners.

★ **Votive Stupas**
Located in the courtyard surrounding Temple 3, these have plaster images of standing Bodhisattvas and seated Buddhas.

0 metres 50
0 yards 50

A View of the Monasteries
Monks' cells surround a courtyard in each of the 11 monasteries. The ruins display skilful brickwork.

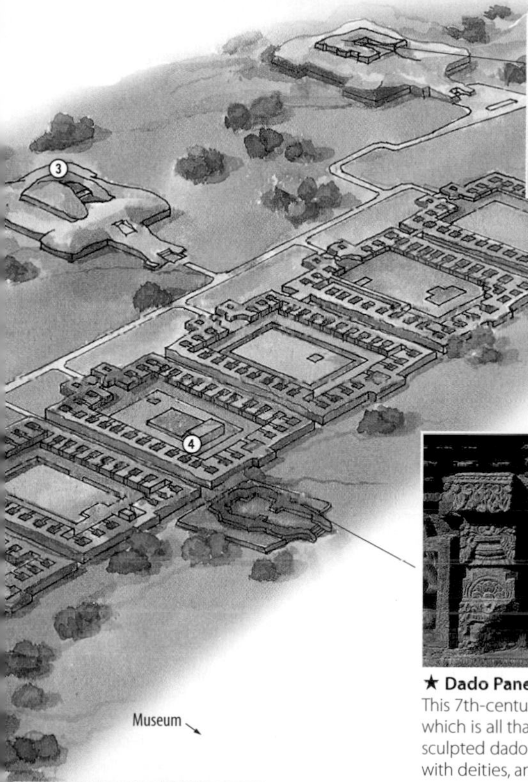

Temple 14
Traces of painting can be seen here in a niche with a pedestal, where a large image of the Buddha once stood.

Museum ↘

★ Dado Panels from Temple 2
This 7th-century temple's basement, which is all that remains, has an elaborately sculpted dado with over 200 panels carved with deities, animals and floral motifs.

Brickwork
Layers of much earlier construction, some of it dating back to the 3rd century BC, are visible in the brickwork at Nalanda.

Hiuen Tsang in Nalanda

The great Chinese scholar-monk, Hiuen Tsang, travelled across forbidding deserts and mountains to come to Nalanda in the early 7th century AD. He spent 12 years both studying and teaching here, and was dazzled by Nalanda's "soaring domes and pinnacles, pearl-red pillars carved and ornamented, and richly adorned balustrades". On his return to China he settled down at the Big Goose Pagoda in Xian, where he translated into Chinese the Buddhist scriptures he had brought back with him from Nalanda.

Chinese print of Hiuen Tsang

Hot sulphur springs at Rajgir, surrounded by temples and rest houses

❽ Rajgir

Nalanda district. 110 kms (68 miles) SE of Patna. 🏛 33,700. 🚗 🚌 ℹ️ Bihar Tourism, Kund Market, (06112) 25 273.

Surrounded by five holy hills, the picturesque little town of Rajgir is important for Buddhists as well as Jains. Both Buddha and Mahavira, founder of Jainism, spent many months meditating and preaching here. The hills around are dotted with Jain temples, the ruins of monasteries and meditation caves. Dominating Rajgir is the large Japanese-built marble and sandstone **Vishwa Shanti Stupa** on Ratnagiri Hill, with its four gilded statues of the Buddha. The 38-m (125-ft) high stupa was built in 1969 by the Nipponzan Myohoji Buddhist sect. Visitors can go up to the stupa by chairlift. From here, a path leads to the adjoining **Griddhakuta Hill** ("Vulture's Peak"), a site much venerated by Buddhists. Two rock-cut caves here were a favourite retreat of the Buddha, and it was on this hill that he preached two of his most famous sermons. The incident of the Buddha subduing a wild elephant, a scene often depicted in Buddhist art, also took place in Rajgir.

To the west of Griddhakuta Hill is **Vaibhara Hill**, at the foot of which are hot sulphur springs, crowded with people seeking a medicinal dip. On top of the hill are the seven **Saptaparni Caves** where the First Buddhist Council met soon after the Buddha's death to record his teachings. Below them on the hill is the **Pippala Watchtower**, a curious rock and stone structure, with cells for guards. It dates to the 5th century BC, when Rajgir was the capital of the Magadha Empire *(see p46)*, ruled by King Bimbisara who became a devotee of the Buddha. The remains of the great drystone cyclopean wall he built can still be seen on Rajgir's hills.

Environs
Pawapuri, 38 km (24 miles) east of Rajgir, is sacred to Jains as the place where the founder of their faith, Mahavira, died in 500 BC. A lotus-filled tank, with the marble Jalmandir Temple in the middle of it, marks the site of his cremation.

❾ Gaya

Gaya district. 100 km (62 miles) S of Patna. 🏛 383,200. 🚗 🚌 ℹ️ Bihar State Tourist Office, Railway Station, (0631) 232 155.

Stretching along the banks of the Phalgu river, Gaya along with Varanasi and Allahabad, is regarded as one of the three most sacred sites for performing Hindu funeral rites. It is believed that Vishnu himself sanctified Gaya, decreeing that prayers for departed souls, performed here, would absolve all their earthly sins. Dominating the religious life of the city is the **Vishnupad Temple**, which is not open to non-Hindus, but no such restrictions apply to the picturesque ghats and shrines along the river front.

Environs
The **Barabar Caves**, cut deep into a granite hill, are 24 km (15 miles) north of Gaya, along a bumpy jeep road. They were the inspiration for the Marabar Caves in EM Forster's famous novel, *A Passage to India*. Dating to the 3rd century BC, these are the earliest examples of rock-cut caves in India. Of the four caves, built for ascetics on the orders of the Mauryan emperor Ashoka, the two most impressive are the **Lomas Rishi** and **Sudama Caves**. They are remarkable for the highly lustrous polish on the stone, and for the way in which the caves have been shaped to imitate the rounded wood and bamboo dwellings which were common at that time. Even the interior walls have perpendicular grooves cut into the stone, in imitation of bamboo strips. The façade of the Lomas Rishi Cave has fine lattice-work carving, and a charming row of elephants paying homage to stupas. These caves were used by the Ajivika sect of ascetics, who were contemporaries of the Jain and Buddhist orders.

It is unsafe to explore this wild and rugged area without reliable guides, recommended by the Bihar Tourism office at Gaya's railway station.

Rituals being performed at the Phalgu Ghat in Gaya

In the Buddha's Footsteps

The Buddha was born in 566 BC as Siddhartha Gautama, prince of the kingdom of Kapilavastu. Though born in Lumbini, in Nepal, all the places associated with his life and his teachings are in Bihar and Uttar Pradesh. These are now part of a well-travelled circuit for Buddhist pilgrims, who follow in the Buddha's footsteps from Bodh Gaya, where he attained enlightenment; to Sarnath where he preached his first sermon; through other places he visited regularly, and finally to Kushinagar, where he died in 486 BC.

Renouncing his princely life, Prince Siddhartha (represented here by a riderless horse) left his palace and his family at the age of 30, to search for answers to the meaning of human existence and suffering.

Emaciated by fasts and penances while he spent six years living with ascetics and wandering as a beggar, Prince Siddhartha found that such self-mortification gave him no answers.

Enlightenment came at Bodh Gaya where, after meditating for 49 days under the Bodhi Tree, he discovered that the cause of suffering is desire; and that desire can be conquered by following the "Eightfold Path" of Righteousness.

The First Sermon, delivered at Sarnath (see p212), contained the essence of his teachings. Eschewing asceticism, rituals, caste and class distinctions, his Eightfold Path prescribed Right Thought, Understanding, Speech, Action, Livelihood, Effort, Concentration and Contemplation.

The Buddha's Death took place in 486 BC. He fell ill after eating wild mushrooms prepared by one of his followers, and died in a grove of *sal* trees at Kushinagar, where a stupa marks the site of his cremation.

The Buddhist Trail attracts Buddhists from all over the world, including countries such as Japan and Thailand. Many stupas and temples along the pilgrimage circuit owe their existence to these devotees. This Buddha image was built by the Japanese.

Buddhist Pilgrim Sites

See also the features on Little Tibet (p127) and Buddhist Iconography (p145).

The Thai Monastery in Bodh Gaya, built like a traditional *wat* (temple)

⑩ Bodh Gaya

Gaya district. 115 km (71 miles) SE of Patna. 🚶 30,900. 🚉 Gaya, 13 km (8 miles) N of town centre, then taxi or bus. 🚌 ℹ️ Bihar Tourism, 34 Mahabodhi Market Complex, (0631) 240 0672. 🎭 Monlam Chenmo Prayers (Jan/Feb), Buddha Jayanti (May).

The holiest site for Buddhists from all over the world, Bodh Gaya is the place where the Buddha attained enlightenment. The focal point of the town is the **Mahabodhi Temple**, whose soaring pyramidal spire dominates the landscape. The temple is enclosed on three sides by a 1st-century BC stone railing, carved with lotus medallions and scenes from the Buddha's life, and includes the sacred **Bodhi Tree**, under which the Buddha meditated before he attained enlightenment.

The original temple at this spot was a circular stupa, built by the Mauryan king Ashoka in the 3rd century BC, but a major reconstruction in the 7th century AD gave the temple its present form. In the 12th century, it was severely damaged by Muslim invaders, but faithfully restored in the 14th century by Burmese kings, who also added the replicas of the main spire at each corner of the temple. Then, as Buddhism went into near eclipse in northern India, the temple site was flooded and silted over, and effectively "lost" for centuries. Some Burmese Buddhists redis-covered it in the late 19th century. The temple ruins were then excavated and restored.

Today, Bodh Gaya once again flourishes as an international centre for Buddhism. Temples and monasteries built by various countries, including China, Japan, Sri Lanka, Vietnam, Thailand, Taiwan, Korea, Bhutan and Nepal, dot the town. The **Thai Temple** is the most picturesque, while the modern **Japanese Temple** is remarkable for the 25-m (82-ft) high Buddha statue that towers in front of it. The **Bhutanese** and **Tibetan Monasteries** are filled with colourful murals and prayer wheels, and both are always thronged by red-robed monks.

In the courtyard around the Mahabodhi Temple, monks meditate at the stupas, novitiates have their heads shaved, and pilgrims pray before the Bodhi Tree. For three weeks during the winter, a tented city springs up around the temple, as thousands of monks and pilgrims congregate here for the Monlam Chenmo Prayers, often presided over by the Dalai Lama and other venerated figures from the Buddhist world. Across the street, the **Archaeological Museum** has fragments of the beautiful original 3rd-century BC temple railing, and bronze and stone images from the 8th to 12th centuries, which were excavated during the restoration of the temple.

The 25-m (82-ft) Buddha statue, erected by the Japanese

🏛 **Archaeological Museum** Open Sat–Thu. 📷

Beautifully carved stupas in the temple courtyard

The Sacred Bodhi Tree

According to local lore, the original Bodhi Tree (*Ficus religiosa*) was cut down by Emperor Ashoka's wife because she was jealous of the time he spent at his Buddhist devotions. The emperor then revived the tree by nurturing its roots with gallons of milk, and built a protective stone railing around it. The tree that stands today is said to come from the same stock as the original tree. Ashoka's son Mahinda took a sapling from the original tree to Sri Lanka on one of his proselytizing missions. The tree flourished there, and its sapling was later brought back to be planted at Bodh Gaya after the original tree had died.

Pilgrims gathered around the Bodhi Tree

Bodh Gaya: Mahabodhi Temple

The Mahabodhi Temple complex, a UNESCO World Heritage monument, marks the site where, more than 2,500 years ago, Prince Siddhartha meditated on the causes of human suffering, found the answers he was seeking under the Bodhi Tree, and became the Buddha – the Enlightened One. The best time to visit the complex is at dusk, when thousands of oil lamps bathe the temple in a golden light, and the sound of Buddhist prayers fills the air.

The Buddha
This gilded stone image (late 10th century) in the main sanctum has an aura of great serenity. The pedestal is carved with alternating lions and elephants.

The Spire, 52 m (171 ft) high, is carved in tiers and capped by an umbrella-like finial.

The Torana
The gateway to the temple is made of granite and covered with inscriptions from the Buddha's teachings. It dates from the 8th century.

The Bodhi Tree under which the Buddha spent 49 days.

The entrance
leads to the main sanctum with the Buddha image.

The Cankamana or Jewel Walk
Carved with lotuses, this sacred promenade was where the Buddha walked, meditating on whether to spread his message to the world.

The Vajrashila
The red sandstone seat beneath the Bodhi Tree marks the spot where the Buddha sat. It probably dates to the 3rd century BC.

⓫ Parasnath

Giridih district. 179 km (111 miles) NE of Ranchi. 🚉 🚌 Madhuban.

An important destination for Jain pilgrims, Parasnath is named after Parsvanatha, the 23rd Jain *tirthankara (see p400)*, who is believed to have attained nirvana here. Clustered on top of Sikayi Hill, the highest peak in Jharkhand at 1,400 m (4,593 ft), are 24 Jain shrines and two temples, each one dedicated to one of the Jain *tirthankaras*. The temple on the highest point is dedicated to Parsvanatha. Pilgrims begin their climb from Madhuban, a stopover at the foot of the hill, and it takes over three hours, through forested slopes. Palanquins are available to carry those who do not want to walk. The views from the top are magnificent.

⓬ Hazaribagh National Park

Hazaribagh district. 135 km (84 miles) N of Ranchi. 🚉 Hazaribagh Rd Station, 67 km (42 miles) S of Pokharia, the main entry point, then bus. 🚌 ℹ️ Tourist Office, near bus stand, Hazaribagh town, located 16 km (10 miles) S of Pokharia. For permission, contact Divisional Forest Officer, Hazaribagh, (06546) 223 340.

Set in the undulating Chhota Nagpur Plateau at an average altitude of 615 m (2,018 ft), covered with tropical deciduous forests, this national park is 16 km (10 miles) from Hazaribagh. Hazaribagh means "Thousand Tigers" and this quiet town's environs were once famous for their tiger population. However, as a result of deforestation, most of the tigers are gone, and

En route to Netarhat, through the picturesque Chhota Nagpur Plateau

spotting a tiger from one of the ten viewing platforms is now rare. The 190 sq-km (73 sq-mile) park, established in 1954, is bisected by the Ranchi-Kolkata Highway which, with its heavy traffic, has driven away many animals to other habitats. But there are plenty of wild boar, nilgai and leopard, and its thick forests are a haven for birdlife.

Leopard at Palamau Park

⓭ Palamau Wildlife Sanctuary

Palamau district. 170 km (106 miles) W of Ranchi. 🚉 Daltonganj, 24 km (15 miles) NW of Betla, the main entry point. 🚌 ℹ️ Tourist Office, Betla, (06562) 256 513. For permits contact the Deputy Director, Palamau National Park, Daltonganj. Jeeps are available at Betla. 🏨

Also known as Betla National Park, the Palamau Wildlife Sanctuary, on the northwestern edge of the Chhota Nagpur Plateau, is set in hilly tribal country, with the Koel and Burha rivers flowing through it. The sanctuary is also home to the

Palamau Tiger Reserve. The sanctuary is dotted with bamboo, *sal (Shorea robusta)* groves, towering *mahua (Madhuca indica)* trees from whose pale yellow flower the area's tribal people (Oraons and Mundas) make a potent liquor, and grassland. It is inhabited by wild elephants, deer, leopards, tigers (44 at last count in 1997) and several bird species. There are numerous watchtowers and hides that have been strategically placed around the water holes. The picturesque ruins of two 16th-century forts, hot springs and a few tribal villages also lie within the park.

⓮ Netarhat

Latehar district. 160 km (99 miles) W of Ranchi. 🚌

The only hill station in Bihar and Jharkhand, Netarhat is situated at an altitude of 1,158 m (3,799 ft) and lies deep within the forested Chhota Nagpur hills, just off the Ranchi-Hazaribagh Highway. There are several pleasant rambles in the hills around this little town, and fine views of the surrounding countryside from **Magnolia Point**. The scenic **Burha Ghagh, or Burha Falls** make an enchanting picnic spot. A curious building here is a huge wooden Swiss-style chalet, formerly the country retreat of the British governors of Bihar, and now a boarding school for boys. The school authorities usually welcome visitors.

Watchtower in the Hazaribagh Wildlife Sanctuary

Fields on the outskirts of Ranchi

⓯ Ranchi

Ranchi district. 289 km (180 miles) E of Patna. 🚉 846,500. ✈ 5 km (3 miles) S of town centre. 🚌 🚍 ℹ Birsa Vihar Tourist Complex, Main Rd, (0651) 230 1230. 🛍 daily. 🎊 Kath Yatra (Jun/Jul).

The capital of the state of Jharkhand, Ranchi is a good base from which to explore the natural beauty of the Chhota Nagpur Plateau. The summer capital of Bihar in the days of the British Raj, Ranchi still attracts visitors keen to escape the heat and dust of Bihar's plains. The town's main attraction is the 17th-century **Jagannath Temple**, perched on a hill in the southwestern outskirts. Like the Jagannath Temple at Puri (see p317), this temple also holds an annual chariot festival.

The Chhota Nagpur Plateau is the home of the forest-dwelling Munda and Oraon tribes. The wide-ranging exhibits and collections of artifacts in the **Ranchi Museum** provide a comprehensive picture of their lifestyles and social structures.

Oraon tribal girls dancing

🏛 **Ranchi Museum**
Open Mon–Sat. **Closed** public hols.

Environs

Hundru Falls, 45 km (28 miles) east of Ranchi, is a picturesque picnic spot. This is the point where the Subarnarekha river drops down dramatically from the Chhota Nagpur Plateau to form a 100-m (328-ft) water-fall, which splashes into the pools below. The sleepy town of **McCluskiegunj**, 40 km (25 miles) northwest of Ranchi, is a quaint relic of the Raj. It was established as a settlement for Eurasians who felt they belonged neither to British nor to Indian society, and wanted a haven of their own. Today, only a handful of the original settlers now have emigrated to Australia), living out their old age in cottages crammed with their treasured collections of English china ornaments, and adorned with pictures of the British royal family.

⓰ Jamshedpur

East Singbhum district. 130 km (81 miles) SE of Ranchi. 🚉 570,300. ✈ 🚍 ℹ Tourist Information Centre, Bistupur, (0657) 243 2892. 🚌 🛍 daily. 🎊 Founder's Day (Mar).

One of India's major industrial centres, Jamshedpur is a rare oasis of cleanliness and efficiency in this region. The planned township, surrounded by lakes, rivers and the pretty Dal Hills, was established in 1908 by the Parsi tycoon, Sir Jamshedji Tata (see p450). He is regarded as the father of industrial development in India. The Tata Iron and Steel Company (TISCO) was set up by him in this area because of the rich deposits of iron ore and coal found here. The Tata empire continues to flourish, and several of its research, educational and cultural institutes here are open to visitors.

Festivals of Bihar & Jharkhand

Maner Urs (Feb), Maner. This festival honours the Sufi saint Sheikh Yahya Maneri with soulful qawwali singing at his mausoleum, and a lively fair in the town.
Sarhool (Mar/Apr), Jharkhand. The Munda tribals perform tree-worshipping ceremonies, followed by much dancing and feasting.
Jatra (Mar/Apr), Jharkhand. The Oraon tribals hold lively dances during this festival, in which the young people choose their mates.
Buddha Jayanti (May), Bodh Gaya. A fair and special prayers are held to celebrate the Buddha's birth, attainment of enlightenment and nirvana.

Pilgrims with offerings for the Sun God on Chhat

Batsavitri (May/Jun). This festival commemorates the legend of Savitri, who brought her husband Satyavan back from the dead through the sheer intensity of her prayer. It is celebrated by married women who fast and pray, tie strings around banyan trees and offer sweets and fruits to images of Savitri.
Sonepur Mela (Oct/Nov), Sonepur (see p220).
Chhat (Oct/Nov). Flower-shaped pastries called thekua are made in every home during this three-day thanksgiving festival, dedicated to the Sun God, celebrated all over Bihar.

MADHYA PRADESH & CHHATTISGARH

Covering a vast area of 308,252 sq km (119,017 sq miles), Madhya Pradesh and Chhattisgarh constitute the geographic heart of India. Between them, they border on to seven states, have one-third of India's forest cover, and are home to 40 per cent of the country's tribal population. Madhya Pradesh is crossed by the Vindhya and the Satpura mountains, and its main river is the Narmada. In the state's rugged north are the famous Khajuraho temples, while eastern Madhya Pradesh has two of India's finest game sanctuaries, Bandhavgarh and Kanha. The scenic Malwa Plateau in the southwest has the great Buddhist stupa of Sanchi and the romantic 15th–16th century citadel of Mandu. In November 2000, the thickly forested and remote southeast, with its predominantly tribal population, became the new state of Chhattisgarh.

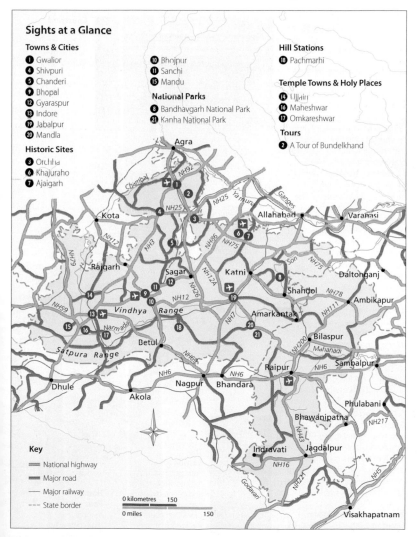

Sights at a Glance

Towns & Cities
1 Gwalior
4 Shivpuri
5 Chanderi
9 Bhopal
12 Gyaraspur
13 Indore
19 Jabalpur
20 Mandla

Historic Sites
3 Orchha
6 Khajuraho
7 Ajaigarh

10 Bhojpur
11 Sanchi
15 Mandu

National Parks
8 Bandhavgarh National Park
21 Kanha National Park

Hill Stations
18 Pachmarhi

Temple Towns & Holy Places
14 Ujjain
16 Maheshwar
17 Omkareshwar

Tours
2 A Tour of Bundelkhand

Key
━━ National highway
━━ Major road
── Major railway
--- State border

0 kilometres   150
0 miles   150

◄ Tigers in Bandhavgarh National Park

For keys to symbols *see back flap*

The Durbar Hall of Jai Vilas Palace with its two gigantic chandeliers

❶ Gwalior

Gwalior district. 321 km (200 miles) S of Delhi. 🚉 827,000. ✈ 14 km (8 miles) N of city centre. 🚌 🚇 🛈 TO Hotel Tansen, MG Rd (0751) 401 0666. 🎭 Tansen Music Festival (Oct/Nov).

Apart from **Gwalior Fort**, the main attraction for visitors to Gwalior is the opulent, Italianate **Jai Vilas Palace**, south of the fort, built for the maharaja of Gwalior by his architect, Colonel Sir Michael Filose, in the late 19th century. Still the residence of the former Scindia rulers, part of the palace has been turned into a museum. The most magnificent room is the Durbar Hall. Hanging from its ceiling are two of the world's largest chandeliers, 13-m (43-ft) high and weighing 3 tonnes each. Before they were hung the strength of the roof was tested by having several elephants stand on it. Also on view is an extraordinary mechanical silver toy train that carried liqueurs around the maharaja's dining table.

North of the fort is Gwalior's old town, which has two interesting Islamic monuments – the 16th-century **Tomb of Mohammed Ghaus**, a Mughal nobleman, which has outstanding stone latticework screens; and the **Tomb of Tansen**, the famous singer who was one of the "nine jewels" of the Mughal emperor Akbar's court (see p184).

🏛 **Jai Vilas Palace Museum**
Closed Wed. **Tel** (0751) 232 2390. 📷

Gwalior Fort: Man Mandir Palace

The massive Gwalior fort stretches for nearly 3 km (2 miles) atop a 100-m (328-ft) high sandstone and basalt hill. Its formidable bastioned walls, 10-m (33-ft) high, enclose exquisite temples and palaces, the most spectacular of which is the Man Mandir Palace. Built between 1486 and 1516 by Raja Man Singh of the Tomar dynasty, this double-storeyed palace is regarded as one of the finest examples of Rajput secular architecture, embellished with superb stone carving and latticework. Brilliant blue, yellow and green tiles depicting parrots and peacocks, rows of ducks, elephants, banana trees and crocodiles holding lotus buds, decorate the Man Mandir's façade.

Courtyard
The interior courtyard with its carved pillars has rooms around it. Two subterranean floors, with fountains and baths, were later used as dungeons.

The Bastions
Rounded bastions, topped with cupolas and decorated with coloured tilework, break the severity of the fort's high walls.

Hathia Paur is the magnificent main gateway.

The lavishly carved and decorated south façade of Man Mandir

Stone Latticework
The oriel window, in the zenana quarters of the palace, is framed against intricately latticed stone battlements. A pair of caparisoned elephants flank the window.

Exploring Gwalior Fort

Described by a 16th-century Persian chronicler as "the pearl in the necklace of castles of Hind", Gwalior Fort has had a turbulent history. Founded in the 8th century AD, it was successively ruled by a series of local Hindu dynasties, followed by the Delhi Sultans, the Mughals and finally the Maratha Scindias *(see p475)*, who became the maharajas of Gwalior in the 18th century. It was also briefly in British hands in the 19th century. The fort is best entered from the **Urwahi Gate** on its western side, where 21 colossal **Jain Sculptures** depicting the *tirthankaras (see p400)* and dating from the 7th to the 15th centuries, are carved into the rock face.

Lying to their left is the richly carved, 25-m (82-ft) high temple, **Teli ka Mandir**, the tallest temple in the fort. Built in the 9th century and dedicated to Vishnu, it has an unusual *shikhara*, rounded at the top. After the Indian Mutiny of 1857 *(see p57)* British soldiers occupied the temple and used it as a soda factory. Situated to its north are a pair of 11th-century Vishnu temples, called the **Saas-Bahu** ("Mother and Daughter-in-Law") **Temples**. They are covered with superb sculptures of dancing girls and deities, though their *shikharas* were destroyed in an attack by Sultan Qutbuddin Aibak *(see p52)* in the 12th century.

North of them is the **Hathia Paur**, entrance gateway to the

Rock-cut Jain sculpture

Man Mandir Palace, its ornate pillars supporting a dome with a richly corbelled arch. At the northeastern edge of the fort is the 15th-century **Gujari Mahal**, built Raja Man Singh for his Gujar (tribal) queen. Now the **Archaeological Museum**, its fine collection of Jain and Hindu sculpture includes the celebrated statue of the *salabhanjika* (wood nymph), originally from the temple at Gyaraspur *(see p247)*.

Gwalior Fort

1 Urwahi Gate
2 Jain Sculptures
3 Teli ka Mandir
4 Saas-Bahu Temples
5 Hathia Paur Gate
6 Man Mandir Palace
7 Gujari Mahal

```
0 metres        700
0 yards         700
```

The 9th-century Teli ka Mandir, the tallest temple in the fort

Women walk past the striking façade of the Khajuraho temple, Madhya Pradesh ▶

❷ A Tour of Bundelkhand

Gwalior and the adjoining region of Bundelkhand, named after the Bundela Rajputs, make up a culturally distinctive area in Central India. Countless forts and monuments, situated in a boulder-strewn landscape of great beauty, still echo with stories of the pageantry of the Bundela Rajput courts, and the valour of warriors such as the Rani of Jhansi *(see p199).* The area's glorious history and refined artistic traditions are reflected in the architectural treasures of Gwalior, the medieval city of Orchha, and the hilltop temples of Sonagiri.

① **Gwalior**
The capital of many dynasties since the 8th century AD, Gwalior *(see p232)* is the most splendid of the "gateways" to the Bundelkhand region.

② **Pawaya**
The remains of an ancient fort can be seen in this capital of the Nag kings (3rd century AD) from the highway at Dabra.

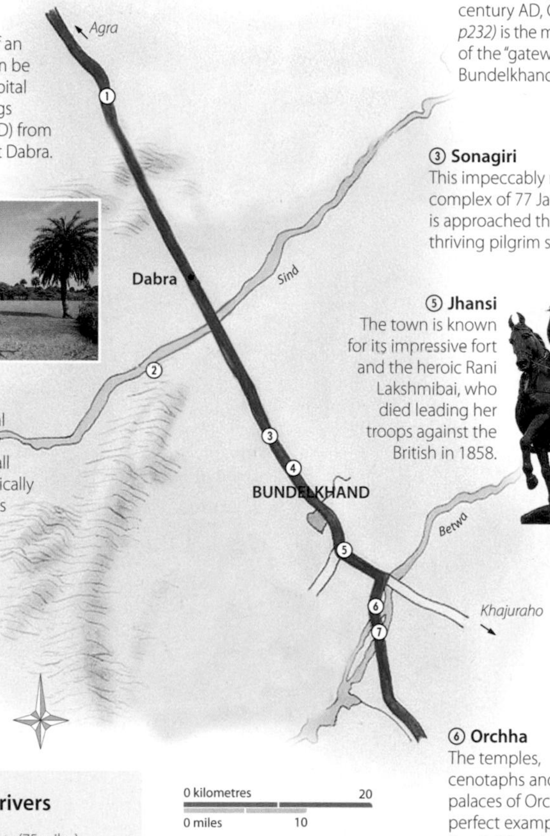

③ **Sonagiri**
This impeccably maintained complex of 77 Jain temples is approached through a thriving pilgrim settlement.

④ **Datia**
This erstwhile Bundela capital surrounded by numerous small lakes, has scenically located palaces on hillocks.

⑤ **Jhansi**
The town is known for its impressive fort and the heroic Rani Lakshmibai, who died leading her troops against the British in 1858.

Key
■ Tour route
= Other roads
≈ River

⑥ **Orchha**
The temples, cenotaphs and tiered palaces of Orchha are perfect examples of Bundelkhand architecture.

Tips for Drivers

Length: 120 km (75 miles).
Stopping-off points: Gwalior, Sonagiri, Datia, Jhansi, Orchha and Taragram provide convenient stopovers. There is a petrol pump at Dabra, after Gwalior. State tourism hotels and guesthouses are available at Gwalior, Datia (Tourist Motel, (07522) 238 125), Jhansi and Orchha. Local buses run between the major stops.

0 kilometres 20
0 miles 10

⑦ **Taragram**
A fascinating handmade paper factory here is an interesting experimental centre aimed at upgrading local craftsmanship.

The marble cenotaph of Madhavrao Scindia at Shivpuri

❸ Orchha

See pp238–9.

❹ Shivpuri

Shivpuri district. 117 km (73 miles) SW of Gwalior. 🚶 146,900. 🚌 🚐
ℹ️ MP Tourism, Railway Station, (0751) 254 0777; Tourist Village, Shivpuri, (07492) 223 760/221 297.

The summer capital of the Scindia rulers of Gwalior, Shivpuri was once a thickly forested region, and a favourite hunting ground of the Mughals. Most of the elephants in Emperor Akbar's army were taken from these forests. Today, the main attractions are the 19th-century white marble cenotaphs of Madhavrao Scindia and his mother, which stand facing each other in a formal Mughal-style garden. With their mix of *shikharas* (spires), domes and cupolas, they epitomize Indo-Islamic architecture. Madhavrao's cenotaph is decorated with *pietra dura* work in lapis lazuli and onyx. There are life-size statues of the ruler and his mother and, in accordance with family tradition, their favourite foods are brought and left here every day. The colonial-style **Madhav Vilas Palace** has airy terraces overlooking the town. The 156-sq km (60 sq-mile) **Madhav National Park** is a mixed deciduous forest with an artificial lake, surrounded by grasslands. **George Castle**, a hunting lodge, was built by Jiyajirao Scindia in honour of King George V, who stayed here in 1911.

❺ Chanderi

Guna district. 227 km (141 miles) S of Gwalior. 🚶 28,300. 🚌 ℹ️ MP Tourism, Tanabana, (07547) 25 2222.

The medieval town of Chanderi is dominated by the **Kirtidurga Fort**, perched 200 m (656 ft) above the Betwa river, and overlooking an artificial lake, Kirtisagar. Built by the Pratihara kings in the 10th century, Chanderi successively fell to the sultans of Delhi and Malwa, the Mughal emperor Babur and finally to the Marathas, becoming part of the Scindia kingdom of Gwalior. The entrance is through the Khuni Darwaza ("Bloody Gateway"), marking the point at which the Mughal emperor Babur broke through the 6-km (4-mile) long granite walls of the fort, when he conquered it in 1528. Cut into the adjacent rock face are

Minaret detail, Kirtidurga Fort

several imposing Jain statues. Most of the structures inside the fort are attributed to Sultan Mahmud of Malwa, and are executed in the graceful provincial Afghan style that distinguishes the buildings of Mandu *(see pp251–3)*. The most ambitious edifice here is the **Koshak Mahal**, built in 1445. The sultan originally planned it as a seven-storeyed palace, but only managed to complete two storeys, each with balconies, rows of windows and beautifully vaulted ceilings. Other notable buildings are the domed and arcaded **Jama Masjid** and the **Badal Mahal** with its elegant gateway. Chanderi was once a flourishing centre of trade, and an exploration of the town reveals large sandstone *havelis*, shops raised on plinths and ruined caravanserais lining the winding lanes. The town is also famous for its gossamer muslin saris and brocades.

Environs
Deogarh Fort, the "Fortress of the Gods", is 25 km (16 miles) southeast of Chanderi. Within it are a splendid display of sculptures from a group of 9th- to 10th-century Jain temples. Just below the fort is the 5th-century Vishnu Dasavatara Temple with its fine sculpture and carved pillars topped by celestial musicians. A statue of Vishnu asleep on Ananta, the cosmic serpent *(see pp28–9)*, is among the early masterpieces of Indian art

Chanderi's fort, the scene of many battles

One of the *chhatris* (cenotaphs) of the Bundela kings at Orchha

❸ Orchha

Tikamgarh district. 120 km (75 miles) SE of Gwalior. 🚉 Jhansi, 19 km (12 miles) NW of Orchha, then taxi or bus. 🚌 Son et Lumière (Chaturbhuj, Jehangir Mahal, & Raj Mahal): Mar–Oct: 7:30–8:30pm (English), 8:45–9:45pm (Hindi); Nov–Feb: 6:30–7:30pm (English), 7:45–8:45pm (Hindi). 🛈 MP Tourism, Sheesh Mahal, (07680) 25 2624; Betwa Retreat, (07680) 25 2618/2402. 🎉 Ramnavami (Apr), Dussehra (Sep/Oct).

Orchha is dramatically positioned on a rocky island, enclosed by a loop of the Betwa river. Founded in 1531, it was the capital of the Bundela kings until 1738, when it was abandoned for Tikamgarh.

Crumbling palaces, pavilions, *hamams*, walls and gates, connected to the town with a 14-arched causeway, are all that remain today. The three main palaces are massed symmetrically together. These are the **Raja Mahal** (1560), **Jahangir Mahal** (1626) and **Rai Praveen Mahal** (mid-1670s), named after a royal paramour.

The old town is dominated by three beautiful temples – the **Ram Raja**, the **Lakshmi Narayan** and the **Chaturbhuj**. A unique blend of fort and temple styles, the Chaturbhuj Temple is dedicated to Vishnu and has huge arcaded halls for massed singing, and a soaring spire.

Lying along the Kanchana Ghat of the Betwa are the 14 beautiful cenotaphs of the Orchha rulers. Along with the many *sati* pillars in Jahangiri Mahal's museum, these serve as reminders of Orchha's feudal past when queens sometimes committed *sati* by jumping into their husband's funeral pyres.

Orchha: Jahangir Mahal

An excellent example of Rajput Bundela architecture, this palace was built by the Bundela king Bir Singh Deo and named after the Mughal emperor Jahangir who spent one night here. The many-layered palace has 132 chambers off and above the central courtyard and an almost equal number of subterranean rooms. The square sandstone palace is extravagantly embellished with lapis lazuli tiles, graceful *chhatris* and ornate *jali* screens. It also has a modest museum.

★ **Entrance Gateway**
The impressive entrance gateway, flanked by stone elephants, leads up to the central courtyard.

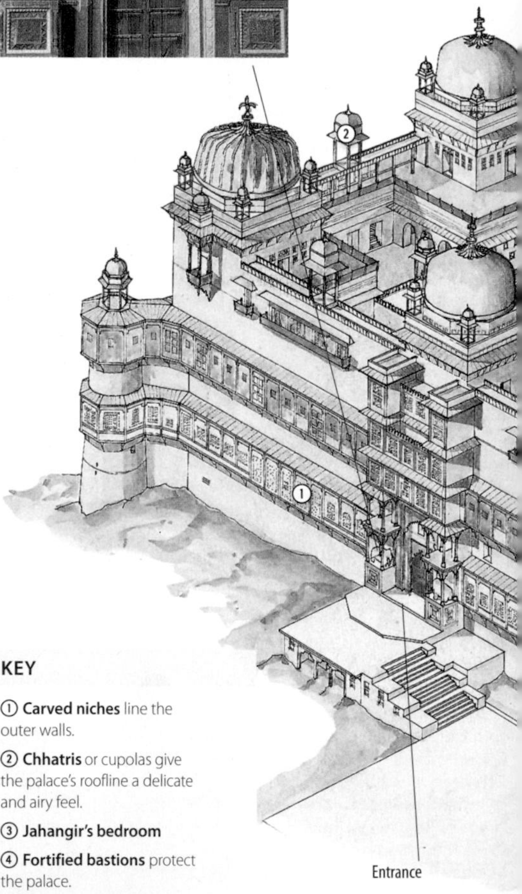

KEY

① **Carved niches** line the outer walls.

② **Chhatris** or cupolas give the palace's roofline a delicate and airy feel.

③ **Jahangir's bedroom**

④ **Fortified bastions** protect the palace.

⑤ **The central courtyard** can be viewed from each part of the palace and has a small museum in a set of rooms that run along it.

Entrance

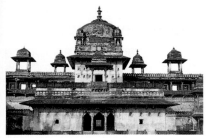

★ Domed Pavilion
A domed pavilion, with an apartment beneath, marks the corners as well as the middle of each side of the palace.

VISITORS' CHECKLIST

Practical Information
Palace Complex.
Open daily. **Closed** public hols.
MP Tourism, Sheesh Mahal, (07680) 252 624.
Museum: **Open** daily.
Closed public hols.

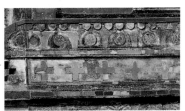

Glazed Tilework
Geometric lapis motifs decorate the outer façade at the top.

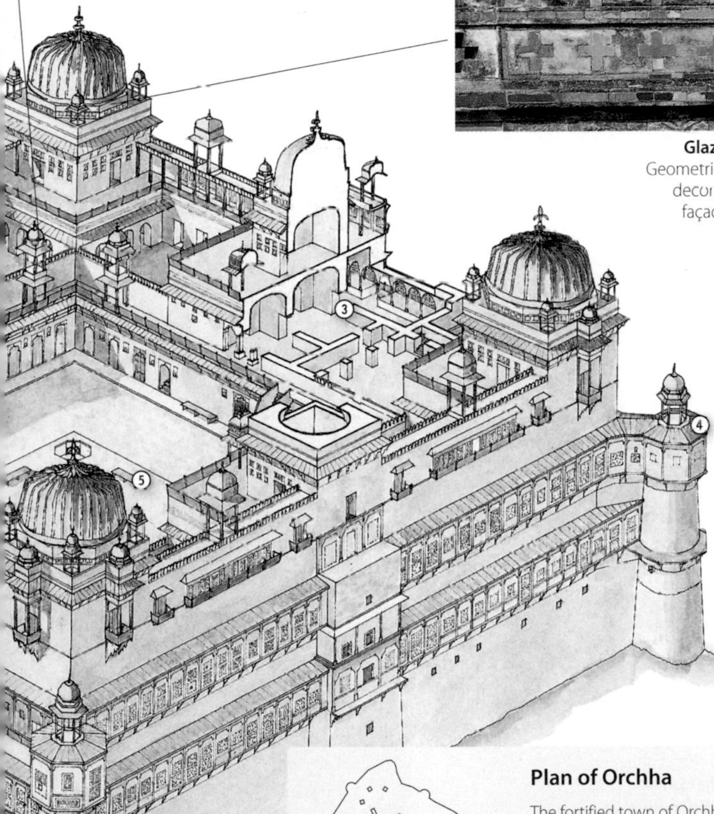

Plan of Orchha

The fortified town of Orchha encloses three major palaces and ruined ancillary structures.

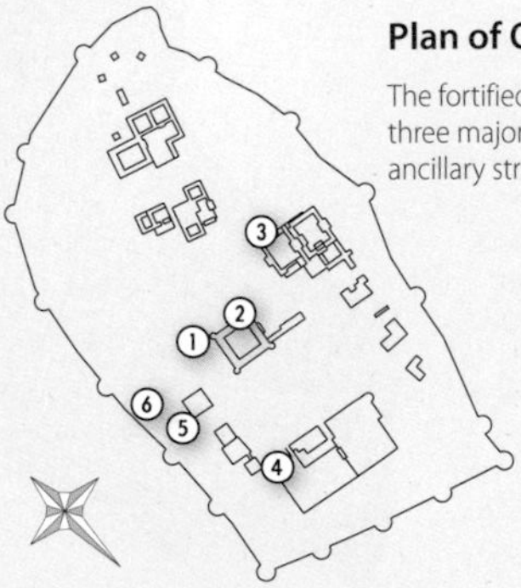

1 Jahangir Mahal
2 Sheesh Mahal
3 Raja Mahal
4 Rai Praveen Mahal
5 *Hamam*
6 Stable

Key

Illustrated area

🟢 Khajuraho: Kandariya Mahadev Temple

The magnificent group of temples at Khajuraho, a UNESCO World Heritage Site, were built between the 9th and 10th centuries by the Chandela dynasty which dominated Central India at that time. The most impressive of the temples is the Kandariya Mahadev, which represents the pinnacle of North Indian temple art and architecture. It is remarkable for its grand dimensions, its complex yet perfectly harmonious composition, and its exquisite sculptural embellishment. Over 800 sculptures cover the temple, depicting gods and goddesses, beasts and warriors, sensuous maidens, dancers, musicians and, of course, the erotic scenes for which the Khajuraho temples are famous.

View of the Kandariya Mahadev temple, built 1025–1050

★ Apsaras
Often carved as support-bracket figures, the celestial nymphs reveal the sculptors' mastery of the female form. Full of natural charm and sensuous grace, they are shown as dancers, attendants of the deities, or simply engaged in everyday activities.

KEY

① **The Ardha Mandapa** or east-facing entrance porch has an exquisite *makara torana* (ceremonial arch) flanked by two crocodile heads, and covered with floral tracery.

② **The Maha Mandapa** features carved pillars, nymph-brackets, a corbelled ceiling and balconied windows, which add to the sumptuousness of the central hall's interior.

③ **The first tier** above the terrace is carved with processional friezes and goddesses.

★ Main Shikhara
The main spire soars to 30 m (98 ft), while 84 smaller spires rise in a crescendo towards it, to create the impression of a mountain range – more specifically, Mount Kailasa, the abode of Shiva.

★ Erotic Panels
The largest erotic panels are on the northern and southern facades, between the balconies. The erotic sculptures are variously believed to celebrate the marriage of Shiva and Parvati, serve as a love manual, or simply express an exuberant celebration of life and creation.

Garbhagriha
The dark and plain garbhagriha *(inner sanctum)*, symbolizing a womb, houses a linga, the phallic symbol and principal object of worship in all Shiva temples. The sanctum is entered through a richly carved door frame.

Exploring Khajuraho

The 25 temples at Khajuraho represent the brilliant burst of artistic flowering that took place under the generous patronage of the powerful Chandela rulers, who made Khajuraho their peacetime capital. The remoteness of the temples' location saved them from the ravages of Islamic raiders, but also led to their being abandoned after the decline of the Chandelas in the 13th century. Hidden in a dense forest for 700 years, they were "rediscovered" in 1838 by Captain TS Burt of the Bengal Engineers. According to local tradition there were originally 85 temples, and ongoing excavations have unearthed extensive ruins in the area.

The polished stone image of Varaha, Vishnu's boar incarnation

The Khajuraho temples are divided into three groups. The most important are in the **Western Group** which, apart from the Kandariya Mahadev (see pp240–41), includes the **Lakshman** and the **Vishwanath Temples**. Both are similar to the Kandariya Mahadev in composition, sculptural embellishments and themes, but they also have individual features.

The superb ceiling of the entrance porch and the female bracket figures inside the Lakshman Temple (built in AD 930) are worth special notice. The pair of street singers on the south façade are also remarkable, with their expressions of intense absorption. The master architect and his apprentices are exquisitely sculpted on the subsidiary shrine in the temple's eastern corner.

Opposite the Lakshman Temple is a pavilion with a magnificent statue of Varaha, the boar incarnation of Vishnu (see p683), covered with carvings of several deities.

In the Vishwanath Temple, dating to AD 1002, the apsara plucking a thorn from her foot (on the south façade) is outstanding, as is the apsara playing the flute, which can be seen in the interior chamber.

The **Matangeshwar Temple** (built AD 900), with its plain circular interior, is the only one still in everyday use (see p247).

The **Archaeological Museum**, near the entrance to the Western Group, has a fine collection of sculptures found in the area, including a dancing Ganesha,

Apsara applying kohl

and a fascinating frieze showing the construction of the Khajuraho temples, with scenes of stone being cut and transported.

A short distance away is the **Eastern Group** of temples. The Jain **Parsvanatha Temple**, built in AD 950, is the most remarkable, for the intricately carved ceiling pendants in its entrance porch. Three exquisite sculptures here show apsaras applying kohl around their eyes, painting their feet (both on the south façade), and fastening ankle bells (on the north façade).

The last phase of temple-building in Khajuraho is seen in the **Southern Group**. The **Chaturbhuj Temple** (built AD 1090) has a superb, four-armed image of Shiva in the inner sanctum. It is the only major temple in Khajuraho without any erotic sculptures.

📼 **Archaeological Museum**
Open 8am–5pm Sat–Thu. **Tel** (07686) 272 320.

An image of Vishnu in the Lakshman Temple

Environs
Raneh Falls, 17 km (11 miles) south of the town of Khajuraho, provide a cool retreat. The 19th-century **Rajagarh Palace**, 25 km (16 miles) southeast of Khajuraho, is in the same Bundela style as the palaces at Datia and Orchha (see pp238–9). Situated 32 km (20 miles) southeast of Khajuraho, the **Panna National Park** has leopards, herds of deer and the scenic Pandav Falls. A favourite tourist spot in the park is Gille's Tree House restaurant, perched 20 m (66 ft) above the ground.

❼ Ajaigarh

Panna district. 75 km (45 miles) E of Khajuraho. **Open** daily.

This great Chandela citadel, built in the 9th century AD and perched 500 m (1,640 ft) above the plains, is now a spectacular ruin. The steep path up to the top goes past gigantic sculptures carved into the sheer cliff face, including a particularly enchanting one of a cow and calf. Within the fort lie the ruins of once-magnificent palaces, broken fragments of statues, and several poignant sati pillars, marking the self-immolation of countless Rajput widows. The fort also houses the Ajay Pal ka Talao, a famous lake, and the ruins of a Jain Temple. Today, the fort can be accessed by its two gates: Darwaza, to the north and Tarhaoni, to the southeast.

❽ Bandhavgarh National Park

One of India's most important Tiger Reserves, the Bandhavgarh National Park sprawls across an area of 625 sq km (241 sq miles). Apart from some 50 tigers, the park's wildlife includes 250 species of birds, leopards, deer, jungle cats and packs of *dhole* (Indian wild dog). Great rocky hills, lush deciduous forests, marshes and meadows make Bandhavgarh one of India's most scenic areas. A picturesque hilltop fort with fine sculptures is part of the park's attractions.

VISITORS' CHECKLIST

Practical Information
Shahdol district. 237 km (147 miles) SE of Khajuraho. **Tel** (07627) 265 406. ℹ️ MP Tourism, White Tiger Lodge, Tala **Open** Oct–Jun. Extra charges for photography. Jeep safaris available.

Transport
Umaria, 33 km (21 miles) SW of Tala, the main entry point.

Sheshasaya Statue
A 11-m (36-ft) long statue of the reclining Vishnu, guarded by a seven-headed snake, is at the base of the fort.

The Fort
The ramparts of Bandhavgarh's fort, whose foundations date back to the 1st century AD, are a good place for birdwatching.

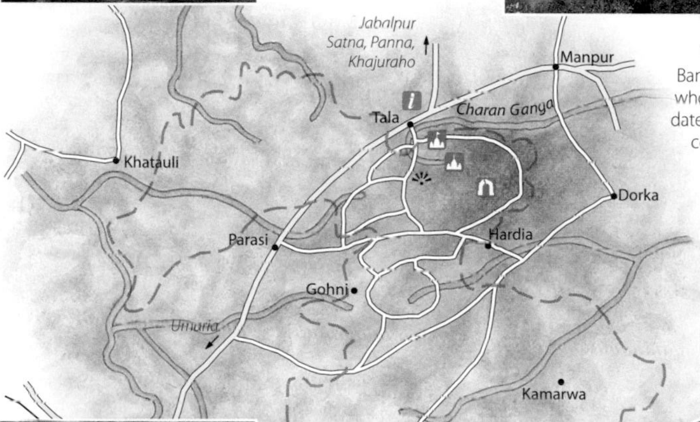

Jabalpur Satna, Panna, Khajuraho

Manpur

Tala

Charan Ganga

Khatauli

Dorka

Parasi

Hardia

Gohnj

Umaria

Kamarwa

Johilla

Crested Serpent Eagle
This large eagle preys on snakes and lizards.

Dhole
The Indian wild dog has a distinctive whistling call, to assemble the pack. It has a red coat, large upright ears and a bushy tail.

0 kilometres 5

0 miles 5

Key

– – Park boundary

═══ Major road

═══ Minor road

The White Tiger of Rewa

In 1951, the maharaja of Rewa captured a white tiger in these forests. Named Mohan, he was mated in captivity with several tigresses, and all the white tigers in zoos across the world today are Mohan's descendants. A pair can be seen in the Bhopal zoo *(see p245)*. Since 1951, no other white tiger has been seen in the Bandhavgarh region. The white tiger is an "evolutionary colour aberration" and not an albino, nor a separate sub-species.

The white tiger, very rare in the wild

❾ Bhopal

The capital of Madhya Pradesh, Bhopal was founded in the 11th century by Raja Bhoj of the Paramara dynasty. By the 18th century, it was held by a Muslim dynasty whose rulers included several remarkable women, the Begums of Bhopal. The city, ringed by hills, stretches along the shores of two artificial lakes, the Upper and Lower Lakes. The old quarter, north of the Lakes, is a maze of narrow lanes, bazaars and mosques. To the south is the new city, with its leafy suburbs and industrial enclaves. In December 1984, a toxic gas leak from the Union Carbide factory claimed the lives of 15,000 people, in one of the world's worst industrial disasters. With the wounds of this tragedy now healing, Bhopal is a good base for visiting some of the state's fascinating sites.

Fountain and tank inside the 19th-century Moti Masjid

◗ Taj-ul-Masjid

Hamidia Rd. **Open** daily. **Closed** to non-Muslims on Fri & on Muslim festivals.

The most imposing monument in Bhopal, this large, pink-washed mosque was begun by Sultan Jehan Begum in 1878 but was left unfinished for almost a century before being completed in 1971. A progressive ruler, the begum established the city's postal system and hospitals, but virtually bankrupted the royal treasury as a result of her ambitious schemes. The enormous courtyard of the mosque has a *dukka* (water tank) for ritual ablutions, and the vast prayer hall is striking for its rows of pillars. This grandiose mosque is surmounted by three white domes and flanked by two 18-storeyed minarets. Its general ambience is majestic rather than beautiful.

▦ The Chowk

Bazaar: **Open** Tue–Sun. Jama Masjid: **Open** daily. **Closed** to non-Muslims on Fri & on Muslim festivals.

Situated in the centre of the old quarter is the Chowk (literally, main square). Streets radiate out from it, each one specializing in a particular type of goods – the Bhopali *batuas* (elaborately beaded purses) for which Bhopal is famous, tussar silk, caps, drums and spices. *Havelis* line the streets, with wooden fronted shops on the ground floor, and elaborate wrought-iron balconies above. Dominating the area is the **Jama Masjid** with its gold finials,

Bhopali *batua*

built in 1837 by Qudsia Begum, another of Bhopal's female rulers. It is surrounded by shops selling silver jewellery.

South of the Chowk is another mosque, the **Moti Masjid** ("Pearl Mosque") built in 1860 by Qudsia Begum's daughter and successor. With its striped dome and tapering sandstone minarets, it looks like a smaller version of the Jama Masjid in Delhi *(see p90)*.

Also worth visiting in this area is the **Shaukat Mahal**, a 19th-century Indo-Saracenic cum Rococo palace. Built by a French mercenary who claimed to be a descendant of the Bourbons, it now houses government offices, though visitors are usually allowed inside by the guards.

▥ Bharat Bhavan

Shamla Hills. **Tel** (0755) 266 0239. **Open** Feb–Oct: 2–8pm; Nov–Jan: 1–7pm. **Closed** Mon & public hols.

A large cultural complex, Bharat Bhavan was established in 1982 to showcase and promote India's rich tribal and folk art heritage. To the right of the entrance is the Tribal Art Gallery, a superb collection that includes votive objects, terracotta figures, masks, wall paintings, woodcarvings, and the distinctive metal sculptures created by craftsmen from Bastar *(see p257)*. A gallery across the courtyard exhibits contemporary Indian art. Bharat Bhavan is also the venue for regular performances of theatre, music and dance in the evenings.

▥ State Museum

Shamla Hills, Banganga Marg. **Tel** (0755) 266 1856. **Open** 10am–5pm Tue–Sun.

A collection of 12th-century Jain bronzes, found in Dhar district in western Madhya Pradesh, form the highlight of this museum's collection. It also has a series of striking stone sculptures, mostly from the 6th to 10th centuries. Older pieces include *yakshis*

The Taj-ul-Masjid, Bhopal's most imposing monument

For hotels and restaurants see pp696–7 and p710

Replica of a tribal hut in the Indira Gandhi Rashtriya Manav Sangrahalaya

(female attendants) dating to 200 BC, and a Standing Buddha in black granite. The museum shop has good plaster replicas of some sculptures for sale.

🏛 Indira Gandhi Rashtriya Manav Sangrahalaya (Museum of Man)

Shamla Hills. **Open** Mar–Aug: 11am–6.30pm; Sep–Feb: 10am–5:30pm. **Closed** Mon & public holidays. 📷

Set in the hills overlooking the Upper Lake, this open-air museum re-creates the tribal habitats of various Indian communities. The Himalayan Village, Coastal Village and Desert Village all feature actual-size dwellings built by the tribal people themselves. Among the highlights are 32 rock shelters decorated with prehistoric paintings. An indoor museum displays utensils, jewellery, ritual objects, musical instruments, murals, tools and costumes of cultures from all over the country.

🏞 Van Vihar National Park

Open 7am–7pm. **Closed** Fri. 📷

The most famous inhabitants of this large park, near the Upper Lake, are the white tigers (see p243). A good time to see these rare creatures is at about 4pm, when they come to the edge of their enclosure for their evening meal. The zoo is also home to lions, leopards and Himalayan bears.

🏛 Birla Museum

Near Lakshmi Narayan Temple. **Tel** (0755) 255 1388. **Open** 9:30am–5pm daily. 📷

This museum has a collection of stone sculptures dating from the 7th to 12th centuries. Shiva, Vishnu and various goddesses are shown in their different incarnations. Particularly impressive are Vishnu in his boar (Varaha) incarnation, Goddess Durga in her ferocious Chamunda form, and Shiva and his consort Parvati in their celestial home on Mount Kailasa. Next to the museum is the large and brightly painted Lakshmi Narayan Temple, overlooking the Lower Lake.

Bhopal City Centre

① Taj-ul-Masjid
② The Chowk
③ Bharat Bhavan
④ State Archaeological Museum

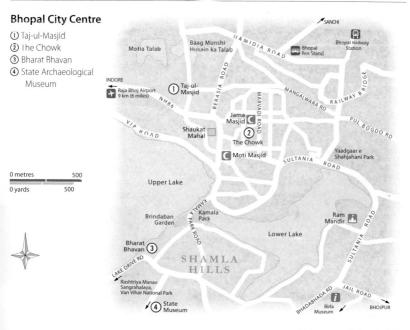

For keys to symbols see back flap

Sculpture from the incomplete Bhojeshwar Temple, Bhojpur

⑩ Bhojpur

Bhopal district. 28 km (17 miles) SE of Bhopal. 🚌 ℹ MP Tourism, Bhopal, (0755) 277 4342/8383.

Founded by the 11th-century Paramara king, Raja Bhoj, who also established Bhopal (see p244), Bhojpur is dominated by the monumental, though incomplete **Bhojesh-war Temple**. Impressive sculptures cover parts of its unfinished corbelled ceiling and its entrance doorway.

Inside, on a tiered platform, is an enormous stone Shivalinga, 2.3-m (8-ft) high and 5.3 m (17 ft) in circumference. Etched on the paving stones and rocks in the forecourt, are the architect's detailed plans for the finished temple, while on the northeast side are the remains of a massive earthen ramp used to haul stone up to the roof.

Environs
The **Bhimbetka Caves** is a UNESCO World Heritage Site. Their prehistoric paintings, dating back some 12,000 years, are about 17 km (11 miles) south of Bhojpur.

⑪ Sanchi

Raisen district. 46 km (29 miles) NE of Bhopal. 🚉 🚌 ℹ Gateway Retreat, (07482) 26 6723. 🎭 Chaityagiri Vihara Festival (Nov).

The tranquil hill of Sanchi contains one of India's best preserved and most extensive Buddhist sites. From the 3rd century BC to the 7th century AD, this was a thriving Buddhist establishment of stupas and monasteries. The complex of buildings at Sanchi therefore show the development of Buddhist art across different periods, stretching over more than a 1,000 years.

Founded by Emperor Ashoka (see p46) whose wife came from nearby Vidisha, Sanchi grew and prospered under subsequent dynasties, largely through the generous patronage of the rich merchants of Vidisha. By the 14th century, Buddhism was on the wane in India and Sanchi was deserted and half forgotten, until it was "rediscovered„ in 1818 by General Taylor of the Bengal Cavalry. Between 1912 and 1919 it was extensively restored by the Archaeological Survey of India

Votive stupa with Buddha image

(ASI) under Sir John Marshall. It was declared a World Heritage Site by UNESCO in 1989. Most of Sanchi's buildings are within an enclosure at the top of the 91-m (299-ft) hill, dominated by the **Great Stupa** and its four superb gateways (see pp248–9). Nearby, to its north, is the smaller **Stupa 3** (built 2nd century BC), with its single gateway, which contained the relics of two of the Buddha's closest disciples, Sariputra and Maudgalayana.

Also within the enclosure are several monasteries, which are located on the eastern, western and southern sides. Of these the 10th-century **Monastery 51** is the most interesting, with its courtyard surrounded by a colonnade, behind which are 22 monks' cells. **Temple 17**, on the eastern side, dates to the 5th century AD. A flat-roofed structure with columns surmounted by double-headed lions, this is the earliest well-preserved example of an Indian stone temple, and its style and features con-siderably influenced the later development of temple architecture.

Located below the Great Stupa, just outside the enclosure, is **Stupa 2** (2nd century BC), whose railings are carved with lotus medallions and mythical beasts. Also depicted is a horse with stirrups. Near the South Gateway of the Great Stupa lies the broken shaft of an Ashokan Pillar, made of highly polished stone. It was

The Bhimbetka Cave Paintings

In 1957, the Indian archaeologist VS Wakanker discovered over 1,000 rock shelters in a sandstone ridge near Bhimbetka village, surrounded by thick deciduous forest. More than 500 of these were covered with paintings done in bold, fluent lines, with the same power and energy as the cave paintings in Lascaux, France, or the Kalahari paintings in Africa. The earliest paintings, from the Upper Paleolithic period, are of large animals such as bison and rhino, done in red pigment, with humans drawn in green. The largest number of paintings are from the Mesolithic period (8000 to 5000 BC), and depict vignettes of daily life, hunting scenes and a range of animals including, curiously, a giraffe. Later caves (1st century AD) show battle scenes and Hindu deities. It was declared a UNESCO World Heritage Site in 2003.

Cave shelter at Bhimbetka

Mesolithic period cave painting from Bhimbetka

Stupa 3, which originally contained the relics of the Buddha's disciples

used as a sugarcane press by a local landlord in the 19th century. Its four-headed lion capital, similar to the one at Sarnath (see p212) but not as fine, can now be seen in the Sanchi **Archaeological Museum**. Some other notable exhibits here include a pair of winged Mauryan lions, sculptural friezes from the gateways and statues of the Buddha and Bodhisattvas.

Environs
Besnagar, situated 10 km (6 miles) northeast of Sanchi, on the confluence of the Beas and Betwa rivers, was once a prosperous centre of trade. A unique relic of its past is the **Heliodorus Column**, with its fluted bell-shaped capital, dating to 113 BC. Dedicated to the god Vasudeva, it was erected by the envoy of the Greek king of Taxila (now in Pakistan), to commemorate his conversion to Hinduism.

Udayagiri, 20 km (12 miles) north of Sanchi, has fine examples of 5th-century AD rock-cut caves, carved into the hillside. Most notable is **Cave 5**,

Sculpture of Varaha, Vishnu's boar incarnation, from Cave 5, Udayagiri

with its impressive sculpture of Varaha, the incarnation of Vishnu as a boar, rescuing the earth goddess from the churning ocean.

Raisen Fort straddles a hill-top 23 km (14 miles) southeast of Sanchi. Its 13th-century gates, palaces, temples and pavilions have lain in ruins ever since a devastating attack in the 16th century by the Sultan of Gujarat, but the site is still hauntingly atmospheric.

Udayapur, 70 km (42 miles) northeast of Sanchi, has the exquisite 11th-century red sandstone **Nilkanteshwar Temple**, dedicated to Shiva. It is comparable in scale and sculptural beauty to the Khajuraho temples (see pp240–42). The symmetry of its graceful *shikhara*, rising in a crescendo of delicately carved stone, is broken by a curious figure that seems to dangle in space. According to local legend, this figure represents the architect, trying to climb to the heavens.

⑫ Gyaraspur
Vidisha district. 64 km (40 miles) NE of Bhopal. 🚉 🛈 MP Tourism, Bhopal, (0755) 277 4340.

The ornately carved 9th-century **Maladevi Temple** at Gyaraspur is built on a hillside. Partly carved out of a rock, it is now in ruins, and much of its superb sculpture has been pillaged. The exquisite statue of the *salabhanjika*, which is now the pride of the Archaeological Museum at Gwalior Fort (see p233), was salvaged from here.

Festivals of Madhya Pradesh & Chhattisgarh
Shivratri (Feb/Mar), Khajuraho. The celestial wedding of Shiva and Parvati is celebrated with colourful processions and an elaborate nightlong re-enactment of the wedding ritual in the Matangeshwar Temple.

Dance Festival (Feb/Mar), Khajuraho. During this week-long festival, India's leading classical dancers perform in front of the Kandariya Mahadeva Temple. The postures and grace of the dancers are echoed in the exquisite stone sculptures of *apsaras* in the temple.

Classical dancer at Khajuraho Dance Festival

Dussehra (Sep/Oct), Chhattisgarh. This ten-day festival in honour of Rama is celebrated with great gaiety in the Bastar tribal heartland of Chhattisgarh. Along with lively dramatized episodes from the *Ramayana* (see p31) there are also colourful tribal fairs with dancing, cock-fights and spirited bartering of goods.

Chaityagiri Vihara Festival (Nov), Sanchi. Buddhists from all over the subcontinent gather at Sanchi to view the relics of two of the Buddha's closest disciples.

Tansen Music Festival (Nov/Dec), Gwalior. Named after the great musician Tansen, one of the "nine jewels", at the court of Mughal emperor Akbar, this festival brings together the best classical musicians and singers from all over the country.

Sanchi: The Great Stupa

India's finest surviving Buddhist monument and World Heritage Site, the Great Stupa at Sanchi, was built in the 2nd century BC. Its hemispherical shape is variously believed to symbolize the upturned alms bowl of a Buddhist monk, or an umbrella of protection for followers of the Buddhist dharma. The stupa's main glory lies in its four stone *toranas* (gateways), added in the 1st century BC. Their sculptures replicate the techniques of wood and ivory carving, and cover a rich variety of Buddhist themes.

West Gateway
This animated scene from the Jataka Tales shows monkeys scrambling across a bridge to escape from soldiers.

Circumambulatory Paths
The paths have balustrades carved with medallions of flowers, birds and animals, and the names of donors who funded them.

South Gateway
The Wheel of Law, being worshipped by devotees, symbolizes the Buddha.

Detail of Architrave
The intricate carving on the architraves is believed to be the work of ivory and wood carvers.

For hotels and restaurants see pp696–7 and p710

★ **North Gateway**
Sujata, the village chief's daughter, offers the Buddha (represented by the Bodhi Tree) *kheer* (rice pudding), as the demon Mara sends the temptress to seduce him.

The Great Stupa and its West Gateway
Enclosing a smaller brick stupa built by Emperor Ashoka in the 3rd century BC, the Great Stupa is capped by a three-tiered stone umbrella, symbolizing the layers of heaven.

★ **Salabhanjika**
Supporting the lowest architrave of the East Gateway is this sensuous, voluptuous tree nymph, gracefully positioned under a mango tree.

KEY

① **The four gateways** show scenes from the Buddha's life, and episodes from the Jataka Tales. The Buddha is not depicted in human form, but only through symbols such as a Bodhi Tree, footprints or a wheel.

② **The *vedika* (railings)** are an impressive recreation in stone of a typical wooden railing design. They were the inspiration for the stone railings around Sansad Bhavan or the Parliament House *(see p78)* in New Delhi.

③ **East Gateway** shows a royal retinue at the palace of Kapilavastu, which was Lord Buddha's home, just before he renounced his princely life.

④ **Statues** of the Buddha meditating, added in the 5th century AD, face each of the gateways.

⓭ Indore

Indore district. 187 km (116 miles) W of Bhopal. 🚹 1,597,400. ✈ 10 km (6 miles) W of town. 🚌 🚎 𝒊 Indore Regional Office, 42 Residency Area, opposite St Paul High School, (0731) 249 9566. 🏪 Mon–Sat. 🎭 Ganesha Chaturthi (Aug/Sep).

The bustling commercial centre of Madhya Pradesh, Indore was a princely state until 1947, ruled by the Maratha Holkar dynasty.

At the heart of the city, surrounded by a lively bazaar, is the **Rajwada Palace**, now just an imposing façade following a fire in 1984. A short walk west of it stands the **Kanch Mandir** ("Glass Temple"), an opulent 19th-century Jain temple, decorated with mirrors, chandeliers, and murals on glass.

On the southwestern edge of Indore is the opulent Lalbagh Palace, built by the rulers of Indore in the early 20th century. Now a museum called the **Nehru Centre**, its gilded Rococo interiors house galleries of miniature paintings, medieval coins and tribal artifacts. In the garden is a statue of Queen Victoria, looking distinctly unamused.

🏛 **Nehru Centre**
Lalbagh Palace. **Tel** (0731) 247 3264. **Open** Tue–Sun. 🚫

Environs
Dewas, 35 km (22 miles) northeast of Indore, was the setting for EM Forster's book *The Hill of Devi* (1953).

Sacred ghats on the Shipra river in Ujjain

⓮ Ujjain

Ujjain district. 56 km (35 miles) NW of Indore. 🚹 429,900. 🚌 🚎 𝒊 MP Tourism, Shipra Residency, (0734) 255 1495/96. 🎭 Kumbh Mela (every 12 years), Shivratri (Feb/Mar).

On the banks of the Shipra river, Ujjain is one of India's seven sacred cities, and one of the four sites of the Kumbh Mela *(see p214)*. In the 4th–5th centuries AD it was the second capital of the Gupta Empire *(see p47)*, with the celebrated Sanskrit poet Kalidasa as one of its leading lights. Its glory was, however, eclipsed in the 13th century after it was sacked by the Delhi Sultans *(see p52)*.

The focal point of the town is the **Mahakaleshwar Temple** (an 18th-century reconstruction on the site of the original), with its much-venerated Shivalinga. In the main square is the **Gopal Temple**, whose silver doors are believed to be from the Somnath Temple in Gujarat, ransacked by Mahmud of Ghazni in the 11th century. A similar pair of doors are at the Golden Temple in Amritsar *(see pp110–11)*. **Ram Ghat**, the largest of sacred ghats on the banks of the river, is the site of the Kumbh Mela (the next Ardh Kumbh here is due in 2022).

On the opposite bank is the **Chintaman Ganesha Temple** whose carved pillars, dating to the 11th century, are the only relics of the original temple. At the southwestern edge of the city is the **Vedh Shala Observatory**. Built in 1730 by Sawai Jai Singh II of Jaipur, the Mughal-appointed governor of Malwa, it is a smaller version of the one at Jaipur *(see pp362–3)*.

Environs
The charming 15th-century **Kaliadeh Palace**, 8 km (5 miles) north of Ujjain, on an island in the Shipra, was built by the sultans of Malwa.

The glittering interior of the Kanch Mandir in Indore

The Hill of Devi

The famous British writer Edward Morgan Forster (1879–1970) spent several months in the princely state of Dewas as private secretary to its eccentric and charming maharaja. *The Hill of Devi*, based on his letters home, provides a delightful inside view of life at a provincial court with its festivities, intrigues and complicated protocol. Dewas is dominated by a hill with the temple of the goddess Chamunda Devi, hence the title of the book. Curiously, tiny Dewas was divided and ruled by two brothers, each with his own palace, army and anthem. Forster was at the court of the elder maharaja. The experience also provided Forster with material for his best-known novel, *A Passage to India* (1924).

Devi image in the temple at Dewas

⑮ Mandu

Dhar district. 105 km (65 miles)
W of Indore. 🚌 🚗 ℹ️ Malwa Resort,
(07292) 263 235.

Perched on a crest of the Vindhya
Mountains is the deserted citadel
of Mandu, one of India's most
romantic and picturesque sites.
Enclosed within its winding
parapet walls, and surrounded
by steep, wooded ravines, are
palaces, mosques, lakes and
pleasure pavilions, built between
1401 and 1529, by the sultans of
Malwa (see p53), who referred to
it as Shadiabad, the "City of Joy".
Mandu is spread over a 23-sq km
(9-sq mile) area, but its major
monuments are clustered in
three groups – the Royal Enclave,
the Village Group and the Rewa
Kund Group.

A row of lofty arches in the Hindola Mahal or Swinging Palace, Mandu

🏛 Royal Enclave

Open daily. 📷
Dominating the Royal
Enclave are the **Jahaz
Mahal** (see pp252–3)
and the majestic
T-shaped **Hindola
Mahal** ("Swinging
Palace"), whose massive inward
sloping walls give the impression
that the building is swaying. Built
in the late 15th century as the
royal assembly hall, its austere
façade is lightened by delicate
tracery work on its arched
windows. Next to it is a well, the
Champa Baoli, connected to a
series of subterranean rooms
cooled by flowing water, where
the ladies of the harem spent hot

Detail from Hoshang
Shah's tomb

summer days. To its east are **Gada
Shah's House and Shop**, which
belonged to an ambitious Rajput
chieftain at the court of Mandu.
The so-called "Shop" was actually
an audience hall, while the house,
a luxurious double-storeyed
structure with water
channels and fountains,
still has traces of two fine
paintings of the chieftain
and his wife. The earliest
of the monuments in
the Royal Enclave is
Dilawar Khan's
Mosque, built by the
first Malwa sultan in 1405, using
the stones and pillars of Hindu
and Jain temples that had stood
here earlier.

🏛 Village Group

Open daily.
The first marble tomb to be built
in India, **Hoshang Shah's Tomb**
(1440) is a perfectly proportioned
structure, where Malwa's most
powerful sultan is buried. It has

an inscription on the door
recording the visit of four of
Emperor Shah Jahan's architects
in 1659.

Opposite it is the magnificent
Jama Masjid (built in 1454). It
is said to have been inspired by
the great Mosque at Damascus.
Three large domes and 58 smaller
ones surmount its colonnades,
and the *mihrab* is decorated with
beautiful calligraphy. Next to it
is the **Ashrafi Mahal** *madrasa*
with the ruins of a seven-storeyed
Victory Tower, acclaimed in
contemporary accounts as
Mandu's finest structure. It was
built by Sultan Mahmud in 1443,
to mark his battle with the
maharana of Mewar. Interestingly,
the latter also built a Victory
Tower at Chittorgarh (see p406)
after the same battle.

The Rewa Kund Group lies
4 km (2.5 miles) to the south, and
comprises of Mandu's ruler Baz
Bahadur's Palace and the beautiful
singer, Rupmati's Pavilion.

Plan of Mandu

1 Delhi Gate
2 Hindola Mahal
3 Champa Baoli
4 Gada Shah's House
5 Jahaz Mahal
6 Hoshang Shah's Tomb
7 Ashrafi Mahal
8 Jama Masjid
9 Malik Mugith's Mosque
10 Dai ka Mahal
11 Baz Bahadur's Palace
12 Rupmati's Pavilion
13 Neelkanth Mahal

0 metres   800
0 yards   800

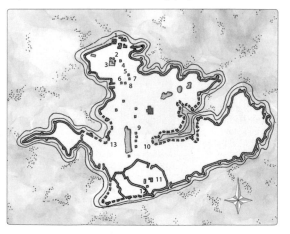

Mandu: Jahaz Mahal

The Jahaz Mahal ("Ship Palace") was built by the fifth sultan of Malwa, Ghiyasuddin (r.1469–1500). Lying on a long, narrow strip of land between two of the many man-made lakes, Munja Talao and Kapur Talao, the palace gives the impression of an anchored ship, especially during the monsoon when the lakes are full. This pleasure palace was staffed entirely by the hedonistic sultan's harem of 15,000 women, who also served as his bodyguard.

The Pavilions
The juxtaposition of conical and domed roofs over the pavilions adds great charm to the Jahaz Mahal's silhouette.

Tilework
Blue and yellow tiles decorated the pavilions.

Entrance →

KEY

① **The terrace pool**, similar in design to the one on the ground floor, is fed by a water channel.

② **Narrow rooms** lie at either end of the ground floor, with its three large halls.

The Terrace
The most spacious part of the palace, the terrace, with its pavilions and kiosks, overlooks the lakes.

Exploring Mandu

Between the Village Group of monuments and Sagar Talao, Mandu's largest lake, are several monuments worth visiting. **Malik Mugith's Mosque**, built in 1432, has carved pillars taken from ruined Hindu temples. To its south are two impressive buildings in a pretty, wooded area – **Dai ki Chhoti Bahen ka Mahal** (the "Nurse's Younger Sister's Palace") and **Dai ka Mahal** (the "Nurse's Palace"). The two women were clearly royal favourites and the pretty, octagonal-domed houses show traces of blue and yellow tilework.

Southeast of Sagar Talao, down a winding road to the edge of a cliff, are the Rewa Kund Group of Monuments, associated with the legendary romance between Sultan Baz Bahadur and the beautiful singer Rupmati. Beside the Rewa Kund Stepwell, fed by an underground stream whose waters are said to be sacred, is **Baz Bahadur's Palace**, constructed between 1508 and 1509. Its most charming feature is an octagonal pavilion overlooking a garden, now covered with weeds.

Located just south of the palace is **Rupmati's Pavilion**, with its lovely fluted domes, from where there is a

Shivalinga at Neelkanth Mahal

spectacular view of the surrounding countryside.

Baz Bahadur, the last sultan of Malwa, was defeated in battle by the Mughals in 1561. After this, Mandu fell into decline, as the Mughal emperors only used it as a halting place on their journeys to the Deccan. In 1616, Mandu briefly came to life again, when the Mughal emperor Jahangir spent seven months here, renovating the palaces and giving lavish parties at the Jahaz Mahal. Accompanying him was Sir Thomas Roe, the Elizabethan ambassador to the Mughal court. He has left a fascinating account of royal festivities and exciting lion and tiger hunts at Mandu. A short distance west of Sagar Talao, a flight

★ **Water Channels**
The intricate spiral designs of the water channels are characteristic of the simple elegance of Mandu's architecture.

★ **Bathing Pool**
The beautiful pool at the northern end is surrounded on three sides by colonnades.

of steps leads down a ravine to **Neelkanth Mahal**. This palace, with its many water channels and cascades, was built in 1574 on the site of an ancient Shiva shrine, for the Mughal emperor Akbar's Hindu wife. The main room, overlooking the valley, is once again in use as a Shiva temple, even though its walls are covered with fine Arabic calligraphy.

Environs
The **Bagh Caves**, lying 50 km (31 miles) west of Mandu, date from AD 400–700. Built by Buddhist monks, they have murals similar in style to those at Ajanta (see pp484–5), but unfortunately these are in a very poor state of preservation.

Baz Bahadur and Rupmati

One day while out hunting, Sultan Baz Bahadur (r.1554–61) spotted a Hindu girl, Rupmati, singing as she bathed in the

An 18th-century miniature of Rupmati and Baz Bahadur

Narmada river. Bewitched by her beauty and her voice, Baz Bahadur persuaded her to live with him in Mandu. Thereafter, he spent his time in the pursuit of love and music, leaving his kingdom vulnerable to attack. When Emperor Akbar's general, Adham Khan, attacked Mandu in 1561, he won an easy victory. Baz Bahadur fled the battlefield, deserting Rupmati who was captured. But the courtesan proved more courageous than the king. Even as the Mughal general waited outside her room to claim her, she committed suicide by swallowing poison.

View of Maheshwar's fort, shrines and ghats, along the Narmada

⑯ Maheshwar

West Nimar district. 90 km (56 miles) SW of Indore. ⛰ 19,600. 🚉 Barwaha, 39 km (24 miles) E of town centre, then taxi or bus. 🚌 ℹ MP Tourism, Narmada Resort, (07283) 27 3455. 🪷 Panchkosi Yatra (Mar).

Picturesquely sited on the banks of the Narmada, Maheshwar is an important Hindu pilgrimage centre. It was the site of the ancient city of Mahishmati, mentioned in classical Sanskrit texts. Maheshwar's beautiful temples and ghats were erected by Queen Ahilyabai of the Holkar dynasty *(see p250)*, in the mid-18th century.

Statue of Queen Ahilyabai

The 1.5-km (1-mile) long river front is dotted with shrines, ghats and the elegant cenotaphs of the Holkar rulers, and is usually thronged with pilgrims taking a dip. A magnificent fan-shaped stairway leads from the river front to Maheshwar Fort's royal enclosure, and the **Ahilyeshwar Temple**, built in 1798. The richly carved courtyard, leading on to the palace, has an impressive statue of Ahilyabai. This benevolent queen, who also built the Vishwanath Temple *(see p209)* in Varanasi, was described by a British colonial official, Sir John Malcolm, as "one of the purest and most exemplary rulers that ever lived".

Also within the fort is the Rehwa Weavers' Society, where the famous gossamer-fine Maheshwari cotton and silk textiles are woven.

⑰ Omkareshwar

East Nimar district. 77 km (48 miles) S of Indore. 🚉 🚌 🚏 ℹ MP Tourism, Narmada Resort, (07280) 271 455. Sri Omkar Mandhata Temple: **Open** 7am–6pm daily. Siddhnath Temple: **Open** 5am–6pm daily. 🪷 Shivratri (Feb/Mar), Kartika Purnima (Oct/Nov).

The island of Omkareshwar, at the confluence of the Narmada and Kaveri rivers, is one of India's most enchanting pilgrimage towns. Seen from above, it is shaped like the sacred *Om* symbol. The island is 2-km (1.3-mile) long and 1-km (0.6-mile) wide, with jagged cliffs on its southern and eastern sides. It is dotted with temples, sadhus' caves and bathing ghats, and filled with the sound of chanting.

A circumambulatory path circles the island, marking out the pilgrim trail. Omkareshwar is linked to the mainland by a concrete causeway, though visitors can also come on the flat bottomed barges that ply the river. The island is dominated by the towering white *shikhara* of the **Sri Omkar Mandhata** ("Bestower of Desires") **Temple**, within which is a particularly sacred Shivalinga, one of 12 *jyotirlingas* (natural rock lingas said to have miraculously emerged from light) in the country.

At the eastern end of the island is the 13th-century **Siddhnath Temple** which has beautiful sculptures of *apsaras*. The northern end has a cluster of Hindu and Jain temples. Overlooking them is a ruined palace, part of a fortified township that stood here until it was sacked by Muslim invaders in the 11th century.

A pilgrim praying on the banks of the Narmada at Omkareshwar

The Narmada Dam Controversy

Since the mid-1980s, an ambitious scheme to dam the Narmada has been embroiled in controversy. The Narmada Valley Authority claim that the Sardar Sarovar Dam will bring electricity, irrigation and drinking water to millions of people. Environmental activists opposing the dam, who include Medha Patkar, leader of the "Save the Narmada" movement, and Arundhati Roy, the 1997 Booker Prize-winning author, say that the dam will inundate some 37,000 ha (91,429 acres) of forest, and displace more than 200,000 villagers, most of them poor tribal people whose distinctive culture and means of livelihood will be wiped out along with their lands. The Supreme Court of India has now ruled that work on the dam can continue. When completed, it will be the second largest in the world, after the Three Gorges Dam in China.

Anti-dam activists at a protest meeting

The Narmada River

Rising in the Amarkantak Plateau, where the Vindhya and Satpura ranges meet, the Narmada flows westward for 1,247 km (775 miles), across the states of Madhya Pradesh and Gujarat before entering the Arabian Sea. One of India's seven sacred rivers, the Narmada, according to Hindu mythology, was born of Lord Shiva's sweat when he performed his cosmic dance *(see p570)*. The Narmada is also believed to be the embodiment of purity, and a legend holds that every year the polluted Ganges comes in the guise of a dark woman, and takes a purifying dip in the Narmada. Sugarcane, cotton and bananas grow along the river, whose banks are lined with temples.

Dhuandhar Falls are a scenic spot, where the river drops 25 m (82 ft) down from the Amarkantak Plateau. The name Dhuandhar means "Stream of Smoke".

Narmada Kund at Amarkantak ("Neck of Shiva"), marks the source of the river. It is surrounded by 16th-century temples.

Maheshwar has beautifully carved river front temples and 28 bathing ghats.

Omkareshwar is an Om-shaped island at the confluence of the Narmada and the Kaveri.

Chausath Yogini Temple which dates to the 10th century, is on a hilltop near the Marble Rocks.

Jabalpur
Bhedaghat
Dhuandhar Falls
Chausath Yogini Temple
Amarkantak
Hoshangabad
Mandla

GUJARAT
Maheshwar
Omkareshwar
MADHYA PRADESH

Sardar Sarovar Dam

At Mandla, the river takes a sharp turn.

MAHARASHTRA

Arabian Sea

Sethanighat Temple at Hoshangabad has an image of the Goddess Narmada.

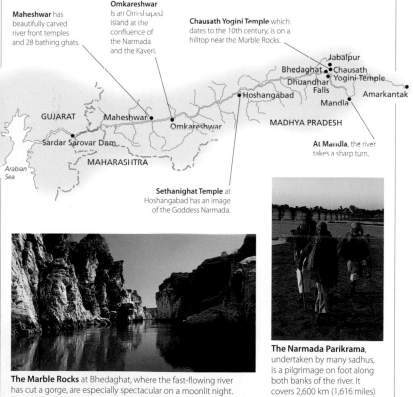

The Marble Rocks at Bhedaghat, where the fast-flowing river has cut a gorge, are especially spectacular on a moonlit night. Boat rides are the best way to experience their beauty.

The Narmada Parikrama, undertaken by many sadhus, is a pilgrimage on foot along both banks of the river. It covers 2,600 km (1,616 miles) and takes about three years.

Pachmarhi's Christ Church, built in 1875, a relic of the Raj

⑱ Pachmarhi

Hoshangabad district. 210 km (130 miles) SE of Bhopal. 🚉 11,400. 🚌 Pipariya, 47 km (29 miles) N of Pachmarhi, then taxi or bus. 🛈 Tourist Motel, Pipariya, (07578) 22 2299. 🚊 🛈 MP Tourism, Amaltas Complex Station, (07578) 25 2098. 🎭 Shivratri (Feb/Mar).

This delightful hill station, at an altitude of 1,067 m (3,501 ft), lies in the verdant hills of the Satpura Range. Its attractions include waterfalls and pools, and caves with prehistoric art. In 1857, Captain James Forsyth of the Bengal Lancers spotted this saucer-shaped plateau, and it was quickly developed into a sanatorium and army station by the British.

The town retains a genteel, Raj-era ambience, and among its colonial relics are the **Christ Church**, built in 1875, with beautiful stained-glass windows, and the **Army Music School** which still begins the day with rousing English martial tunes such as the Colonel Bogey March.

Pachmarhi means "Five Houses", and the town takes its name from the five ancient **Pandava Caves**, set in a garden south of the bus stop. From the caves, paths lead to the scenic **Apsara Vihar** ("Fairy Pool") and the **Rajat Prapat Waterfalls**.

The wooded hills around Pachmarhi, home of the Gond and Korku tribes, are dotted with cave shelters, some of them with paintings dating back 10,000 years. The most accessible of them is the **Mahadeo Cave**, 6 km (4 miles)

from the Jai Stambh ("Victory Pillar") in the centre of town. The **Jatashankar Cave Temple**, dedicated to Shiva, is a short excursion, 2 km (1.3 mile) from the main bus stop. At the Shivratri festival, a colourful gathering of pilgrims and sadhus takes place here. En route to it is the **Harper's Cave**, so called because it has a painting of a man playing an instrument that looks like a harp.

⑲ Jabalpur

Jabalpur district. 330 km (205 miles) E of Bhopal. 🚉 951,500. ✈ 14 km (8 miles) W of town centre. 🚌 🚊 🛈 MP Tourism, Railway Station, (0761) 267 7690; Kalchuri Residency, (0761) 267 8491/92.

The gateway to Bandhavgarh (see p243) and Kanha (see pp258–9), two of India's finest wildlife sanctuaries, Jabalpur was from the 12th to 16th centuries the capital of a powerful Gond tribal kingdom, whose most famous ruler was a brave and able woman, Rani Durgavati. In 1817 the British made it an army cantonment and administrative centre, to deal with the growing menace of gangs of highway bandits known as *thuggees*, who would rob travellers. In the 1830s, Colonel William Sleeman launched his famous campaign against the *thuggees*, and in a few years had wiped them out. The word thug (from *thuggee*), though, seems to have found a permanent place in the

Detail from a Gond tribal house

English language. In the bazaar is the **Rani Durgavati Museum** with stone sculptures and Gond tribal artifacts. The ruined **Madan Mahal Fort**, built by a Gond king in 1116, overlooks the town from a hill to the west.

🏛 **Rani Durgavati Museum** **Open** 10am–5pm Tue–Sun. **Closed** Mon & public hols.

🏯 **Madan Mahal Fort** 🛈 (0761) 267 7290. **Open** 8am–6:30pm daily. 🎫

Environs The **Marble Rocks**, the **Chausath Yogini Temple** and the **Dhuandhar Falls** are 22 km (14 miles) southwest of Jabalpur.

⑳ Mandla

Mandla district. 95 km (59 miles) S of Jabalpur. 🚌 🚊 🛈 MP Tourism, Tourist Motel, (07642) 26 0599. 🖂 daily.

This sleepy town is situated on a loop in the Narmada river, which provides a natural moat for the 17th-century Gond Fort, now in ruins. Mandla is a sacred city for Gond tribals, whose warrior queen, Durgavati, committed suicide here in 1564 when she was defeated by the Mughal emperor Akbar's army. Temples and ghats line the banks of the river, where the Gonds perform their funeral rites. The main bazaar, near the bus stand, is interesting to explore with its shops selling tribal silver jewellery and bell metal.

The Narmada river at Mandla, lined by temples and ghats

The Folk Art of Bastar

Bastar district, in the newly-created state of Chhattisgarh, is a remote, thickly forested area, predominantly inhabited by tribal people and small communities of craftsmen. They live close to nature, and their arts and crafts have been inspired by the beauty, rhythm and vigour of forest creatures and plants. Animal, bird and plant motifs embellish many of the utilitarian, decorative and ritual objects that they fashion out of clay, wood, metal and cotton yarn. These can be seen at the weekly tribal markets held in Madhya Pradesh and Chhattisgarh, as well as in handicrafts shops in Delhi.

Wooden walking sticks, toys and ritual objects are carved out of the soft wood of roots and stems. The ingenious walking sticks make an eerie whistling sound, meant to scare away wild animals and evil spirits in the forest.

A newly-wed tribal couple in Bastar

Combs in wood and metal are exchanged between young tribal boys and girls of Bastar as tokens of love. The wooden combs are decorated with simple geometric motifs, while the brass ones are more ornately carved.

Iron lamps, embellished with leaf forms and lively animal and bird figures, are a speciality of Bastar's *lohars* (blacksmiths), who also make agricultural tools.

A brass comb, carved with the image of a deity

Tribal potters make fascinating clay ritual figures of mythical animals, horses and elephants. The materials used are the red and black clay from river banks, known for their strength and elasticity.

Bronze images, made by the Ghadva community of metalsmiths, using the lost wax technique, include this guardian deity of a Bastar village.

Textiles for festive occasions are woven from thick unbleached cotton by the Panka community of weavers. The motifs, always inspired by nature, are woven in red madder-dyed yarn.

㉑ Kanha National Park

Often described as India's finest game sanctuary and a model for wildlife conservation, Kanha's magnificent landscape combines grassy meadows and flat-topped hills with meandering streams and lush deciduous forests. The setting for Rudyard Kipling's famous *The Jungle Book*, Kanha is today an important Project Tiger *(see p293)* Reserve. Along with Bandhavgarh *(see p243)*, it is one of the best places to spot these elusive creatures. The rich variety of wildlife found within this 1,954-sq km (754-sq mile) park, once the exclusive hunting ground of the British viceroys, includes deer, leopard, hyena, sloth bear, pythons and nearly 300 species of birds.

Common Mongoose
This ferret-like animal is a fierce fighter, particularly known for its masterly combats with snakes.

Dadars and Deer
Grassy meadows, known as dadars, characterize much of Kanha. They provide an ideal habitat for herbivores such as the spotted deer.

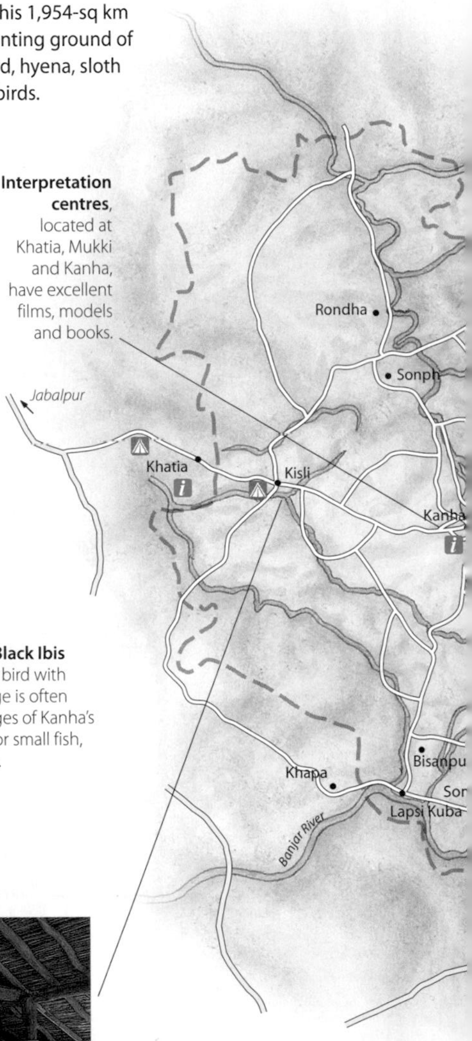

Interpretation centres, located at Khatia, Mukki and Kanha, have excellent films, models and books.

Jabalpur

Rondha

Sonph

Khatia

Kisli

Kanha

Black Ibis
This elegant bird with glossy plumage is often found at the edges of Kanha's waterholes, looking for small fish, frogs and earth-worms.

Khapa

Bisanpu

Sor

Lapsi Kuba

Banjar River

Kipling Camp
This British-run complex, close to the park entrance at Kisli, has pleasant chalets, surrounded by forest. The camp arranges guided safaris.

For hotels and restaurants see pp696–7 and p710

Shravantal
This tranquil waterhole attracts several water birds, such as the lesser whistling teal and the shoveller. There are viewing platforms located nearby.

| 0 kilometres | 3 |
| 0 miles | 3 |

Tiger
Kanha's tigers now number about 100. Park guides expertly track them through pug marks and the alarm calls of deer and langurs.

Central Indian Barasingha
Conservation has increased the numbers of this rare species, which was close to extinction 30 years ago.

Bilaspur

• Bahmnidadar

Mukki

Kipling's Jungle Book
The English writer Rudyard Kipling (1865–1936) was born in Bombay (Mumbai), and though he spent little time in India, the country provided the setting for many of his books. Among his most enduring works is *The Jungle Book*, which features delightful stories of animal behaviour and the law of the jungle. Set in the Seonee Forests of Kanha, their endearing hero is the wolf-reared boy Mowgli; and the many

Jacket for Disney's version of *The Jungle Book*

enchanting animal characters include Rikki-tikki-tavi, the mongoose, Shere Khan, the tiger, Kaa, the python, and Baloo, the bear.

Key

- - - Park boundary
=== Major road
=== Major road

EASTERN INDIA

Introducing Eastern India

Kolkata, India's second largest city, is the best known destination for visitors to Eastern India. Apart from this endlessly fascinating metropolis, the region offers an astonishing diversity of landscapes, peoples and cultures. These include the steamy mangrove forests along the Bay of Bengal, habitat of the Royal Bengal tiger, the spectacular mountain vistas of Darjeeling (officially Darjiling) and Sikkim, and Odisha's magnificent temples and beaches. Further east are Assam and the northeastern states, home to many different tribal communities, whose distinct cultures flourish in areas of pristine natural beauty.

An agile Nishi tribesman of Arunachal Pradesh crossing the Siang, a tributary of the Brahmaputra river, on a tightrope

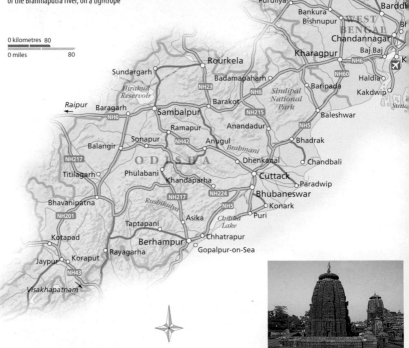

0 kilometres 80

0 miles 80

The 10th-century Mukteshwar Temple complex in Bhubaneswar

◀ Picturesque view from Tshangu Lake

Key

- National highway
- Major road
- Other road
- State border
- International border
- Main railway
- Minor railway
- △ Summit

Tea gardens in Darjeeling, nestling in the foothills of the Eastern Himalayas

Getting Around

Kolkata, Guwahati and Bhubaneswar, the three major cities in this region, are well connected by air and rail to most parts of India. From Kolkata and Guwahati, there are regular flights to all the northeastern states. The hill station of Darjeeling, and Sikkim's capital, Gangtok, are accessible by air or rail up to Bagdogra-Siliguri, from where buses and taxis complete the journey up to the hills on National Highway 31. The delightful Himalayan Toy Train (see p298) also runs from Siliguri to Darjeeling, providing panoramic views of the Himalayas en route. From Kolkata, most destinations in West Bengal are reached on National Highway 34. In Odisha, the major sights are connected by National Highway 5. The gateway to the northeast, Guwahati in Assam, has good road links to the other six states on National Highways 37, 40 and 52. Visitors require travel permits for some destinations in the northeast (see p734).

For keys to symbols see back flap

A PORTRAIT OF EASTERN INDIA

The peoples and cultures found in India's eastern states are as varied as the landscape itself. Stretching from the crowded metropolis of Kolkata to the remote tribal settlements of Arunachal Pradesh, which border on China and Myanmar, the region includes mountainous Sikkim, tropical Odisha, and the lush valleys of Assam, watered by the mighty Brahmaputra river.

West Bengal, the largest and most densely populated of the eastern states, offers the visitor a kaleidoscope of images. These range from the mangrove swamps of the Sunderbans, home of the Royal Bengal tiger, to the misty tea gardens of Darjeeling, and the unique vitality of the state capital Kolkata (formerly Calcutta).

Orchid from Meghalaya

Kolkata is a city that evokes extreme reactions: novelists exhaust metaphors trying to describe it, filmmakers are defeated by it, and even the average non-Bengali agrees that something about the city defines that abstract entity – "culture". As a headquarter of the East India Company, and later, the capital of British India, the city played an early host to crucial Western influences, especially English education. It witnessed the phenomenon popularly described as the Bengal Renaissance, a complex dynamic of socio-religious reform, and literary and artistic efflorescence, with a strong nationalistic undercurrent. Kolkata thus became a nodal point in the formation of a colonial consciousness. Rabindranath Tagore *(see p296)*, its most famous son, lives on through his much-loved stories, poems, plays and songs. Another cultural icon is the film director Satyajit Ray, whose work has had a profound impact on Asian art cinema. Since 1977, West Bengal has been under Communist rule. However, in 2011 the Left Front, including the Communist Party of

A village pond in Odisha, with a small Hindu temple on its banks

Statues being transported during Durga Puja, Kolkata's biggest festival

cultural and religious life still revolves around its serene and beautiful Buddhist monasteries.

In the extreme eastern corner of India are Assam and the six northeastern states of Arunachal Pradesh, Meghalaya, Manipur, Mizoram, Nagaland and Tripura, connected to the rest of the country only by a thin corridor of land.

India, lost the assembly elections. The culture of flag-waving processions, however, blends flawlessly with the typical Kolkata pastime of *adda* – a lively mix of heated political debate, highbrow analyses and lowbrow gossip. This is all played out against a backdrop of crumbling vestiges of some splendid colonial architecture.

From Kolkata, many visitors travel south to the beaches and exquisitely sculpted temples of Odisha. The highpoint of Odisha's cultural and religious year is the spectacular annual Rath Yatra, a festival held in the temple town of Puri *(see p316)*. The state pays a price for its scenic location on the Bay of Bengal – it is often hit by devastating cyclones during the monsoon. In recent years, Odisha's people, who include many forest-dwelling tribal groups, have enjoyed increasing prosperity, with its growing tourism industry. However, many major schemes to develop the state's rich mineral resources and several developmental projects proposed by the government have failed to materialize.

North of Kolkata lies Sikkim, its skyline dominated by the snow-capped peaks of India's highest mountain, Kanchendzonga *(see p306)*, which soars to a height of 8,598 m (28,209 ft). Sikkim's culture borrows much from neighbouring Tibet and Nepal, and many people practice the Tibetan form of Buddhism, introduced in the 15th century by its former rulers, the Chhogyals, who came from Tibet. Much of Sikkim's

Dancer at monastery festival, Sikkim

This region is home to dozens of tribal communities, each with its own language and culture *(see pp340–41)*.

Tea dominates the economy of Assam, which produces more than half the tea grown in India, as well much of the country's oil. The other six states have rich agricultural and forest resources, and little industry. The isolation of the Northeastern states, and their shared borders with Bangladesh, Bhutan, China and Myanmar, has led to violent separatist move-ments in some areas. Visitors need special permits *(see p35)* for this region, whose main attraction is its pristine natural beauty and rare flora and fauna.

An Assamese woman pounding grain

The Story of Indian Tea

India is the world's second-largest producer of tea, perhaps the world's most popular drink. The tea plant *(Camellia sinensis)* is indigenous to Northeast India, and though tea was cultivated and drunk for centuries by the Singpho tribe of Arunachal Pradesh as a stimulant and medicinal brew, tea plantations for commercial exploitation were only established in the mid-19th century. Today, the Indian tea industry employs over a million people, half of whom are women, and produces about 1,135 million kg (2,502 million lb) of tea every year, most of which is grown in Assam, northern Bengal and Darjeeling (Darjiling).

Darjeeling's tea gardens are a picturesque sight, covering terraced hill slopes upto an altitude of 1,950 m (6,398 ft).

Shade trees

Fresh tea leaves are plucked from April to December. A skilled picker can harvest 37 kg (82 lbs) of leaves a day, enough to yield 20 kg (44 lbs) of processed tea

Pickers in a Tea Garden

The tea bush, with its bright green oval leaves, is regularly pruned to keep its height low, allowing for convenient picking. Left wild, the plant can grow into a tree up to 10 m (33 ft) tall.

The withering process blows warm air over the leaves, reducing their moisture content by half. The leaves are then rolled, pressed, fermented, and finally dried again.

Fresh tea leaves · Dried tea leaves

The CTC or crush, tear and curl method, is used to process a more robust, granular Assam tea. The leaves are crushed to release their enzymes, before they are fermented and dried.

Tea tasters tell the quality of a tea by breathing on to leaves clutched in their fist, and inhaling the warmed aroma. To fix the base price at auctions, they also sample the brew, swilling the liquid round their tongues, in the manner of wine tasters.

A 1950s poster advertising a brand of Indian tea

Darjeeling tea logo

Assam tea logo

Darjeeling and Assam teas are the best known Indian varieties. Darjeeling teas are famous for their delicate muscatel flavour, and the best ones have been sold at auction for up to US$220 for 1 kg (2.2 lbs). Assam tea has a stronger taste and darker colour.

Women's supple fingers are preferred for the delicate task of plucking just the top two leaves.

Tea bush

Basket for carrying plucked tea leaves

Bronze tea kettles with dragon-shaped handles and elephant trunk spouts, are typical of the Darjeeling and Sikkim region.

Masala tea

Herbal tea

Assam Tender Buds

Green tea

Darjeeling Golden Tips

Assam Superior Buds

Different types of Indian tea include green (unfermented) tea which is drunk in Kashmir, and *masala* tea spiced with cardamom and ginger. Long leaves give a superior brew, while broken leaves and tea dust go into tea bags.

Tea Estates

In the early 19th century, the British began looking for a site in India, suitable for growing tea for the British market. They soon discovered wild tea plants growing in the northeast, and by 1850, vast tracts of tiger-populated jungle had been cleared in Assam, northern Bengal and Darjeeling to establish tea gardens. Today India has over 25,000 tea estates of varying size, each a self-contained world with its own school, shops and medical clinic. At its heart is the plantation manager's gracious bungalow, and a club where the planters used to meet for tennis and sundowners.

A typical tea planter's bungalow in northern Bengal

The Flavours of Eastern India

This region, watered by the rivers of the Gangetic Delta and washed by the sea, is a land of plenty, with an abundance of fresh vegetables, coconut and fish. Rice is the staple food and the region produces a wide variety. Freshwater fish is popular all across this riverine land. Pork and beef are eaten in most of the Northeastern states, while in Sikkim, the food is largely Tibetan with bamboo shoots and steamed dishes featuring on the menu. This region, with its large tea estates in the Himalayan foothills, is also the home of India's finest teas, especially from Darjeeling.

Green chillies and lime

Bay leaves, chillies and other spices on sale at a weekly market

Basic Dishes

In the delta and coastal areas of Bengal and Odisha, five spices – mustard, aniseed, fenugreek, cumin and black cumin seeds – are used to flavour the food while mustard oil is the preferred cooking fat. The two cuisines are similar, except that the Bengalis pride themselves on having a more sophisticated palate. *Dalma* is

Odisha's signature dish and is a combination of vegetables and *arhar dal* (red gram). Vegetables, such as potatoes and aubergines (eggplant), are fried *(bhaja)*, mashed *(bharta)* and lightly or heavily spiced as in *dalna*, made with peas and cauliflower. Classic dishes include *shukto* (mixed vegetables with bitter gourd) and *mochar ghonto*, made from the banana flower.

Fish and Seafood

It is fish that brings out the genius of cooking in this region. Every part is eaten – the head makes a delicious curry *(muri ghonto)* and the roe an excellent cocktail snack *(macher dimer bora)*. Popular fish of the region are *rahu* (carp), *betki* and the much-loved *hilsa* or *ilish* fish which floods the rivers during the monsoon. *Hilsa* is cooked in

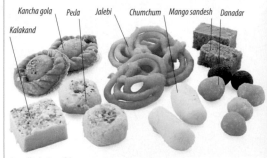

Kancha gola   Peda   Jalebi   Chumchum   Mango sandesh   Danadar

Kalakand

A small selection of the many varieties of sweets from Bengal

Local Dishes and Specialities

This region's cuisine is varied. Historically, Calcutta (now Kolkata) has been a melting pot and the traditional Bangla *ranna*, which combines the Bengali fish-based, delicately spiced food, the Muslim mutton dishes and the many-layered Dacci *parantha*, was enriched by the flavours of its Jewish, Armenian, Indo-Portuguese and English settlers. Fish is the centrepiece of both the Bengali and Oriya meal, and can be cooked with vegetables, as in *besar maacch*. Often, dried prawns are added to vegetables to enchance the flavour. Rice, a *dal* (lentils), vegetable preparations, sweet and sour chutneys, green chillies and slices of lime accompany the meal. In the Northeast, pork is a favourite. It is cooked with bamboo shoots, wild mushrooms or with ground rice and herbs in a one-pot dish called *onla*.

Tomato chutney

Momos, Tibetan dumplings, are eaten with a fiery sauce of dried red chillies and a bowl of chicken broth.

Women working in paddy fields in Odisha

mustard, fried crisp, smoked to melt its innumerable bones, steamed in a banana leaf *(ilish macher paturi)* or cooked in a light sauce of yoghurt and ginger *(doi maach)*. Other great regional inventions are the delicate *daab chingri*, where prawns are cooked in a tender coconut *(daab)* and *chingri malai* curry (prawns cooked in coconut milk).

Other Favourites

Sikkim's distinctive cuisine is influenced also by Nepal and Bhutan. Some popular dishes are the Tibetan-style *thupka* (thick noodle soup), *momos* and the diverse ways of cooking local cottage cheese *(churpi)*. Assamese food combines pungent ingredients with fermented foods, such as the Manipuri *iromba*, made with

fermented fish, vegetables and bamboo shoots. Other dishes include *akshi aong* (a delicious pork curry heavily seasoned with chillies) and *anok pongsuem* (steamed fish from Nagaland).

In Kolkata, food from the Raj still reigns supreme among

Basket of freshly caught fish being carried to the market

other cuisines. Typical dishes are prawn cocktail, roast lamb with mint sauce and the ever-popular caramel custard.

Sweets

Both Odisha and Bengal are known for their infinite variety of milk-based sweets. *Sandesh*, made from *chenna* (an Indian ricotta), is by far the most popular. Cottage cheese and syrup are also used to create many varieties of sweets including *kancha gola*, *chumchum* and *danadar*. *Peda* and *kalakand* are made with condensed milk and chopped nuts.

ON THE MENU

Bhapa hilsa *Hilsa* marinated with mustard and chillies and steamed in a banana leaf.

Chholar dal Yellow split peas seasoned with cumin seed and *garam masala*.

Kamla kheer A pudding with oranges and thickened milk.

Kosha mangsho A spicy mutton curry eaten with rice or fluffy fried breads *(luchi)*.

Mishti doi Yoghurt sweetened with molasses and garnished with chopped nuts.

Saag bhaja Stir-fried spinach, garnished with coconut.

Shorshey maachh Fish cooked in a mustard sauce.

Prawn malai curry has prawns cooked in coconut cream with crushed mustard seeds and red chillies.

Aloo posto, common to both Bengal and Odisha, are potatoes cooked with a paste of poppy seeds.

Caramel custard, a Raj favourite, is a milk mixture baked in a dish with sweet caramel lining its base.

KOLKATA

One of the world's great cities, Kolkata or Calcutta as it used to be known, has been through many incarnations. From an obscure village on the banks of the Hooghly river, it evolved into the capital of Great Britain's Indian empire. Today, this vibrant city with its distinct imperial flavour is the capital of the state of West Bengal.

In 1690, an English merchant, Job Charnock, established a trading post in the riverside village of Sutanuti which, together with neighbouring Govindapur and Kolikata, grew into the city of Calcutta. Over the next 200 years, the city became a flourishing commercial centre with imposing Victorian Gothic buildings, churches, and boulevards. Simultaneously, intellectual and cultural life bloomed, with a renaissance of Bengali art and literature, and the growth of a strong nationalist reform movement that led to the founding of the Brahmo Samaj, an enlightened off-shoot of Hinduism, and the establishment of Presidency College, then the foremost centre of English education. The decision to shift the capital to New Delhi in 1911 and the urban decay of the 1960s diminished some of the city's affluence, but never quenched its effervescence.

In 2001, Calcutta became Kolkata, the Bengali pronunciation of its name. The city is crowded and dirty in places, but is nevertheless full of character. The teeming life of the waterfront along the Strand, the noisy jumble of bazaars and pavement stalls, the residential streets with their once gracious mansions, all make for an electric, cosmopolitan atmosphere, rarely found in other Indian cities. Kolkata's charms straddle the decaying grandeur of the imperial capital and the smart restaurants and boutiques of Park Street. These coexist with the traditional Bengali world of Rabindranath Tagore's mansion at Jorasanko, the Kalighat temple and the potters' village of Kumartuli, and with the lively politics of the Coffee House and the Maidan, dominated by the Victoria Memorial, a spectacular symbol of imperial high noon.

View of the Hooghly river and the Howrah Bridge, the third longest cantilever bridge in the world

◀ Statue of the young Queen Victoria in the central hall, Victoria Memorial

Exploring Kolkata

The city of Kolkata lies in a long strip, with the river to its west and the wetlands to its east. Along the river front, the Strand, is the city centre with the Maidan, a large 400-ha (988-acre) park where Kolkata's residents play football, hold political rallies or enjoy the cool evenings. On the other side of the park is the city's main thoroughfare, the Chowringhee or Jawaharlal Nehru Road with shops, hotels, offices and residential buildings. The southern part of the city has the middle-class residential areas, while north Kolkata is the older part of the city, its maze of narrow lanes crowded with houses, cheek-by-jowl with shops and offices.

WB 19
A 7141
WMT
4159
A street scene at New Market with Kolkata's distinctive taxis

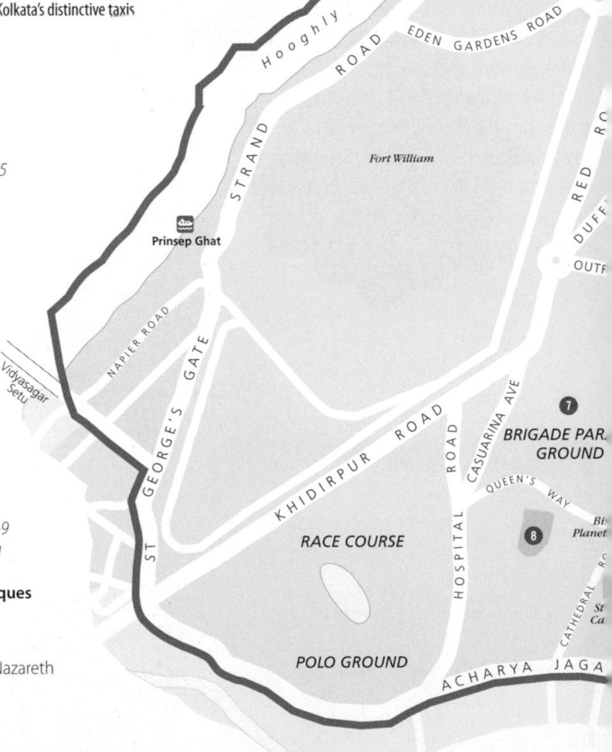
MILLENNIUM PARK
STRAND
HARE
Chandpal Ghat
KIRON SHANKAR R
High Court
Town Hall
ESPLANADE ROW WEST
SHAHID KHUDIRAM BOSE RD
Assembly House
GOVT PLACE
EDEN GARDENS
Babu Ghat
EDEN GARDENS ROAD
Hooghly
ROAD
STRAND
Fort William
RED
DUFF
OUTR
Prinsep Ghat
NAPIER ROAD
Vidyasagar Setu
ST GEORGE'S GATE
KHIDIRPUR ROAD
ROAD
CASUARINA AVE
7
BRIGADE PAR
GROUND
QUEEN'S WAY
HOSPITAL
RACE COURSE
8
Planet
CATHEDRAL
POLO GROUND
ACHARYA JAGA

Sights at a Glance

Historic Buildings, Areas & Neighbourhoods

Museums

Churches, Temples & Mosques

Parks & Gardens

For hotels and restaurants see p697 and pp710–11

Key

- Sight
- National Highway (Inset map)
- Major road (Inset map)

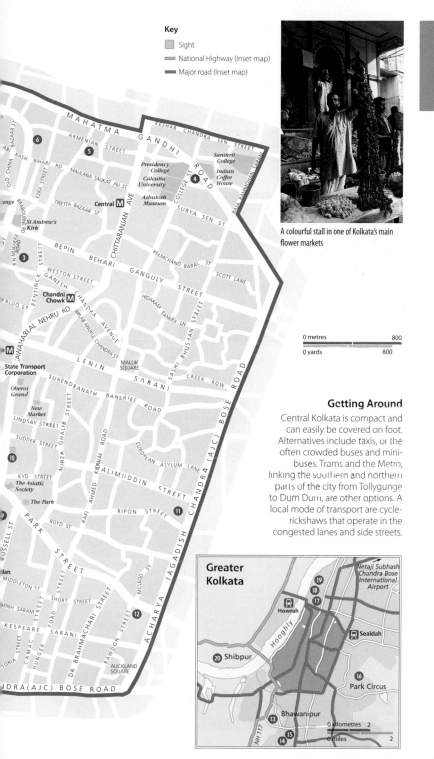

A colourful stall in one of Kolkata's main flower markets

MAHATMA GANDHI ROAD

ABI BAZAAR ST
RASH BIHARI RD
OLD CHINA
EZRA STREET
ARMENIAN STREET
MAULANA SAUKAT ALI ST
TIRETTA BAZAAR ST
KESHAB CHANDRA SEN STREET

6
5

Presidency College
Calcutta University
Ashutosh Museum

Sanskrit College
Indian Coffee House

4

COLLEGE ST
RAJA RAMMOHAN SARANI
SURYA SEN ST

Central Ⓜ

St Andrew's Kirk
R N MUKHERJI ROAD
BEPIN BEHARI GANGULY STREET
PREMCHAND BARAL ST
SCOTT LANE

BENTINCK STREET
BRABOURNE RD
WESTON STREET
GANESH CHANDRA AVENUE
CHITTARANJAN AVE
HIDARAM BANERJI LN
SASHI BHUSAN STREET

3

Chandni Chowk Ⓜ

WATERLOO ST
BIPLAB ANUKUL CHANDRA ST
JAWAHARLAL NEHRU RD
LENIN SARANI
MALLIK SQUARE
CREEK ROW

Ⓜ
State Transport Corporation

Oberoi Grand
SUKENDRANATH BANERJEE ROAD
New Market
LINDSAY STREET
MIRZA GHALIB STREET
SUDDER STREET

BOSE ROAD

10
KYD STREET
The Asiatic Society
KIDWAI ROAD
EUROPEAN ASYLUM LANE
ALIMUDDIN STREET
The Park

RAFI AHMED KIDWAI ROAD
RIPON STREET

CHANDRA (AJC)

11

PARK STREET
RUSSELL ST
ROYD ST
STREET

9
Maidan
MIDDLETON ST
MINH SARANI
SHORT STREET
FORD STREET
McLEOD ST

DR BRAHMACHARI STREET

ACHARYA JAGADISH

KESPEARE SARANI
VICTORIA STREET
CAMAC STREET
HUNGER FORD ST
RAWDON STREET

12

AUCKLAND SQUARE

NDRA(AJC) BOSE ROAD

| 0 metres | | 800 |
| 0 yards | | 800 |

Getting Around

Central Kolkata is compact and can easily be covered on foot. Alternatives include taxis, or the often crowded buses and mini-buses. Trams and the Metro, linking the southern and northern parts of the city from Tollygunge to Dum Dum, are other options. A local mode of transport are cycle-rickshaws that operate in the congested lanes and side streets.

Greater Kolkata

Netaji Subhash Chandra Bose International Airport

19
18
17

🚉 Howrah

Hooghly

🚉 Sealdah

20 Shibpur

16
Park Circus

Bhawanipur
13

NH 117

15
14

| 0 kilometres | 2 |
| 0 miles | 2 |

For keys to symbols see back flap

❶ Street-by-Street: Around BBD Bagh

This is the "heart" of Kolkata and was the site of the original Kolikata, one of the villages from which the city grew. In 1930, three young Indian freedom fighters, Binay, Badal and Dinesh, shot the British inspector-general of police inside the Writer's Building. The square, now named after them, is ringed by British colonial buildings, dating to the 18th and early 19th centuries. These were once the centres of British administrative and commercial control.

Job Charnock's Tomb
Job Charnock is believed to have laid the foundations of the English settlement in Kolkata.

★ St John's Church
The design of this church (see p276) was based on London's St Martin-in-the-Fields. The constructing engineers wanted the spire to be higher, but desisted fearing the soggy sub-soil.

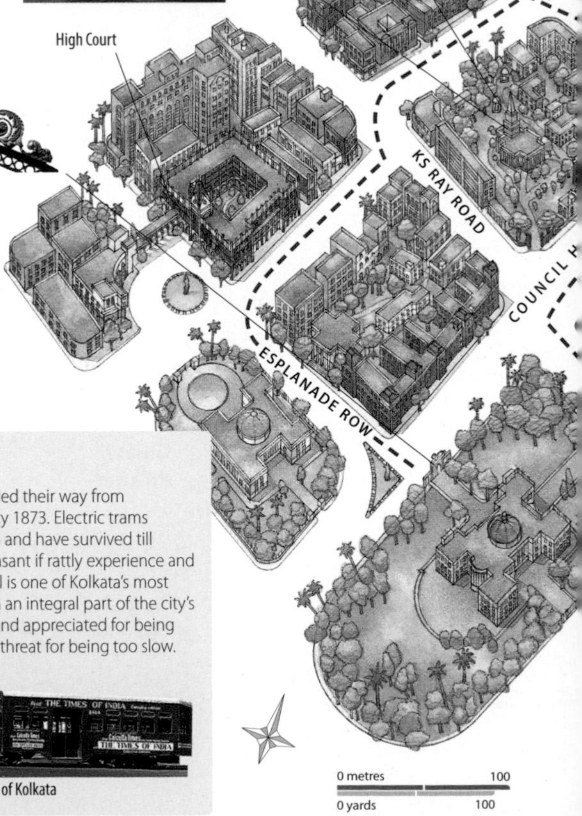

STRAND ROAD

HARE STREET

High Court

KS RAY ROAD

COUNCIL H

Gates of Raj Bhavan
Magnificent Neo-Classical gateways lead to the old Government House, built in the mid-18th century. This is now the residence of the state governor, and can be viewed from across the road.

ESPLANADE ROW

Trams in Kolkata

Horse drawn trams first trundled their way from Sealdah station on 24 February 1873. Electric trams were introduced in June 1905 and have survived till today. Riding in them is a pleasant if rattly experience and the tram's slowly clanging bell is one of Kolkata's most characteristic sounds. Though an integral part of the city's transport network (see p273) and appreciated for being pollution free, they are under threat for being too slow.

An electric tram plying on the streets of Kolkata

| 0 metres | | 100 |
| 0 yards | | 100 |

★ GPO
Kolkata's General Post Office is housed in this building with its impressive rotunda. Designed by Walter Granville and built in the 1860s, it stands on the site of the old mud fort.

Locator Map
See Kolkata Map pp272–3

St Andrew's Kirk
Consecrated in 1818, the church has a soaring steeple, a magnificent organ and a beautifully carved pulpit.

FAIRLIE PLACE

SUBASH ROAD

LYONS RANGE

T STREET

NETAJI

BBD BAGH NORTH

BBD BAGH SOUTH

ROSS PLACE

OLD COURT HOUSE STREET

RN MUKHERJI ROAD

Old Currency House

ATERLOO STREET

Key

— Suggested route

★ Writers' Building
The hub of colonial India from 1777, this imposing building with its Corinthian façade derives its name from the "writers" (clerks) of the East India Company who worked here. The building used to house several state government offices, however, many of the offices have shifted due to restoration work.

View Across Lal Dighi
The East India Company's seat of administration, their courts of justice and the churches for their Sunday services were set up around this small tank, fed by springs.

View of St John's Church with its soaring spire

❷ St John's Church

2/2 Council House St. **Tel** (033) 2243 6098. **Open** 8am–5pm. ⛪ 8am Sun (with Holy Communion).

The first parish church in Kolkata, St John's Church was established in 1787. It boasts an impressive stained-glass panel of *The Last Supper*, in which the artist Johann Zoffany gave the 12 disciples the faces of British personalities famous in the city at the time.

St John's has many associations with the history of the English East India Company. Warren Hastings, Governor of Bengal, was married here. In the churchyard is a memorial to Lady Canning, the vicereine who died in 1861. Her name lives on in popular memory because she was much addicted to a fried, syrupy sweetmeat, which was named after her (it is pronounced "leddy-kenny" in Bengali). The mausoleum of Job Charnock *(see p274)* also stands here.

A short distance away is the memorial to the victims of the notorious "Black Hole Tragedy", an event which became one of the favourite horror stories of the Raj. When Siraj-ud-Daula, the Nawab of Bengal, captured the old British fort which stood on the site of the present General Post Office *(see p275)* in 1756, he imprisoned over 100 British inhabitants in a small, airless cell. Only 23 people were found alive the next morning – the rest had died of asphyxiation and thirst.

❸ Nilhat House

Behind Old Mission Church. Auctions held from 9am–6:30pm Tue–Thu. Prior permission required from brokerage houses, J Thomas. **Tel** (033) 2248 6201.

A tea auction centre, Nilhat House stands on the site of an indigo trading house (*nil* means indigo, while *hat* is market). It dates to 1861; only the tea auction houses in London are older. Tea has always played an important role in the state's economy, especially in the colonial period. But even today, the bidding for teas from Darjeeling and the Dooars in northern Bengal and Assam *(see pp266–7)* is brisk. The auction prices are determined by the opinions of tea tasters, whose highly trained palates can immediately distinguish the type, plantation and year of each brew. Visitors can view and participate in these animated proceedings with prior permission.

❹ College Street

Bidhan Sarani, North Kolkata. Ashutosh Museum: **Tel** (033) 2241 0071. **Open** 10:45am–4:30pm Mon–Fri. 📷

As the location of Kolkata's elite educational institutions, College Street is the heart of Bengali intellectual life. The pavements are crowded with stalls selling textbooks, exam guides, classics and second-hand books of all kinds – some people even claim to have discovered valuable first editions. Many of Kolkata's best bookshops are also found here.

The **Presidency College** was established here in 1817 and was then known as the Hindu College. Started as an institution for the city's rich who wanted their sons to receive a Western-style education, it boasts great scholars, scientists and writers such as film director, Satyajit Ray (1922–92)

and economist Amartya Sen, who won the Nobel Prize for Economics in the year 1998.

Across the road is the dark, cavernous **Indian Coffee House**, the favourite haunt of the city's intelligentsia since it opened in 1942. Even today, waiters in shabby cummerbunds serve endless cups of strong coffee to teachers, students, writers and poets.

Down a lane opposite Presidency College is the **Sanskrit College**, founded in 1824 to promote the study of ancient Indian languages, history and culture. Its ground floor has a small display of medieval Hindu sculpture and palm-leaf manuscripts.

Next to Presidency College are the buildings of **Calcutta University**, founded in 1857. Today, the gracious 19th-century main structure is dwarfed by modern high-rise additions, through which the old edifice, with its Ionic pillars and symmetrical proportions, is barely visible.

On the ground floor, the **Ashutosh Museum** specializes in the art of Eastern India. The exhibits include a fine collection of terracottas, bronzes, coins, old manuscripts and some exquisite examples of *kantha* (a quilting technique) and Kalighat paintings, or *pats* *(see p283)*.

A second-hand bookstore on College Street

Detail of the ornamental entrance of Nakhoda Mosque

❺ Nakhoda Mosque

1, Zakaria St. **Tel** 990 370 8808.
Open daily. with permission.

The city's largest mosque, Nakhoda Mosque is based on the design of Akbar's tomb at Sikandra *(see p182)*. Built in 1926, it is surmounted by a dome and faced with red sandstone, with minarets that rise to a height of 46 m (151 ft). It can accommodate over 10,000 people for prayer, but on major religious occasions, people spill out on to the street. Nearby is the **Hotel Royal**, famous for its rich *biryani* and *chaanp* (goat's ribs cooked in spiced gravy). This is a fascinating neighbourhood with 19th-century mansions, old bazaars and temples.

❻ Armenian Church of St Nazareth

Armenian St, near Brabourne Rd.
Open daily.

Built by Armenian traders in 1724, the Armenian Church of St Nazareth stands on the site of the original 1688 wooden church, which had burnt down in 1707. Immigrants from Isfahan in Persia, the Armenians were among the earliest foreign traders to settle in Kolkata. Once a thriving community, today their numbers have dwindled. The church has a unique rounded spire, and its grounds house several graves with ornate tombstones.

❼ Maidan

Bounded by Strand Rd, AJC Bose Rd, Cathedral Rd & Eden Gardens Rd.
St Paul's Cathedral: **Open** daily.
🕐 7:30am, 8:30am, 10:30am & 6pm Sun.

In the heart of the city, this 400-ha (988-acre) park stretches from the Hooghly river in the west to Chowringhee in the east, and contains several interesting areas and buildings. In the early 18th century, a dense jungle was cut down to build **Fort William**, after the earlier mud fort was destroyed in 1756. The present fort, a squat, irregular octagon, was completed in 1781. Today, it is the headquarters of the Indian Army's Eastern Command and not usually open to the public.

To the north of the fort are the pleasantly laid out **Eden Gardens**, where international cricket matches are held. They were conceived and designed in 1841 by Emily and Fanny Eden, the sisters of the governor general, Lord Auckland. At the northern corner of the Maidan is the **Burmese Pavilion** set in a small lake. This was brought here by Lord Dalhousie from Prome in Myanmar in 1854.

To its east is the **Shahid Minar**, literally "Martyrs' Memorial", originally called Ochterlony

Stained glass, St Paul's Cathedral

Monument. It was named after Sir David Ochterlony, one of the Raj's daredevil soldiers, who had led the British armies to victory in the Anglo-Nepal War in 1816. The monument is a fluted Doric column, 48 m (157 ft) high with a cupola for a roof. To its south is the Maidan's most impressive building, the **Victoria Memorial** *(see pp278–9)*.

A short distance from the Memorial is **St Paul's Cathedral**. It was designed by Major WN Forbes in 1847 and its spire, modelled on Britain's Canterbury Cathedral, was added after the earlier one was destroyed in the 1934 earthquake. Its grounds are lined with trees and the interior is notable for a superb stained-glass window, designed by Edward Burne-Jones in memory of the viceroy, Lord Mayo. The **Race Course** is on the southwestern corner of the Maidan. Racing is popular in Kolkata and races are held throughout the year. Polo is played here for a few weeks in the winter season. The city's two famous football clubs, Mohun Bagan and East Bengal, are based in the Maidan.

On Sunday afternoons, a lively fair with acrobats, magicians and jugglers takes place at the northern end of the Maidan. This is also the venue for large political rallies

Eden Gardens, the site of many cricket matches

❽ Victoria Memorial

The city's most celebrated landmark, this monument to imperial self-confidence was the brainchild of Lord Curzon (1859–1925), one of British India's most flamboyant viceroys. The domed Classical structure, completed in 1921, was constructed with marble from Makrana, which also supplied marble for the Taj Mahal, and financed by "donations" from princes and ordinary citizens. Now a museum, its 25 galleries are spread over the ground and first floors. The collection, which covers a fascinating selection of Raj memorabilia, includes the Calcutta Gallery, with oil paintings and watercolours of the city's history.

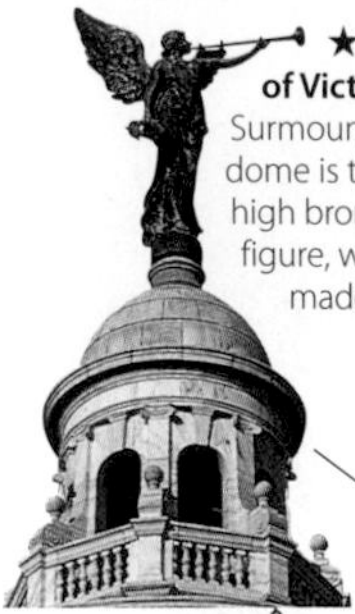

★ Angel of Victory
Surmounting the dome is this 6-m (20-ft) high bronze revolving figure, with a trumpet, made in Italy.

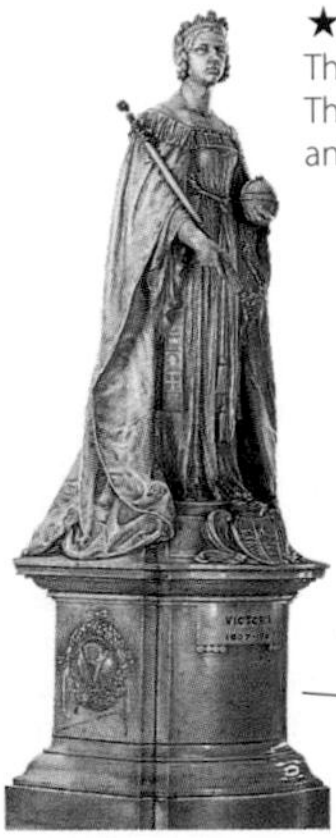

★ Statue of the Young Queen Victoria
The queen, sculpted in marble by Thomas Brock in 1921, holds an orb and a sceptre.

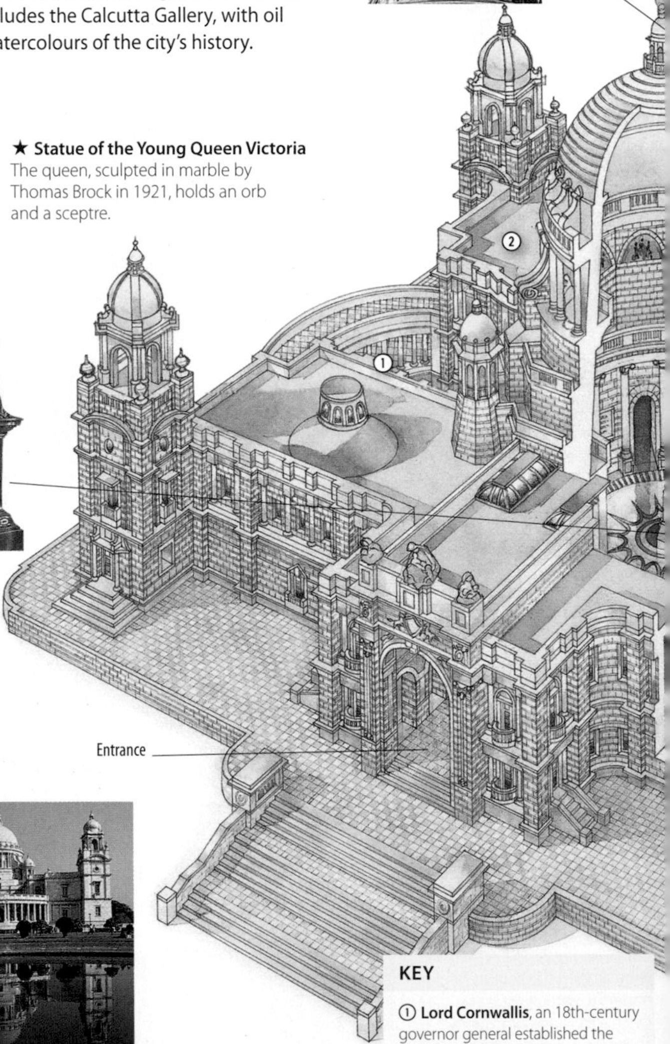

Entrance

General View
The impressive marble façade of the Victoria Memorial.

KEY

① **Lord Cornwallis**, an 18th-century governor general established the Raj's administration.

② **Durbar Hall**

③ **Picture Gallery**

Bronze Panel
Two bronze panels depicting a viceregal procession decorate the bridge at the northern entrance to the Memorial.

Dome
Skylights in the marble rotunda allow light to filter through to illuminate the lobby below.

Calcutta Gallery
This gallery has an excellent collection of landscapes painted by 18th-century British artists.

Exploring the Victoria Memorial
The foundation stone of this impressive structure was laid by the Prince of Wales, later King George V, during his visit to India in 1906. Designed by William Emerson, President of the British Institute of Architects, the building stands in spacious grounds, dotted with ornamental palms, ponds and statues. The museum contains over 10,000 artifacts that represent various facets of the Raj, such as a desk owned by Queen Victoria, embellished with paintings of Indian birds. Among the fine collection of paintings are works by the 18th-century landscape artists, Thomas Daniell and his nephew William Daniell, whose aquatints and lithographs of Indian scenes virtually determined the way India was perceived in 19th-century Britain. The collection also includes paintings by Johann Zoffany (1733–1810), portraits of imperial stalwarts, records of the East India Company, an exquisite set of Persian manuscripts, and paintings that depict Kolkata's history.

A majestic bronze statue of Queen Victoria by Sir George Frampton

❾ Chowringhee

JL Nehru Rd. The Asiatic Society:
1, Park St. **Tel** (033) 2229 0779.
Library: **Open** 10am–5pm Mon–Sat.
Museum: **Open** 10am–6pm Mon–Fri.
w asiaticsocietycal.com

Now called Jawaharlal Nehru
Road, Chowringhee was a
fashionable promenade during
the Raj. This thoroughfare
derives its name from a fakir
(holy man), Jungle Giri
Chowringhee, who once lived
here. At its northern end is
the **Oberoi Grand** (see p703).
Established in the 1870s, and
known as the Grand Hotel, it
was considered "the most
Popular, Fashionable and
Attractive Hotel in India".
  Behind the Oberoi Grand is
New Market (see p286), built in
1874. Surmounted by a clock
tower, shops here are placed
along many interconnected
corridors. One of the oldest is
the Jewish confectionery and
bakery, Nahoum's, which has
a beguiling variety of cookies,
fudge and spiced cakes.
  At its southern end, on Park
Street, is **The Asiatic Society**,
founded in 1784 by Sir William
Jones, a formidable Oriental
scholar. He was the first to
establish the common origins
of Latin and Sanskrit, and called
Sanskrit the "mother of all
languages". The Society's
Museum and **Library** have a
large collection of over 60,000
old and rare manuscripts in
Sanskrit, Arabic and Persian,
as well as artifacts such as a
3rd-century BC stone edict, and
17th- century folios from the
Badshahnama, Abdul Hamid
Lahori's history of the Mughal
emperor Shah Jahan's rule.

The well-preserved period façade of
Chowringhee building

❿ Indian Museum

The oldest and largest museum in India, the Indian
Museum was founded in 1814. The imposing building,
designed by Walter Granville, also the architect of the
General Post Office (see p275), dates to 1878. The museum's
impressive collection is noted for artifacts from the 2,500
BC Indus Valley Civilization, sculpture from Gandhara, the
superbly sculpted railings from the 2,000-year-old Bharhut
Stupa, and a fine collection of 5th-century Gupta coins.

Pala Bronze
This 12th-century Bodhisattva
(an enlightened being) figure
shows the fluid grace and
beauty of Pala sculpture.

Chandela Sculpture
Dating to the 10th–11th
century, this sensuous maiden
from Khajuraho holds a baby
in her arms while two small
children cling to her knees.

Nautch Party
This 19th-century Company School Painting of *nautch* or dancing girls, combines European and Indian techniques of art.

First floor

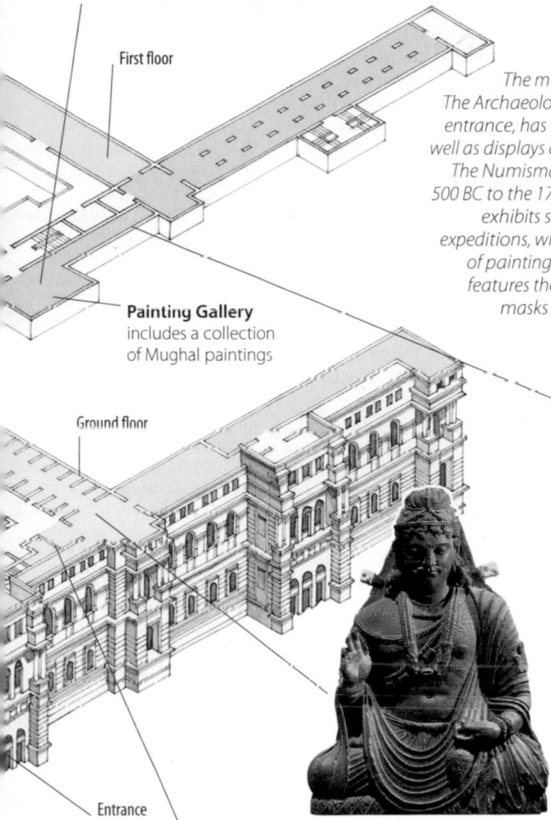

Gallery Guide

The museum is built around a courtyard. The Archaeology Gallery, to the right of the main entrance, has railings from the Bharhut Stupa as well as displays of ancient and medieval sculpture. The Numismatics Gallery has coins dating from 500 BC to the 17th century. The Zoological Section exhibits stuffed birds from British zoological expeditions, while the Art Gallery has a collection of paintings and miniatures. The second floor features the Mask Gallery. The gallery exhibits masks from West Bengal, Odisha, Assam, Karnataka and Bhutan.

Painting Gallery
includes a collection of Mughal paintings

Ground floor

Kalighat Painting
Painted in the folk style of the 19th-century Kalighat school, this represents the Vaishnava saint Chaitanya.

Entrance

★ Gandhara Sculpture
Dating to the 3rd century, this image of Maitreya, the Future Buddha, shows a strong Greek influence in the way the folds of the robe are sculpted.

★ Bharhut Railings
Episodes from Buddhist scriptures, events from the Buddha's life and scenes from daily life are carved on these railings.

Key to Floorplan

- Art and Textile Gallery
- Geology Section
- Botany Section
- Zoological Section
- Anthropology Section
- Archaeology Gallery
- Egyptian Gallery
- Numismatics Gallery
- Library

A Sister of Charity outside the Mother House

⓫ Mother House

54A, AJC Bose Rd. **Tel** (033) 2217 2277.
Open Fri–Wed. **W** mother teresa.
org Donations: are tax-exempt.

The city of Kolkata is inextricably linked to the name of Mother Teresa. At first a teaching nun at Loreto Convent, the death and devastation she witnessed in the city during the famine of 1943, and Partition of India in 1947 *(see p60)*, made her leave this cloistered world and dedicate her life to the poor. The Missionaries of Charity was a new order she formed in 1950, with the Mother House as its headquarters. This simple building is today also her final resting place. Her grave is on the ground floor in a hall. It has no ornamentation, only a Bible placed on it. On a board on the wall are two words, "I thirst".

⓬ Park Street Cemetery

Bounded by Rawdon St & Park St.
Open Mon–Fri.

A romantic, overgrown haven of Raj nostalgia in the middle of the city, the Park Street Cemetery was opened in August 1767 to receive the body of John Wood, an official in the Custom House of the East India Company. From that date till the first half of the 19th century, it served as the resting place of many important Europeans who died in Kolkata. It was this graveyard which gave Park Street its original name, Burial Ground Road. Its name Park Street was derived from the park that Elijah Impey, the Chief Justice of the Supreme Court, established in the area. His grave is in this cemetery as well. William Jones, the great scholar and founder of The Asiatic Society, lies under a pyramid-shaped tomb. Henry Vansittart, one of the first governors of Bengal, is also buried here; so too is Henry Louis Vivian Derozio (1809-1831), a Eurasian teacher at Hindu College in the mid-19th century, who died at the young age of 23. Derozio inspired his students to question all established traditions and was one of the pioneers of what has come to be known as the Bengal Renaissance *(see p264)*. The best known tomb is that

of Rose Aylmer, an early love of the poet Walter Savage Landor. Her tomb, an unpretentious spiralled obelisk, is inscribed with lines by Landor. Also buried here is Colonel Kyd, founder of the Botanical Gardens *(see p285)*.

⓭ Alipore

Bounded by AJC Bose Rd, Belvedere Rd & Alipore Rd. Alipore Zoological Gardens: **Open** 9am–5pm Fri–Wed. **Closed** Thu except on public hols, when the following Friday is closed.. 🏛 National Library: **Tel** (033) 2479 1384. **Open** daily. **Closed** public hols. 🏛 Agri Horticultural Society: **Tel** (033) 2479 3580. **Open** 7–10am & 2–6pm Mon–Sat (only to members and their guests). **W** agrihorticultureindia. com 📷 Flower Show (Jan, Feb, Nov).

Best described as the city's most fashionable address, the suburb of Alipore in south Kolkata is a sylvan world of tree-lined avenues, with palatial houses surrounded by well-kept lawns. Kolkata's zoo, the **Alipore Zoological Gardens**, was established here in 1875 and has a large collection of birds and mammals. Situated nearby, the Belvedere Estate has a broad expanse of lawn and also houses the **National Library**. This is the country's largest library with over two million manuscripts and books. The library has been shifted to the Bhasha Bhawan,

Weathered tombs in the tree-shaded Park Street Cemetery

The National Library in Alipore, with its colonnaded verandah

another building on the same grounds. Built in the Italian Renaissance style, the original building, Belvedere, was once the residence of the lieutenant governors of Bengal.

Further down are the lush gardens of the **Agri Horticultural Society**, founded in 1820 by the missionary William Carey (see p291) to develop and promote agriculture and horticulture in India. In the first 40 years of its existence, seeds, bulbs and ornamental plants were imported from England, South Africa and Southeast Asia. Since then the Society has amassed a varied collection of rare flowering trees and herbs. It's also an excellent place to buy winter annuals.

⑭ Kalighat

Ashutosh Mukherjee Rd **Open** daily.

Kolkata's oldest pilgrimage site, Kalighat finds mention in numerous medieval poems and ballads. Legend has it that the god Shiva, in a fury of grief at

Kalighat painting of two wandering mendicants

the death of his wife, Sati (an incarnation of Parvati), slung her body on his shoulders and danced the terrible *tandava nritya* (dance of death), destroying everything in his path. To stop the carnage, Vishnu flung his magic *chakra* (discus) at Sati's body, and the dismembered pieces scattered across the land. The spot where the little toe fell became Kalighat, and some believe that the name Kolkata is derived from this.

The present Kali Temple dates to the early 19th century, but this has been a sacred spot for much longer. The image of the goddess in the dark inner sanctum is of a wild, untamed figure, with tangled tresses and wide, ferocious eyes. Her extended tongue has a gold covering which is changed every day. The temple is always crowded, especially on Tuesdays and Saturdays.

Kalighat has, over the years, become synonymous with Kalighat

The brick-and-mortar spire of the Kali Temple at Kalighat

pats, a distinctive painting style adopted by the scroll-painters of Bengal. They use paper and water-based paints, instead of tempera, to depict contemporary subjects. A good collection of Kalighat *pats* is on display at the Indian Museum (see pp280–81).

⑮ Nirmal Hridaya

251, Kalighat Rd. **Tel** (033) 2464 4223. **Open** 8–11am & 3–5pm daily.

Mother Teresa's home for the destitute, Nirmal Hridaya ("Pure Heart"), is near the Kali Temple. The site was probably chosen as this holy place teems with poor and old people, who come here to die and attain *moksha*. A large, clean hall is full of beds for the sick and dying who are cared for by nuns, in their characteristic white and blue saris. Visitors who want to work as volunteers must first register at Mother House.

Mother Teresa (1910–1997)

Mother Teresa, born Agnes Gonxa Bojaxhiu in Albania, came to Calcutta in 1929 to begin life as a teacher. The poverty and suffering she saw impelled her to leave the convent. She set up the order of the Missionaries of Charity and her indefatigable work among the lepers, the terminally ill, the unwanted and the poor earned her universal respect and love. To the people of Kolkata she was just "Mother" and their love for her transcended boundaries of religion, class and community. She was awarded the Nobel Peace Prize in 1979.

Mother Teresa on a postage stamp

Kim Li Loi, a family-run Chinese restaurant in Tangra

⑯ Tangra

Off the Eastern Metropolitan Bypass.
🎌 Chinese New Year (Feb).

This eastern suburb is the city's new Chinatown. Chinese immigration to Kolkata began in the 18th century, and today large numbers of this still significant community have settled here. Tangra preserves the rich and varied culture of its immigrant population. A Chinese newspaper and journal are published from here, and there are many tiny restaurants, mostly extensions of family kitchens. "Tangra Chinese", with its discernibly Indian taste, is today as distinct a cuisine as Szechwan and Cantonese. Many of the city's leather tanneries are based at Tangra as, traditionally, the Chinese were involved with the very lucrative shoe trade.

⑰ Marble Palace

46, Muktaram Babu St. **Tel** (033) 2269 3310. **Open** 10am–3:30pm Tue, Wed & Fri. **Closed** Mon & Thu. 📷 🚫 Entry permit: Contact Tourism Centre, 3/2 BBD Bagh, (033) 2248 8271.

This opulent mansion was built in 1835 by Raja Rajendra Mullick, a wealthy *zamindar* (landowner). His descendants still live here, but most of the house is open to visitors. Rajendra Mullick, who had travelled extensively in Europe, brought back an eclectic collection of Venetian chandeliers, Ming vases and Egyptian statuary that he housed in his Classical-fronted mansion, built around a colonnaded courtyard. Today, the Marble Palace provides a wonderful glimpse into the life of a rich 19th-century Bengali household. Nearly a 100 varieties of marble have been used on the floors and the dark halls are hung with paintings by European artists. In the courtyard is the family temple, while the grounds have a rock garden and aviary, home to mynahs and peacocks.

⑱ Jorasanko

6/4, Dwarkanath Tagore Lane. Rabindra Bharati Museum: **Tel** (033) 2269 6610. **Open** 10am–5pm Mon–Fri, 10am–2pm Sat & Sun. 🎭 Son et Lumière: 7pm (English). **Closed** Mon & Thu. 🎭 🎌 Rabindranath Tagore's birthday (May).

A major centre of Bengali art and culture in the 19th century, Jorasanko is the ancestral home of Bengal's favourite son, Rabindranath Tagore *(see p296)*. Built in 1785, this simple three-storeyed, red brick structure housed the lively and cultivated Tagore family, many of whose members were prominent intellectuals and social reformers. The lane on which the house is located is named after Dwarkanath Tagore (1784–1846), the poet's father and a wealthy entrepreneur.

Today, the old house has been expanded and turned into **Rabindra Bharati University**, which specializes in the study of Bengali cultural forms. The house itself has been preserved as the **Rabindra Bharati Museum**. Beginning with the room in which Rabindranath Tagore died, it traces the history of the illustrious Tagore family with a large collection of art and memorabilia. There is an entire section devoted to paintings by Rabindranath.

The red brick Rabindra Bharati University, at Jorasanko

Final touches being given to a Durga image

⑲ Kumartuli

North Chitpur Rd.

Literally, the "Area of the Potters", Kumartuli is a maze of alleys, where images of various Hindu gods and goddesses are made. The best time to visit is late August and early September as this is when potters create the idols for the ten-day-long Durga Puja. It is fascinating to watch them at work, moulding the clay, strengthened by straw and pith, to create images of the fish-eyed goddess Durga, her face often modelled on popular Hindi film actresses and her hair long and flowing.

Nearby is an ancient temple dedicated to Shiva, known as the **Buro Shiva** or "Old Shiva Temple". This is probably the only extant terracotta temple in the city, embellished with terracotta tablets in the frieze below the roof. Further away is Kolkata's celebrated landmark, the giant **Howrah Bridge** (now called Rabindra Setu), an airy, elegant mesh of steel that appears to float above the turgid Hooghly river *(see p271)*. The sunset behind the bridge is one of the loveliest sights in the city. Built in 1943 to replace the old pontoon bridge, this is the sixth longest cantilever bridge in the world, with a central span of 457 m (1,500 ft). The bridge links Kolkata with Howrah (Haora), the city's main railway station on the opposite bank, and is always clogged with traffic. To its south is the impressive Vidyasagar Setu. This massive cable-stayed suspension bridge was built in 1993 to connect South Kolkata with Shibpur and Howrah station.

⑳ Botanical Gardens

W bank of the Hooghly river, Shibpur. 🚢 from Babu Ghat. **Tel** (033) 2668 9970. **Open** daily. The Palm House: **Open** 10am–5pm daily. Note: Visitors should plan morning visits as the house may be closed in the afternoon for security reasons. The National Herbarium: **Open** Mon–Fri. **Closed** public hols.

The Botanical Gardens, in the Shibpur suburb of Howrah, were established in 1787 by Colonel Kyd, an official of the East India Company. It has an astonishing array of flora including ferns, cacti and palms, and boasts of plants from every continent. The chief attraction is the magnificent banyan tree *(Ficus bengalensis)*. Claimed to be the largest banyan tree in the world, it is more than 200 years old and its branches, giving rise to nearly 300 aerial roots, spread over 60 m (197 ft). The central trunk was, however, struck by lightning in 1919 and was subsequently removed. The sight of this tree alone is worth the long journey.

The gigantic leaves of the *Victoria amazonica* lily, Botanical Gardens

The Durga Puja

Image of the ten-armed Durga, slaying Mahisha

Durga Puja is West Bengal's favourite annual ritual in which simply everyone participates. Usually held between September and October, it heralds the advent of autumn and the new harvest. Each locality sets up its own *puja*, organized by local clubs and associations, financed through public subscriptions, though some of the old Bengali families perform their own *puja* in their ancestral houses. Brightly illuminated *pandals* (bamboo structures), often shaped like famous monuments such as the White House or the Taj Mahal, are erected on roads and in parks, and an image of the goddess Durga *(see p29)* is installed within. The goddess is elaborately decorated and in traditional Bengali homes, real jewellery is used. Presents are exchanged and great feasts are prepared. On the final day, the images are immersed in the Hooghly, to the frantic beating of drums and cries of "Jai Ma Durga!" ("Hail to Mother Durga!").

Shopping & Entertainment in Kolkata

Kolkata is a delightful place to shop, even though it lacks the fashionable boutiques of Delhi or Mumbai. There are several old-style bazaars and street hawkers, and fewer glitzy shopping malls. Many shops stock a wide variety of goods, such as those in New Market; others cater to special niches. In certain places one needs to drive hard bargains – the shopkeepers both expect and enjoy this process. Kolkata was once famous for its auction houses, but sadly most of these have now shut down. This is also a culturally vibrant city, with regular performances of theatre, music and film shows. Exhibitions by well-known contemporary artists are also held throughout the year.

Shops and Markets

Kolkata's **New Market** *(see p280)*, on Lindsay Street, is the city's most famous shopping centre. Officially the Sir Stuart Hogg New Municipal Market, established in 1874, this is still a shopper's paradise, where one can find everything from Chinese sausages and fortune cookies to Tibetan curios and gold jewellery. **Sudder Street**, behind the Indian Museum, is another popular shopping centre. Each locality has its own bazaar; the best known of these are Gariahat, Bhowanipore (or Jadubabu's Bazaar), Bowbazaar and Maniktola. Wandering through bazaars offers a glimpse of street life, but be prepared for touts and beggars.

Shops usually open from 10am to 7pm and remain closed on Sundays and public holidays. New Market and some markets also close after 2pm on Saturday, so do check the timings in advance.

Saris and Textiles

The best shops for saris unique to West Bengal are **Ananda**, **Meera Basu** and **Tantuja Bengal Handloom**. Ananda also has an excellent selection of dhotis and *kurtas*. The upmarket boutique **Ritu's** has superb garments designed by Ritu Kumar, one of India's top designers. Exquisite hand-embroidered table linen and children's clothes are available at **Good Companions**. Carpets and *dhurries* are available at **Calcutta Carpets**.

Handicrafts and Gifts

Handicrafts special to West Bengal such as the terracotta Bankura horse *(see p295)*, are on sale at **Manjusha Emporium**. The **Crafts Council of West Bengal** is another fascinating outlet that sells traditional saris as well as artifacts, while **Sasha** has a wide range of curios and bric-a-brac. Tea of the finest quality is available at **Dolly's Tea Shop** in the Dakshinapan shopping complex. This complex also has numerous other state handicraft emporia.

Books and Music

This city of intellectuals and Nobel laureates, such as Rabindranath Tagore and Amartya Sen, is heaven for those willing to search for second-hand bargains in the shops that line the pavements of **College Street** *(see p277)* and **Free School Street**. Many of these shops have a good selection of rare and out of print books. **Dasgupta & Co** has a large choice, though there is no place to browse. The **Seagull Bookstore**, on the other hand, encourages browsing and is the best place for serious literature and academic books. **Starmark** too, has a large stock that ranges from thrillers to encyclopedias. The centrally located **Oxford Bookstore**, is also well-stocked and has a good café.

Music aficionados are advised to try **m3** which has a good selection of Indian and Western CDs and audio cassettes. On Chitpur Road towards Nakhoda Mosque *(see p277)*, are music shops selling sitars, *sarods, veenas*, flutes and violins. Free School Street is about the only place in India where record albums of 1950s Elvis Presley and Jerry Lee Lewis or 1960s Beatles and Rolling Stones are easily available.

Sweets

West Bengal's sweets are famous. The variety is bewildering, but the two most popular are *sandesh* and *rosogulla (see p268)*. The latter is on sale in every sweetshop, but those in **KC Das & Sons**, the family which invented this delicacy, are the best. *Sandesh*, made of cottage cheese and sugar (molasses or *gur* in the winter months), are of two kinds, those that are soft and those that have a harder outer crust. Both are widely available, but the best are found in **Nakur Nandy & Girish Chandra Dey**, **Makhan Lal Das & Sons** and **Balaram Mullick**.

Entertainment Guides, Tickets and Venues

The *Sunday Telegraph* magazine and other English language dailies list the day's entertainment on their engagements page. Other useful sources of information are *Cal Calling* and *Kolkata: This Fortnight*, which is distributed by the West Bengal Tourist office. Information on tickets as well as reviews of plays and concerts also appear with the announcements.

Kolkata's cultural centre is just off the Maidan. The **Rabindra Sadan Complex**, named after Rabindranath Tagore, includes the **Academy of Fine Arts**. Next door is **Nandan**, where retrospectives of films by Satyajit Ray and other renowned directors, are regularly held. Other venues around the city include **INOX**, **Gorky Sadan**, **Fame** and the well-known **British Council**. Exhibitions by well-known as well as up and coming artists are held at the city's many art galleries, especially the **Birla Academy of Art and Culture**,

CIMA Gallery and **Chitrakoot Gallery**. CIMA Gallery also has a gift shop.

Music and Theatre

Performances of West Bengal's well-established classical and folk theatre (*jatra*) are staged throughout the year by semi-professional and amateur groups. Bengali theatre is perhaps the most vibrant in the country. Its rich repertoire includes plays with historical and socially relevant themes as well as translations of Greek, European, Sanskrit and Hindi classics. *Jatra*, on the other hand, was introduced by the Vaishnava saint, Chaitanya Mahaprabhu, in the 16th century, and is based on musical plays that revolve around the Krishna legend (*see p183*). Characterized by dramatic acting interspersed with song and dance, the plays cater to both rural and urban audiences.

Another popular form of entertainment is Rabindra Sangeet. These melodious songs composed by Tagore include folk songs that are traditionally sung by boatmen who ply the Ganges. Regular concerts are held in the city, and attract audiences who continue to revere Tagore.

Clubs and Nightlife

Kolkata is a city of clubs which date to colonial times and are open only to members. Sometimes temporary membership can be arranged, particularly at the popular **Tollygunge Club** (*see p703*) which has huge grounds with rare trees and birds. Visitors can stay at the club, which offers all the comforts of a top hotel but at reasonable rates.

Kolkata's once glittering and lively nightlife dwindled during the political upheavals of the 1960s. It is reviving now and affluent youth throng hotels where the city's hip nightclubs and discotheques, such as **Shisha Reincarnated**, **Someplace Else**, **Tantra** and **Big Ben**, are situated.

DIRECTORY

Saris and Textiles

Ananda
13, Russell St.
Tel (033) 2229 2275.

Calcutta Carpets
209A, AJC Bose Road.
Tel (033) 3028 3940.

Good Companions
13 C, Russell St.
Tel (033) 3292 9612.

Meera Basu
8, Dr Sarat Banerjee Rd.
Tel (033) 6634 3691).

Ritu Kumar
South City Mall.
Tel (033) 2422 5422.

Tantuja Bengal Handloom
Ground Floor, Dakshinapan Complex, Dhakuria.
Tel (033) 2423 7433.

Handicrafts and Gifts

Crafts Council of West Bengal
13, Chowringhee Terrace.
Tel (033) 2223 9422.

Dolly's Tea Shop
G-62, Dakshinapan Complex, Dhakuria.
Tel (033) 2423 7838.

Manjusha Emporium
Dakshinapan Complex, Dhakuria.
Tel (033) 2423 7099,

Sasha
27, Mirza Ghalib St.
Tel (033) 2252 1586.

Books and Music

Dasgupta & Company
54/3, College St.
Tel (033) 2241 4609.

m3
20 H, Park St.
Tel (033) 4006 1850.

Oxford Bookstore
17, Park St.
Tel (033) 2229 7662.

Seagull Bookstore
31, SP Mukherjee Rd.
Tel (033) 2476 5869.

Starmark
3, Lord Sinha Rd.
Tel (033) 4006 3310.

Sweets

Balaram Mullick
2, Puddapukur Rd.
Bhowanipur.
Tel (033) 2454 0281.

KC Das & Sons
11, Esplanade East.
Tel (033) 2248 5920.

Makhan Lal Das & Sons
313, Rabindra Sarani.
Tel (033) 2555 8182.

Nakur Nandy & Girish Chandra Dey
56, Ramdulal Sarkar St.
Tel (033) 2241 0048,

Entertainment Venues

Academy of Fine Arts
2, Cathedral Rd.
Tel (033) 2223 4302.

Birla Academy of Art and Culture
108, Southern Ave.
Tel (033) 2466 2843.

British Council
16, Camac St.
Tel (033) 2282 5370.

Chitrakoot Gallery
55, Gariahat Rd.
Tel (033) 2461 8812.

CIMA Gallery
Sunny Towers, 43, Ashutosh Chowdhury Ave. **Tel** (033) 2485 8717.

Fame
Metropolis Mall, Hiland Park, 925 Chak Garia.
Tel (033) 4010 5555.

Gorky Sadan
3, Gorky Terrace.
Tel (033) 2283 2742.

INOX
South City Mall.
Tel (033) 2422 5265.

Nandan
1/1, AJC Bose Rd.
Tel (033) 2223 1210.

Rabindra Sadan
Cathedral Rd.
Tel (033) 2223 9917.

Clubs and Nightlife

Big Ben
The Kenilworth, Little Russell St.
Tel (033) 2282 3939.

Shisha Reincarnated
22, Camac Street, Block D, 6th Floor
Tel (033) 2281 1313.

Someplace Else
The Park Hotel, Park St.
Tel (033) 2249 9000.

Tantra
The Park Hotel, Park St.
Tel (033) 2249 9000.

Tollygunge Club
120, Deshpran Sasmal Rd.
Tel (033) 2417 6022.

WEST BENGAL & SIKKIM

West Bengal has three distinct types of landscape. In the west, the red soil gives its rich colour to the terracotta temples of Bishnupur. The Ganges Delta in lower Bengal has dense, tangled mangrove swamps where Royal Bengal tigers roam, while the charming, Raj-era hill stations of Darjeeling and Kalimpong are located in the foothills of the Himalayas in the northern part of the state. The neighbouring state of Sikkim, which also borders Bhutan, Nepal and China, is ringed by mountains. In its tranquil valleys, richly ornamented Buddhist monasteries stand amidst emerald-green terraced tea fields. The world's third highest mountain, Kanchendzonga (8,586 m/28,169 ft), dominates the skyline and the life of Sikkim's people. The two states have a combined population of 81 million.

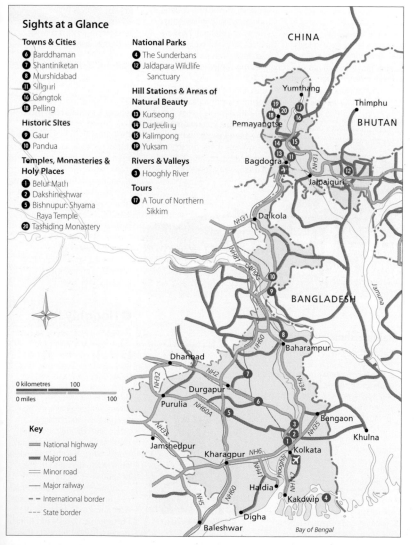

Sights at a Glance

Towns & Cities
6 Barddhaman
7 Shantiniketan
8 Murshidabad
11 Siliguri
16 Gangtok
18 Pelling

Historic Sites
9 Gaur
10 Pandua

Temples, Monasteries & Holy Places
1 Belur Math
2 Dakshineshwar
5 Bishnupur: Shyama Raya Temple
20 Tashiding Monastery

National Parks
4 The Sunderbans
12 Jaldapara Wildlife Sanctuary

Hill Stations & Areas of Natural Beauty
13 Kurseong
14 Darjeeling
15 Kalimpong
19 Yuksam

Rivers & Valleys
3 Hooghly River

Tours
17 A Tour of Northern Sikkim

Key
━━ National highway
━━ Major road
═══ Minor road
── Major railway
– – International border
--- State border

◄ The ten-armed goddess Durga, elaborately adorned for the Durga Puja festival

For keys to symbols *see back flap*

❶ Belur Math

Howrah district. 10 km (6 miles) N of Kolkata. 🚕🚌 or taxi from Kolkata. **Open** daily. Conservative dress appreciated.

Just outside Kolkata, on the west bank of the Hooghly river, is Belur Math, the headquarters of the Ramakrishna Mission. The order was established in 1897 by the dynamic, reformist Hindu crusader Swami Vivekananda (see p619), Ramakrishna Paramhansa's foremost disciple. The modern temple within the sprawling complex was built in 1938 and embodies Ramakrishna's philosophy, based on the unity of all faiths. The ground plan is in the shape of a cross, the windows have arches reminiscent of Mughal buildings, the gate shows Buddhist influence, and Hindu architectural motifs decorate the façade. Smaller temples and dormitories for the monks belonging to the order surround it. The place is spotlessly clean, and the atmosphere contemplative and calm. Today, the Mission has centres across the world.

❷ Dakshineshwar

24 Parganas district. 12 km (8 miles) N of Kolkata. 🚌🚇 or taxi from Kolkata. **Open** daily. Conservative dress appreciated.

North of Belur Math, on the east bank of the Hooghly river, stands the temple of Dakshineshwar, one of Bengal's most popular pilgrimage spots. The temple, built in 1855 by a rich and pious widow, Rani Rashmoni, was initially opposed by orthodox religious interests as she was not a Brahmin (the highest Indian caste). No Brahmin was therefore willing to be the temple priest. Only Ramakrishna Paramhansa, then still a boy, agreed, and he spent many years there, preaching and developing his philosophy of the essential oneness of all

The curved *bangaldar* roof of the Kali temple, Dakshineshwar

faiths. His room in the temple complex is still preserved in its original state.

The impressive whitewashed temple is set on a high plinth and topped by nine cupolas. The roof, with its line of rounded cornices, stands out impressively against the sky. Inside the sanctum is an image of Bhabatarini, an incarnation of the goddess Kali.

Within the large compound, strung along the river bank, are 12 smaller temples, each dedicated to the god Shiva. Crowds of pilgrims visit the Dakshineshwar temple daily, lending the sprawling temple complex a cheerful and bustling atmosphere.

❸ Hooghly River

Hooghly district. 24 km (15 miles) N from Kolkata to Shrirampur. 🚉🚌🚇 River cruises. ℹ Babu Ghat (near Eden Gardens) or Tourist Office, (033) 2248 7302.

When the Ganges enters the lower Gangetic Plains in West Bengal, the river breaks up into many channels. The main distributary, the Hooghly (now Hugli), flows 260 km (162 miles) from Murshidabad to the Bay of Bengal.

Between the 15th and 19th centuries, this easily navigable river attracted Dutch, French, Portuguese, Danish and British traders. The settlements they

Belur Math, on the west bank of the Hooghly river

Ramakrishna Paramhansa (1836–86)

Ramakrishna, one of modern India's greatest spiritual teachers, was born into a poor family of priests in 1836. He became a priest at Dakshineshwar, where he began a life of prayer and meditation. His philosophy was lucid – there is an inherent truth in all religions and a simple life is a pure life. A mystic who claimed to speak directly to God, he could explain complex and abstruse theological issues in the simplest language, which appealed to the poor and rich alike. His teachings were carried to the USA and to Britain by his main disciple Swami Vivekananda (1863–1902) who set up many Ramakrishna Mission centres abroad for education and religious studies.

Ramakrishna Paramhansa

Visitors praying at the Church of Our Lady of Bandel

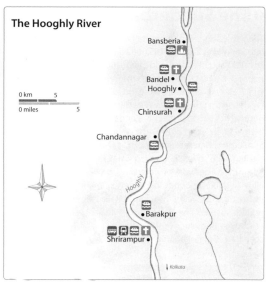

The Hooghly River

Bansberia

Bandel
Hooghly

Chinsurah

Chandannagar

Barakpur

Shrirampur

↓ Kolkata

0 km   5
0 miles   5

established transformed the river banks into a mini Europe the remnants of which can be best explored today by taking one of the river cruises.

Up river from Kolkata is **Shrirampur** (Serampore), a Danish colony until 1845. Dr William Carey, the first Baptist missionary in India *(see p283)*, set up the earliest printing press here in 1799 and translated the Bible into several Indian languages, including Bengali, marking the beginnings of modern Bengali prose. He also founded the first theological college, today Shrirampur College, in 1818. Its library houses a priceless collection of 18th- and 19th-century books.

On the east bank is **Barakpur** (Barrackpore), the site of the British viceroys' once gracious country house. The mansion, locally referred to as Lat Bagan ("Governor's or Lord's Garden"), was built by Lord Wellesley, the governor general in the early 19th century.

Chandannagar (Chandernagore), a French settlement from 1673 until 1952, still retains a Gallic ambience. The public benches on the waterfront (previously Quai Dupleix) are replicas of those found in Paris parks. The elegant Administrator's Residence, built in the 18th century, is now the Institut de

Chandernagore, a library and museum, and contains an interesting collection of French-era documents and artifacts. The Église du Sacré Cœur has a statue of Joan of Arc and a Lourdes grotto.

North of Chandannagar is **Chinsurah** (Chunchura), an Armenian settlement, taken over by the Dutch in 1625 and later by the British. The Armenian Church was built in 1697, though the steeple was added a century later. The town of **Hooghly**, to the north, has an impressive *imambara* (mosque) built in 1836. Further upriver is **Bandel**, founded by the Portuguese in 1580. The

Armenian Church, Chinsurah

Church of Our Lady of Bandel, consecrated in 1599, is the oldest in Eastern India. After being refaced in granite, it has, however, lost some of its charm. People of all faiths still pray at the statue of Our Lady of Happy Voyages, an icon with an interesting history. In 1632, while the city was being sacked by the Mughal emperor Shah Jahan, the icon was lost in the river, but later reappeared miraculously on the banks in front of the church.

Further north is **Bansberia**, site of several terracotta temples. The Ananta Vasudeva Temple, built in 1679, has a panel of warriors carved above the entrance, while the Hanseshwari Temple, built in 1814, has a fabulous array of Kremlin-like onion domes and an elaborately carved façade.

The French Administrator's Residence in Chandannagar

For keys to symbols *see back flap*

❹ The Sunderbans

The vast Ganges-Brahmaputra Delta stretching into Bangladesh covers 105,000 sq km (40,541 sq miles) and has the world's largest tropical mangrove forest. The Sunderbans Reserve, which spreads across 2,585 sq km (998 sq miles), created within the delta was declared a Tiger Reserve in 1973 to protect the endangered Royal Bengal tiger. A part of the reserve houses the Sundarbans National Park, a UNESCO World Heritage Site covering 1,330 sq km (513 sq miles). The intricate network of waterways, creeks and alluvial islands abounds in a variety of marine life, including crustaceans and dolphins, as well as reptiles such as Olive Ridley turtles and estuarine crocodiles. Birds such as the waterfowl can be seen here. Guided boats are available.

Fiddler Crabs
Male fiddler crabs have a large claw resembling a bow and fiddle, which they use to attract females and deter enemies.

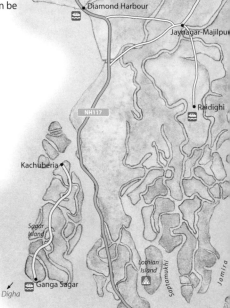

Mangrove Forests
Renowned for their variety of mangroves, the Sunderbans were once dominated by the *sundari* tree (*Heritiera fomes*), now nearly extinct due to rampant timber poaching. Mangroves have ingeniously adapted to flooding and salinity, using breathing roots or pneumatophores.

Country Boats
Small rowboats, available from Sajnakhali, take visitors along the reserve's many waterways. These craft are preferable to the noisier motorboats that tend to scare away wildlife, especially the rich variety of waterfowl.

For hotels and restaurants see pp697–8 and p711

More to See

The western boundary of the Sunderbans boasts a number of popular beaches and reserves, all of which can be reached by road or boat. **Ganga Sagar** on Sagar Island, is the spot where millions of pilgrims gather for the annual Ganga Sagar Mela *(see p299)* during Makar Sankranti in January. **Diamond Harbour** is a popular picnic spot, while **Bakkhali** and **Digha** have beautiful beaches and are popular resorts. Bakkhali is also a haven for birdlife.

Estuarine or Saltwater Crocodile
Saltwater crocodiles, known as "salties", grow up to a length of
8 m (26 ft). They feed on small mammals and have occasionally
been known to attack humans.

Royal Bengal Tiger
According to the census (2001–2), the
Indian stretch of the Sunderbans has
245 Royal Bengal tigers. The only tigers
known to live in mangrove forests,
they have adapted remarkably to
the environment, becoming expert
swimmers and feeding on fish.

Tale of the Tiger

The tiger plays a major role in India's cultural history as a symbol of
power and kingship. In Hindu iconography, Shiva wears a tiger skin,
while the fearsome Goddess Durga is often portrayed riding a tiger.
Tiger images can also be seen in vibrant murals in Buddhist
monasteries in Arunachal Pradesh, Sikkim and Ladakh. In the
Sunderbans, ritual offerings are made to the forest deity, Banbibi, to
seek protection from the tiger. Yet statistics belie the tiger's mythic
status. In 1900, India's tiger
population was about
40,000; by 1972 it had fallen
to 1,800. Alarmed, the Indian
government launched
Project Tiger. Numbers seem
to have grown, and a tiger
census is under way. India
has about 60 per cent of the
world's tiger population,
protected in 28 Project Tiger
Reserves across the country.

A play re-enacting Banbibi protecting a mother
and child from the tiger

Key

══ Minor road

▪▬▪ Park boundary

▪▪▪ International border

══ National Highway

══ Major road

0 kilometres   10

0 miles   10

❺ Bishnupur: Shyama Raya Temple

Bishnupur, capital of the Mallabhumi kingdom between the 17th and the mid-18th centuries, is renowned for its elaborately adorned terracotta temples, made of the local red clay. The most imposing of these is the Shyama Raya Temple, built in 1643. It is richly decorated with scenes from Lord Krishna's life as well as episodes taken from the epic *Ramayana (see p31)*. Other motifs in the temple include scenes of hunting, boating and military processions.

Front façade of the Shyama Raya Temple

KEY

① **The inner chamber**, called *thakurbari* (god's house), has a finely decorated altar at one end.

② **The cornice** echoes the contours of thatched village huts.

③ **Shikharas**, or the design of the five spires is inspired by the temple tradition of nearby Odisha *(see p310)*.

④ **The curved cornice** deflects rain water.

Arched Façade
The arches, supported by squat, ornamented pillars, lead to a vaulted corridor.

For hotels and restaurants see pp697–8 and p711

VISITORS' CHECKLIST

Practical Information
Bankura district. 132 km (82 miles) NW of Kolkata. 🏛 128,811. **Open** daily. 🎭 Jhapan (Aug).

Transport
🚉 🚌

Terracotta Friezes
Scenes from the epics alternate with scenes from daily life. Here, Krishna plays his flute for the gopis (milkmaids).

The twin hut-like roofs of the Keshta Raya Temple, Bishnupur

Exploring Bishnupur's Temples

The terracotta temples of Bishnupur are scattered over a 3-km (2-mile) radius, and stand out vividly against the vibrant green and ochre colours of the landscape.

The **Rasa Mancha Temple**, built by the ruler Bir Hambir in the late 16th century, has 108 pillars and a pyramidal roof. Images of Krishna and Radha were displayed here for the Rasa Festival, a tradition that still continues today.

North of the Rasa Mancha Temple is the large **Keshta Raya (Jor Bangla) Temple**, built in 1655. It has joined twin roofs, literally *jor bangla*. Floral motifs, scroll work and scenes from the *Ramayana* and *Mahabharata* embellish the friezes on the walls.

The **Madan Mohan Temple** further north, was built in 1694 and has friezes showing events from the life of Krishna.

To the northwest, the 19th-century **Shridhara Temple** has nine spires or *nav ratna*. The frieze at the entrance shows the god Shiva dancing.

❻ Barddhaman

Barddhaman district. 125 km (78 miles) NW of Kolkata. 🚌 🎭 Barddhaman Festival (Jan).

The Rajas of Barddhaman (Burdwan) were once powerful landlords and great patrons of the arts. Today, the small, nondescript town is a gateway to some interesting sites. The rajas built several temples at **Kalna**, 50 km (31 miles) to the east, in the 18th and 19th centuries. The Shiva temple, with 108 minor shrines, is the most impressive. **Nabadwip**, 20 km (12 miles) to the north of Kalna, was the birthplace of Sri Chaitanya (1486–1533), founder of the movement that revived the Krishna cult (see p183). It is a charming town, with a few old houses built of the narrow red brick, unique to pre-British Bengal. Pilgrims singing *kirtans* throng the Gauranga Temple. Nearby, in **Mayapur**, is the large and modern Chandrodaya Temple, headquarters of ISKCON (International Society for Krishna Consciousness).

Interior Arch
This doorway has rich carvings of creepers, foliage and flowers.

Bankura Horses

Bankura district's vibrant tradition of folk art includes a variety of clay handicrafts. The district's most famous product is the Bankura horse, a very stylized figure with a long neck and elongated ears, in warm terracotta colours. Artisans have used the same techniques of hollow clay moulding and firing for generations. Sizes vary from minute, palm-sized toys to gigantic creations over 1 m (3 ft) high. The horses are votive figures and are usually placed in front of local deities.

Bankura clay horse

Students attending open-air classes at Visva Bharati University

❼ Shantiniketan

Birbhum district. 213 km (132 miles) NW of Kolkata. 🚉 Bolpur, 3 km (2 miles) S of Shantiniketan, then rickshaw. 🚌 Bolpur. 🎭 Kendulimela (Jan), Paush Mela (Dec).

This serene settlement was founded by Debendranath Tagore in 1863. In 1901, his son Rabindranath started a school here, which became a university in 1921. Rabindranath's aim was to establish an institution that followed the traditional Indian *gurukul* system of instruction, where gurus would teach while sitting on the grass under trees. The university also stressed the importance of community living, and specialized in all branches of the arts and humanities, with a special emphasis on Bengali culture.

Today the **Visva Bharati University**'s structure is more conventional, but certain traditions, such as open-air lessons, remain sacrosanct. The place is still hallowed ground for admirers of Tagore.

In the campus is the Uttarayan Complex, where the poet lived and worked for many years. Other departments include **Kala** (Fine Arts) **Bhavan, Sangeet** (Music) **Bhavan** and **China Bhavan**, specializing in Chinese studies. Shantiniketan's association with contemporary Indian art is evident by the works on display by many of the country's leading artists, such as Binode Bihari Mukherjee (1904–80), Nandalal Bose (1882–1966) and

Ram Kinkar Baij (1910–80). The **Vichitra Museum** has memorabilia from the poet's life, including his paintings, developed from the sketches he made in the margins of his written work. Excellent performances of Rabindra Sangeet (songs written and set to music by Tagore) can be heard at the campus every evening.

The village of **Kenduli**, nearby, is the birthplace of the medieval poet, Jayadeva, who composed the *Gita Govinda,* a paean to Krishna. Every year in January the Bauls, wandering minstrels known for their soulful songs, gather here for Kendulimela, a festival where they sing without pause for three days.

🏛 **Visva Bharati University**
Tel (03463) 262 626/261 531.
Open Thu–Tue. 🚫 📷 Vichitra Museum: **Open** daily. 📷 🚫

❾ Murshidabad

Murshidabad district. 200 km (124 miles) N of Kolkata. 🚉 🚌

The former capital of the nawabs of Bengal, Murshidabad lies in the green and gold Bengal countryside. This city, on the banks of the Bhagirathi river, was founded in 1704 by Nawab Murshid Quli Khan, governor of the Mughal emperor Aurangzeb. His grave lies beneath the stairs of the impressive **Katra Mosque**, built in 1724 along the lines of Kartalab Khan's Mosque at Dhaka. The nawab chose this site because he wanted the footsteps of the faithful to pass over him.

Hazarduari ("A Thousand Doors"), the nawabs' palace, was built in the 1830s by General Duncan McLeod of the Bengal Engineers who, inspired by

The grand façade of Hazarduari Palace in Murshidabad

Rabindranath Tagore (1861–1941)

Tagore was India's ultimate Renaissance man and his influence is still felt in all branches of the arts, particularly in Bengal. Born in 1861 into the rich and cultivated Tagore family *(see p284)*, he became a poet, lyricist, novelist, short story writer, essayist, painter, choreographer, actor, dramatist and singer – as well as the author of India's national anthem. Following the translation of his poem *Gitanjali* into English by WB Yeats, he was awarded the Nobel Prize in 1913. He was knighted by the British government, but returned the honour in protest against the massacre at Jallianwala Bagh *(see p60)*. Mahatma Gandhi called him Gurudev ("Great Teacher"). Tagore died in August 1941, but his memory is still deeply revered by Bengalis and his portraits, if not his books, occupy pride of place in nearly all middle-class Bengali homes.

Nobel laureate Tagore, in 1930

Italian Baroque, gave it a banquet hall lined with mirrors and a striking circular Durbar Hall. The palace is now a museum with many fine exhibits, such as a gigantic chandelier, presented by Queen Victoria, which was hung directly over the nawabs' solid silver throne. The library has over 10,000 books, among them some beautiful illuminated Korans. Other items on display are a motley collection of arms and armour, including a cannon which was fired at the crucial Battle of Plassey in 1757 *(see p56)*, when Robert Clive defeated the nawab, Siraj-ud-Daulah – a battle which eventually paved the way for the establishment of the British Empire in India. The town declined after Kolkata grew in importance.

🏛 **Hazarduari Museum**
Open Sat–Thu.

❾ Gaur

Malda district. 325 km (202 miles) N of Kolkata. 🚆 Malda, 12 km (7.4 miles) N of Gaur, then taxi or bus. 🚌 Monuments: **Open** daily.

The impressive ruins of Gaur are an indication of its former glory, when the city caught the imagination of the second Mughal emperor Humayun who called it Jinnatabad ("Abode of Paradise"). This abandoned city, spread over 52 sq km (20 sq miles), dates to the 15th and 16th centuries, though the area has a much older history. The Buddhist Pala kings ruled here from the 8th century onwards until they were ousted by the Senas, Bengal's last Hindu

The carved terracotta façade of the Eklakhi Mausoleum, Pandua

dynasty, in the 12th century. Thereafter, it was ruled by a series of Muslim sultans, including the Ilyas Shahi dynasty. Gaur was sacked by Sher Shah Sur *(see p83)* in 1539, and ravaged by plague in 1575, after which it became part of the Mughal Empire.

The oldest structure is the **Sagar Dighi**, a large tank built in the 12th century. On the eastern bank of the Bhagirathi river are the ramparts of a fort, within which is a brick wall that once enclosed a palace. The northern gate, the **Dakhil Darwaza**, built in 1459, has a soaring entrance archway and corners embellished with carving. To its north are the remains of **Sona Mosque**, built in 1526, and Gaur's largest mosque. Other interesting buildings include the many-arched **Qadam Rasul Mosque**, built in 1530 to enshrine an impression of the Prophet Mohammad's footprint, the brick **Tantipara Mosque** and

The Gumti Darwaza, Gaur

the **Lattan Mosque** with remnants of blue, green, yellow and white tiles. The **Gumti Darwaza**, the eastern entrance to the city of Gaur, still stands.

❿ Pandua

Malda district. 360 km (224 miles) N of Kolkata. 🚆 Malda, 18 km (11 miles) S of Pandua, then taxi or bus. 🚌

The creeper-covered ruins of Pandua lie on either side of a 10-km (6-mile) stretch of an old paved brick road. In the 1300s, Pandua replaced Gaur as the capital of Bengal's Muslim rulers. At the northern end, the 14th century **Adina Mosque**, built by Sultan Sikandar Shah, imitates the design of the great mosque at Damascus. Once the largest mosque in India, it contains Sikandar Shah's tomb. Further south is the early 15th-century **Eklakhi Mausoleum** which contains the grave of Sultan Jalal-ud-din. This stucture, built at great cost, was one of the earliest square brick tombs to be constructed in Bengal. The octagonal inner chamber, unusually, has an image of Ganesha, the Hindu elephant god, carved over the entrance archway. The **Qutb Shahi Mosque**, to the south, is sometimes called the "Golden Mosque" as its minarets were once topped with yellow tiles. It was built in 1582 by Sultan Makhdum Shah, whose grave lies adjacent to the mosque.

The Dakhil Darwaza in Gaur, built with small, red bricks

Tea plantations lining the road between Bagdogra and Siliguri

⓫ Siliguri

Darjeeling district. 79 km (49 miles) SE of Darjeeling. 🏙 470,300. ✈ Bagdogra, 12 km (7 miles) W of Siliguri, then taxi or bus. 🚉 New Jalpaiguri, 60 km (37 miles) SE of Siliguri, then taxi or bus. 🚌 ℹ Tourist Office, Siliguri, (0353) 251 1974.

Siliguri, in the foothills of the Eastern Himalayas, was once a calm, provincial town, with quiet streets and well-equipped shops where tea planters would come to stock up on provisions. Today, much of the town is a vast trucking depot, though it has some lively bazaars, such as the one on **Tenzing Norgay Road**. The Tibetan woollens on sale here are good bargains, and cane furniture, a speciality of the area, is widely available. In the winter, Siliguri hosts international Buddhist conferences and also serves as the transit point for travellers to the Jaldapara Wildlife Sanctuary.

Environs
Clustered close to Siliguri are **New Jalpaiguri**, the railhead for the area, and **Bagdogra**, which has the airport. Along with Siliguri, these towns act as gateways to the hill stations of Darjeeling, Kurseong and Kalimpong, as well as to Bhutan and Sikkim. The drive between these towns goes past beautiful green acres of tea plantations.

⓬ Jaldapara Wildlife Sanctuary

Jalpaiguri district. 200 km (78 miles) E of Siliguri. 🚉 Madarihat, the entry point, then taxi. 🚌 Madarihat. ℹ For general enquiries and bookings for the Hollong Forest Lodge, contact Tourist Office, Siliguri, (0353) 251 1974. **Open** mid-Sep–mid-Jun. 📷 Extra charges for photography. 🏨 Hollong.

The region around the Jaldapara Wildlife Sanctuary, in the richly forested Dooars Valley, was once the hunting ground of the kings of Bhutan. Today, it is one of the biggest reserve forests in West Bengal, covering an area of 216 sq km (83 sq miles). Established in 1941, the reserve sprawls over lush,

The Darjeeling Himalayan Railway (DHR)

The most attractive way to travel to Darjeeling from Siliguri is by the Darjeeling Himalayan Railway (DHR), also known as the "toy train". The narrow gauge train gasps its way up from New Jalpaiguri (NJP) to Darjeeling, 2,128 m (6,982 ft) above sea level. The journey takes nine hours, and the track rises a total of 2,088 m (6,850 ft) over its length of 80 km (50 miles). Built between 1879 and 1881, the train line is now a UNESCO World Heritage Site. The line makes wide loops as it zigzags up the hill, requiring the train to backtrack for certain stretches. Each of the steam engines, one of which dates to 1892, hauls up three carriages. If nine hours sounds daunting, try journeying to Kurseong by train and taking a bus to Darjeeling, or travelling only the last stretch (from Ghoom to Darjeeling) by train. Tickets are available at NJP and Darjeeling stations. The NJP–Darjeeling train leaves at 9am; the Darjeeling–NJP train departs at 9:15am. In peak season, there is an 8:30am NJP–Kurseong train and a Kurseong–NJP train at 2:30pm. For more details, *see p753*.

The toy train pulled by steam engines

For hotels and restaurants see pp697–8 and p711

deciduous forests and dense scrubland, with the Torsa river flowing through it. This is one of the few places in India where the great Indian one-horned rhinoceros *(see p334)* can be easily spotted. About 50 of these magnificent animals live in the sanctuary, protected from poachers who hunt them for their horns, which are believed to be powerful aphrodisiacs. The sanctuary is home to various other rare and endangered species as well, including the leopard, tiger, hispid hare, hogbadger, and sloth bear.

Large numbers of hog deer, spotted deer, barking deer and gaur (Indian bison) can also be seen at Jaldapara. Bird species include the lesser pied hornbill, and the Bengal florican with its mottled and streaked plumage. In addition, there are eight species of freshwater turtles in Jaldapara's ponds.

The northern part of the sanctuary, known as Totopara, is located along the banks of the Torsa river. It is home to the Toto tribe, now only 1,300 strong, whose members have consistently refused to succumb to the comforts of civilization.

A delightful way to explore the Jaldapara Sanctuary is to take an early morning elephant safari through the park. The elephants belong to the forest department and spend their entire lives within the confines of the sanctuary. Quite often, the elephants taking visitors on safaris are accompanied by

their calves, which gambol along closely beside them. The many waterholes in the sanctuary, where animals come to drink in the evenings, are excellent spots for wildlife sightings.

The elegant, colonial-style **Hollong Forest Lodge** within the sanctuary offers food and accommodation.

⓳ Kurseong

Darjeeling district. 50 km (31 miles) N of Siliguri. 🚆 🚌

Halfway between Siliguri and Darjeeling, on the Darjeeling Himalayan Railway line, secluded Kurseong has a quiet charm. It is smaller than Darjeeling, with a milder climate because of its lower altitude. Set amid tea gardens, with lush vegetation and a picturesque lake, Kurseong is known for its natural beauty. According to local legend, the place gets its name from *kurson rip*, a beautiful wild orchid found in the area. Kurseong is a walkers' paradise.

Jungle fowl, found in large numbers at Jaldapara

The trek from **Mirik** to Kurseong *(see p307)*, which takes about eight hours, runs through tea estates, orange orchards, cardamom plantations and small villages, and provides spectacular views of the valley. Similarly, the five-hour walk to **Ghoom** is also beautiful, winding along a ridge which runs through a thick, but well shaded, forest.

Festivals of West Bengal & Sikkim

A priest conducting prayer services at a Saraswati Puja *pandal*

Ganga Sagar Mela *(mid-Jan)*, Sagar Island. Thousands of pilgrims assemble for a fair, and a dip at dawn at the point where the Ganges enters the sea.

Saraswati Puja *(Jan/Feb)*. Saraswati is the Goddess of Learning and her image is always dressed in pale yellow. School and college girls dress in yellow too, and place their books at the feet of the goddess during this festival, celebrated all over Bengal.

International Flower Festival *(Apr/May)*, Gangtok. Held at the height of the flowering season, this festival showcases Sikkim's rare orchids, rhododendrons and other beautiful flowers.

Saga Dawa *(May)*, Gangtok. Sacred scriptures are carried from monasteries through the streets by stately processions of lamas during this festival, which celebrates the Buddha's birth, his enlightenment and his attainment of nirvana.

Durga Puja *(Sep/Oct)* *(see p285)*.

Burra Din *(25 Dec)*, Kolkata. Otherwise known as Christmas, Burra Din is celebrated by Christians and non-Christians alike. Kolkata's main shopping streets are lit up and little plastic pine trees, decorations and thickly iced fruit cakes are on sale at every local market.

Gaur (Indian bison) roaming the scrubland at Jaldapara

A view of Darjeeling with Mount Kanchendzonga in the background

⑭ Darjeeling

Darjeeling district. 79 km (49 miles) NW of Siliguri. 🚉 107,600. ✈ Bagdogra, 90 km (56 miles) S of city centre, then bus or taxi. 🚌 🚕 ℹ Government Tourist Office, 1, Nehru Road, Chowrasta, (0354) 225 4050.

The name Darjeeling derives from the monastery of Dorje Ling (meaning Place of the Thunderbolt) that once stood on Observatory Hill. The British chose this sunny, west-facing ledge of the Himalayan foothills to build a sanatorium in the mid-19th century. Subsequently, it became Bengal's summer capital and the government would move up here when the plains grew too hot. Today, much of Darjeeling's Raj splendour is still in evidence and contrasts with its Tibetan, Nepali and Bengali character.

This picturesque town squats rather precariously on the hillside, and has three main thoroughfares, **Hill Cart Road**, **Laden Road** and **The Mall**. The Mall is the hub of Darjeeling, leading to the crowded **Chowrasta** (crossroads), lined with bookshops such as the **Oxford Book and Stationery**, which has a wide range of books on India. Other shops sell teas, curios and souvenirs. Vendors offer sets of bright, out-of-focus postcards and guided tours. A rather jolting ten-minute pony ride round the Chowrasta is also available.

Nearby is the **Bhutia Busty Monastery**, built in 1879. The cult text, *The Tibetan Book of the Dead*, was found in the library attached to this shrine, and was translated into English in 1927. The murals in the temple are beautiful – but visitors should ask for permission before entering.

The presence of **Kanchen-dzonga** (8,586 m/28,169 ft), India's highest peak *(see p306)*, dominates the town. Some of the best views of the entire snow-clad range of the Eastern Himalayan peaks can be enjoyed from the windy, prayer flag-lined **Observatory Hill**.

At **North Point**, in the northwest corner of Darjeeling, is India's first passenger ropeway, a cable car connecting Darjeeling to **Singla Bazaar** in the Little Rangeet Valley. The hour-long journey provides a good view of the mountains and the tea gardens that cling to the sides and bottom of the valley.

The **Himalayan Mountain-eering Institute** is to the south of North Point on Birch Hill. Its Mountaineering Museum has a fascinating contour model of the Himalayan peaks, while the Everest Museum *(open Fri–Wed)* gives a history of the various attempts to climb Everest and other Himalayan peaks. The **Himalayan Zoo** is adjacent, and is famous for its high-altitude fauna, including snow leopards, Siberian tigers and red pandas. To the south, the **Lloyds Botanical Gardens** are home to an interesting and varied collection of Himalayan flora – the hundreds of species of orchids in its Orchid House

The carved and painted façade of the Yiga Choeling Monastery

are particularly lovely. The town also has some well-preserved colonial churches. **St Andrew's Church**, west of Observatory Hill, was built in 1843, though the clock tower was added later. **St Columba's Kirk**, near the train station, was built in 1894 and is worth a visit for its magnificent stained-glass windows.

Some of the best preserved examples of Raj-era grandeur in India are Darjeeling's hotels and clubs. Just above Observatory Hill is the rattan- and-chintz-decorated **Windamere Hotel** (see p698). Open fires heat the sedate lounge where, to the accompaniment of a string quartet playing genteel tunes, maids in starched aprons serve sandwiches and Darjeeling tea to visitors and guests.

Ghosts of colonial planters can be sensed at the **Planters' Club**. Old hunting prints hang on the walls and visitors can sit in front of coal fires while bearers, who must have been robust young men in 1947, serve drinks in slow motion.

Bhutia Busty Monastery
Chowrasta. **Open** daily.

Himalayan Mountaineering Institute
Birch Hill Park, entrance on Jawahar Rd West. **Tel** (0354) 225 4083. **Open** Mon-Fri. Extra charges for photography.

Himalayan Zoo
Open Fri–Wed.

Environs

Those interested in Buddhism should visit the **Yiga Choeling Monastery**, 8 km (5 miles) south of Darjeeling, established in 1875 by the Gelugpa (Yellow Hat) sect. The monastery has murals of Buddhist deities and beautiful, if faded, frescoes in the prayer hall. Ask for permission before entering the shrine. The 5 m (15 ft) statue of the Maitreya (Future) Buddha is the highlight at this monastery. **Tiger Hill**, 11 km (7 miles) south of Darjeeling, offers spectacular views of the mighty **Everest** (8,848 m/ 29,029 ft) and other peaks in the Eastern Himalayan Range, including **Makalu** (8,475 m/ 27,805ft) and **Janu** (7,710 m/ 25,295 ft), as they catch the first

Women tea pickers in northern Bengal's tea gardens, around Darjeeling

rays of the sun. Early risers can take a pre-dawn drive to Tiger Hill (about 45 minutes in a jeep).

Senchal Lake, 5 km (3 miles) west of Tiger Hill, is a lovely mountain lake, but tends to be crowded with local tourists. For visitors who come to Darjeeling during the plucking season (April to November), the **Happy Valley Tea Estate**, just beyond the town, is a pleasant tea garden to visit.

Mural, Zangdopelri Fo-Brang Monastery

Yiga Choeling Monastery
Open daily. Donations welcome.

⑮ Kalimpong

Darjeeling district. 51 km (32 miles) E of Darjeeling. 43,000.

Kalimpong was once part of Sikkimese and then Bhutanese territory, before it became part of British India in the 19th century. It was at the head of the ancient trade route to Tibet and still has the feel of a frontier town. Its market sells a mix of the exotic and the mundane, from fern shoots to plastic buckets. Memories of the Raj are recalled by the charming stone cottages and the quaint ambience of the **Himalayan Hotel** (see p699), once a family home.

The **Thongsa Monastery** is Kalimpong's oldest monastery. It was built in 1692, and is a brisk hour's walk above the town. To the south of the town, the **Zong Dog Palri Fo Brang Monastery**, blessed by the Dalai Lama in 1976, has some interesting three-dimensional mandalas.

The town's many nurseries produce a large number of exotic orchids, gladioli, amaryllis lily and cactii. A good one to visit is the **Udai Mani Pradhan Nursery**.

Tenzing Norgay (1914–86)

Tenzing Norgay and Sir Edmund Hillary were the first two men to stand on top of Mount Everest. Tenzing Norgay was born in Tsa-chu, Nepal, into the Sherpa community, and later made his home in Darjeeling. He undertook his first climb as a porter with a British expedition in 1935 and climbed many mountain peaks before his successful one with Hillary in 1953, when he was the sherpa sirdar (head sherpa). Tenzing won the George Medal and later became the head of Darjeeling's Himalayan Mountaineering Institute. Tenzing's life highlighted the contributions, earlier seldom acknowledged, that sherpas make to Himalayan expeditions.

Statue of Tenzing, Himalayan Mountaineering Institute

Stupa at Gangtok's Namgyal Institute of Tibetology

⓰ Gangtok

East Sikkim district. 110 km (68 miles) N of Siliguri. 🏠 29,200. ✈ Bagdogra, 123 km (76 miles) S of city centre, then taxi or bus. 🚃 Siliguri, 107 km (66 miles) S of city centre, then taxi or bus. 🚌 🚹 Sikkim Tourism, MG Marg, (03592) 221 634. 🎭 Losar Festival (Feb/Mar), Enchey Monastery Festival (Aug & Dec). Travel permits: required to enter Sikkim (see p307).

The capital of Sikkim, Gangtok reflects this tiny state's extraordinary ethnic diversity. In the crowded city, which spills precariously down a ridge, Lepchas (the region's original inhabitants) live alongside Tibetans, Bhutias, Nepalis and Indians from the plains. Though now full of modern structures, Gangtok's "Shangrila" aspects can still be experienced in pockets of the city and in its alpine environs.

Until 1975, Sikkim was a kingdom, with the status of an Indian Protectorate. It was ruled by the Chogyals, Buddhists of Tibetan origin, whose dynasty began in the 17th century. However, the British Raj's policies of importing cheap labour from neighbouring Nepal for Sikkim's rice, cardamom and tea plantations drastically changed Sikkim's demography. Soon Nepali Hindus constituted 75 per cent of the state's population. In 1975 the population of Sikkim voted to join the Indian Republic, ending the rule of Palden Thondup Namgyal, the last Chogyal.

At the town's northern edge is the early 20th-century **Enchey Monastery**, whose large prayer hall is full of murals and images, representing the pantheon of Mahayana Buddhist deities (see p145). Enchey's festivals feature spectacular masked dances. At the southern end is the **Namgyal Institute of Tibetology**. Established in 1958, it has a rare collection of medieval Buddhist scriptures, bronzes and embroidered thangkas.

🏯 Enchey Monastery
Open daily. Photography only allowed outside the monastery.

🏛 Namgyal Institute of Tibetology
Open Mon–Sat. **Closed** 2nd Sat & public hols. 🚗 🌐 tibetology.net

Environs
Saramsa Orchidarium, situated 14 km (9 miles) south of Gangtok, displays many of the 450 orchid species found in Sikkim. They flower from April to May, and again in October.

Rumtek Monastery, 24 km (15 miles) southwest of Gangtok, is the headquarters of the Kagyupa (Black Hat) sect, one of the oldest Tibetan Buddhist sects, and the seat of its head, the Gyalwa Karmapa. The 16th Karmapa fled Tibet in 1959 after the Chinese invasion, and built a replica here of his monastery

Guardian of the East at Rumtek

at Tsurphu in Tibet. Rumtek is an impressive complex, its flat-roofed buildings topped with golden finials, and filled with treasures brought from the monastery in Tibet. Especially splendid is the reliquary chorten of the 16th Karmapa, behind the main prayer hall, made of silver and gold and studded with corals, amber and turquoise. Since the 16th Karmapa's death in 1981, however, there have been two claimants to his title (and the monastery's legendary treasures), including one who dramatically escaped from Tibet into India in 2000. Until this dispute is resolved, the armed guards that surround the monastery will remain. Rumtek's main festivals are in February/March and in May/June.

Tsomgo Lake, 34 km (21 miles) northeast of Gangtok, lies at an altitude of 3,780 m (12,402 ft). Visitors to the lake require a special permit from the Sikkim Tourism office in Gangtok. The drive to Tshangu Lake, close to the border with China, is spectacular. The lake is impressive both in spring and summer, when it is surrounded by alpine flowers, and in winter when it's frozen. Visitors can go for rides on the shaggy black yaks that stand docilely on the lake's

🏯 Rumtek Monastery
Tel (03592) 252 329. **Open** daily. Photography only allowed outside the monastery. 🌐 rumtek.org

The richly decorated prayer hall of Rumtek Monastery

Flora and Fauna of the Eastern Himalayas

The Eastern Himalayas and their foothills in northern Bengal, Sikkim and the northeastern states are exceptionally rich in rare flora and fauna. This region receives the brunt of the Southwest Monsoon winds as they rise over the Bay of Bengal and hit the Eastern Himalayas with full force, gradually losing impetus as they travel westward. The resulting high moisture content in the air and soil has helped create a habitat of dense virgin forests, fertile hillsides and lush alpine pastures. Among the plants that can be seen in this region are over 50 species of rhododendron, 500 species of orchid and several varieties of primula and bamboo. Typical fauna of the region include yaks, blue sheep and red pandas. Local folklore adds another – the elusive Yeti or Abominable Snowman, glimpsed by many mountaineers.

The blue poppy (*Meconopsis betonicifolia*), which attracted famous 19th-century plant hunters such as Joseph Hooker to the Eastern Himalayas, grows above the tree-line, in alpine pastures where yaks graze.

The cardiocrinum lily (*Cardiocrinum giganteum*) is highly scented. It grows in temperate forests of oak, maple and rhododendron in Sikkim.

Orchids, such as this beautiful yellow *Dendrobium* species, festoon the forests of Arunachal Pradesh, Meghalaya, Manipur, Nagaland and Sikkim.

Magnolia campbelli with its lovely white blossom, blooms profusely in early spring in the temperate forests of the Darjeeling hills and Sikkim.

The great pied hornbill, (*Buceros bicornis*) with its huge yellow and black beak, is common in the forests of Arunachal Pradesh, where several tribes sport its black and white feathers in their headdress.

The red panda (*Ailurus fulgens*), also called the cat-bear, is a bright chestnut colour with white-rimmed ears and a bushy tail. One of its favourite foods is dwarf bamboo, which grows in the temperate forests of Arunachal Pradesh and Sikkim. The red panda is the state animal of Sikkim.

The yak is greatly prized in Sikkim. It serves as a pack animal, and also provides milk, meat and wool from its shaggy coat.

⓱ A Tour of Northern Sikkim

Northern Sikkim is an area of unspoilt natural beauty, framed by snowcapped Himalayan peaks. This tour, following the valley of the Teesta river, goes past tranquil monasteries and villages, through forests of rhododendron, to Yumthang where yaks graze in meadows filled with alpine flowers. Along the way there are charming rural markets, and superb views of the world's third highest peak, Mount Kanchendzonga.

Tips for Drivers

Length: 149 km (93 miles).
Stopping-off points: The tour can be done in 2–3 days. Phodong, Mangan-Singhik and Lachung are stopping-off points.
Permits: Visitors require special permits for this region, issued by the Department of Tourism in Gangtok, (03592) 221 634. Travel is permitted in groups of two or more persons. For more details, see p307.

⑥ **Yumthang** The Lachung-Yumthang road crosses rhododendron forests, which bloom between April and June. Yumthang, at 3,597 m (11,800 ft), also has hot sulphur springs.

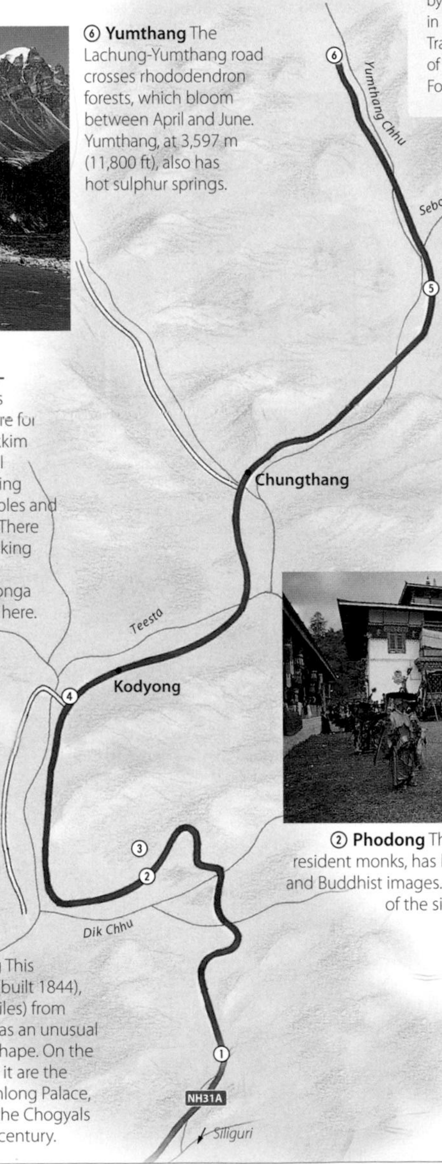

⑤ **Lachung** Just 15 km (9 miles) from Tibet, with which it used to trade before 1959, Lachung is a pretty village on both banks of the Lachung river.

④ **Mangan-Singhik** This market centre for northern Sikkim attracts local villagers selling oranges, apples and cardamom. There are breathtaking views of the Kanchendzonga Range from here.

Chungthang

Key

▬ Tour route
▬ National highway
═ Minor road

Teesta

Kodyong

② **Phodong** This serene monastery, with 260 resident monks, has beautiful murals, woodcarving and Buddhist images. It was built in 1740 and is one of the six major monasteries in Sikkim.

0 kilometres   5
0 miles   5

③ **Labrang** This monastery (built 1844), 4 km (2.5 miles) from Phodong, has an unusual octagonal shape. On the track below it are the ruins of Tumlong Palace, the seat of the Chogyals in the 19th century.

Dik Chhu

① **Gangtok** Built on a high ridge above the Ranikhola river, Gangtok (see p302) is a bustling town, at an altitude of 1,780 m (5,840 ft).

NH31A

↓ Siliguri

⓲ Pelling

West Sikkim district. 143 km (89 miles) W of Gangtok. 🚌 Gezing, 9 km (6 miles) S of city centre, then local bus or taxi. 🛈 Pelling Information Centre, 943 463 0876 (mobile); Gangtok Information Centre, (03592) 221 634. 📅 Pemayangtse Festival (Feb/Mar). Travel permits: required (see p307).

Situated on a ridge, at an altitude of 1,859 m (6,100 ft), with excellent views of the peaks and glaciers of the Kanchendzonga Range, Pelling is a fast growing town. It is a convenient base from which to explore western Sikkim and embark on treks (see pp306–307). This is the state's most beautiful and unspoilt region, with expanses of forest, green river valleys, superb trekking trails, and Sikkim's oldest monasteries. Pelling is a day's drive from Gangtok, and is accessible from Darjeeling (72 km/45 miles south).

Detail of a door, Pemayangtse

The main attraction here is the monastic complex of **Pemayangtse**, built in 1705, on a ridge a half-hour's walk from the town. Surrounded by picturesque monks' quarters and outhouses, the austere three-storeyed main monastery is a treasure house of beautiful *thangkas*, murals and images, with a breathtakingly intricate model of Zangdopelri, the seven-storeyed celestial home of Guru Padmasambhava (see p143), on the top floor. Pemayangtse has an annual festival, with spectacular masked dances. Sikkim's second oldest monastery, **Sangachoeling** (built in 1697),

is a steep 40-minute hike through thick forests above Pemayangtse. It has exquisite murals. The ruins of Sikkim's 17th-century capital, built by the second Chogyal (see p302), are at **Rabdentse**, 3 km (2 miles) south of Pelling.

Environs
Khecheopalri Lake, 25 km (16 miles) north of Pelling, is an enchanting spot that is sacred to both Buddhists and Hindus, who come here to make a wish. Seen from above, the lake is shaped like the footprint of Buddha. Though surrounded by a forest, it does not have a single leaf floating on its surface, and according to local belief, a holy bird swoops down and removes each leaf as it falls on the water.

⓳ Yuksam

West Sikkim district. 162 km (101 miles) W of Gangtok. 🚌 🛈 Pelling Information Centre, 943 463 0876 (mobile); Gangtok Information Centre, (03592) 221 634. Travel permits: required (see p307).

Yuksam was the first capital of Sikkim, where the first Chogyal of Sikkim was crowned in 1641 by three learned lamas. A stone throne and some *chortens* mark this historic spot. Below it is **Kathok Lake**. **Dubdi Monastery**, built in 1701, with its exquisite Buddhist images and meditation cave, is a steep half-hour climb above. Yuksam is the starting point for the trek to Dzongri (see p306).

Mani stones being carved at Tashiding Monastery

⓴ Tashiding Monastery

West Sikkim district. 145 km (90 miles) W of Gangtok. **Open** daily. 📅 Bumchu Festival (Feb/Mar). Travel permits: required (see p307).

Built in 1716, Tashiding Monastery stands on the summit of a heart-shaped hill, where Guru Padmasambhava is said to have shot an arrow and then meditated on the spot where it fell. Surrounded by *chortens*, *mani* stones, water-driven prayer wheels, and the Ratong and Rangeet rivers, with Mount Kanchendzonga looming behind the hill, this is a magical spot. During the annual Bumchu Festival it attracts large crowds from all over Sikkim.

During this festival, sacred water, said to have been put into a sealed jar by a 17th-century Buddhist saint, is mixed with river water and distributed as a powerful blessing to devotees. Miraculously, the supply of sacred water never runs dry, and each year when the jar is unsealed, oracle priests can predict the future of Sikkim from the water level in it – too much or too little water augurs ill for Sikkim's peace and prosperity. Tashiding also has the **Thongwa Rangdol Chorten**, a mere glimpse of which is supposed to wipe away all sins. The main temple, rebuilt in 1987, has large images of the Buddha and the Bodhisattvas.

Prayer flags fluttering near Yuksam, the first capital of Sikkim

Trekking in West Bengal & Sikkim

The eastern Himalayas, spanning Tibet, Nepal, West Bengal and Sikkim, have some of the world's highest peaks such as Kanchendzonga, Everest, Lhotse and Makalu, and offer a variety of trekking options amidst lush hills bursting with orchids and rhododendron blossoms. The region is also alive with legends of the Abominable Snowman or Yeti, a huge, ape-like creature, who allegedly lives above the snowline. West Bengal's most popular trails are centred around the Singalila Ridge near Darjeeling, with views of Nepal's great massifs, while most of Sikkim's trails are dominated by the mighty Kanchendzonga. The best seasons are between October and November, and February and May.

Locator Map

▮ Area shown below

The Singalila Ridge
The Singalila Ridge, which begins near Darjeeling and extends to Kanchendzonga, has several trails. The Sandakphu-Phalut route beginning at Manebhajan has spectacular views of Everest, Lhotse, Makalu and Kanchendzonga, with plenty of lodges along the way. The 60-km (37-mile) path ends at the roadhead at Rimbik.
Duration: 6 days
Altitude: 3,636 m (11,929 ft)
Level of difficulty: Moderate

0 kilometres   5
0 miles   5

Mount Kanchendzonga

Mount Kanchendzonga, the third highest peak in the world at 8,598 m (28,209 ft), dominates the skyline of Sikkim and West Bengal's Darjeeling district. Its name means "Five Treasures of the Snows", and the Sikkimese believe that the five summits of the Kanchendzonga Range conceal four treasures – gold and gems, grain, silver and holy scriptures. This magnificent mountain is revered as the guardian deity of Sikkim and is worshipped all over the state during the Pang Lhabsol festival, which takes place in the seventh month of the Tibetan calendar (between August and September). Prayers, rituals and masked dances are performed at monasteries – with the massif represented by a red mask crowned with skulls – to ensure that the land is protected in the year to come. Such is the awe in which the Sikkimese hold the peak that in 1999, an Austrian expedition to scale it was cancelled after widespread public protest that this would dishonour the deity and bring catastrophe to Sikkim.

A panoramic view of Mount Kanchendzonga from Dzongri Peak

The Dzongri Trail
One of Sikkim's most popular treks, the trail from Pemayangtse to Dzongri covers 35 km (22 miles) one way. It leads past Yuksam and Tsokha through forests of rhododendron to Dzongri, with clear views of Kanchendzonga. The return to Yuksam takes two days.
Duration: 6–7 days
Altitude: 4,030 m (13,222 ft)
Level of difficulty: Moderate to tough

Rafting and Kayaking
Rafting is very popular on the Teesta and Rangeet rivers, and is possible between October and November. Kayaks can be hired from the West Bengal Tourism office in Darjeeling.

Key

- – – The Singalila Ridge
- – – Kurseong to Mirik
- – – The Dzongri Trail
- ═══ National highway
- ▬▬▬ Major road
- ═══ Minor road
- - - - State border

Practical Tips

Be prepared: Acclimatization is essential for altitudes over 3,000 m (9,843 ft). See p743 for information on altitude sickness. Guides and porters can be hired in Gangtok and Darjeeling. The region is hit hard by the monsoon and trekking between early June and late September is not advisable. For more details on trekking, see p727.

On the trek: Sikkim's trekking trails have suffered deforestation and littering, so ensure that all litter is carried back with you. Drink plenty of water and carry a first aid kit and cooking fuel. Never burn wood, which is a scarce resource. Put out all fires properly, leaving no burning embers. Some trails have leeches (see p743), so carry salt which, when sprinkled on a leech, causes it to fall off.

Permits: Foreign visitors require travel permits for Sikkim, issued for a 15-day period from the District Magistrate's Office in Darjeeling, (0354) 225 4233, or the Sikkim Tourism offices in Delhi, (011) 2611 5346, Kolkata, (033) 2281 5328, and Siliguri, (0353) 221 6502. A 14-day extension is permitted, issued by the Department of Tourism in Gangtok, (03592) 221 634, who also issue special permits for restricted areas such as Dzongri, Yumthang and Tsomgo Lake. Travel to these areas is permitted in groups of two or more persons. Trekking permits for Sikkim are available from the Department of Tourism in Gangtok, and Sikkim Tourism in Delhi. All treks must be arranged by a registered agency. For general information, see p734

Equipment hire & operators: Himalayan Adventures in Darjeeling, (0354) 225 4004, and Sikkim Trekking and Tours in Gangtok, (03592) 203 638, are reputed agencies. For more details, see p731.

Kurseong to Mirik
A great introduction to the West Bengal hills, this gentle 18-km (11-mile) hike goes past numerous villages and local tea estates.
Duration: 1 day
Altitude: 1,767 m (5,797 ft)
Level of difficulty: Easy

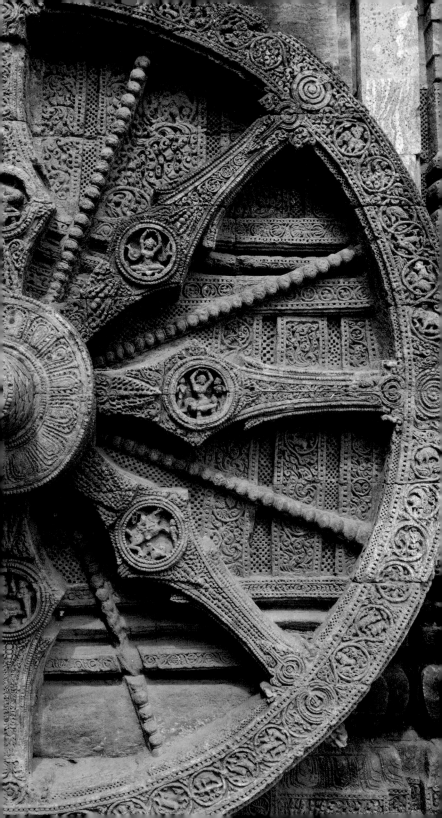

ODISHA

Bounded on the west by the thickly forested hills of the Eastern
Ghats, and on the east by nearly 500 km (311 miles) of coastline
on the Bay of Bengal, Orissa, also known as Odisha, covers an
area of 156,000 sq km (60,232 sq miles). Its most famous sights are
clustered together in a compact triangle on the eastern coast, in
the fertile delta of its major river, the Mahanadi. These include the
magnificent 13th-century Sun Temple at Konark, a UNESCO World Heritage
Site, and other outstanding temples at Bhubaneswar and Puri. To recover from
sightseeing fatigue, there are beaches within easy reach at Puri, Konark and
Gopalpur-on-Sea, fringed by coconut groves and fishing villages. Just south of this
triangle is Chilika Lake, Asia's largest lagoon and a paradise for birdwatchers. The
hinterland of the coast is lush with green paddy fields, dotted with ancient Buddhist
ruins and tranquil hamlets, where Odisha's beautiful traditional crafts flourish. The
spectacular, unspoilt landscape of northern Odisha includes Simlipal National Park,
with its wealth of wildlife, and settlements of tribal people who form nearly a
quarter of Odisha's population of 35 million.

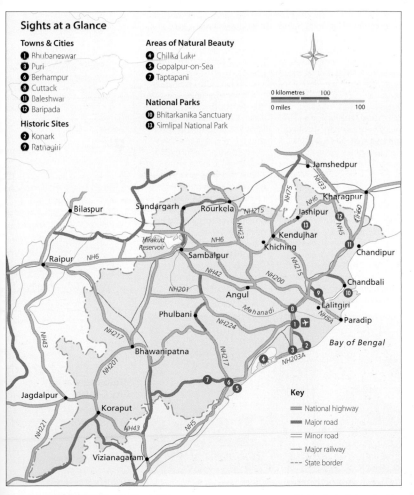

Sights at a Glance

Towns & Cities
1 Bhubaneswar
3 Puri
6 Berhampur
8 Cuttack
11 Baleshwar
12 Baripada

Historic Sites
2 Konark
9 Ratnagiri

Areas of Natural Beauty
4 Chilika Lake
5 Gopalpur-on-Sea
7 Taptapani

National Parks
10 Bhitarkanika Sanctuary
13 Simlipal National Park

0 kilometres   100
0 miles   100

Jamshedpur
Bilaspur
Sundargarh
Rourkela
NH75
NH6
Kharagpur
Jashipur
NH215
NH23
NH6
Kendujhar
Khiching
NH5
Chandipur
Hirakud Reservoir
Sambalpur
NH6
Raipur
NH42
NH200
NH215
Chandbali
Angul
NH201
Mahanadi
Lalitgiri
NH5A
Phulbani
NH224
Paradip
NH43
NH217
Bhawanipatna
NH217
Bay of Bengal
Jagdalpur
NH201
Koraput
NH43
NH5
NH221
NH203A
Vizianagaram

Key
▬ National highway
▬ Major road
═ Minor road
— Major railway
--- State border

◄ Ancient carved wheel at the Konark Sun Temple, Odisha

For keys to symbols *see back flap*

❶ Bhubaneshwar

The capital of Odisha, Bhubaneswar is famous for its superb Hindu temples. Most of these are in the older, southern part of the city, while the new town, with its modern administrative buildings and wide tree-lined avenues, is in the north. The temples date from the 7th to the 13th centuries, a period which saw the waning of Buddhism and a revival of Hinduism under the successive dynasties that ruled Odisha: the Shailodbhavas and Bhauma Karas in the 7th–8th centuries; the Somavamshis in the 9th–11th centuries; and the Eastern Gangas in the 12th–13th centuries.

Devotees bathing in the sacred waters of Bindusagar

Exploring the temples

More than 400 temples remain of the 7,000 that are said to have once embellished Bhubaneswar, earning it the title, the "City of Temples". A distinctive version of the North Indian style of temple architecture evolved in Odisha over the centuries *(see p25)*, under the patronage of the different dynasties. As the power and prosperity of these dynasties grew, the temples became bigger and more elaborate. Most of the temples have two main components – a convex curvilinear spire locally known as the *deul* (elsewhere called the *shikhara*), which towers over the inner sanctum where the deity's image is kept; and an entrance porch or assembly hall called the *jagamohan,* with a stepped pyramidal roof. Some of the bigger temples have two or three of these porches. Several smaller shrines and bathing tanks often surround the main temple, which is enclosed in a walled compound.

The magnificent 11th-century **Lingaraj Temple** represents the high point of the Orissan style,

where both sculpture and architecture have evolved in perfect harmony. Its grandeur lies in its towering 54-m (177-ft) high *deul* (spire) with dramatic vertical ribs, and in the consummate artistry with which each sculpture and embellishment is executed. The female figures, animals, and friezes of ceremonial processions are full of grace and exuberance. The temple's large courtyard has more than 100 smaller shrines. The main deity here is Shiva as Tribhuvaneswar ("Lord of the Three Worlds"), from which the city takes its name. The intriguing image of a rampant lion springing on a crouching elephant is a powerful motif in this temple, as in many others in Odisha, and some scholars believe it is a royal emblem. Non-Hindus cannot enter the Lingaraj Temple, but can view it from a platform near its northern gateway. The other temples are open to visitors.

North of the temple is the large **Bindusagar Tank** with a pavilion in the middle. It is believed to contain water from every sacred river in India. The main deity of the Lingaraj

Temple is brought here for a ritual bath *(see p313)* every year. The 8th-century **Vaital Deul Temple**, to the west of

Bhubaneswar City Centre

① Lingaraj Temple
② Bindusagar Tank
③ Vaital Deul Temple
④ Parasurameshwar Temple
⑤ Mukteshwar Temple
⑥ Rajarani Temple
⑦ Odisha State Museum

The impressive spire of the 11th-century Lingaraj Temple

Bindusagar, is an unusual temple with eerie interior carvings. These indicate that it was probably used for macabre tantric rites, including human sacrifice. The main deity here is a terrifying, eight-armed Chamunda (a Tantric form of Durga), with a garland of skulls, seated on a corpse, flanked by a jackal and an owl.

Built in the 7th-century, the **Parasurameshwar Temple**, on the road to Puri, is the best preserved and most lavishly sculpted of the earliest group of temples. The square-towered shrine has a rectangular *jagamohan* adjoining it, decorated with wonderfully animated bands of dancers and musicians on its west window. The main entrance to the *jagamohan* also has a fine carving of domestic

elephants capturing wild ones, to the left of the lintel. Set into the outer walls of the shrine are images of deities, among them a superb potbellied Ganesha, and his brother Karttikeya sitting on his vehicle, the peacock.

The nearby 10th-century **Mukteshwar Temple**, one of the jewels of Orissan temple architecture, is notable for its exquisite sculptures and elegant proportions. Its beautiful *torana* (gateway) is decorated with langorously reclining female figures. The *jagamohan* is illuminated by diamond-shaped latticed windows on the north and south walls, their outermost frames depicting enchanting scenes of frolicking monkeys. A unique feature of the *jagamohan* is the decorated ceiling, carved into a lotus with eight petals. The sculptures of female figures in this temple are remarkable for their expressive faces, with hairstyles and jewellery shown in exquisite detail. The octagonal wall surrounding the temple has a number of niches, each containing a wheel, a lotus medallion or a delicate scroll. Many of the sculptures here also depict scenes from the famous *Panchatantra* tales.

Set amidst paddy fields, just off the main road, is the 11th-century **Rajarani Temple**. It

Guardian figures, Rajarani Temple

has a particularly striking spire decorated with miniature replicas of itself, rising in continuous tiers around the tower. This temple is renowned for its fine sculptures of *dikpals* (the guardians of the eight cardinal directions) perched on lotus flowers. Of these, Agni, the God of Fire on a ram, and Varuna, God of the Oceans seated on a crocodile, are particularly impressive. Also remarkable are the tall and slender female figures, carved in high relief on the walls of the temple.

🏛 Odisha State Museum

BJB Nagar. **Open** Tue–Sun. **Closed** public hols. 🛇

The highlight of this interesting museum is its rich collection of Buddhist and Jain sculptures, coins, and painted palm-leaf manuscripts. There are also collections of tribal art, traditional jewellery and musical instruments.

Environs

The **Nandan Kanan Zoo** and botanical gardens, 20 km (12 miles) north of Bhubaneswar, is famous for its white tigers *(see p243)*. The zoo, surrounded by a thick forest, enables the animals to live in natural surroundings. Panthers and gharials *(Gavialis gangeticus)* have been successfully bred in captivity here.

⚡ Nandan Kanan Zoo

Open Tue–Sun. 🛇
🖵 ♿

VISITORS' CHECKLIST

Practical Information
Bhubaneswar district. 480 km (298 miles) S of Kolkata.
🚇 647,350. ℹ Odisha Tourism, BJB Nagar, (0674) 243 2177.
🎏 Tribal Mela (Jan), Ashokashtami (Mar/Apr).

Transport
✈ 4 km (2.5 miles) NW of city centre. 🚊 🚌

CUTTACK, Nandan Kanan Zoo

🚉 Railway Station 1km (0.6 mile)

PURI CUTTACK RD

KAUPANI CUTTACK RD

KALPANA SQUARE

KALPANA RD

ℹ

⑦ Odisha State Museum

BJB NAGAR FC

LEWIS ROAD

BJB NAGAR RD

TANKAPANI RD

Mukteshwar Temple
ar Park
eshwar

⑥ Rajarani Temple

Daya River

LEWIS ROAD

ROAD

0 metres 500
0 yards 500

Chausath Yogini Temple, PURI, KONARAK, DHAULI & PIPLI

The beautifully sculpted *torana* of Mukteshwar Temple

Exploring Bhubaneswar's Surroundings

Many sites of historical and architectural significance lie close to Bhubaneswar. They include Jain monastic caves, Hindu temples, Buddhist stupas and ancient rock inscriptions, dotting the lush green landscape around the city. Dating from the 3rd century BC (when the area was part of the great kingdom of Kalinga) to the 13th century AD, these sites bear witness to the region's political and religious importance for a continuous period of over 1,000 years.

Bagh Gumpha at Udaigiri, shaped like the open mouth of a tiger

🏛 Udaigiri and Khandagiri Caves

7 km (5 miles) W of Bhubaneswar. **Open** daily. 🏛 📷 Sadhu Convention (Jan).

The twin hills of Udaigiri ("Sunrise Hill") and Khandagiri ("Broken Hill") were honeycombed to make retreats for Jain monks in the 1st century BC. Located just off the highway that runs from Bhubaneswar to Kolkata, the hills rise suddenly from the flat surrounding plains, and are separated from each other by the highway.

Carvings at Udaigiri Caves

As one approaches from Bhubaneswar, **Udaigiri** is the hill on the right, and is best explored first as it has the more interesting caves. The most impressive of its 18 caves is the double-storeyed **Rani Gumpha** or "Queen's Cave" (Cave 1), which has lavishly sculpted friezes of women dancing and playing music, kings and queens in courtly splendour, elephants, monkeys and foliage. The sculpture is remarkable

for its expressive animation, and has been compared with the famous sculpted gateways at Sanchi (see pp248–9).

Other notable caves are **Chhota Hathi Gumpha** or "Small Elephant Cave" (Cave 3), with six superb elephants flanking its entrance; **Ganesh Gumpha** (Cave 10) whose sculptures include an intriguing battle scene with a woman riding an elephant while soldiers in kilts chase her, and **Bagh Gumpha** or "Tiger Cave" (Cave 12), its front ingeniously shaped

like a tiger's head with the mouth open. The most significant cave historically is **Hathi Gumpha** or "Elephant Cave" (Cave 14). On the rock above its entrance is an inscription from the 1st century BC. It records that the caves were carved by Kharavela, third king of the powerful Chedi dynasty, whose conquests included large parts of Bihar, the Deccan and South India. The inscription also states that King Kharavela rebuilt his capital, Kalinganagar, after it was destroyed by a cyclone. Even today, Odisha remains vulnerable to cyclones, the last one having devastated the state in October 1999. On the summit of Udaigiri stands a ruined apsidal structure, probably used as a place of worship by the monks.

Across the highway, on **Khandagiri**, are 15 caves with carvings of sacred Jain symbols. The **Ananta Cave** (Cave 3), with its figures of twin serpents on the arches above the doorways, is the most important and has superb ornamentation and lively friezes, including one of boys chasing lions, bulls and other animals. Another enchanting carving in this cave shows the goddess Lakshmi in a lotus pool, being bathed with water from pitchers held by two elephants (see p28). Three of the caves – numbers 5, 8 and 9 – have impressive carved figures of the Jain tirthankaras in high relief.

Unlike Buddhist caves such as those at Ajanta (see p483) and Ellora (see p482), most of the Udaigiri and Khandagiri caves are so low that it is impossible

Khandagiri, the site of a Jain monastery with rock-cut chambers

Hirapur's Chausath Yogini Temple, open to the sky

to stand upright in them. This was in keeping with the self-mortification and asceticism that Jain monks were expected to practise. The site still attracts sadhus, who gather here every year in January to meditate in the caves. A lively fair springs up below the hills to entertain the crowds that gather to seek the sadhus' blessings.

🏛 Dhauli
8 km (5 miles) S of Bhubaneswar.
A stark white Buddhist stupa in the middle of serene green paddy fields on the banks of the Daya river marks the site of the bloody battle of Kalinga, fought by one of India's greatest rulers, the Mauryan emperor Ashoka (see p46) in 260 BC. He won the war but the carnage and misery it inflicted on the people filled the emperor with remorse and brought about a dramatic change of heart. After this battle, he gave up digvijaya (military conquest) for dharmavijaya (spiritual conquest), embraced Buddhism, and publicized his new maxims in rock edicts, installed in different parts of his empire. One of these is here, at the base of Dhauli Hill, in which the emperor declares, "All men are my children", and enjoins his officials to ensure impartiality, non-violence, justice and compassion in administration. The top of the rock is sculpted into an imposing elephant's head, symbolizing the Buddhist dharma. This is one of the earliest sculptures found in the subcontinent. The huge white Shanti Stupa ("Peace Pagoda") at the top of the hill was built by Japanese Buddhists in the early 1970s.

🏛 Chausath Yogini Temple
13 km (8 miles) SE of Bhubaneswar.
This 9th-century, circular temple is dedicated to the chausath yoginis or 64 manifestations of the goddess Shakti, who symbolizes female creative energy. All the images, each about 0.6 m (2 ft) tall and carved out of black chlorite stone, are placed in niches in the inner enclosure. The presiding deity, a graceful 10-armed yogini, is in the 31st niche. The temple is located in the pretty village of Hirapur.

Garden umbrella from Pipli, with appliqué-work

Environs
Pipli, 20 km (12 miles) south of Bhubaneswar, on the highway to Puri, is a village of artisans famous for their colourful appliqué-work fabrics. The craft originated to serve temples, providing intricately stitched awnings and covers for deities, and hangings in vivid hues for festival days. Today, garden umbrellas, cushion covers, wall hangings and bags are made in Pipli using the same techniques, in which cloth is cut into bird, flower, animal and other decorative shapes, and stitched on to fabric of a contrasting colour. Shops selling these line both sides of the highway as it passes through Pipli, enveloping it in a blaze of colour.

Festivals of Odisha
Tribal Mela (Jan), Bhubaneswar. Odisha's large and varied tribal population exhibit their dances, music, arts and crafts at this colourful week-long festival

Makar Mela (14 Jan), Chilika Lake. Pilgrims bring offerings to a cave and temple devoted to the goddess Kali on a rocky island called Kalijai in Chilika Lake.

Magha Saptami Chandrabaga Mela (Jan/Feb), Konark. To honour Surya, the Sun God, pilgrims come for a purifying dip in the sea before they worship at the temple. A colourful fair is held, with stalls selling food and gifts.

Ashokashtami (Mar/Apr), Bhubaneswar. The image of Shiva, the main deity of the Lingaraj Temple, is taken in procession in a chariot for a ritual bath in the sacred Bindusagar Tank.

Chaitra Parba (Apr), Baripada. This spring festival is marked by displays of the spectacular martial dance known as Mayurbhanj Chhau.

Rath Yatra (Jun/Jul), Puri (see p317).

Konark Dance Festival (1–5 Dec), Konark. Classical dancers perform on an open air stage near the Sun Temple during this five-day festival.

A dancer performing during Rath Yatra celebrations

❷ Konark: The Sun Temple

One of India's great architectural marvels, this temple to the Sun God, Surya, was conceived as a gigantic chariot, with 12 pairs of wheels to carry the Sun God on his daily journey across the sky. Built in the 13th century by King Narasimhadeva of the Eastern Ganga dynasty *(see p48)*, the temple is also remarkable for its superb sculptures. Gods and demons, kings and peasants, elephants and horses jostle for space on its walls with dozens of erotic couples. Konark is now a UNESCO World Heritage Site.

Maiden with Bird
Statues of graceful maidens in a variety of poses are carved on the temple's façades.

★ **Surya**
The majestic image of the Sun God stands on a chariot, flanked by his wives, and other deities.

KEY

① **Court Scene**, is an enchanting relief of the king being presented with a giraffe. This indicates the existence of maritime trade between Odisha's Eastern Ganga kings and Africa.

② **Amalaka**

③ **The three-tiered roof** is shaped like a stepped pyramid and crowned with a round fluted stone called an *amalaka*. The terraces between each tier are covered with sculptures.

★ **Wheels of the Chariot**
The 12 pairs of exquisitely carved wheels represent the months in a year, while the eight large spokes mark the division of the day into three-hour sections. The seven horses pulling the chariot represent the days of the week.

The Konark Sun Temple, on the shores of the Bay of Bengal

The Cymbal Player
This sculpture is in a row of wonderfully
animated dancers, musicians and drummers
on the terrace of the pyramidal roof.

Medallion
Deities and dancers decorate
the medallions on the hub and
the spokes of the wheels.

Erotic Sculpture
A demure snake
goddess provides
a contrast to the
amorous couple
beside her. The
erotic sculptures
at Konark are
a celebration of
the joys of life.

Bhogmandir

Main entrance

Bhogmandir
The ruined "Hall of Offerings"
has gigantic rampant lions on
cowering elephants.

Exploring Konark

The Sun Temple at Konark originally had a towering *deul* (spire), 70 m (230 ft) high, over its main sanctuary. Visible far out at sea, the temple was an important navigational aid for European sailors headed for Calcutta (Kolkata), who called it the Black Pagoda. Over time, the temple's easily weathered khondalite stone was progressively corroded by seawinds and sand, and by the 19th century the great tower had completely collapsed. Only its base still remains. The temple's Bhogmandir or "Hall of Offerings", is now roofless, but its plinth and pillars remain, carved with figures of dancers, depicting the poses still used in classical Odissi dance *(see p32)*.

The chariot-shaped *jagamohan* or assembly hall was buried for nearly two centuries under drifting sand. It was only unearthed and restored by the Archaeological Survey of India (ASI) in the early 20th century. Its many remarkable sculptures include no less than 1,700 elephants in animated motion, carved on the plinth; and several enchanting *alasa kanyas* (maidens at leisure), playing with a pet bird, holding a mirror, or leaning against a doorway.

Three life-size images of the Sun God, Surya, made of contrasting coloured chlorite stone, are positioned so that the sun's rays fall on their faces, turn by turn, at dawn, noon and sunset.

In the northeast corner of the compound is the **Shrine of the Nine Planets**, a large stone slab carved with the deities of the nine planets. Colossal sculptures of war horses and elephants stand at the north and south. Near the compound is the **Archaeological Museum** with fine sculptures recovered from the site. The beach is 3 km (2 miles) from the temple, but is unsafe for swimming because of treacherous undercurrents.

Puri's Jagannath Temple, topped with Vishnu's wheel and flag

❾ Puri

Puri district. 62 km (39 miles) S of Bhubaneswar. 🚉 157,650. 🚌 🚐 ℹ️ Odisha Tourism, Station Rd, (06752) 222 740/222 562. 🛒 daily. 🎪 Rath Yatra (Jun/Jul). Jagannath Temple: **Open** daily. **Closed** to non-Hindus.

Hand-painted *ganjifa* playing card from Puri

One of India's most important pilgrimage centres, this seaside town is dominated by the towering Jagannath Temple. Early European sailors, for whom its 65-m (213-ft) high spire was an important landmark, called it the White Pagoda, to differentiate it from Konark's Sun Temple which they named Black Pagoda.

The **Jagannath Temple** was built in the 12th century by King Anantavarman of the Eastern Ganga dynasty *(see p48)*.

Surrounded by a 6-m (20-ft) high wall, its main gate is guarded by a pair of brightly painted stone lions. Non-Hindus are not allowed in, but can get a good view of the complex, with its multitude of small shrines and its courtyard thronged with pilgrims, from the roof of the Raghunandan Library across the street from the main gate.

The temple is similar in design to the Lingaraj Temple in Bhubaneswar *(see p310)*, with three smaller shrines adjoining its tall sanctuary tower. The elegant stone column near the entrance, topped with the figure of Arun, charioteer of the Sun God, was brought here from the Sun Temple at Konark in the 18th century.

From the temple, Puri's main street, **Bada Danda**, runs through the town, crammed with pilgrims' rest houses and shops selling food, religious souvenirs and handicrafts. Local specialities are the colourful *pattachitra* paintings and round *ganjifa* playing cards painted with religious themes.

Puri's beach is its other attraction, though not always safe for swimming because of dangerous undercurrents. The long beach front is crowded with stalls and groups of pilgrims along Marine Parade. Sunbathers and swimmers should therefore head to the eastern end, which is cleaner and more secluded, or to the beaches attached to the better hotels. Local fishermen wearing conical hats serve as lifeguards on the beach, and take visitors out to sea in their boats to watch the sunsets.

A family picnic on Puri Beach

The Jagannath Cult

A unique cult has grown around Jagannath (Lord of the Universe), an incarnation of Vishnu. At Puri's Jagannath Temple, 6,000 resident priests perform the elaborate daily rituals of bathing, dressing and worshipping the image of Jagannath, together with those of his brother Balbhadra and sister Subhadra. Sumptuous meals are offered to the three deities five times a day, prepared daily by 400 temple cooks. During the spectacular Rath Yatra (chariot festival) in June/July, the deities are taken out in a procession in mammoth wooden chariots, pulled by thousands of devotees. The word juggernaut (large truck) is derived from the size and unstoppable force of Lord Jagannath's chariot.

Temple offerings are sold at numerous stalls at the gates of the temple.

Devotees try to spend at least three days paying obeisance to Jagannath.

Balbhadra has a white face and rides in a chariot with 14 wheels and four horses.

Subhadra has a yellow face and rides in a red chariot.

Puri cityscape

Jagannath's chariot is 1,370 m (4,495 ft) tall and has 16 wheels.

Jagannath Temple

Policeman

Musicians and drummers

Temple priests

Pattachitra Painting of the Rath Yatra

The Rath Yatra marks Lord Jagannath's annual journey to his birthplace, the Gundicha Temple, just over 2 km (1.3 miles) away. Over 200,000 people, including priests pilgrims, musicians and drummers, join the procession.

Temple dancers, young boys known as *gotipuas*, perform the classical Odissi dance *(see p32)* before the deities every night. They are accompanied by musicians singing verses from the *Gita Govinda*, a 12th-century epic poem *(see p296)*.

Balbhadra, Subhadra and Jagannath, the three deities, are believed to be of tribal origin, but have been absorbed into the Hindu pantheon. They have huge, all-seeing eyes, and outstretched arms to protect and bless all mankind.

A view of Chilika Lake, a haven for water birds and dolphins

❹ Chilika Lake

Puri, Ganjam & Khordha districts. 50 km (31 miles) SW of Puri. 🚉 Balugaon, then taxi or bus. 🚌 Balugaon & Satpada. 🛈 Odisha Tourism, Barkul, (06756) 211 078. 🎉 Makar Mela (Jan). Satpada and Nalabana Islands: 🚤 hired from Barkul, Balugaon, Satpada & Rambha.

A great, shallow lagoon covering 1,100 sq km (425 sq miles), Chilika is separated from the Bay of Bengal by a sandy ridge, with just a narrow channel connecting it to the sea. Believed to be the largest brackish water lake in Asia, Chilika is recognized as one of the most important wetlands in the world because of the phenomenal variety of aquatic and birdlife it supports. From November to February, the lake and its reed islands teem with nesting birds, including several winter migrants, such as the golden plover, the flamingo, the purple moorhen and the osprey. A major attraction at Chilika are dolphins, which are often spotted off **Satpada Island**, located at the confluence of the lake and the sea.

Nalabana Island, at the core of the lake, is the best place for birdwatching. Odisha Tourism arranges boat trips to both the islands. **Kalijai Temple**, built on a small rocky island, is a pilgrimage spot which attracts festive crowds during the Makar Mela in January. The lake also supports the local people who earn their living from Chilika's prawns, crabs and fish.

❺ Gopalpur-on-Sea

Ganjam district. 172 km (107 miles) SW of Bhubaneswar. 🚉 Berhampur 18 km (11 miles) E of town centre, then taxi or bus. 🚌 🛈 Odisha Tourism, Berhampur Railway Station, (0680) 224 3931.

This quiet seaside town was, in ancient times, a great seaport for Odisha's maritime trade with Indonesia (see p322). The British later developed it as a beach resort and it now has a sleepy charm, except during the Durga Puja holidays (see p285) in October, when it swarms with tourists from Bengal. Swimming in the sea is not safe because of treacherous undercurrents. But the beach, lined with bungalows and dotted with casuarina groves, is a good place to spend the day, watching the fishing boats and the sunset.

❻ Berhampur

Ganjam district. 170 km (106 miles) SW of Bhubaneswar. 🚉 🚌 🛈 Odisha Tourism, Railway Station, (0680) 228 0226.

The main commercial centre in southern Odisha, Berhampur is famous for its beautiful handwoven ikat silk, available in its bustling bazaar where weavers sit at their looms. The railhead for the seaside town of Gopalpur-on-Sea, Berhampur is also a convenient base for visiting **Jaugarh**, 35 km (22 miles) north of the city. Jaugarh has a 3rd-century BC rock edict erected by the Emperor Ashoka following the Battle of Kalinga, after which he had a change

Painted panel from the 17th-century temple at Buguda

Floral offering to a goddess of fertility at Taptapani's hot springs

of heart. The edict is similar to the one at Dhauli (see p313), in which Ashoka declares "All men are my children" and spells out his ethical code. A short distance away, at **Buguda**, is the Biramchinarayan Temple, built in the 17th century, with beautiful murals depicting scenes from the Ramayana.

❼ Taptapani

Ganjam district. 51 km (32 miles) W of Berhampur. 🚌 🛈 Odisha Tourism, Taptapani, (06814) 211 631.

Picturesquely located on a forested hill in the Eastern Ghats, this spa is renowned for its hot springs. The boiling, sulphurous water bubbles out of a crevice in the hillside and is piped to a pool in a clearing. Near the pool is a small shrine to a tribal goddess of fertility as, apart from being beneficial for various chronic ailments, the hot springs are also believed to cure infertility. A tree with seed pods overhangs the pool, and women seeking the infertility cure are supposed to pick up seeds from the tree that have fallen to the muddy bottom of the pool – a difficult feat, especially since the water is too hot for more than a quick dip. The Saora tribal women (see p325), whose villages are nearby, can often be seen taking the cure. The most comfortable way to enjoy the hot springs is by renting a room in the Odisha Tourism rest house just below the pool, which has hot water from the springs piped directly into its bathtubs.

The Odisha Weaver's Art

Odisha has a long and rich tradition of handwoven textiles. Over 300,000 people work in the state's textile industry producing a range of materials, from the simple cotton weaves of tribal areas, to the elaborate painted textiles for use in temples. Odisha's forests yield a wealth of wild silk cocoons, which are now supplemented by mulberry plantations. The state is famous for its silk ikat weaves, an intricate technique in which warp and weft threads are tie-dyed in such a way as to produce patterns when woven. Typical motifs include birds, animals, fish, seashells, holy *rudraksh* beads and temple spires.

Vriksha Pattachitra shows a contemporary minimalist version of the traditional painted textile, used as a temple hanging. The tree is painted on natural-coloured wild silk *(tussar)*.

The *bomkai* cotton sari from Ganjam district was traditionally woven for the local aristocracy. Its distinguishing features are the temple spire pattern on the border, and the rich end piece with its elaborate ikat motifs.

The *kotpad* sari from the Koraput tribal region has a simple elegance, with unbleached cotton offset by a rich red madder-dyed border.

The *ekphulia* (one flower) sari achieves a striking effect by repeating the one-flower and fish motifs.

The conch-shell motif in this silk ikat panel with its delicate, curvilinear pattern, is an example of the fine sense of design and colour that Odisha's weavers have.

The fish motif in this *tussar* silk textile symbolizes prosperity and luck. Below the fish are a row of *damroos* (hand-held drums).

The *jotai* ikat sari is inspired by the finger-painted patterns, called *jotai*, that adorn the walls of many village homes in Odisha. The rich red colour of the sari, and the rows of stylized trees and temple spires on the borders, add to the sumptuous effect.

❽ Cuttack

Cuttack district. 35 km (22 miles)
N of Bhubaneswar. 🗺 535,150.
🚉 🚌 ℹ️ Odisha Tourism, Arunodaya
Market Building, Link Rd, (0671) 231
2225. 🎏 Bali Yatra (Oct/Nov).

Situated on the Mahanadi
Delta, Cuttack is Odisha's most
populous city, and was its
capital from the 10th century
onwards until 1956, when
the capital was moved to
Bhubaneswar (see p310). There
is little evidence today of the
city's historic past. The gateway
and moat of the 13th-century
Barabati Fort, in northwest
Cuttack, are all that remain of
this great citadel which once
had a nine-storeyed palace.
The eastern part of town is
more interesting, with silversmiths' shops in **Balu Bazaar**
and **Nayasarak**, where Cuttack's
famous silver filigree jewellery
is made. Nearby, in the shops
on **Jail Road**, the full range of
Odisha's beautiful handicrafts
are available, including ikat
silk, carved hornware
and paintings.

In this area, a cluster of
green domes marks the
18th-century **Kadam Rasul
Mosque**, where the Prophet
Mohammed's footprints are
carved on a round stone.

The 18th-century Kadam Rasul Mosque in Cuttack

The Indonesian Connection

From the 4th century BC to the 14th century AD, the power and
wealth of successive kingdoms in Odisha derived from their rich
maritime trade, especially with Bali, Java and Sumatra. Indeed, ever
since the 10th century, the word *kling*, derived from Kalinga which
was the ancient name of Odisha, has been used in Indonesia to
refer to India and Indians. With the trading links came cultural
influences, which are still visible in Odisha's crafts. The state's
weavers originally learned the intricate art of ikat weaving (see p321)
from Indonesia, and later were especially commissioned to weave
all the silks for ceremonial use in the royal courts and temples of
Indonesia. Another Odisha craft that originally came from Indonesia
was the silver filigree work that is still being done in Cuttack. Today,
Odisha's old maritime links
with Bali, Java and Sumatra
are commemorated in a
festival called Bali Yatra
(Bali Journey) held in
Cuttack during the full moon
of Kartik (October/
November). A colourful fair is
held on the banks of the
Mahanadi river, and tiny
boats made of banana bark
are lit with clay lamps and
floated in the river.

The colourful entrance gate to the Bali Yatra
fair at Cuttack

❾ Ratnagiri

Cuttack district. 70 kms (44 miles) NE
of Cuttack. 🚌 ℹ️ Odisha Tourism,
Link Rd, Cuttack, (0671) 231 2225.

The three Buddhist sites of
Ratnagiri, Udaigiri and Lalitgiri,
situated close to each other, are
most conveniently visited on
a day trip from Cuttack or
Bhubaneswar, driving through a
beautiful landscape of low hills
and lush paddy fields. The most
impressive of the three sites is
Ratnagiri ("Hill of Jewels") which,
between the 7th and the 11th
centuries, was a major Buddhist
university and monastic
establishment, described by the
7th-century Chinese traveller
Hiuen Tsang (see p223). Located
on top of a mound, crowned by
a large stupa, the best-preserved
structure here is a monastery
with a central courtyard and an
impressive colonnade around
the monks' cells. A beautiful
4-m (13-foot) high image of
the seated Buddha can be seen
inside, together with other
Buddhist divinities, and the
entrance doorway is superbly
carved. A small **Archaeological
Museum** displays other
sculptures found at the site.

Udaigiri ("Sunrise Hill"), 10 km
(6 miles) south of Ratnagiri,
is still being excavated and
seems to have better preserved
sculptures. The western spur of
the hill has a row of rock-cut
sculptures, while the northern
spur is covered with the ruins

The serene 7th-century meditating Buddha
image at Ratnagiri

Flocks of waders amidst the mangroves at Bhitarkanika Sanctuary

of brick stupas. A colossal sculpture of the Buddha here has an inscription dating it to the 8th century.

Lalitgiri ("Hill of Grace"), about 10 km (6 miles) south of Udaigiri (and directly connected by bus to Cuttack), is believed to be the oldest of the sites. The ruins, spread over two adjacent hills, include a terraced stone platform, a gallery of life-size Bodhisattva figures and an apsidal temple. Some of the better-preserved sculptures and a carved doorway have been incorporated into a modern Hindu temple. At the foot of a hill is a village of stone-carvers, who keep alive Odisha's fine tradition of stone

🏛 **Ratnagiri Archaeological Museum**
Open Sat–Thu. 📷

⓾ Bhitarkanika Sanctuary

Kendrapara district. 106 km (66 miles) NE of Cuttack. Entry points: Chandbali, Rajnagar. 🚆 Bhadrakh, 50 km (31 miles) NW of Chandbali, then bus. 🚌 to Rajnagar. 🚢 from Rajnagar or Chandbali to Dangmal, Ekakula & Habalikhati. 🛈 For permits and bookings contact Bhubaneswar, (06786) 220 397 or Rajnagar, (06729) 272 460. **Open** mid-Oct–mid-Apr. 📷

Famous as the nesting ground of the Olive Ridley turtle, this 145-sq km (56-sq mile) sanctuary is situated on the delta of the Brahmani and Baitarani rivers on the Bay of Bengal. It also has the largest mangrove forests in the

country after the Sunderbans in West Bengal (see pp292–3), with 63 of the 72 known mangrove species found here.

Encompassing 12 offshore islands, long sandy beaches and numerous rivulets and creeks, Bhitarkanika is home to an impressive range of fish, more than 170 species of birds such as storks, egrets, ibis and migratory ducks, and the largest number of estuarine crocodiles in the country. Bagagahana

and Saribana are the spots to visit for birdwatching in Bhitarkanika.

Accommodation is available at a forest rest house at Chandbali, the entry point to the sanctuary, as well as deep within the sanctuary at Dangmal, Habalikhati and Ekakula (all three are accessible by boat). Odisha Tourism in Bhubaneswar and Cuttack organize tours and the necessary Forest Department permits for Bhitarkanika.

The Olive Ridley Turtle

Every year, in an awe-inspiring phenomenon, hundreds of thousands of Olive Ridley turtles arrive from as far away as South America, to nest at Gahirmatha, a 10-km (6-mile) stretch of beach near the mouth of the Brahmani river in Bhitarkanika Sanctuary. The world's largest *arribada* (Spanish for "the great arrival") occurs in February and March, when some 200,000 nesting females congregate here, each laying between 50 and 200 eggs in deep

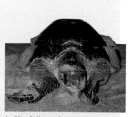

An Olive Ridley turtle nesting at Gahirmatha Beach

hollows they excavate in the sand. After a two-month incubation with the sun's heat, the hatchlings emerge in millions and scamper out to the sea at night. Sadly, less than 0.1 per cent survive to adulthood, as dogs, seagulls, sharks as well as human poachers take an enormous toll

Olive Ridley hatchlings heading for the sea

on their numbers. The absence of *arribadas* in 1997 and 1998 caused much alarm among conservationists, until in March 2000 a record 700,000 Olive Ridleys arrived at Gahirmatha. Since the turtles return each year to nest at the spot where they were born, the cycle continues. Motorboats can be hired from Dangamala to visit Gahirmatha and see the world's largest-known rookery of Olive Ridley turtles.

⓫ Baleshwar

Baleshwar district. 214 km (133 miles) NE of Bhubaneswar. 🚗 🚌
i Odisha Tourism, SPA Complex, Station Square, (06782) 262 048.

Once a bustling seaport, Balasore or Baleshwar was established by the British in 1642. It was later in the possession of the French and the Dutch, but had lost its importance by the 18th century, with the silting up of the port. Its colonial past is visible in the ruins of some Dutch tombs, and what are said to be the remnants of old canals which led to the sea. Today Baleshwar is a sleepy town, surrounded by paddy fields and villages, and renowned for the pretty hand-crafted lacquer boxes and brass fish made locally.

Environs
The tranquil seaside village of **Chandipur**, 16 km (10 miles) east of Baleshwar, is easily reached by a short taxi or scooter ride from the town. Here, the sea recedes up to 5 km (3 miles) at low tide, leaving an expanse of clean white sand. Odisha Tourism offers accommodation in a picturesque old bungalow a short distance from the beach, with the day's fresh catch served at dinner. The only blot on this peaceful landscape is the Indian Army's test firing range for rockets, just outside Chandipur village, against which environmentalists and villagers have been campaigning for many years.

Brass fish, Baleshwar

⓬ Baripada

Mayurbhanj district. 178 km (111 miles) NE of Bhubaneswar. 🚗 🚌 *i* (06792) 252 710. 🛏 daily. 🎭 Chaitra Parba (Apr), Rath Yatra (Jun/Jul).

The main market town of northeastern Odisha, Baripada is the headquarters of Mayurbhanj district, which is rich in forests and has a large population of tribal people. Baripada is also the gateway to Simlipal National Park. The town holds a Rath Yatra (chariot festival) in June/July, which takes place around the **Jagannath Temple**. This festival is a small-scale version of the one that is held in Puri *(see p316)*, but is equally lively and vibrant, as the entire town joins in the procession. A unique feature in Baripada is that the chariot of the female deity, Subhadra, is pulled only by women.

Another colourful festival held here is Chaitra Parba (in April), when tribal groups perform the vigorous Chhau dance wearing fabulous costumes. It was originally performed by warriors just before they went on to the battlefield. In the eastern part of town, **Baripada Museum** has fine sculptures, pottery, and coins found in the area.

🏛 **Baripada Museum**
Open Tue–Sun. 📷

Environs
Haripur, 16 km (10 miles) southeast of Baripada, has the evocative ruins of palaces and temples built by the rulers of the Bhanja dynasty who made this their capital in the 15th century. The most impressive ruins are of the brick-built Rasikaraya Temple, and the Durbar Hall of the Bhanja kings.

⓭ Simlipal National Park

Mayurbhanj district. 320 km (199 miles) N of Bhubaneswar. Entry points: Lulung & Jashipur. 🚗 Baripada, 50 km (30 miles) E of the park, then bus or taxi. 🚌 to Lulung (via Baripada) & Jashipur. *i* For bookings and permits contact Field Director, Simlipal Tiger Reserve, Baripada, (06792) 255 939. **Open** Nov–mid-June. 📷 Extra charges for photography. 🚙 Jeeps available in the park.

This extraordinarily beautiful park is located amidst the pristine forests and hills of northeast Odisha. Stretching over an area of 2,750 sq km (1,062 sq miles), Simlipal comprises dense *sal (Shorea robusta)* and rosewood forests, broken by lush grasslands. Numerous rivers such as the Budhabalanga, Khairi, Salandi, Palpala and cascading rapids traverse the forest, creating spectacular waterfalls, similar to

Women tending their paddy fields near Baleshwar

A waterfall cascading down the hills at Barehipani, Simlipal National Park

those at Joranda (150 m/492 ft) and Barehipani (400 m/1,312 ft) at Simlipal.

Originally the maharaja of Mayurbhanj's private hunting ground, Simlipal was declared a wildlife sanctuary in 1957. A total of 1,076 types of mammals and 29 species of reptiles reside in Simlipal. One of the earliest tiger reserves in India, it is home to about 100 tigers, as well as an impressive range of other fauna including elephants, leopards, deer, gaur (Indian bison) and pangolins (or scaly anteaters). These curious-looking animals, covered with large overlapping scales, feed exclusively on termites and ants, tearing open anthills with their powerful claws and scooping up the insects with their long tongues. When threatened, the pangolin rolls up into an impenetrable armoured ball. Over 230 species

Pangolin at Simlipal

of birds can also be seen at Simlipal.

The rare *muggers* (marsh crocodiles) can be spotted in rivers or basking on the banks where they dig tunnels to keep cool. At Jashipur, the western entry point to the park, there is a **Crocodile Sanctuary** where the reptiles can be observed at close quarters. One of the park's best spots for viewing wildlife is located in the grasslands at **Bacchuri Chara**, which are a favourite haunt of elephant herds. Another good area for sightings is at **Manghasani Peak** (1,158 m/3,799 ft), one of the highest in the park. Basic food

and accommodation are available in forest rest houses at Lulung, Barehipani, Chahala, Joranda and Nawana.

Environs
The capital of the Bhanja kings in the 10th and 11th centuries, **Khiching** has some of the finest examples of temple sculpture to be seen in Odisha. It is 20 km (12 miles) west of Jashipur, the western entry point to Simlipal National Park, and 150 km (93 miles) west of Baripada. The main sight here is the towering Khichakeshwari temple, reconstructed in the early 20th century entirely from the ruins of the original temple that stood here. The temple is adorned with superb images of several deities, including a vibrant dancing Ganesha. A number of other temples, together with the ruins of two forts built by the Bhanja kings, dot this hamlet.

The small **Archaeological Museum** is well worth visiting. Among its highlights are outstanding life-size statues of Shiva and his consort Parvati, and exquisite sculptural panels from now fallen temples.

IIII Archaeological Museum
Open Tue–Sun. **Closed** public hols.

Tribes of Odisha

More than 60 different tribes, descended from the original, pre-Aryan inhabitants of the land, live in Odisha. Many still inhabit hills and forests in the remote interior of the state, relatively untouched by outside influences. The Saoras, who live in the vicinity of Taptapani *(see p320)*, are agriculturists whose mud houses are beautifully painted and decorated with carved doors and lintels. Further west live the Koyas, whose customs decree that their women must only marry considerably younger men. The dominant tribe in Odisha are the Kondhs, who used to perform human sacrifice to ensure the fertility of their land, until the British stamped out this practice in the mid-19th century. Today the Kondhs are renowned for their knowledge of medicinal herbs, and their beautiful metal jewellery. The Odisha government is now promoting tours of some tribal areas. Interested visitors should contact Odisha Tourism in Bhubaneswar, (0674) 243 2177, for information about the necessary permits, as well as accommodation in areas that have few facilities for travellers. For more details, see pp730–31.

Kondh girl in her tribal jewellery

An 11th-century sculpture of Shiva and Parvati, Khiching

ASSAM & THE NORTHEAST

Assam and the six northeastern states, often called the Seven Sisters, make up the most geographically isolated and least visited part of India. This region, which has international borders with China, Myanmar (Burma), Bhutan and Bangladesh, has an unusually rich diversity of ethnic groups, languages, religions, climates and landscapes. The largest of the Seven Sisters is Arunachal Pradesh, spread along the valley of the Brahmaputra river, and famous for its tea gardens and for the rare one-horned rhinoceros. The rolling green hills of Meghalaya boast the delightful hill station of Shillong, as well as one of the wettest places on earth, Cherrapunji. Arunachal Pradesh, Nagaland, Manipur, Mizoram and Tripura are home to more than 100 different tribes, with distinct and fascinating cultures. The Northeast is also a naturalist's paradise, with a wealth of rare flora and fauna.

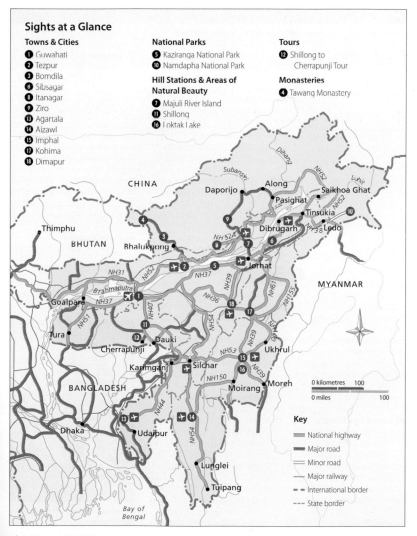

Sights at a Glance

Towns & Cities
1 Guwahati
2 Tezpur
3 Bomdila
6 Sibsagar
8 Itanagar
9 Ziro
13 Agartala
14 Aizawl
15 Imphal
17 Kohima
18 Dimapur

National Parks
5 Kaziranga National Park
10 Namdapha National Park

Hill Stations & Areas of Natural Beauty
7 Majuli River Island
11 Shillong
16 Loktak Lake

Tours
12 Shillong to Cherrapunji Tour

Monasteries
4 Tawang Monastery

Key
National highway
Major road
Minor road
Major railway
International border
State border

◀ Buddhist art in Khinmey Nyingma Monastery, Tawang, Arunachal Pradesh   For keys to symbols *see back flap*

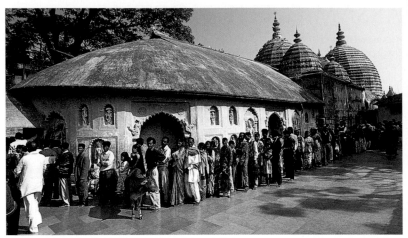

Devotees at Guwahati's Kamakhya Temple, a major centre of pilgrimage for Hindus

❶ Guwahati

Kamrup (Metro) district. 1,081 km (672 miles) NE of Kolkata. 🕅 818,809. ✈ Borjhar, 25 km (16 miles) W of city centre, then bus or taxi. 🚇 🚌 ℹ️ Assam Tourism, Station Rd, (0361) 254 7102. 🎉 Rongali Bihu (Apr), Ambubachi (Jun), Assam Tea Festival (Jan).

The capital of Assam, Dispur, lies in Guwahati city. Guwahati is also the gateway to Northeast India. Ringed by the Nilachal Hills, the city stretches along both banks of the broad Brahmaputra river. An ancient seat of tantric Hinduism, with a number of interesting temples in its environs, Guwahati is now a busy commercial centre for Assam's tea and oil industries. Its outer fringes are dotted with the slender, graceful betelnut palm trees from which Guwahati (literally "Betel Nut Market") derives its name.

Brass utensil for serving betel leaf

🛕 Kamakhya Temple
Perched on Nilachal hill, 8 km (5 miles) northwest of the city, this temple is one of India's most important pilgrimage destinations. The present structure with its typically Assamese beehive-shaped *shikhara* dates to the 17th century, after the original temple was destroyed

by Muslim invaders. According to legend, as a furious and grieving Shiva carried the corpse of his wife, Sati (also known as Parvati) around the skies, parts of her dismembered body fell to the earth *(see p283)*. All these sites have been sanctified by major temples. Kamakhya is believed to mark the place where her vagina fell, and is therefore said to have special powers associated with energy and creation. In accordance with tantric rituals, a goat is sacrificed here every day, and offered to the goddess. The giant turtles in the temple ponds look forward to being fed by visitors. The colourful annual Ambubachi festival, which marks the end of the earth's menstrual cycle, attracts pilgrims here from all over India, to be blessed by the goddess.

🛕 Navagraha Temple
On Chitranchal hill, in northeast Guwahati, is the Navagraha ("Nine Planets") Temple, believed to mark the site of the ancient city of Pragjyotishpur, Guwahati's old name, which was famous as a centre of astronomy. Beneath its red beehive-shaped dome is a dark chamber with nine lingas representing the nine planets.

🛕 Umananda Temple
Peacock Island. 🚤 Umananda Ghat, 1 km (0.6 miles) N of railway station.

Enchantingly located on the lush green Peacock Island in the middle of the Brahmaputra, this 16th-century temple is also dedicated to Shiva's wife. The island, swarming with friendly langur monkeys, is an excellent place to stand and watch the river, deceptively slow on the surface but with swift undercurrents.

🏛 State Museum
GN Bordoloi Rd. **Tel** (0361) 254 0651. **Open** Mar–Sep: 10am–4:30pm; Oct–Feb: 10am–3:45pm daily. 📷

This interesting museum, just east of the railway station, has fine reconstructions of tribal

Umananda Temple, on a pretty island in the Brahmaputra

villages, a comprehensive collection of local handicrafts and a gallery of medieval stone and bronze sculptures, which were excavated from Ambari, an archaeological site in the heart of the city.

🐾 Zoo & Botanical Gardens

RG Baruah Rd. **Open** Sat–Thu.
📷 Extra charges for photography.

The well-maintained zoo is in the eastern part of the city. Clouded leopards, hornbills and, of course, the native one-horned rhinos, can be seen in spacious, moated enclosures. The Botanical Gardens adjoin the zoo.

Vashishtha Temple, on a wooded hill surrounded by streams

Environs

The **Vashishtha Temple**, 12 km (7 miles) southeast of Guwahati, stands in a pretty spot that marks the confluence of three streams, with a waterfall and groves of trees around it. This is said to be the site of the ashram of the sage Vashishtha, a character in the *Ramayana (see p31)*.

Sualkuchi, 32 km (20 miles) west of Guwahati, is a major weaving centre for Assam's famous golden-hued *muga*

and *paat* silk. Several houses here have women working at their looms, and they are happy to welcome visitors.

Hajo, 32 km (20 miles) northwest of Guwahati, is a pilgrimage site for Buddhists, Hindus and Muslims. The 16th-century Hayagriva Madhava Temple, on Monikut Hill, is sacred to Hindus and Buddhists, who believe that the Buddha died here. Fine bas-reliefs of scenes from the *Ramayana* decorate

its walls. Below the temple is a pond, home to Hajo's most famous resident – a giant turtle. On another hill is the Poa Mecca ("Quarter of Mecca") Mosque, established by an Iraqi prince who visited Assam in the 12th century. A pilgrimage here is believed to be equivalent to a quarter of the piety attained by a Haj pilgrimage to Mecca.

The spectacular temple ruins at **Madan Kamdev** are 50 km (31 miles) northwest of Guwahati. Exuberantly erotic carvings of deities and celestial nymphs lie strewn on a small hillock here. They date from the 10th to 12th centuries, when the area was ruled by the Pala dynasty *(see p48)*.

The Brahmaputra river at dawn

The Mighty Brahmaputra

The Son of Brahma, Creator of the Universe, is the name of this majestic river which dominates life in Assam and much of Arunachal Pradesh. Curiously, it is the only Indian river to have a male name. The Brahmaputra begins its 2,900-km (1,802-mile) course from near the holy mountain of Kailasa in Tibet, where it is known as the Tsang Po. Plunging down from a height of 5,200 m (17,060 ft), it then carves a straight, deep 1,100-km (684-mile) long furrow through the Tibetan Plateau. As it continues, the river makes a great sweeping turn around the eastern end of the Himalayas, before plummeting through the deep gorges of upper Arunachal Pradesh where it is called the Siang. Here, the river is crossed by a group of frighteningly fragile-looking bridges made of rope, including the 367-m (1,204-ft) long suspension bridge at Kamsing, one of the longest in the world.

The Brahmaputra enters the plains near the Assam-Arunachal border, and then flows westward through Assam for 724 km (450 miles), broad and tranquil, except during the monsoon when it swells enormously, flooding flat land and forests, and sweeping away homes, crops and animals in an annual ritual of destruction. Just before the end of its course, the Brahmaputra merges with the Ganges to create the huge Bengal delta, before emptying into the Bay of Bengal in Bangladesh.

Sculpture of a goddess from the temple ruins at Madan Kamdev

The ruins of Tezpur's Da Parbatia Temple, dating to the 5th–6th centuries AD

❷ Tezpur

Sonitpur district. 180 km (112 miles) NE of Guwahati. 🚍 100,477. ✈ Salonibari, 10 km (6 miles) N of town centre, then bus or taxi. 🚌 🚐 ℹ Tourist Office, Zenkins Rd, (03712) 221 016.

A picturesque town on the north bank of the Brahmaputra river, Tezpur is surrounded by undulating green valleys covered with tea gardens. The hills of northern Arunachal provide a scenic backdrop to the town, and for visitors, Tezpur is a convenient stop and a take-off point for trips to parts of Arunachal Pradesh.

Tezpur means "City of Blood", and this gory name is derived from its legendary past as the capital of the Hindu demon kings, the Asuras, said to have been vanquished here by Lord Krishna in a bloody battle. More recently, in 1962, Tezpur was close to another bloodbath when the invading Chinese army reached its outskirts before suddenly declaring a ceasefire *(see p61)*.

The ruins of the **Da Parbatia Temple**, 5 km (3 miles) west of the city, dating from the 5th to 6th centuries AD, bear testimony to Tezpur's ancient past, and represent the earliest example of sculptural art in Assam. All that is left of the temple are some sculptures and an exquisitely carved door frame, with images of the river goddesses Ganga and Yamuna on either side. **Chitralekha Udyan**, close to the Tourist Lodge, is Tezpur's prettiest spot, with a beautifully landscaped garden near a lake. It is embellished with 9th- and 10th-century sculptures unearthed in the city. A charming 19th-century colonial church stands behind the Tourist Lodge.

Environs

Scenic **Bhalukpong**, 58 km (36 miles) northwest of Tezpur, is set in green foothills that mark the border of Assam and Arunachal Pradesh. The Kameng river flows past it. Added attractions are medicinal hot springs, and an Orchid Centre, located 7 km (4 miles) away at **Tipi**, with some 500 varieties of orchids native to Arunachal. **Nameri National Park**, 35 km (22 miles) north of Tezpur, covers 200 sq km (77 sq miles). The Jia Bhoroli river winds through its deciduous forests,

Epiphytic orchid

which are home to clouded leopards, *mithuns* (Indian bison) and the rare white- winged wood duck. Nameri can be explored on elephant back. The Potasali Eco-Camp on the river, run by the Forest Department, organizes white-water rafting and *mahseer* fishing trips for visitors. **Orang National Park**, 65 km (40 miles) northwest of

Tezpur, is often described as a mini-Kaziranga *(see pp334–5)* since it has a similar landscape of marshes, streams and grassland, the favoured habitat of the one-horned rhinoceros. This little sanctuary is also home to the Asiatic wild buffalo and the Hoolock gibbon.

🚩 Nameri Sanctuary

Permits: Divisional Forest Officer, Western Assam Wildlife Division, Dolabari, Tezpur, (03712) 268 054 **Open** Nov–Apr. 📷 Extra charges for photography. 🛶 🏠 Potasali Eco-Camp 09435 145 563, 09435 250 025.

🚩 Orang Wildlife Sanctuary

Permits Divisional Forest Officer, Mangaldoi, (03713) 230 022. **Open** Oct–Apr. 📷 🛶

❸ Bomdila

West Kameng district. 140 km (87 miles) NW of Tezpur. 🚐 🎉 Losar (Feb/Mar). Travel permits: required *(see p734)*.

The scenic road from Tezpur winds steeply up through thick forests to this pleasant town, at an altitude of 2,530 m (8,301 ft). The headquarters of Arunachal's West Kameng district, Bomdila has Buddhist monasteries surrounded by apple orchards, with views of snowcapped peaks, terraced paddy fields and waterfalls. The **Crafts Centre** is famous for its carpet weaving. The town's inhabitants belong largely to the Monpa and Sherdukpen tribes, who combine Tibetan Buddhism with some of their original animist rituals and beliefs. They wear a curious black cap with five "tails" projecting from its rim, that serve to drain rainwater away from the face.

Monpas celebrating their New Year with a Yak Dance near Bomdila

Rows of prayer wheels at the 17th-century Tawang Monastery

❶ Tawang Monastery

Tawang district. 325 km (202 miles) NW of Tezpur. 🚌 🚩 Losar (Feb/Mar). Travel permits: required (see p734).

The largest Buddhist monastery in India, Tawang is situated in Arunachal Pradesh at an altitude of 3,050 m (10,007 ft). As the road ascends from Bomdila, the scenery becomes alpine, lush with pine, oak and rhododendron forests, and a short, high-altitude bamboo which is the favourite food of the red panda (see p303). Past the Dirang Valley with its old dzong (fort), the road climbs sharply to the **Sela Pass**. At 4,249 m (13,940 ft), this is the second highest motorable pass in the world; the highest is in Ladakh (see p147). This barren, desolate landscape is softened by a serene lake that lies below the Sela Pass.

Beyond a memorial to a valiant Indian soldier who held up the advancing Chinese army during the India-China conflict of 1962, the road descends to a beautiful, wide valley. The monastery, dramatically located on a spur surrounded by snowcapped peaks, dominates the valley. When the Dalai Lama fled Tibet in 1959, his route into India was through Tawang, and he still visits the area regularly to hold special prayers.

Founded in 1645 by a lama from Merak in neighbouring Bhutan, this Gelugpa (Yellow Hat) establishment (see p143) has over 500 resident monks. It was also the birthplace of the sixth Dalai Lama. The three-storeyed dukhang (assembly hall) has a magnificent 8-m (26-ft) high statue of the Buddha. The ancient library, leading onto the main courtyard, has an excellent collection of thangkas and valuable Buddhist manuscripts.

The **Bramdungchung Nunnery**, associated with Tawang Monastery, is located 12 km (7 miles) northwest of Tawang. The road to the monastery, which can be reached by jeep, reveals a stunning alpine landscape of snowpeaks, Monpa hamlets with stone houses, and juniper and dwarf rhododendron bushes. Fluttering prayer flags and a long prayer wall mark the approach to the nunnery, guarded, as are most of the monasteries in this region, by fierce Tibetan mastiffs.

An intricately painted Wheel of Life mural at Tawang Monastery

Festivals of Assam & the Northeast

Losar (Feb/Mar), Bomdila and Tawang. The Monpa and Sherdukpen tribes of Arunachal Pradesh celebrate their New Year with feasts, masked dances and special prayer sessions at monasteries.

Dancers at the Rongali Bihu Festival, Assam

Rongali Bihu (Apr), Guwahati. The Assamese New Year is celebrated across the state with exuberant singing, drumming and dancing. The women perform a gracefully sinuous dance, while the men accompany them on horns and drums. The liveliest festivities are in Guwahati.

Weiking Dance (Apr/May), Shillong. This three-day festival to usher in the spring features processions, prayers and dances. Khasi virgins, wearing crowns and clan jewellery, dance in a circle, while young men dressed as warriors, with shields, bows and arrows, form a ring around them.

Lai Haraoba (Apr/May), Imphal and Moirang. This Manipuri spring festival honours the many pre-Hindu nature deities revered in the region. Special prayer ceremonies, dazzling displays of Manipuri martial arts and graceful ritual dances are performed to appease the deities. The most beautiful celebrations take place at Moirang.

❺ Kaziranga National Park

Assam's magnificent Kaziranga National Park, declared a World Heritage Site by UNESCO, is the home of the Indian one-horned rhinoceros. Beautifully situated on the banks of the Brahmaputra, the 430-sq km (166-sq mile) park's landscape is characterized by vast grasslands and swamps, dotted with patches of semi-evergreen forest. The Mikir Hills, where several animals migrate during the monsoon, form its southern boundary. Kaziranga's rich variety of wildlife includes almost 100 tigers, large numbers of the Asiatic wild buffalo, herds of wild elephants, Hoolock gibbons, pythons and 300 species of birds, including the rare Bengal florican.

Exploring Kaziranga
Visitors on elephant-back are safe from charging rhinos and wild buffaloes.

Asiatic Wild Buffalo
Kaziranga has India's largest population of this mammoth-horned buffalo which likes to wallow in the park's swamps.

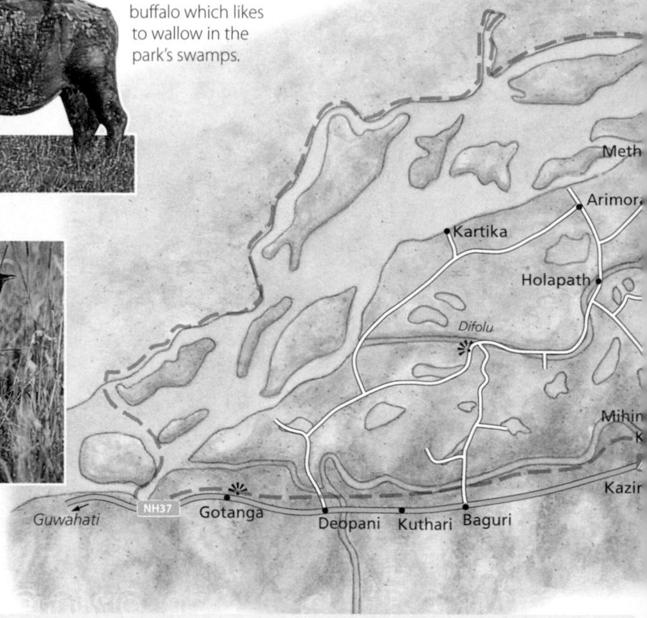

Bengal Florican
This rare bird has beautifully streaked plumage.

Meth
Arimor
Kartika
Holapath
Difolu
Mihin
K
Kazir
Guwahati

NH37
Gotanga
Deopani Kuthari Baguri

The Indian One-horned Rhinoceros

Kaziranga is one of the last refuges of the Indian one-horned rhinoceros *(Rhinoceros unicornis)*, an endangered species that was close to extinction at the beginning of the 20th century. Successful conservation measures have seen their numbers rise to 2,500 (across Assam and the foothills of Nepal), of which 1,500 are in Kaziranga. Once found extensively across the subcontinent, the rhino population dwindled dramatically because of widespread poaching for its horn, a prized ingredient in Chinese medicine. Actually a mass of closely matted hair, each rhino horn fetches an exorbitant price in Southeast Asia, where it is believed to have great medicinal and aphrodisiac properties.

A rhino mother and her baby in Kaziranga's vast grasslands

Beel **(Shallow Lake)**
Floods inundate the park every monsoon, leaving behind
beels and marshes as they recede. These attract herds of
wild elephants, and many other animals and water birds.

VISITORS' CHECKLIST

Practical Information
Golaghat district. 215 km
(134 miles) NE of Guwahati.
Tel (03776) 26 2423. 🛈 Bonani
Tourist Lodge, Kohora. **Open** Nov–
Apr. 📷 Extra charges for photo-
graphy. 🚙 Jeeps available. 🏠

Transport
✈ Jorhat, 96 km (60 miles) NE of
Kohora, the entry point, then taxi.
🚉 Furkating, 75 km (47 miles) E
of Kohora, then taxi. 🚌

Hog Deer
These animals, closely
related to the spotted
deer (chital), are found in
large numbers in the
park's riverine grasslands.

Boralimara
Rajamari
Dhansirimukh
Ageratoli
Jorhat
Bokakhat
Methoni
Idgrass Resort
bhangri
mola
Bheel
NH37

Wildgrass Resort
Located 5 km (3 miles) east of
Kohora, just outside the park,
this eco-friendly resort
(see p700) arranges elephant
rides and trips to nearby tea
plantations *(see pp266–7).*

0 kilometres   8
0 miles   8

Key
━━ Park boundary
▭▭ National highway
═══ Minor road

Hoolock Gibbon
This 1-m (3.3-ft) ape can
be recognized by the
distinctive silvery band
above its eyebrows, and its
loud whooping hoot, which
resounds through the forest.

For keys to symbols *see back flap*

❻ Sibsagar

Sibsagar district. 370 km (230 miles) NE of Guwahati. 62,500. Jorhat, 60 km (37 miles) S of city centre, then taxi or bus. Assam Tourism, near Shivadol Temple, (03772) 222 394. Shivratri (Feb/Mar).

At the heart of Assam's tea and oil-producing region, Sibsagar is also the state's most historic city, as the seat of the Ahom dynasty (see p53) which ruled Assam for 600 years. Originally from Myanmar (Burma), the Ahoms converted to Hinduism and gradually indigenized after conquering Assam in 1228. The Ahoms were defeated by the Burmese in 1817, and their kingdom became part of the British Indian Empire in 1826.

The Ahoms were great builders, as is evident from the ruins in and around Sibsagar. Dominating the town is the enormous 103-ha (255-acre) man-made **Sibsagar Lake**, with three temples on its banks. Especially impressive is the towering **Shivadol Temple** with its 33-m (108-ft) high gilded spire, built by an Ahom queen in 1734. About 4 km (2 miles) south of the town are the ruins of two 18th-century brick palaces, **Kareng Ghar** and **Talatal Ghar**. Both are seven storeys high, and the latter also has three underground floors and a warren of secret tunnels. To its northeast is the elegant **Rang Ghar**, the oval, double-storeyed royal sports pavilion, constructed in 1746.

Vaishnavite mask, Majuli

❼ Majuli River Island

Jorhat district. 314 km (195 miles) NE of Guwahati. Neamati Ghat, 13 km (8 miles) N of Jorhat. from Neamati Ghat to Majuli, then bus to Garamur. On arrival, foreigners must register with the Sub-Divisional Officer, Majuli, who also handles bookings.

Perhaps the largest inhabited river island in the world, Majuli covers an area of 929 sq km (359 sq miles). It is easy to forget that Majuli is an island, holding within it hills, rivulets and little islands of its own. This amorphous landmass is constantly being sculpted into new dimensions and shapes by the Brahmaputra. Every year during the monsoon, the river submerges large tracts of land, forcing the inhabitants to move to higher ground. After the floods recede, leaving behind fertile, freshly silted land, the people return to cultivate the area.

As interesting as Majuli's distinctive landscape are its satras, unique monasteries founded in the 15th century by the Vaishnavite reformer-philosopher, Srimanta Sankardeva. The satras are rich repositories of traditional Assamese arts and crafts, and regularly stage dance-dramas in praise of Vishnu. Majuli's main settlement is at **Garamur** which has two satras. About 20 others are scattered across the island. Visitors can stay in the satras, and should offer to make a donation towards overnight stays or meals.

❾ Itanagar

Papum Pare district. 420 km (261 miles) N of Guwahati. 150,000. Lakhimpur, 60 km (37 miles) NE of town centre, then taxi or bus. Directorate of Tourism, Itanagar, (0360) 221 4745. Travel permits: required (see p734).

Until it became the capital of Arunachal Pradesh in 1971, Itanagar was a settlement of the Nishi tribe, one of the

Bamboo forests in the vicinity of Itanagar, in Arunachal Pradesh

Apatani woman in the rice fields near Ziro

largest among the 26 major tribes that inhabit the state. A few traditional Nishi longhouses still remain, now all but swamped by Itanagar's newly constructed government buildings. The Nishis are easily recognizable – they sport black and white hornbill feathers in their cane headgear, wear their hair in a bun on their foreheads and often carry bearskin bags.

The **Nehru Museum**, near the Secretariat, offers a comprehensive look at the arts and crafts of all the tribes of Arunachal Pradesh. Cane and bamboo artifacts, textiles, jewellery, and totem objects are on display here. A pretty but bumpy 6-km (4-mile) drive north from Itanagar leads to the lovely, emerald-green **Gyakar Sinyi Lake**, surrounded by dense forests. Many of the tall trees are festooned with orchids.

🏛 **Nehru Museum**
Siddharth Vihar. **Tel** (0360) 221 2276.
Open Sun–Thu. 📷 Extra charges for photography.

❾ Ziro

Lower Subansiri district. 150 km (93 miles) NE of Itanagar. 🚗 50,000. 🚌 *i* Deputy Commissioner's Office, (03788) 224 255. Travel permits: required (*see p734*).

The picturesque town of Ziro in central Arunachal Pradesh, lies in a large, flat valley, surrounded by low pine-covered hills. This area, better known as the Apatani

Plateau, is the home of the prosperous Apatani tribe who practise a unique system of cultivation that combines rice-growing with pisciculture. The flooded paddy fields are stocked with fingerlings, the two staples of Apatani diet thus coming from the same plot of land. Like the Nishis, the Apatanis wear their hair in a bun on their foreheads, held with a brass skewer. Both

Adi longhouse near Along

the men and women are tattooed, and the women sport huge bamboo nosepluqs. Northeast of Ziro, three other areas – **Daporijo**, **Along** and **Pasighat** – are now open to foreigners (with permits). The latter two are situated on the Brahmaputra river and are inhabited by the Adi tribe (*see p340*). The drive from Ziro to Pasighat (300 km/186 miles) is wonderfully scenic, through dense virgin forest and tribal villages with thatched longhouses.

❿ Namdapha National Park

Changlang district. 380 km (236 miles) NE of Itanagar. 🚌 Margherita, 64 km (40 miles) SW of Miao, the entry point. *i* Director, Project Tiger, Miao, (03807) 222 249. **Open** Oct–Mar. 📷 Travel permits: required (*see p734*).

This superb park in remote eastern Arunachal Pradesh, bordering Myanmar, covers 1,985 sq km (766 sq miles). Rising from the plains to 4,500 m (14,764 ft) in the Himalayas, it covers a variety of habitats, and is the only reserve in India where all the four big cats of the Himalayas – tiger, leopard, clouded leopard and the rare snow leopard are found. It was declared a Tiger Reserve in 1983. Other wildlife includes the great Indian hornbill, the red panda (*see p303*), and the Hoolock gibbon (*see p335*).

Environs
The legendary Burma Road (or Stilwell Road) begins at **Ledo**, 60 km (37 miles) south-west of Miao. This 1,700-km (1,056-mile) road, of great strategic importance in World War II, connected Ledo, via the forbidding jungles and mountains of Arunachal Pradesh and Northern Myanmar, to Kunming in China's Yunnan province. Supervised by the American General Joseph Stilwell and built in two years at enormous human cost, it has now fallen into disrepair, but is still used by locals travelling on foot.

Tribal people of eastern Arunachal Pradesh on the Burma Road

Locally made bamboo baskets on sale in Shillong's Bara Bazaar

⓫ Shillong

East Khasi Hills district. 127 km (79 miles) S of Guwahati. 260,000. Meghalaya Tourism, 3rd Secretariat, Lower Lachumiere, (0364) 250 0736. Weiking Dance (Apr/May).

Capital of the tiny state of Meghalaya, Shillong, with its mist-shrouded hills, pine forests, lakes and waterfalls, is sometimes described as the "Scotland of the East". Lying at an altitude of 1,496 m (4,908 ft), it was chosen as the headquarters of the British administration in Assam in 1874. It soon developed into a popular hill station, providing refuge from the searing heat of the plains.

The town still retains a distinctly colonial ambience, with its mock-Tudor bungalows, churches, polo ground and beautiful 18-hole golf course. It is also the home of the matrilineal Khasi tribe. The idyllic countryside around the town can be easily explored in short excursions.

Bara Bazaar

Bara Bazaar Rd. **Open** Mon–Sat.

This sprawling market offers a vivid glimpse of Khasi tribal society. The stalls are piled high with produce from the surrounding villages – honey, pineapples, piglets, dried fish, wild mushrooms, raw betel nut and bamboo baskets. The market is dominated by Khasi women, who run most of the stalls. Dressed in their traditional tunic-like *jainsems* and tartan-checked shawls, these cheerful matriarchs can drive a hard bargain.

Museum of Entomology

Umsohsun Rd. **Open** 10am–5pm Mon–Sat.

This small private museum, situated north of Bara Bazaar, was established in the 1930s by the Wankhar family, and boasts a collection of rare butterflies and insects found in Meghalaya. Among them are huge stick insects, iridescent beetles, and the giant yellow and black birdwing butterfly which cloaks itself in a deadly poison to protect itself from predatory birds. The family also runs a breeding centre for rare species.

Ward Lake & Lady Hydari Park

Park: **Open** daily. Extra charges for photography.

In the centre of town, the horseshoe-shaped Ward Lake has pleasant promenade paths around it, paddle boats for hire and a café. A short distance to its south is Lady Hydari Park, with a pretty Japanese garden and a mini zoo which includes fauna native to Meghalaya's forests, such as hornbills, leopard cats, and the aptly named slow loris, a ferret-like creature that crawls around as though heavily drugged.

Environs

The beautiful **Bishop** and **Beadon Falls** are 3 km (2 miles) north of Shillong, just off the Guwahati-Shillong Highway. Along the same route, 17 km (11 miles) north of Shillong, is **Umiam Lake**, a large artificial reservoir set among forested hills. It offers facilities for angling, kayaking and water-skiing, and has an orchidarium in the adjacent park. The scenic **Elephant Falls** are 11 km (7 miles) south of Shillong. The road to **Mawphlang**, 24 km (15 miles) southwest of Shillong, is richly forested with pine and oak, and is a good place to see some of Meghalaya's rare species of orchids in their natural habitat.

The Elephant Falls, flowing over ferns and rocks

The Khasis

The Khasis are the predominant tribe in the Shillong area. Believed to have originated in Southeast Asia, their language belongs to the Mon-Khmer group. It is not known when they migrated to this region. Today, the majority of Khasis are Christians, their ancestors converted by British missionaries in the 19th century. Nevertheless, they retain many of their tribal customs. Chief among these is their matrilineal social structure, which dictates that landed property can only be inherited by females, with the youngest daughter given a special position as custodian of the family house and the clan's traditional rituals.

Khasi matriarch at her stall in Shillong's main market

⓬ Shillong to Cherrapunji Tour

The road to Cherrapunji through the East Khasi Hills winds through dense pine and oak forests, full of ferns and orchids. En route are dramatic gorges and ravines, waterfalls and limestone caves. Cherrapunji is one of the wettest places on earth, and established a world record of an incredible 2,621 cm (1,032 in) of rain in 1861. It continues to record an average rainfall of 1,143 cm (450 in) in the monsoon months of July to September.

Cherrapunji's famous oranges

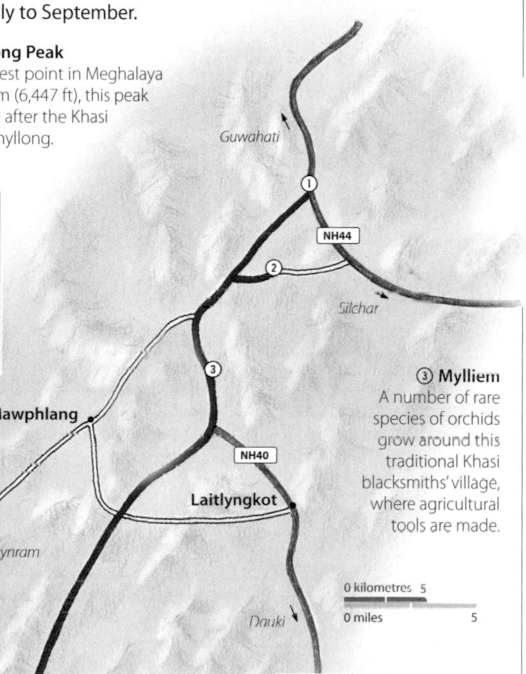

① Shillong
Ward Lake marks the centre of the town.

② Shillong Peak
The highest point in Meghalaya at 1,965 m (6,447 ft), this peak is named after the Khasi deity, Ushyllong.

Guwahati

NH44

Silchar

④ Cherrapunji
Surrounded by groves of orange and banana trees, this little town has a lively weekly market and is famed for its delicious orange-flower honey.

Mawphlang

NH40

Laitlyngkot

③ Mylliem
A number of rare species of orchids grow around this traditional Khasi blacksmiths' village, where agricultural tools are made.

Mawsynram

0 kilometres 5

0 miles 5

⑤ Nohkalikai Falls
These are the second highest falls in India. Tall Khasi memorial stones dot the area around them.

Dauki

Tips for Drivers

Length: 120 km (75 miles).
Stopping-off points: The tour takes between 6–7 hours. Shillong Peak, Cherrapunji (meals, toilets available), Nohsngithiang Falls, Nohkalikai Falls and Mawsmai Caves are the best places to stop.
Getting around: Meghalaya Tourism, (0364) 250 0736, and several travel agencies run daily tours from Shillong to Cherrapunji. Take a torch to explore the caves.

⑥ Mawsmai Caves
Some of these limestone caves run more than 4 km (2 miles) deep.

Key
- ▬ Tour route
- ═ Other roads
- ▬ National highway

⑦ Nohsngithiang Falls
On a clear day, there is a fine view of the plains of Bangladesh from these impressive falls, also known as the Seven Sisters Falls.

Tribal Peoples of the Northeast

Northeast India is home to an extraordinary diversity of tribal peoples. Arunachal Pradesh alone has 26 major tribes, while Nagaland has 16. Dozens of others inhabit Assam, Manipur, Mizoram, Meghalaya and Tripura. Though living in the same region, they have been geographically isolated from each other by steep mountain ridges, rivers and gorges, and have therefore retained their distinct cultural identities and languages.

Pipes of wood and metal are smoked by tribes in Arunachal Pradesh.

Gigantic stone megaliths can be seen all over the state of Meghalaya. They were erected by the Khasi tribe as memorials to the dead.

Intricate beadwork, crafted by the Wanchos of Arunachal

The Adis of Arunachal Pradesh are famous for their engineering skills and construct superb bridges, such as this tube of canework over the Brahmaputra river.

The Konyaks of Nagaland, who perform spirited martial dances, wear colourful costumes, with hornbill feathers, wild boar tusks and painted canework caps.

The Thankuls of Manipur are skilled at weaving, producing a distinctive red and white textile with a silken sheen.

A chief's house in Nagaland has crossed gables and is decorated with his tribe's symbols. The *mithun* (bison species) skull in the foreground symbolizes power and prosperity.

This Naga chief used to be a headhunter. The wooden heads on his basket indicate how many heads he took.

The Cheraw dance is performed at tribal festivals in Mizoram. The Mizos love music and dancing, and the Cheraw dance requires women to step agilely between rapidly moving bamboo poles.

Ujjayanta Palace in Agartala, built in 1901

⓭ Agartala

West Tripura district. 600 km (373 miles) S of Guwahati. 🚶 367,800. ✈ 12 km (7 miles) N of town centre, then bus or taxi. 🚌 ℹ Tripura Tourism, Swet Mahal, Palace Compound, (0381) 222 3893.

The capital of Tripura, a former princely state bordered by Bangladesh, Agartala is a pleasant little town, its lush tropical greenery dotted with red-brick civic buildings. Dominating the town is the sprawling white **Ujjayanta Palace**, built in 1901 in Indo-Saracenic style. Now the State Legislature, the palace's opulent interior includes a tiled Chinese Room with a magnificent ceiling crafted by Chinese artisans. It is open to visitors when the Assembly is not in session (5–7pm). Tripura is renowned for its exceptionally fine cane and bamboo work, freely available in the market.

Cane basket from Tripura

Environs
Neermahal Water Palace, 55 km (34 miles) south of Agartala, on an island in Rudrasagar Lake, was the summer home of the former maharajas of Tripura. Built in white marble and red sandstone, this fairy-tale palace has a profusion of pavilions, balconies, turrets and bridges, and part of it is open to the public. **Udaipur**, 58 km (36 miles) south of Agartala, is renowned for the 16th-century **Tripurasundari Temple** with its distinctive Bengal-style roof.

⓮ Aizawl

Aizawl district. 480 km (298 miles) SE of Guwahati. 🚶 228,300. ✈ 35 km (22 miles) W of town centre, then bus or taxi. 🚌 ℹ Mizoram Tourism, Bungkawn, (0389) 233 3475. Travel permits: required *(see p734)*.

Perched along a ridge, its houses and churches standing out against the green hillside, Aizawl is Mizoram's capital, and home of the Mizo tribes, said to have migrated here from Myanmar's Chin Hills 300 years ago. In the centre of town is the lively **Main Market**, where local farmers congregate. Almost the entire population of Mizoram (as of Nagaland and Meghalaya) is now Christian, converted by missionaries who first came here in 1891. As a result of the schools they started, Mizoram has the second highest literacy rate in India. Blue jeans are more commonly seen today than tribal dress among the men, but the women still wear their elegant *puans* (long, narrow skirts). Visitors can see these being woven at the **Weaving Centre** in Luangmual, 7 km (4 miles) away.

Aizawl, stretching across a ridge

Fish sellers at Imphal's Ima Keithel

⓯ Imphal

Imphal district. 484 km (301 miles) SE of Guwahati. 🚆 217,300. ✈ 6 km (4 miles) S of city centre. 🚌 ℹ️ Manipur Tourism, next to Hotel Imphal, (0385) 224 603/220 802. 🎭 Yaosang (Feb/Mar), Lai Haraoba (Apr/May). Travel permits: required *(see p734)*.

The capital of Manipur (the "Jewelled Land"), Imphal lies in a broad oval valley enclosed by forested hills. Its inhabitants mostly belong to the Meitei tribe. The liveliest part of the town is the **Ima Keithel** ("Mothers' Market") where more than 3,000 women congregate daily to sell fresh produce, fish, grain, canework and handicrafts, including the elegant striped textiles worn by the Meitei women. These formidable Imas, who sport *tikas* of sandalwood paste on their noses, have formed a powerful union and pride themselves on charging fair prices.

Imphal's main temple, the **Govindaji Temple**, stands east of the Bazaar, and on festivals associated with Lord Krishna the graceful Manipuri dance *(see p33)* is performed here. Sagol Kangjei, Manipuri polo, is a favourite sport in Imphal (they claim to have invented the game), and an opportunity to see a match should not be missed – the Polo Ground is in the centre of the town. It is a fast and furious game, with the players dressed in dhotis and often riding bareback on the agile Manipuri horses. Two well-tended **Commonwealth War Graves Cemeteries** are on the northern and eastern outskirts of town. Buried here are the men who died fighting the Japanese during the invasion of Manipur in World War II. Also worth visiting is an impressive **Orchidarium** displaying various indigenous species. It is 12 km (7 miles) north of the town.

Manipuri dancer

Environs

Moirang, 45 km (28 miles) south of Imphal, with its ancient temple to the pre-Hindu god, Thangjing, is the spiritual home of the Meiteis, who celebrate Lai Haraoba *(see p331)*. During World War II, Moirang was the headquarters of the Indian National Army (INA), led by Subhash Chandra Bose, which fought against the Allies.

⓰ Loktak Lake

Bishnupur district. 48 km (30 miles) S of Imphal. 🚌 ℹ️ For bookings on Sendra Island, contact Manipur Tourism, (0385) 224 603/220 802. 🏨 Travel permits: required *(see p734)*.

Loktak Lake is one of the most enchanting places in the northeast. Almost two-thirds of this huge expanse of freshwater is covered by unique floating saucer-shaped islands of reed and humus, locally called *phumdi*, which are home to a community of fishermen. The southern part of the lake forms the **Keibul Lamjao National Park** where contiguous masses of *phumdi* form the very special habitat of the endangered Manipur brow-antlered deer called *sangai*. These deer have divided hooves, specially adapted to their floating habitat, and elegantly curved antlers. Only a 100 or so of these graceful animals are now left, found in the wild only in an area of 6 sq km (2 sq miles) within the park. **Sendra Island**, at the heart of the park, provides a magnificent view of the lake, its islands and its rich birdlife.

Floating islands of reed and humus with fishermen's houses and moored boats, on Loktak Lake

The Baptist Church in Kohima, one of many churches in the area

Boat rides are also offered. However, due to current political instability, only day-trips to Loktak Lake are possible.

⑰ Kohima

Kohima district. 339 km (211 miles) E of Guwahati. 🗺 92,100. 🚇 Dimapur, 74 km (46 miles) NW of Kohima, then taxi or bus. 🚌 ℹ️ Nagaland Tourism, (0370) 224 3124. Travel permits: required *(see p734)*.

The capital of Nagaland, Kohima, at an altitude of 1,500 m (4,921 ft), is a small, pleasant town surrounded by hills which are dotted with villages. Kohima is famous in World War II history for the decisive battle, fought on the tennis court of the British deputy commissioner's house, that finally stopped the Japanese advance into India in April 1944.

War Cemetery, Kohima

Those who fell in the battle are buried in the beautifully kept **War Cemetery** covering a terraced hillside. A poignant inscription at the base of one of the two large crosses here reads: "When you go home tell them of us and say, For your tomorrow we gave our today". The **Cathedral of Reconciliation**, which overlooks the cemetery, was built in 1995, partly funded by the Japanese government.

Kohima's main bazaar is a good place to encounter the handsome Naga people *(see pp340–41)* in their colourful woven shawls, who come from surrounding villages to sell their produce. The market also offers visitors a glimpse of the diet that supposedly made the Nagas such formidable warriors – bees' larvae and dog meat are favourites.

The **State Museum**, 2 km (1.2 miles) north of the bazaar, has an excellent anthropological collection of Naga masks, textiles, jewellery and totem pillars from all the 16 Naga tribes. Particularly intriguing is a large ceremonial drum that looks like a dugout canoe, kept in a shed outside the museum. The drum is engraved with stylized waves, and has gongs that look like paddles. This and other factors, such as the use of seashells in their costumes, has led some anthropologists to conjecture that the Nagas were originally a seafaring people, possibly from Sumatra. Today, a high percentage of Nagas are Christians and a church can be found in almost every corner of the state.

The original village of Kohima, **Bara Basti**, is a settlement of the Angami Naga tribe, located on a hill overlooking the town. Though now considerably modernized, it still has its ceremonial gateway, and a large traditional community house, the *morung*, with crossed horns surmounting its gable. A less modernized Angami Naga village is **Khonoma**, 20 km (12 miles) southwest of Kohima, with its wooden houses, carved gateway and surrounding stone wall. The villagers are known for their agricultural skills – terraced paddy fields cover the hillside, growing 20 varieties of rice, and a system of bamboo pipes irrigates the fields.

🏛 **State Museum**
Tel (0370) 226 0133. **Open** Mon–Sat.
Closed public hols. 🈲

⑱ Dimapur

Kohima district. 74 km (46 miles) NW of Kohima. 🗺 135,900. 🚇 🚌 ℹ️ Tourist Office, near Nagaland State Transport Office. Travel permits: required *(see p734)*.

This bustling town in the plains functions as a gateway to the rest of Nagaland. It was founded by the Kachari rulers, a Tibeto Burmese people who were displaced from their territories in Assam in the 13th century by the invading Ahoms *(see p336)*. Some of the ruins of their old capital can be seen in the heart of the town. Most notable are 30 carved megaliths, believed to be fertility symbols. About 5 km (3 miles) from the city centre, on the road to Kohima, is the **Ruzaphema Bazaar** which displays a fascinating range of tribal handicrafts.

Carved monoliths in Dimapur erected by the Kachari kings

WESTERN INDIA

Introducing Western India

This region has some of India's most popular destinations. In Rajasthan, the desert forts of Jaisalmer and Jodhpur, the palaces and lakes of Udaipur, and the Ranthambhore National Park evoke all the romance and splendour of the state's princely past. Gujarat's Jain temples and intricately designed stepwells are architectural marvels, while its natural wonders can be enjoyed on the beaches of Diu and at the lion sanctuary at Gir. The landscapes in this region range from the sand dunes of Rajasthan to the vast salt flats of Kutch, to the urban bustle of the two state capitals, Jaipur and Ahmedabad.

Rajasthani women in festive dress at the Pushkar Fair

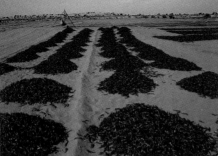

Chillies drying in the desert sun near Osian, Rajasthan

Getting Around

Jaipur, Jodhpur, Udaipur and Ahmedabad are linked by air to Delhi and Mumbai as well as to each other. Trains travel between all the major cities, with fast trains connecting Delhi and Jaipur. Two luxury trains, the Palace on Wheels and the Royal Rajasthan on Wheels *(see p753)*, offer a more romantic way to explore Rajasthan and Gujarat. Within Rajasthan, a network of national highways links most major destinations by road, while National Highways 8, 14 and 15 continue on to Gujarat.

◀ Cameleers in the Thar Desert, Jaisalmer, Rajasthan

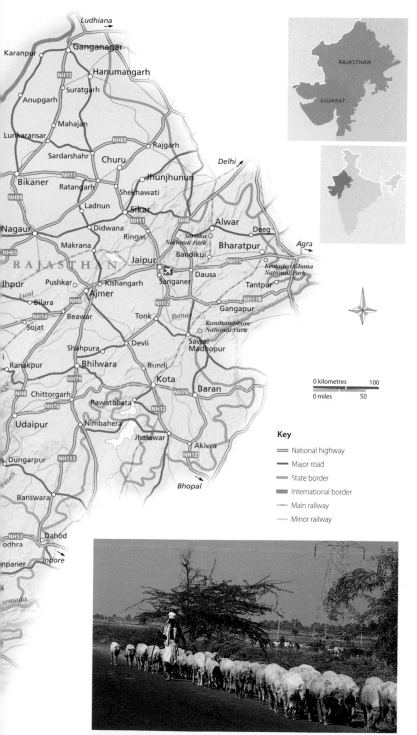

Ludhiana

Karanpur   Ganganagar
NH15
      Hanumangarh
Anupgarh   Suratgarh
Lunkaransar   Mahajan
Sardarshahr   NH65   Rajgarh
Bikaner   Churu
NH11   Ratangarh
NH89   Jhunjhunun
Ladnun   Shekhawati
Nagaur   Didwana   Sikar
NH65   NH11
Makrana   Ringas   NH8   Alwar   Deeg
        Sariska
        National Park   Bharatpur   Agra
Ihpur   Pushkar   Kishangarh   Jaipur   Bandikui
Luni   Ajmer   Sanganer   Dausa   Keoladeo Ghana
Bilara   NH8   National Park
NH14   Beawar   Tonk   Banas   Tantpur
Sojat   NH11B
                Gangapur
        Shahpura   Devli   Ranthambhore
Ranakpur   National Park
        Bhilwara   Bundi   Sawai
NH79   Madhopur
NH8   Chittorgarh   Kota
          Rawatbhata   Baran
Udaipur   Nimbahera   NH76
              NH12
Dungarpur   NH113   Jhalawar   Aklera
                      NH12
              Bhopal
Banswara

RAJASTHAN

NH53   Dahod
odhra
npaner   Indore
        rmada

RAJASTHAN

GUJARAT

0 kilometres   100
0 miles   50

Key

═══ National highway
━━━ Major road
▪▪▪ State border
███ International border
╌╌╌ Main railway
─── Minor railway

A Rabari nomadic shepherd with his flock in Gujarat

For keys to symbols *see back flap*

A PORTRAIT OF WESTERN INDIA

The Great Thar Desert and the Arabian Sea have been two dominating influences in the history and culture of Rajasthan and Gujarat. Both these states have boundaries with Pakistan and, before 1947, contained a number of princely states. In most other respects, however, the two states are a study in contrasts.

A many-splendoured land of fairy-tale palaces and vibrant fairs and festivals, Rajasthan fulfills everyone's favourite fantasies about India. Until Independence in 1947 Rajasthan, literally "the Land of Kings", was indeed just that. It was made up of more than 20 princely states, bastions of royal opulence and feudal pageantry. They were ruled by Rajput clans such as the Kachhawahas of Jaipur, the Rathores of Jodhpur and the Sisodias of Udaipur. Their legacy has helped make the state one of the country's most popular tourist destinations.

A desert nomad's shelter in Rajasthan

Today, Rajasthan's once-impregnable forts are open to visitors, and many of the old princely palaces and feudal castles have been converted into delightful hotels, often run by the erstwhile ruling families. Tourism has helped restore these historic buildings, and breathed new life into them. Apart from becoming successful hoteliers, many former princes have found new roles for themselves in politics, representing their constituencies in India's parliament. Rajasthan's traditional arts and crafts have also been revived, with tourists replacing maharajas as the new patrons.

Eighty per cent of Rajasthan's population still lives in rural areas, engaged in agriculture and livestock herding. The rhythm of life in the villages continues much as it has for hundreds of years, the drudgery of the daily grind broken every few weeks by religious festivals and cattle fairs, such as those at Pushkar (see pp378–9) and Nagaur (see p380). These wonderfully colourful events provide Rajasthani villagers with an occasion for feasting, socializing, trading, and enjoying traditional entertainments such as camel races and puppet shows. The fairs have become a major attraction for visitors as well, offering a close and memorable encounter with the people and culture of rural Rajasthan.

Rajasthani society is still socially very conservative, with great value placed

Camels for sale at the Pushkar Fair

on ancient feudal codes of conduct and honour. As recently as 1987, an incident of *sati* took place here, when a young widow burnt herself on her husband's funeral pyre, while the whole village watched in admiration. But things are changing: female literacy in Rajasthan, which was just 20 per cent in the early 1990s has increased to over 50 per cent in 2013, and women now head many village government councils. Rural development schemes have brought schools, hospitals and water to remote desert villages. What has still not changed, however, is the old-world courtesy and hospitality encountered everywhere in Rajasthan, be it in a princely palace or a mud hut in the desert.

In sharp contrast with Rajasthan, Gujarat is one of the most industrially advanced and urbanized states in the country – nearly 50 per cent of its population lives in cities. The Gujaratis' legendary business acumen has helped make the state one of the most prosperous in India.

While the forbidding expanses of the Thar Desert had for centuries effectively insulated Rajasthani society, Gujarat's 1,600 km (992 miles) of coastline on the Arabian Sea have helped foster contacts with other lands and cultures, and bred an adventurous spirit in the people. Since ancient times, Gujarat has traded with Arabs and Persians, East Africa, China, and Indonesia, through its ports at Surat *(see p424)* and Mandvi *(see p433)*, while from the 16th century onwards European traders established their bases along the coastline. In the late 19th and early

The Tarnetar Fair in Gujarat

20th centuries, many Gujaratis sailed to far off lands in search of new opportunities, and today their descendants (many of them with the surnames Patel and Shah) are flourishing – be it as hoteliers in America, retail traders in Britain, industrialists in Nigeria or lawyers in South Africa.

Gujaratis have been deeply influenced by Jainism *(see p402)*, which took hold in the region in the 11th century, during the reign of the Solanki kings and thrived together with Hinduism in Gujarat. Jainism's emphasis on non-violence, community service, simple living and high thinking was an integral part of the philosophy of Gujarat's most famous son, Mahatma Gandhi, who led India's struggle for independence *(see p60)*. Ordinary mortals too try to follow this creed in their daily lives. Most Gujaratis, whether at home or abroad, are strict vegetarians, known for their toughness and self reliance, and for their thrift and philanthropy. These qualities were especially evident after the devastating earthquake that hit Gujarat in January 2001 *(see p432)*, from which the state has made a remarkable recovery.

Rajasthani women preparing lunch

Forts and Palaces

The spectacular forts of Rajasthan were originally forbidding, defensive citadels, but by the mid-16th century, when most Rajput states had made peace with the Mughals, luxurious palaces, pleasure pavilions and gardens were added to them, displaying many Mughal-inspired features. In the late 19th and early 20th century there was another spate of palace-building in both Rajasthan and Gujarat. As a result of increasing contact between the British Raj and the princely states, a marked European influence in both architecture and decor is visible in these palaces.

Sileh Khanas (armouries) store a variety of weapons, from ceremonial jewelled swords to sharp knuckle-dusters, and even special armour for war elephants.

Cannons to defend the fort are mounted on the bastions, which tower high above the surrounding area.

Ramparts follow the contours of the hill.

Rana Kumbha's Palace

Entrance gates are high enough for elephants to pass through. Their doors have huge spikes to prevent enemy elephants from storming them.

Water reservoirs, often fed by underground springs, are found in forts in the arid areas of Rajasthan and Gujarat.

Types of Forts

Ancient Indian treatises list six types of forts for good defences. While *giri durgs* (hill forts) such as Chittorgarh are the most impregnable, other effective types are *dhanva durg*, protected by desert, such as Jaisalmer *(see pp392–3)*; *vana durg*, protected by forest, such as Ranthambhore *(see p410)*; *mahi durg*, protected by thick mud walls, such as Bharatpur's Lohagarh *(see p371)*; *jala durg*, protected by water, such as Ghagron *(see p407)*; and *nara durg*, a city fort such as Nagaur *(see p380)*, protected mainly by trusted men.

Ghagron Fort in Rajasthan, an example of a fort protected by water

Palaces

Palaces built by maharajas during the Raj, unlike those in the old forts, had modern plumbing, drawing rooms and dining halls suitable for entertaining British dignitaries.

Lalgarh Palace in Bikaner *(see p383)* was built in 1902. It beautifully combines Rajput decorative features with European elements, such as banquet halls and billiard rooms.

Wankaner Palace *(see p431)* was built in 1907. Construction finished in 1928. The ruler's travels in Europe gave him a taste for Italianate pillars and Gothic arches, crowned here with Mughal pavilions.

The Victory Tower was built in 1458 after a successful battle. Each of its nine storeys is a temple.

Corridors and staircases, that connect the private chambers in Rajput palaces, are often narrow and twisting to confuse enemy invaders.

Temples were built by rulers and merchants, who believed their deities protected the fort.

Forts

Chittorgarh (see p406), founded in AD 728 but added to at various times until the 16th century is, like many Rajput forts, built on a commanding height above the plains. Its massive ramparts encircle palaces, temples, stables and reservoirs.

Sheesh Mahals ("Halls of Mirrors") are ceremonial halls inlaid with mirror mosaic. One candle, reflected in the myriad mirrors, makes the whole room glitter.

Zenanas (women's quarters) have secluded courtyards and exquisite stone latticework (*jali*) screens. These let in ,0light and air, yet maintain privacy. Most zenanas are large, because they also housed the rulers' many concubines.

The Flavours of Western India

Rajasthan, largely scrub and desert and dominated by hill forts of stone, has a simple cuisine dictated by the landscape and climate. As a result, the food here is more robust and strength-giving, as is evident by the creative use of cereals and lentils. The varied palate of Gujarat has emerged from its contact with the different communities who have settled in this state. What is commonly called Gujarati food is vegetarian with the regional variations of North and South Gujarat, Kathaiwar and Kutch. It is a delicate balance of the spicy and sweet and its infinite variety of dishes can be sampled in the Gujarati *thali* (platter).

Bunch of fenugreek

An array of tangy savouries, very popular among Rajasthanis

Rajasthan

The best-known dish here is *dal-baati*, a lentil curry with wheat-dough balls which can be buried in the sand to bake. The same *baati*, when crumbled and garnished with raisins and almonds, is transformed into a rich sweet called *chorma*. This food can be carried for days through the parched landscape. In the desert districts, milk, *ghee* (clarified butter) and buttermilk

are used to make up for the water scarcity. Other substitutes are *amchur* or dried mango powder, used instead of tomatoes, and asafetida to enhance taste. Desert plants such as *sangri (Prosopsis cineraria)* beans and *khair (Capparis decidua)* have great nutritional value. These are dried and cooked with oil and spices to make *khair-sangri*. Mint, turmeric, mango and garlic chutneys are popular accompaniments.

The cuisine of the martial Rajput clans includes highly seasoned meat dishes. The most famous is *lal maas*, a lamb dish cooked with *ghee* and red chillies. A variation is the *safed maas*, a "white" curry with yoghurt and nuts. *Khud khargosh*, is a summer special where wild hare is stuffed with spices, sealed in dough and roasted in cloth.

Spicy lentils, split peas, peanuts and puffed rice are used in crunchy savoury snacks,

Khakra (wheat wafer) | Puri (deep-fried bread) Naan | Missi roti (spicy wheat wafer) | Lachha paratha (layered bread) | Pudina paratha (layered bread, with mint)

A selection of breads from Rajasthan and Gujarat

Local Dishes and Specialities

Vegetarian food dominates the cuisine of Rajasthan and Gujarat, both states having been strongly influenced by Jainism and Vaishnavism, which forbid animal slaughter. Rajasthan's cereal-based diet includes *kadhi* (lentil and yoghurt soup), types of *khichdi* (rich rice preparations) and breads made from *bajra* (millet) and *jowar* (sorghum maize). Gujarati cuisine uses a wide range of protein-rich lentils, cereals and vegetables, distinguished by wonderfully subtle seasoning. Pickles, often made of *kairi* (green mango), are a basic part of it. Sweets include the seasonal *aamras* (mango fool) and *doodh pak*, made with thick sweetened milk, dried fruit and nuts.

Khandvi and dhokla

Undhiyo, a Gujarati *thali* dish, consists of yams, potatoes and aubergines (eggplant) roasted in an earthenware pot.

Women selling fresh vegetables in a Rajasthan village

such as *bhujia*, *dal-moth* and *khatta-meetha sev*. *Lachha paratha* (layered bread)

Gujarat

Gujarat has large vegetarian communities of Hindus and Jains who, as practitioners of non-violence, have developed an extremely refined vegetarian cuisine, rated as one of India's most sophisticated. A typical *thali* contains innumerable small bowls *(katoris)*, filled with vegetables, lentils, *farsaans* (savoury snacks), pickles, chutneys, breads and sweets. This meal allows a person to savour the delicate balance of flavours – sweet and sour, salty and spicy, crisp and soft, low fat and deep-fried.

Bajra (millet) is the staple grain of the Saurashtra peninsula and Kutch district in Gujarat and is used to make the *rotlis* (baked bread) that are eaten with most

meals. Another bread is *thepla*, a savoury griddled bread made from chickpea flour. Rice specialities, such as *khichdi* (a nourishing mixture of rice and five kinds of lentils), *vangi bhat*, (rice with aubergines and coriander) and *masala bhat* (spicy rice) are made more

Young girls gathering red chillies that have been sun-dried

tempting by the addition of a dollop of *ghee* at the end. Jaggery or sugar is used to sweeten every dish and the food is usually seasoned with mustard, asafetida and fenugreek, used both for flavour and digestion.

Integral to a meal are crisp *farsaans*, particularly *dhokla* (steamed spongy cakes of chickpea flour and yoghurt), *khandvi* (chickpea flour rolls filled with coconut), *mirchi pakora* (green chilly fritters) and *khakra* (wafers).

Saurashtra is famous for pickles and *methia masala*, made from powdered fenugreek, chillies and salt and used as a salad dressing, while from the bakeries of Surat come wonderful local biscuits, *nankhatais*.

ON THE MENU

Batata nu shak A dry spicy potato preparation.

Besan halwa A sweet made from chickpea flour.

Dahi pakora Lentil dumplings in yoghurt.

Kadhi A light curry made with chickpeas and lentils.

Makki soyta Corn kernels in a spicy sauce.

Mattar ki kachori Fried bread stuffed with peas.

Mula ni kadi Yoghurt curry with white radish.

Paunk Mixed vegetables seasoned with lime and jaggery, a winter dish, popular in Surat.

Gatta curry has steamed dumplings made from chickpea flour cooked in a spiced yoghurt sauce.

Sulas, a speciality of Rajput clans, is barbecued meat softened with a paste made from a melon-type fruit.

Shrikhand is a dessert made from yoghurt flavoured with saffron, cardamom, nuts and dried fruits.

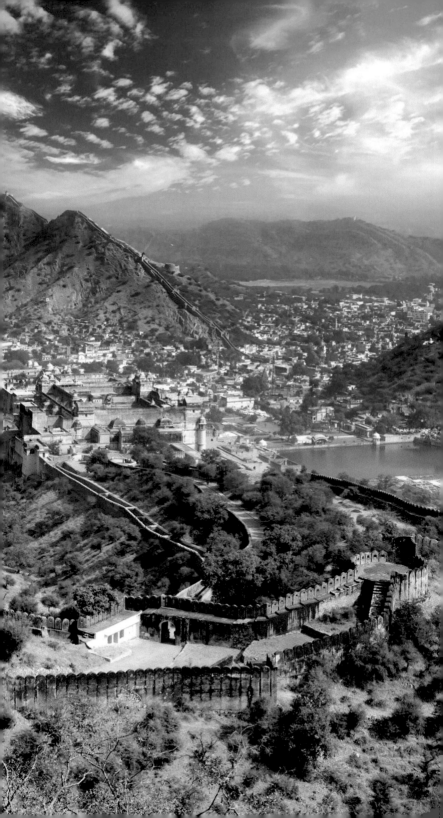

RAJASTHAN

No state in India is as rich in magnificent palaces and forts, colourful festivals and bazaars, as Rajasthan. Stretching over 342,000 sq km (132,047 sq miles), the state is bisected by the Aravalli Range, which runs diagonally from the northeast to the southwest. Its main river is the Chambal. The Thar Desert, which covers western Rajasthan, was once ruled by three great kingdoms – Jaisalmer, Jodhpur and Bikaner. Shekhawati, with its painted *havelis*, is in the semi-arid north while the eastern plains have the bustling state capital, Jaipur, and the Ranthambhore National Park, famous for its tigers. In the hilly, wooded south are the fairy-tale palaces, lakes and forts of Udaipur, and the spectacular Jain temples at Ranakpur, and Dilwara in Mount Abu.

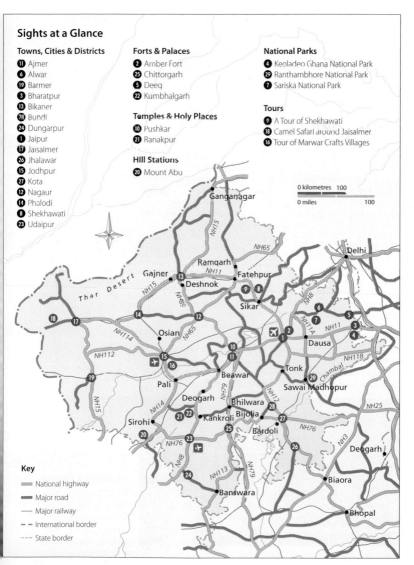

Sights at a Glance

Towns, Cities & Districts
11 Ajmer
6 Alwar
19 Barmer
3 Bharatpur
13 Bikaner
28 Bundi
24 Dungarpur
1 Jaipur
17 Jaisalmer
26 Jhalawar
15 Jodhpur
27 Kota
12 Nagaur
14 Phalodi
8 Shekhawati
23 Udaipur

Forts & Palaces
2 Amber Fort
25 Chittorgarh
5 Deeg
22 Kumbhalgarh

Temples & Holy Places
10 Pushkar
21 Ranakpur

Hill Stations
20 Mount Abu

National Parks
4 Keoladeo Ghana National Park
29 Ranthambhore National Park
7 Sariska National Park

Tours
9 A Tour of Shekhawati
18 Camel Safari around Jaisalmer
16 Tour of Marwar Crafts Villages

Key

⎯ National highway
▬ Major road
⎯ Major railway
‑ ‑ International border
‑ ‑ ‑ State border

◀ Panoramic view of the historic Amber Fort in Jaipur

For keys to symbols *see back flap*

❶ Jaipur

A labyrinth of fascinating bazaars, opulent palaces and historic sights, Jaipur is often called the "Pink City" because its prominent buildings are washed in this colour. Tradition and modernity exist side by side here. On its colourful streets, motorbikes jostle for space with camels, and turbaned village elders rub shoulders with youngsters in jeans. Jaipur's old walled area has the City Palace, an astronomical observatory and bazaars that sell everything from shoes to jewellery. Recent additions include a multi-arts centre, but the focal point remains the Hawa Mahal.

Govind Dev Temple, dedicated to Krishna

🏛 City Palace Museum
See pp360–61.

🕌 Govind Dev Temple
Jaleb Chowk (behind City Palace). **Open** daily. 🎊 Holi (Mar), Janmashtami (Aug/Sep), Annakut (Oct/Nov).

The presiding deity of this unusual temple is the flute-playing Lord Krishna (also known as Govind Dev). The image of this god originally came from the Govindeoji Temple in Brindavan *(see p183)*. It was brought to Amber *(see pp368–9)*, then the capital of Jaipur's ruling family, in the late 17th century to save it from the iconoclastic zeal of the Mughal emperor Aurangzeb.

It is believed that this temple was once a garden pavilion called Suraj Mahal where Sawai Jai Singh II lived while his dream-city, Jaipur, was being built. Legend has it that one night the king awoke from his sleep to find himself in the presence of Krishna who demanded that his *devasthan* ("divine residence") be returned to him. Jai Singh then moved

to the Chandra Mahal, at the opposite end of the garden, and installed the image as the guardian deity of Jaipur's rulers.

Just behind the temple is the 18th-century **Jai Niwas Bagh**, a Mughal-style garden with fountains and water channels. Towards the north is the Badal Mahal, an enchanting hunting pavilion.

🏟 Chaugan Stadium
Brahmpuri. **Open** daily.

This large open area near the City Palace derives its name from *chaugan*, an ancient Persian form of polo played with a curved stick. The area was once used for festival processions and wrestling matches, as well as elephant and lion fights. Today the stadium, with its viewing pavilions, is the venue for the famous Elephant Festival *(see p375)* held at the same time as the Holi celebrations.

🏰 Hawa Mahal
Sireh Deori Bazaar. **Tel** (0141) 261 8862. **Open** daily. **Closed** public hols. 📷 Extra charges for photography.

A whimsical addition to Rajasthan's rich architectural vocabulary, the fanciful Hawa Mahal or "Palace of Winds" was erected in

Sights at a Glance
① City Palace Museum
② Govind Dev Temple
③ Chaugan Stadium
④ Hawa Mahal
⑤ Albert Hall Museum
⑥ Jantar Mantar

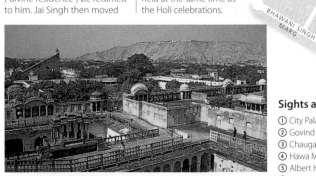

A view of the walled city of Jaipur

1799 by the aesthete Sawai Pratap Singh (r.1778–1803). Its ornate pink façade has become an icon for the city. The tiered Baroque-like composition of projecting windows and balconies with perforated screens is five storeys high but just one room deep, its walls not more than 20 cm (8 inches) thick. Built of lime and mortar, the structure was designed in this way to enable the veiled ladies of the harem to observe unnoticed the lively street scenes below. Dedicated to Lord Krishna, the Hawa Mahal, seen from afar, looks like the *mukut* (crown) that often adorns the god's head.

Visitors can climb up the winding ramp to the top, and a gateway towards the west leads into the complex. Within are administrative offices and the interesting **Archaeological Museum**, which houses a small collection of sculptures and local handicrafts, including some utensils dating back to the 2nd century BC.

VISITORS' CHECKLIST

Practical Information
Jaipur district. 261 km (162 miles) SW of Delhi. 2,324,500. Paryatan Bhavan, Mirza Ismail Rd, (0141) 511 0596. Mon–Sat. Kite Flying Festival (14 Jan), Elephant Festival (Mar), Gangaur (Mar/Apr), Teej (Jul/Aug).

Transport
15 km (9 miles) S of city centre.

🏛 Albert Hall Museum

Ram Niwas Bagh. **Tel** (0141) 256 5124. **Open** Sat–Thu. **Closed** public hols. free on Mon.

This grand, multi-layered museum was designed by Sir Samuel Swinton Jacob, a master of the Indo-Saracenic style *(see p26)*. The ground floor displays decorative shields, embossed salvers and local glazed pottery. A 9-m (30-ft) long *phad* (painted cloth scroll) depicts the life of Pabuji, a 14th-century folk hero *(see p385)*. The museum's greatest treasure, however, is one of the world's largest Persian garden carpets (dating from 1632). This can be viewed on request in the Durbar Hall. The museum also has an extensive collection of paintings dating back to the 16th century.

🛕 Jantar Mantar
See pp362–3.

MAP

0 metres 500
0 yards 500

Jal Mahal, GAITOR
Jaigarh & Amber Fort

RAMGARH

Talkatora
Chaugan Stadium ③
Jai Niwas Bagh
Joriwar Singh Gate

Govindji Temple
MOTI KATRA BAZAAR

City Palace Museum ①

Jantar Mantar ⑥
Hawa Mahal ④

THE PINK CITY

TRIPOLIA BAZAAR
RAM GANJ BAZAAR

Jami Masjid

GAITA

Ajmeri Gate
New Gate
Sanganeri Gate

Albert Hall Museum ⑤

Sisodia Rani ka Bagh, AGRA

Ram Niwas Bagh

SMS Hospital

Jawahar Kala Kendra & Moti Doongri Palace

Key

Street-by-Street area: *see pp358–9*

Caparisoned elephant at a festival

The Building of Jaipur

Sawai Jai Singh II was a keen scholar, statesman and patron of the arts. He was awarded the title of "Sawai" ("one-and-a-quarter"), a metaphor for one who is extraordinary, by the Mughal emperor Aurangzeb when he was just 11 years old. With the help of a gifted Bengali engineer, Vidyadhar Chakravarty, Jai Singh built a new capital south of Amber and named it Jaipur ("City of Victory"). Work began in 1727 and took six years to complete. Surrounded by a crenellated wall pierced by seven gates,

Sawai Jai Singh II (r.1700–43)

Jaipur is laid out in a geometric grid of streets and squares and is one of India's finest examples of a planned city.

Street-by-Street: Around Badi Chaupar

The Badi Chaupar ("Large Square") is at one end of the colourful Tripolia Bazaar. Few changes have been made to the original 18th-century plan of streets and squares. Branching out of the main streets are narrow pedestrian lanes where artisans fashion puppets, silver jewellery, and other local handicrafts in tiny workshops. Behind are the *havelis* of eminent citizens, some used as schools, shops and offices. The area is a hub of activity, rich with pungent smells and vibrant colours, with temple bells adding to the cacophony of street sounds.

★ Jantar Mantar
Jai Singh II's observatory of astronomical instruments looks like a series of futuristic sculptures (see pp362–3).

Ishwar Lat
Ishwari Singh built this tower in 1749 to commemorate his victory over his stepbrother, Madho Singh I.

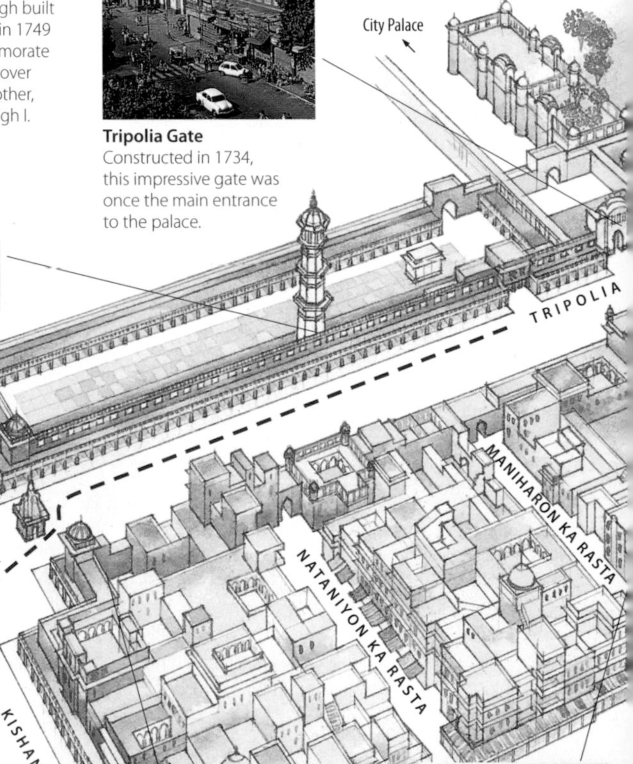

Tripolia Gate
Constructed in 1734, this impressive gate was once the main entrance to the palace.

City Palace

TRIPOLIA

MANIHARON KA RASTA

← Chandpol

Chhoti Chaupar
("Small Square") leads to Kishanpol Bazaar, famous for its shops selling rose-, saffron-, almond- and vetiver-flavoured sherbets.

NATANIYON KA RASTA

KISHANPOL BAZAAR

Maharaja Arts College

Flower Sellers
Marigolds and other flowers are made into garlands and used as offerings to beloved deities in temples and roadside shrines.

Lac Bangles
Maniharon ka Rasta is full of tiny workshops of lac bangle makers.

★ **Hawa Mahal**
A view of Hawa Mahal's unusual rear façade can be seen from the City Palace.

★ **Johari Bazaar**
Vegetable sellers sit at one end of this street where many big gem dealers also have their offices and shops.

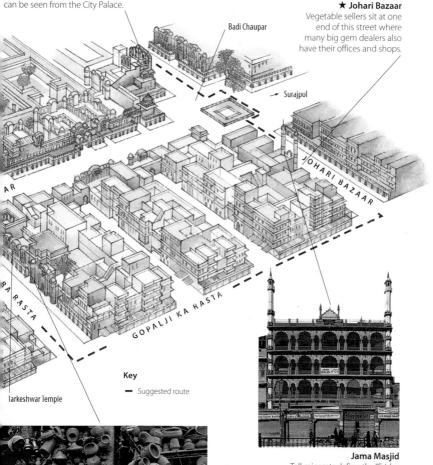

Badi Chaupar

Surajpol

JOHARI BAZAAR

AR

RASTA

GOPALJI KA RASTA

Key

— Suggested route

Jarkeshwar Temple

Jama Masjid
Tall minarets define the "Friday Mosque", its three storeys fronted by arched screens.

Pottery Shop
Large terracotta urns, pots of all sizes, bells, statues, foot-scrapers and oil lamps made by traditional craftsmen are sold here.

0 metres 100
0 yards 100

Jaipur: City Palace Museum

Occupying the heart of Jai Singh II's city, the City Palace has been home to the rulers of Jaipur since the first half of the 18th century. The sprawling complex is a superb blend of Rajput and Mughal architecture, with open, airy Mughal-style public buildings leading to private apartments. Today, part of the complex is open to the public as the Maharaja Sawai Man Singh II Museum, popularly known as the City Palace Museum. Its treasures, which include miniature paintings, manuscripts, Mughal carpets, musical instruments, royal costumes and weaponry, provide a splendid introduction to Jaipur's princely past, and its fascinating arts and crafts.

★ **Pritam Chowk**
The "Court of the Beloved" has four delicately painted doorways representing the seasons.

Sileh Khana
The erstwhile armoury houses the museum's collection of weapons, among the finest in India. Some pieces, such as this shield, are lavishly decorated.

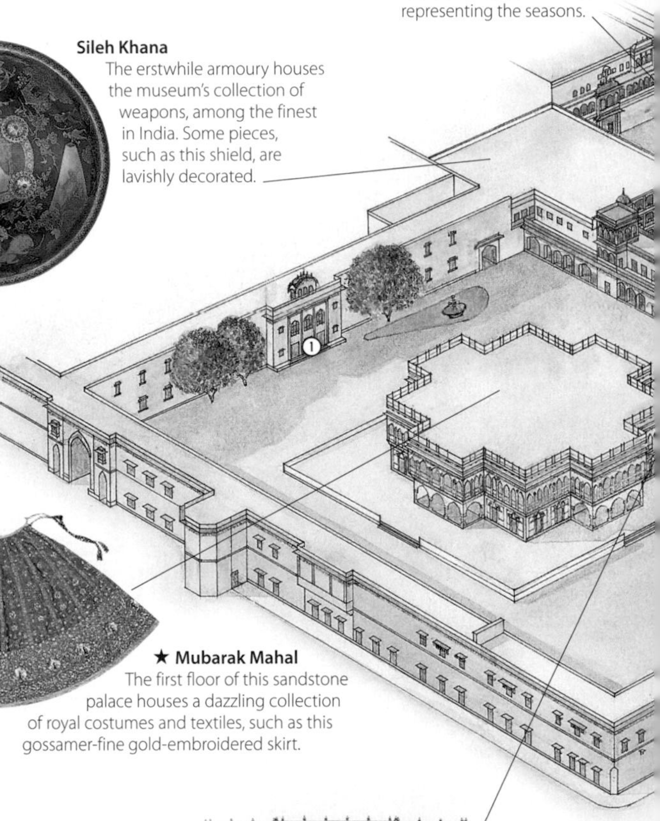

★ **Mubarak Mahal**
The first floor of this sandstone palace houses a dazzling collection of royal costumes and textiles, such as this gossamer-fine gold-embroidered skirt.

KEY

① Crafts demonstration area

② Riddhi-Siddhi Pol

③ Shops

④ Transport gallery

⑤ Ticket counter

★ **Rajendra Pol**
Flanking this gateway are two large elephants, each carved from single blocks of marble.

Chandra Mahal
Each floor of this seven-storeyed palace is extravagantly decorated and has a specific name according to its function. The palace is closed to the public.

VISITORS' CHECKLIST

Practical Information
City Palace Complex.
Tel (0141) 260 8055. .
Open daily. **Closed** public hols.
🏛 Museum and Jaigarh Palace only. Photography allowed for façades only, extra charges for video photography. 📷 📸 Crafts demonstration area: **Open** daily. **Closed** public hols.

★ Silver Urns
The two giant silver urns in the Diwan-i-Khas, listed in the Guinness Book of Records as the world's largest silver objects, carried sacred Ganges water for Madho Singh II's visit to London in 1901.

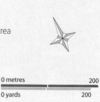

Diwan-i-Aam
The former ceremonial hall now displays rare Mughal and Rajput miniature paintings, as well as carpets, manuscripts, a superbly crafted silver throne and an ivory elephant howdah.

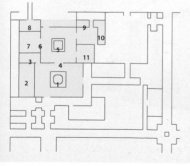

The City Palace

1 Mubarak Mahal
2 Crafts Demonstration Area
3 Sileh Khana
4 Rajendra Pol
5 Diwan-i-Khas
6 Riddhi-Siddhi Pol
7 Pritam Chowk
8 Chandra Mahal
9 Shops
10 Transport Gallery
11 Diwan-i-Aam

0 metres	200
0 yards	200

Key

☐ Area illustrated

Jaipur: Jantar Mantar

Of the five observatories built by Sawai Jai Singh II, the one in Jaipur is the largest and best preserved; the others are in Delhi *(see p82)*, Ujjain, Mathura and Varanasi. A keen astronomer himself, Jai Singh kept abreast of the latest astronomical studies in the world, and was most inspired by the work of Mirza Ulugh Beg, the astronomer-king of Samarkand. Built between 1728 and 1734, the observatory has been described as "the most realistic and logical landscape in stone", its 16 instruments resembling a giant sculptural composition. Some of the instruments are still used to forecast how hot the summer months will be, the expected date of arrival, duration and intensity of the monsoon, and the possibility of floods and famine.

Narivalaya Yantra
Inclined at 27 degrees, these sundials represent the two hemispheres and calculate time by following the solar cycle.

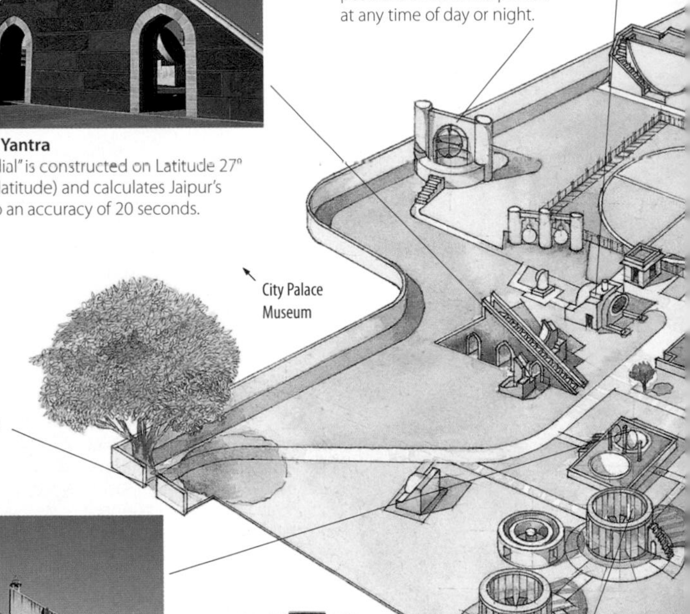

Unnatansha Yantra
was used to determine the positions of stars and planets at any time of day or night.

Laghu Samrat Yantra
This "small sundial" is constructed on Latitude 27° North (Jaipur's latitude) and calculates Jaipur's local time up to an accuracy of 20 seconds.

City Palace Museum

Entrance

Chakra Yantra
A brass tube passes through the centre of these two circular metal instruments. They can be used to calculate the angles of stars and planets from the equator.

★ Ram Yantra
Vertical columns support an equal number of horizontal slabs in the two identical stone structures that comprise this instrument. Its readings determine the celestial arc from horizon to zenith, as well as the altitude of the sun.

A view of Jantar Mantar
The complex of stone and metal instruments was repaired with the addition of marble inlay comissioned by Madho Singh II in 1901.

★ Samrat Yantra
Jai Singh believed that gigantic instruments would give more accurate results This 23-m (75-ft) high sundial forecasts the crop prospects for the year.

Hawa Mahal

Rashivalaya Yantra
This is composed of 12 pieces, each of which represents a sign of the zodiac and therefore faces a different constellation. This *yantra* (instrument), used by astrologers to draw up horoscopes, is the only one of its kind.

★ Jai Prakash Yantra
These two sunken hemispheres map out the heavens. Some historians believe that Jai Singh invented this instrument himself, to verify the accuracy of all the other instruments in the observatory.

Jaipur: South of the Walled City

By the end of the 19th century, Jaipur had expanded far beyond the boundaries of the walled city established by Sawai Jai Singh II. Many new pleasure palaces, hunting lodges and mansions came up on its outskirts, making the city a harmonious blend of old and new.

Lakshmi Narayan Temple, a white marble addition to the Pink City

🏛 Moti Doongri Palace
Jawaharlal Nehru Marg.
Closed to the public.

Moti Doongri palace, perched on a low hillock, owes its florid exterior to Sawai Man Singh II, who converted the old fort of Shankargarh into a palace, and added turrets in the style of a Scottish castle. In 1940 he married the beautiful Princess Gayatri Devi of Cooch Behar, and this palace with its modernized interior became the venue for glittering parties hosted by the glamorous couple.

At the foot of Moti Doongri is the white marble **Lakshmi Narayan Temple**, a popular place of worship, admired for its elaborate carvings.

🏛 Rambagh Palace
Bhawani Singh Rd. **Tel** (0141) 221 1919. 🛇 open to non-residents.

The Rambagh Palace, now a splendid hotel, has a colourful past. Built in 1835, it was originally a small garden pavilion for Ram Singh II's wet nurse, but was used as a hunting lodge after she died in 1856. Later, on his return from England, Ram Singh II's son Madho Singh II transformed it into a royal playground with squash and tennis courts, a polo field and an indoor swimming pool. In 1933, it became the official residence of Madho Singh's adopted heir, Man Singh II, who hired

Hammonds of London to redo the interiors. New additions included an exotic red and gold Chinese room, black marble bathrooms, Lalique crystal chandeliers and an illuminated dining table. Surrounded by fairy-tale gardens, it became a hotel in 1957, when Man Singh II moved to the smaller Raj Mahal Palace.

🏛 Raj Mahal Palace
Sardar Patel Marg. **Tel** (0141) 510 5665. 🛇 open to non-residents.

Now a grand heritage hotel, this pleasant 18th-century palace, less opulent than the Rambagh

Palace, occupies a special place in the history of Jaipur. Built in 1739 for Sawai Jai Singh II's favourite queen, Chandra Kumari Ranawatji, it was used as a summer resort by the ladies of the court. In 1821, it was declared the official home of the British Resident in Jaipur. However, the most memorable phase of its history dates to the time when Man Singh II and Gayatri Devi moved here from Rambagh Palace in 1956. Among the celebrities they entertained were Prince Philip, the polo player like Man Singh II, and Jackie Kennedy.

🏛 Jawahar Kala Kendra
Jawaharlal Nehru Marg.
Tel (0141) 270 5879. **Open** daily.
💻 🏛

Designed by the Indian architect Charles Correa in 1993, this remarkable building pays vivid tribute to

Jawahar Kala Kendra

contemporary Indian design. Imaginatively patterned after the famous grid system of the city, each of its nine squares or courts houses a small *mahal*, or palace, named after a planet. Each one displays selected exhibits of textiles, handicrafts and weaponry, while in the centre there is a wonderfully conceived open-air plaza where performances of traditional Rajasthani music and dance are held.

The luxurious interior of Rambagh Palace, now a hotel

For hotels and restaurants see p699 and pp712–13

Jaipur Jewellery

Be it the fabulous rubies and emeralds sported by former maharajas and their queens or the splendid silver and bone ornaments worn by peasants, jewellery is an integral part of Rajasthani culture. Even camels, horses and elephants have specially designed anklets and necklaces. Jaipur is one of the largest ornament-making centres in India, and *meenakari* (enamel work) and *kundankari* (inlay work with gems) are the two traditional techniques for which it is most famous. In the 16th century, Man Singh I *(see p368)*, influenced by the prevailing fashions of the Mughal court, brought five Sikh enamel workers from Lahore to his state. Since then, generations of highly skilled jewellers have lived and worked here. Jaipur caters to every taste, from chunky silver ornaments to more sophisticated designs intricately set in gold with precious stones.

A jewelled trinket box with a *kundankari* lid; the lower portion of this box is worked in fine *meenakari* and has traditional floral patterns in red, blue, green and white.

Sarpech, the cypress-shaped turban ornament, was a fashion statement introduced by the Mughal emperors in the early 17th century to display their finest gems. Rajput rulers, impressed by Mughal flamboyance, sported similar dazzling ornaments such as this piece of enamelled gold set with emeralds, rubies, diamonds and sapphires, finished with a pearl drop.

The skill of stone-setting can be seen in the crowded alleys of Haldiyon ka Rasta, Jadiyon ka Rasta and Gopalji ka Rasta. An inherited art, the jewellery trade is in the hands of artisans' guilds.

Meenakari embellishes the obverse side of *kundan* jewellery, for the Rajasthani love of adornment decrees that even the back of a piece of jewellery *(left)* must be as beautiful as the front *(right)*.

Kundankari uses highly refined gold as a base, which is then inlaid with lac and set with precious and semi-precious stones to provide colour and design. Purified gold wire outlines the design and also conceals the lac background.

Jaipur is now a centre of lapidary, specializing in cutting emeralds and diamonds from Africa, South America and various regions of India. Gem-cutters learn their skill by cutting garnets.

Exploring Jaipur: Outer Sites

A parallel range of hills runs along Jaipur's eastern periphery, from Sanganer in the south up to Amber and beyond, enclosing a narrow valley. Consisting of thickly wooded slopes and rocky terrain, this was the area where the nobility built temples, gardens, pavilions and palaces. Perched high above the city are the dramatic fortresses of Nahargarh and Jaigarh that guarded the approach to both Amber and the new capital of Jaipur. The surrounding region also has the remains of fortified walls, temples, *havelis* and the marble cenotaphs of the Kachhawaha kings of Amber and Jaipur.

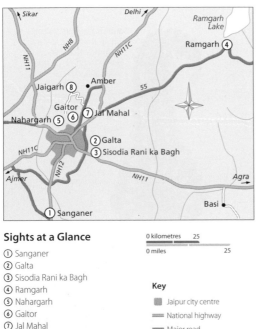

Sights at a Glance

① Sanganer
② Galta
③ Sisodia Rani ka Bagh
④ Ramgarh
⑤ Nahargarh
⑥ Gaitor
⑦ Jal Mahal
⑧ Jaigarh

0 kilometres   25
0 miles   25

Key

▬ Jaipur city centre
━ National highway
━ Major road
═ Minor road

Marble statue of a Jain *tirthankara* at Sanganer's Sanghiji Temple

For hotels and restaurants see p699 and pp712–13

Sanganer

Jaipur district, 15 km (9 miles) SW of Jaipur.

This colourful town is famous for its blockprinted cotton. Today most of its printers and dyers belong to a guild, with retail outlets selling reasonably priced fabrics. Sanganer owes its success as a printing centre to a rivulet whose waters have a mineral content that fixes dyes. Sanganer is also a centre of handmade paper, and of Jaipur's renowned, hand-painted Blue Pottery, of which vases and tiles with delicate Persian, Turkish and Indian designs are made. Tucked away in the old walled town is the impressive 11th-century Jain **Sanghiji Temple**, lavishly decorated with carvings. Sanganer is now a busy suburb of Jaipur city and houses the city's airport.

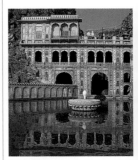

A sacred tank in Galta

🏛 Galta

Jaipur district. 10 km (6 miles) E of Jaipur.

This picturesque gorge cradles Galta Kund, an 18th-century religious site with two main temples and a number of smaller shrines. Its seven sacred tanks, fed by natural spring water, are said to have curative powers. Two pavilions on either side of the complex have well-preserved frescoes. The Surya Temple, high on the ridge, provides spectacular views of Jaipur.

🔆 Sisodia Rani ka Bagh

Jaipur district. Purana Ghat. 6 km (4 miles) E of Jaipur. **Tel** (0141) 264 0594. **Open** daily. 📷

This terraced garden was laid out in the 18th century for

The picturesque Jal Mahal, seemingly afloat during the monsoon

Sawai Jai Singh II's second wife, who married him on the condition that her son would succeed to the throne. To escape the inevitable palace intrigues, the queen moved to a more private home outside the walled city. Her little double-storeyed palace, decorated with lively murals, is surrounded by beautiful gardens. It is today a popular location for Indian films.

🏯 Ramgarh
Jaipur district. 40 km (25 miles) E of Jaipur.

Ramgarh is the site of one of the earliest Kachhawaha fortresses. The fort was built by the dynasty's founder, Duleh Rai (r.1093–1135), who also built a temple dedicated to the goddess Jamvai Mata, now visited by thousands of devotees. Ramgarh Lodge, on the northern bank of a man-made lake, is an elegant French villa-style hunting lodge built in 1931 for the Jaipur royal family. It is now a pleasant heritage hotel. The lake, which was used for water-based sports during the 1982 Asian Games is now dry and the polo ground is no longer operational, but the hotel remains popular as a spa resort near Jaipur.

🏯 Nahargarh
Jaipur district. 9 km (6 miles) NW of Jaipur. **Tel** (0141) 518 2957. **Open** daily. **Closed** public hols.

The forbidding hill-top fort of Nahargarh ("Tiger Fort") stands in what was once a densely forested area. The fierce Meena tribe ruled this region until they were defeated by the Kachhawahas. Its fortifications, strengthened by Sawai Jai Singh II, were subsequently expanded by successive rulers. Madho Singh II added a

lavish palace called Madhavendra Bhavan for his nine queens. Laid out in a maze of terraces and courtyards, it has a cool, airy upper chamber from which the ladies of the court could view the city. Its walls and pillars are an outstanding example of *arayish*, a form of plaster work that is hand-polished with a piece of agate to produce a marble finish.

🏯 Gaitor
Jaipur district. 8 km (5 miles) N of Jaipur. **Open** daily. **Closed** public hols.

The marble cenotaphs of the Kachhawaha kings are enclosed in a walled garden just off the Amber road. This area was chosen by Sawai Jai Singh II as the new cremation site after Amber (*see pp368–9*) was abandoned. Ornate carved pillars support the marble *chhatris* erected over the platforms where the maharajas were cremated. One of the most impressive cenotaphs in the complex is that of Jai Singh II himself. It has 20 marble pillars carved with religious and mythological scenes and is

topped by a white marble dome. The most recent cenotaph was erected in 1997 in memory of Jagat Singh, the only son of Sawai Man Singh II and Gayatri Devi.

🏯 Jal Mahal
Jaipur district. 8 km (5 miles) N of Jaipur. **Open** daily.

During the monsoon, water fills the Man Sagar lake, and the Jal Mahal ("Water Palace") seems to rise from it like a mirage. Built in the mid-18th century by Madho Singh I, it is inspired by the Lake Palace at Udaipur, where the king spent his childhood. It was later used for royal duck-shooting parties, and a variety of water birds are still seen here. The terraced garden, enclosed by arched passages, has elegant semi-octagonal towers capped by cupolas in each corner.

🏯 Jaigarh
Jaipur district. 12 km (8 miles) NW of Jaipur. **Tel** (0141) 267 1848. **Open** 9am–4:30pm. **Closed** public hols. 🏯

Legendary Jaigarh, the "Victory Fort", watches over the old capital of Amber. One of the few surviving cannon foundries is located here. Its most prized possession is the monumental 50-tonne Jai Van, cast in 1726 and said to be the world's largest cannon on wheels. Ironically, despite its impressive size, the cannon has never been fired.

The famous Jai Van

Other interesting sights are the Diva Burj, a seven-storeyed tower where a huge oil lamp was lit on the king's birthday, two temples and a palace built over 200 years ago.

The ramparts of Jaigarh Fort, a feat of military engineering

❷ Amber Fort

The fort palace of Amber was the Kachhawaha
citadel until 1727, when their capital moved to Jaipur.
Successive rulers continued to come here on important
occasions to seek the blessings of the family deity, Shila
Devi. The citadel was established in 1592 by Man Singh I
on the remains of an old 11th-century fort, but the various
buildings added by Jai Singh I (r.1621–67) are what
constitute its magnificent centrepiece.

Elephant ride on the cobbled
pathway to the fort

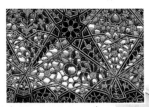

★ Sheesh Mahal
The flame of a single candle,
reflected in the tiny mirrors
embedded in this chamber,
transforms it into a starlit sky.

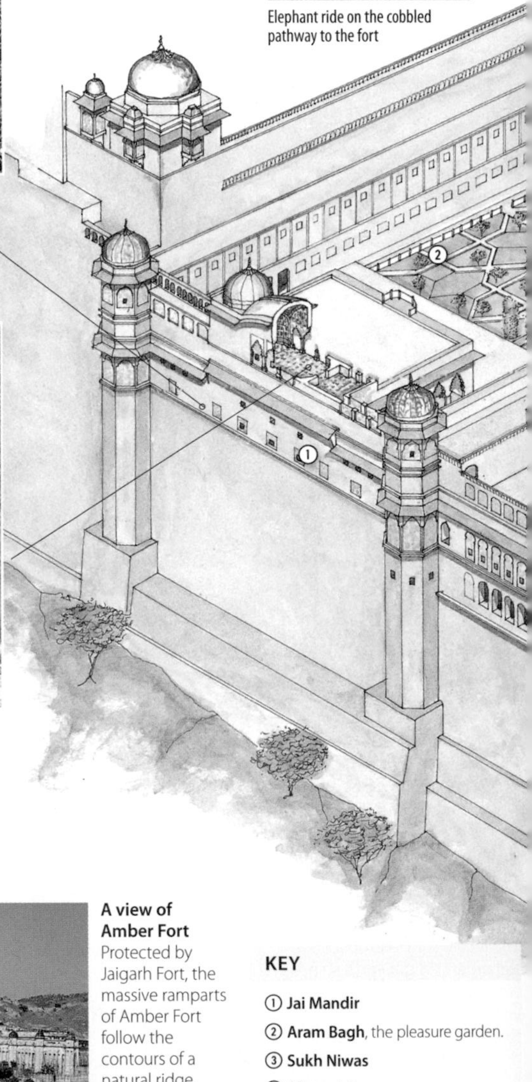

Jas Mandir
This Hall of Private Audience has
latticed windows, a floral ceiling
of elegant alabaster relief work
and glass inlay. A marble screen
here overlooks the Maota Lake
and allows in cool air.

**A view of
Amber Fort**
Protected by
Jaigarh Fort, the
massive ramparts
of Amber Fort
follow the
contours of a
natural ridge.

KEY

① **Jai Mandir**

② **Aram Bagh**, the pleasure garden.

③ **Sukh Niwas**

④ **Diwan-i-Aam**

⑤ **Sattais Katcheri**

VISITORS' CHECKLIST

Practical Information
Jaipur district. 11 km (7 miles)
N of Jaipur.
Tel (0141) 253 0293. **Open** 8am–
5:30pm daily. **Closed** public hols.

★ Ganesh Pol
This shimmering three-storeyed gateway,
built in 1640, is connected to the private
apartments by the screened
uppermost level, meant for
ladies in purdah.

★ Shila Devi Temple
This ornately carved silver
door is the entrance to the
Shila Devi Temple.

Shila Devi
Temple

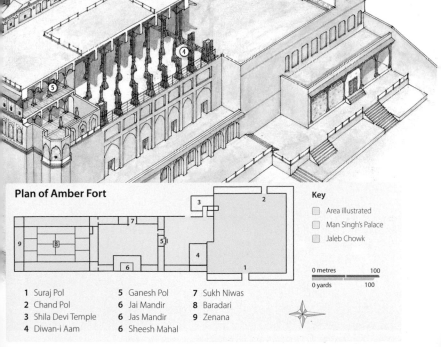

Plan of Amber Fort

Key

- Area illustrated
- Man Singh's Palace
- Jaleb Chowk

0 metres   100
0 yards   100

1 Suraj Pol	5 Ganesh Pol	7 Sukh Niwas
2 Chand Pol	6 Jai Mandir	8 Baradari
3 Shila Devi Temple	6 Jas Mandir	9 Zenana
4 Diwan-i Aam	6 Sheesh Mahal	

Exploring Amber (the Old Capital)

Crowning the crest of a hill, Amber Fort offers a panoramic view of Maota Lake and the historic old town at the base of the hill, which was the early seat of the Amber kings before they made the fort their capital. Several havelis, stepwells, and temples can be seen below the fort, pointing to the existence of a self-sufficient township, where the Mughal emperor Akbar used to stop on his annual pilgrimage to Ajmer *(see p380)*.

Sattais Katcheri, where the revenue records were written

The Fort Complex

The main entrance to the historic Amber Fort is through the imposing **Suraj Pol** ("Sun Gate"), so called because it faces the direction of the rising sun, the Kachhawaha family emblem. The gate leads into a huge courtyard, **Jaleb Chowk**, lined on three sides with souvenir and refreshment shops. A flight of steps leads to the **Shila Devi Temple**, which has silver doors, silver oil lamps, grand pillars carved to look like banana trees, and contains the Kachhawaha family deity, a stone *(shila)* image of the goddess Kali. The next courtyard is the **Diwan-i-Aam**, the space for public audience. Near it is the **Sattais Katcheri**, a colonnade of 27 *(sattais)* pillars, where scribes once sat to record revenue petitions.

The magnificent **Ganesh Pol** is the gateway to three pleasure palaces, each with special features, built around a Mughal-style garden, **Aram Bagh**. Maota Lake, which provided water to the fort, is surrounded by two exquisite gardens. The **Kesar Kyari Bagh** has star-shaped flower beds once planted with saffron *(kesar)* flowers, while **Dilaram Bagh**, built in 1568 as a resting place for Akbar on his way to Ajmer, is a clever pun on the name of its architect, Dilaram ("Heart's Ease"). A small Archaeological Museum is located nearby. The farthest and oldest end of the fort was converted into the zenana (women's quarters), with screens and covered balconies for the seclusion of the royal ladies in purdah. Faint traces of frescoes are still visible on the walls. In the centre of the courtyard is a pavilion with 12 pillars, the **Baradari**.

Marble carving of a Hindu deity

The Township

The **Chand Pol** ("Moon Gate"), directly opposite Suraj Pol, leads to the old town outside the fort. The beautiful **Jagat Shiromani Temple** with its remarkable *torana* (gateway) is one of the many temples that lies along this route. It also has a water tank, **Panna Mian ka Kund**. To the east lies **Sagar**, a popular picnic spot with two terraced lakes. The Jaipur-Delhi Highway cuts across the town, and Amber's main market and bus stand are located on this road. Further north stands the **Akbari Mosque**, built by Emperor Akbar in 1569, and towards the east is **Bharmal ki Chhatri**, a walled enclosure containing a group of memorials. This was the old cremation site for the rulers of Amber until a new spot was chosen at Gaitor *(see p367)*, near Jaipur.

Kesar Kyari Bagh, named after the rare saffron flowers once planted in its star-shaped flower beds

❸ Bharatpur

Bharatpur district. 181 km (112 miles) E of Jaipur. 🚉 204,500. 🚌 ℹ️ RTDC Hotel Saras, (05644) 223 790. 🎭 Jaswant Mela (Oct).

Most famous for its bird sanctuary, the kingdom of Bharatpur was founded by the fearless Jats, a community of landowners. Their most remarkable

The moat and ramparts of Lohagarh

leader, Raja Suraj Mal (r.1724–63), fortified the city of Bharatpur in 1733 and used the loot from Mughal buildings to embellish the forts and palaces of his kingdom.

In the centre of the town is **Lohagarh** ("Iron Fort"), a masterpiece of construction. Its massive double ramparts of packed mud and rubble surrounded by impressive moats withstood repeated attacks by the Marathas and the British until it was finally captured by Lord Lake in 1805. Three palaces built in the fort display a fine mix of Mughal and Rajput stylistic detail. One is now the site of

a pharmaceutical college, while the other two, around the Katcheri Bagh, house the **State Museum**. Its artifacts include a rare collection of 1st- and 2nd-century stone carvings. An interesting sunken *hamam* (bath) is close by. In 1818, Bharatpur became the region's first princely state to sign a treaty with the East India Company.

🏛 **State Museum**
Tel (05644) 22 8185. **Open** Fri–Wed. **Closed** public hols. 🎭 free on Mon. Extra charges for photography.

❹ Keoladeo Ghana National Park

See pp372–3.

❺ Deeg

Bharatpur district. 36 km (22 miles) N of Bharatpur. 🚌 ℹ️ RTDC Hotel Saras, Bharatpur, (05644) 22 3700. 🎭 Holi (Mar), Jawahar Mela (Aug). Water Palace: **Open** daily. **Closed** the day after Holi (Mar). 🎭

Once the capital of the Jat kings of Bharatpur, Deeg rose to prominence after the decline of the Mughal empire in the 18th century. Its square fort and fortified town, once filled with grand mansions and gardens, now lie unkempt and forlorn.

Deeg's Raja Suraj Mal and his son, Jawahar Singh, were keen builders of lavish pleasure palaces and the most remarkable of these is the **Deeg Water Palace**, a romantic summer retreat for the Jat kings. The magic of the monsoon inspired a lyrical composition of sand-stone and marble pavilions replete with gardens and pools. A skilful cooling system drew water from a huge reservoir and used a number of innovative special effects to simulate monsoon showers and even

Sawan Pavilion, Deeg Water Palace

produce rainbows. The coloured fountains are now used only during the Jawahar Mela.

Deeg Water Palace

Sawan Pavilion is shaped like an upturned boat. Its ingenious water system created a semi-circle of falling water.

Nand Bhavan

Keshav Bhavan had heavy lithic balls placed on its roof, that rolled and produced "thunder" when water gushed up the hollow pillars and pipes inside the arches.

Entrance

Gopal Bhavan's numerous overhanging kiosks and balconies are reflected in Gopal Sagar from which it seems to rise. The interior still retains the original furnishings and objets d'art.

The roof-top reservoir had water drawn to it from four wells. Pipes leading from its sides supplied water to the chutes and fountains.

❹ Keoladeo Ghana National Park

A UNESCO World Heritage Site regarded as one of the world's most important bird sanctuaries, Keoladeo Ghana derives its name from a Shiva temple (Keoladeo) within a dense forest *(ghana)*. This once-arid scrubland was first developed by Bharatpur's rulers in the mid-18th century by diverting the waters of a nearby irrigation canal to create a private duck reserve. Extravagant shooting parties for British viceroys and other royal guests were held here, and horrifying numbers of birds were shot in a single day. Today, the park spreads over 29 sq km (11 sq miles) of wetlands, and attracts a wide variety of migrant and water birds who fly in each winter from places as distant as Siberia. Keoladeo's dry area has mixed deciduous and scrub vegetation and is home to many animals, including the famed nilgai.

Shallow wetlands, one of the world's finest heronries

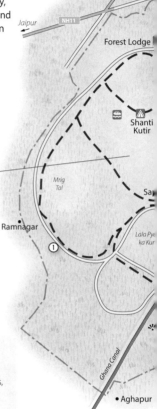

Jaipur NH11

Forest Lodge

Shanti Kutir

Mrig Tal

Sa

Ramnagar

①

Lala Pyo ka Kur

Ghana Canal

Aghapur

Getting Around the Park
Expert boatmen navigate the wetlands and point out bird colonies. Bicycles and cycle-rickshaws are also available for touring the forest paths.

The male Sarus crane dances to attract his mate

Birds, Resident and Migrant

The park attracts over 375 bird species belonging to 56 families. Egrets, darters, cormorants, grey herons and storks hatch nearly 30,000 chicks every year. The park's most eagerly awaited visitor is the Siberian crane, now an endangered species. Other birds include the peregrine falcon, steppe eagle, garganey teal, snake bird and white ibis. Among the large variety of storks are the open-bill stork, the painted stork and the black-necked stork, considered to be the world's tallest stork. Standing on coral-coloured legs, the bird is 2 m (7 ft) tall, with a wingspan of 2.5m(8ft). The Sarus crane, a symbol of fidelity in Indian mythology, woos its partner for life with an elaborate mating dance.

Baby cormorants

Key

▬▬ National highway
▬▬ Main road
▬▬ Minor road
·—·— Park boundary
▬ ▬ Foot path/cycle trail
▢ Marshland

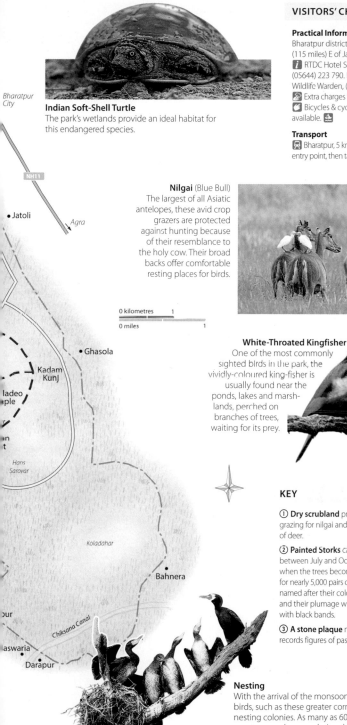

Indian Soft-Shell Turtle
The park's wetlands provide an ideal habitat for this endangered species.

Bharatpur City

NH11

● Jatoli

Agra

Nilgai (Blue Bull)
The largest of all Asiatic antelopes, these avid crop grazers are protected against hunting because of their resemblance to the holy cow. Their broad backs offer comfortable resting places for birds.

0 kilometres 1

0 miles 1

● Ghasola

Kadam
Kunj

ladeo
ple

n
t

*Hans
Sarovar*

White-Throated Kingfisher
One of the most commonly sighted birds in the park, the vividly-coloured king-fisher is usually found near the ponds, lakes and marsh-lands, perched on branches of trees, waiting for its prey.

Koladahar

Bahnera

KEY

① **Dry scrubland** provides good grazing for nilgai and other species of deer.

② **Painted Storks** can be seen between July and October. This is when the trees become nesting sites for nearly 5,000 pairs of these birds, named after their colourful beaks and their plumage which is "painted" with black bands.

③ **A stone plaque** near the temple records figures of past bird shoots.

Chiksana Canal

bur

aswaria
Darapur

Nesting
With the arrival of the monsoon, thousands of birds, such as these greater cormorants, set up nesting colonies. As many as 60 noisy nests on one tree may be seen during this season.

For keys to symbols *see back flap*

Gate of the Tomb of Fateh Jang

❻ Alwar

Alwar district. 150 km (93 miles) NE of Jaipur. 🚂 260,300. 🚍 ☷ 𝑖 RTDC, Nehru Marg, opp railway station, (0144) 234 7348. 🎪 Jagannathji Fair (Mar/Apr).

The former princely state of Alwar is now a dusty, provincial town, visited by few tourists except those on their way to the Sariska National Park. Nevertheless it has some remarkable monuments, built by its wealthy rulers in the 18th century, that are worth seeing. The most significant of these is the **City Palace**, whose architectural features include a profusion of curved *bangaldar* roofs and *chhatris* (pavilions) as well as delicate Mughal floral tracery and *jalis*. The palace, built in 1793, now houses the District Collectorate and Police Head-quarters, and is best viewed from the central courtyard with its lovely marble pavilions. The lavishly decorated Durbar Hall and the Sheesh Mahal, on the first floor, can only be viewed with special permission.

A door to the right of the courtyard leads to the **City Palace Museum**, spread over three halls on the palace's upper storey. Its treasures, which bear witness to the opulent lifestyles

of Alwar's maharajas, include rare and exquisite copies of the Persian poet Sa'adi's *Gulistan* (written in 1258) and the *Babur Nama* or "Memoirs of Babur" (1530), superb Mughal and Rajput miniatures and an awesome armoury. Particularly intriguing is a macabre coil called *nagphas*, used for strangling enemies. Another unique exhibit is a silver dining table with dividers, through which shoals of metal fish can be seen swimming.

The cenotaph of Maharaja Bakhtawar Singh (r.1790–1815) lies behind the palace, across a magnificent *kund* (tank). It is locally known as **Moosi Maharani ki Chhatri**, after his mistress who committed *sati* here after he died. An elegant monument that blends brown sandstone with white marble, its ceilings are adorned with gold leaf paintings.

On a steep hill above the city is the rugged **Bala Qila**, a fort with extensive ramparts, massive gateways and some spectacular views from the top. Originally a 10th-century mud fort, it was added to by the Mughals and Jats, and captured by Pratap Singh of Alwar in 1775. Within the fort is a pretty frescoed palace, the Nikumbh Mahal, in the courtyard of which a police wireless station is, rather inappropriately, sited. Also visible are the ruins of the Salim Mahal, named after Jahangir (Salim),

A page from famous Persian poet Sa'adi's *Gulistan*

Mughal emperor Akbar's heir who was exiled here after he plotted to kill Abu'l Fazl, the emperor's official historian. Near Alwar's railway station is another fine monument, the **Tomb of Fateh Jang**, one of Emperor Shah Jahan's ministers, built in 1647. Dominated by an enormous dome, the walls and ceiling of this magnificent five-storeyed structure have raised plaster reliefs.

Alwar's green lung, **Company Bagh**, is a lovely garden with a greenhouse.

🏛 **City Palace**
Near Collectorate. **Open** daily. 📷

🏛 **City Palace Museum**
Open Sat–Thu. **Closed** public hols.
📷 🚫

🏛 **Moosi Maharani ki Chhatri**
Open Sat–Thu. **Closed** public hols.
📷

🏛 **Bala Qila**
Open daily. Written permission not required anymore. The visitor's name is entered in a register at the office of the Superintendent of Police, City Palace.

🏛 **Tomb of Fateh Jang**
Near railway station.
Open daily.

The elegant marble pavilion at Moosi Maharani ki Chhatri

Sariska Palace, a luxury hotel just outside the Tiger Reserve

❼ Sariska National Park

Alwar district. 37 km (23 miles) NE of Alwar. 🚌 ℹ️ Field Director, Project Tiger Sanctuary, Sariska (0144) 284 1333. **Open** Sep–Jun. 🚗 Extra for personal vehicles or jeeps. 📷 🌿

Designated a Tiger Reserve under Project Tiger (see p293) in 1979, Sariska National Park, formerly the private hunting ground of the princely state of Alwar, sprawls over 800 sq km (309 sq miles), with a core area of 480 sq km (185 sq miles). The Aravalli Range branches out at Sariska, forming low plateaus and valleys that harbour a wide spectrum of wildlife.

Silk cotton in bloom

The tiger population at Sariska is now believed to be between 20 and 30. However, spotting one is a rarity. It was reported by the media that not a single tiger survived in the reserve. Nevertheless, forest guides keep track of where a tiger was last seen and can sometimes lead visitors to spot this elusive predator.

There are a series of watering holes in Sariska, at Pandupol, Bandipol, Slopka, Kalighati and Talvriksha, that make good vantage points to view wildlife, especially at sunset when hoards of animals flock to them to quench their thirst. The gentle chital or spotted deer is commonly sighted at the park's watering holes, while the *chausingha* (four-horned antelope), unique to Sariska, can be spotted around Pandupol. Other species that

can be seen here are panthers and black-faced langur monkeys, jackals and hyenas, nilgai or blue bulls, wild boars and porcupines.

Among the birds that can be spotted are the crested serpent eagle, the great Indian horned owl, woodpeckers, kingfishers and partridges.

The dry deciduous forests of Sariska come to life during the brief spring and early summer when the flowering *dhak (Butea monosperma)* and laburnum bloom. The date palm begins to bear fruit, while berries known locally as *kair (Capparis decidua)* appear on the bushes.

The **Kankwari Fort**, dating to the 17th-century, and temple ruins, such as those of the **Pandupol Temple**, lie within the park. The **Sariska Palace**, built at the end of the 19th century as a hunting lodge for Alwar's rulers, is now a luxury hotel, with a collection of vintage *shikar* photographs.

Black-faced Hanuman langurs, a common sight at Sariska

Festivals of Rajasthan

Nagaur Cattle Fair (Jan/Feb), Nagaur. Camel races, puppet shows, folk music and dance mark this week-long fair (see p380).

Gangaur (Mar/Apr). This 18-day festival celebrates the marital bliss of Shiva and Parvati and is a major event all over Rajasthan, though celebrated with special verve in Udaipur. Women perform the swirling *ghoomar* dance, and carry images of the goddess in colourful processions through the streets, as they pray for their husbands' wellbeing.

Gangaur celebrations, Udaipur

Elephant Festival (Mar), Jaipur. Processions of splendidly caparisoned elephants and an elephant polo tournament are the highlights of this festival.

Mewar Festival (Mar), Udaipur. Mewar's heritage is celebrated with cultural shows and fireworks.

Teej (Aug/Sep). Girls all over Rajasthan wear new clothes, sing and dance joyously to celebrate this festival venerating Parvati, goddess of marital harmony. Teej also heralds the arrival of the monsoon.

Urs (Oct), Ajmer. The mesmerising music of qawwali singers is a highlight of the 13-day-long death anniversary ceremonies for the Sufi saint, Khwaja Moinuddin Chishti.

Pushkar Fair (Oct/Nov), Pushkar (see pp378–9).

❽ Shekhawati

Sikar & Jhunjhunu districts. 115 km
(72 miles) NW from Jaipur to Sikar.
🚌 🎭 Gangaur Festival (Mar/Apr),
Dussehra (Sept/Oct).

A view of the impressive Char-Chowk Haveli, Lachhmangarh

This region, named after its
15th-century ruler Rao Shekha,
has a number of fascinating
small towns with well-preserved
painted *havelis*, forts and temples.
Among the most interesting are
Lachhmangarh and **Fatehpur**
with their grand *havelis*, and
Dundlod, with its well-restored
fort. Especially worth visiting
is **Ramgarh**, 20 km (12 miles)
north of Fatehpur. Famous for
its Shani Temple which has an
ornate interior of mirrorwork
and gilt, the town also has the
Ram Gopal Poddar Chhatri,
covered with more than 400
paintings. The main bazaar is
crowded with "antique" dealers,
who sell carved doors and
windows from derelict *havelis*.
Many of these are extremely
skilful new copies of the originals.
Mahansar, 15 km (9 miles)
northeast of Ramgarh, has the
splendid Sone ki Dukan Haveli,
abundantly worked in gold leaf.
The paintings on its vaulted
ceiling, depicting the incarnations
of Vishnu, are perhaps the finest
in the area.
Bissau, 10 km (6 miles)
northwest of Mahansar, has

the 18th-century Keshargarh
Fort, which provides an excellent
view of the sand dunes to the
north and west. It also has ten

Impressive interiors of the Dundlod
Fort, Shekhawati

richly painted *havelis*. During
Dussehra, Ramlila performances
take place every evening,
with the actors wearing masks
and costumes made by local
sadhvis (female ascetics) who
started this tradition in the
19th century.
Churu, 12 km (8 miles)
northwest of Bissau, is in the
desert. Though not actually
part of the Shekhawati region, it
is included in the painted *haveli*
circuit, as many merchants had
homes here too. The Surana
Double Haveli, with its imposing
proportions and 1,111 windows,
is the main attraction. The Banthia
Haveli, east of the vegetable
market, has interesting if bizarre
frescoes, including one of Jesus
smoking a cigar.

The Painted Havelis of Shekhawati

The ancestral homes of some of India's leading industrialist families,
such as the Birlas and Goenkas, can be seen in the many little towns
of Shekhawati. These sprawling old *havelis* with their exuberantly
frescoed walls were built between the late 18th and early 20th
centuries by local Marwari merchants who had migrated to the

Fresco of a group of turbaned
Rajput chieftains

The entrance to Biyani Haveli, Sikar

port- cities of Bombay (Mumbai)
and Calcutta (Kolkata) to seek their
fortunes. Their interaction with the
British and exposure to modern urban
and industrial trends influenced their
lifestyles. Consequently, their homes
grew increasingly grand, reflecting the new ideas they brought
back with them, as well as their new-found wealth and social status.
The style and content of the Shekhawati frescoes are a telling comment
on the urbanization of a traditional genre. The local artists still followed
the one-dimensional realism of traditional Rajput painting *(see p409)*,
but juxtaposed among the gods, goddesses and martial heroes are
images from a changing world. In their celebration of contemporary
"pop" themes, the frescoes of British ladies, top-hatted gentlemen, brass
bands and soldiers, trains, motor cars, aeroplanes, gramophones and
telephones, symbolize the industrial society emerging in the late
19th century.

A Tour of Shekhawati

Situated along the old camel caravan trade route, northwest of Jaipur, the Shekhawati ("Garden of Shekha") region resembles an open-air museum. A network of excellent roads through semi-arid scrubland connects numerous towns and villages, known for minor forts, *baolis* and the painted *havelis* of India's leading merchant families, still standing in all their evocative splendour.

A wall in the Poddar School, Nawalgarh, depicting gods and goddesses flying kites

④ Mandawa
This fort-palace is now a charming hotel and a convenient base from which to visit neighbouring towns.

⑤ Dundlod
Its fort-palace and two splendid Goenka *havelis* are worth a visit

③ Fatehpur
This picturesque mid-15th century town is best known for the Singhania, Goenka and Jalan *havelis*.

Key

▬ Tour route

╌ Road

≈ River

② Lachhmangarh
An old fort towers above this 19th-century town. The Char Chowk ("Four Courtyards") Haveli, owned by the Ganeriwala family, is said to be the grandest in the region.

⑥ Nawalgarh
The Poddar and the Aath ("eight") *havelis* are renowned for their frescoes.

Tips for Drivers

Length: 111 km (69 miles).
Stopping-off points: Mandawa, Dundlod, Mukundgarh, Fatehpur and Nawalgarh have good hotels.
Getting around: Petrol pumps are at regular intervals on the main road. A number of lesser roads lead off from NH11 towards Jhunjhunu. All of them have roadside eateries which sell mineral water, hot and cold drinks and snacks.

① Sikar
Sikar's charm lies in its colourfully painted *havelis*, bazaars and rural ambience.

⑩ Street-by-Street: Pushkar

A peaceful pilgrim town of lakes and 400 temples, Pushkar derives its name from *pushpa* (flower) and *kar* (hand) after a legend that claims its lakes were created from the petals that fell from the divine hands of Brahma the Creator. Today, life revolves around its lakeside ghats, temples and vibrant, colourful bazaars, and it is this harmonious mix of the spiritual and commercial that draws people to Pushkar.

Villagers at the Fair
Hundreds of thousands of people, camels and cattle attend the annual fair, said to be one of the largest in Asia.

Residential area

Dhanna Bhagat Temple

SADAR BAZAAR

Savitri Temple →

Fair

PARIKRAMA MARG

★ **Brahma Temple**
This is one of the few temples in India dedicated to Brahma who, according to myth, was cursed by his wife Savitri when, in her absence, he invited Gayatri, a tribal girl, to take her place in an important ritual.

Badi Ganeshji Temple

Parasurama Temple

VISITORS' CHECKLIST

Practical Information
Ajmer district. 144 km (90 miles) SW of Jaipur.
Tel (0145) 277 2040
⊠ 14,800. *i* RTDC Hotel Sarovar. ⊟ daily. ⊠ Pushkar Fair (Oct/Nov). No eggs, meat or alcohol is available or allowed in Pushkar.

Transport
⊟

Key
— Suggested route

Pushkar Lake
On top of a hill, by the sacred lake of Pushkar, is the temple of Savitri. Across the lake, on another hill, is the Gayatri Temple.

Rangji Temple
This temple is conspicuous for its South Indian style of architecture (see p24). Its *gopura* (gateway), carved with over 360 images of deities, towers over the area.

Women at Sadar Bazaar

Camel at the Pushkar Fair

The Pushkar Fair
In the Hindu month of Kartik (October/November), ten days after Diwali, this peaceful town and its environs come alive as the much anticipated annual cattle fair begins. Tents and campsites suddenly spring up to accommodate the thousands of pilgrims, tourists and villagers with herds of cattle, horses and camels who come here to participate in this spectacular event.

Pushkar has always been the region's central cattle market for local herdsmen and farmers who buy and sell camels and indigenous breeds of cattle. Over the years, this trade in livestock has greatly increased in volume. The Pushkar Fair is now one of Asia's largest cattle fairs, and it transforms the quiet little village into a bustling market.

In the vast, specially-built amphitheatre on the outskirts of the town, numerous camel, horse and donkey races and contests take place amid lusty cheers from the spectators. A festive, carnival atmosphere prevails in Pushkar during the fair's two-week duration. Giant Ferris wheels and open air theatres offer amusement, while food stalls do a brisk trade, as do the shops that sell a fascinating variety of goods. In the evenings, people huddle round campfires, listening to the haunting strains of Rajasthani folk ballads. The fair reaches a crescendo on the night of the full moon (*purnima*), when pilgrims take a dip in the holy lake. At dusk, during the beautiful *deepdan* ceremony, hundreds of clay lamps on leaf boats are lit and set afloat in a magical tableau.

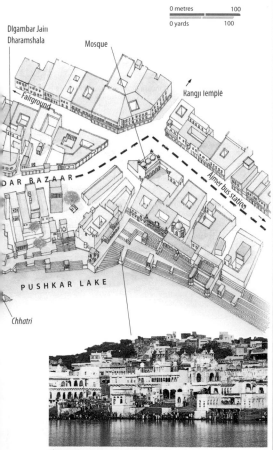

0 metres 100
0 yards 100

Digambar Jain Dharamshala

Mosque

Fairground

Rangji Temple

SADAR BAZAAR

Ajmer bus station

PUSHKAR LAKE

Chhatri

★ Ghats
Pushkar has 52 ghats. Devout Hindus make at least one pilgrimage to Pushkar and bathe at the holy ghats to wash away their sins, thereby earning themselves a place in heaven.

⓫ Ajmer

Ajmer district. 135 km (84 miles) SW of Jaipur. 🚉 485,200. 🚌 🚐 i Rajasthan Tourism, near Khadim Hotel, (0145) 262 7426. 🎭 Urs (Oct).

Ajmer is famous throughout the subcontinent for the holy Muslim shrine, **Dargah Sharif**, the tomb of the great Sufi saint, Khwaja Moinuddin Chishti (1143–1235). Located in the southwest corner of the city, the saint's marble-domed tomb is at the heart of the Dargah complex, which is virtually a township in itself. It includes a bazaar and two marble mosques, built by the Mughal emperors Akbar and Shah Jahan in the 16th and 17th centuries. Akbar was Chishti's most famous devotee, and once walked barefoot all the way from Agra to Ajmer, a distance of 363 km (226 miles), as thanksgiving after the birth of his son Salim, the future Emperor Jahangir.

Millions of pilgrims come to Ajmer for the saint's annual Urs (death anniversary) in October, when spirited Sufi musicians sing the saint's praises in front of his tomb. A special rice pudding, cooked in giant iron cauldrons in the Dargah's courtyard, is offered to devotees.

West of the Dargah Sharif is Ajmer's architectural gem, the **Adhai-Din-ka-Jhonpra**, or "Hut of Two-and-a-Half Days". This strange name is said to derive from the duration of a religious fair that used to be held here. Though in ruins, the early 13th-century mosque complex, built into a hillside, is most impressive. Its main glory is its exquisite seven-arched screen in front of the colonnaded hall. Each

Pilgrims at Ajmer's Dargah Sharif, India's holiest Muslim shrine

arch is different, and the numerous columns have elaborate carvings.

In the southeast corner of Ajmer is **Mayo College**, one of India's best public schools. An excellent example of Indo-Saracenic architecture, it was set up in 1875 by the viceroy, Lord Mayo, as an "Eton of the East" for Rajput princes. Its early students came accompanied by family retainers and private tutors, and some, like the prince of Alwar, even brought along their own elephants. Behind the 19th-century **Nasiyan Temple**, in the heart of the old city, is the Svarna Nagari Hall, vividly decorated with coloured-glass mosaics and large gilded wooden figures, recreating scenes from Jain mythology.

Calligraphy, Adhai-Din-ka-Jhonpra

The **Rajputana Museum**, also in the old city, is located in Emperor Akbar's fort and palace. Its exhibits include impressive sculptures dating from the 4th to the 12th centuries.

Around **Anasagar Lake**, to the northwest of the city, are elegant marble pavilions built by Emperor Shah Jahan in the 17th century. They are set on the lake's banks, in a pretty garden called Daulat Bagh. North of the city, on the summit of Beetli Hill, is the ruined 12th-century **Taragarh Fort**, which affords spectacular views of Ajmer and the surrounding

🛕 **Nasiyan Temple**
SM Soni Marg. **Open** daily. 📷

🏛 **Rajputana Museum**
Near bus stand. **Open** daily. 📷

⓬ Nagaur

Nagaur district. 137 km (85 miles) NE of Jodhpur. 🚉 83,400. 🚌 🎭 Cattle Fair (Jan/Feb).

This little desert town, midway between Jodhpur and Bikaner, is dominated by **Ahichhatragarh Fort**, dating to the 12th century. In the mid-18th century, the ruler of Jodhpur received the fort as a gift from the Mughals and embellished it with a charming pleasure palace. Several of its chambers have exquisite frescoes, now being carefully restored. The palace also has lovely water channels decorated with fish-scale patterns and ornamental spouts, as well as an ingenious system of airducts that used to supply the inner rooms with cool air.

The Nagaur Cattle Fair rivals the Pushkar Fair (see p379), and is a dazzling kaleidoscope of animals, crafts and people, including Nagaur's famous puppeteers whose dramatic shows bring alive popular Rajasthani legends and folklore.

The exuberantly decorated seven-arched screen at the Adhai-Din-ka-Jhonpra, Ajmer

Ships of the Thar Desert

The desert dwellers of Rajasthan could not survive without their camels. In the sandy, inhospitable expanse of the Thar Desert, it is their only means of transport, their beast of burden, as well as an important source of nourishment (camel's milk, slightly salty in taste, is drunk throughout Rajasthan's deserts). The hardy camel demands little in return. It can do without food and water for up to a month in winter, and a week in summer, tanking up on 70 litres (148 pints) of water at one go. The Rajasthani's affection for his camel is evident at all the desert fairs, where camels are given pride of place, resplendent in their colourful tassels and jewellery.

Varieties of Camel

Three varieties of camel inhabit Rajasthan. All of them have two rows of eyelashes which help keep the sand out of their eyes. Their humps contain a thick layer of fat, which shields their bodies from the scorching desert sun.

Gujarati camels are darker-haired and adept at traversing marshy areas such as the Rann of Kutch.

Bikaneri camels have hairy ears, and great load-bearing capacity and stamina.

Jaisalmeri camels, with longer legs, can cover up to 22 km (14 miles) an hour.

Camel carts, ingeniously equipped with old aircraft wheels, are a common sight in Rajasthan's cities.

Dhola and Maru, star-crossed lovers in Rajasthani folklore who eloped on their trusty camel, are a favourite theme in paintings.

Camelskin handicrafts include beautiful embossed water bottles. Bags, slippers, and lacquer-painted lampshades are other camelskin products.

Camel races at fairs test the evenness of a camel's gait by seeing how far it can carry a pot of milk without spilling any.

Camel cavalry regiments of the Indian Army have their origin in the camel regiments of the maharaja of Bikaner, which fought in Egypt in World War I. Today they patrol the desert borders.

⑬ Bikaner

Bikaner district. 361 km (224 miles) NW of Jaipur. 🚗 529,000. 🚉 🚌 ℹ️ Dhola Maru Hotel, Pooran Singh Circle, (0151) 252 9621. 🐫 Camel Festival (Jan), Jambeshwar Festival (Feb/Mar), Kolayat Fair (Nov).

Along with Jodhpur and Jaisalmer, Bikaner was one of the three great Desert Kingdoms of Rajasthan and, like them, prospered because of its strategic location on the overland caravan trade route to Central Asia and China. It was founded in 1486 by Rao Bika, the disgruntled younger son of Rao Jodha, the ruler of Jodhpur (see pp384–5), who left home in search of new territory to conquer.

The imposing ramparts of the 16th-century Junagarh Fort

Somewhat over-shadowed by the splendours of Jodhpur and Jaisalmer, Bikaner nevertheless has a great deal to offer visitors, with its old walled town where camels saunter past colourful stalls, its many temples and palaces, and the magnificent Junagarh Fort, perhaps the best preserved and most ornately decorated of all the forts in Rajasthan.

Maharaja's swing at Junagarh Fort

🏛️ Junagarh Fort

Open Sat–Thu. 📷 🎫 Extra charges for photography. Museum: **Open** daily. 📷

Constructed between 1587 and 1593 by the third ruler of Bikaner, Rai Singh, Junagarh Fort is protected by a 986-m (3,235-ft) long sandstone wall with 37 bastions, a moat and, most effectively of all, by the forbidding expanse of the Thar Desert. Not surprisingly, the fort has never been conquered, a fact which explains its excellent state of preservation. Within the fort's austere stone walls are no less than 37 profusely decorated palaces, temples and pavilions, built by its

successive rulers over the centuries, though in a harmonious continuity of style. The most outstanding is the **Anup Mahal**, built by Maharaja Anup Singh in 1690 as his Hall of Private Audience. It was sumptuously decorated between 1787 and 1800 by Maharaja Surat Singh. In an ingenious imitation of Mughal *pietra dura* work at a fraction of the cost, the lime-plaster walls of the Anup Mahal have been polished to a high lustre. They are covered with red and gold lacquer patterns, further embellished with mirrors and gold leaf. The **Karan Mahal** (built between

Interior with ornamental lacquer work, Anup Mahal

1631 and 1669) is the Hall of Public Audience and is ornamented in a similar if somewhat less lavish style.

Two other gorgeous, heavily decorated palaces are the 17th-century **Chandra Mahal** ("Moon Palace") and **Phool Mahal** ("Flower Palace"). The latter contains Rao Bika's small, low bed with curved silver legs, on which he slept with his feet touching the ground. The bed was so designed to enable Rao Bika to jump quickly to his feet and fight off murderous intruders. The Chandra Mahal, which was the queens' palace, has carved marble panels depicting the Radha-Krishna legend, and both palaces have superb stone carving and *jalis*. The blue-and-gold **Badal Mahal** ("Cloud Palace") is covered with paintings of clouds, yellow streaks of lightning and rain showers – a favourite fantasy in this arid land. The **Hawa Mahal** ("Palace of Winds") has a huge mirror positioned over the maharaja's bed, which apparently enabled him to view the courtyard below, thus alerting him to approaching danger. The oldest palace in the fort is **Lal Niwas**, dating to 1595, and decorated with floral motifs in red and gold. The newest palace is the huge **Durbar Niwas** ("Coronation Palace"), built in the early 20th century by Bikaner's most progressive ruler Sir Ganga Singh (r.1887–1943), who gave Bikaner its railway link and built the Ganga Canal which brought precious irrigation water to his kingdom. He was also famous for hosting elaborate *shikars* (hunting expeditions) for visiting British dignitaries. The Durbar Niwas now houses the fort museum, whose armoury section includes such fascinating exhibits as a 56-kg (124-lb) suit of armour, a dagger with a pistol built into it, and swords with lion-shaped handles. Other exhibits include the fragrant sandalwood throne of the rulers, said to date back to their 5th-century ancestors who were the kings of Kannauj (Uttar Pradesh), and a curious half-spoon for soup, used by the maharaja to ensure that his luxuriant moustache remained pristine during mealtimes.

Coat of arms of Bikaner's rulers

🏬 Walled City

West end of MG Rd.
Shops: **Open** daily.

In the old walled city, entered through Kote Gate, is the bazaar, where excellent local handicrafts can be found, such as rugs and carpets, painted lampshades made of camel hide, and beautiful miniatures in the Bikaneri style. Savoury snacks *(bhujias)* are another local speciality, and Bikaneri *bhujias* are renowned throughout India, as are the sweets made of camel's milk. The grand 17th- and 18th-century *havelis* of Bikaner's wealthy merchants line the narrow lanes in the vicinity around Rampuria

One of the two cannons flanking the entrance to Lalgarh Palace

Street. Two of the most ornate are the **Rampuria** and **Kothari Havelis**. The former is now a delightful heritage hotel. In the southwestern corner of the walled town are two Jain temples, dating from the early 16th century, the **Bhandeshwar** and **Sandeshwar Temples**. Both are ornately carved and are embellished with frescoes, mirrorwork and gold leaf scrollwork inside. They were built by two brothers who, having no children, constructed these masterpieces for posterity.

🏛 Lalgarh Palace

N of city centre. **Tel** (0151) 254 0201.
Museum: **Open** Thu–Tue. 🎟 ✉

Lalgarh Palace, outside the walled town, is a sprawling extravaganza of carved friezes, *jalis*, pillars and arches in the distinctive reddish-pink local sandstone (which resulted in Bikaner being dubbed the "Red City"). Constructed between 1902 and 1926, it was designed by Sir Samuel Swinton Jacob (*see p357*) in a style that combines traditional Rajput and Renaissance European features with Art Nouveau decor inside. Part of it has been converted into a hotel, and another section into a museum with vintage photographs and wildlife trophies. Lalgarh Palace's museum and beautiful gardens are open to visitors.

Environs

The **Camel Breeding Farm**, 9 km (6 miles) southeast of Bikaner, is best visited in the late afternoon when the camels return from grazing. Set up in 1975, the farm breeds nearly half the camels found in India, including those for the camel regiment of the Indian Army.

Gajner, 30 km (19 miles) northwest of Bikaner, has the red sandstone Summer Palace of the maharajas, now a luxury hotel, and the Gajner National Park, home to blackbucks, wild boars, desert foxes and a large

number of migratory birds. The 17th-century **Karni Mata Temple** at Deshnok, 30 km (19 miles) southeast of Bikaner, is also known as the Rat Temple, because of the hundreds of rats that swarm around the temple and its precincts. The rats are considered sacred and are fed sweets and milk by the priests and visitors, who believe that they are reincarnated holy men. The temple is dedicated to Karni Mata, an incarnation of Durga, and is entered through intricately carved silver doors, presented by Sir Ganga.

🐪 Camel Breeding Farm
Open Mon–Sat. 🎟 📷

🛕 Karni Mata Temple
Open daily. 📷 Karni Mata Festival (Mar/Apr & Sep/Oct).

Devotee feeding milk to rats at Karni Mata Temple, Deshnok

❶ Phalodi

Jodhpur district. 150 km (93 miles) SW of Bikaner. 🚌

This large town attracts visitors because of the lovely hamlet of Khichan, 4 km (2.5 miles) to its east. Khichan is famous for the demoiselle cranes that gather around its lake between September and March. The birds migrate here from the Mongolian steppes for the winter. Every day, the villagers spread grain on the fields for the birds, and as a result the number of cranes that come here has increased substantially over the years. At last count, 7,000 cranes spent the winter at Khichan.

⑮ Jodhpur

With the majestic Mehrangarh Fort towering over opulent palaces, colourful bazaars and the sands of the Thar Desert, Jodhpur epitomizes all the romance and feudal splendour of Rajasthan. Now the second largest city in the state, Jodhpur was founded in 1459 by Rao Jodha, the Rathore ruler of the kingdom of Marwar. Strategically located on the overland trade route, it soon became a flourishing trade centre. Its merchant class, known as the Marwaris *(see pp376)*, have retained their entrepreneurial skills and continue to run many of India's leading business houses. The special riding breeches, known the world over as jodhpurs, were designed here.

🏛 Mehrangarh Fort
See pp386–7.

🏬 Sardar Bazaar
Open daily.

Jodhpur's bazaar lies in the heart of the old city, which is surrounded by a 10-km (6-mile) wall, pierced by eight gates. Clustered around a clock tower (built in 1912), the bazaar is a fascinating area to explore, with its little shops selling silver jewellery, lacquer bangles, tie-dyed fabrics, soft camel leather shoes, puppets, clay figurines and colourful heaps of sweets and spices. The pavements are lined with henna artists who decorate women's palms with intricate, lacy patterns.

An interesting building in this area is the early 17th-century **Taleti Mahal**, its carved balconies supported by temple pillars. Built for a favourite royal concubine, it now houses a school. There are several other beautiful houses in the bazaar area, mostly made of red sandstone and heavily carved.

🏛 Jaswant Thada
Open daily. 📷

This elegant pillared marble memorial with fine lattice

Blue-washed houses around Jodhpur's Mehrangarh Fort

carving is the *chhatri* (cenotaph) of Maharaja Jaswant Singh II (r.1878–95), whose innovative irrigation schemes brought water and prosperity to this parched land. Local people, who believe the maharaja has retained his healing touch, come regularly to offer prayer and flowers at his shrine. Cenotaphs of subsequent rulers and members of the royal families are also located here, though earlier rulers have their memorials at Mandore.

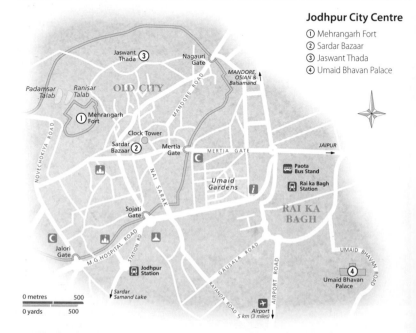

Jodhpur City Centre

① Mehrangarh Fort
② Sardar Bazaar
③ Jaswant Thada
④ Umaid Bhavan Palace

For keys to symbols *see back flap*

Umaid Bhavan Palace, a fusion of Rajput, Jain and Art Deco styles

🏛 Umaid Bhavan Palace
Open daily.

This immense palace, built of creamy-pink sandstone and marble, is a prime example of princely India's opulence. Its 347 rooms include eight dining halls, two theatres, a ballroom, several lavishly decorated reception halls and a vast underground swimming pool. A 60-m (197-ft) dome covers the cavernous central hall which, at its inauguration, seated 1,000 people for dinner.

The palace was commissioned by Maharaja Umaid Singh, apparently to create jobs for his famine-stricken subjects. Begun in 1929, it took 3,000 men 15 years to complete; 19 km (12 miles) of railway tracks were also laid to bring the sandstone from the quarry. HV Lanchester, the architect of the Central Hall of Westminster in London, created a pleasing fusion of Rajput, Jain and European Art Deco styles for his royal patron.

Umaid Singh's grandson, Gaj Singh, still lives in a section of the palace, while the rest has been turned into a luxury hotel. The palace museum is open to visitors and has an impressive collection of decorated weapons, watches and fantastically-shaped clocks, paintings, French furniture and porcelain.

The road in front of it, leading to the smaller Ajit Bhavan Palace, is lined with antique shops.

Environs
Mandore, 9 km (6 miles) north of Jodhpur, was the capital of the Rathore kings of Marwar until the 15th century, when Rao Jodha built a new capital at Jodhpur. Set around terraced garden on a hillside are the red sandstone *chhatris* of Jodhpur's earlier rulers. The most imposing is that of Ajit Singh with its towering temple-like spire. When he died in 1724, his six wives and 58 concubines committed *sati* on his funeral pyre. The Hall of Heroes has 15 life-size statues of religious deities and folk heroes. Further up the hill are the queens' cenotaphs (Raniyon ki Chhatri) and the tall and narrow 17th-century Ek Thamba Mahal Palace.

Balsamand, 6 km (4 miles) north of Jodhpur, has the 19th-century red sandstone water palace of the maharajas beside a large artificial lake. The **Sardar Samand Lake**, 55 km (34 miles) south of Jodhpur, attracts several water birds including egrets, ibis and pelicans. On its shores is the maharajas' Art Deco-style hunting lodge. The drive here passes through interesting Bishnoi villages (*see p389*).

Jaswant Thada, the 19th-century cenotaph of Maharaja Jaswant Singh II

Bhopa Balladeers

Like the troubadours of medieval Europe, the nomadic Bhopa tribe of western Rajasthan enjoys a lively tradition of storytelling through song and dance. A long painted scroll (known as a *phad*) is, rather like a comic strip, crammed with paintings depicting dramatic events in the life of a Marwar hero, the brave warrior Pabuji. The Bhopa unrolls his scroll, and narrates the story through songs, highlighting relevant pictures on the scroll with a lantern, while his wife brings the tale to life with animated dance sequences. The Bhopas' performances draw enthusiastic crowds at fairs and festivals across the Marwar region.

Painted scroll used by Bhopas

Jodhpur: Mehrangarh Fort

Rising sheer out of a 125-m (410-ft) high rock, Mehrangarh is perhaps the most majestic of Rajasthan's forts. Described by an awe-struck Rudyard Kipling as "the creation of angels, fairies and giants", Mehrangarh's forbidding ramparts are in sharp contrast to the flamboyantly decorated palaces within. Founded by Rao Jodha in 1459, the sandstone fort was added to by later rulers, mostly between the mid-17th and mid-19th centuries. The royal apartments within the fort now form part of an outstanding museum.

The Ramparts
The bastioned walls, parts of which are hewn out of the rock itself, are in places 24-m (79-ft) thick and 40-m (131-ft) high. Perched on them are old cannons.

★ Phool Mahal
Built between 1730 and 1750, this is the fort's most opulent chamber, richly gilded and painted. It was used for royal celebrations.

Shringar Chowk
This courtyard has the coronation throne of the Jodhpur rulers, made of white marble. Every ruler after Rao Jodha was crowned on it.

The blue-washed houses of Brahmapuri village, clustered below the ramparts of Mehrangarh Fort

VISITORS' CHECKLIST

Practical Information
Tel (0291) 254 8790. Mehrangarh Fort and Museum: **Open** daily. Museum Trust. Extra charges for photography.

★ Moti Mahal
Built between 1581 and 1595, this magnificent room was the Hall of Private Audience. Its ceiling is decorated with mirrors and gold leaf, and crushed seashells were mixed with plaster to give its walls a lustrous sheen.

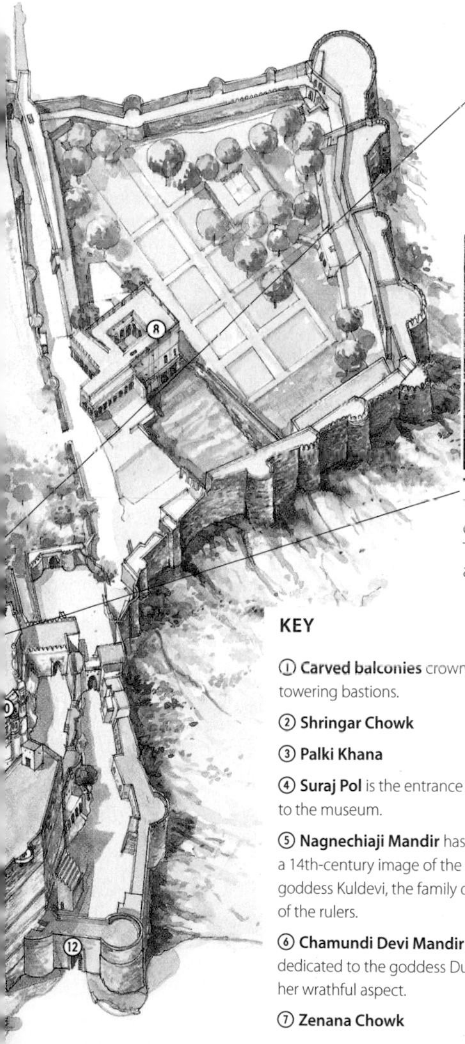

Takhat Mahal
This exuberantly painted room with a wooden ceiling was the favourite retreat of Maharaja Takhat Singh (r.1843–73), who had 30 queens and numerous concubines.

KEY

① **Carved balconies** crown the towering bastions.

② **Shringar Chowk**

③ **Palki Khana**

④ **Suraj Pol** is the entrance to the museum.

⑤ **Nagnechiaji Mandir** has a 14th-century image of the goddess Kuldevi, the family deity of the rulers.

⑥ **Chamundi Devi Mandir** is dedicated to the goddess Durga in her wrathful aspect.

⑦ **Zenana Chowk**

⑧ **Chokelao Palace**, now under restoration, was a pleasure palace built around a sunken garden.

⑨ **Jhanki Mahal** is a long gallery with exquisite latticed stone screens.

⑩ **Phool Mahal**

⑪ **Sileh Khana's** exceptional collection of weapons includes damascened Mughal daggers, gem-studded shields, and special armour for war elephants.

⑫ **Jai Pol**, one of the seven fortified gates to the fort, is now the main entrance. It was built in 1806 by Maharaja Man Singh to commemorate a victory in battle.

Exploring Mehrangarh Fort Museum

The Mehrangarh Fort Museum is justly regarded as the best of the many palace museums in Rajasthan. Its rich and varied collection includes a golden throne, fine miniature paintings, traditional costumes and fascinating weapons. Particularly magnificent are the skilfully restored royal chambers, which present a vivid picture of princely life and culture in Rajasthan.

Maharaja's cradle with a mechanical rocking system, in Jhanki Mahal

The entrance to the museum is through the Suraj Pol on the fort's southeastern side. Inside, to the right, is the **Palki Khana** with a collection of richly gilded palanquins. Along with the impressive elephant howdahs on display in the **Howdah Gallery** next door, these reflect the importance of grand processions in courtly life. Particularly impressive is a 17th-century howdah made of solid silver, a gift from the Mughal emperor Shah Jahan. Another treasure is a spectacular palanquin covered in gold leaf, dating to 1730. This stands in the **Daulat Khana** (Treasury Hall), just before the **Sileh Khana** with its superb collection of weapons.

A gem-studded rhino-hide shield

From here, steps lead up to the **Umaid Mahal**, which exhibits miniature paintings of the Jodhpur School. Heavily influenced by the Mughal style, these paintings provide fascinating vignettes of life at court – the rulers riding camels with their courtesans, playing polo and leading ceremonial processions. Here too is a grand silk canopy, that was used by the rulers for outdoor camps.

The next chamber, on the floor above, is the splendidly gilded, 18th-century **Phool Mahal** ("Flower Palace"), the Hall of Public Audience. It also has superb miniatures, including a set of 36 *Ragamala* paintings that depict the moods of various musical ragas.

The 19th-century **Takhat Mahal**, the chamber of a pleasure-loving ruler, is exuberantly painted with murals of Radha and Krishna and dancing maidens. The glass Christmas tree balls hanging from the ceiling were added in the 1930s. **Sardar Vilas**, just below Takhat Mahal, showcases Jodhpur's fine woodwork. Particularly striking is a door inlaid with ivory.

The next chamber is **Jhanki Mahal** or "Peeping Palace", so called because the women of the royal zenana could peep through its latticed stone screens to observe the ceremonies and festivities in the courtyards below. It now has a collection of royal cradles, including one with an ingenious mechanical rocking system, surmounted by guardian angels. From here a courtyard leads to the 16th-century **Moti Mahal** or "Pearl Palace". A palmist sits in the courtyard to foretell the futures of visitors.

The museum also has a fine collection of Rajasthani turbans and folk music instruments. Rooms displaying costumes, royal tents and special treasures are under preparation.

Environs

Osian, 64 km (40 miles) northwest of Jodhpur, is the site of 16 outstanding Jain and Hindu temples. Built by wealthy traders between the 8th and 12th centuries, when Osian was an important stop on the caravan trade route to Central Asia, they represent the earliest phase of temple architecture in Rajasthan.

Famous for the rich variety and exuberance of their sculptural decoration are the 11 temples at the southern and western edge of Osian village. Of these, the most impressive is the 8th-century **Mahavira Temple** with a superb ceiling and 20 carved pillars holding up the main portico. Equally beautiful are the classically elegant 10th-century **Sun Temple** and the profusely sculpted **Vishnu** and **Harihara Temples**, from the 8th–9th centuries.

The other temples are on a hill east of the village, dominated by the 12th-century **Sachiya Mata Temple**, approached through a series of beautifully carved arches. This temple is particularly popular with infertile women who believe that Sachiya Mata, an incarnation of Durga, has special powers to help them bear children.

The entrance to the Sachiya Mata Temple, Osian

⑯ Tour of Marwar Crafts Villages

The arid countryside south of Jodhpur is dotted with villages, their mud and thatch huts inhabited by the Bishnois and communities of potters and weavers. A daylong tour of this area provides a memorable opportunity to observe the rhythm of daily life in these hamlets, experience the warm hospitality of the villagers, and see beautiful traditional crafts being practised.

Tips for Drivers

Length: 55 km (34 miles).
Getting around: Allow 6–7 hours for the trip. Refreshments are available at Gudda Bishnoi, Salawas and Kakuni. The heritage hotels at Rohet and Luni (Fort Chanwa) offer good food and are pleasant places for a break. Hotels and travel agencies in Jodhpur can arrange taxis. A four-wheel drive is recommended.

① Jodhpur
This historic and beautiful city is on the edge of the Thar Desert.

② Gudda Bishnoi
The Bishnois in this hamlet tend camels and goats. The men wear only white, but the women wear vivid colours and silver jewellery.

③ Salawas
The villagers here are skilled weavers of *dhurries* (rugs) in traditional geometric patterns and vegetable colours. They are made of cotton or camel hair.

Jaisalmer

Ajmer

Khejarli

Mogra

Luni

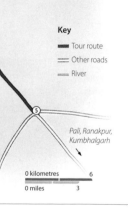

⑤ Rohet
The 17th-century palace-fort here is now a heritage hotel surrounded by villages of leather craftsmen.

④ Kakuni
This village, 26 km (16 miles) south of Jodhpur, is famous for its pottery, made of the fine local clay.

Key
━━ Tour route
═══ Other roads
── River

Pali, Ranakpur, Kumbhalgarh

The Bishnois

The Bishnois, passionate environmentalists, are followers of a 15th-century sage, Jambeshwar, whose creed is contained in 29 (*bis noi*) principles. Most of these focus on environmental protection, and the Bishnois' faith bids them to protect every living being, if necessary with their lives. Thus, the otherwise timid blackbuck can be seen roaming freely near Bishnoi villages, confident that it will be unharmed. Bishnois believe they will be reborn as deer.

Bishnoi woman

0 kilometres 6
0 miles 3

⑰ Jaisalmer

Today a remote outpost in the Thar Desert, Jaisalmer was founded in the 12th century by Maharawal Jaisal of the Bhatti Rajput clan. It was once a flourishing trade centre, strategically located on the busy caravan trade route to Afghanistan and Central Asia. Its earlier rulers grew rich by looting gems, silk and opium from the caravans, but by the 16th century Jaisalmer had become a peaceful town, whose wealthy traders and rulers vied with each other to beautify their austere desert surroundings with splendid palaces and *havelis*. Made of the local golden-yellow sandstone, they are the most spectacular examples of the Rajasthani stonemason's art. In the 18th century, with the growth of sea ports at Surat and Bombay (Mumbai), Jaisalmer's importance dwindled. But the buildings from its golden age still stand, clustered around a magnificent fort *(see pp392–3)*.

VISITORS' CHECKLIST

Practical Information
Jaisalmer district. 285 kms (177 miles) W of Jodhpur. 58,300. 𝒊 Tourist Reception Centre, Station Rd, (02992) 25 2406. 📷 Desert Festival (Feb), Gangaur Festival (Mar/Apr).

Transport
🚆 🚌

cupolas cap the roof. The rear portion of this *haveli* was, sadly, damaged during the Gujarat earthquake in January 2001, but visitors are still allowed in.

🏛 Manik Chowk

Located at the entrance to the fort, this is the main marketplace, where caravans used to halt in the past. The tiny shops sell camel hair blankets and gorgeous embroidered textiles. Desert nomads and their camels add to the bazaars' colour.

🏛 Badal Vilas

Near Amar Sagar Gate. **Open** daily.
This late 19th-century palace is distinguished by its multi-tiered tower in the shape of a *tazia* – the ornately decorated tower of wood, metal and coloured paper, carried by Shia Muslims at Muharram *(see p673)*. The Tazia Tower of Badal Vilas, built in the mid-20th century, was a parting gift to the maharawal from the town's Shia stonecarvers, many of whom moved to Pakistan after Independence.

🏞 Gadisagar Lake

SE of the city walls.
This rainwater reservoir, built in 1367, was once the city's sole source of water. Lined with ghats and temples, it comes alive during the Gangaur festival (March/April), when the maharawal leads a procession here. The beautiful gateway leading to the tank was built by a royal courtesan, Telia, whose audacity so enraged the queens that they demanded its instant demolition. The quick-witted Telia immediately had a statue of Krishna installed on top, thereby ensuring not only that the gateway would stand, but that everyone would bow before passing through it.

🏛 Salim Singh's Haveli

Near the Fort entrance. Local guides can arrange visits for a fee.
This *haveli* was built in 1815 by a powerful prime minister of Jaisalmer. Narrow at the base, its six storeys grow wider at each level, and all its 38 balconies have different designs. Peacocks dance between the arches on the topmost balcony, and blue

Jaisalmeri smoking a hookah

🏛 Nathmalji's Haveli

Near Gandhi Chowk. Local guides can arrange visits for a fee.
Built in 1855 by another prime minister of Jaisalmer, the particular charm of this five-storeyed mansion is that the two sides of its façade were carved by two craftsman-brothers, Hathu and Lallu. Though at first glance they seem identical, the details on each side are actually quite different. Besides the usual floral, geometric and animal patterns, this *haveli's* motifs also reflect new influences – a European-style horse and carriage, bicycles and steam engines.

🏛 Patwon ki Haveli

E of Nathmalji's Haveli. **Open** daily.
This enormous and very elaborate *haveli* was built between 1805 and 1855 by Guman Chand Patwa, one of Jaisalmer's richest merchants and bankers, who dealt in silk, brocade and opium, and had a chain of trading stations stretching from Afghanistan to China. This six-storeyed mansion has five adjoining apartments for each of his sons, and 66 balconies. The curved eaves on the balconies suggest a fleet of sailing boats, and the numerous latticed windows are carved with breathtaking intricacy.

Gadisagar Lake, lined with ghats

The Jaisalmer Haveli

After the fort, Jaisalmer's *havelis* are its greatest attraction. Built in the 19th century by the town's merchants and ministers, these mansions dominate its labyrinthine lanes. The *havelis* of Salim Singh, Nathmalji and Patwon are the finest examples of this type of architecture, their golden stone façades so finely carved that they could be made of lace. Several generations of an extended family lived together in these huge mansions, which usually contained secluded women's quarters that outsiders could not enter. Jaisalmer's stonemasons still practise their art, doing restoration work in the fort, and working abroad for wealthy new patrons in the Gulf and Saudi Arabia.

The entrance of most *havelis* is on a plinth, raised high above street level, to prevent the desert sand from blowing into the rooms. The ground floor had no living rooms, and was usually used as a warehouse or storeroom.

The inner courtyard, found in all *havelis*, was a protected place for children to play in, and for women to attend to their daily chores in privacy.

Jharokhas, or projecting balconies, have curved *bangaldar* eaves. Their purpose was more decorative than functional, and they gave the stonemasons an opportunity to display the full range of their creativity and skill.

Jalis, or latticed stone screens, display a rich variety of patterns. They keep out the harsh desert sun but let in fresh air. They also enabled women to observe street life without being seen.

Yellow sandstone lends itself particularly well to fine carving. Soft when newly quarried, the stone gradually becomes harder with exposure.

Narrow streets in the neighbourhood of Patwon ki Haveli, lined with intricately carved façades, retain their traditional ambience.

Jaisalmer Fort

Jaisalmer Fort rises like a fabulous mirage out of the sands of the Thar Desert, the awesome contours of its 99 bastions softened by the golden hue of the stone. Built in 1156 by Maharawal Jaisal, and added to by his successors, this citadel stands on the peak of the 80-m (263-ft) high Trikuta Hill. In medieval times, Jaisalmer's entire population lived within the fort and even now, thousands of people reside here, making it India's only living fort. Royal palaces, a cluster of Jain temples, mansions and shops are all contained within its walls.

The southern ramparts, built of stone without any mortar

KEY

① **The ramparts**, with an inner parallel wall, have huge cannonballs perched on top, ready to crush invaders.

② **Intricate sandstone carvings** are found in these seven temples dedicated to the Jain *tirthankaras*, including Rishabdeo, Sambhavnatha Parsvanatha and others.

③ **Gyan Bhandar**, in the basement of the Sambhavnatha Temple, is a library of illustrated Jain palm-leaf manuscripts, some of them dating to the 11th century.

④ **Annapurna Bhandar** was originally the fort's granary. Its ground floor has a temple.

⑤ **Moti Mahal**

⑥ **Naqqar Khana**, or "Drummers' Gallery", has a richly carved octagonal balcony.

⑦ **Rani Mahal**

★ **Jain Temples**
Exquisitely carved Jain temples were built in the 15th and 16th centuries by the town's wealthy traders.

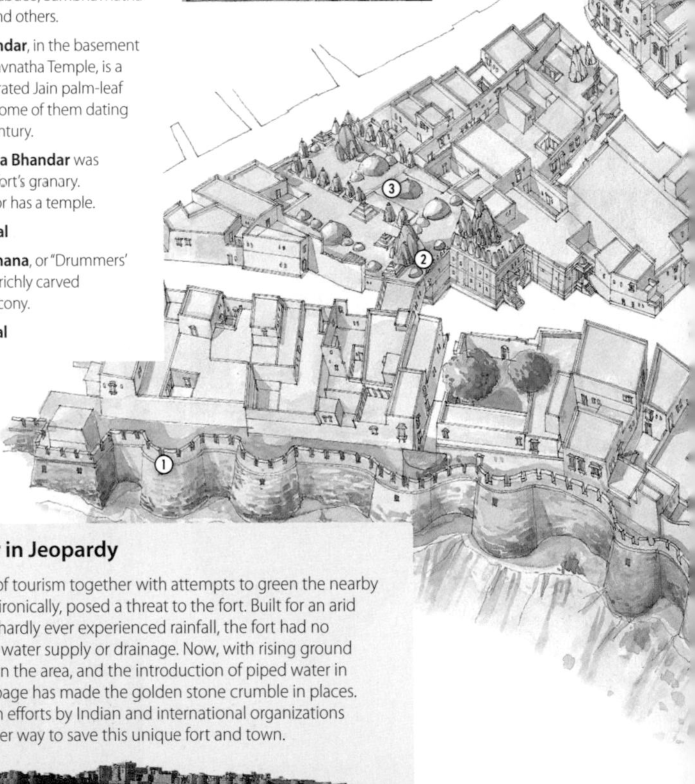

Jaisalmer in Jeopardy

The growth of tourism together with attempts to green the nearby desert have, ironically, posed a threat to the fort. Built for an arid climate that hardly ever experienced rainfall, the fort had no provision for water supply or drainage. Now, with rising ground water levels in the area, and the introduction of piped water in the fort, seepage has made the golden stone crumble in places. Conservation efforts by Indian and international organizations are now under way to save this unique fort and town.

The 12th-century Jaisalmer Fort, threatened by rising damp

Royal Complex
The seven-storeyed palace complex consists of several interconnected palaces, built between the 16th and 19th centuries.

VISITORS' CHECKLIST

Practical Information
Jaisalmer Fort: ℹ️ Rajasthan Tourism, Station Rd. **Tel** (02992) 25 2406. **Open** daily. 🅿️ Extra charges for photography. 📷 👟 ✏️ 🏠 Jain Temples: **Open** daily. Extra charges for photography. Gyan Bhandar: **Open** daily.

Sarvottam Vilas
Brilliant blue tiles and glass mosaic work decorate this mid 18th century palace.

★ **Moti Mahal**
Floral paintings and carved doors embellish this 18th-century palace

★ **Dussehra Chowk**
Festivals, royal performances and parades took place in this open plaza, framed by the palace complex. The rulers' marble throne overlooks the plaza.

Exploring Jaisalmer's Outer Sights

The environs of Jaisalmer are dotted with sites of both architectural and natural beauty. These include beautiful temples, the haunting ruins of the old capital, a fascinating desert village, rolling sand dunes, and the habitat of a rare desert bird, the great Indian bustard.

Manganiyar musicians, whose ballads recount Jaisalmer's history

🏯 Bhattiani Rani Temple
2 km (1.3 miles) S of fort. **Open** daily.
This secluded Hindu shrine was built in honour of a 19th-century Jaisalmer princess who, surprisingly, committed *sati* on her brother-in-law's funeral pyre. A clan of Muslim musicians, the Manganiyars, are the caretakers of the temple, and recount this story, with its intriguing undertones, in their soulful ballads about Jaisalmer's history.

🏯 Bada Bagh
7 km (4 miles) N of fort.
The royal cenotaphs, with elaborately carved ceilings and fine equestrian statues of the rulers, are set in a green oasis. Next to them is the Bhaironji Temple, frequented by childless women who offer their silver girdles to the deity, in the hope that he will cure their infertility.

🏯 Lodurva
15 km (9 miles) NW of Jaisalmer.
The capital of the Bhatti Rajputs before they built the fort at Jaisalmer, Lodurva was abandoned after it was sacked by Muslim invaders in the 11th century. A group of Jain temples dominates this site, where the remains of many other fine buildings lie

concealed beneath the desert sands. A beautiful *torana* leads to the main temple, which houses a metal sculpture of the Kalpavriksha ("Celestial Tree"). It is believed to have wish-fulfilling powers.

🏯 Akal Fossil Park
17 km (11 miles) SE of Jaisalmer. **Open** daily.
Extraordinary fossilized tree trunks, some of them 180 million years old, can be seen in this park. They bear witness to the fact that this arid area was once covered with dense forest.

Great Indian bustard

🏯 Khuri
40 km (25 miles) SW of Jaisalmer.
Set among sand dunes, this little village is a superb example of desert architecture. Functional as well as beautiful, the village houses have thick mud walls that provide

protection against the fierce desert heat and winds, while the paintings that decorate their exteriors bring colour and beauty to the brown, parched environs.

🏯 Desert National Park
43 km (27 miles) W of Jaisalmer.
For permission, contact Collector's Office, Jaisalmer, (02992) 25 2201.
Jeep & Camel safaris.

This fascinating park is spread over 3,162 sq km (1,221 sq miles) of scrub and sandy wasteland, close to the border with Pakistan. Its star attraction is the great Indian bustard (*Choriotis nigriceps*), a large bird with a height of 1.2 m (4 ft). The bustard had been hunted almost to extinction, and only about 1,000 remain now, but sightings are likely here. Other wildlife includes sand grouse, several species of falcon and vulture, desert fox, and *chinkara* (Indian gazelle).

⑲ Barmer

Barmer district. 160 km (99 miles) SE of Jaisalmer. 🚉 🚌 ❶ Rajasthan Tourism, Khartal, (02982) 22 2956.
🎪 Tilwara Cattle Fair (Jan/Feb), Thar Desert Festival (Mar).

This remote desert town, whose arid soil cannot support agriculture, has become a major centre for desert handicrafts. Woodcarving, blockprinted textiles, embroidery and carpet weaving are the main source of livelihood for its people. They also lavish their skills on their mud huts, which are beautifully decorated with geometric and floral patterns. Barmer buzzes with activity during the annual Tilwara Fair (January/February), one of the many large cattle fairs in Rajasthan.

Visitors on a camel safari near Jaisalmer

⊕ Camel Safari Around Jaisalmer

The fascinating desertscape around Jaisalmer is best explored on a camel safari. A two-day excursion takes in historic sights and villages of sheep and camel herders. Overnight stays in tents offer magical dawns and sunsets amid the dunes. Cushions are provided, but riders are advised to carry an extra one, to help soften the effects of the camel's lurching gait.

Tips for Riders

Duration: Two days and two nights. **Day 1:** Jaisalmer to Lodurva via Bada Bagh and Ramkunda, 18 km (11 miles). **Day 2:** Lodurva to Sam via Kahala and Kanoi, 20 km (12 miles); Sam to Jaisalmer (by jeep), 45 km (28 miles). **Overnight stays:** Camps at Lodurva and Sam. For more details on safaris, see p727; for tour operators, see p731.

② Bada Bagh
The cenotaphs of the maharawals (rulers) of Jaisalmer are surrounded by green mango groves and thorny khejri (Prosopsis cineraria) trees.

① Jaisalmer
The camels set off from the First Gate of Jaisalmer's magnificent 12th-century fort.

③ Ramkunda
A picnic lunch is served at this little village with a 15th-century Shiva temple.

Kishangarh

Baramsar

Damodara

NH15 — Bikaner

NH15 — Barmer

Kuldhera

⑥ Kanoi
The older houses in this village are painted with flowers, animals and birds. The village craftsmen make elaborately carved camel saddles inlaid with brass.

⑤ Kahala
This hamlet of mud houses is inhabited by herders of goats and sheep. They also weave attractive blankets.

④ Lodurva
The night is spent at the old capital of the maharawals, which has lovely Jain temples. Dinner is served under a star-studded sky.

0 km   5
0 miles   5

Key

▬▬ Tour route
══ Other roads
▬▬ National highway

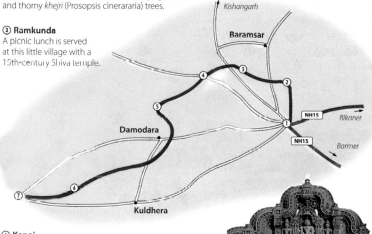

⑦ Sam
Rippling sand dunes stretch as far as the eye can see. The 45-km (28-mile) journey back to Jaisalmer the next morning is by jeep.

View of the historic Mehrangarh Fort, Jodhpur ▶

The intricately carved Vimala Vasahi Temple

⓴ Mount Abu

Sirohi district. 185 km (115 miles) W of Udaipur. 🗺 22,100. 🚉 Abu Rd, 20 km (12 miles) SE of town centre, then bus. 🚌 ℹ opp main bus station, (02974) 23 5151. 🎭 Summer Festival (Jun).

Rajasthan's only hill station, Mount Abu has one of India's most spectacular sights – the **Dilwara Jain Temples**. This group of five marble temples is situated on a hill 3 km (2 miles) northeast of the town. The two most outstanding are the **Vimala Vasahi Temple** and the **Luna Vasahi Temple** which have incredibly intricate and delicate carvings. The sculptural details on the various doorways, archways, pillars and ceilings of both these temples are simply breathtaking, the marble worked so finely that in places it is almost translucent.

The Vimala Vasahi Temple, dedicated to the first Jain *tirthankara*, Adinath, was built in 1031 by Vimala Shah, a wealthy prime minister of the Solanki kings of Gujarat. A statue of him seated on an elephant is in a pavilion to the right of the entrance. Inside, graceful nymphs and musicians, spirited horses and elephants adorn the arches and pillars, and the superb 11-tiered domed ceiling in the main hall. The inner sanctum has a statue of Adinath in tranquil meditation, while 52 carved niches contain images of the other *tirthankaras*. The Luna Vasahi Temple, dedicated to

Neminath, the 22nd Jain *tirthankara*, dates to 1231 and is even more ornately carved. Its most glorious feature, the main hall, has a magnificent lotus-shaped, tiered pendant carved from a single block of marble, descending from its domed ceiling. Behind the main shrine is the fascinating Hall of Donors, with a series of figures mounted on elephants, some in black marble. There are also life-size statues of the donors and their wives, with every detail of their dress and jewellery exquisitely and painstakingly carved.

The focal point of Mount Abu town is **Nakki Lake**, ringed by colonial mansions dating to the late 19th century, and the summer palaces of Rajput rulers. The curiously shaped **Toad's Rock** overlooks the lake, and **Sunset Point**, southwest of the lake, offers some spectacular views from a stone terrace.

About 4 km (2.5 miles) below Mount Abu, just off the main highway leading to the town, is the historic **Gaumukh** ("Cow's Mouth") **Temple** with a natural spring flowing from the mouth of a marble cow.

🗝 Dilwara Jain Temples

Open daily. **Closed** to menstruating women. Leather articles are not allowed inside.

Environs

Achalgarh, 8 km (5 miles) beyond Dilwara, has the ruins of a 15th-century fort, and a Shiva temple. The latter has a statue of Nandi made with over 4,000 kg (8,819 lbs) of gold, silver, brass and copper. A five-minute walk from the temple is **Guru Shikhar**, Rajasthan's highest point at 1,721 m (5,646 ft). It is marked by a small but exquisite Vishnu temple.

⓺ Ranakpur

Rajsamand district. 90 km (56 miles) NW of Udaipur. 🚌 Temple Complex: **Open** daily. **Closed** to menstruating women. Leather articles are not allowed inside.

Set in a secluded, wooded valley of the Aravalli Hills, the 15th-century Ranakpur temple complex, dominated by the great **Adinath Temple**, is one of the five great holy places of the Jain faith. The grand scale and sheer architectural complexity of the white marble temple distinguish it as perhaps the single most impressive example of Western Indian temple architecture *(see pp400–401)*. The temple has an unusual four-sided plan, with four separate entrances. Each entrance leads through a veritable forest of columns, and a number of beautifully ornamented halls and chapels, to the central sanctum containing a four-faced image of Adinath.

Dancer, Luna Vasahi Temple

Each of the temple's 1,444 pillars is carved with different patterns of floral motifs, and the play of light and shadow on

View of the Jain temple complex at Ranakpur

The winding ramparts of the indomitable Kumbhalgarh Fort

the pillars, as the sun moves from east to west each day, is one of the glories of this monument. Equally stunning is the superb filigree carving on the concentric ceiling pendants, and the exuberant grace of the goddesses who form the support brackets. On one of the columns facing the sanctum, a carved panel with two figures on it depicts Dharna Shah, the builder of the temple, who was a minister of the maharana of Mewar, and his architect, Depa.

A wall topped with spires surrounds this serene temple complex, which also has a Hindu Sun Temple, and two other Jain temples. Of these, the 15th-century Parsvanatha Temple is distinguished by the exceptionally fine pierced stonework on its windows.

㉒ Kumbhalgarh

Rajsamand district. 63 km (39 miles) N of Udaipur. 🚉 Kankroli, 35 km (21 miles) SE of Kumbhalgarh, then bus. 🚌 ✍

Like a gigantic brown snake, the great ramparts of Kumbhalgarh Fort wind along the rugged contours of the Aravalli Hills for 36 km (22 miles). This massive 15th-century fort, strategically located at a height of 1,050 m (3,445 ft) along the border between Marwar (Jodhpur) and Mewar (Udaipur), was known as "The Eye of Mewar", because it

offered a commanding view of the countryside for miles around. Built by Maharana Kumbha (r.1433–68), who also built the great fort of Chittorgarh *(see p334)*, Kumbhalgarh was justly reputed to be the most impregnable fort in Rajasthan. Its ramparts are wide enough for six horsemen to ride a-breast, and seven fortified gates, studded with threatening spikes, lead to its entrance.

The crenellated walls of the fort enclose the smaller fortress of Kartargarh, several palaces and temples now in ruins, fields, water reservoirs and stables. Standing at the highest point of the fort is the **Badal Mahal**, a 19th-century addition with airy chambers and fine wall paintings of hunting scenes. The 15th-century **Neelkantha Temple**, which also lies within the fort, has a huge Shivalinga and is still in use.

A deity on the fort wall, believed to prevent evil happenings

Another interesting temple, the **Navachoki Mamdeva Temple**, is in a gorge to the east of Kartargarh. It contains several slabs of black granite inscribed with the history of Mewar, the earliest slab dating to 1491. Next to it is the cenotaph of Maharana Kumbha.

Kumbhalgarh was also the birthplace of Maharana Pratap (1540–97), a great warrior king famous for his heroic stand against the armies of the Mughal emperor Akbar.

Environs
The **Kumbhalgarh Wildlife Sanctuary** covers 578 sq km (223 sq miles) of the Aravalli Hills, west of the fort, on the leeward side. Panther, flying squirrel, wolf and many bird species can be seen here.

Kankroli, 35 km (21 miles) southeast of Kumbhalgarh, has the 17th-century Dwarkadhish Temple on the southern shore of Rajsamand Lake. The western shore is lined with lovely marble pavilions and ghats.

The charming little town of **Deogarh**, 55 km (34 miles) north of Kumbhalgarh, set among lakes and hills, has the 17th-century Rajmahal Palace with exquisite wall murals, and the Anjaneshwar Mahadev Temple in a cave in the hillside. Deogarh is also a popular base for horse safaris which explore this picturesque part of Mewar.

Marblework in Jain Temples

Rajasthan's most outstanding Jain temples, at Ranakpur and at Dilwara in Mount Abu *(see p398)*, are breathtaking in the wealth and variety of their sculptural ornamentation. Made of white marble quarried at Makrana, which also provided the marble for the Taj Mahal, the Ranakpur and Dilwara temples are architectual marvels. Above all, they are testimony to the incredible artistry of the marble carvers who created these masterpieces. Visitors should use binoculars to fully appreciate the astounding work on the ceilings and pillars.

This four-faced image of Adinath, the first *tirthankara*, stands in Ranakpur's main sanctum. It faces the four cardinal directions.

The Jain Religion

Jain nuns with covered mouths

Jainism, founded in the 6th century BC, is based on a doctrine of non-violence towards all living beings. Jains are strict vegetarians, and the more orthodox ones cover their mouths to avoid inadvertently swallowing living organisms. Jains believe in 24 *tirthankaras* or crossing-makers, enlightened beings who guide others across the "river of transmigration" (the journey of the soul from one life to the next). The first of the *tirthankaras* was Adinath, also known as Rishabdeo, and the last was Mahavira (born in 540 BC). Regarded as the religion's founder, his 2,600th birth anniversary was celebrated in 2001. Jainism attracted many followers among the wealthy traders and merchants of Western India, who were also politically powerful as financiers and ministers in Rajput princely states. As acts of devotion and penance, they financed the building of several elaborately carved temples in Gujarat and Rajasthan.

Hall of Pillars

A forest of carved columns connected by wavy arches leads to the main sanctum at Dilwara's Vimala Vasahi Temple. It was built in the 11th century.

Exterior
The uncarved exterior of Ranakpur's 15th-century Adinath Temple contrasts sharply with the profuse decoration inside. This symbolizes the Jain belief in the insignificance of outward forms, and the importance of a rich inner life.

Corbelled Ceilings

The ceilings are carved in concentric tiers to symbolize the Jain view of the universe as a series of cosmic cycles. Marble carvers were paid in gold according to the weight of the marble shavings they presented at the end of each day's work.

Dancers and deities, gracefully sculpted, are the struts that support the ceiling.

This Ranakpur ceiling is a typical example of the Rajasthani marble carvers' art. It is so finely worked that the marble is translucent in places.

Sculptured panels at Ranakpur show dancers full of grace and movement.

Pillars in Dilwara are densely carved with floral motifs and figures in niches. No two pillars are identical in their ornamentation.

Kalpavalli medallions, with their exquisite patterns of foliage, tendrils and flowers, feature at both Dilwara and Ranakpur.

The Parsvanatha plaque shows the 23rd *tirthankara* protected by a multi-headed cobra. It is set into the southern wall of the Adinath Temple at Ranakpur.

㉓ Udaipur

This fairy-tale city, with its marble palaces and lakes surrounded by a ring of hills, was founded by Maharana Udai Singh in 1559, and became the capital of Mewar after the fall of Chittorgarh in 1567 *(see p406)*. The rulers of Mewar, who belonged to the Sisodia clan of Rajputs, traced their dynasty back to AD 566. Fiercely independent, they refused matrimonial alliances with the Mughals, and took great pride in their reputation as the prime defenders of Rajput honour. The city is dominated by the massive City Palace, which overlooks Lake Pichola with its romantic island palaces. Picturesque *havelis*, ghats and temples line the lake front, with the lively bazaars of the old walled city stretching behind them.

A view of Lake Pichola, with the Jag Mandir Palace on an island

Jag Niwas, or the Lake Palace, in its magical setting on Lake Pichola

🏛 City Palace
See pp404–405.

🏛 Jag Mandir
Lake Pichola. **Open** daily. 🚢 City Palace Jetty. 🚢 Jag Niwas: **Tel** (0294) 252 8016. 🚫 open to non-residents.

Jag Mandir, with its lush gardens and marble chambers exquisitely inlaid with coloured stone, was built in 1620. Eight stone elephants stand solemn guard at its entrance. Between 1623 and 1624, this island palace provided refuge to Prince Khurram (who would later become the Mughal emperor Shah Jahan) while he rebelled against his father. It is believed to have inspired many of his ideas for the Taj Mahal.

Jag Niwas, or the Lake Palace, built between 1734 and 1751, was once a royal summer retreat and is now one of the world's great hotels. It is also a popular location for film shoots (including James Bond's *Octopussy*). Both palaces can be seen on a boat tour of Lake Pichola.

🏛 Jagdish Mandir
Moti Chhohta Rd. **Open** daily. Bagore ki Haveli: Gangaur Ghat. **Tel** (0294) 252 2567/241 0539. 🚫

This 17th-century temple, just north of the City Palace's main gate, has an enormous black stone image of Vishnu in its profusely carved main shrine. The entrance is flanked by stone elephants, and a superb bronze image of Garuda (the mythical bird who is Vishnu's vehicle) stands in front of the temple. Nearby, at Gangaur Ghat, is the 18th-century **Bagore ki Haveli**, now a museum exhibiting Udaipur's traditional arts and crafts, costumes, musical instruments and marblework. Folk music and dance performances are held here every evening at 7pm.

Pichhwai painting

The old walled city, a jumble of shops and houses, many with beautifully painted façades, lies east of the Jagdish Mandir. In its narrow, lanes are the **Bapu** and **Bara Bazaars**, selling wooden toys, puppets, textiles, jewels and *pichhwais*.

🌊 Fateh Sagar Lake
Fateh Sagar Rd.
North of Lake Pichola is Fateh Sagar Lake, with a garden café on its island. Overlooking it is Moti Magri Hill with a statue of Udaipur's great 16th-century warrior, Maharana Pratap, and his valiant steed, Chetak.

🌸 Saheliyon ki Bari
Saheli Marg. **Open** daily. 🚫
This delightful 18th-century retreat in the north of the city (its name means "Garden of the Maids of Honour") has ornamental fountains, a lotus pool and a rose garden. It was built for a queen of Udaipur, whose dowry included 48 maids.

🏛 Ahar
Ashok Nagar Rd. Museum: **Open** Sat–Thu. **Closed** public hols. 🚫
Located 3 km (2 miles) east of Udaipur, Ahar has the impressive cenotaphs of 19 Mewar rulers, and a small archaeological museum.

Environs
Shilpgram, 8 km (5 miles) northwest of Udaipur, is a lively ethnographic crafts village, with

Pavilion in the Saheliyon ki Bari, an 18th-century queen's garden

Nagda's Saas-Bahu Temples, seen through the finely carved *torana*

VISITORS' CHECKLIST

Practical Information
Udaipur district. 269 km (167 miles)
S of Jodhpur. 389,400.
Rajasthan Tourism, Suraj Pol, (0294)
241 1535. Gangaur Festival
(Mar/Apr), Mewar Festival (Apr).

Transport
25 km (16 miles) E of city
centre.

artisans, folk performers, and replicas of traditional houses. Camel rides are also available. **Eklingji**, 22 km (14 miles) northeast of Udaipur, is a complex of 108 temples and shrines, dedicated to Lord Shiva. It marks the site where the founder of the Mewar ruling dynasty, Bappa Rawal, received special blessings from a sage who lived here. The main temple dates to the 16th century. Built of marble and granite, it includes an impressive pillared hall and a four faced image of Shiva crafted in black marble, with a silver Nandi facing it. **Nagda**, a short distance away from Eklingji, is worth a visit for the Saas-Bahu

Temples ("Mother and Daughter-in-law Temples"), twin structures dedicated to Vishnu. The 11th-century temples are entered through a finely carved *torana* and are renowned for their elaborate sculptures depicting amorous couples and scenes from the epic *Ramayana*.

One of Rajasthan's main pilgrimage sites is the 18th-century Shrinathji Temple at **Nathdwara**, 48 km (30 miles) northeast of Udaipur. The main deity is Lord Krishna, known locally as Shrinathji. His black stone image was brought here from Mathura *(see p156)* to save it from destruction by the Mughal emperor Aurangzeb in the 17th

century. Beautiful painted cloth hangings known as *pichhwais* are hung behind it. Non-Hindus cannot enter the temple, but Nathdwara town's picturesque bazaar, with its *pichhwai* painters at work, is worth a visit. *Pichhwais*, one of the most vibrant forms of Indian painting, are done on stiff cloth in vegetable and mineral colours. They depict 24 scenes from the Krishna legend, each linked with a particular festival or holy day. At the centre of each painting is a stylised image of Lord Krishna, with dusky skin, slanting eyes and intricate jewellery, set against a background of verdant foliage, birds, animals and skyscapes. Around the deity are cows, milkmaids and devotees.

Udaipur City Centre

① City Palace
② Jag Mandir
③ Jagdish Mandir
④ Fateh Sagar Lake
⑤ Saheliyon ki Bari

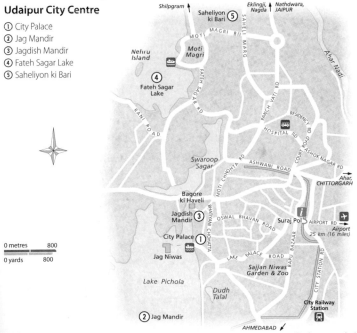

For key to symbols *see back flap*

Udaipur: City Palace

Stretching along the eastern shore of Lake Pichola, Udaipur's City Palace is a fascinating combination of Rajput military architecture and Mughal-style decorative techniques. Its stern, fortress-like façade, topped by a profusion of graceful balconies, cupolas and turrets, has been aptly described by one writer as a massive plain cake topped with fabulous icing. The largest palace in Rajasthan, covering an area of 2 ha (5 acres), the City Palace is actually a complex of several palaces, built or added to by 22 different maharanas between the 16th and 20th centuries. Much of it is now a museum, and parts of it are luxury hotels.

Fateh Prakash
This early 20th-century palace, now a hotel, has a magnificent Durbar Hall and a gallery of crystal furniture.

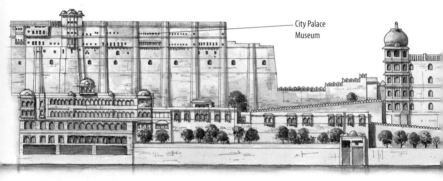

City Palace Museum

Rajya Angan Chowk, with a temple to the goddess Dhuni Mata

Exploring the City Palace

The older section of the City Palace complex dates from 1568. Behind its fortified walls is a maze of royal apartments, reception halls and courtyards. They are linked to each other by narrow passages and steep staircases – a feature typical of Rajput palaces of that period, designed to confuse invaders.

The superb **City Palace Museum** is spread out through several palaces in this section, and is entered through the imposing **Tripolia Gate** (built in 1713). Above the entrance is the Mewar crest – a large Sun face (reinforcing the Sisodia clan's claim to be descended from the Sun), flanked by Rajput and Bhil warriors (the tribal Bhils,

skilled archers, played a heroic role in Mewar's great battles). Beyond this is the **Ganesh Deorhi Gate** where entrance tickets for the museum are checked. It leads into a courtyard decorated with frescoes of horses and elephants, and a marble relief of the god Ganesha surrounded by dazzling mirror and glass inlay.

The next courtyard is the **Rajya Angan Chowk**, from where steps lead to the **Chandra Mahal** (built in 1620). One of the loveliest palaces in the complex, it has beautiful columns, fretwork windows and striking marble reliefs of Rajput women, one of whom carries a shield. There is a magical view of Lake Pichola and its island palaces from here.

Another flight of steps from here leads to the charming **Bari Mahal** (built in 1699). Perched 27 m (89 ft) above the ground, it is built on a terraced hillside that is completely enclosed within the palace walls. Deep

A view of the City Palace, on the eastern shore of Lake Pichola

VISITORS' CHECKLIST

Practical Information
City Palace Complex.
Tel (0294) 252 8016. **Open** daily.
🚫 Photography restricted. 🏛
Museum: Extra charges for photo-
graphy. 🍴 📷 Fateh Prakash:
🅿 open to non-residents. Shiv
Niwas: 🅿 open to non-residents.

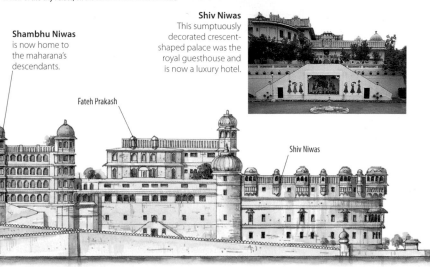

Shiv Niwas
This sumptuously decorated crescent-shaped palace was the royal guesthouse and is now a luxury hotel.

Shambhu Niwas
is now home to the maharana's descendants.

Fateh Prakash

Shiv Niwas

Kanch Burj, with its dazzling decoration of red and silver glass

halls with receding rows of carved arches open into an enchanting courtyard with a marble pool in the middle. Tall *neem* trees stand around it, providing dappled shade.

The Bari Mahal leads to the **Dilkhushal Mahal** (built in 1620) with two remarkable chambers – the Kanch Burj ("Glass Turret") inlaid with red and silver glass, and the Krishna Niwas which exhibits outstanding Mewar miniature paintings (*see p409*). This was the room of 16-year-old Princess Krishna Kumari, who committed suicide in 1807 when rival suitors from Jodhpur and Jaipur threatened to go to war over her hand.

To the left of this palace is the ornate **Moti Mahal**, the chamber of the dissolute Maharana Jawan Singh (r.1828–38), who once promised a dancing girl half his kingdom if she could walk a tightrope across Lake Pichola. The girl had almost reached when the maharana's alarmed courtiers cut the rope, and the dancer

Mosaic of dancing peacock in the Mor Chowk

drowned. Still further left is the **Mor Chowk** ("Peacock Courtyard") with its brilliantly coloured 19th-century mosaics of three dancing peacocks. The southern end of the City Palace complex has three other opulent palaces built in the late 19th and early 20th centuries – **Shambhu Niwas** where the descendants of the rulers now live; **Fateh Prakash** with its magnificent Durbar Hall, fine portraits and gallery of crystal furniture; and the semi-circular **Shiv Niwas** built as the royal guesthouse (Queen Elizabeth II once stayed here). Fateh Prakash and Shiv Niwas are now luxury hotels, but are open to non-residents for tours and meals.

A colourfully painted chamber in Juna Mahal, Dungarpur

❷❹ Dungarpur

Dungarpur district. 110 km (68 miles)
S of Udaipur. 42,550.
Vagad Festival (Jan/Feb),
Baneshwar Festival (Feb).

This remote, relatively unknown
town boasts some unexpected
artistic treasures. Dominating
Dungarpur is the seven-storeyed
Juna Mahal, built in the 13th
century on a large rock. The
interior of this palace-fort, in
contrast to its rather battered
exterior, glows with exuberant
ornamentation, and contains
some of the most beautiful
frescoes to be seen in Rajasthan.
Remarkably well-preserved,
these include a series of erotic
paintings from the *Kama Sutra*
in the erstwhile ruler's bedroom,
on the top floor of the palace.

The 19th-century **Udai Vilas
Palace** beside a lake, is built of
local grey-green granite in a
blend of Rajput and Mughal
styles. Rising from the centre of
its courtyard is a fantastic four-
storeyed pavilion with cusped
arches, densely carved friezes,
and a profusion of canopies and
balconies. The large room on its
top storey is inlaid with a variety
of semi-precious stones.

❷❺ Chittorgarh

Chittorgarh district. 115 km (72 miles)
NE of Udaipur. Janta Avas
Graha, Station Rd, (01472) 24 1089.
Meera Utsav (Oct).

The great, battle-scarred
Chittorgarh Fort epitomizes
in its tragic history the valour,
romance, chivalry and strict
death-before-dishonour code
glorified in Rajput myths and
legends. Sprawling across 280
ha (692 acres), atop a steep
180-m (591-ft) high rocky hill,
Chittorgarh's ruined palaces,
temples and towers bear
witness to its illustrious and
turbulent past, when it was
the capital of the Sisodia rulers
of Mewar, between the 12th
and 16th centuries.

As Rajasthan's mightiest fort,
it was the target of successive
invaders. The first siege, in 1303,
was by Sultan Alauddin Khilji *(see
p52)*, whose goal was to capture
not only the fort but also the
queen, Rani Padmini, whose
legendary beauty the sultan had
glimpsed reflected in a mirror.
When defeat seemed inevitable,
Rani Padmini along with 13,000
women committed *jauhar* – a
ritual form of mass suicide by
immolation, practised by Rajput
women to escape dishonour at
the hands of their enemies. It is
said that 50,000 Rajput warriors
died in the ensuing battle.
Alauddin's army then proceeded
to sack the fort and destroyed
many of its buildings. Within a
few years, however, the ruler's
grandson had regained it for
the Sisodia dynasty.

The next great battle, this time
against Sultan Bahadur Shah of
Gujarat in 1535, saw the Queen
Mother, Rani Jawaharbai, lead
a cavalry charge and die on the
battle-field along with the flower
of Rajput youth. Once again,
thousands of women inside the
fort committed *jauhar*. The third
and final assault on Chittorgarh
was led by the Mughal emperor
Akbar, who was able to capture
it in 1567. Chittorgarh was
abandoned thereafter, and the
Sisodias moved their capital
to Udaipur *(see pp402–403)*.

Seven massive spiked gates
lead to the fort. The first building
to the right is **Rana Kumbha's
Palace** (built between 1433
and 1468), probably the earliest
surviving example of a Rajput
palace. Its northern side has a
profusion of richly carved
balconies, and a unique
stepped wall. Elephant

A view of the impressive Chittorgarh Fort, spread over a rocky hill

stables and a council chamber comprise its public areas, while the private apartments are a maze of small rooms, including a zenana section. Near it are the 20th-century **Fateh Prakash Palace**, which now houses a museum of sculpture found on the site; the **Kumbha Shyam Temple**, dating to the 15th-century, with a fine sculpture of Vishnu in his Varaha (boar) incarnation; and the **Meerabai Temple**, built in 1440 by Meerabai, (see p53) another remarkable Mewar queen. A mystic and a poetess, she defied Rajput convention and devoted her life to the worship of Lord Krishna.

The main street runs south of this temple towards the nine-storeyed **Vijay Stambh** ("Victory Tower"), built by Maharana Kumbha between 1458 and 1468, to commem-orate his victory over Sultan Mahmud of Malwa (see p251). The view from the top of this extraordinary 36-m (118-ft) high sand-stone structure, richly carved with gods and goddesses, is magnificent.

Vijay Stambh

The main street continues further south past noblemen's mansions to the **Gaumukh Reservoir**, fed by an underground spring, and the 16th-century **Kalika Mata Temple**, built over the original Sun Temple which was destroyed during the devastating siege of 1303.

Opposite this temple stands the 19th-century reconstruction of **Padmini's Palace** with a lake pavilion adjacent to it. The palace contains the mirror in which Alauddin Khilji supposedly saw her reflection. Standing further south, past some Jain temples, is the **Kirti Stambh**. This seven-storeyed tower is dedicated to the first Jain tirthankara, Adinath.

🏛 **Fateh Prakash Museum**
Open Sat–Thu. 🎫 free on Mon.

The 11th-century temple of the Sun God, in Jhalrapatan

㉖ Jhalawar

Jhalawar district. 323 km (201 miles) S of Jaipur. 🚉 48,100. 🚌 🚕 ℹ Hotel Chandrawati, (07432) 23 0081. 🎪 Chandrabhaga Cattle Fair (Oct/Nov).

This delightful little town, surrounded by orange groves and poppy fields, is dominated by a 19th-century fort, the seat of the erstwhile princes of Jhalawar. It now houses govern-ment offices. An incongruous yet charming part of the fort is the **Bhavani Natya Shala Theatre** (built in 1921), which was modelled on the grand opera houses the maharaja had seen on his European tours. The old walled town of **Jhalrapatan** ("City of Bells"), 6 km (4 miles) south of the fort, has a splendid cluster of 11th-century temples. Of these the most impressive is the **Surya Temple** with its stunning image of the Sun God. About 1.5 km (1 mile) south of this temple, on the banks of the Chandrabhaga river, stands the superbly carved 7th-century **Chandra Mauleshwar Temple**.

Environs
The 14th-century **Ghagron Fort**, 10 km (6 miles) west of Jhalawar, is situated amid a landscape of hills, woods and fields, and surrounded on three sides by the Kali, Sindh and Ahu rivers.

The lush forests, cliffs and grasslands of **Darrah Wildlife Sanctuary**, 70 km (44 miles) west of Jhalawar, look just as they do in the famous Kota paintings (see p409) of hunting scenes – only the tigers and princes are now missing.

㉗ Kota

Kota district. 261 km (162 miles) S of Jaipur. 🚉 696,000. 🚌 🚕 ℹ Hotel Chambal, (0744) 232 6527. 🎪 Dussehra Mela (Sep/Oct).

The imposing façade of Kota's fortified **City Palace**, which dates back to 1625, stretches along the banks of the Chambal river, recalling the princely past of this now heavily industrialized city. Kota's artistic heritage is well-represented in the palace apartments – every available surface is covered with miniature paintings, mirrorwork, murals and mosaics. Particularly resplendent is the Durbar Hall, with its ebony-and-ivory doors, and paintings depicting Kota's history. Many of the royal apartments now form part of the excellent **Rao Madho Singh Museum**, which has a fine collection of weapons and royal regalia.

On Kishorsagar Lake, in the middle of the town, is the charming island palace known as **Jag Mandir**, built in the 18th century by a Kota queen who yearned for her childhood home in Udaipur (see p402).

🏛 **Rao Madho Singh Museum**
Open Sat–Thu. 🎫

Environs
Bardoli, 55 km (34 miles) southwest of Kota, has one of Rajasthan's most beautiful temple complexes. The 9th-century Ghateshwar Mahadev temple has an outstanding sculpture of Nataraja (the dancing Shiva) on the door of its sanctum.

Ebony-and-ivory door in the 17th-century City Palace, Kota

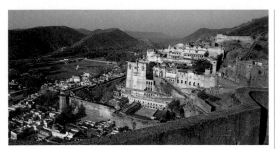
View of Bundi, nestled in a narrow valley of the Aravalli Hills

❷❽ Bundi

Bundi district. 215 km (134 miles) S of Jaipur. 🚉 88,350. 🚌 🚗 ℹ️ Rajasthan Tourism, Tourist Reception Centre, (0747) 244 3697. 🏤 daily. 🎭 Gangaur (Mar/Apr).

Bundi is often described as the undiscovered jewel of Rajasthan. Surrounded on three sides by the rugged, thickly forested Aravalli Hills, this walled town has retained much of its historic character. The **Taragarh Fort** crowns the crest of a steep hill overlooking the town, while the **Garh Palace** spills picturesquely down the hillside. This palace is Bundi's – and Rajasthan's – jewel. Lieutenant Colonel James Tod, (1782–1835), the British Political Agent and author of the authoritative *Annals and Antiquities of Rajasthan*, wrote that "the *coup d'oeil* of the castellated palace of Boondi, from whichever side you approach it, is the most striking in India".

The state of Bundi was founded in 1341 by Rao Deva of the "fire-born" Hada Chauhan Rajput clan, and the massive, square Taragarh Fort dates to his reign. Work on the palace began in the 16th century, and it was added to by successive rulers over the next 200 years, at different levels on the hillside. Unlike most other palaces in Rajasthan, there is very little Mughal influence in its architecture. The Garh Palace

Painting from the Chitrashala

represents a rare example of the pure Rajput style, with curved roofs topping pavilions and kiosks, a profusion of temple columns and ornamental brackets, and typically Rajput motifs such as elephants and lotus flowers. Unusually, the palace is not built of the sandstone favoured by most other Rajput kingdoms, but of a hard, green-tinged serpentine stone, quarried locally. This stone, unlike sandstone, does not lend itself to fine carving. Instead, Garh Palace was embellished by superb paintings. The palace is entered through the imposing **Hathia Pol** ("Elephant Gateway"), flanked by two towers and topped by a pair of huge painted elephants. The most spectacular parts of the palace are the **Chattar Mahal** (built in 1660), and the **Chitrashala**, an arcaded gallery (built between 1748 and 1770) overlooking a hanging garden. The murals in these are regarded as among the finest examples of Rajput painting. The themes they cover include scenes from religious ceremonies, hunting scenes and other princely amusements. The colours are predominantly blue and green, with touches of deep red and yellow. In the middle of the town is the **Naval Sagar**

Lake, with a little temple on an island in its centre. The fort and palace reflected in the lake make a pretty sight.

Bundi has over 50 stepwells, of which the most beautiful is the 46-m (151-ft) deep **Rani-ki-Baori**, also in the centre of town. Built in the 17th century, it is strikingly similar to Adalaj Vav in Gujarat *(see pp418–19)*, with richly decorated archways and sculptures of Vishnu's ten avatars *(see p683)*.

Situated at the northern edge of the town is the 18th-century **Sukh Niwas Mahal**, a romantic summer palace overlooking **Jait Sagar Lake**. Standing at the opposite end of the lake are the royal cenotaphs, and at its western edge is an elegant hunting tower, the **Shikar Burj**.

Environs

Bijolia, 50 km (31 miles) southwest of Bundi, on the road to Chittorgarh, has a group of three beautiful 13th-century temples, dedicated to Shiva. **Menal**, lying 20 km (12 miles) further along the same road is a delightful wooded spot with 11th-century temples standing near a gorge.

Tonk, 113 km (70 miles) north of Bundi, was once the capital of the only Muslim princely state in Rajasthan. Founded in the early 19th-century, its main attraction is the splendid Sunehri Kothi ("Golden Mansion") within the palace complex, every inch of its interior covered with gold leaf, lacquer-work, moulded stucco and striking mirrorwork. Stained-glass windows bathe this opulent hall in glowing colours. Tonk's Arabic and Persian Research Institute has rare, illuminated medieval Islamic manuscripts.

The gilded interior of Sunehri Kothi in Tonk

Rajasthani Miniature Painting

The intricate and vivid paintings of Rajasthan's princely states grew out of illustrated Jain and Hindu sacred texts. Originally, they depicted mainly religious themes, in bold lines and bright primary colours. After the 17th century, however, the influence of the more sophisticated Mughal-Persian art tradition brought greater delicacy of line, and a wider range of colours and themes into Rajasthani art. By the 18th century, many princely states such as Kishangarh, Mewar, Bundi and Kota had developed their own distinctive styles. In most schools of Rajasthani painting, however, human figures are shown in profile, and different colours, seasons, flowers and animals are used symbolically to express a variety of moods. These various schools of miniature painting continue to flourish in Rajasthan today.

The Maharana Celebrating Gangaur (1715)

Jain religious text, early 17th century

Mewar Paintings

Large, detailed compositions, showing scenes from the lives of the maharanas of Udaipur, are characteristic of the Mewar School. The paintings depict festivals, grand processions, historic battles and religious ceremonies. The intricate detail was achieved by using just a single squirrel hair as a brush.

Bundi and Kota Paintings

The neighbouring princely states of Bundi and Kota produced outstanding miniatures. Bundi specialized in depicting palace life and scenes from Krishna's life, executed in soft blues and greens. Kota is renowned for its superb hunting scenes, set in dramatic forested landscapes, with wonderful depictions of animals and foliage. An 18th-century court painter named Sheikh Taju created many of them.

Bundi miniature depicting a palace scene

Kishangarh Paintings

Famous for his fine portraits, the 18th-century Kishangarh artist, Nihal Chand, found a favourite model in the royal courtesan, Bani Thani Radha, with her elegantly elongated features and enigmatic expression. He was also known for his lyrical depictions of skyscapes and seasons.

Bani Thani Radha, often called the Indian Mona Lisa

Maharao Durjan in the Kota Forest (1730)

㉙ Ranthambhore National Park

This park lies in the shadow of the Aravalli and Vindhya mountain ranges and covers a core area of 275 sq km (106 sq miles). Its razor-sharp ridges, deep boulder-filled gorges, lakes and jungles are the habitat of carnivores such as the caracal, panther, jackal and hyena, numerous species of deer, and a rich variety of resident and migratory birds. The most famous resident, however, is the endangered tiger, and it is a unique experience to catch glimpses of this majestic animal. Like other parks in the region, this was originally the hunting ground of Jaipur's maharajas and it only became a Project Tiger Reserve in 1973.

Rajbagh Talao
Ruined pavilions stand on the banks of Rajbagh Talao, one of the three lakes in the park.

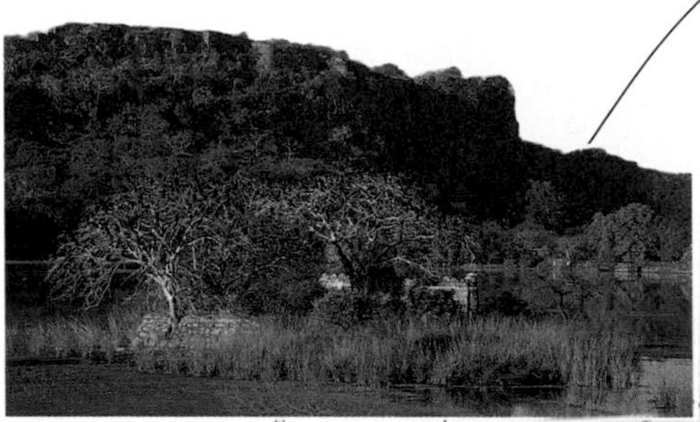

Ranthambhore Fort
The park derives its name from this great Rajput forest fort that is 1,000 years old and stands at a height of 215 m (705 ft).

Sambar
Large herds of sambar (*Cervus unicolor*) are seen around the lakes, wallowing in the water and feeding on aquatic plants, unperturbed by jeeps and visitors.

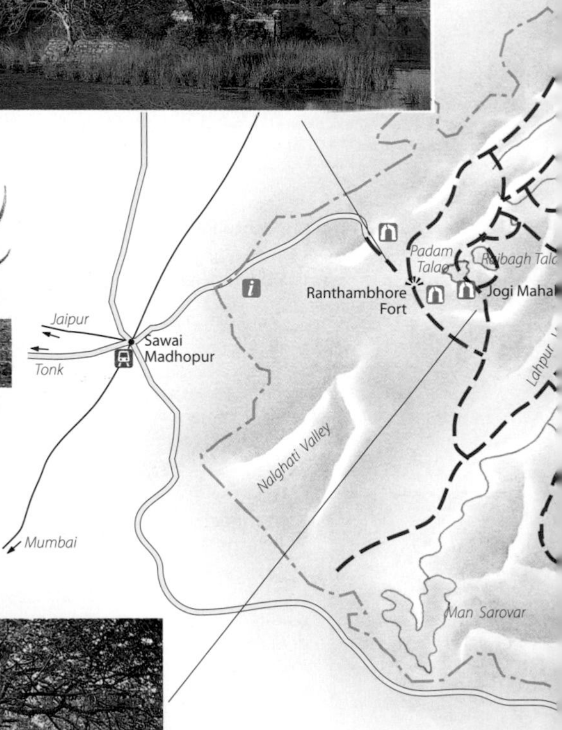

Jaipur
Tonk
Sawai Madhopur
Mumbai
Padam Talao
Rajbagh Talao
Ranthambhore Fort
Jogi Mahal
Nalghati Valley
Lahpur
Man Sarovar

Banyan Tree
This enormous banyan tree (*Ficus bengalensis*) lies in the grounds of Jogi Mahal. Its many spreading branches are all supported by roots.

Delhi
Banas
Semli Valley
Gilai Sagar
Khandar Fort
0 kilometres 5
0 miles 2
Key
Major road
Railway
Park border
Trail

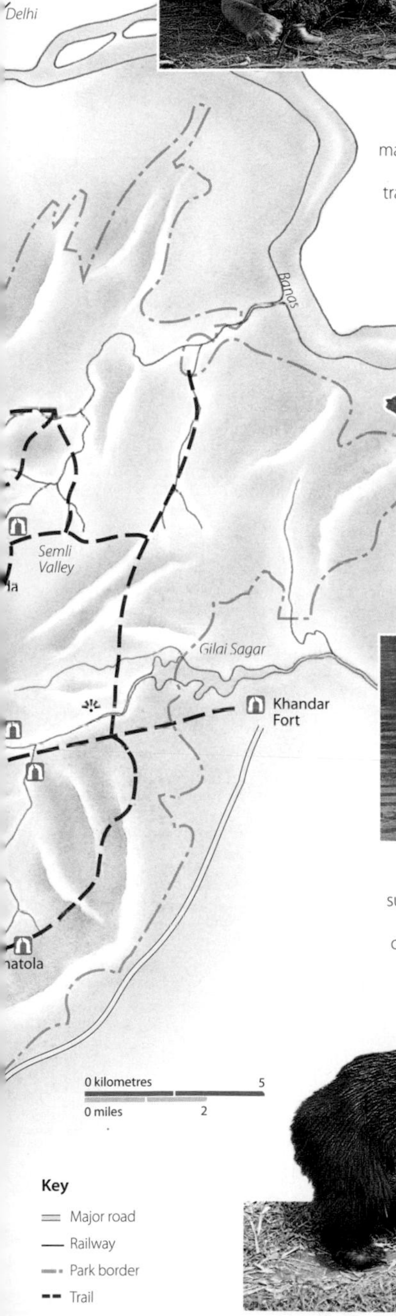

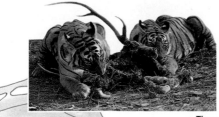

Tiger
Sighting the park's main predator is a matter of chance, but one can often find traces of its activities.

VISITORS' CHECKLIST

Practical Information
Sawai Madhopur district. 180 km (112 miles) SE of Jaipur. RTDC Hotel Vinayak, Sawai Madhopur, (07 462) 221 333. **Open** Oct–Jun. Extra charges for photography. compulsory. Walking is strictly prohibited. Only jeeps hired from the Project Tiger Office, (07462) 220 479, near the railway station, are allowed inside the park. The Dastkari Kendra, (07462) 222 892, opp Kutalpura village on the way to Kundera.

Transport
Sawai Madhopur, 10 km (6 miles) E of entry point, then taxi. Sawai Madhopur.

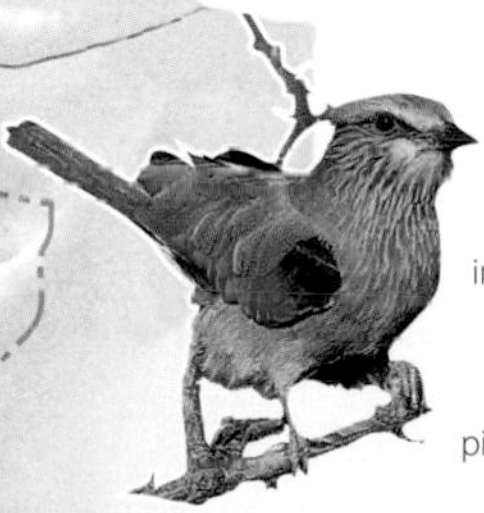

Indian Roller Bird
This is one of the many species of birds found in the park. The others include birds of prey such as the crested serpent eagle and Bonelli's eagle, and many species of pigeons, flycatchers, storks and water birds.

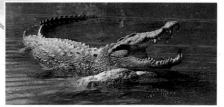

Marsh Crocodile
Muggers, or marsh crocodiles, are commonly seen submerged in water or basking on the shores of the lakes. Ungulate species are their main prey, and sometimes a crocodile can be glimpsed dragging the carcass of a deer into the water. Monitor lizards and pythons are some of the other reptiles found in the park.

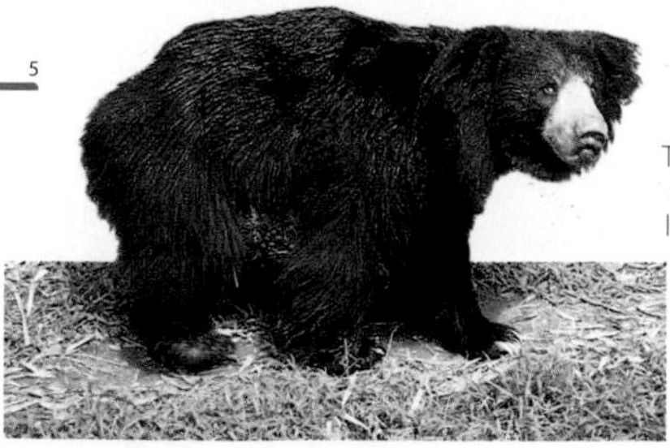

Sloth Bear
This shaggy bear with short hind legs and a long muzzle emerges at duskto feed. During the day it shelters in the rocky outcrops and is difficult to sight.

For keys to symbols *see back flap*

GUJARAT

The state of Gujarat has three distinct regions – a corridor running north to south which is the industrial mainland, a peninsula known as Saurashtra, and Kutch, which is partly desert and partly marshland. The state's 1,666-km (1,035-mile) coastline has attracted sea-farers through the ages, lured by the rich prospects of trade. The Arabs, Portuguese, Dutch, Mughals and British, as well as Parsis fleeing their native Iran, have all left their mark on Gujarat's culture. Fascinating archaeological sites, superb Jain, Hindu and Islamic architecture, exquisite crafts and rare wildlife, including the Asiatic lion, are among Gujarat's attractions, as are its hardworking, enterprising people. In January 2001, an earthquake hit Gujarat and devastated the region of Kutch. But with their legendary capacity to overcome hardship and disaster, the people lost no time in rebuilding their lives out of the debris around them.

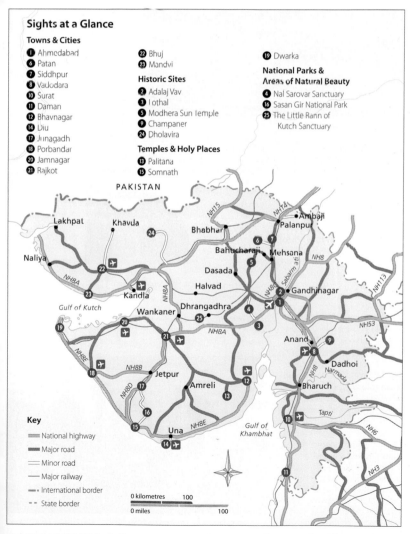

Sights at a Glance

Towns & Cities
1 Ahmedabad
6 Patan
7 Siddhpur
8 Vadodara
10 Surat
11 Daman
12 Bhavnagar
14 Diu
17 Junagadh
18 Porbandar
20 Jamnagar
21 Rajkot

22 Bhuj
23 Mandvi

Historic Sites
2 Adalaj Vav
3 Lothal
5 Modhera Sun Temple
9 Champaner
24 Dholavira

Temples & Holy Places
13 Palitana
15 Somnath

19 Dwarka

National Parks & Areas of Natural Beauty
4 Nal Sarovar Sanctuary
16 Sasan Gir National Park
25 The Little Rann of Kutch Sanctuary

Key
National highway
Major road
Minor road
Major railway
International border
State border

◀ Striking façade of the Mahabat Maqbara, Junagadh

For keys to symbols *see back flap*

❶ Ahmedabad

Gujarat's leading city, Ahmedabad was the state capital until 1970. This bustling industrial and commercial centre also has a fascinating old quarter, redolent with Gujarat's traditional culture and history. Legend has it that the city owes its foundation to Sultan Ahmed Shah (r.1411–42), who, while out hunting, encountered a warren of rabbits on the banks of the Sabarmati river. Astonishingly, the rabbits turned fiercely on his hounds and defended their territory. Viewing this as an auspicious sign, the sultan built his new capital at this site and named it after himself – Ahmedabad.

A view of the crowded banks of the Sabarmati river

🏛 The Old City

Bounded by Lady Vidyagauri Rd, Sardar Patel Rd & Kasturba Gandhi Rd. Heritage Walking Tours: **Tel** (079) 2657 4335.

A maze of crowded bazaars, *pols* (large gateways, leading to residential quarters), exquisitely carved façades, temples, mosques and sub-terranean stepwells (*vavs*) mark the 3-km (2-mile) square that makes up the Old City. This area is best explored on foot, and the Ahmedabad Municipal Corporation organizes a daily Heritage Walking Tour through the atmospheric bylanes.

Built at the site of the original city, **Bhadra Fort** has panoramic views of the surrounding streets. Southwest of the fort is **Ahmed Shah's Mosque**, a simple place of worship, built in 1414 on the site of an early 13th-century Hindu temple.

Perhaps Ahmedabad's most photographed monument, **Siddi Saiyad's Mosque** (also known as Siddi Saiyad Ni Jaali), in the northeast corner of Bhadra Fort, is renowned for its superb yellow stone latticework. Made by a slave of Ahmed Shah in 1572, the twin *jalis* on the western

wall depict the intertwining branches of a tree, carved with extraordinary delicacy.

Southeast of the fort, the **Teen Darwaza** ("Triple Gateway") straddles the road, which is lined with shops selling block-prints, silverware and bric-à-brac. Close by, along Mahatma Gandhi Road, is the **Jama Masjid**, which Sultan Ahmed Shah built in 1423, to enable the faithful to congregate

Tree of Life *jali* in Siddi Saiyad's Mosque

for Friday prayers. The masons who constructed this yellow sandstone structure ingeniously used pieces retrieved from demolished Hindu and Jain temples – the black slab close to the main arch is said to be the base of an inverted Jain idol. The mosque's 15 domes are supported by 260 pillars covered with intricate carvings. The interior is illuminated by natural light filtered through latticework screens.

Outside the east entrance of the Jama Masjid, close to the jewellery bazaar in Manek Chowk, is the **Tomb of Ahmed Shah**, with elegant pillared verandahs, where the sultan, his son and grandson are buried. In the heart of the market, echoing the plan and layout of the sultan's tomb, lies **Rani-ka-Hazira**, the mausoleum of his many queens.

To the southeast of Manek Chowk is **Rani Sipri's Mosque**, also known as Masjid-e- Nagina ("Jewel of a Mosque") because of its elegant proportions and slender minarets. Northwest of Manek Chowk is **Rani Rupmati's Mosque**, dedicated to the sultan's Hindu wife. Built in the mid-15th century, the mosque incorporates elements of Hindu and Islamic design, with perforated stone screens to provide privacy for women.

The city's famous Shaking Minarets, which are located next to the railway station, are closed to visitors.

Traffic moving through the Teen Darwaza thoroughfare

Outside the Old City
N of the Old City.

Situated outside the Delhi Gate, the **Hatheesing Temple** was built in 1850 by Huthising Kesarising, a Jain merchant. This intricately carved marble temple is dedicated to Dharmanath, the 15th Jain *tirthankara*. A paved courtyard has 52 cubicles, housing shrines dedicated to different *tirthankaras*.

A fine example of Gujarat's stepwells is the **Dada Harir Vav** lying to the northeast of the old city. Built in 1500 for Bai Harir Sultani, a lady from the sultan's harem, its walls and pillars are beautifully decorated with elaborate carvings.

New Ahmedabad
W of Sabarmati river.

Across the Sabarmati river, modern Ahmedabad has some fine examples of contemporary architecture designed by Le Corbusier (*see p97*) and the American architect, Louis Kahn. The **Sanskar Kendra**, designed by Le Corbusier, has a rare collection of miniature paintings. The Indian Institute of Management (IIM), India's top college for business studies, is in a campus designed by Louis Kahn. Close by, the **LD Institute of Indology** houses ancient manuscripts and paintings, and the **Calico**

Museum (*see pp342–3*) displays an outstanding collection of textiles. The prestigious National Institute of Design is on the south bank of the river.

Sabarmati Ashram
Open 8:30am–7pm daily.
Closed mid-Jun–mid-Oct.

A spartan colony of tiled houses, the **Sabarmati Ashram** was a second home to Mahatma Gandhi. It was from here that he orchestrated the final struggle for India's freedom. His cottage, Hriday Kunj, has been maintained much as he left it, and contains some personal items such as his round eyeglasses, wooden slippers, books and letters.

Gandhi's room in the Sabarmati Ashram, with his spinning wheel

Environs
About 4 km (2.5 miles) south of the city is the **Vishala Complex** with a museum displaying traditional utensils. It also has an excellent outdoor restaurant for Gujarati cuisine, set in an attractive rural ambience (*see p615*). A short distance to the southwest is the **Sarkhej Roja**, a beautiful complex of tombs and pavilions around an artificial lake, built as a retreat for Gujarat's rulers between 1445 and 1461. Its tombs include that of Ahmed Shah's spiritual advisor, Sheikh Ahmed Khattu. Finely carved brass latticework is a unique feature of this site. Built in the late 1960s, the state capital, **Gandhinagar**, is 25 km (16 miles) north of Ahmedabad. Spread over 60 sq km (23 sq miles), this planned township has the state's administrative complex at its centre.

Ahmedabad Old City Centre

① Bhadra Fort
② Ahmed Shah's Mosque
③ Siddi Saiyad's Mosque
④ Teen Darwaza
⑤ Jama Masjid
⑥ Tomb of Ahmed Shah
⑦ Rani-ka-Hazira
⑧ Rani Sipri's Mosque
⑨ Rani Rupmati's Mosque

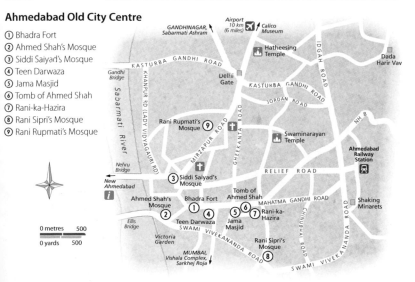

Ahmedabad: The Calico Museum

A major centre of India's textile trade and industry since the 15th century, Ahmedabad is an appropriate location for this outstanding museum. Its collection of rare textiles includes royal tents, carpets and costumes; religious paintings on cloth; embroideries, brocades and silk weaves; and Kashmir shawls. The exhibits, most of which date to the 17th and 18th centuries, are displayed in a beautiful old *haveli*. The museum was established in 1949 by the Sarabhai family, textile mill owners and leading philanthropists of Gujarat.

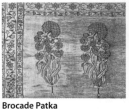

Brocade Patka
This 18th-century gold brocade waistband, patterned with pink poppies, was part of a royal costume.

★ **Mughal Tent**
This sumptuous 17th-century tent is made up of intricately hand-painted cotton panels in the *kalamkari* technique *(see p684)*. Mughal kings used these tents during military campaigns, on hunting expeditions and while touring their kingdom.

Ground floor

★ **Sharad Utsav Pichhwai**
Lord Krishna plays the flute in this exquisite 18th-century *pichhwai* from Nathdwara *(see p403)*. It was hung in the temple on the autumn full moon, when nectar is believed to fall from heaven. Note the delightful cow licking Krishna's leg.

Gallery Guide

The museum, set in the verdant Shahi Bagh gardens, is spread over 12 rooms on two floors of the haveli. The exhibits are displayed with great imagination, and each gallery presents the craft of a region, a tribal group or a religious sect. Within the museum compound, housed in another fine haveli, are the Sarabhai Foundation Galleries, with a fine collection of bronze icons and paintings.

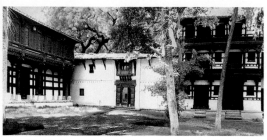

A view of the Calico Museum, showing the richly carved wooden façade of the old *haveli* in which it is housed

VISITORS' CHECKLIST

Practical Information
Sarabhai Foundation, Shahi Bagh, N of Delhi Gate.
Tel (079) 2286 5995.
calicomuseum.com
Open Thu–Tue. **Closed** public hols. 10:30am–12:30pm, 3–5pm. Garden tour by appointment only.
Sarabhai Foundation Galleries: **Open** Thu–Tue. **Closed** public hols.

Transport
San Marco.

First floor
Entrance
0 metres 2
0 yards 2
Outer gate

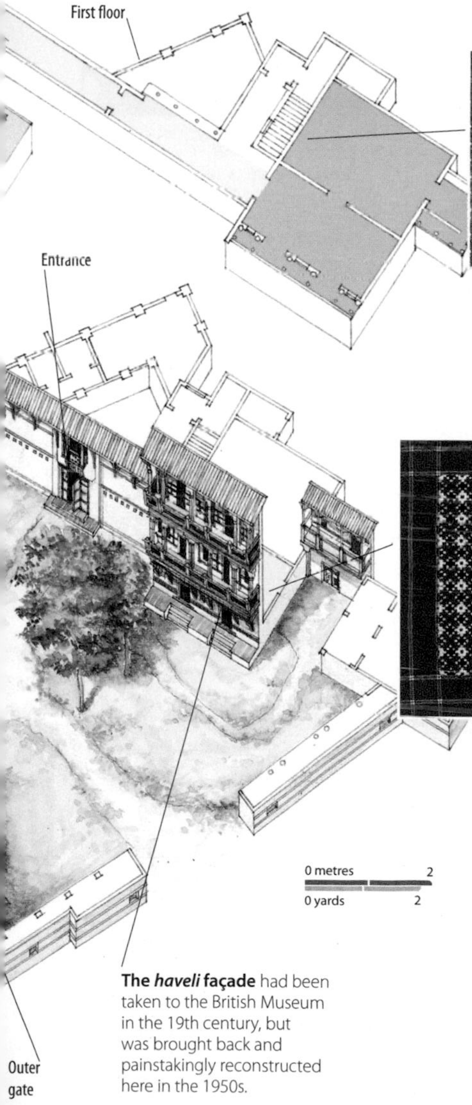

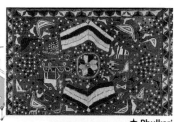

★ Phulkari
Elaborately embroidered with cotton thread and floss silk, this 19th-century piece from Punjab was part of a bride's dowry.

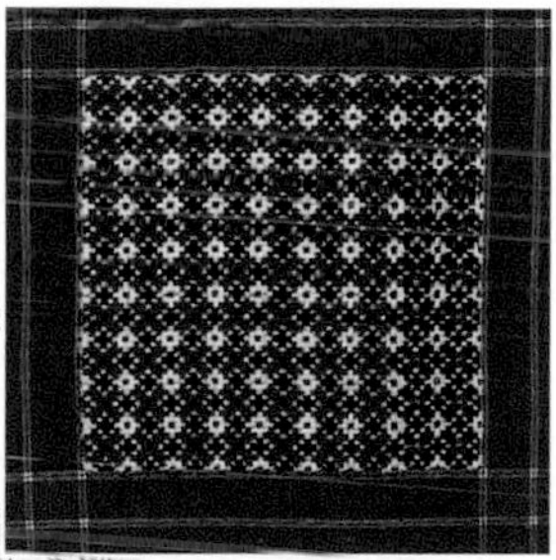

Telia Rumal
This cotton kerchief from Andhra Pradesh is made by a unique technique, where the yarn is oiled before being dyed and woven.

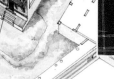

The *haveli* façade had been taken to the British Museum in the 19th century, but was brought back and painstakingly reconstructed here in the 1950s.

Key to Floorplan

- Export textile galleries
- Court textiles
- Gallery of shawls
- Mughal costumes
- Jain and Vaishnav textiles
- Kutch and Sindh embroidery
- Kathiawar embroidery
- Textiles of Odisha
- Madhubani quilts
- Phulkari from Punjab, Kantha from Bengal
- Tie-and-dye gallery

❷ Adalaj Vav

The stepwells (vavs) of Gujarat are an
ingenious answer to the water scarcity in
this arid region. Many of these elaborately
ornamented, underground wells are dedicated
to deities, acknowledging the hand of God
in providing life-sustaining water. Adalaj Vav,
perhaps Gujarat's finest stepwell, was built in
1499 by Rudabai, the wife of a local chieftain,
to conserve water and provide a cool and
pleasant ambience for social interaction.
A series of beautiful platforms and galleries
are built into the sides of the stepwell, all
the way down to its subterranean depths.

Local women at the stepwell, which is still used
for rest and recreation

The Stepped Corridor
The main corridor leads down five
storeys to a depth of 30 m (98 ft),
through pavilions whose walls,
pillars and niches are covered
with sculptures.

★ The First Well
Adalaj has an intermediate tank, 7 m
(23 ft) in diameter, just before the
main well. The octagonal well-
shaft is entirely covered with
fine carvings.

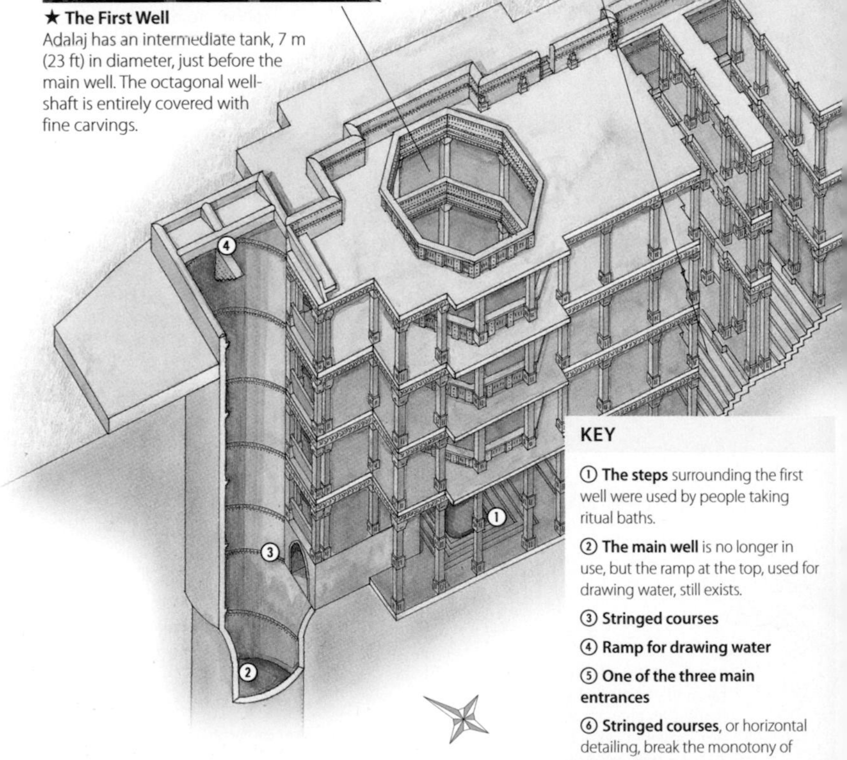

KEY

① **The steps** surrounding the first
well were used by people taking
ritual baths.

② **The main well** is no longer in
use, but the ramp at the top, used for
drawing water, still exists.

③ **Stringed courses**

④ **Ramp for drawing water**

⑤ **One of the three main
entrances**

⑥ **Stringed courses**, or horizontal
detailing, break the monotony of
plain walls.

Ornamental Detail
The well-shafts are profusely carved with intricate floral and geometric motifs, interspersed with figurines.

★ **The First Landing**
Balconies, windows, doors and shrines line the first landing – a large underground platform. Adalaj is best viewed at noon, when sunlight filters down to the bottom.

The Pavilions
The pavilions, supported by rows of carved pillars, are flooded with diffused light and provide ideal resting places.

★ **Wall Niches**
Niches feature in all the pavilions, carved with motifs of pots, horses, flowers and leaves.

Other Stepwells in Gujarat

The 11th-century **Rani ni Vav** in Patan *(see p421)* is among the most elaborately carved stepwells, with some 800 sculptures. Built in 1499, **Dada Harir Vav** *(see p415)* in Ahmedabad, is one of the finest examples of a *vav* from the Muslim period in Gujarat. The 15th-century **Ambarpur Vav**, 18 km (11 miles) from Ahmedabad, is one of the few *vavs* still in use.

Rani ni Vav in Patan, one of India's largest stepwells

The dry dock at Lothal, dating to 2500 BC

❸ Lothal

Ahmedabad district. 75 km (47 miles) SW of Ahmedabad. 🚉 Lothal–Burkhi station, 6 km (4 miles) SW of Lothal, then local transport. 🚌 to Burkhi. **Open** Sat–Thu. 🏛 📷

Excavations at Lothal have unearthed the remains of a remarkable city of the Indus Valley Civilization (see p45) that existed 4,500 years ago. Located 6 km (4 miles) northwest of the confluence of the Sabarmati and Bhogavo rivers, Lothal (literally, "Mound of the Dead") had a navigable estuary to the sea through the Gulf of Cambay (now Gulf of Khambat), which made it a flourishing port that once traded with Egypt, Persia and Mesopotamia.

The site reveals the foundations of a well-planned city with blocks of houses, paved drains, channels and wells, and 12 public baths. Other finds include beautifully made beads and pottery decorated with bird and animal motifs. Seals with intriguing, pictographic writing (as yet undeciphered), and weights and measures were also found here. The city was surrounded by a mud brick embankment, to protect it from the perennial floods which, in all probability, caused the city's destruction around 1,900 BC.

Among the prize exhibits in the **Archaeological Museum** are a copper figurine and a gold-bead necklace.

In 2001, Indian oceanographers carrying out water pollution tests in the Gulf of Cambay nearby, made an astonishing discovery. They found the foundations of two cities under the sea, complete with streets, houses, staircases and temples. Objects recovered from the seabed, such as a stone slab covered with mysterious markings (which could be the earliest form of writing yet discovered), and carved wooden logs, have been carbon-dated to 7,500 BC. The discovery of this site, which has been dubbed "Asia's Atlantis", has excited historians and archaeologists all over the world, as it suggests that civilization may have started 5,000 years earlier than previously believed. They surmise that the city may have been submerged as sea levels rose at the end of the Ice Age in about 8000

🏛 Archaeological Museum
Open Sat–Thu. 🏛 📷

❹ Nal Sarovar Sanctuary

Ahmedabad district. 60 km (37 miles) SW of Ahmedabad. 🚉 Viramgam, 35 km (22 miles) N of entry point, then taxi. 🚌 Viramgam. 🛈 Conservator of Forests (Wildlife), Gandhinagar, (079) 952717–223 500. 🏛 📷 permit: needed from Forest Department to enter sanctuary, (079) 372 3500.

Nal Sarovar sanctuary is one of the largest bird sanctuaries in the country. The 115-sq km (44-sq mile) Nal Lake and the surrounding swamp forests are best visited between November and February, when they attract as many as 250 species of waterfowl, including geese, flamingoes, cranes, pelicans, storks, cormorants, ibis and spoonbills. Winter migrants from as far as Siberia, such as the bluish-grey

Reed beds on Nal Lake

demoiselle crane, also gather here in hundreds, and can be observed at fairly close quarters. A perennial resident is the Sarus crane, the largest species of crane in the world. Believed to pair for life, Sarus cranes enact a spectacular courtship ritual, performing a synchronized dance that involves bowing with outstretched wings. Unfortunately, pressures on the habitat from the resident fishing communities, and from growing numbers of tourists, are slowly depleting the Nal Lake's rich variety of birdlife.

Graceful flamingoes, a regular sight at the Nal Sarovar Sanctuary

Exquisitely carved images of Hindu deities at Rani ni Vav, Patan

❺ Modhera Sun Temple

See pp422–3.

❻ Patan

Mehsana district. 125 km (78 miles) from Ahmedabad. ⚐ 112,050. 🚉 🚌
🎏 Jatar Fair (Sep/Oct).

The town of Patan was the capital of this region between the 8th and 15th centuries, before Sultan Ahmed Shah moved base to Ahmedabad *(see pp414–15)* in 1411. The ruins of the old capital, Anhilwada, lie 2 km (1.3 miles) northwest of Patan, and include an impressive stepwell, **Rani ni Vav**, and a water tank. The seven-storeyed stepwell ranks with Adalaj Vav *(see pp418–19)* as the finest in Gujarat. This splendid piece of architecture from the Solanki period (10th–14th centuries), now painstakingly restored, boasts some 800 individual, elaborately carved sculptures. Constructed in the 11th century by Queen Udaymati as a memorial to her husband, Bhimdeva, its unique feature is its direct as well as lateral series of steps leading to the water's edge. At the base are 37 niches, with the elephant god Ganesha carved into them. Nearby, the **Sahastralinga Talav**, a water tank with 1,000 shrines dedicated to the god Shiva, stands on the banks of the Saraswati river.

Patan also boasts more than 100 beautifully carved Jain temples, of which the **Panchasara Parsvanatha Temple** is the most striking. The town also has numerous traditional *havelis* with intricately carved façades.

Another attraction for many visitors is the beautiful *patola* sari. This lavish fabric is woven in Patan by a single family who have passed the craft down from one generation to the next. They are available locally and in major cities.

❼ Siddhpur

Mehsana district. 128 km (80 miles) N of Ahmedabad. ⚐ 53,600. 🚉 🚌

Lying along the Anjuni river, Siddhpur was once famous for the Rudra Mala Complex of Shiva temples, dating from the 10th century. It was later destroyed by Muslim invaders in the 13th century. Historical accounts describe a three-storeyed complex, profusely carved in stone and supported by 1,600 pillars, with 11 smaller shrines and three 40-m (131-ft) tall gateways. Two porches and four columns from the main shrine are all that remain today, together with a well-preserved, carved gateway with two high columns. An exploration of the town reveals interesting wooden *havelis* and pillared mansions, built by Muslim traders in the 19th century.

Environs

This region has the popular temple towns of **Ambaji**, 88 km (55 miles) north of Siddhpur, and **Bahucharaji**, 55 km (34 miles) southwest of Siddhpur. Both temples are dedicated to the goddess Amba (a reincarnation of Shiva's consort, Parvati) and they attract large crowds of devotees during the four main full-moon festivals each year in March, June, September and November. The pilgrims have their heads shaved *en masse* at both temples.

Traditional houses in Siddhpur with finely carved façades

Patola Weaving

Patola is an intricate silk weaving technique practised in Patan. The warp and weft threads are coloured in parts by tie-dyeing, and then woven to form clear designs in a method called double ikat *(see p672)*. Typical motifs include jewels, flowers, animals and dancing women, interspersed with geometric forms. The craft is laborious – a month's work goes into weaving one sari length (5.5 m/6 yards) – and its product is highly prized, especially in a bridal trousseau. This exquisite fabric was exported to Indonesia where it became the cloth of the royal court.

Detail of a typical *patola* sari

❺ Modhera Sun Temple

The Sun Temple at Modhera was built in 1026 by King Bhima I of the Solanki dynasty. It is so precisely laid out in an east-west direction that the sun's rays course through its chambers and strike the centre of the inner sanctum at high noon every day. The carvings, both inside and on the exterior, are extraordinarily detailed, depicting a pantheon of Hindu deities as well as scenes from everyday life. An impressive tank dominates the forecourt. The juxtaposition of a tank with a Sun Temple is inspired by Vedic scriptures, which say that the sun was born from the depths of a primordial ocean.

The Entrance Hall
This hall has 12 representations of Surya, that depict the phases of the sun in each month of the year.

Shrines
The tank is surrounded by miniature shrines, topped by curved *shikharas*.

KEY

① **The Kund** or tank is shaped like an inverted pyramid. Flights of stairs create a ripple effect down to its base.

② **Sabha Mandapa,** the assembly hall, was reserved for religious discourses and socio-cultural ceremonies.

❻ Vadodara

Vadodara district. 113 km (70 miles) SE of Ahmedabad. 🏔 1,306,100. ✈ 8 km (5 miles) NE of town centre. 🚌 🚄 𝑖 Gujarat Tourism, (0265) 242 7489. ⬤ Vadodara Municipal Corporation, (0265) 243 3116/3118.

Situated on the Vishwamitri river, Vadodara owes much of its splendour to Sayajirao Gaekwad III (1875–1939), a former ruler who transformed his principality into a progressive centre of culture, education and industry. Today Vadodara, also known as Baroda, is a vibrant city with many interesting buildings,

museums and parks. The **Laxmi Vilas Palace,** an Indo-Saracenic pile, was designed by the English architect Major Charles Mant *(see p472)* and completed in 1890. It is still the residence of the erstwhile ruling family, though there are

plans to convert parts of it into a luxury hotel. The grounds already host a golf club. The **Maharaja Fateh Singh Museum,** also within the grounds, has a rare collection of paintings by the famous Indian artist Raja Ravi

The magnificent façade of the Laxmi Vilas Palace

The Torana
All that survives of the *torana* or arched gateway are these two intricately carved columns leading into the temple.

VISITORS' CHECKLIST

Practical Information
Mehsana district. 119 km (74 miles) NW of Ahmedabad.
i (02734) 28 4334.
Open daily. 🎫 📷 🏛
Modhera Dance Festival (Jan).

Transport
🚆 Mehsana, 25 km (16 miles) away, then taxi or bus. 🚌

Garbhagriha
The walls and pillars of the inner sanctum are richly carved with images of deities, in strict order of their celestial hierarchy.

Nritya Mandapa
This hall, which leads from the assembly hall towards the inner sanctum, was used for dance performances.

Varma (1848–1906). **Sayaji Bagh**, a beautiful park in the heart of the city, houses a zoo, a planetarium and the **Vadodara Museum and Picture Gallery**, which has an eclectic collection of Mughal miniatures, European oil paintings and royal artifacts. Pride of place goes to its collection of 68 striking bronzes from Akota, a centre of Jain culture in the 5th century. Other notable sights are the **Kirti Mandir**, the *samadhi* (memorial) of Vadodara's royal family; and

Radha and Madhava by Raja Ravi Varma

the **Nyaya Mandir**, an Indo-Saracenic building that is now a law court. The city also has the Maharaja Sayajirao University's **College of Fine Art**, an institute of national eminence.

🏛 **Laxmi Vilas Palace**
Tel (0265) 243 1819.
Open Tue–Sun, by appt.
Golf Club:]**Tel** (0265) 655 5999.

🏛 **Maharaja Fateh Singh Museum**
Tel (0265) 242 6372.
Open Tue–Sun.

🏛 **Vadodara Museum and Picture Gallery**
Tel (0265) 79 359. **Open** 10:30am–5pm Tue–Sun.

Environs
The famous Amul Dairy is located in **Anand**, 38 km (24 miles) northwest of Vadodara. Synonymous with the "White Revolution" that made India self-sufficient in milk, it helped pioneer India's dairy cooperative movement, and now procures one million litres of milk every day from 1,000 milk cooperative societies. It is open daily to visitors from 3 to 5pm.

Jain Temple in Pavagadh Fort, near Champaner

❾ Champaner

Vadodara district. 52 km (32 miles) NE of Vadodara. 🚌 🚶 Mahakali Festival (Mar/Apr).

The deserted city of Champaner, a UNESCO World Heritage Site, is situated at the foot of Pavagadh Hill. Originally the seat of a Rajput Chauhan dynasty, Champaner was conquered by the Muslim ruler Mahmud Begada in 1484. He spent 23 years rebuilding the citadel, adding mosques, palaces and tombs within its massive walls, guarded by huge gateways. Champaner remained the capital of Gujarat until 1535, when it was conquered by the Mughal emperor Humayun. Thereafter, it fell into gradual decline.

Much of Champaner lies in ruins today, with the remains of many old mosques and palaces reflecting a blend of Islamic and Jain traditions. The **Jama Masjid**, built in 1523, is a large, symmetrical structure with a perfectly proportioned dome. Its richly ornamented exterior with 172 pillars and 30-m (98-ft) high minarets, makes it one of the finest Islamic monuments in western India. Another elegant mosque here is the 16th-century **Nagina Masjid**.

The **Pavagadh Fort**, at the crest of the 820-m (2,690-ft) high Pavagadh Hill, is 4 km (2.5 miles) to the southwest of Champaner. It has a cluster of Muslim, Hindu and Jain shrines, and the ruins of an ancient fortification, reflecting its chequered past. On the way up the hill are the ruins of the **Sat Mahal**, the seven-storeyed palace of the Chauhan kings. The kings were slain when they refused to embrace Islam after the Muslim conquest, and their women and children committed *jauhar*. There are also two domed granaries, the Makai Kothar and the Naulakha Kothar.

Environs
Dabhoi Fort, 75 km (47 miles) south of Champaner, was constructed in the 13th century by the Solanki Rajputs (10th–14th centuries). It is an interesting example of Rajput military architecture, with four gates, a water tank fed by an aqueduct and fields within the fort to provide food during a siege.

Detail from the Jama Masjid

Ruins of the 16th-century Jama Masjid in Champaner

❿ Surat

Surat district. 234 km (145 miles) S of Ahmedabad. 🗺 5,374,400. 🚉 🚌 ℹ 1/847 Athugar St, Nanpura, (0261) 247 6586. 🏛 Mon–Sat.

Strategically located on the coast, Surat was once a prosperous port and many powers battled to control it between the 16th and 18th centuries. At various times the Portuguese, Dutch, Mughals, Marathas and British held sway here, but its importance began to wane after 1837, when it was ravaged by flood and fire. Many of Surat's Hindu and Parsi merchants *(see p451)* left for Bombay (Mumbai), which then gradually overtook Surat as the premier port on the western coast. Though no longer a port of any consequence, Surat is today a major industrial centre.

The 16th-century **Surat Castle**, beside the Tapti Bridge, is the town's oldest structure. Built by Khudawan Khan, an Albanian Christian who embraced Islam, the castle has 12-m (39-ft) high battlements and 4-m (13-ft) thick walls. Iron strips were used to bind its various elements and all its joints were filled with molten lead, to make it as impenetrable as possible. Especially noteworthy is the imposing gateway in its eastern wing, with a menacingly spiked exterior, and a delicately carved interior. Sadly, sundry offices now housed within the castle have robbed it of its historic ambience.

Northeast of the castle, just beyond Kataragama Gate, are the English, Dutch and Armenian cemeteries, that bear witness to the city's cosmopolitan past. Though now overgrown, they are worth exploring for the intriguing personal histories recounted on the tombs' epitaphs. Particularly impressive is the mausoleum of Sir George Oxinden, a governor of the Surat Port, and his brother, in the British cemetery. The tomb of Baron Adriaan van Reede, built in the 17th century, in the Dutch cemetery has an enormous double cupola.

Modern Surat is known for its flourishing textile industry which produces the famous *tanchoi* (brocade) silk. It also specializes in jewellery and is a major diamond-cutting centre for suppliers from all over the world. During the 1980s, the city had, unfortunately, become a byword for urban squalor, and in 1994 suffered an outbreak of plague. This galvanized the city's administration into a massive clean-up drive, which has resulted in the revival of Surat as a prosperous commercial centre.

⑪ Daman

Daman Union Territory. 390 km (242 miles) S of Ahmedabad.
🚉 35,750. 🚆 Vapi, 10 km (6 miles) SE of Daman, then taxi or bus. 🚌
🛈 Nani Daman, (0260) 225 5104.
🌐 damantourism.com

Tucked away in the southern tip of Gujarat, adjoining Maharashtra, is the tiny enclave of Daman which was a Portuguese colony until 1961. The Damanganga river, which flows into the Arabian Sea, divides the town into two distinct parts – Nani Daman (Little Daman) which is dotted with hotels and bars, and Moti Daman (Big Daman), the old Portuguese township.

Moti Daman is enclosed within the massive **Daman Fort**. Its ten bastions and two gateways date to 1559, and it is ringed by a moat linked to the river. Daman's well-preserved churches include the large **Bom Jesus Cathedral**, built

The gateway to St Jerome's Fort in Nani Daman

in 1603, which has a richly carved portal and an ornamental altar. The smaller **Rosario Chapel**, outside the fort walls, has exquisitely carved wooden panels, depicting scenes from the life of Jesus. The lighthouse, to the north of the fort, affords fine views of the Gulf of Cambay.

St Jerome's Fort, in Nani Daman, is less grand than Daman Fort but houses the lovely chapel of Our Lady of the Sea. The chapel has a delicate, classical façade of 12 columns crowned with a cross.

Liquor flows freely in Nani Daman's dingy bars, attracting crowds of tipplers from the rest of Gujarat where alcohol is prohibited. Those who want to take in local colour would be well advised to avoid the bars and explore the farmers' market or the riverside fish market instead.

The Devka and Jampore beaches, 5 km (3 miles) north and south of Daman respectively, are not spectacular, but offer tranquil retreats among casuarina groves.

View of the harbour below St Jerome's fort in Nani Daman, Daman

Festivals of Gujarat

Uttarayan *(14 Jan)*. Coinciding with Makar Sankranti which marks the height of winter, this colourful festival fills the sky all over Gujarat with thousands of beautifully crafted kites.

Modhera Dance Festival *(Jan)*, Modhera Sun Temple. This three-day festival of Indian classical dance is a unique opportuniy to enjoy these dance forms in the setting in which they were originally performed.

Bangles on sale at Tarnetar Fair

Tarnetar Fair *(Sep)*, Tarnetar, 8 km (5 miles) from Thangadh. This unique matchmaking *mela* sees prospective grooms promenading the fairgrounds, holding colourful umbrellas, as young women wearing multi-pleated skirts swirl around in dance. A girl indicates her preference by approaching a youth for a chat, leaving it to the elders to settle matrimonial details.

Navratri *(Sep/Oct)*. Navratri or "nine nights" is celebrated throughout Gujarat and is marked by nine nights of dancing in honour of the mother goddess. Women perform the *garba* dance, whirling around in a circle, clapping their hands. The exhilarating *dandia ras* is the highlight, when men and women strike small lacquered batons to a beat that gets faster and faster till it finally breaks in a frenzied crescendo.

⑫ Bhavnagar

Bhavnagar district. 200 km (124 miles) SW of Ahmedabad. 🏙 511,000. ✈ 8 km (5 miles) SE of city centre. 🚇 🚌

For most visitors, Bhavnagar is little more than a convenient base for exploring the magnificent temple town of Palitana. Yet Bhavnagar itself is not without charm – its old bazaar, dotted with merchants' *havelis*, has shops specializing in tie-dye textiles and gold and silver jewellery. In the southeast corner of the city, on the road to the airport, is the semi-circular **Barton Museum** (built in 1895). It houses the private collection of coins, weapons and *objets d'art* of a British officer, Colonel Barton, who served here in the 19th century.

The **Nilambagh Palace**, once the former rulers' residence, was built in 1859 and is now a luxury hotel with a great banquet hall and peacocks in the garden.

🏛 **Barton Museum**
Tel (0278) 242 4516.
Open 10am–6:30pm Mon–Sat.
Closed public hols. 🚫 📷

🏨 **Nilambagh Palace**
Ahmedabad Rd. **Tel** (0278) 242 4241.

Environs
The flat grasslands of the 36 sq-km (14 sq-mile) **Velavadar National Park** (65 km/40 miles north of Bhavnagar) are home to over 1,000 blackbucks. Blackbucks were protected by the Bishnoi community *(see p389)* until the state took over this role. A walk through the park at dusk provides a glimpse of the wolves that hunt this Indian antelope, and of the nilgai that congregate at the park's watering holes.

🏞 **Velavadar National Park**
ℹ Forest Dept, Bhavnagar, (0278) 288 0222. **Open** mid-Oct–May. 📷 Extra charges for photography. 🎫

⑬ Palitana

Bhavnagar district. 52 km (32 miles) SW of Bhavnagar. ℹ (02848) 25 2327. 🚇 🚌 🎉 Falgun Suth Tera (Feb/Mar).

An extraordinary cluster of 1,008 Jain temples crowns the twin summits of Palitana's Shatrunjaya Hill and covers the saddle linking them. The first Jain *tirthankara*, Adinath *(see p400)*, is said to have visited this hill, while his chief disciple, Pundarika, is believed to have attained enlightenment here. Most of the temples date to the 16th century – earlier temples on this site were destroyed by Muslim invaders in the 14th and 15th centuries. The temples are grouped into nine fortified clusters called *tuks*, and named after the wealthy devotees who paid for their construction. Each *tuk* has a main shrine surrounded by several smaller ones. The most impressive of the main shrines is the 17th-century **Adinath Temple**, on the hill's northern ridge. Its ceilings, walls and supporting brackets are covered

Detail from the door of a temple in Palitana

Sculptures of Jain *tirthankaras* along a temple corridor, Palitana

with carvings of saints, dancers, musicians and lotus blossoms. Many images of Adinath are enshrined inside. The southern ridge is dominated by the 16th-century **Adishvara Temple**, with its richly ornamented spire. The main image within portrays Rishabhnath. It has eyes made of crystal and is adorned with necklaces and a magnificent gold crown.

The 4-km (2.5-mile) ascent to the summit of the hill takes about two hours, a task made lighter by the spectacular silhouette of hundreds of temple spires and domes against the sky. From the top, there is a panoramic view of the Gulf of Cambay and the countryside.

⑭ Diu

Diu Union Territory. 495 km (308 miles) S of Ahmedabad. 🏙 21,600. 🚇 Delwada, 8 km (5 miles) N of town centre. 🚌 ℹ Diu Jetty, (02875) 252 653.

The little island of Diu covers an area of just 39 sq km (15 sq

The 19th-century Nilambagh Palace in Bhavnagar, set in a huge garden

The abandoned seaside fort at Diu, dating to the 16th century

miles). Once known as the "Gibraltar of the East", it was a flourishing Portuguese colony from the 16th century onwards. It was ceded to India in 1961 and is today a Union Territory, administered by the Central Government. The majestic **Diu Fort** on the eastern end of the island dominates the town. Built in 1535 when the Portuguese took control of Diu, it is worth a visit for its impressive double moat, its old cannons and for the superb views of the sunset it offers.

Diu town, sandwiched between the fort to the east and the city wall to the west, retains a distinctly Portuguese atmosphere in its churches and its many mansions. The **Nagar Seth Haveli** is particularly outstanding, with carved balconies and stone lions. The **Church of St Paul** (built in 1610) has a lovely, carved wooden altar, statues of the saints and a sonorous old organ. Its impressive Gothic façade was rebuilt in 1807. Nearby, the **St Thomas Church** (built in 1598) houses a museum of religious artifacts and stone inscriptions

linked to the island's history. The beach at **Nagoa**, 7 km (4 miles) from the town, has a long stretch of sand fringed with palm trees. Other beaches within easy reach of Diu are Jallandhar and Chakratirth which has a sunset viewpoint. As a Union Territory, Diu is not subject to Gujarat's prohibition laws. This explains the profusion of bars in the town, and the invasion, on weekends, by thirsty Gujaratis.

ⓖ Somnath

Junagadh district. 406 km (252 miles) SW of Ahmedabad. 🚍 🖂

Situated on the coast with a commanding view of the Arabian Sea, the **Somnath Temple** is revered as one of the 12 most sacred sites dedicated to Lord Shiva. The temple's legendary wealth made it the target of successive plundering armies, beginning with Mahmud of Ghazni in 1026, who is said to have made off with camel-loads of gold and precious gems, leaving the edifice in ruins. The cycle of pillage and

reconstruction at Somnath continued over the next seven centuries. The present temple, made of stone, was built in 1950.

East of the temple, at the confluence of three rivers, is **Triveni Tirth**. The ghats going down to the sea at this spot are said to mark the place where Lord Krishna's funeral rites were performed, after a hunter mistook him for a deer and killed him.

ⓖ Sasan Gir National Park

Junagadh district. 368 km (229 miles) SW of Ahmedabad. Entry point: Sasan Gir. 🚗 🚍 🛈 For permits contact Field Director, Sinh Sadan, Sasan Gir (02877) 28 5541. **Open** mid-Oct–mid-Jun. 📷 Extra charges for photography. 🚙 Jeeps available.

Until a century ago, the Asiatic lion roamed vast areas of India, from Gujarat all the way to Bihar in the east. Now, the Sasan Gir National Park is the only habitat left of the lion outside Africa. Asiatic lions are smaller than African lions, with a fold of skin along the belly. The males have shorter manes. About 320 lions live in Gir's 259 sq km (100 sq miles) of dry scrub forest. By the early 1900s, the Asiatic lion had been hunted and poached almost to the point of extinction. Their remarkable resurgence in Gir is attributed to the conservation efforts of the erstwhile nawab of Junagadh (see p430) and, subsequently, the Gujarat state government.

A number of rivers wind through Gir, making it a haven for a range of wildlife, including the caracal, the *chausingha* (four-horned antelope), the blackbuck and a substantial leopard population.

The Moon God and Somnath

Legend weaves an interesting tale around the origins of the temple at Somnath. Som, the Moon God, was wedded to the 27 daughters of Daksha, a son of Brahma, but he loved only one of them, Rohini, causing great frustration to the other sisters. An infuriated Daksha cursed his son-in-law, causing him to lose his lustre. In despair, Som turned to Shiva and served him with such zealous devotion that Shiva gave him respite from the curse – he would wax for half the month and wane for the rest. In gratitude the Moon God built a Shiva temple at Somnath.

The Somnath Temple, visited by devotees of Shiva

An Asiatic lioness basking in the sun in Sasan Gir Sanctuary

Cluster of Jain temples on the Shatrunjaya Hill, Palitana, ▶

The impressive Jain temple complex on Girnar Hill, just outside Junagadh

⑰ Junagadh

Junagadh district. 393 km (244 miles) SW of Ahmedabad. ⨪ 168,700. ⊞ ⊞ ⓘ Majwadi Darwaza, (0285) 265 1170. ⊟ Mon–Sat. ⧉ Bhavnath Fair (Feb/Mar), Kartik Mela (Oct/Nov).

Junagadh, which means "Old Fort", takes its name from the ancient fort of Uparkot, built in the 4th century on a plateau at the eastern edge of the town. The fort is surrounded by massive walls, over 20 m (66 ft) high in places, and a 90-m (295-ft) deep moat inside the walls. This once teemed with crocodiles that were fed on criminals and political enemies. An ornate, triple-arched gateway marks the entrance to the fort. Inside, a cobbled path leads past Hindu temples to the now deserted **Jama Masjid** at the top of the plateau. Its carved stonework and pillars show that it was constructed on the remains of a destroyed Hindu temple. Nearby are a cluster of Buddhist caves dating to the 2nd century. The fort also has two fine 11th-century stepwells, the Navghan Kuan and the Adi Charan Vav.

In the mid-19th century, the nawabs of Junagadh moved down from the old fort into new colonial-style palaces in the city. The **Durbar Hall** of the City Palace, built in 1870, houses a museum with the typical trappings of royalty – palanquins, silver thrones and old armour. A complex of royal

Intricate carving on Mahabat Maqbara

mausoleums can be seen near the city's railway station, the most notable of which is the **Mahabat Maqbara** with splendid silver doors.

Junagadh's main attraction, however, is **Girnar Hill**, 6 km (4 miles) east of the city. An extinct volcano, this has been a holy site for Buddhists, Jains and Hindus since the 3rd century BC. Over 4,000 steps lead to the top of the 1,080-m (3,543-ft) high hill. En route is an **Ashokan Rock Edict**, dating to 250 BC *(see p46)*, that conveys Emperor Ashoka's message of non-violence and peace. Halfway up the hill are a cluster of beautiful Jain temples. Most notable among them is the **Neminath Temple**, enshrining a black marble image of the 22nd Jain *tirthankara (see p400)* who is believed to have

died here. The 12th-century **Amba Mata Temple**, at the summit, is very popular with newlyweds, who come seeking blessings for conjugal bliss.

🏛 **Durbar Hall Museum**
Tel (0285) 262 1685. **Open** Thu–Tue. **Closed** 2nd & 4th Sat. ⧉

⑱ Porbandar

Porbandar district. 404 km (251 miles) SW of Ahmedabad. ⨪ 133,100. ⊞ ⊞ ⊟ Mon–Sat. ⓘ (0286) 224 5475. Extra charges for photography.

Once a major port on the Arabian Sea, Porbandar is today famous as Mahatma Gandhi's birthplace. The house where Gandhi was born in 1869 still stands in a small alley, in the western part of the city. Next door is the **Kirti Mandir Museum** with photographs from the Mahatma's life, and extracts from his speeches and writings. The city has little else

---

The Nawab of Junagadh and His Dogs

The 11th Nawab of Junagadh (1900–59), like his forebears, had a passion for breeding dogs, and these pedigreed pooches, 800

Portrait of the Nawab with his favourite dog

of them, were housed in luxury with separate rooms and personal attendants. The Nawab even held elaborate banquets to celebrate their "nuptials". On the eve of India's Independence, when the princely states were given the option of either remaining in India or becoming a part of Pakistan, the Nawab's decision to accede to Pakistan was thwarted by popular protest. The Nawab, however, decided to leave Junagadh. When the time for departure came, the Nawab, true to form, boarded the aircraft with his dogs, leaving behind his entire harem of concubines.

to attract visitors; in addition, it has the dubious distinction of housing local mafia dons. Interestingly, large sections of Gujarat's diasporic population originated from this district.

Entrance to the Kirti Mandir Museum, Porbandar

⓵ Dwarka

Jamnagar district. 453 km (282 miles) W of Ahmedabad. 🚊 🚌 📷 Janmashtami (Jul/Aug). 🛈 (02892) 23 4013.

Legend has it that about 5,000 years ago, Lord Krishna *(see p683)* forsook his kingdom at Mathura *(see p182)* and came to live on the seafront at Dwarka, where he founded a glittering new city. It is believed that the city was subsequently submerged under the sea. Whether or not this is myth or fact, excavations of the seabed have indeed established the existence of a submerged city in the vicinity of Dwarka.

Hindu pilgrims flock to Dwarka throughout the year. The city's main temple is the towering **Dwarkadhish Temple**, dating to the 16th century. Built of granite and sandstone on a plinth area of 540 m (1,772 ft), it is supported by 60 pillars and rises seven storeys to an impressive height of 51 m (167 ft).

Situated a short distance to its east is the small, lavishly carved **Rukmini Temple**. Built in the 12th century, it is dedicated to Krishna's wife.

⓴ Jamnagar

Jamnagar district. 308 km (191 miles) SW of Ahmedabad. 🏠 447,800. ✈ 10 km (6 miles) W of city. 🚊 🚌 🛈 (0288) 266 3922. 🗓 Mon–Sat.

Founded by a local prince, Jam Rawal, in 1540, Jamnagar's old walled city is dominated by the **Lakhota Fort**, the original seat of its rulers, and the **Ranmal Lake** which surrounds it. The fort was badly damaged during the earthquake in January 2001, though visitors are still allowed inside. The museum in the fort has fine sculptures from nearby excavation sites, dating from the 9th to 18th centuries. Close by is the Kotha Bastion which once stored the rulers' arsenal.

In the heart of the old town is the circular **Darbar Gadh** where the Jamsahebs (as the rulers were called) held public audiences. This structure was also damaged heavily in the 2001 earthquake, but the ground floor is safe for visitors. The lanes leading off from here are worth exploring as the city is famous for its tie-dye fabric and silver jewellery. In this area are two Jain temples, the **Shantinath** and **Adinath Temples**, entirely covered with mirrorwork, gold leaf, murals and mosaics. Close to them is the 19th-century **Ratanbai Mosque**, its doors inlaid with mother-of-pearl. In the early 20th century, Jamnagar was ruled by the famous cricketer KS Ranjit Sinhji (r.1907–33). The city acquired several elegant public buildings and parks under his able administration.

🏛 **Lakhota Fort Museum**
Open Thu–Tue. **Closed** 2nd & 4th Sat. 📷 📹

Environs
The **Marine National Park**, in the Gulf of Kutch, is 30 km (19 miles) from Jamnagar. An archipelago of 42 islands, the park's marine life is best viewed from the island of Pirotan.

🗒 **Marine National Park**
🚤 Jamnagar jetty. For permits contact the Park Director, Jamnagar, (0288) 255 2077. 📷

⓶ Rajkot

Rajkot district. 216 km (134 miles) W of Ahmedabad. 🏠 966,700. ✈ 1 km (0.6 miles) NW of city centre. 🚊 🚌 🛈 Bhavnagar House, (0281) 223 4507. 🗓 Mon–Sat.

The headquarters of the Saurashtra region (southwest Gujarat) during the British Raj, modern Rajkot is a commercial and industrial town. The centre of the region's groundnut trade, it is also reputed for its handicrafts.

Rajkot's many 19th-century buildings give it a distinctly colonial flavour. The **Watson Museum** in Jubilee Bagh, named after a British Political Agent, has a fine collection of portraits of local rulers, tribal artifacts, archaeological finds from Harappan sites and a large statue of Queen Victoria. The impressive **Rajkumar College**, established by the British for the sons of the Gujarat nobility, remains a prestigious public school.

🏛 **Watson Museum**
Tel (0281) 222 3065. **Open** 9am–1pm, 3–6pm Thu–Tue. **Closed** 2nd & 4th Sat. 📷 Extra charges for photography.

Environs
Wankaner Palace, 39 km (24 miles) northeast of Rajkot, is an eclectic mix of Mughal, Italian and Victorian-Gothic styles. Though still inhabited by the former royal family, a portion is now a luxury hotel. **Halvad**, 125 km (78 miles) north of Rajkot, has a 17th-century lakeside palace.

Statue of the first principal, Rajkumar College, Rajkot

Rabari women near Bhuj, bringing water home

㉒ Bhuj

Kutch district. 217 km (135 miles) W of Ahmedabad. ♦ 121,100. ✈ 7 km (4 miles) N of city centre. 🚌 🚐 ℹ Gujarat Tourism, Toran Rann Resort, Mirzapur Bhuj, (02832) 224 910. ♦ Ashadhi Bij (Jul/Aug).

Until the earthquake of January 2001 reduced much of Bhuj to rubble, this was a fascinating walled city, with beautiful palaces and *havelis*, and a bazaar famous for its rich handicrafts and jewellery. Bhuj was the capital of the prosperous princely state of Kutch, whose wealth derived from its sea trade with East Africa and the Persian Gulf ports. African slaves were an important part of Kutch's maritime trade, and their many descendants still live in the city. The town's main attraction was the **Darbargadh Palace** complex, which houses the fabulous **Aina Mahal** or "Palace of Mirrors". Built in 1752, it was damaged in the 2001 earthquake but has now been extensively renovated. The palace and its contents are linked to the remarkable life of its Gujarati architect, Ramsinh Malam. Shipwrecked off the East African coast as a 12-year-old, he was rescued by a Dutch ship and taken to the Netherlands, where he spent the next 17 years. There, he blossomed as a craftsman, mastering Delft tile-making, glass-blowing, enamelling and clock-making. When he returned home, the ruler of Kutch, Rao Lakha, gave him an opportunity to display these skills. The Aina Mahal was thus decorated with Venetian-style chandeliers, Delft blue tiles, enamelled silver objects and chiming clocks – all made locally under Ramsinh's supervision. At the same time, local crafts of the highest quality were also displayed, such as a superb ivory-inlaid door, jewelled shields and swords, and a marvellously detailed 15-m (49-ft) long scroll painting of a royal procession, complete with African pageboys. All these form a part of the palace museum.

The royal cenotaphs, the Swaminarayan Temple and the bazaar are now unfortunately in ruins, but the excellent **Folk Arts Museum** still stands. It has a choice collection of Kutch textiles and local crafts, and a reconstructed village of Rabari *bhoongas (see p434)*.

🏛 **Folk Arts Museum**
Mandvi Rd. **Tel** (02832) 220 541.
Open Mon–Sat. 🖼 📷

Earthquake in Gujarat

On 26 January 2001, at 8:46am, as India celebrated its Republic Day, a devastating earthquake struck Gujarat. Its epicentre was in Kutch. Measuring 7.7 on the Richter Scale, it destroyed most of Bhuj, the headquarters of Kutch district, as well as Anjar, the second largest town in Kutch, and razed 450 villages in the district to the ground. Among the 20,000 people killed in the earthquake were 400 schoolchildren of Anjar, who were crushed under the rubble of falling buildings in a narrow street as they marched jauntily through town in the Republic Day Parade. In the state capital, Ahmedabad, most of those killed were trapped in recently-built highrise apartment buildings, which collapsed like houses of cards while, ironically, centuries-old historic monuments throughout the state suffered relatively little damage. An exception was the spectacular 18th-century Darbargadh Palace in Bhuj, with its richly decorated interiors showcasing the finest Gujarati craftsmanship. Much of the damage it suffered is irreparable, however, after some necessary renovation it is open to visitors yet again. In contrast, the traditional, round mud *bhoongas* of the semi-nomadic Rabaris of Kutch withstood the earthquake remarkably well. Gujarat, and in particular Kutch, has always been an area of seismic activity, and some historians believe this is one reason that cities of the Indus Valley Civilization *(see p45)*, such as Dholavira and Lothal, declined around 1900 BC. In more recent times, 1,100 people died in the 1819 earthquake and 7,000 in the 1956 earthquake. The disaster of 2001 made more than 250,000 people homeless. A massive rehabilitation effort began almost immediately. Besides the Gujarat government and the Indian Union, over 150 countries readily came forward to provide assistance. Above all, it was the resilience of the residents that brought life back to normal.

Labourers at an earthquake relocation center, Bhuj

The tranquil seafront at Mandvi, once a busy port

㉓ Mandvi

Bhuj district. 60 km (37 miles) SW of Bhuj. ⬛ 14,300. 🚌

This old port town has fine beaches, good swimming, and camel and horse rides along the shore. Close to the beach is the **Vijay Vilas Palace**, an impressive Indo-Edwardian pile built in the 1940s as a royal summer retreat. Its lovely garden, drawing room and rooftop terrace are open to visitors and provide beautiful views of the sea. In the town is the curious 18th-century **Old Palace** of the Kutch rulers (now a girls' school). Architecturally a blend of local and European styles, its façade is decorated with cherubic Dutch boys holding wine goblets – architect Ramsinh Malam's touching salute to his adopted country.

🏛 **Vijay Vilas Palace**
Open Thu–Tue. 📷 Extra charges for photography.

㉔ Dholavira

Bhuj district. 250 km (155 miles) NE of Bhuj. 🚌 ℹ️ For permission contact the Superintendent of Police, Bhuj, (02832) 25 0444. **Open** daily.

Dholavira is a small village where archaeologists have unearthed extensive remains of a city that dates back to about 3000 BC. Lying on Khadir island in the Rann of Kutch it is, along with Lothal (see p420), the largest known Indus Valley settlement in India. The site reveals evidence of a remarkable, planned city with broad roads, containing a central citadel, a middle town

with spacious dwellings, a lower town with open spaces for markets and festivities, and two stadia. An intriguing ten-character inscription (which is still to be deciphered) is on the citadel's northern gate. The presence of large reservoirs and a dam reflect the existence of sophisticated systems for harvesting water.

㉕ The Little Rann of Kutch Sanctuary

Kutch district. Entry points: Dhrangadhra, 130 km (81 miles) W of Ahmedabad, & Dasada, 117 km (73 miles) NW of Ahmedabad. 🚉 Dhrangadhra, 20 km (12 miles) S of park. 🚌 Dhrangadhra & Dasada, then bus or jeep. ℹ️ Gujarat Tourism, Ashram Rd, Ahmedabad, (079) 2657 8046. For permits & tours contact Forest Office, Dhrangadhra. 📷 Extra charges for photography.

An expanse of salt flats and grasslands in northwest Gujarat, the Little Rann of Kutch has a stark and unforgettable beauty – in sunlight, the salt crystals in the sand glitter like diamonds, while at night they bathe the landscape in an eerie blue haze. Every year, during the monsoon, when the sea and rivers flood the region, the salt flats are transformed into great marshy swamps, with patches of higher ground forming grassy islands known as bets. Some 4,841 sq km (1,869 sq miles) of this unique ecosystem, which supports a variety of rare fauna, form a wildlife sanctuary which is one of the last refuges of the Asiatic

wild ass (Equus hemionus khur), known locally as ghorkhur. Akin to the Tibetan kiang, the ghorkhur is distinguished by a dark stripe along its back. Only about 1,000 of them now remain. Known for its speed (up to 60 km or 37 miles per hour), the wild ass lives in herds led by a stallion, and survives by migrating between the grassy bets through the seasons, in search of food.

The sanctuary also has a large population of nilgai (blue bull), blackbuck, chinkara (Indian gazelle), wolves, and the rare caracal. Birdlife includes migratory demoiselle cranes, pelicans and flamingoes who come to the salt marshes during the winter months.

The Asiatic wild ass, found in Kutch

Dhrangadhra and Dasada are both interesting bases from which to visit the Little Rann of Kutch Sanctuary. Dasada has a 15th-century fort and a village where potters and textile printers practise their craft. The family of Dasada's former feudal chiefs arrange accommodation and guided tours of the Rann. Dhrangadhra, capital of a former princely state, has a fine 18th-century palace, and a bazaar with interesting colonial buildings. Tours of the sanctuary can be arranged through the Forest office here. Accommodation is available in the government rest house.

Salt pans in the Rann, a major source of livelihood in Kutch

Rural Life and Art in Kutch

Kutch is home to several pastoral communities, many of them semi-nomadic herders of camels and sheep. Among them are the Rabaris, whose round houses *(bhoongas)* with conical roofs are a distinctive feature of the Kutch landscape. These communities are skilled in a variety of crafts, the vibrant hues and forms of their creations adding beauty to their stark surroundings. Anjar, which used to be the crafts centre of Kutch, was tragically destroyed in the January 2001 earthquake, as were many of the crafts villages near Bhuj. Despite this, the intrepid craftspeople continue to work and sell their creations at shops in Mumbai, Ahmedabad and Delhi.

A typical toadstool-shaped Rabari house in Kutch

The Rabari Bhoonga

The bhoongas of the Rabaris, superbly designed for the hot, arid climate of Kutch, are also structurally solid. Most of them withstood the 2001 earthquake. A typical cluster of bhoongas, their beautifully decorated interiors displaying the artistic skills of the Rabaris, can be seen at Tunda Vandh, 15 km (9 miles) east of Mandvi.

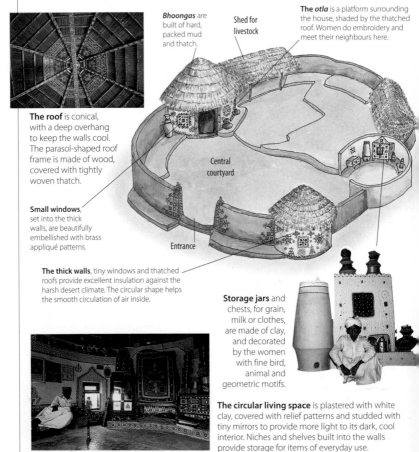

Bhoongas are built of hard, packed mud and thatch.

Shed for livestock

The otla is a platform surrounding the house, shaded by the thatched roof. Women do embroidery and meet their neighbours here.

The roof is conical, with a deep overhang to keep the walls cool. The parasol-shaped roof frame is made of wood, covered with tightly woven thatch.

Central courtyard

Small windows, set into the thick walls, are beautifully embellished with brass appliqué patterns.

Entrance

The thick walls, tiny windows and thatched roofs provide excellent insulation against the harsh desert climate. The circular shape helps the smooth circulation of air inside.

Storage jars and chests, for grain, milk or clothes, are made of clay, and decorated by the women with fine bird, animal and geometric motifs.

The circular living space is plastered with white clay, covered with relief patterns and studded with tiny mirrors to provide more light to its dark, cool interior. Niches and shelves built into the walls provide storage for items of everyday use.

Rabari women dress in black wool, dramatically offset with silver jewellery. They also sport tattoos of peacocks and camels, as well as small crosses to keep away the evil eye.

Rabari men, in contrast to the women, wear only white, with fine embroidery at the back of their pleated *kediyans* (jackets). White and red woven shawls and voluminous turbans complete their attire.

People

The pastoral communities of Kutch include Jaths, Ahirs, Meghwals, Bharwads and Sodhas, as well as Rabaris. While the men wander with their flocks, the women, children and elders stay at home, adding to the family income with their crafts skills.

Rabari girls wear the family's finest heirlooms. They begin embroidering their trousseau dresses as soon as they can hold a needle.

Craft

Crafts are not just a means of earning and employment for the rural people of Kutch. They are also a proud and creative expression of each community's distinct culture and identity, through which utilitarian objects like cupboards, quilts, shoes, cowbells or clay dishes are transformed into art forms.

Embroidery is done by most semi-nomadic communities. This section of a large wall hanging shows the work of a Rabari woman.

Rogan, a speciality of Niruna village near Bhuj, is a unique technique by which cloth is decorated with intricate, embossed lacquer-work patterns.

Leather objects are made by Meghwal men. They are embellished with bright tassels and embroidery.

Pottery dishes such as this large platter are used at village feasts. They are made by the men of the Kumbhar (potter) community.

Patchwork in vivid colours, using scraps and waste material, is done by Bharwad women to make items such as quilts, awnings and camel saddle covers.

Silverwork is crafted by the Sodha community, who also make jewellery to order in traditional designs, for the other pastoral communities.

SOUTHWESTERN INDIA

Introducing Southwestern India

Encompassing the three states of Maharashtra, Goa and Karnataka, Southwestern India contains the central Deccan Plateau, the narrow Konkan coastline and the craggy Western Ghats that run parallel to the coast. Its major city is Mumbai (Bombay), India's vibrant commercial capital. The region's varied attractions include Goa's idyllic beaches and Portuguese churches, the ancient caves and temples of Ajanta and Ellora, and the magnificent ruins of Hampi. Further south are Bengaluru, often described as Asia's Silicon Valley, the former princely state of Mysore, and the great Hoysala temples of Belur and Halebid.

Maharashtrian farmers with their oxen, often colourfully decorated

Getting Around

This region has three international airports, at Mumbai, Bengaluru and Dabolim in Goa. With domestic airports at Pune, Aurangabad, Nagpur and Mangalore, the region is well connected by air. The Indian Railways also cover the region extensively. Fast trains run between the large cities, and air-conditioned trains also connect most medium-sized cities and townships. The spectacular Konkan Railway runs 760 km (472 miles) along the coast, from Mumbai to Thiruvananthapuram (in Kerala), over 2,137 bridges, 140 rivers and through 83 km (52 miles) of tunnel. At 160 km (99 miles) per hour, it is India's fastest line. The hinterland is crisscrossed with numerous national highways, major and minor roads, and is well-connected by bus. Private operators run luxury coaches on the more popular routes, including the Mumbai-Goa-Hampi stretch.

Key

— National highway

— Major road

— State border

— Main railway

— Minor railway

◀ Wooden outrigger fishing boats at Asvem Beach, Goa

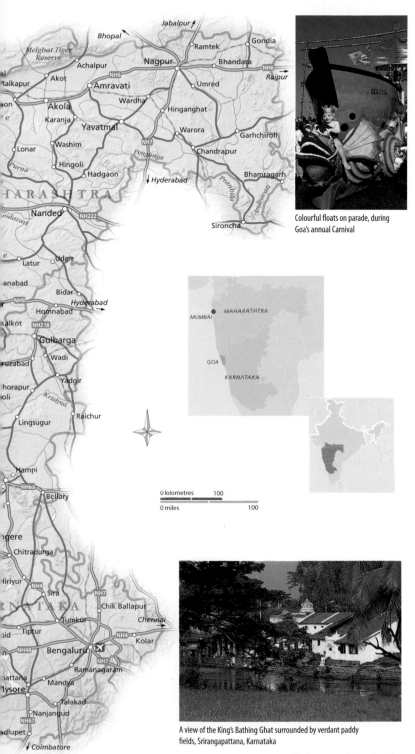

Melghat Tiger
Reserve
Achalpur
Akot
Amravati
Wardha
Akola
Karanja
Yavatmal
Washim
Lonar
Hingoli
Hadgaon
↓ Hyderabad
Nanded
Latur Udgir
anabad
Bidar
Homnabad
Gulbarga
Wadi
Yadgir
Lingsugur
Raichur
Hampi
Bellary
Chitradurga
Sira
Chik Ballapur
Tumkur
Tiptur
Kolar
Bengaluru
Ramanagaram
Mandya
Talakad
Nanjangud

Jabalpur
Bhopal
Ramtek
Gondia
Nagpur
Bhandara
Umred
Raipur
Hinganghat
Warora
Garhchiroli
Chandrapur
Bhamragarh
Sironcha
Hyderabad
Chennai

MUMBAI MAHARASHTRA
GOA
KARNATAKA

0 kilometres   100
0 miles   100

Colourful floats on parade, during
Goa's annual Carnival

A view of the King's Bathing Ghat surrounded by verdant paddy
fields, Srirangapattana, Karnataka

For keys to symbols *see back flap*

A PORTRAIT OF SOUTHWESTERN INDIA

The southwest is a region of many and varied splendours. Its three states, Maharashtra, Goa and Karnataka, contain golden beaches, wooded hills, serene villages along the picturesque Arabian Sea coastline, and two of India's most cosmopolitan and dynamic cities – Mumbai (formerly Bombay) and Bengaluru.

Mumbai, capital of Maharashtra, is India's largest and most populous city, as well as its commercial and financial capital. It is also home to the world's largest cinema industry, popularly known as Bollywood. The city presents extraordinary and sometimes shocking contrasts – the glamorous world of film stars and business tycoons exists side by side with the squalor of slums and shantytowns, where over three million people (nearly one-third of Mumbai's population) live. The dominant image, however, is that of an upbeat, street-smart city full of dynamism and *joie de vivre*.

Mumbai's population includes Marathi-speaking Hindus, a sizeable number of Muslims and Christians, as well as Jews, Parsis and other communities from different parts of India, drawn by its vibrant entrepreneurial culture, and often, by dreams of making it big in films. While this makes Mumbai remarkably cosmopolitan, it has on occasion led to sectarian strife, especially over the past decade, since the rise of the militant Hindu rightwing Shiv Sena Party. Maharashtra is a vast state, its population of over 96 million making it politically important, and major industries based on cotton, sugar, engineering goods and processed foods lending it economic vitality. Strawberry fields and grape vineyards dot its rich agricultural hinterland, but the most prized crop remains the Alfonso mango, a particularly sweet and luscious variety, which is exported across the world. Central Maharashtra has two World Heritage sites to its

Green coconut

Little fishing boats in Mumbai's harbour, against a backdrop of the city's skyscrapers

Goan women on their way to Sunday Mass

credit, at Ajanta and Ellora *(see pp480–85)*. The murals and sculptures found here testify to the common, ancient roots of Hinduism and Buddhism.

Many visitors travel by train from Mumbai to the tiny neighbouring state of Goa. The Konkan Railway which connects the two, and continues southwards to Karnataka, is a wonderful way to see the lush coastal scenery of coconut groves, spice plantations and fishing villages. Goa was a Portuguese colony from 1510 until 1961, when it was liberated by the Indian Army. The Portuguese departed peacefully, leaving behind a rich cultural legacy in cathedrals and mansions, music, dance, and in its distinctive cuisine. Another legacy of 450 years of Portuguese rule is in religion – almost one-third of Goa's population is Roman Catholic. Tourism and related industries are today a major source of livelihood here. Visitors from all over the world throng the beautiful beaches, which offer secluded palm-fringed retreats, as well as lively resorts buzzing with bars, cafés and discos.

Karnataka is often described as the geographical and cultural meeting point between India's Dravidian south and its Indo-Aryan north. The state's varied landscape and architecture both reflect this unique melange. Karnataka's narrow strip of fertile coastland is backed by the green hills of the Western Ghats, covered with forests of fragrant sandalwood and teak. These slope down to a vast plateau, watered by the Kaveri and Krishna rivers. This is the state's historic and cultural heartland, dotted with architectural treasures in an extraordinary variety of styles. They were built by local Hindu and Muslim dynasties, as well as by ambitious rulers from the north, Maratha warriors and medieval Islamic chieftains, all of whom had once established kingdoms here.

Bengaluru, the state capital, presents a sharp contrast to Karnataka's historic sites. As the ebullient centre of India's burgeoning computer software industry, this once laid-back town has been transformed into a globalized, high-tech showcase for contemporary India. Several multinational corporations have opened offices here, while pubs and shopping malls line its streets, catering to a young, cosmopolitan population.

A Hanuman statue in Nasik, Maharashtra

The lush landscape along Karnataka's coastline

The Konkan Coast

All along the Konkan Coast, from Mumbai to the south of Mangalore, are villages where, for over 2,000 years, fishing communities have harvested the fruits of the sea. A distinctive culture has developed in this area, protected by the forested hills of the Western Ghats. Beyond the coastline are fertile paddy fields, and plantations of coconut, cashew, betel nut, rubber, pepper and other spices. This is also India's monsoon land, where the Southwest Monsoon is at its heaviest, and where Arab merchants, drawn by the monsoon winds, came to trade long before the Europeans.

Locator Map
🟦 Extent of Area

Harvesting ripe paddy is a full-time occupation for the entire village.

Paddy Cultivation

In wet paddy cultivation, seedlings are raised in a nursery and then transplanted in waterlogged fields when they are 30 cm (12 in) high.

Pepper, cashew and betel nut are some of the major cash crops that this region grows in abundance.

A rubber plantation bungalow is festooned with strips of cured rubber hanging out to dry.

Fisherfolk of the Coast

Coastal people belong to different communities, speak their own dialects and celebrate local festivals. Strong and hard-working, their lives are ruled by natural forces.

Fishermen prepare their boats before they cast off just before dawn. The boats return by late morning.

A basket of freshly caught fish is carried to the shore to be sold directly to waiting customers.

Coastal dwellings have sloping roofs made of tiles to deflect the heavy rains during the monsoon.

These women from Mumbai's small Koli fishing community are dressed in bright festival finery.

Small boats moored in the Konkan backwaters

Flowers are a common form of adornment and are picked each morning by girls and women for their hair.

Konkan Coast

The narrow coastal strip that runs along the Arabian Sea is sheltered by the verdant slopes of the Western Ghats. This region can be explored either by road or on the Konkan Railway (see p438).

Monsoon clouds herald the onset of the monsoon, when the coast is lashed by torrential rain from June to early September.

The Western Ghats, or the Sahyadri Range, run in an unbroken line along the coast.

Dried fish is eaten during the monsoon when heavy rains prevent fishing.

Local fish markets sell a large variety of freshly caught produce.

Boat building is done by expert artisans who repair old boats using traditional methods, as well as build new ones from locally procured wood.

The Flavours of Southwestern India

A large part of this region lies on the shores of the Arabian Sea and consequently fish, coconut and rice are the dominant ingredients. Mumbai is a metropolis, home to many groups of people, and the city's cuisine reflects its myriad influences. Further south, along the Konkan Coast to Goa and Mangalore, the fish and rice diet has regional variations. Interior Maharashtra has a large number of vegetarian communities especially around Pune, although spicy mutton curries are a speciality of the state. Karnataka's food is a mosaic of distinct communities such as the coastal Udipi vegetarian fare and the meat-based food of Kodagu.

Custard apple

A local woman selling bananas, coconuts and other fruit

Basic Dishes

In Maharashtra, rice, wheat, lentils and *jowar* (sorghum maize) form the backbone of the people's diet. This accompanies the *bhaji* (a vegetable dish) or *rassa*, (curried vegetables cooked in groundnut oil). The food is distinguished by a blend of spices, coriander, sesame, cumin seeds and dried coconut (*goda*) and *kalaa masalas*. *Koshimbirs* (relishes freshly made with cucumber or carrots) perk up the meal.

In Karnataka, the three staples are rice, *jowar* and *ragi* (finger millet). In rural areas, *ragi* is steam-cooked, rolled into balls and served with hot chutney or *huli* (a spicy lentil dish). Variations of the *dosa* (see *pp558–9*) are also eaten here with coconut chutney and potatoes.

Coastal Fare

Along the Konkan Coast, coconuts, cashew nuts and fresh vegetables are in abundance. However, sea-food predominates and the types of fish available range from the flat pomfret,

Prawns · Mackerel · Lobster · Squid · Pomfret · Mussels · Sardines
Selection of seafood available along the Arabian Sea coastline

Local Dishes and Specialities

The culinary choices in this region are varied and range from stalls selling spicy savouries, such as *bhelpuri, pani-puri* and *pav-bhaji*, to beach shacks and specialist restaurants. Tastes are eclectic and reflect flavours imported from as far off as Iran (Parsi) and Portugal (Goa). Karnataka's and Maharashtra's vegetarian food is complemented by the fish, pork and chicken dishes from the Konkan Coast, Goa, Mangalore and Coorg. This fertile region yields fruits, such as *chikoo* (sapodilla plum) custard apple, mango, papaya and grapes, as well as crops such as sugarcane and cashew, and spices, particularly pepper. During the mild winters in south Maharashtra, jaggery is made, and with it, a peanut or sesame toffee (*chikki*).

Cashew nuts

Akuri, spicy scrambled eggs cooked with tomatoes and onions and garnished with coriander, is a Parsi delicacy.

Fishermen unloading the catch of the day, Goa

salmon *(rawas)* and mackerel to prawns, lobsters and clams. Fish is grilled, fried or cooked as curries with fresh coconut and spices. *Kokum* (a dried sour plum), tamarind, raw mango or the local Goan vinegar are used as souring agents. *Kokum* and coconut milk are also used to make a drink, *sol kadi*.

Although the coastal area has several culinary features in common, particularly in the preparation of seafood, Goa's cuisine is different as it combines Portuguese and local flavours. Some typical dishes include *peixe a Portuguese* (a fish curry with olive oil) and *ambot-tik* (a tangy fish curry with tamarind). Goan chillies are famed for their colour and are used to make the *recheio masala*, which is added to fish, pork and mutton curries.

Malvan fish dishes are equally tasty, especially the *mori chi aamti* (a spicy shark curry) and *bangda* (whole mackerel fried with spices).

Other Favourites

The cuisine of the Parsis of Mumbai reflects their Persian ancestory. Their food is mainly non-vegetarian and includes *patra ni machhi* (fish steamed in a banana leaf), *jardaloo sali*

Coffee berries from a plantation in Coorg, Karnataka

boti (mutton with apricots), and the popular *dhan sak* (a meat and lentil casserole).

The Kodavas of Coorg have a distinct culture and cuisine and are the only Hindu community that allows non-vegetarian food and alcohol to be served at weddings. *Pandi* (pork) curry is a favourite and is eaten with steamed rice balls *(kadum-buttu)*. *Koli* curry, a chicken curry, and *bembla* curry, made from bamboo shoots, are other specialities, as are their wonderful rice preparations, such as *noolputtu* (rice noodles) or *oduputtu* (rice pancakes), enjoyed by other communities too.

ON THE MENU

Amti Sweet and sour lentils.

Balachão Prawns or chicken cooked with pickling spices.

Bebinca A multi-layered cake.

Kesari bhath Sweet made of semolina, sugar and saffron.

Kolhapuri mutton Mutton with chillies, coconut, aniseed and poppy seed.

Moru kolumbu Vegetables in a yoghurt sauce.

Patra ni macchi Fish with a coriander-coconut chutney, steamed in banana leaves.

Suran Steamed yam garnished with dry red chillies and curry leaves.

Vindaloo a dish of pork cooked in a marinade of vinegar, red chillies and other spices, is Goa's signature dish.

Fugad is finely sliced, stir fried cabbage garnished with coconut and chillies. Beans can also be used.

Bisibele huliyana, a delicious preparation of lentils, rice and vegetables, is a one-dish meal from Karnataka.

MUMBAI

Mumbai (formerly Bombay), capital of Maharashtra, is India's most dynamic, cosmopolitan and crowded city. The country's financial centre and its busiest port, Mumbai is also home to the world's biggest cinema industry, popularly known as Bollywood. Some 20 million people, from billionaire tycoons to homeless pavement dwellers, live in this teeming megalopolis.

Consisting of seven swampy islands when the Portuguese acquired it in 1534, Bombay (from the Portuguese Bom Bahia or "Good Bay") came to the British Crown in 1661 as part of the dowry of Catherine of Braganza when she married Charles II. Finding little use for the islands, the British leased them to the East India Company, which quickly realized their potential as an excellent natural harbour in the Arabian Sea. The rise of Bombay began in the late 1600s, when the company relocated its headquarters here. By the 18th century, Bombay had become the major city and shipbuilding yard on the western coast, and by the 19th century, land reclamations had joined the islands into the narrow promontory that it is today. The promise of commercial opportunities lured communities of Gujaratis, Parsis *(see p451)* and Baghdadi or Sephardic Jews to Bombay, giving the city its vibrant multicultural identity. The city has reverted to its local name, Mumbai, from Mumba-Ai (Mother Mumbai), the eight-armed goddess worshipped by the Koli fishermen who were the islands' original inhabitants.

Mumbai is a city of striking contrasts. Skyscrapers stand next to stately Victorian and Art Deco buildings, traditional bazaars adjoin glittering shopping malls, and opulent neighbourhoods are surrounded by sprawling slums. Swelling Mumbai's population are migrants from all over the country who continue to flock to this "land of opportunities" in search of fame, fortune, or just a bit part in a Bollywood movie.

Swirling traffic around Flora Fountain in the heart of Mumbai

◀ The Gateway of India, Mumbai's signature landmark

Exploring Mumbai

Mumbai is a long, narrow promontory covering 603 sq km (233 sq miles), which juts into the Arabian Sea. Its downtown is the historic Fort area in South Mumbai, that derives its name from earlier colonial fortifications. This is the city's nerve centre, with the best-known sights, hotels and restaurants. The posh residential area of Malabar Hill lies along the western coastline, just north of Marine Drive. Suburban Mumbai, with its sprawling modern developments, stretches northwards from Bandra.

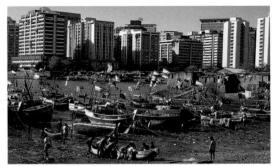

Fishing boats, decorated for Holi, at the seafront in South Mumbai

Sights at a Glance

Historic Buildings, Streets & Neighbourhoods

- ⑩ *Victoria Terminus pp458–9*
- ① Gateway of India
- ② Wellington Fountain
- ③ Colaba Causeway
- ④ *Kala Ghoda pp452–3*
- ⑥ Town Hall
- ⑦ Horniman Circle
- ⑧ Mumbai Stock Exchange
- ⑨ Flora Fountain
- ㉑ Bandra
- ⑬ Ballard Estate

Historic Sites

- ⑱ Khotachiwadi
- ⑭ General Post Office
- ⑮ Marine Drive
- ⑫ Shahid Bhagat Singh Marg
- ⑯ Malabar Hill
- ㉕ Elephanta Island

Museums

- ⑤ *The Prince of Wales Museum pp454–5*

Temples & Mosques

- ⑰ Banganga
- ⑳ Haji Ali Mosque
- ⑲ Mahalaxmi Temple

Beaches & Parks

- ㉒ Juhu Beach
- ㉔ Sanjay Gandhi National Park

Shops & Markets

- ⑪ Crawford Market

Entertainment

- ㉓ Film City

For hotels and restaurants see p700 and pp714–15

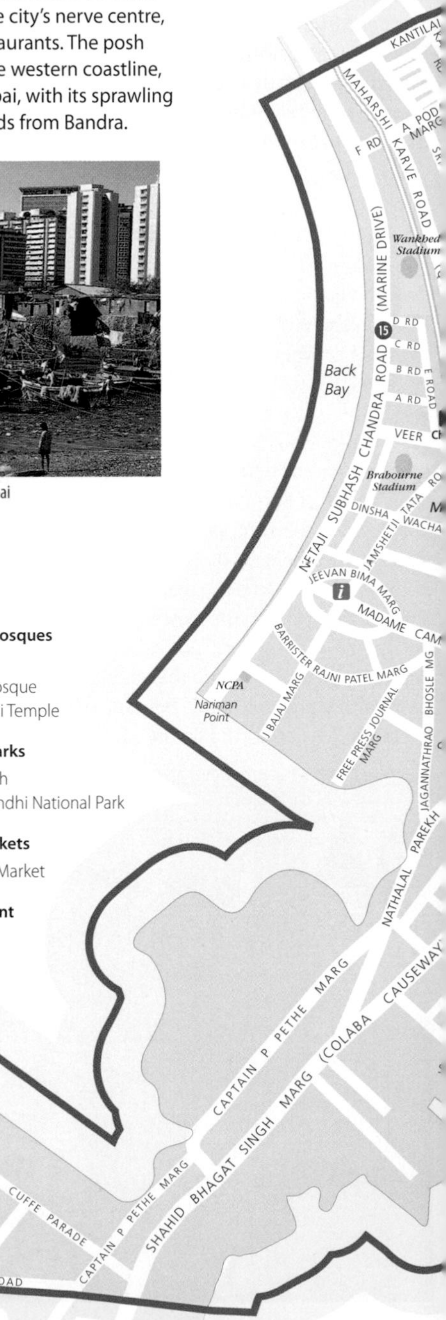

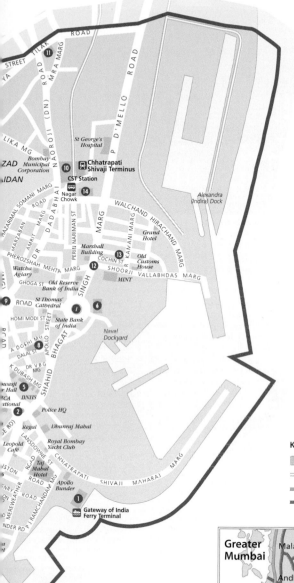

ROAD

STREET

TILAK

MRA MARG

(DN)

ROAD

NAOROJI

D'MELLO

ROAD

LIKA MG

St George's
Hospital

Bombay
Municipal
Corporation

ZAD

IDAN

10

11

Chhatrapati
Shivaji Terminus

CST Station

14

Nagar
Chowk

Alexandra
(Indira) Dock

MAZARIMAL SOMANI MARG

WALCHAND HIRACHAND MARG

ROAD

DADABHAI

AMRIT MARG

DR

MARG

SINGH

PERIN NARIMAN ST

KAMANI MARG

Grand
Hotel

HARZABAN

Marshall
Building

COCHIN ST

Old
Customs
House

PHEROZSHAH

MEHTA MARG

SHOORJI VALLABHDAS MARG

13

12

Watcha
Agiary

GHOGA ST

Old Reserve
Bank of India

MINT

9

ROAD

St Thomas'
Cathedral

HOMI MODI ST

State Bank
of India

6

Naval
Dockyard

A DOSHI MG

DALAL ST

DR V B G
MG

8

K DUBASH MG

SHAHID

BHAGAT

APOLLO

CHHATRAPATI

uwasji
r Hall

DNHS

CA
ational

5

2

Police HQ

E RD)

LANSDOWNE ST

Regal

Dhunraj Mahal

Leopold
Café

Royal Bombay
Yacht Club

ISTON

ROAD

Taj
Mahal
Hotel

SHIVAJI MAHARAJ MARG

ENRY VEAHIR

ROAD

Apollo
Bunder

1

J RAMCHANDAN MG

MEREWATHER

Gateway of India
Ferry Terminal

NDER RD

0 metres 400
0 yards 400

Doubledecker bus at Victoria
Terminus *(see pp458–9)*

Key

◻ Sight
═ Railroad
━ National Highway (Inset map)
━ Major road (Inset map)

**Greater
Mumbai**

Thane

Malad **24**

23

Andheri

22

NH8

✈ CSI

Santa
Cruz

✈

NH3

New
Mumbai

Trombay

21

Arabian
Sea

20

19

16 **18**

17

25

Nhave

Mumbai

0 kilometres 10
0 miles 10

Getting Around

Three suburban railway lines link the
northern suburbs to the city centre and
the southern tip. A taxi, private car or the
red BEST buses are convenient ways to
get around within the city. In the suburbs,
you can only use the auto-rickshaws.

For keys to symbols *see back flap*

The Gateway of India with the red-domed Taj Mahal Hotel behind it

● Gateway of India

Apollo Bunder, Chhatrapati Shivaji
Marg & PJ Ramchandani Marg.

Mumbai's most famous landmark, the Gateway of India, was the first sight to greet travellers to Indian shores during the heyday of the British Raj. Ironically, it also became the exit point for British troops after India gained independence in 1947. It was built to commemorate the visit of King George V and Queen Mary in 1911, en route to the Delhi Durbar, but in fact, the King and Queen were met with a mock cardboard structure – the actual Triumphal Arch, built in honey-coloured Kharodi basalt, was completed only in 1924, years after the royal visit. This monumental structure, with two large reception halls, arches and minarets, and embellishments inspired by 16th-century Gujarati architecture, was designed by the Scottish architect George Wittet in Indo-Saracenic style. The Gateway commands a spectacular view of the sea and looks particularly impressive at night when it is illuminated, with the inky black sea stretching into the horizon beyond it. This is the heart of Mumbai's tourist district, the city's most popular gathering place, and is always teeming with with locals, visitors, vendors and boatmen. Boats and barges moored here provide regular services across the bay and to islands such as Elephanta (*see p465*). They can also be hired for leisurely trips down the Mumbai coastline.

Statue of Chhatrapati Shivaji opposite the Gateway

North of the Gateway of India, towards Wellington Fountain, is Chhatrapati Shivaji Road. Formerly Apollo Pier Road, it has been renamed after Shivaji (*see p475*), Maharashtra's great warrior-hero. Shivaji's equestrian statue is placed here in a pleasant garden, in line with the Gateway. Standing nearby is the statue of the 19th-century Hindu philosopher and reformist Swami Vivekananda (*see p619*).

Around the Gateway are some majestic buildings dating from the colonial era. These include the old **Yacht Club**, which now houses the offices of the Atomic Energy Commission (entry restricted), the **Royal Bombay Yacht Club**, originally built as a residential annexe to the Old Yacht Club, and the **Taj Mahal Hotel**, behind which lies the busy Colaba Causeway.

The stately, red-domed Taj Mahal Hotel was built in 1903 by a prominent Parsi industrialist, Jamshedji Tata (*see p229*) who, it is said, decided to construct this magnificent hotel when he was barred from entering the "Whites Only" Watsons Hotel. The Taj, with its splendid Moorish arches and columns, majestic stairways and galleries, remains one of Asia's grandest hotels, while Watsons, also known as "Esplanade Mansion", is now a dilapidated building, the hotel having closed down long ago.

The eastern sea face stretching in front of the Gateway of India is Mumbai's favourite promenade. Called **Apollo Bunder**, it was once the traditional dockyard of the local Koli fishermen, the islands' original inhabitants. Today, snake charmers and performing monkeys, astrologers and ear-cleaners hustle for business among the strollers. Dozens of yachts, fishing boats and ferries are moored in the waters beyond.

The Royal Bombay Yacht Club, a relic of the British Raj

The entrance to Cusrow Baug, a Parsi enclave along Colaba

❷ Wellington Fountain

Bounded by MG Rd, Shahid Bhagat Singh Marg, Chhatrapati Shivaji Marg & Madame Cama Rd.

Built to commemorate the Duke of Wellington's visit to Bombay in 1801, Wellington Fountain (now renamed Shyama Prasad Mukherjee Chowk) is encircled by some magnificent colonial buildings. These include the old **Majestic Hotel** (now the government-owned Sahakari Bhandar) with its mock minarets and Gujarati balconies, and the elegant Art Deco **Regal Cinema**, designed by Charles Stevens and completed in 1933. His father, Frederick William Stevens, designed the imposing grey stone Indo-Gothic **Sailors' Home**, with a bas-relief of Neptune on its front gable, in 1876; it is now the Maharashtra State Police Headquarters. Equally impressive are the Edwardian Cowasjee Jehangir Hall by George Wittet, now the **National Gallery of Modern Art** (see p453), and the Indo-Saracenic **Prince of Wales**

Museum (see pp454–5). Adjoining it is Hornbill House, the headquarters of the Bombay Natural History Society (BNHS), a prestigious institution established in 1883.

❸ Colaba Causeway

Shahid Bhagat Singh Marg. Afghan Memorial Church: **Open** daily.
🕐 7am & 4:30pm, Sun.

Constructed by the British in 1838, Colaba Causeway helped integrate the main city with Colaba, its southernmost spur. Today, the posh Causeway, also known as Shahid Bhagat Singh Road (see p460), is an eclectic mix of shops, restaurants and residential enclaves. Among them is the charming Parsi housing colony of **Cusrow Baug**, built in 1934, where the distinct culture and lifestyle of this dwindling community is preserved. The Causeway's many restaurants include one that has become an institution, the **Leopold Café and Bar**, established in 1871, and a

popular meeting place ever since. Further south are the **Sassoon Docks**, worth visiting early in the morning when they are buzzing with activity. This is when the fishermen bring in their catch and a wholesale fish market is set up by the lively, and thoroughly professional Koli fishwives.

At the southern end of Colaba is the **Afghan Memorial Church of St John the Evangelist**, built between 1847 and 1858 (see p25). This grand Neo-Gothic structure with its tall spire and imposing front porch in buff basalt stone, was built in memory of the soldiers who died in the First Anglo-Afghan War (1843), and the church is full of poignant memorial stones. It has superb stained glass, especially on its west windows, where an outstanding panel depicts the Crucifixion. A memorial to the martyrs stands in the garden.

Fishermen bringing in the day's catch at Sassoon Docks

The Parsi Community in Mumbai

Conductor Zubin Mehta, a Mumbai-born Parsi

Mumbai's cosmopolitan, progressive culture owes a great deal to the contribution of the Parsi community. Originally from Iran, where they followed the ancient Zoroastrian faith, they migrated to India in the 10th century AD when the advent of Islam brought with it the religious persecution of Zoroastrians. They settled along the west coast of Gujarat, absorbing many local traditions, and later moved to Mumbai where they made their name as brilliant financiers and traders. Often, they adopted the name of their trade, and so one finds Parsi surnames such as Mistry (mason) and Vakil (lawyer), or even Readymoney! A wealthy and talented community that has produced several leading industrial houses, such as the Tatas and the Godrejs, Parsis are also renowned for their philanthropy and have founded several cultural, educational and medical institutions in Mumbai.

❹ Street-by-Street: Kala Ghoda

Kala Ghoda, or "Black Horse", was named after an equestrian statue of King Edward VII that once stood at the intersection of Mahatma Gandhi Road and K Dubash Marg. The statue was removed in 1965, but the name persists in public memory, thanks in part to the large mural of a black horse that commemorates it. Stretching from Wellington Fountain at the southern end of Mahatma Gandhi Road, to Bombay University at the north, and flanked by the Oval Maidan and the naval base at Lion Gate, this area is a hub of cultural activity. It houses a number of art galleries, restaurants and fine shops and boutiques.

David Sassoon Library
The garden behind the library serves as a reading area.

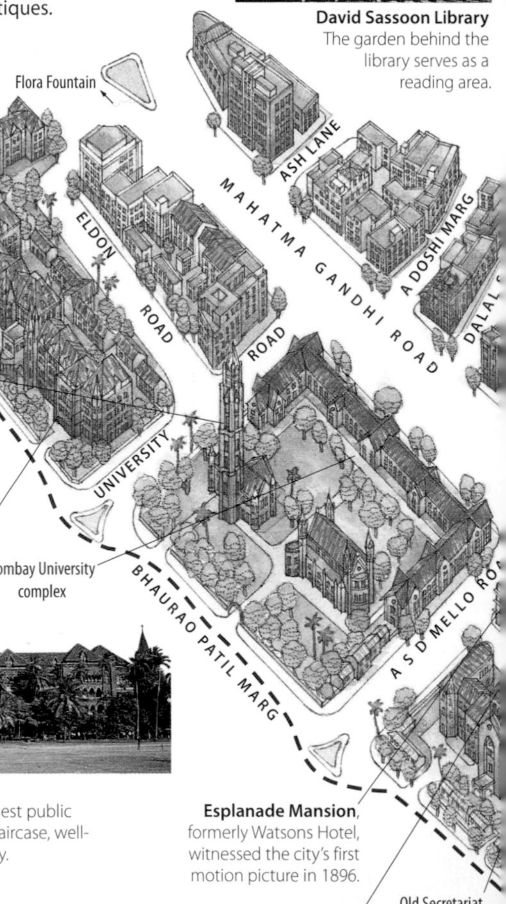

Flora Fountain

Victoria Terminus

ELDON ROAD

MAHATMA GANDHI ROAD

ASH LANE

A DOSHI MARG

DALAL

UNIVERSITY

Bombay University complex

BHAURAO PATIL MARG

A S D MELLO ROAD

★ Rajabai Clock Tower
This 85-m (280-ft) high tower in Bombay University is adorned with figures representing different Indian communities.

★ High Court
This fortress-like building, the second largest public building in the city, has a grand central staircase, well-appointed court rooms, and a large library.

Esplanade Mansion,
formerly Watsons Hotel, witnessed the city's first motion picture in 1896.

Old Secretariat

0 metres   50
0 yards   50

Army & Navy Building
The Neo-Classical Army & Navy Building, a departmental store in the early 1900s, is home to several offices of the Tata Group.

Kenneseth Eliyahoo Synagogue
This is the oldest Sephardic synagogue in the city, donated by the Sassoon family. It is used for prayer by Mumbai's Baghdadi and Bene Israeli Jewish community.

Locator Map
See Mumbai Map pp448–9

Key

— Suggested route

Elphinstone College
Part of this delightful Venetian Gothic building houses the State Archives.

Kenneseth Eliyahoo Synagogue

K DUBASH MARG

Lion Gate

Hornbill House

★ Prince of Wales Museum
Mumbai's most prestigious museum has a good collection of Rajput miniatures and sculptures *(see pp454–5).*

Police Headquarters

Wellington Fountain

Gateway of India

The National Gallery of Modern Art, an Edwardian building, has the most impressive exhibition space in Mumbai.

Regal Cinema

David Sassoon Library

Jehangir Art Gallery
This gallery exhibits paintings by leading contemporary Indian artists, and also has a popular café.

❺ The Prince of Wales Museum

Renowned for its superb sculptures and miniature paintings, the Prince of Wales Museum is housed in a grand Indo-Saracenic building designed by George Wittet. Its foundation stone was laid by the Prince of Wales (the future George V) in 1905. During World War I, it served as a military hospital, and was formally inaugurated in 1923 by Lady Lloyd, wife of Governor George Lloyd. Generous gifts from discerning private collectors have enabled the museum to build a collection of rare quality.

Japanese Cloisonné
This 19th-century vase forms part of an impressive collection of Far Eastern art.

Second floor

Ivory Statuette
A Parsi girl, Bai Aimai Wadia, is depicted in traditional dress in this 19th-century piece from the Decorative Arts gallery.

Arms and Armour include the finely decorated swords and shields of the Mughal emperors.

★ Jahangir Giving Alms
This early 17th-century Mughal miniature shows Jahangir giving alms to Sufi mendicants at the Dargah Sharif in Ajmer. The gallery has over 200 miniatures.

The Coomaraswamy Hall hosts seminars and temporary exhibitions.

Key to Floorplan

- Pre- and Proto-History Gallery
- Key Gallery
- Indian Sculpture
- Natural History Section
- Decorative Arts
- Miniature Paintings
- Bronzes
- Nepalese and Tibetan Art
- Maritime History
- European Paintings
- Far Eastern Art
- Arms and Armour
- Premchand Roychand Gallery

Gallery Guide

The museum, now renamed the Chhatrapati Shivaji Maharaj Vastu Sangrahalaya, has galleries on three floors. The ground floor houses sculpture (including Gandhara masterpieces), the Pre- and Proto-History Gallery, and the Natural History Section. On the first floor are miniature paintings, decorative arts, Nepalese and Tibetan Art, and the Premchand Roychand Galleries. The second floor has European paintings, arms and armour.

VISITORS' CHECKLIST

Practical Information
159/61 MG Rd, Fort Area
Tel (022) 2284 4484
w csmvs.in
Open Tue–Sun. **Closed** public
hols.

Key Gallery
The central hall on the ground floor offers a sampling of the museum's treasures, with prize exhibits from different galleries.

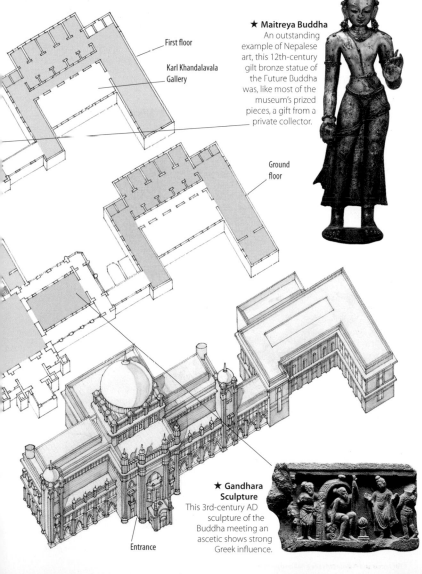

First floor

Karl Khandalavala Gallery

Ground floor

★ **Maitreya Buddha**
An outstanding example of Nepalese art, this 12th-century gilt bronze statue of the Future Buddha was, like most of the museum's prized pieces, a gift from a private collector.

★ **Gandhara Sculpture**
This 3rd-century AD sculpture of the Buddha meeting an ascetic shows strong Greek influence.

Entrance

The Town Hall, Mumbai's most elegant public building

❻ Town Hall

Shahid Bhagat Singh Marg, Fort Area.
Tel (022) 2266 0956. **Open** Mon–Sat.
Closed public hols. The Asiatic
Society: **Tel** (022) 2266 0956.
Open Mon–Sat.

In recognition of Mumbai's
importance as a burgeoning
commercial centre in the 1820s,
the city was bestowed with a
Town Hall, facing the vast open
space of Cotton Green (now
Horniman Circle). Designed by
Colonel Thomas Cowper and
completed in 1833, the Town Hall
is considered to be among the
finest Neo-Classical buildings in
India, and is one of the earliest
surviving colonial buildings in
Mumbai. Its impressive façade
of pedimented porticoes
surmounts a row of fluted Doric
columns. A grand flight of 30
steps leads into a magnificent
Assembly Hall, the venue for
public meetings during the Raj.

The Town Hall's north wing
houses **The Asiatic Society**,
founded in 1804 by Sir James
Mackintosh, with its imposing
high ceiling, teak-panelled walls,
and elegant cast-iron balustrades.
This institution's extensive library
has a priceless collection of
800,000 volumes, including a first
edition of Dante's *Divine Comedy*,
ancient Sanskrit manuscripts and
old Bombay gazetteers. It also
holds fragments of what is
believed to be Gautama Buddha's
begging bowl. On the first floor
are marble statues of Mumbai's
founding fathers, among them
two governors, Mountstuart
Elphinstone and Sir Bartle Frere,
and the Parsi philanthropist Sir
Jamsetjee Jeejeebhoy.

❼ Horniman Circle

Veer Nariman Rd, Fort Area. St Thomas'
Cathedral: **Tel** (022) 2202 0121.
Open daily. ✝ 8am & 4:30pm, Sun.

The central green, the old
Cotton Green where traders
used to buy and sell bales
of cotton, was laid out
as a public garden in
1872. Later known
as Elphinstone Circle,
it was renamed after
Independence in
honour of Benjamin
Guy Horniman, a former
editor of the *Bombay
Chronicle* who was
an active supporter
of India's Freedom
Movement. Today,
the garden remains a
delightful spot, much
frequented by students
and office workers who
relax here before the
long commute back to
their homes in the

Stained glass,
St Thomas'
Cathedral

Greek-inspired keystone at
Horniman Circle

distant suburbs. The garden is
also the venue for open-air
theatrical performances and
cultural events in the winter.

The elegant circle of Neo-
Classical buildings around the
garden was built in the 1860s,
and fashioned after acclaimed
English examples such as Royal
Crescent in Bath. Designed
by James Scott, the buildings
around the garden share a
uniform façade with pedestrian
arcades and decorative terracotta
keystones from England, and
represent the earliest planned
urban compositions in Mumbai.

Anchoring the western edge
of the flower-filled green patch
of Horniman Circle is **St Thomas'
Cathedral**, the city's oldest
church, which was consecrated
in 1718. Like many of Mumbai's
great edifices, this too was
funded by public
donations, collected in
large part by a young
East India Company
chaplain named Richard
Cobbe. The church has
an imposing bell tower
and flying buttresses,
and some fine
19th-century stained
glass. The cathedral's
spacious interior is
especially remarkable
for its splendid marble
memorials to heroes
of the Raj. An
exceptionally fine one
is the monument to
Governor Jonathan
Duncan, which depicts
him being blessed by Hindus for
his efforts to stop infanticide. In
front of the entrance porch is a
charming Neo-Gothic fountain.
Designed by Sir George Gilbert
Scott, it was donated by the
Parsi financier, Sir Cowasjee
Jehangir Readymoney.

Opposite the Cathedral are
some lovely buildings – the Neo-
Gothic **Elphinstone Building**,
built in the late 19th century, and
the Neo-Classical **British Bank of
the Middle East**. Across the road
is the **Readymoney Mansion** with
its detailed timberwork, carved
balconies, and Mughal arches.
Reminiscent of a Rajasthani
haveli, it was also designed by
George Wittet (*see p454*).

The Mumbai Stock Exchange, India's financial epicentre

❽ Mumbai Stock Exchange

Dalal Street, Fort Area.
Closed to public.

India's financial epicentre, the **Mumbai Stock Exchange** towers above Dalal Street. This is Mumbai's Wall Street and derives its name from the many stockbrokers (dalals) in the area. The presence of close to 50 banks on a short stretch underlines the frenetic pace of its commercial activity. Just before lunchtime, the area swarms with dabbawallahs (see p461) who bring home-made lunchboxes to the thousands of office workers in the area.

❾ Flora Fountain

Junction of Veer Nariman Rd, MG Rd & Dr Dadabhai Naoroji Rd, Fort Area

Standing at the intersection of three major streets is **Flora Fountain**, the quintessential icon of Mumbai. Sculpted out of Portland stone by James Forsythe and shipped out from England, the fountain is surmounted by the Roman goddess Flora who stands above exuberantly carved seashells, dolphins and mythical beasts. Erected in 1869 in what was then a spacious open plaza, Flora Fountain is now swamped in a sea of traffic, and over-shadowed by a **Martyrs' Memorial** put up by the Maharashtra state government in 1960. The area has now

been renamed Hutatma Chowk ("Martyrs' Square"). This area marks the western ramparts of the now-vanished old Fort, built by the East India Company in 1716, which covered the southern part of the city. The Fort was demolished in the 1860s by the governor, Sir Bartle Frere, to allow the city to expand, and to accommodate the grandiose new civic and commercial buildings he had planned. All these buildings were designed with pedestrian arcades, which today are crowded with hawkers selling a wide range of goods, from old books to clothes and electronic gadgets.

North of Flora Fountain, leading towards Victoria Terminus, is Dadabhai Naoroji (DN) Road, lined with some magnificent Victorian and later colonial structures such as the **Capitol Cinema** with its classical detailing, the **JN Petit Institute and Library** (1898) with its Venetian Neo-Gothic façade, and the Art Deco **Watcha Agiary** (Parsi Fire Temple) with its Assyrian-style carvings, built in 1881. Other interesting structures include the Indo-Saracenic **Times of India Building** and the fanciful **Municipal Corporation Building**, with its Islamic minarets, Gothic towers and onion domes.

❿ Victoria Terminus

See pp458–9.

Flora Fountain, a favourite Mumbai landmark

⓫ Crawford Market

Dr Dadabhai Naoroji Rd & Lokmanya Tilak Rd. Shops: **Open** daily.

Built on the orders of Sir Arthur Crawford, Bombay's first Municipal Commissioner (1865–71), Crawford Market, now known as Mahatma Jyotiba/Jyotirao Phule Market, lies to the north of Victoria Terminus. Designed by William Emerson and completed in 1869, this architectural extravaganza of Moorish arches and half-timbered gables, topped by a clocktower, consists of a large central hall with two wings. Tiers of wooden stalls display nearly 3,000 tonnes of fresh produce daily, from fruit and flowers to fish and exotic birds. The floor is paved with stone from Caithness in Scotland, which remains cool through the day. The lamp brackets are shaped like winged dragons. Above the entrance doors, the charming marble bas reliefs depict scenes from market life. They were carved by Lockwood Kipling (see p114), father of the writer Rudyard Kipling, as was the fountain in the courtyard exuberantly decorated with Hindu river goddesses and animals.

Just west of the market is **Zaveri Bazaar**, where diamond, gold and silver merchants have their opulent stores. Northwest of the market, on Mutton Street, is **Chor Bazaar** ("Thieves' Market"), with its fascinating antique and bric-a-brac shops.

Vegetable stall at Crawford Market

⑩ Victoria Terminus

The most impressive example of Victorian
Gothic architecture in India, Victoria Terminus
Railway Station (now renamed Chhatrapati
Shivaji Terminus) is a rich extravaganza
of domes, spires and arches. Designed by
Frederick William Stevens and decorated
by local art students and craftsmen, it was
completed in 1888 and named to commemorate
Queen Victoria's Golden Jubilee. Now the
headquarters of the Central Railway, over 1,000
trains and two million passengers, including
crowds of suburban commuters, pass through
the station daily. In 2004, it was declared a
UNESCO World Heritage Site.

Victoria Terminus, often mistaken for a grand
palace or cathedral

The Gables
The gables are crowned
by sculptures representing
Engineering, Agriculture
and Commerce.

★ Booking Hall
A Neo-Gothic vaulted roof with
wooden ribs covers the hall. Stained
glass, colourful tiles and decorative
iron grilles add to its beauty.

KEY

① **Entrance** gate piers are topped
by stone sculptures of a lion and
a tiger, symbolizing Britain and
India, respectively.

② **A majestic staircase** of blue
stone, with beautiful iron railings,
sweeps up beneath the dome.

③ **Water spouts** shaped like
animal heads jut out from the
base of the dome.

The Central Dome
A 4-m (13-ft) high statue of "Progress", holding a torch, crowns the colossal dome, which has eight decorated ribs.

VISITORS' CHECKLIST

Practical Information
Dr Dadabhai Naoroji Rd,
Fort Area.
Tel (022) 2265 6565.
🖼 of the interiors. ⊘ ⚹ 📷

Stained Glass
Set into the octagonal tower below the dome are brilliantly coloured stained-glass windows, decorated with a locomotive and foliage.

Portrait Medallion
Studded into the façade are busts of Raj-era personalities, such as Sir Bartle Frere *(see p456)*.

★ Stone Carvings and Sculptures
An exquisite peacock carving decorates this window. Other carved screens and friezes feature elephants, monkeys and snakes.

The Ruttonsee Mulji fountain, elaborately carved and embellished

⑫ Shahid Bhagat Singh Marg

Fort Area.

This busy street, also known as Colaba Causeway (see p451) towards its southern end, is the bustling commercial and administrative hub of the so-called Fort area (see p457). Virtually no traces of this historic structure remain, but the area still offers a fascinating glimpse into the continuities between colonial and present-day Mumbai.

The **Reserve Bank of India**, which stands on the site of an old military barracks, is India's leading banking institution. Built in 1939 and designed by JA Ritchie, its grand Art Deco entrance, flanked by two impressive columns, enhances its air of respectable solidity. There are attractive cast-iron grilles in the window panels. The modern highrise offices of the Reserve Bank, across the road, stand in the grounds of the old **Mint**. This is a majestic Classical-fronted building, designed and built in 1827 by Major John Hawkins, a member of the Bombay Engineers' Regiment. Entry into the Mint is restricted, but visible from its compound is a stone gateway erected by the Portuguese, now inside the naval establishment, INS Angre.

West of the Mint, occupying a corner site at the intersection of Pherozeshah Mehta and Shahid Bhagat Singh roads, is the imposing **Gresham Assurance Building**. This Art Deco structure has an impressive basalt façade, with two grand pillars and a dome.

The **Marshall Building**, directly opposite, has a Florentine dome, and was constructed in 1898 to accommodate the warehouse and offices of a British engineering firm. Its façade, embellished with a medley of angels, portholes and pediments, is a wonderful example of how contemporary European architecture was successfully transplanted to eastern settings.

Drinking water fountains or pyavs were set up across the city by local philanthropists to provide respite from the hot Indian summer. At the point where Shahid Bhagat Singh Marg meets Mint Road is the **Ruttonsee Mulji Drinking Water Fountain** designed by FW Stevens, the leading architect of Victorian Bombay, who also designed the Municipal Corporation Building and the Victoria Terminus (see pp458–9). This fountain was erected in 1894 by a local trader, in memory of his only son, whose statue stands beneath the dome. Made of limestone and red and blue granite, it is decorated with projecting elephant heads, whose trunks spout water. The dome, supported by columns made of blue granite, is crowned by the figure of a young boy. The fountain also has a special trough from which animals can drink.

Further down Mint Road, just before its junction with Walchand Hirachand Marg, is another pyav and the **Kothari Kabutarkhana**. Literally "Pigeon House", the Kabutarkhana is an ornate stone structure, constructed in the 18th century by a Jain merchant, Purushottamdas Kothari, and added to in the 19th and early 20th centuries. Jains, like Buddhists, believe that all living beings have souls, and that kind acts towards all life forms will earn the giver merit in the next life.

At the western end of Walchand Hirachand Marg is **Nagar Chowk**, an oasis of green in the midst of swirling traffic. It has an impressive statue of Sir Dinshaw Manekji Petit, a baronet, captain of industry and leading Parsi philanthropist of the early 20th century. The statue was sculpted by Sir Thomas Brock and the surrounding garden is a good place from which to view some of Mumbai's grand Victorian buildings – among them Victoria Terminus, the Bombay Municipal Corporation building and the General Post Office. Shahid Bhagat Singh Marg eventually runs into D'Mello Road, formerly known as Frere Road. This area lay under water until the 1860s, when it was reclaimed by the Port Trust. Today the road is lined with popular eateries.

Gresham Assurance Building

Pigeons at the Kothari Kabutarkhana pecking at their daily supply of grain

⑬ Ballard Estate

Bounded by Shahid Bhagat Singh Marg, Walchand Hirachand Marg & Shoorji Vallabhdas Marg.

This entire area was once part of the sea until it was reclaimed by the Bombay Port Trust and converted into a business district. Planned between 1908 and 1914 by George Wittet, architect of the Gateway of India, the area was developed according to the strict guidelines set by him, maintaining a restrained elegance in contrast to the over-ornamentation of the Victorian edifices in the Fort area. The district's broad pavements and neat tree-lined avenues are lined with stone buildings of uniform height and style, giving the Estate an atmosphere of calm tranquillity, unusual in a business quarter.

A convenient point of entry into Ballard Estate is from Shoorji Vallabhdas Marg, near the imposing Marshall Building. Among the most impressive buildings on this street is the **Customs House**. Designed by Wittet himself, it has a grand entrance portico in stately Renaissance style, framed by two columns rising to the height of the building. Next to it is the **Bombay Port Trust** also designed by George Wittet. Two striking ships in full sail are

The General Post Office, combining European and Indian styles

sculpted on its basalt façade. Further down the road, to the east, is the **Port Trust War Memorial**, honouring the memory of port officers who died in World War I. The memorial has a single, fluted column shaft in stone, surmounted by a lantern. The **Grand Hotel** dominates the corner of Walchand Hirachand Marg and Ram Gulam Marg. Another of George Wittet's designs, it has a striking central atrium. The grandiose **Mackinnon & Mackenzie Building** has an impressive portico, columns and statues. This, and other beautiful Edwardian buildings, such as **Darabshaw House** and **Neville House**, make Ballard Estate a uniquely elegant business district.

Port Trust Memorial

⑭ General Post Office

Walchand Hirachand Marg.
Open Mon–Sat.

Completed in 1913, this fantastic composition of minarets, domes and arches was designed by John Begg and supervised by George Wittet. A prime example of the Indo-Saracenic style, the General Post Office (GPO) building combines elements of Indian architecture, most notably an Islamic dome inspired by the Gol Gumbad in Bijapur *(see p547)*, with classical European traditions. Mumbai's main post office, the GPO has a lofty three-storeyed rotunda inside, which leads to its various departments. Business is transacted from behind delightful old-fashioned wooden counters.

The Dabbawallahs of Mumbai

Among Mumbai's most characteristic sights are the *dabbawallahs*, men who pick up freshly cooked lunches from over 200,000 suburban homes and deliver them to offices all over the city. Most office workers spend an average of two hours travelling to work. Hot, home-cooked lunches therefore would normally be an impossible luxury – if it weren't for the *dabbawallas*. They pick up the meals, usually *rotis*, vegetables and *dal*, packed in three or four round stainless-steel containers, known as tiffin boxes or *dabbas* (hence the name *dabbawallah*) from each

Dabbawallahs delivering home-cooked lunch to office workers

house, colourcode the office addresses onto the lids, thread the *dabbas* onto long poles and cycle off to the nearest station. Here the *dabbas* are handed over to other *dabbawallas*, who deliver them to the right offices. Lunches rarely go astray, and empty *dabbas* are delivered back home by late afternoon. *Dabbawallahs*, traditionally migrants from the neighbouring city of Pune, consider themselves descendants of Mawle warriors, associated with King Chhatrapati Shivaji Maharaj. They provide one of Mumbai's most efficient services.

Marine Drive, sweeping in an arc along the sea, connecting the northern and southern ends of Mumbai

ⓕ Marine Drive

Netaji Subhash Chandra Rd.

Known as the "Queen's Necklace" after the glittering string of streetlights lining the road, Marine Drive (renamed Netaji Subhash Chandra Road) sweeps along a sea-facing promenade which runs from **Nariman Point** to **Malabar Hill**. Built on land reclaimed from the sea in the 1920s, it is also the main arterial link between the suburbs and the city's prime commercial and administrative centres, Nariman Point and the Fort area *(see p457)*. Situated at its eastern periphery is the **Oval Maidan**, nursery of such legendary Indian cricketing heroes as Sachin Tendulkar (b.1973) and Sunil Gavaskar (b.1949).

The buildings of Marine Drive are characterized by a strong Art Deco flavour, popular in Mumbai during the 1930s and 1940s. With the advent of electric elevators, and with concrete replacing the earlier stone and brick, the apartment blocks on the seafront were built to a uniform height of five floors, making this the most fashionable residential area of the time.

The best way to enjoy Marine Drive during the day is from the upper floor of a red double-decker bus, which provides panoramic views of the sea and the city's skyline. In the evening, it swarms with people taking their daily walks, couples meeting after work and families gathering around the vendors selling coconut water and

bhelpuri (see p445). **Chowpatty Beach** is the city's most popular promenade and the southern-most of Mumbai's beaches. Earlier cluttered with food stalls and hawkers, the area has now been substantially cleaned up in a drive by the civic authorities. An inexpensive evening destination for the city's residents, it remains lively till late at night. It is also the venue for Mumbai's largest festival, Ganesha Chaturthi *(see p471)*, when huge crowds gather at Chowpatty Beach to immerse images of Ganesha, the elephant-headed god, in the Arabian Sea.

The **National Centre for Performing Arts (NCPA)**, at the southern tip of Marine Drive, is the city's most active venue for music, dance and theatre performances. Its Tata Theatre and Experimental Theatre stage works by international and Indian playwrights with the best of local talent, while India's finest musicians and dancers perform regularly in its other auditoriums *(see pp466–7)*.

ⓖ Malabar Hill

Bounded by Napean Sea Rd,
Ridge Rd & Walkeshwar Rd.

This posh residential area, once dotted with bungalows set in large, forested compounds, is today crowded with highrise apartment blocks, home to Mumbai's rich and famous. The Parsi **Towers of Silence** are also located in this area. Parsis *(see p451)*, who believe that the elements of earth, water, air and fire are sacred and should not be defiled, place their dead in these tall, cylindrical stone towers to be picked clean by vultures. This, they believe, is one of the most environmentally friendly ways of disposing of the dead. A fall in Mumbai's vulture population, however, remains a cause of worry. A high wall and a thick belt of trees surround the Towers, which are closed to visitors.

The **Hanging Gardens** provide a pleasant open space in the vicinity, with good views of the city.

The Hanging Gardens, rising in tiers on Malabar Hill

⑰ Banganga

Walkeshwar, Malabar Hill.

Hidden amidst the soaring skyscrapers of Malabar Hill is the small settlement of Banganga, set around a sacred tank. According to legend, Rama, hero of the *Ramayana (see p31)*, pausing here while on his way to rescue his abducted wife Sita, shot an arrow into the ground and a spring gushed forth. This is the origin of the tank, and devotees take regular ritual dips in it. The site has several temples – the **Jabreshwar Mahadev**, at the tank's corner, is the prettiest, while the **Walkeshwar Temple**, built in the 18th century, has a linga said to have been built by Rama himself. Around the tank and temples are rest houses *(dharamsalas)* for pilgrims.

Khotachiwadi's narrow lanes and balconied houses

⑱ Khotachiwadi

Bounded by Jagannath Shankarshet Rd & Raja Ram Mohan Roy Rd, Girgaum.

In the narrow bylanes of Girgaum in central Mumbai is the old-fashioned neighbourhood of Khotachiwadi (literally, "Headman's Orchard"). Khotachiwadi grew as a suburban settlement, north of the Fort, in the 19th century, and retains the sleepy quality of a coastal village. The low, tile-roofed cottages have timber eaves and open verandahs with cast-iron balconies, the focal point for most daytime activities. The inhabitants were converted to Christianity by Portuguese missionaries

The Mahalaxmi Temple, dedicated to Lakshmi, the Goddess of Wealth

and adopted names such as Fernandes, D'Costa and D'Lima. Anant Ashram, a tiny eatery in Khotachiwadi's bylanes, serves excellent prawn curry and rice.

⑲ Mahalaxmi Temple

Mahalaxmi Temple Lane, off Bhulabhai Desai Rd.

Devotees, both rich and poor, throng this temple dedicated to Lakshmi, the Goddess of Wealth and Prosperity, who is also known as Laxmi in Maharashtra and in parts of Gujarat *(see p423)*. The approach is lined with stalls selling religious offerings, such as coconuts, flowers and small plastic icons. The temple's history dates to the 18th century, when an embankment being constructed along the bay was repeatedly washed away. The contractor dreamt that if a temple was built to Laxmi, the wall would hold. And this actually happened. Nearby is the **Mahalaxmi Race Course**,

next to Mahalaxmi Station, which has horse races every weekend from November to April. In its crowded stands the city's fashionable set rub shoulders with the poor and hopeful.

⑳ Haji Ali Mosque

Off Lala Lajpat Rai Marg. **Open** daily.

Approached by a long causeway which gets submerged at high tide, is the *dargah* (tomb) of a rich merchant, Haji Ali Shah Bukhari, who gave up his wealth after a pilgrimage to Mecca. The *dargah* dates to the 15th century, but the dazzling white mosque was built in the early 20th century and seems to float on its small island in the Arabian Sea. The causeway, usually lined with beggars, leads to a huge marble courtyard. The tomb lies at its centre and devotees touch their heads to the heavily embroidered *chador* (ceremonial cloth) covering it. Female devotees sit behind a *jali* (stone screen).

Haji Ali Mosque, built on an island linked to the shore by a causeway

㉑ Bandra

N of Mahim Bay. Mount St Mary Basilica: Mount Mary Rd. **Tel** (022) 2642 3152. **Open** daily. 🎪 Bandra fête (Sep).

The prosperous suburb of Bandra, in the north of Mumbai, is connected to the city by the Mahim Causeway. Amidst its modern apartment blocks, swanky boutiques and restaurants, are vestiges of its past as a small Portuguese enclave. The quiet lanes with tile-roofed bungalows are inhabited by a community of local East Indian Christians, whose ancestors were converted by the Portuguese. A number of Roman Catholic churches, too, were built by the Portuguese, who retained Bandra until the late 18th century. The most important of these is the **Mount St Mary Basilica**, which attracts devotees of all faiths. Outside the church is a bizarre market selling wax models of various body parts. Devotees with ailing limbs buy the appropriate model and solemnly place it on the altar before the Virgin Mary in the belief that she will effect a miraculous cure. A deserted Portuguese fort, **Castella de Aguada**, on a hill, offers spectacular views of the sea and the hinterland.

Bandra's plush **Pali Hill** locality, which has the villas of several Bollywood stars, draws crowds of star-struck Indian tourists. Its other attractions are the seafront promenades at **Bandstand** and **Carter Road**, especially popular with the local youth. Also situated here is a small Koli fishing village.

A vendor on Mumbai's crowded Juhu Beach

㉒ Juhu Beach

N of Bandra.

The sandy coastline of Juhu Beach lies north of the city centre. This is not a beach for leisurely sunbathing, though, since it is always crowded. On weekends, especially, it is packed with families of picnickers playing cricket on the beach, paddling tentatively in the water and enjoying the sea breeze. Vendors offering snacks, toys and fairground rides add to the *mela* (fair) atmosphere. Juhu also has several luxury hotels that serve as weekend retreats for Mumbai's tycoons and Bollywood film stars.

The **Prithvi Theatre**, on Juhu Church Road, was founded in 1978 by one of Bollywood's leading families, the Kapoors. It stages plays in Hindi, Gujarati and English, and has a lively café, popular with Mumbai's arty crowd. A theatre festival is held in November *(see p466)*.

㉓ Film City

Goregaon East. 🛈 Contact Film City's Public Relations Office (022) 2840 1533.

Built in 1978 to meet the needs of Mumbai's booming Hindi film industry, better known as Bollywood *(see pp36–7)*, Film City sprawls over 140 ha (346 acres) in the city's northern outskirts. Bollywood produces some 800 feature films a year, making it the world's largest film industry, rivalled only by South India's Telugu and Tamil film industries. Film City is where many Bollywood blockbusters are shot, as are most TV soaps and serials. Song-and-dance routines, scenes of tear-jerking melodrama and action-packed fight sequences take place simultaneously on Film City's dozen shooting stages, against outsize backdrops of medieval forts, dense jungles and opulent cardboard palaces. In between takes, mythological heroes rub shoulders with rifle-toting bandits and skimpily clad vamps.

㉔ Sanjay Gandhi National Park

Borivili. 🛈 Conservation Education Centre, near elephant gate Goregaon, (022) 2842 1174. **Open** Tue–Sun. 🚫 🎫 Kanheri Caves: **Open** Tue–Sun. 🚫

An hour's train ride north of Mumbai, this national park is one of the few in India within the limits of a city. Surrounded by rolling hills, its deciduous forests harbour a wealth of birdlife and fauna, wild boar, cobras, as well as the occasional tiger. Tiger and Lion Safaris are offered in fenced-off sections of the park.

In a picturesque wooded area of the park is an extra-ordinary complex of 109 Buddhist caves, the **Kanheri Caves**, dating from the 1st to the 9th centuries AD. The 6th-century **Cave 3** is the most impressive, with its colossal Buddhas, richly carved pillars and brackets and hemispherical stupa. The caves are best approached through the Park's northern entrance.

Dancers practising a song sequence for the film, *Ready* at Film City

㉕ Elephanta Island

Located on an island off Mumbai's eastern shore, the 6th-century AD Elephanta cave temples, chiselled into a rocky cliff and dedicated to Shiva, contain some great masterpieces of Indian sculpture. Originally called Gharapuri, or "Island of Caves", the island was renamed Elephanta by the Portuguese after a huge stone elephant that once stood here. This is now in the garden of the Bhau Daji Lad Museum in Mumbai's Byculla area. A UNESCO World Heritage Site, the Elephanta cave temples can be visited on a day trip by boat from Mumbai.

Plan of Elephanta Caves

1 Northern Entrance	6 Marriage of Shiva-Parvati
2 Mahesamurti	7 Shiva spearing Andhaka
3 Ardhanarishvara	8 Eastern Entrance
4 Gangadhara	9 Shiva and Parvati
5 Western Entrance	Playing Dice

VISITORS' CHECKLIST

Practical Information
9 km (6 miles) NE of Mumbai.
🛈 for ferries, (022) 2202 6364.
Open Wed–Mon. 🛈 🛈
🎭 Elephanta Music & Dance
Festival (Feb).

Transport
🚢 from Gateway of India
at 9am

The Elephanta caves, cut into the cliff high above the water

Exploring Elephanta

The origins of the cave temples at Elephanta are lost in obscurity, but in all probability they date to the 6th century AD and represent the period of Brahmanical revival after Buddhism began to decline. From the pier, where visitors disembark from the boats, a long flight of 125 steps leads to the temple's main **Northern Entrance**. This is a huge square hall with sides measuring 40 m (131 ft), supported by two dozen massive pillars. Here, in a deep recess against the rear (south) wall, is the huge triple-headed Shiva statue, the **Mahesamurti**, also known as Trimurthy. This is the glory of Elephanta, and few visitors can fail to be moved by this powerful, compelling image, hailed by art historian Percy Brown as "the creation of a genius". The three faces represent Shiva in his different manifestations. The central face, with its elaborate crown, depicts Shiva the Preserver, sublimely serene and introspective. The one facing west represents Shiva the Creator, gentle, solicitous and graceful. The head facing east, with its cruel mouth, fiercely hooked nose and serpents adorning the hair, shows Shiva as the Destroyer. On either side of the statue are other superb sculptures. The one on the east shows Shiva as **Ardhanarishvara** – the Lord who is both Male and Female, and thus symbolizes the Divine Unity in which all opposites

are resolved. The image on the west is of Shiva as **Gangadhara**, helping the river goddess Ganga descend to earth (see p167) while his consort Parvati and other deities look on.

Contrasting images of peace and violence, joy and fury, can be seen in exquisite sculptures throughout the temple. Thus, one sculpture near the **Western Entrance** lyrically depicts the marriage of Shiva and Parvati, while opposite it is a powerful panel showing Shiva brutally impaling the demon Andhaka. The **Eastern Entrance** has Shiva and Parvati contentedly playing dice in their mountain abode, as the demon-king Ravana tries to destroy their home by shaking the mountain.

The 5.5-m (18-ft) high Mahesamurti, dominating the cave temple

Shopping & Entertainment in Mumbai

Mumbai is one of India's best shopping destinations. Large malls, department stores and exclusive boutiques stocking international brand names, coexist with traditional bazaars and pavement stalls selling everything from diamonds to dentures. Mumbai also has a vibrant nightlife, with more discotheques and pubs than any other Indian city. As the home of the Hindi film industry, Bollywood, Mumbai often holds gala premiere nights at its many cinema halls. The city's crowded cultural calendar also includes several concerts, exhibitions, theatre shows and festivals. But perhaps the best entertainment the city offers is the non-stop circus on its bustling streets and sidewalks.

Shops and Markets

South Mumbai's main shopping areas include Colaba Causeway, Kemp's Corner, and the shopping arcade in the Oberoi Hotel at Nariman Point. The traditional market for fresh produce is Crawford Market (see p457), while Bhuleshwar and Kalbadevi, north of the Fort area, are popular haunts for textiles and jewellery. Atria and Crossroads, near the Haji Ali Dargah, are two popular shopping malls. Further out, Inorbit (at Malad), Oberoi (in Goregaon East) and the Palladium (in Lower Parel, at Phoenix Mills) also draw large crowds of shoppers.

Antiques and Jewellery

A good place for antiques is Chor Bazaar, or "Thieves' Market", near Crawford Market. This warren of shops is crammed with colonial furniture, Victorian bric-a-brac and Chinese porcelain, along with a lot of junk and fakes. Very good bargains can still be found here. **Phillips Antiques**, on Shyama Prasad Mukherjee Chowk, stocks a fine collection of old postcards, prints and Raj-era lithographs. Note that strict rules govern the export of antiques (see p734).

Central Mumbai's Zaveri Bazaar is lined with jewellers' shops, **Tribhovandas Bhimji Zaveri** being the most famous. **Nayaab Jewels**, in Khar, has a great collection of antique jewellery. The shopping arcades at the **Oberoi** and **Taj Hotels** (see p700 & p700) are also good places to shop for jewellery.

Textiles and Fashion

Mumbai is a fashion-conscious city, and most Indian designers have outlets here. Exclusive boutiques include **Ensemble**, **Melange** and **Tarun Tahiliani**, while casual ready-made garments are available at **Cotton World**. The Oberoi Hotel (see p700) houses, exclusively, Gucci and Jimmy Choo stores. **Fantasia**, **Indian Textiles** and **Fabindia** specialize in traditional Indian textiles and weaves, including silk saris, home furnishings and accessories. For good quality handwoven home furnishings and floor coverings, the best shop is **Shyam Ahuja**.

Handicrafts and Gifts

Handicrafts from all over India are available in Mumbai. The widest range and best quality can be found at the **Cottage Industries Emporium**, **Contemporary Arts and Crafts** and **Bombay Store** in the Fort area. **Chimanlal's** has a good selection of handmade paper, while **Inshallah Maashallah** stocks pure perfume essence (attar) in tiny glass bottles capturing the fragrances of rose, vetiver and jasmine.

Mumbai is renowned for its high quality leather goods at reasonable prices. **Rasulbhai Adamji** at Colaba, and many shops in the Oberoi Shopping Centre have a good range of jackets, handbags, wallets and luggage, some of it "inspired" by Gucci, Prada and Louis Vuitton. **Joy Shoes** at the Taj Hotel has high quality shoes and leather accessories. Books, CDs and audio cassettes of both Indian and Western music, are available at various outlets throughout the city, including hotel bookshops. However, one of the best shops for music is **Rhythm House**.

Entertainment Guides, Tickets and Venues

Daily newspapers list the day's entertainment and events on their engagements page. Other good sources of information are the magazines *TimeOut Mumbai* and *Know Your City Mumbai*. A useful website which offers online information on cultural events and entertainment is *www.explocity.com* Tickets for most concerts and plays can be bought at **Rhythm House** or at the venue itself. The major venues for Mumbai's cultural events are the **NCPA** or National Centre for the Performing Arts (see p462), the **Nehru Centre** auditorium and **Shanmu khananda Hall**. **Prithvi Theatre** in Juhu (see p464) is a lively centre for stage productions. Other active exhibition venues include the **Jehangir Art Gallery**, the **NGMA** (National Gallery of Modern Art) and the Artists' Centre, located at Kala Ghoda (see pp452–3).

Performing Arts

Mumbai is a great centre of classical Indian music, and many well-known performers can be heard here. This cosmopolitan city also has many enthusiasts of jazz and Western classical music (conductor Zubin Mehta received his early training in Mumbai) and frequent concerts are held by both local and visiting international groups. Classical and folk dance performances from different parts of the country also feature regularly on the cultural calendar. Mumbai has a vibrant theatre tradition, with productions in

English as well as Marathi, Gujarati and Hindi. These are often staged in the open at **Horniman Circle Gardens** *(see p456)*. The cultural high season is from November to April, though performances take place through the year.

Cinema

As the capital of the Hindi film industry, Mumbai hosts a number of film-related events. Most of the film studios are located in the suburbs as are the private residences of most screen celebrities. Great fanfare precedes the release of big-budget blockbusters, and glittering premieres are held at popular cinema halls such as **Sterling**, **Regal** and **Fun**

Cinemas. These draw star-struck fans who spend hours standing outside, waiting for a glimpse of their favourite stars. Film festivals, documentary film screenings, lectures, talks and exhibitions are also held throughout the year at various venues, such as the **British Council**.

Heritage Tours

The Maharashtra Tourism Development Corporation (MTDC), offers guided tours of Mumbai on double-decker buses. **Bombay Heritage Walks**, organized by a group of young architects, take visitors through historical districts such as Banganga, Khotachiwadi and the Fort area, on weekends, except during the monsoon

(June to September). Prior booking is necessary.

Nightclubs and Bars

Mumbai's nightlife is more active than that of any other Indian city. While nightclubs and bars open and close at regular intervals, some have remained consistently popular. One of the liveliest is **Hard Rock Café**, ingeniously housed in a mill compound in Worli. In south Mumbai, **Pizza by the Bay** has live music Wednesday through Saturday. Most hotels have their own bars and nightclubs, such as **Enigma** at the JW Marriott, which attracts Bollywood's A-list stars. Another favourite haunt of Mumbai's jetset is **Ghost**, one of the city's trendiest nightspots.

DIRECTORY

Antiques and Jewellery

Nayaab Jewels
490, 17th Road Khar, Khar.
Tel (022) 2648 0633.

Phillips Antiques
SP Mukherjee Chowk, Colaba. **Tel** (022) 2202 0564.

Tribhovandas Bhimji Zaveri
Zaveri Bazaar.
Tel (022) 4046 5001.

Textiles and Fashion

Cotton World
Mandlik Rd, Colaba.
Tel (022) 6634 5555.

Ensemble
Great Western Bldg, Shahid Bhagat Singh Marg. **Tel** (022) 2287 2883.

Fabindia
Oberoi Shopping Centre.
Tel (022) 2842 9272.

Fantasia
Oberoi Shopping Centre.
Tel (022) 2284 6362.

Indian Textiles
Taj Hotel, Apollo Bunder.
Tel (022) 2202 8783.

Melange
Altamount Rd.
Tel (022) 2385 4492.

Shyam Ahuja
Crossroads Mall.
Tel (022) 2495 3435.

Tarun Tahiliani
Ramchandani Marg, Apollo Bunder. **Tel** (022) 2287 0895.

Handicrafts and Gifts

Bombay Store
Western India House, PM Rd, Fort Area.
Tel (022) 4066 9999.

Chimanlal's
Fort Area.
Tel (022) 2207 7717.

Contemporary Arts and Crafts
Napean Sea Rd.
Tel (022) 2363 0740.

Cottage Industries Emporium
Chhatrapati Shivaji M Rd.
Tel (022) 2282 8876.

Inshallah Maashallah
Colaba.**Tel** (022) 2204 9495.

Joy Shoes
Taj Hotel, Apollo Bunder.
Tel (022) 2202 8696.

Rasulbhai Adamji
Colaba. **Tel** (022) 2202 1267.

Rhythm House
Kala Ghoda.
Tel (022) 2284 2835.

Entertainment Information

w explocity.com

Entertainment Venues

British Council
Nariman Point.
Tel (022) 2282 3530.

Jehangir Art Gallery
Fort Area.
Tel (022) 2284 3989.

NGMA
Kala Ghoda.
Tel (022) 2285 2457.

NCPA
Nariman Point.
Tel (022) 2283 4500.

Nehru Centre
Worli. **Tel** (022) 2496 4676.

Prithvi Theatre
Janaki Kutir, Juhu.
Tel (022) 2614 9546.

Shanmukhananda Hall
King's Circle.
Tel (022) 2401 5164.

Cinema

Fun Cinemas
Andheri West.
Tel 921 993 5050.

Regal
Shyama Prasad Mukherjee Chowk.
Tel (022) 2202 1017.

Sterling
Hazarimal Somani Marg.
Tel (022) 2207 5187.

Heritage Tours

Bombay Heritage Walks
Tel (022) 2369 0992.

Nightclubs and Bars

Enigma
JW Marriott, Juhu.
Tel (022) 6693 3000.

Ghost
Minoo Desai Marg, Colaba.
Tel (022) 2287 6305.

Hard Rock Café
Bombay Dyeing Mill Compound.
Tel (022) 2438 2888.

Pizza by the Bay
Marine Drive.
Tel (022) 2284 3646.

MAHARASHTRA

Verdant hills, scenic coastal plains and busy industrial centres make up the varied landscape of Maharashtra, which covers an area of 308,000 sq km (118,920 sq miles). The hills of the Western Ghats, source of many rivers, run parallel to the narrow Konkan Coast, while cradled in the centre is the Deccan Plateau, formed from black volcanic lava 70 million years ago. This area saw a great flowering of art and architecture from the 2nd century BC onwards, and two famous UNESCO World Heritage sites are located here – the Buddhist caves at Ajanta and the rock-cut temples at Ellora. The rocky terrain around Pune is dotted with the massive forts built by the 17th- century Maratha leader, Shivaji, who launched successful guerrilla campaigns against the Mughals. His cult-like status is today perpetuated by the Shiv Sena, a nationalist political party. Modern Maharashtra is a prosperous, highly industrialized region, with a strong agrarian base. Cotton and tobacco are widely cultivated, as are a variety of fruits including oranges, *chikoos* (sapodilla) and mangoes.

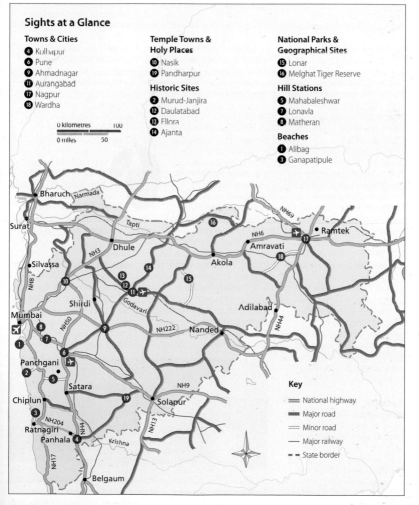

Sights at a Glance

Towns & Cities
- ④ Kolhapur
- ⑥ Pune
- ⑨ Ahmadnagar
- ⑪ Aurangabad
- ⑰ Nagpur
- ⑱ Wardha

Temple Towns & Holy Places
- ⑩ Nasik
- ⑲ Pandharpur

Historic Sites
- ② Murud-Janjira
- ⑫ Daulatabad
- ⑬ Ellora
- ⑭ Ajanta

National Parks & Geographical Sites
- ⑮ Lonar
- ⑯ Melghat Tiger Reserve

Hill Stations
- ⑤ Mahabaleshwar
- ⑦ Lonavla
- ⑧ Matheran

Beaches
- ① Alibag
- ③ Ganapatipule

0 kilometres 100
0 miles 50

Bharuch — Narmada
Surat
Tapti
Silvassa
NH3
Dhule
NH8
⑩
Shirdi
⑬ ⑫ ⑭
⑪
Godavari
Mumbai
⑧
NH50
⑦
⑨
① ⑥
Panchgani
② ⑤
Satara
Chiplun
③
NH204
Ratnagiri
Panhala ④
Krishna
NH17
Belgaum

NH69
⑯
NH6
Amravati ⑰ Ramtek
Akola ⑱
⑮
Adilabad
NH222 Nanded
NH44
NH9
Solapur
⑲
NH13

Key
═ National highway
▬ Major road
═ Minor road
— Major railway
- - State border

View of the imposing Janjira Fort, built on an island

❶ Alibag

Raigarh district. 108 km (67 miles) S of Mumbai. 🚌 🚢 from Gateway of India, Mumbai, to Mandve, 18 km (11 miles) N of Alibag, then bus.

The port of Alibag was developed by the Marathas in the 17th century to protect their kingdom from the Dutch, Portuguese and the increasingly powerful British. Alibag is today a quiet town, just across the bay from Mumbai. Its most impressive sight is its beach, a 5-km (3-mile) stretch of soft silver sand, lined by a stand of coconut and casuarina trees.

Kolaba Fort, constructed on an island in 1662 by the Maratha ruler Chhatrapati Shivaji (see p475), looms over the skyline. It is a forbidding grey mass of lead, steel and stone, built on a rock jutting from the sea, and can be reached on foot during low tide. Within its high ramparts are enclosed a temple dedicated to Lord Ganesha, and next to it a sweet-water well that must have been useful during sieges. There are two main entrances to the fort, one from the shore and another from the sea. The enormous shore-side doorway is decorated with sculptures of tigers, elephants and peacocks.

Environs
Kihim Beach, 9 km (6 miles) north of Alibag, is a tranquil getaway, with woods brimming with birds and wild flowers. It was the favourite haunt of the famous Indian ornithologist Salim Ali (1896–1987), author of the finest book on Indian birds.

❷ Murud–Janjira

Raigarh district. 165 km (103 miles) S of Mumbai. 🚌 from Gateway of India, Mumbai to Mandve, 120 km (74 miles) N of Murud, then bus. 🚢 from Rajpuri to Janjira Fort.

A sleepy coastal town with Indo-Gothic houses and meandering pathways, Murud has a picture-perfect beach that promises lazy, sunny afternoons and cool dips in the clean sea. The little village of Rajpuri, 4 km (2.5 miles) south of the main Murud town, is the gateway to the Janjira Fort, the strongest island-fort in the Konkan, still enduring the surge and retreat of the Arabian Sea. Boats are available at Rajpuri to take visitors to the fort.

Also evocatively known as the Jazeere Mehboob or "Moon Fort", it was built in 1511 by the Siddis, who originally arrived in the Deccan from Abyssinia as slave-traders. The fortress, with its high ramparts, 22 bastions and granite walls jointed with lead to withstand the onslaught of the sea, proved invincible against attacks by the Portuguese and British, and even against the great Maratha leader, Shivaji.

Steps lead to a sturdy stone gate, where a stone engraving of a lion holding six diminutive elephants in captivity, represents six successive Siddi victories. Rusty cannons point outwards through niches in the ramparts. The palaces, gardens and mosques lie in silent ruin, and luxurious vegetation grows around the palace of the Siddi ruler, Sirul Khan.

❸ Ganapatipule

Ratnagiri district. 375 km (233 miles) S of Mumbai. 🚉 Ratnagiri, 22 km (14 miles) S of Ganapatipule, then bus. 🚌 🎪 Gauri Ganapati (Sep/Oct).

The small coastal village of Ganapatipule is named after the 400-year-old temple of Swayambhu Ganapati. Here, the self-originated idol of Ganapati (the local name of Lord Ganesha) is revered by Hindus as one of the eight sacred sites, or "Ashtha Ganapatis", in India. Devotees show respect to the deity by performing a *pradakshina*, a walk around the hill near the temple. The beach has long stretches of pristine white sands and clear waters. Beyond the coast lie groves of fruit trees, including mango, banana, jackfruit, coconut and betel nut.

Alphonso mango

Environs
Ratnagiri, 25 km (16 miles) south of Ganapatipule, is famous for its groves of delicious Alphonso mangoes, locally known as *hapus*. Ratnagiri's fortress, Bala Qila, is situated along the coast, and is intact, with a notable Bhagavati temple within its walls.

The Swayambhu Ganapati Temple, at the base of a hill in Ganapatipule

Ganesha, the Remover of Obstacles

Lord Ganesha, the elephant-headed son of Shiva and Parvati, is the most auspicious and popular deity in India, and especially beloved in Maharashtra. Images of the endearing, potbellied god are found in every household, on temple doorways and shop entrances, on letterheads and wedding invitations. No task or enterprise is ever begun without invoking him, as he is the Lord of New Beginnings. Worshipped in many guises, he is Vighneshvara, the Remover of Obstacles, and Siddhidata, the God of Prosperity and Success. Ganesha is above all a friend, lovable and benign, and his festival, Ganesha Chaturthi, crosses all social boundaries uniting the people of Maharashtra in a frenzied ten-day celebration.

Lord Ganesha

Lord Ganesha's four arms hold his various attributes. Two of these, his broken tusk and a round sweetmeat called modaka, appear consistently. In the other two hands, he sometimes holds a lotus blossom, an elephant goad, an axe or prayer beads. According to legend, Ganesha gained his elephant head after Shiva, in a state of fury, cut his son's head off and then, in remorse, stuck on the head of a passing elephant.

Elephant goad

A half halo indicates his divinity.

The broken tusk, used as a pen to write the *Mahabharata*, was the result of an encounter with Parasuram *(see p683)*.

Modaka

A rat is the vehicle of Ganesha

Intricate clay images of Ganesha are made and consecrated on the first day of Ganesha Chaturthi *(see p477)*. These are then enshrined in *pandals* or decorated stages, and worshipped continuously for ten days amidst Hindi and Marathi recitations and musical performances.

Colourful floats, accompanied by folk dancers, lead the serpentine processions that fill the streets, amidst chants and drumbeats. The processions end at the water's edge, where hundreds of idols are immersed in rivers, lakes or the sea. This final immersion on the tenth day marks the deity's return to his abode.

See also features on Hindu Mythology *(see pp28–9)*, Shiva *(see p570)* and Vishnu *(see p683)*.

Colourful fishing boats docked off the Malvan coast

❹ Kolhapur

Kolhapur district. 396 km (246 miles) S of Pune. 🏔 493,200. 🚗 🚌 ⓘ Maharashtra Tourism, (0231) 265 2935.

Situated on the banks of the Panchganga river, the city of Kolhapur is a thriving commercial centre, noted today for its flourishing dairy industry. It is also one of Maharashtra's most important pilgrimage sites, associated from early times with the worship of Shakti (the Mother Goddess). Ruled by the Hindu Yadava dynasty between the 10th and 13th centuries, it was later occupied by the Mughals. In 1659, Kolhapur was finally seized by the Maratha chief Shivaji (see p475), and was later inherited by his younger son. The state remained with the Bhonsles (one of the four Maratha princely families) until Independence.

Of the numerous temples in Kolhapur, the **Shri Mahalakshmi** or Amba Bai Temple, dedicated to the Mother Goddess, is the most venerated. Built in the 7th century by the Chalukya king Karnadeva, the temple's idol, said to be a *swayambhu*, or naturally occurring monolith, is encrusted with diamonds and other precious stones. The *mandapa* has a finely carved ceiling. Behind the temple are the remains of the **Old Palace** or Rajwada, where members of the former maharaja's family still live.

Kolhapuri chappals

Its huge entrance hall was once used for large public wedding ceremonies. Situated near the palace gates are the town's wrestling grounds, where young men practise traditional Indian wrestling, known as *kushti*.

The **New Palace**, 2 km (1.3 miles) north of the city centre, was completed in 1881 and designed by Major Charles Mant (see p422), who merged European, Jain, Hindu and Islamic elements to create a style which widely

The Malvan Coast

Fishing boat, Malvan coast

The Southern Konkan coastline in the Sindhudurg district, known as the Malvan Coast, is dotted with marine forts and pretty fishing villages that are worth visiting. **Vijaydurg Fort**, 525 km (326 miles) south of Mumbai, stands on the site of an 11th-century fort, rebuilt by the Bijapur sultans (see pp546–7) in the 16th century. In 1654, it was further renovated by Shivaji, who added three layers of fortifications, 27 bastions and 300 guns. It became the main naval base for the great Maratha admiral Kanhoji Angre, who used the fort to plunder European ships in 1698. It fell to the British in 1756; a platform stands within the grounds, where British astronomers set up their telescopes to study a solar eclipse. About 74 km (46 miles) south of Vijaydurg, **Sindhudurg Fort**, built by Shivaji in 1664, lies deserted on an island known as Kurte. With its 10-m (33-ft) high ramparts, it was a Maratha stronghold until power shifted to Vijaydurg. Shivaji's palm and feet impressions are preserved in mortar near the entrance. The fort contains the only temple of Shivaji in the world and is the only place in Maharashtra where a statue of Shivaji depicts him without a beard. The small port of **Malvan**, 4 km (2.5 miles) north of Sindhudurg, lends its name to this stretch of coast. It is being developed into a beach resort, as is **Vengurla**, 56 km (35 miles) to the south.

Savantwadi, 23 km (14 miles) east of Vengurla, was the capital of the Bhonsle kings. The art of making *ganjifa* cards (painted, circular playing cards) was developed here. The town is also known for its wooden toys and lacquer work. **Amboli**, 25 km (16 miles) northeast of Savantwadi, is a pretty hill station.

A view of Vijaydurg Fort, overlooking fishing boats in the bay

became known as the Indo-Saracenic style of architecture. The palace is today the **Shahaji Chhatrapati Museum** and displays a collection of royal memorabilia, including garments, hunting photographs and one of Mughal emperor Aurangzeb's swords.

The **Town Hall**, another structure designed by Charles Mant, has a small museum with a number of artifacts from nearby excavation sites. Kolhapur is also famous for its hand-crafted leather slippers, known as Kolhapuri *chappals*.

Old Palace
Open daily.

New Palace
Open daily. Shahaji Chhatrapati Museum: **Open** Tue–Sun.

Environs
One of the most important forts in the Deccan is at **Panhala**, a hill station 19 km (12 miles) northwest of Kolhapur. Situated on a steep hillside, the fortress is well protected by three impressive double walled gates, and 7-km (4 mile) long ramparts. Within its walls stand two temples, one dedicated to Amba Bai and the other to Maruti, the Wind God. The most interesting monuments are the huge stone granaries, the largest of which, Ganga Kothi, covers 948 sq m (10,204 sq ft). Established in the 12th century by Raja Bhoja II, the fortress fell successively to the Yadavas, the Adil Shahis of Bijapur, Shivaji, Emperor Aurangzeb and the British. There are many private homes

Panhala Fort in the picturesque Sahyadri Hills, after the monsoon

Panchgani, with spectacular views of the Krishna river

in Panhala as well, including that of the famous Indian singer Lata Mangeshkar (*see p507*).

❺ Mahabaleshwar

Satara district. 115 km (72 miles) SW of Pune. 12,800. Cycles available.

The largest hill station in Maharashtra, Mahabalesh-war is situated 1,372 m (4,501 ft) above sea level. In 1828, Sir John Malcolm, Governor of Bombay, chose this beautiful spot as the site for the official sanatorium. Soon after, the wooded slopes were covered with typical colonial structures, among them **Christ Church**, **Frere Hall**, **Government House** (which was the grand residence of the governor), the **Mahabaleshwar Club**, and the ever-popular polo grounds and race course.

Water spout, Krishna Temple

Due to its high altitude, the town has a cool climate and offers many pleasant walks. There are also several lookout points such as **Bombay Point**, from where the sea can be seen on a clear day, and **Arthur's Seat**, which affords panoramic views of the Konkan Coast. **Venna Lake** has facilities for boating.

In the old town is the sacred **Krishna Temple**, supposedly built on the legendary site of the Panchganga, or source of five rivers – the Koyna, Savitri, Venna, Gayatri and the mighty Krishna. The latter covers 1,400 km (870

miles), stretching from this spot to the Bay of Bengal on the east coast. The temple has a much venerated, naturally occurring Shivalinga, and a small tank. There are two other temples here, dedicated to Hanuman and Rama. There are also several berry farms close by, where visitors can help to pick strawberries, raspberries and mulberries.

Environs
The hill station of **Panchgani**, 18 km (11 miles) east of Mahabaleshwar, is surrounded by five hills. The town is the starting point for many scenic trekking trails (*see p477*). It is also dotted with some charming old British and Parsi bungalows, some of which can be visited. The majestic hill-top forts of **Pratapgarh** and **Raigad**, 18 km (11 miles) west and 70 km (44 miles) northwest of Mahabaleshwar respectively, were both Maratha strongholds. They offer commanding views of the surrounding countryside.

About 111 km (69 miles) south of Mahabaleshwar is **Chiplun**, lying on the banks of the Vashishti river, whose waters supply Koyna Lake, a large man-made reservoir. The town is well-known for its irrigation scheme, developed in the 1980s, that provides water to the coastal fringe between the Sahyadri Hills and the sea. This quiet place offers splendid views of the Vashishti river as it winds through the hills.

The sprawling campus of Pune University

❻ Pune

Pune district. 163 km (101 miles) SE of Mumbai. 🚗 3,530,000. ✈ 12 km (7 miles) NE of city centre, then taxi or auto. 🚉 🚌 ℹ Maharashtra Tourism, I Block, Central Bldg, (020) 2612 6867. 🎉 Ganesha Chaturthi (Aug/Sep).

The fast-growing, industrial city of Pune is situated on the Deccan Plateau, at the confluence of the Mutha and Mula rivers, and is bounded by the Sahyadris in the west. Its pleasant climate and proximity to Mumbai made it the perfect monsoon capital for the British in the 19th century. Then called Poona, it became an important administrative centre and military cantonment. Even today, the Indian army's Southern Command is based here.

Pune was also the childhood home of the Maratha leader, Shivaji. From 1750 until 1817, it was the capital of the Maratha Confederacy and was ruled by the Peshwas. The remains of their **Shaniwar Wada Palace** is in the old city. Built in 1736, the palace was razed in a fire in 1828. Only its outer walls and the main entrance with large spikes, designed to deter the enemy's elephants, survive. Further south is **Vishram Bagh Wada**, a beautiful Peshwa palace with an elaborate wooden façade.

For many visitors, Pune is synonymous with the famous **Osho International Commune** founded by Bhagwan Rajneesh or Osho, and situated at Koregaon Park in the north of the city.

The flamboyant pop mystic, or "sex guru" as he was called, had a meteoric rise in the West. Even after his demise in 1990, his well-appointed ashram continues to attract devotees from Europe and America. Housed in a traditional Maratha house or *wada*, is the charming privately owned **Raja Dinkar Kelkar Museum**. On display is a collection of beautiful everyday objects such as pots, lamps, pens, ink stands, nutcrackers, and other utilitarian items. An interesting piece is a Maharashtrian Chitrakathi scroll painting, used in folk theatre performances.

The **Tribal Museum**, east of the railway station, showcases the state's tribal cultures, especially from the Sahyadri and Gondwana regions.

The **Aga Khan Palace**, across the Mula river to the north of the city, is where Mahatma Gandhi was imprisoned by the British for two years; today, it is the Gandhi National Memorial. Gandhi's wife, Kasturba, died here and her ashes have been interred in a memorial in the gardens.

Other places of interest in the city include St Mary's Church, a fine garrison structure consecrated in 1825; the rock-cut Pataleshwar Cave Temple, dating from the 8th century; the Parvati Temple perched on a hilltop; and fine gardens, such as Empress

A Warli painting from Raja Dinkar Kelkar Museum

Botanical Gardens and Bund Gardens. Pune is the centre of Maratha culture, with a lively tradition of theatre, classical music and dance. It is also an important university town and is home to the prestigious government-run Film and Television Institute and the National Film Archives.

Environs

About 24 km (15 miles) south-west is the **National Defence Academy**, the training school for army, navy and air force cadets, at Khadakvasla. Further southwest are the forts of **Rajgad** and **Sinhgad** (the "Lion Fort"). The latter is associated with Shivaji's general, Tanaji Malasure. According to legend, he tied strong ropes to monitor lizards, made the creatures stick to the fort walls with their adhesive foot pads, and thus scaled the walls and captured the fort.

🏛 **Osho International Commune**
Tel (020) 6601 9999. **Open** daily. 🚫 📷

🏛 **Raja Dinkar Kelkar Museum**
1378, Shukrawar Peth.
Tel (020) 2447 4466. **Open** daily.
Closed public hols. 🚫

🏛 **Tribal Museum**
28 Gardens, off Koregaon Rd.
Open daily.

🏛 **Aga Khan Palace**
Ahmadnagar Rd. **Tel** (020) 2688 0250. **Open** Mon–Sat.
Closed 2nd & 4th Sat, public hols. 🚫

Vishram Bagh Wada, a Peshwa palace in the heart of the old city

Shivaji and the Marathas

Maharashtra's greatest hero, Shivaji, was born in 1627 to Shahji Bhonsle, a chieftain from Pune who served the sultans of Bijapur *(see pp546–9)*. Daring, ambitious and restless since his boyhood, by the age of 19 he had become the head of a band of intrepid fighters. Soon, Shivaji's brilliant guerrilla tactics against Emperor Aurangzeb and the powerful Mughal army, and his swift conquests of mountain and sea forts, enabled him to establish a separate Maratha kingdom. In 1674, he was crowned Chhatrapati, the traditional title of a Hindu monarch, at his capital, Raigad. When he died in 1680, at the age of 53, he left behind a powerful Maratha state, which continued to play an important role in Indian history for the next 100 years.

Waghnakh ("tiger's claw"), a deadly hand weapon, was used by Shivaji to overcome and kill Afzal Khan, the Bijapur general, in a "friendly" meeting at Pratapgad.

Maratha horsemen were feared for their lightning raids which wrought havoc on enemy territory. The Deccan Plateau's hilly terrain aided their guerrilla tactics against the Mughals.

जय भवानी

Shivaji is revered all over Maharashtra as a god-like hero. A fearless soldier and charismatic leader, he united the Marathas into a formidable force that defied the mighty Mughals. Today, he has become a symbol for the Hindu revivalist movement.

Fortresses, such as Rajgad and Raigad *(see p473)* and the sea forts *(see p472)* along the west coast, were the key to Maratha strategy and success. Shivaji's conquest of the crucial Purandhar Fort in 1649 compelled the sultan of Bijapur to condemn him as a rebel.

Shaniwar Wada was the former residence of the Peshwas, who came to power after Shivaji's grandson's death. The other main clans of the Maratha Confederacy – which was a significant power in the 18th century – were Holkars *(see p250)*, Scindias *(see pp232–3)*, Gaekwads *(see p423)* and Bhonsles *(see p472)*.

The Buddhist *chaitya griha* at Karla Cave, near Lonavla

❼ Lonavla

Pune district. 62 km (39 miles) NW of Pune. 🚂 55,700. 🚉 🚌 Karla Cave: 🛈 Maharashtra Tourism, Karla, (02114) 282 230. **Open** daily. 🏛 Bhaja Caves: 🏛

Situated on the main train line from Mumbai to Pune, Lonavla was once a sleepy hill station famous for its *chikki*, a type of caramelized sweet. It has now become an extremely popular weekend getaway for city-dwellers from nearby Mumbai. Spread around the bustling main street, lined with souvenir shops, the town offers pleasant walks and is a convenient base for exploring the surrounding hills.

Environs

About 8 km (5 miles) northwest of Lonavla is **Khandala**, another pretty town with panoramic views of the scenic Western Ghats. The famous Buddhist rock-cut **Karla Cave**, 11 km (7 miles) east of Lonavla, dates from the 2nd to 1st centuries BC. The splendid *chaitya griha* (*see p24*), the largest and best preserved of the early Buddhist caves in the Deccan, is the most significant sight here. It has a magnificently sculpted courtyard, a towering 14-m (46-ft) high façade with a horseshoe shaped window, and a large pillared hall with a monolithic stupa. The 20-odd **Bhaja Caves**, located 3 km (2 miles) off the Karla road, are the oldest in the region, dating from the 2nd century BC. Cave 12, a *chaitya griha*, still contains the remains of wooden beams on its ceiling. On either side of the façade are carvings of multistoreyed structures with windows and balconies.

Statue of a divine couple, Karla Cave

The **Bedsa Caves**, situated 9 km (6 miles) southeast of Bhaja, date to the 1st century AD. The roof of the main cave bears faint traces of paintings.

❽ Matheran

Raigarh district. 118 km (73 miles) NW of Pune. 🚂 5,200. 🚉 From Neral Junction, take the toy train to Matheran (2 hrs). 🚌 🛈 Opp railway station.

The closest hill station to Mumbai, Matheran (meaning "Mother Forest" or "Forest on Top") lies at a height of 803 m (2,635 ft) above sea level. This picturesque town is situated in the forested Sahyadri Hills. In 1855, Lord Elphinstone, the governor of Bombay, visited Matheran, and the town soon became fashionable. The stately **Elphinstone Lodge** that he built became his weekend retreat. A railway line was laid in 1907, and a quaint toy train (*see p753*) still winds its way slowly through hills and forests from the junction at Neral. All motor vehicles are completely banned within the limits of the town, making it uniquely peaceful, despite the burgeoning crowds of visitors, particularly on weekends.

Matheran has as many as 33 lookout points. **Porcupine Point** or Sunset Point, a favourite with sightseers, is known for its spectacular sunsets. **Louisa Point** has views of the ruined Prabal Fort and a mountain trail called Shivaji's Ladder. By far the most impressive viewpoint is **Hart Point**, from where it is possible, on a clear day, to see as far as Mumbai. St Paul's Anglican Church, the pretty Lord's Mountain and Valley Resort and the Roman Catholic Church are among the many Raj-era buildings in Matheran.

Splendid views at Porcupine Point, also known as Sunset Point, Matheran

Intricate carved stonework seen in Damri Mosque

❾ Ahmadnagar

Ahmadnagar district. 140 km (87 miles) NE of Pune. ⛰ 307,500. 🚋 🚌

The seat of a powerful Muslim kingdom in the 16th century, Ahmadnagar was founded in 1490 by Ahmad Nizam Shah Bahri, the son of a Hindu convert. In 1599, the Mughals, led by Akbar, invaded the city after his favourite commander Abu'l Fazl murdered the ruling sultan. However, the sultan's sister, Chand Bibi, ably defended the kingdom. The succeeding years saw the rise of Malik Ambar, a former African slave who fought successful battles against neighbouring Bidar

(see p549) and Golconda (see pp670–71). In 1636, the kingdom finally submitted to Mughal rule.

The rulers of the Nizam Shahi dynasty were great builders, and their style of architecture shows an unmistakeable Persian influence. The **Ahmadnagar Fort**, 4 km (2.5 miles) northeast of the station, was built in 1490, though the impressive stone walls were added in 1563. Its palace, the only surviving structure, consists of a large hall with a series of domes. In 1942 it housed an important political prisoner, Jawaharlal Nehru, who wrote his famous book, *The Discovery of India*, here. The **Jama Masjid** dates to the same period. Nearby is the ornate **Damri Mosque**. Built in 1568, it has a cut-out trefoil parapet and finials topped by miniature pavilions.

Emperor Aurangzeb died in Ahmadnagar in 1707, and his body rested briefly at the small **Alamgir Dargah**, near the cantonment, before being interred at Khuldabad (see 479).

To the west of the town lies **Bagh Rauza**, a walled garden complex. It contains the mausoleum of Ahmad Nizam Shah Bahri, which has a lavishly decorated interior.

Festivals of Maharashtra

Janmashtami (Aug/Sep). The birth of Lord Krishna is celebrated enthusiastically all over the state. Pots of butter are strung high in the streets and human pyramids attempt to reach them, imitating the god's childhood pranks.

Janmashtami in Mumbai

Naga Panchami (Aug/Sep). Snakes, considered powerful creatures and revered across India, are worshipped during this festival. After being fed cupfuls of milk, they are taken out in colourful processions and later released into the fields.

Ganesha Chaturthi (Jul/Aug). This is the most significant festival in Maharashtra, celebrated with particular fervour in Pune and Mumbai. Clay idols of Lord Ganesha (see p471) are made and then worshipped over 10 days, amidst lively festivities. After this they are led in colourful processions to the closest water body and immersed.

Kalidasa Festival (Nov), Nagpur. Some of the most renowned exponents of classical music and dance gather at this festival, organized to honour the 4th-century Sanskrit dramatist and poet, Kalidasa.

Ellora Festival (Jan), Ellora. This festival presents a variety of classical performing arts against the evocative setting of the famous Kailasanatha Temple.

Hiking in the Sahyadris

The Western Ghats, also known in Maharashtra as the Sahyadris, run parallel to India's west coast and stretch across the states of Maharashtra, Karnataka, Tamil Nadu and Kerala. Formed from volcanic rock, the hills are a maze of ridges and valleys. In Maharashtra, the many popular hill stations serve as excellent starting points for a number of scenic walking trails. **Mahabaleshwar** and **Panchgani** are particularly well-marked with hiking routes that lead through lush forests and valleys. These hills also have a wealth of craggy rock-faces perfect for climbing and **Lonavla** is a favourite base for rock climbing enthusiasts. **Matheran** has a much-trodden path known as Shivaji's Ladder, which leads from One Tree Hill down to the valley below. The Sahyadri Hills are particularly beautiful in September after the rains, when the hills are carpeted with wild flowers and cascading waterfalls seem to appear at every turn.

The rugged ranges of the Sahyadri Hills

The holy tank of Ramkund, Nasik

⑩ Nasik

Nasik district. 187 km (116 miles) NE of Mumbai. ⚐ 1,077,000. 🚆 🚌 *i* Maharashtra Tourism, (0253) 257 0059. 📷 Kumbh Mela (every 12 years).

The town of Nasik is one of India's most holy sites. A bustling temple town, built on both banks of the Godavari river, it has almost 200 shrines. The ghats that line the river front are the venue for the spectacular Kumbh Mela *(see p215)*. Legend says that Rama, hero of the *Ramayana (see p31)*, lived here during his 14-year exile. **Ramkund**, the centrally located tank and the town's focal point, is believed to mark the spot where Rama and his wife Sita bathed. The ashes of the dead are also immersed here.

Most of Nasik's temples date to the 18th century. The **Kala Rama Temple**, east of Ramkund, is built in black stone with a 25-m (82-ft) high *shikhara*. It supposedly marks the spot where Sita was abducted by Ravana. The **Rameshwar Temple** has carvings on the roof of its hall, while the **Muktidham Temple**, close to the station, carries inscriptions from the *Bhagavad Gita* on its walls.

Environs

Pandu Lena, 8 km (5 miles) south of Nasik, has 24 Buddhist caves dating to the 1st and 2nd centuries BC. The oldest is Cave 10, a *vihara* (monastery) which has splendid sculptures and

inscriptions above its entrance. Cave 18, an early *chaitya griha*, has a beautifully carved exterior. Other fine caves include Caves 3 and 20. The sacred **Trimbakeshwar Temple**, 33 km (21 miles) west of Nasik, is built on the site of one of Shiva's 12 naturally-occurring *jyotirlingas* (lingas of light). It is surrounded by a large paved platform and has a carved *shikhara*. Though closed to non-Hindus, visitors can still get a good view of the courtyard and the shrine leading off it.

About 65 km (40 miles) south of Nasik is **Shirdi**, the temple complex of the first Sai Baba, Maharashtra's most popular saint, who died in 1918.

⑪ Aurangabad

Aurangabad district. 404 km (251 miles) NE of Mumbai. ⚐ 873,000. ✈ 10 km (6 miles) E of town centre, then taxi. 🚆 🚌 *i* Maharashtra Tourism, Station Rd East, (0240) 233 1513.

The largest city in northern Maharashtra, Aurangabad is the nearest air-link to the splendid caves at Ellora and Ajanta *(see pp480–85)*. It was founded in 1610 by Malik Ambar, prime minister of the Nizam Shahi rulers of Ahmadnagar *(see p477)*. In 1653 it became the headquarters of Aurangabad, the last great Mughal emperor. It was from this city – which he renamed

after himself – that he conquered the Deccan states.

The city's most famous monument is the **Bibi ka Maqbara**. Located outside the walled city, this imitation of the Taj was built in 1678 by Aurangzeb's son, Azam Shah, in memory of his mother Rabia Durrani. Standing in the middle of a large Mughal garden, it has four disproportionately large minarets at the ends of its raised platform. Like the Taj, it uses white marble and stucco, but there is none of the fine *pietra dura* work that distinguishes Shah Jahan's creation *(see pp176–7)*.

Aurangzeb's walled city makes up the central part of the town, although a few structures from Malik Ambar's older city remain, including the **Naukonda Palace**, or Naukhanda Palace, (largely in ruins) and the **Jama Masjid**. On the left bank of the Khan river is the **Dargah of Baba Shah Musafir**, a Sufi saint who was Aurangzeb's spiritual guide. The complex contains a small mosque, a *madrasa* (theological college), a law court, the zenana (women's quarters) and a water mill (Panchakki), fed by a rectangular tank.

Also within the old city, close to Zafar Gate, is the **Himroo Factory**. Aurangabad is famed for its ancient art of weaving brocade, using silk and gold threads, known as *kamkhab*. When the city's prosperity declined, the weavers began using less expensive

Detail of the entrance door, Bibi ka Maqbara

Bibi ka Maqbara in Aurangabad, an imitation of Agra's Taj Mahal

An ornately carved pillared hall in Cave 3,
Aurangabad Caves

cotton and silver threads,
producing *himroo*, which literally
means similar. A variety of such
shawls and saris are available
in showrooms across town.
The factory also produces rich
Paithani saris, intricately woven
with gold thread.

Environs

About 3 km (2 miles)
north are the
Aurangabad Caves.
Mainly excavated
during the Vakataka
and Kalachuri
periods (6th and 7th
centuries), these caves
can be divided into
two groups. Of the
five caves in the
western group, the
oldest is Cave 4, dating
to the 1st century AD. It is a fine
chaitya griha with a monolithic
stupa. Carved on the rock face
outside is a superb image of
the Buddha, seated on a lion
throne. Cave 3 (5th century)
has an ingeniously designed
pillared hall that is acoustically
sensitive and amplifies sound.
Inside the inner sanctum, a
Seated Buddha is flanked by
devotees with floral offerings.

The eastern group, nearby,
comprises four caves. Cave 6 has
delicately sculpted Bodhisattvas,
surrounded by flying figures.
The most splendid of the caves
is Cave 7, a sumptuous shrine
with large sculptures of Tara and
Avalokitesvara *(see p145)*. Its inner
sanctum has a superb frieze of a
female dancer accompanied by
seven musicians.

⑫ Daulatabad

Aurangabad district. 13 km (8 miles)
E of Aurangabad. 🚌 Bus tours
are offered by Maharashtra Tourism,
Aurangabad, (0240) 233 1513.
Taxis & jeeps also available from
Aurangabad. **Open** daily.

Perched on a granite outcrop
of the Deccan Plateau, this
formidable fort has witnessed
some of the greatest carnage in
the region. Originally known as
Deogiri, it was captured in 1296
by Alauddin Khilji, the Deccan's
first Muslim invader from Delhi.
He was followed by Muhammad
bin Tughluq, who annexed the
fort in 1328 and renamed the
town Daulatabad ("City of
Fortune"). In a fit of misguided
reasoning, he decided to shift
his capital here, and compelled
Delhi's entire population to
march across 1,127 km (700
miles). Thousands died of
starvation or disease along the
way, and when the
move failed, the
sultan and his court
marched back to
Delhi. Daulatabad was
successively
conquered by the
Deccani Bahmani
sultans, the Nizam
Shahis, the Mughals,
the Marathas and
finally the Nizam
of Hyderabad –
each conquest
proving more bloody and
savage than the last.

Himroo fabric,
Aurangabad

The pyramid-shaped hill,
on which the imposing fort
is built, stands apart from the
surrounding ranges, and towers
to a height of 183 m (600 ft).
This made Mughal emperor
Shah Jahan's chronicler note
that "neither ant nor snake could
scale it". Four solid concentric
walls protect the fort. The first
of its three zones is **Ambarkot**,
the outer fort. Within, stands the
60-m (197-ft) high victory tower,
Chand Minar, built in 1435 by
Alauddin Bahmani to celebrate
his conquest of the fort. In the
nearby **Jama Masjid**, 106 pillars
from Jain and Hindu temples
separate the main hall into 25
aisles. A triple gateway studded
with iron spikes provides access

into **Kataka**, the inner fort.
Gateways lead through fortified
walls into the base of the citadel,
known as **Balakot**, separated
by a moat once infested
by crocodiles.

Near the innermost gate lies
the blue and white tiled **Chini
Mahal**, where the last sultan of
Golconda was imprisoned by
Aurangzeb in 1687. On a nearby
bastion is the enormous bronze
cannon, the **Qila Shikhan** or
"Fort Breaker". This 6-m (20-ft)
long cannon has a splendid ram's
head, and Persian inscriptions
along its length refer to it as
the "Creator of Storms". A series
of dark tunnels lead to the heart
of the citadel and end near a
pillared pavilion, **Baradari**, a
late Mughal building. The fort's
ramparts offer sweeping views.

Environs

The walled village of **Khuldabad**
("Heavenly Abode") is 10 km
(6 miles) north of Daulatabad.
The Alamgir Dargah, dedicated
to the Muslim saint, Sayeed
Zain-ud-din, (d.1370), is its most
famous monument. Also known
as Rauza, this religious complex,
established by Sufi saints in the
14th century, was considered
so sacred that several Deccani
sultans chose to be buried here.
Emperor Aurangzeb, who died
in the Deccan in 1707, is buried
in a simple tomb in the courtyard.
The beautiful tomb of Malik
Ambar *(see p477)*, is a short
distance to the north.

The Chand Minar, once covered in glazed
Persian tiles, Daulatabad

⑬ Ellora: Kailasanatha Temple

The finest of the Ellora group of rock-cut caves is the magnificent Kailasanatha Temple (Cave 16), a UNESCO World Heritage Site. Commissioned by the Rashtrakuta king Krishna I in the 8th century, this mammoth complex, spanning 84 m (276 ft) by 47 m (154 ft), was carved out of a huge rocky cliff face. Sculptors chiselled through 85,000 cubic metres (approximately 3 million cubic ft) of rock, beginning at the top of the cliff and working their way down. The resulting marvel, embellished with huge sculptural panels, was meant to depict Mount Kailasa, the sacred abode of Lord Shiva.

★ **The Roof**
The *mandapa* (assembly hall) roof is embellished by a lotus carved in concentric rings, topped by four stone lions.

KEY

① **Courtyard** has two life-size elephants on either side.

② **The Nandi Pavilion**

③ **The tower** rises 32.6 m (107 ft), and was once covered in white plaster, to replicate Mount Kailasa's snowy peaks.

④ **Rock-cut monasteries**

⑤ *Ramayana* panels flank the south wall, while the north wall has *Mahabharata* and Krishna legends.

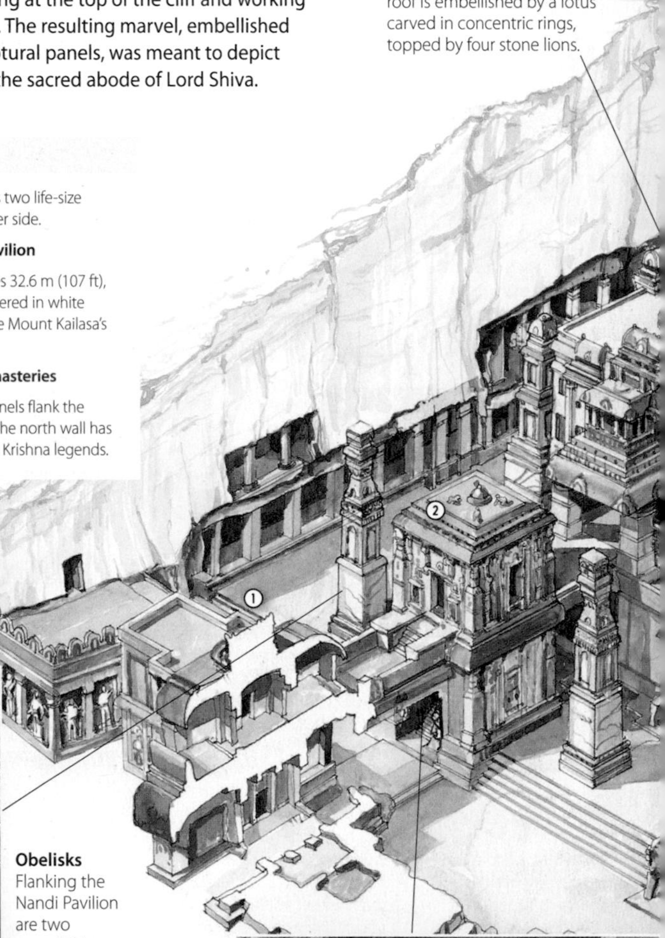

Obelisks
Flanking the Nandi Pavilion are two monolithic pillars, 17 m (56 ft) high, with carvings of lotus friezes and garlands.

★ **Lakshmi with Elephants**
Facing the entrance, the ornate Gajalakshmi panel in the Nandi Pavilion depicts Lakshmi seated in a lotus pond and being bathed by elephants bearing upturned pots in their trunks.

Supporting Elephants
Elephants with lotuses in their trunks are carved all along the lower storey, and appear to support the structure.

VISITORS' CHECKLIST

Practical Information
Aurangabad district. 30 km (19 miles) NW of Aurangabad Open Wed–Mon (all caves). Flash photography is prohibited. Light is best in the afternoon. Take packed lunch, a torch, wear comfortable shoes and a sun hat. Ellora Festival (Dec).

Transport
Jeeps are also available at Aurangabad & tour operators also organize trips.

★ Ravana Shaking Mount Kailasa
A large panel depicts Ravana (the demon king in the *Ramayana*) shaking Mount Kailasa in order to disturb Shiva and Parvati in their mountain home.

| 0 metres | | 10 |
| 0 yards | | 10 |

Three Goddesses
The Hall of Sacrifice contains life-size images of Durga, Chamunda and Kali, as well as of Ganesha, Parvati and the seven mother goddesses.

Exploring Ellora

The 34 caves at Ellora, hewn from a 2-km (1.3-mile) long escarpment, are among the most splendid examples of rock-cut architecture in India.

The emergence and growing importance of Ellora coincided with the decline of Buddhism, and a Hindu renaissance under the Chalukya and Rashtrakuta dynasties (7th–9th centuries AD). Ellora was situated on an important trade route that ran between Ujjain in Madhya Pradesh and the west coast. It was the revenue from this very lucrative trade that sustained 500 years of excavation at Ellora, as the older Ajanta caves began to be abandoned.

The caves at Ellora fall into three distinct groups – Buddhist, Hindu and Jain – and they are numbered from the southern end. The **Buddhist Caves** (1 to 12) date from the Chalukya period, between the 7th and 8th centuries. The first nine are variations of *viharas* or monasteries, and are filled with fine Buddha figures, Bodhisattvas and scenes from Buddhist mythology. The most splendid is **Cave 10**, or Vishwakarma ("Carpenter's Cave"), named after the celestial carpenter. A striking *chaitya griha* (*see p24*), it is dominated by a figure of the Teaching Buddha

View of the dramatic Ellora escarpment with its seasonal waterfall

carved in front of a votive stupa, placed under a vaulted roof. It is so intricately carved that it seems to be made of wood. Other important caves are **Cave 11**, or Do Thal (two-storeyed), and **Cave 12**, or Tin Thal (three-storeyed). The upper hall of Cave 12 has large Bodhisattvas carved on its walls, while rows of seven Buddha figures flank the entrance to the antechamber.

The **Hindu Caves** (13 to 29), were carved out between the 7th and 9th centuries, and represent the peak of Ellora's development. **Cave 14**, or Ravana ki Khai, contains impressive sculptures of deities from the Hindu pantheon, such as Durga slaying the buffalo demon, and Vishnu as the boar-headed Varaha. **Cave 15**, or Dashavatara, also has superb sculptural depictions. **Cave 21**,

or Rameshvara, and **Cave 29**, or Dhumar Lena, are other impressive caves.

The **Jain Caves** (30 to 34) date from Ellora's last stage, in the 9th century, and are simpler than the Hindu ones. **Cave 32**, or Indra Sabha, is the finest of the group. A monolithic shrine, it has carvings of elephants, lions and *tirthankaras* (*see p402*) on the courtyard walls. **Cave 30**, or Chhota Kailasa, is a small, incomplete replica of the Kailasanatha Temple (*see pp480–81*) and has sculptures of various *tirthankaras* and Mahavira on a lion-throne.

Environs

The 18th-century **Grishneshvara Temple**, nearby, is one of the 12 *jyotirlinga* shrines dedicated to Shiva, built by Rani Ahilyabai of Indore (*see p254*).

The upper-storey hall, Vishwakarma (Cave 10)

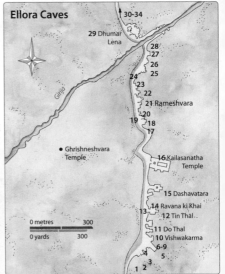

Ellora Caves

30–34
29 Dhumar Lena
28
27
26
25
24
23
22
21 Rameshvara
20
19
18
17
16 Kailasanatha Temple
● Ghrishneshvara Temple
15 Dashavatara
14 Ravana ki Khai
13
12 Tin Thal
11 Do Thal
10 Vishwakarma
6–9
5
4
3
2
1

Griha

0 metres   300
0 yards   300

Façade of Cave 19, Ajanta, with a large
horseshoe-shaped window

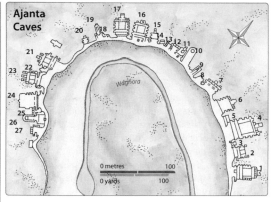

Ajanta Caves

⑭ Ajanta

Aurangabad district. 110 km
(68 miles) NE of Aurangabad.
🚌 from Aurangabad. **Open** Tue–Sun.
📷 Flash photography is prohibited.
🎫 🚫 Organized tours & taxis
are also available from Aurangabad.
Take a packed lunch, bottled water,
torch, and wear comfortable
shoes and a sun hat.

A UNESCO World Heritage Site,
the 30 extraordinary rock-cut
caves at Ajanta lie within a
horseshoe-shaped escarpment,
overlooking the narrow Waghora
river gorge. At its head is a
waterfall that drops into the
Saptakunda pool. The caves were
occupied for only a short period
and, over time, the surrounding
jungle concealed their existence.
They were "rediscovered" quite
accidentally in 1819, when
John Smith, of the 28th Madras
Cavalry, suddenly saw the top
of the façade of Cave 10 while
on a tiger hunt.

Ajanta's caves fall into two
groups. The early group belongs
to the more austere Hinayana
phase of Buddhism (2nd–1st
century BC), during which the
Buddha was not represented
in human form but only by
symbols such as a Wheel of
Law or a Bodhi Tree. The second
group dates from the Mahayana
period (5th–6th centuries AD),
carved out during the rule of the
Vakataka dynasty, when artistic
expression was more exuberant.
The caves were inhabited by
monks, artists and craftsmen,
who used them as *varsh-vatikas*
or monsoon shrines. Stylistically

they are of two types – *chaitya
grihas* (prayer halls) and *viharas*
(monasteries). The *chaityas* have
vaulted ceilings and octagonal
columns that divide the space
into a central hall with a votive
stupa, the object of veneration.
The side aisles that run around
the hall were used for ritual
circumambulation. The Mahayana
chaityas also have Buddha
images. *Viharas* typically have a
verandah, a hall surrounded by
cells, and an inner shrine with
enormous Buddha figures.

Of the seven Mahayana caves,
dating from the 5th century AD,
Cave 1 is famous for its splendid
murals (*see pp484–5*). Above its
verandah are friezes of scenes
from the Buddha's life, while its
ceiling is supported by 20 carved
and painted pillars. **Cave 2** has
a superb façade carved with
images of Naga kings, and their
attendants (*ganas*), while its
main shrine has a magnificent
painted ceiling.

Caves 8, 9, 10, 12, 13 and 15 are
Hinayana caves. **Cave 9**, a *chaitya*

griha, has a façade adorned with
windows and lattice-work. The
large Buddha figures along the
sides were a later addition (5th
century) and its murals are from
both periods. **Cave 10** is thought
to be Ajanta's oldest cave and
is one of its finest *chaitya grihas*.

Caves 15 to 20 are late
5th-century Mahayana caves.
Cave 16 has sculptures of
beautiful maidens flanking the
doorway, while in **Cave 17** the
entrance to the inner shrine
is ornamented with Buddha
figures, goddesses and lotuses.

Caves 21 to 27 (7th century),
make up the final group. **Cave
26** displays the full magnificence
of Ajanta's sculptural art.
Especially remarkable are two
splendid panels – one depicts
the Temptation of the Buddha
by the Demon Mara, while the
Parinirvana is a 7-m (23-ft)
image of the reclining Buddha,
with his eyes closed as if in sleep.
His disciples mourn his passing,
while above, celestial beings
rejoice in his salvation.

The moving Parinirvana, depicting the passing of the Buddha, Cave 26

The Ajanta Murals

The earliest and finest examples of Buddhist painting in India can be seen at the Ajanta caves. Executed between the 2nd century BC and the 5th century AD, the murals show scenes from the Buddha's life, and from the Jataka Tales, which recount stories of the Buddha's previous incarnations as an enlightened being or Bodhisattva. Magnificent, detailed compositions, the murals include depictions of court scenes, princes and musicians, and offer fascinating glimpses of daily life in the 5th century. The colours, derived from plants and minerals, are in rich shades of ochre, lime, black, green and lapis lazuli.

Avalokitesvara, also identified as Vajrapani, is the most venerated Bodhisattva in the Mahayana pantheon, and can be seen to the right of the antechamber doorway.

Cave 1
This late 5th-century vihara (monastery) contains some of Ajanta's most evocative murals.

The Miracle of Sravasti, on the antechamber's right wall, depicts a famous miracle when the Buddha multiplied himself a thousand-fold.

Padmapani (Lotus-Holder), the Bodhisattva of Compassion, can be seen on the wall to the left of the antechamber doorway. He is surrounded by celestial beings and air-borne figures.

The *Mahajanaka Jataka,* to the left of the antechamber, recounts the life of Prince Mahajanaka, who renounced the world to become an ascetic. Here, the prince is surrounded by female attendants.

A scene depicting a king, possibly the Vakataka ruler Harisena, greeting a Persian embassy

Scenes from the *Mahajanaka Jataka*, from left to right, depict Prince Mahajanaka, Queen Shivali enticing the prince, palace maids, and a dancing girl.

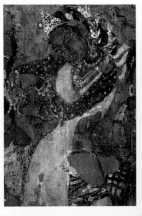

Cave 2

Similar in design to Cave 1, this 5th-century vihara is profusely painted in lustrous colours. The walls, columns, capitals and ceiling are covered in scrollwork, geometric and floral patterns, and numerous Jataka panels, including stories connected with the Buddha's birth.

The large *mandala* (circular diagram) dominates the elaborately painted ceiling of this remarkable cave. A depiction of the cosmos, its outer ring is filled with lotus motifs.

Cave 10

Considered to be Ajanta's oldest cave, this chaitya griha dates to the 2nd century BC. The left wall has its oldest mural, a frieze depicting a prince worshipping a Bodhi Tree.

Numerous figures of the Buddha embellish some of the octagonal pillars (39 in all), that separate the aisles from the central nave in Cave 10.

Cave 16

Outstanding paintings in this cave depict the conversion of Nanda, the Buddha's half-brother, and show his wife swooning when she hears the news of his becoming a monk.

Nanda's wife, Sundari, fainting upon hearing of his conversion

Cave 17

This cave has the largest number of paintings. Among the finest are a vast panel depicting Simhala's shipwreck and encounter with a man-eating ogress; and a lady at her toilet, gazing intently into a mirror.

Eight seated Buddha figures are depicted above the doorway in the verandah, with a row of amorous couples directly below them.

This detail of an *apsara* (celestial maiden) adoring the Buddha, is part of a larger mural on the verandah to the right of the door. The Ajanta murals are renowned for their exquisite portrayal of women.

A panel from the *Visvantara Jataka*, to the left of the doorway, depicts Prince Visvantara and his wife drinking wine. They then move to the city gate and give alms to the needy.

The enormous meteorite crater at Lonar, partially filled by a lake

⓫ Lonar

Buldana district. 130 km (81 miles) E of Aurangabad. 🚉 Jalna, 83 km (52 miles) W of Lonar, then bus. 🚌 from Aurangabad, taxis also available.

The tiny village of Lonar, is famous for its remarkable meteorite crater. Thought to be the only hyper-velocity impact crater in basaltic rock in the world, the mammoth crater, 2 km (1.3 miles) in diameter and 700 m (2,297 ft) deep, is estimated to be about 50,000 years old. Scientists believe that the meteorite is still buried beneath the southeastern edge of the crater. A lake fills the bottom and the ruins of some Hindu temples stand on its shores. The crater is rich in birdlife, and monkeys and herds of deer can also be seen. There are a few rest houses that offer rooms and the village has some eateries as well.

⓰ Melghat Tiger Reserve

Amravati district. 400 km (249 miles) NE of Aurangabad. 🚉 Amravati, 100 km (62 miles) SE of entry point. Maharashtra Tourism, organizes buses or jeeps from Amravati to the park. 🛈 For bookings contact the Field Director, (0721) 266 2792. **Open** daily. 🐾

The Project Tiger Reserve of Melghat, which means "Meeting Place of the Ghats", spreads across the Gawilgarh Hills in the southern part of the Satpura Mountains. Its highest altitudes are approximately 1,178 m (3,865 ft) above sea level. These hills have a dense canopy of the country's finest deciduous teak and bamboo forests, which

are now threatened by rampant commercial exploitation for timber. Along with its elusive 70 tigers, the reserve is home to about 50 leopards, *chausingha* (four-horned antelope), *dhole* (Indian wild dog), jungle cats, hyenas and a rich variety of birds. The sanctuary also supports the state's largest concentration of *gaur*, the endangered Indian bison.

The best time to visit is from December to May, when the park is pleasantly cool. Its five rivers, the Khandu, Khapra, Sipna, Garga and Dolar, dry out in summer, and the few remaining pools of rainwater are highly prized as watering holes.

Environs
Chikhaldhara, lying 25 km (16 miles) northeast of Melghat, is a quaint hill station established by the British in 1839.

A tiger resting in a tree at the Melghat Tiger Reserve

⓱ Nagpur

Nagpur district. 520 km (323 miles) NE of Aurangabad. 🚹 2,130,000. ✈ 10 km (6 miles) S of city centre, then bus or taxi. 🚉 🚌 🛈 Maharashtra Tourism, (0712) 253 3325. 🎭 Pola (Jun/Jul), Kalidasa Festival (Nov).

Situated on the banks of the Nag river, Nagpur lies exactly in the centre of India. The capital of the Central Provinces until it became part of Maharashtra state after Independence, it is a fast developing industrial city and the country's orange-growing capital. Historically, it was the capital of the aboriginal Gond tribals until it was captured by the Maratha Bhonsles (*see p472*) in 1743, and finally by the British in 1861.

In October 1956, the city witnessed an event of great social importance, when Dr BR Ambedkar, writer of the Indian Constitution and a freedom fighter born into a lower caste Hindu family, converted to Buddhism in a stand against the rigid Hindu caste system. Nearly 200,000 people followed him, and the movement gathered great momentum, resulting in about three million conversions.

Nagpur town is built around **Sitabaldi Fort**. In the eastern part of the city are the remains of the **Bhonsle Palace**, which was destroyed by fire in the 19th century. South of the old city lie the **Chhatris**, or memorials of the Bhonsle kings, while a number of colonial buildings are situated in the western part of Nagpur. Among them are the High Court and the Anglican Cathedral of All Saints (1851).

Environs
Ramtek, 40 km (25 miles) northeast of Nagpur, is associated with the 14-year exile of Rama, Sita and Lakshman, as told in the epic *Ramayana (see p31)*. It was the capital of the Vakataka dynasty between the 4th and the 6th centuries, and the fort on the Hill of Rama dates to this period. Its walls, however, were built in 1740, by the founder of Nagpur's Bhonsle dynasty, Raghoji I.

Baskets of juicy oranges on sale in Nagpur's thriving market

Tadoba-Andhari Tiger Reserve, also known as the Jewel of Vidharba, lies 208 km (129 miles) south of Nagpur. The best time to visit this reserve is between February and May.

⓲ Wardha

Wardha district. 493 km (306 miles) NW of Aurangabad. from Nagpur to Wardha, then bus or auto to Sevagram. **Tel** (07152) 284 753.

Most visitors to Wardha are en route to Mahatma Gandhi's historic **Sevagram Ashram**, now a national institution, 8 km (5 miles) northwest of Wardha town. Established by Gandhi in 1936, Sevagram ("Village of Service") was based on Gandhi's philosophy of rural economic development. It became the head-quarters of India's National Movement, where Gandhi lived and worked for more than 15 years. Spread over 40 ha (99 acres) of farmland, the ashram has numerous *kutirs* or rural dwellings and several research centres. Gandhi's personal effects, such as his spinning wheel and spectacles, are on display, and khadi, the coarse home-spun cotton that Gandhi made famous as the symbol of India's freedom struggle, is also on sale. A photo exhibit opposite the main entrance depicts scenes from Gandhi's life, while a hospital catering to the needs of local villagers, is located on the main road. Prayers are held daily at 4.30am and 6pm under a pipal tree planted by Gandhi, which visitors can attend.

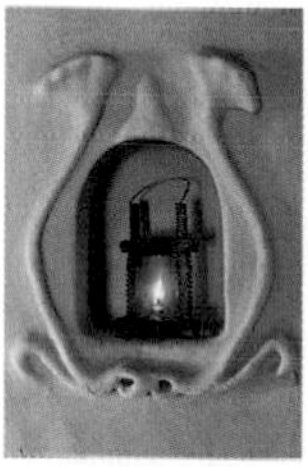

An oil lamp in a niche, Sevagram

Environs

The ashram of Gandhi's disciple, Vinobha Bhave, is 10 km (6 miles) north of Sevagram at **Paunar**. Bhave started the successful Bhoodan Movement (which literally means "land donation") that sought to persuade wealthy landowners to give portions of their holdings to the poor.

⓳ Pandharpur

Sholapur district. 250 km (155 miles) SE of Pune. 91,500. Ashadh Ekadashi Fair (Jul).

The spiritual capital of Maharashtra, Pandharpur is situated on the banks of the Chandrabhaga river and is the site of the sacred shrine of Vithoba, an incarnation of Lord Vishnu. The temple was built in 1228 and is the focal point of a sacred pilgrimage which draws thousands of Varakaris (members of one of the state's most popular religious sects) here every July to attend the Ashadh Ekadashi fair. *Dindis* or group processions travel to Pandharpur from every village in the area, accompanied by devotional singing. The river front, lined with numerous bathing ghats, comes alive with crowds of people, who gather here for their ritual dip.

The spartan interior of Mahatma Gandhi's ashram at Sevagram, near Wardha

GOA

This tiny state, along the Konkan Coast, covers 3,702 sq km (1,429 sq miles) and consists of just two districts, North and South Goa. Goa's distinct culture is a legacy of its colonial past. In 1510, Alfonso de Albuquerque established a small but powerful Portuguese enclave here. Though Goa became a part of the Indian Union in 1961, evidence of the 400-odd years of Portuguese rule is still apparent in the people's dress, language, religion and cuisine, and in their music, a fusion of the plaintive *fado* with the lilting rhythms of local Konkani folk songs. Today, Goa is one of India's most popular holiday destinations, with its idyllic beaches, lush paddy fields, coconut plantations and villages dotted with pretty whitewashed churches and grand mansions. Its other attractions include the Hindu temples around Ponda, built between the 15th and 18th centuries, and the magnificent cathedrals of Old Goa. Goa's friendly, easy-going people go out of their way to make visitors feel at home.

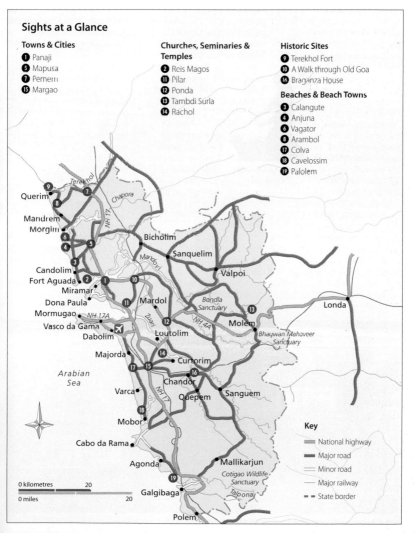

Sights at a Glance

Towns & Cities
1. Panaji
5. Mapusa
7. Pernem
15. Margao

Churches, Seminaries & Temples
2. Reis Magos
11. Pilar
12. Ponda
13. Tambdi Surla
14. Rachol

Historic Sites
9. Terekhol Fort
10. A Walk through Old Goa
16. Braganza House

Beaches & Beach Towns
3. Calangute
4. Anjuna
6. Vagator
8. Arambol
17. Colva
18. Cavelossim
19. Palolem

Key
━━ National highway
━━ Major road
═══ Minor road
──── Major railway
╌╌ State border

0 kilometres 20
0 miles 20

◀ Pretty interior of the Royal Chapel of St Anthony

For keys to symbols *see back flap*

❶ Panaji

Goa's capital, Panaji, situated at the mouth of the Mandovi river, is reminiscent of a provincial Mediterranean town. Earlier a port of the Adil Shahi kings of Bijapur *(see p546)*, it became a military landing stage and warehouse after the arrival of the Portuguese in 1510. In 1759, after a series of epidemics in Old Goa, the viceroy was forced to move his residence to Panaji, or Panjim as it was then called. However, it was only in 1843 that the town became the official capital of Portuguese territories in India. Today, Panaji has a relaxed and friendly ambience, especially along the leafy avenues of the old town *(see pp492–3)*. The newer commercial hub, laid out on a grid, has concrete structures interspersed with colonial buildings and churches.

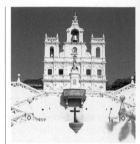

The Church of Our Lady of the Immaculate Conception

🏛 Old Secretariat

Avenida Dom Joao Crasto. **Tel** (0832) 222 2701. **Closed** for renovations.

The riverfront edifice that housed the State Legislative Assembly until the year 2000 is one of Panaji's oldest buildings. It was once the summer palace of Yusuf Adil Shah, Goa's 16th-century Muslim ruler, and fell to the Portuguese in 1510, despite a formidable battery of 55 cannons and a salt-water moat that protected it.

Rebuilt in 1615, its strategic location made it a point of entry for ships and a stopover for viceroys and governors en route to Old Goa *(see p505)*. In 1760, after Old Goa was abandoned in favour of Panaji, the Idalcaon's Palace (a corruption of Adil Shah's or Khan's Palace), as it was then known, became

The 19th-century statue of Abbé de Faria

the official residence of the viceroys – until 1918, when the residence moved to the Cabo Palace, southwest of Panaji. Extensive renovations have transformed the original Islamic structure into the colonial building it is today, with a sloping tiled roof, wide wooden verandahs and cast-iron pillars. The Ashoka Chakra or the Buddhist Wheel of Law, the emblem of the Indian government, has replaced the Portuguese viceroys' coat of arms, above the entrance to the building.

Standing west of the Secretariat is the arresting statue of Abbé de Faria. This Goan priest, who was born in Candolim in 1756, underwent theological training in Rome. After his ordination, he moved

to Paris, where he won acclaim as the father of modern hypnosis.

🏛 Church of Our Lady of the Immaculate Conception

Church Square. **Tel** (0832) 242 6939. **Open** daily. 🏛 (English) 8am, Mon–Sat; 8.15am, Sun.

Overlooking Largo da Igreja or "Church Square", Panaji's main square, is the Church of Our Lady of the Immaculate Conception, the town's most important landmark. Portuguese sailors used to come to the original chapel, consecrated in 1541, to offer thanksgiving prayers after their long and treacherous voyage from Lisbon.

The present church, with its Baroque façade framed by twin towers, was built in 1619. Its most striking feature, the double flight of stairs leading up to the church, was added in 1871. The central pediment was built at the same time, as was the belfry to accommodate the huge bell brought from Old Goa's

View of the the riverside Secretariat at Panaji, with its tiled roof and colonial façade

For hotels and restaurants see p701 and pp715–16

Augustinian monastery *(see p500)*. The chapel in the south transept has fine reredos (altar panels) retrieved from the viceroy's chapel in the Secretariat. The Baroque splendour of the main altar and the two transept altars is in sharp contrast to the otherwise simple interior.

⛪ Menezes Braganza Institute
Malacca Rd.
Tel (0832) 222 4143.
Open Mon–Sat.

An excellent example of 19th-century Portuguese civic architecture, the Institute Vasco da Gama was

The central pavilion, Azad Maidan

built to impart knowledge in the arts and sciences. It was later renamed after the philanthropist Luis de Menezes Braganza (1878–1938), whose family home is in Chandor *(see p512)*.

Today, this is Goa's Central Library, with a good collection of rare books. The superb mural in blue painted ceramic tiles *(azulezos)* was added to the entrance lobby in 1935, and depicts scenes from the epic *Os Lusiadas* (Lusiada, meaning the "people of Portugal", is derived from Lusitania, Portugal's old name). Written by the 16th-century Portuguese poet, Luis Vaz de Camões, this recounts the history of the Portuguese presence in Goa. The institute used to have an art gallery with works by late 19th- and early 20th-century European artists. These exhibits are now housed in the State Museum.

The grassy square in front of the Institute, **Azad Maidan**, is lined on one side by the Police Headquarters, built in 1832 with stones from Old Goa's abandoned buildings. The pavilion in the centre was made in 1847, using Corinthian pillars taken from a Dominican church, dating to the mid-16th century. Inside, a memorial to the freedom fighter Dr Tristao de Braganza Cunha has replaced an earlier statue of the first viceroy, Alfonso de Albuquerque, now in the Archaeological Museum in Old Goa *(see p504)*.

🏛 State Museum
Patto. **Tel** (0832) 243 8006.
Open Mon–Fri. **Closed** public hols.
This museum houses a rather modest collection of pre-colonial artifacts, including statues, *sati* stones, antique furniture and carvings from ravaged Hindu temples, as well as some Christian icons.

Environs
Panaji's nearest beach, **Miramar**, is 3 km (2 miles) west. **Dona Paula**, 7 km (4 miles) southwest of Panaji, is near the headland dividing the estuaries of the Zuari and Mandovi rivers. It is named after a viceroy's daughter who, the story goes, jumped into the sea when she wasn't allowed to marry a local fisherman. The jetty offers fine views of Fort Aguada across the bay. Jet skis are available for rent and visitors can also take a ferry-ride to Vasco da Gama harbour.

A scene from *Os Lusiadas*, depicting Vasco da Gama's arrival in Goa

Goan River Cruises

A delightful way to spend an evening in Goa is to take one of the many sunset cruises along the Mandovi river, organized by the Goa Tourism Development Corporation, (0832) 243 8750, and also by private operators. Most of the cruises begin from the jetty at the foot of Mandovi bridge, every day between 6 and 7pm (tickets are available at the jetty). Entertainment is provided by troupes of Goan dancers and musicians. On full moon nights, an excellent dinner is also provided on board. Some operators, such as Goa Tourism's Backwater Thrills, (0832) 242 4001, organize specialized tours through the backwaters, a vibrant mangrove habitat and home to marsh crocodiles and migratory birds. Focussing on culture and food, Pascoal Organic Spice Village, (0832) 234 4268, takes visitors to the sylvan settings of spice plantations, which attract flocks of beautiful birds.

An evening cruise down the Mandovi river

Street-by-Street: Panaji Old Town

Tucked away between Ourem Creek and Altinho Hill in Panaji are the old residential quarters of Fontainhas and São Tomé, built on reclaimed land in the 19th century. Fontainhas was named after the fountain of Phoenix, a spring that provided the quarter's only source of water, while São Tomé takes its name from the São Tomé Church. This old-world precinct, characterized by a jumble of painted, tile-roofed houses, has streets lined with taverns offering authentic Goan cuisine and *feni* (cashewnut liqueur), and bakeries serving *bebinca*, the delicious local cake. Many of the residents still speak Portuguese.

A priest in the doorway of St Sebastian's Chapel

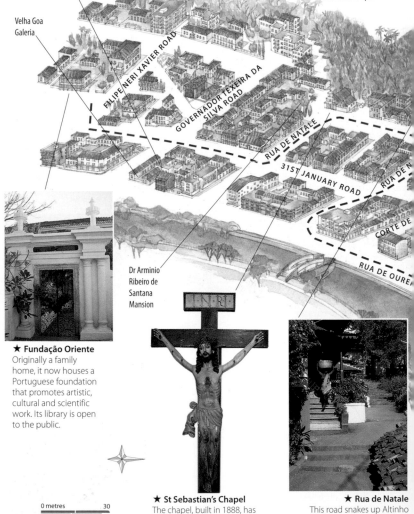

Panjim Inn

Velha Goa Galeria

FILIPE NERI XAVIER ROAD

GOVERNADOR TEIXEIRA DA SILVA ROAD

RUA DE NATALE

31ST JANUARY ROAD

RUA DE N

CORTE DE

RUA DE OURE

Dr Arminio Ribeiro de Santana Mansion

★ **Fundação Oriente**
Originally a family home, it now houses a Portuguese foundation that promotes artistic, cultural and scientific work. Its library is open to the public.

0 metres   30
0 yards   30

★ **St Sebastian's Chapel**
The chapel, built in 1888, has a life-size crucifix that used to hang in the Palace of the Inquisition in Old Goa.

★ **Rua de Natale**
This road snakes up Altinho Hill and has steps laid out to help pedestrians negotiate the gentle climb.

VISITORS' CHECKLIST

Practical Information
Fontainhas & São Tomé.
St Sebastian's Chapel: **Open** am
only. São Tomé Church: **Open** am
only. Fundação Oriente Library:
Tel (0832) 223 0728. **Open** Mon–
Fri. Velha Goa Galeria: **Tel** (0832)
242 6628. **Open** Mon–Sat.

Ourem Creek
The picturesque Rua de Ourem faces Ourem Creek. Behind it, colourful
houses dot the slopes all the way up Altinho Hill.

Altinho Hill

Key
— Suggested route

Venite Restaurant
This first-floor restaurant,
overlooking the street
below, has a wonderful
ambience and serves
excellent European and
Goan food.

31ST JANUARY ROAD

GOMES PEREIRA ROAD

LUIS DE MENEZES ROAD

SÃO TOMÉ STREET

São Tomé, a tiny
church built in
1849, was once
the focus of a
busy square. The
nearby Mint marks
the Inquisition's
execution site.

MAHATMA GANDHI ROAD

Ourem Creek

Pato Bridge

Streetscape
Most houses are painted yellow, ochre, green
or indigo with a white trim – in keeping with
the old Portuguese building code.

Reredos behind the main altar, Reis Magos Church

❷ Reis Magos

North Goa district (Bardez taluka). 3 km (2 miles) NW of Panaji. 🚍 🎪 Feast of Three Kings (Jan).

The fort at Reis Magos was built in 1551 by Don Alfonso de Noronha, the fifth viceroy, as a second line of defence after the forts at Aguada and Cabo (the tip of Dona Paula). It once housed a prison, which was moved to Mormugao in 1996. Adjacent to the fort is the Reis Magos Church. Constructed in 1555, this is one of Goa's earliest churches, and has the royal Portuguese coat of arms on its façade.

Soccer game in progress, Calangute

Environs
Fort Aguada, 4 km (2.5 miles) west of Reis Magos, was built in 1612 as a defence against the Marathas and the Dutch. Its church, dedicated to St Lawrence, the patron saint of sailors, was built in 1630, while the huge lighthouse dates to 1864. Some buildings within the fort now house the state prison. The local beach, Sinquerim, is known for its luxury resorts.

❸ Calangute

North Goa district (Bardez taluka). 16 km (10 miles) NW of Panaji. 🚍 🛈 Kingstork Beach Resort, (0832) 227 5120.

The centre of the hippie scene in the 1960s and 1970s, Calangute is Goa's most popular beach. During the day, it is packed with sunbathers, hawkers, masseurs, hair-braiders and ear-cleaners. The entire stretch of sand right up to the adjacent Baga Beach is lined with resorts, trinket stalls, bars and beach shacks such as Reggie's Bar and Souza Lobo, which serve excellent Goan food. **Atlantis Water Sports**, offers a diverse range of water sports. Rides on fishing boats are also available at bargain prices. Calangute's church, **St Alex**, topped by a large dome, is on the road to Mapusa. Its Rococo-style white-and-gold interior has pretty, shell-shaped niches.

🎇 Atlantis Water Sports
Calangute. **Tel** 09890-47272.

Environs
Extending north of Calangute, **Baga Beach** is far less crowded, although its expanse of soft, white sand has its share of guesthouses and bars. It hosts the leisurely Saturday Night Ingo's Bazaar – a great alternative to the Wednesday flea market at nearby Anjuna. Tito's Bar, which has the only dance floor on the entire beach, is the hub of Baga's nightlife. **Candolim Beach**, 2.5 km (2 miles) south of Calangute, stretches all the way to Fort Aguada. Popular with large tour groups, the once peaceful waters now resound with the whir of speedboats and jet skis. **Saligao**, 2 km (1.3 miles) east of Calangute, has the pretty Church of Mae de Deus, in Neo-Gothic style, as well as a seminary which prepares boys for theological studies at Rachol Seminary (see p508).

❹ Anjuna

North Goa district (Bardez taluka). 18 km (11 miles) NW of Panaji. 🚍 🚆 Flea Market (Wed).

Anjuna has now replaced Calangute as a haven for backpackers. It is better known for its full-moon rave parties and sprawling flea market than for its beach. The popular flea market, held every Wednesday, is crowded with hawkers from all over India selling everything from Balinese batik, silver jewellery and papier-mâché boxes, to Tibetan prayer wheels, Rajasthani mirrorwork and Kerala woodcarvings. Fluorescent rave gear and trendy beachwear round off the selection, while added attractions are performing monkeys and fortune-telling Nandi bulls.

A woman selling sarongs at the Anjuna flea market

Beaches and Beach Life

Goa's splendid beaches stretch over 106 km (66 miles), from Querim in the north to Mobor in the south. Each beach has its own individual character, though in general, South Goa's beaches are far less developed than those in North Goa. The entire Goan coast is a popular tourist destination. To cater to the growing number of visitors, many beaches now have shacks serving beer, snacks and seafood, lively flea markets, and vendors offering a variety of services from head massages to dolphin-watching trips.

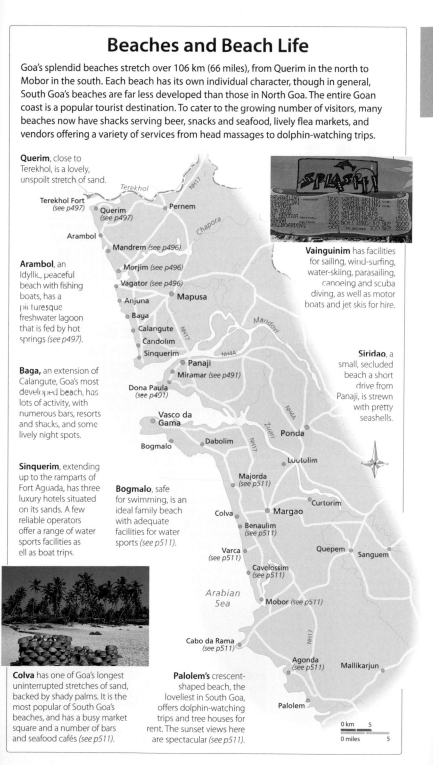

Querim, close to Terekhol, is a lovely, unspoilt stretch of sand.

Terekhol Fort (see p497)

Querim (see p497)

Terekhol

Arambol

Arambol, an idyllic, peaceful beach with fishing boats, has a picturesque freshwater lagoon that is fed by hot springs (see p497).

Mandrem (see p496)

Morjim (see p496)

Vagator (see p496)

Anjuna

Baga

Calangute

Candolim

Mapusa

Chapora

Pernem

NH17

Vainguinim has facilities for sailing, wind-surfing, water-skiing, parasailing, canoeing and scuba diving, as well as motor boats and jet skis for hire.

Baga, an extension of Calangute, Goa's most developed beach, has lots of activity, with numerous bars, resorts and shacks, and some lively night spots.

Sinquerim

Panaji

Miramar (see p491)

Dona Paula (see p491)

Vasco da Gama

Bogmalo

Mandovi

NH4A

Dabolim

Zuari

NH17

Ponda

Loutolim

NH4A

Siridao, a small, secluded beach a short drive from Panaji, is strewn with pretty seashells.

Sinquerim, extending up to the ramparts of Fort Aguada, has three luxury hotels situated on its sands. A few reliable operators offer a range of water sports facilities as ell as boat trips.

Bogmalo, safe for swimming, is an ideal family beach with adequate facilities for water sports (see p511).

Majorda (see p511)

Colva

Benaulim (see p511)

Varca (see p511)

Cavelossim (see p511)

Margao

Curtorim

Quepem

Sanguem

Arabian Sea

Mobor (see p511)

Cabo da Rama (see p511)

Agonda (see p511)

Mallikarjun

Palolem

Colva has one of Goa's longest uninterrupted stretches of sand, backed by shady palms. It is the most popular of South Goa's beaches, and has a busy market square and a number of bars and seafood cafés (see p511).

Palolem's crescent-shaped beach, the loveliest in South Goa, offers dolphin-watching trips and tree houses for rent. The sunset views here are spectacular (see p511).

0 km   5

0 miles   5

The façade of St Jerome's Church (Our Lady of Miracles), Mapusa

❺ Mapusa

North Goa district (Bardez taluka).
13 km (8 miles) N of Panaji.
🚍 40,150. 🚉 🚌 *i* GTDC Hotel,
(0832) 226 2794. 🛥 Fri. 🎪 Feast
of Our Lady of Miracles (Apr).

The largest town in northern Goa, Mapusa's main point of interest is the colourful Friday market, with its tantalizing aromas of dried fish, spices, chillies, vinegar, local toddy and the spicy Goan sausages, *chouriça*. The region's famous cashewnuts are also much in demand. Hawkers peddle a range of beachwear, including cheap T-shirts and summer dresses, in the covered colonnades in front of the rows of shops. In the lanes leading off from the main market are stalls selling handicrafts and souvenirs from all over the country.

St Jerome's Church, also known as the Church of Our Lady of Miracles, was rebuilt twice, first in 1719 and again in 1838, after it was destroyed by fire. Its main altar, with the image of Nossa Senhora de Milagres, has some grand ornamental screens, salvaged from a church in Old Goa.

Interestingly, both Hindus and Catholics celebrate the Feast of Our Lady (held 16 days after Easter) with equal fervour. At the end of the festival Hindu devotees, accompanied by Catholics, take the holy oil from St Jerome's church back to the nearby Shanteri Temple.

Environs
Mayem Lake, 14 km (9 miles) southeast of Mapusa, is an ideal picnic spot, with boating facilities and a good resort.

❻ Vagator

North Goa district (Bardez taluka).
17 km (11 miles) N of Panaji.
🚍 Chapora village.

A beautiful bay sheltered by rocky outcrops at both ends, Vagator consists of a number of small beaches fringed by shady coconut palms. Rarely crowded, it is the perfect place to discover Goa's unspoilt beauty.

The southernmost cove of **Ozran** lies below a steep cliff, where a freshwater stream empties into a clear pool, ideal for swimming. **Little Vagator**, to the north, is a secluded stretch of sand popular with more discerning visitors. **Big Vagator Beach** is dominated by the red laterite **Chapora Fort** situated on top of a hill at its northern tip. Now in ruins, this fort was

Brightly coloured fishing nets

built by the Portuguese in 1717 on the remains of an older bastion erected by the Adil Shahi sultans. Its name, Chapora, is derived from "Shahpura", or "Town of the Shah", as the village was once known. In 1739, Sambhaji, the son of the Maratha chief Shivaji *(see p475)*, occupied the fort for a short time until it was returned to the Portuguese in exchange for Bassein, near Mumbai. Its ramparts, now desolate, offer sweeping views of the coast. Chapora village, below the fort, has many pleasant cafés.

Environs
The many fishing villages along the northern coastline can only be reached by taking a ferry across the Chapora river from Siolim, 10 km (6 miles) from Chapora village. The area around the village of **Morjim**, 5 km (3 miles) north of Chapora village, is ideal for birdwatching. **Mandrem** is another quiet village with a beautiful location and glorious beach, 12 km (7 miles) north of Chapora village.

❼ Pernem

North Goa district (Pernem taluka).
29 km (18 miles) N of Panaji.
🚍 🚌 every half hour from Siolim.

The headquarters of Goa's northern most *taluka*, or sub district, Pernem was occupied by the Portuguese in the mid-18th century. It was one of the last conquests they made between 1764 and 1788 – a period during which they expanded their territory to include Pernem, Bicholim and Satari in the north, and Ponda *(see p506)*, Sanquem, Quepem and Canacona in the south. By this time, the fervour for conversions that existed during the period of the early conquests had waned, and these areas remained predominantly Hindu.

The brightly painted **Bhagavati Temple**, in the bazaar, stands on a 500-year-old site,

Shack restaurant on Morjim Beach, a common sight in Goa

A fisherman casting his net off Querim Beach

although the present structure dates to the 18th century. It is dedicated to the eight-armed Bhagavati, an incarnation of Shiva's consort Parvati. Its elaborate gateway is framed by two life-size elephants. A short distance from the bazaar is the palatial **Deshprabhu House**, the 19th-century mansion of the wealthy Hindu Deshprabhu family, who fought for Goa's liberation in 1961. This sprawling property, built around 16 courtyards, has a private temple and a museum displaying family portraits and antiques.

Deshaprabhu House
Tel (0832) 242 1594 to arrange a visit.

❽ Arambol

North Goa district (Pernem taluka). 50 km (31 miles) N of Panaji. every half hour from Siolim.

Also known as Harmal, Arambol is the only fishing village in North Goa that has some basic facilities for visitors. Situated along one of Goa's less commercial beaches, it still retains all the charm of a traditional fishing village,

except for the occasional gypsy selling bright scarves and skirts. Unlike in central Goa, the Hindu influence is apparent here; the numerous cafés and guesthouses are called Ganesha or Namaste instead of Pete's or Johnny's.

At the northern end, a rocky footpath leads to a second beach, entirely surrounded by cliffs. This sandy cove has a freshwater lagoon fed by hot springs and lined with sulphurous mud. A 5-km (3-mile) long path, heading north, leads to **Querim Beach** (pronounced "keri") – a pristine strip of white sand, backed by casuarina trees.

❾ Terekhol Fort

North Goa district (Pernem taluka). 42 km (26 miles) N of Panaji. every half hour from Querim.

Across the Terekhol river from Querim is the little hamlet of Terekhol, with Terekhol (Tiracol) Fort situated on a plateau above it. The early 18th-century fort was captured by the Portuguese in 1776 from the Bhonsles, a Maratha clan. It was the scene of an uprising in 1954, when a group of *satyagrahis* (freedom fighters) hoisted the Indian flag on its ramparts in an act of civil disobedience against colonial rule. The fort's high battlements face the sea, looking across the waters to Fort Aguada, Arambol and Chapora. The tiny chapel within the fort, with a statue of Christ in the courtyard, is usually closed but the atmospheric Terekhol Fort Heritage Hotel offers some excellent views.

Carnival king on a float

Festivals of Goa

Jatra *(Jan)*, Quepem. A colourful festival *(jatra)* honouring local temple deities is celebrated at the Shantadurga Temple *(see p506)*. Other such festivals take place through the year at various temples in Ponda.

Carnival *(Feb)*, Panaji. Goa's grandest festival marks the beginning of Lent. "King Momo", who personifies fun and frolic, orders his subjects to forget their troubles, and leads a colourful parade through the streets. Three days and nights of non-stop revelry follow.

Masked dancers, Carnival

Shigmotsav (Shigmo) *(Mar)*. This joyous Hindu spring festival is celebrated acoss the state. Festivities continue for five days and include colourful street floats (in the larger towns), local folk theatre, sword dances and the lively spraying of coloured powder.

All Saints Procession *(Apr)*, Goa Velha, Pilar. Large crowds of devotees carry statues of 26 saints in procession from St Andrew's Church, in this small village near Pilar.

Feast of St Francis Xavier *(3 Dec)*, Old Goa. The feast of Goa's patron saint is held on the anniversary of his death (1552). Attended by Catholic pilgrims from all over the world, the feast is preceeded by novenas (nine days of prayer).

A holy cross on top of a knoll, Arambol Beach

⑩ A Walk through Old Goa

A magnificent complex of cathedrals, churches and monasteries, spread along a 1.5-km (1-mile) stretch, marks the site of Old Goa, the Portuguese capital until the mid-18th century. The walk through this area, now a UNESCO World Heritage Site, takes in two of Goa's most important religious monuments, the Basilica de Bom Jesus and the grand Sé Cathedral, and ends on Holy Hill, where some of Goa's oldest churches are located. Most of these buildings, designed by Italian or Portuguese architects, encompass a range of European styles, from sober Renaissance to exuberant Baroque and Portuguese Manueline *(see p505).*

④ **Sé Cathedral**
This is thought to be Asia's largest church. The gilded high altar has six splendid panels depicting the life of St Catherine of Alexandria.

⑦ **The Chapel of St Catherine**, like Our Lady of the Rosary, was built to celebrate Albuquerque's victory in 1510 and served as Goa's only cathedral until the Sé Cathedral was built.

⑬ **Our Lady of the Rosary** was built on top of Holy Hill in 1526 by Alfonso de Albuquerque. He had watched Yusuf Adil Shah's defeat in 1510 from this very spot and vowed to build a church here.

⑫ **Royal Chapel of St Anthony**
St Anthony, Portugal's national saint, was also considered the Captain of the army.

Panaji ⑬ ...... RUA DAS NAUS DE ORMUZ

Holy Hill ⑩ ⑫ ⑪ ⑨

⑩ **Convent of St Monica**, dating to the mid-17th century, will house Asia's first Museum of Christian Art, currently being relocated from Rachol *(see p508).*

⑪ **Church and Monastery of St Augustine**
The 46-m (151-ft) high laterite belfry dominates the remains of what was once India's largest church.

⑨ **Church and Convent of St John of God**
Rebuilt in 1953, this convent dates back to 1685 when it was built by the Order of the Hospitallers of St John of God to tend to the sick.

② Gateway of Adil Shah's Palace

The gate, comprising a lintel and basalt pillars, is all that survives of Adil Shah's palace, also used as the viceroys' residence from 1554 to 1695.

① Viceroy's Arch

Over 1,000 ships a year brought new arrivals to Goa in the 17th century. They passed under this laterite archway, built by Francisco da Gama (viceroy 1597–1600).

VISITORS' CHECKLIST

Practical Information
North Goa district (Tiswadi taluka). 9 km (6 miles) E of Panaji.
ℹ GTDC, Old Goa Tourist Hotel, behind Police Station, near MG Statue, (0832) 228 5327. 🎏 Feast of St Francis Xavier (3 Dec). The Archaeological Survey of India's booklet on Old Goa is available at the Archaeological Museum.

Transport
🚇 Karmali, 9 km (6 miles) S of Old Goa. 🚌 or taxi from Panaji.

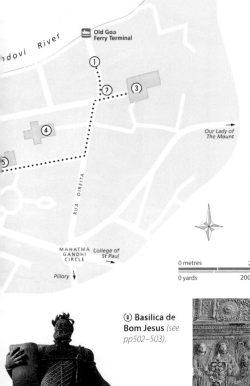

Old Goa Ferry Terminal

ndovi River

Our Lady of The Mount

RUA DIREITA

MAHATMA GANDHI CIRCLE — College of St Paul

Pillory ↓

0 metres 200
0 yards 200

③ Church of St Cajetan

Built by Italian friars in 1651, this church is renowned for the exuberant woodcarvings on its high altar and pulpit.

⑧ Basilica de Bom Jesus (see pp502–503).

⑤ Archaeological Museum

A bronze statue of the poet Luis Vaz de Camões, holding his epic *Os Lusiadas* (see p491), stands in the museum, now housed in the converted convent of St Francis of Assisi, adjoining the church.

⑥ Church of St Francis of Assisi

Built by the Franciscan friars in 1521, this is one of Old Goa's most important churches. Its carved and gilded main altar depicts the crucified Jesus, four Evangelists, St Francis, and Our Lady with the baby Jesus.

Old Goa: Basilica de Bom Jesus

The Basilica de Bom Jesus is revered by Roman Catholics all over the world since it houses the mortal remains of Goa's patron saint, Francis Xavier. It was the first church in South Asia to be granted the status of Minor Basilica, by Pope Pius XII in 1946. Built by the Jesuits in 1594, this grand Baroque structure blends Corinthian, Doric, Ionic and composite styles in its magnificent three-tiered façade. The Duke of Tuscany, Cosimo III, donated the elaborate tomb of St Francis in exchange for the pillow that lay under the saint's head. The tomb took the Florentine sculptor Giovanni Foggini ten years to build; it was finally assembled in 1698. The adjoining Professed House (1589) was used as the priests' quarters until it was damaged by a fire in 1633.

Doorway to Sacristy
An exquisitely carved wooden door leads to the sacristy.

★ Main Altar
The gilded reredos has a statue of St Ignatius of Loyola and another of the Infant Jesus. Local craftsmen, used to decorating temples, made plump, typically Hindu looking cherubs on the altar.

St Francis Xavier (1506–1552)

Francis Xavier was sent to Goa by the Portuguese king, Dom Joao III. He arrived in May 1542, aged 36, and worked tirelessly over the next few years, converting nearly 30,000

people. He died while on voyage off the coast of China in 1552, and was temporarily buried on an island. When his body was dug up three months later to transfer his bones, it showed no signs of decay. A year later, when his remains were enshrined in the Basilica in Goa, his body was still in pristine condition. This was declared a miracle, and in 1622 he was canonized. Expositions of his relics take place every ten years or so, the last one was in 2004–2005.

St Francis Xavier, Art Gallery

Catholic nuns at the entrance to the Basilica

★ **Tomb of St Francis Xavier**
The marble and jasper tomb has four bronze plaques depicting scenes from the saint's life. Built in a mixture of Italian and Indian styles, the silver reliquary containing the sacred relics is surmounted by a cross with two angels.

Sacristy

KEY

① **Chapel of the Blessed Sacrament**

② **Altar of Our Lady of Hope**

③ **Altar of St Michael**

④ **Basalt Stone Tablet** features the Jesuit motto, IHS or *Iaeus Hominum Salvator*, means "Jesus the Saviour" in Greek.

★ **Wooden Pulpit**
The figures of Jesus and several Evangelists are beautifully carved on the pulpit.

Façade
This is the only Goan church not covered in lime plaster. Its original coat was removed in 1956, exposing the soft red laterite beneath. Each of the three doorways and six windows is flanked by elegant pillars and basalt detailing.

Exploring Old Goa

Portugal's Goa Dourada ("Golden Goa") was once a vast city, inhabited by more than 30,000 people. In the 16th century, it attracted missionaries and soldiers, merchants and horse-traders, and its elegant palaces and mansions were much praised by contemporary visitors. However, by the mid-18th century, a series of epidemics and the silting up of the Mandovi river forced the viceroy to move his residence downstream to Panaji (*see p490*). Thereafter, decline set in and, by the 19th century, the city was finally abandoned and its houses demolished. Today, Old Goa is a mere shadow of its former self, but the few churches and cathedrals that remain are considered to be among Goa's most significant monuments.

Rows of pillars on either side of the central nave, Sé Cathedral

🏛 Church of St Cajetan

E of Viceroy's Arch. **Open** daily.
In the 17th century, Pope Urban III sent Italian priests from the Theatine Order to Golconda (*see pp670–71*). When refused entry, they settled in Old Goa. Here, in 1651, they erected a church dedicated to their founder, St Cajetan, designed along the lines of St Peter's in Rome. The distinctive dome and interior, laid out in the shape of a Greek cross, embody the majesty of Italian Baroque. The adjacent monastery is today a college of theology.

Detail of altar, Church of St Cajetan

🏛 Sé Cathedral

Senate Square. **Tel** (0832) 228 4710. **Open** daily. 🕑 7am Mon–Sat (Konkani), 6am Sat (Eng), 7:30am, 10am & 4pm Sun (Konkani).

Ordered by the government in Portugal to build a church worthy of their mighty empire, Francis Coutinho (viceroy, 1561–4) envisaged a magnificent cathedral that would be the largest in Asia. The result is the Renaissance-style Sé Cathedral, designed in the 16th century by Julio Simao and Ambrosio Argueiro, and built over 80 years. Its 30-m (98-ft) high Tuscan-style façade was flanked by two square bell towers, only one of which survives. In it hangs the Golden Bell, known for its melodic tones, which rang out during the dreaded *auto da fé* trials, held in the cathedral's front square.

The interior, with intricate Corinthian detailing, has a 76-m (249-ft) long central nave. As many as 15 altars grace the interior, but the *pièce de résistance* is the gilded high altar, dedicated to St Catherine of Alexandria, with panel paintings depicting scenes from her life. Two of the eight chapels, the Blessed Sacrament and the Cross of Miracles, have delicate filigree work on their screens. The font, used by St Francis Xavier to baptize converts, is near the entrance. The sacred relics of his body, kept in the Basilica de Bom Jesus (*see pp502–503*), are brought to the cathedral during the expositions held every ten years.

🏛 Archaeological Museum

Convent of St Francis of Assisi. **Tel** (0832) 228 5333. **Open** Sat–Thu. 🖼
Once Goa's largest monastery, the Convent of St Francis of Assisi (built in 1517) now houses the Archaeological Museum. A huge bronze statue of Alfonso de Albuquerque, moved from Panaji, dominates the entrance hall. Among the objects of interest are a finely carved

From right to left, Sé Cathedral, Church of St Francis of Assisi and Church of Our Lady of the Rosary in Old Goa

image of Vishnu and a Surya statue, dating to the Kadamba period (11th–12th centuries), and stone inscriptions in Marathi and Persian, relics of earlier ruling dynasties. Other exhibits include Hindu *sati* stones, a model of *São Gabriel* (the ship in which Vasco da Gama sailed to India in 1498), and a bronze statue of St Catherine in the courtyard. The Portrait Gallery on the first floor has 60 paintings of Goa's viceroys and governors.

⌂ Church of St Francis of Assisi

W of Sé Cathedral. **Open** daily.
Built by the Franciscan friars in 1521, and rebuilt in 1661, this church has a beautifully carved doorway (taken from the original building). This is a rare example of the Portuguese Manueline style, which uses many nautical motifs,

Façade with two octagonal towers, Church of St Francis of Assisi

and was developed during the reign of King Dom Manuel (r.1469–1521). A pair of

Detail of memorial, St Augustine's ruins

navigator's globes and a Greek cross (the emblem of all Portuguese ships) embellish the door. The superb Baroque interior has floral frescoes on the walls and ceiling, and the floor is paved with the sculpted tombstones of Portuguese nobility. The gilded altar has figures of St Francis and Christ. Other noteworthy features are the pulpit, which is carved in floral designs and the painted panels in the chancel, which depict various scenes from the saint's life.

⌂ Church and Monastery of St Augustine

Holy Hill.
Once the largest church in India, with a grand five-storeyed façade, St Augustine's now lies in ruins. Erected by the Augustinian order in 1512, the Gothic-style church was abandoned in 1835, and its roof caved in seven years later. Excavations begun in 1989 revealed eight chapels, four altars, wall sculptures and more than 100 splendid granite tombstones. According to contemporary descriptions, the church also had grand staircases and galleries, and a library that rivalled the one at Oxford (England), in the 17th century. Today, all that remains of St Augustine's is its soaring bell tower *(see p500).*

⌂ Church of Our Lady of the Rosary

Holy Hill. **Open** daily.
With its castle-like turrets and simple altar painted with baskets of flowers, this is one of Goa's earliest Manueline-style churches. The tomb of Dona Catarina, wife of Garcia de Sá (viceroy from 1548-9) and the first Portuguese woman to migrate to Goa, also lies here.

Further Afield

A few buildings of interest lie in Old Goa's southeastern corner. Marking the end of the Rua Direita, Old Goa's main street, is a desolate basalt pillar on a raised platform, the remains of the terrible **Pillory**. Criminals and heretics were strung up here as punishment, in the centre of the city square. Close by, on the road to Ponda, lies the **College of St Paul**. Founded by the Jesuits in 1541, it had 3,000 students, making it the largest Jesuit school in Asia. It also housed Asia's first printing press. St Francis Xavier stayed and preached here; the chapel further up the road was also used by him, and was later dedicated to his memory.

The **Church of Our Lady of the Mount**, built in 1510, sits on top of a hill and is reached by a lane that leads off the Cumbarjua Road. Built by Alfonso de Albuquerque after his victory over Yusuf Adil Shah, the church offers magnificent views over Old Goa's towers and turrets.

Altar in the Church of Our Lady of the Rosary, on Holy Hill

The Goa Inquisition

At the request of Francis Xavier *(see p502)*, a tribunal of Jesuits arrived in 1560 and took over Adil Shah's secondary palace (of which few traces now remain), to the south of Sé Cathedral. Their mission was to curb the libertine ways of the Portuguese settlers and convert "infidels". During the Inquisition in 1567, all Hindu ceremonies were banned, temples were destroyed and Hindus forcibly converted. Those who refused were locked away in the dungeons of the "Palace of the Inquisition" (as Adil Shah's palace was known) to await the *auto da fé* (acts of faith) trial. The condemned were burnt alive in front of a congregation of dignitaries. Over the next 200 years, 16,000 trials were held and thousands killed, and it was not until 1812 that the Inquisition was finally dissolved.

Mural of a proselytizing priest

17th-century painting of St Cecilia, patroness of church choirs, Pilar

⓫ Pilar

North Goa district (Tiswadi taluka). 12 km (7 miles) SE of Panaji.

Set on a hilltop, **Pilar Seminary** was originally built by the Capuchins (a Franciscan order) in 1613, on the site of an old Hindu temple. Abandoned in 1835, when all religious orders were disbanded, it was reopened by the Carmelites in 1858. In 1890, the Society of Pilar set up a mission college here, and classes are still held in the old seminary building.

The adjoining **Church of Our Lady of Pilar** has an elaborately carved stone doorway with a figure of St Francis of Assisi above it. Inside is a statue of Our Lady of Pilar, brought here from Spain. The tomb of Agnelo D'Souza (seminary director, 1918–27) lies adjacent to the church. The **New Seminary**, built in 1946, stands close by. Its museum displays Christian art, Portuguese coins and a stone lion, the symbol of the Kadamba dynasty.

🏛 Museum
Tel (0832) 221 8521. **Open** daily (Sun and public hols by appointment).

Environs
Goa Velha, 2 km (1.3 miles) southwest of Pilar, marks the site of Govapuri, the port-capital of the Kadamba rulers between the 11th and 13th centuries, of which few traces now remain.

⓬ Ponda

South Goa district (Ponda taluka). 28 km (17 miles) SE of Panaji. 17,700. Urs of Shah Abdullah (Feb).

The town of Ponda is a busy commercial centre, and its main sight is the **Safa Shahouri Mosque**, 2 km (1.3 miles) to the west. Built by Ibrahim Adil Shah (a successor of Yusuf Adil Shah) in 1560, it is a rectangular structure, with window arches, topped by a slanting tiled roof. A ritual tank to the south has the same designs as those on the *mihrabs* (arched niches).

Ponda also lends its name to the *taluka* (sub-district) of the same name, which is renowned for its numerous Hindu temples, tucked away in thick forests. As the Portuguese expanded their territory in central Goa, they destroyed over 550 temples. Hindu priests fled with their religious artifacts to regions that lay outside Portuguese control, especially the area around Ponda town, where they built new temples in the 17th and 18th centuries.

More than half of Goa's population is Hindu, and Goan temples, unlike those elsewhere in India, are a fascinating blend of European Baroque, Muslim and Hindu architectural styles. Their basic plan remains Hindu, but often Muslim domes replace the usual *shikharas* (spires) over the main

Brass lamp tower, Shri Mahalsa Temple

sanctum, and the prayer halls are decorated with ornate European chandeliers.

The **Shantadurga Temple**, 3 km (2 miles) southwest of Ponda at Kavlem, is Goa's most popular shrine. Built by Shahu, the grandson of the Maratha chief Shivaji *(see p475)*, the russet and cream coloured temple has an unusual pagoda-style roof, dominated by a five-storeyed octagonal lamp tower, unique to Goa. Grand chandeliers hang from the gilded roof in the huge central hall, and embossed silver screens shield the main sanctuary, which holds the silver deity of Shantadurga (a form of Shiva's consort Parvati), brought from Mormugao *taluka*. Also of interest are the huge *rathas* (chariots) that are used during the Jatra in January *(see p497)*. The **Shri Ramnath Temple**, a short walk away, is noted for the grand silver screen embossed with animal and floral motifs, in front of its sanctum. Its linga, originally from Loutolim, is worshipped by devotees of both Shiva and Vishnu.

The **Shri Nagueshi Temple**, 4 km (2.5 miles) west of Ponda at Bandora, dates to 1780, though a temple may have stood here earlier. Built for the worship of Nagesh (Shiva as Lord of the Serpents), it is one of the oldest temples in this region. Its entrance hall has

The large 18th-century water tank at the Shri Mangesh Temple

carved wooden friezes depicting scenes from the epics *Ramayana* and *Mahabharata (see pp30–31)*.

The 18th-century **Shri Lakshmi Narasimha Temple** is situated in Velinga village, 5 km (3 miles) northwest of Ponda. Its majestic image of Narasimha, Vishnu's man-lion incarnation *(see p683)*, was brought here from Mormugao in the 1560s. Surrounded by forest, it is one of Goa's most attractive temples, with a sacred tank and an elaborate gateway. A tower standing close by houses the temple's musicians during the annual Jatra festival, held here in May.

Dedicated to Vishnu, the **Shri Mahalsa Temple** is 7 km (4 miles) northwest of Ponda, in Mardol village. The main deity (either a female form of Vishnu or his consort Lakshmi) was taken from Verna. The temple's distinguishing feature is an exceptionally tall brass pillar, 21 tiers in all, rising from a figure of Kurma (Vishnu's incarnation as a turtle), with Garuda (his vehicle) perched on top. The pillar symbolizes Mount Kailasa which, according to Hindu mythology, was placed on Kurma's back and was used to churn the primordial ocean. The original shrine is a wooden structure with a sloping roof, and the entrance porches have carvings of musicians and warriors. Its main hall has intricately carved pillars, while the central part of the ceiling is raised, with painted

A procession during the Shigmo Jatra, at the Shri Mahalsa Temple

images of gods set in niches. A short distance to the northwest, at Priol, lies Goa's wealthiest temple, the 18th-century **Shri Mangesh Temple**, dedicated to Shiva. The courtyard has a sacred *tulsi* (basil) plant growing in a bright green urn, a characteristic Goan feature. There is a large sacred tank and a seven-storeyed lamp tower. Dance-dramas are performed here during the Jatra festivities in April and May. A vividly painted elephant on wheels stands at the entrance to the white and yellow temple. Inside, 19th-century Belgian chandeliers hang from the ceiling, while the main sanctum has a linga transferred from Mormugao. The childhood home of Lata Mangeshkar (b.1929), India's most famous singer of film songs, was near the temple.

About 4 km (2.5 miles) northeast of Ponda town, near the village of Khandepar, is a cluster of **Hindu Rock-cut Caves** from the 10th–13th centuries, with carved lotus decorations on the ceiling, simple door frames and niches for oil lamps.

A few spice gardens that grow aromatic spices such as cardamom, nutmeg and cinnamon, make interesting day trips from Ponda. The Pascoal Plantation, 8 km (5 miles) east, and the Savoi Spice Garden at Savoi Verem, 12 km (7 miles) north, are easy to reach.

The Kadamba-period Tambdi Surla Temple, set on the banks of a stream

⑬ Tambdi Surla

South Goa district (Sanguem taluka). 73 km (45 miles) E of Panaji. Taxis from Panaji or Ponda are the best option.

Hidden away in the forests of Tambdi Surla, stands the oldest existing Hindu temple in Goa, dating from the Kadamba period (between the 11th and 13th centuries). Built in black basalt and dedicated to Shri Mahadeva (Shiva), the temple probably survived because of its remote location. The symmetrical structure is made of stone slabs fitted neatly into each other, without using mortar. Set on a low plinth, the entrance hall has ten pillars, and the *shikhara* (spire) above the sanctum has a miniature relief and fine carvings of Brahma, Vishnu, Shiva and his consort, Parvati.

Detail, Tamdi Surla Temple

Environs

The **Bhagwan Mahaveer Sanctuary**, 20 km (12 miles) southeast of Tamdi Surla, covers an area of 240 sq km (93 sq miles) and is home to leopards, deer and the Indian bison. The 600-m (1,969-ft) high **Dudhsagar Waterfalls** on the Goa-Karnataka border are its main attraction. The small **Bondla Sanctuary**, 30 km (19 miles) east of Tambdi Surla, is known for its variety of birds.

🦌 **Bhagwan Mahaveer Sanctuary**
Open daily. 🏞

🦌 **Bondla Sanctuary**
Open Sep-Jun: Fri-Wed.
🏞

Altar, Church of St Ignatius Loyola, Rachol

⑭ Rachol

South Goa district (Salcete taluka).
52 km (32 miles) SE of Panaji. 🚌

The small hamlet of Rachol occupies the site of an old fortress built by the Bijapur sultans *(see p546)*, which was ceded to the Portuguese in 1520. A laterite archway and a dry moat are the only remnants of the bastion – once fortified with 100 cannons – that used to guard the southern borders of the Portuguese territories. The pretty **Church of Nossa Senhora das Neves** (Our Lady of the Snows), in the village, was built in 1576.

Today, **Rachol Seminary**, built in 1606, is probably the most important of Goa's seminaries. First established in Margao in 1574, and known as the College of All Saints, the earlier seminary included a hospital, a school for the poor and a printing press. It was relocated here after the Margao institution was destroyed in a Muslim raid in 1579. For generations, this was Goa's most prestigious educational institution, both for secular and religious studies, offering a seven-year course in theology and philosophy, to prepare young seminarians for the priesthood. Spectacularly located on the summit of a

Silver reliquary, museum collection

hill, the building has a grand fort-like façade, flanked by imposing watchtowers. The seminary's vast entrance hall is covered with impressive murals and opens on to a central courtyard, surrounded by cloistered rooms made of solid teak, each one with an adjoining wood-panelled study. The grand staircase is adorned with Hindu sculptures, excavated from the ancient Hindu temple on the site of which the seminary was constructed. This leads to the first floor and the library, which has a rare collection of Latin and Portuguese books, and portraits of Goa's archbishops.

Attached to the seminary is the **Church of St Ignatius Loyola**, dedicated to the eponymous saint. It has an ornately carved and gilded altar with a painting of St Constantine, the first Roman emperor to convert to Christianity. According to legend, a few bone fragments and a vial of his blood were brought to Rachol in 1782, and are supposedly enshrined near the entrance. The choir stall has delicate murals of the founding saints of various religious orders. On the first floor balcony is a beautiful 16th-century pipe-organ from Lisbon. Until mid-2001,

Rachol Seminary also housed the renowned Museum of Christian Art, established in 1991 by the Indian National Trust for Art and Cultural Heritage (INTACH) and the Gulbenkian Foundation of Portugal. The entire collection is currently being shifted to the Convent of St Monica in Old Goa *(see p500)*, and will be set up in the Chapel of the Weeping Cross, adjacent to the convent. Its impressive collection of 17th- and 18th-century religious objects includes silver and ivory ornaments, ornate clerical robes, processional crosses and holy water sprinklers. Particularly charming is a portable altar for travelling missionaries, with candle stands and a mass kit.

⑮ Margao

South Goa district (Salcete taluka).
33 km (21 miles) S of Panaji. 🚇 78,500. 🚉 🚌 ℹ Margao Residency, (0832) 271 5528. 📷 Feast of the Holy Spirit (May).

Margao (Madgaon), Goa's second most important city after Panaji, is the administrative and commercial capital of the South Goa district. This bustling town also serves as the area's main trading centre for local fish and farm produce.

The town square, **Praça Jorge Barreto**, has the large, colonial Municipal Building, which houses the library on its southern side, and a popular café called Longinhos nearby. Just behind the Municipal Building, to the south, are

A view of the hilltop Seminary and Church at Rachol

Margao's lively bazaars, selling the day's catch of fish and fresh fruit and vegetables. The **Covered Market**, close by, sells just about everything, including piles of soap flakes, pulses, dried fish, pickles, spicy pork sausages, tamarind, flower garlands, jaggery and crockery. A row of shops to the north sells locally brewed wines, and the lane just outside the market has a number of cloth merchants.

Abbé de Faria Street, winding north from the town square, is lined with some well-preserved colonial mansions, and leads to Margao's old Latin Quarter. Its central square, **Largo de Igreja**, is also surrounded by colourful 18th- and 19th-century town houses, with tiled roofs, wrought-iron balconies and balustrades. In the centre of the square is a monumental, 16th-century cross, overlooked by the towering Baroque **Church of the Holy Spirit**. Built in 1565 on the site of a ravaged Hindu temple, the church and the adjoining Jesuit College of All Saints were ransacked numerous times by Muslim raiders. While the seminary was moved to Rachol, the church was rebuilt in 1675. Its whitewashed façade is flanked by two towers topped with domes and embellished with lanterns, though its side walls have been left unusually bare of

The red and white Municipal Building, Praça Jorge Barreto, Margao

lime-plaster. The grand interior has a stucco ceiling, a gilded pulpit decorated with carvings of the apostles, a Rococo altar, and elegant Baroque altar-pieces in the transepts. Just behind the church, Agostinho Lorenço Street leads east to the imposing mansion called **Sat Burnzam Gor**, or "Seven Gables" *(see p510)*, named after the original seven gables or pyramidal crests on its roof. It is the only surviving example of a house with pyramidal roofs in Goa. Built in 1790 by Ignacio da Silva from his earnings as the viceroy's secretary, the huge, impressive salons are filled with richly carved rosewood furniture and priceless porcelain, and its private chapel was the first that was permitted in Goa. From the intersection lying east of the church, a road winds up to **Monte Hill**. Although one

Monumental cross in Largo de Igreja

cannot enter the tiny chapel at the top, the views across Margao's rooftops of the entire southern coast are spectacular.

Sat Burnzam Gor
Only by prior appointment; contact Mrs de Silva.

Environs
The pretty villages around Margao have a number of colonial country mansions, dating to the prosperous period from the 18th to the 19th centuries, when local landlords began to profit from Portugal's control over the maritime trade routes from Africa to Malacca (in Malaysia). Many of these homes were also owned by Goans, who held high posts in the Portuguese government and were granted land in exchange for their services.

Loutolim, 10 km (6 miles) to the northeast, was once an important Portuguese administrative centre, and has a cluster of stately homes, all situated fairly close to the main church square. The Goa Tourism office, and the Houses of Goa museum, (0832) 241 0711, located at Salvador do Mundo, can organize visits to these buildings. **Chandor**, 13 km (8 miles) east of Margao, has the palatial Braganza house, Goa's largest private dwelling *(see pp512–13)*. **Chinchinim**, 10 km (6 miles) south of Margao, and **Benaulim**, 6 km (4 miles) southwest of Margao, also have fine mansions, with typical Goan *balcaos* (porches) and terracotta-tiled sloping roofs.

Fresh prawns, sardines, mackerel and salmon, Margao bazaar

Goa's Colonial Mansions

Goa's countryside is dotted with grand colonial mansions, built by the wealthy land-owning Goan gentry, who prospered in the 18th and 19th centuries. The homes of these local aristocrats were built in the traditional style of the region, with central courtyards, deep porches and window shutters made of oyster-shell. The furniture and interior decor, however, were largely European. Today, the Belgian chandeliers, Venetian cut-glass and gilded mirrors, Baroque-style rosewood furniture and Chinese porcelain, displayed inside, provide a fascinating picture of the tastes and lifestyles of a vanished era.

Oyster-shell window shutters line the façade of Sat Burnzam Gor ("Seven Gables") in Margao. A unique feature of 16th- and 17th-century Goan architecture, oyster shells were used in place of glass panes and effectively kept out the heat and glare.

A typical pyramidal balcao, or porch, graces the entrance of the Figueredo House in Loutolim. Chairs were often placed under the *balcao*, as it was customary to socialize at the front door.

This antique rosewood carving from Goa's grandest mansion, Braganza House in Chandor *(see pp512–13)*, is a typical example of Indo-Portuguese Baroque.

European-style salons, such as the regal ballroom in the Dr Alvaro Loyola Furtado Mansion in Chinchinim, built in 1833, have crystal chandeliers and elegant furniture.

Carved antique furniture at the Casa dos Mirandos

Where to See Goan Houses

Loutolim has four houses of interest – Salvador da Costa House, Roque Caetan Miranda House, Figueredo House and Casa dos Mirandos, which is the finest. *Margao* has the Sat Burnzam Gor, *Chinchinim* has the Loyola Furtado Mansion, and *Chandor* has the Braganza House. For more details see page 509.

⑰ Colva

South Goa district (Salcete taluka).
6 km (4 miles) W of Margao. 🚌
ℹ️ GTDC Colva Residency, (0832) 278
8047. 🎭 Fama de Menino Jesus (Oct).

Colva's proximity to Margao makes it an ideal summer retreat for Margao's residents. It is one of South Goa's oldest and most developed beach resorts, and its 25-km (16-mile) long sandy beach, from the Mormugao peninsula in the north to Mobor in the south, is the longest uninterrupted stretch in the state.

Today, Colva draws vast numbers of visitors, who spend the day enjoying the lively atmosphere of its many beach shacks, set high on stilts and backed by shady palms. These serve delicious grilled lobster and other sea-food specialities. Numerous top-end and mid-range hotels stand on the main beach road, while the southern extremities have more pristine stretches. Fisherfolk haul in their catch on the beach front, which also plays host to full-moon rave parties.

A cheerful waiter, Mobor

Standing a short distance from the sea, Colva's **Church of Our Lady of Mercy**, built in 1630, has an attractive Baroque interior and houses the famous statue of Menino (baby) Jesus, holding an orb and a flag, revered for its miraculous healing powers.

Environs
Majorda, 7 km (4 miles) north of Colva, has a wide beach dotted with luxury hotels.

Bogmalo Beach, 20 km (12 miles) northwest of Colva, is a popular venue for wind-surfing.

Tourism has spilled over from Colva to the quiet fishing village of **Benaulim**, 2 km (1.3 miles) south, whose roads are lined with small guesthouses, restaurants and bars. **Varca Beach**, 5 km (3 miles) further south, has many plush hotels, as well as a parish church with an imposing façade.

⑱ Cavelossim

South Goa district (Salcete taluka).
15 km (9 miles) S of Margao. 🚌

A favourite with Indian celebrities, Cavelossim has an enchanting 2-km (1.3-mile) stretch of sand. It also has a golf course, luxury resorts and excellent seafood restaurants, such as the Seaways Bar. The ornate **Church of the Holy Cross**, is situated in a pretty square.

Environs
Mobor, 5 km (3 miles) south of Colva, is an idyllic spot, with its backdrop of hills and the pretty fishing village of **Betul** nestling near the Sal river. The Leela Beach Resort is located here. **Cabo da Rama** ("Cape Rama"), the promontory just south of Betul, is named after Rama, hero of the *Ramayana*, who supposedly hid here during his 14-year exile *(see p31)*. It has the ruins of a Hindu fortress that fell to the Portuguese in 1763.

A thatch-roofed beach shack,
Palolem Beach

⑲ Palolem

South Goa district (Salcete taluka).
37 km (23 miles) S of Margao. 🚌

Famous for its spectacular sunsets, this bay is enclosed by a rocky outcrop at one end, and Canacona Island, a good camping site, at the other. Palolem's remote location, away from the crowded beaches of central Goa, makes it an ideal for a quiet holiday. A special attraction are the boat rides offered by fishermen, who take visitors out to sea for dolphin watching trips.

Environs
Southern Goa is for the most part isolated and unspoilt by tourism. **Agonda**, 7 km (4 miles) north of Palolem, is even quieter than its neighbour **Galgibaga**, 8 km (5 miles) south of Palolem, has a beautiful stretch of virgin sand, shaded by eucalyptus trees rather than palms. The remote **Cotigao Wildlife Sanctuary**, 18 km (11 miles) west of Palolem, is worth visiting for its tranquil beauty.

Visitors cycling on the sands at Colva, Goa's longest beach

⑯ Braganza House

The awesome scale of Braganza House, and the magnificence of its interior, make it Goa's grandest colonial mansion. This 17th-century building is still occupied by two branches of the Braganza family. The descendants of Antonio Elzario Sant'Anna Pereira occupy the east wing, while Francisco Xavier de Menezes Braganza's descendants live in the west wing. Both men received royal titles and a coat of arms from the king of Portugal in the late 19th century. The top floors of their private apartments have the splendid ballroom, library and chapel, and fine collections of 18th-century furniture and Chinese porcelain.

Dining Hall
A long table fills the first floor dining hall of this sprawling mansion.

★ **The Chapel**
The Baroque-style chapel has a diamond-encrusted fingernail of St Francis Xavier on its altar.

KEY

① **The East Wing** is owned by the Braganza Pereiras.

② **Guest Bedroom** is dominated by a large rosewood four-poster bed. At its foot is a rosewood two-seater.

③ **The West Wing** is occupied by the Menezes Braganzas.

④ **The Library** has Goa's finest private collection, with over 5,000 leather-bound books.

★ **The Ballroom**
A rosewood armchair with the Braganza coat of arms, and a gilded mirror are in the mansion's grandest room. The walls as well as the floors are of marble, and chandeliers hang from its floral-patterned zinc ceiling.

Menezes Braganza Salon
A collection of exquisite Chinese porcelain is displayed in one of the salons, where a large vase takes pride of place.

VISITORS' CHECKLIST

Practical Information
Church Square, Chandor (Salcete taluka). 20 km (12 miles) E of Margao.
Tel (0832) 278 4201.
Admission to both wings only by prior appointment.
🏛 Donations appreciated.

Transport
🚌 🚐

Portrait of Francisco Xavier de Menezes Braganza
A portrait of the grandfather of renowned journalist, Luis de Menezes Braganza *(see p491)*, hangs in the ballroom of the west wing.

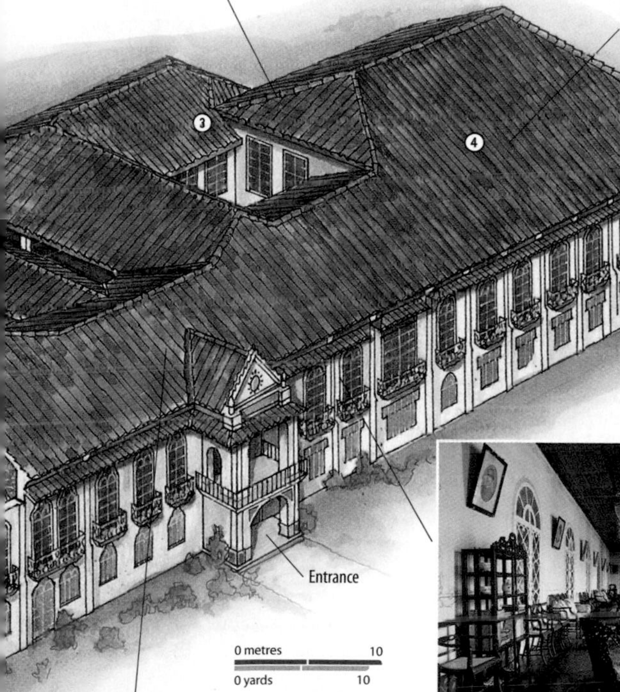

Entrance

0 metres   10
0 yards   10

★ **The Hallway**
A long and elegantly furnished hallway lies just behind the façade of the house. It is lined with 28 bay windows and overlooks a well-maintained garden.

Stairway
The monumental double staircase forms the core of the house, connecting the lower entrance level to the furnished top floors.

KARNATAKA

Extending from the Arabian Sea and the fertile forested ridges of the Western Ghats, with their thriving plantations of coffee, spices and fruit, to the drier, boulder-strewn region of the Deccan Plateau, Karnataka's scenic diversity is striking. Equally varied are its historical monuments. These range from the 6th–8th century Hindu temples at Badami, Pattadakal and Aihole, the earliest to be found in South India, to Tipu Sultan's 18th-century, European-style island fort at Srirangapattana, and the extravagantly turreted, early 20th-century palace in Mysore. Other sights include the superb temples at Halebid and Belur, the colossal Gommateshvara monolith at Sravana Belgola and the magnificent ruins of Hampi, the site of the great citadel of Vijayanagar. In northern Karnataka are the medieval citadels of the Deccan sultans at Bijapur, Gulbarga and Bidar, their walls enclosing mosques, audience halls and royal tombs.

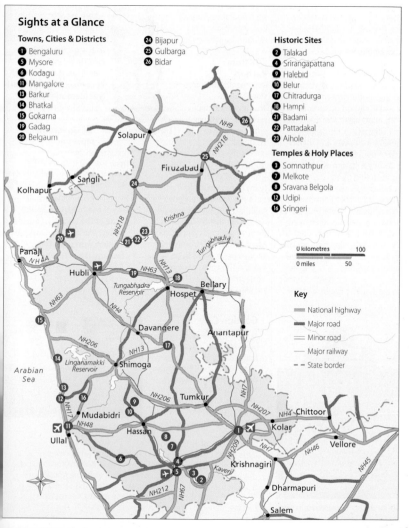

Sights at a Glance

Towns, Cities & Districts
- **1** Bengaluru
- **5** Mysore
- **6** Kodagu
- **11** Mangalore
- **13** Barkur
- **14** Bhatkal
- **15** Gokarna
- **19** Gadag
- **20** Belgaum
- **24** Bijapur
- **25** Gulbarga
- **26** Bidar

Historic Sites
- **2** Talakad
- **4** Srirangapattana
- **9** Halebid
- **10** Belur
- **17** Chitradurga
- **18** Hampi
- **21** Badami
- **22** Pattadakal
- **23** Aihole

Temples & Holy Places
- **3** Somnathpur
- **7** Melkote
- **8** Sravana Belgola
- **12** Udipi
- **16** Sringeri

Key
- National highway
- Major road
- Minor road
- Major railway
- State border

◀ The ancient Virupaksha Temple in Hampi

For keys to symbols *see back flap*

❶ Bengaluru

Often described as Asia's Silicon Valley because of its thriving information technology industry, Bengaluru is India's fifth-largest and fastest-growing city. Until its high-tech boom began in the late 1980s, it was known as the Garden City, with greenery flourishing in its pleasant, temperate climate. Today, with a growing population of young professionals, it has acquired a vibrant, cosmopolitan air. Bengaluru was founded in the 16th century by a local chieftain, Kempe Gowda, but derives its name from the Kannada word *benda kaluru*, or "boiled beans", which an old woman gave a 10th-century Hoysala king when he turned up hungry at her doorstep.

🏛 Vidhana Soudha
Dr Ambedkar Rd.
Closed to the public.
Built of granite and porphyry, this imposing building houses the Secretariat and the State Legislature of Karnataka. Constructed in 1956 after the transfer of power from the ruling Wodeyar dynasty to the central government, it was designed by Kengal Hanumanthaiah, the then chief minister, who intended it to "reflect the power and dignity of the people". It is capped by a 20-m (66-ft) dome, which is surmounted by the four-headed Ashokan lion, symbol of the Indian state. With Rajasthani *jharokhas*, Indo-Saracenic pillars and other decorative elements, the Vidhana Soudha exemplifies the Neo-Dravidian style of post-Independence Bengaluru. The woodwork inside is noteworthy, especially the sandalwood door to the Cabinet Room, and the

Speaker's Chair made of rosewood from Mysore. The building looks spectacular on Sunday evenings when it is beautifully illuminated.

🏛 Attara Kacheri
Opposite Vidhana Sabha.
Open Mon–Fri.
This graceful, two-storeyed building with Corinthian columns, was completed in 1864 and housed the Public Offices from 1868 until 1956. These were later moved to the Vidhana Soudha, and this building became the High Court. On the ceiling of its Central Hall is a portrait of Sir Mark Cubbon, commissioner of Mysore from 1834 to 1861. Behind the building is an equestrian statue of him by Baron Marochetti.

🌳 Cubbon Park
Cantonment. **Open** daily.
Laid out in 1864 by Richard Sankey, the chief engineer of Mysore, and named in honour of the commissioner, Cubbon Park extends over 135 ha (334 acres). Its partly formal landscaping imaginatively integrates natural rock outcroppings with groves of trees and giant bamboos.

The park is liberally dotted with statues, such as that of the 19th-century ruler Chamarajendra Wodeyar (1868–94), overlooking the pond near an octagonal, cast-iron bandstand. There are also marble statues of Queen Victoria and Edward VII. In the middle of the park, a red-painted, Neo-Classical building known as the **Sheshadri Iyer Memorial** houses a public library.

Chamarajendra Wodeyar

🏛 Government Museum
Kasturba Gandhi Rd.
Open 10am–5pm Tue–Sun. 📷
Venkatappa Art Gallery: **Tel** (080) 2286 4483. **Open** 10am–5pm Tue–Sun. 📷
Established in 1866, this is one of the oldest museums in the entire country. Housed in a red stucco Neo-Classical building with Corinthian columns, it has three sections, with a fine collection of wooden sculptures and exotic paintings.

Garden City

The Cantonment in Bengaluru was established in 1809, to house British troops quartered here during the 19th century. With its orderly streets, houses with characteristic "monkey top" eaves, and its lawns, trees, flowers and shrubbery, Bengaluru was eventually christened the "Garden City of India". Two large parks, Cubbon Park and Lalbagh, along with numerous smaller ones such as the Kensington Gardens, act as the lungs of this verdant city. These gardens provide a welcome retreat from Bengaluru's crowded streets and give a refreshing sense of space. The city is particularly charming in January and August when dahlias, marigolds and roses bloom in abundance.

A corner of Cubbon Park

The magnificent Vidhana Soudha, housing the Karnataka Secretariat

For hotels and restaurants see pp701–702 and pp716–17

Mysore painting from Venkatappa Art Gallery

The **Venkatappa Art Gallery**, named after K Venkatappa, an early 20th-century artist patronized by the Wodeyar rulers of Mysore, forms one wing of this museum. In addition to a number of works by Venkatappa himself, the gallery has watercolours and paintings made in the Mysore style. These works still retain a greenish coating, imparted by a finishing rub with jade. The gallery also has a collection of leather puppets made of deer- and goat-skin, and fine sculptures from the Satvahana, Hoysala and Vijayanagar periods.

St Mark's Cathedral

Mahatma Gandhi Rd. **Open** Tue–Sun.
This simple, Neo-Classical cathedral was completed in 1812 and consecrated by the Bishop of Calcutta in 1816. An elegant, cream-coloured structure, it has an imposing portico in front and an apsidal recess at the rear. A shallow dome marks the internal crossing.

Bengaluru Palace

N of Vidhana Soudha. **Tel** (080) 2336 0818. **Open** Mon–Sat.
Built in 1880 at the exorbitant cost of one million rupees, the Bengaluru Palace was modelled on Windsor Castle, complete with fortified towers and turreted parapets. It stands amid undulating lawns, partly converted into a formal garden with axial paths. Spread over 13,700 sq m (147,466 sq ft), the palace fell into disrepair after 1949 when it was at the centre of an ownership dispute between the government and the ruling Wodeyars. It has since been restored to the Wodeyars and is now rented out as a popular venue for functions such as weddings and music concerts, and film shoots. No Kannada movie is considered complete if a scene is not shot here.

Bengaluru City Centre

① Vidhana Soudha
② Attara Kacheri
③ Cubbon Park
④ Government Museum
⑤ St Mark's Cathedral

0 metres 800
0 yards 800

Exploring Old Bengaluru

In spite of rapid development, vestiges of the city's historic past are still found in the streets of Old Bengaluru, south of the city centre. In contrast to the relentless modernization of the rest of Bengaluru, this area contains monuments from the period of the Gowdas to that of Haider Ali and Tipu Sultan, and bears witness to the city's history from the 16th to the 19th centuries.

Tipu Sultan's Palace

Albert Victor Rd.
Tel (080) 2670 6836.
Open daily.

Within the original citadel, a mud-brick fort built by Kempe Gowda in 1537, lies Tipu Sultan's Palace, dating from about 1790. Made mostly out of wood with finely embellished balconies, pillars and arches, this two-storeyed structure, a replica of the Daria Daulat Bagh in Srirangapattana *(see p520)*, served as a summer retreat of Tipu Sultan. He endearingly called it Rashk-e-Jannat, or the "Envy of Heaven". Although now dilapidated, it is still a hauntingly atmospheric place retaining the original elegant teak pillars.

The palace housed the public administrative offices from 1831, until they were shifted to the Attara Kacheri in 1868 *(see p516)*. It now has a museum with artifacts from the Haider Ali–Tipu regime.

Dahlia bloom, Lalbagh

The **Venkataramana-swamy Temple**, nearby, dates from the early 18th century and was built by the Wodeyar kings.

Lalbagh

Lalbagh Rd.
Tel (080) 2657 0181.
Open daily. free
6–9am & 6:30–7:30pm daily.
Flower Show (Jan & Aug).

Regarded as one of the most richly diverse botanical gardens in South Asia, Lalbagh, in the southern part of the city, was laid out by Haider Ali in 1740. Spread over 97 ha (240 acres) of parkland, many of its tropical and subtropical plants were brought here by Haider Ali's son, Tipu Sultan. Later, John Cameron, the Gardens' Superintendent in the 1870s, imported several more rare species from Kew Gardens in London. Cameron was also responsible for initiating work on Lalbagh's famous Glass House, modelled on London's Crystal Palace and conceived as a venue for horticultural shows. Surrounded by *champaka* trees and pencil cedars, the Glass House has played host to several visiting dignitaries. An Annual Flower Show is still held here.

The entrance to the park is marked by an equestrian statue of Chamaraja Wodeyar of Mysore. Another popular attraction is the surreal Floral Clock, surrounded by Snow White and the seven dwarfs; this was a gift from Hindustan Machine Tools, leading Indian manufacturers of watches.

Gavi Gangadhareshvara Temple

W of Lalbagh. **Open** daily.
Makar Sankranti (Jan).

One of Bengaluru's oldest temples, the Gavi Gangadhareshvara Temple was built inside a natural cave in Gavipuram by Kempe Gowda in the 16th century. Legend has it that Kempe Gowda built this temple in gratitude after being released from his five-year imprisonment by Rama Raya.

Highlights include granite pillars, two of which support huge discs representing the sun and the moon, while the other two are topped by a Nandi and a trident. Devotees gather here during the Makar Sankranti festival to witness a unique phenomenon – the evening sun's rays passing between Nandi's horns and falling on the linga inside the cave.

The spacious, 19th-century Glass House at Lalbagh, with its intricate cast-iron frame

For hotels and restaurants see pp701–702 and pp716–17

The Glitter of Gold

The ancient seers of India referred to gold by many names – synonyms for life, longevity, and beauty. Indians considered this metal auspicious and believed that wearing gold ornaments would ensure a long life. Craftsmen traditionally drew inspiration for their designs and motifs from nature, and also from the splendid temples with their ornately carved façades. The Kolar and Hatti mines in Karnataka were the repositories of the largest deposits of gold in ancient India. Due to the high price of gold, craftsmen mastered the technique of beating a minuscule quantity of gold into thin sheets and then transforming them into exquisite jewellery.

Bangles

Earrings

Hair ornament

Decorative Ornaments

Gold ornaments were designed to be worn on practically every part of the body, from the crown of the head to the tips of the toes, to decorate and protect the wearer. Plants, animals and astral bodies inspired many of the shapes.

A Lady, late 19th-century painting by Raja Ravi Varma showing a woman in her finery

A large cobra head, set with rubies, emeralds and diamonds and edged with emerald beads, is tied to a plait to prevent it from unravelling. The snake form, as a symbol of fertility, occurs in many ornaments.

Temple deities are often adorned with ritual ornaments. These pieces display some of the forms and techniques used by ancient Indian jewellers, and show the evolution of their craft.

Pavan Sara, a necklace made of coins, is a piece of jewellery found all over the country. As an instrument of savings, the coins were redeemed for cash when the need arose.

Devotees congregating at the Vaidyeshvara Temple, Talakad

❷ Talakad

Mysore district. 45 km (28 miles) SE of Mysore. 🚌 🚶 Panchalinga Darshana (every 12 years).

The historic city of Talakad, situated on the north bank of the Kaveri river, now lies partly buried under shifting sand dunes. From the 5th to the 10th centuries it was the capital of the Ganga dynasty (see p526), but only two modest temples survive from that period. The largest edifice at this site is the 12th-century **Vaidyeshvara Temple**, dedicated to Shiva. Nearby is the more modest Kirti Narayana Temple, where the 3-m (10-ft) high image of Vishnu is still worshipped. A festival, the Panchalinga Darshana, is celebrated here at intervals of 12 years.

❸ Somnathpur

Mysore district. 36 km (22 miles) E of Mysore. 🚌

One of the finest representations of Hoysala architecture (see p528), the **Keshava Temple** is the highlight of this obscure little village. Built in 1268 by Somnatha, a general of King Narasimha III, its design is attributed to the celebrated sculptor and architect, Janakacharya. The temple is accessed from the east,

through a doorway with an open portico, where a slab records Somnatha's generous donations. Unlike the other Hoysala temples at Halebid and Belur (see p527), this is well preserved and has complete towers. The temple has three star-shaped shrines that lead off a pillared hall; both the shrines and the hall stand on a high plinth. The basements of the inner sanctums and hall are profusely carved with animal and floral patterns, while images of deities under foliage canopies occupy the walls above. The interior of the hall is remarkable for its splendid columns and the elaborate ceilings which display lobed motifs, pendant buds and looped bands.

The three shrines house fully modelled, life-size images of Krishna playing the flute (south) and Janardana, a form of Vishnu (north). The Krishna image in the western shrine is a modern replacement of the original.

Also in Somnathpur is the ruined granite **Panchalinga Temple**, built in 1268 as a memorial in honour of Somnatha's family.

🏛 **Keshava Temple**
Open daily. 📷

❹ Srirangapattana

Mandya district. 16 km (10 miles) N of Mysore. **Tel** (08232) 238 377. 🚉 from Mysore. 🚌 from Mysore. Autos and cycles available.

Known to the British as Seringapatam, this island fortress in the Kaveri river enjoys historical significance as the site of the battles between the British and Tipu Sultan, the "Tiger of Mysore". The British finally stormed the citadel in 1799, killing Tipu and consolidating their power in South India. Today, none of the structures within the fort survive, barring the bridges across the two arms of the Kaveri river, from which the bathing ghats and the ramparts can be seen.

To the east and the south, a broad moat surrounds the polygonal bastions and turreted parapets constructed by the French engineers employed by Tipu. The Mysore Gate and Elephant Gate, to the south, are flanked by guardrooms. Sultan Battery, the dungeons where Tipu used to keep British prisoners, is to the north; nearby is the Water Gate, where Tipu was killed.

The **Sri Ranganatha Temple**, after which the island is named, is a large complex that was substantially restored in the 19th century. The inner sanctum

Insignia engraved on a horse-cart, Srirangapattana

Representations of Hindu deities at the Keshava Temple

Mural depicting a battle at the Daria Daulat Bagh, Srirangapattana

enshrines an image of the reclining Vishnu and is approached through pillared halls and an open courtyard with a gilded lamp column.

The fort's eastern end has the **Jama Masjid**, erected by Tipu in 1787. It has an elevated prayer chamber.

The **Daria Daulat Bagh**, Tipu Sultan's summer palace, built in 1784, stands in the middle of a beautiful garden near the river, a short distance south of the fort. Each of its sides has three arched openings in the centre and the whole palace is surrounded by a pillared verandah. The east and west walls of the verandah are both covered with murals, restored in 1855. On the west wall are scenes of battle, one of which illustrates Haidar Ali's victory over the British at Pollilur (1780), while the east wall depicts courtly scenes. The carved woodwork and the elegant painted floral designs on the wall reveal Mughal influence. The palace is now a museum, with paintings, maps and Tipu memorabilia on display. Further south, past the Church of the Abbé Dubois (where the learned French Jesuit priest and author lived between 1799 and 1823) and the British Cemetery, is the **Gumbaz** – the tombs of Haidar Ali and Tipu Sultan. The walls of the chambers are decorated with the tiger-stripes motif (bubri) favoured by Tipu. The ebony and ivory doors were a gift from the viceroy, Lord Dalhousie, in 1855. The sangam (confluence) of the two arms of the Kaveri river is further south.

Snake shrine, Srirangapattana

🏛 **Daria Daulat Bagh Museum**
Tel (08326) 252 045. **Open** daily. 📷

(see p535)

Festivals in Karnataka

Banashankari Temple Fair (Jan/Feb), Badami. This 20-day festival combines religious rites with the excitement of a funfair. An annual cattle fair, specializing in white bulls, is held at the same time.

Hoysala Mahotsava (Mar), Belur and Halebid. A festival of dance and music unfolds against the spectacular backdrop of these historic temples.

Royal Dasara (Sep/Oct), Mysore. This grand, 10-day festival, known as Dussehra in North India, celebrates the victory of the goddess Chamundeshvari (Durga) over the buffalo demon, Mahishasura; it owes its origin to the Mahanavami festival (see p535). A royal elephant carrying an image of the goddess leads a splendid display of military bands, sports and parades, while religious ceremonies worship the elephant, the horse and weapons such as the State sword. Firework displays, concerts and wrestling matches liven up the evenings. A descendant of the former ruling Wodeyars plays a pivotal part and the famous golden throne, generally not on display, is used for the rituals.

Hampi Festival (Nov), Hampi. Well-known dancers and musicians from around the country participate in this lively event.

Tipu Sultan: "Tiger of Mysore"

Tipu Sultan, the ruler of Mysore, stands head and shoulders above the many Indian rulers who were his contemporaries.

He was a shrewd diplomat, expert soldier, excellent scholar and accomplished poet, and his military and administrative skills were complemented by his dream of a modern industrial state. The latter found expression in his cultivation of European contacts and employment of French engineers. The Sultan's main adversaries were the British who had conquered part of his father Haider Ali's territory and wealth in the first two Mysore Wars (1767–9 and 1780–84). Tipu waged two further wars against them, culminating in the fall of Srirangapattana in May 1799, where he died fighting.

Portrait of Tipu Sultan (1750–99)

Caparisoned elephant at the Dasara celebrations, Mysore

Mysore: Amba Vilas Palace

The magnificent Amba Vilas Palace, a treasure house of exquisite carvings and works of art from all over the world, was built by the Wodeyar rulers. The main block of this Indo-Saracenic building, with domes, turrets, arches and colonnades, was designed by Henry Irving in 1898. It replaced an earlier structure that was destroyed by a fire. During weekends and festivals, thousands of light bulbs enliven the palace's stern grey exterior.

Public Durbar Hall
This richly decorated gold-and-turquoise hall, on the second floor, exudes royal splendour. A series of paintings on the rear wall shows the goddess Durga in her various forms.

Amba Vilas Hall
The Private Durbar Hall is smaller than, but as sumptuous as, the Public Hall. It is roofed with stained glass imported from Glasgow. The central part of its ceiling is supported by cast-iron columns and arches.

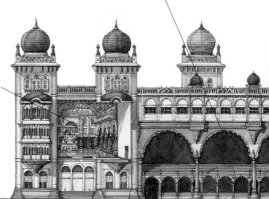

❺ Mysore

Mysore district. 140 km (87 miles) SW of Bengaluru. 🚊 2,641,000. ✈ 10 km (6 miles) S of city centre. 🚌 🚍 *i* KSTDC Transport Wing, Hotel Mayura Yatri Niwas, 2 Jhansi Laxmi Bai Rd, (0821) 242 3652. 🎭 Vairamudi Festival (Mar/Apr), Feast of St Philomena (Aug), Royal Dasara (Sep/Oct).

Situated among fertile fields, and skirted by wooded hills, Mysore was the capital of the Wodeyar rulers, who were governors of southern Karnataka under the Vijayanagar kings. The Wodeyar dynasty ruled almost uninterrupted from 1399 until Independence, except for the 38-year rule of the Muslim warlord Haider Ali and his son, Tipu Sultan, in the 18th century (*see p521*). Modern Mysore is the creation of Tipu Sultan who, in 1793, levelled the old city and built the present town. Today, Mysore is an important cultural centre, with the largest university in Karnataka. It is also renowned for its ivory work, silk-weaving, sandalwood incense and carvings.

Several elegant public buildings, erected under the Wodeyars, enhance the wide, tree-lined streets. In the heart of the city is the **Amba Vilas Palace**. To its west is **Jaganmohan Palace**, built in 1861 to mark the coronation ceremony of Krishnaraja III. It partly obscures a Neo-Classical structure, now the **Chamarajendra Art Gallery**, which houses an interesting collection of disparate objects including antique furniture, musical instruments, ceramics and ivory. On its top floor is a splendid collection of musical instruments, as well as magnificent paintings by the renowned 19th-century artist from Kerala, Raja Ravi Verma.

Near the northwestern corner of Amba Vilas Palace is **Krishnaraja Circle**, where a statue of Krishnaraja Wodeyar

The crouching Nandi on Chamundi Hill

View of the Amba Vilas Palace, Mysore

Golden Throne
Originally made of fig-wood overlaid with ivory, this jewelled throne was later plated with gold and silver. It is now brought out only during the Dasara celebrations.

Seating gallery for viewing the annual Mysore Dasara procession *(see p521)*.

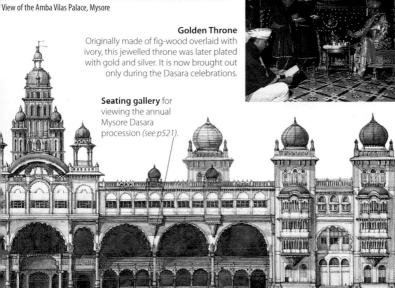

stands beneath a pavilion. The **Sayyaji Rao Road** that leads out from this circle is the principal shopping centre of the town. A short distance away is the Government House, the seat of the British Residents from 1805. Nearby, the **Cathedral of St Philomena**, with a stained-glass interior, is a Neo-Gothic structure that was completed in 1959.

In the western part of the city is the Neo-Classical **Manasa Gangotri**, the campus of Mysore University. The **Oriental Research Institute** here houses a collection of Sanskrit manuscripts, while the **Folklore Museum** has one of the most important ethnographic collections of South Indian toys, puppets and household objects, as well as two wooden chariots. On the way to **Chamundi Hill**, 8 km (5 miles) southeast of

Mysore, is **Lalitha Mahal Palace**, built in 1930. Formerly a private royal guest house, it is now a hotel. About halfway up the hill is the Nandi monolith, dating to 1659. Carved out of a single boulder, it is 7.5 m (25 ft) long and 5 m (16 ft) high. The richly decorated bull is depicted crouching. The **Chamundeshvari Temple**, at the summit of the hill, was built in the 17th century by the Wodeyars and was later refurbished. It houses a beautifully decorated idol of Chamundeshvari, the family deity of the Wodeyar kings.

Environs
The picturesque **Brindavan Gardens** are 16 km (10 miles) to the north of the city. This popular picnic spot was laid out below the Krishnarajasagar Dam by

Krishnaraja Wodeyar. The numerous fountains are illuminated every evening with beautiful multi-coloured lights.

Striking façade of the Cathedral of St Philomena

Wildlife Sanctuaries of Karnataka

The Nilgiri Biosphere Reserve, encompassing six contiguous wildlife sanctuaries, spans the states of Karnataka, Kerala and Tamil Nadu. Created to protect the extraordinary biodiversity of the last surviving tracts of tropical evergreen and deciduous forests of the Western Ghats, it includes the area over which the notorious sandalwood smuggler and bandit, Veerappan, once held sway. This reserve, along with the adjacent Mudumalai Sanctuary *(see p608)*, forms one of the most important migratory corridors for animals such as the Asian elephant and the Indian bison. These parks are within convenient reach of Bengaluru *(see pp516–17)* and Mysore *(see pp522–23)*.

The Ranganthittoo Bird Sanctuary covers 675 sq km (261 sq miles) of riverine islands in the middle of the Kaveri river and attracts a large number of water birds during the nesting season, especially from June to November.

Bandipur, declared a wildlife sanctuary in 1931 by the then Maharaja of Mysore, has many *chausingha* (four horned antelope), and is also a Project Tiger Reserve *(see p293)*. It spreads over 875 sq km (338 sq miles).

The BRT Wildlife Sanctuary, east of the Nilgiri Biosphere Reserve, is a corridor between the Western and Eastern Ghats. Covering an area of 540 sq km (209 sq miles), it supports a variety of birdlife, including storks.

The Nagarhole Wildlife Sanctuary's profusion of rivers and swampy grasslands keep it green all year. Established in 1983, the park has 645 sq km (249 sq miles) of deciduous vegetation. Its wildlife includes the bonnet macaque. It is located around 50 km (31 miles) from Mysore.

The Kabini Reservoir, separating Bandipur from Nagarhole, offers fine views. The Kabini River Lodge nearby is an excellent place for sighting wildlife, and a good place to stay.

Locator Map
■ Wildlife Sanctuaries

Coffee plantation in Madikeri

❻ Kodagu

Kodagu district. 120 km (75 miles) S of Mysore. 🚌 *i* Department of Tourism, Madikeri, (08272) 228 580. 🎭 Keil Poldu (Jun–Sep), Cauvery Shankaramana (Oct), Huthri (Nov).

Picturesquely set amid the forested mountains of the Western Ghats, the district of Kodagu (or Coorg) was an independent state until it was incorporated into the newly formed state of Karnataka in 1956. **Madikeri**, the district headquarters, situated 1,500 m (4,921 ft) above sea level and surrounded by rolling coffee and orange plantations, is a charming hill town, and a convenient base from which to explore Kodagu.

Madikeri (or Mercara) was once the capital of the Hindu Lingayat kings, who ruled for over 200 years from 1600, except for a brief period when Tipu Sultan seized power. The **Fort**, at the centre of the town, was built by the third Lingayat king in 1812. Within its stone ramparts, it contains the simple, unpretentious palace of the Lingayat rulers, along with a temple, an old church, a museum and the local prison.

The famous **Omkareshvara Shiva Temple**, situated in a hollow east of the Fort, was built by Linga Raja II in 1820 and dedicated to Vishnu and Shiva. The temple complex consists of brick buildings in the Indo-Saracenic style set in courtyards surrounded by pillared verandahs. Other notable monuments in Madikeri are the **Royal Tombs** of Raja Dodda Vira, his wife and his son, Linga Raja II. Curiously, these display a distinct Islamic influence, with onion-shaped domes, minarets and trellis work.

Kodagu remains pleasantly cool all year round, and the hills are at their most lush after the heavy monsoon showers when they make for delightful hikes. The walk up to **Abbey Falls**, 8 km (5 miles) from Madikeri, is popular and takes trekkers through forests and coffee plantations. Kodagu is renowned for its sprawling coffee plantations, first introduced in the mid-19th century by the British. The Kodava people bought back their land after Independence, but several estates still retain their British names. Kodagu produces some of the world's finest varieties of mild coffee; in fact, it is Karnataka's richest district because it accounts for the majority of coffee exports from the state. Coffee bushes are grown in the benevolent shade of large trees such as oak and rosewood, and in mixed plantations with crops of oranges, pepper vines and cardamom.

Nisargadhama, 27 km (17 miles) from Madikeri, is a beautiful forest retreat on a riverine island on the Kaveri. The bamboo cottages built here by the forest department are ideal for viewing wildlife.

Talakaveri, 45 km (28 miles) southwest of Madikeri, at an altitude of 1,276 m (4,186 ft), is the source of the Kaveri, one of India's seven sacred rivers (*see p604*); there is a small shrine built around the spring. At **Bhagamandala**, 36 km (22 miles) southwest of Madikeri, the Kaveri meets its two tributaries, Kanike and Sujoythi. Several shrines dot the area near the confluence – also the site of the striking Bhandeshvara temple, built in the Kerala style (*see p25*).

The Talakaveri shrine, a place of great religious significance

The Kodavas

The people of Kodagu, known as Kodavas, are a distinct ethnic group, and have their own language, Coorgi. The Kodavas are proud of their martial origins and the country's armed forces have had a fair number of generals from this community. They may no longer live in the huge four-winged homes called *ain mane*, but their many traditional festivals, celebrated with great elan, still bring them together. Coorgi weddings are unique, in that there are no priests and they are solemnized by elders. The men dress in traditional *kupyas*, or long black coats tied at the waist by a gold- and red-tasseled sash, while women wear Coorgi-style saris with pleats at the back. Their distinctive cuisine includes tangy pork curry served with rice dumplings.

A Kodava couple in traditional dress

❼ Melkote

Mandya district. 54 km (34 miles) N of Mysore. 🛈 Tourist Office, (08232) 238 377 🚌 🎭 Vairamudi (Mar/Apr).

A picturesque hill town of shrines and monasteries, Melkote is a major pilgrimage centre for devotees of Vishnu; it is also associated with Ramanuja, the renowned Hindu philosopher and social reformer who died in 1137. Ramanuja is worshipped along with Vishnu in the **Narayana Temple**, in the southern part of town. South of the temple stands a solitary gopura, while perched on the summit of a hill to the northeast of the town, is the small **Narasimha Shrine**, overlooking the large Kalyani Tank.

Daily life in Melkote revolves around temple rituals, and the tradition of religious learning introduced by Ramanuja survives in its many institutions, of which the Academy of Sanskrit Research is most famous.

Narasimha Shrine overlooking the Kalyani Tank at Melkote

❽ Sravana Belgola

Hassan district. 140 km (87 miles) NW of Bengaluru. 🚌 🛈 Tourist Office, (08176) 257 254. 🎭 Mahamastakabhisheka (every 12 years; last one was in 2006).

This small town, situated between two granite hills, Indragiri and Chandragiri, is the most important Jain site in South India. It is dominated by the colossal 17.7-m (58-ft) high monolithic **Statue of Gommateshvara**, also known as Bahubali, son of the first Jain tirthankara (see p400). On the summit of the 143-m (469-ft) high Indragiri Hill, the north-

The head-anointing ceremony at Sravana Belgola

facing statue of the naked saviour stands on an anthill staring impassively ahead. Entwined around his legs and arms are creepers, indicating the length of time he stood immobile in meditation. An inscription at the base records its consecration in AD 981 by Chamundaraya, the powerful minister of Rajamalla IV, one of the Ganga kings.

The town, which lies at the base of the hill, has a large tank as well as a number of Jain temples (bastis). Perhaps the most interesting of these is the matha, near the steps leading to Indragiri Hill. The walls of its courtyard have a series of vivid 18th-century murals illustrating the past and present births of Parsvanatha, the 23rd tirthankara, as well as scenes from the annual fair held here. Some fine Jain bronzes are displayed in the sanctuary that opens off the courtyard. On Chandragiri Hill, to the north of the town, is

another cluster of bastis established by the 10th–12th century Ganga kings and their powerful ministers. The **Neminatha Basti**, commissioned by Chamundaraya, enshrines an image of Neminatha, the 22nd tirthankara. The adjoining **Chandragupta Basti** has miniature panels carved on perforated stone screens depicting episodes from the life of Bahubali and his royal disciple, Chandragupta. A 5-m (16-ft) high sculpture of Parsvanatha, the 23rd tirthankara, is enshrined in another nearby basti.

Every 12 years, Jainism's most important festival, the spectacular Mahamastaka-bhisheka (head-anointing ceremony) is held here. The festival commemorates the consecration of the Bahubali monolith, and attracts thousands of monks, priests and pilgrims. A special scaffold is erected behind the statue so that priests can ritually bathe the god with milk, water from the holy rivers, ghee, saffron, sandalwood paste, vermilion and flower petals. At the last ceremony, held in 1993, a specially-hired helicopter flew overhead, showering the statue with 20 kg (44 pounds) of gold leaf, 200 litres (423 pints) of milk, marigolds and jewels, to the delight of the assembled crowds.

Environs
The village of **Kambadahalli**, 15 km (9 miles) east of Sravana Belgola, is another Jain settlement. The 10th-century Panchakuta Basti houses a trio of tirthankaras in three separate shrines.

A view of Chandragiri Hill above Sravana Belgola

A columned Nandi pavilion in the Hoysaleshvara Temple, Halebid

❾ Halebid

Hassan district. 213 km (132 miles) W of Bengaluru. 🚉 Hassan, 34 km (21 miles) S of town centre, then bus or taxi. 🚌 Cycles available on hire. ℹ️ Tourist Office, (08177) 273 224.

Set amid a lush agricultural landscape ringed by distant hills, this isolated site was the Hoysala capital in the 12th and 13th centuries. While the palace has yet to be excavated, the stone ramparts that once surrounded the city can still be seen. Outside the ramparts, to the east, is the vast tank known as Dorasamudra, which was also the city's original name.

A magnificent seated Nandi at Halebid

Today, the principal attraction of Halebid is the **Hoysaleshvara Temple**, begun in 1121 by King Vishnuvardhana, but never finished. This structure comprises a pair of identical temples, each with its own east-facing linga sanctuary opening on to a hall and a screened porch. Each temple is also preceded by a pavilion with a huge statue of Nandi, the bull-vehicle of Shiva. As the two halls are joined together to create a spacious columned interior, the temples function as a single monument. The outer walls are elevated on friezes of naturalistic and fanciful animals, interspersed with animated carvings of scenes from the *Ramayana* and *Mahabharata* (*see pp30–31*). Among the finest wall panels here are those of Shiva dancing on the outstretched skin of the elephant demon he had slain, Krishna playing the flute and Krishna holding up Mount Govardhan, on the south face of the southern sanctuary. On the north face of the northern sanctuary is a splendid Nataraja (Shiva as the Lord of Dance) and a panel depicting a crouching multi-armed and -headed Ravana creeping up on Shiva and Parvati seated on Mount Kailasa. Set on the plinth on which the temple is raised is a three-dimensional composition of a warrior plunging his sword into a leonine beast with a ferocious head, interpreted as the dynastic symbol of the martial Hoysala rulers. The landscaped garden in front of the Hoysaleshvara Temple serves as an **Archaeological Museum**. A panel here shows a majestic seated Ganesha. A short distance south of the complex is a group of 12th-century Jain *bastis*.

🏛️ **Archaeological Museum**
Tel (08177) 273 227. **Open** 8am–5pm Sat–Thu. 🚫 ♿ 🌐 **asi.nic.in**

❿ Belur

Hassan district. 17 km (11 miles) SW of Halebid. 🚉 Hassan, 34 km (21 miles) SE of town centre, then bus or taxi. 🚌 ℹ️ Tourist Office, (08177) 222 209.

One of the jewels of South Indian architecture, Belur's **Chennakeshava Temple** was built in 1117 by Vishnuvardhan to commemorate the Hoysala triumph over the Cholas (*see pp50–51*). At the end of the town's main street, a towered *gopura*, erected by the kings of Vijayanagar (*see p534*) in the 16th century, marks the entrance to the temple. Inside is a spacious paved courtyard, surrounded by subsidiary shrines and colonnades. In the centre is the main temple, a single star-shaped sanctuary opening onto a columned hall fronted by a screened porch.

The entire surface of the grey-green schist structure is covered with richly textured relief carvings. The lintels have foliate frames running between open-mouthed aquatic monsters (*makaras*) with exuberantly foliated tails. The stone grilles that filter light into the porch are raised on friezes of elephants, lotus stems, garlands and amorous couples. Brackets fashioned as female dancers, musicians and huntresses, standing gracefully under perforated trees, support the sloping eaves above the grilles. Many bear the artists' signatures, a sign of their elevated status under the Hoysalas. Even finer bracket figures can be seen inside the temple.

🏛️ **Chennakeshava Temple**
Tel (08177) 222 218. **Open** daily. **Closed** to non-Hindus.

Belur's Chennakeshava Temple, in the centre of a large courtyard

Hoysala Art and Architecture

The temples of the Hoysala kings (12th–13th centuries) and their powerful ministers are among the wonders of South Indian art and architecture. They embody a fusion of the curving towers *(shikharas)* of North India with the columned *mandapas* of the south, and are characterized by their unique star-shaped plan and their rich surface decoration. The dense imagery of the basement friezes and wall panels, sculpted with religious and mythological scenes, as well as the exquisite bracket figures, are fashioned out of grey-green schist, a material that permits beautifully intricate carving.

Gods seated with their consorts, such as this remarkable rendering of the Lakshmi-Narayana theme from Belur, are carved in full detail and set into the outer walls of Hoysala temples.

Flowing foliate patterns, derived from lotus stems and leaves, run continuously around the basements of Hoysala temples.

Bracket figures, fashioned as beautiful female dancers, are the highlights of Hoysala temples. This sculpture of a female drummer from Belur has an engraving of the artist's signature.

Mandapa interiors have spacious aisles lined with massive, highly polished lathe-turned columns, with undulating profiles and sharp ridges. A good example is this magnificent Nandi pavilion opposite the main shrine at Halebid.

The Somnathpur Temple

The perfectly proportioned triple-sanctuaried Keshava Temple at Somnathpur (see p520), built in 1268, was the last of the great Hoysala temples.

Towers over Hoysala sanctuaries have small spires arranged in tiers.

The stepped outlines of the plinth echo the complex star-shaped plan of the sanctuary.

Miniature shrines flank the entrance steps.

Terracotta-tiled rooftops in Mangalore

⓫ Mangalore

South Kanara district. 357 km (222 miles) W of Bengaluru. 🚹 399,000. ✈ 20 km (12 miles) N of city centre, then taxi or bus. 🚉 🚌 🚖 Karnataka Tourism, Hotel Indraprastha, Light House Hill Road, (0824) 244 2926.

This thriving port on the estuary of the Netavati and Gurpur rivers is the largest city in Dakshina (South) Kanara, the coastal district famous for its coffee, cashewnut and pepper plantations. Rich harvests of these crops have attracted traders through the ages. Arab merchants first came here in the 13th and 14th centuries, and were later followed by the Portuguese and the British.

Mangalore today, presents a panorama of terracotta-roofed houses, whitewashed churches, temples and mosques, nestling amid groves of coconut palms. Among its historic monuments is the old watchtower, known as **Sultan's Battery**, built of laterite in 1763 by Haider Ali of Mysore (see p522).

Mangalore's 19th-century churches include the domed Church of the Most Holy Rosary and the Jesuit College of St Aloysius. Situated at the foot of Kadiri Hill, 3 km (2 miles) north of the city, is the 17th-century **Manjunath Temple**, with some superb bronze images of the Buddha, dating to the 10th–11th centuries, installed in the porch.

Environs
The pleasant beach resort at **Ullal** is just 12 km (7 miles) south of the city. Numerous Jain temples and monasteries dot the villages around Mangalore. The finest is the elaborate 15th-century Chandranatha Basti at **Mudabidri**, 35 km (22 miles) to the northwest. Dominating the summit of a hill at **Karkala**, 18 km (11 miles) further north, is the 13-m (43-ft) high Gommateshvara monolith (1432), an obvious imitation of the larger and earlier one at Sravana Belgola (see p526). The 16th-century Chaturmukha Basti, a perfectly symmetrical temple with a central chamber enshrining 12 tirthankaras, stands at the base of the hill. The pilgrimage town of **Dharmasthala**, 75 km (47 miles) to the east, is well-known for its Shiva temple. Its Gommateshvara statue was installed in 1973.

⓬ Udipi

Udipi district. 58 km (36 miles) N of Mangalore. 🚹 113,100. 🚉 🚖 Tourist Office, Krishna Building, Car Street, (0820) 252 9718. 📷 Pargaya (Jan), Chariot Festival (Aug).

All roads in Udipi lead to the large open square in the city centre where the **Krishna Temple** is located. This is the focal point of all activity, spiritual and commercial, in this bustling pilgrim town. The famous 13th-century Vaishnava teacher, Madhava, is believed to have founded the temple by installing an image of Krishna he had rescued from a shipwreck. Parked outside the temple are the festival chariots with dome-like towers made of bamboo and covered with colourful textiles. After passing through the entrance gate, pilgrims bathe in the tank before entering the main sanctuary with its silver doors and viewing window. Surrounding the square are other temples and the eight mathas associated with the Krishna Temple, built in the typical Kanara style with wooden verandahs and sloping roofs.

Udipi also lends its name to the inexpensive eateries that originated here. Catering to a local clientele, the menu concentrated on traditional South Indian vegetarian food, such as the masala dosa and idli (see pp558–9). These restaurants, with their affordable rates, quick turnover and simple but good food, are now found all over India.

Environs
About 5 km (3 miles) west of Udipi is **Malpe Beach**, where fishing boats can be hired for excursions. **Manipal**, 4 km (2.5 miles) to the east, is an industrial and educational centre. The **House of Vijayanath Shennoy** in Manipal, now a museum, is an example of a traditional home, with a fine collection of everyday objects.

🏛 **House of Vijayanath Shennoy** Open Mon–Sat.

Priests performing rituals during the Chariot Festival at Udipi

Shop selling religious paraphernalia at Barkur

⑬ Barkur

Udipi district. 71 km (44 miles)
N of Mangalore. 🚉
🎭 Navaratri (Sep/Oct).

The coastal town of Barkur was a flourishing port in the 15th and 16th centuries until its river silted up. Today, the town's main attractions are its many temples with their typical sloping terracotta-tiled roofs. The largest is the **Panchalingeshvara Temple**, situated at the southern end of the town. Devotees gather at the stepped tank near the temple for a ritual bath before worshipping at the two east-facing linga shrines. The other temples include one dedicated to both Shiva and Ganesha, and the smaller Someshvara and Somanatheshvara temples.

Environs
The little hamlet of **Mekkekattu**, 8 km (5 miles) north of Barkur, has shrine of painted *bhuta* figures (local spirits). These are copies of the originals, which were removed to New Delhi's Crafts Museum (*see pp84–5*) and the Folklore Museum in Mysore (*see p523*), after the shrine's renovation in the 1960s. The vividly painted deity Nandikeshvara, (the winged bull) stands in the lower shrine while his consort occupies the upper one. Fierce guardian deities crowd a side chamber.

⑭ Bhatkal

North Kanara district. 165 km (102 miles) N of Mangalore. 🚗 31,800. 🚉
🎭 Navaratri (Sep/Oct).

Located along a picturesque highway that follows the coastline, this town was an important port during the 16th and 17th centuries. The many beautiful Jain and Hindu stone temples found here date from those days of prosperity. Standing in the town's main street are the Chandranatheshvara and Parsvanatha *bastis*. Situated 2 km (1.3 miles) to the east, on the other side of the highway, is the **Khetapai Narayan Temple**, built in 1540. Its sanctuary and hall are enclosed within stone screens fashioned to imitate wood. Finely sculpted guardian figures flank the doorway.

Detail of a stone panel, Bhatkal

Environs
Tucked away in the forested hills at **Kollur**, 35 km (22 miles) southeast of Bhatkal, is a shrine dedicated to the goddess Mukambika. This is a very popular pilgrimage.

India's highest waterfalls, the **Jog Falls**, lie 60 km (37 miles) northeast of Bhatkal. They can be seen at the head of the Sharavati river, framed by jagged pinnacles of rock.

⑮ Gokarna

North Kanara district. 200 km (124 miles) N of Mangalore. 🚉 ℹ️
Tourist Office, Main Rd, Karwar, (08382) 221 172. 🎭 Shivratri (Feb/Mar).

Spectacularly situated by the Arabian Sea, Gokarna is a favourite with visitors in search of sun, sea and sand. A charming little town with two principal streets and clusters of traditional tile-roofed brick houses, Gokarna is also an important centre of Sanskrit learning.

The **Mahabaleshvara Temple**, at the western end of the main street, was destroyed by the Portuguese in 1714 and then rebuilt later in the 18th century. In the sanctuary is a stone linga, encased in brass, placed on a coiled stone serpent. The floor of the hall in front has an intricate engraving of a giant tortoise. Shiva's birthday (Feb/Mar) is celebrated here with great fanfare. The two great temple chariots lead a procession through the town's narrow streets, while priests chant hymns in praise of Shiva.

Beaches Around Gokarna

Long stretches of beautiful, unspoilt beaches extend along the western coast from Gokarna to Karwar, a seaside town 60 km (37 miles) to the north. South of Gokarna are the Half Moon and Paradise beaches, while nearer Karwar are the lovely Binaga and Araga beaches. The gently curving bays, fringed by palms, are still occupied by small fishing villages where life revolves around the sea and the daily catch. Tourism remains unknown and only a few simple shacks offer basic food and shelter.

Waves breaking against rocks at a beach near Karwar

The two-storeyed Vidyashankara Temple at Sringeri

⑯ Sringeri

Chikmagalur district. 100 km (62 miles) NE of Mangalore. 🚆 🚌 🎭 Navaratri (Sep/Oct).

The small settlement of Sringeri, tucked away in the forested ranges of the Western Ghats, is today an important pilgrimage centre and one of the most powerful seats of orthodox Hinduism in South India. This was where Shankaracharya, *(see p652)*, the great 9th-century philosopher and social reformer, established the first of his four *mathas*, the other three are at

Floral offerings at Sringeri's temple

Joshimath in the Himalayas *(see p191)*, Puri *(see p316)* to the east and Dwarka *(see p431)* to the west. Today, his successors (also known as Shankaracharyas) wield tremendous influence in both religious and temporal

matters, while the *mathas* still function as centres of spiritual learning.

Standing on a paved terrace are two temples overlooking the Tunga river, crammed with sacred fish. The smaller temple, dedicated to Sharada, a popular form of the goddess Saraswati, is the principal destination for local pilgrims. Next to it is the 16th-century **Vidyashankara Temple**, where the Shankaracharya is worshipped in the form of a linga. This stone structure, which stands raised on a high platform, is laid out on an almost circular star-shaped plan. Friezes depicting the many forms of Shiva and Vishnu embellish the faceted walls. The hall that precedes the inner sanctum has massive piers carved as rearing *yalis* (mythical leonine beasts).

⑰ Chitradurga

Chitradurga district. 200 km (124 miles) N of Bengaluru. ℹ️ Kamana Bhavi Extension, 8th Ward Fort Rd; (08194) 234 466. 🚆 🚌

Located at the base of a rugged chain of hills, this town was a prominent outpost of the Vijayanagar Empire *(see pp534–5)*. Later, in the 17th–18th centuries, it became the headquarters of a line of local chiefs known as Bedas, until it was occupied by Haider Ali *(see p521)* in 1799 and then by the British.

The **Fort**, defined by walls of huge granite blocks, rises above the town. A series of three gates leads to the irregular inner zone, strewn with striking granite boulders. There are several small temples here, as well as a number of ceremonial gateways erected by the Bedas. The platforms and pavilions within the compound of the Sampige Siddheshvara Temple mark the spot where the Bedas were crowned. The remains of rubble and mud-built granaries and residences, and a large circular well can be seen nearby.

In the town below, the local **Government Museum** displays artifacts from surrounding sites. On the main street, the 17th-century Ucchalingamma Temple should not be missed.

🏰 **Fort**
Open daily. 📷

🏛️ **Government Museum**
Tel (08194) 224 202.
Open 9am–5pm Tue–Sun. 📷

The fort at Chitradurga, with gateways and shrines dotting the boulder-strewn landscape

A spectacular view of the magnificent Mysore Palace ▶

⑱ Hampi

A UNESCO World Heritage Site on the south bank of the Tungabhadra river, Hampi boasts the evocative ruins of Vijayanagar or the "City of Victory". The capital of three generations of Hindu rulers for more than 200 years, Hampi reached its zenith under Krishnadeva Raya (r.1510–29) and Achyuta Raya (r.1529–42). The site, which comprises the Sacred and Royal Centres, has a superb location, with rocky ridges and granite boulders acting as natural defences. The urban core of the city was fortified and separated from the Sacred Centre by an irrigated valley, through which ancient canals and waterways still run.

King's Balance
Ruling kings were weighed on this balance against gold or grain, for distribution to the Brahmins.

KEY

① **Krishna Temple** was erected by Krishnadeva Raya in 1513 to commemorate his victory over Odisha. It is no longer a place of worship.

② **The Queen's Bath**, an open-air structure, seems to have been designed for royal recreation.

③ **The Mahanavami Platform** was used by kings during the Mahanavami festival *(see p521)*, and for pre-war ceremonies.

Vitthala Temple *(see pp536–7)*

Tiruvengalanatha Temple

Matanga Hill

Bazaar Street

Tungabhadra

Hemakuta Hill

★ **Virupaksha Temple**
The ancient temple of Virupaksha, dedicated to the goddess Pampa and her consort Shiva, is dominated by a 53-m (174-ft) high *gopura*. This is the principal place of worship in Hampi.

★ **Narasimha Monolith**
Carved out of a single boulder in 1528, this awe-inspiring image of Vishnu shows him in his half man-half lion incarnation *(see p683)*.

Chariot Festival
The bustling Bazaar Street is the main centre of activity and the venue for the colourful Chariot Festival. The temple chariot carries the main deity through the streets so it can be publicly honoured.

VISITORS' CHECKLIST

Practical Information
Bellary district. 364 km (266 miles) NW of Bengaluru.
Tel (08394) 228 537.
Bazaar St. Virupaksha Temple: **Open** daily. Lotus Mahal: also covers the Vitthala Temple. Chariot Festival (Feb), Hampi Festival (Nov). Foreigners must register at Virupaksha Temple Police Station.

Transport
Hospet, 13 km (8 miles) W of site.

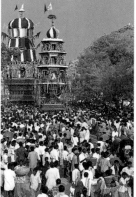

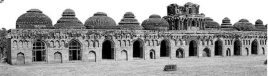

Elephant Stables
An imposing structure of 11 chambers, this once housed the royal elephants. Especially noteworthy are the polygonal roofs, alternating with smooth or ribbed domes.

0 metres 500
0 yards 500
Hazara Ramachandra Temple
Ruined Palaces
3 Great Bath
2
Hospet
Archaeological Museum

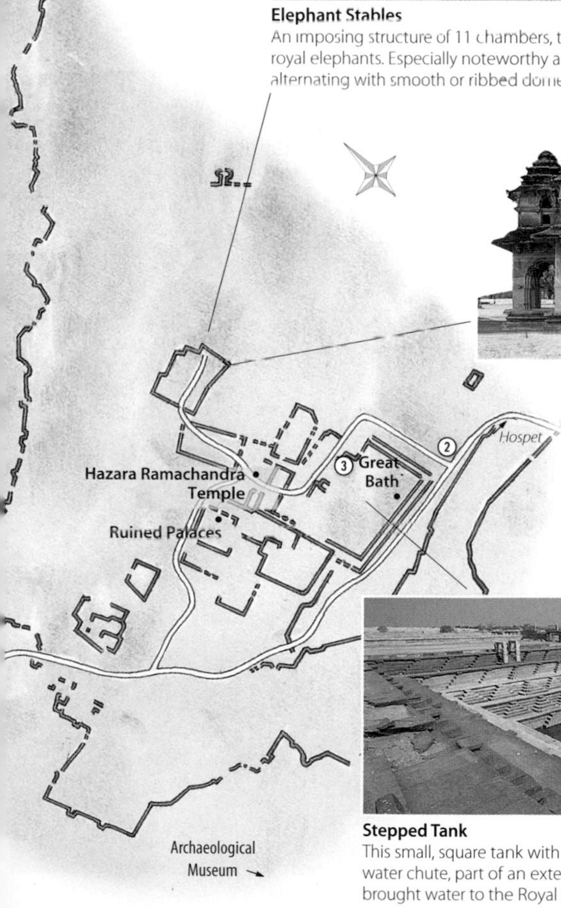

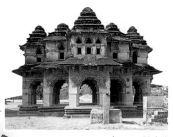

★ Lotus Mahal
A skilful blend of Hindu and Islamic architecture, this building may have served as a socializing area for the women in the royal family.

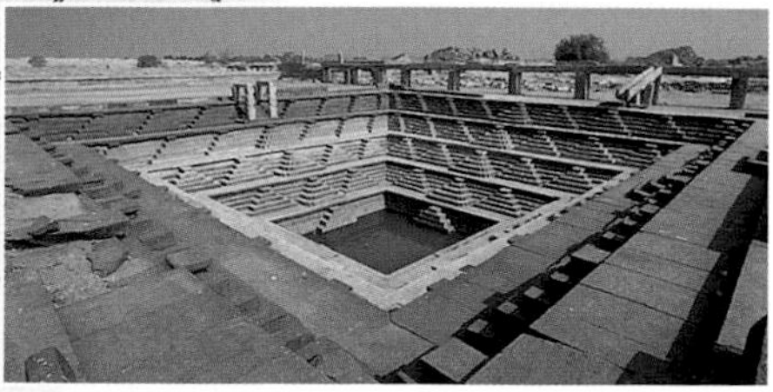

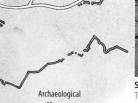

Stepped Tank
This small, square tank with multiple steps was fed by a water chute, part of an extensive "hydraulic system" that brought water to the Royal Centre.

Hampi: Vitthala Temple

The grandest of all the religious monuments in the Sacred Centre, the Vitthala Temple represents the high point of Vijayanagar art and architecture. Though its founder remains unknown, it was enlarged in the 16th century by two of Vijaynagar's greatest rulers, Krishnadeva Raya and Achyuta Raya. Preceding the main shrine is the great open hall, or *mahamandapa*, built on a low platform and supported by intricately carved pillars. This was the gift of a military commander in 1554, just 11 years before the city was sacked and abandoned.

★ Yalis
Leaping *yalis* (mythical leonine beasts), many with riders, adorn the outer piers of the temple.

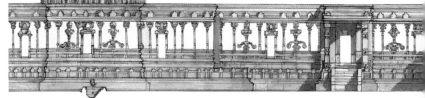

Reconstruction of the Tower
This shows the pyramidal vimana (tower), over the main sanctuary of the Vitthala Temple, as it looked when it was built in the 16th century.

Relief
A niche in a stone pillar has a superb rendering of Garuda, the eagle mount of Vishnu.

Exploring Hampi

The fabled city of the Vijayanagar kings (*see pp534–5*), covering an area of around 20 sq km (8 sq miles), sprawls across a spectacular barren and boulder-strewn landscape.

The **Sacred Centre**, on the southern bank of the Tungabhadra river, is dominated by the impressive **Virupaksha Temple**. It is dedicated to a form of Shiva (Virupaksha), known here as Pampapati (the "Lord of Pampa"), and commemorates his wedding to Pampa, the goddesss of the Tungabhadra. In front is the colonnaded **Bazaar Street** that dates mainly from the 16th to the mid-17th centuries, when it teemed with pilgrims and travellers in search of exotic wares. A path beside the river leads past the **Kodandarama Temple**, with its figures of Rama, Sita and

Lakshman carved on to a boulder inside the sanctuary. The bathing ghats here are considered to be the holiest at the site.

Beyond lies the **Temple of Achyuta Raya**, one of the major Hindu complexes at Hampi, dating from 1534 and dedicated to Tiruvengalanatha, the form of Vishnu that is venerated at Tirupati (*see p682*). Its perfect plan of two concentric enclosures, each entered by a towering gopura to the north, is clearly visible from the summit of **Matanga Hill**. The riverside path continues to the Vitthala Temple, from where a road proceeds to the

village of **Kamalapuram**, where the **Archaeological Museum** is located. En route is a gateway with a damaged façade of windows and battlements.

The road that runs south from Hampi village, through the Sacred Centre, leads up **Hemakuta Hill**, scattered with numerous pre- and early Vijayanagar shrines, many with small pyramidal towers. A large image of the elephant god, Ganesha, carved on a boulder,

A view of Matanga Hill

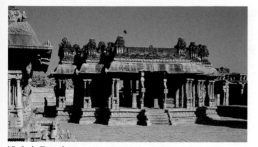

Vitthala Temple
This striking temple with its elaborate *mandapas* (columned halls) is dedicated to Vitthala, an incarnation of Vishnu the Preserver, the second god in the Hindu Trinity.

VISITORS' CHECKLIST

Practical Information
E of the Sacred Centre.
Open daily. free on Fri.

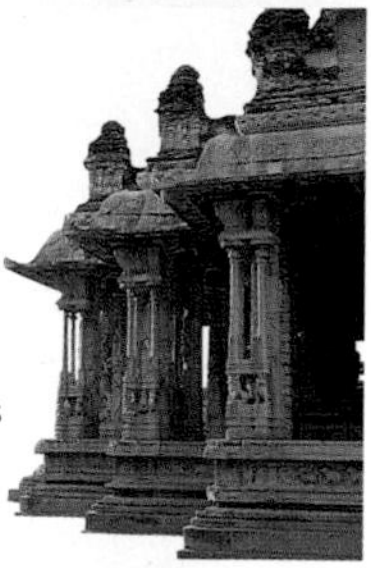

Musical Columns
Small hollow columns emit different tones when lightly tapped.

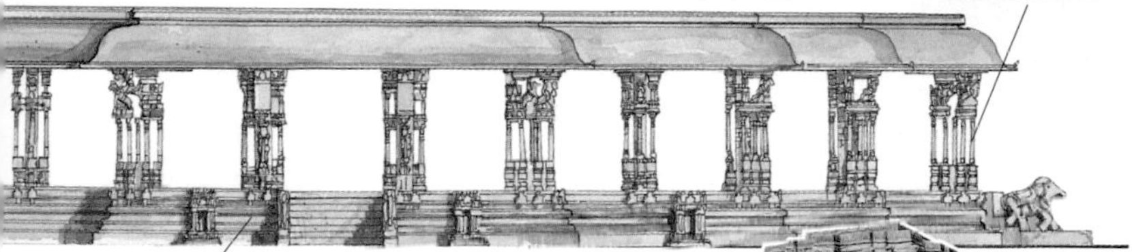

Chariot

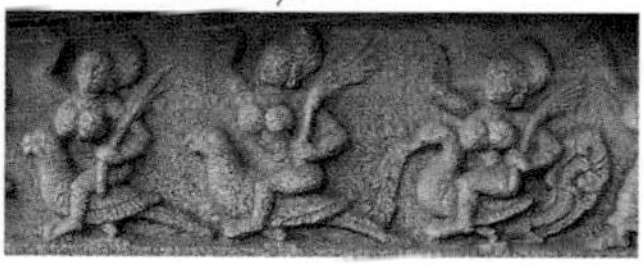

Frieze Detail
This panel depicts a trio of celestial nymphs riding on parrots.

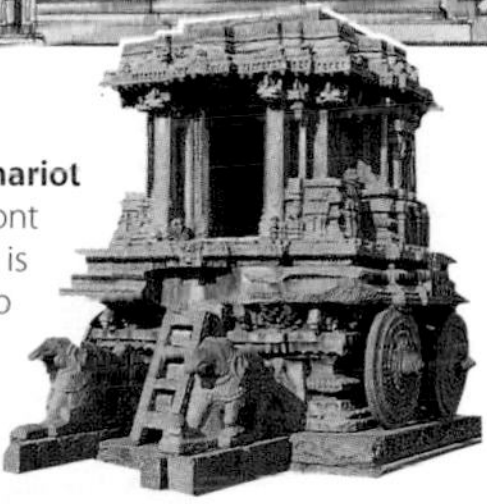

★ Chariot
This shrine in front of the temple is dedicated to Garuda and is fashioned as a stone chariot.

marks the top of the ridge. Further south is the **Krishna Temple**, erected in the early 16th century during the reign of Krishnadeva Raya. It is entered through a massive, though partly ruined gopura. The colonnaded street to the east now runs through fields of sugarcane, while the square tank nearby still stores water. As it continues south, the road travels past the tremendous Narasimha Stone Monolith, a representation of Vishnu's man-lion incarnation *(see p683)*.

Fortified walls enclose the **Royal Centre**. At the latter's core is the superb **Hazara Rama Temple**, built by Deva Raya I, a Vijayanagar king of the 15th century. Its outer walls are covered with friezes that depict ceremonies of the Mahanavami festival. Reliefs of episodes from the Ramayana can be seen here.

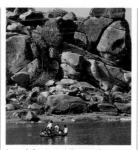

A coracle ferrying people across the Tungabhadra river

Around the temple are excavated remains of palaces, baths and a hundred-columned audience hall, while to its north are the Elephant Stables and the **Lotus Mahal**.

Archaeological Museum
Kamalapuram. **Tel** (08394) 241 561.
Open 8am–5pm Sat–Thu.
asi.nic.in

Environs

The historic village of **Anegondi** lies on the opposite bank of the Tungabhadra river. Until a bridge under construction becomes operational, it can be reached only on the coracles that have plied the river for centuries.

An important settlement before the establishment of Vijayanagar, Anegondi's now dilapidated palaces, temples and bathing ghats still preserve vestiges of their former glory. The Kalyan Mahal, a palace-like building reminiscent of Hampi's Lotus Mahal *(see p535)*, stands in the central square. Nearby are a temple and a 14th-century gateway. The massive walls and rounded bastions of Anegondi's citadel enclose the rocky hills lying west of the main town. Anegondi is also of interest for its traditional mud-clad houses.

An outer wall of Gadag's Someshvara Temple, with temple towers in relief

⓳ Gadag

Gadag district. 450 km (280 miles) NW of Bengaluru. 🚉 🚌 *i* Hotel Durga, Vihar Complex. ⌚ daily.

An important cotton collection centre, the sleepy little town of Gadag comes to life during the cotton season in May and June. During these months, the cotton market hums with activity and is well worth a visit.

A number of late Chalukyan monuments (11th–12th centuries) in the city indicate its historic past. Standing to the south is the **Trikuteshvara Temple**, remarkable for its three sanctuaries facing a common, partly open hall. Inclined slabs that serve as balcony seats are decorated with figurative panels, and are overhung by steeply angled eaves. Inside the hall, the columns have figures arranged in shallow niches. The east sanctuary accommodates three lingas, while the one to the south is dedicated to the goddess Saraswati.

In the middle of the city stands the **Someshvara Temple**. Though abandoned and now in a dilapidated state, its intricate carvings are fairly well preserved. Look for the doorways to the hall, which have densely carved figures and foliation.

Sculpted figures

Environs

The small village of **Lakkundi**, 11 km (7 miles) southeast of Gadag, has temples dating from the 11th–12th centuries, built of grey-green chloritic schist. Surrounded by mud houses, a number of such temples are tucked away down narrow streets. Jain Basti, the largest temple, has a five- storeyed tower. Its basement is adorned with friezes of elephants and lotus petals. Lathe-turned columns are seen on the porch. The nearby Kashi Vishvanatha Temple has a pair of sanctuaries facing each other across a common porch. Relief carvings of a pair of *makaras* or aquatic monsters, sitting on the walls, are typical motifs of late Chalukyan art.

⓴ Belgaum

Belgaum district. 502 km (312 miles) NW of Bengaluru. 🚉 🚌 *i* Tourist Office, Ashoka Nagar, (0831) 247 0879.

This bustling city, on the border with Maharashtra, was an important garrison town under the British. Even today, the cantonment, with its bungalows and barracks, has a significant military presence. Earlier, in the 16th and 17th centuries, Belgaum was a provincial centre under the Adil Shahi rulers of Bijapur (see p546), the Marathas of Pune (see p475), as well as the Mughals when they occupied this part of Karnataka. The **Fort** to the east is unusually elliptical in layout and its stone walls incorporate many reused temple blocks. The **Safa Mosque** nearby was built in the first half of the 16th century by Asad Khan, the governor of Belgaum. The town also has three temples that date to the late Chalukyan period.

The elliptical fort at Belgaum

Performing Arts of Karnataka

Karnataka has a rich and vibrant performing arts tradition. Story telling, with the help of media such as paintings and leather puppets, was among the most popular folk entertainments in the northern and northeastern part of the state, and in neighbouring Andhra Pradesh, before the advent of the cinema. Itinerant folk performers would delight rural audiences with stirring tales of good and evil, based on mythological episodes. A number of dance-dramas, such as the Yakshagana, developed in South Kanara, the region of Karnataka that borders Kerala. As in Kathakali (see p661), Yakshagana actors dress in awe-inspiring costumes to perform a heavily mimetic dance, while the singer recites the story to the accompaniment of music.

Karnataka's Leather Puppets

Huge figures made of goatskin are punched with holes of various shapes to allow light to filter through, thus creating the interplay of light and coloured shadow, so essential to shadow theatre. The chief puppeteer recites the story, while his assistants provide musical accompaniment.

Figures are etched on the prepared skin with a sharp instrument, then cut along the outline and coloured.

The chief puppeteer manipulates the puppet with the help of an attached stick.

Performances take place at night. A light is placed behind a thin cotton screen, so that the audience, sitting in front, sees the moving shadows.

Perforations on the figure allow light to pass through.

Bright colours and outlines are combined to create striking effects.

A stick is attached for manipulation.

Hanuman, the Monkey God, a major character in the *Ramayana*

Yakshagana

This folk dance-drama originated in the early 16th century. An all-male cast consisting of about 20 actors and musicians act out a repertoire that is inspired mainly by episodes from the great epics (see pp30–31), especially the *Mahabharata*. All-night performances, organized at the behest of a wealthy patron on special occasions, take place in the open, and no particular props are needed. Yakshagana's spectacular costumes are enhanced by tall headgear, a profusion of ornaments and elaborate make-up.

A man creating the elaborate headgear

Actors performing a scene from the *Mahabharata*

㉑ Badami

Dramatically situated within a horseshoe of red sandstone cliffs, overlooking the green waters of a large lake, this historic town was the capital of the powerful early Chalukya kings, who ruled the Deccan during the 6th–7th centuries AD. These rulers also held sway at Pattadakal (*see pp542–3*) and Aihole (*see pp544–5*). Among the rock-cut and structural monuments, the most richly decorated are the cave temples, which are carved into the cliff on the southern side. Of these, Cave 1 is dedicated to Shiva, Caves 2 and 3 to Vishnu, and Cave 4 to the Jain saints.

Columned verandah, Cave 3

A linga sanctuary is carved into the rear wall.

CAVE 1

A flight of steps in this cave leads up to a pillared verandah, behind which is a square, columned hall with a small sanctuary carved into the rear wall. The highlights here are the Nataraja panel and the carved panels on the ceiling.

Cave 2
This Vaishnava cave has a superb frieze of Varaha, the boar incarnation of Vishnu, on one end of the porch. A row of dwarfs is carved below it.

Cave 3
The verandah of this large and beautiful cave has an enormous four-armed figure of Vishnu seated on Adisesha, the serpent whose five hoods spread protectively over his crown. At his feet is the bird Garuda, his mount. This is the only cave with an inscription, dated AD 578.

Nataraja Panel
This 12-armed dancing Shiva is one of the earliest and finest depictions of the Nataraja in Karnataka.

Cave 4
Standing and seated Jain *tirthankaras* cover the walls and columns in Cave 4, on top of a cliff. Some of these were added in the 11th and 12th centuries, when this part of Karnataka was governed by a later line of Chalukya rulers.

Exploring Badami

Most of Badami's temples are situated on the imposing cliff that lies north of the man-made Agastya Lake. The boulder-strewn landscape and the large lake acted as natural defences of the site. Standing on the embankment is the 11th-century **Yellamma Temple**, with its multi-storeyed tower. Further away, inside the village, is the **Jambulinga Temple**, dating to AD 699, with triple shrines dedicated to Brahma, Vishnu and Shiva opening off a common *mandapa*. The **Bhutanatha Temple** is scenically located at the end of the lake and was built in several phases. The core shrine, with a pyramidal tower, is from the 6th–7th centuries, while the porch, embellished with angled eaves and overlooking the water, dates to the 11th century. Several boulders lying around the temple have reliefs of a sleeping Vishnu, and a seated Jain figure. Lesser shrines nearby show the pyramidal layered towers that are typical of the late Chalukya style.

The **Archaeological Museum**, on the north side of the lake, displays a magnificent triangular panel depicting Brahma surrounded by elaborate foliage; this piece must have once surmounted a free-standing portal. Other items of interest include a squatting female divinity with a lotus head, and two panels showing Shiva – spearing a demon and shooting arrows as he rides in a chariot.

Steps ascend through a rugged gorge to the 7th-century **Upper Shivalaya Temple** that crowns the cliffs rising to the north of the town. Only the walls of the passageway and the multi-storeyed tower capped with a square-domed roof still stand; the *mandapa* in front has been dismantled. Its simple basement mouldings and wall pilasters are typical

The tower of the Upper Shivalaya Temple

of early structural architecture under the Chalukyas. Diminutive scenes of Krishna holding up Mount Govardhana, and Narasimha disembowelling his victim, are carved intricately on the walls. Perched on top of an isolated boulder near the main road north of the town, is the **Mallegitti Shivalaya Temple**, a well-preserved 7th-century structure. Perforated stone windows flank sculptured panels of Vishnu and Shiva, topped with garlands.

Environs

A popular Devi shrine, facing a large tank dating from the 18th century, is situated at **Banashankari**, 5 km (3 miles) east of Badami. At **Mahakuta**, 8 km (5 miles) to the east, a group of 7th-century temples built in contrasting North- and South-Indian styles *(see p24)*, are clustered around a small tank.

The Bhutanatha Temple overlooking the tank

㉒ Pattadakal

The sacred complex at Pattadakal is picturesquely situated on the banks of the Malprabha river. A UNESCO World Heritage Site, its superb 8th-century temples are a fitting climax to the artistic achievements of the Chalukya kings, as seen in neighbouring Badami *(see pp540–41)* and Aihole *(see pp544–5)*. While these towns were important ancient settlements, Pattadakal, with only a small resident population, was mainly used for royal festivities and coronation ceremonies.

Shiva appearing out of the fiery linga, Virupaksha Temple

Exploring Pattadakal

The main temple complex is situated in landscaped gardens next to the small village. Built in a combination of the North Indian and South Indian temple styles *(see p24)*, these striking structures reveal a great deal about the evolution of temple architecture in South India.

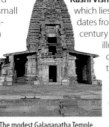

The modest Galaganatha Temple, built of sandstone

cut tiers of horseshoe-shaped motifs and a ribbed finial. The **Kashi Vishvanatha Temple**, which lies to the west, dates from the mid-8th century and further illustrates the developments in the North Indian temple style. Its faceted tower is entirely covered with a mesh design of interlocking horseshoe-arched motifs. The columns inside the small vestibule preceding the sanctum are carved with a variety of mythological scenes.

North Indian-style Temples

Characterized by their curved towers *(shikharas)* over the inner sanctum, North Indian-style temples are exemplified in the **Kadasiddeshvara** and **Jambulinga Temples**, which are situated near the entrance. These are unassuming sandstone structures with damaged wall sculptures and curving tiered towers. The larger but incomplete **Galaganatha Temple** nearby has a well-preserved tower with sharply

South Indian-style Temples

South Indian temple towers *(vimanas)* rise in a stepped pyramidal formation, as in the **Sangameshvara Temple**, the earliest in the complex. It was erected by the Chalukya king, Vijayaditya, who died in AD 733 before the structure was completed. Its multi-storeyed tower is capped with a square domed roof. The

incomplete hall in front has been restored.

The largest temples are the twin **Virupaksha** and **Mallikarjuna Temples** to the south. Both are dedicated to Shiva and were constructed in AD 745 by two sister queens of the powerful Chalukya king, Vikramaditya II, to commemorate his victory over the Pallava rulers of Tamil Nadu. These temples represent the climax of early Chalukya architecture and are said to be based on the Kailasanatha Temple in Kanchipuram *(see p586)*. They also served as the inspiration for the colossal Kailasanatha monolith at Ellora *(see pp480–82)*.

Today, the Virupaksha Temple is the only functioning shrine in this complex. In front is a Nandi pavilion with a magnificently carved bull covered by a cloth. The temple

View of the twin Virupaksha and Mallikarjuna Temples, Pattadakal

Nataraja, ceiling panel from the Papanatha Temple

itself consists of a spacious, columned hall with triple porches leading to the linga sanctum, surrounded by a passageway. The ornately carved pillars and ceilings portray mythological and religious stories. The finest reliefs are on either side of the east porch and include one of Shiva as *lingodbhavamurti*, appearing out of a fiery linga, and a depiction of Vishnu as Trivikrama, traversing the Universe in three steps.

The Mallikarjuna Temple, though identical, is smaller and more compact. The interior hall has a number of Shaivite sculptures. The walls surrounding the temple, and the Nandi pavilion in front of it, are incomplete.

A path from the Virupaksha Temple gateway along the river leads to the **Papanatha Temple**. This early 8th-century temple was extended several times, as can be seen in the unusual arrangement of double halls leading to the sanctuary, and in the later addition of passageway walls with porches on three sides. The exterior combines South Indian-style pilastered wall niches with North Indian-style mesh patterns and curvilinear towers. Battle scenes from the *Ramayana (see p31)*, carved on the east wall, conclude with Rama's coronation, shown on the column of the main porch. Both the halls have central aisles, with pot and foliage motifs carved on the capitals. Ornate brackets and beams support ceiling panels, the finest of which show a coiled *naga* (snake) deity

Battle between Arjuna and Shiva, Virupaksha Temple

and a Dancing Shiva (Nataraja), in the inner hall.

Jain Temple
To the west of the village, is a 9th-century Jain Temple built by the Rashtrakuta rulers, who succeeded the Chalukyas in the middle of the 8th century. A spacious open porch with peripheral lathe-turned columns is overhung with angled eaves. Some remarkable carvings of life-size elephant torsos are placed beside the doorway that leads into the inner hall.

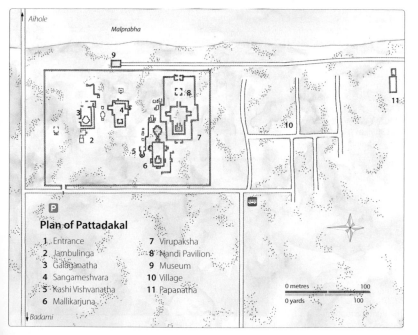

Plan of Pattadakal

1. Entrance
2. Jambulinga
3. Galaganatha
4. Sangameshvara
5. Kashi Vishvanatha
6. Mallikarjuna
7. Virupaksha
8. Nandi Pavilion
9. Museum
10. Village
11. Papanatha

A view of the Gaudar Gudi with the Ladkhan Temple behind it, Aihole

❷❸ Aihole

Bagalkote district. 44 km (27 miles) NE of Badami. 🚉 Badami, 46 km (29 miles) SW of town, then bus or taxi. 🚌 📷 Ramalinga Temple Chariot Festival (Feb/Mar).

Time seems to have stood still in this small, dusty town, situated on the Malprabha river, about 14 km (9 miles) downstream from Pattadakal (see pp542–3). Fortifications encircle much of the town. Within are ancient sandstone temples of varying types, some of which were used as dwellings and are named after their former inhabitants. The temples are associated with both the early and later Chalukya rulers of Badami (see pp540–41), and date from the 6th–11th centuries.

Most visitors begin their tour of Aihole at the **Durga Temple**. Nearby is a small complex with the **Ladkhan Temple**. This building is recognizable by the tiers of sloping slabs that roof the spacious hall as well as the adjoining entrance porch. River goddesses and amorous couples are carved on the columns of the porch, while images of deities can be seen on the side walls of a small chamber at the rooftop level. The adjacent **Gaudar Gudi** comprises a small sanctuary set within an open *mandapa*, with balcony seating on four sides. The ruined Chakra Gudi is near the stepped tank. The **Kunti Group**, a quartet of temples conceived as open

columned halls with interior sanctuaries, lies to the south. The temple to the southeast, probably the first to be built, has superbly carved ceiling panels portraying the Hindu Trinity of Brahma, Vishnu and Shiva. A similar trio of ceiling panels can be seen in the Hucchapayya Math, lying a short distance beyond.

A stepped path leads to the top of the hill southeast of the town, passing by a two-storeyed Buddhist temple. At the summit of the hill stands the serene **Meguti Temple** built in AD 634, the earliest dated structural monument in Karnataka. The temple's clearly articulated basement, plastered walls and eaves show the South Indian style of temple architecture (see p24) in its earliest phase. An impressive seated Jain figure is installed in the sanctuary. Prehistoric megalithic tombs are located to the rear of the temple.

The road, going downhill, follows the curving fortifications and passes the Jyotirlinga Group, until it ends at the Durga Temple. To the north of the Durga Temple is the **Chikki Gudi**, with exquisitely carved columns, beams and ceiling panels. A path to the right, leads to the small **Hucchimalli Gudi**, with a North Indian style tower, and an unusual icon of Karttikeya, Shiva's son, carved on the ceiling of the front porch.

Nearby lies the rock-cut **Ravala Phadi Cave**, dating to the late 6th century. Its interior is enhanced with splendid carvings of Hindu divinities. These include a Dancing Shiva in a subshrine; Ardhanarishvara, Harihara and Shiva with Ganga, on the walls of the main hall; and Varaha and Durga in the antechamber preceding the small linga sanctuary. Tiny shrines and a fluted column stand in front.

The exuberant Dancing Shiva relief in Ravala Phadi Cave

Aihole: Durga Temple

The largest and finest monument at Aihole, the Durga Temple is also the most unusual because of its apsidal sanctuary surrounded by an open colonnade. The temple is elevated on a lofty plinth, with steps at one end leading to a porch with elaborate carvings of sensuous couples and guardians on its columns. Other sculptural masterpieces, of Shiva with Nandi, Narasimha, Vishnu with Garuda, Durga and Harihara, are placed in the niches lining the colonnade. The interior of the hall is plain by contrast and the circular plinth within the sanctuary empty. The temple's name is a misnomer, as the identity of the image that was once worshipped here remains unknown.

A view of the semi-circular sanctuary of the Durga Temple

Naga Ceiling
A ceiling panel in the *mandapa* depicts a *naga* with a coiled serpent body.

The entrance porch
has columns embellished with intricate carvings.

The capstone
(*amalaka*), a ribbed disc, has fallen down from the tower.

Durga
This niche shows a multi-armed Durga slaying the buffalo demon.

Shikhara
Little remains of the tower that once rose above the inner sanctum.

Column Carving
This depiction of an amorous couple, carved on one of the columns in the porch, is a masterpiece of Chalukyan art.

㉔ Bijapur

Bijapur district. 530 km (329 miles) NW of Bengaluru. 246,000. 🏢 🚌 ℹ Karnataka Tourism, Station Rd, (08352) 250 359. 🎵 Bijapur Music Festival (Feb/Mar), Gagan Mahal Urs Festival (Sep).

After the fall of the Bahmanis (see p548), the Adil Shahi sultans emerged as the principal rulers of the Deccan in the 16th and 17th centuries. Their capital, the fortified city of Bijapur, was protected by ramparts with prominent bastions; many of the original cannons are still in place. The Malik-i-Maidan ("Lord of the Plain"), reputedly the largest cannon of the period in India, still guards the western entrance. Within the fort's walls are splendid mosques, palaces and tombs built by a succession of enlightened rulers.

🏛 The Citadel

The Citadel, in the heart of the city, is defined by its own fortified walls and surrounded by a wide moat. The south gate, the only one surviving, leads into what was once the palace complex. This ceremonial centre of Bijapur, surrounded by arcades, is known as the **Quadrangle**, and is today occupied by municipal offices. To its northwest stands the **Sat Manzil**, the seven-storeyed pleasure palace from the top of which the whole city could once be seen. Of this, only five storeys now remain. It overlooks an exquisitely ornamented

The arcaded prayer hall of the Jama Masjid

miniature pavilion called the **Jal Mandir**. A short distance to the north are the **Gagan Mahal**, the audience hall of Ali Adil Shah I, with an arched façade facing an open space, and the **Anand Mahal**, or the "Palace of Joy", where the ladies of the seraglio lived. Other fine structures include the **Mecca Masjid**, a charming little mosque to the east of the Citadel, and **Karimuddin's Mosque** near the south gate, built with temple materials pillaged in 1310 by Alauddin Khilji (see p52).

Medallion at Jama Masjid

🏛 Outside the Citadel

The walled city, outside the Citadel, is scattered with monuments built by the Adil Shahi sultans. To the east of

the Citadel is the double-storeyed **Asar Mahal**, built in 1646 as the hall of justice, and later converted into a sacred reliquary to house two hairs of the Prophet. Chambers on the upper level are decorated with murals depicting floral themes and courtly scenes with European-style figures. A short distance away is the elegant **Mihtar Mahal**, belonging to the period of Ibrahim II (1580– 1626) and entered through a triple-storeyed gateway. Balconies projecting over the street are supported on angled struts carved as if they were made of wood. The gateway leads to a small mosque.

The grandly conceived **Jama Masjid**, to the southeast, was begun by Ali Adil Shah I in 1576, but never finished. The marble floor of the capacious prayer hall has been divided into some 2,250 rectangular bays to resemble prayer mats. Even today, the mosque attracts more than 2,000 worshippers during Friday prayers. To the north and west are more tombs and mosques, including the Taj Baoli, a large square tank surrounded by steps.

🕌 Ibrahim Rauza

Open daily. 📷 Extra charges for photography.

This exquisite mausoleum, often described as the finest Islamic building in the Deccan, was built by Ibrahim II for his wife. In fact, he predeceased her and is buried here too. The funerary complex consists of a tomb and a mosque, raised on a plinth in the middle of a formal garden. A huge tank nearby is named after his wife, Taj Sultana. The walls of the tomb, as seen within an arcaded verandah, are embellished with superb calligraphic and geometric designs. The tomb chamber is roofed by a flat vault with curving sides.

Ibrahim Rauza, the beautifully proportioned tomb of Ibrahim II

Bijapur: Gol Gumbad

Bijapur's most celebrated building, the monumental tomb of Muhammad Adil Shah (1627–56), second son and successor of Ibrahim II, is commonly known as the "Round Dome", or Gol Gumbad. The slightly bulbous dome, the largest in the world after St Peter's in Rome, rises on a base of petals to form a fitting climax to the whole composition. Completed in 1656, the tomb stands in the middle of a formal garden. On the west side is a small mosque with five arches flanked by slender minarets.

Circular gallery

Minaret

VISITORS' CHECKLIST

Practical Information
Station Rd.
Tel (08352) 204 737.
Open daily. 🎫 free on Fri.
Autos & cycles available.

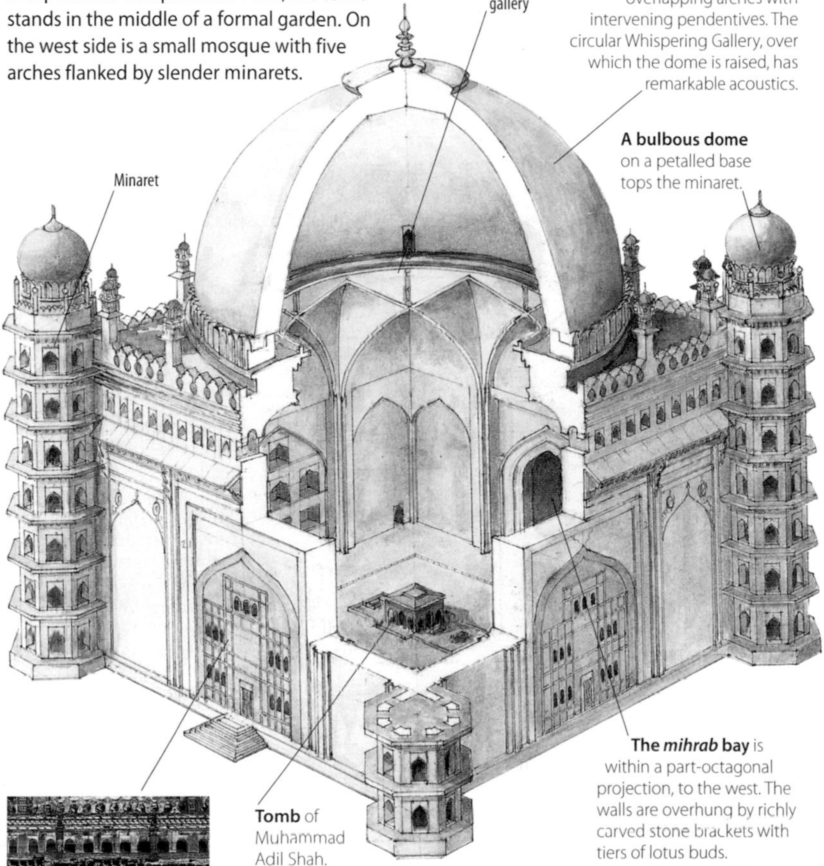

The dome is nearly 43 m (141 ft) in diameter. It is carried on eight overlapping arches with intervening pendentives. The circular Whispering Gallery, over which the dome is raised, has remarkable acoustics.

A bulbous dome on a petalled base tops the minaret.

The *mihrab* bay is within a part-octagonal projection, to the west. The walls are overhung by richly carved stone brackets with tiers of lotus buds.

Tomb of Muhammad Adil Shah.

Entrance Arch
The entrance façade has a wide, lofty arch in the centre, pierced with small windows on either side.

Deccani Painting

The Muslim rulers of the Deccan, especially of Golconda *(see pp670–71)* and Bijapur, during the 14th and 15th centuries, encouraged art and established a Deccani School of Painting. This was influenced first by direct contact with Central Asia and Persia, and later by the Mughals. At the court of Bijapur, elements of European Renaissance and Persian art were assimilated into the classical Indian tradition, to create a distinctive Deccani style.

Chand Bibi Playing Polo, a Deccani painting

The vaulted hall of the Jama Masjid at Gulbarga

㉕ Gulbarga

Gulbarga district. 160 km (99 miles) NE of Bijapur. 🚉 428,000. 🚌 🚕 *i* Gulbarga Tourist Office, (08472) 220 644. 🎋 Urs (Mar).

This small provincial town contains some of the earliest examples of Islamic architecture in Karnataka. These date to the 14th and 15th centuries, when Gulbarga flourished as the capital of the Bahmani sultans *(see p53)*, the first of the great Muslim kingdoms to dominate the Deccan.

The **Dargah of Gesu Daraz** (d.1422), to the northeast of the present town, is one of South India's holiest Muslim shrines. Khwaja Gesu Daraz, or Bande Nawaz as he was affectionately

Devotees at the gateway to the Dargah of Gesu Daraz, Gulbarga

known, was a Sufi mystic from the Chishti sect *(see p380)*. He fled from North India and sought refuge here at the court of Firuz Shah Bahmani, a pious and enlightened ruler. His simple tomb stands in the middle of a large, sprawling complex comprising a group of lesser tombs, mosques and *madrasas*, and is a major pilgrimage centre. The Dargah of Shah Kamal Mujarrad, another saint who lived in Gulbarga, lies further south

A complex of seven royal tombs, known as the **Haft Gumbad**, lies to the west of the *dargah*. Firuz Shah Bahmani, who also died in 1422, is buried here in the largest and most elaborate of all the mausoleums. Immediately west of the city are the desolate ruins of the forbidding fort, almost circular and protected by a wide moat. Little of the royal centre remains intact today. Near the entrance gateway is the Bala Hisar, a solid keep dating from the 17th century, when the Adil Shahis *(see pp546–7)* occupied the city. The most interesting structure, however, is the large **Jama Masjid** nearby. Built in 1367, to commemorate Gulbarga's status as the capital, this is one of the earliest mosques in South India, and the only one without an open courtyard. To its rear is the 14th-century Bazaar Street, lined

with small chambers now converted into dwellings. This leads to a series of gateways shielded by walls that protrude outwards from the fort walls. To the west of the fort are the derelict tombs of the early Bahmani sultans.

Another 14th-century monument is the **Shah Bazaar Mosque**, to the north of the fort. Its domed entrance chamber leads into a courtyard with a prayer hall beyond. A street from here proceeds westwards to an arcaded portal flanked by lofty minarets. Behind this portal lies the Dargah of Sheikh Sirajuddin Junaydi, a simple tomb with arcaded recesses and a flattish dome.

Environs
The picturesque ruins of **Firuzabad**, the palace city founded in 1400 by Firuz Shah Bahmani on the east bank of the Bhima river, are located 28 km (17 miles) south of Gulbarga. The massive stone walls with quadrangular bastions and arched gateways define an approximately square zone, almost 1,000 m (3,281 ft) wide. The best preserved structures are the Jama Masjid and a two-storeyed audience hall. Among the remains are the royal baths *(hamams)*, with pyramidal vaults and fluted domes, said to be the oldest in the Deccan.

㉖ Bidar

Bidar district. 120 km (75 miles) NE of Gulbarga. 🚌 Autos & cycles available.

Bidar became the Bahmani capital in 1424, when Firuz Shah's brother and successor, Ahmad Shah, moved his court here. With the collapse of the Bahmani dynasty at the end of the 15th century, control of the region passed into the hands of the Baridis. The city was included in the World Monuments Fund in 2014.

Bidar's **Fort**, built in 1428 by Ahmed Shah Bahmani, occupies a promontory that is defended by double rings of walls and a moat partly carved out of the bedrock. A trio of arched gates, one with polychrome tilework,

The walled road leading to the entrance gateway of Bidar's fort

another with a prominent dome, leads into what was once the royal enclave. To the left is the Rangin Mahal, an exquisite palace built by Ali Shah Barid in the 16th century. The hall, with its original wooden columns displaying ornate brackets and beams, and the rear chamber adorned with magnificent tile mosaics and inlaid mother-of-pearl decoration, are especially striking. Nearby is the unusual Solah Khamba Mosque, with massive circular columns, built by the Tughluqs (see p52) in 1327. In front is the Lal Bagh, a walled garden with a central lobe-fringed pool. A short distance to the south is the ruined Diwan-i-Am, the Public Audience Hall, and the Takht Mahal, a monumental portal with traces of hexagonal tiles decorated with tiger and sun emblems in the spandrels.

The old walled town sprawls beneath the ramparts of the fort. On one side of the main north-south street is the **Takhti-i-Kirmani**, a 15th-century gateway embellished with bands of foliate and arabesque designs. Further south is the magnificent late 15th-century **Madrasa of Mahmud Gawan**, named after the erudite prime minister who was the virtual ruler of the Bahmani kingdom. This used to be a famous theological college,

and at one time boasted a huge library, well-stocked with scholarly manuscripts. A superb example of Central Asian-style architecture, it has four arched portals that stand against a background of domes facing a central court. A pair of minarets flanks its façade. Tile mosaics on the exterior still survive, including a finely worked calligraphic band in rich blue and white. Still further south, the **Chaubara** marks the intersection of the two principal streets running through Bidar.

The **Mausolea of the Baridi rulers** lie west of Bidar. The largest is the Tomb of Ali Shah Barid (1577). This lofty, domed chamber, open on four sides, stands in the middle of a symmetrical four-square garden. Blank panels above the arches once contained tile mosaic, examples of which are preserved inside. The black polished basalt sarcophagus is still *in situ*.

Bidar is also known for a special type of encrusted metalware, often mistaken for damascening, known as *bidri* (see p669). Introduced in the mid-17th century by artisans from Iran, the craft flourished under court patronage. The style, characterized by intricate floral and geometric designs, inlaid in gold, silver or brass onto a matt black surface, was used to embellish various objects,

Tile mosaic at Bidar's madrasa

including platters, boxes, *huqqa* bases and trays. Today, the finest pieces are housed in museums, and only a handful of artisan families still practise this craft in the town of its origin.

Environs

The Bahmani necropolis stands in the open countryside near **Ashtur**, a small village 3 km (2 miles) northeast of Bidar. The oldest and grandest of the tombs is the early 15th-century Tomb of Ahmad Shah. Splendid murals embellish the interior walls as well as the huge dome. The adjacent tomb of Alauddin Ahmad II, his successor, has coloured tile mosaics. Just outside is the Chaukhandi, the modest tomb of the saint Khalil Allah (d.1460), which has superb calligraphic panels over the doorways.

Façade of the Madrasa of Mahmud Gawan in Bidar

SOUTH
INDIA

Introducing South India

South of the Vindhya range, India's Dravidian heartland has all that a visitor could look for. Dramatic coastlines, both on the Arabian Sea and the Bay of Bengal, meet at Kanniyakumari on the Indian Ocean. Isolated beaches, dense forests and game reserves are among its natural wonders. Tamil Nadu has some of India's most magnificent ancient temples, still active centres of religious practice. A different culture prevails in Puducherry, which retains a strong French influence. Kerala is rich in beautiful scenery as well as in cultural heritage, while Andhra Pradesh has some of the region's most fascinating historic sites.

Fisherman at a sluice gate on the Kaveri river

A class in progress in a traditional Vedic school, Tamil Nadu

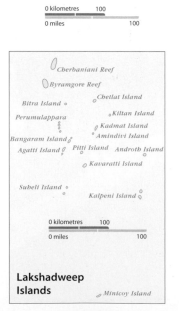

| 0 kilometres | 100 |
| 0 miles | 100 |

Cherbaniani Reef

Byramgore Reef

Chetlat Island

Bitra Island

Perumulappara

Kiltan Island

Kadmat Island

Aminidivi Island

Bangaram Island

Agatti Island

Pitti Island

Androth Island

Kavaratti Island

Suheli Island

Kalpeni Island

| 0 kilometres | 100 |
| 0 miles | 100 |

Lakshadweep Islands

Minicoy Island

◄ Wooden boat cruise in the backwaters jungle in Kochin, Kerala

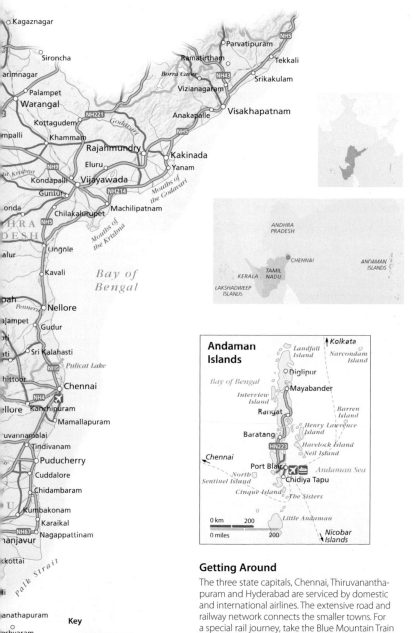

Kagaznagar

Sironcha

arimnagar

Palampet

Warangal

Kottagudem

mpalli

Khammam

Rajahmundry

NH9

Eluru

Kondapalli

Vijayawada

Guntur

onda

Chilakalurupet

NH5

HRA
DESH

Ungole

alur

Kavali

Parvatipuram

Ramatirtham

Borra Caves NH43

Vizianagaram

Anakapalle

Srikakulam

Tekkali

Visakhapatnam

NH221

Godavari

Kakinada

Yanam

Machilipatnam

Mouths of
the Godavari

Mouths of
the Krishna

Bay of
Bengal

Pennar

Nellore

ajampet

Gudur

ati

Sri Kalahasti

NH18

Pulicat Lake

hittoor

Chennai

NH4

ellore

Kanchipuram

Mamallapuram

uvannamalai

Tindivanam

Puducherry

Cuddalore

Chidambaram

U

Kumbakonam

Karaikal

NH67

Nagappattinam

hanjavur

kottai

Palk Strait

anathapuram

eshvaram

Andaman Islands

Landfall
Island

Kolkata

Narcondam
Island

Diglipur

Bay of Bengal

Mayabander

Interview
Island

Rangat

Baratang

Barren
Island

Henry Lawrence
Island

HN223

Havelock Island

Neil Island

Chennai

Port Blair

North
Sentinel Island

Chidiya Tapu

Andaman Sea

Cinque Island

The Sisters

0 km   200

0 miles   200

Little Andaman

Nicobar
Islands

ANDHRA
PRADESH

CHENNAI

KERALA

TAMIL
NADU

ANDAMAN
ISLANDS

LAKSHADWEEP
ISLANDS

Key

— National highway

— Major road

— State border

-- Main railway

— Minor railway

Getting Around

The three state capitals, Chennai, Thiruvanantha-puram and Hyderabad are serviced by domestic and international airlines. The extensive road and railway network connects the smaller towns. For a special rail journey, take the Blue Mountain Train from Coimbatore to Ooty *(see pp608–609)*. There are regular flights from Kolkata and Chennai to the Andaman Islands, and from Kochi (Kerala) to Agatti (Lakshadweep). Cruises to Lakshadweep are available from Kochi, and to the Andamans from Chennai, Kolkata and Visakhapatnam.

For keys to symbols *see back flap*

A PORTRAIT OF SOUTH INDIA

The term "South India", though it conveys a sense of geographical unity, also encompasses a multitude of differences. While the three states – Tamil Nadu, Kerala and Andhra Pradesh – share, to some extent, an ancient heritage, they speak different languages, and each has its distinct artistic, cultural and political tradition.

A popular view holds that while the history of North India is one of wars and invasions, the south remained cocooned in peaceful stagnation. In actual fact, the three states witnessed bloody conflicts between Jainism and Buddhism on the one hand, and Brahminical Hinduism on the other. They saw the rise and fall of powerful kingdoms, who fought many wars to establish their dominance. In the beginning of the colonial period, South India was also a battleground between the Europeans and the regional kingdoms. All these upheavals have left their mark on the region.

Tamil Nadu, the heartland of Dravidian India has, for over three decades, been

Wooden effigy, Thiruvananthapuram

ruled by two regional parties. Though arch-rivals, they share a common platform, based on a strong advocacy of Tamil language and culture. Tamil is the oldest surviving Dravidian language, with a literature that goes back to AD 300. This period, known as the Sangam era, derives its name from the Tamil Sangams, gatherings of poets and writers, which produced countless poems, remarkably secular in nature, of which over 2,000 have survived. Another enduring expression of Tamil culture is visible in Tamil Nadu's Hindu temples – it has no less than 30,000 of them. A more modern face of Tamil Nadu

A 16th-century Catholic church, overlooking a little fishing village at Kanniyakumari

A portrait of film star-turned-politician Jayalalitha

development indices that are exceptional among Indian states – the country's highest literacy rate (the language spoken here is Malayalam), a low population growth rate, the lowest infant mortality rate, and a near-perfect record in communal harmony. Culturally, Kerala boasts spectacular dance forms such as Kathakali *(see p661)*, and the martial *kalaripayattu (see p630)*. Today, its renowned Ayurvedic health resorts *(see p633)* are also a major draw for international travellers.

Telugu-speaking Andhra Pradesh is South India's largest state, with its capital, Hyderabad, located in the heart of the Deccan Plateau. This city was once the seat of the powerful Nizams *(see p664)* whose wealth was legendary. Their legacy has given Hyderabad a unique flavour, rich in manifestations of an Islamic culture – in its architecture and cuisine, and in the widespread use of Urdu.

can be seen in the state capital, Chennai, a vibrant commercial and political centre that still retains its traditional values. Here, classical Carnatic music concerts draw as large and enthusiastic crowds as raucous political rallies. Many coastal areas in Tamil Nadu were devastated by the December 2004 tsunami, which took a toll of over 10,000 lives. Kerala and Andhra Pradesh were also affected, though to a much lesser extent.

A truck overloaded with hay

Andhra Pradesh shares with Tamil Nadu a penchant for film stars-turned-politicians. For many years it was ruled by Telugu cinema's most loved actor, NT Rama Rao, who specialized in playing mythological heroes. His son-in-law, Chandrababu Naidu, as chief minister, chose a more down-to-earth way of winning popular support, with his schemes to modernize the state. As a result, Hyderabad now vies with Bengaluru for the title of India's information technology capital.

In Kerala, separated from Tamil Nadu by the magnificent forested hills of the Western Ghats, the main attraction is not temples (though it has those too), but natural beauty. It is easy to understand why this narrow strip of land between the Arabian Sea and the Western Ghats, with its verdant landscape of palm trees, paddy fields and coffee plantations, criss-crossed by enchanting waterways, has been dubbed "God's own country".

Modern-day Kerala, with a strong leftist political tradition, boasts of

Tamil Brahmin boys performing a religious ritual

Temple Towns

Srirangam *(see p605)* is typical of many towns in South India, especially in Tamil Nadu, that are dominated by sanctuaries dedicated to Hindu deities who protect the city and its population. Conceived as a vast religious complex, the town is enclosed by high fortress-like walls, and entered through towering gateways *(gopuras)*. The temple itself consists of multiple walled enclosures, often in concentric arrangements, surrounded by streets that echo the temple's layout. Though Srirangam is the most perfect in layout, other such towns include Chidambaram *(see p594)* and Madurai *(see pp612–15)*.

Puja items being sold outside the temple enclosure

Kalyana Mandapas (marriage halls) have raised platforms in the middle. Portable images of the deities are placed here during the ritual marriage ceremonies and festivals that are conducted annually, in the presence of thousands of devotees.

Kitchens produce food for priests and thousands of pilgrims during festivals that take place in the complex. Nearby are stores and granaries.

Subsidiary shrines of other deities, such as Garuda and Hanuman in Vishnu temples, and Ganesha, Nandi and Subrahmanya or Murugan in Shiva temples, are also venerated within the complex.

Banners are hoisted on slender, brass-clad wooden columns in the middle of the enclosure. Here, too, are small altars.

The outer enclosures of temple complexes are packed with houses to accommodate the priestly community, which presides over the religious life of temple towns.

The main sanctum, where the principal deity is enshrined, forms the nucleus of the whole complex. This is the *garbhagriha*, or womb chamber. The main doorway into the sanctuary is opened only during prayer time, to allow worshippers to make offerings to the deity within.

Wooden chariots covered with carved panels are parked outside the main gates. During festivals they are pulled by devotees through the streets of the town.

Tanks and wells provide water for ritual bathing, cooking and general washing. Temple tanks have steps on four sides for bathers to descend to the water. Small pavilions in the middle are used for special festivals.

The inner enclosures, constituting the most sacred precincts, are filled with subsidiary shrines, pillared halls, flag columns, altars, kitchens, rest houses, tanks and wells.

Axial *mandapas* and corridors direct worshippers from the outer *gopuras* towards the main sanctuary. Sculptures on columns embellish these passageways. Bronze images are also displayed here.

Gopuras, or ceremonial gateways, with soaring, pyramidal towers, are set into four sides of each of the concentric sets of walls that define the sacred complex. Their hollow brick towers are covered with brightly painted plaster sculptures. Barrel-vaulted roofs at the tops of the towers are crowned by gilded pot finials, visible from all over the town.

Mandapas are columned halls which sometimes take on vast proportions, especially the so-called thousand-pillared halls. These can accommodate large numbers of visitors who come to listen to sermons or to enjoy performances of classical music and dance.

The Flavours of South India

Rice preparations dominate South Indian cuisine, of which the best known are *dosai* (rice pancakes served with spiced potatoes), *idli* (steamed rice dumplings), *vadai* (deep-fried lentil doughnuts) and *uttapam* (a spicy pancake). All are eaten with *sambhar* (lentil broth) and chutneys made with coconut, garlic and chillies. These are "tiffin" or breakfast foods, and specialist restaurants can be found all over India and abroad. Despite the commonalities, each state's cuisine has its own flavour, dictated by regional tastes and locally grown ingredients, as is evident in Hyderabad's sophisticated Muslim cuisine.

Sprig of curry leaves

Fresh green coconuts, providing a refreshing drink on a hot day

Kerala

Kerala, the land of spices, particularly pepper, inspired the European race for an empire in the East. An abundance of spices, such as cloves, mace, cardamoms and cinnamon, have infused the cuisine with a range of exotic aromas. Added to this are coconuts, used in the preparation of almost all dishes.

The different communities have distinctive cuisines. The Hindu Brahmins specialize in vegetarian food, while the Muslims and Christians excel in mutton and poultry dishes. Foreign influences are apparant and the classic *moilee*, a term used for fish or vegetable curries, is a corruption of the Portuguese *molho* or sauce.

The staple food is rice and the best-known dish is the *appam*, a steamed rice pancake. A typical middle-class meal comprises boiled rice accompanied by pulses, a vegetable curry, a dry vegetable, pickles, poppadams, and a meat or fish dish for non-vegetarians. The *sadya*, a festive meal eaten at Onam, is always served on a banana leaf.

Tamil Nadu

Six tastes – sweet, sour, salty, bitter, peppery and astringent – define

Spiced potatoes · Vada · Coconut chutney · Chilli chutney · Rava dosa · Uttapam · Sambhar · Plain dosa · Idli

Selection of South Indian rice preparations and other accompaniments

Local Dishes and Specialities

The common culinary heritage leans heavily on rice, lentils, coconut and spices. Vegetable preparations are diverse and range from the steamed or stir-fried *poriyal*, which is tempered with spices and curry leaves, to *avial* (mixed vegetables in thick coconut sauce) and *mirchi ka salan* (a curry with whole green chillies). Interestingly, the word curry is a derivative of *kari*, a spicy dish from Kerala and Tamil Nadu, while *rasam*, integral to a meal as an appetizer and digestive, was the base of the Anglo-Indian mulligatawny soup. Chicken, lamb and fish also feature on the menu, particularly the seafood curries from Kerala and Andhra Pradesh and the delicious *biryanis* and wide range of *kebabs* from Hyderabad.

Coconuts

Appams and stew, a popular dish, consists of fermented rice pancakes served with a vegetable or chicken stew.

Chinese fishing nets, an iconic sight in Fort Cochin, Kerala

Tamilian food. A traditional meal includes all six to balance nutrition, the appetite and digestion. The special flavour of the food comes from a combination of curry leaves, ginger, coconut, garlic, coriander, asafetida, tamarind, pepper, chillies, cloves, cumin, cinnamon and cardamom.

Meals consist of cooked rice served with an array of vegetable dishes, *sambhar*, *rasam* (watered down version of sambar with pepper, herbs and tomatoes) and chutneys. Crisp poppadams or *appalam* (rice wafer) complete a meal. Desserts include the warm milky rice *payasam* or sweet *pongal*, also made from rice.

Non Brahmin communities, such as the Chettiars from Chettinad, are meat eaters. Their hot and spicy cuisine has several interesting fish, mutton and chicken dishes, of which pepper chicken is considered the best.

Andhra Pradesh

The liberal use of red chilli and tamarind make Andhra food one of the country's spiciest. Rice and vegetables form the basis of a meal. Some common dishes include *pulihora* (sour/tamarind rice), *pesarattu* (a

View of a street vegetable market in rural Tamil Nadu

variation of the *dosai*, made with lentils and rice), *dhapalam* (a vegetable curry) and *pachidi* (a curd-based relish).

In contrast is the cuisine of Hyderabad with its distinct Muslim influences. Savoury mutton or chicken *biryanis* are accompanied by *kebabs*, lamb, chicken or vegetable curries *(salans)*, vegetables and breads. Some specialities include *pathar gosh* (lamb cooked on a stone), *haleem* (a pounded wheat and lamb dish eaten during the fasting months of Ramzan or Ramadan) and desserts such as *shahi tukra* and *kubani ka meetha*, made with dried apricots and cream.

ON THE MENU

Aadu olathiayathu Fried cubes of lamb garnished with coconut and curry leaves.

Meen varuval *Masala* fried fish from Chettinad, served with sliced onions and lime.

Sambhar A spicy lentil broth with mixed vegetables, a must for all meals.

Tahari A rice and mincemeat *pulao*, a Hyderabad special.

Tamatar pappu A spicy tomato and lentil curry.

Thengai saadham Coconut rice, seasoned with red chillies and curry leaves.

Upma A savoury semolina breakfast dish.

Bagharey baingan, whole aubergines stuffed with spices, are Hyderabad's most famous vegetarian dish.

Meen moilee, a speciality of the Christian community of Kerala, is a lightly spiced coconut fish curry.

Payasam is a creamy dessert made from rice and milk and garnished with cashew nuts and raisins.

CHENNAI

Chennai, formerly known as Madras, is the state capital of Tamil Nadu and the gateway to the rich and varied culture of the South Indian peninsula. Originally a cluster of fishing hamlets along the Coromandel Coast, the city developed its cohesive shape under the British. Today, it is South India's commercial and cultural capital, and the fourth largest metropolis in India.

A modern capital, with the appearance of a gracious garden city, Chennai was once a group of villages set amidst palm-fringed paddy fields, until two English East India Company merchants, Francis Day and Andrew Cogan, established a factory-cum-trading post here. Completed on St George's Day, 23 April 1640, this fortified settlement came to be known as Fort St George. Outside its walls was George Town, the so-called "native town", whose crowded lanes, each devoted to a particular trade, serviced the British colonists. Colonial rule linked the various villages, including the settlement founded in the 16th century by the Portuguese at San Thomé, the sacred site associated with St Thomas the Apostle. Several centuries before the Europeans arrived, the great 7th-century Pallava port was at Mylapore; its Kapalesvara Temple, along with the

Parthasarathi Temple at Triplicane, bear testimony to the city's antiquity.

Colonial rule marked the beginning of the city's growth as a major commercial centre. Today, most of the large business houses have their offices in George Town, while Fort St George is the power centre of the Tamil Nadu state government. Extending across 174 sq km (67 sq miles), Chennai today is a dynamic mix of the old and the new, its stately colonial structures juxtaposed with modern high-rises. Its rich cultural heritage of Tamil literature, music and dance is perpetuated in universities and performing arts centres. It is also a highly political city, as can be seen from the many grandiose memorials to politicians that line Marina Beach. A huge hoarding depicting Jayalalitha, a Tamil Nadu political leader, looming above Marina promenade

A huge hoarding depicting Jayalalitha, a Tamil Nadu political leader, looming above Marina promenade

◄ The distinctive towering steeple at St Andrew's Kirk

Exploring Chennai

A conglomeration of several overgrown villages, Chennai has no single centre, but can be divided into a numerous urban districts, connected by four main roads. George Town is to the northeast of Periyar EVR High Road (Poonamallee High Road), while Triplicane and Mylapore are to the south. The city's main thoroughfare, Anna Salai (Mount Road), links Fort St George with Mount St Thomas, to the south. Chennai's other main roads, Rajaji Salai (North Beach Road) and Kamarajar Salai (South Beach Road), run along the seafront, along the popular Marina promenade towards Kalakshetra.

An early morning scene at a flower shop at Parry's Corner

Sights at a Glance

Historic Buildings, Areas & Neighbourhoods
1 Fort St George
2 George Town
4 Egmore
6 Anna Salai
8 Triplicane

Churches & Holy Places
3 *St Andrew's Kirk pp566–7*
9 Mylapore & San Thomé
14 Little Mount & Mount of St Thomas

Walk
7 *A Walk along the Marina pp572–3*

Museums
5 Government Museum Complex

Parks & Gardens
13 Guindy National Park

Entertainment
11 Kalakshetra
12 MGR Film City

For hotels and restaurants see p702 and p717

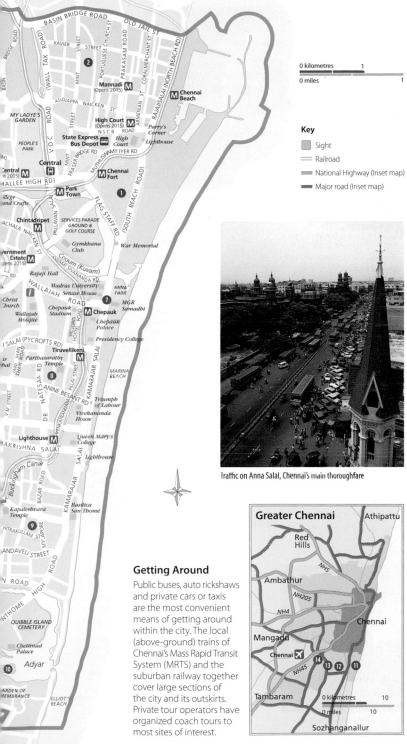

BASIN BRIDGE ROAD

OLD JAIL ST

BRIDGE ROAD

BASIN

(WALL TAX ROAD)

XAVIER STREET

STREET

PORTUGUESE CHURCH ST

PRAKASAM ROAD

CORALMERCHANT ST

RAJAJISALAI (NORTH BEACH RD)

2

Mannadi Ⓜ
(Opens 2015)

Ⓜ **Chennai Beach**

AUDIAPPA NAICKEN ST

MINT

MY LADYE'S GARDEN

VOC ROAD

ARMENIAN ST

High Court Ⓜ
(Opens 2015)
N S C B ROAD

Parry's Corner

PEOPLE'S PARK

STREET

State Express Bus Depot 🚌

MINT

FRASER BRIDGE RD

MUTHUSWAMY IYER RD

High Court

Lighthouse

entral Ⓜ **Central** 🚉
s 2015)

MALLEE HIGH RD)

Ⓜ **Chennai Fort**

ollege
and Crafts

Ⓜ **Park Town**

1

Chintadripet Ⓜ

ACHALA NAICKEN ST

PILLAIYAN SALAI

FLAG STAFF RD

(SOUTH BEACH ROAD)

SERVICES PARADE GROUND & GOLF COURSE

vernment Estate Ⓜ
pens 2015)

Gymkhana Club

War Memorial

RD

Rajaji Hall

COOUM (KUVAM)
SWAMI SIVANANDA RD

7

Christ Church

WALLAJAH ROAD

Madras University Senate House

ANNA PARK

Chepauk Stadium

Ⓜ **Chepauk**

MGR Samadhi

VICTORIA HOSTEL ROAD

Chepauk Palace

Wallajah Mosque

Presidency College

SALAI (PYCROFTS RD)

Tiruvellikeni

JHAN JHAN RD

bal

Parthasarathy Temple

0

ANINE BESANT RD

PILJI STREET

KAMARAJAR SALAI

MARINA BEACH

DR

NATESAN RD

VENKATRAMAN ST

Triumph of Labour

Vivekananda House

VM STREET

Lighthouse Ⓜ

Queen Mary's College

AKRISHNA SALAI

Lighthouse

KAMARAJAR SALAI

Buckingham Canal

ai

BAZAR ROAD

Basilica San Thomé

Kapaleshvara Temple

9

HITRAKULLAM ST

MYLAPORE

ANDAVELI STREET

HIGH ROAD

V ROAD

NTHOME

QUIBBLE ISLAND CEMETERY

Chettinad Palace

10

Adyar

ARDEN OF
EMEMBRANCE

ELLIOT'S BEACH

0 kilometres 1

0 miles 1

Key

◻ Sight

═ Railroad

▬ National Highway (Inset map)

▬ Major road (Inset map)

Traffic on Anna Salai, Chennai's main thoroughfare

Getting Around

Public buses, auto rickshaws and private cars or taxis are the most convenient means of getting around within the city. The local (above-ground) trains of Chennai's Mass Rapid Transit System (MRTS) and the suburban railway together cover large sections of the city and its outskirts. Private tour operators have organized coach tours to most sites of interest.

Greater Chennai

Athipattu

Red Hills

NH5

Ambathur

NH205

NH4

Chennai ✈

14 **13** **12** **11**

Mangadu

NH45

Tambaram

0 kilometres 10

0 miles 10

Sozhanganallur

For keys to symbols see back flap

The Secretariat at Fort St George, the seat of Tamil Nadu's government

❶ Fort St George

Bounded by Sir Muthuswamy Iyer Rd, Flag Staff Rd & Kamarajar Salai (South Beach Rd). Fort Museum: **Tel** (044) 2538 4510. **Open** daily. **Closed** public hols. 📷

Britain's first bastion in India, the nucleus from which an empire grew, was established in a banana grove owned by a farmer called Madrasan. The official grant for the land, however, was given by Venkatadri Nayak, the deputy of the Raja of Chandragiri *(see p684)*. The first factory within the fortified enclosure was completed on St George's Day, 23 April 1640, and named Fort St George. This was the East India Company's main settlement until 1772, when Calcutta, now Kolkata, was declared the seat of the government.

The sloping ramparts, |with battlements for gun emplacement that can still be seen today, were designed by Bartholomew Robins in 1750, after the original walls were

destroyed by the French army in 1749. These ramparts form an irregular pentagon, further reinforced by a ring of earthen walls that slope down to a moat surrounding the entire complex. The drawbridges that once led to the Fort's five main gates have now been replaced by roads. Note that most buildings in the fort have restricted access; only St Mary's Church and the Fort Museum are open to the public.

The first building to be seen on entering the Fort through the Sea Gate is the Neo-Classical **Secretariat**, which is today the seat of the government of Tamil Nadu. Behind it lie the **Legislative Council Chambers**. With their handsome classical lines and façades embellished with gleaming black pillars, these impressive buildings (built 1694–1732) are said to be among the

oldest surviving British constructions in India. The 45-m (148-ft) tall flagstaff was erected by Governor Elihu Yale in 1687 to hoist the Union Jack for the first time in India. Today, the Indian tricolour flies in its stead. Yale began his career as a clerk with the East India Company and later founded Yale University in the USA.

Standing to the south of the Legislature building is **St Mary's Church**, the oldest Anglican church in Asia. It was built between 1678 and 1680 by Streynsham Master, then the governor of Madras. Memorials, paintings, antique Bibles (including one printed in 1660) and silver are displayed in the church, and speak of its vibrant history. Both Elihu Yale and Robert Clive were married in this church, and the three daughters of Job Charnock *(see p271)* were baptized here before the family moved to Bengal. Arthur Wellesley, who later became the Duke of Wellington and triumphed at Waterloo, and Robert Clive, both lived in Fort St George. Their residences, Wellesley House and Clive House, still stand, albeit in a somewhat dilapidated condition, across from the church.

To the north is the **Parade Ground**, formerly Cornwallis Square, which was laid out in 1715. Magnificent parades and rallies were held here. To its east are ministerial offices, and

The altar in St Mary's Church with a painting of the Last Supper

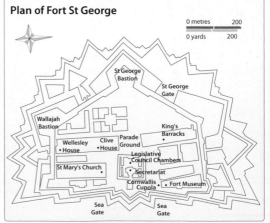

Plan of Fort St George

0 metres 200
0 yards 200

St George Bastion
St George Gate
Wallajah Bastion
King's Barracks
Wellesley House
Clive House
Parade Ground
Legislative Council Chambers
St Mary's Church
Secretariat
Cornwallis Cupola
Fort Museum
Sea Gate
Sea Gate

barracks for regiments. Near the southeast corner of the Parade Ground is the **Fort Museum**, built in the 1780s. A treasure trove of colonial memorabilia, the museum is housed in what was built to be the Public Exchange. It has paintings of British royalty, 18th-century weaponry, emblems and other relics from the British era. Among its prized possessions are a scale model of the Fort and a painting of King George III and Queen Charlotte. There are lithographs on the second and third floors that provide fascinating perspectives of old Madras and other parts of South India.

Near the museum's southern end, and overlooking its cannon, is the **Cornwallis Cupola**, which originally stood in the Parade Ground. It is the largest one built to house the statue of the governor-general, Lord Cornwallis, sculpted in 1800. It shows him accepting the two young sons of Tipu Sultan *(see p521)* as hostages.

❷ George Town

Bounded by Rajaji Salai (North Beach Rd) & NSC Bose Rd.

In the 1640s, weavers and dyers from Andhra Pradesh were settled in this enclave to manufacture cloth for the East India Company's textile trade. The British referred to the settlement as "Black Town",

The General Post Office, George Town

while its inhabitants called it Chennapatnam, from where Chennai gets it name. After the entire area was rebuilt 100 years later, it was renamed George Town. During this period, most of the city's commercial activity was concentrated within this 5-sq km (2-sq mile) area. It still remains a busy hive of activity with public institutions in the south, trade and commercial premises in the centre, and residential quarters in the north. The first feature of interest is the 38-m (125-ft) high **Lighthouse** on Rajaji Salai, whose beacon was visible 25 km

Fruit vendors on the pavements of George Town

(16 miles) out at sea. The adjacent red-brick **High Court**, designed by Chisholm in the Indo-Saracenic style, with stained glass and carved furniture, was opened in 1892, while the nearby **General Post Office** with its archways and square towers, is another fine Indo-Saracenic building. **Parry's Corner**, at the junction of NSC Bose Road and Rajaji Salai, is named after Parry and Company. Founded by Thomas Parry in 1790, it is the oldest British mercantile company still operating in Chennai. **Dare House**, the present headquarters of this 200-year-old company, now stands at the site.

The area's longest street, **Mint Street**, gets its name from the authorized mint that was set up here in 1841 to produce gold coins for the British as well as for various local rulers. The mint buildings are now part of the government printing press. The 17th-century houses lining George Town were once the residences and business centres of Indian as well as Portuguese, Armenian and other foreign traders. **Armenian Street** is named after the many Armenians who lived here, while **Coral Merchant Street** housed a small Jewish community that traded in corals.

Today, each street in George Town is dominated by a particular trade. Anderson Street specializes in paper, grain merchants operate from Audiappa Naicken Street, while textile wholesalers have their warehouses on Govindappa Naicken Street and Godown Street. Some streets, such as Kasi Chetty Street and Narayanamudali Street, are lined with shops selling fancy goods and imported bric-a-brac.

A portrait of Robert Clive by Nathaniel Dance (1773)

Robert Clive (1725–74)

One of the most flamboyant personalities in the history of British India, Robert Clive was only 19 when he began his career as a clerk for the East India Company at Fort St George. Soon tiring of paperwork, he became a soldier and fought many successful battles *(see p56)*, including the Carnatic Wars, which established the Company's rule in South India. Clive was given the stewardship of Fort St George and later become Governor of Bengal. The wealth he amassed in India led to his trial, in England, on charges of corruption. Clive committed suicide in 1774.

❸ St Andrew's Kirk

A magnificent example of Neo-Classical architecture, St Andrew's Kirk was consecrated in 1821. Inspired by St Martin- in-the-Fields in London, it was designed and executed by Major Thomas de Havilland and Colonel James Caldwell of the Madras Engineers, at a cost of £20,000. The body of the church is a circle, with rectangular compartments to the east and west. The circular part, 24.5 m (80 ft) in diameter, is crowned by a shallow masonry dome coloured a deep blue. This is painted with golden stars and supported by 16 fluted pillars with Corinthian capitals.

A view of St Andrew's Kirk with its towering steeple

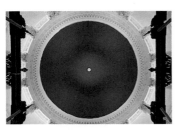

★ Dome
An architectural marvel, the dome has a framework of brick supported by an annular arch and is filled in by pottery cones. Its blue interior is formed by crushed sea shells mixed with lapis lazuli.

Stained glass
The stained-glass windows above the altar, in warm, rich colours, are among the glories of the church.

KEY

① **Mahogany Pews** and a pulpit furnish the interior. From 1839, the pews were let out to prominent citizens; the brass fittings that once held their name cards can still be seen.

② **Sixteen fluted Corinthian columns** support the dome, lending beauty and balance to the design.

③ **The steeple** is 50 m (164 ft) high, 4 m (13 ft) taller than its inspiration, St Martin-in-the-Fields in London. On top of the slim pyramidal spire is a distinctive bronze weathercock.

④ **A double colonnade** of 12 polished Ionic columns is surmounted by a pediment.

VISITORS' CHECKLIST

Practical Information
Egmore.
Tel (044) 2561 2608.
Open daily. ⛪ 7am, 9am & 6pm
Sun. ⚔ St Andrew's Day (Nov).

The Wells of St Andrew's Kirk

Because of sandy soil and a site prone to flooding during the monsoon, the church's foundations are actually a series of wells sunk to depths ranging from 4 m to 15 m (13 ft to 49 ft) below ground level. This example of engineering ingenuity is based on a structural practice followed by most indigenous buildings in the area. The wells are constructed either of specially made curved bricks, or pottery cylinders. These are placed so as to ensure maximum compaction of the soil, allowing the water to rise within them and thus protecting the main structure. The 150 wells were dug by a group of itinerant well-sinkers, the Mumvutties.

0 metres 10
0 yards 10

Entrance

★ **Pipe Organ**
Dominating the altar is the handsome pipe organ in dull green and burnished gold. Installed in 1883, this instrument was built in Yorkshire, England.

A view of Egmore Railway Station, one of the city's major landmarks

❹ Egmore

Bounded by Periyar EVR High Rd & Pantheon Rd. ℹ️ Egmore Railway Station, (044) 2819 4579.

The entire area south of Periyar EVR High Road (earlier known as Poonamallee High Road) and the curve of the Cooum river is known as Egmore. This was originally a small village that the East India Company acquired in the late 17th century, as it began to expand its territories. Egmore was also one of the earliest residential localities, where wealthy Company merchants built palatial homes surrounded by luxuriant gardens – the so-called "garden houses" that were extremely popular in colonial Chennai.

The **Government College of Arts and Crafts**, founded in 1850, stands on EVK Sampath Salai. This striking Gothic building and its art gallery were built by Robert Fellowes Chisholm *(see p573)*, who was also appointed its superintendent (principal) in 1877. Its first Indian principal, Debi Prasad Roy Chowdhary, was a renowned painter and sculptor in the 1950s. The artists' village at Cholamandal *(see p582)* was established by bis successor, Dr KCS Panicker. Today the prestigious Government College is one of India's foremost art schools. Its gallery has regular exhibitions of contemporary painting and sculpture by artists and students.

To its west is the **Egmore Railway Station**, another of Chisholm's architectural gems. This is a handsome building,

constructed in Indo-Saracenic style, with unconventional flattish domes and pointed arches. The station, operational since the early 20th century, connects Chennai with the rest of Tamil Nadu and the south.

Today Egmore is the up-market commercial heart of Chennai, a concrete jungle of offices, department stores, boutiques and hotels. On Pantheon Road are the largest showrooms of Co-Optex *(see p578)*, a unit of the Tamil Nadu Handloom Textiles Cooperative, which sells handwoven silk and cotton saris and fabrics from the state.

❺ Government Museum Complex

Pantheon Rd. **Tel** (044) 2819 3778. **Open** Sat–Thu. **Closed** public hols. 🚫 📷 Connemara Public Library: **Tel** (044) 2819 1842. **Open** daily.

Standing Buddhas from Amravati

This complex of cultural institutions used to house the Public Assembly Rooms in the 18th century. At the time, its spacious tree-lined grounds were the venue for all public entertainment in the city. The Indo-Saracenic **Government Museum**, with its faded red walls and labyrinth of staircases and interconnecting galleries, spread over five sections,

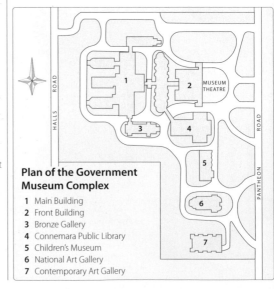

Plan of the Government Museum Complex

1 Main Building
2 Front Building
3 Bronze Gallery
4 Connemara Public Library
5 Children's Museum
6 National Art Gallery
7 Contemporary Art Gallery

The façade of the National Art Gallery, built in Neo-Mughal style

each with a specific collection of objects. The 30,000-odd exhibits range from rocks and fossils to books and sculptures.

The Archaeological Section, in the main building, is noted for its exceptional collection of South Indian antiquities. The exhibits include stone and metal sculpture, woodcarvings and manuscripts. Its rare collection of Buddhist antiquities numbers over 1,500 pieces. A major section comprises artifacts from Amravati (see p679), that were brought here in the early 1800s by an intrepid Englishman, Colonel Colin Mackenzie. On display are sculptural reliefs, panels and free-standing statues. Objects include a 2nd-century votive slab with a rendering of a stupa, and numerous stone panels with episodes from the Buddha's life depicted in low relief.

The Numismatics Section has a large collection of coins, particularly South Indian and Mughal coins. There are also some gold Gupta coins with Sanskrit inscriptions.

The Government Museum was one of the earliest institutions in India where ethnology and prehistoric archaeology were represented as museum subjects. The Anthropology Section, in the front building, has a good collection of prehistoric antiquities, including cooking utensils and hunting tools, among them the first palaeolith

Parvati, 9th century, Chola period

in India, discovered in 1863 by Bruce Foote. The Zoological Section, in the main building, is one of the largest sections of the Museum. Although its scope is limited to South Indian fauna, a few non-indigenous animals and birds, such as the macaw, mandarin duck, and golden pheasant, have been added to enrich the collection. There is also an 18.5-m (60-ft) long whale skeleton on display. The adjoining 19th-century Museum Theatre, a semi-circular structure also built in Indo-Saracenic style, was initially used as a lecture hall. It is now a venue for public performances.

Some of the finest examples of South Indian bronze casting are on display in the **Bronze Gallery**. Its superb collection of almost 700 bronzes, specifically from the Pallava and Chola periods (between the 9th and 13th centuries) have been retrieved from temples and sites in the region. There are many impressive sculptures of the Nataraja – the depiction of Shiva performing his cosmic dance of creation (see p570). Another outstanding piece is an 11th-century Chola Ardhanarisvara, a composite figure where Shiva and his consort Parvati

are joined together to form a holistic entity. Bronzes of other gods and goddesses in the Hindu pantheon, include Rama, Sita and Ganesha. The panorama of images also includes various Buddhist bronzes from Amravati, a Chola Tara and Maitreya Avalokitesvara, and 11th century images of various Jain tirthankaras.

Opposite is the imposing **Connemara Public Library**, inaugurated in 1896. This structure, with its profuse stucco decoration, woodwork and stained-glass windows, was named after a dissolute brother of the viceroy, Lord Mayo. It is one of India's four national libraries and contains every book published in the country. Its oldest and most prized possession is a Bible, dated 1608.

The **National Art Gallery** (closed for renovation) is perhaps the finest building in the complex. Designed by Henry Irwin, one of the city's most celebrated architects, it was constructed in 1909 in Neo-Mughal style with a pink sandstone finish. Its immense door echoes the monumental gateways of Fatehpur Sikri (see pp184–7). On display are more Chola bronzes, including two fine images of Rama and Sita, and a superb 11th-century Nataraja.

Nearby, the **Contemporary Art Gallery** has a collection of contemporary Indian art, with works by renowned South Indian artists, among them Raja Ravi Varma (see p630).

A 2nd-century stupa panel from Amravati

Shiva, the Cosmic Dancer

Bronze sculptures depicting gods and goddesses, are the glory of South Indian art. Strict iconographic guidelines determine the proportions of each image and the symbolic meaning of every stance, hand gesture, weapon, and adornment. Master sculptors working within these rules were able, nevertheless, to create images of extraordinary individuality, power and grace. Among the most remarkable bronze sculptures are those of Shiva as Nataraja, the Cosmic Dancer, and his wife Parvati. Richly symbolic in their iconography, they were made during the Chola period, from the 9th to the 13th centuries.

Nataraja

The Nataraja figure of Shiva as the Cosmic Dancer symbolizes nature's cycle of evolution and transmutation, and displays the Chola artists' mastery of form and expression.

A tiny crescent moon, a symbol of the passage of time, balances in his hair.

Goddess Ganga is shown among Shiva's flying locks since it was Shiva who eased her descent to earth *(see p167)*.

The fire in the left hand symbolizes destruction.

The drum in his right hand symbolizes the rhythm of creation.

An open palm grants freedom from fear.

The left palm pointing to the foot symbolizes salvation from ignorance.

The left leg is lifted up in an animated dance movement.

The ring of flames symbolizes the cosmos.

The right leg tramples Apasmara, a dwarfish figure representing ignorance.

The marriage of Shiva and Parvati is a beautiful example of Chola art. It shows Shiva, standing regal and tall, tenderly holding his bashful bride Parvati's hand. Vishnu, as the brother of Parvati, is shown as an onlooker.

Bronze images representing the main temple deity are taken out in processions on festive occasions. These images are clad in silk and decked with sandalwood paste and floral garlands.

See also features on Hindu Mythology *(see pp28–9)*, Ganesha *(see p471)* and Vishnu *(see p683)*

The multi-arched façade of the Thousand Lights Mosque

❻ Anna Salai

From Cooum Island to Little Mount.
Rajaji Hall: **Tel** (044) 2536 5635.
Open daily.

A long arterial road leading from north Chennai to Little Mount at its southern end *(see p577)*, Anna Salai (or Mount Road) is the city's main thoroughfare. The "garden houses" that belonged to Chennai's elite stood on either side of it until well into the early years of the 20th century. Today, it is a modern commercial road, lined with hoardings depicting film stars, and the expansive homes of the past have been replaced by multistoreyed buildings.

Anna Salai begins on an island in Cooum Creek, just south of Fort St George. The site is watched over by the statue of Sir Thomas Munro, the governor of the Madras Presidency from 1819 to 1826. Nearby, set in an expanse of greenery, is the prestigious **Gymkhana Club**. Sited close to the army headquarters, this was an exclusive facility for military officers. Until 1920, its membership was restricted to garrison officers only and, even today, the club grounds belong to the armed services.

The **Old Government Estate**, southwest of the Gymkhana Club, houses the mansion where the governors of Madras once lived in regal splendour. Though the main building is falling apart, the banqueting hall, built in 1802 by the second Lord Clive, the eldest son of Robert Clive, retains its grandeur. It was named **Rajaji Hall** after the first Indian governor general, C Rajagopalachari, popularly known as Rajaji.

Inside this elegant Neo-Classical building, an impressive broad staircase leads up to the vast banqueting hall, which has beautiful panelling and chandeliers.

Anna Salai then enters its commercial stretch. Along this length of the road are some of the city's oldest commercial landmarks, including one of India's largest bookshops, **Higginbotham's** *(see p578)*, **Spencer's**, an international department store, and the **Taj Connemara**, one of the city's finest hotels.

Nearby is the 19th-century **Thousand Lights Mosque** further down, gets its name from the tradition of lighting 1,000 oil lamps to illuminate the Assembly Hall that once occupied the site. Standing further south is **St George's Cathedral**, planned by James Lillyman Caldwell and built by Thomas de Havilland in 1814. Its distinctive 42 m (138 ft) tall spire is one of Chennai's major landmarks.

Main altar in St George's Cathedral, built in the early 19th century

Film Stars and Politics

The South Indian film industry, particularly Tamil and Telugu cinema, is credited with having been the breeding ground of many politicians. The first chief minister from the Dravidian Party (then called DMK), the late Dr CN Annadurai, as well as his immediate successor, M Karunanidhi, were both scriptwriters with large followings. However, the most remarkable actor-turned-politican was Marudur Gopalamenon Ramachandran, whose portrayal of a swashbuckling hero made him the embodiment of righteousness. Popularly known as MGR, he acquired a cult status in the region and was chief minister of Tamil Nadu from 1977 to 1987. His co-star and protégée, Jayalalitha, another charismatic chief minister, was ousted on charges of corruption in 2001, but was reinstated later that year. Current heroes, such as Rajnikant and Kamalahassan, have more macho images that depend heavily on daredevil stunts. They, too, have fans throughout South India.

Hoardings depicting popular South Indian heroes

❼ A Walk along the Marina

Chennai's seashore hosts one of India's largest urban beaches, stretching for 13 km (8 miles) along the city's eastern flank. The Marina, connecting Fort St George with San Thomé Basilica almost 5 km (3 miles) away, was built by Mounstuart Elphinstone Grant-Duff, the governor between 1881 and 1886. Described by architectural historian Philip Davies as "one of the most beautiful marine promenades in the world", it is a favourite place for Chennai's citizens to escape the humid heat of the city and enjoy the sea breezes. The walk along Kamarajar Salai (earlier known as South Beach Road) takes in parks, tree-lined cobbled streets and spectacular colonial and Indo-Saracenic buildings.

The Indo-Saracenic Presidency College, nucleus of Madras University

Anna Park

The walk starts from the Victory War Memorial ① which marks the north end of Kamarajar Salai. This memorial originally commemorated the victory of the Allied armies during World War I, and was later dedicated to the memory of those soldiers from the Madras Presidency who lost their lives in World War II. To its south, in Anna Park, is the Anna Samadhi ②, a memorial erected in honour of CN Annadurai, the former chief minister of Tamil Nadu, who introduced significant political and social reforms in the state. Further south is the MGR Samadhi ③, a commemorative garden with gateways and pathways, built in honour of the popular Tamil film icon and chief minister, MG Ramachandran (see p571). An array of souvenir shops and eateries can be found along this stretch of the

Victory War Memorial, Kamarajar Salai

beach, attracting tourists from the rest of the state. Particularly interesting is the Sunday market, with its curious jumble of goods.

North Marina

Across Kamarajar Salai is a series of imposing red brick buildings, built in a combination of architectural styles, which include Indian and Moorish features. The Indo-Saracenic Madras University ④ was founded in 1857, making it one of the oldest universities in India. An architectural marvel, the Senate House ⑤ was designed by Robert Chisholm in a mixture of Byzantine and Saracenic styles. This became the headquarters of Madras University in 1879. These buildings now stand in what was once the sprawling estate of the old Chepauk Palace ⑥. This splendid Indo-Saracenic

structure, on Wallajah Road, was once the home of the Nawab of Arcot. Though the palace was built in 1768, Chisholm added the extensions, including the tower that once connected the two wings. It now houses government offices. Chepauk Stadium, Chennai's famous cricket ground, lies behind the palace. Further down the road is Presidency College ⑦, the first institution in South India for higher education, founded in 1840. This rather austere structure has a ribbed dome with four clocks on its surface. Among the famous alumni of the college are the first Indian governor-general, C Rajagopalachari, and the Nobel Prize-winning physicists, CV Ramanand his nephew, S Chandrasekhar.

South Marina

Further south, an impressive landmark on Kamarajar Salai is the statue *Triumph of Labour* ⑧.

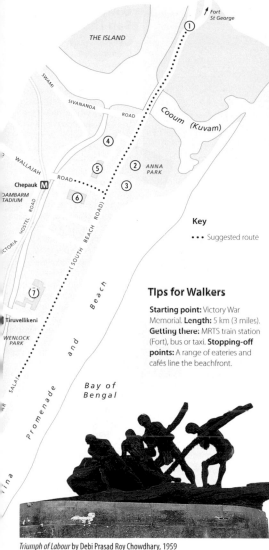

THE ISLAND

Fort St George

①

SWAMI

SIVANANDA ROAD

Cooum (Kuvam)

WALLAJAH ROAD

④

⑤

② ANNA PARK

③

Chepauk Ⓜ

⑥

CHIDAMBARM STADIUM

VICTORIA HOSTEL ROAD

(SOUTH BEACH ROAD)

⑦

Tiruvellikeni

WENLOCK PARK

SALAI

Promenade

Tina

Beach

Bay of Bengal

Key

••• Suggested route

A busy evening scene on the Marina Beach

This sculpture was created by Debi Prasad Roy Chowdhary (*see p568*), who became the first Indian principal of the Madras School of Arts and Crafts in 1929.

West of the main road, off Annie Besant Road, is the Ice House ⑨, formerly a women's hostel known as Vivekananda House. In the 1840s, this circular building, with a stone pineapple perched on its roof, was a storehouse for ice, which was imported all the way from New England (USA). It was also the site from which Swami Vivekananda (*see p619*) delivered his speeches when he visited the city. It has now been handed over to the Ramakrishna Mission which has plans to restore it. Further south is Queen Mary's College ⑩, today the Madras College for Women. Opened in July 1914, this was Chennai's first women's college. A bust of the queen still graces the entrance of the building.

An imposing lighthouse ⑪ marks the southern end of the Marina.

Tips for Walkers

Starting point: Victory War Memorial. **Length:** 5 km (3 miles). **Getting there:** MRTS train station (Fort), bus or taxi. **Stopping-off points:** A range of eateries and cafés line the beachfront.

Triumph of Labour by Debi Prasad Roy Chowdhary, 1959

Robert Chisholm's Legacy

Robert Fellowes Chisholm (1845–84) was among the most talented architects in India in the mid-19th century. In 1864, Chisholm's designs for the proposed Presidency College and Senate House won a competition, and he was appointed the consulting architect to the Madras government. The next 15 years saw considerable building activity along the Marina, where many innovative buildings were erected. Chisholm's designs blended Italian and Saracenic features so that the new structures would harmonize with the existing Chepauk Palace. For many years he was the head of the School of Industrial Art, founded in 1855 and now known as the Government College of Fine Arts.

Senate House, Robert Chisholm's signature building, completed in 1873

Fruits on sale at Triplicane Market

❽ Triplicane

Off Kamarajar Salai (South Beach Rd).
Parthasarathi Temple: **Open** daily.
🎏 Neeratu Utsavam (Dec).

The crowded suburb of
Triplicane was among the first
villages to be acquired by the
East India Company in the
1670s. It derives its name from
the sacred lily tank *(tiru-alli-keni)* that once stood here. One
of the oldest temples in the
city, the historic **Parthasarathi
Temple**, is situated in Triplicane.
Built in the 9th century, the
temple is dedicated to Krishna
(or Partha) in his role as Arjuna's
divine charioteer *(sarathi)* in
the epic, the *Mahabharata
(see p30)*. The temple festival, in
December, attracts thousands
of devotees. At one time, the
residences of the priestly
Brahmin caste were clustered
in the narrow lanes around the
temple. Among them were
the homes of the mathematical
genius, Srinivasa Ramanujan
(1887–1920), and the early
20th-century nationalist
poet, Subramania Bharati.
Triplicane was once part of

the kingdom of Golconda
(see pp670–71), and as a result
this quarter has the largest
concentration of Muslims in
the city. The Nawab of Arcot,
Muhammad Ali Wallajah
(1749–95), an ally of the British
in their struggle for power
against the French, contributed
generously to the
construction of a
large mosque here
in 1795. Known
as the **Wallajah
(Big) Mosque**,
this beautiful grey
granite structure
with slender
minarets is situated
on Triplicane High
Road. The adjoining
graveyard contains
the tombs of
various Muslim
saints. The nawab's
descendants still
live in Triplicane, in a
stately mansion known as
Amir Mahal. Constructed in
1798, it became their residence
after the Chepauk Palace *(see
p572)* was taken over by
the British.

❾ Mylapore & San Thomé

S of Triplicane. Kapaleswarar Temple:
Open daily. Basilica of San Thomé:
Open daily. Luz Church: **Open** daily.

The site of a great Pallava port
in the 7th and 8th centuries,
Mylapore is today one of the
busiest parts of the city. This
traditional quarter, with its
religious organizations, tiny
houses and lively bazaars,
is dominated by the
Kapaleswarar Temple, the
largest in Chennai. The main
deity, Shiva, is symbolized
as a peacock *(mayil)*, thus giving
the area its original name,
Mayilapura, the "Town of the
Peacocks". According to legend,
Shiva's consort, Parvati, assumed
the form of a peahen to worship
Shiva, represented here by his
linga. A sculptural panel in a
small shrine in the courtyard

The Gothic-style Basilica
of San Thomé

depicts the legend.
The present temple
was built after the
original was
destroyed by the
Portuguese in the
16th century.
Mylapore's links
with Christianity
date to the 1st
century AD, to the
time of St Thomas
(see p577). In the
10th century, a
group of Nestorian
Christians from
Persia (Iran)
discovered the saint's burial site
and built a church and tomb.
The Portuguese, following the
trail of the saint, established
the settlement of San Thomé
in the early 16th century. The
present **Basilica of San Thomé**,
over the tomb of the saint, is an
impressive Gothic-style structure
built in 1898. It has an ornate
interior with magnificent
stained-glass windows and a
towering steeple. The crypt
is said to contain a small bone
from the saint's hand and the
weapon that killed him.
Nearby is the **Luz Church**,
which was built by a Franciscan
monk in 1516, making it the
oldest Catholic church in Chennai.

The graceful façade of Wallajah Mosque, with its flanking minarets

For hotels and restaurants see p702 and p717

⑩ Adyar

S of San Thomé, across Adyar river.
Theosophical Society: **Tel** (044) 2491
2474. **Open** Mon–Fri & (Sat morn).
Brodie Castle: **Open** daily.

Few places in Chennai offer greater serenity than the sprawling gardens of the **Theosophical Society**, situated in the city's Adyar neighbourhood, on the banks of the Adyar river. Founded in New York in 1875, the Society moved here seven years later when it acquired Huddlestone Gardens. Built in 1776 by John Huddlestone, a wealthy civilian, this large mansion is today the world headquarters of the Society. Its magnificent 108-ha (270-acre) estate comprises several 19th-century buildings, one of which is the former home of its founder Colonel Henry S Olcott.

The main building houses the Great Hall, almost spartan in its simplicity, where prayer meetings are held. Bas-reliefs, representing the different faiths, and engravings of verses taken from the holy books of all world religions can be seen here. There are also marble statues of the founders, Colonel Olcott and Helena Petrovna Blavatsky, as well as one of Annie Besant, who became president in 1907.

The Adyar Library and Research Centre, founded by Olcott in 1886, is one of the finest libraries in India. Its collection of 165,000 books and 20,000 palm-leaf and parchment manuscripts has made it a valuable repository for Indological research. The surrounding tranquil gardens have shrines dedicated to various faiths. The greatest

The 400-year-old banyan tree in the gardens of the Theosophical Society

attraction here, however, is the 400-year-old banyan tree, whose spreading branches cover an immense area of 4,180 sq m (44,993 sq ft). Over the decades, many of the Society's meetings and spiritual discourses were held under its canopy. Unfortunately, a terrible storm in 1989 destroyed its main trunk.

Brodie Castle, north of the Theosophical Society, is an imposing white structure on the banks of the Adyar. Now known as Thenral, it houses the prestigious College of Carnatic Music. Built in 1796 by James Brodie, an employee of the East India Company, it is said to be among the first "garden-houses" built in the city. These spacious, airy houses with broad pillared verandahs, set in sprawling wooded gardens, were characteristic of colonial Chennai. This house later became the home of the first Chief Justice of the Madras High Court.

Further north of Brodie Castle is the **Madras Club**, built by George Moubray, who came to India as an accountant in 1771. He acquired 42 ha (104 acres) of land on the banks of the Adyar, and built a house with a central cupola, surrounded by a beautiful garden. Known as Moubray's Cupola, this was once the exclusive preserve of the city's European population. Indians were only allowed membership in 1964, after it merged with the Adyar Club.

The pillared entrance of Brodie Castle in Adyar

The Theosophical Society

In the 1870s, Colonel Henry S Olcott, a veteran of the American Civil War, met the Russian aristocrat and clairvoyant, Madame Helena Petrovna Blavatsky in Vermont (USA) at the farm of the Christian Scientist, Mary Baker Eddy. Soon after, they launched a movement to foster the spirit of universal brotherhood, aiming to create a Utopian society in which people of all castes, creeds and colour could live in harmony. The movement attracted great

Theosophical Society

thinkers and intellectuals, among them Dr Annie Besant, president of the Indian National Congress in 1917. The idea of forming a national political party was, in fact, first voiced in the 1890s at the Society's headquarters in Adyar, under the banyan tree, by the British civil servant AO Hume. The famous philosopher Jiddu Krishnamurti was also associated with the Society.

A Bharat Natyam dance lesson in progress at Kalakshetra

⑪ Kalakshetra

Thiruvanmiyur, East Coast Rd.
or taxi. **Tel** (044) 2452 1844.
Open Mon–Sat. **Closed** college hols.
Kalakshetra Arts Festival (Dec/Jan).

This pioneering institution for classical dance, music and the fine arts, established in 1936, was the brainchild of Rukmini Devi. A protégée of Annie Besant, she was deeply influenced by the progressive views of the Theosophical Society (see p575). At 16, she scandalized conservative society by marrying George Sydney Arundale, the 40-year-old Australian principal of the Society's school. The couple's extensive travels exposed Rukmini to the world of Western culture, specially dance, inspiring her to study ballet under the great Russian ballerina Anna Pavlova. Back in Chennai, she again defied tradition by learning and performing the classical *dasi attam*, hitherto the domain of *devadasis* (temple dancers). The International Centre for the Arts, which she set up for the revival of this dance form, now called Bharat Natyam, (see p33), is today Kalakshetra, the "Temple of Art".

The school is set in a vast 40-ha (99-acre) campus, where classical music and dance are taught according to the traditional methods, by which a guru imparts knowledge to a small group of students. Some of India's best known dancers, including Yamini Krishnamurti, and the institute's current director, Priyadarsini Govind,

were trained here. At the end of each year, a festival is held and performances are staged in an auditorium designed like a *koottambulam*, the traditional theatre of Kerala temples (see p643).

⑫ MGR Film City

Near Indira Nagar. **Open** daily.
Extra charges for photography.

One of Chennai's major attractions is a film city, dedicated to the memory of the hugely popular matinée idol, MG Rama-chandran (see p571). This is now the most popular location for Chennai's flourishing Tamil film industry, which is second only to Mumbai (see pp36–7) in film production. A fantasy world of extravagant sets and hi-tech equipment, Film City attracts starstruck fans from all over Tamil Nadu, who come here to catch a glimpse of their favourite film stars.

A film set in MGR Film City

⑬ Guindy National Park

S Chennai. Sardar Vallabhbhai Patel Rd. Guindy station.
Tel (044) 2432 1471 (wildlife warden).
Open Wed–Mon. Raj Bhavan: **Closed** to public.

Once a distant suburb which was nearly twice its current size, Guindy has now been engulfed by the fast growing metropolis of Greater Chennai. Originally part of the private forest surrounding Guindy Lodge, a portion was officially declared the Guindy National Park in 1977. This predominantly dry deciduous scrub jungle of acacia is interspersed with larger trees such as sandalwood (*Santalam album*), banyan (*Ficus bengalensis*) and jamun (*Syzygium cumini*). Its most famous residents are the herds of endangered blackbuck (*Antelope cervicapra*), introduced in 1924. Among its 130 species of birds are raptors such as the honey buzzard and the white-bellied sea eagle. Winter is the best time for birdwatching, when migrant birds visit the forest. Also located within the park is the **Madras Snake Park**, established in the 1970s by Romulus Whitaker, the American zoologist, who also set up the Crocodile Bank outside Chennai (see p582). Today, the well-maintained Snake Park houses numerous species of snakes, among them king cobras, vipers and pythons. Other reptiles include crocodiles, turtles and

A song-and-dance sequence being shot on location for a Tamil movie

lizards. Large information boards, strategically placed, provide interesting details on the habitat and behaviour of the various species. For those who are interested, there are live demonstrations of venom extraction; the venom is used as an antidote for snake bites.

The historic 300-year-old Guindy Lodge, to the west of the Park, is now the **Raj Bhavan**, the residence of the governor of Tamil Nadu. Built as a weekend retreat for the city's British rulers, this handsome white building was renovated and expanded in the mid-1800s by the then governor, Grant-Duff.

Today, Guindy has some of the city's most prestigious institutions. The area also has many impressive memorials to modern India's leaders, Mahatma Gandhi, K Kamaraj and C Rajagopalachari.

The Masonry Cross, engraved on a rock in the cave, Little Mount

Façade of the Church of Our Lady of Expectations, Mount of St Thomas

⓮ Little Mount & Mount of St Thomas

SW Chennai. Near Marmalog Bridge.
🚉 St Thomas Mount station. 🚌

A rock-hewn cave on Little Mount is believed to be the place where, in AD 72, the mortally wounded St Thomas sought refuge. Near the modern **Church of Our Lady of Good Health** is the older **Blessed Sacrament Chapel** built by the Portuguese over the cave. Inside the cave is the opening through which the fleeing saint is said to have retreated, leaving behind a still visible imprint of his hand near the entrance. At the rear end of the cave is the Masonry Cross before which St Thomas is said to have prayed. By the **Church of the Resurrection** is a perennial spring with curative powers. Legend claims that the spring originated when St Thomas struck the rock with his staff to provide water for his thirsty congregation.

About 3 km (2 miles) southwest of Little Mount is the 95-m (312-ft) high Mount of St Thomas or Great Mount. A flight of 132 steps leads to the summit and the **Church of Our Lady of Expectations**, built by the Portuguese in the 16th century. The most important relic here is the ancient stone cross embedded into the wall of the altar. Said to have been engraved by the saint himself, this is the legendary "bleeding cross" that miraculously bled between 1558 and 1704.

Below the eastern flank of the Mount is the **Cantonment** area, with its shady streets lined with 18th-century Neo-Classical bungalows.

St Thomas in India

According to legend, St Thomas or Doubting Thomas, one of the 12 apostles, came to South India soon after Jesus Christ died. He is said to have arrived in Cranganore (*see p653*) in AD 52 and spent the next 12 years along the Malabar Coast, spreading the Gospel and converting the local population. He gradually moved eastwards and finally settled in Mylapore (*see p574*). He spent the last years of his life in a cave on Little Mount, from where he would walk every day to the beach, resting for a while and preaching in the groves. It is said that one day in AD 72, while praying on the Mount of St Thomas, he was mortally wounded by a lance, and fled to Little Mount, where he died. His body was carried by his converts to San Thomé, where he was buried in the crypt of the small chapel he had built. This is today the Basilica of San Thomé, and the large stained-glass window depicts his story. The Portuguese colonized Mylapore in the early 16th century, lured by accounts left by the 13th-century Venetian traveller, Marco Polo, who had visited the early Nestorian chapel here. The saint holds a special place in the hearts of Indians, and was decreed the Apostle of India in 1972.

Portrait of St Thomas

Shopping & Entertainment in Chennai

As the capital of Tamil Nadu, Chennai has an excellent selection of handicrafts and handwoven textiles from the state. From shimmering silks in glowing colours and finely woven cottons to jewellery and replicas of Chola bronzes, the choice is enormous. The city's shopping centres include up-market department stores, malls and trendy boutiques, as well as the vibrant local bazaars which sell a wide range of merchandise. Chennai is also the cultural capital of South India, where performances of classical dance and music take place throughout the year. The height of the cultural season is from mid-December to mid-January, when the city hosts the prestigious Marghazhi Festival.

Shops and Markets

The best shopping in Chennai can be found in the more traditional areas, such as Panagal Park, Pondy and Burma bazaars, and the lanes around the temple at Mylapore. These were small street markets that have now grown into mini shopping malls, where everything is available at bargain prices. Chennai's oldest department store, Spencer's, partially burned down in the 1980s, and has now been rebuilt as a modern mall. It houses shops selling merchandise as varied as groceries and imported Swiss watches. Next door is the city's oldest landmark, **VTI** (Victoria Technical Institute), where handicrafts and a range of good quality linen are sold. This charitable organization supports South Indian Christian missions that specialize in exquisite hand-embroidery.

Most shops are open Monday to Friday, from 9:30am to 7pm. Bazaars, however, keep more flexible hours.

Jewellery and Antiques

The best place for high quality traditional South Indian gold jewellery is **Vummidi Bangaru Jewellers**. They also stock excellent reproductions of the gem-encrusted costume jewellery worn by classical dancers. **Prince Jewellery**, in Panagal Park, has jewellery from Kerala and also specializes in light weight gold ornaments. Modern and traditional silverware and jewellery are available at **Sukhra** and **Amethyst**.

Genuine antiques are hard to find. However, **Rani Arts & Crafts** stocks copies of old artifacts, including brass and metal images and objects, Tanjore (Thanjavur) paintings *(see p601)* and lacquerware.

Textiles and Saris

Tamil Nadu is renowned for the richness and variety of its silk and cotton textiles, a good selection of which is available in Chennai. **Radha Silks**, **Kumaran Silks** and **Sundari Silks** are famous all over India for their wonderful range of fabrics and silk saris from Kanchipuram *(see p587)*. **Nalli's**, a huge multistoreyed shop, has the widest range of Kanchipuram saris, and is always packed with local shoppers, particularly during the festival and wedding seasons. Other outlets are **Man Mandir** and **Shilpi**, a small boutique that sells saris and home furnishings. **Fabindia** too, stocks furnishings and ready-made garments. A good variety of textiles can be found at **Co-optex**, the large Tamil Nadu Cooperative of Textiles showroom. This pioneering society has encouraged the revival of handlooms.

Handicrafts and Gifts

A fine selection of handi-crafts can be found at **Poompuhar**, the Tamil Nadu State Emporium. VTI also sells handicrafts, though hand-embroidered linen and nightwear are their main specialities. **Cane and Bamboo** is another interesting little shop with an assortment of gift items and souvenirs.

Apparao Galleries not only stocks paintings by contemporary Indian artists, but also has an accessory shop for gifts and home products. Their boutique sells trendy designer-wear.

Naturally Auroville specializes in natural products made in the Puducherry Ashram and Auroville *(see pp590–92)*. The merchandise includes pottery, handmade paper, perfumed candles, incense sticks and aromatherapy oils and lotions.

Chennai is also a good place to shop for handcrafted musical instruments, such as the violin, *mridangam* and *veena*. While these are found at many outlets in the city, the best selections are available at **Musee Musicals** and **Sapthaswara Music Store**. **Music World** stocks a wide range of CDs and audio cassettes by well-known Carnatic musicians. The city also has a number of excellent bookshops. Of these, the oldest and most well-stocked is **Higginbotham's**, established in 1844.

Entertainment Guides, Tickets and Venues

Announcements of performances of Carnatic music *(see p599)* and classical dance such as Bharat Natyam *(see p32)*, appear regularly in the entertainment columns of local newspapers. The city guides *Hallo! Madras* and *Chennai This Fortnight* list entertainment venues and information on tickets.

Performances of music and dance are held throughout the year. However, the peak season is from 15 December to 15 January, when the Chennai Festival, organized by the city's *sabhas* (cultural societies), takes place. During this period more than 500 concerts are held. The most prestigious cultural centre is the **Music**

Academy. Other venues are **Narada Gana Sabha**, **Sri Krishna Gana Sabha** and **Karthik Fine Arts**. Classical dance, music and theatre performances are also held at the **Museum Theatre** in the Pantheon Complex *(see p568)* and the auditorium at **Kalakshetra** *(see p576)*.

Music and Dance

Since the 1920s, Chennai has been the leading centre of Carnatic music and classical dance. The first music festival took place in December 1927 during the Madras session of the Indian National Congress. A year later, the Music Academy was established to promote Carnatic music, and in 1936,

Rukmini Devi set up Kalakshetra to popularize Bharat Natyam, the dance form once performed only in temples. Today, these two institutions along with the many *sabhas* are the major sponsors of music and dance events in the city.

During the season, music lovers gather in Chennai to hear India's top performers as well as promising new talent. Concerts of Carnatic music, both vocal and instrumental, begin in the morning and often last till midnight. Dance recitals are also held. Recently, some dancers have experimented with the traditional repertoire to create a contemporary form that is a fusion of Indian folk and classical forms with Western themes.

Cinema

The choice of films that show at Chennai's many cinemas, such as **Devi**, **Ega** and the **Sathyam Cineplex**, ranges from popular Bollywood and Tamil blockbusters to the latest commercial Hollywood releases. Tamil films are very similar to those produced in Mumbai's Bollywood, with song and dance sequences and a great deal of melodrama. But they play a role far beyond mere entertainment – their themes often have a social message and their charismatic actors, with their political links *(see p571)*, make them a potent medium of communication, especially among rural audiences.

DIRECTORY

Jewellery and Antiques

Amethyst
14 Padmavathi Rd,
Jeyapore Colony,
Gopalapuram.
Tel (044) 2835 1627.

Prince Jewellery
13 Nagaeswara Rao Rd,
Panagal Park. **Tel** (044)
2436 3137. 769 Spencer
Plaza, Anna Salai.
Tel (044) 2849 5817.

Rani Arts & Crafts
8 Nowrojee Rd, Chetpet.
Tel (044) 4232 7888.

Sukhra
42 North Mada St,
Mylapore. **Tel** (044) 6555
5555 or (044) 2464 0699.

Vummidi Bangaru Jewellers
Rani Seethai Hall, 603
Anna Salai. **Tel** (044) 2829
2003/ 2004/1573/1574.

Textiles and Saris

Co-optex
Pantheon Rd, Egmore.
Tel (044) 2819 2394.

Fabindia
Illford House, 3 Woods Rd,
off Anna Salai.
Tel (044) 4216 8346.

Kumaran Silks
12 Nageswaran
Rd, T Nagar.
Tel (044) 2434 3544.

Man Mandir
15 Khader Nawaz Khan
Rd, Nungamabakkam.
Tel (044) 2833 3350.

Nalli's
9 Nageswaran Rd, T
Nagar. **Tel** (044) 2434
4115.

Radha Silks
Sannathi St, Mylapore.
Tel (044) 2464 1319.

Shilpi
1 GG Minar, 23 College
Rd, Nungambakkam.
Tel (044) 2828 2603.
29, CP Ramaswamy Rd.
Tel (044) 2499 7526.

Sundari Silks
54–55 North Usman
Rd, T Nagar.
Tel (044) 2814 3093.

Handicrafts and Gifts

Apparao Galleries
7 Wallace Garden, 3rd St,
Nungambakkam. **Tel**
(044) 2833 0726/2226.

Cane and Bamboo
20 C-in-C Rd, Ethiraj Lane.
Tel (044) 2821 1649.

Higginbotham's
116 Anna Salai.
Tel (044) 2851 3519.

Musee Musicals
67 Anna Salai.
Tel (044) 2849 2717.

Music World
Spencer's Plaza.
Tel (044) 2833 0517.

Naturally Auroville
30 Khader Nawaz Khan
Rd, Nungambakkam.
Tel (044) 2821 7517.

Poompuhar
818 Anna Salai. **Tel** (044)
2852 0624.

Sapthaswara Music Store
165 Royapetta H Rd,
Mylapore.
Tel (044) 2499 6498.

VTI
New 180, Anna Salai.
Tel (044) 2858 6779.

Entertainment Venues

Kalakshetra
Kalakshetra Foundation,
Thiruvanmiyur.
Tel (044) 2491 1844.

Karthik Fine Arts
New 16, Bhimanna
Garden St, Alwarpet.
Tel (044) 2499 7788.

Museum Theatre
Pantheon Rd, Egmore.
Tel (044) 2819 3778.

Music Academy
168 TTK Rd, Alwarpet.
Tel (044) 2811 5162.

Narada Gana Sabha
314 TTK Rd, Alwarpet.
Tel (044) 2499 3201.

Sri Krishna Gana Sabha
8 Maharajapuram
Santhanam Salai, T Nagar.
Tel (044) 2814 0806.

Cinema

Devi
48 Anna Salai.
Tel (044) 2855 5660.

Ega
810 Poonamallee High
Rd. **Tel** (044) 4343 6363.

Gaiety
1, Blackers Rd, Anna Salai.
Tel (044) 2841 5154.

Sathyam Cineplex
Sathyam Theatre
Complex, 8, Thiru Vi
Ka Rd, Royapettah.
Tel (044) 4224 4224.

TAMIL NADU

The cradle of ancient Dravidian culture, Tamil Nadu extends from the Coromandel Coast in the east to the forested Western Ghats in the west. At its heart is the fertile Kaveri valley, a land of rice fields and spectacular temples. This is the site of ancient Cholamandalam, where the Chola kings built magnificent temples at Thanjavur and elsewhere. Great temples also stand at Madurai and Chidambaram, which witnessed an efflorescence of dance, music and literature under their enlightened rulers. The 7th-century port-city of Mamallapuram with its spectacular rock-cut temples is now a World Heritage Site, while the former French enclave of Puducherry, and British forts and churches reflect the state's colonial history. Many towns in Tamil Nadu have the prefix "Tiru", which means sacred, and indicates the presence of a major religious site.

Sights at a Glance

Towns, Cities & Districts

4 Vellore
7 Puducherry
14 Tiruchirapalli
19 Coimbatore
23 Chettinad
24 Ramanathapuram
26 Tuticorin

Historic & Cultural Sites

1 Dakshina Chitra
2 Mamallapuram
6 Gingee Fort

Temples & Temple Towns

3 Kanchipuram
5 Tiruvannamalai

8 Chidambaram
10 Gangaikondacholapuram
11 Kumbakonam
12 Tiruvaiyaru
13 Thanjavur
15 Srirangam
20 Palani
22 Madurai
25 Rameshvaram
27 Tiruchendur
28 Tirunelvelli
29 Suchindram
30 Kanniyakumari

Tours

9 Coromandel Driving Tour
18 Tour of the Nilgiris

National Parks

17 Mudumalai Wildlife
   Sanctuary

Hill Stations

16 Yercaud
21 Kodaikanal

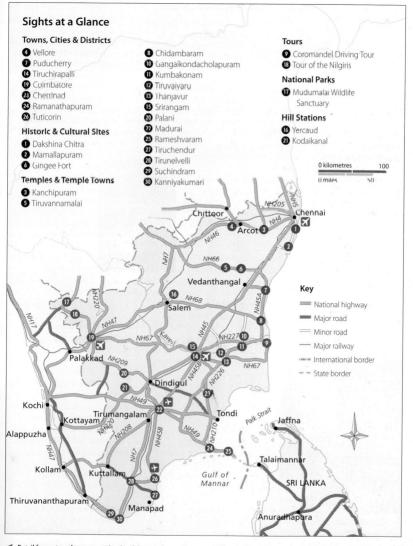

Key

— National highway
— Major road
— Minor road
— Major railway
·=·=· International border
– – State border

◀ Detail from a temple *gopura* with colourful stucco figures, Sarangapani Temple, Kumbakonam   **For keys to symbols** *see back flap*

❶ Dakshina Chitra

Chingleput district. 26 km (16 miles) S of Chennai. 🚌 **Tel** (044) 2491 8943. **Open** Wed–Mon. 🖼 🛍 ⛲ 📷

This heritage village, on the Coromandel Coast, provides a fascinating glimpse into the homes and lifestyles of the people of South India. The village features reconstructions of traditional houses, including, so far, six from Tamil Nadu, three from Kerala and one from Karnataka. The handsome Chettiar mansion *(see p616)* on view, with its elaborately carved wooden door, reflects the wealth of the Chettiar merchant community, while the homes of priests, farmers, weavers and potters are simple yet elegant structures. Within the complex is an Ayyanar shrine *(see p609)* and an open courtyard, where folk and classical dance performances and craft demonstrations are held.

Environs

Cholamandal Village, 12 km (7 miles) north of Dakshina Chitra, is an artists' village established in 1966 and the first of its kind in India. For nature lovers, the **Crocodile Bank**, founded by an American zoologist, Romulus Whitaker, is 15 km (9 miles) south of the village. It includes a snake farm and a cooperative of Irulas, a community of rat-catchers.

🏛 **Cholamandal Village**
Tel (044) 2449 0092. **Open** daily.

🏛 **Crocodile Bank**
Tel (044) 2747 2447. **Open** Wed–Mon. 📷 Extra charges for photography.

A colourful sign announcing the entrance to the Crocodile Bank

The sculpted relief at Mamallapuram, depicting Bhagiratha's Penance

❷ Mamallapuram

Kanchipuram district. 58 km (36 miles) S of Chennai. 🚌 ℹ️ Covelong Rd, (044) 2744 2232. **Open** daily. 🛍 📷 ⛲ 🎭 Dance Festival (Jan/Feb).

The UNESCO World Heritage Site of Mamallapuram (or Mahabalipuram) was once a major port-city, built in the 7th century by the Pallava king, Narasimha Varman I, also known as Mamalla, the "Great Wrestler". This spectacular site, situated on the Bay of Bengal, extends across a boulder-strewn landscape and comprises rock-cut caves and monolithic shrines *(see pp584–5)*, structural temples and huge bas-reliefs that are considered the greatest examples of Pallava art. The stone-carving tradition that created these wonders is still alive in the many workshops scattered around the village.

Krishna's Butter Ball, a natural boulder

The spectacular **Shore Temple**, perched dramatically on a promontory by the sea, has survived the ravages of time and erosion. It was built by Mamalla for Vishnu, while the two Shiva shrines were added by Mamalla's successor Narasimha Varman II, more popularly known as Raja Simha. The temple has a low boundary wall, with rows of seated Nandis surrounding it. Placed inside are a reclining Vishnu, a 16-faceted polished linga and reliefs of Somaskanda – a composite form of Shiva with his consort, Parvati and sons, Skanda and Ganesha. Inland from the Shore Temple, in the village centre, is the celebrated bas-relief **Bhagiratha's Penance**, also known as Arjuna's Penance or the Descent of the Ganges. Carved on an immense rock with a natural vertical cleft, symbolizing the Ganges, the panel depicts in great detail the story of the sacred river's descent from the sky *(see p167)*. This divine act, made possible by the penance of the sage Bhagiratha, is witnessed on the panel by celestial and semi-celestial beings, ascetics, and animals. The symbolism is best understood during the monsoon, when rainwater flows down the cleft and collects in the tank below.

Nearby are the unfinished **Panch Pandava Cave Temple**, and **Krishna's Butter Ball**, a natural boulder perched precariously on a slope.

South of Bhagiratha's Penance is the **Krishna Mandapa**, a huge bas-relief showing the god lifting Mount Govardhan to protect the people from torrential rains, as well as performing his tasks as a cowherd. The **Olakkanatha Temple**, above the *mandapa*, was once used as a lighthouse.

On the ridge southwest of Bhagiratha's Penance are three cave temples. The **Mahishasuramardini Cave Temple** has a graceful portrayal of Goddess Durga on her lion mount, subduing the buffalo-headed demon, Mahisha, on the northern wall. This panel seems to emanate life and motion, in contrast to the one on the southern wall, where Vishnu reclines in deep meditation before creating the earth.

The **Trimurti Cave Temple**, northwest of Bhagiratha's Penance, is dedicated to three gods – Shiva, Vishnu and Somaskanda. The shrines are guarded by statues of graceful doorkeepers. A sculpture of Durga standing on Mahisha's head is on an outer wall. To its south, the **Varaha or Adi Varaha Cave Temple** has beautifully moulded lion pillars, while the relief sculptures of Lakshmi, Durga and Varaha, the boar incarnation of Vishnu, are among the masterpieces of Pallava art. It also features interesting panels of Pallava rulers with their consorts. The Lion Throne, on top of a hill further west, is a raised platform with a seated lion, discovered near the piles of brick rubble thought to be the remains of the palace of

the Pallavas. The two-storeyed, rectangular **Ganesha Ratha**, further south, is attributed to Parameshvara Varman I (r.669–90). The temple, originally dedicated to Shiva, has beautifully carved inscriptions listing the royal titles of Parameshvara Varman.

A small **Archaeological Museum**, with sculptures and fragments excavated from the site, lies to its east.

🏛 **Archaeological Museum**
West Raja St. **Open** daily. 🖼
Shore Temple: 🖼 also covers
Panch Rathas.

Environs
The **Tiger's Cave**, 4 km (2.5 miles) north, is a shallow cave framed by a large boulder, with heads of *yalis* (mythical leonine beasts). It was probably a stage for outdoor performances.

The Vedagirisvara Temple, dedicated to Shiva, at the top of a hill in the village of **Thirukazhukundram**, 17 km (11 miles) west, is famous for the two eagles that swoop down at noon to be fed by the temple priests. According to legend, these birds are saints who fly from Varanasi *(see pp206–212)* to Rameshvaram, stopping here to rest.

Fishermen with their boats off the beach at Mamallapuram

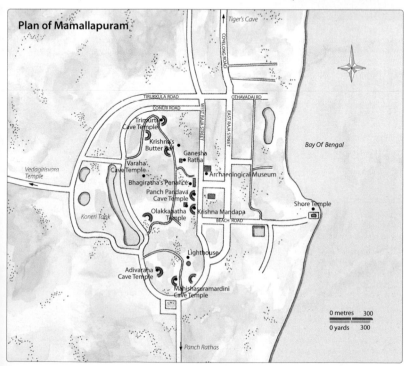

Plan of Mamallapuram

Mamallapuram: Panch Rathas

This 7th-century complex of monolithic rock-cut shrines called the Panch (five) Rathas (processional temple chariots) is named after the five Pandava brothers, heroes of the epic *Mahabharata (see p30)*, and their queen Draupadi. Although unfinished, these impressive temples are a tribute to the genius of the stone-cutters who carved these large boulders *in situ*. In an ambitious experiment, the styles and techniques of wooden architecture were imitated in stone, to create a variety of forms that later came to influence South Indian temple design.

Arjuna Ratha, Draupadi Ratha and Nandi

Arjuna Ratha
This two-storeyed temple has a graceful portrayal of Shiva leaning on his mount, the bull Nandi. Royal couples and other elegantly carved figures in the niches embellish the outer walls.

★ Durga Panel
A four-armed Durga is carved on the rear wall of the Draupadi Ratha's sanctum, with kneeling devotees in front. One of these is shown in the process of cutting his head off, as a supreme act of self-sacrifice.

KEY

① **Draupadi Ratha**, a stone replica of a thatched tribal shrine, is the smallest *ratha* of the group, and is dedicated to the goddess Durga.

② **Nandi**, carved out of a single rock, faces the Arjuna Ratha.

③ **Dharmaraja Ratha**, an imposing three-storeyed *ratha*, is crowned by an octagonal domed roof. Sculpted panels are carved on the upper storeys.

④ **Bhima Ratha**, a gigantic, rectangular *ratha* with a barrel-vaulted roof and unfinished lower level, is named after the Pandava brother famed for his strength.

★ Standing Lion
The mount of Durga is placed in front of the Draupadi Ratha.

King Narasimha
The Pallava king Narasimha Varman I, the patron of this complex and after whose title, Mamalla, the site is named, is shown wearing a crown, a silk garment and jewellery.

VISITORS' CHECKLIST

Practical Information
1.5 km (1 mile) S of
Mamallapuram village.
Tel (044) 2744 2232.
Open daily. 🎫 🚫 ℹ️ Tamil
Nadu Tourism, Covelong Rd.

★ Harihara
Niche figures on the lower level include beautiful sculptures of Harihara, a composite form of Vishnu and Shiva *(see p51)*. The right side of the body with matted locks of hair is Shiva, and the left is Vishnu, with a smooth, tapering cylindrical crown.

Nakul Sahdeva Ratha
Named jointly after the Pandava twins, this *ratha* is unique for its apsidal form, known in architectural terms as *gajaprishta* (back of an elephant). As if to emphasize this, a perfectly sculpted elephant, carved from a single stone, stands next to it.

Vaishnavite priests, Varadaraja Temple

❸ Kanchipuram

Kanchipuram district. 76 km (47 miles) SW of Chennai. 🔁 162,500. 🔁 🔁 ℹ️ Hotel Tamil Nadu, 78, Kamakshi Amman Sannathi St, (044) 2722 2553/2554. 🗓 Shivratri (Feb/Mar), Panguni Uthiram Festival (Mar/Apr), Brahmotsava (May/Jun).

The small temple town of Kanchipuram, or Kanchi, as it is popularly known, is one of the seven sacred cities of the Hindus. From the 6th to the 8th centuries, it was the capital of the Pallavas (see p582), who built numerous temples here and founded universities for higher learning. Royal patronage from the succeeding Chola, Pandya and Vijayanagar dynasties further consolidated the city's reputation as a religious and commercial centre.

Kanchipuram is sacred to Shaivites (devotees of Shiva) as well as to Vaishnavites (worshippers of Vishnu). The town is thus divided into two distinct zones, with the Shaivite temples to the north and the Vaishnavite temples to the southeast.

It also has an important Devi (goddess) temple, the **Kamakshi Temple**, situated northeast of the bus stand. Dedicated to Kamakshi, or the "loving-eyed" Parvati, the temple was rebuilt in the 14th century, during the Vijayanagar period. It has four colourful *gopuras* and the main sanctum has a gold-plated roof. The **Kailasanatha Temple**, to the west of the bus stand, is the oldest and grandest structure in the town. Built in the early 8th century by Rajasimha, the last great Pallava king, this Shiva temple is surrounded by 58 smaller shrines, each with splendid carvings of the various representations of Shiva. The frescoes here are the earliest in South India. The sanctum has a circumambulatory passage with great symbolic meaning – seven steps (indicating seven births) lead to a dark passage (indicating the journey of life) and a narrow outlet (indicating death).

The great **Ekambareshvara Temple** on Car Street, constructed originally by the Pallavas, has a 16-pillared *mandapa* in front of it, that was added later by the Vijayanagar kings. This is one of the five *panchalinga* shrines (see p588) and houses a linga made of earth (*prithvi*). Legend says that the goddess Kamakshi, as part of her penance for disturbing Shiva's meditation, created this linga with earth taken from under a mango tree. Lingas abound in the corridors of the temple complex, while on the western side of the shrine stands the sacred mango tree, said to be 3,000 years old.

The **Vaikuntha Perumal Temple**, near the railway station, is one of the 18 temples dedicated to Vishnu. Erected by the Pallava king Nandi Varman II (r.731–96), this unique structure has three main sanctums, built one on top of the other. Each of them enshrines an image of Vishnu in a different form – standing, sitting and reclining. The hall in the lower shrine has panels depicting the genealogy, coronations and martial conquests of the Pallava kings.

The **Varadaraja Temple**, on Gandhi Road, is the town's main Vishnu temple. The chief deity is a form of Vishnu known as Varadaraja (the "King who Bestows Benediction"). It is believed that the temple stands on the site where Brahma performed a *yagna* (sacrifice) to invoke Vishnu's presence. Among the temple's jewels is a valuable gold necklace, said to have been presented by Robert Clive (see p565).

Kanchipuram, famous for its silk, is also the seat of one of the four Shankaracharyas. They belong to the long line of head priests of the *matha* (religious centre) founded by the much-respected 9th-century philosopher-saint Adi Shankaracharya (see p652).

Environs

The bird sanctuary of **Vedanthangal**, 30 km (19 miles) southeast, attracts more than 30,000 migratory birds. Species such as cormorants, egrets, white ibis, and grey wagtails can be seen between October and February. The sanctuary has been looked after by locals for well over 250 years.

View of Kailasanatha, Kanchipuram's oldest temple

Kanchipuram Silk

Initially, Kanchipuram was a weaving and trade centre for cotton textiles. But from the 19th century, with the increase in availability of mulberry silk from neighbouring Karnataka, the craftsmen turned entirely to silk weaving. Today, the silk fabric and saris created by the city's weavers and dyers are ritually offered to the gods before being sold. Kanchipuram silks, an essential part of every Indian bride's trousseau, are renowned for their lustre, and for their elegant combination of contrasting colours on the borders and end pieces *(pallavs)*.

Cocoons of the silkworm *(Bombyx mori)* are reared on bamboo frames before being dropped into boiling water to preserve the length of the fibre.

Yarn being sorted and graded before dyeing

Dyeing is done by a special community which is skilled in this technique. The dyer first dips the yarn into a cauldron of colour and then dries the hanks in the sun.

Warp and weft yarns are prepared by family members. More than 5,000 families are involved in this very lucrative handloom industry.

Classic Kanchipuram saris are woven from twisted yarn, which makes them extremely durable. They are embellished with motifs such as temple spires, holy *rudraksha* beads, lotus flowers and peacocks, often woven in gold thread.

Weavers' dwellings are simple structures built around a courtyard, and serve as both a home and a work place. The loom is the main feature and occupies a large portion of the living area. Weaving skills are passed from generation to generation within families.

❹ Vellore

Vellore district. 145 km (90 miles) W of Chennai. ⛰ 3,936,331. 🚉 Katpadi, 5 km (3 miles) N of town centre, then bus or auto. 🚌 🛵 daily.

Surrounded by a deep artificial moat, the 16th-century **Vellore Fort** dominates the heart of this town. An impressive example of military architecture, the fort has a turbulent history. This formidable structure has withstood many battles, including an ill-fated mutiny led by the son of Tipu Sultan *(see p521)* in 1806 against the British East India Company. Today, part of the fort houses some government offices, including the Archaeological Survey of India (ASI), district courts and a prison. A museum within has a small but good collection of historical objects found in the area.

The only major structure to survive in the fort is the magnificent **Jalakanteshvara Temple**, constructed by the Nayakas, governors of the region under the Vijayanagar kings, in the mid-16th century. This Shiva temple is located near the fort's northern wall. It is surrounded by a low-lying boundary wall and contains a tank and subsidiary shrines. In the early 20th century, the temple was used as a garrison and its linga was removed from the sanctum. This was reinstated in 1981, after which worship recommenced. In the outer

The broad moat surrounding the quadrangular Vellore Fort

courtyard is the ornate Kalyana Mandapa. Its pillars are carved with magnificent horses and *yali* riders.

Vellore is renowned for its prestigious Christian Medical College, set up in 1900 by the American Dr Ida Scudder. This instiution specializes in research on tropical diseases.

🏛 Vellore Fort
Open daily. Museum:
Open Sat–Thu. **Closed** 2nd Sat of every month. Jalakanteshvara Temple: **Open** daily.

Environs
Arcot, 27 km (17 miles) east of Vellore, is best known for its flamboyant nawabs *(see p574)* and their resistance to the British and French forces in the late 18th century. Some derelict tombs and a Jama Masjid are all that remain from that period.

❺ Tiruvannamalai

Tiruvannamalai district. 85 km (53 miles) S of Vellore. 🚉 🚌 🛵 Karthigai Deepam (Nov/Dec).

One of the most sacred cities of Tamil Nadu, this pilgrim town is the place where Shiva is believed to have appeared as a column of fire *(sthavara* linga*)* in order to assert his supremacy over Brahma and Vishnu. Arunachala Hill (the "Red Mountain"), which forms a backdrop to the town, is said to be the site where the fire manifested itself, and is thus perceived as the light of god himself. On the day of the Karthigai Deepam festival *(see p593)*, an enormous *deepa* (lamp), using 2,000 litres (528 gallons) of ghee and a 30-m (98-ft) wide wick, is lit on the hill, and burns for days. On a full moon night, pilgrims perform a 14-km (9-mile) long circumambulation on foot around the hill.

The Five Elemental Lingas

Hindu belief holds that five essential elements – air, water, fire, earth and ether – created man and the universe. Shiva, one of the three main gods of the Hindu Trinity, is represented as the embodiment of these five elements in five different places. At Sri Kalahasti in Andhra Pradesh *(see p684)*, he is represented as air; in Tiruvanaikka *(see p605)* he takes the form of water, so the linga (phallic symbol) in the main sanctum is partly immersed in water. At Tiruvannamalai, Shiva represents fire, while in the Ekambareshvara Temple at Kanchipuram *(see p586)*, the linga is made of earth. Finally, at Chidambaram *(see p594)* Shiva represents ether, the most sacred of the five elements.

Nataraja Temple, Chidambaram, housing the ether linga

The 16th-century Arunachaleshvara Temple at Tiruvannamalai

Arunachaleshvara Temple, the town's most important structure, is one of the five elemental shrines of Shiva, where the linga, encased in gold, represents fire. Covering a vast area of 10 ha (25 acres), this is also one of the largest temple complexes in India, parts of it dating to the 11th century. It has nine imposing towers, huge *prakaras* (walled and cloistered enclosures), the large Shivaganga Tank and a vast thousand-pillared hall.

Tiruvannamalai is also where Sri Ramana Maharishi, the famed 20th-century saint, spent 23 years in meditation. The **Sri Ramana Maharishi Ashram**, near Arunachala Hill, is an internationally renowned spiritual centre that attracts devotees from all walks of life.

Arunachaleshvara Temple Open daily. **Closed** to non-Hindus. inside the sanctum.

The Krishna Temple and Durbar Hall on Krishnagiri Hill, Gingee Fort

(1 mile) from north to south. Built by the local Nayaka governors, feudatories of the Vijayanagar kings, in the 15th and 16th centuries, the fort was occupied by Bijapur's Adil Shahi Sultans *(see p546)*, the Marathas *(see p475)*, the French and finally the British.

This once-great fortress city is dotted with dilapidated arcaded chambers, mosques, *mandapas*, small shrines, tanks and granaries. Many temples, mostly dedicated to Vishnu, survive as well. These include the deserted temple in the main citadel on the 242-m (794-ft) high Rajagiri Hill. The most prominent, however, is the great **Venkataramana Temple**, in the foothills of the outer fort, near Puducherry Gate. This was constructed by Muthialu Nayaka in the 17th century. Its original pillars were removed by the French and used in the Government Square at Puducherry *(see p590)*. Near the gateway are panels depicting scenes from the *Ramayana (see p31)* and the

Vishnu Purana. A Ranganatha Temple and a Krishna Temple, both smaller than the Venkataramana Temple, are located on Krishnagiri Hill, as is the **Durbar Hall**. The Durbar Hall has balconies extending to the edge of the hill which provide good views of the surrounding countryside.

The fort's finest monument is the **Kalyana Mahal**, a square hall built for the ladies of the court. The building has a central eight-storeyed pyramidal tower with a single large room on each floor.

There are also traces of a network of natural springs and tanks that provided an excellent supply of water to the citadel. One of the tanks, Chettikulam, has a platform where Raja Thej Singh, a courageous 18th-century Rajput chief and vassal of the Mughal emperor, was cremated. Tamil folk songs glorify Gingee and Raja Thej Singh, who was killed in a heroic battle against the Nawab of Arcot.

Kalyana Mahal with Rajagiri Hill in the background, Gingee

❻ Gingee Fort

Viluppuram district. 37 km (23 miles) E of Tiruvannamalai. Open daily.

Gingee (locally called Senji) Fort, is a remarkable example of military engineering. Its three citadels, dramatically perched atop three hills – Krishnagiri to the north, Rajagiri to the west and Chandrayandurg to the southeast – are enclosed by solid stone walls to form a vast triangular-shaped area extending more than 1.5 km

Gingee Fort sprawling across three hills

❼ Street-by-Street: Puducherry

The former capital of French territories in India, Puducherry was established in 1674 by François Martin, the first director of the French East India Company. The town is laid out in a grid pattern, with parallel streets cutting across each other at right angles. Its main promenade, the 3-km (2-mile) long Goubert Salai running along the Bay of Bengal, formed part of the French Quarter, with its elegant colonial mansions, tree-lined boulevards, parks, bars and cafés. Beyond this was a canal, now dry, that demarcated the Tamil Town, where the local populace once lived.

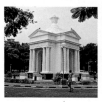

Government Square A pavilion stands in the centre of this tree-lined square.

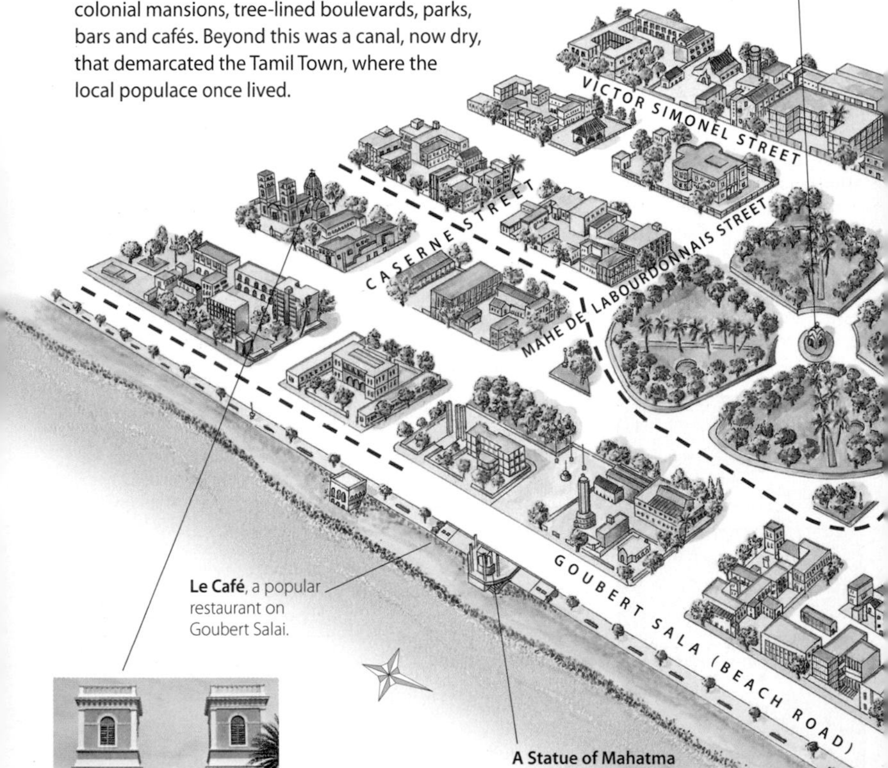

VICTOR SIMONEL STREET
CASERNE STREET
MAHE DE LABOURDONNAIS STREET
GOUBERT SALA (BEACH ROAD)
0 metres 80
0 yards 80

Le Café, a popular restaurant on Goubert Salai.

A Statue of Mahatma Gandhi, 4 m (13 ft) high, stands on a pedestal surrounded by eight stone pillars.

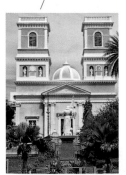

★ Church of Our Lady of the Angels Built in 1865, this striking church boasts a rare oil painting of Our Lady of the Assumption, a gift from the French emperor, Napoleon III.

Joseph François Dupleix

Puducherry's colonial past is intricately interwoven with the life of the redoubtable Marquis Joseph François Dupleix, governor between 1742 and 1754. This energetic statesman tried valiantly to prevent British supremacy by forming alliances with local princes. This power struggle was aggravated by the War of Austrian Succession in Europe between England and France. With the final defeat of the French in the Second Carnatic War, Dupleix relinquished his governorship and returned in disgrace to Paris. His memorial statue is on Goubert Salai.

Dupleix (1697–1764)

For hotels and restaurants see pp702–703 and pp717–18

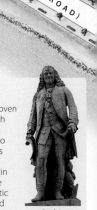

Raj Nivas
A harmonious fusion of French and Indian styles of architecture, Dupleix's palatial home is now the Lieutenant Governor's official residence.

VISITORS' CHECKLIST

Practical Information
Union Territory of Puducherry. 160 km (99 miles) S of Chennai. 🏣 220,800. 🚹 Puducherry Tourism, Goubert Salai, (0413) 233 9497. 🎫 🏛 Mon–Sat. 🎊 Masimagam (Feb/Mar), Ganesha Chaturthi (Aug/Sep).

Transport
🚆 🚌 🚐

General Hospital

Manakula Vinayakar Temple
Dedicated to Ganesha, this temple has a golden spire, and walls portraying 40 different forms of Ganesha.

MANAKULA VINAYAKAR

KOIL STREET

FRANCOIS MARTIN STREET

LAW DE LAURISTON STREET

CAMPAGNIE ST

MARINE STREET

STREET

Key

━ Suggested route

★ Aurobindo Ashram
Named after Sri Aurobindo (see p592), this serene ashram organizes regular meditation sessions to which all are welcome.

Puducherry
Museum's collection ranges from ancient Roman artifacts and Chola bronzes to beautiful snail shells.

★ View of the Seafront
Goubert Salai, the boulevard along the Bay of Bengal, is lined with grand colonial buildings.

Exploring Puducherry

Often described as a sleepy French provincial town, Puducherry (originally named Pondicherry) retains a distinct Gallic flavour. French is still spoken among the older residents, while stately colonial mansions stand in tree-lined streets that are still known by their colonial names. Even the policemen continue to wear the military-style caps, known as kepis. Located on the east coast of Tamil Nadu, it is the administrative capital of a Union Territory that includes the former French enclaves of Mahe in Kerala *(see p659)*, Yanam in Andhra Pradesh and Karaikkal in Tamil Nadu.

🏛 Puducherry Museum
49, Rue St Louis. **Tel** Director Art & Culture, (0413) 233 6236. **Open** Tue–Sun.

Located in the lovely old Law Building, near Government Park, the Puducherry Museum has an outstanding collection of artifacts from the French colonial period. The rooms in one section are furnished in French style, and are decorated with marble statuary, paintings, mirrors and clocks. Prized exhibits include the bed that Dupleix slept in when he was the governor, and a *pousse-pousse*, an earlier version of the rickshaw.

The museum also displays rare bronzes and stone sculptures from the Pallava and Chola periods. Among the artifacts excavated from nearby Arikamedu, an ancient port that had trade links with Imperial Rome, are beads, amphorae, coins, ornamented oil lamps, funerary urns and fragments of pottery and china.

Inside the same compound is the **Romain Rolland Library**. Established in 1872, the library now has a rich collection of more than 300,000 volumes, including many rare editions in both French and English. Its mobile library service takes more than 8,000 books in a bus to nearby villages. The reference section, on the second floor, is open to the public.

🖥 Romain Rolland Library
Tel (0413) 233 6426. **Open** Mon–Sat.

⛪ Basilica of the Sacred Heart of Jesus
South Boulevard. **Open** daily.

A serene atmosphere cloaks this brown and white Neo-Gothic basilica, built in the 1700s. Its most interesting features are its large stained-glass panels depicting incidents from the life of Jesus Christ, and the handsome arches that span the nave. Further along the southern boulevard is the cemetery, which has tombs with ornate marble decorations.

Stained glass, Basilica of the Sacred Heart

🌳 Botanical Gardens
S of City Bus Stand.

Lying at the far western end of the old Tamil Town, the Botanical Gardens, laid out in 1826, were designed in the formal French style with clipped trees, flower beds, gravel walks and fountains. The French introduced many unusual and exotic trees and shrubs from all over India and the world, many of which are still here. With its 1,500 species of plants, this is one of the best botanical gardens in South India. An interesting little aquarium displays some of the more spectacular marine species from the Coromandel Coast.

🖥 House of Ananda Rangapillai
Ananda Rangapillai St. **Tel** (0413) 233 5756 for permission to visit.

This lavishly furnished house, once the home of an 18th-century Indian nobleman, offers fascinating glimpses into a vanished lifestyle. Now a museum, the house was owned by Ananda Rangapillai, Dupleix's favourite courtier and *dubash* (translator). A perceptive observer and commentator, he maintained a series of diaries between 1736 and 1760, recording his views of the fluctuating fortunes of the French in India. However, he displeased Madame Dupleix, who eventually ousted him from his post.

Sri Aurobindo Ghose

The firebrand Bengali poet-philosopher, Aurobindo Ghose, who joined the struggle for freedom in the early 1900s, was known for his extremist views. To escape from the British, he took refuge in the French territory of Puducherry, where he was drawn into the spiritual realm. It was here that he studied, wrote about and popularized the principles of yoga. His disciple, Mirra Alfassa, known later as "The Mother", was a Parisian mystic, painter and musician, who first came to Puducherry with her husband during World War I. Sri Aurobindo's philosophy so inspired her that she stayed on, and was later instrumental in the establishment of the Aurobindo Ashram.

Sri Aurobindo (1872–1950)

The verdant courtyard of the École Française d'Extrême-Orient

⊞ École Française d'Extrême-Orient
16 & 19, Rue Dumas.
Tel (0413) 233 2504.
An internationally renowned research institution, the 19th-century École Française d'Extrême-Orient is noted for its research in archaeology, history and sociology.

⊞ French Institute of Indology
11, St Louis St. **Tel** (0413) 233 4539.
The prestigious French Institute of Indology was established in the mid-1950s by an eminent French Indologist, Dr Jean Fillozet. Originally set up for the study of local language and culture, this institute now has links with many French universities and research organizations.

⊞ Aurobindo Ashram
Rue de la Marine.
Tel (0413) 223 3604. **Open** daily.
Puducherry's best-known landmark, the Aurobindo Ashram dominates life in this town.

Founded by Sri Aurobindo in 1926, the Ashram is a peaceful retreat with tree-shaded courtyards. The flower-festooned *samadhi* (memorial) of Sri Aurobindo and The Mother lies under a frangipani tree in the main courtyard. This memorial, with two chambers, one above the other, is the focal point for all disciples and followers.

Environs
Auroville, or the "City of Dawn", 8 km (5 miles) northwest of Puducherry, was designed by French architect Roger Anger in 1968. Conceived as a utopian paradise by The Mother, Mirra Alfassa, it was planned as a futuristic international city, where people of goodwill would live together in peace. The International Commune, with 40 settlements with names like Grace, Serenity and Certitude, and 550 permanent residents, was meant to bring people from different castes, religions and nations under one roof, where they could live in harmony. Two important settlements, Fraternité and Harmonie, sell handicrafts made by local artisans. The Matri Mandir, a meditation centre set in an area of 25 ha (62 acres), reflects The Mother's spiritual beliefs. This spherical marble chamber has a crystal placed inside it, reflecting the sun's rays. The concentrated light acts as a focal point to aid meditation.

Matri Mandir, the spiritual and physical centre of Auroville

Festivals of Tamil Nadu

Pongal (*mid-Jan*). A thanksgiving festival in praise of the sun, land and cattle, Pongal is celebrated all over Tamil Nadu. A sweet rice pudding (*pongal*) is the main offering. The southern districts organize a bull fight, a popular martial event known as *manju virattal*.

Chitirai (*mid-Apr*). The Tamil New Year is celebrated all over the state with offerings of food to the gods. In Madurai, the marriage of Minakshi (Parvati) and Sundareshvara (Shiva) is celebrated with much pomp.

Adi Perukku (*Jul/Aug*). Sweets and different kinds of rice preparations are offered to the rivers of Tamil Nadu to mark the onset of the monsoon.

Navaratri Gollu (*Sep/Oct*). Exclusively for women, this nine-day festival marks the victory of Goddess Durga over the buffalo demon Mahisha. Houses are decorated with *gollu* dolls, which depict gods and goddesses, as well as with contemporary secular icons.

Karthigai (*Nov/Dec*), Tiruvannamalai. People decorate their homes with lights to celebrate the birth of Murugan, son of Shiva (*see p588*).

Tamil women making preparations for Pongal

The gold-plated roof of the main sanctum, Nataraja Temple, Chidambaram

8 Chidambaram

Thanjavur district. 60 km (37 miles) S of Puducherry. 59,000. Hotel Tamil Nadu, Railway Feeder Rd, (04144) 238 739. Dance Festival (Feb/Mar), Arudhra (Dec/Jan).

Sacred Chidambaram, where Shiva is believed to have performed his cosmic dance, the *tandava nritya*, is a traditional temple town where history merges with mythology to create a deeply religious ambience. All ancient Hindu beliefs and practices are zealously observed here, manifested in an endless cycle of rites and rituals.

The focal point of the town is the awe-inspiring **Nataraja Temple**, built by the Cholas *(see pp50–51)* in the 9th century to honour their patron deity, Shiva as Nataraja, the "Lord of Dance" *(see p570)*. The temple has an unusual hut-like sanctum with a gold-plated roof, the huge, colonnaded Shivaganga Tank, and four colourful *gopuras*. The most interesting is the eastern *gopura* which features detailed sculptures of the 108 hand and feet movements of Bharat Natyam *(see p33)*, and is considered a veritable encyclopaedia of this classical temple dance.

Within the temple's three enormous enclosures are five major halls *(sabhas)*, each conceived for a special purpose. In the outer enclosure, next to the Shivaganga Tank, is the Raja Sabha ("Royal Hall"), a beautiful thousand-pillared hall, built as a venue for temple rituals and festivals. Many Chola kings were crowned here in the presence of the deity. In the central enclosure is the Deva Sabha ("Divine Hall"), where the temple bronzes are housed, and administrative functions performed. The adjacent Nritya Sabha ("Dance Hall") has a superb collection of sculptures, the finest being the **Urdhava Tandava**. The innermost enclosure, the holiest part of the complex, contains the Chit Sabha or Chitambalam ("Hall of Bliss"), from which the town derives its name. This is the main sanctum, housing one of the five elemental lingas of Shiva *(see p588)*, the *akasha* linga, which represents ether, the all-pervading element central to human existence. The inner sanctum containing the linga is hidden behind a black curtain, symbolizing ignorance, which is removed only during prayer time. There is a certain aura of mystery to this veiled sanctum and it is often called the Sacred Secret of Chidambaram (Chidambara Rahasyam). Finally, the fifth hall, in front of the Chit Sabha, is the Kanaka Sabha ("Golden Hall"), where Shiva is supposed to have performed his cosmic dance.

Other areas of interest in the complex are the **Govindarajaswamy Shrine**, housing the reclining Vishnu, the **Shivakamasundari Shrine**, dedicated to Shiva's consort, Parvati, and the **Subramanyam Shrine**, in which Murugan is worshipped.

Religious traditions in the temple are preserved by a group of hereditary priests whose ancestors came to Chidambaram 3,000 years ago. Known as the *dikshitars*, they are easily recognized by their top-knots. Chidambaram's other claim to fame is the modern **Annamalai University**, which is located to the east. Founded by a philanthropist over 50 years ago, it is Tamil Nadu's first residential university, specializing in South Indian studies.

Urdhava Tandava, Nataraja Temple

Nataraja Temple
Near bus stand. **Open** daily.

Environs
Located 16 km (10 miles) east of Chidambaram, **Pichavaram's** maze of picturesque backwaters, with mangrove forests and 1,700 islands in 4,000 canals, can be explored in rowboats.

⑨ Coromandel Driving Tour

Named after Cholamandalam ("the Realm of the Cholas"), the Coromandel Coast extends from the Godavari Delta in Andhra Pradesh in the north, to Point Calimere in the south. This spectacularly beautiful strip of land played a significant role in the maritime history of India. Its great ports have, through the ages, attracted traders and merchants in search of textiles and spices.

Dansborg Fort at Tarangambadi

① Tirumullaivasal
A magnificent shrine to Shiva dominates this small, coastal town.

② Poompuhar
This historic port city once had trade links with ancient Greece and Rome. An interesting museum here recreates stories of its past glory in bas-reliefs.

③ Tarangambadi
More popularly known as Tranquebar, this little town was a Danish settlement In the 17th century. It has an impressive fort, churches and a beautiful brick gateway, the Town Gate.

Key

🔲 Tour route

— Other roads

0 kilometres   10

0 miles   10

④ Karaikal
This former French town has many 19th-century mansions and a Neo-Gothic church.

⑥ Nagapattinam
An old Chola port, this was also a major Buddhist centre till the 13th century. It was later occupied by the Portuguese, the Dutch and finally the British.

⑤ Nagore
The 16th-century tomb of Hazrat Sayyid Shahul, a Muslim saint who died in Nagore, attracts devotees of all religions, castes and creeds.

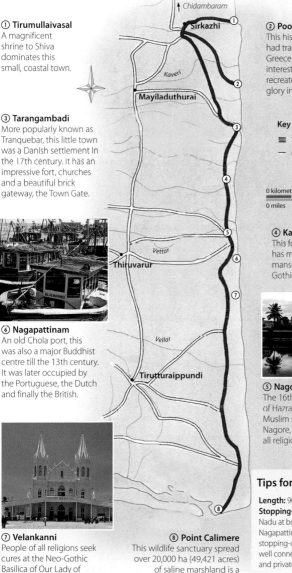

Tips for Drivers

Length: 90 km (56 miles).
Stopping-off points: Hotel Tamil Nadu at both Poompuhar and Nagapattinam are convenient stopping-off points. The route is well connected by government and private buses.

⑦ Velankanni
People of all religions seek cures at the Neo-Gothic Basilica of Our Lady of Good Health.

⑧ Point Calimere
This wildlife sanctuary spread over 20,000 ha (49,421 acres) of saline marshland is a haven for migratory birds.

Map labels: Chidambaram, Sirkazhi ①, ② Poompuhar, Kaveri, Mayiladuthurai, ③, ④, Vettar, Thiruvarur, ⑤, ⑥, ⑦, Vellar, Tirutturaippundi, ⑧

The superb Nataraja sculpture at Gangaikondacholapuram

⑩ Gangaikon-dacholapuram

Tiruchirapalli district. 40 km (25 miles) SW of Chidambaram. 🚌 from Chidambaram or Kumbakonam.

Grandly titled Gangaikon-dacholapuram, "The City of the Chola who Took the Ganges", this now modest village was the capital of the powerful Chola dynasty *(see pp50–51)* during the reign of Rajendra I (r.1012–44). A great military commander like his father Rajaraja I, Rajendra I was the first Tamil ruler to venture northwards. He built this city to commemorate his successful campaign across the Ganges. According to an inscription, he then ordered the defeated rulers to carry back pots of sacred Ganges water on their heads to fill the Chola-Ganga tank, a victory memorial.

Except for the magnificent **Brihadishvara Temple**, little remains of his capital city. Built as a replica of Thanjavur's Brihadishvara Temple *(see pp602–603)*, the towered sanctum of this granite Shiva

temple is shorter than the one at Thanjavur. Adorning the lower walls, columns and niches are many remarkable sculptural friezes. One of the most outstanding is the panel depicting Shiva blessing Chandesha, a pious devotee sculpted to resemble Rajendra I himself. The sculptures of the *dikpalas* (guardians of the eight directions), *ekadasas* (the 11 forms of Shiva), Saraswati, Kalyanasundara and Nataraja *(see p570)* are also splendid examples of Chola art. Steps near the small Durga shrine in the courtyard lead past a

sculpture of a seated lion to a well, believed to have been filled with Ganges water for daily rituals.

The small **Archaeological Museum**, near the temple, exhibits Chola artifacts from neighbouring sites.

🏛 **Brihadishvara Temple**
Open daily. Museum: **Open** daily.

⑪ Kumbakonam

Thanjavur district. 74 km (46 miles) SW of Chidambaram. 🚹 140,100. 🚉 🚌 *ℹ* Thanjavur tourist office, (04362) 231 325. 🎉 Nageshvara Temple Festival (Apr/May), Mahamaham Festival (every 12 years).

Like Kanchipuram *(see p586)*, Kumbakonam is one of the most sacred cities in Tamil Nadu. Located on the southern bank of the Kaveri river, this is an ancient city where, as legend says, Shiva's arrow shattered the cosmic pot *(kumbh)* containing the divine nectar of creation *(amrit)*. This myth has given Kumbakonam both its name and sanctity. Today, the city represents the traditional cultural values of the Tamil heartland. It is also the region's main commercial and craft centre, famous for its textiles, jewellery, bronze casting and the superior quality of its locally grown betel leaves.

It is believed that when the divine nectar emerged from the pot, it filled the huge **Mahamaham Tank**. This is Kumbakonam's sacred centre and the site of the great Mahamaham Festival, held every 12 years (the last one

The 17th-century Adikumbheshvara Temple, Kumbakonam

was held in 2004). At the auspicious time, thousands of devotees enter the tank for their holy dip. This is when the purifying power of the water is said to be at its height. The devout believe that all of India's nine sacred rivers (Ganges, Yamuna, Saraswati, Sarayu, Godavari, Narmada, Kaveri, Payokshini and Kanniyakumari) also bathe in the tank to cleanse themselves of the sins of humanity accumulated in their waters.

The tank, renovated by the Nayakas in the 17th century, has steps at the four cardinal points, and 16 ornate pavilions in honour of the 16 *mahadanas* (great gifts bestowed by a ruler on a spiritual centre). A fine example of Nayaka art is a relief depicting a king being weighed on a balance against gold (a ceremony known as *tulapurushadeva*), carved on the roof of a 16-pillared *mandapa* that stands at the northwest corner of the tank. To the north is the **Kashivishvanatha Temple**, which has a small shrine facing the water; this is dedicated to the nine sacred rivers, personified as goddesses. The shrine representing the Kaveri river occupies the central position.

To the east of the tank is the 17th-century **Adikumbheshvara Temple**, built on the legendary spot where Shiva shattered the pot. A unique feature here is the depiction of 27 stars and the 12 zodiac signs carved on a large block of stone in the Navaratri Mandapa. It also has a superb collection of silver *vahanas* (vehicles) which are used during festivals to carry the temple deities. The grand, 12-storeyed **Sarangapani Temple**, to the east, is the most important Vaishnavite shrine in the city.

Nearby is the 9th-century **Nageshvara Temple**, a fine example of early Chola architecture. The town's oldest temple, this is the site of an annual festival that celebrates the worship of the linga by the sun. Niches on the sanctum walls contain exquisitely carved figures depicting the

Temple chariots at Kumbakonam's Adikumbheshvara Temple

forms of Shiva, and scenes from the *Ramayana*.

Environs
The spectacular Airavateshvara Temple at **Darasuram**, 4 km (2.5 miles) west of Kumbakonam, was built by the Chola king, Rajaraja II (r.1146–73). This temple is dedicated to Shiva, who is known here as Airavateshvara, the "Lord of Airavata". Legend claims that after Airavata, the white elephant of Indra, the God of the Heavens, regained his lost colour, he worshipped Shiva at this spot.

Shiva's wedding procession, Darasuram

The four-tiered temple has a sanctum and three halls, of which the finest is the Rajagambira Mandapa, conceived as a stone chariot drawn by caparisoned horses, with Brahma as its driver. The outer walls have fine friezes and carvings of musicians, dancers and acrobats as well as depictions from the *Periya Puranam*, a Tamil treatise on

the 63 Shaivite poet-saints, the Nayannars *(see p49)*. The late Chola temple at **Tirubhuvanam**, 8 km (5 miles) northeast of Kumbakonam, is dedicated to Kumbheshvara, the "God who Removes Fear". This is also an old silk weaving centre. About 8 km (5 miles) west of Kumbakonam is **Swamimalai**, one of the six sacred shrines devoted to Lord Murugan *(see p29)*, who, legend says, propounded the meaning of "Om", the sacred mantra, to his father Shiva, and thus assumed the title Swaminatha ("Lord of Lords"). The temple, situated on a hill, has an impressive statue of Murugan in the sanctum; interestingly, he has an elephant as his vehicle instead of the typical peacock. This small village is also an important centre for bronze casting, where artisans still use traditional methods to create beautiful images for temples *(see p598)*.

Small votive shrines outside the Airavateshvara Temple, Darasuram

The College of Music at Tiruvaiyaru, on the Kaveri river

⑫ Tiruvaiyaru

Thanjavur district. 13 km (8 miles)
N of Thanjavur. 🗺 185,737. 🚌
🎵 Thyagaraja Music Festival (Jan).

The fertile region watered by the Kaveri river and its four tributaries is known as Tiruvaiyaru, the sacred *(tiru)* land of five *(i)* rivers *(aru)*. For nearly 2,000 years the Tamil people have regarded the Kaveri as the sacred source of life, religion and culture. As a result, many scholars, artists, poets and musicians settled in this region, under the enlightened patronage of the rulers of Thanjavur *(see pp600–601)*. Among them was Thyagaraja (1767–1847), the greatest composer-saint of Carnatic music. The history of this small town is thus deeply linked with the growth and development of South Indian classical music.

The little **Thyagaraja Temple**, in the town, was built to commemorate the last resting place of the celebrated composer-saint. A musical festival is held here every year on the anniversary of his death,

which falls, according to the Tamil calendar, in January. Hundreds of musicians and students of Carnatic music gather in the town and sing Thyagaraja's songs from morning till midnight for a whole week.

As dawn breaks over the river, a procession of musicians makes the short journey from Thyagaraja's house to the temple, singing continuously all the way. Music lovers wait eagerly at the shrine, seated on the mud floor of the thatch-roofed auditorium. To the sacred chants of priests, the stone image of Thyagaraja is ritually bathed with milk, rosewater, sandalwood and honey. The five songs known as the *pancha ratna* ("five gems") of Thyagaraja, which are considered unequalled masterpieces of Carnatic music, are sung in a grand chorus by all the assembled musicians. This ceremony is an annual reaffirmation of devotion to the composer and to a great tradition of music. For music lovers from all over India, it

can be a magical experience. Also in the town is the 9th-century **Panchanandishvara Temple** ("Lord of the Five Rivers"), built by the Cholas. Dedicated to Shiva, the shrines of Uttara (north) Kailasha and Dakshina (south) Kailasha, on either side of the main temple, were built by the wives of Rajaraja I and Rajendra I *(see pp50–51)*. The temple's huge *prakara* (boundary) walls, pillared *mandapas* and the Mukti Mandapa are immortalized in the songs of the Nayannars, a sect of 7th-century poet-saints *(see p49)*.

Environs

Pullamangai village, 12 kms (7 miles) northeast of Tiruvaiyaru, is noted for the **Brahmapurishvara Temple**, dating to the 10th century. The temple features elegant depictions of various gods and goddesses.

Cows being bathed in the waters of the Kaveri, Tiruvaiyaru

Thanjavur Bronzes

The Thanjavur region's wealth of artistic traditions includes the creation of exquisite bronze images through a process known as *cire perdue* or the "lost wax" technique. A model of the image is first made  in wax and then coated with layers of clay to create a mould, which is heated to allow the melting wax to flow out through a hole at the base. A molten alloy of five metals *(panch loha)* is poured into the hollow. When it cools, the mould is broken and the image is finished and polished. Finally, the image's eyes are sealed with a mixture of honey and ghee and then ritually "opened" by a priest, using a golden needle. Even today, traditional artisans, known as *sthapathis*, create these images according to a fixed set of rules and guidelines laid down in the *Shilpa Shastra*, an ancient treatise on art. The main centre for bronze casting in Tamil Nadu is Swamimalai *(see p597)*.

Artisan adding finishing touches to bronze idols

Carnatic Music

The classical music of South India is known as Carnatic music. Though based on the general concepts of raga (melody) and *tala* (rhythm) found in Hindustani music *(see pp32–3)*, Carnatic music differs in many respects. It is almost exclusively devotional in character, uses different percussion and musical instruments, and develops the melody in a more structured manner. It also lays more emphasis on rhythm. Some of the greatest Carnatic music was composed between 1750 and 1850, by the musical trinity of Thyagaraja, Syama Sastri, and Muthuswami Dikshitar who, between them, wrote over 2,500 songs in Sanskrit and Telegu, modifying and refining features that are now essential to the genre.

Accompanying Instruments

Traditional South Indian instruments such as the veena, the nadasvaram, the flute and the thavil are used for accompaniment, along with Western instruments such as the violin and saxophone.

Mridangam (two-headed drum)

Saraswati veena

Flute

The violin, a bow-string instrument of Western origin, is played in a seated position.

The ghatam, a mere clay pot, can produce fabulous rhythms in the hands of an accomplished performer.

Bombay Jayashri is a leading vocalist.

Tanpura

Ghatam

Violin

Music festivals are often held in large cities, where concerts take place in small auditoriums, called *sabhas*. Most performers are accompanied by a violinist and two percussionists. A typical concert lasts for about three hours, during which a series of songs, usually in Telugu, are sung. The lyrics are as important as the melody, and many are devotional in nature.

The nadasvaram, which is a wind instrument, is a must at temple festivals, weddings and auspicious occasions. The *thavil* (drum) player performs complex rythmic improvisations to accompany the melody.

The veena, which resembles the more widely seen sitar, is a beautifully hand-crafted string instrument.

⑬ Thanjavur

The city of Thanjavur, or Tanjore, lies in the fertile Kaveri Delta, a region often referred to as the "rice bowl of Tamil Nadu". For nearly a thousand years, this great town dominated the political history of the region as the capital of three powerful dynasties – the Cholas (9th–13th centuries), the Nayakas (1535–1676) and the Marathas (1676–1855). The magnificent Brihadishvara Temple *(see pp602–603)*, is the most important Chola monument, while the Royal Palace dates to the Nayaka and Maratha periods. Today, Thanjavur's culture extends beyond temples and palaces, to encompass classical music and dance. It is also a flourishing centre for bronze sculpture and painting.

Seven-storeyed observation tower of the Royal Palace, Thanjavur

🏯 Shivaganga Fort
Off Hospital Rd. **Open** daily.
The quadrangular Shivaganga Fort, southwest of the old city, was built by the Nayaka ruler, Sevappa Nayaka, in the mid-16th century. Its battlemented stone walls, which enclose an area of 14 ha (35 acres), are surrounded by a partly rock-cut moat. The square **Shivaganga Tank** in the fort was excavated by Rajaraja I, and later renovated to provide drinking water for the city. The fort also contains the great Brihadishvara Temple, Schwartz Church, and a public amusement park.

Maratha ruler Serfoji II
(r.1798–1832)

🏛 Brihadishvara Temple
See pp602–603.

🏯 Schwartz Church
Off West Main Rd. **Open** daily.
The 18th-century Christ Church or Schwartz Church, a legacy of Thanjavur's colonial past, stands to the east of the Shivaganga Tank. This church was founded by the Danish missionary, Reverend Frederik Christian Schwartz, in 1779. When he died in 1798, the enlightened Maratha ruler, Serfoji II, donated a striking marble tablet to the church. This tablet, made by John Flaxman, has been placed at the western end of the church. It depicts the dying missionary blessing his royal patron, surrounded by ministers and pupils from the school that he established.

🏛 Royal Palace
East Main Rd. **Open** daily. 🖼
📷 Extra charges for phtography.
Resembling the shape of a flying eagle, this palace was built originally by the Nayaka rulers as their royal residence, and was subsequently remodelled by the Marathas. A large quadrangular courtyard leads into the palace complex, at one end of which is a pyramidal, temple-like tower. Outside the palace complex stands the seven storeyed, arcaded observation tower, now without its capping pavilion.

The splendid Maratha Durbar Hall, built by Shahji II in 1684, has elaborately painted and decorated pillars, walls and ceiling. A wooden canopy embellished with glittering glass pieces and supported by four wooden pillars stands above a green granite slab on which the royal Maratha throne once stood. The other buildings include the Sadir Mahal, which is still the residence of the erstwhile royal family, and the Puja Mahal.

The **Rajaraja Museum and Art Gallery**, in the Nayaka Durbar Hall, was established in 1951 and has an impressive collection of bronze and stone idols dating from the 7th to the 20th centuries. Particularly noteworthy are the images of Shiva, such as the Kalyanasundaramurti, which depicts the wedding of Shiva and Parvati *(see p570)*, and the Bhikshatanamurti, which shows Shiva as a wandering mendicant, carrying a begging bowl and accompanied by a dog.

Next to the Rajaraja Museum is the **Saraswati Mahal Library**, constructed by the Maratha rulers. This is one of the most important reference libraries in India, with a fine collection of rare palm-leaf manuscripts and books collected by the versatile and scholarly Serfoji II. An adjoining **Museum** displays some of these valuable works. The **Royal Museum** occupies

Mural at the entrance of Saraswati Mahal, Royal Palace, Thanjavur

part of the private quarters of the Maratha Palace, and exhibits the personal collection of Serfoji II. Nearby is the Sangeeta Mahal (Music Hall), built by the Nayakas, and specially designed with acoustic features for musical gatherings.

🏛 Rajaraja Museum and Art Gallery

Tel (04362) 239 823. **Open** daily. **Closed** Sun & public hols. 🖼

Vithoba fresco in the Art Gallery, Royal Palace, Thanjavur

🏛 Saraswati Mahal Library
Open to public.
Museum: **Closed** Thu–Tue.

🏛 Royal Museum
Open daily. 🖼

Environs
Lying 55 km (34 miles) east of Thanjavur, Thiruvarur is famous for its Thyagaraja Temple dedicated to the Somaskanda form of Shiva (see p582). The temple has four gopuras. Its ceiling is covered with 17th-century paintings of scenes from the Shiva legend.

Thanjavur Paintings

A distinctive school of painting emerged during the rule of the Marathas, patronized by Serfoji II. This highly ornamental style was characterized by vibrant colours as well as decoration with gold leaf and precious and semi-precious stones. The themes are mostly religious, and the symbolic colour palette of red, black, blue and white depicts each deity in a specific colour. The subjects usually have rotund bodies and almond-shaped eyes. A favourite image is Krishna portrayed as a chubby infant.

Baby Krishna with his mother, Yashodhara

Thanjavur City Centre

① Shivaganga Fort
② Brihadishvara Temple
③ Schwartz Church
④ Royal Palace

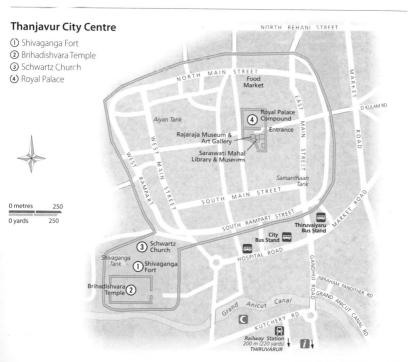

0 metres 250
0 yards 250

Thanjavur: Brihadishvara Temple

This monumental granite temple, the finest example of Chola architecture, is now a UNESCO World Heritage Site. Completed in AD 1010 and dedicated to Shiva, it was built by Rajaraja Chola I *(see pp50–51)* as a symbol of the unrivalled power and might of the Cholas. The temple basement is covered with inscriptions that give details of the temple's administration and revenue, and provide valuable historical information on Chola society and government.

★ Vimana
The 66-m (217-ft) high pyramid-shaped *vimana*, over the sanctum, is a 13-storeyed structure. Its gilded finial was presented by the king.

★ Dvarapala
Two gigantic *dvarapalas*, or doorkeepers, at the eastern entrance, direct devotees to the sanctum with their pointed fingers.

KEY

① **Linga shrine**

② **The passageway** is circumambulatory and built on two levels, owing to the colossal height of the 4-m (13-ft) linga.

③ **An octagonal cupola**, beautifully carved out of a massive block of granite weighing 80 tonnes, crowns the *vimana*.

Frescoes
Chola frescoes adorn the passage around the sanctum. They were discovered when the 17-century Maratha paintings covering them began to disintegrate.

General View of the Temple
The Brihadishvara Temple stands in
the middle of a rectangular court,
surrounded by subsidiary shrines. On
the southern side of the courtyard is an
Archaeological Museum which displays,
among other things, photographs of
the temple before restoration.

★ Nandi Mandapa
Carved out of a single block
of granite weighing 25
tonnes, this huge Nandi
figure is 6 m (20 ft) long, and
faces the inner sanctum.

**Priests Outside
the Temple**
Although under the
jurisdiction of the
Archaeological Survey
of India, the temple
is open for worship.

Nandi Mandapa

Shiva-Parvati
Granite divinities occupy the wall
niches of the sanctum.

Tiruchirapalli's Rock Fort looming above the city

⓮ Tiruchirapalli

Tiruchirapalli district. 60 km (37 miles) W of Thanjavur. ▨ 2,418,400. ✈ 7 km (4 miles) S of town centre, then bus or taxi. 🚆 🚌 ℹ Hotel Tamil Nadu, 101 Williams Rd, (0431) 241 4346. ✦ Teppakulam Float Festival (Mar).

Situated at the head of the fertile Kaveri Delta, this city is named after the fierce three-headed demon *(tirusira)* who attained salvation after being slain by Shiva. The town's history is interwoven with the political fortunes of the Pallavas, Cholas, Nayakas and finally the British, who shortened its name to Trichy. Today, Tiruchirapalli is Tamil Nadu's second largest city.

Dominating the town is the massive **Rock Fort**, perched dramatically on a rocky outcrop that rises 83 m (272 ft) above the flat plains. This impregnable fortress was constructed by the Nayakas of neighbouring Madurai, who made Tiruchirapalli their second capital in the 16th and 17th centuries. They also expanded the Shiva temple, where the god is worshipped as Thayumanavar (the "God who Became a Mother"). Legend says that when a flash flood prevented a mother from coming to her pregnant daughter's aid, Shiva assumed her form and helped in the childbirth. Further up, on the summit, is a small Ganesha Temple from where there are spectacular views of the sacred island of Srirangam.

At the base of the southern rock face is the first of the two cave temples. The lower one dates to the 8th century, and the upper one to the reign of the great Pallava ruler, Mahendra Varman (r.600–630). This contains one of the great wonders of Pallava art, the Gangadhara Panel, depicting Shiva holding a lock of his matted hair to receive the River Ganga as she descends from the heavens *(see p167)*. Much of the present town dates to the 18th and 19th centuries, when the British constructed the cantonment and numerous civic buildings and churches. Many of these buildings are located around the large Teppakulam Tank at the base of the fort – a busy area surrounded by fruit, vegetable and flower markets.

Among the town's earliest churches are Christ Church (1766), founded by Reverend Frederick Christian Schwartz *(see p600)*, to the north of the tank; the Neo-Gothic **Cathedral of Our Lady of Lourdes** (1840), to the west of the tank; and the Jesuit St Joseph's College, also to the west of the tank. In the cantonment, which lies to the southwest of the fort, is the Church of St John (1816).

🏰 Rock Fort
Open daily. ⏷ Extra charges for photography.

The Cathedral of Our Lady of Lourdes at Tiruchirapalli

The Kaveri River

Shrine depicting the legend of Goddess Kaveri

One of the nine sacred rivers of India, the Kaveri covers a length of 785 km (488 miles) from its source at Talakaveri in Karnataka *(see p525)* to Poompuhar on the Bay of Bengal. Myths glorify the Kaveri as the personification of a female deity (in some versions, Brahma's daughter), who erupted from the sage Agasthya's *kamandala* (water pot). From the early centuries of the Christian era, the Kaveri has been central to Tamil culture, especially under the Cholas, who ruled the region between the 9th and 13th centuries. The great temple cities that developed along its course became centres of religion, dance, music and the arts. Farsighted water management schemes in the delta, instigated by the Cholas, transformed the Thanjavur region into the "rice bowl" of Tamil Nadu, and even today, devotees offer rice to the river goddess on the 18th day of the Tamil month Adi (July/August). Unfortunately, the river has now become the subject of a bitter dispute over water distribution between the Tamil Nadu and Karnataka governments.

Environs

At **Kallanai**, 24 km (15 miles) northeast of Tiruchirapalli, is a 300-m (984-ft) long earthen dam across the Kaveri river, the Grand Anicut. This formed part of the huge hydraulic system created by the Cholas (*see pp50–51*) to divert water from the river into a vast network of irrigation canals. The original no longer exists and the dam in operation today was rebuilt by British engineers in the 19th century.

Other places of interest are the 7th-century Shiva temple at **Narthamalai**, 17 km (11 miles) to the south, and the 2nd-century BC Jain cave temples at **Sittanavasal**, 58 km (36 miles) to the southeast. Faded paintings here portray dancing girls, and a lotus tank with swans and fishes.

⓯ Srirangam

Tiruchirapalli district. 9 km (6 miles) N of Tiruchirapalli. 🚌 🛕 Vaikuntha Ekadashi (Dec/Jan), Chariot Festival (Jan).

The sacred 3-km (2-mile) long island of Srirangam, formed by the Kaveri and Kollidam rivers, is one of the most revered pilgrimage sites in South India. At its core is the majestic **Ranganatha Temple** (*see pp556–7*). Dedicated to Vishnu, this is one of the largest temple complexes in Tamil Nadu and covers an enormous area of 60 ha (148 acres).

The complex as it exists today has evolved over a period of four centuries. Extensive reconstruction first took place in 1371, after the original 10th-century temple was destroyed by the Delhi Sultan, Alauddin Khilji (*see p52*). Its present form, however, includes extensions added in the 17th century by the Nayaka rulers, whose second capital was in neighbouring Tiruchirapalli. The last addition was in 1987, when the unfinished southern gateway was finally completed.

Dominated by 21 impressive *gopuras* (gateways), the complex has seven *prakara* (boundary) walls defining its seven enclosures. The outer three comprise residences for priests, hostels for pilgrims, and small restaurants and shops selling religious books, pictures and sundry temple offerings. The sacred precinct begins from the fourth enclosure, beyond which non-Hindus are not allowed. This is where the temple's most important shrines are located. Among these are the spacious Thousand-Columned Mandapa, where images of Ranganatha and his consort are enthroned and worshipped during one of the temple's many festivals, and the magnificent **Seshagirirayar Mandapa**, with its rearing stone horses with mounted warriors

A coracle ride on the Kaveri, Srirangam

attacking fierce animals and *yalis* (mythical leonine beasts). A small museum close by has a good collection of stone and bronze sculptures.

The core of the complex is the sanctum, with its gold plated *vimana*, where an image of Vishnu as Ranganatha, reclining on the cosmic serpent, Adisesha, is enshrined. This temple is also the place where the great 11th-century philosopher Ramanuja (*see p526*) developed the bhakti cult of personal devotion into a formalized mode of worship.

Horse, Seshagirirayar Mandapa

Today, a constant cycle of festivals glorifying Vishnu are celebrated throughout the year.

East of the Ranganatha Temple is the mid-17th-century **Jambukeshvara Temple** in the village of Tiruvanaikka. The main sanctum contains one of the five elemental lingas (*see p588*), representing Shiva as the manifestation of water. Legend says that the linga was created by Shiva's consort, Parvati, and in homage to her, the priest wears a sari when performing the *puja*. Non-Hindus can view the outer shrines in the complex, but not the main sanctum.

🛕 **Sri Ranganatha Temple**
Open daily. **Tel** (0431) 243 2246. 🏛 for viewpoint on top. 📷 Extra charges for photography. Museum: **Open** daily.

🛕 **Jambukeshvara Temple**
Open daily. 📷 Extra charges for photography.

One of the impressive gateways at the Ranganatha Temple, Srirangam

Intricately carved pillars at the Minakshi Sundareshvara Temple, Madurai ▶

Yerikadu Lake, from which Yercaud derives its name

⑯ Yercaud

Salem district. 32 km (20 miles) NE of Salem. 🚉 Salem, then bus. 🚌 ℹ️ Hotel Tamil Nadu, Yercaud Ghat Rd, (04281) 223 334. 🎭 Shevaroyan Temple Festival (May).

This attractive hill station, situated in the Shevaroy Hills, was established in the early 1800s by the British, who introduced the coffee plant here. Today, this is one of the state's most productive areas, and its surrounding slopes are entirely covered with plantations of coffee, tea, jackfruit and plantains.

The man-made **Yerikadu Lake** and the **Killiyur Falls** are two of the area's most scenic spots, while **Lady's Seat**, near the lake, offers delightful views of the surrounding countryside. The town and its environs have several apiaries that produce delicious honey. The **Horticultural Research Station** has an interesting collection of rare plants.

⑰ Mudumalai Wildlife Sanctuary

Nilgiris district. 64 km (40 miles) W of Udhagamandalam. 🚌 Theppakadu, the main entry point. ℹ️ Tourist Office, Theppakadu, (0423) 244 3977. For bookings contact Wildlife Warden's Office, Ooty, (0423) 244 5971. **Open** daily (may be closed during Feb–Mar). 🎫 🎥 Jeeps available. 🏠

Mudumalai or "Ancient Hill Range", situated at the base of the Nilgiri Hills, is separated from Karnataka's Bandipur National Park (see p524) by the Moyar river.

This sanctuary is an important constituent of the 5,500-sq km (2,124-sq mile) Nilgiri Biosphere Reserve of the Western Ghats. Along with adjacent Bandipur and Nagarhole, it provides one of the most important refuges for the elephant and the Indian gaur in India. The park encompasses 322 sq km (124 sq miles) of undulating terrain, and rises to 1,250 m (4,101 ft)

⑱ Tour of the Nilgiris

The picturesque *nila giri* or "Blue Mountains", at the junction of the Eastern and Western Ghats, are so named because the shrub *kurunji (Strobilanthes kunthianus)* turns the hills blue with its blossoms every 12 years. Covered with high altitude grasslands and *sholas* (montane evergreen forests), they are of special interest to botanists and entomologists. This tour offers enchanting glimpses of lush green valleys, hill stations and hamlets inhabited by tribal people.

Jacaranda in full bloom in the Nilgiris

Tips for Drivers

Length: 90 km (56 miles).
Getting around: Avalanche and Pykara can only be reached from Ooty, as there are no road links from Coonoor. The route is well covered by public & private buses. An exciting alternative is the *Nilgiri Blue Mountain Train*, which runs from Mettupalayam to Ooty, via Coonoor (see p753).

⑥ **Pykara**
Dams, fenced *sholas*, green meadows and conical-shaped Toda houses can be seen here.

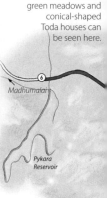

Madhumalai

Pykara Reservoir

⑤ **Avalanche**
This natural paradise has dense forests and a beautiful lake.

| 0 km | 3 |
| 0 miles | 3 |

Makurti Lake

Key

━━ Tour route
═══ Other roads

at Moyar Betta. The lowest point of the sanctuary is at the picturesque **Moyar Waterfalls**. Its topography is as varied as the vegetation, which ranges from dense deciduous forests of teak, laurel and rosewood in the west, to scrub jungle towards the east, interspersed with grassland, swamps and bamboo brakes. The sanctuary provides a habitat for a rich diversity of wildlife, including the Nilgiri tahr *(see p23)*, sambar, tiger, leopard, spotted deer, flying squirrel, Malabar civet and Nilgiri langur. Over 120 species of birds, resident and migratory, can be seen here as well. These include the scops owl and the crested hawk eagle.

⓭ Coimbatore

Coimbatore district. 96 km (60 miles) NE of Chennai. 🚇 924,000. ✈ 10 km (6 miles) NE of city centre, then bus. 🚆 🚌 ℹ Hotel Tamil Nadu, Dr Nanjappa Rd, (0422) 230 2176. 🏨 Mon–Sat. 🎏 Thaipoosam (Jan/Feb), Karthigai (Nov/Dec).

Tamil Nadu's third largest city, Coimbatore is a major industrial centre and the state's commercial capital, with huge textile mills and engineering units. It is also a convenient base for visiting the Nilgiri hill stations. The city has a reputed Agricultural College, and two famous temples. The **Perur Temple** on the Noyyal river and the popular **Muruga Maruthamalai Temple**, on top of a hillock, are dedicated to Lord Shiva and his son, Murugan, respectively. They are visited by thousands of devotees during temple festivals.

The **Siruvani Waterfalls** are beautiful, and Siruvani water famed for its purity and taste.

Guardian Deities

Huge figures made of burnt clay can be seen on the outskirts of villages in the southern districts of Tamil Nadu. They are worshipped as the guardians of the villages. The most prominent folk deity is Ayyanar, also known as Ayyappa, the son of Shiva and Vishnu. This mustachioed god, with prominent eyes, wears short trousers and carries a sword. His horse stands by his side so that he can ride through the night, keeping evil spirits at bay. Other deities are Munisami, who holds a trident and shield and rides a lion, and the black-hued Karuppusami, the nocturnal avenger who punishes thieves.

Guardian deities outside a village shrine

---

① Ooty
Officially known as Udhagamandalam, this Queen of Hill Stations was originally inhabited by the Todas *(see p611)*. The century-old Blue Mountain Train terminates here.

② Dodda Betta
The highest peak in the Nilgiris (2,623 m/8,606 ft) has fantastic views of the hills, valleys and plateaux.

③ Kotagiri
Known for its salubrious climate, this hill station is situated in the shadow of Dodda Betta Peak.

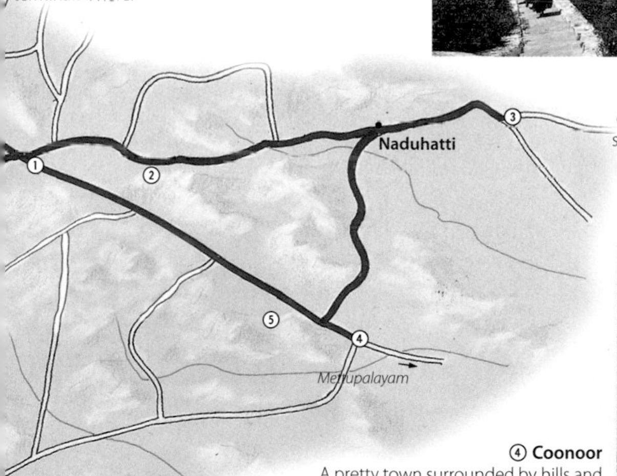

Naduhatti

Mettupalayam

④ Coonoor
A pretty town surrounded by hills and tea and coffee plantations, Coonoor hosts an annual fruit and vegetable show in May, at Sim's Park.

Tree-lined avenue in Kodaikanal

they created a sanatorium-cum-retreat here. They also established Kodai's International School in 1901.

This picturesque town is today spread out around the man-made, star-shaped **Kodai Lake**, created by the dam built by Sir Vere Henry Levinge in 1863. The 3-km (2-mile) long trail around the lake makes for a pleasant walk. On the shore is a Boat House, built in 1910. East of the lake is **Bryant Park**, famous for its plant collection (including over 740 varieties of roses) and its annual flower show, held in May.

Beyond the city centre are a number of scenic areas, such as Pillar Rocks, Silver Cascade and Green Valley View (originally known as Suicide Point), which offer enchanting picnic spots and views of the deep valley. Kodai also has many opportunities for cycling, riding and long, rambling walks. A trail following the hillside, called **Coaker's Walk**, provides a panoramic view of the hill station. The walk ends at the Church of St Peter, built in 1884, which has fine stained-glass windows. Nearby is a small **Telescope House**.

Some 3 km (2 miles) northeast of the lake is the **Kurunji Andavar Temple**, dedicated to Murugan. It is named after the amazing *kurunji* flowers *(see p653)*, associated with the god. The Chettiar Park nearby, laid out along the hillside, is where the *kurunji* blooms every 12 years.

⑳ Palani

Madurai district. 120 km (75 miles) NW of Madurai. ✈ Madurai, 119 km (74 miles) SE of town centre, then bus or taxi. 🚌 🚐 🚆 Thaipoosam (Jan/Feb), Karthigai (Nov/Dec).

A major pilgrimage centre, Palani is situated on the edge of the great Vyapuri Tank. Its hilltop **Subrahmanyam Temple** is the most famous of the six abodes of Murugan, the son of Shiva, who is said to have come here disguised as a mendicant after quarreling over a fruit with his brother, Ganesha. Popularly known as Dandayutha Pani ("Bearer of the Staff"), Murugan is depicted with a clean shaven head, holding a stick. His image is made of medicinal herbs, mixed together to create a wax-like substance. During the Thaipoosam festival, the temple attracts thousands of pilgrims, many of whom shave their heads as an expression of devotion. An electric cable car takes devotees up the 600 steps to the hill shrine.

Palani is also a base for hikes in the surrounding hills.

㉑ Kodaikanal

Madurai district. 120 km (75 miles) NW of Madurai. 🚌 Palani, 65 km (40 miles) N of town centre, then bus or taxi. 🚐 𝒊 Tamil Nadu Tourism, (04542) 241 675. 🕐 Mon–Sat. 🎉 Summer Festival (May), Flower Show (May), Winter Festival (Dec). 🏊

Lush green valleys, terraced plantations and a pleasant climate make Kodaikanal one of Tamil Nadu's most popular hill stations. Kodaikanal, or Kodai as it is commonly called, was first "discovered" by American missionaries in the 1840s. Drawn by its bracing climate and clean environs,

Religious offerings for sale in Palani

Hiking in the Nilgiris

Short excursions around Ooty offer many opportunities to explore the Nilgiris *(see pp608–609)* on foot. There are scenic trails in the grasslands around Mukurthi, an extinct volcano known to the Todas as the "Gateway to the Dead",

Waterfall in the Nilgiris

and in the windswept Avalanche region, which consists of rolling, grassy downs, *shola* trees and rhododendrons. The western edge of this region falls away into the dense tropical jungles of Kerala. The eastern half of the range, largely deprived of the Southwest Monsoon, is dominated by dry scrub and volcanic rock.

The Todas

The Nilgiris are home to 18 tribal groups, among whom the Todas are the most remarkable. A pastoral community, the Todas are wheatish in complexion, curly haired, and are strict vegetarians. Their language, though of Dravidian origin, has no script. According to their creation myth, Goddess Teikirshy and her brother On first created the buffalo by waving a magic wand, and then created the Toda man. The first Toda woman was created from the right rib of the man. The Todas' first contact with civilization occurred when the East India Company annexed the Nilgiris in 1799. In 1823, John Sullivan, the then Collector of Coimbatore, built the first stone house in Ooty on land purchased from the Todas. Today, there are only about 1,100 Todas left.

The dairy temple, conical in shape, is decorated with sun, moon, serpent and buffalo head motifs. Only men are allowed to go inside.

Toda buffaloes, pale brown with long horns, are deeply revered. A buffalo is often sacrificed after a funeral to accompany the deceased's soul in the afterlife.

Homespun cotton shawls called *puthikuzhi* have black-and-red embroidered motifs. Worn by both Toda men and women, they are tied around the waist, with one end thrown over the shoulder, almost like a Roman toga.

Elders are treated with great respect, and greeted by lifting their right foot and putting it on one's head for their blessings.

Dairy ceremonies are festive occasions, generally celebrated with dance and music. The lively songs consist of simple stanzas, describing important events from the Todas' past.

The barrel-shaped huts, made of bamboo, grass and cane, consist of a single room. Entry is through a carved wooden door, so small that one has to crawl through it to enter. Several of these windowless bamboo huts make up a Toda village, which is called a *mund*.

㉒ Madurai

One of South India's great temple towns, Madurai is synonymous with the celebrated Minakshi Temple *(see pp614–15)*. This ancient city on the banks of the Vaigai river has, over the centuries, been a rich repository of Tamil culture. Some 2,000 years ago, it hosted the famous Sangams (gatherings of writers and poets), which were to provide Tamil literature with some of its most enduring works. From the 7th to 13th centuries, as the capital of the Pandyas, it saw art and trade with Rome and China flourish. It later became part of the Vijayanagar Empire, and was the Nayaka capital in the 16th–17th centuries. Today, religion and culture remain a vibrant part of the city's daily life.

The grand pillared hall in the Thirumalai Nayakar Palace

🏛 Minakshi Sundareshvara Temple
See pp614–15.

🏯 Thirumalai Nayakar Palace
1.5 km (1 mile) SE of Minakshi Temple. **Open** daily. 🎭 Son et Lumière: (English): 6.45pm, daily. 🎭

The power and wealth of the Nayakas is evident from the remains of this once grand palace, built by Thirumalai Nayaka in 1636. The building, with its interesting Islamic influences, was partially restored in the 19th century by Lord Napier, governor of Madras between 1866 and 1872. Today, only the spacious rectangular courtyard called the Swarga Vilasam ("Heavenly Pavilion")

and a few adjoining buildings survive, their awesome scale evoking the grandeur of a vanished era. The courtyard measures 3,900 sq m (41,979 sq ft), and is surrounded by massive circular pillars. To its west lies the Throne Chamber, a vast room with a raised, octagonal dome. This room leads to the Dance Hall, which now houses a display of archaeological objects.

🏯 Theppakulam
E of Minakshi Temple. **Open** daily. ⛴
Madurai's great tank is another marvel attributed to Thirumalai Nayaka. The square tank has steps, flanked by animal- and bird-shaped balustrades, leading down to the rippling

waters. This is the venue of the annual Theppam (Float) festival, celebrating the marriage of Shiva and Minakshi, when their images are taken in illuminated boats to the small pavilion in the centre of the tank.

🏛 Koodal Alagar Temple
1 km (0.6 miles) SW of Minakshi Temple. **Open** daily. **Closed** to non-Hindus.

One of the 108 sacred Vaishnavite shrines, this glorious temple has three superimposed sanctuaries, of diminishing size, housing Lord Vishnu. From bottom to top, the images show Vishnu in the seated, standing and reclining position. The outer wall has beautiful sculptures and stone screens.

⛪ Anglican Cathedral
Off W Masi St. **Open** daily.
A fine example of Neo-Gothic architecture, this church was designed by Robert Fellowes Chisholm *(see p573)*, and consecrated in 1881.

🕌 Tombs of the Madurai Sultans
N of the Vaigai river. **Open** daily.
The sultans of Madurai ruled the city after the invasion in 1310 by Malik Kafur, a general of Alauddin Khilji *(see p52)*. They lie buried to the north of the city. The complex includes Alauddin's Mosque, with its flat-roofed prayer hall and tapering octagonal towers, and the tomb of a local Sufi saint, Bara Mastan Sada, built in the 16th century.

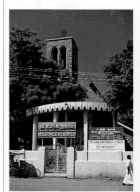

Entrance to the Anglican Cathedral at Madurai

A mural depicting a scene from the *Ramayana*, Alagarkoil Temple

VISITORS' CHECKLIST

Practical Information
Madurai district. 498 km
(309 miles) SW of Chennai.
923,000. *i* Tourist Office,
West Veli Road, (0452) 233 4757.
Mon–Sat. Theppam
Festival (Jan/Feb), Avanimoolam
(Aug/Sep), Navaratri (Sep/Oct).

Transport
12 km (7 miles) S of city
.

Environs

Thiruparankundram, 6 km
(4 miles) southwest of Madurai,
is a small town known for its
sacred granite hill. Regarded as
one of the six sacred abodes of
Murugan, the son of Shiva, the
hill was the site of his marriage
to Devayani, the daughter of
Indra. There is a rock-cut temple
here, built by the Pandyas in
the 8th century. The temple is
approached through a series
of 17th- and 18th-century
mandapas, at ascending levels,
linked by stone steps. The
entrance *mandapa* has typical
Nayaka period pillars with horse
and *yali* riders, while portraits of
Nayaka rulers are carved on the
columns. The temple's main
sanctum contains five shrines.

The 14-day temple festival,
in March/April, celebrates the
victory of Murugan over the
demon Suran, his coronation,
and his subsequent marriage
to Devayani.

The temple at **Alagarkoil**, 21
km (13 miles) north of Madurai,
is dedicated to Kallalagar, a form
of Vishnu who is regarded as
Minakshi's brother. According
to legend, when Kallalagar went
to give his sister in marriage
to Sundareshvara, he stayed
on the banks of the Vaigai river
during the ceremony. This event
is celebrated every year, in
April/May.

On the summit of the hill
is Palamudircholai, the last of
the six abodes of Murugan,
marked by a shrine, while
further away is Nupura Ganga,
a perennial spring, used for
all rituals in the temple, and
believed to have emerged
from Vishnu's ankle.

Madurai City Centre

① Minakshi Sundareshvara Temple
② Thirumalai Nayakar Palace
③ Koodal Alagar Temple
④ Anglican Cathedral

0 metres 500
0 yards 500

Madurai: Minakshi Sundareshvara Temple

This enormous temple complex is dedicated to Shiva, known here as Sundareshvara (the "Handsome God"), and his consort Parvati or Minakshi (the "Fish-eyed Goddess"). Originally built by the early Pandyas (7th–10th centuries), it was extensively added to by succeeding dynasties, especially between the 14th and 18th centuries. The temple complex is within a high-walled enclosure, at the core of which are the two sanctums for Minakshi and Sundareshvara, surrounded by a number of smaller shrines and grand pillared halls. Especially impressive are the 12 *gopuras*. Their soaring towers rise from solid granite bases, and are covered with stucco figures of deities, mythical animals and monsters, painted in vivid colours.

Guardian Deities
Fierce monster images, with protruding eyes and horns, mark the arched ends of the vaulted roofs, and serve as guardian deities.

Gopura

Pyramidal gates (gopuras) rise to a height of more than 50 m (164 ft). These towering gateways indicate the entrance to the temple complex at the four cardinal points, while lesser gopuras lead to the sanctums of the main deities.

Stucco Work
The figures of deities on the tower are repaired, repainted and ritually reconsecrated every 12 years.

Openings in the middle of the long sides allow light to enter the hollow chambers at each level.

The profusely carved pillars of the Thousand-Pillared Hall

Exploring the Minakshi Temple

The temple is entered from the eastern side through the **Ashta Shakti Mandapa** or the "Hall of Eight Goddesses", with sculpted pillars representing the various aspects of the Goddess Shakti. Next to this hall is the **Minakshi Nayaka Mandapa**, a spacious

columned hall used for shops and stores. This hall has a votive lamp-holder with 1,008 lamps, which are lit on festive occasions and present a spectacular sight.

The adjacent seven-storeyed **Chitra Gopura**, is the tallest tower in the complex. Next to it is the **Potramarai Kulam**, or "Golden Lotus" Tank, with steps leading down to the water. It is surrounded by pillared corridors that once bore

Kalyana Sundara, Vishnu giving Minakshi to Shiva

paintings from the Vijayanagar period. To the west of this tank is the **Minakshi Shrine**, one of the two main shrines, comprising two concentric corridors and many halls and galleries. Here lies the bed to which Minakshi's "husband", in the form of Sundareshvara's image, is brought every night from his own shrine, the **Sundareshvara Shrine**, which stands to the

north. The god resides in this, the second main shrine, amid columns that bear the fish motifs emblematic of his wife. The 16th-century "Flagpole Hall" or **Kambattadi Man-dapa**, in front of this shrine, has a pavilion with a seated Nandi, a gilded flagpole and ornately carved pillars depicting the 24 forms of Shiva. To its east is the **Thousand-Pillared Hall** with 985 beautifully decorated columns. Dating to the 16th century, this hall is now a museum, which displays bronze and stone images. A set of pillars, a marvel in stone, produce the seven notes of Carnatic music. The **Kalyana Mandapa**, to the south of the pillared hall, is where the marriage of Shiva and Parvati is celebrated every year during the Chitirai Festival in mid April.

Pudumandapa, the 100-m (328-ft) long "New Hall" with portrait sculptures of the Nayaka rulers, is outside the main temple complex. Built by Tirumalai Nayaka in 1635, it now houses a market selling saris, jewellery and spices.

Minakshi Sundareshvara Temple Complex

1 Ashta Shakti Mandapa
2 Minakshi Nayaka Mandapa
3 Chitra Gopura
4 Potramarai Kulam
5 Minakshi Shrine
6 Sundareshvara Shrine
7 Kambattadi Mandapa
8 Thousand-Pillared Hall
9 Kalyana Mandapa

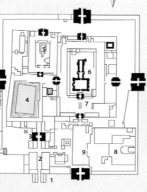

0 metres 100
0 yards 100

The Potramarai Kulam, surrounded by a colonnade

Chettiar Mansions

The arid region encompassing the towns of Karaikudi, Devakottai and their neighbouring villages, collectively known as Chettinad, is distinguished by large ornate mansions which are the ancestral homes of the Chettiars, Tamil Nadu's rich merchant community. Like the Marwaris of Shekhavati *(see pp376–7)*, the Chettiars were astute businessmen who travelled far to make their fortunes. The wealth they acquired in Burma, Sri Lanka, Malaysia, and Vietnam was used to build these elaborate mansions. Today, the Chettiars are prominent bankers and industrialists based in Chennai and Bengaluru.

Chettiar Houses

Built in the early 20th century, these houses reflect the social, ritual and kinship needs of the community, as well as its economic status. Though now unoccupied for most of the year, they are still used for family celebrations.

The splendid Chettinad Palace, Kanadukathan

A long verandah with wooden pillars leads to a series of open courtyards, surrounded by rooms to accommodate the growing family.

The first pillared hall, where each pillar is made from an entire tree trunk of Burma teak, is reserved for the men of the house to receive guests and conduct business.

The formal reception room has marble floors, stained-glass windows, painted cornices, teak and rosewood furniture and ornate chandeliers.

Elaborate marble floors, well-polished doorways, carved wooden beams, granite pillars, and other decorative elements in a Chettiar house display the skills of the Tamil craftsmen.

Intricately carved wooden doorway

㉓ Chettinad

Chettinad district. 82 km (51 miles) NE of Madurai. 🚌 🚐 🏠 daily. 🎭 Bullock Races (Jan/Feb).

Karaikudi, the heart of the Chettinad area, has several temples, including the 7th-century **Pillaiyarpati Temple** dedicated to Lord Ganesha. It also has fine Chettiar mansions, and antique shops stocked with treasures from these mansions. Chettinad is famous for its hot, spicy, non-vegetarian cuisine – pepper chicken is one of the most popular dishes. The food is prepared in copper vessels and served on plantain leaves.

㉔ Ramanathapuram

Ramanathapuram district. 117 km (73 miles) SE of Madurai. 🚹 62,000. 🚌 🚐 🏠 daily. 🎭 Urs at Erwadi Dargah (Dec).

This ancient town is associated with the Setupatis, local rulers who rose to prominence in the late 17th century under the Madurai Nayakas. They derived prestige and income by controlling the isthmus that led to Rameshvaram island. A century later, their rule came to an end when they surrendered to the East India Company in 1792.

To the west of the present town is the palace complex of the Setupatis. Though little remains, the 17th-century **Ramalinga Vilas**, on the north side of the palace complex, still has well-preserved wall paintings. These depict the epics as well as battle scenes, business transactions and royal ceremonies. The upper chambers depict more private royal scenes, such as family gatherings, music and dance recitals, and hunting expeditions. A small shrine, facing north, is dedicated to the family goddess of the Setupatis, Rajarajeshvari. It stands immediately south of the Ramalinga Vilas.

On the outskirts of the town is the 400-year-old **Erwadi Dargah**, housing the tomb of Ibrahim Syed Aulia, a Muslim saint. It attracts devotees from all over India, as well as from Sri Lanka,

The longest corridor at Ramanathaswamy Temple, with sculpted pillars

Malaysia and Singapore during its annual festival in December.

㉕ Rameshvaram

Ramanathapuram district. 163 km (101 miles) SE of Madurai. 🚹 38,050. 🚌 🚐 ℹ️ Tourist office, East Car Street, (04573) 221 064. 🎭 Ramalinga (Jun/Jul).

A major pilgrimage site, the sacred island of Rameshvaram juts out into the Gulf of Mannar, the narrow body of water separating Tamil Nadu from Sri Lanka.

The **Ramanathaswamy Temple**, in the middle of the island, is dedicated to Shiva. It houses the linga that Lord Rama, the hero of the epic *Ramayana (see p31)*, is said to have installed and worshiped after his victory against Ravana in Lanka. Founded by the Chola rulers but expanded extensively during the Nayaka period,

Devotees taking a dip in the holy waters of the Agni Tirtha

in the 16th to 18th centuries, this massive temple is enclosed within a high wall with five *gopuras*. The most remarkable feature of this temple is the **Sokkattan Mandapa**, so called because it resembles a *sokkattan* (dice) in shape. It surrounds the core of the temple on four sides in a continuous corridor, and is the largest and most elaborate of its kind, with 1,212 pillars extending 197 m (646 ft) from east to west and 133 m (436 ft) from north to south. The complex also has a staggering 22 *tirthas* (tanks) for ritual ablutions; it is believed that a dip in the Agni Tirtha, in front of the temple, removes all sins. The installation ceremony of the linga by Rama and Sita is celebrated every year.

Standing on **Gandamadana Hill**, the highest point of the island, 3 km (2 miles) northwest of the Ramanathaswamy Temple, is a two-storeyed *mandapa* that is said to shelter the footprint of Rama.

Dhanushkodi ("Rama's Bow"), the southern-most tip of Rameshvaram, about 18 km (11 miles) from the main temple, has a spectacular beach. From here, a series of boulders, known as Adam's Bridge, or Rama Setu can be seen extending far into the horizon. These are believed to be the ruins of a bridge constructed by Lord Rama's *varnara sena* (army of monkeys) after Hanuman reported Sita's captivity in Ravana's Palace. The Kodandarama Temple, on the shore, is said to be where Ravana's brother, Vibeeshna was coronated. Miraculously, the temple survived a devastating cyclone in 1964.

❷⑥ Tuticorin

Tuticorin district. 148 km (92 miles) S of Madurai. 🚇 1,750,176. 🚉 🚌 🎎 Golden Chariot Festival (Aug).

This is Tamil Nadu's second largest natural harbour, and the main port of call for ships from Southeast Asia, Australia and New Zealand. Tuticorin is also a major industrial centre with thermal power stations, spinning mills and salt extraction units.

The city's other important commercial activity is pearl fishing. Since the early centuries of the Christian era, this region's pearls have been in demand throughout the world. Ancient Tamil literature mentions a flourishing trade with the Romans, who bought Tuticorin pearls in exchange for gold and wine.

Today the government, which has set up a society of divers, strictly regulates pearl fishing, in order to protect the oyster beds – sometimes pearl fishing is allowed only once in ten years. The pearl fishers still use traditional methods, diving to a depth of up to 70 m (230 ft) without oxygen to extricate the pearls. Most divers can remain underwater for more than a minute; their only safeguard against accidents or natural danger is to dive in pairs.

Tuticorin was occupied by the Portuguese in the 17th century and later by the Dutch and the British. Its colonial past is visible in two elegant churches, the Dutch **Sacred Heart Cathedral**, built in the mid-18th century, and the beautiful 17th-century **Church of the Lady of the Snows**, built by the Portuguese.

Corridor of the Kanthimathi Nellaiyappar Temple, Tirunelvelli

❷⑦ Tiruchendur

Tuticorin district. 210 km (130 miles) S of Madurai. 🚉 🚌 from Madurai, Tirunelvelli, Tuticorin & Nagercoil. 🎎 Annual Temple Festival (Jun/Jul).

This beautiful coastal town, one of the six sacred abodes of Shiva's son, Murugan *(see p610)*, has the impressive **Subramanyam Temple**. Dating to the 9th century, it was renovated in the 20th century. The temple, entered through the towering Mela *gopura*, is built on a rocky promontory overlooking the Gulf of Mannar, and provides lovely views. On the seashore there are many caves and rock-cut sculptures.

Environs
Manapad, 18 km (11 miles) south, has one of the oldest churches in India, the Church of the Holy Cross. Built in 1581, it preserves a fragment of the "True Cross", brought from Jerusalem. An annual festival held every September attracts pilgrims from all over the region. St Francis Xavier visited this coastal village in 1542.

❷⑧ Tirunelvelli

Tirunelvelli district. 154 km (96 miles) SW of Madurai. 🚉 🚌 *i* Tamil Nadu Tourism, Tirunelvelli Junction, (0462) 250 0104. 🎎 Chariot Festival (Jun/Jul).

Situated in the fertile tract by the Tamaraparani river, Tirunelvelli is dominated by the **Kanthimathi Nellaiyappar Temple**, parts of which date to the 13th century. This complex of twin temples, dedicated to Shiva and Parvati, has two huge rectangular enclosures connected by a long corridor. The Shiva temple is to the north, while the Parvati temple is to the south. The elaborate *mandapas* here include the Somavara Mandapa, which contains two pillars carved like *gopuras*; the Rishaba Mandapa, with exquisitely carved sculptures of Manmatha, the God of Love, and his consort Rathi; and the Mani Mandapa, with a set of stone pillars that produce the melodic notes of Carnatic music *(see p599)* when tapped.

Every summer, the temple's wooden chariots are led in procession through the town during the annual Chariot Festival, which attracts thousands of devotees.

Environs
Courtallam (Kuttalam) Falls, at an elevation of 170 m (558 ft), are 59 km (37 miles) northwest of Tirunelvelli. This picturesque spot is famed for its exotic flora and the medicinal properties of its waters.

The Church of the Holy Cross in Manapad

Sthanumalaya Temple at Suchindram, overlooking the temple tank

㉙ Suchindram

Kanniyakumari district. 247 km
(154 miles) S of Madurai. 🚉 Nagarcoil,
5 km (3 miles) NW of town centre,
then bus. 🚌 🎭 Arudhra Festival
(Dec/Jan).

This small temple town is
closely linked with the legend
of Kumari, the Virgin Goddess
(an incarnation of Parvati). It is
believed that Shiva rested at this
quiet spot by the banks of the
Pelayar river, while the goddess
Kumari performed her penance
at Kanniyakumari.

Suchindram's unique
Sthanumalaya Temple is
dedicated to the Hindu Trinity
of Brahma, Vishnu and Shiva.
The rectangular complex has
enormous, brightly coloured
gopuras dating from the
17th–18th centuries, which
depict stories from the great
epics *(see pp30–31)*. One of the
two main shrines, built in the
13th century, contains the
Sthanumalaya linga, which
symbolizes Brahma, Vishnu
and Shiva. The other is
dedicated to Vishnu, whose
image is made of a special
kind of jaggery and mustard.

The temple also boasts a set
of musical pillars made from
single blocks of granite. When
tapped, each pillar produces a
different musical note. Other
highlights are a 5-m (16-ft) high
statue of Hanuman placed
opposite the Rama shrine, and
the exquisite sculptures in the
Vasantha Mandapa. A special
puja is held here every Friday
evening, with music and a
procession. In the complex is
an ancient banyan tree, and a
sculpture of Shiva's bull, Nandi,
which locals believe actually
continues to grow.

㉚ Kanniyakumari

Kanniyakumari district. 235 km (146
miles) S of Madurai. 🚉 19,700. 🚉 🚌
ℹ️ Tamil Nadu Tourism, Beach Rd,
(04652) 246 257. 🎭 Chaitra Purnima
(Apr), Navaratri (Sep/Oct).

The southernmost tip of the
Indian subcontinent, where the
Indian Ocean, the Arabian Sea
and the Bay of Bengal meet,
Kanniyakumari enchants visitors
with its spectacular views,
especially at sunrise and sunset.
The most breathtaking of these
occurs on Chaitra Purnima (the
full moon night in April) when
both sunset and moonrise
occur at the same time.

Kanniyakumari is believed
to be the abode of Kumari, the
Virgin Goddess, who is supposed
to have done penance here so
that she could marry Shiva. The
marriage, however, did not take
place, since it was deemed that
she remain a virgin in order to
save the world. Her temple,
the **Kumari Amman Temple**, a
popular pilgrimage centre on
the seashore, was built by the
Pandya kings in the 8th century
and was extensively renovated
by the Chola, Vijayanagar and
Nayaka rulers. A magnificent

structure, the temple has a
Navaratri Mandapa with a
beautifully painted panel of
Mahishasuramardini (Durga
killing the demon Mahisha). An
18th-century shrine within the
temple contains the footprints
(sripadaparai) of the goddess
Kumari, who performed her
penance at this spot.

The **Gandhi Memorial**, near
the temple, is where Mahatma
Gandhi's ashes were kept before
immersion. The building is
designed so that every year
on October 2nd (Gandhi's
birthday), at midday, the rays
of the sun fall on the exact spot
where his ashes were placed.

Just off the coast, on a rocky
island, the **Vivekananda
Memorial** marks the spot where
the great Indian philosopher,
Swami Vivekananda *(see p290)*
meditated before attending
the World Religious Conference
in Chicago in 1893. Near the
memorial is the imposing
40-m (131-ft) high statue of
Tiruvalluvar, the 1st-century BC
Tamil poet, who wrote the epic
Tirukural, often referred to as
one of the greatest classics
of Tamil literature.

The **Church of Our Lady
of Joy**, which was founded by
St Francis Xavier in the 1540s,
is located at the southern edge
of the town. Other attractions
include the sandy beaches
and the multi-coloured
granite rocks.

🏯 **Kumari Amman Temple**
Open daily. **Closed** Sanctum
closed to non-Hindus.
🏛️ **Vivekananda Memorial**
Open Wed–Mon. 🚫 🚢 every 30 min.

The beach at Kanniyakumari with its three memorials

ANDAMAN ISLANDS

An archipelago of 572 idyllic islands in the Bay of Bengal, about 1,000 km (620 miles) from the mainland, the Andamans and the neighbouring Nicobar Islands are actually the peaks of a submerged mountain range which extends from Myanmar to Indonesia. They encompass three distinct ecosystems – tropical forests, mangroves and coral reefs, which support a staggering variety of plant and animal life. Foreign visitors require a permit *(see p734)*, and are not allowed on the Nicobar Islands. Many parts of the Andamans, too, are off-limits, to preserve their rare biodiversity and protect the six tribal groups, some of whom are fiercely independent. Their hostility was probably the reason why Marco Polo described the islands as being inhabited by cannibals. The Andamans acquired the sinister name Kala Pani ("Black Waters") in the 19th century, when the British established a penal colony here. The islands were severely hit by the tsunami waves in December 2004. Their permanent population includes migrant Indians, Bangladeshis, Sri Lankans and Karens from Myanmar. The surrounding reefs are ideal for water sports.

Sights at a Glance

Towns & Villages
1 Port Blair
5 Chidiya Tapu

Islands
3 Ross Island
6 Cinque Island
7 Ritchie's Archipelago
8 Middle Andaman
9 North Andaman

National Parks
2 Mount Harriet National Park
4 Wandoor Marine National Park

Key
— National highway
— Major road
— Minor road
--- Ferry route

0 kilometres 100
0 miles 100

◀ Children playing near the Havelock Island jetty

For keys to symbols *see back flap*

An aerial view of the capital, Port Blair

❶ Port Blair

South Andaman Island. 1,190 km
(739 miles) E of Chennai. 🚹 100,200.
✈ 3 km (2 miles) S of town centre,
then bus or taxi. 🚌 ℹ Govt of India
Tourist Office, Junglighat Rd, (03192)
236 348; Department of Information,
Publicity and Tourism (INPT), (03192)
232 694. Travel permits: required for
the Andaman Islands *(see p734)*. 📷
Island Tourism Festival (Dec/Jan).
🌐 andamans.gov.in

The capital, Port Blair, is located
to the southeast of South
Andaman Island. The town is a
base from which to
travel around the
archipelago, and is
well equipped with
hotels, banks, tour
operators and sports
complexes.
   The town's
tumultuous history
began in 1789, when
Lieutenant Archibald
Blair of the British
East India Company
conducted a survey
to identify a safe
harbour for the Company's
vessels. He chose the site of what
is now Port Blair. Fifty years later
the islands became a penal
colony. Those incarcerated were
political activists involved in the
Indian Mutiny of 1857 *(see p57)*;
by 1864, the number of prisoners
had grown from 773 to 3,000. In
1896, the construction of the
Cellular Jail began; it soon
became an infamous symbol of
colonial oppression. Designed
specifically for solitary confine-
ment, it earned the Islands the
dreaded name of Kala Pani or

A row of tiny cells,
Cellular Jail

"Black Waters", reflecting the
atrocities that awaited the
prisoners. It remains Port Blair's
most prominent landmark.
   Of the original seven wings
laid out around a central
watchtower, only four remain;
three have been converted into
a hospital and are lined with
cells, each 3 by 3.5 m (10 by 11
ft) in size. Daily rations consisted
of two cups of drinking water
and two cups of rice. Executions
were frequent and many were
made to undergo hard labour.
Japanese troops, who occupied
the Islands during
World War II,
destroyed part of the
prison. In 1945, the
British moved back,
re-established their
headquarters at Port
Blair and closed
the jail. It is now
a memorial to the
political prisoners;
a moving sound and
light show is held
here every evening.
The town's other
places of interest are scattered
around Aberdeen Bazaar, on
the east side of town. The
Anthropological Museum, west
of the bazaar, sheds light on the
islands' tribal inhabitants and has
a collection of rare photographs
taken in the 1960s. The Aquarium,
also known as the **Fisheries
Museum**, at the eastern end of
MG Road, displays hundreds of
species of unusual fish, corals
and shells. Next door, the
Andaman Water Sports Complex
hires out row boats, jet skis and
paddle boats. The **Samudrika**

Marine Museum, run by the
Indian Navy, has five galleries
devoted to the history, geography
and anthropology of the Islands,
and has a superb display on marine
life. The tiny zoo at Haddo has
successfully bred saltwater
crocodiles and returned them
to the wild.
   Chatham Sawmills on Chatham
Island, 5 km (3 miles) north, is one
of the oldest and largest saw mills
in Asia. Established by the British
in 1836, this is where many of
the Islands' fast disappearing
species of trees, including the
towering *padauk* (Andaman
redwood), are processed.

Environs
The nearest beach from Port Blair
is the crescent shaped **Corbyn's
Cove**, 6 km (4 miles) south of the
capital. **Viper Island**, named after
a 19th-century British shipping
vessel that was wrecked off its
shore, can be reached via a cruise
from Port Blair. Its sinister history
involves the local prison, built in
1867, whose macabre gallows and
torture posts can still be seen.
Only daytime visits are allowed
as the island has no inhabitants.
About 14 km (9 miles) from Port
Blair lies **Sippyghat Farm**, where
many varieties of spices and
indigenous plants and shrubs
are grown.

🏛 **Cellular Jail**
Open 8:45am–12:30pm, 1:30–5pm
Tue–Sun. Son et Lumière: 6pm &
7:15pm daily (Hindi); 7:15pm Mon,
Wed, Fri (English). 📷

The day's catch, a boatful of fresh fish,
clams and crayfish

🏛 **Anthropological Museum**
Tel (03192) 232 291. **Open** Fri–Wed.
Closed Mon & public hols.

🏛 **Fisheries Museum**
Tel (03192) 231 848. **Open** 9am–1pm,
2–4:45pm. **Closed** 2nd Sat of month,
Wed & public hols. 🖼

🏊 **Andaman Water
Sports Complex**
Tel (03192) 232 694.
Open daily.

🏛 **Samudrika
Marine Museum**
Tel (03192) 248 327 (ext. 2437).
Open Tue–Sun. 🖼

Chatham Sawmills
Open 8:30am–2:30pm Mon–
Sat, mornings are best. 🖼

❷ Mount Harriet National Park

South Andaman Island. 70 km
(44 miles) N of Port Blair. 🚌 From
Chatham Wharf or Phoenix Bay
Jetty (Fisheries Jetty) in Port Blair to
Bamboo Flats Jetty, then taxi to park
entry point. Tickets for day visits
are available at entrance. 🖼

Some of the Andamans'
highest peaks are in Mount
Harriet National Park, lying
across the inlet from Phoenix
Jetty in Port Blair. Mount
Harriet, at 365 m (1,198 ft),
is surrounded by evergreen
forests that support a
remarkable biodiversity,
predominantly birds such
as the great black
woodpecker and the
green imperial pigeon.
Well-marked hiking
trails include the 2-km
(1-mile) walk to
Kalapathar, and the
16-km (10-mile) trail
to Madhuban Beach,
where elephants are
trained for lumbering.
Beware of leeches
during the monsoon.
    The **Forest Guest
House**, on top of Mount
Harriet, offers fine views
of Port Blair and Ross
Island. Visits and overnight
stays are possible with
permission from the
Chief Conservator of
the Forest, (03192) 230
152 or 233 270.

❸ Ross Island

Ross Island. 2 km (1 mile) E of Port
Blair. 🚢 from Aberdeen Jetty. Travel
permits: required for the Andamans
(see p734). Only day trips allowed.

A short ferry ride from Port
Blair leads to Ross Island, which
served as the administrative
capital for most of the
Andaman Islands from 1858
until 1941. Ross Island's
history, however, is
much older, for it
was the home of the
indigenous Great
Andamanese *(see p627)*.
Within 20 years of British
occupation, diseases

Orchid

such as syphilis and measles
virtually wiped out the tribe,
whose numbers dropped from
5,000 to just 28. Ross Island
was also the base for the British
administrators of the penal
colony in Port Blair, and was
equipped with swimming pools
and bungalows. In 1941, the
Japanese converted the site
into a POW camp, and built war
installations, remnants of which
can still be seen. It now lies
deserted, and the few signs
of its colonial glory, such as the
chief commissioner's house
and the Anglican church, are
dilapidated and overgrown. The
area is now under the Indian
Navy, whose museum, Smritika,
records the lives of those
imprisoned here.

The rare Narcondam hornbill

Snorkelling and Scuba Diving

Snorkelling, a popular way to explore
marine life

Snorkelling
Snorkels can be hired out
for around ₹100 per day from
numerous tour operators.
Popular venues are Corbyn's
Cove, Wandoor, Chidiya Tapu,
Neil and Havelock Islands.

Scuba Diving
There are several registered
dive centres on Havelock
Island. Andaman Bubbles,
(03192) 282 140, is well
established, and charges
₹3,000 for a couple of dives
near Port Blair, ₹3,500 for
areas further than Wandoor.
It also runs diving courses.
Andaman Dive Club, (09474)
224 171, also offers diving
courses. In addition, Gold
India, (993322384) and
Barefoot Scuba (9474263120)
are also registered diving
centres on the island. The
Andaman Scuba Club, also
on Havelock Island, is a
pretty resort on the beach.
www.andamanscubaclub.com

Eco-friendly Diving
Coral reefs are sensitive
and even the gentlest touch
can kill them. It is important
that you avoid touching or
treading on them, and be
careful with your fins. Practise
descending into the sea
before the actual dive, as
descent is often too fast,
leading to collision with
reefs. Do not use anchors
near reefs.

❹ Wandoor Marine National Park

Created in 1983 to preserve the tropical ecosystems of 15 uninhabited islands in the Andamans, the Mahatma Gandhi Marine National Park at Wandoor stretches over 281 sq km (108 sq miles). It encompasses myriad lagoons, bays, coral reefs, rainforests and mangrove creeks. Ferries from Wandoor village skirt lagoons with kaleidoscopic sea beds, and are often chased by schools of playful dolphins. Most of the islands are protected and thus inaccessible; however, their coasts reveal a fascinating transition from towering tropical canopies to stilted mangroves. The only islands that allow visits are Jolly Buoy Island (open 15 Nov–15 May), which is ideal for snorkelling, and Redskin Island (open May–Nov), with a well-marked nature trail. Unfortunately, the 2004 tsunami caused widespread destruction of coral reefs in Jolly Buoy.

Types of Coral
Corals are of two broad types – either hard or soft. The colourful soft coral has no outer skeleton.

Angelfish
The angelfish is one of the reef's most vividly coloured fish. Its bright hues help to camouflage it as well as to advertise its territory.

Lion or Scorpion Fish
Measuring up to 40 cm (16 in), this ornate fish has deadly venom in its rays, which can be fatal for humans.

Giant Robber Crab
One of the largest and rarest crabs in the world, its powerful claws help it to climb trees such as the coconut palm, and break the hard shell of its fruit.

Grouper Fish
Among the most commonly found species, groupers can change their colour to match the rocks and surrounding reefs.

The Coral Reef
Referred to as rainforests of the sea, the multi-coloured reefs are delicate ecosystems that support an amazing variety of marine life (see p651), and over 200 species of coral.

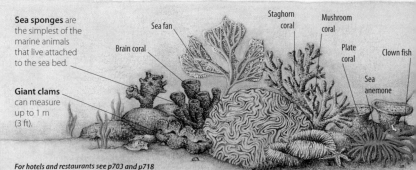

Sea sponges are the simplest of the marine animals that live attached to the sea bed.

Giant clams can measure up to 1 m (3 ft).

Sea fan

Brain coral

Staghorn coral

Mushroom coral

Plate coral

Clown fish

Sea anemone

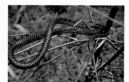

Green Tree Snake
One of the 40-odd species found here, this harmless snake has no fangs and eats reptiles and frogs.

VISITORS' CHECKLIST

Practical Information
South Andaman Island. 29 km (18 miles) SW of Port Blair.
Chief Wildlife Warden, Van Sadon, Haddo, Port Blair, (03192) 233 270. For tours to Jolly Buoy & Redskin islands, (03192) 232 694.
Open daily, subject to weather. Best time: Dec–Mar. Forest Lodge has 4 suites. Snorkelling & scuba diving.

Transport
from Wandoor village.

Gurjan trees make up the emergent layer, which towers above the canopy at 60 m (197 ft).
Padauk, or Andaman redwood, grows up to 36 m (118 ft).
The second layer, known as the canopy, with trees such as the *padauk*, absorbs most of the sunlight.
Orchids
Bamboo
Toung Pienne tree
Pandanus forms part of the understorey layer.
Ferns
Mushrooms

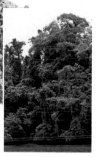

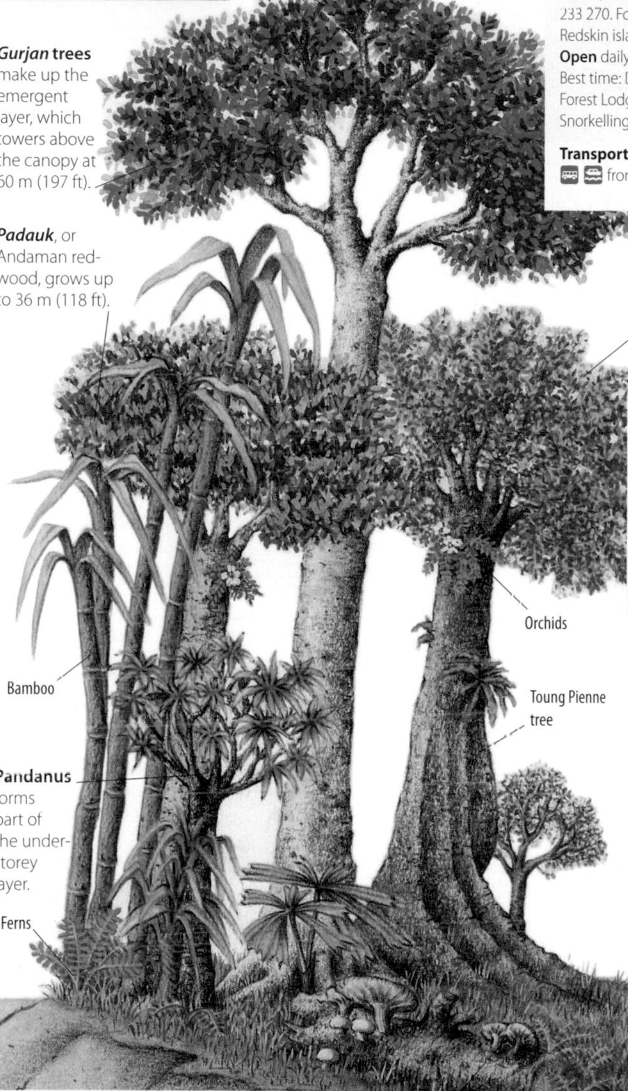

Tropical Rainforest

The multi-layered tropical rainforests include giant trees such as the gurjan and padauk, a rich undergrowth of epiphytes and climbers, and over 120 species of ferns.

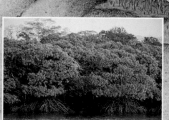

Mangroves
Dense mangrove forests grow along the waterlogged creeks of Wandoor's islands, and support a variety of fauna such as snakes, crabs, crocodiles and waterfowl.

A boat gliding across the glass-like surface of a lagoon, Andamans

❺ Chidiya Tapu

South Andaman Island. 25 km (15 miles) S of Port Blair. 🚌 🚢 from Port Blair. Taxis available from Port Blair.

The fishing village of Chidiya Tapu ("Bird Island"), at the southern-most tip of South Andaman Island, is an hour's drive from Port Blair. Its white beaches, skirting a large bay, make it a popular day trip with visitors.

Forest trails through the surrounding tropical undergrowth are a birdwatcher's delight, as they teem with a vast variety of species, including rare sunbirds, kingfishers, woodpeckers and eagles. Its beaches, especially the picturesque **Munde Pahar Beach**, are excellent for snorkelling, and there are good camping facilities as well. The forest department is setting up a biological park, to house the animals from Port Blair's zoo (see p622).

❻ Cinque Island

Cinque Island. 39 km (24 miles) S of Port Blair. 🚢 motor boats from Port Blair & Wandoor, ferries from Chiriya Tapu. Travel permits: required for the Andamans (see p734). Only day visits are allowed.

The volcanic Cinque Island is perhaps the most beautiful of the entire Andamans group, as it has had little human interference over the years and is mostly uninhabited. Comprising two islands, North and South Cinque, connected by a sand bar, it was declared a sanctuary in 1987. The surrounding reefs of rare coral and varied marine life offer

some of the best snorkelling and scuba diving in the Andamans. The sandy shores are also among the last refuges of the hawksbill and green sea turtles, which nest here annually in their hundreds.

Environs
Tiny groups of islands known as the **Sisters** and the **Brothers**, lying 12 km (7 miles) and 32 km (20 miles) south of Cinque respectively, can be visited only with a professional diving group. Large tracts of the remote southern island of **Little Andaman**, 120 km (74 miles) and eight hours by ferry from Port Blair, are a reserve for the 119 surviving members of the Onge tribe. It is not advisable to try and make contact with them. Part of northern Little Andaman is open to visitors.

A hermit crab digging a temporary home

Little Andaman
🚢 check website for schedule.
🌐 **www.and.nic**

❼ Ritchie's Archipelago

The group of islands lies between 20 km (12 miles) & 40 km (25 miles) E of South Andaman. 🚢 from Port Blair & Rangat Bay (Middle Andaman), Long Island: 6:15am Mon, Wed & Sat from Port Blair, 7:15am Tue, Thu, Sun return to Port Blair. Travel permits: required for the Andamans (see p734).

This cluster of tiny islands is for the most part protected as a national park to preserve its remarkable biodiversity. Only three islands are open to visitors, and they are connected to Port Blair by ferry daily; note that ferries to Long Island do not operate on Thursdays and Sundays.

Neil Island, 36 km (22 miles) northeast, is the closest to the capital and is inhabited by settlers from Bengal. The interior is lush with paddy fields and plantations; the island is the region's main producer of fresh fruit and vegetables. The beaches offer superb snorkelling opportunities.

Havelock Island, 54 km (34 miles) northeast of Port Blair, is the most popular among visitors. MV Makruzz (www.makruzz.com) runs a daily catamaran to the island, which is well equipped, with guesthouses and a well-stocked bazaar. Coastal cruise (www.coastalcruise.in) also offers boats. Try out the tented accommodation on Radhanagar Beach, at the western tip of the island, where dolphins, dugongs and turtles can be spotted from the long

A colourful sea fan and a grouper fish

Elephants, indispensable to the islands' lumber trade

stretches of white sand. The elephants found on the island were originally brought here to work the timber trade. Bikes and scooters are available and are the best way to explore.

The northernmost island in the archipelago, **Long Island**, 82 km (51 miles) north of Port Blair, attracts few visitors, perhaps because of the six-hour journey to get there. It nevertheless has attractive beaches. There is just one rest house and virtually no public transport available, although bicycles can be hired. North Passage Island, 55 km (34 miles) south of Port Blair, has a beautiful white sandy beach at Merk Bay.

A vividly coloured local pineapple

Environs
Barren Island, 132 km (82 miles) northeast of Port Blair, has the only active volcano in India. After lying dormant for nearly 200 years, it erupted twice at the end of the 20th century, In 1991 and 1994. Rising sharply from the sea, its enormous crater continues to spew smoke. The island is now a wildlife sanctuary. There is no public ferry service and only chartered ferries make the 20-hour journey from Port Blair. Landing on the island is not permitted, so divers are the only visitors, drawn by the rich marine life.

Indigenous Tribes

Until the 18th century, the Andaman and Nicobar Islands were inhabited by 12 distinct groups of aboriginal tribes. Now, overwhelmed by the immigrant population and threatened by disease and loss of land, their numbers have fallen from 5,000 to just 800. The Mongoloid Nicobarese and Shompen tribes of the Nicobars probably migrated from Myanmar, while the origins of the four Negrito tribes, the Jarawas, Great Andamanese, Onges and Sentinelese, continue to baffle anthropologists. Of these, only the largest – the Nicobarese – have partially integrated into the mainstream, while the Onges and the Great Andamanese, now increasingly dependent on subsidies, live in tribal "reserves". The Sentinelese from North Sentinel Island, are still hostile, fending off strangers with showers of arrows. The Shompens of Great Nicobar are as wary of outsiders. Most tribal groups survived the December 2004 tsunami, by following their own early warning systems. As the last representatives of truly independent indigenous peoples, perhaps their only chance of survival remains in self-imposed isolation.

A Jarawa tribesman

❽ Middle Andaman

Middle Andaman Island. 170 km (106 miles) N from Port Blair to Rangat. 🚢 from Port Blair. Travel permits: required for the Andamans (see p734).

This is literally the middle island among the Andamans trio. Large tracts of its interior are part of the highly protected Jarawa Tribal Reserve. The Jarawas, traditional hunter-gatherers, are probably the last racially pure tribe left in India. The Andaman Trunk Road winds along the island's spine, running from Port Blair through Bharatrang Island, famous for its mud volcano and limestone caves, to Middle Andaman. With the welfare of the Jarawas in mind, there is restricted public transport. The area around **Rangat** is lush with tropical forests; the town itself has only a few provision stores. **Rangat Bay** is the point of departure for ferries to Port Blair and Havelock and Long Islands. Just 15 km (9 miles) away, **Cuthbert Bay** is a sanctuary for hundreds of marine turtles, which arrive here annually to nest. **Mayabander**, at the northern tip, 71 km (44 miles) from Rangat, is a beautiful spot. Some of its beaches, such as **Karmatang**, are famous for their spectacular sunrises, and are also nesting grounds for marine turtles.

❾ North Andaman

North Andaman Island. 290 km (180 miles) N from Port Blair to Diglipur. 🚢 from Port Blair. Travel permits: required for the Andamans (see p734).

North Andaman is the least populated of the three large islands. **Diglipur**, in the northeast, is one of the few places with accommodation. It is known for its beaches – in particular, Ram Nagar and Kalipur – and also has the islands' highest peak, **Saddle Peak** (737 m/2,418 ft), which is a national park. A scenic trail leads to the peak's summit.

From **Aerial Bay**, 9 km (6 miles) northeast of Diglipur, one can visit Smith and Ross Islands (see p623).

KERALA

Nestling between the Western Ghats and the Arabian Sea, Kerala is an enchanting mosaic of coconut groves and paddy fields, wide beaches and labyrinthine backwaters, verdant hills and rainforests. Its diverse culture is enriched by the three great religions that have ancient roots here. Hinduism is the religion of the majority, practised here with a rare rigour that prohibits non-Hindus from entering most temples. Christianity, followed by a quarter of the population, was brought here by the Apostle St Thomas, while Islam was introduced by Arab traders in the 7th century. The architectural treasures of the state include the beautiful wooden palace at Padmanabhapuram, stately colonial buildings and a 16th-century synagogue in Kochi. This politically conscious state, where power alternates between Left and Centrist parties, boasts the highest literacy rate in India. Many of its people work in the Middle East, their remittances home adding greatly to Kerala's prosperity.

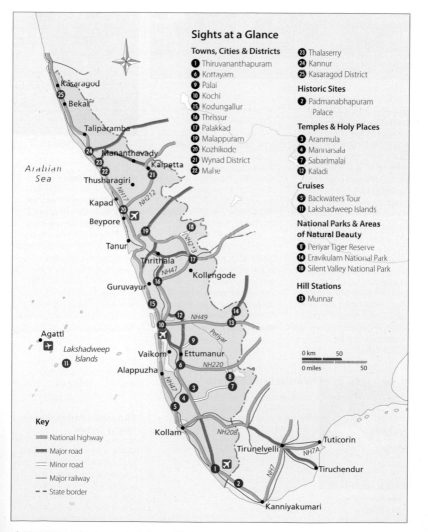

Sights at a Glance

Towns, Cities & Districts
1. Thiruvananthapuram
6. Kottayam
9. Palai
10. Kochi
15. Kodungallur
16. Thrissur
17. Palakkad
19. Malappuram
20. Kozhikode
21. Wynad District
22. Mahe
23. Thalaserry
24. Kannur
25. Kasaragod District

Historic Sites
2. Padmanabhapuram Palace

Temples & Holy Places
3. Aranmula
4. Mannarsala
7. Sabarimalai
12. Kaladi

Cruises
5. Backwaters Tour
11. Lakshadweep Islands

National Parks & Areas of Natural Beauty
8. Periyar Tiger Reserve
14. Eravikulam National Park
18. Silent Valley National Park

Hill Stations
13. Munnar

Key
- National highway
- Major road
- Minor road
- Major railway
- State border

◀ A houseboat moored on the enchanting backwaters of Kerala

For keys to symbols *see back flap*

❶ Thiruvananthapuram

Kerala's capital, known until 1991 as Trivandrum, was the seat of the former royal family of Travancore from 1750 to 1956. The magnificent Anantha Padmanabhaswamy Temple has given the city its name, Thiruvananthapuram – literally the "Holy City of Anantha", the sacred thousand-headed serpent on whom Vishnu reclines. Built across seven hills, the city's old quarter clusters around the temple, while along busy Mahatma Gandhi Road are colonial mansions, churches and modern high-rises.

The Napier Museum, built in the 19th century

🏛 Government Arts and Crafts (Napier) Museum

Museum Rd. **Closed** Mon, (Wed am) & public hols for all museums. 📷 covers all museums. Kanakakunnu Palace: **Tel** (0471) 231 4615.

Located in a well-planned compound is a complex of museums and the city's zoo. The Government Arts and Crafts Museum, earlier known as the Napier Museum after John Napier, a former governor of Madras, is in a red-and-black brick Indo- Saracenic structure, designed by Robert Fellows Chisholm *(see p573)* in the 19th century. It exhibits a rare collection of bronzes, stone sculptures, exquisite ivory carvings and a temple chariot, all fashioned in the territories of the former kingdom of Travancore.

To the north of the Museum, is the **Shri Chitra Art Gallery**, housed in a beautiful building that incorporates the best elements of local architecture. The pride of its collection are the works of Raja Ravi Varma (1848–1906) and his uncle Raja Raja Varma, both pioneers of a unique academy style of painting in India. Raja Ravi Varma was considered the finest Indian artist of his time, and his mythological paintings have inspired the popular religious prints found in many Indian homes. The **Natural History Museum**, to the east, has a fine replica of a typical Kerala Nair wooden house, *naluketu*,

detailing the principles of its construction.

The **Kanakakunnu Palace**, where the Travancore royal family once entertained their guests, is adjacent to the complex, on top of a hill.

A short drive down the road from the complex leads to Kowdiar Junction, a round-about of walls and ornate railings facing the Kowdiar Palace, the former maharaja's official residence.

A painting by Raja Ravi Varma in Sri Chitra Art Gallery

Mahatma Gandhi Road

The city's main road runs from the Victoria Jubilee Town Hall to the Anantha Padmanabha-swamy Temple. Among the many impressive buildings that line this road are the Secretariat, headquarters of the state government, the University College and the Public Library. The latter, founded in 1829, has a collection of more than 250,000 books and documents in Malayalam, Hindi, Tamil and Sanskrit. To the north, beyond the charming Connemara Market, are the Jama Masjid, St Joseph's Cathedral and the Neo-Gothic building of Christ Church.

🏯 Anantha Padmanabha-swamy Temple

Fort area. **Tel** (0471) 246 4606. **Closed** to non-Hindus. Special rules for clothing apply *(see p738)*.

Located within the fort that encircles the old town, this is the only temple in the state with a towering seven-storey *gopura*, commonly seen in

---

Kalarippayat practice, CVN Kalari Sangham

Martial Arts of Kerala

Constant warfare in the 11th century gave rise to *kalaripayattu*, Kerala's martial arts. From it emerged two streams – the *chavverpada*, suicide squads, and the *chekavan*, warriors who fought duels to the death, in order to settle the nobility's disputes. Students learn to use weapons such as swords, spears, daggers, the *urumi*, (a flexible metal sword) and wooden poles. In the final stage, the student is taught how to defeat an opponent by applying pressure to nerve points.

The imposing *gopura* of the Anantha Padmanabhaswamy Temple

Tamil Nadu's temple architecture. The restrained ornamentation, however, is typical of Kerala. A flagstaff encased in gold stands in the huge courtyard. The main corridor, which runs around four sides of the courtyard, has 324 columns and two rows of granite pillars, each embellished with a woman bearing a lamp (*deepalakshmi*). The hall also has mythological animals, sculpted with rotating stone balls in their jaws. Rich murals adorn the outer walls of the inner shrine, where the 6-m (20-ft) long reclining Vishnu resides, with his head towards the south and feet towards the north.

🏛 Kuthiramalika Palace Museum

Fort area. **Open** Tue–Sun. 📷 Extra charges for photography. 🎞 📸 Carnatic Music Festival (Jan/Feb).

This interesting museum (also known as Puthen Malika) is housed in an 18th-century palace, built by Raja Swathi Thirunal Balarama Varma, a statesman, poet, musician and social reformer. A fine example of Kerala architecture, this wooden palace has a sloping tiled roof. The wood carvings are particularly noteworthy, especially the 122 horses lining the eaves of the building. On display are various artifacts from the royal collection, including a solid crystal throne given by

the Dutch, and another carved out of the tusks of 50 elephants.

🏛 CVN Kalari Sangham

East Fort area. **Tel** (0471) 247 4182. **Open** Mon–Sat. 📷 🎞

This training centre for *kalaripayattu* was established in 1956 to revive Kerala's martial arts tradition. Each morning, students collect at the gymnasium (*kalari*) to perform a series of exercises that will help them develop the necessary combat skills. The centre also has a shrine to the deity of martial arts, Kalari Paradevata, and an Ayurvedic clinic where students are given oil massages.

Thiruvananthapuram City Centre

① Government Arts and Crafts (Napier) Museum
② Mahatma Gandhi Road
③ Anantha Padmanabhaswamy Temple
④ Kuthiramalika Palace Museum
⑤ CVN Kalari Sangham

For keys to symbols *see back flap*

Exploring Thiruvananthapuram's Environs

Thiruvananthapuram is the gateway to the southern tip of India. South of the city, along the Lakshadweep Sea, are many beach resorts, the most famous of which is Kovalam. The Padmanabhapuram Palace *(see pp634–5)*, the former residence of the Travancore kings, is to the southeast, while to its north and east are tranquil hill stations located picturesquely in the densely forested Cardamom (Ponmudi) Hills. Thiruvananthapuram also houses many important institutions, including the meteorological station, which performs the task of plotting the arrival of the Southwest Monsoon. The city is also one of Kerala's main centres of Ayurveda.

A young boy flaunts his catch, Kovalam Beach

Lighthouse Beach, one of the many idyllic beaches in Kovalam

🚉 Kovalam
Thiruvananthapuram district. 16 km (10 miles) S of Thiruvananthapuram. 🚌 *i* Tourism Office, (0471) 248 0085.

Until the 1960s, Kovalam was just a sleepy fishing village with narrow lanes and thatched dwellings with wide courtyards for drying fish. However, once its spectacular beach and shallow, crystal clear waters were discovered, it became a favourite with hippies and backpackers, and over the years acquired the reputation of being a shabby, downmarket resort. Today, however, it also attracts the rich and famous, who come here in private planes. As a result, the beaches are dotted with both luxury and budget resorts, as well as cafés and several government-approved Ayurveda centres that offer anything from a simple massage to three-week treatments. Hawkers, too, have set up stalls selling

handicrafts and inexpensive beachwear. Despite the onslaughts of mass tourism, Kovalam retains an inherent charm that makes it one of India's finest and most popular beach resorts.

Kovalam's sheltered natural bay is ringed by two rocky headlands. Its three beaches – Grove Beach, Eve's Beach and Lighthouse Beach, all within short walking distance of each other – provide visitors with their fill of sun, sea and sand. While the beaches to the south of the promontory are more crowded, the ones to the north offer ample secluded space for sunbathing, safe swimming in the placid blue waters, catamaran trips, and water sports.

🚉 Varkala
Thiruvananthapuram district. 40 km (25 miles) N of Thiruvananthapuram. 🚌 *i* Tourist Information Centre, near the helipad.

This beautiful little beach town is better known among locals as a major pilgrimage centre. According to legend, the sage Narada flung a cloth made from the bark of a tree into the air, and it landed at the spot where the small town of Varkala now stands. Narada then directed his disciples to pray for salvation at the newly created beach, which came to be known as Papanasham Beach or the "Beach of Redemption". Since then, this beach has been associated with ancestor worship, as Hindus immerse the ashes of their dead here.

At the heart of the town is the sacred **Janardhana Swamy Temple**, believed to be more than 2,000 years old. This temple, dedicated to Krishna, attracts many pilgrims. One of the bells in the temple is said to have been given in gratitude by the captain of a 17th-century Dutch sailing ship, after his prayers were answered. Varkala's other pilgrimage centre is the hilltop **Memorial of Sree Narayana Guru** (1855–1928) at Sivagiri, 3 km (2 miles) east of the temple. Every day, countless devotees flock to the memorial of this great saint and social reformer who advocated "one caste, one religion, one god for

Bananas and other fruit on sale, Varkala

A view of the long sandy beach at Varkala

mankind". With its backdrop of red laterite cliffs overlooking the beach, Varkala has now emerged as a popular resort and spa. The town is famous for its natural springs with therapeutic qualities, and is also a centre for Ayurvedic treatment and yoga. To the south is the desolate Anjengo Fort, the main garrison of the Dutch East India Company in the 17th and 18th centuries.

🎋 Ponmudi

Thiruvananthapuram district. 61 km (38 miles) NE of Thiruvananthapuram. 📷 *i* Government Guest House, (0472) 289 0230.

Ponmudi, literally "Golden Crown", rises to a height of 915 m (3,002 ft) from the base of a thick tropical forest. Surrounded by tea estates and forested hills, this hill station is still unspoilt, refreshingly cool and mist shrouded for most of the year. Its narrow winding paths and verdant environs offer pleasant walks. Wild flowers grow in abundance on the banks of gurgling brooks, adding to the charm of this peaceful place.

🎋 Agasthyarkoodam

Thiruvananthapuram district. 60 km (37 miles) NE of Thiruvananthapuram. Trekking permits: Contact the Office of the Wildlife Warden, Thiruvananthapuram, (0471) 236 0762.

At an elevation of 1,890 m (6,201 ft), Agasthyarkoodam is the highest peak in southern Kerala. It forms part of the Western Ghats and the Agasthyavanam Forest, designated a sanctuary in 1992.

The mountain is revered by both Buddhists and Hindus, as it is believed to be the abode of the Bodhisattva Avalokitesvara (*see p145*), as well as of the sage Agastya, a disciple of Shiva. Women are not allowed here. The hills are rich in medicinal herbs, and harbour many species of birds and wildlife. Trekking to the top – a distance of 28 km (17 miles) – takes two days and is permitted only between December and April. The summit provides fine views of the lake created by the Neyyar Dam.

Festivals of Kerala

Vishu (*Apr*). The first day of the Malayali New Year is celebrated with zest throughout the state. It is believed that looking upon a group of auspicious objects at dawn ensures a year of peace and prosperity.

Thrissur Pooram (*Apr/May*), Thrissur. The highlight of this festival is the ceremonial procession of two *devis* (goddesses) on caparisoned elephants to the Vadakunnathan Temple. The parasols held above the elephants are changed in an exciting synchronized ritual, accompanied by *chendamelam*, an orchestra of percussion instruments. A display of fireworks marks the climax.

Onam (*Aug/Sep*). The most popular of Kerala's festivals. It honours Mahabali, a selfless ruler whose subjects were so content that envious gods tricked him into losing his life and kingdom. His last wish was to visit his people once a year to ensure that they were happy. During Onam, an aura of plenty is created to gladden Mahabali's heart. Great feasts are prepared, new clothes worn, and courtyards are decorated with floral patterns (*athapookkalam*). The Nehru Trophy Boat Race (*see p40*) is held at this time.

Caparisoned elephants and musicians, Thrissur Pooram

Ayurveda Therapy

A classical text on medicine, the *Ashtangahridaya*, is the foundation of Ayurveda in Kerala. Its author, Vagbhata, was the disciple of a Buddhist physician, and received little recognition in the rest of India. It is believed that a few Nampoothiri (Brahmin) families were the original Ayurvedic physicians, and their descendants still carry the honorific title of *ashtavaidyan*. Today, this holistic science of healing is practised throughout India. However, the Kerala method is famous for its five-pronged treatment, *panchakarma*, in which medicated oils, herbs, milk, massage and a special diet are used to cure all types of ailments.

Ayurvedic treatment in progress

❷ Padmanabhapuram Palace

Set amid lush hills, verdant paddy fields and perennial rivers, Padmanabhapuram Palace is the finest example of Kerala's distinctive wooden architecture. Laid out in a sequence of four adjoining walled compounds, comprising public and private zones, the palace has richly carved wooden ceilings, sculpted pillars, slatted windows, and pagoda-like tiled roofs. From 1590 to 1790, Padmanabhapuram was the home of the the former princely state of Travancore, which straddled parts of present-day Tamil Nadu as well as Kerala. By some quirk of fate, this beautifully kept palace now falls in Tamil Nadu but is maintained by the government of Kerala.

Detail from a carved rosewood door

★ Prayer Hall
The prayer hall, on the third floor of the King's Palace, has exquisite murals on its walls. A medicinal bed here, carved from 64 different types of wood, was a gift from the Dutch.

Entrance Hall
The entrance hall has a profusely carved wooden ceiling with 90 different inverted flowers, a polished granite bed and an ornate Chinese throne.

KEY

① **Main Gate** to the palace complex entrance is reached after crossing a large courtyard. This gate has a decorated gabled roof.

② **The clock tower's** chimes could be heard from a distance of 3 km (2 miles).

③ **The Lady's Chamber** houses two large swings, a pair of enormous Belgian mirrors and a royal bed.

④ **The Bath House** is a small airy room, where the male members of the royal family were given a massage before they descended, down covered steps, to a private tank to bathe.

⑤ **The dining hall**, laid out over two storeys, could seat 2,000 guests.

⑥ **The palace museum** houses artifacts including furniture, wooden and granite statues, weapons and utensils.

Entrance

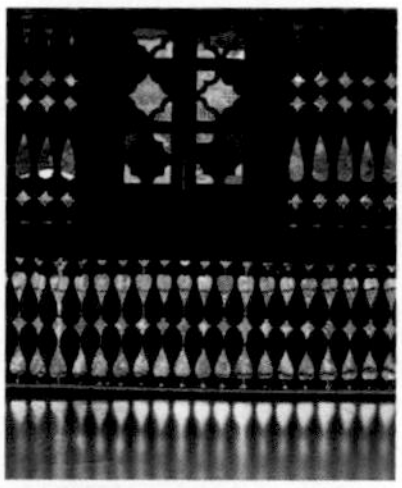

Carved bay window for watching processions

VISITORS' CHECKLIST

Practical Information
Tamil Nadu state. Kanniyakumari district. 52 km (32 miles) SE of Thiruvananthapuram.
Tel (04651) 250 255.
Open Tue–Sun. Extra charges for photography.

Transport

Guest house
4
5
0 metres 20
0 yards 20

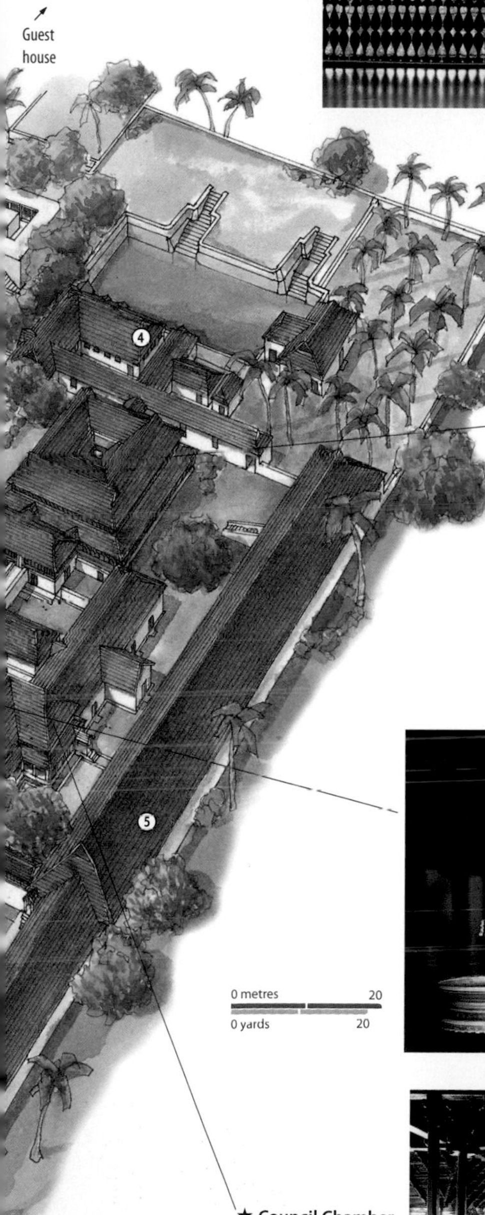

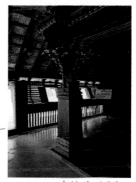

★ Mother's Palace
Built in 1550, this is the oldest building in the complex. It contains intricately carved wooden pillars fashioned from the wood of the jackfruit tree. The floor was polished to a red gloss with hibiscus flowers.

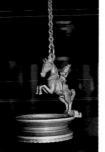

Lamp
A horse lamp (the horse is a symbol of valour) in the entrance hall, hangs suspended from a special chain that keeps the lamp perfectly balanced.

★ Council Chamber
The king's council chamber has wooden louvres to let in light and air. The gloss on the floor was achieved with a mixture of lime, sand, egg white, coconut water, charcoal and jaggery.

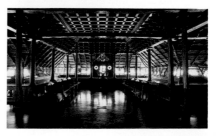

An elephant being led down the steps of Aranmula's Parthasarthy Temple

❸ Aranmula

Pathanamthitta district. 125 km (78 miles) NW of Thiruvananthapuram. **i** (0468) 232 6409. 🚌 🚤 from Alappuzha. 🚣 Onam Boat Regatta (Aug/Sep).

This picturesque village on the banks of the Pampa river is famous as the venue for Kerala's magnificent snake boat races. The boat race festival has its origins in the legend of a devotee who once gave food to a Brahmin, believed to be Vishnu in disguise. However, the Brahmin, before disappearing, advised him to send his offering to Aranmula instead. Since then, during the festival, a ceremonial boat, carved out of a single block of wood, carries a consignment of food from a nearby village to the temple at Aranmula. On the last day of Onam *(see p663)*, this ceremonial boat leads a procession of about 30 snake boats to the temple. On this day, there is no racing and all the boats arrive together, as Krishna is said to be present on each boat at the same time.

The **Parthasarathy Temple**, one of the state's five most important temples, is dedicated to Krishna, and has an image of the god as Parthasarathy, the Divine Charioteer in the great epic, the *Mahabharata*. The image was brought here on a raft made of six bamboos, and this is what the town's name signifies – in Malayalam *aaru* means six and *mula*, bamboo.

Aranmula is also known for its unique metal mirrors made from an alloy of silver, bronze copper and lead. These mirrors were traditionally used as part of the arrangement of auspicious objects during Vishu, the Malayali New Year, in April *(see p633)*.

Environs

The 14th-century **Thiruvamundur Temple**, near Chengannur, 7 km (4 miles) west of Aranmula is dedicated to Krishna and attributed to Nakul, one of the five Pandava brothers *(see p30)*. Near Chenganacherry, 27 km (17 miles) northwest of Aranmula, is the **Tirukkodittanam Temple**. This 11th-century temple is dedicated to Sahadev, Nakul's twin brother, and has lovely murals adorning its walls. It is a temple vibrant in traditional art and music.

Metal mirror, Aranmula

❹ Mannarsala

Alappuzha district. 132 km (82 miles) NW of Thiruvananthapuram, (0479) 241 3788. 🚌 🚤 Thulam (Oct/Nov).

The custom of worshipping snakes in Kerala reaches a climax at Mannarsala, the best known of the four main Naga temples in the state. According to legend, a woman from a family of great Naga devotees gave birth to two sons, one of whom was a serpent-child, who asked his family to worship him and vanished. The temples at Mannarsala, dedicated to the King of Snakes, Nagaraja, and his consort, Sarpayakshini, are situated in a thick grove of tall trees and dense bushes, surrounded by thousands of hooded stone serpents of various styles and sizes.

In Kerala, the ancestral home *(tharavad)* of every upper-class Namboothiri and Nair family is supposed to have a *sarpa-kavu* or snake-grove, housing a *nagakal* or snake stone. If a *tharavad* cannot afford to maintain its own shrine, the snake stones are offered to this temple.

The holy rites at Mannarasala are conducted by a priestess *(amma)*, a vestal virgin, who lives on the premises and is supported in her religious duties by her family.

Childless couples place a bell metal vessel *(uruli)* face down in front of the deities, to seek their blessings.

Sacred Serpent Shrines

In Kerala, the sacred serpent plays a significant role in belief and ritual. Malayali folklore speaks of a wooded, rural land inhabited mainly by Nagas (snakes) – the Lords of the Underworld – who were overthrown by the Brahmin settlers brought here by Parasurama *(see p683)*, the sixth incarnation of Vishnu. This mythological incident is the origin of snake worship in Kerala since, after their defeat, Parasurama ordered that snakes be accorded divine status. Most temples thus have a niche for a snake god, amid dense sacred groves of ancient trees. The old ancestral homes *(tharavads)* also have private temples or groves for a snake deity.

Sacred grove with snake *(naga)* images, Mannarsala Temple

Boats of Kerala

Kerala's ancient boat-building industry is a specialized part of its rich wood-working tradition, that also includes architecture *(see p642)*. Boats built at Beypore *(see p657)* were highly prized and used by Arab merchants. The construction of a boat is always begun on an auspicious day in the Malayalam calendar, and is marked by an invocation to the gods. The most sought-after wood is *anjili (Artocarpus hirsuta)*, though teak is also used. Racing boats of various sizes and shapes participate in the annual Onam regatta at Aranmula. Of these, the most magnificent is the long, narrow *chundanvallam*, or snake boat.

Boat Building

A master craftsman, assisted by a team traditionally drawn from different religions, builds the boat. No nails or metal pieces are used; only wooden pegs and joints hold the parts together.

Snake Boat Races

Snake boats (chundanvallam), once used to carry warriors, now participate in what is believed to be the world's largest team sport. The Nehru Trophy Boat Race (see p40), introduced in 1952, is the most famous.

Rowing is perfectly synchronized to the pulsating rhythm of *vunchipattu* (boatmen's songs). Their themes are devotional, mythological, or related to rural life.

The prow of the boat is normally manned by four boatmen.

Oarsmen

Singers

Amaram, the stern, is decorated with brass studs and inlay work.

Kettuvallams are now often converted into houseboats. *Kettu* means a bundle, while *vallam* is a big boat. Originally, these were used as ferries or to carry rice.

Canoes, usually made from a single log of wood, can carry no more than one or two people. They are commonly used to transport light cargo, such as coir fibre.

❺ Backwaters Tour

A cruise along the backwaters is one of the most enchanting experiences that Kerala offers. Exploring this labyrinthine network of waterways, which weave through villages set amidst lush vegetation, offers glimpses of Kerala's unique rural lifestyle, where land and water are inseparable. The most popular backwaters tour is from Kollam (Quilon), situated between Ashtamudi Lake and the Arabian Sea, to Alappuzha (Alleppey) on the edge of Vembanad Lake. The choice of transport ranges from local ferries and speedboats to *kettuvallams (see p637)*.

Locator Map

Water hyacinths are the cause of a serious ecological problem since untamed growth has clogged the waterways of Kuttanad, the rice bowl of Kerala.

Children going to school by boat are a common sight. Various types of boats are used as transport along the backwaters, connecting the small villages with the mainland.

Coconut palms fringe the waterways. In addition to coconuts, rice is cultivated extensively in Kuttanad, the area between Kottayam and Alappuzha.

Houses along a canal have jetties with moored boats. The ground and water levels are often equal, which makes flooding a problem during the monsoon.

Coconut Lagoon is a wonderful resort on Vembanad Lake, near the bird sanctuary in Kumarakom.

Toddy tappers are expert at scaling coconut palms. The local brew, made from fermented coconut palm sap, is sold in shacks along the waterways. The first brew is light and delicious – however, potency levels rise with subsequent fermentation.

Tips for Passengers

Route 1: Kollam to Alappuzha
Dep: 10:30am. Maximum
Duration: 8 hrs. *i* District
Tourism Promotion Council
(DTPC), Kollam, (0474) 274 5625.
Route 2: Alappuzha to Kollam
Dep: 10:30am. Maximum
Duration: 8 hrs. *i* DTPC,
Alappuzha, (0477) 225 3308.
For more details, see p757.

Chinese fishing nets along the backwaters are used to trap fish. A popular fish in Kerala, *karimeen* (pearl spot), is found in these waters.

Children with banana trunks playing in the water

Backwaters

According to legend, Parasurama, the sixth incarnation of Vishnu, created Kerala by throwing his battle axe into the sea. The abundance of canals, lagoons and lakes in the state seem to reinforce this legend of a land born from the sea.

In this coir-producing village, women beat the husk and spin the fibre to make ropes or floor coverings. The fibre is often dyed to create brightly coloured mats with geo-metric designs.

Coconut husks soak in the shallow waters near the banks. This softens the husks before they are beaten to produce the fine fibre that is turned into coir. The flesh is converted into oil, or used in cooking.

6 Kottayam

Kottayam district. 160 km (99 miles) N of Thiruvananthapuram. 🚇 1,974,551. 🚍 🚌 *i* District Tourist Promotion Council, (0481) 256 0479. 🎭 Drama Festival (Jan).

Enclosed by the blue waters of Vembanad Lake and the paddy fields of Kuttanad to its west, and by the lush hills of the Western Ghats to its east, Kottayam is one of Kerala's most beautiful districts. Its climate and landscape have combined to make the region prosperous. Kottayam town is surrounded by extensive plantations of rubber, and other valuable cash crops such as tea, coffee, cardamom and pepper. The first town in India to attain 100 per cent literacy, it is also the birthplace of Kerala's publishing industry and home to many Malayalam newspapers and magazines. A popular writers' co-operative society, the Sahitya Pravarthaka Sahakarana Sangham, which was set up here more than 50 years ago, has played a cardinal role in fostering the growth of Malayalam literature.

Kottayam also has an old Christian tradition that has been preserved by its large Syrian Christian population. It was one of the first towns to be patronized by St Thomas *(see p577)* in the 1st century AD. Of the many fine churches and seminaries that dot the landscape, the best known are the two Syrian Orthodox churches, **Valia Palli** and **Cheria Palli**, both dating to the mid-16th century. The churches

Mural from the stately Shiva temple at Ettumanur

stand on a hillock, about 2 km (1.2 miles) north of the city centre, and have colourful frescoes adorning their walls. The Nestorian cross at Valia Palli is said to have come from Kerala's first church, founded by St Thomas at Kodungallur *(see p653)*. Cheria Palli has lovely painted panels behind its main altar, depicting scenes from the life of the Virgin Mary.

Nestorian cross at Valia Palli Church, Kottayam

Environs
Mannanam, 8 km (5 miles) north of Kottayam, is a pilgrimage centre for Syrian Christians, who gather in their thousands each January to attend a religious convention, one of the largest in Asia.

Kumarakom, a bird sanctuary on the banks of Vembanad Lake, is 12 km (7 miles) west of Kottayam. A great variety of birds can be observed from vantage points.

A large temple dedicated to Shiva at **Ettumanur**, 12 km (7 miles) north of Kottayam, has beautiful murals, similar to those found at Mattancherry Palace in Kochi *(see p646)*. The 11th-century Mahadeva Temple at **Vaikom**, 40 km (25 miles) northwest of Kottayam, is famous for its elephant pageants and traditional dance performances, which take place between November and December each year. It is also the site where Mahatma Gandhi led an important *satyagraha* (civil disobedience movement) to make temples accessible to untouchables.

Wooden Architecture in Kerala

The importance of wooden architecture in Kerala is evident in legends that glorify the master carpenter, Perunthachhan. Palaces, temples, mosques and homes all have characteristic sloping tiled roofs to drain away the heavy rains during the monsoon. Roofs are generally hipped, often with decorated gables, topped by brass pot finials. To achieve height, they rise in two or more superimposed tiers to create steeply pyramidal profiles. Joints and wooden pegs, instead of nails, are used.

Brackets are often carved as *yalis* or figures of gods and goddesses.

Temple with pyramidal roof

Wooden pillars are ornate. These are decorative as well as functional, as they support the roof.

The Baroque façade of St Thomas Church, at Palai

❼ Sabarimalai

Pattanamthitta district. 191 km (119 miles) N of Thiruvananthapuram. 🚌 to Pamba, then by foot. **ℹ** (04735) 202 048. 🎊 Mandalam (Dec/Jan), Makaravilakku (mid-Jan).

One of India's most famous pilgrimage centres, Sabarimalai lies in the Western Ghats at an altitude of 914 m (2,999 ft). The final 14-km (9-mile) approach from Pamba, through dense forest, is made on foot.

The focus of devotion here is the temple dedicated to the popular deity, Ayyappa. The temple stays open from November to mid-January, in April and during the first five days of each month of the Malayalam calendar. People of all religions can worship here, but women between the ages of 10 and 50 are restricted from entering. The final 18 sacred steps (each representing a sin that a devotee renounces on setting foot on it) are sheathed in *panchaloha*, an alloy of five

metals, and lead to the sanctum. Only those who have observed 41 days of penance (celibacy, wearing black and and not shaving) are entitled to undertake the pilgrimage.

❽ Periyar Tiger Reserve

See pp644–5.

❾ Palai

Kottayam district. 175 km (109 miles) N of Thiruvananthapuram. 🚌 **ℹ** (0481) 256 0479. 🎊 Epiphany (6 Jan). St Thomas Church: **✝** (Malayalam) 6am daily.

The prosperous town of Palai is surrounded by thick rubber plantations. The small, 16th-century **St Thomas Church** is its main attraction. Constructed in the traditional style of early Christian churches in Kerala, it has a quaint wooden pulpit with a fish-like base, an elaborately carved main altar and two simpler side altars. A stone slab carries inscriptions in Syriac. Attractive glass candelabra are suspended from wall brackets, while a chandelier hangs from the ceiling. There is a wooden balcony at the rear. Services are still held in the church. Adjoining this building is a modern church, also dedicated to St Thomas.

The Ayyappa Cult

A Dravidian deity worshipped throughout Kerala, Ayyappa (or Sastha), was born out of the union between Shiva and Vishnu (who had transformed himself into a woman, Mohini). The baby, found on the banks of the Pamba river, was adopted by the childless king of Pandalam. Ayyappa later revealed his divine status when he destroyed a demon. Before returning to his heavenly abode, however, the god shot an arrow into the air which landed near the ashram of the sage Sabari, where a temple was built. Ayyappa's warrior friend, Vavar, is a Muslim saint whose *dargah* nearby is visited by both Muslims and Hindus.

Ayyappa devotees, Sabarimalai

Ceilings are divided into panels carved with lotus designs or Hindu deities, such as Brahma, surrounded by *dikpalas* (guardian figures).

Koottambulams, traditional theatres, are usually situated in the precincts of large temples and palaces. They serve as the venue for staging Koodiyattam (dance-drama) performances.

Interiors of *koottambulams* have tall wooden pillars and *jalis* on three sides for ventilation. The roof is specially designed to provide excellent acoustic quality.

❽ Periyar Tiger Reserve

The construction of the Mullaperiyar Dam across the Periyar river at Thekkady, in 1895, submerged large tracts of land and created a huge lake, covering an area of 26 sq km (10 sq miles). Years later, in 1935, the then Maharaja of Travancore declared 600 sq km (232 sq miles) of forest surrounding the lake a wildlife sanctuary. The Periyar Lake now forms the nucleus of the ecosystem of the sanctuary which, over the years, has been expanded to 777 sq km (300 sq miles). Declared a Tiger Reserve in 1978, the sanctuary is a rare example of human interference having enhanced rather than damaged an ecosystem.

Visitors viewing wildlife from a boat on Periyar Lake

Lake Palace
The former hunting lodge of the Maharaja of Travancore is now a delightful hotel inside the sanctuary.

Birdlife
The petrified tree trunks that jut out from the lake make convenient perches for birds looking out for fish.

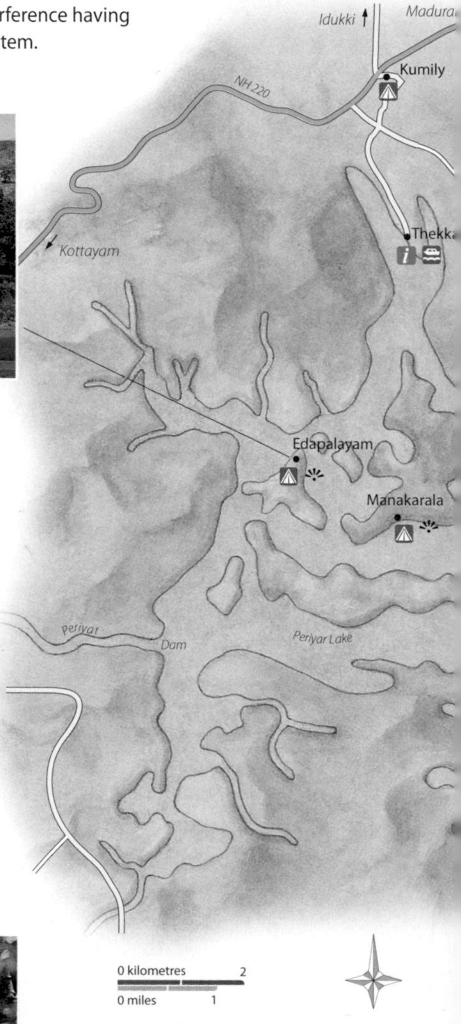

Idukki ↑   *Madura*

Kumily

NH 220

← *Kottayam*

Thekk

Edapalayam

Manakarala

Periyar   *Dam*   *Periyar Lake*

0 kilometres   2

0 miles   1

Wildlife
The deciduous forests, grasslands and tropical evergreen interiors of Periyar are the habitat of the endangered lion-tailed macaque *(left)*, as well as Indian bison *(gaur)*, sloth bears and the slender loris.

For hotels and restaurants see p703 and pp718–19

Herds of Elephants
The lake, a year-round source of water, and the abundant grassland make the sanctuary an ideal habitat for elephants, which now number approximately 800.

VISITORS' CHECKLIST

Practical Information
Idukki district. 190 km (118 miles) N of Kochi. 🛈 Forest Divisional Office, Kumily (04869) 22 2028, Tourist Information Centre, Kumily (04869) 224 571.
w keralatourism.org

Transport
🚌 🚢

The Mangaladevi Temple, 15 km (9 miles) east of Thekkady, lies at a height of 1,337 m (4,387 ft), and offers excellent panoramic views of the forested hills of the Ghats.

Mangaladevi Temple

Indian Giant Squirrel
This agile squirrel can make amazing leaps that cover about 6 m (20 ft). It is found in Periyar's deciduous and evergreen forests.

Mullakady

Periyar Lake
Two-hour boat cruises on the mist-shrouded lake offer excellent opportunities for spotting wildlife, especially herds of elephants.

Thannikudi

Periyar

Key
━━ National highway
━━ Major road
━━ Minor road

Orchids
Periyar is known for its many species of flowering plants, including nearly 150 species of orchids. The rare orchid *Habeneria periyarancis*, named after the region, is found only here.

For keys to symbols *see back flap*

⑩ Kochi

Kochi, better known as Cochin, is Kerala's most cosmopolitan city. It is also its main trading centre for spices and seafood. Built around a saltwater lagoon of the Arabian Sea, Kochi is in fact a collection of narrow islands and peninsulas. While mainland Ernakulam boasts of concrete shopping malls and glitzy apartment buildings, Mattancherry and Fort Kochi have an old world charm, with their blend of Dutch, Portuguese and English bungalows and quaint narrow streets (see pp648–9). The scenic location of Kochi's natural harbour, surrounded by palm groves, green fields, inland lakes and backwaters, has enchanted visitors from across the globe for centuries.

Brahma emerging from Vishnu's navel, mural, Mattancherry Palace

🏛 Mattancherry Palace

Jew Town. **Tel** (0484) 222 6085.
Open daily.

The Mattancherry Palace, constructed by the Portuguese in the mid-1550s, was given to the ruler of Cochin as a token of goodwill in exchange for trading rights. It was later renovated by the Dutch, and so gained the misnomer, Dutch Palace. The two-storeyed structure, built around a courtyard with a small shrine to the goddess Bhagavati, is today a museum with a rare collection of murals and royal artifacts.

In the central Durbar Hall, where coronation ceremonies were once held, is the portrait gallery of the Kochi rulers; it also displays palanquins and textiles. The adjacent bedrooms and chambers are renowned for their fine 17th-century murals, representative of Kerala's temple art. Painted in rich, warm shades of red, yellow, black and white, they depict religious and mythological themes as well as episodes from the Ramayana.

✡ Paradesi Synagogue

Jew Town. **Tel** (0471) 232 1132.
Open Sun–Fri.

Nestling in a cul-de-sac at the end of a narrow lane, in the heart of Jew Town, is India's oldest synagogue. The first Jewish settlers are said to have reached Kodungallur (see p653) in the 1st century AD. Their settlement, then known as Shingly, prospered over the centuries.

However, persecution by the Portuguese in the early 16th century forced them to migrate to Cochin, where they settled on land given by the raja, and built a synagogue in 1568. Cochin's Jewish community was divided into two distinct groups – the so-called Black or Malabari Jews, who claimed to be descendants of the original settlers, and the White or Paradesim Jews, who came here from the Middle East, and after whom the synagogue

Kochi City Centre

① Mattancherry Palace
② Paradesi Synagogue
③ Kochi International Pepper Exchange
④ St Francis Church
⑤ Willingdon Island
⑥ Bolghatty Island

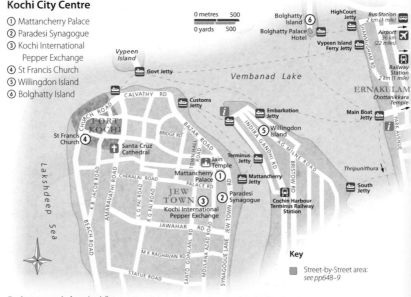

Key

Street-by-Street area: see pp648–9

Main hall with brass pulpit and blue-tiled floor, Paradesi Synagogue

is named. A third, smaller group, the Brown or Meshuhurarum Jews, descended from converted slaves, many of whom were in the spice trade. In 1940, there were 2,500 Jews in Kerala, but today only a dozen families remain, the rest having migrated to Israel.

The present synagogue, with its tiled roof and clock tower, was rebuilt in 1664 with Dutch help, after the Portuguese destroyed it in 1662. The synagogue's treasures include beautiful silver and gold Torah scrolls, a multitude of hanging oil lamps and crystal chandeliers, and a superbly crafted brass pulpit. The floor is covered with exquisite hand-painted blue willow pattern tiles, which were brought from Canton in the mid-18th century by a powerful merchant, Ezekiel Rahabi.

The narrow lanes around the synagogue are crammed with Dutch-style residences.

Today, most of these house antique shops.

🗒 Kochi International Pepper Exchange

Jew Town. **Tel** (0484) 222 4263. Passes required to enter hall. **Open** Mon–Sat.

This unique establishment reverberates with voices, seemingly raised in anger, as one ascends the stairs. However, nothing prepares the visitor for what lies within – the small hall is lined with tiny cubicles, each with a man talking animatedly on a telephone. Theatrical gestures accompanied by a loud cacophony of sounds mark the drama of each day's pepper auction.

🏛 St Francis Church

Fort Kochi. **Open** Mon–Sat.
🕐 (English) 8am, daily.

Established in the early 1500s by the Portuguese (who called it Santo Antonio) this is one of India's earliest European churches, with a simple façade that became the model for later churches. Taken over by the Dutch and then the British, it is today affiliated to the Church of South India.

Within are numerous gravestones with inscriptions, the earliest a Portuguese epitaph, dated 1562. Vasco da Gama *(see p657)* was buried here in 1524 until his body was taken to Portugal 14 years later.

Willingdon Island

This man-made island, named after the viceroy, Lord Willingdon, was created in the 1920s out of silt dredged to deepen Kochi port. Situated between Fort Kochi,

VISITORS' CHECKLIST

Practical Information
Ernakulam district. 222 km (138 miles) N of Thiruvananthapuram. 🚉 596,500. 🛈 Tourist Information Centre, (0484) 236 0502; TRC, near Ernakulam jetty (0484) 235 3234. 🎎 Onam (Aug/Sep), Utsavam (Nov/Dec).

Transport
✈ 36 km (22 miles) E of city centre, then bus or taxi. 🚃

Mattancherry and Ernakulam, it has some good hotels, as well as the main harbour, the Port Trust building, the customs house and the railway station. It is also an important naval base.

Bolghatty Island

Bolghatty Palace Hotel: **Tel** (0484) 275 0500. 🚫 open to non-residents.

A narrow strip of land, this beautiful island with breath-taking views of the bay, is the location of Bolghatty Palace. Set in 6 ha (15 acres) of lush green lawns, this palatial structure was originally built by the Dutch in 1744 and later became the home of the British Resident. It has now been converted into a hotel run by the Kerala Tourism Development Corporation.

Environs

Kochi's bustling business centre, **Ernakulam**, is 10 km (6 miles) east of Fort Kochi. The Hill Palace at **Thripunithura**, 10 km (6 miles) southeast of Ernakulam, was built in 1895 and was the official residence of the former rulers of Cochin. The palace, set in spacious grounds, is now a museum with a fairly good collection of paintings, manuscripts and royal memorabilia. The exquisite floor tiles differ from room to room, and the sweeping wooden staircases have a grandeur all of their own. The 10th-century **Chottanikkara Temple**, dedicated to the mother goddess Bhagavati, one of Kerala's most popular deities, is 16 km (10 miles) northeast of Ernakulam.

🏛 Thripunithura Museum

Tel (0484) 278 1113. **Open** Tue–Sun.

Antique shops lining the narrow lanes in Jew Town

Street-by-Street: Fort Kochi

Kochi's natural harbour, created by a massive flood in 1341, attracted imperialists and merchants from all over the world. In the 16th century, the Portuguese built a fort here, which was later occupied by the Dutch and then the British. Today, this quarter, with its mixture of architectural styles, encapsulates Fort Kochi's tumultuous history. The most important building here is St Francis Church, erected by the Portuguese in 1502 and considered to be among the oldest churches built by Europeans in India. This area has now been declared a Heritage Zone to preserve its many historic buildings.

★ **Santa Cruz Cathedral**
Built in 1887, this cathedral has impressive murals on its ceiling.

Kashi Art Café
This charming restaurant, in an old Dutch building, houses an art gallery.

TOWER ROAD

BASTION STREET

PRINCESS STREET

Mattancherry

RIVER ROAD

CHURC

Koder House
The residence of Satu Koder, patriarch of Kochi's Jews, was built by his ancestors in 1808. It has now been converted into a boutique hotel.

★ **Chinese Fishing Nets**
First erected between 1350 and 1450, these cantilevered fishing nets indicate trade links with China.

For hotels and restaurants see p703 and pp718–19

Peter Celli Street
Many hotels and shops
are located here.

Bishop's House
Once the Portuguese governor's
house, this 16th-century structure
is now home to Kochi's bishop.

United Club, once a British
club, now houses a school.

→ Bishop's
House

Malabar House Residency
This historic house is now a
wonderful hotel.

LLI STREET

RIUSDALE ROAD

PARADE ROAD

ROAD

NEW SEA WALL

The Dutch
cemetery

★ **St Francis Church**
Vasco da Gama was
buried here in 1524,
before his body was
taken to Portugal.

Key

— Suggested route

⑪ Lakshadweep Islands

Formerly the Laccadives, the
Lakshadweep Islands are an archipelago
of 36 exquisite coral islands, with
untouched beaches and verdant coconut
groves, scattered off the Kerala coast in
the Arabian Sea. With a total land area of
only 32 sq km (12 sq miles), Lakshadweep
(which means 100,000 islands) is the
smallest Union Territory in India. The
atolls enclose shallow lagoons harbouring
India's richest diversity of coral varieties,
and a multitude of colourful reef fish. Only
two islands – Bangaram and Kadmat –
are open to foreign visitors, while Indian
visitors have a choice of six; all offer
superb snorkelling and scuba-diving.

Cherbaniani Reef

LAKSHADWEEP
ISLANDS

Byramgore Reef

Chetlat Island

Bitra Island

Kiltan Island

Perumulappara

Kadmat Island

Bangaram Island

Amindivi Island

Agatti Island

Pitti Island   Androth Island

Kavaratti Island

Suheli Island

Kalpeni Island

Wind-surfing in the Lakshadweep Islands

0 kilometres   100
0 miles   50

Minicoy Island

Kavaratti Island

450 km (280 miles) W of Kochi.
🚤 **Open** to Indian passport
holders only. ⚓

Lakshadweep's administrative
headquarters, Kavaratti is the
busiest island, and home to a
large number of mainlanders,
most of whom work for the
government. It has beautiful
white beaches and its crystal-
clear lagoon is popular with
water sports enthusiasts.

There are 52 mosques
on the island that cater to
the predominantly Muslim
population. The **Ujra Mosque**
(restricted entry) has an ornate
ceiling, carved from driftwood.
The island also has a **Marine
Aquarium**, which displays a
variety of tropical fish and corals.

Huts at Bangaram Island Resort

Agatti Island

55 km (34 miles) NW of Kavaratti
Island. 🛫 🚤 **Open** to Indian
passport holders only. ⚓

Lakshadweep's only airport is
on Agatti Island. It has a fine
lagoon and offers easy access
for day visits to the uninhabited
islands of Bangaram, Tinnakara
and Parali I and II. Although
all visitors arriving by plane
must go through Agatti, the
island itself is not open to
foreign visitors.

Bangaram Island

58 km (36 miles) NW of Kavaratti.
🚤 ⚓

The uninhabited Bangaram
Island is covered with dense
groves of coconut palms and
has lovely sandy beaches.

The **Bangaram Island Resort**,
run by Casino Hotels of Kochi,
has about 30 rooms as well
as a restaurant and bar. Its
lagoon, rich with corals and
tropical fish, is excellent for
scuba diving and snorkelling.
Visitors can also choose from
the variety of water sports

available, including sailing. A
health certificate from a doctor
is required for diving.

Kadmat Island

70 km (44 miles) N of Kavaratti
Island. 🚤 ⚓

Thickly covered with palm trees,
Kadmat Island has two fine
lagoons, to the east and west.
The **Water Sports Institute**
offers canoeing, kayaking and
glass-bottomed boat rides, and
the **Lacadives Dive School**, on
the same premises, offers

Snorkelling in Lakshadweep Islands'
crystal-clear waters

Fisherfolk picking mussels among reefs in the shallows

snorkelling and scuba diving
and has qualified instructors.

Water Sports Institute
SPORTS Office, Kochi.
Tel (0484) 266 8387.

Lacadives Dive School
Tel Mumbai, (022) 6517 7381; Kochi,
(0484) 236 7752. **W** lacadives.com

Kalpeni Island
125 km (78 miles) SE of Kavaratti
Island. 🚢 **Open** to Indian passport
holders only.

The clear, shallow lagoon
of Kalpeni Island is the largest
in Lakshadweep. With
excellent reefs,
Kalpeni is ideal
for diving and
snorkelling. Coral
debris, deposited by
a storm in 1847, has
formed raised banks
on the eastern and
southern shores.

A hermit crab coming
out of a shell

Kalpeni's inhabitants were
among the earliest islanders to
send girls to school, paving the
way for other islanders who had
traditionally kept their girls and
women confined to the home.

Minicoy Island
250 km (155 miles) S of Kavaratti
Island. 🚢 **Open** to Indian
passport holders only.

Lakshadweep's southernmost
island, Minicoy has a unique
culture influenced by the
neighbouring Maldives. Mahl,
spoken here, is a dialect of the
Maldivian Dhivehi,
which is related to
the Indo-Persian
languages with a
script written from
right to left. Minicoy
is often referred to as
"Women's Island", as
its ten villages are
matrilineal. It is also

rich in the performing arts;
the traditional Lava dance
is performed on festive
occasions. Tuna fishing has
become an important activity,
with the establishment of
a tuna canning factory.
Minicoy has a grand lagoon,
and is the only island in the
archipelago with a stretch
of mangroves along its
shores. A large lighthouse,
built by the British in 1885,
commands an impressive
view of the sea.

Marine Life in the Coral Reefs
The Lakshadweep Islands are a conglomeration of atolls – ring-shaped coral reef formations – that are
the richest coral reefs found in India. Formed over thousands of years, they are made up of billions of
minute organisms called polyps. Related to sea anemones, polyps build their skeletons outside their
body. As they grow, their limestone skeletons become elaborate coral formations, with new colonies
spreading over dead ones, and eventually turn into formidable reefs. The complex and fragile reef
ecosystem is alive with an extraordinary range of plants and marine life. Over 600 species of reef fish,
such as clown fish and parrot fish in a dazzling array of colours, giant clams with purple lips, delicate
sea fans and sea anemones, ink-blue starfish, dolphins, harmless sharks and marine turtles, make up
the spectacular diversity of the underwater world. (For tips on eco-friendly diving, see p623.)

Parali Island, one of Lakshadweep's many atolls

Corals of a 100-odd
varieties, including the
boulder-like porites, the
ridged brain (right), and the
branched staghorn, can be
seen here. The myriad
colours are produced by
the variety of algae that
grow on them.

The nine-tiered tower dedicated to Shankaracharya, Kaladi

⑫ Kaladi

Ernakulam district. 35 km (22 miles) NE of Kochi. 🚌

This quiet town on the banks of the beautiful Periyar river is celebrated as the birthplace of the great saint and philosopher, Shankaracharya. Two shrines, built in 1910 on the river bank, honour his memory. One is dedicated to him and the other to the goddess Sharada, and both are maintained by the Sringeri Matha (see p531).

Nearby is a spot known as Brindavan, where the Shankaracharya's mother, Aryamba, was cremated. The old Shri Krishna Temple, near the Sharada Temple, has an image of the deity, said to have been installed by Shankaracharya himself. On the road to the Krishna Temple is a 46-m (151-ft) tall, nine-tiered octagonal tower, the Shri Adi Shankaracharya Kirti Stambha Mandapa. Each of its floors commemorates the life and works of Shankaracharya.

Environs

The **Malayattor Church**, 8 km (5 miles) east of Kaladi, is said to be where St Thomas erected a cross. The 1,000-year old rock-cut **Kalil Temple**, 22 km (14 miles) southeast of Kaladi, was originally a Jain temple. It is now dedicated to the mother goddess. Unlike at other temples, a female elephant is used in all ceremonial rituals.

⑬ Munnar

Idukki district. 130 km (81 miles) N of Kochi. 🚌 ℹ️ Tourist Information Centre, Munnar, (04865) 231 516. 🚇 daily.

The picturesque little town of Munnar lies at a height of about 1,800 m (5,906 ft), in a part of the Western Ghats known as the High Ranges. The name Munnar (which means "Three Rivers" in Tamil) is derived from its location at the confluence of three mountain streams – Kundala, Mudrapuzha and Nallathanni.

Located in 24,000 ha (59,305 acres) of sprawling tea estates, first established by the British in 1878, Munnar was once a summer resort for the British government in South India. The most important plantation in the High Ranges today belongs to Tata Tea, which oversees almost every public facility in the vicinity. The quaint High Range Club, made of wicker and teak, still serves as a social centre for Munnar's planters and, with its customary "gentlemen's bar", retains an old-world atmosphere.

Munnar remains a popular destination for visitors from Tamil Nadu and Kerala. Because of this, the town and its environs have witnessed a proliferation of hotels, restaurants and shopping centres. However, areas further away from the city centre remain relatively unspoilt, and the gentle hills offer excellent cycle rides and walks.

Environs

Mattupetty Lake, 13 km (8 miles) north of Munnar, is surrounded by semi-alpine scenery. A cattle-breeding centre is located nearby, and it is also possible to go boating or ride elephants.

A view of the tea plantations around Munnar

Adi Shankaracharya (AD 788–820)

Adi Shankaracharya, only 32 when he died, travelled the length and breadth of India, wrote erudite commentaries on Hindu scriptures, and composed devotional poems and prayers. The core of his monist philosophy is that there is only one reality and that is Brahman, the all-pervading cosmic force of which the human soul is a part, while all material objects are mere illusions (maya). The Buddhist elements in his philosophy provoked, during his lifetime, the orthodox Brahminical charge that he was a "Buddha in disguise". His historical importance lies in the fact that he provided an intellectual basis to Hindusim.

The philosopher Adi Shankaracharya

The captivating landscape of Eravikulam National Park

⑭ Eravikulam National Park

Idukki district. 16 km (10 miles) NE of Munnar. 🚌 or auto-rickshaw from Munnar to Rajamalai, the entry point. ℹ️ For information, contact Divisional Forest Officer, Munnar, (04865) 23 1587. **Open** Aug–May. 🎫

The rolling high-altitude grasslands, a striking contrast to the dense *sholas* or tropical montane forests of the valleys, are unique to the mountain landscape of the Western Ghats. Easily the best preserved stretch of this extraordinarily beautiful landscape is the Eravikulam National Park, spread across an area of 97 sq km (38 sq miles) at the base of the **Anaimudi Mountain**.
With a height of 2,695 m (8,842 ft), this has the distinction of being the highest peak south of the Himalayas. Anaimudi, which means "Elephant Head", not surprisingly resembles one. The peak and its environs provide good hiking territory.

The park, on the border of Kerala and Tamil Nadu, was established in 1978 with the specific aim of conserving the endangered Nilgiri tahr, a rare breed of mountain goat (see p23). Today, the park is home to about 3,000 tahr, the single largest population of this slate-grey goat in the world. Extremely agile, it inhabits the rocky slopes, and can be observed at surprisingly close quarters. The park is also home

Kurunji flower in full bloom

to macaques, leopards, and packs of *dhole*, the rare Indian wild dog. Its streams contain trout, and there are also more than 90 species of birds, including song birds such as the laughing thrush.

Eravikulam is regarded as one of the best-managed national parks in the country. The Muduvan tribals, who live at the periphery of the park, are employed to assist in its conservation. Their traditional method of selectively burning parts of the grassland prevents large forest fires, and also helps regenerate the tender grass on which young tahr feed. Eravikulam is also famous for the *kurunji (Strobilanthes kunthianus)*, the blue flowers that suddenly bloom en masse every 12 years and transform the rocky landscape into a sea of blue. The *kurunji* is next expected to bloom here in 2018.

⑮ Kodungallur

Thrissur district. 32 km (20 miles) N of Kochi. 🚌 🚗 Id (Feb/Mar), Bharani Festival (Mar/Apr).

Known as Muziris to the Greeks, and Cranganore to the Europeans, Kodungallur was the historic capital of the Cheraman Perumals, monarchs of the Chera empire (see p47). Situated at the mouth of the Periyar river, this was the Malabar Coast's main port until a flood tide in 1341 silted up the harbour. After this catastrophe, Kochi (see p646) became the main port.

The town is today a major destination for Hindus, Christians and Muslims alike. The **Bhagavati Temple**, in the city centre, is the venue of a three-day festival of erotic song and dance. This temple was originally the shrine of a Dravidian goddess. It was then taken over by either the Buddhists or the Jains. The festival marks the reclaiming of the site for the goddess.

St Thomas (see p577) is said to have landed here in AD 52. The **Mar Thoma Pontifical Shrine** houses a sacred relic that was brought from the Vatican in 1953 to celebrate the anniversary of the saint's arrival 1,900 years earlier.

The **Cheraman Mosque**, 2 km (1.3 miles) from the city centre, was built in AD 629 by Malik Bin Dinar, who introduced Islam to Kerala. Perhaps the first mosque in India, it resembles a Hindu temple.

Kerala's Matrilineal Family System

Called *marumakkathayam* in Kerala, the matrilineal family system, whereby inheritance is determined through the female line, is believed to have evolved in the late 10th century. This was a period of internecine warfare, and by placing women at the core of the inheritance, men could go to battle, knowing that their children's material well-being was protected. Children thus bear their mother's family name, and are identified as members of her family, with her brothers performing the role of the father figure. The Nairs are best known for this system, since warriors traditionally came from this community. Anthropologists, however, have traced its origin to the cult of the mother goddess widely prevalent in Kerala.

A Nair matriarch from Kerala

The Asian Elephant

Literature, art and culture in India celebrate the elephant. Ganesha, the elephant-headed son of Shiva and Parvati, is the Remover of Obstacles, and his name is invoked before any important task is undertaken *(see p471)*. Unlike in the rest of India, Ganesha is a minor deity in Kerala. Yet, elephants play a major role in the daily life and festivals of the people of Kerala, who have a uniquely close and affectionate relationship with elephants. Though mainly used as draught animals, elephants also participate in temple rituals, where they carry the deity in sacred processions. For such occasions, elephants are splendidly caparisoned with ornaments of gold. The wealthier temples have their own elephants.

The tusker (a male with large tusks) faces great danger from poaching, despite the ban on ivory.

Asian Elephant
Denizen of the forests and floodplains of the Himalayan foothills, Central India and the southern highlands, the Asian elephant (Elephas maximus) is not as tall as the African elephant, and has smaller ears.

This 19th-century print shows how trained elephants were used to capture wild ones by driving them into *khedas* (corrals).

Temple elephants are usually bought at the Sonepur Mela in Bihar *(see p220)*. The mahout devotes hours every day to grooming and training them for temple festivals. All commands are given in Malayalam.

In Kerala, elephants are often seen carrying their own feed. Most people allow mahouts to cut as many fronds of palm as the animal needs – up to 200 kg (441 lb) a day.

Icons and motifs depicting the elephant are common in Indian art, as they are an integral part of Hindu mythology and pageantry.

View of the Catholic Lourdes Cathedral in Thrissur

⓰ Thrissur

Thrissur district. 80 km (50 miles) N of Kochi. 🚗 312,1200. 🚌 🚐 🛈 Tourist Office, Govt Guest House, (0487) 232 0800. 🎭 Thrissur Pooram (Apr/May), Kamdassamkadavu Boat Races (Aug/Sep).

This town, built around an elevated area called The Round, was planned during the reign of Raja Rama Varma, the ruler of Cochin (Kochi) in the 18th century. In the heart of The Round is the multi-roofed **Vadakkunnathan Temple**. This great Shiva temple was built in the 9th century, and has superb woodcarvings and rich decorative murals. The splendid Pooram festival is held here each year, with the main activities taking place outside the temple walls (non-Hindus are not permitted inside the shrine). Northeast of the temple is the State Museum, displaying a good collection of murals, woodcarvings, sculpture and antique ornaments. The Archaeological Museum housed in the Shakthan Thampuran Palace features rare stone engravings recovered from the forests of Thrissur.

Thrissur is often dubbed Kerala's cultural capital as the town is home to two prestigious state-run cultural institutions. These are the Kerala Sangeetha Nataka Academy (for music and theatre) and the Kerala Sahitya Academy (for literature).

The town suffered political upheavals for centuries, having been successively ruled by the Zamorins of Kozhikode *(see p657)*, Tipu Sultan of Mysore and the rulers of Kochi. The Dutch and the British have also made their presence felt in the history of this district, as is evident from the many impressive churches, such as the late 19th-century **Lourdes Cathedral**, around the town.

Environs

Guruvayur, 29 km (18 miles) west of Thrissur, has Kerala's most popular temple. Legend has it that the 16th-century Shri Krishna Temple was created by Guru ("Instructor of the Gods"),

Entrance, Shri Krishna Temple

and Vayu ("God of the Winds"). The temple's elephant sanctuary is within the compound of an old palace nearby. It houses more than 40 elephants that belong to the deity – it is customary to present an elephant as an offering here.

The renowned performing arts and teaching centre, the **Kerala Kala Mandalam**, is 32 km (20 miles) northeast of Thrissur. Founded in 1930 by the famous Malayali poet, Vallathol Narayan Menon, at Cheruthuruthy, it offers intensive training in Kathakali, Mohiniattam and Koodiyattam dance forms. Instrumental and vocal music forms are taught here as well. The complex also has a large *natyagriha* (dance hall) for performances.

🏛 **Kerala Kala Mandalam**
Tel (04884) 26 2305 for permission. **Open** Mon–Fri. **Closed** public hols, Apr/May.

Vadakkunnathan Temple in Thrissur

The Pooram Festival

A *pooram* (meeting) is a temple festival marked by the ceremonious congregation, at a particular temple, of deities from various other temples. Though a number of *poorams* are held throughout Kerala, Thrissur's Pooram is the most spectacular. Held between April and May, it celebrates the processional arrival of two goddesses before Shiva, after whom the town is named. Through a sea of devotees and the hypnotic beat of percussion instruments, two rows of elephants, with the central ones carrying the deities, move majestically towards each other. A firework display ends the celebrations.

Elephants at the Pooram festival

🔞 Palakkad

Palakkad district. 99 km (62 miles)
N of Kochi. 🔲 2809934. 🚇
ℹ️ Tourist Information Centre, near
Children's Park, (0491) 253 8996.
🎪 Chariot Festival (Oct/Nov).

Situated at the base of the
Western Ghats, Palakkad (Palghat)
derives its name from the dense
forests *(kadu)* of *pala (Alsteria
scholaris)* trees that once covered
the land. Today, however, paddy
fields and tobacco plantations
have taken their place.

Tipu's Fort, in the heart of
the town, was built by Haider
Ali of Mysore in 1766; it was
subsequently occupied by the
British after they defeated his
son and successor, Tipu Sultan
(see p521), some 30 years
later. This sombre, granite
structure now houses various
government offices.

The large **Vishwanatha
Temple**, on the banks of
the Kalpathy river, is famous
for its chariot procession.

On the outskirts of town are
the extensive **Malampuzha
Gardens**, laid out above a huge
irrigation dam built across the
Malampuzha river. Pleasant boat
cruises are possible on a large
lake, nestling in the foothills.

Environs

The town of **Kollengode**
is 19 km (12 miles)
south of Palakkad
and is set in pastoral
surroundings. The
Vishnu Temple and
Kollengode Palace are worth a
visit. **Thrithala**, 75 km (47 miles)
west of Palakkad, has a Shiva
temple and the ruins of a mud
fort. Its most important
sight, the Kattilmadam
Temple, is a granite
Buddhist monument
dating from the
9th–10th centuries.

Silent Valley, a haven of rare plants and herbs

🔞 Silent Valley National Park

Palakkad district. 88 km (55 miles) NW
of Kochi. 🚌 Mannarkkad, the entry
point. Jeeps available to Mukkali.
ℹ️ For permits and reservations
(compulsory), contact the Wildlife
Warden, Mannarkkad, (04924) 222
056. 🆆 silentvalley.gov.in

The Silent Valley National Park,
spread over an area of 90 sq
km (35 sq miles), preserves
what is perhaps the country's
last substantial stretch of virgin
tropical evergreen forest. An
important part of the Nilgiri
Biosphere Reserve *(see
p524)*, it represents
some of the spec-
tacular biodiversity of
the Western Ghats. The
park is renowned for its
rare plants and herbs,
which include over 100
species of orchids. Wildlife
includes tigers, elephants, the
Nilgiri langur, the sloth bear,
the shy nocturnal slender loris
and the endangered lion-tailed
macaque. A variety of
birds, as well as
100 species of
butterflies and

Slender loris

400 species of moths, is also
found here. Visitors can trek to
the source of the Kunthipuzha
river, which flows through
this valley.

Accommodation is available
at the forest lodge in Mukkali,
just outside the park.

🔞 Malappuram

Malappuram district. 153 km (95
miles) N of Kochi. 🚌 ℹ️ (0483) 273
1504. 🏛️ daily. 🎪 Valiya Nercha (Feb/
Mar), Shivratri (Feb/Mar).

This "land atop hills" stands at the
entrance to the Malabar region,
and is crossed by three major
rivers – the Chaliyar, the Kadalundi
and the Bharatapuzha. A military
centre of the Zamorins of Calicut,
it was the scene of fierce fighting
between British forces and the
Mopplahs (Muslim peasants),
known as the Mopplah Revolt.
The most serious uprising
occurred in 1921, after which
many rebels were exiled to the
Andamans *(see pp622–3)*. The
old British barracks, on a hilltop
overlooking the Kadalundi
river, now houses the district
administration. Malappuram is
also an important seat of both
Hindu and Islamic learning.

Environs

Kerala's pioneering Ayurvedic
institution *(see p633)* is at
Kottakkal, 12 km (7 miles)
southwest of Malappuram.
Started in 1902, the Kottakkal
Arya Vaidyasala is based in
a splendid building, and has

The desolate ruins of Tipu's Fort at Palakkad

Arya Vaidyasala, at Kottakkal

a research centre and hospital. **Tirur**, 32 km (20 miles) southwest of Malappuram, was the 16th-century birthplace of the father of Malayalam literature, Tunchat Ramanuja Ezhuthachan. He also taught the Malayalam alphabet to children, a practice that continues at a shrine dedicated to him.

One of the earliest Portuguese settlements on the Malabar Coast was at **Tanur**, 34 km (21 miles) southwest of Malappuram. St Francis Xavier *(see p502)* is said to have come here in 1546.

⓴ Kozhikode

Kozhikode district. 254 km (158 miles) N of Kochi. 🅰 436,600. ✈ Karipur, 25 km (16 miles) S of city centre. 🚊 🚌 𝒊 District Tourism Promotion Council, (0495) 272 0012. 🎭 Shivratri Utsavam (Feb/Mar).

This busy commercial town, better known throughout the world as Calicut, was the capital of the kingdom of the powerful Zamorins (a Portuguese corruption of their title, Samoothiri). Under them the town prospered as a major centre of the Malabar trade in spices and textiles, and it was from Calicut that the word calico originated as the term for white, unbleached cotton. It was in Calicut, too, that Vasco da Gama, the Portuguese explorer who discovered the sea route to India, was first received by the Zamorin in his palace in May 1498. Dominating the city centre is the large Manamchira Tank, flanked by the Town Hall and the Public Library, both fine examples of traditional architecture. A striking Roman Catholic cathedral also stands near the Manamchira Tank.

The town's Muslim heritage is indicated by its numerous mosques, remarkable for their massive size and elaborate wood carvings. Among these, the Mishqal Palli, near the port, is the most impressive, with a five-tiered tiled roof. Note that this mosque is not open to non-Muslims.

The **Pazhassirajah Museum** exhibits wood and metal sculptures and reconstructions of megalithic monuments. The Art Gallery next door has paintings by Raja Ravi Varma, the 19th-century painter who belonged to a princely family from Travancore *(see p630)*. Kozhikode's busy shopping area, the quaintly named **Sweetmeats Street**, was once lined with shops selling the famous Calicut *halwa*, a brightly coloured sweet made of flour and sugar. Today, SM Street, as it is popularly known, has only a few shops that sell *halwa*. Court Road, leading off SM Street, houses the bustling Spice Market. Kozhikode is today the storage and trading centre for hill produce from Wynad *(see p658)*; spices such as cloves, cardamom, pepper, turmeric and coffee are sorted and packaged in the old warehouses along the waterfront.

🏛 **Pazhassirajah Museum**
East Hill. **Tel** (0495) 238 4382. **Open** Tue–Sun.

Environs
A short 18-km (11-mile) drive north of the city leads to the small village of **Kappad**, where a stone plaque on the beach commemorates the spot where Vasco da Gama is supposed to have landed in 1498.

The historic village of **Beypore**, 10 km (6 miles) south of Kozhikode, is believed to be the fabled Ophir, referred to in ancient Greek and Roman texts. Artisans still follow the traditional methods of their forefathers at this shipbuilding centre *(see p637)*. The type of dhows that were built here for Arab merchants more than 1,500 years ago are still in demand in West Asia. Old vessels are also brought here to be repaired. Visitors should make reservations in advance.

Thusharagiri, 50 km (31 miles) away from Kozhikode, is a plantation town that abounds in rubber, arecanut, pepper, ginger and spices. It is also a trekking and rock climbing destination. The surrounding hills offer some exciting trails. One of the most popular is a 12-km (7.5-mile) long trek that crosses three lovely waterfalls, one of which falls from a height of 75 m (246 ft), and climbs up through dense evergreen forests, where a variety of birds and animals can be spotted. The nearest airport is at Karipur, about 23 km (14 miles) from Kozhikode.

Fishermen with colourful nets in the harbour of Beypore

The Tree House in Wynad, blending into the sylvan landscape

㉑ Wynad District

280 km (174 miles) NE from Kochi to Kalpetta. 🚌 ⓘ Tourist Information centre, Kalpetta, (04936) 204 441.

A remote region of virgin rainforests and mist-clad mountain ranges, Wynad provides the ideal climatic conditions for Kerala's extensive plantations of cardamom, pepper, coffee and rubber. Relatively untouched by modernization, this is the homeland of large groups of indigenous tribal communities, such as the cave-dwelling Cholanaikens, and the down-trodden Paniyas, who until 50 years ago were sold as bonded labour to plantation owners. It is also the favoured habitat of animals such as the Nilgiri langur, wild elephants and the giant Malabar squirrel.

The gateway to Wynad is **Lakkidi**, at its southern end. An ancient tree on the main highway, ominously draped with a heavy iron chain, presents a curious sight. Local legend claims that it binds the angry spirit of a Paniya tribal who showed a group of British surveyors the path through the dense forest. Instead of being rewarded, he was killed here and his spirit apparently haunted the highway until it was exorcised.

Kalpetta, the district headquarters, is 15 km (9 miles) to the north. Once a major Jain centre *(see p400)* this has two Jain temples situated nearby. The Anantanatha-swami Temple is at Puliyarmala, 6 km (4 miles) away, while the Glass Temple of Koottamunda, dedicated to the third Jain *tirthankara*, Parsvanatha, is on the slope of Vallarimal Hill, 20 km (12 miles) to the south. The area's tallest peak, Chembara Peak (2,100

Coffee blossoms in a Wynad plantation

m/6,890 ft) is 14 km (9 miles) southwest of Kalpetta, and is excellent for trekking and birdwatching.

Sulthan's Bathery (Sultan's Battery), 10 km (6 miles) east of Kalpetta, derives its name from Tipu Sultan of Mysore *(see p521)*, who built a fort here in the 18th century. The **Edakkal Caves** are 12 km (7 miles) away. Their inscriptions and carvings of human and animal figures are said to date to prehistoric times; some believe that these caves were the refuge of Jain monks. The caves' environs abound in megaliths. The **Wynad (Muthanga) Wildlife Sanctuary**, 16 km (10 miles) east of Sulthan's Battery, was established in 1973 and is part of the Nilgiri Biosphere Reserve *(see p524)*.

Mananthavady, 35 km (22 miles) north of Kalpetta, was the scene of a long guerrilla war between the local king, Pazhassi Raja, and British troops, led by Lord Arthur Wellesley, the future Duke of Wellington who defeated Napoleon at Waterloo. About 32 km (20 miles) to the north is the Vishnu Temple at Thirunelli, built beside the Paapanassini river. This is a major pilgrimage site, where Hindus perform funeral rites.

🏛 **Edakkal Caves**
Open daily. 📷 📹

🦌 **Wynad Sanctuary**
📷 📹 Extra charges for photography. Permits from Wildlife Warden, Sulthan Bathery, (04936) 220 454.

The remains of Tipu's fort, Sulthan's Battery

㉒ Mahe

Union Territory of Puducherry.
Mahe district. 48 km (30 miles)
N of Kozhikode. 🚍 **ℹ** Govt
Tourist Home, (0495) 270 2304.
🎭 St Theresa's Feast (Oct).

Situated on the Mayyazhi river,
this former French enclave is
named after the French admiral,
Mahe de La Bourdonnais, who
landed here in November 1741.
A French colony until 1954, it is
today part of the Union Territory
of Puducherry (see p590). Only
some traces of Mahe's colonial
heritage remain, among them
the beautiful old residence
of the French administrator,
at the mouth of the river. It is
now the office-cum-residence
of the Indian government's
administrator. Mahe's main church,
the whitewashed, Baroque
St Theresa's Church, is situated
on the highway. The town's
main "industry" seems to centre
around the supply of cheap
alcohol, attracting truck drivers
and motorists who come here
from nearby areas to stock up.

㉓ Thalaserry

Kannur district. 255 km (158 miles)
N of Kochi. 🚍 🚍

Fishing and agriculture are
the major occupations in
Thalaserry (once known as
Tellicherry), and observing
the bartering of the day's
catch can be an enjoyable
experience. The British East
India Company established

Fishmongers awaiting the daily catch at Thalaserry

one of their first trading posts
at Thalaserry at the end of the
17th century. In 1708, they
built the enormous laterite
fort on the coast. An old
lighthouse still stands on its
ramparts, and there are also
two secret tunnels, one of
which leads into the sea.

The Thalaserry Cricket Club,
founded in 1860, is one of
the oldest in India, as cricket
was introduced here in
the late 18th century.

This region is one
of the main centres
of *kalaripayattu (see
p630)*, a fact that has
made it a training
ground for circus
artistes as well. It is a
common sight to see
young men in the
kalari (gymnasium),
exercising to tone
their muscles and practising
with wooden weapons.
Many images of deities
adorn the *kalari*, giving it
a sacred character.

façade of the fort,
Thalassery

㉔ Kannur

Kannur district. 66 km (41 miles)
N of Kochi. 🚇 🚍 **ℹ** District Tourism
Promotion Council, Taluk Office
Campus, (0497) 270 6336. 🚢 daily.

This scenic coastal town,
called Cannanore by European
settlers, was an important
maritime centre in the 14th
and 15th centuries. The
Portuguese built **St
Angelo Fort**, 5 km (3
miles) south of
the city, in 1505. This
enormous laterite
structure overlooks
the fishing harbour
and is protected
by the sea on three
sides. It was later
occupied by the
British, who
established a large
military garrison here.
Muzhapilangad Beach, 15 km
(9 miles) south of Kannur, is
a serene spot with a 4-km
(2.5-mile) long sandy beach,
safe for swimmers.

Theyyam, Kerala's Spectacular Dance-ritual

A Theyyam dancer clad in a
colourful costume

This dance-ritual, particular to the north Malabar region, was originally aimed
at appeasing ancient village deities, the mother goddess, folk heroes,
ancestors and spirits. With the advent of Brahminism, Hindu divinities
replaced many of the earlier ones, and the Theyyam pantheon shrank from
300 to around 40. The Theyyam presentation begins with the singing of the
thottam (song) in praise of the deity relevant to that particular ritual. This is
followed by the dance, the steps and postures of which show the strong
influence of Kerala's martial arts tradition, *kalaripayattu*. Drums, pipes and
cymbals provide the accompaniment. The performers, all male, wear masks,
body paint, colourful costumes and imposing headgear (*mudi*), which often
rises to a staggering height of more than 2 m (7 ft). The tender leaves of the
coconut palm are cut to various designs and shapes to form part of the
elaborate costume of the dancer. Theyyams, usually annual rituals, are held
between December and May. However, at the Parassinikadavu Temple, 20 km
(12 miles) north of Kannur, Theyyam is performed every day.

The laterite ramparts of Bekal Fort, outside Kasaragod town

㉕ Kasaragod District

400 km (249 miles) S from Kochi to Kasaragod. 🚌 🚐 ℹ Tourism Promotion Council (04994) 256 450.

Kerala's northernmost district, flanked by the Western Ghats to the east and the Arabian Sea to the west, is a fertile region of thickly forested hills and meandering rivers. The district is named after its main town, Kasaragod, a bustling centre of the coir and handloom industries. About 8 km (5 miles) north of Kasaragod, is the **Madhur Temple**. This beautiful temple, with its copper-plate roofing, has a commanding location overlooking the Madhuvahini river.

Situated 16 km (10 miles) south of Kasaragod is **Bekal Fort**, the largest and best-preserved fort in Kerala. This enormous, circular structure is built with large blocks of laterite, and its outer wall rises majestically from the sea to a height of 39 m (128 feet). Inside is a cunningly concealed tunnel that leads directly to the sea. The fort's origins are shrouded in mystery, though it is generally thought to have been built in the mid-1600s by a local chieftain Shivappa Nayak, whose fiefdom was in neighbouring Karnataka. The scene of much conflict, the fort was eventually occupied by the British

after the defeat of Tipu Sultan (see p521).

Many beautiful beaches lie to the north and south of the fort. The closest, **Pallikere Beach**, provides a spectacular view of the fort. The Kerala government, along with the Bekal Resorts Development Corporation, have plans to develop this area as a major tourist complex. About 6 km (4 miles) north of Bekal, **Kappil Beach** is a secluded area, ideal for swimming. Kodi Cliff, at one end of the beach, is a scenic spot with wonderful views of the sunset on the Arabian Sea.

The **Chandragiri Fort**, on the banks of the Chandragiri river, is 10 km (6 miles) north of Bekal. This 17th-century fort is also attributed to Shivappa Nayak, who built it to defend his kingdom against the Vijayanagar rulers (see pp534–5). The imposing Malik Dinar Mosque, nearby, is said to have been founded by Malik Ibn

A typical temple lamp

Dinar, a disciple of the Prophet Muhammad, who introduced Islam to Kerala in about AD 664. The grave of Malik Ibn Muhammed, a descendant of Malik Ibn Dinar, lies here.

The 9th-century **Ananthapura Temple**, 30 km (19 miles) north of Bekal, is the only temple in Kerala erected in the centre of a lake. It is said to be the original abode of Ananthapadmanabha, the presiding deity of the Anantha Padmanabhaswamy Temple in Thiruvananthapuram, the state capital (see p631).

The small hill station of **Ranipuram** is situated 80 km (50 miles) east of Kasaragod. Set amid acres of rubber and spice plantations, it offers good opportunities for trekking.

This region is also the centre for a number of performing arts, such as Theyyam (see p659) and Yakshagana, the elaborate folk art form from Karnataka (see p539).

Ananthapura Temple, built in the middle of a lake

Kathakali: Kerala's Classical Dance-Drama

Literally meaning "story-play", Kathakali is a highly evolved classical form of dance, drama and music (both vocal and instrumental), that is almost 400 years old. Male actor-dancers, in voluminous colourful skirts, elaborate headdresses and jewellery, enact stories from the Puranas and epics, mainly the *Mahabharata (see p30)*. The story unfolds simply at first, before building to a dramatic climax. The frenetic drumming, the emotive singing and the rhythmic movements of the dancers reach a crescendo, as the many scenes of love and valour culminate in the triumph of good over evil. These are traditionally all-night performances, held in temple courtyards during religious festivals. Modern performances are shorter.

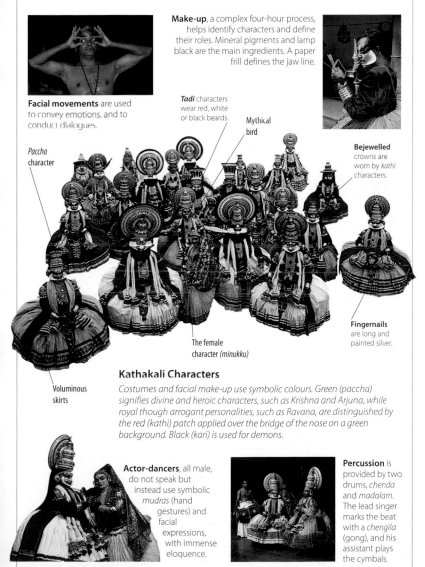

Make-up, a complex four-hour process, helps identify characters and define their roles. Mineral pigments and lamp black are the main ingredients. A paper frill defines the jaw line.

Facial movements are used to convey emotions, and to conduct dialogues.

Tadi characters wear red, white or black beards.

Mythical bird

Paccha character

Bejewelled crowns are worn by *kathi* characters.

Fingernails are long and painted silver.

The female character *(minukku)*

Voluminous skirts

Kathakali Characters

Costumes and facial make-up use symbolic colours. Green (paccha) signifies divine and heroic characters, such as Krishna and Arjuna, while royal though arrogant personalities, such as Ravana, are distinguished by the red (kathi) patch applied over the bridge of the nose on a green background. Black (kari) is used for demons.

Actor-dancers, all male, do not speak but instead use symbolic *mudras* (hand gestures) and facial expressions, with immense eloquence.

Percussion is provided by two drums, *chenda* and *madalam*. The lead singer marks the beat with a *chengila* (gong), and his assistant plays the cymbals.

ANDHRA PRADESH

From the unspoilt beaches of Visakhapatnam along the Coromandel Coast, to the emerald green paddy fields of Nellore district, much of Andhra Pradesh is occupied by the rocky Deccan Plateau which rises 1,000 m (3,281 ft) above the fertile coastal plains. This is South India's largest state, covering an area of 275,070 sq km (106,205 sq miles). The main language spoken by its 76 million people is Telugu, though Urdu is also spoken in the state capital, Hyderabad. This vibrant city was, until 1947, the seat of the fabulously wealthy royal family, the Asaf Jahi Nizams. Andhra Pradesh's varied cultural heritage is visible in its monuments. These include the ancient Buddhist site at Nagarjunakonda, the great Islamic fort of Golconda and the hilltop Hindu temple at Tirupati, which attracts more pilgrims than any other temple in India. The state's distinctive handicrafts include superb woven ikat textiles, pearl jewellery and inlaid metal *bidri* work.

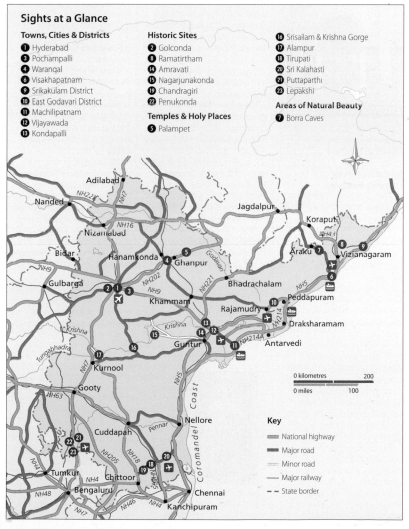

Sights at a Glance

Towns, Cities & Districts
1. Hyderabad
3. Pochampalli
4. Warangal
6. Visakhapatnam
9. Srikakulam District
10. East Godavari District
11. Machilipatnam
12. Vijayawada
13. Kondapalli

Historic Sites
2. Golconda
8. Ramatirtham
14. Amravati
15. Nagarjunakonda
19. Chandragiri
22. Penukonda

Temples & Holy Places
5. Palampet

16. Srisailam & Krishna Gorge
17. Alampur
18. Tirupati
20. Sri Kalahasti
21. Puttaparthi
23. Lepakshi

Areas of Natural Beauty
7. Borra Caves

Key

— National highway
— Major road
--- Minor road
— Major railway
- - State border

◀ Charminar or Four Towers, Hyderabad's signature landmark | **For keys to symbols** *see back flap*

❶ Hyderabad

The fifth largest city in India, Hyderabad was founded in 1591 and planned as a grid with the Charminar *(see pp666–7)* at its centre. It has now grown well beyond the confines of the original walled city, to include another town north of the Musi river, the military cantonment at Secunderabad, and a burgeoning high-tech estate, nicknamed "Cyberabad". The city's sights include the grand palaces of its erstwhile rulers, the Nizams, and the colourful bazaars and mosques of the old city.

The Neo-Classical façade of the 19th-century Purani Haveli

🏛 Purani Haveli (Nizam's Museum)

Near Mir Alam Mandi Rd. **Tel** (040) 2452 1029. **Open** 10:30am–5pm Sat–Thu.

This sprawling complex of mid-19th-century Neo-Classical buildings was the main residence of the sixth Nizam, Mahbub Ali Pasha. A glimpse of his lavish lifestyle can be seen in the eastern wing of the main building, in the Massarat Mahal. This has the Nizam's gigantic wooden wardrobe, a 73-sq m (786-sq ft) room with closets on two levels, and a mechanical elevator affording access to the upper tier. Its contents once included 75 identical tweed suits – the Nizam liked the pattern so much that he bought the Scottish factory's entire stock of it.

Purani Haveli also houses the Nizam's Museum, which displays china, silver objets d'art, and several fascinating photographs that capture the legendary opulence of the Nizam and his court.

🏛 Salarjung Museum

Near Naya Pul. **Tel** (040) 2457 6443. **Open** Sat–Thu. **Closed** public hols.

This eclectic collection of over 40,000 objects once belonged to Salarjung III, Prime Minister of Hyderabad between 1912 and 1914. Salarjung's highly individual taste ranged from objects of sublime beauty to some bordering on kitsch, which is what makes this museum so fascinating.

The pride of the museum is the outstanding Mughal jade collection, which includes an exquisite, translucent leaf-shaped cup. Miniature paintings are also well represented, including those of the local Deccani School *(see p547)*, as are Indian stone and bronze sculpture, inlaid ivory objects and medieval Islamic manuscripts. A prized 13th-century Koran has the signatures of three Mughal emperors. Salarjung's rather florid taste in European art is represented

Portraits of Salarjung III and his son, painted on ivory

by some 19th-century statuary, while the collection of oil paintings include a Canaletto, a Guardi and a Landseer.

🏛 Osmania General Hospital

Afzalganj. **Tel** (040) 2460 0121. **Open** daily.

A spectacular stone building with soaring domes, Osmania General Hospital was built in 1925 as part of the seventh Nizam's modernization plan after a catastrophic flood in 1908. Opposite it, across the river, are the **Boys' High School** and the **High Court**, built in pink granite and red sandstone. An imaginative blend of Islamic decorative detail and Western interior layouts, all three buildings, as well as the city's Railway Station, were constructed between 1914 and 1936, and

The Nizams of Hyderabad

Hyderabad was India's biggest and richest princely state, as large as England and Scotland together. Its rulers, known as the Nizams, belonged to the Asaf Jahi dynasty, founded in 1724 by Nizam-ul-Mulk who first came to Hyderabad as the Mughal governor of the Deccan, and then established his independence as Mughal power in Delhi

Portrait of the last Nizam (r.1911–48)

waned. The Nizams' fabulous wealth derived largely from their legendary hoard of emeralds and their diamond mines near Golconda, and many tales are told of their extravagance and eccentricities. The seventh and last Nizam, Osman Ali Khan, was the richest man in India but, unlike his ancestors, he was a notorious miser who smoked cigarette butts and wore the same set of shabby, patched clothes for weeks on end. After Independence in 1947, the Nizam resisted joining the Indian Union. However, riots broke out and Indian Army action to restore order finally led to the state's accession.

are the work of the British architect Vincent Esch.

🏛 Badshahi Ashurkhana

Patthergatti Rd. **Open** daily, with permission of the caretaker.

This historic building, the Ashurkhana or "Royal House of Mourning", was built in 1595 by Muhammad Quli Qutb Shah, the fifth Qutb Shahi ruler *(see p671)*, as a congregation hall for Shias during the month of Muharram. It houses beautiful silver and gold *alams* (ceremonial standards) studded with precious stones, which are carried in procession during Muharram *(see p673)*, and are on display here through the year, on Thursdays.

Exquisite enamel-tiled mosaics adorn the central niche and the western wall, in glowing yellow, orange and turquoise. The outer hall with wooden colonnades was added

🏛 Charminar
See pp666–7.

🕌 Mecca Masjid
See pp666–7.

Splendid 17th-century tiled mosaics in the Badshahi Ashurkhana

🏛 Falaknuma Palace

Near Naya Pul. **Tel** (040) 6629 8585. **Open** daily.

The most opulent of the Nizams' many palaces, Falaknuma Palace was built in 1872. The front façade is in Palladian style, while the rear is a jumble of Indo-Saracenic domes and cupolas, added on to house the zenana. The lavish interior has tooled leather ceilings created by Florentine craftsmen, furniture and tapestries ordered from France, and marble imported from Italy.

The Nizams' most important guests, including King George V, stayed at Falaknuma, but after the death of the sixth Nizam here in 1911 (after a bout of drinking), the palace fell into disuse. Acquired by the Taj Group in 1995, it has been converted into one of the country's top luxury hotels.

Hyderabad City Centre

1. Purani Haveli (Nizam's Museum)
2. Salarjung Museum
3. Osmania General Hospital
4. Badshahi Ashurkhana
5. Charminar
6. Mecca Masjid

Key

Street-by-Street area: *see pp666–7*

For keys to symbols *see back flap*

Hyderabad Street-by-Street: Charminar

In the heart of the Old City, Charminar ("Four Towers") is Hyderabad's signature landmark. It was built in 1591 by King Muhammad Quli Qutb Shah of the Qutb Shahi dynasty *(see p670)* and, according to legend, marks the spot where he first saw his lover, the beautiful Hindu dancer Bhagmati. Another story says he built it as thanksgiving at the end of a deadly plague epidemic. Today, Charminar is the hub of a busy commercial area, where the grand mosques and palaces of the erstwhile rulers are surrounded by lively bazaars selling everything from pearls and perfumes to cabbages and computers.

Caps on sale on the pavement outside Mecca Masjid

Chowmahalla Palace

SHAH ALI BANDA ROAD

★ Mecca Masjid
Built between 1617 and 1694, this huge mosque has bricks from Mecca embedded in its central arch. Several Nizams are buried here.

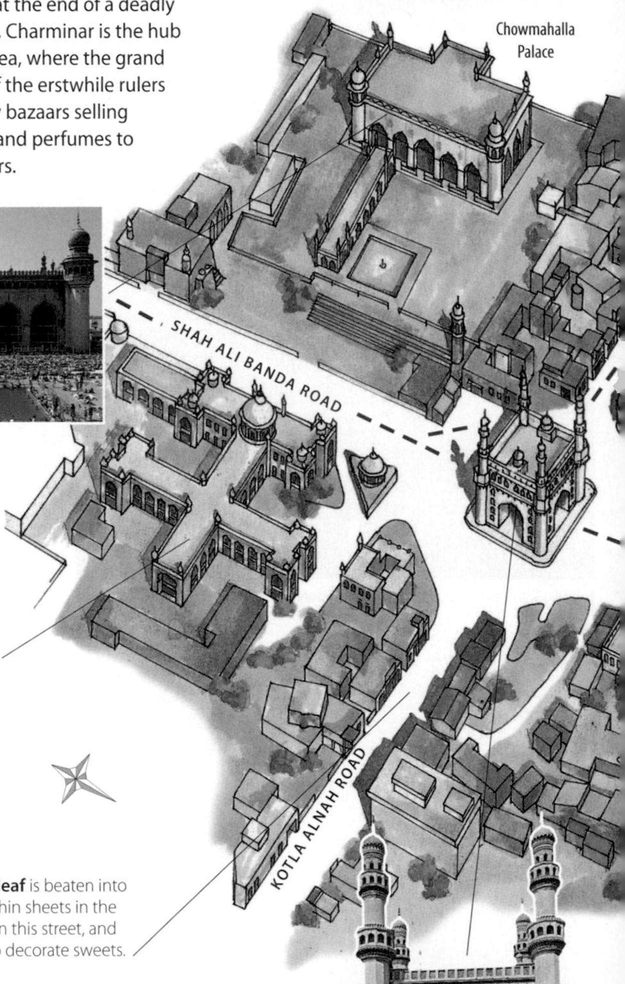

Nizamia Unani Ayurvedic Hospital was built by the last Nizam in the 1920s for the practice of traditional Graeco-Arab medicine.

Silver-leaf is beaten into wafer-thin sheets in the shops in this street, and used to decorate sweets.

KOTLA ALNAH ROAD

| 0 metres | 50 |
| 0 yards | 50 |

Key

— Suggested route

★ Charminar
Grand arches frame Charminar's four sides. On the top floor is the city's oldest mosque. The minarets soar to 49 m (160 ft).

★ Laad Bazaar
Bangles, tinsel, embroidery, brocade turbans for bridegrooms, henna, herbal potions, and everything else needed for a bride's trousseau, are sold in this colourful bazaar.

Attar Shop
Perfume oils, sold in tiny bottles, include a local speciality called *gil*, which captures the scent of wet earth after the first rainfall of a scorching summer.

Char Kaman
served as the entrance to the royal mosque inside Charminar. Nearby are shops selling pearls.

Sher-e-dil Kaman
leads to shops selling gorgeous brocades and antique silk saris.

Machhli Kaman
This is one of four ceremonial arches, built in 1594, around an open area where parades were held. It is carved with the auspicious fish symbol denoting prosperity.

GULZAR HAUZ ROAD

MITLI KA SHER ROAD

PANJERSHAH ROAD

PATHERGATTI

ROAD

Naya Pul

Jama Masjid
This simple whitewashed mosque, built in 1597, is the second oldest in Hyderabad.

Exploring Hyderabad & Secunderabad

By the 19th century, Hyderabad had begun to expand beyond the crowded confines of the old quarter, clustered on both banks of the Musi river. New palaces, and the British military cantonment of Secunderabad, were now built on the city's outskirts.

🏛 Birla Archaeological Museum

Opposite Ravindra Bharathi, Saifabad. **Tel** (040) 2324 1067. **Open** daily. 📷

Previously located in the Asmangarh Palace, once a 19th-century hunting lodge of the sixth Nizam, the Birla Archaeological Museum is now housed in a large complex on Naubat Pahad. The museum has a number of galleries that display bronze artifacts, arms and armour, sculptures, art and objects from excavation sites, including items found at Vaddamanu that date from as far back as 100 BC. The complex also houses a science museum, planetarium, modern art gallery and the Birla Mandir temple.

🏛 The Residency

Koti. **Open** Mon–Sat.

This elegant Palladian mansion, now the University College for Women, was built in 1805 by the third Nizam as a gift for the British Resident at his court, James Kirkpatrick. It was decorated in style, with a painted ceiling, and mirrors and chandeliers from Brighton Pavilion in England. The pediment above the portico still bears the East India Company's lion-and-unicorn coat of arms.

In the grounds is a small replica of the main building, which Kirkpatrick built for his aristocratic Hyderabadi wife, Khairunissa Begum – a liaison that created a great scandal at the time. There is a small British cemetery in a corner of the grounds.

🏛 State Archaeological Museum

Assembly Rd, N of Railway Station. **Tel** (040) 2323 2267. **Open** Sat–Thu. **Closed** Fri & public hols. 📷

Two large Norman-style gateways mark the entrance to the Nampally Public Gardens, which contain the State Archaeological Museum. It has a large collection of Buddhist art, some fine Chola bronzes, Roman coins, and even an Egyptian mummy. There are also replicas of murals and sculptures from the Ajanta and Ellora caves *(see pp480–85)*. Nearby is the **State Legislative Assembly** (built in 1913), a domed complex modelled on a Rajasthani palace.

Hussain Sagar, with a gigantic statue of the Buddha

🌊 Hussain Sagar

This huge lake, created in 1562, lies off Mahatma Gandhi Road, which bisects Hyderabad and Secunderabad. The 3-km (2-mile) stretch of road along its southern boundary is Hyderabad's most popular promenade; it is lined with statues of eminent figures from Andhra Pradesh's history. At the centre of the lake is a rock, on which stands a 17-m (56-ft) high monolithic statue of the Buddha, weighing 350 tonnes. Completed in 1986, it sank to the bottom of the lake when the ferry carrying it capsized. It was finally salvaged (intact) seven years later and installed on the rock in 1994.

🏙 Secunderabad

Northeast of Hussain Sagar along the Tank Bund Road, Secunderabad was established in 1806 as a cantonment to house British troops. It has since grown into a teeming city which is an extension of Hyderabad. At its centre is the **Parade Ground**, overlooked by **St Andrew's Church** and the imposing colonial-style **Secunderabad Club**. The Neo-Gothic **Holy Trinity Church** (built in 1848) is 6 km (4 miles) north of the Parade Ground, and has beautiful stained-glass windows, elegant steeples on its square tower and a British cemetery.

The walled compound of the **Paigah Palaces**, where the Hyderabadi aristocracy lived, is 2 km (1.3 miles) west of the Parade Ground, opposite Begumpet Airport. The most imposing palace is Vicar Manzil, built by the leading nobleman at the sixth Nizam's court, Sir Vicar-ul-Umra; he had built the magnificent Falaknuma Palace *(see p665)* for himself but had to move out when the Nizam decided to acquire it. At its entrance is the **Spanish Mosque** (built in 1906), with Moorish arches and octagonal spires.

The Spanish Mosque at the entrance of Vicar Manzil, Secunderabad

Hyderabadi Culture

Sultan Muhammad Quli Qutb Shah, who founded Hyderabad in 1591, was an enlightened ruler, and a poet, scholar and patron of the arts. His kingdom was also a flourishing centre of trade, especially in pearls, diamonds and horses. At his court and in his bazaars, Hyderabadis rubbed shoulders with traders, scholars and artisans from different lands. This cosmopolitan tradition, and the culture of courtly elegance and etiquette, continued with the next dynasty – that of the Asaf Jahi Nizams, which ruled from 1724 until 1947. As a result, Hyderabad has a uniquely composite culture, a mélange of Hindu and Muslim customs, mingled with Arab, Persian and Turkish influences, evident in its language, food, manners and arts.

Bidriware uses a technique introduced by Persians in the 16th century, by which black gunmetal is intricately inlaid with silver in floral and geometric patterns.

Hyderabad's distinctive cuisine includes dishes of Persian and Turkish origin such as *haleem* (minced meat cooked with wheat) and *lukmi* (puff pastry squares filled with meat).

Falaknuma Palace *(see p665)*, photographed towards the end of the 19th century by the court photographer Lala Deen Dayal, captures the opulence of the Nizam of Hyderabad's lifestyle.

The Nizams' jewels were legendary, and included fabulous pieces such as this 19th-century turban ornament, set with rubies from Burma and diamonds from their mines at Golconda *(see pp670–71)*.

Muharram *(see p673)* is observed by processions of Shia Muslims carrying decorated tazias through the city. Hyderabad's Shia population is mostly descended from Persians who settled here several generations ago.

Golconda miniatures often depict the city's sophisticated, cosmopolitan culture. This 18th-century painting shows merchants from many lands calling on a lady.

❷ Golconda

Sprawling across a boulder-strewn plateau, Golconda ("Shepherd's Hill") Fort was the citadel of the Qutb Shahi dynasty, which ruled the Hyderabad region from 1518 to 1687. The earlier 12th-century mud fort that stood here was transformed between 1518 and 1580 into a splendid fortified city of grand palaces, mosques and gardens by successive Qutb Shahi rulers. Golconda Fort was also famous for its great hoard of diamonds, mined nearby, which included the celebrated Kohinoor diamond, now part of the British Crown jewels. The colossal ruins of Golconda cover an area of 40 sq km (15 sq miles).

Bala Hisar Gate, entrance to the royal complex at Golconda Fort

🏛 Golconda Fort
This great fortress is protected by three formidable lines of defence. The first, an outer fortification made of enormous blocks of granite, encircles the citadel and its entire township. The middle wall surrounds the base of the hill, while the innermost one follows the contours of the highest ridge. Visitors enter through the **Fateh Darwaza** ("Victory Gate"), on the east side, which has a Hindu deity carved above its arch. Huge iron spikes are studded into the gate to prevent it from being stormed by elephant cavalries. From the Fateh Darwaza, the road curves past the

Archaeological Museum (the old Treasury), and through the bazaar, once a famous centre for cutting and polishing diamonds. Beyond are the two massive arches of the **Habshi Kaman Gate**, with rooms on top. These used to house a drummers' gallery and the sultans' Abyssinian guards. This gate leads to the middle fortification wall.

To its north is the austere, domed **Jama Masjid**, built in 1518 by Sultan Quli Qutb Shah, the founder of the dynasty; he was murdered here while at prayer by his son Jamshed in 1543. Beyond is the ceremonial arch, the **Bala Hisar Gate**, decorated with various Hindu motifs, including *yalis* (fantastic leonine beasts). This is the entrance to the inner citadel, known as the **Bala Hisar Complex**, where the royal palaces, assembly halls, workshops and an armoury are located. North of the Bala Hisar is a walled enclosure, begun in 1652, and planned as an extension to the inner fort. **Hathion ka Jhaad** ("Elephant Tree"), in the Naya Qila, is an extra- ordinary 700-year-old Baobab tree (*Adansonia*

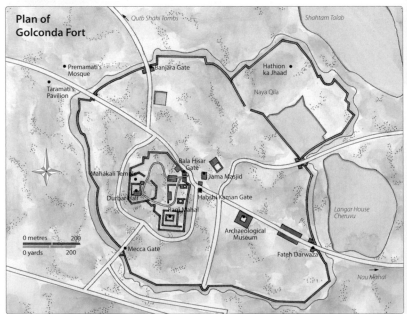

Plan of Golconda Fort

Qutb Shahi Tombs

Shahtam Talab

Premamati's Mosque

Banjara Gate

Hathion ka Jhaad

Taramati's Pavilion

Naya Qila

Bala Hisar Gate

Mahakali Temple

Jama Masjid

Durbar Hall

Habshi Kaman Gate

Rani Mahal

Langar House Cheruvu

Archaeological Museum

0 metres 200
0 yards 200

Mecca Gate

Fateh Darwaza

Nau Mahal

The royal bath near Rani Mahal, Golconda Fort

digitata), said to have been brought to Golconda by the sultans' Abyssinian guards.

The large-domed **Grand Portico** behind the Bala Hisar Gate is a good place to test the remarkable acoustics that were an important feature of the fort's defences. A soft handclap here can be heard in the king's chambers at the summit of the hill.

West of the Grand Portico are the ruins of the Qutb Shahi palaces. The most impressive of these is the **Rani Mahal**, a vaulted hall on a raised terrace, decorated with lovely floral arabesques. Hollows in these carvings were once inlaid with Golconda's famous diamonds and other precious stones. To the west of the Rani Mahal, a steep flight of 200 steps winds past royal baths, granaries, treasuries, water tanks and the remains of gardens, to the summit of the hill. Traces of the elaborate water supply system which carried water to the top of the citadel are visible along the route.

Just below the summit is a graceful mosque built by Sultan Ibrahim Qutb Shah, the third sultan, and the ancient Hindu **Mahakali Temple**, built into a cave.

At the summit of the hill is the three-storeyed **Durbar Hall** ("Throne Room"), with a rooftop pavilion. From here there are wonderful views of the entire fort and its surroundings, which include two pretty structures on hillocks – **Taramati Baradari** and **Premamati's Mosque**.

These are named after the two dancers who were royal favourites, and said to be so lightfooted that they could dance all the way from the pavilion to the Bala Hisar on a tightrope. Standing outside the fort, east of the Fateh Darwaza, is the **Nau Mahal** ("Nine Palaces"), where the Nizams of Hyderabad held court whenever they came to Golconda.

🎧 Qutb Shahi Tombs

1 km (0.6 miles) NW of Golconda Fort. This royal necropolis, where seven of the nine Qutb Shahi rulers are buried, is laid out in gardens with water channels, pools and tree-lined pathways. The tombs, built by each king in his lifetime, display a distinct and eclectic architectural style – they have large onion domes, Persian arches, Turkish columns and Hindu brackets and motifs. Built of grey granite and plaster, each tomb's dome is set on a petalled base, with a richly ornamented gallery and small minarets surrounding it. The **Tomb of Muhammad Quli Qutb Shah**, the founder of the city of Hyderabad, is the most impressive. It is surrounded by a spacious terrace, where poetry and music festivals and Hyderabadi food festivals are occasionally held. Traces of brilliant turquoise and green enamelled tiles, which once

Ceiling decoration, Bala Hisar Gate

The elegant tomb of Muhammad Quli Qutb Shah, Golconda

covered the façades of all the tombs, still remain. Other remarkable monuments are the **Tomb of Queen Hayat Baksh Begum**, the wife of Mohammed Quli Qutb Shah, and the mosque behind it (both mid-17th century), decorated with exquisite floral designs and calligraphy.

At the centre of the complex is the simple but beautifully proportioned **Royal Mortuary Bath**. The bodies of the deceased kings were ritually bathed before burial on the inlaid, 12-sided platform; the surrounding 12 water tanks symbolize the 12 Shia Imams.

A panoramic view of Golconda Fort

❸ Pochampalli

Nalgonda district. 41 km (26 miles) E of Hyderabad. 🚌 🛕 daily.

Andhra Pradesh's ikat belt, where intricate tie-and-dye textiles are woven, borders Hyderabad. Pochampalli, the name by which most of the state's ikat fabric is known, is the largest centre for this craft. The technique in its present form was first introduced in the 19th century in Chirala, in Guntur district, from where the fabric was exported to Africa.

Pochampalli's main street is lined with busy workshops where the various stages of production take place. Ikat weavers first tie the yarn according to the pattern and then dye them in great vats. A special oil-based technique is used to restrict the dye to those parts of the yarn that need to be coloured. The dyed yarn is then dried in the sun and finally woven on large hand-operated looms, to produce a cloth called *telia rumal (see p417)*. The state cooperative warehouses, as well as several shops, sell a wide range of beautiful silk saris and fabrics.

Environs
The neighbouring village of **Choutuppal**, 20 km (16 miles) southeast of Pochampalli, produces mainly cotton ikat fabrics. **Narayanpur**, another major weaving centre, is about 36 km (23 miles) further down the Vijaywada Highway, again to the southeast.

Khush Mahal, the audience hall at Warangal Fort

❹ Warangal

Warangal district. 148 km (92 miles) NE of Hyderabad. 🚉 🚌 ℹ APTDC, Kazipet, (0870) 245 9201.

A major *dhurrie*-weaving centre today, Warangal was described by the 13th-century Venetian traveller, Marco Polo, as one of the principal cities of South India. It was the capital of the Hindu Kakatiya kings, who dominated this region until the beginning of the 14th century.

An ancient fort at the edge of the modern town is all that remains of this once grand city. Built during the reign of the Kakatiya queen Rudramadevi (r.1262–89), its striking circular plan, with three concentric rings of walls, is still intact. The outer two rings, both of mud, define a circle 1.2 km (1 mile) in diameter. The innermost ring is made of stone, with four massive gateways at the cardinal points. At its geometric centre, four ornate *toranas* (gateways), marking the sacred precinct, are the only remains of a great Shiva temple that once stood here. The *toranas* themselves are remarkable for their size and beauty.

A short distance to the west is the **Khush Mahal**, an audience hall that was built by Muslim invaders in the 14th century. Massive angled walls with slit windows define a lofty interior with vaulted arches, though the roof is quite damaged. It is remarkably similar to the Hindola Mahal in Mandu *(see p251)*.

Environs
Hanamkonda, the site of the first Kakatiya capital before it moved to Warangal, is 3 km (2 miles) northwest of Warangal. The magnificent Thousand-Pillared Temple here, dedicated to Shiva, was erected in 1163 by Rudradeva (r.1158–95), the first great Kakatiya king.

This grey-green basalt temple, known as the *trikuta* or triple shrine, consists of a trio of shrines dedicated to Shiva, Vishnu and Surya. They are connected to a *mandapa*, now roofless, by a platform with a magnificently polished Nandi bull. The columns have sharply cut, lathe-turned shafts. A ceiling panel carved with an image of Nataraja *(see p570)* covers the central bay. The temple's gardens contain several small linga shrines, and an ancient well.

The magnificent Thousand-Pillared Temple at Hanamkonda, near Warangal

The 13th-century Ramappa Temple at Palampet

❺ Palampet

Warangal district. 213 km (133 miles) NE of Hyderabad. 🚌

This village is dominated by the **Ramappa Temple**, the best preserved example of Kakatiya architecture. Dedicated to Shiva, it was built in 1213 by Recherla Rudra, a general of the ruler Ganapatideva (r.1199–1262). Like the temple at Hanamkonda, it too has a spacious *mandapa* with beautifully sculpted black basalt columns. This *mandapa*, cruciform in plan, also has porches with balcony seats on three sides. The eaves sheltering the peripheral columns are supported by angled struts, many

Carving, Gana Puram

of which are fashioned as three-dimensional maidens with graceful bodies in dancing poses. Other similar but smaller relief figures, as well as scenes from the epics, are seen in the central ceiling panel within the *mandapa*.

The exterior of the sanctuary, in contrast, is devoid of any carvings. The restrained ornamentation and simple modelling are typical of the elegance of Kakatiya art. A stone pavilion sheltering a Nandi, smaller in size than the one at Hanamkonda, but as exquisitely carved, stands in front of the temple.

South of the Ramappa Temple is **Ramappa Cheruvu**, a vast artificial lake created by Recherla Rudra, and surrounded by picturesque hills.

Environs

More Kakatiya temples can be seen at **Gana Puram**, a little village 13 km (8 miles) northwest of Palampet. The largest consists of a pair of Shiva shrines, both with *mandapas* and balcony seats. The main shrine has delightful female *dvarapalas* (doorkeepers), dancing maidens and finely carved brackets. Other minor shrines dot the walled compound.

Traditional Andhra Dhurries

Although lustrous silk and wool carpets from Persia and Turkey embellished the palaces of the Nizams of Hyderabad, Andhra Pradesh has long had a local tradition of carpet weaving in Warangal and Eluru. Commonly known as *dhurries*, the rugs are made in both cotton and wool, in a variety of designs and colours. The cotton *dhurries* from Warangal are usually woven into geometric patterns, while the woollen carpets of Eluru (274 km/170 miles southeast of Warangal) sport floral designs that hint at a Western influence. The more expensive *shatranjis* (a chessboard-like pattern) are made with heavy cotton thread and produced on horizontal looms. The *kalamkari* craftsmen of Sri Kalahasti (see p684) make rugs in traditional designs on a jute base, using vegetable dyes.

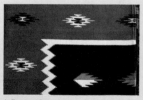

A *dhurrie* with geometric patterns

A view of the Visakhapatnam harbour on the Bay of Bengal

❻ Visakhapatnam

Visakhapatnam district. 354 km
(220 miles) NE of Vijayawada.
🚠 3,591,811. ✈ 12 km (7 miles)
W of town centre, then bus or taxi.
🚉 🚌 ℹ APTDC, RTC Complex,
(0891) 278 8820. 🏖 daily.

India's second busiest port
after Mumbai, Visakhapatnam,
also known as Vizag, is rapidly
becoming the largest shipyard
in the country. It is an important
industrial town and naval base
as well. The town makes a
convenient point from which
to visit some of the beautiful
beaches along the Bay of
Bengal and the many pic-
turesque temple towns of the
northern coastal districts of
Andhra Pradesh.

Named after Visakha,
the Hindu God of Valour, Visakhapatnam was once part of the
Mauryan emperor Ashoka's vast
empire (see p46). Later, it was
ruled by the Andhra kings of
Vengi, and other South Indian
dynasties, including the Pallavas,
Cholas and Gangas. In the
15th century, it became part
of the Vijayanagar Empire
(see pp534–5). It finally came
into British hands in the 17th
century, after which it was
developed into a major port.

Looming above the port is
a hilly ridge with three crests,
each with a religious shrine.
On the southernmost one,
Venkateshvara Konda, is a
temple dedicated to Balaji
(Krishna); in the middle is
Ross Hill, with a mid-19th-
century church; the third,

Dargah Konda, has a shrine
dedicated to a Muslim
saint, Ishaque Madina.

Along the southern coastline
is **Dolphin's Nose**, a 358-m
(1,175-ft) long rocky outcrop
that rises 175 m (574 ft) above
the sea. On it stands
a lighthouse with a
beam that can be
seen 64 km (40
miles) out at sea.
Vestiges of the city's
colonial past are
visible here in an
old Protestant
church, a fort,
barracks and an arsenal, all
dating to the 18th century.

Idyllic beaches, set on the
fringes of the Eastern Ghats
and bounded by forested hills
and rocky cliffs, include the
Ramakrishna Mission Beach,
now being developed as
a tourist resort by Andhra
Pradesh Tourism, **Rishikonda
Beach** and **Lawson's Bay**.

Towards the north of the
town, beyond Lawson's Bay, is
Kailasagiri, a forested hill which

Dutch heraldry,
Bheemunipatnam

has several lookout points for
a panoramic view of the city
and harbour. The twin town of
Waltair, once a health resort
for British officers, is north of
the bay. Andhra University, one
of the largest campuses in the
state, is also situated here,
along with a number of pretty
19th-century churches.

Environs
Simhachalam, the "Lion's Hill"
Temple, dedicated to Lord Varaha
Narasimha, an incarnation of
Vishnu (see p683), stands at the
summit of the thickly forested
Ratnagiri Hill, 16 km (10 miles)
northwest of Visakhapatnam.
A flight of steps leads to the
northern gateway, an elaborately
decorated gopura that is the
main entrance to the temple.
Inside the compound is a
tall dvajasthambha (flagpole).
Similar in style to
Konark's Sun Temple
(see pp314–15),
the temple was
constructed in
the 9th or 10th
century, and was
extensively rebuilt
during the 13th
century. It is
believed that the presiding
deity was originally Shiva, but
he was replaced by this
incarnation of Vishnu after the
reformer-saint, Ramanuja (see
p526), visited the site in the
11th century.

Bheemunipatnam is a 38-km
(24-mile) drive northeast from
Visakhapatnam, along one of the
longest stretches of beach road
in the country. This quiet fishing
village, situated at the mouth of
the Gosthani river, was a Dutch

Obelisk-shaped Dutch tombs at Bheemunipatnam

settlement in the early 17th century. Bimlipatam, as it was then known (locally referred to as Bhimli), was the site of Maratha attacks and Anglo-Dutch wars throughout the 17th and 18th centuries. Its Dutch legacy can be seen in some of the old colonnaded houses, the ruined fort, and the Dutch cemetery, which has unusual, obelisk-shaped tombstones.

A fascinating stalactite formation inside the Borra Caves

❼ Borra Caves

Visakhapatnam district. 90 km (56 miles) N of Visakhapatnam. 🚌
Open daily 📷

Close to the northern border of Visakhapatnam district are these magnificent limestone caves, discovered in 1807 by William King of the Geological Survey of India. The extensive underground chambers, lined by stalactites and stalagmites, are now being developed by

the state tourism department as a major attraction for visitors. Some smaller stalagmites are worshipped as lingas, with Nandi bulls placed in front of them. The local people believe that the water trickling from the roof of the caves is from a mountain spring which is the source of the Gosthani river.

Environs
About 22 km (14 miles) northeast of Borra is the **Araku Valley**, home of several tribal communities, the state's original inhabitants. The road to Araku goes past

Tribal women from Araku Valley

forests and coffee plantations, and the valley, with its woods, waterfalls and bracing climate, offers pleasant walks.

❽ Ramatirtham

Visakhapatnam district. 72 km (45 miles) NE of Visakhapatnam. 🚌

Ruins from the Ikshvaku period (3rd to 4th centuries AD), when Buddhism flourished in this area, can be seen at Ramatirtham. Just outside the village is a group of structures on a hill known as Gurubhaktakonda ("Hill of the Devoted Disciple"). On a narrow rocky ledge about 165 m (541 ft) above the surrounding plains are the ruins of a stupa, monasteries, and prayer halls enclosing smaller stupas. Close by, on another hill called Durgakonda, is a similar set of ruins, along with carvings of Jain *tirthankaras* (see p400) that date from the 8th and 9th centuries.

❾ Srikakulam District

108 km (67 miles) NE from Visakhapatnam to Srikakulam. 🚌

The headquarters of Andhra Pradesh's northernmost district, Srikakulam is located on the banks of the Swarnamukhi river. On the outskirts of the town, at **Arasavalli**, is a sun temple, ingeniously constructed at such an angle that the sun's rays fall directly on the deity's feet twice a year. The **Sri Kurmanadha Temple** at Srikurman, 13 km (8 miles) east of Srikakulam, is dedicated to Kurma, the tortoise incarnation of Vishnu. It was built by the Chalukya kings in the 10th century but was substantially rebuilt by the Cholas in the 12th and 13th centuries. The colonnade around the main shrine has 19th century murals of Krishna and Vishnu.

Mukhalingam, 48 km (30 miles) north of Srikakulam, was the first capital of the Eastern Ganga kings, before they moved to Odisha (see p48). The temples here date to their reign, between the 9th and 13th centuries. The best preserved is the 9th-century Madhukeshvara Temple, with magnificent sculptures of Shiva and friezes of scenes from the Krishna legend. The 10th-century Someshvara Temple, at the entrance to the town, has beautiful statues of river goddesses and other deities, flanking the main doorway.

Mural showing Krishna surrounded by *gopis*, at Sri Kurmanadha Temple in Srikakulam district

Ripening fields of paddy with the Eastern Ghats in the background, near Rajahmundry

⑩ East Godavari District

398 km (247 miles) E of Hyderabad to Rajahmundry. ✈ 10 km (6 miles) from Rajahmundry. 🚉 Rajahmundry. 🚌

The Godavari, one of South India's most sacred rivers, swells to a wide torrent (at places 6 km/ 4 miles across), just north of **Rajahmundry** town. Lush paddy fields and sugarcane plantations characterize the countryside.

Rajahmundry, the largest town in East Godavari district, is best known for the many Chalukya temples in its vicinity, and for the 2,743-m (8,999-ft) long bridge that spans the river. The lookout points on **Dowleswaram Dam** (built 1848–52), 10 km (6 miles) downstream, offer spectacular views of the river. Every 12 years, the Dakshina Pushkaram festival – the Kumbh Mela (see p215) of the South – takes place here.

Peddapuram, famous for its fine handwoven silk and cotton, is 43 km (27 miles) northeast of Rajahmundry, on the road to Visakhapatnam.

Annavaram, 81 km (50 miles) to the northeast of Rajahmundry, is the site of the Satyanarayana Temple, on Ratnagiri Hill, renowned for its 4-m (13 ft)-high statue of the Hindu Trinity, and its ancient sundial.

The **Godavari Gorge** begins 80 km (50 miles) north of Rajahmundry. A drive or boat ride along the Gorge, which cuts through the hilly Eastern Ghats, offers views of spectacular scenery, with a series of lakes that many find reminiscent of Italy and Scotland.

Ryali, 37 km (23 miles) south of Rajahmundry, has a Chalukya temple dedicated to Vishnu. It houses a stone image of the Goddess Ganga (see p167), from which flows a continuous trickle of water.

Draksharamam, 46 km (29 miles) southeast of Rajahmundry, is famed for its 10th-century Bhimeswara Swamy Temple, which combines the Chalukya and Chola styles of architecture, and houses a 5-m (16-ft) high linga. The Godavari is said to have been split into seven streams by the Saptarishis (seven great sages) of Hindu mythology and three of these streams are believed to have gone underground here. Close to the town is an old Dutch cemetery, locally known as Ollandu Dibba ("Holland Mound"), with gravestones dated between 1675 and 1728, some with very elaborate designs.

Antarvedi, on the banks of the Vashishta river, a branch of the Godavari, is 112 km (70 miles) south of Rajahmundry. It is best reached by boat from Narsapur on the south bank. The Sri Laxmi Narasimha Swamy Temple (built in 1823), with its brightly painted tower, stands on the river bank and is usually thronged with pilgrims who come for a dip in the holy river.

⑪ Machilipatnam

Krishna district. 340 km (211 miles) SE of Hyderabad. 🚉 🚌 🚗 daily.

One of the first European settlements on India's eastern coast, Machilipatnam ("City of Fish") was a thriving port and textile centre in the 17th and 18th centuries. It was also the headquarters of the English East India Company on the Coromandel Coast. The French and the Dutch briefly established themselves here as well. The Dutch cemetery, with its ornate tombstones, are all that remain from that period.

Machilipatnam was hit by a giant tidal wave in 1864, which drowned more than 30,000 people. It was caused by a volcanic eruption at Mount Krakatoa, 5,000 km (3,107 miles) away. After that it lost its importance as a port, but it remains famous for its kalamkari textiles (see p684).

A kalamkari blockprinter at work in Machilipatnam

Trade Textiles: Tree of Life

Between the 17th and 18th centuries, the Coromandel Coast, with Machilipatnam as its trade centre and port, was one of the main producers and exporters of cotton textiles to Western Europe. At first just items of barter, they soon became fashionable in Europe, increasing the demand for the region's dye-painted cotton *kalamkari* (*see p684*) fabric, known in Europe as chintz. Special designs were commissioned, among them the Tree of Life, which absorbed techniques and aesthetics from India, Persia, China and Europe. Valued for their richness of colour and design, they were widely used as hangings and spreads in European homes.

Tree of Life

The Tree of Life was a very popular motif in textiles from the Coromandel Coast. Based on ancient nature myths that deified plants and trees, and inspired largely by Persian miniatures, its central flowering tree, rising from a rocky mound, linked earth to heaven and symbolized creation.

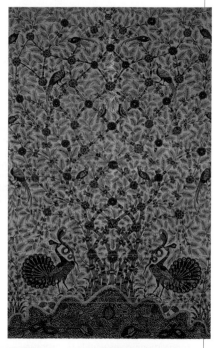

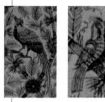

Birds, real and mythical, inhabit the thickly foliated upper branches of the tree. Standing on the mound are two stylized peacocks holding snakes in their beaks.

Aquatic creatures, such as fish and tortoise, are depicted to show marine life in the holy waters below the Sacred Mound. Shades of indigo have been used to create the effect of rippling waves and flowing water.

A bamboo thicket, composed as a single Tree of Life, rises from the Sacred Mound. The painted and printed flowers and feathery leaves suggest nature's exuberance.

A view of the Prakasam Barrage, built over the Krishna river at Vijayawada

⑫ Vijayawada

Krishna district. 267 km (166 miles) SE of Hyderabad. 🚗 1,048,240. 🚉 🚌 ℹ APTDC, (0866) 257 1393. 🛒 daily.

The third largest city in the state, Vijayawada is a busy commercial town with one of the largest railway junctions in the country. In a picturesque spot on the northern bank of the Krishna river, it is bounded on three sides by the Indrakiladri Hills. The area around the river banks is a pleasant contrast to the noisy, crowded town.

Within the city limits, on a low hill to the east, is the **Kanaka Durga Temple**, dedicated to the goddess Lakshmi. The **Victoria Museum**, on Bunder Road, houses a fine collection of Buddhist and Hindu relics from the 2nd and 3rd centuries. Especially impressive are the white limestone Standing Buddha from the nearby Buddhist site of Alluru (3rd or 4th century), and the powerful depiction of Durga slaying the buffalo demon Mahisa (2nd century).

On the outskirts of town is the 1-km (0.6-mile) long **Prakasam Barrage**, first built in 1855 and extensively reconstructed in 1955. It irrigates nearly 1.2 million ha (3 million acres) of land, turning the Krishna Delta into the richest granary in Andhra Pradesh. **Bhavani Island**, a scenic picnic spot, is just upstream, reached by launch from the river bank.

▥ Victoria Museum
Open Sat–Thu. Extra charges for photography.

Environs
Mogalrajapuram, 3 km (2 miles) east of Vijayawada, and **Undavalli**, 4 km (2.5 miles) to the south, on the other side of the river, are famous for their rock-cut temples (5th–7th centuries).

Mangalgiri, 12 km (7 miles) south of Vijayawada, is a textile village, specializing in fine cotton saris and striped and checked fabrics. It also has the impressive 14th-century Lakshmi Narasimha Temple complex, with a small Garuda shrine in front of it.

⑬ Kondapalli

Krishna district. 20 km (12 miles) NW of Vijayawada. 🚌

This pretty village, famous for its painted wooden toys, is dominated by the 8th-century Hill Fort built by the Eastern Chalukya dynasty. Encircled by ramparts and towers, the fort was an important stronghold in the Krishna Valley under the Qutb Shahis of Hyderabad (see p670), in the 16th century. At the crest of the hill, a steep climb up, is the ruined Tanisha Mahal palace. The path descends past a deep tank, the granary and the armoury, to the Golconda Gate, which faces northwest towards Hyderabad.

Kondapalli Toys

Lord Krishna

The craft of toy-making has been passed down for many generations in Kondapalli. In the hands of the deft artisans, the light yet strong and flexible *poniki* wood is fashioned into distinctive figures of gods and goddesses, fruits and vegetables, which adorn many Andhra homes during festivals. Each part of the toy is whittled into shape, and then glued together using a special tamarind-seed glue. The piece is then covered with lime glue, which gives it a smooth finish. It is allowed to dry before being brightly painted in vivid blues, greens, reds and yellows, with touches of black.

A toy being painted in bright colours

The Maha Chaitya at Amravati, now only a low earthen mound

⑭ Amravati

Guntur district. 37 km (23 miles) W of Vijayawada. 🚍 from Guntur. 🚍 from Hotel Krishnaveni, Vijayawada. 🚗 run by AP Tourism, Vijayawada. 🛈 Haritha Hotel, (08643) 224 616.

Renowned for its **Maha Chaitya**, or "Great Stupa", Amravati was once the most impressive of the many Buddhist religious settlements along the Krishna Valley. Today, nothing remains of this stupa except a low earthen mound, but in its day it was reputed to be the largest and most elaborate stupa in South India. It was built by the Satavahanas, the great Andhra dynasty, in the 3rd and 2nd centuries BC (see p47).

The Maha Chaitya was enlarged several times by the Ikshvaku kings, who succeeded the Satavahanas, reaching its final form between the 3rd and 4th centuries AD. Clad in the local white limestone, the Maha Chaitya was an earthen hemispherical mound about 45 m (148 ft) in diameter and more than 30 m (98 ft) in height, including its supporting drum and capping finial. It was surrounded by a 6-m (20-ft) high railing with posts and cross pieces, and lofty entrance gateways at the cardinal points, all exuberantly carved.

In the 5th century, when South India saw a revival of Hinduism,

the stupa was abandoned, and remained so until a British official, Colonel Colin Mackenzie, began excavating the site in 1796. Unfortunately, by the time a thorough investigation of the ruins began in the mid-19th century, most of the limestone portions had been pillaged, many fine pieces having been shipped to Britain.

Nevertheless, a great deal of fine sculpture remains at the site, and is on display at the **Archaeological Museum**, next to the Maha Chaitya. Unlike the stupa at Sanchi (see pp248–9), where the Buddha is represented through symbols such as the Bodhi Tree or footprints, the Amravati sculptures show him in human form. The museum's display includes large Standing Buddha images, some more than 2 m (7 ft) high, whose natural poses and elegantly fluted robes suggest the influence of late Roman classical art. The second gallery has a remarkable life-sized ceremonial bull, reconstructed from

fragments discovered in 1980. A part of the stupa's railing, decorated with scenes from the Buddha's life, is reconstructed in the courtyard. Other exhibits include an instructive model of the original monument and superb sculptures of the Bodhi Tree, under which the Buddha is said to have meditated.

🏛 **Archaeological Museum**
Open Sat–Thu. Extra charges for photography.

Environs

Overlooking the Krishna river, just north of the museum, is the **Amaralingeswara Swamy Temple**. Built during the 10th and 11th centuries, it was renovated in the 18th century by a local chief whose statue stands in the outer hall. The sanctuary and the open-columned hall are in a walled compound. A basement, reached by a flight of stairs, is believed to conceal the remains of a stupa, suggested by the pillar-shaped linga in the sanctuary, which was probably part of the stupa dome.

Ceremonial bull, Amravati Museum

The Amravati Sculptures

The surviving limestone carvings from the Maha Chaitya are now divided between the Archaeological Museum at Amravati, the Government Museum in Chennai (see p569) and the British Museum in London. These reliefs testify to the vitality of early Buddhist art traditions in South India. Posts and railings show ornate lotus medallions, friezes of garlands carried by dwarfs, and Jataka Tales (see p484) illustrated with vivid scenes of crowds, horse riders and courtiers. Drum panels are adorned with pots filled with lotuses, model stupas with serpents wrapped around the drums, and flying celestials above the umbrella-like finials.

Amravati limestone carving with a scene from the Jataka Tales

Limestone carving, Amravati Museum

⑮ Nagarjunakonda

Guntur district. 189 km (118 miles)
W of Vijayawada. 🚉 Macherla,
22 km (14 miles) SE of site, then
bus to Vijayapuri. 🚌 🚢 daily from
Vijayapuri, except Fri. 🛈 Vijay Vihar,
(08680) 277 362. 🎭 from Hyderabad.

Nagarjunakonda or "Nagarjuna's
Hill", on the banks of the Krishna
river, was named after Nagarjuna
Acharya, the 2nd-century
Buddhist theologian and founder
of an influential school of philosophy. Once a sophisticated
Buddhist settlement, with large
monasteries and stupas, wide
roads and public baths, it was
established in the 3rd and 4th
centuries, when the area
flourished under the rule of
the powerful Ikshvaku kings.

Thereafter, Nagarjunakonda
was ruled by a succession of
dynasties, culminating with the
Vijayanagar rulers, who built a
fort around the Buddhist ruins.
When the Vijayanagar Empire
declined, the area was abandoned.
It was rediscovered only between
1954 and 1961.

In the early 1960s, when the
huge Nagarjuna Sagar Dam was
being constructed across the
Krishna, a number of these
rediscovered ancient Buddhist
settlements were threatened
with submersion. However, the
Archaeological Survey of India
salvaged and reconstructed
many of them, brick by brick, on
top of the hill where the citadel
once used to stand.

Today, most of the hill, and the
secluded valley in which these

View of the hemispherical stupa, Bodhishri Chaitya, Nagarjunakonda

settlements once stood, have
been submerged by the waters
of the Nagarjuna Sagar lake.
Only the top of the hill, where
the rescued remains have been
reassembled, juts out like an
island. The island is accessible
by launches, which leave
regularly from the small
village of Vijayapuri, on the
banks of the lake.

On the island, the path from
the jetty leads first to the **Simha
Vihara 4**. This comprises a
stupa built on a high
platform with a pair of
chaitya grihas (prayer
halls) adjoining it. While
one of the *chaitya
grihas* houses a
second stupa, the
other enshrines a
monumental
sculpture of the
Standing Buddha. The **Bodhishri
Chaitya**, opposite it, has a raised
stupa contained within a semi-
circular-ended brick structure. To
its west is the **Maha Chaitya**
stupa which, with a diameter of

Detail of a carving,
Nagarjunakonda

27.5 m (90 ft), was one of the
largest at Nagarjunakonda. Its
internal rubble walls radiate
outwards like the spokes of a
wheel, and are filled with earth.
Just ahead of it is the **Swastika
Chaitya**, named after the Indian
swastika emblem formed by
its rubble walls.

Near the citadel walls is a stone
megalith, some 2,000 years old. It
conceals a simple burial chamber
that once contained four skulls.

To its east is the
**Archaeological
Museum**, which
houses superb
Buddhist sculptures
from the ruins of
Nagarjunakonda. They
include limestone
reliefs and panels
carved with seated
Buddhas, flying
celestial beings and miniature
replicas of stupas. Friezes from
the railings which surrounded the
stupas depict scenes from the
Buddha's life. Among the free-
standing sculptures are dignified
Buddha figures dressed in
elegant robes.

🏛 **Archaeological Museum**
Open Sat–Thu. 📷 🚫

Environs
More structures from the
Ikshvaku period are
reassembled at a site 15 km (9
miles) south of Vijayapuri. These
include a Stadium, with tiered
galleries around a central court,
possibly used for musical and
theatrical performances and
sporting events. The adjacent
Monastic Complex has shrines
and *chaitya grihas* as well as a
refectory, store and baths.

A giant-sized statue of the Standing Buddha in Nagarjunakonda

For hotels and restaurants see p703 and p719

⑯ Srisailam & Krishna Gorge

Kurnool district. 213 km (133 miles) S of Hyderabad. 🚌 daily from Hyderabad. 🛈 Haritha Hotel, APTDC, (08643) 224 616; Punnami Hotel, Srisailam, (08524) 288 888. 🎎 Shivaratri (Feb/Mar).

The pretty temple town of Srisailam, situated in the thickly wooded Nallamalai Hills, overlooking the deep Krishna Gorge, is a popular pilgrimage spot. Dominating the town is the **Mallikarjuna Swamy Temple**, whose white tiered *gopuras*, standing atop fortress-like walls, are visible from a great distance. The temple, which houses one of the 12 *jyotirlingas* (naturally formed lingas said to contain the light of Shiva), is believed to date to pre-Vedic times, though the present structure was built in the 15th century. The carvings on the walls represent Shiva in his many forms. A pillared hallway leads to the inner shrine, guarded by a monolithic Nandi bull.

Further up the hill is the **Hatakesvara Temple**, said to be the spot where the philosopher-saint Shankaracharya (see p652) wrote one of his celebrated treatises. A small Shiva temple at the summit, **Sikharam**, offers breathtaking views of the valley.

The dammed waters of the Krishna power a huge hydroelectric project at Srisailam. When the waters are high enough, a luxury launch, the *Zaria*, ferries visitors from the reservoir at Nagarjuna Sagar to Srisailam Dam. For almost half the distance between the reservoir and Srisailam Dam, the river passes through a thick forest reserve, habitat of the tiger, panther and hyena. The river, which runs very deep at Srisailam, is known here as the Patal Ganga ("Underground Ganges") – according to legend, it springs from an underground tributary of the Ganges. On the ghats close to the dam, boatmen offer enchanting rides on their basin-shaped reed and bamboo boats.

The Sangameshvara Temple outside Alampur village

⑰ Alampur

Mahboobnagar district. 215 km (134 miles) S of Hyderabad. 🚗 🚌

This village, on the northern bank of the Tungabhadra river, is the site of the earliest Hindu temples in Andhra Pradesh. Constructed by the Chalukyas of Badami (see pp540–41) in the 7th and 8th centuries, the nine red sandstone shrines are collectively known as the **Navabrahma Temples**, and are dedicated to Shiva. The layout conforms to a standard scheme – each temple faces east, has an inner sanctum, a pillared *mandapa*, and is surrounded by a passage. The tower over the inner sanctum, capped by an *amalaka* (circular ribbed stone), shows the distinct influence of North Indian temple architecture (see p24).

Detail from the Padmabrahma Temple

The later temples in the group have porches with perforated stone screens on three sides of the passageways, as in the **Svargabrahma Temple**, built in AD 689. This beautiful temple

Naga (Snake deity) from the Archaeological Museum, Alampur

has outstanding sculptures, including a complete set of *dikpalas* (guardian figures) in the corner niches, and icons of Shiva in various forms. Some columns in the interior have been elaborately carved, such as those in the **Padmabrahma Temple**. The pillars here have seated lions at the base, fluted shafts and ribbed pot-shaped capitals. The **Balabrahma Temple** is the only one of the group, still in use. The **Archaeological Museum**, next to the complex, has a fine collection of early Chalukya sculptures. Just outside the village is the reconstructed **Sangameshvara Temple**, removed from a site that was submerged by the damming of the Krishna, 15 km (9 miles) to the north. Standing on a high terrace, it is similar to the Navabrahma group, except that the sculptural details have eroded.

Just southwest of the Navabrahma Temple complex are the **Papanashanam Temples** (9th–10th centuries). These temples have imposing multi-tiered pyramidal roofs but little external decoration, though the interior columns are ornately carved. One of the temples has a fine ceiling panel of Vishnu's incarnations (see p683), and another has a powerful image of Durga.

🏛 **Archaeological Museum**
Open Sat–Thu. 🖼

View of Tirupati, with the gold-gilded *vimana* of the temple

⑱ Tirupati

Chittoor district. 558 km (347 miles) S of Hyderabad. 🏨 228,202. ✈ 12 km (7 miles) S of the city centre, then taxi. 🚌 🚃 *i* Andhra Pradesh Tourism, Sridevi Complex (0877) 228 9120. 🎉 Brahmotsavam (Sep/Oct).

The most popular destination for Hindu pilgrims in India, Tirupati is the site of the **Shri Venkateshvara Temple**, situated in the Tirumala Hills, 700 m (2,297 ft) above the town. The seven "sacred hills" of Tirumala are believed to symbolize the seven-headed serpent god Adisesha, on whose coils Vishnu sleeps. The temple dates to the 9th century, although it has often been expanded and renovated from the 15th century onwards.

Lord Venkateshvara, the presiding deity at Tirupati

The aura that surrounds Lord Venkateshvara (a form of Lord Vishnu, who is also known as Balaji) as the "Bestower of Boons" has made his temple the most visited and the richest in India. It eclipses Jerusalem and Rome in the number of pilgrims it attracts – around 25,000 a day, and up to 100,000 on festival days. The gold *vimana* and flagpole, and the gold-plated doorway into the inner sanctum, proclaim the temple's wealth. The jet-black stone image, 2-m (7-ft) high, stands on a lotus and is adorned with rubies, diamonds and gold. The deity also wears a diamond crown, believed to be the singlemost precious

ornament in the world. He is flanked by his consorts, Sridevi and Bhudevi. The entrance portico has superb life-size images of the Vijayanagara king and queens (*see pp534–7*), who worshipped Venkateshvara as their protective deity.

The entire complex is built to accommodate the huge influx of pilgrims, who come to seek favours from Lord Venkateshvara. This is one of the few temples in South India where non-Hindus are allowed into the inner sanctum. Devotees wait patiently in long queues for a special *darshan*, and make offerings of money, gold and jewellery that net the temple an annual income of nearly 1.5 billion rupees. The Tirumala Tirupati Deva-sthanam (TTD), which runs the temple, employs a staff of 6,000 to see to the pilgrims' needs and maintain temple premises.

The temple complex includes a ritual bathing tank, and a small **Art Museum** with images of deities, musical instruments and votive objects. Surrounding it are green valleys and the Akash Ganga waterfall, which is the source of the holy water used for bathing the deity.

A unique feature at Tirupati is that many devotees offer their hair to the deity, and there are separate enclosures for this purpose. It is believed that since hair enhances a person's

appearance, shaving it off sheds vanity as well. This offering is usually made after the fulfilment of a wish. The hair-offerings are later exported to the United States and Japan where they are made into wigs.

Most pilgrims stop at the small Ganesha shrine in the foothills, and at the **Govinda-rajaswamy Temple** in Tirupati town, before driving up the hill to the Tirumala shrine. This temple, which dates to the 16th–17th century, is dedicated to both Krishna and Vishnu. Built by the Nayakas, the successors to the Vijayanagar rulers, it is approached through a massive, grey outer *gopura* that dominates Tirupati's skyline, and is carved with scenes from the *Ramayana* (*see p31*). An exquisite pavilion in the inner courtyard has carved granite pillars, an ornate wooden roof, and impressive sculptures of crouching lions. The temple has a magnificent image of the reclining Vishnu, called Ranganatha, coated with bronze armour. A short distance north of the temple is the **Venkateshvara Museum of Temple Arts**, with temple models, photographs and ritual objects.

🏛 **Shri Venkateshvara Temple**
Open daily. Darshan: 6–11am. Extra charges to join the shorter queue for special darshan of the deity.

The main gateway to the Govindarajaswamy Temple

Avatars of Vishnu

Vishnu, the second god in the Hindu Trinity, personifies the preserving power of nature. Seen as the most "human" of the gods and the redeemer of humanity, he is said to have appeared on Earth in several avatars or incarnations, whenever the cosmic order was disturbed. From the 2nd century, a new devotional worship of Vishnu's incarnation as Krishna developed in South India, and, by AD 1000, Vaishnavism had become widespread. At his most famous temple, in Tirupati, Vishnu is worshipped as Venkateshvara, the God who Fulfills Desires. Lakshmi, the Goddess of Wealth, is his consort.

The Ten Incarnations

Vishnu descends to earth periodically, in order to redress the balance between good and evil. He is said to have ten main avatars, of which nine have already appeared; the tenth is yet to come.

Main image of Vishnu

Kavad is a portable wooden shrine, which shows Vishnu in his Krishna avatar, protected by the serpent Adisesha, and with his brother Balrama.

Krishna, who came to free the world from oppression.

Matsya, the fish and first avatar, rescued Manu (the first man) and the Vedas from a flood.

Rama, the seventh avatar, is the embodiment of goodness.

Buddha, is the ninth avatar *(see p225)*.

Kurma, the tortoise and second avatar, churned the ocean to produce *amrita*, the divine nectar.

Krishna

Vamana, the dwarf priest and the fifth avatar, saved the world from a demon

Parasurama, the sixth avatar, came to subdue the Kshatriyas who were overpowering the Brahmins.

Varaha, the boar and third avatar, saved the earth from drowning in the ocean by lifting it up on his tusks.

Narasimha, the half-man, half-lion fourth avatar, killed the demon Hiranyakshipu and delivered the earth from his evil deeds.

Kalki, the tenth avatar, is still to come. Vishnu will then appear for the final destruction and will recreate the world in perfect purity.

See also features on Hindu Mythology *(see pp28–9)*, Ganesha *(see p471)* and Shiva *(see p570)*

Rani Mahal, roofed by stepped pyramidal towers, at Chandragiri

⑲ Chandragiri

Tirupati district. 18 km (11 miles) SW of Tirupati. 🚌 from Tirupati.

This small village was once an important outpost of the Vijayanagar kings. It later became the capital of the Aravidu ruler, Venkatapatideva (r.1586–1614), whose reign saw the decline of the Vijayanagar Empire.

Chandragiri's once glorious past is reflected in the massive walls of its late 16th-century fortress and some abandoned palaces. The most important of these is the **Raja Mahal**, which has an arcaded Durbar Hall and a domed pleasure pavilion. It was here that Sir Francis Day of the East India Company was granted land in 1639, in order to set up a factory in what later came to be known as Madras (see p561). Nearby is the **Rani Mahal**, with its striking pyramidal towers, and its façade decorated with foliate and geometric motifs.

A temple next to the ruined palaces at Chandragiri

⑳ Sri Kalahasti

Chittoor district. 41 km (26 miles) E of Tirupati. 🚌 from Tirupati. 🎦 Temple Festival (Sep/Oct).

Located between two steep hills, on the southern bank of the Svarnamukhi river, this town is one of the most important pilgrimage centres in Andhra Pradesh. Dominating one end of the crowded main street is a 36.5-m (120-ft) high free-standing *gopura*, erected in 1516 by Emperor Krishnadeva Raya of Vijayanagar (see pp534–7). The royal emblems of the dynasty, depicting the boar and the

Flower seller at Sri Kalahasti

sword together with the sun and the moon, are intricately carved on to the walls of this seven-storeyed towered gateway.

Nearby, similar but smaller *gopuras* provide access to the **Kalahastishvara Temple**, the town's main attraction, surrounded by a paved rectangular compound. A doorway to the south leads into a crowded enclosure of columned halls, pavilions, lamp columns and altars, connected by a maze of colonnades and corridors. Some of the columns are carved as rearing animal figures. In the north corridor are a set of bronzes of the 63 Shaivite saints called Nayannars (see p49). The inner sanctum, opening to the west, enshrines the *vayu* (air) linga, one of the five elemental lingas of Shiva (see p590) in South India. It is a curiously elongated linga protected by a cobra hood, made of brass. According to a local legend, a spider, a cobra and an elephant worshipped the linga in their own special way. The spider first spun a web around it to

Kalamkari Fabrics

Deriving their name from the word *kalam* for pen and *kari* for work, these brightly coloured cotton fabrics are produced at Machilipatnam (see p676) and Sri Kalahasti. Using a mixture of painting and dyeing techniques, figures of gods, goddesses, trees and birds are first drawn on the fabric, and then painted with a "pen" made of a bamboo stick padded at one end with cotton cloth. The traditional natural colours of ochre, soft pink, indigo, madder red and iron black are characteristic of *kalamkari* textiles. *Kalamkaris* from Sri Kalahasti were part of temple ritual and, like temple murals, depict mythological themes, with gods, goddesses and other celestial beings. The ones from Machilipatnam display a distinct Persian influence (see p677) and once formed part of a lucrative trade with Europe, dating back to the 17th century.

Kalamkari depicting Shiva and Parvati

View of Sri Kalahasti town, with its towering *gopuras* and the Kannappa Temple on a hillock

protect it from the sun's rays. The cobra, when he reached the shrine, was so upset to see the linga covered with dirty cobwebs that he cleaned and covered it with little stones. The last to arrive was the elephant, who removed the stones and decorated the linga with flowers. This continued for some time until the three devotees, each sure that his way of worship was the purest and that the others had committed sacrilege, decided to confront each other. In the fight that ensued, they collapsed and Lord Shiva, pleased by their devotion, blessed them and named the shrine after them – Sri (spider), Kala (cobra) and Hasti (elephant).

Sri Kalahasti is also linked to the legend of Kannappa, the hunter, through its **Kannappa Temple**. One of the 63 Nayannars, Kannappa plucked out his eye in a frenzy of devotion and offered it to Shiva. A shrine commemorating him stands on the summit of the hillock that rises to the east.

Worshippers have thronged to this temple for generations to seek relief from the "evil effects" of Saturn. Some pilgrims also come here with their unmarried daughters in the hope that a special *puja* at the temple will help them find good husbands.

㉑ Puttaparthi

Ananthapur district, 437 km (272 miles) S of Hyderabad. ✈ 6 km (4 miles) SW of ashram, then taxi. 🚌 Dharmavaram, 40 km (25 miles) N of Puttaparthi, then bus. 🚌 ℹ APTDC, (040) 3048 8365. 🎉 Sai Baba's Birthday (23 Nov).

As the birthplace of Sri Satya Sai Baba, the "godman" who preaches religious tolerance, universal love and service to others, Puttaparthi has a very special significance for his vast number of devotees from all over the world. Sai Baba's ability to produce *vibhuti* (sacred ash), seemingly miraculously out of thin air, is considered by his devotees to be an important symbol of his god-like status and powers. From a very young age,

Sri Satya Sai Baba
(1926–2011)

Sai Baba, born as Satyanarayana Raju in this village on 23 November 1926, claimed divine powers. When he was only 14, he declared that he was the reincarnation of a celebrated saint, Sai Baba from Shirdi in Maharashtra, who died in 1918. He passed away in 2011. It is believed that he will return after his death as another saint called Prem Sai Baba. In 1950 Satya Sai Baba established an ashram for his followers, whose numbers had swollen to gigantic figures. Known as **Prasanthi Nilayam** or the "Abode of Highest Peace", it is today a large complex with guesthouses, dormitories, kitchens and dining halls. Over the years, several buildings have appeared around the ashram – schools, colleges, residential complexes, hospitals, a planetarium, a museum and recreation centres, transforming this tiny village into a cosmopolitan township. Outside the ashram, at the lower end of the village, rural life continues, seemingly unaffected by the ashram's activities. The countryside around is very fertile, with stretches of well-irrigated fields.

Women working in the fields, Puttaparthi

The ornate *mihrab* of the Sher Shah Mosque, Penukonda

② Penukonda

Anantapur district. 425 km (264 miles) S of Hyderabad. 🚌 🚃 Babayya Fair (Dec).

A rocky hill dominates Penukonda, or the "Big Hill", with walls rising up its steep sides to form an almost triangular fort. A strategic Vijayanagar citadel from the 14th and to 16th centuries, Penukonda was the capital of the succeeding Aravidu rulers until it was captured, first by the Qutb Shahis, and then by, the Mughals followed by the Marathas. Today, gateways, watchtowers, dilapidated halls and shrines skirt the path to the summit.

At the foot of the hill is the walled city, with its main gateways in the northern and eastern sides. To the south is a large tank. The main monuments are situated along the city's north-south road. The **Parsvanatha Jain Temple** here contains a remarkable sculpture, dating from the Hoysala period (12th–13th centuries), of the Jain saint Parsvanatha (*see p400*) standing in front of an undulating serpent. The 16th-century **Sher Shah Mosque**, nearby, has an arcaded façade and a bulbous dome.

Further south, standing next to each other, are two granite temples dedicated to Rama and Shiva. The pilastered façade walls of the **Rama Temple** are brought to life by carvings depicting episodes from the *Ramayana (see p31)* and the Krishna legend, while scenes from the Shiva mythology are sculpted on the walls of the **Shiva Temple**.

The adjacent **Gagan Mahal** is a palatial structure dating to the Vijayanagar period. An arcaded verandah leads to a vaulted hall with rear chambers. The domed pavilion above is topped by a pyramidal octagonal tower. A similar, smaller tower tops the adjoining staircase. To its east is a square pavilion with curving eaves, a pierced parapet and an octagonal pyramidal tower. The interior has traces of intricate plasterwork. Nearby is a well with an ornate entrance shaped like a lion.

A short distance north of the walled city is the **Dargah of Babayya**, the shrine of a 16th-century Muslim saint. A popular pilgrimage place which was much patronized by Tipu Sultan (*see p521*), it holds a big fair in December.

② Lepakshi

Anantapur district. 478 km (297 miles) S of Hyderabad. 🚌 🚃 daily. 🚃 Shivratri (Feb/Mar).

An enormous monolith of Nandi, Shiva's bull, stands 1 km (0.6 miles) east of Lepakshi, welcoming visitors to this important pilgrimage town.

Lepakshi's top attraction is the **Virabhadra Temple**, which stands on a rocky outcrop. It was built in the mid-16th century, under the patronage of two brothers, Virupanna and Viranna, governors of Penukonda under the Vijayanagar empire.

The temple is an important repository of the styles of sculpture and painting that evolved during this period. Dedicated to Virabhadra (Shiva in his ferocious

Monolithic *naga*, Virabhadra Temple

form), the temple stands in the middle of two concentric enclosures, built on three levels. It is entered through a *gopura* on the north side. On either side of the inner entrance are figures of the river goddesses Ganga and Yamuna, with a background of foliage. Among the other notable sculptures here are the carvings on the massive pillars that define the central space in the open hall; the deities, guardians and sages carved on to the piers of the unfinished Kalyana Mandapa; and the imposing monolithic seven-headed *naga* (serpent) sheltering a granite linga, to the southeast of the main shrine. Paintings in vibrant vegetable and mineral colours cover the ceilings of the two adjoining *mandapas* (one open and the other walled in), the walls of the Ardha Mandapa and some subsidiary shrines. Gods and goddesses, groups of donors and worshippers, and scenes from myths and legends, bear witness to the superb pictorial art of the Vijayanagar empire.

A gory legend connected to the Virabhadra Temple says that Virupanna misused state funds to build this shrine, and then forestalled royal punishment by blinding himself. The two dark reddish spots on the western wall of the inner enclosure are said to be the marks left by his eyes.

Carved pillars at the Virabhadra Temple

Lepakshi Paintings

The glory of Lepakshi lies in the magnificent frescoed ceilings of the Virabhadra Temple, where a series of exquisite paintings illustrate in lively fashion episodes from the epics and the *Puranas*. The figures are shown in profile, with prominent eyes and sharply chiselled noses and chins. The frescoes are characterized by elegant black linework, set out against an orange-red background. Particularly striking are the beautiful costumes and the detailed rendering of hairstyles, textile patterns, and jewellery. The palette of colours is limited to white, green, black and various shades of ochre and brown, applied to a stucco surface specially treated with lime. Some of the most beautiful paintings are on the ceiling of the open *mandapa*, arranged in long strips along the surrounding bays.

Ravana Nandi Shiva Parvati Brahma officiating as the priest Garuda, Vishnu's bird-vehicle

The Marriage of Shiva and Parvati
This is Lepakshi's most spectacular fresco, and echoes the murals at Ajanta (see pp484–5) in its colours, detailed depiction of costumes and jewellery, and graceful female figures.

Dakshinamurti (Shiva as a Divine Teacher) is shown seated on a hillock, expounding on mysticism and philosophy to sages gathered at his feet.

Parvati, with her maids, is shown getting ready for the wedding. Flat figures in stylized poses, often arranged in rows, characterize these paintings.

The Boar Hunt shows a wild boar charging at Arjuna and Shiva, who are preparing to shoot him.

TRAVELLERS' NEEDS

WHERE TO STAY

Visitors to India have a wide choice of accommodation available – from traditional hospitality in grand old palaces and home stays, to modern western-stye deluxe hotels, budget hotes and tourist bungalows. Prices vary depending on the quality of services offered, and the location. Star-rated luxury hotels, speciality hotels, health spas and heritage hotels are expensive, but the amenities they offer more than justify the high room rates. The moderately priced mid-range hotels, often managed by state tourism departments, may lack the glamour of a five-star, but they are clean and offer excellent value for money. Cheaper accommodation is available at guesthouses, youth hostels and even spartan pilgrim abodes, such as *dharamshalas* and *ashrams*. Hotel rates fluctuate with the season and are usually cheaper during the off-season from April to September. The hotel listings on pages 694–703 provide a selection of some of the best hotels throughout India, to suit every taste and budget.

Grading and Facilities

At the top of the scale are the five-star deluxe hotels. Most of these are part of international and Indian hotel chains, such as the Hilton, **Oberoi**, **ITC Hotels** or **Taj Group**. Next, are the four- and three-star hotels, some of them run by the state governments, followed by the guesthouses. Heritage hotels offer the opportunity to stay in beautifully restored forts, palaces and stately homes.

Pricing and Booking

Accommodation in the bigger cities is generally more expensive. The most expensive establish-ments are the five-star and five-star deluxe hotels as well as the exclusive heritage hotels, although smaller properties among the latter can be cheaper. State-run hotels, which have a good nationwide network, are more economical, though their rates can differ. Price categories for guesthouses also vary. Tariffs are based on the European system of room rent only, although in some places breakfast is included. Flexible prices dominate the market during the off-season and in some cases may drop by almost 50 per cent. It is worth negotiating for a good discount.

Some hotels have a dual tariff policy (for foreigners and Indians), which means that foreigners have to pay a dollar room rate plus any additional taxes on the listed price. This is payable either in foreign currency or Indian rupees. Hotel rates are usually revised every October, at the beginning of the tourist season. It is advisable to book well in advance during the peak tourist season (Oct–Mar). Since the classifications of hotels can be bewildering, it is best to get a complete description of what to expect in terms of both room and service quality. While making reservations, especially for mid-range and budget hotels, check which credit cards are accepted. Note that some hotels demand payment in advance and will refund only part of the amount if the booking is cancelled.

Check-out time is usually 12pm noon, though some hotels are more flexible and allow a 24-hour departure, or accept a small fee for a few hours' extension. Smaller hotels may allow a later check out, for free. When paying, scrutinize the bill thoroughly and retain all receipts on departure.

Taxes

The hotel bill includes taxes levied by the federal and state governments. The federal government charges a uniform 10 per cent hotel expenditure tax (on room rent only), which is imposed on all hotels with a tariff of ₹3,000 and above. States levy a luxury tax on the rack rate of a room as well; this varies from 5 to 25 per cent. There may also be local taxes such as sales tax, service tax and special taxes on alcohol. Some hotels also levy a service charge.

Hidden Costs

Be prepared to pay extra for breakfast, mini bar, mineral water, telephone calls, laundry, room service (if this is not a regular service), business centre usage, heaters in cold locations, concierge services and even pay channels on television. Transfers to and from the hotel are complimentary only for up-market package tours.

For non-local and international telephone calls,

Bedroom interiors at the Taj Mahal Palace and Tower *(see p700)*, Mumbai

◀ Flea market shop with handmade goods on display in Hampi

Picturesque setting of the Neemrana heritage hotel in Alwar

check if there is an in-house ISD/STD facility, though it is cheaper to get a local sim card *(see p746)*. Small hotels, with no running hot water, often charge extra for buckets of hot water.

Luxury Hotels

India's luxury hotels are comparable with the best anywhere in the world. They offer capacious suites and rooms, fine service and a host of amenities. These usually include a travel desk, state-of-the-art conference facilities, shopping arcades, swimming pools, modern fitness centres and multi-cuisine restaurants. The staff are polite and attentive and can help plan itineraries and make arrangements for activities such as tennis, golf or riding. Reservations should be made in advance, especially during the peak season.

Heritage Hotels

Several palaces, forts and havelis, particularly in Rajasthan, Madhya Pradesh, Himachal Pradesh and Gujarat, have been restored, modernized and converted into plush, luxury hotels. These establishments have a gracious, old-world charm, and many are still run by former princely families, who treat visitors like honoured guests.

Bookings can be made through private agencies, such as the **HRH Group of Hotels**, **Neemrana Hotels** and **WelcomHeritage**. Bookings at these hotels can also be made through reputed travel agents.

Middle-range Hotels

The four- and three-star hotels offer a scaled-down version of five-star luxury and are less expensive. Levels of comfort, cleanliness and professional services are, however, high. Rooms are air conditioned and have en-suite bathrooms. In addition, there are restaurants, gift shops, business centres and sometimes extensive gardens.

Budget Hotels and Tourist Lodges

Budget hotels are often found around bus stands and railway stations. They are inexpensive, with simple decor, Indian or Western-style toilets, ceiling fans and basic food options in a dining hall. The tariff in major cities is higher than in smaller towns.

An excellent option, particularly in lesser-known tourist destinations, is the countrywide network of tourist bungalows and lodges run by the state tourism departments. Moderately priced, they offer

both independent rooms with en-suite baths and dormitory accommodation.

Dak Bungalows

Government-run dak bungalows (inns with very basic facilities) are cheap, clean and conveniently located. Although they are not easily available for public use, visitors can contact the local or district authorities for help in making reservations. Book in advance as priority usually goes to visiting officials.

Guesthouses, Paying Guests and Home Stays

In some states, such as Goa, Tamil Nadu, Rajasthan and Madhya Pradesh, family cottages and old mansions have been converted into guesthouses. While these usually fall into the mid-range or budget categories, the number of amenities, quality of service and price can be erratic. Look at the rooms before checking in, as the difference between two rooms of the same price can be substantial.

Staying with local families is a popular option. It is best to check with the state tourism offices *(see p737)* for a list of establishments under their Paying Guest Scheme. Rajasthan Tourism has a comprehensive list, as does Madhya Pradesh Tourism. For Kerala, **Sundale Vacations** is a reliable resource. The UK-based **Munjeeta Travels** or **Home & Hospitality** also organize home stays.

Lounge of the Lakkhotaa Lodge *(see p699)*, Shillong

Dharamshalas and Ashrams

Religious centres, among them dharamshalas, ashrams, gurudwaras and monasteries, offer basic but clean accommodation all over the country. For most, prior booking is not essential and stay is often free, although donations are appreciated. It is wise to abide by the rules of the house and not offend any sentiments. Some ashrams in the older sections of towns usually provide only a mattress on the floor, which should suffice if the stay is just for a night. Be prepared to share rooms and bathrooms.

Popular ashrams such as **Sri Aurobindo Ashram** and the **Sivananda Ashram**, have branches spread across the country. Bookings must be made in advance. Their head offices can be contacted for details.

In Ladakh, many monasteries run hotels fairly close to their premises. Lamayuru Monastery Hotel is among the best and has a great setting within the compound (see p142).

National Parks and Camping Sites

National parks and wildlife sanctuaries usually have forest rest houses with basic facilities. Since most of these are often reserved for forest officials, many of the larger parks have private resorts located on their periphery. The most popular among these are in Ranthambhore (Sher Bagh), Corbett (Infinity Resorts), Kaziranga (Wildgrass) and

Luxury campsite at Pushkar during the annual cattle fair

Nagarhole (Kabini River Lodge). Reservations can be made through **Wild World India**, or through travel agencies. Camping is not allowed inside wildlife sanctuaries, and as a rule, it is not safe to venture out for unguided walks.

Tented camps are provided by operators who organize adventure tours, such as river rafting on the Ganges (see p189), or those that specialize in camping holidays (see p728). Check the arrangements in advance, as some may not provide mosquito nets or mineral water. In Rajasthan, some hotels offer guests the option of staying in luxury tents set in spacious gardens. During the Pushkar and Kumbh *melas* (fairs), the state governments provide tented accommodation on site.

Special Hotels

The rising interest in holistic health and well-being has spawned a number of exclusive health spas and specialized resorts. The most popular are those that offer herbal treatments,

such as Ayurveda and yoga. Other services include massage therapies, such as aromatherapy and reflexology and meditation. Usually, a strict diet is part of the spartan regime, although rules at the top-end resorts are flexible. The **Oberoi Group** and Ananda are world-class spas. An entirely different accommodation is provided on board Kerala's kettuvallams. These traditional rice boats are luxurious and provide a unique experience of the scenic backwaters. Trips can be organized by **Tourindia**.

Youth Hostels

India has an outstanding network of youth hostels. Though these offer rooms at very low rates, they also tend to be packed. Members of the **Youth Hostel Association of India** and Youth Hostel International get priority bookings, but non-members can get a room for a higher price. Both room and dorm-style accommodation is available. The **YMCAs** are better equipped, though more expensive and located in fewer towns.

Touts

Visitors with no prior bookings should contact tourist counters at the airport, railway station or bus stand to avoid being harassed by touts, who also operate as taxi and auto-rickshaw drivers. Many are very persuasive and offer incredible discounts, all for a commission. Some, however, are genuinely helpful, and if there is no other option, keep the driver waiting

Riceboat or *kettuvallam*, Kerala backwaters

until you are sure about the lodgings. Speak to a policeman if they become too persistent.

Facilities for the Disabled and Children

Though there are few facilities for the disabled, hotel staff are generally considerate. The government has initiated a move to add wheelchair ramps, special lifts and bathrooms wherever possible, although older properties, even the five-star hotels, may find it difficult to accommodate them.

Most hotels have no special amenities for children. However, Indian hotel staff are usually good with children and provisions can be made for extra beds. Only a few, select hotels offer baby-sitting services.

Tipping

Despite the inclusion of service charges in the bill, tips are expected in most places. The amount is discretionary. A tip of ₹10 is fine for parking attendants, room service and porters, but waiters expect 10 per cent of the bill. Taxi drivers don't need to be tipped. However, tipping is a great way to get things done quickly.

Recommended Hotels

The options featured in this guide have been carefully selected and are among the best places to stay in the country in their respective categories. These categories highlight accommodations that are unique to India, such as palace hotels and safari lodges near national parks. The choices reflect new boutique hotels opening up throughout the country, which provide an alternative to the established luxury of large five-star chains. In areas where choice is limited, the list emphasizes places offering good value for money, including government-run lodges, which maintain acceptable and

Simple interiors of Dhole's Den *(see p701)*, a boutique safari lodge in Bandipur

comfortable standards. In the metropolises, the full spectrum of accommodation is presented, from self-contained five-star resorts to small locally-managed B&Bs. The DK Choice category draws attention to establishments that are exceptional, either for their outstanding location, their emphasis on sustainability, or their heritage credentials.

DIRECTORY

Hotel Chains

Ashok Group
ITDC, 7 Jeevan Vihar,
3, Sansad Marg, Delhi.
Tel (011) 2374 8165.
W theashokgroup.com

ITC Hotels
Tel (011) 2611 2233.
W itchotels.in

Oberoi Group
Tel (011) 2389 0507.
W oberoihotels.com

Taj Group
Tel (022) 2202 5515.
W tajhotels.com

Heritage Hotels

HRH Group of Hotels
City Palace, Udaipur.
Tel (0294) 252 8016.
W hrhhotels.com

Indian Heritage Hotels Association
Sansar Chandra Rd, Jaipur.
Tel (0141) 237 1194.
W indianheritage hotels.com

Neemrana Hotels

A-20, Feroze Gandhi Marg,
Lajpat Nagar-II, Delhi.
Tel (011) 4666 1666.
W neemranahotels.com

WelcomHeritage
25, Community Centre,
Basant Lok, Vasant Vihar,
Delhi. **Tel** (011) 4603 5500.
W welcomheritage hotels.in

Guesthouses, Paying Guests & Home Stays

Home & Hospitality
Tel 0207) 503 6204.
W homeand hospitality.co.uk

Munjeeta Travels
12 Cavendish Rd, Woking,
Surrey, GU22 0EP, UK.
Tel (01483) 773 331.
W munjeetatravel.com

Sundale Vacations
Tel (0484) 235 9127.
W sundale.com

Dharamshalas & Ashrams

Niranjana Hotel
Next to Lamayuru
Monastery, Ladakh
district, Jammu
& Kashmir.
Tel (01982) 224 555.

Sivananda Ashram
Divine Life Society,
PO Shivanandanagar,
249192, Tehri Garhwal
district, Uttarakhand.
Tel (0135) 243 0040.
W sivanandaonline.org

Sri Aurobindo Ashram
W sriaurobindo ashram.org

National Parks & Camping Sites

Wild World India
2, Hauz Khas
Village, Delhi.
Tel (011) 4602 1018.
W wildworldindia.com

Special Hotels

Tourindia
PO Box 163, Near SMV
High School, Mahatma
Gandhi Road,
Thiruvananthapuram.
Tel (0471) 233 1507.
W tourindiakerala.com

Youth Hostels

YMCA
YMCA Hostel,
1 Jai Singh Rd,
Connaught Place, Delhi.
Tel (011) 2336 3187.
W newdelhiymca.org/

Youth Hostels Association of India
Tel (011) 2687 1969.
W yhaindia.org

Where to Stay

Delhi

Blue Triangle Family Hostel (YWCA) ®®
Great Value
Ashoka Rd, Connaught Place, 110001
Tel *(011) 2336 0133*
Ⓦ ywcaofdelhi.org
Basic accommodation in a great location, recommended by female travellers. Free breakfast.

Hotel Broadway ®®
Heritage
4/15A Asaf Ali Rd, 110002
Tel *(011) 4366 3600*
Ⓦ hotelbroadwaydelhi.com
Atmospheric hotel in Old Delhi. Comfortable rooms, restaurant and heritage walking tours.

Prince Polonia ®®
Comfort lodging
2325/26 Tilak Gali, off Main Bazaar, Paharganj, 110055
Tel *(011) 4762 6600*
Ⓦ hotelprincepolonia.com
Good budget option in a busy area. Popular with travellers.

Amarya Haveli ®®®
Boutique
P5 Hauz Khas Enclave, 110016
Tel *(011) 4175 9268*
Ⓦ amaryagroup.com
Urban oasis with stylish rooms, a lovely lounge and a roof terrace.

Claridges ®®®
Luxury
12 Aurangzeb Rd, 110011
Tel *(011) 3955 5000*
Ⓦ claridges.com
Elegant hotel with sumptuous rooms and beautiful artwork. Pool and tapas restaurant.

Poolside view of the stylish Claridges hotel in Delhi

Jor Bagh 27 ®®®
Comfort lodging
27 Jor Bagh, 110002
Tel *(011) 2469 4430*
Ⓦ jorbagh27.com
Peaceful guesthouse near Lodhi Gardens with pleasant rooms.

Maidens ®®®
Heritage
7 Sham Nath Marg, 110054
Tel *(011) 2397 5464*
Ⓦ maidenshotel.com
One of Delhi's oldest hotels with classic style and great views of the Delhi Ridge.

Palace Heights ®®®
Boutique
D26–28 Connaught Place, 110001
Tel *(011) 4358 2610*
Ⓦ hotelpalaceheights.com
Small but stylish rooms in a superb location. Glass-roofed restaurant, Zaffran, on site.

Sheraton New Delhi ®®®
Business
District Centre, Saket, 110017
Tel *(011) 4266 1122*
Ⓦ starwoodhotels.com
Sandwiched between two upmarket malls. Stylish interiors and a good business centre.

The Ashok ®®®
Luxury
50-B Chanakyapuri, 110021
Tel *(011) 2611 0101*
Ⓦ theashok.com
Palatial Mughal architecture and the famous Amatrra spa.

DK Choice

The Imperial ®®®
Heritage
1 Janpath, 110001
Tel *(011) 2334 1234*
Ⓦ theimperialindia.com
This elegant hotel with alluring interiors and award-winning restaurants is one of the best ways to experience both Colonial and modern Delhi. Designed as part of Lutyens grand vision of Delhi, the hotel hosted Gandhi and Nehru as they discussed India's independence and partition.

The Manor ®®®
Boutique
77 Friends Colony West, 110065
Tel *(011) 2692 5151*
Ⓦ themanordelhi.com
Stylish hotel where designer Terence Conran stays. Acclaimed restaurant – Indian Accent.

Price Guide
Prices are based on one night's stay in for a standard double room, inclusive of service charges and taxes.

®	up to INR1,000
®®	INR1,000–5,000
®®®	over INR5,000

The Oberoi ®®®
Luxury
Dr Zakir Hussain Marg, 110003
Tel *(011) 2436 3030*
Ⓦ oberoihotels.com
The height of luxury in the heart of the city. Great service and fantastic Sunday brunch.

The Taj Mahal Hotel ®®®
Luxury
1 Man Singh Rd, 110001
Tel *(011) 2302 6162*
Ⓦ tajhotels.com
Mughal-inspired decor and lovely grounds. The superb Varq is one of the many restaurants on site.

Tree of Life B&B ®®®
Boutique
D-193 Saket, 110017
Tel *(0) 98102 77699*
Ⓦ tree-of-life.in
Stylish and friendly B&B close to Saket metro and Qutb Minar.

Haryana and Punjab

AMRITSAR: Le Golden ®®
Comfort lodging
Clock tower Ext, 143001
Tel *(0183) 255 8800*
Ⓦ hotellegolden.com
Good rooms with great views of the Golden Temple and Akal Takht from the roof.

AMRITSAR: Ranjits Svaasa ®®®
Heritage
47-A The Mall Rd, 143001
Tel *(0183) 256 6618*
Ⓦ welcomheritagehotels.in
Set in a restored *haveli*. Great food and an ayurvedic spa.

CHANDIGARH: Kaptain's Retreat ®®
Boutique
Sector 35-B, 160022
Tel *(0172) 500 5599*
Ⓦ nivalink.com
Stylish rooms with lots of cricket memorabilia in a hotel owned by the legendary Kapil Dev.

CHANDIGARH: Taj Hotel ®®®
Luxury
Block 9a, Sector 17, 160017
Tel *(0172) 551 3000*
Ⓦ tajhotels.com

Taj-style luxury with all the mod cons close to the city's business and shopping areas.

GURGAON: Trident Hilton ⓇⓇⓇ
Luxury
443 Udyog Vihar, Phase V, 122001
Tel *(0124) 245 0505*
Ⓦ tridenthotels.com
Stunning design and ultra-modern facilities. Popular restaurants on site.

Himachal Pradesh

DALHOUSIE: Grand View Hotel ⓇⓇⓇ
Rural retreat
Near Dalhousie Club, 700001
Tel *(01899) 242 823*
Ⓦ grandviewdalhousie.in
Stylish rooms with spectacular views of the Pir Panjal range.

DHARAMSALA: Chonor House ⓇⓇ
Boutique
Thekchen Choeling Rd, Mcleod Ganj, 176219
Tel *(01892) 246 406*
Ⓦ norbulingka.org
Beautiful hotel with traditional Tibetan furniture and paintings. Excellent restaurant.

DHARAMSALA: Grace Hotel ⓇⓇ
Heritage
558 Old Chari Rd, Kotwali Bazaar, 176215
Tel *(01892) 223 265*
Ⓦ welcomheritagehotels.in
Set in a stunning, beautifully-restored 200-year-old manor house. Superb local food.

KULLU: Neeralaya ⓇⓇⓇ
Eco-friendly
Raison Village, 175101
Tel *(01902) 245 725*
Ⓦ neeralaya.com
Beautiful resort in a scenic location with cottages and villas overlooking the Beas river

MANALI: Baikunth Magnolia ⓇⓇⓇ
Boutique
Circuit House Rd, Mall, 175131
Tel *(01902) 250 118*
Ⓦ baikunth.com
Lovely stone and wood building with spacious rooms and balconies. Romantic vibe.

MANALI: Banon's Resort ⓇⓇⓇ
Comfort lodging
Near Circuit House, 175131
Tel *(01902) 252 335*
Ⓦ banonresortmanali.com
Characterful hotel with spacious rooms. Good restaurant and a very popular bar.

Warm and inviting interiors of the Banjara Camp in Sangla

DK Choice

SANGLA: Banjara Camp ⓇⓇⓇ
Rural retreat
Sangla, 172106
Tel *(0) 98169 59904*
Ⓦ banjaracamps.com
An urban escape with epic mountain scenery next to the rushing Baspa river. Choose from beautiful rooms in a stone cottage or deluxe tents. Head out for a relaxing and picturesque walk and return to delicious food.

SARAHAN: Shrikhand ⓇⓇ
Comfort lodging
Sarahan Village, 172102
hptdc.nic.in
Opposite the Bhimakali Temple. Basic accommodation surrounded by mountains.

SHIMLA: Hotel Combermere ⓇⓇ
Comfort lodging
The Mall, 171001
Tel *(0177) 265 1246*
Ⓦ hotelcombermere.com
Comfortable rooms and two good in-house restaurants.

SHIMLA: Wildflower Hall ⓇⓇⓇ
Heritage
Chharabra Village, 171012
Tel *(0177) 264 8686*
Ⓦ oberoiwildflowerhall.com
Former weekend retreat of Lord Kitchener. Ultimate luxury with an amazing heated pool.

Ladakh, Jammu & Kashmir

ALCHI: Alchi Resort ⓇⓇ
Rural retreat
Alchi, 194101
Tel (01982) 227 177
Ⓦ alchiresort.tripod.com
Well-appointed whitewashed chalets in a flowery garden.

KARGIL: Hotel D'zojila ⓇⓇ
Comfort lodging
Baru, Biamathang, 194103
Tel *(22) 6150 6363*
Ⓦ nivalink.com
Peaceful spot on the Suru river, with a pleasant garden. Two km (1.3 miles) from town centre.

LEH: Ladakh Residency ⓇⓇ
Comfort lodging
Changspa, 194101
Tel *(01982) 258 111*
Ⓦ ladakhresidency.com
Traditional touches, including wall paintings, and modern amenities. Rooftop restaurant.

LEH: Oriental Guesthouse ⓇⓇ
Eco-friendly
Changspa, 194101
Tel *(01982) 253 135*
Ⓦ oriental-ladakh.com
Family-run with rooms for all budgets. Great organic food.

LEH: Yak Tail ⓇⓇ
Comfort lodging
Fort Rd, 194101
Tel *(01982) 252 118*
Ⓦ hotelyaktail.com
Convenient for the bazaar and restaurants. Appealing wood rooms; some with balconies.

NUBRA: Hotel Yarab Tso ⓇⓇ
Rural retreat
Tiger, Nubra, BPO Sumur Nubra
Tel *(01982) 252 480/ 9622820661*
Ⓦ hotelyarabtso.com
Friendly farmhouse vibe with large rooms; most enjoy mountain views. Great food.

SRINAGAR: The Lalit Grand Palace ⓇⓇⓇ
Heritage
Gupkar Rd, 190001
Tel *(0194) 250 1001*
Ⓦ thelalit.com
The maharaja's former residence, a palace of great charm and history. Gorgeous furnishings and grounds dotted with chinar trees.

For more information on types of hotels *see page 693*

SRINAGAR: Vivanta by Taj - Dal View ⊗⊗⊗
Luxury
Kralsangri, Brein, 191121
Tel *(0194) 246 1111*
Ⓦ vivantabytaj.com
Lake views, sprawling gardens, fantastic dining and chic decor.

ULEYTOKPO: Ule Ethnic Resort ⊗⊗
Eco-friendly
Uleytopko, 194101
Tel *(01982) 253 640*
Ⓦ uleresort.com
High-quality chalets and canvas huts beside an orchard. Organic meals and solar power.

Uttar Pradesh and Uttarakhand

AGRA: Taj Plaza ⊗⊗
Comfort lodging
Taj East Gate Rd, 282001
Tel *(0562) 223 2515*
Ⓦ hoteltajplaza.in
Close to the Taj Mahal with rooftop views and good rooms.

AGRA: Amar Vilas ⊗⊗⊗
Luxury
Taj Fast Gate Rd, 282001
Tel *(0562) 223 1515*
Ⓦ amarvilas.com
The height of all luxury and the only hotel where every room has view of the Taj Mahal.

LUCKNOW: Vivanta by Taj ⊗⊗⊗
Luxury
Vipin Khand, Gomti Nagar, 226010
Tel *(0522) 671 1000*
Ⓦ vivantabytaj.com
Colonial-style building with luxurious rooms and grounds. Live *ghazals* in the evenings.

NAINITAL: The Palace Belvedere ⊗⊗⊗
Heritage
Awagarh Estate, Mallital, 263002
Tel *(05942) 237 434*
Ⓦ thepalacebelvedere.com

Live like a king at this former palace with beautiful, spacious rooms and incredible views.

RISHIKESH: Rainforest House ⊗⊗
Eco-friendly
Badrinath Rd, Brahmpuri, 249175
Tel *(0) 80067 79298*
Ⓦ rainforest-house.com
Calm oasis with stylish rooms, yoga and a café serving Italian classics and healthy local food.

TEHRI GARHWAL: Ananda in the Himalayas ⊗⊗⊗
Luxury
Narendra Nagar, 249175
Tel *(0124) 451 6650*
Ⓦ anandaspa.com
Award-winning spa resort with yoga, holistic treatments and superlative views.

VARANASI: Scindhia Guest House ⊗⊗
Comfort lodging
Scindia Ghat, 221001
Tel *(0542) 239 3446*
Ⓦ scindhiaguesthouse.com
Simple rooms with home-cooked food and friendly vibe.

VARANASI: Hotel Ganges View ⊗⊗⊗
Heritage
Asi Ghat, 221005
Tel *(0542) 329 0289*
Ⓦ hotelgangesview.com
Characterful early 19th-century home right on the ghats; serves delicious vegetarian food.

Bihar and Jharkhand

BODH GAYA: Kundan Bazar Guest House ⊗
Great value
Bhagalpur Village, 824231
Tel *(0631) 220 0049*
Ⓦ kundanbazar.com
Perfect budget option with cheerful rooms, free cycles, bike rental, rooftop café and gift shop. Short walk from centre of Bodh Gaya.

BODH GAYA: Mahayana Guest House ⊗⊗
Comforte lodging
PO Box 04, 824231
Tel *(0631) 220 0756*
Run by the Tibetan monastery with rooms around airy courtyards. Close to Mahabodhi Temple.

PATNA: Hotel Chanakya ⊗⊗
Business
R-Block, Beerchand Patel Marg, 800001
Tel *(0612) 222 3141*
Ⓦ chanakyapatna.com/
Centrally located with good facilities and two restaurants.

PATNA: Maurya Patna ⊗⊗⊗
Business
South Gandhi Maidan, 800001
Tel *(0612) 220 3040*
Ⓦ maurya.com
Tasteful accommodation in the heart of the commercial district.

RAJGIR: Indo Hokke Hotel ⊗⊗
Boutique
Near Viraytan, 803116
Tel *(06119) 255 245*
Ⓦ theroyalresidency.net
Popular with international Buddhist tourists. Japanese design with a bathhouse.

RANCHI: Chanakya BNR Hotel ⊗⊗
Heritage
Station Rd, 834001
Tel *(0651) 246 1211–4*
Ⓦ chanakyabnrranchi.com
Modern, four-star hotel with a 1905 wing full of old-world charm.

Madhya Pradesh and Chhattisgarh

BANDHAVGARH: Samode Safari Lodge ⊗⊗⊗
Rural retreat
Bandhavgarh, 484661
Tel *(0124) 405 7795*
Ⓦ samode.com
This is a stunning eco-property in the heart of the jungle.

BANDHAVGARH: Skays Camp ⊗⊗⊗
Eco-friendly
129 Tala Village, 484661
Tel *(0)94253 31209*
Ⓦ skayscamp.in
Beautiful place to stay close to the jungle. Run by naturalists.

BHOPAL: Noor-us-Sabah Palace ⊗⊗⊗
Luxury
VIP Rd, Koh-e-Fiza, 462030
Tel *(0755) 422 7777*
Ⓦ noorussabahpalace.com
Literally 'the light of day'.

Picturesque setting of the Vivanta by Taj in Srinagar

Key to Price Guide *see page 694*

Atmospheric and elegant palace with beautiful rooms.

GWALIOR: Usha Kiran Palace ⊛⊛⊛
Heritage
Jayendraganj, Lashkar, 474009
Tel *(0751) 244 4000*
🌐 tajhotels.com
Beautifully restored 120-year-old palace with rooms, suites and villas with private pools

KANHA: Infinity Kanha Wilderness ⊛⊛⊛
Rural retreat
Baherakhar, District Balaghat
Tel *(07636) 290 290*
🌐 infinityresorts.com
Tents and villas with wooden decks. Village and wildlife tours.

KHAJURAHO: Casa Di William ⊛
Comfort lodging
Opposite Temples, 471606
Tel *(07686) 274 244*
🌐 casadiwilliam.com
Well-decorated spacious rooms and rooftop views. A short walk to the temples.

KHAJURAHO: Taj Chandela ⊛⊛⊛
Luxury
Sevagram, 471606
Tel *(7686) 2723 5564*
🌐 tajhotels.com
Old fashioned Taj property amid landscaped gardens.

MAHESHWAR: Ahilya Fort ⊛⊛⊛
Heritage
Ahilya Fort, 451224
Tel *(011) 4155 1575*
🌐 ahilyafort.com
Stunning historic fort of one of the most celebrated women rulers of the 18th century.

DK Choice

ORCHHA: Sheesh Mahal ⊛⊛
Heritage
Inside the Fort, 472246
Tel *(07680) 252 618*
🌐 mptourism.com
Stay right inside the atmospheric fort for an exceptional experience. The two antique-filled suites recall bygone grandeur. Guests enjoy unparalleled views across the atmospheric fort courtyard. There is an excellent restaurant on site.

UJJAIN: Grand Tower ⊛⊛
Comfort lodging
1, Vikram Marg, Near Clock Tower
Tel *(0734) 255 3699*
🌐 hotelgrandtower.com
Pleasant business hotel convenient for the riverside ghats of Ujjain.

Simple and minimalist decor at The Bodhi Tree, Kolkata

Kolkata

Broadway Hotel ⊛
Great value
27A Ganesh Chandra Ave, 700013
Tel *(033) 2236 3930*
🌐 broadwayhotel.in
Centrally located with a great bar. Airy rooms have retro furnishings from 1937.

Fairlawn Hotel Pvt Ltd ⊛⊛
Heritage
13A Sudder St, 700016
Tel *(033) 2252 1510*
🌐 fairlawnhotel.com
Quirky hotel near New Market with old-fashioned charm. Simple but comfortable rooms.

DK Choice

The Bodhi Tree ⊛⊛
Boutique
48/44 Swiss Park, Rabindra Sarobar, 700033
Tel *(033) 2424 6534*
🌐 bodhitreekolkata.com
A haven of calm in Kolkata's chaos, this B&B has six rooms, each uniquely furnished, be it in Bengali, Tibetan or Rajasthani style. The Art Café in the courtyard serves delicious meals amid plants and paintings, and a restful homely atmosphere pervades throughout.

ITC Sonar ⊛⊛⊛
Luxury
JBS Halden Ave, 700046
Tel *(033) 2345 4545*
🌐 itchotels.in
Resort-feel hotel close to the airport with five-star facilities.

Oberoi Grand ⊛⊛⊛
Luxury
15 Jawaharlal Nehru Rd, 700013
Tel *(033) 2249 2323*
🌐 oberoihotels.com
Colonial grande dame with classic rooms, pool and spa.

Taj Bengal ⊛⊛⊛
Luxury
34B Belvedere Rd, Alipore, 700027
Tel *(033) 2223 3939*
🌐 tajhotels.com
Mix of traditional and modern furnishings, grand public areas and top-notch restaurants.

The Kenilworth ⊛⊛⊛
Business
1 & 2 Little Russell St, 700071
Tel *(033) 2282 3939*
🌐 kenilworthhotels.com
Elegant rooms in a period building, English-style pub and spa.

Tollygunge Club ⊛⊛⊛
Heritage
120 Deshapran Sasmal Rd, 700033
Tel *(033) 2417 6022*
🌐 thetollygungeclub.com
Colonial nostalgia and an 18-hole golf course.

West Bengal and Sikkim

DARJEELING: Cedar Inn ⊛⊛⊛
Heritage
Jalapahar Rd, 734101
Tel *(0354) 225 4446*
🌐 cedarinndarjeeling.com
Victorian-Gothic building boasting Kanchendzonga views. Wood-panelled interiors.

DARJEELING: Glenburn Tea Estate ⊛⊛⊛
Luxury
Glenburn Tea Estate, 734101
Tel *(0) 98300 70213*
🌐 glenburnteaestate.com
High-class suites and excellent service amid tea gardens.

GANGTOK: Elgin Nor-Khill ⊛⊛⊛
Heritage
Paljor Stadium Rd, 737101
Tel *(03592) 205 637*
🌐 elginhotels.com
Former retreat of Sikkim's rulers with traditional furnishings.

For more information on types of hotels *see page 693*

KALIMPONG: Himalayan Hotel ₹₹
Heritage
Upper Cart Rd, 734301
Tel *(03552) 255 248*
w himalayanhotel.biz
Heritage property adorned with photographs and Tibetan art.

DK Choice

KURSEONG: Cochrane Place ₹₹
Heritage
132 Pankhabari Rd, Fatak, 734203
Tel *(0) 99320 35660*
w imperialchai.com
This refurbished Colonial home has lush gardens and Kangchenzonga views. Deluxe rooms have antique furniture and oodles of character. The annex has a Swiss-chalet feel. Walks, spa and tea estate tours on offer.

RUMTEK: Bamboo Retreat ₹₹₹
Rural retreat
Sajong Village, 737101
Tel *(0392) 252 516*
w bambooretreat.in
Set amid paddy fields with meditation, massage and organic food; half-board.

SHANTINIKETAN: Mark & Meadows ₹₹
Rural retreat
Sriniketan Rd, 731204
Tel *(03463) 264 8701–2*
w markandmeadows.com
Red-tiled cottages in landscaped grounds. Family-friendly.

SUNDERBANS: Sunderban Jungle Camp ₹₹
Eco-friendly
Bali Island, 24 Parganas South
Tel *(033) 2455 0917*
w helptourism.com
Ethnic mud huts. Packages include travel from Kolkata, boat trips, park fees, and meals.

Odisha

BHUBANESWAR: Mayfair Lagoon ₹₹₹
Luxury
8-B Jayadev Vihar, 751013
Tel *(0674) 666 0101*
w mayfairhotels.com
Blend of modern design and traditional Kalinga art.

BHUBANESWAR: The Trident ₹₹₹
Luxury
CB-1 Nayapalli, 751013
Tel *(0674) 230 1010*
w tridenthotels.com

Bright, colourful lounge at Cochrane Place, Kurseong

Elegant property with orchards. Restaurant and games room inspired by city's temples.

GOPALPUR-ON-SEA: Mayfair ₹₹₹
Luxury
Ganjam, 761002
Tel *(0680) 282 021*
w mayfairhotels.com
Lovely grounds and stunning swimming pool.

DK Choice

GOUDAGUDA: Chandoori Sai ₹₹
Rural retreat
Kakiriguma, Koraput District
Tel *(0) 94433 42241*
w chandoorisai.com
Rustic guesthouse in the heart of Odisha's tribal belt. The rooms are inspired by the architecture of the Poraja and Kondha tribes.

KONARK: Yatri Niwas ₹
Comfort lodging
AT/PO Konark, 752111
Tel *(06758) 236 821*
w panthanivas.com
No frills, government-run place right next to the Sun Temple.

PURI: Hotel Gandhara ₹₹
Great value
Chakratirtha Rd, 752002
Tel *(06752) 224 117*
w hotelgandhara.com
Courtyard pool, spacious rooms and pretty gardens, all in a great location for sightseeing.

Assam and the Northeast

AGARTALA: Welcome Palace ₹₹
Business
HG Basak Rd, 799001
Tel *(0381) 238 4940*
w hotelwelcomepalace.in

Spacious rooms, friendly service and restaurant serving Thai, Indian and Chinese.

AIZAWL: Chaltlang Tourist Lodge ₹
Great value
Chaltlang, 796012
Tel *(0389) 234 1083*
w mizotourism.nic.in
Government lodge atop a steep ridge with views. 4 km (2.5 miles) from the city markets.

GUWAHATI: Baruah Bhavan ₹₹
Heritage
40, MC Rd, Uzanbazar, 781001
Tel *(0) 9954024165*
w heritagehomeassam.com
Assamese bungalow with verandahs and a roof terrace.

IMPHAL: The Classic Hotel ₹₹
Business
North AOC, 795001
Tel *(0385) 244 3967/9*
w theclassichotel.in
Modern hotel with functional rooms. Near markets and Kangla.

ITANAGAR: Hotel Donyi Polo Ashok ₹₹
Comfort lodging
C-Sector, 791111
Tel *(0360) 221 2626*
w theashokgroup.com
Old-fashioned but pleasing rooms with views, plus a bar.

KAZIRANGA NATIONAL PARK: Wild Grass Resort ₹₹
Rural retreat
Bochagaon, 785109
Tel *(03776) 262 085*
w oldassam.com
Long-standing resort. Guided tours to the park and villages, restaurant and cultural events.

KOHIMA: Razhü Pru ₹₹
Heritage
Mission Compound, Kohima Vill
Tel *(0370) 229 0291*
Old Naga-style bungalow in wood, with handcrafted furniture.

SHILLONG: Hotel Pinewood ⊛⊛
Heritage
Rita Rd, European Ward, 793001
Tel *(0364) 222 3116*
🅦 meghalayatourism.org
Raj-era, mock-Tudor bungalow
with fireplaces and a fine bar.

DK Choice

**SHILLONG: Lakkhotaa
Lodge** ⊛⊛⊛
Luxury
Mawpun, Polo Hills, 793001
Tel *(0364) 259 0523–4*
🅦 lakkhotaalodge.com
Opulent interiors with luxurious
furnishings follow feng shui
principles. The owners have
hand-picked every design and
detail. A memorable place to
stay with great food and service.

Rajasthan

BIKANER: Bhairon Vilas ⊛⊛
Boutique
Near Fort, 334001
Tel *(0151) 254 4751*
🅦 hotelbhaironvilas.com
Quirky rooms and a fantastic bar
with Rajasthani memoribilia.
Great rooftop views.

**DEOGARH: Deogarh
Mahal** ⊛⊛⊛
Heritage
Deogarh Village, 313331
Tel *(02904) 252 777*
🅦 deogarhmahal.com
Palace with labyrinthine
corridors, sumptuous rooms and
breathtaking views.

**DUNGARPUR: Udai Bilas
Palace** ⊛⊛⊛
Heritage
Udai Bilas Palace, 314001
Tel *(02964) 230 808*
🅦 udaibilaspalace.com
Rooms on the waterfront,
restaurant around a lotus pond
and an auto-themed bar.

JAIPUR: Samode Haveli ⊛⊛⊛
Luxury
Ganga Pole, 302002
Tel *(0141) 263 2407*
🅦 samode.com
Sophisticated decor, stunning
dining room and lovely pool.

JAISALMER: Nachana Haveli ⊛⊛
Heritage
Gandhi Chowk, 345001
Tel *(02992) 252 110*
🅦 nachanahaveli.com
Lovingly restored *haveli* with
heaps of character. Popular
rooftop restaurant, Saffron.

DK Choice

JODHPUR: Raas ⊛⊛⊛
Boutique
*Tunwar Ji Ka Jhalara, Makrana
Mohalla, 342001*
Tel *(0291) 263 6455*
🅦 raasjodhpur.com
Inspired by the landscape of
Jodhpur, this magnificent hotel
blends seamlessly with the red-
sandstone Meherangarh Fort
that towers over the city. Stylish
rooms that look out onto the
pool or gardens.

**KUMBHALGARH:
The Aodhi** ⊛⊛⊛
Luxury
Kelwara, 313325
Tel *(02954) 242 341*
🅦 eternalmewar.in
Old, stone home, surrounded by
nature, below the atmospheric
fort. Horse safaris and walks.

NAGAUR: Ranvas ⊛⊛⊛
Boutique
Nagaur Fort, 341001
Tel *(01582) 241 271*
🅦 ranvasnagaur.com
Stay inside Nagaur fort in
the converted *havelis* of the
Maharajahs' 16 wives.

**PUSHKAR: Inn Seventh
Heaven** ⊛⊛
Great value
Next to Mali ka Mandir, 305022
Tel *(0145) 510 5455*
🅦 inn-seventh-heaven.com
Restored *haveli* with themed
rooms and rooftop restaurant.

**SAWAI MADHOPUR: Sher
Bagh** ⊛⊛⊛
Rural retreat
Sherpur-Khiljipur Village, 322001
Tel *(07462) 252 120*
🅦 sujanluxury.com
Luxurious tented safari camp
with huge beds. Nightly bonfire.

**SHEKAWATI: Mandawa
Haveli** ⊛⊛
Heritage
Near Sonthaliya Gate
Tel *(01592) 223 088*
🅦 hotelheritagemandawa.com
Incredible frescoes inside this
restored *haveli*. Comfortable
rooms around a courtyard.

UDAIPUR: Udai Vilas ⊛⊛⊛
Luxury
Lake Pichola, 313001
Tel *(0294) 243 3300*
🅦 oberoihotels.com
Elegant palatial hotel looking out
over lake and city's palaces.

Gujarat

DK Choice

**AHMEDABAD: House of
Mangaldas Girdhardas** ⊛⊛⊛
Heritage
*Opposite Sidi Sayid Mosque, Lal
Darwaza, 38001*
Tel *(079) 2550 6946*
🅦 houseofmg.com
House of MG, as it is affectionately
dubbed, is a stunningly
atmospheric heritage property
with sweeping staircases,
beautifully decorated halls
and luxurious rooms. There is a
lovely shop and two fantastic
restaurants. The heritage walks,
especially the nighttime walk,
are recommended.

DIU: Radhika Beach Resort ⊛⊛
Family-friendly
Nagoa, near the beach, 362520
Tel *(02875) 252 555*
🅦 radhikaresort.com
This beach resort with lovely
spacious rooms, a large pool
and good restaurant is ideal
for families.

Intimate dining at the well-reviewed House of Mangaldas Girdhardas, Ahmedabad

For more information on types of hotels *see page 693*

KACHCCH: Shaam-e-Sarhad ⊛⊛
Eco-friendly
Hodka Village, 370510
Tel *(02832) 574 124*
🕸 hodka.in
Eco resort run by a village co-op, with huts and tents. Campfire, live music and delicious food.

SASAN GIR: Gir Birding Lodge ⊛⊛
Rural retreat
1.5 km north of Sasan, 362135
Tel *(02877) 295 514*
🕸 girbirdinglodge.com
Set in a mango orchard. Lions can often be heard at a distance.

VADODARA: WelcomHotel ⊛⊛⊛
Business
RC Dutt Rd, Alkapuri, 390007
Tel *(0265) 233 0033*
🕸 itcwelcomgroup.in
Right in the main shopping hub with a popular restaurant.

Mumbai

Hotel Lawrence ⊛
Great value
Saibaba Rd, Kalaghoda, Fort, 400001
Tel *(022) 2284 3618*
Basic well-kept rooms, shared bathrooms, and helpful owner.

Sea Shore Hotel ⊛
Great value
1/49, Kamal Mansion, Arthur Bunder Rd, Colaba, 400005
Tel *(022) 2287 4238*
Simple but cared for lodge offers Taj-like views at a fraction of the price. Shared bathrooms.

Bentley's Hotel ⊛⊛
Great value
Oliver St, Colaba, 400001
Tel *(022) 2288 0442*
🕸 bentleyshotel.com
The best rooms here are large and cool, with windows opening onto gulmohar trees.

Residency Hotel ⊛⊛
Comfort lodging
Rustom Sidhwa Marg, Fort, 400001
Tel *(022) 6667 0555*
🕸 residencyhotel.com
One of the best deals downtown with clean rooms and friendly staff.

YWCA International Centre ⊛⊛
Great value
18 Madam Cama Rd, 400001
Tel *(022) 2202 0598*
🕸 ywcaic.info
Neat and pleasant ensuite rooms in a sociable collegiate lodge. Breakfast and dinner are included.

Ascot Hotel ⊛⊛⊛
Comfort lodging
38 Garden Rd, Colaba, 400001
Tel *(022) 6638 5566*
🕸 ascothotel.com
Graceful 1930s hotel with chic wood-panelled rooms. Good amenities and an ace location.

Hotel Sea Princess ⊛⊛⊛
Comfort lodging
Juhu Beach, 400049
Tel *(022) 2646 9500*
🕸 seaprincess.com
Long-established hotel with both renovated and old-world rooms overlooking Juhu Beach.

Orchid Hotel ⊛⊛⊛
Eco-friendly
Nehru Rd, Vile Parle East, 400099
Tel *(022) 26164040*
🕸 orchidhotel.com
Large rooms, attentive service and eco-friendly features. Very handy for the domestic airport.

Regency Hotel ⊛⊛⊛
Comfort lodging
73, Nepean Sea Rd 400006
Tel *(022) 6657 1234*
🕸 regencymumbai.com
Well-kept secret. Small but flawless rooms in a quiet spot at the base of posh Malabar Hill.

Suba Galaxy ⊛⊛⊛
Business
NS Phadke Rd, Andheri E, 400069
Tel *(022) 2682 1188*
🕸 hotelsubagalaxy.com
Small but good-value rooms in a sleek business hotel close to airports.

DK Choice

Taj Mahal Palace and Tower ⊛⊛⊛
Luxury
Apollo Bunder, 400001
Tel *(022) 6665 3366*
🕸 tajhotels.com
An icon of Indian hospitality since 1903. The restored and shining Palace Wing is Mumbai's ultimate luxury address, with elegant and tech-savvy rooms and cavernous suites offering front row views of the Gateway of India. Superb restaurants include the clubby Sea Lounge.

The Oberoi ⊛⊛⊛
Luxury
Nariman Point, 400021
Tel *(022) 6632 5757*
🕸 oberoihotels.com
Top-class restaurants, 24-hour spa and rooms with iPod docks and glass-walled bathrooms.

Maharashtra

AURANGABAD: Oberoi Hotel ⊛⊛
Great value
Railway Station Rd, New Osmanpura, 431005
Tel *(0240) 232 3841*
No relation to the luxury hotel chain; this well-run lodge is Aurangabad's best bargain.

AURANGABAD: Taj Residency ⊛⊛⊛
Luxury
8-N - 12, CIDCO, Rauza Bagh, 431003
Tel *(0240) 661 3737*
🕸 tajhotels.com
A modern palace with domes, huge rooms, gardens and pool. Great base for the caves.

DK Choice

GANPATIPULE: Atithi Parinay ⊛⊛
Rural retreat
Kolagewadi, Ratnagiri, 415617
Tel *(0) 90499 81309*
🕸 atithiparinay.com
Tucked away in the coastal hinterland, this peaceful and organic farm-homestay offers an introduction to village life in Maharashtra. Rooms vary from rustic cottages with traditional earthen floors to safari-style tents and a tree-house. Trails lead to a nearby creek, and quiet beaches are a short drive away.

KHOLAPUR: Opal ⊛⊛
Great value
Old Pune-Bengaluru Rd, 416005
Tel *(0231) 253 6767*
🕸 hotelopal.co.in
Basic rooms behind an Art Deco façade. Superb local dishes.

Quaint tree-house at Atithi Parinay in Ganpatipule

LONAVLA: The Machan ⊛⊛⊛
Eco-friendly
Lonavala, 401401
Tel *(022) 3063 5133*
🅦 themachan.com
Secluded rustic luxury in timber and glass treehouses. Breezy balconies overlook the forest.

MAHABALESHWAR: Brightland ⊛⊛⊛
Rural retreat
Kates Point Rd, 412806
Tel *(02168) 260 700*
🅦 brightlandholiday.com
Mountain-top resort with great views and an ayurvedic centre.

NAGPUR: Radisson Blu ⊛⊛⊛
Business
93/7 Wardha Rd, 440015
Tel *(0712) 666 5888*
🅦 radissonblu.com
Spacious accommodation in this efficient hotel near the airport.

NASHIK: Hotel Rajmahal ⊛⊛
Great value
Sharanpur Rd, 422002
Tel *(0253) 329 0888*
🅦 hotelrajmahalnashik.com
Quiet and well-kept rooms a few steps from the bus station.

PUNE: Sunderban ⊛⊛⊛
Heritage
19 Koregaon Park, 411001
Tel *(020) 2612 4949*
🅦 tghotels.com
Charming rooms with antique leather lounges in the Art Deco wing. Fine Italian restaurant.

WARDHA: Sevagram Ashram Yatri Niwas ⊛
Great value
Sevagram Ashram, 442102
Tel *(07152) 284 753*
🅦 gandhiashramsevagram.org
Spartan but spotless ashram guesthouse with a bookshop. Serves vegetarian meals.

Goa

BAGA: Cavala ⊛⊛⊛
Beachside
Saunta Vaddo, 403516
Tel *(0832) 227 6090*
🅦 cavala.com
Family-friendly resort with pool and themed music nights.

BARDEZ: Nilaya Hermitage ⊛⊛⊛
Boutique
60, Bhatti Arpora, 403515
Tel *(0832) 226 9793*
🅦 nilaya.com
Epic hilltop property with stylish rooms, pool, and a music room.

Elegant bedroom interiors, Siolim House, Siolim

CALANGUTE: Pousada Tauma ⊛⊛⊛
Boutique
Porba Vaddo, 403516
Tel *(0832) 227 9061*
🅦 pousadatauma.com
Made with local laterite stone. Has a good ayurvedic centre.

CHORLA GHATS: Wildernest ⊛⊛⊛
Eco-friendly
Sankhali, 416512
Tel *(0) 93411 12721*
🅦 wildernest-goa.com
Stunning eco-resort with infinty pool and nature walks.

MAJORDA. Alila Diwa ⊛⊛⊛
Luxury
Adao Waddo, 403713
Tel *(0832) 274 6800*
🅦 aliladiwagoa.com
Stunning resort with spacious rooms, spa and lovely infinity pool.

MANDREM: Beach Street ⊛⊛
Beachside
Junas Vaddo, 403527
Tel *(0) 94238 82600*
🅦 beachstreet.in
Lovely rooms in a 1920s palace as well as secluded beach huts.

PALOLEM: Ordo Sounsar ⊛⊛
Beachside
North Palolem Beach, 403702
Tel *(0) 98224 88769*
🅦 ordosounsar.com
Tented huts on a quiet stretch of beach. Delicious Goan food.

PANAJI: Panjim Inn ⊛⊛
Heritage
31 January Rd, 403001
Tel *(0832) 222 6523*
🅦 panjiminn.com
Goa's first heritage hotel – all four-poster beds and antiques.

SINQUERIM: Taj Holiday Village ⊛⊛⊛
Beachside
Dando, Candolim, 403519
Tel *(0832) 664 5858*
🅦 tajhotels.com

Beautifully laid out with Goan-style cottages, massive pool and three great restaurants.

DK Choice

SIOLIM: Siolim House ⊛⊛⊛
Heritage
Opp Vaddy Chapel, 403517
Tel *(0832) 227 2138*
🅦 siolimhouse.com
This 350-year old Portuguese mansion once belonged to the governor of Macau. Romantic rooms, an airy living room and a beautiful pool make this the perfect getaway. Popular beaches and markets are just a short drive away.

Karnataka

DK Choice

BANDIPUR: Dhole's Den ⊛⊛⊛
Eco-friendly
Kaniyanapura, 571126
Tel *(0) 94444 68376*
🅦 dholesden.com
Set in grassland on the edge of Bandipur National Park, this boutique safari lodge comes with mountain views. Bright, TV-free rooms, with showers open to the sky, are powered by the wind and sun; veggies are picked from the organic garden. Safaris are led by a naturalist.

BENGALURU: Sri Lakshmi Comforts ⊛⊛
Comfort lodging
117 MG Rd, 560001
Tel *(080) 2555 9388*
🅦 slcomforts.in
One of the city's best budget deals with spartan but well-maintained rooms, friendly staff and a good *thali* restaurant.

For more information on types of hotels *see page 693*

Impressive teak-pillared courtyard at Chettinadu Mansion, Chettinad

**BENGALURU: Taj West
End**   ⓇⓇⓇ
Luxury
23 Race Course Rd, 560001
Tel *(080) 6660 5660*
Ⓦ tajhotels.com
Charming 1887 property set amid
gardens. Suites with balconies.

BIJAPUR: Hotel Pearl   ⓇⓇ
Comfort lodging
Station Rd, 586101
Tel *(08352) 256 002*
Ⓦ hotelpearlbijapur.com
Well-kept hotel with pastel rooms.
Good vegetarian restaurant.

COORG: Palace Estate   ⓇⓇ
Rural retreat
Kakkabe, 571212
Tel *(08272) 238 446*
Ⓦ palaceestate.co.in
Lovely homestay on a spice farm
among forested hills.

GOKARNA: Nirvana Café   Ⓡ
Great value
Om Beach
Tel *(08386) 329 851*
Bamboo huts and a cottage
attached to café on beach.

HAMPI: Mowgli Guest House Ⓡ
Great value
Virupapur Gaddi, 583234
Tel *(08533) 287 033*
Ⓦ mowglihampi.com
Mud huts and bright rooms that
open onto green paddy fields.

HOSPET: Malligi   ⓇⓇ
Comfort lodging
6/143 Jambunatha Rd, 583201
Tel *(08394) 228 101*
Ⓦ malligihotels.com
Modern hotel with functional
rooms, restaurant and pool.

MYSORE: Green Hotel   ⓇⓇ
Heritage
2270 Vinoba Rd, 570012
Tel *(0821) 242 2668*
Ⓦ hotelritzmysore.com

Beautiful palace with sustainable
tourism ethos. Croquet lawns
and good restaurant.

**NAGARHOLE NP: Kabini River
Lodge**   ⓇⓇⓇ
Rural retreat
Karapur
Tel *(080) 4055 4055*
Ⓦ junglelodges.com
Iconic resort set in a former
royal hunting lodge. Daily tiger
safaris organized.

Chennai

Karpagam International   Ⓡ
Good value
*41 South Mada St, Mylapore,
600004*
Tel *(044) 2495 9984*
Basic, yet atmospheric lodge
with front rooms overlooking
a temple pond.

DK Choice

Footprint B&B   ⓇⓇ
Boutique
*16 Sriram Nagar South St, off TTK
Rd, Alwarpet, 600018*
Tel *(0) 98400 37383*
Ⓦ footprint.in
This peaceful and intimate city
retreat has stylish but unfussy
rooms, decorated with handmade
paper from Auroville. Indian
and continental breakfasts are
prepared to order. The owner,
Rucha, is a wealth of information on the best places to see,
eat and shop in Chennai.

Oriental Inn   ⓇⓇ
Comfort lodging
71 Cathedral Rd, 600086
Tel *(044) 2811 4941*
Ⓦ orientalinn.in
Spacious studios and many
restaurants in a central spot.

Savera Hotel   ⓇⓇ
Business
146 Dr Radhakrishnan Rd, 600004
Tel *(044) 2811 4700*
Ⓦ hotelsavera.com
Good-value central hotel with a
pool and rooftop restaurant.

Raintree   ⓇⓇⓇ
Eco-friendly
636 Anna Salai, Teynampet, 600035
Tel *(044) 2830 9999*
Ⓦ raintreehotels.com
Understated rooms, choice of
restaurants and a rooftop pool.

**Vivanta by Taj -
Connemara**   ⓇⓇⓇ
Heritage
Binny Rd, 600002
Tel *(044) 6600 0000*
Ⓦ tajhotels.com
Elegant Art Deco touches and
supremely comfortable rooms.

Tamil Nadu

DK Choice

**CHETTINAD: Chettinadu
Mansion**   ⓇⓇⓇ
Heritage
Kanadukathan
Tel *(04565) 273 080*
Ⓦ chettinadumansion.com
Dating back to 1902, this
traditional Chettiar house
sprawls across half a block, its
soaring ballroom giving way
to a succession of teak-pillared
courtyards. Huge rooms on the
second floor come with private
rooftop sit-outs.

**KANYAKUMARI: Hotel Tamil
Nadu**   Ⓡ
Great value
Beach Rd, 629702
Tel *(04652) 246 257*
Ⓦ ttdconline.com
Quiet government place with
sea-facing terraces and gardens.

**KODAIKANAL: Carlton
Hotel**   ⓇⓇⓇ
Comfort lodging
Boat Club Rd, 624101
Tel *(04542) 248 555*
Ⓦ carlton-kodaikanal.com
Spacious hotel with private
terraces overlooking the lake.

**MADURAI: Heritage
Madurai**   ⓇⓇⓇ
Luxury
*11 Melakkal Main Rd,
Kochadai, 625016*
Tel *(0452) 238 5455*
Ⓦ heritagemadurai.com

Huge villas come with plunge pools and a private chef.

MAHABALIPURAM: Sri Harul Guest House ₹
Great value
181 Bajanai Koil St, 603104
Tel *(0) 93846 20173*
Simple guesthouse right on the beach. Relaxed rooftop café.

MUDUMALAI: Jungle Retreat ₹₹
Rural retreat
Bokkapuram, 643223
Tel *(0423) 252 6469*
W jungleretreat.com
Stone cottages, romantic treehouses or bamboo huts.

OOTY: YWCA Anandagiri ₹
Heritage
Ettines Rd, 643001
Tel *(0423) 244 2218*
W ywcaagooty.com
High-ceilinged cottages with fireplaces, set in pine-shaded gardens. Fantastic value.

PUDUCHERRY: Hotel de l'Orient ₹₹
Heritage
17 rue Romain Rolland, 605001
Tel *(0413) 234 3067*
W neemranahotels.com
Antique-furnished rooms in an 18th-century schoolhouse.

TIRUCHIRAPPALLI: Grand Gardenia ₹₹
Business
22-25 Mannarpuram Jn, 620020
Tel *(0431) 404 5000*
W grandgardenia.com
Well-equipped hotel with big rooms and rooftop restaurant.

Andaman Islands

HAVELOCK: Barefoot at Havelock ₹₹₹
Eco-friendly
Beach No 7, SH 4, 744211
Tel *(0) 98402 38042*
W barefoot-andaman.com

Spectacular interiors of the famous Taj Falaknuma Palace, Hyderabad

Thatched Nicobari-style villas and cottages, rustic restaurant and a short stroll to the beach.

PORT BLAIR: Fortune Resort Bay Island ₹₹₹
Comfort lodging
Marine Hill, 744101
Tel *(03192) 234 101*
W fortunehotels.in
Built with local *padoauk* wood. Imaginatively done rooms and open-deck Nico Bar.

Kerala

DK Choice

ALAPPUZHA: Purity ₹₹₹
Luxury
Muhamma, 688525
Tel *(0184) 221 6666*
W malabarescapes.com
This Italianate villa is ultimate in discreet Backwaters luxury. Huge rooms with sunken baths, artworks and antique beds. Bicycles and canoes for exploring the Backwaters.

FORT COCHIN: Delight Homestay ₹₹
Heritage
Ridsdale Rd, 682001
Tel *(0484) 221 7658*
W delightfulhomestay.com
Grand old house with airy, spotless rooms, shady terrace and orchid-filled gardens.

KOVALAM: Niraamaya ₹₹₹
Luxury
Pulinkudi, Kovalam, 695521
Tel *(0471) 226 7333*
W niraamaya.in
Ancient Keralite cottages on a clifftop overlooking beaches. Good for ayurveda and yoga.

KOZHIKODE: Alakapuri Hotel ₹
Great value
MM Ali Rd, 673004
Tel *(0495) 272 3451*
Roomy cottages are set around a broad, grassy courtyard.

MUNNAR: Tea Sanctuary ₹₹
Rural retreat
Kanan Devan Hills Plantation
Tel *(04865) 230141*
W theteasanctuary.com
Stay in quaint cottages dotted around a tea plantation.

THEKKADY: Coffee Inn ₹
Good value
Lake Rd, Kumily, 685509
Tel *(04869) 222 763*
W coffeeinnthekkady.com

Bamboo huts in a lush garden or swish rooms. Great location.

VARKALA: Mektoub ₹₹
Boutique
Odayam Beach, 695311
Tel *(0) 94479 71239*
Peaceful rustic-mystic hideaway with a charming owner. Short stroll to uncrowded sands.

WAYANAD: Aranyakam ₹₹
Rural retreat
Valathur, Meppadi–Vaduvanchal Rd, 673577
Tel *(04936) 280 261*
W aranyakam.com
Coffee plantation B&B with cool rooms in the bungalow or a treehouse overlooking ravines.

Andhra Pradesh

HYDERABAD: Taj Mahal ₹₹
Great value
4 1-999 Abid Rd, 500001
Tel *(040) 2475 8250*
W hoteltajmahalindia.com
A characterful budget hotel that is palatial outside, big and bright within.

DK Choice

HYDERABAD: Taj Falaknuma Palace ₹₹₹
Heritage
Engine Bowli, Falaknuma, 500054
Tel *040 6629 8585*
W tajhotels.com
A luxurious palace hotel set (610 m) 2,000 ft above Hyderabad. Suites are decked out with antiques, and cavernous chambers feature dining tables that stretch for miles. Faultless service, a health spa and superb restaurants make staying here a memorable experience.

VIJAYAWADA: Mamata ₹
Good value
Eluru Rd, 520002
Tel *(0866) 257 1251*
W mamatahotel.com
Standard budget hotel with reasonably well kept rooms and friendly staff.

VISAKHAPATNAM: Dolphin ₹₹
Comfort lodging
Dabagardens, 530020
Tel *(0891) 662 2444*
W dolphinhotelsvizag.com
Large, well-equipped and friendly hotel. Smart rooms, and good restaurants.

For more information on types of hotels *see page 693*

WHERE TO EAT AND DRINK

Indian cuisine is as rich in variety as the country itself. The delicate flavours of the classic cuisines that developed in the imperial courts of Delhi, Kashmir, Hyderabad and Lucknow are complemented by a vast range of regional specialities, made with a variety of exotic ingredients. From the arid desert of Rajasthan come robust chilli-hot curries, whereas fish dominates the cuisine of the lush, coastal areas of West Bengal, Goa and, to some extent, Kerala. Eating habits in urban India are undergoing considerable change, triggered by rapidly changing lifestyles and the introduction of Western fast-food chains. Though most Indians relish food cooked at home, eating out is becoming increasingly popular in the larger cities. Restaurants now offer anything from pizzas and burgers to sophisticated multi-course meals alongwith local and imported wines. The restaurants listed on pages 706–719 have been selected for their quality, variety, service and price range.

Etiquette

Indians are overwhelmingly hospitable and many hotels and restaurants strive to follow a similar ethos. While it is customary for Indians to eat with their fingers, eateries do provide cutlery. There is usually a basin for washing hands before and after a meal, and restaurants often provide finger bowls with warm water and lemon for this purpose. Eating beef is taboo among Hindus, as is pork for Muslims.

Visitors savour a meal at one of Mumbai's many restaurants

Restaurants

Changing lifestyles are mostly responsible for the proliferation of eating places, in smaller towns as well as big cities. These range from luxurious gourmet restaurants to small cafés and roadside stalls, offering an eclectic mix of food, from Indian to Italian to Japanese. Most urban restaurants are air conditioned and the more expensive ones boast decor and service that is of international standards. Traditional eating places, especially those that cater to a local clientele, are large, noisy halls, often with special "family rooms". Simple and wholesome, mainly vegetarian, meals, are served here.

International chains, such as Dominos and McDonalds, have outlets in most big towns. Special menus have been introduced to suit local tastes.

Most restaurants open by about 11am and close by midnight. In larger cities, it is best to book a table in advance for weekends and holidays, especially at the more popular restaurants.

Speciality Restaurants

The growing appreciation for international cuisine has led to a rise in upmarket speciality restaurants in most big cities. Authentic Thai, Chinese, Mexican, Japanese and Italian dishes, prepared by expert chefs using imported ingredients, are enthusiastically patronized by discerning gourmands.

Regional Indian specialities, too, are in demand. Restaurants specializing in barbecued *tandoori* kebabs and breads, as well as cuisine from Goa, Kerala, Kashmir, Lucknow, Hyderabad, West Bengal and Rajasthan, now offer a wide range of dishes derived from traditional family recipes. Restaurants offering fusion food have begun to attract diners in search of unusual tastes and flavours. Here, inspired chefs experiment with recipes and ingredients from India and abroad, to create exciting new menus.

Coffee Shops

Luxury hotels have 24-hour coffee shops, where it is possible to grab a late dinner or early breakfast. Many local cafés and restaurants serving beverages and light snacks also keep flexible

A cook deftly prepares a paper-thin, plate-sized *rumali roti*

An improvised eatery in Rajasthan's Thar Desert

hours. Small, bistro-type establishments now appear in many shopping malls and at tourist sites. These are perfect places to relax over sandwiches and a cup of tea.

Roadside and Market Food Stalls

For a glimpse of the original Indian fast-food industry, a journey through the country's roadside and market food stalls is ideal. Improvised stalls or carts, equipped with stoves and other cooking appliances, dish out tasty meals with speed and efficiency. The choice ranges from vegetarian snacks, such as spicy *samosas*, *dosas* and *idlis*, to *tandoori* chicken, kebabs, "fish fry" and Indian-style Chinese chowmein. Indian sweets, fruit, ice cream and a variety of drinks are also available. Unpretentious eateries also serve good food. These include the North Indian *dhabas* (which serve both non-vegetarian and vegetarian food), the Goan beach shacks (which specialize in fish curries with rice) and the South Indian Udipi restaurants (which serve only vegetarian meals). For health precautions, *see pages 740–43*.

Vegetarian Food

India's excellent vegetarian food emanates from the country's largely vegetarian population. A simple, but delectable meal of fresh seasonal vegetables, *dal* (lentil curry) and a wide choice of *rotis* and rice preparations can be enjoyed anywhere. Often these are served all together on a *thali* (platter) and are great value. The food's quality is endorsed by the displayed signs "Cooked in pure

ghee" or "Cooked in *ghee* made from cow's milk".

Alcohol

The serving of alcohol is restricted, and some states, such as Gujarat, are officially "dry". Liquor is sold through government-approved shops and licensed restaurants. Prices vary across the country because of the difference in taxes between states. Foreign wines are available at most liquor shops, pubs and restaurants, where you will also find Indian Made Foreign Liquor (IMFL), such as beer, whisky and vodka. The quality of Indian wines and champagne is improving, and some brands are even exported. Carrying alcohol for consumption in a restaurant is not permitted, nor is drinking in public places. National holidays and notified election days are "dry days", when alcohol is unavailable.

Prices and Tipping

Prices are fixed everywhere, be it in a luxury hotel or at a market stall. Luxury hotels also levy a Food and Beverage Tax (though

the amount varies), which can escalate costs considerably. Check your bill before paying. Even though a service charge is usually included, waiters do expect to be tipped – 10 per cent of the bill is acceptable. Roadside eateries and street vendors are extremely cheap and don't expect to be tipped.

Paying

Credit cards are accepted in most upmarket restaurants and bars, particularly those in luxury hotels. However, always keep some Indian rupees on hand to pay for meals at eateries in small towns or roadside stalls and cafés.

Recommended Restaurants

The restaurants on the following pages have been carefully selected to provide a variety of cuisine options from across the sub-continent. You'll find everything from regional specialities to street food staples. Classic *tandoori* restaurants alongside those specializing in the less familiar South Indian cuisine. Quality international establishments have been highlighted, as well as restaurants that have adopted neighbouring cuisines such as Tibetan or Chinese. The DK Choice restaurants are extra special. These are the truly exceptional establishments that boast a unique menu, superb cuisine, presentation, service or location, or just offer something unique that simply has to be experienced.

Afternoon tea in a resort in the backwaters of Kerala

Where to Eat and Drink

Delhi

Karim's ®
North Indian
16 Jama Masjid, 110006
Tel *(011) 2326 9880*
Celebrating it's 100th year in
2013, Karim's is an institution in
Old Delhi, with tasty kebabs and
an unmatched *tandoori*
leg of lamb.

Naivedyam ®
South Indian vegetarian
1 Hauz Khas Village, 110016
Tel *(011) 2696 0426*
Fantastic *thalis*, delicious *dosas*
and Malabar *paranthas* with
kurma (coconut-based stew) –
all in a beautiful restaurant
with murals.

Saravana Bhavan ®
South Indian vegetarian
46 Janpath, 110001
Tel *(011) 2331 7755*
Hugely popular diner with great
thalis and *dosa*. The mini-tiffin
with a taste of everything is
fantastic. Also in P block CP.

Triveni Tea Terrace ®
North Indian
*205 Tansen Marg, near Connaught
Place, 110001*
Tel *(0) 99996 11209*
Peaceful atmosphere and
delicious *palak paneer*, kebabs
and *paranthas*. The building has
an art gallery and amphitheatre.

Amour ®®
Mediterranean
30 Hauz Khas Village, 110016
Tel *(0) 92121 26687*
Terrace for open-air dining plus
stylish indoor restaurant. Serves
Italian and Mediterranean fare in
hip Hauz Khas Village.

Baci ®®
Italian
23 Sunder Nagar Market, 110003
Tel *(011) 4150 7445*
Popular café-style Italian eatery
offering all the usual pasta
favourites and dishes like pan-
seared pork or grilled salmon.

Chor Bizarre ®®
Kashmiri
*Hotel Broadway, 4/15A Asaf
Ali Rd, 110002*
Tel *(011) 4366 3600*
Atmospheric decor,
complete with a vintage car.
Fantastic Wazwan food to be
had; try the *gushtaba* (meat
balls cooked in yoghurt).

Diva ®®
Italian
*M-8A, M Block Market,
GK 2, 110048*
Tel *(011) 2921 5673*
Ritu Dalmia has a love affair
with Italian food. Try the beaten
chicken with butter balsamic
sauce. Latitude 28 in Khan Market
is a sister restaurant.

Kwality ®®
North Indian
*7 Regal Building, Connaught
Place, 110001*
Tel *(011) 2374 2310*
Serving up rich North Indian fare
including *tandoori* items and
kebabs. Everyone raves about
the delicious *chhola bhatura*
(spicy chickpeas).

Smokehouse Deli ®®
Fusion
17 Khan Market, 110003
Tel *(011) 4356 2820*
Global tastes such as lamb and
chipotle patties, prawn and
sambal skewers and curried veg
burger. Branches in Hauz Khas
and Vasant Kunj too.

Bukhara ®®®
North Indian
*Maurya Sheraton, Sardar
Patel Marg, 110021*
Tel *(011) 2611 2233*
Northwestern frontier cooking
right out of the *tandoor* oven in
the open kitchen. Rich flavours.

Dum Pukht ®®®
North Indian
*Maurya Sheraton, Sardar
Patel Marg, 110021*
Tel *(011) 2611 2233*

Diners enjoying a meal at Delhi's most
famous restaurant, Bukhara

Stunning restaurant voted one
of the best in the world by
Condé Nast. Delicious *biryani*,
shahi nihari (slow-cooked lamb)
and *kheer* (rice dessert).

DK Choice

Indian Accent ®®®
Modern Indian
*The Manor, 77 Friends
Colony West, 110065*
Tel *(011) 4323 5151*
Giving a new spin to Indian
classics, celebrity chef Manish
Mehrotra changes his menu
seasonally. Sample the *masala*
wild mushrooms paper *dosa*,
tuna *bhel* ceviche or tamarind
glazed *tandoori* pork ribs. For
dessert go for the dark and
white chocolate *kulfi* lolipops.

Kainoosh ®®®
Modern Indian
*122–124 DLF Promenade Mall,
Vasant Kunj, 110070*
Tel *(0) 95607 15544*
Thalis with nutmeg-infused lamb
kofti or cardamom and saffron
chicken. Atmospheric Keya bar
next door.

Lodi Restaurant ®®®
Mediterranean
*Lodi Gardens, opp Mausam
Bhavan, 110003*
Tel *(011) 2465 5054*
Garden restaurant strewn with
lanterns; the menu includes lamb
tagine, and pumpkin ravioli with
burnt butter and sage.

Magique ®®®
Multi-cuisine
*Garden of Five Senses,
Saket, 110044*
Tel *(0) 97175 35533*
A sprawling, romantic space with
delicious Mediterranean, Thai,
Japanese and Italian fare.

Olive at the Qutb ®®®
Mediterranean
*One Style Mile, Haveli 6,
Mehrauli, 110016*
Tel *(011) 2957 4444*
Stylish restaurant serving up
grilled *basa*, foie gras and blue
cheese *gnochi*. Great Sunday
brunch and amazing views.

Spice Route ⊗⊗⊗
South East Asian
The Imperial, Janpath, 110001
Tel *(011) 4111 6605*
Stunning decor inspired by a South Indian temple. The food comes by way of Thailand, Vietnam and Sri Lanka.

Threesixty° ⊗⊗⊗
Fusion
The Oberoi, Dr Zakir Hussain Marg, 110003
Tel *(011) 2436 3030*
Legendary Sunday brunch aside, Threesixty° offers up superb Japanese food and wood-oven pizzas.

Wasabi ⊗⊗⊗
Japanese
The Taj Mahal Hotel, 1 Man Singh Rd, 110001
Tel *(011) 6651 3585*
Live cooking with a teppanyaki and grill counter, a sushi bar that serves fish flown in daily from Tokyo, and a stylish sake bar.

Contemporary decor at Wasabi, one of Delhi's best Japanese restaurants

Haryana and Punjab

AMRITSAR: Punjabi Rasoi ⊗
North Indian
Near Jallianwala Bagh, Shastri Market, 143001
Tel *(0183) 254 0140*
Close to the Golden Temple and Jallianwala Bagh, this great little place offers good Punjabi and South Indian dishes.

AMRITSAR: Crystal ⊗⊗
North Indian
Crystal Chowk, Queen's Rd, 143001
Tel *(0183) 222 5555*
Top-notch North Indian food – from *murgh makhani* (butter chicken) to *palak paneer*. Busy on weekends.

CHANDIGARH: Elevens ⊗
North Indian
Kaptains Retreat, Sector 35-B, 160022
Tel *(0172) 500 5599*
Enjoy *malai kofta* and chicken dishes while surrounded by cricket memorabilia.

CHANDIGARH: Barbeque Nation ⊗⊗
International
SCO 39, Madhya Marg, Sector 26, 160019
Tel *(0172) 606 0000*
Popular chain restaurant where you can cook your own dinner! Each table has its own BBQ, so guests choose their ingredients and get going.

CHANDIGARH: Bombay Chopstick ⊗⊗
Chinese
Sector 10, 160011
Tel *(0172) 463 0666*
Thai as well as Chinese favourites. There is also a pleasant outdoor seating area.

CHANDIGARH: Pashtun ⊗⊗
North Indian
SCO 333–334, Sector 35–B, 160036
Tel *(0172) 260 7728*
This place offers up excellent North Indian vegetarian and meat classics.

CHANDIGARH: Mehfil ⊗⊗⊗
Multi-cuisine
SCO 183–185, Sector 17–C, 160017
Tel *(0172) 270 3539*
One of the oldest restaurants in town serving up tastes from around the world; good Mughlai.

Himachal Pradesh

CHAIL: Palace Hotel's Restaurant ⊗⊗
Himachali
Palace Hotel, 173217
Tel *(01792) 248 141*
Delicious local specialities. Yoghurt is used liberally in many preparations.

CHAMBA: Iravati Hotel ⊗⊗
Himachali
Iravati Hotel, 176310
Tel *(01899) 222 671*
Try the *achari* chicken or the *guchi madara* (spicy mushroom and peas). Great mountain views.

DHARAMSALA: Lung Ta ⊗
Japanese
Jogibara Rd, Mcleod Ganj, 176219
Closed *Sun*
Japanese diner with sushi on Tuesdays and Fridays; other specials during the rest of the week. All profits go to charity.

DHARAMSALA: Nick's Italian Kitchen ⊗
Multi-cuisine
Kunga Guesthouse, Bhagsu Rd, 176219
Tel *(01892) 221 180*
A Tibetan-run eatery with good range of pastas, and Tibetan staples like *momos* and *thukpa*.

DHARAMSALA: Seven Hills of Dokebi ⊗⊗
Korean
Jogibara Rd, Mcleod Ganj, 176219
Closed *Mon*
Exceptional Korean food in a beautiful restaurant, with low seating upstairs. Korean sushi, tofu hot pots and *kimchi*.

MANALI: Chopsticks ⊗
Chinese
The Mall, 175131
Tel *(01902) 252 639*
Well-loved Chinese restaurant that also serves Tibetan *momos* and *gyakok* (hot pot).

MANALI: Johnson's Café ⊗⊗
Multi-cuisine
Johnson's Hotel, Circuit House Rd, 175131
Tel *(01902) 253 764*
Great trout specialties as well as good pastas. Lovely gardens.

DK Choice

MANALI: La Plage ⊗⊗⊗
Fusion
Behind Club House, Old Manali, 175131
Tel *(0) 98053 40977*
Effortlessly chic restaurant amid apple orchards. The food is as good as the stunning views. Sesame chicken with wasabi mashed potatoes, trout with almonds and the chocolate *thali* are must-haves. If visiting in summer, don't miss the craft market held on the weekends.

For more information on types of restaurants *see page 705*

SHIMLA: Baljees ®
Multi-cuisine
The Mall, opp Town Hall, 171003
Tel *(0177) 281 4054*
A hardy perennial that serves all
the familiar South Indian and
North Indian classics.

SHIMLA: Ashiana ®®
Multi-cuisine
The Ridge, 171001
Great location and a circular
design to catch the views.
Good food and a bar.

SHIMLA: Cecil ®®®
Multi-cuisine
Chaura Maidan, 171004
Tel *(0177) 280 4848*
Wood-panelled dining room in
the 100-year-old Oberoi Cecil
hotel. Expect top-notch food.

Ladakh, Jammu & Kashmir

**ALCHI: Zimskhang
Restaurant** ®®
Multi-cuisine
On the lane to the monastery
Tel *(01982) 227 086*
Best choice in town with an
extensive and reliable menu and
a pleasant tree-shaded courtyard.

**JAMMU: The Terrace – Sky
Lounge Restaurant** ®®
Multi-cuisine
KC Residency, Residency Rd, 180001
Tel *(0191) 252 0770*
Fantastic open-air terrace with
panoramic views and high-
quality food. A good bar and
revolving restaurant on site too.

LEH: Amdo Cafeteria ®®
Tibetan and Chinese
Main Market, 194101
Tel *(01982) 253 114*
Rooftop with views of the palace
and fort. Delicious noodles,
spring rolls and more.

LEH: Chopsticks Noodle Bar ®®
Asian & Ladakhi
Raku Complex, Fort Rd, 194101
Tel *(0) 99069 70496*
Trendy spot in a central
but quiet location serving up
Asian and local dishes.

**LEH: Mentokling
Garden Restaurant** ®®
Multi-cuisine
Zansti, 194101
Tel *(01982) 252 992* **Closed** *Nov–
Feb*
Pretty, garden restaurant with
a mellow vibe and lots of
apple trees.

LEH: Omasila Restaurant ®®
Multi-cuisine
Hotel Omasila, Changspa, 194101
Tel *(01982) 252 119*
Well-established restaurant
offering regional and Western
fare, served indoors or in the
pleasant courtyard.

**LEH: Open Hand Espresso
Bar & Bistro** ®®
International
Off Old Fort Rd, 194101
Tel *(0) 98719 09777* **Closed** *Nov–
Mar*
Fully organic, healthy meals,
great cakes and coffee. There
is a fairtrade shop and adjoining
vegetable gardens.

**LEH: Penguin Garden Restaurant
& German Bakery** ®®
International
Fort Rd, 194101
Tel *(01982) 251 523* **Closed** *Oct–
May*
Leafy courtyard restaurant with
a German bakery. Background
music and laid-back vibe.

**LEH: Summer
Harvest Restaurant** ®®
Multi-cuisine
Fort Rd, 194101
Tel *(01982) 252 226* **Closed** *Nov–
Mar*

Modest eatery with mainly
Tibetan dishes and a sprinkling
of Western fare.

SRINAGAR: Latitude ®®®
Multi-cuisine
Vivanta by Taj – Dal View, 191121
Tel *(0194) 246 1111*
All-day dining in Modernist
interiors or alfresco with sublime
lake views.

Uttar Pradesh and Uttarakhand

AGRA: Dasaprakash ®
South Indian vegetarian
*9 Bansal Nagar,
Fathehabad Rd, 282002*
Tel *(0562) 223 0089*
Tasty *dosas* and generous *thali*.
Try the Mysore *masala dosa*.

AGRA: Esphahan ®®®
Mughlai
Amar Vilas, Taj East Gate, 282001
Tel *(0562) 223 1515*
Stunning restaurant at the
Oberoi with exquisite Mughlai
food. Try the *thali*.

AGRA: Peshawri ®®®
North Indian
ITC Mughal, 282001
Tel *(0562) 402 1700*
Delicious kebabs and a
renowned Dal Bukhara at
this village-style restaurant.

ALLAHABAD: El Chico ®®
Multi-cuisine
24 MG Road, Civil Lines, 211001
Tel *(0532) 242 0075*
Deservedly popular restaurant
serving good Indian and Western
food. Also has a bakery.

**FATEHPUR SIKRI: Navratan
Restaurant** ®
Multi-cuisine
Gulistan Tourist Complex, 283110
Tel *(0561) 328 2490*
Great pit stop while sightseeing,
with good views and great Indian
and Western food.

HARIDWAR: Fun and Food ®
North Indian
Rani Pur More, 249401
Tel *(0) 78300 00953*
North and South Indian dishes
served out in the garden area.
There is an area for children to
play in as well.

LUCKNOW: Tunde Ke Kebab ®
North Indian
Aminabad Chowk, 226018
A must-visit restaurant with a
great reputation for melt-in-the
mouth minced meat kebabs.

Modern dining area at Latitude in Srinagar

Key to Price Guide *see page 706*

LUCKNOW: Vvanjan ℗
North Indian vegetarian
Vinay Palace, 10 Ashok Marg, 226001
Tel *(0522) 228 8220*
Superb vegetarian fare; try the *jeera aloo* and *palak paneer*.

LUCKNOW: Falaknuma ℗℗℗
North Indian
Clarks Avadh, 8 MG Rd, 226001
Tel *(0522) 262 0131*
Rooftop restaurant featuring Avadhi food – traditional *Dum Pukht* cuisine. Live music adds.

LUCKNOW: Oudhyana ℗℗℗
North Indian
Vipin Khand, Gomti Nagar, 226010
Tel *(0522) 239 3939*
Elegant dining room in the Taj specializing in slow-cooked marinated Avadhi cuisine; try the *nihari ghost* (lamb).

MATHURA: Best Western Radha Ashok ℗℗
Multi-cuisine
Best Western Radha Ashok, Masani Bypass Rd, 281001
Tel *(0565) 253 0395*
Decent multi-cuisine food as well as typical North Indian fare in a relaxed garden setting.

MUSSOORIE: Whispering Windows ℗℗
North Indian
Library Bazaar, The Mall, 248179
Tel *(0135) 263 2020*
Good views of the Mall from this popular eatery. Go for the butter chicken and fluffy *naan*.

RISHIKESH: Chotiwala ℗
North Indian vegetarian
Swarg Ashram, across Shivanand Jhula, 249201
Tel *(0135) 243 0070*
A Rishikesh institution that is extremely popular and atmospheric; try the *aloo poori*.

DK Choice

RISHIKESH: Ramana's Garden ℗
Multi-cuisine vegetarian
Nr Tapovan Resort, 249192
Tel *(0135) 243 5558* **Closed** *monsoon months*
Ramana's Garden restaurant was set up to give the children from Ramana's Orphanage a vocational education, and they are involved in all aspects including the baking and tending the garden. Organic salad from the garden, Tibetan *momos*, cannelloni and amazing cakes to be sampled.

Entrance to the popular Chotiwala restaurant in Rishikesh

RISHIKESH: Glasshouse on the Ganges ℗℗℗
Multi-cuisine
Badrinath Rd, 249303
Tel *(0) 9412076420*
Great food in a beautiful Neemrana property on the banks of the Ganges.

VARANASI: Keshari Restaurant ℗
North Indian vegetarian
Teri Neem, Godowlia, off Dasavamedha Rd, 221010
Tel *(0542) 240 1472*
Popular place with fantastic *thalis*. Good portions of North and South Indian fare.

VARANASI: Lotus Lounge ℗℗
Fusion
Mansarovar Ghat
Tel *(0) 98385 67717* **Closed** *Sun*
Everything from *momos* and Thai curries to grilled eggplant and salads. Views of the Ganga.

VARANASI: Pizzeria Vaatika ℗℗
Multi-cuisine
Assi Ghat, 221005
Tel *(0) 98380 94111*
Great location right on the ghats serving up good wood-oven pizzas.

VARANASI: Raga ℗℗
Korean
Marnikarnika Ghat
Tel *(0542) 240 2945*
Follow the hand-painted signs through the back streets to find this fantastic Korean restaurant.

Bihar and Jharkhand

BODH GAYA: Café Om ℗
International
Near Bank of India, 824231
Casual eatery that offers a range of Western, Indian, Japanese and Tibetan fare. Tourists and pilgrims – all are welcome.

BODH GAYA: Lotus Restaurant ℗
International
Nr Birla Dharamshala, 824231
A well-prepared, tasty and varied menu at this simple, reliable and safe budget establishment.

PATNA: Bansi Vihar ℗
South Indian
Fraser Rd, 800001
Bright and modern canteen-style family restaurant. Excellent *dosas*, *idli*, *uttapam*, plus a few Chinese options.

DK Choice

PATNA: Pind Balluchi Revolving Restaurant ℗℗
Punjabi
16-18th Floor, Biscoman Towers, Gandhi Maidan, 803110
Tel *(0) 99343 04634*
A revolving restaurant, Pind Balluchi offers phenomenal city views. This upmarket chain, with origins in Punjab, is especially renowned for the kebabs. The rustic village theme and the well-stocked bar are added bonuses.

PATNA: Samarat ℗℗
Multi-cuisine
Hotel Chanakya, 800001
Tel *(0612) 222 3141*
Freshly prepared Indian, Chinese and Western dishes served in a restful dining room. This was Patna's first elite restaurant and it remains a popular stalwart.

RAJGIR: Lotus Restaurant ℗℗
Japanese
Indo Hokke Hotel, 803116
Tel *(06119) 255 245*
Authentic – the chefs are all trained in Japan; the ambience underlined by green mats, teak furniture and exotic lampshades.

For more information on types of restaurants *see page 705*

Gently lit interiors at Baan Thai, Kolkata

RANCHI: Kaveri Restaurant ℝℝ
North Indian vegetarian
11 GEL Church Complex,
Main Rd, 834001
Tel *(0651) 233 0330*
Best-known vegetarian place in
town with generous portions of
simple, wholesome food.

RANCHI: The Oriental
Kitchen ℝℝ
Chinese
Chanakya BNR Hotel,
Station Rd, 834001
Tel *(0651) 246 1211-4*
Relaxing restaurant that serves
Chinese food with an Indian twist.

Madhya Pradesh
and Chhattisgarh

BANDHAVGARH: Dining Room
at Infinity ℝℝℝ
North Indian
Infinity Wilderness, Bijharia
Tel *(07627) 265 395*
Buffet or à la carte menu in this
rustic restaurant with outdoor
seating. Excellent service.

BHOPAL: Winds n Waves ℝ
Multi-cuisine
Van Vihar Rd, Nr Boat Club, 462002
Tel *(0755) 266 1523*
With great views of the lake,
this MP tourism venture offers a
range of cuisines and live music.

BHOPAL: La Kuchina ℝℝℝ
Mediterranean
Hotel Jehan Numa Palace, 157
Shamla Hills, 462002
Tel *(0755) 266 1100*
Sicilian style decor, quality pasta
dishes and wood-oven pizza. The
hotel buffet is good too.

GWALIOR: Daawat ℝℝ
North Indian
Hotel Gwalior Regency, 411776
Tel *(0751) 234 0670*
Specializes in Mughlai and

Punjabi food, with a good bar.
A favourite with families and
business travellers alike.

INDORE: Earthen Oven ℝℝℝ
North Indian
Hotel Fortune Landmark, Near
Meghdoot Gardens, 452010
Tel *(0731) 2398 8444*
Great kebabs and other North
Indian specialities in a pleasant
dining room.

KANHA: Earth Restaurant ℝℝℝ
Multi-cuisine
Kanha Earth Lodge, 481661
Tel *(0124) 422 2657*
Indian and Continental served
in a beautiful setting; drinks by
the bonfire in the evenings. Only
open to residents.

KHAJURAHO: Mediterraneo ℝℝ
Italian
Jain Temples Rd, 471606
Tel *(07686) 272 246*
Excellent value Italian restaurant
with wood-fired pizzas and a
great range of pastas. Lovely
outdoor seating.

DK Choice

KHAJURAHO: Raja Café ℝℝ
Multi-cuisine
Opp Western temples, 471606
This legendary eatery is blessed
with an excellent location – the
terrace affords superb views
of the temples. Great Indian
and Continental food, good
thalis, Hungarian *goulash* and
delicious Italian coffee.

ORCHHA: Sheesh Mahal ℝℝ
North Indian
Hotel Sheesh Mahal,
472246
Tel *(07680) 252 624*
Atmospheric dining room in a
beautiful fort with lots of
antiques. Good North Indian
and an excellent buffet.

UJJAIN: Shree Ganga ℝ
North Indian
50, Amar Singh Marg,
Freeganj, 456010
Tel *(0) 94250 91192*
Old restaurant with impeccable
service and good food. The South
Indian *dosas* and traditional
sweets are recommended.

Kolkata

Anand ℝ
South Indian
19 Chittaranjan Ave, 700072
Tel *(033) 2212 9757* **Closed** *Wed*
Superb South Indian food in
the city centre, in an attractive
ambience. Packed on weekends.

Chung Wah ℝ
Chinese
13 A&B Chittaranjan Ave, 700072
Tel *(033) 2237 7003*
Established in 1920, this
boisterous place serves Indian-
style Chinese; try the chilli
chicken and *chopsuey*.

Suruchi ℝ
Bengali
89 Elliot Rd, 700016
Tel *(033) 2229 1763* **Closed** *dinner*
daily.
Basic little place run in aid of
destitute women, popular with
office crowd; try the prawn *malai*.

Banana Leaf ℝℝ
South Indian
73-75 Rash Behari Ave, 700026
Tel *(033) 2464 1960*
Family restaurant with a huge
pure-veg menu, daily specials
and set meals; the mini-*idli* and
lassis (yoghurt drink) are a must.

Baan Thai ℝℝℝ
Thai
The Oberoi Grand Hotel, 15
Jawaharlal Nehru Rd, 700013
Tel *(033) 2249 2323*
Top-quality feast of Thai
delicacies. The "Khuntock"
seating arrangement, as well
as tables, are available.

Charnock's ℝℝℝ
Multi-cuisine
KB-26, Sector 3, Salt Lake, 700098
Tel *(033) 2335 1349*
Pleasant atmosphere and a
great variety of food to suit all
tastes. Good views of the city's
outer fringes

Fire and Ice ℝℝℝ
Italian
Kanak Building, 41 Jawaharlal Nehru
Rd, 700071
Tel *(033) 2288 4073*

Authentic pizzas and Italian dishes that really hit the mark. Laid-back restaurant with Hollywood and Bollywood posters.

DK Choice

Kewpie's ⊗⊗⊗
Bengali
2 Elgin Lane, 700020
Tel *(033) 2486 9929* **Closed** *Mon*
Intimate dining in a quaint 100-year old residence that has been attractively refurbished. Kewpie's has great charm and authentic Bengali food to match. The *thali* has a wide range of dishes, including famous local fish dishes as well as unusual vegetarian cuisine.

Mainland China ⊗⊗⊗
Chinese
3A Gurusaday Rd, 700019
Tel *(033) 2283 7964*
Outstanding food in a pristine setting try the skewered jumbo prawns and "drunken chicken" in Shaoxing wine.

Mirch Masala ⊗⊗⊗
Multi-cuisine
49/2 Gariahat Rd, 700019
Tel *(033) 2461 8900*
Lively atmosphere and whacky decoration that includes vivid murals and ambassador taxis. The food is rich and substantial, and the beer cool and refreshing.

Oh! Calcutta ⊗⊗⊗
Bengali
Forum Mall, 10/3 Elgin Rd, 700020
Tel *(033) 2283 7161*
Award-winning restaurant that does a fresh take on Bengali cuisine – wonderful fish and seafood in a classy setting.

Zaranj & Jong's ⊗⊗⊗
Multi-cuisine
26 Jawaharlal Nehru Rd, 700087
Tel *(033) 2249 0369*
The two share an entrance; Zaranj specializes in Punjabi dishes while Jong's serves Burmese, Japanese and other southeast Asian fare.

West Bengal and Sikkim

DARJEELING: Kunga ⊗
Multi-cuisine
51 Gandhi Rd, 734101
Tel *(0354) 225 3971*
Cosy family-run eatery serving amazing hearty soups and huge *momos*. Has a traveller clientele.

DARJEELING: Glenary's ⊗⊗
Multi-cuisine
15 Nehru Rd, 734101
Tel *(0354) 225 7554*
A fun restaurant, with a bar and bakery that's a Darjeeling mainstay. Kanchendzonga views on clear days.

DARJEELING: The Park Restaurant ⊗⊗
International
41 Laden La Rd, 734101
Tel *(0354) 225 5270* **Closed** *mid-Jan–mid-Feb*
Excellent international dishes, including decent Thai food, and inviting decor.

GANGTOK: Café Live & Loud ⊗⊗
Café
Enchey Compound, Tibet Rd, 73/101
Tel *(03592) 205 024*
Tasty snacks, served out on the verandah at this relaxed place where live music is the main draw.

GANGTOK: Snow Lion Restaurant ⊗⊗
Multi-cuisine
Hotel Tibet, Paljor Stadium Rd, 73/101
Tel *(03592) 203 468*
Furnished in Tibetan-style, with an eclectic menu; good place to sample Sikkimese dishes.

GANGTOK: Tangerine ⊗⊗
Multi-cuisine
Hotel Chumbi Residency, Tibet Rd, 737101
Tel *(03592) 226 618*
The *tandoor* oven is a particular draw, along with the twinkling lights of Rumtek Hill at night. Enjoy a casual meal by the bar.

GANGTOK: The Oyster Restaurant ⊗⊗
Multi-cuisine
Hotel Sonam Delek, Tibet Rd, 737101
Tel *(03592) 202 566*

Magnificent views of Kanchendzonga. Great variety on the menu; guests are partial to a breakfast of French toast and pancake.

KALIMPONG: Gompu's Bar and Restaurant ⊗⊗
Multi-cuisine
Dambar Chowk, 734301
Tel *(03552) 255 818*
Bustling restaurant that is a long-standing Kalimpong favourite. Mainly meat-based options and beer available.

KURSEONG: Pankasari ⊗⊗
Multi-cuisine
Cochrane Place,132 Pankhabari Rd, 734101
Tel *(0) 99320 35660*
Inventive dishes use fresh-from-the-garden ingredients. Candle-lit dinners and a tea boutique.

SILIGURI: Amrapali ⊗⊗
Multi-cuisine
Hotel Cinderella, 3rd Mile, Sevoke Rd, 734401
Tel *(0353) 254 7136*
A vegetarian restaurant with courteous staff and a well-stocked bar.

Odisha

BHUBANESWAR: Hare Krishna ⊗
Vegetarian
Laichand Market Complex, Janpath, 751001
Tel *(0674) 253 4188*
Come here for fresh Jain vegetarian food and superb *lassis*. Well-decorated eatery.

BHUBANESWAR: Tangerine ⊗⊗
Asian
Station Square, Janpath, 751001
Tel *(0674) 253 3009*
Popular; serves mostly Thai and Chinese plus some Indian dishes.

Daab Chingri (prawns with chilli paste and coconut cream), Oh! Calcutta, Kolkata

For more information on types of restaurants *see page 705*

DK Choice

BHUBANESWAR: Nakli Dhaba ₹₹₹
North Indian
*Mayfair Lagoon, 8–B
Jaydev Vihar, 751013*
Tel *(0674) 666 0101*
Set up like a roadside dhaba, this colourful, atmospheric place specializes in northwest frontier food; fantastic *tandoori* pomfret, mutton *rogan josh*, and some vegetarian options too.

CHIKLA LAKE: Panthanivas ₹
Multi-cuisine
Balugaon, Khurda, 752030
Tel *(06756) 227 488*
Lake-side location run by Odisha Tourism. Serves decent Indian as well as regional dishes.

GOPALPUR-ON-SEA: Sea Shell ₹
Seafood
Beachfront
One of many beach shacks serving the catch of the day. Good Chinese and cold beer.

GOPALPUR-ON-SEA: Crab Station ₹₹₹
Seafood
Mayfair Hotel, 761002
Tel *(0680) 282 021*
Delicious seafood; the crab dishes at this hotel-restaurant are particularly good.

KONARK: Gitanjali R
Multi-cuisine
OTDC, near Sun Temple, 752111
Tel *(06578) 235 831*
An Odisha Tourism restaurant with flavours from across the world; good seafood and Odishan dishes.

The vibrant and colourful Nakli Dhaba in Bhubaneswar

PURI: Peace ₹₹
Multi-cuisine
CT Rd, 752002
A relaxed garden setting plus good portions of travellers' staples including muesli and fruit.

PURI: Wildgrass ₹₹
Oriya
VIP Rd, Beach Area, 752001
Tel *(0) 94370 23656*
Expect fantastically fresh seafood, delicately spiced curries and local Odishan food.

PURI: Xanadu Garden ₹₹
International
CT Rd, 752002
Tel *(06752) 227 897*
Friendly garden place with fish dishes and flavours from around the world. Try the Indonesian *gado-gado*. Great breakfasts too.

Assam and the Northeast

AGARTALA: Rajdarbar ₹₹
Multi-cuisine
Hotel Rajdhani, BK Rd, 799001
Tel *(0381) 222 3387*
Popular place with cane and bamboo furnishings inspired by Tripura craftsmanship.

AIZAWL: David's Kitchen ₹₹
Multi-cuisine
David's Hotel Clover, Chanmari-Chaltlang Rd, 796007
Tel *(0389) 230 5736*   **Closed** *Sun*
A popular social spot with cheerful interiors, free Wi-Fi and an interesting menu.

DIMAPUR: Hotel Tragopan ₹₹
Multi-cuisine
Circular Rd, 797112
Tel *(03862) 230 351*
Sample traditional Naga cooking such as fish and pork steamed in bamboo shoot. The Tragopan Special is a popular fish, or chicken, curry.

GUWAHATI: Paradise ₹
Assamese
GNB Rd, 781003
Tel *(0361) 266 6904*
A local haunt specializing in the lightly-spiced flavours of Assamese cuisine. Order the *thali* to sample a range of dishes.

GUWAHATI: Mainland China ₹₹₹
Chinese
4th Floor, Dona Planet, GS Rd, 781005
Tel *(0361) 246 6222*
Atmospheric, modern restaurant with generous buffets and spicy Chinese food.

IMPHAL: Classic Hotel ₹₹
Multi-cuisine
North AOC, Near Guwahati High Court, 795001
Tel *(0385) 244 3967*
Choose between Classic Café and Rita's Café – both stylish, with good snacks plus mains.

ITANAGAR: Bhismak Restaurant ₹₹
Multi-cuisine
Hotel Donyi Polo Ashok, C-Sector, 791111
Tel *(0360) 221 2611*
Sumptuous dishes and a panoramic view. Local cuisine prepared on special request.

KOHIMA: Shilloi ₹₹
Multi-cuisine
Hotel Japhu, PR Hills, 797001
Tel *(0370) 224 0211*
Hilltop setting and charming dining area add to the perfectly-cooked dishes at Shilloi.

SHILLONG: Café Shillong - Heritage ₹₹₹
International
Royal Heritage - Tripura Castle Hotel, Tripura Castle Rd, 793003
Tel *(0364) 250 1111*
Funky café-restaurant in a 1920s heritage hotel. Continental favourites by the fireplace or on the terrace with amazing views.

TEZPUR: Gabharu ₹₹
Multi-cuisine
Hotel Luit, Ranu Singh Rd, 784001
Tel *(03712) 224 708*
The varied menu, friendly staff and pleasing surroundings make this Tezpur's most reliable option.

Rajasthan

BIKANER: Harasar Haveli ₹₹
North Indian
Hotel Harasar Haveli, opp Karni Singh Stadium, 334001
Tel *(0151) 220 9891*
Great rooftop restaurant with live music, dance and delicious Rajasthani dishes.

BIKANER: Hotel Bhanwar Niwas ₹₹₹
North Indian
Rampuria St, Old City, 334001
Tel *(0151) 252 9323*
Step back in time at this elegant dining room that does a fantastic North Indian buffet.

JAIPUR: Peacock ₹
Multi-cuisine
Hotel Pearl Palace, Hari Kishan Somani Marg, Hathroi Fort, 302001
Tel *(0141) 237 3700*

Super popular with excellent croissants in the morning and great views at night.

JAIPUR: Anokhi ®®
Fusion
KK Square Shopping Complex, Prithviraj Rd, 302001
Tel *(0141) 400 7244*
A little café serving great salads, veggie dishes and coffee, next to the Anokhi store.

JAIPUR: Diggi Palace ®®
North Indian
SMS Hospital Rd, 302004
Tel *(0141) 237 3091*
Great North Indian food in a dining area that spills out into the garden. Have their own cookbook and cookery workshops.

JAIPUR: LMB ®®
North Indian vegetarian
Johari Bazar, 302003
Tel *(0141) 256 5844*
Jaipur institution famous for its sweets and egg-free bakery. Serves a range of vegetarian meals.

JAISALMER: Shahi Palace ®
Multi-cuisine
Shiv St, near SBBJ bank, 345001
Tel *(02992) 255 920*
Rooftop restaurant with great views of the fort. Fantastic Rajasthani dishes such as *kadhai pakoda*.

JAISALMER: Jaisal Italy ®®
Fusion
Inside Fort Gate, 345001
Tel *(02992) 253 504*
Ethnic decor and superb fort views. As the name suggests they have good Italian food and coffee.

JODHPUR: Café Sheesh Mahal ®®
Multi-cuisine
Nr Pal Haveli, Clocktower, 342001
Enjoy sandwiches, snacks, brownies and cappuccino, and watch the world go by.

DK Choice

JODHPUR: Indique ®®
North Indian
Pal Haveli, Clocktower, 342001
Tel *(0291) 329 3328*
With recipes passed down for generations, Indique does good *thalis* plus an à la carte menu. It is an atmospheric place with views of the busy market and of Mehrangarh fort. Live music and Rajasthani dance every night.

JODHPUR: Kalinga ®®
North Indian
Opposite station, 342001

Picturesque outdoor seating at the Chokelao Restaurant, Jodhpur

The tasty *lal maas* (red lamb) and aubergine and okra dishes have to be tried. Good breakfasts.

JODHPUR: Chokelao Restaurant ®®®
North Indian
Mehrangarh Fort, 342006
Tel *(0291) 255 5389*
Towering above Jodhpur with good, but pricey North Indian *thalis*. Book in advance.

PUSHKAR: Sunset Café ®
Multi-cuisine
Close to Pushkar Palace, 305022
Tel *(0145) 277 2725*
Especially atmospheric at sunset, this café serves up traveller fare from muesli to veggie burgers.

PUSHKAR: Sixth Sense ®®
Multi-cuisine
Inn Seventh Heaven, Mali Ka Mandir, 305022
Tel *(0145) 510 5455*
Salads, jacket potatoes, pastas and great desserts – all at this beautiful rooftop restaurant.

UDAIPUR: Food Club ®®
Multi-cuisine
Bada Ramayan Chowk, 313001
Tel *(0) 93523 20103*
Atmospheric place with lake-side seating in a courtyard. Good North Indian food.

UDAIPUR: Savage Garden ®®
Mediterranean
22 Chandpole, Gangaur Ghat, 313001
Tel *(0294) 242 5440*
A small doorway leads to a royal blue courtyard where fish, *mezze* and pastas can be had.

UDAIPUR: Upre by 1559AD ®®
Multi-cuisine
Lake Pichola Hotel, Hanuman Ghat, 313001
Tel *(0294) 243 1197* **Closed** *lunch daily*
Elegant rooftop eatery with lake views and excellent Rajasthani delicacies.

UDAIPUR: Ambrai ®®®
North Indian
Amet Haveli, Nr Leela Palace, 313001
Tel *(0294) 243 1085*
Popular lakeside restaurant. Tasty North Indian food. Book ahead for lakeside tables.

Gujarat

AHMEDABAD: Sankalp ®
South Indian
Samir Building, CG Rd, 380009
A popular South Indian chain with several outlets. Tasty food and amazing chutneys.

AHMEDABAD: Swati Snacks ®
Gujarati
Thakorbhai Hall, Law Garden, 380006
Tel *(079) 2640 5900*
Rice pancakes cooked in banana leaf, *patra* and *musala khichdi* in a swish diner.

AHMEDABAD: Green House ®®
Gujarati
House of MG, opp Sidi Sayid Mosque, Lal Darwaza, 380001
Tel *(079) 2550 6946*
Gujarati snacks and light dishes in this atmospheric courtyard. Amazing saffron anise *kulfi*.

AHMEDABAD: Ikobo ®®
North Indian
Drive In Rd, 380054
Tel *(079) 3006 0770*
Sizzlers are the speciality here, but also does a good range of kebab and *shashlik*.

AHMEDABAD: Mangaldas Ni Haveli ®®
Café
Lakha Patel ni Pol, 380001
Tel *(079) 2550 6946* **Closed** *Sun*
Beautiful café housed in a stunningly restored *haveli*; does great breakfasts. This is also the starting point for guided walks.

For more information on types of restaurants *see page 705*

DK Choice

AHMEDABAD: Vishalla ℝℝ
Gujarati
Opp Vasna Tol Naka, 5 km (3 miles) outside the city, 380007
Tel *(079) 2660 2422*
Sample Gujarati delicacies off a banana leaf and drink from clay cups at this village-themed restaurant. Traditional *garba* dancing and folk songs add to the atmosphere and there is a village museum on-site as well.

DIU: Apana ℝℝ
Seafood
Old Fort Rd, 362520
Tel *(02875) 253 650*
Huge platters of seafood, including lobster, plus dishes from North and South India.

DIU: O'Coqueiro ℝℝ
Seafood
Firangiwada Rd, 362520
Tel *(0) 98246 81565*
Garden restaurant with top notch Portuguese-style fish dishes and curries; superb grilled fish with coriander potatoes.

VADODARA: Mandap ℝℝ
Gujarati
RC Dutt Rd, 390007
Tel *(0265) 305 5000*
With 15 dishes in the Gujarati *thali*, this is a great place to taste local food. Cake shop too.

Mumbai

Bademiya ℝ
Street food
Tulloch Rd, Colaba, 400001
Tel *(022) 2202 1447*
Mumbai's ultimate late-night kebab stall, with fresh and safe meat and vegetarian kebabs.

Kailash Parbat ℝ
Street food and North Indian
1st Pasta Lane, Colaba, 400005
Tel *(022) 2284 1972*
Popular diner with two branches: one does North Indian, the other street food – *pav bhaji, pani puri* – and great sweets. No seating space.

Legacy Of Mumbai ℝ
Vegetarian
SV Rd, Chincholi Naka, Malad West, 400050
Tel *(022) 4222 1000*
Renowned for its vegetarian cuisine, this eatery is a favourite with students. The steaming hot *idli sambar* is a must-have. Suitable for take-away orders.

Convival atmosphere at the popular Leopold Café, Mumbai

Kamat Samarambh ℝ
South Indian vegetarian
Opp Electric House, Colaba Causeway, 400005
Tel *(022) 2287 4734*
Buzzing café serving South Indian classics – *idli, uttapam* and *thalis* – to a mixed crowd.

DK Choice

Britannia & Company ℝℝ
Persian
Sprott Rd, Ballard Estate, Fort, 400001
Tel *(022) 2261 5264* **Closed** *Sun*
An authentic and eccentric Parsi restaurant, whose one-of-a-kind *berry pulao* is a Mumbai must-try. Owner Boman Kohinoor still works the floor at 91 years of age; he'll drop by to show you his letters from Buckingham Palace. End with the delicious caramel custard.

Café Churchill ℝℝ
Continental
Opposite Cusrow Baug, Colaba Causeway, 400005
Tel *(022) 2284 4689*
Tiny café crammed with patrons. Club sandwiches, fish and chips, lasagne, Irish stew and cakes.

Café Mondegar ℝℝ
Continental
Shahid Bhagat Singh Rd, 400039
Tel *(022) 2202 0591*
Round-the-clock service, friendly ambience topped with a juke box. Busy on weekends.

Candies ℝℝ
Continental
Pali Hill, St. Andrews Rd, Bandra West, 400050
Tel *(022) 2642 4124*
A sprawling multi-storied eatery with enchanting interiors. Good multi-grain tuna sandwiches, mutton mince rolls and desserts.

Gajalee ℝℝ
Seafood
Hanuman Rd, Vile Parle E, 400057
Tel *(022) 2616 6470*
This is the place to try *bombil* (Bombay Duck) and chilli-laden clam and crab *masalas*.

Koyla ℝℝ
North Indian
Hotel Gulf, Arthur Bunder Rd, Colaba, 400005
Tel *(022) 6636 9999*
Open air lounge-restaurant serving *tandoori* platters. Hookahs and great views.

Leopold Café ℝℝ
International
Colaba Causeway, 400076
Tel *(022) 2282 8185*
Colaba icon with clinking beer glasses and raucous chatter over plates of steak and fried chicken.

Out of the Blue ℝℝ
Continental
14 Union Park, Off Carter Rd, Khar West, 400052
Tel *(022) 2600 3000*
Secluded candlelit restaurant, serving risottos and sizzler plates. Live music most nights.

Soul Fry Casa ℝℝ
Goan
Silver Croft, Pali Mala Rd, Bandra West
Tel *(022) 2604 6892*
This Goan restaurant creates a toes-in-the-sand vibe. Excellent seafood and vindaloo dishes, plus dancing to live music.

Theobroma ℝℝ
Patisserie
Cusrow Baug, Colaba Causeway, 400039
Tel *(022) 2288 0101*
Sophisticated bakery-café with superb coffee, baguettes and a range of chocolate cakes.

Key to Price Guide *see page 706*

The Yoga House ⑨⑨
Vegetarian fast food
Sherly Rajan Rd, Bandra West
Tel *(022) 6554 5001*
Fresh vegetarian delights; "The
Yogi's Breakfast" is a must-try.
Yoga classes in the morning.

Dome ⑨⑨⑨
Lounge
Intercontinental Hotel,
Marine Drive, 400020
Tel *(022) 3987 9999*
Tapas-size tasting plates are
incidental to the cocktail menu.
Stunning view up Marine Drive.

Indigo ⑨⑨⑨
Continental
4, Mandlik Rd, Colaba, 400001
Tel *(022) 6636 8980*
Meet the Bollywood A-list at this
bungalow-restaurant. Exquisite
east-meets-west food. Terrace for
alfresco dining.

Le Pain Quotidien ⑨⑨⑨
Continental
Dhanraj Mahal, CSM Rd,
Colaba, 400039
Tel *(022) 6615 0202*
Lovely ambience, lively staff and
freshly-baked desserts; try the
delectable pastries.

Ling's Pavilion ⑨⑨⑨
Chinese
19/21, Mahakavi Bhushan Marg,
Colaba, 400039
Tel *(022) 2285 0023*
Go for the sugarcane prawns and
mushroom-stuffed chicken, or
ask for the picks of the day.

Olive Bar and Kitchen ⑨⑨⑨
Mediterranean
14 Union Park, Pali Hill, 400052
Tel *(022) 2605 8228*

Diners at the stylish yet informal
Latitude in Aurangabad

Favourite hangout of Mumbai's
elite, serving everything from
French to Turkish. Excellent
Sunday brunch.

Maharashtra

AURANGABAD: Naivedya ⑨
Vegetarian
Jalna Rd, CIDCO, 431003
Tel *(0240) 248 4191*
Clean, vegetarian *thali* place with
a choice of spicy Rajasthani and
sumptuous Gujarati specialities.

AURANGABAD: Latitude ⑨⑨⑨
International
Vivanta by Taj, 8–N - 12, CIDCO,
Rauza Bagh, 431003
Tel *(0240) 661 3737*
Known for its fastidiously-
prepared regional Indian
specialities and attentive
service. Relaxing garden views.

CHIPLUN: Riverview
Restaurant ⑨⑨
Seafood
Dhamandivi Taluka Khed, 415707
Tel *(02355) 259 081*
Set in a tranquil resort with valley
views. An eclectic menu, but the
Konkani seafood specials are a
good choice.

KOLHAPUR: Padma Guest
House ⑨
Regional
1550 C Ward, Laxmipuri,
416002
Tel *(0231) 264 1387*
This humble eatery serves
authentic Kolhapuri cuisine –
spicy, delicious, and heavy
on the mutton. Excellent *thalis.*

MAHABALESHWAR:
Grapevine ⑨⑨⑨
International
Masjid Rd, 412806
Tel *(02168) 260 101*
The meat-heavy menu here ranges
from European to Indian. Great
Parsi veg *dhansak* and *salli boti*
(meat curry with potato sticks).

NAGPUR: Nanking ⑨⑨
Chinese
Residency Rd, Sadar, 440001
Tel *(0712) 253 1850*
Nagpur's best Chinese place with a
menu that includes Hakka noodles
and garlic-and-chilli paneer.

NAGPUR: Ashoka ⑨⑨⑨
International
Mount Rd, Sadar, 440001
Tel *(0712) 253 1141*
A fixture on the fine-dining scene
since 1956. Superb sizzlers and
some Indian dishes.

NASHIK: Soma ⑨⑨⑨
Indian
Sula Vineyards, Govardhan, 422222
Tel *(0253) 302 7777*
Classic Indian dishes, matched
with quality wines from the
surrounding vines.

DK Choice

PUNE: Hotel Shreyas ⑨
Vegetarian
1242 B, Apte Rd, Deccan
Gymkhana, 411004
Tel *(020) 2553 1228*
Shreya's lays out Pune's best
Maharashtrian *thali.* Waiters
patrol the dining hall ladling
out endless helpings of veg
curry, rice, roti and sweets.

PUNE: Malaka Spice ⑨⑨
Asian
Lane 5, North Main Rd, Koregaon
Park, 411001
Tel *(020) 3057 0433*
A smart eatery with varied Asian
fare: Thai curries, tempura
vegetables and dim sums.

PUNE: Touché the Sizzler ⑨⑨
Multi-cuisine
7, Clover Centre, Moledina Rd, Camp
Area, 411001
Tel *(020) 2613 4632*
Sizzling hot plates, piled with
steak, seafood or vegetables.

Goa

ANJUNA: Anand ⑨⑨
Goan
Siolim Rd, 403509
Wait in line here for amazingly
fresh seafood: crab *masala*,
mussel fry and fish curry rice.

ASSAGAO: Villa Blanche ⑨⑨⑨
Fusion
Badem Church Rd, 403507
Tel *(0) 98221 55099*
Courtyard-restaurant serving
salads and German meatballs.
Don't miss the Sunday brunch.

ASHWEM: La Plage ⑨⑨⑨
French
Ashwem Beach, 403527
Tel *(0) 98221 21712*
French-run place with tuna with
wasabi mash, pumpkin ravioli
and the delicious chocolate *thali.*

BAGA: Britto's ⑨⑨
Multi-cuisine
Baga Beach, 403516
Tel *(0832) 227 7331*
Exceptional crab *masala,*
fish caldin and delicious
calamari *vindaloo.*

For more information on types of restaurants *see page 705*

BAGA: Fiesta ⊕⊕⊕
Fusion
Tito's Lane, 403516
Tel *(0832) 227 9894*
Beautiful decor, lovely garden
and delicious food. Great steaks,
pastas and plenty of seafood.

CALANGUTE: Souza Lobo ⊕⊕
Goan
Calangute Beach, 403516
Tel *(0832) 228 1234*
An institution, with favourites
such as crab *xacuti*, prawn curry
rice, pork *sorpotel* and *vindaloo*.

CANDOLIM: Stone House ⊕⊕
Multi-cuisine
Fort Aguada Rd, 403515
Tel *(0832) 247 9909*
Popular, with nightly live music,
fresh fish dishes, and North
Indian and Continental food.

CANDOLIM: Bomra's ⊕⊕⊕
Burmese
247 Fort Aguada Rd, 403515
Tel *(0) 97675 91056*
Stylish yet relaxed, with amazing
food including spicy rare beef
salad, snapper with lemongrass
and the Burmese *khao suey*.

MAJORDA: Martin's Corner ⊕⊕
Multi-cuisine
Binwaddo, Betalbatim, 403713
Tel *(0832) 288 0413*
Has a varied menu, but go
for the Goan dishes such as pork
vindaloo and chicken *cafreal*.

MANDREM: Café Nu ⊕⊕
Fusion
Junas Waddo, 403527
Tel *(0) 98506 58568*
In a garden setting with fusion
food – fish in banana leaves, fig
salad and lemongrass martinis.

DK Choice

MORJIM: Sublime ⊕⊕⊕
Fusion
Morjim Beach, 403512
Tel *(0) 98224 84051*
Celebrity chef Chris Saleem
Agha Bee is at the helm of this
restaurant serving up flavours
from around the world. Choose
from Asiatic beef medallions
with wasabi mash, mustard-
encrusted fish or the mega-
organic salad.

MORJIM: Sur La Mer ⊕⊕⊕
Multi-cuisine
Morjim Beach, 403512
Tel *(0) 98500 56742*
Eat by the pool or in a pretty
dining area. Delightful dishes
include three-cheese *filo* parcels
and lobster thermidor.

Key to Price Guide *see page 706*

PALOLEM: Ourem 88 ⊕⊕
Fusion
Ourem, 403702
Tel *(086) 9882 7679*
Stylish café with beer-battered
fish, seafood pastas and steaks
with rocket mash on the menu.

PANJIM: Hotel Venite ⊕⊕
Seafood
31 January Rd, Althino, 403001
Tel *(0832) 242 5537* **Closed** *Sun*
Old-world eatery with bags of
Portuguese charm and a range
of fish dishes. Sit by the window.

PANJIM: Viva Panjim ⊕⊕
Goan
31 January Rd, Fontainhas, 403001
Tel *(0832) 242 2405* **Closed** *Sun
lunch*
Goan Portuguese food and tasty
seafood – great prawn chilli fry,
Goan sausage *palao* and home-
made desserts.

QUEPEM: Palacio del Deao ⊕⊕
Goan
Nr Holy Cross Church, 403705
Tel *(0832) 266 4029*
Quintessential Goan experience
at this lovely 200-year-old
mansion. Expect many courses.
Booking essential.

SINQUERIM: Banyan Tree ⊕⊕⊕
Thai
*Taj Holiday Village, Fort
Aguada Rd, 403519*
Tel *(0832) 664 5858*
Set in the gardens of the
lovely Taj property, this is
a renowned Thai restaurant
serving all the usual curry
favourites and fresh seafood.

UTORDA: Zeebop ⊕⊕
Seafood
Nr Kenilworth Resort, 403713
Tel *(0832) 275 5333*
Right on the beach; has superb
fresh seafood. Great fish curry
rice and crab *papads*.

Karnataka

**BENGALURU: Mavalli Tiffin
Rooms** ⊕
South Indian vegetarian
14, Lalbagh Rd, Mavalli, 560027
Tel *(080) 2222 0022* **Closed** *Mon*
This 1924 institution is the place
to taste traditional food such as
bisi bele bath and *rawa idli*.

BENGALURU: Blue Ginger ⊕⊕⊕
Vietnamese
*Taj West End, Race
Course Rd, 560001*
Tel *(080) 6660 5660*
The city's most romantic diner
with authentic Vietnamese
soups, salads and stir fries in a
garden overflowing with ferns.

BENGALURU: Ebony ⊕⊕⊕
International
Barton Center, MG Rd, 560001
Tel *(080) 4178 3344*
Stunning views and excellent
North Indian, Thai and French
fare. Buffet on weekdays.

BIJAPUR: Kamat ⊕
Vegetarian
Hotel Kanishka, Station Rd, 586104
Tel *(0835) 224 3131*
Cheerful vegetarian eatery next
to the Gol Gumbaz, serving good
snacks and *thalis*.

CHIKMAGALUR: Peaberry ⊕⊕⊕
International
Gateway Hotel, KM Rd, 577101
Tel *(08262) 660 660*
Wide selection of regional, Italian
and seafood dishes.

MANGALORE: Gajalee ⊕⊕
Seafood
*Circuit House Compound,
Kadri Hills, 575004*
Tel *(0824) 222 1900*
Offshoot of the famous Mumbai
eatery, dishing up great prawn
biryani and fish *masala* fry.

Romantic dining area at Blue Ginger in Bengaluru

MYSORE: Hotel Mylari ⓥ
South Indian
769 Nazarbad Main Rd, 570010
Tel *(0) 99800 13292*
A Mysore institution – both
adjacent Mylaris serve divinely
crispy, paper-thin *dosas*.

DK Choice

MYSORE: Green Hotel ⓥⓥ
North Indian
2270 Vinoba Rd, 570012
Tel *(0821) 425 5000*
This garden restaurant is a
great place to relax. Order from
the North Indian menu, then
explore the halls or play croquet
on the trimmed lawns. Acres of
space for kids to play. Also in the
grounds, Malgudi Café serves
great cakes.

MYSORE: Parklane Hotel ⓥⓥ
International
2720 Sri Harsha Rd, 570001
Tel *(0821) 400 3500*
Courtyard hangout with fairy
lights and live Indian classical
music. Tasty *biryanis* and *curries*,
weekend BBQs and beer.

UDUPI: Mitra Samaj ⓥ
South Indian
Car St, 576101
Tel *(0820) 252 0502*
Full of pilgrims, this small place
churns out endless plates of *idli*,
vada and a variety of *dosas*.

Chennai

Mathsya ⓥ
South Indian vegetarian
1, Halls Rd, Egmore, 600008
Tel *(044) 2819 1900*
Traditional staples served in a
cosy dining room. The house
thali comes with ace tamarind
and coconut *dosas*.

Nair Mess ⓥ
South Indian
*22 Mohammed Abdullah 2nd St,
Chepauk, Triplicane, 600005*
Tel *(044) 2842 0850*
Busy Kerala joint, serving
limitless portions of rice, fish
and prawn curry, and flaky
parotta bread.

Saravana Bhavan ⓥ
South Indian vegetarian
N Mada St, Mylapore, 600004
Tel *(044) 2461 1177*
This locally owned chain has
branches all over Chennai,
all offering clean, reliably tasty
and cheap South Indian food.
Superb ice creams.

Annalakshmi ⓥⓥ
Vegetarian
*18/3, Rukmani Lakshmipathy Rd,
Egmore, 600008*
Tel *(044) 2852 5109*   **Closed** *Mon*
Named after the goddess of food,
this charity-run place does one of
the best *thalis* and Indian buffets
in town. Book ahead.

Minar – Savera Hotel ⓥⓥ
Mughlai
Savera Hotel, 146 RK Salai, 600004
Tel *(044) 2811 3475*
Try the rich cuisine of Lucknow at
this top-floor restaurant, decked
out palace-style.

Tuscana Pizzeria ⓥⓥ
Italian
*19 3rd St, Wallace Garden
Rd, Nungambakkam, 600006*
Tel *(044) 4503 8008*
Excellent for thin crust
wood-fired pizzas, *carpaccios*,
cannelonis, plus good desserts.

Benjarong ⓥⓥⓥ
Thai
146, TTK Rd, Alwarpet, 600018
Tel *(044) 2432 2640*
Waiters float through this dimly
lit room with aromatic bowls of
chilli-roasted crab, tom yum and
pandanus-wrapped chicken.

Dakshin at ITC ⓥⓥⓥ
South Indian
*Sheraton Park Hotel, TTK Rd,
Alwarpet, 600018*
Tel *(044) 2499 4101*
Refined versions of home-style
Keralan, Tamil and Andhra
cooking. Live sitar and tabla.

DK Choice

Royal Vega ⓥⓥⓥ
Vegetarian
*ITC Grand Chola Hotel, 63 Mount
Rd, Guindy, 600032*
Tel *(044) 2220 0000*
After a ceremonial *aarthi* greeting,
guests choose one of five
distinct palace-themed rooms
to dine in. Feast on exquisite
vegetarian dishes drawn from
royal kitchens across India.
To experience it all order the
magnificent *thali*, served on
a silver platter.

Tamil Nadu

**KANYAKUMARI: Ocean
Restaurant** ⓥⓥ
International
*Seashore Hotel,
East Car St, 629702*
Tel *(04652) 246 704*

Grand interiors of the Royal Vega restaurant
in Chennai

North Indian, Chinese and seafood
served against the awe-inspiring
backdrop of the ocean.

DK Choice

**KARAIKUDI:
The Bangala** ⓥⓥⓥ
South Indian
Devakottai Rd, Senjai, 630001
Tel *(04565) 220 221*
The banquet hall of this heritage
hotel is one of the best places
to taste Chettinad cuisine. Lunch
is served *thali*-style on banana
leaves. Expect signature Chettinad
specials such as chicken pepper
fry, crunchy banana *vadas* and
coconut pudding on the daily
changing menu.

MADURAI: Surya ⓥⓥ
South Indian
110 W Perumal Maistry St, 625001
Tel *(04522) 343 151*
Rooftop views of the Meenakshi
Temple, excellent Andhra
cooking and cold beer.

**MAMALLAPURAM: Golden
Palate** ⓥⓥ
Vegetarian
*Mamallaa Heritage Hotel, 104 East
Raja St, 603104*
Tel *(0) 93801 26188*
This clean and bright hotel
restaurant serves fresh North
Indian comfort food, including
rich paneer and lentil dishes.

OOTY: Chandan Vegetarian ⓥ
North Indian vegetarian
*Nahar Nilgiris Hotel, 52-A
Charing Cross, 643001*
Tel *(0423) 244 5797*
Roomy restaurant serving North
Indian and Chinese food. In the
same hotel, the lawnside Garden
Café does excellent *dosas*.

For more information on types of restaurants *see page 705*

Traditional Alleppey Fish Curry at the Harbour Restaurant, Alappuzha

PUDUCHERRY: Rendezvous ⓦⓦ
French
30 Rue Suffren, 605001
Tel *(0413) 222 7677* **Closed** *Tue*
Classic French food served on a breezy terrace. The seafood is particularly good.

PUDUCHERRY: Palais de Mahe ⓦⓦⓦ
Indian
4 Rue de Bussy, 605001
Tel *(0413) 234 5611*
Rooftop restaurant in the heart of the French quarter, famous for its modern-Indian cooking.

THANJAVUR: Sathars ⓦ
North Indian
167 Gandhiji Rd, 613001
Tel *(04362) 231 041*
Humble eatery serving the best *tandoori* and *biryani* in town.

Andaman Islands

DK Choice
HAVELOCK ISLAND: Full Moon Café ⓦⓦ
Multi-cuisine
Beach No 3, 744211
Tel *(03192) 282 222*
Undoubtedly, the best food on the islands, with a beachside setting with funky lanterns beneath palm trees. A range of Indian food, with a special focus on Maharashtrian cuisine, and sublime seafood on offer. Global fare from the Levant to China, plus desserts and coffee that are the real deal.

HAVELOCK ISLAND: Barefoot ⓦⓦⓦ
Multi-ciusine
Beach No. 7, Radhanagar, 744101
Tel *(0) 98402 38042*

Drinks and dinner by candle-light. Reliable and varied food in a romantic jungle setting.

HAVELOCK ISLAND: Red Snapper ⓦⓦⓦ
Multi-cuisine
The Wild Orchid, Vijaynagar, 744211
Tel *(03192) 28 2472*
Slick joint with seafood, Asian, Continental and vegetarian dishes, plus a good bar.

PORT BLAIR: Annapurna ⓦ
South Indian
Aberdeen Bazar, 744101
Family eatery serving vegetarian set meals and light dishes in cool dim interiors.

PORT BLAIR: Salt n Pepper ⓦⓦ
Multi-cuisine
Sea Shell Hotel, 744101
Tel *(03192) 242 773*
The rooftop lounge-bar has magical views, and the restaurant has the tastiest multi-cuisine food in town.

Kerala

ALAPPUZHA: Harbour Restaurant ⓦⓦ
Seafood
Beach Rd, 688012
Tel *(0477) 223 0767*
Sociable beachfront place serving good fish dishes at a leisurely pace – perfect for enjoying beer and sunset views.

ALAPPUZHA: Chakara ⓦⓦⓦ
Seafood
Raheem Residency, Beach Rd, 688012
Tel *(0477) 223 0767*
Smart rooftop restaurant serving freshly caught fish in South Indian and Continental styles. Try the Alleppey fish curry.

KANNUR: MVK ⓦ
South Indian
SM Rd, 670001
Tel *(0497) 276 7192*
A Kannur institution offering great chilli chicken and some of the best *biryanis* in north Kerala.

KOCHI: Caza Maria ⓦⓦ
South Indian
6/125 Jew Town Rd, Mattancherry, 682002
Tel *(0) 98460 50901*
Authentic Kerala fish curries served in an antique-filled Colonial building in the Jewish Quarter's spice market.

KOCHI: Dal Roti ⓦⓦ
North Indian
1/293 Lilly St, Fort Kochi, 682001
Tel *(0484) 221 7655*
Queues stretch down the block for the *kathi* rolls and Mughlai stuffed *parathas* dished up by amiable Ramesh and his family.

KOCHI: Kashi ⓦⓦ
Café
Burgher St, Fort Kochi, 682001
Tel *(0484) 221 5769* **Closed** *Jun*
Serene art gallery-café, spread over plant-shaded courtyards. Good coffee and cakes.

DK Choice
KOCHI: Fort House ⓦⓦⓦ
Seafood
2/6A Calvathy Rd, 682001
Tel *(0484) 221 7103*
Hidden away in a modest hotel, Fort House has Kochi's most unforgettable location – tables line up along a jetty with fishing boats, herons and the occasional dolphin drifting by. Refined dishes include stir-fried calamari and fish cooked in clay pots.

KOZHIKODE: Sagar Hotel ⓦ
South Indian
Mavoor Rd, 673572
Tel *(0495) 272 0152*
This packed, multi-storey café is famous for its *biryanis*. Good *dal* (lentils) and flaky Kerala *parotta*.

KOVALAM: Rockholm ⓦⓦ
International
Light House Rd, Vizhinjam, 695523
Tel *(0471) 248 0306*
This terrace restaurant offers stunning sea views and Indian, Chinese and Continental dishes.

KUMARAKOM: Baker's House Taj ⓦⓦⓦ
International
Vivanta by Taj, 686566
Tel *(0481) 252 5711*

At dusk, brass lamps twinkle around this 120-year-old bungalow serving pan-global high-end cuisine.

MUNNAR: Saravana Bhavan ⊛
South Indian vegetarian
MG Rd, 685612
Tel *(0486) 230 418*
Clean and friendly place serving *dosas* and huge Kerala-style *thalis* on banana leaves.

THEKKADY: Our Place ⊛
British
Rosappukandam Kumily, 685509
Tel *(0) 93888 63003*
Run by a British-Indian couple, this cosy café serves comfort English food, along with Indian vegetarian options.

THEKKADY: Falling Leaves ⊛⊛⊛
International
Shalimar Spice Garden Resort, Murikkady, 685535
Tel *(04869) 222 132*
Atmospheric dining room in a jungle-shaded resort. Indian and Italian options, and Kerala *thalis* served on banana leaves.

THRISSUR: Hotel Bharat ⊛
South Indian vegetarian
Chembottil Lane, Round South, 680001
Tel *(0487) 242 1720*
Good honest Kerala and South Indian food – *dosas*, *puttu* and *thalis* – served to huge crowds.

TRIVANDRUM: Villa Maya ⊛⊛⊛
International
Airport Rd, Subash Nagar, Enchakkal Westfort Rd, 695024
Tel *(0471) 257 8901*
In an 18th-century villa, with pavilions and fountains. Dishes range from Kerala curries to Israeli and Moroccan specials.

VARKALA: Juice Shack ⊛
Fast food
Behind Tibetan Market, North Cliff, 695141
Tel *(0) 99952 14515*
A backpacker-favourite, this breezy spot offers Western comfort food, juices and salads.

VARKALA: Oottupura ⊛
South Indian
Jicky's Hotel, Near helipad, 695141
Tel *(0) 93881 709571*
This tumbledown shack serves tasty vegetarian curries with fresh *rotis* to mop up.

VARKALA: GAD at Taj Gateway ⊛⊛⊛
International
Janardhanapuram, 695141
Tel *(04706) 673 300*

Superb South Indian food and a great breakfast buffet with relaxing, outdoor areas.

Andhra Pradesh

HYDERABAD: Hotel Shadab ⊛
Hyderabadi
21 High Court Rd, Ghansi Bazaar, 500066
Tel *(040) 3051 2844*
Scruffy old place in old Hyderabad, dishing up arguably the best *biryanis* and kebabs in the city.

HYDERABAD: Paradise Food Court ⊛
Hyderabadi
SD Rd, Paradise Circle, Secunderabad, 500003
Tel *(040) 6666 1199*
Legendary for its *biryani*, it continues to serve fragrant mounds of the iconic Hyderabad dish.

DK Choice

HYDERABAD: Taste of Darkness ⊛⊛
Multi-cuisine
Inorbit Mall, Hitech City, 500058
Tel *(040) 6460 3341* **Closed** *Mon*
A unique concept that is part restaurant, part social commentary. Blind waiters lead you through the pitch black dining room, and you "see" your meal – a simple curry-rice-roti set menu of one to four courses – through the eyes of a blind person. A fascinating insight that only heightens the senses of smell and taste.

HYDERABAD: Firdaus ⊛⊛⊛
Mughlai
Taj Krishna Hotel, Banjara Hills, 500034
Tel *(040) 6666 2323*

First-rate Mughlai cuisine, with the special Hyderabadi *haleem* (meat stew) available year-round.

HYDERABAD: The Water Front ⊛⊛
International
Eat St, Necklace Rd, 500004
Tel *(040) 2330 8899*
Coastal Indian and Chinese fare, but the views over Hussain Sagar are the main attraction.

TIRUPATI: Hyderabad House ⊛
South Indian
Yalamuri Complex, Tuda Rd, 517501
Tel *(0877) 222 3324*
Bustling restaurant offering flavoursome *biryanis* – both vegetarian and meat variants.

VIJAYAWADA: Aromas ⊛⊛
North Indian
LV Manor Hotel, MG Rd, 520010
Tel *(0866) 663 4455*
Slick hotel restaurant with a range of Indian food. The North Indian curries are the highlights.

VISAKHAPATNAM: Infinity ⊛⊛
Asian
Novotel, Beach Rd, 530003
Tel *(089) 1282 2222*
Rooftop place where glass walls reflect fabulous bay views. Great for sizzlers and cold beer.

VISAKHAPATNAM: Zaffran ⊛⊛
North Indian
Novotel, Beach Rd, 530003
Tel *(089) 1282 2222*
Awadhi and northwest frontier cuisine accompanied by ocean views. Private dining rooms too.

WARANGAL: Kadambari ⊛
International
Hotel Ashoka, 6-1-242, Main Rd, Hanamkonda, 506015
Tel *(0870) 257 8491*
Family-friendly hotel-restaurant specializing in Keralite food.

A typical Kerala *thali* served on a banana leaf

SHOPS & MARKETS

India's superb tradition of textiles, arts and crafts makes shopping in this country tremendous fun. The range and quality is diverse – finely crafted bronzes and metalware, lustrous silks, jewellery, miniature paintings and handwoven carpets, as well as delightful, inexpensive tribal artifacts and souvenirs. The kaleidoscope of hues, textures and scents at local bazaars and markets, where flowers, fresh produce and spices are sold, is fascinating, as are the rows of pavement sellers hawking clothes and accessories. Though often a noisy and chaotic experience, browsing through the stalls can often lead to exciting bargains. Traditional bazaars co-exist with the multi-storeyed department stores and shopping malls of urban India, where all manner of goods, both local and imported, are sold under one roof. These are a favourite with local shoppers. For details on shopping in Delhi, see pages 100–101; for Kolkata, see pages 286–7; for Mumbai, see pages 466–7; and for Chennai, see pages 578–9.

Opening Hours

Most shops in the principal shopping areas in urban India are open from about 10am to 7:30pm. Local stores keep longer hours, while markets selling fresh produce are open for business from dawn until late at night. Government emporia have fixed shopping hours, from 10am to 6pm with a lunch break between 1pm and 2pm. Shop timings vary from city to city, as do holidays. Republic Day (26 January), Independence Day (15 August) and Mahatma Gandhi's Birthday (2 October) are national holidays, and by law all shops and markets in the country remain closed.

A shopping mall in Gurgaon

How to Pay

The rupee is accepted everywhere. All the larger stores accept major international credit cards, such as MasterCard and Visa, but it is wise to carry some cash for purchases in bazaars and smaller shops. Some stores accept traveller's cheques as well, though a passport will be required for identification. International currency, too, can be used in certain places. If paying by credit card, ensure that the voucher is filled out in front of you, to avoid fraud. A Value Added Tax (VAT), between 4 to 12.5 per cent, is charged on some items, unless the bill has been paid in foreign currency or with a foreign-based credit card.

Rights and Refunds

When buying expensive items, such as carpets, jewellery or antiques, always insist on a receipt or cash memo. This is important in case damaged goods need to be returned or exchanged, though often in India this is less easy than it sounds. Refunds, too, are difficult. Take particular care when purchases need to be shipped out. Check what costs are involved, including insurance, and ensure that all the paperwork is done correctly. International courier services (see p747) can also be approached to ship out large purchases.

Bargaining

A good way to get the best results when bargaining, is to check out costs and quality at a number of outlets. Usually, the big stores have fixed prices with no scope for bargaining, but haggling in bazaars and smaller shops can be quite rewarding. Try not to quote unrealistically low prices and miss out on a good deal in the process.

Touts

Handle touts firmly and try not to succumb to offers of genuine antiques or fantastic bargains.

Flower-seller displaying garlands on a pavement, Kolkata

They all operate on a commission basis, and taking visitors to shops of their choice is just a means of acquiring extra cash. Tourist coaches often stop at selected stores, but it is not obligatory to purchase anything. Don't be taken in by shops that say "government approved"; these are private enterprises not to be confused with government-run outlets.

Department Stores and Boutiques

Plush, air-conditioned department stores, malls and plazas, and up-market boutiques are now a regular feature in most large towns. They stock a variety of goods, ranging from clothes and leather items to kitchenware. International brands of cosmetics, perfume, fashion accessories, home appliances, glassware and more, are also available here. Boutiques specialize in popular Indian designer labels, including high-fashion Western-style and traditional Indian apparel.

Government Emporia

All state governments have special outlets, with fixed prices, selling textiles and handicrafts from that particular region. These emporia have large premises in all state capitals, and although the range and quality of the items vary, they are good places to shop for gifts and souvenirs. Some of the well-stocked ones that also have branches in most larger cities are Poompuhar (Tamil Nadu), Rajasthali (Rajasthan), Khadi (Delhi) and Gurjari (Gujarat).

Craft Centres and Bazaars

The diversity of traditional Indian crafts is one of the attractions of travelling in this country. Each region, town and village specializes in a particular skill, be it pottery, weaving, metalware or painting. In some smaller villages it is possible to observe artisans at work and

Colourful paper kites on sale in a Rajasthan village

buy directly from them. If a craft centre is not on your itinerary, many cities have arts and craft shops that sell handicrafts made in the region.

Shopping in local bazaars, with their noise and colour, is a unique experience. Located in the heart of old cities, bazaars are typically a maze of tiny shops and pavement stalls, selling a variety of merchandise, from flowers, vegetables and other fresh produce, to cooking utensils, textiles and jewellery.

Specialist Stores

Specialist stores have built their reputation on the quality of merchandise they sell. The passion for antiques has led to a proliferation of shops selling bronzes, stone sculpture and metal artifacts. If buying antiques, check with the Archaeological Survey of India *(see p735)* as objects over 100 years old cannot be taken out of the country. However, excellent reproductions can always be found. Exquisite gold and silver jewellery is readily available, though it is best to visit established jewellers. Jaipur is an excellent place to shop for precious stones, while Hyderabad is known for good-quality pearls.

Rajasthan, particularly Jaipur, Udaipur and Jodhpur, specializes in good quality miniatures, folk paintings and religious *pichhwais* on cloth. Other types of painting, such as Tibetan *thangkas* and the jewel-encrusted Tanjore paintings, are available in Ladakh, Himachal Pradesh and Tamil Nadu.

India's renowned textile tradition ranges from South India's glorious silk saris and Varanasi brocades to fine handwoven cottons, in a wide range of designs and colours. Inexpensive casual wear can be bought at pavement stalls. Boutiques are good places for designer clothes. Carpets and woollen goods, especially the pricey *pashmina* and *jamavar* shawls, should be bought only from reliable shops.

Tea, spices, herbal products and incense are also popular items. Kerala's spices are famous, while tea can be purchased all over the country. Herbal cosmetics and incense are usually sold in general stores, while *attar* (traditional perfume) can be found in most bazaars.

Mumbai's Chor Bazaar, a treasure trove of antiques

What to Buy in India

Shopping in India is a fascinating experience, since the bazaars and boutiques showcase a wide range of the country's decorative arts and crafts. The quality can vary, but the choice is enormous. Superb jewellery, colourful textiles, handicrafts and artifacts, as well as aromatic spices and herbal products, are all available. There are also elegant contemporary interpretations of traditional designs. In many places visitors can watch artisans at work and buy directly from them.

Lacquerware

Bowls and platters in red and black lacquer were originally imported from Burma. Many of these can still be found in Chennai and on Kochi's Jew Street *(see p647).*

Brassware

A wide variety of perfectly proportioned ritual and utilitarian objects, such as boxes and *lotas* (water pots) were once an essential part of every household. They are now freely available in antique shops all over India.

Silverware

The choice of intricately carved and embossed silver artifacts includes salvers, candlesticks, nut bowls and decorative objects. Different parts of India usually specialize in a particular craft. Odisha is well known for its delicate filigree, while in Gujarat and Rajasthan, silversmiths carve elaborate designs on a solid base.

Stoneware

Stoneware is strongly influenced by the pietra dura motifs on the Taj Mahal *(see pp178–9).* Designers have now created a select range of tableware for the modern home that uses white marble as a base with delicate patterns printed in silver and gold foil.

Jewellery

Exquisite gem-encrusted *kundan* and enamelled *meenakari* jewellery from North India *(see p365),* as well as gold ornaments from the south, are available in jewellery shops. Tribal or rural-style silver jewellery is also sold.

Gold necklaces
and bangle

Silver anklets, bracelet and armband

Navratna necklace
and emerald earring

Printed and silk tissue
cushion covers

Light-weight
cotton quilts

Textiles

A dazzling choice of blockprints, silk and cotton woven textiles and gold brocade can be bought by the metre or as ready-made garments, scarves, saris and home accessories. Good-quality paisley *jamavar* and pashmina shawls are also available in select stores.

Paisley
jamavar
shawl

Brocade textile
and scarf

Bamboo and Cane Products

The northeastern states are famous for their fine bamboo and cane work. Besides objects of everyday use, such as large baskets for tea-pluckers, hats and utensils, artisans have now created a variety of trays, baskets, boxes and containers for the contemporary market. Good-quality furniture is also made for local and international buyers.

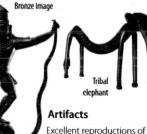

Bronze image

Tribal
elephant

Paintings

Many places, especially Jaipur, Jodhpur and Udaipur in Rajasthan, have shops and ateliers where painters skilfully recreate old miniatures *(see p409)*. Poster colours are now used instead of natural pigments, but the themes are still traditional. These range from court scenes to depictions of religious and mythological stories.

A miniature painting

Artifacts

Excellent reproductions of antique bronzes *(see p598)* are available in many shops. These include images of Hindu deities, such as Krishna and Ganesha, as well as objects made by tribal artisans.

Herbal and Beauty Products

Traditional herbal remedies have been re-invented to suit the modern-day need for eco-friendly soaps and cosmetics, soothing oils and lotions. Aromatherapy is highly popular, and Auroville *(see p593)* has developed a wide range of scented candles and joss sticks.

Aromatherapy
candles from
Auroville

Joss sticks
(agarbatti)

Soaps

Ayurvedic cosmetics

ENTERTAINMENT

Entertainment in India offers fascinating insights into the religious, cultural and social diversity of the country. The vast tradition of performing arts is an ancient one, inextricably linked to religion and mythology. Initially, classical music and dance were performed as part of temple ritual, while the rich repertoire of folk forms emerged as a response to local conditions, the land and community. Today, the choice of entertainment includes classical dance and music, religious dance-dramas, contemporary theatre and colourful temple festivals. There are popular alternatives as well, especially cinemas, where the latest Bollywood blockbusters are shown.

Sources of Information

Local newspapers and magazines are good sources of information, as they carry regular listings and advertisements of events. Often, hotels have in-house publications highlighting the city's sights as well as its entertainment venues and programmes. If not, the travel desk can usually provide the necessary information. In addition, the India Tourism offices and website (see p735) publish an annual calendar of events. Good travel agents can also let visitors know what is happening where, and can help prepare an itinerary of cultural events. For details on entertainment in Delhi, see pages 100–101; for Kolkata, see pages 286–7; for Mumbai, see pages 466–7; and for Chennai, see pages 578–9.

Booking Tickets

For cultural programmes and the cinema, it is best to book tickets in advance at the venue itself. Tele-booking, especially for the more popular shows, is not always reliable. Some stores in the larger cities also have ticket counters; event organizers will indicate where these are in the local newspapers. Hotels or tour operators can often arrange tickets as well.

Classical Music and Dance

Classical music and dance are a dynamic reflection of India's rich cultural heritage (see pp32–3). Regular performances of Odissi, Bharat Natyam, Kuchipudi and Kathakali, the dance-drama from Kerala, are organized by state tourism departments and private cultural organizations at auditoriums and hotels. Dance festivals against the backdrop of historic sites are also popular. Such events are now held at Ajanta and Ellora (see pp480–85), Konark (see pp314–16), Mamallapuram (see pp582–5) as well as Khajuraho (see pp240–42), and offer a unique way to enjoy India's many famed dance forms.

Folk musicians from Rajasthan playing *sarangis* (string instruments)

Concerts of Indian classical music, in the North Indian (Hindustani) and South Indian (Carnatic) styles, draw crowds of music lovers. Concerts by soloists as well as groups are held regularly in the larger cities. There is often a lively interaction between the artists and the audience, who express their appreciation by exclaiming or clapping several times during a concert.

Devotional music, such as Sufi qawwalis and Hindu *bhajans*, also attracts large audiences. Other forms include *ghazals*, lyrical poems in Urdu, and Rabindra Sangeet, songs composed by the great Bengali poet Rabindranath Tagore (see p296).

Folk Theatre, Music and Dance

The traditions of folk and tribal theatre, music and dance are as vibrant as those of the classical forms. At one time, these indigenous forms were restricted to the region of their

A classical dancer performing at the dance festival at Mamallapuram

A movie theatre in Mumbai, with large posters of Bollywood releases

birth. Today, promotion by various cultural organizations has given folk artists greater exposure. As a result urban audiences can watch Chhau, a masked dance performed by men from Odisha, Bihar and West Bengal; balladeers (bhopas) and manganiyars from Rajasthan; the garba from Gujarat; the exuberant Punjabi bhangra; street theatre (jatra) from West Bengal; traditional martial arts from Kerala; and tamasha, a theatre troupe with dancers and musicians from Maharashtra. During the Dussehra festival, Ramlilas – exuberant dramatizations of the epic Ramayana (see p31) – are held all over North India. The most elaborate of these take place by the banks of the Ganges in Varanasi (see p207).

Contemporary Theatre

In the larger cities, good quality performances of Western shows are staged. However there is also a very strong tradition of Indian-language theatre in Marathi, Gujarati, Hindi and Bengali. The range covers adaptations of contemporary works by well-known Indian authors, musicals and political satires. Many of these productions, draw their inspiration from India's rich repertoire of classical and folk forms.

Puppet Shows

Puppetry in India is an ancient tradition, especially in Odisha, Karnataka (see p539), Rajasthan, Tamil Nadu, Andhra Pradesh and West Bengal, where itinerant folk performers use string, rod, glove and shadow puppets to tell mythological tales to a primarily rural audience. Today, many hotels organize cultural programmes for their foreign guests, which often include a traditional puppet show. A contemporary puppet theatre movement dealing with socially relevant themes related to education, health and gender and sexuality, is also becoming popular.

Cinema

The most popular form of entertainment is cinema, especially the extravagant blockbusters from Bollywood (see pp36–7). Some excellent regional-language films, which touch on socially or politically relevant themes, are also made in Kerala, West Bengal, Tamil Nadu and Andhra Pradesh. Select theatres hold special screenings of avante-garde films, or New Wave Cinema, but these lack popular appeal. There are cinema halls in almost every town and large village, whereas the larger cities have multiplexes (with fast food eateries) that offer a mix of

Polo Lounge, a popular bar in the Hyatt Regency Hotel, Delhi

both Bollywood and Hollywood films. Tickets are more expensive here.

Bars and Discos

Nightlife in India is definitely getting livelier. While Mumbai's night spots (see p467), Bengaluru's pub culture and Goa's night-long beach parties and moonlight raves have been much publicized, more conservative towns elsewhere in the country now have at least a few bars, pubs, pool lounges or discotheques.

Indipop

International music channels such as MTV have given a tremendous boost to the Indian pop scene. Known as Indipop, the music of groups such as Indian Ocean and Euphoria, and singers such as Lucky Ali and Alisha Chinai, has made pop stars as popular as film stars. The styles range from fusion music and folk-Inspired bhangra pop to re-mixes of popular Hindi film hits. Some classical singers, such as Shubha Mudgal, have begun to experiment with popular music in order to reach a wider audience, particularly the MTV generation.

Fairs and Festivals

The constant cycle of fairs and festivals is intrinsic to the Indian way of life, (see pp38–41). From Holi, the festival of colour in spring, to Diwali, the festival of lights at the onset of winter, there are a series of colourful celebrations that mark the changing seasons or mytholo-gical events, as well as countless temple festivals. Visitors will usually have ample opportunity to witness these vignettes of the country's cultural and religious heritage, during their travels. Being invited to a home during a festival or a traditional celebration can also be an enjoyable experience.

Each chapter in this book has a column highlighting the main regional festivals.

OUTDOOR ACTIVITIES & SPECIALIST HOLIDAYS

India offers a wide range of sporting and outdoor activities. The larger cities have facilities for golf, tennis, swimming and riding. Winter (Oct–Feb) is the main season for sports, such as polo and cricket. For the more adventurous, there are treks in the Himalayas, tiger tracking in India's many wildlife parks, and a choice of rivers for white-water rafting. Camel or horse safaris offer a memorable way to explore the Rajasthan desert. For the more spiritually inclined, there are yoga and meditation centres, and opportunities to spend time with renowned gurus at their ashrams. An increasing number of visitors are attracted by India's Ayurvedic health spas, and other holistic healing centres, which emphasize nature-based treatments.

Spectator Sports

Indians are cricket-crazy and grab at any chance to watch or play the game. Winter is the main season, when world-class teams tour the country and test matches and one-day internationals are held in cities such as Delhi, Kolkata, Mumbai, Chennai, Bengaluru and Kanpur. The Indian Premier League (IPL), a Twenty20 cricket competition, has made the sport even more popular. Announcements of match schedules and ticket details appear in the national and local newspapers.

Football does not have the high profile that cricket enjoys, but in certain places, such as Kolkata, Goa and Kerala, it is as popular. The game creates great hysteria in Kolkata, and professional clubs such as Mohun Bagan and its rival team East Bengal have mass followings. Check the local press for matches on in the city. Hockey, although a national passion, is not yet big enough to attract international events.

Swimming and Tennis

All five-star hotels have excellent swimming pools with attached fitness centres. Non-residents are allowed to use hotel pools for a fee. In North India, outdoor pools close in winter. Beach resorts have pools as well as access to beaches. Before swimming in the sea, check with the lifeguard that it is safe. Swimming and sunbathing in the nude are strictly prohibited.

Hotels offer grass or hard court tennis facilities and can also arrange games at certain local clubs, especially in the larger cities. India joined the Davis Cup fraternity in 1921, and has hosted the event numerous times. The **RK Khanna Tennis Stadium** also organizes tournaments. Among India's pride are Leander Paes, winner of the 2010 Australian Open mixed doubles, and Mahesh Bhupathi and Sania Mirza, who won the 2009 Australian Open as partners.

Golf

A vast network of clubs with well-maintained courses has made India a popular destination for golfers. The Royal Calcutta Golf Club was set up as early as 1829, and was followed by others in Raj-era hill stations, tea estates and cantonments. Exclusive golf resorts such as the ITC Classic Resort near Manesar, designed by the international golfer Jack Nicklaus, are much frequented, especially by top executives who like to combine a round of golf with negotiating business deals.

The **Indian Golf Union** in Kolkata organizes a choice of activities, ranging from international events to leisurely games. It can also arrange temporary membership at the Royal Calcutta Golf Club and the Delhi Golf Club.

Many towns in India, such as Jaipur, Agra and Ranikhet, have well-maintained, army-run golf courses located in cantonment areas, which are open to foreigners for a fee. It is therefore worthwhile to enquire about facilities when in a new town.

Polo and Riding

Still very much an elitist sport, polo is enjoying a pleasant revival thanks to corporate sponsorships. The **Army Polo and Riding Club** in Delhi is the main centre, and can be

A golfer beneath the ramparts of Jaipur's Moti Doongri Fort

contacted for match schedules and other information. The season is in winter when regular matches are held in Delhi, Kolkata, Jaipur, Jodhpur and Mumbai.

Two of India's leading teams still play under the banners of the erstwhile princely houses of Jodhpur and Kashmir, while the Indian Army continues its long association with polo and fields its own team. Polo is extremely popular in Jaipur, and matches are held at the Rajasthan Polo Club near the Rambagh Palace Hotel. In some hotels in Rajasthan's Shekhawati district, visitors are taught how to play the game. Some variations are elephant and camel polo (both played in Jaipur), while in Ladakh, a rough and ready form of polo is played, with ponies instead of horses.

As for riding, thoroughbred horses can be hired at clubs in Delhi and Kolkata, as well as at the **Royal Equestrian Polo Centre** in Jaipur, after applying for a temporary membership. For joyrides there are always the hack ponies, found in most hill stations or on beaches.

Heli Tourism

For short but delightful package tours, **Deccan Aviation** organizes helicopter trips to many exotic destinations, such as the mountain ranges of the north and northeast, and around Bengaluru and Mumbai. The cost includes food and lodging. While expensive, these are perfect for tourists with plenty of cash but limited time. The government-run **Pawan Hans Helicopters Ltd** also offers heli-trips in collaboration with hotels or tour operators.

Jeep, Camel and Horse Safaris

Often, the best way to explore places that are off the beaten track is to take one of the many safaris on offer. Jeep safaris are popular in Ladakh, especially to the Nubra Valley (see p147) and to the lakes of Tso Moriri and Pangong Tso. Jeep safaris are

Horse safaris, a delightful way of exploring Rajasthan

also popular in Lahaul, Spiti and Kinnaur in Himachal Pradesh. A good base is Manali which has a large number of adventure tour operators. Among them, **Himalayan Adventurers** is a reputable agency that organizes off road jeep safaris as well as other adventure activities such as trekking and rafting. The two-day route from Manali to Leh is a very popular one.

Camel-owners in the Thar Desert in Rajasthan, around Jaisalmer, specialize in camel safaris between October and February. Most safaris last about four days, and the minimum charge is around ₹400 per day (inclusive of meals and blankets, with extra charges for tents). Among the many operators is the **Desert Resort and Camp** at Manvar, which offers top-end safaris in luxury tents. A pleasant alternative is horse safaris around Jodhpur, Shekhawati, Kumbhalgarh and Udaipur. These offer unique glimpses of rural life, taking in forts, palaces

Trekking over the spectacular Shingo-la pass in Zanskar, Ladakh

and remote villages. **Ghanerao Safari Tours** in Jaipur specializes in horse safaris and offers both easy and challenging trips. Many hotels in Rajasthan organize horse safaris. Elephant safaris are also available (see p729).

Trekking

India has a fantastic range of trekking options. Besides the Himalayas, the Nilgiris (see p610) in South India, and the Sahyadris (see p477) in Maharashtra, have many trails for short hikes.

The great Himalayas are a trekker's paradise. **Ibex Expeditions**, a reputable agency, organizes expeditions all over the Himalayas. For more detailed information on trekking and local adventure tour operators in Himachal Pradesh, see pages 118–19; in Ladakh and Zanskar, see pages 156–7; in Garhwal and Kumaon, see pages 192–3; and in West Bengal and Sikkim, see pages 306–307.

This guide divides trails into three types, based on levels of difficulty. "Easy" ones, which involve mildly strenuous walking at mid-high altitudes, are a good introduction. "Moderate" routes cover various terrains and should not be attempted by people with heart problems and serious ailments. Only experienced climbers should attempt "tough" treks, since these go to very high altitudes and require high levels of fitness. It is mandatory to carry a permit (see p734) near international border areas.

Parasailing, popular in Himachal Pradesh and Uttarakhand

Camping and Adventure Sports

Holidays that combine camping and trekking can be particularly enjoyable. **Banjara Camps** specializes in tented holidays in the scenic Sangla Valley in Himachal Pradesh, while **Jungle Lodges and Resorts** organizes well-run luxury camps in Karnataka.

India also provides opportunities to pursue a range of adventure sports. However, it is advisable to take out extra cover on your insurance if you plan on trying any of these activities.

Hang-gliding and parasailing are offered in Himachal Pradesh, especially in Manali and Dharamsala, and near Billing in Kangra. Ooty in Tamil Nadu is another great hang-gliding site, while the Western Ghats in Maharashtra and Goa offer idyllic conditions for parasailing. Local tourism offices in each state organize these sports and can be contacted for bookings and equipment hire.

For mountaineering and rock climbing enthusiasts, the Himalayas offer a number of challenging peaks, many rising above 7,000 m (22,966 ft). Uttarakhand and Himachal Pradesh are India's main mountaineering regions, and Sikkim also offers climbing in the Himalayas. The **Indian Mountaineering Foundation** in Delhi is the central agency; it organizes expeditions and has an active rock climbing fraternity, too. It also provides information on the country's other institutes, such as the

Himalayan Mountaineering Institute in Darjeeling *(see p300)*, and the Nehru Intitute of Mountaineering in Uttarkashi *(see p191)*, both of which offer courses.

Auli in Uttarakhand is the best-equipped ski-centre in India, and is open between January and March. For bookings and skiing information, contact the **GMVN Office** in Dehra Dun, or the **GMVN Tourist Rest House** in Auli, which also hires out gear. Solang Nala, 13 km (8 miles) northwest of Manali, also has ski slopes that are open between February and March. The **Atal Bihari Vajpayee Institute of Mountaineering and Allied Sports** in Manali rents out skiing equipment, offers mountaineering courses, and also organizes kayaking on the Beas river.

Kayaking and River Rafting

The challenge of the fast-flowing rivers of the Himalayas makes India a popular destination for kayaking and white-water rafting. Rivers are graded from levels I to VI; only professionals should attempt rapids that are graded IV and above. The main destinations are the Indus and Zanskar in Ladakh, the Beas and Satluj in Himachal Pradesh, the Ganges, Bhagirathi and Tons in Uttar Pradesh, and the Teesta in Sikkim. The best seasons are between September and December, and again between February and April.

Numerous agencies run organized trips and provide tents, rafts, life jackets and meals. The Ganges near

Rishikesh is a popular site *(see p189)*, as it is just a few hours drive from Delhi. Many companies have set up rafting camps and provide equipment during the season. **Himalayan River Runners**, and **Aquaterra Adventures** are two of the reputable agencies that run various rafting camps in Uttarakhand and Ladakh.

Water Sports

Goa is a popular destination for water sports, where yachting competitions and wind-surfing regattas are attended by enthusiasts from all over the world. Sports such as water-skiing, sailing, wind-surfing and parasailing are offered by local agencies, on beaches such as Baga, Vainguinim, Sinquerim, Anjuna and Bogmalo. The **National Institute of Watersports**, located in Panaji, also offers training courses in wind-surfing, water-skiing, sailing and scuba diving, and hires out boats and equipment as well.

The **Royal Bombay Yacht Club** in Mumbai organizes sailing excursions for visitors every Saturday, while Kerala's popular Kovalam Beach has some facilities for surfing and snorkelling. In Tamil Nadu, a few water sports centres and hotels offer water sports facilities along the coast between Chennai and Mamallapuram.

The Lakshadweep Islands, off the Kerala coast, have excellent centres for wind-surfing, parasailing and water-skiing, as well as snorkelling and scuba diving. **Lacadives** on Kadmat Island has the best equipped centre *(see p651)*. An equally exciting destination for

White-water rafting on the Ganges

Colourful wind-surfing sails, Goa

snorkelling, scuba diving and other water sports is the tropical Andaman Islands in the Bay of Bengal. It is best to check in advance however as some water sports may not be available because of the 2004 tsunami. Quality equipment, including glass-bottomed boats and scuba gear, is on offer at the **Andaman Water Sports Complex** *(see p622)* in Port Blair.

Fishing

India's network of rivers and lakes provides ample opportunity for fishing enthusiasts. All fishing in India requires a permit, which can be obtained from the Fisheries Officer at the various state Fisheries Departments. However, it is simpler to let an agency organize the permits for you. Himalayan River Runners organizes exciting *mahseer* fishing expeditions in the Ganges in February and March.

The best spots in North India are the Ramganga river, outside Corbett National Park; Gangalehri, off the Haridwar-Rishikesh road on the Ganges; and Pong Dam, on the Beas in Himachal Pradesh. This state also offers superb trout-fishing on the Beas river at Katrain, and in the scenic Sangla Valley on the Baspa river.

In South India, **Jungle Lodges and Resorts** *(see p731)* run the Kali River Camp at Dandeli and the Cauvery Fishing and Nature Camp, in Karnataka. These are luxury camps for discerning visitors who wish to combine a fishing holiday with modern comforts.

Wildlife Tourism

A relatively new concept in tourism, combining nature study with conservation activities, is becoming increasingly popular in India. The country has an extraordinary diversity of habitats that support a vast variety of plant and animal life, including many rare and endangered species.

Today, India has 70 protected national parks and over 400 wildlife sanctuaries that cover 4.15 per cent of its total area. Numerous societies are actively involved in environmental issues.

The **World Wide Fund for Nature, India (WWF)**, with its headquarters in Delhi, has a regular programme of activities such as camping trips, film shows and seminars on wildlife. The **Bombay Natural History Society (BNHS)** is one of the foremost nature institutions in India. Its first Indian president was the renowned ornithologist, Dr Salim Ali *(see p470)*. The Society, dedicated to conservation, with special emphasis on bird studies, also organizes workshops. Another eminent institution is the **Madras Naturalists' Society**.

India's many wildlife reserves and game sanctuaries are the best places to see endangered species in the wild. **Ibex Expeditions** organizes eco-friendly trips to parks all over India; **Exotic Journeys** is another reputable agency *(see p693)*. Jungle Lodges and Resorts in Karnataka runs numerous luxury camps, spread across the Nagarhole and BRT Wildlife Sanctuaries *(see p524)*, with coracle boat rides, elephant safaris and film screenings on offer for visitors.

Corbett Park in Uttarakhand *(see pp196–7)*, Kanha in Madhya Pradesh *(see pp258–9)* and the Sunderbans in West Bengal *(see pp292–3)*, are among India's largest Tiger Reserves. Rajasthan's Keoladeo Ghana National Park *(see pp372–3)* attracts a large variety of migratory birds in winter and is a birdwatcher's paradise, while Kaziranga in Assam *(see pp334–5)* is one of the few places in the world where the Indian rhino can be found in the wild. The best park for observing Asian elephants is Periyar in Kerala *(see pp644–5)*, which has the largest population of wild elephants in the country.

A few practical tips should be followed while visiting wildlife reserves. Do not litter, and be especially careful not to drop any plastic and synthetic materials. Carry a pair of binoculars, wear sturdy boots, and never wander off on your own, as this could be dangerous. Do not play loud music or blow horns within park limits since this disturbs the animals. Also, talk softly on safaris to improve the chances of spotting wildlife.

An elephant safari in Kaziranga National Park, habitat of the Indian rhino

A traditional head massage with Ayurvedic oils, Kovalam Beach

Yoga and Healing

Yoga, meditation and Hindu philosophy are taught at ashrams and spiritual centres in most Indian cities. Some of the best are in Rishikesh, where courses are conducted by learned gurus, renowned in their fields. Of these, the **Sivananda Ashram** (see p693) is the most famous. Pune's **Osho International Commune** (see p474), started in the 1960s by the charismatic guru Bhagwan Rajneesh, offers residential courses in meditation and philosophy. The **Ramamani Iyengar Memorial Yoga Institute**, run by the well-known Yogacharya BKS Iyengar is also in Pune, and offers a choice of *hatha* yoga courses. Among India's other reputed yoga and meditation centres are the **Sri Aurobindo Ashram** in Pondicherry (see p693), the **Chinmaya Mission** at Mumbai and the **Ramakrishna Mission** at Belur Math (see p693). Hotels and travel agencies can find out about local branches of many of these centres.

India also has numerous institutes that conduct courses in Buddhist meditation and *vipassana*. Dharamsala and McLeodganj, the home of the Dalai Lama, have some of the best centres. Residential courses are held at the **Tushita Meditation Centre**. Ayurveda and naturopathy rely on the healing powers of herbs and

Logo of a yoga centre in Rishikesh

natural foods, and are widely practised in India. Ayurvedic treatment using special herbal oils, is thought to have originated in Kerala (see p633), and is widely practised there today. Almost all hotels in the state have Ayurvedic centres, especially around Kovalam and Thiruvananthapuram.

The **Kairali Ayurvedic Health Resort** at Palakkad (with branches in Delhi and Khajuraho), and the **Somatheeram Ayurvedic Resort** at Kovalam are among the best centres. For visitors in search of medical advice and treatment, the **Arya Vaidyasala** in Kottakal (see p656) is a pioneer institute.

India also has a handful of luxury spas, which emphasize holistic healing (see p692). The **Jindal Naturecure Institute** in Bengaluru, also known as Jindal's Farm, admits patients for specialized treatments for respiratory and stomach disorders, ulcers, migraines and diabetes.

Other healing practices such as Reiki and Pranic healing (methods that channel positive forces through the body's *chakras* or energy centres), are practised in many larger cities, and it is best to check local city magazines for details. A magazine, published every month, called *Life Positive*, focuses on new-age healing techniques.

Cultural Activities

Indian classical dance and music are taught at renowned institutes all over the country. **Triveni Kala Sangam** (see p79) in Delhi holds courses in classical singing, dance and painting. Dharamsala's **Norbulingka Institute** teaches Tibetan arts and crafts, including *thangka* painting and embroidery. The dance village of **Nrityagram**, near Bengaluru, offers long-term courses in classical dance, choreography, music and painting. **Kalakshetra** in Chennai (see p576) is a premier institute for teaching Carnatic music and classical dance, and the **Kerala Kala Mandalam** (see p655) near Thrissur, is another renowned centre for the performing arts.

A few travel agencies offer special interest tours on subjects such as architecture, rural and tribal culture, traditional arts and crafts, and cuisine. They make itineraries to suit individual tastes. **Incent Tours** focuses on textiles, architecture and food, while **Travel Link** specializes in tribal tours in Odisha.

Various institutions all over the country promote traditional crafts and artisans. The **Crafts Museum** (see pp84–5) in Delhi, and the **Dastkar Craft Centre**, which is near Ranthambhore in Rajasthan, are two places where visitors can observe artisans at work and learn more about their skills and way of life.

Gujarati musicians at the Crafts Museum, New Delhi

DIRECTORY

Sports

Indian Golf Union
24, First floor, Adchini, Delhi.
Tel (011) 2652 5771.
W indiangolfunion.org

RK Khanna Tennis Stadium
Tennis Stadium, Africa Avenue, Delhi.
Tel (011) 2617 6276.

Polo & Riding

Army Polo & Riding Club
Brar Square, Delhi.
Tel (011) 2569 9444/9555.
W armypoloclub.com

Royal Equestrian Polo Centre
Dundlod House, Civil lines, Jaipur.
Tel (0141) 221 1276.
W dundlod.com

Heli-tourism

Deccan Aviation
G11, G Block, Hauz Khas Market, Delhi.
Tel (011) 2652 0035.
W deccanair.com

Pawan Hans Helicopters Ltd.
Safdarjung Airport, Delhi.
Tel (011) 2461 5711.
Fax (011) 2461 1801.
W pawanhans.co.in

Jeep, Camel & Horse Safaris

Desert Resort & Camp, Manvar
261, behind Umaid Bhavan Palace, Jodhpur.
Tel (0291) 251 1600.
Fax (0291) 251 1300.
W manwar.com

Ghanerao Safari Tours
B–II/302 Kamal Apts, Bani Park, Jaipur.
Tel (0141) 220 1209.
Fax (0141) 401 7427.
W horsesafari.com

Himalayan Adventurers
The Mall, Manali.
Tel (01902) 252 750.
Fax (01902) 252 182.
W himalayan adventurersindia.com

Trekking

Ibex Expeditions
30, Community Centre East of Kailash, Delhi.
Tel (011) 2646 0244.
W ibexexpeditions. com

Camping & Adventure Sports

Atal Bihari Vajpayee Institute of Mountaineering & Allied Sports
Manali.
Tel (01902) 252 342.

Banjara Camps
1 A Hauz Khas Village, Delhi.
Tel (011) 2685 5152.
Fax (011) 2686 1397.
W banjaracamps.com

GMVN
74/1 Rajpur Rd, Dehradun.
Tel (0135) 274 6817.
Fax (0135) 274 6847.

GMVN Tourist Rest House, Auli
Tel (01389) 223 208.

Indian Mountaineering Foundation
6 Benito Juarez Marg, Delhi. **Tel** (011) 2411 1211. **W** indmount.org

Jungle Lodges & Resorts
Shrungar Shopping Centre, MG Rd, Bengaluru.
Tel (080) 2558 4111.
Fax (080) 2558 6163.
W junglelodges.com

Kayaking & River Rafting

Aquaterra Adventures
S–507 Greater Kailash II, Delhi. **Tel** (011) 2921 2760. **W** aquaterra.in

Himalayan River Runners
C1, Basement, Community Centre. Safdarjung, Delhi.
Tel (011) 2685 2602.
Fax (011) 2686 5604.
W hrrindia.com

Water Sports

National Institute of Watersports
Sundial Apts, AS Rd, Altinho, Panaji, Goa.
Tel (0832) 243 6550.
W niws.nic.in

Royal Bombay Yacht Club
Apollo Bunder, near Taj Mahal Hotel, Mumbai.
Tel (022) 2202 1880.
W royalbombay yachtclub.com

Wildlife Tourism

Bombay Natural History Society
Hornbill House, Shaheed Bhagat Singh Rd, Mumbai. **Tel** (022) 2282 1811. **W** bnhs.org

Madras Naturalists' Society
8 Janaki Avenue, Abhiramapuram, Chennai.
Tel (044) 2499 5833.
W blackbuck.org.in

World Wide Fund for Nature, India
172–B, Max Mueller Marg, Lodi Estate, Delhi.
Tel (011) 4150 4815.
W wwfindia.org

Yoga & Healing

Arya Vaidyasala
Kottakkal, Kerala.
Tel (0423) 274 2216.
W aryavaidyasala.com

Chinmaya Mission
Central Chinmaya Mission Trust, F-3 Panchsheel, C Road, Churchgate, Mumbai.
Tel (022) 2281 4646.
W chinmayamission. com

Jindal Naturecure Institute
Jindal Nagar, Bengaluru.

Tel (080) 2371 7777.
W naturecure-inys.org

Kairali Ayurvedic Health Resort
D-120 Andheria Modh Mehrauli, Delhi.
Tel 9555156156.
W kairali.com

Osho International Commune
17 Koregaon Park, Pune.
Tel (020) 6601 9999.
W osho.com

Ramamani Iyengar Memorial Yoga Institute
1107 B/1 Hare Krishna Mandir Rd, Model Colony, Shivaji Nagar, Pune.
Tel (020) 2565 6134.
W bksiyengar.com

Tushita Meditation Centre
McLeodganj.
Tel (8988) 160 988.
W tushita.info

Cultural Activities

Dastkar Craft Centre
Kutalpura Village.

Incent Tours
Sushant Tower, Sushant Lok II, Sector 56, Gurgaon, Haryana.
Tel (0124) 4414 7955.
W incent-tours.com

Norbulingka Institute
Sidhpur, Dharamsala.
Tel (01892) 246 405.
W norbulingka.org

Nrityagram
The Dance Village, Hessaraghatta, Bengaluru.
Tel (080) 2846 6313.
Fax (080) 2846 6312.
W nrityagram.org

Travel Link
Metro House, Vani Vihar Square, Bhubaneswar, Odisha. **Tel** (0674) 254 6591. **Fax** (0674) 254 6595. **W** travellink-india.com

SURVIVAL GUIDE

PRACTICAL INFORMATION

India receives over 5 million visitors each year. The peak season is in winter (Oct–Mar), and it is wise to book ahead during this time. English is widely spoken in most parts of the country, so communication is rarely a problem. Tourist infrastructure (transportation, accommodation and restaurants) is of international standard in the larger cities; the remoter areas offer fairly basic accommodation, and some areas are still not equipped to cater to the international tourist, who may seek better banking services or prefer to pay by credit card. The Department of Tourism has offices across the country, *(see p757)* as well as overseas, which provide brochures, itineraries and guided tours. There are many travel agencies in India, but it is wise to approach a reputable one for accommodation, tickets and tours.

When to Go

India's weather is, for most, the key factor in deciding when to visit. The best time is between October and March, when conditions are pleasant across the country. Try to avoid the summer (Apr–Jun), which is unbearably hot in the north, and very sultry in the south. The rainy season (Jul–Sep) is also best avoided, as frequent heavy rainfall can make travel difficult, especially in the southwestern states of Goa, Maharashtra and Kerala. The Himalayan region can be very cold from November to January. The foothills, which provide a welcome escape from the heat of the plains, are at their best between March and June, and again in September (after the rains). Climate and rainfall charts can be found on pages 42–3.

What to Take

The clothes you need will depend on the time of year that you visit. In northern India, from November until February, you will need a warm jacket, sweater and socks, especially after sundown, whereas in the south, the weather is balmy at that time. In February and March, and again in October, bring light woollens. During the summer and monsoon season (Apr–Sep) only loose-fitting cotton clothes are comfortable. Bring footwear that is easy to remove, as you will have to take off your shoes in places of worship. A first aid kit is a must *(see p742)*. A raincoat or umbrella, a hat to protect against the strong sun, and a torch are also useful.

Advance Booking

It is advisable to have confirmed advance bookings for accommodation and travel, especially during the peak season (Oct–Mar). Airline tickets are available at short notice, but as trains are always crowded, bookings should be made ahead – ticket reservations can be made two months in advance. Insist on written confirmations.

Visas and Passport

All visitors to India, except Nepalese and Bhutanese citizens, need a valid visa and passport to enter the country. Indian consular offices around the world issue a standard six-month tourist visa. Tourists can enter the country three times within the stipulated visa period, which is convenient for visiting neighbouring countries such as Nepal and Sri Lanka. Foreigners who arrive in India on this visa do not need to register themselves with a local authority and can travel freely in all areas except the so-called "Restricted Areas", which require special permits.

Visa extensions are sometimes granted for 15 days or, in exceptional cases, for a longer period. The application process is complicated. In Delhi, collect an extension form from the **Ministry of Home Affairs** office; then submit it to the **Foreigners Regional Registration Office (FRRO)**; it will finally be issued by the Ministry of Home Affairs. In Mumbai, Chennai or Kolkata, contact the local FRRO. Visa stamp

Permits

In addition to a visa, you may need special travel permits to visit what are known as "Restricted Areas". Obtaining a permit can be complicated, so it is best to ask a reliable travel agent, at home or in India, to

A Goa café doing brisk business in winter, when the weather is balmy

◀ The popular Darjeeling Toy Train on the Batasia Loop

arrange it for you. This can take up to four weeks, so plan in advance. Permits are also issued by Indian embassies and consular offices abroad; from the FRRO in Delhi, Kolkata, Mumbai and Chennai; and from the Resident Commissioner's offices in Delhi. You will be asked to show these permits when travelling in restricted areas. You will also need trekking permits for the Himalayan regions bordering Pakistan, Tibet and China, and for treks in Uttarakhand (see pp192–3), Himachal Pradesh (see p119), Ladakh (see p146, p147 & p157) and West Bengal and Sikkim (see p307). All visitors to Sikkim require 15-day travel permits, because of its proximity to a sensitive border with China.

Among the seven northeastern states, no permits are required for Assam, Meghalaya and Tripura. However, permits are required for Arunachal Pradesh, Mizoram, Manipur and Nagaland, and can be acquired from any of the state tourist offices. In some areas, permits are issued only to groups of four or more – these are best organised by a travel agent.

Foreign nationals require a permit, valid for 30 days, for the Andaman Islands, but this excludes tribal areas and some islands, including Nicobar. Permits can be obtained on arrival at the immigration counter at Port Blair airport, or at Kolkata and Chennai airports. If travelling by ship, a permit can be obtained on arrival at Port Blair, as well as from the FRRO offices in the four main cities. For permits to travel to the Lakshadweep Islands, (see page 651).

Embassies and Consulates

Most countries have embassies in Delhi, as well as consulates in Mumbai, Kolkata and Chennai. Consular offices can re-issue passports and assist in case of emergencies, such as theft, imprisonment and hospitalization. All city telephone directories and information guides carry detailed listings of embassies and consulates, as does the Indian Ministry of Tourism's website (www.tourindia.com).

Customs Information

When entering India, visitors have a duty-free allowance of 2 litres of liquor or wine and 200 cigarettes. For articles such as jewellery, video cameras, music systems or laptop computers, they must fill in the tourist baggage re-export form, undertaking to take these items back or else pay a fairly heavy duty on them on departure. They must also fill a currency declaration form if the aggregate value of their foreign currency (bank notes and traveller's cheques) exceeds US$10,000 or equivalent. There is a duty of 60 per cent if the baggage value limit is exceeded. Antiques over 100 years old cannot be exported, neither can wildlife products, such as animal pelts, shahtoosh shawls or ivory. Consult the **Archaeological Survey of India (ASI)** and the **Ministry of Environment and Forests** for details of these rules.

Visa stamp

Immunization

Only visitors travelling from certain countries in Africa, South America and Papua New Guinea require a valid vaccination certificate for yellow fever. However, visitors should get vaccinated against tetanus, typhoid and hepatitis A and B. It is also advisable to start a course of anti-malarial tablets before leaving for India, after consulting a doctor (see p743).

Insurance

Take out an insurance policy for medical emergencies as well as theft before leaving home. Travel insurance is also essential to cover any adventure activity or sport that you may undertake on your trip.

DIRECTORY

FRRO

w immigrationindia.nic.in

Delhi
East Block 8, Level 2,
Sector 1, RK Puram.
Tel (011) 2671 1443.

Mumbai
Special Branch Building,
Badruddin Tayabji Lane.
Tel (022) 2262 0446.

Chennai
Shastri Bhavan Annexe, 26
Haddow Rd.
Tel (044) 2354 4970.

Kolkata
237 AJC Bose Rd.
Tel (033) 2283 7034.

Ministry of Home Affairs

Delhi
North Block, Central Secretariat.
Tel (011) 2309 2161.

Travel Agents

Abercrombie & Kent
Tel (011) 4600 1600 (India).
Tel (0044) 01242 547 700 (UK).
w akdmc.com

Cox & Kings
Tel (011) 4129 7900 (India).
Tel (0044) 020 7873 5000 (UK).
w coxandkings.com

Kuoni Travel India
Tel (0124) 470 3400 (India).
w sita.in

Mercury Travels
Tel (011) 2439 5018 (India).
w mercurytravels.co.in

ASI

Janpath, Delhi.
Tel (011) 2301 5954.
w asi.nic.in

Ministry of Environment & Forests

Paryavaran Bhavan, CGO
Complex, Lodhi Rd, New Delhi.
Tel (011) 2436 1669.

General Information

w outlooktraveller.com
w travel.indiamart.com
w tourindia.com

Tourist Information

Tourist information offices run by the **Government of India Department of Tourism** *(see p757)* can be found across the country and abroad. Each state also has its own tourism department, providing reliable and detailed advice and practical information on sightseeing, travel and stay. Tourist brochures and maps are readily available. A number of travel sites on the Internet also provide up-to-date information. There are information counters in the arrival halls of international and domestic airports, as well as information booths at railway and bus stations.

Tourist brochures

Admission Charges

A common entry ticket (₹250 for foreign visitors; ₹10 for domestic ones) allows access to several of India's UNESCO World Heritage sites. The Taj Mahal is not included in this deal. Another common entry ticket covers the monuments run by the Archaeological Survey of India (ASI). Tickets can be purchased from ASI offices and monuments and from branches of the India Tourism Development Corporation (ITDC).

There are often additional fees for cameras, video cameras, and for special shows such as the Son et Lumières. Most places of worship do not have any admission fee, but often have a donation box. If you are of a different religious denomination, it is advisable to ask if you may enter *(see p738)*.

Holidays and Opening Hours

Each year, the government issues a new holiday list *(see p39)* that includes all major religious festivals, whose exact dates may change from year to year. Some are known as "restricted holidays", which means that though the office may be open, the staff may be on leave. Banks, offices and most markets remain closed on the three national holidays: Republic Day (26 January), Independence Day (15 August) and Mahatma Gandhi's birthday (2 October). Monuments and museums are normally open 10am–6pm with an hour's lunch break, and generally closed on Mondays and government holidays. Markets and shops stay open until at least 7pm in most places. Temples tend to close between 1pm and 4pm, when the deity is "at rest". Government offices work from Monday to Friday, from 9:30am to 6pm with, supposedly, a half-hour lunch break.

Guides

All tourist offices, travel agents and hotels can arrange a certified guide for fixed hourly rates. At popular monuments, amateur guides can be a nuisance. Look instead for English-speaking guides who wear a metal badge certifying government tourist department approval. French, Italian, Spanish, German, Russian and Japanese-speaking guides are also available at many popular destinations.

Backpackers

For students and young travellers, most of the larger cities have branches of the **Youth Hostels Association of India (YHAI)** *(see p693)*. Though it is not necessary to be a member of the association to stay, members do get priority and lower rates. **YMCA** hostels in larger cities also provide cheap lodgings for backpackers. Apart from these, plenty of other cheap options are available across the country, including the smaller towns. It is a good idea to buy a strong padlock, as some of the budget hotels have flimsy locks. Many of these are not air conditioned, nor do they have mosquito nets – the latter are essential, and available locally. Do not leave money and important documents in your hotel; keep them with you at all times. Be wary of conmen enticing you with the promise of cheap accommodation and bargain shopping.

Facilities for the Disabled

Facilities for the disabled are still relatively basic across the country and public buildings and places of interest seldom have ramps or rails. However, airports and all main railway stations do have wheelchairs and ramps, and porters are always available to carry luggage. Pavements are difficult to negotiate in a wheelchair as they are often uneven. Few hotels are equipped for the needs of the disabled visitor. The staff, however, will go out of their way to help.

Facilities for Children

Although some luxury hotels do have baby-sitting facilities, these services are not commonly available. However, Indians are generally tolerant of children, who are warmly welcomed in

Visitors on a guided tour of the lake at Ranganthittoo Bird Sanctuary

most places. If travelling with young infants, it is advisable to bring your own supplies of baby food and formula milk. Disposable nappies are widely available in the larger towns.

Language

Though Hindi is the official language of India, there are several regional languages as well. Bengali is spoken in Kolkata and West Bengal, Marathi in Mumbai and Maharashtra, Tamil in Tamil Nadu, Telugu in Andhra Pradesh and Malayalam in Kerala. English has become the most convenient link language and is widely spoken in most Indian cities. It is also the language of commerce, and most people who deal with tourists, such as taxi drivers, guides, hotel staff, shop assistants and officials, speak English. Road signs and numbers are usually in English as well as in the regional language of the particular state.

Electricity

The electrical current in India is 220–240 volts, 50 Hz. The power supply can be very erratic during the summer months, with low voltage, fluctuations and fairly long power cuts.

Triple round-pin sockets are the norm, but adaptors and transformers are easily available at the larger stores. It is advisable to carry a power surge cable to protect laptop computers against voltage fluctuations.

Indian Standard Time and Calendar

In spite of its size, India has only one standard time. India is 5.5 hours ahead of Greenwich Mean Time (GMT) 4.5 hours behind Australian Eastern Standard Time, and 10.5 hours ahead of US Eastern Standard Time. The Western Gregorian calendar is used for all official work as this avoids the confusion of traditional calendars, which vary between religions and regions. For example, in 2011,

the official Indian calendar (Saka era) reads 1933, whereas the old Hindu calendar (Vikram era) reads 2068.

Measurements and Conversion Chart

The metric system is most commonly used all over the country.

Imperial to Metric
1 inch = 2.5 centimetres
1 foot = 30 centimetres
1 mile = 1.6 kilometres
1 ounce = 28 grams
1 pound = 454 grams
1 pint = 0.6 litres
1 gallon = 4.5 litres

Metric to Imperial
1 centimetre = 0.4 inches
1 metre = 3 feet 3 inches
1 kilometre = 0.6 miles
1 gram = 0.04 ounces
1 kilogram = 2.2 pounds
1 litre = 1.8 pints

A range of plugs

Photography

Sophisticated digital, film and colour-processing facilities are readily available, even in smaller towns. Remember to check expiry dates when buying batteries and film. Larger photo shops also have excellent developing and printing facilities and offer quick services.

Taking pictures of women, tribal communities, and places of worship can be sensitive issues and it is best to ask before using your camera. Photographing security-sensitive areas, such as railway stations, dams, airports and military installations, is prohibited. Notice boards indicate where photography is not allowed.

DIRECTORY

State Government Tourist Offices in India

Delhi
18-A, D.D.A. SCO Complex, Defence Colony.
Tel (011) 2464 7005.
[W] delhitourism.gov.in

Goa
Dr Alvarez Costa Rd, Panaji.
Tel (0832) 242 4001.
[W] goa-tourism.com

Himachal Pradesh
The Mall, Shimla.
Tel (0177) 265 2561.
[W] himachaltourism.gov.in

Kerala
Park View Building, Thiruvanthanapuram.
Tel (0471) 232 1132.
[W] keralatourism.org

Madhya Pradesh
Paryatan Bhavan, Bhadbhada Rd, Bhopal. Tel (0755) 277 8383.
[W] mptourism.com

Maharashtra
Opposite LIC Buildings, Madame Cama Rd, Mumbai.
Tel (022) 2204 4040.
[W] maharashtratourism.gov.in

Rajasthan
Paryatan Bhawan, MI Rd, Jaipur.
Tel (0141) 511 0598.
[W] rajasthantourism.gov.in

Tamil Nadu
TN Tourism Complex, No 2, Wallajah Rd, Triplicane, Chennai.
Tel (044) 2538 9857.
[W] tamilnadutourism.org

Uttar Pradesh
C-13, Vipin Khand, Gomti Nagar, Lucknow. Tel (0522) 230 7037.
[W] up-tourism.com

Uttarakhand
Pt. Deendayal Upadhaya Paryatan Bhawan. Near ONGC Helipad, Garhi Cantt, Dehradun.
Tel (0135) 255 9898.
[W] uttarakhandtourism.in

West Bengal
3/2 BBD Bag (East), Kolkata.
Tel (033) 2243 6440.
[W] westbengaltourism.gov.in

Etiquette

India is still a traditional society, governed by strong family values. Though in cities and larger towns you will find youngsters in Western dress with a modern, cosmopolitan outlook, they remain traditional in many ways. And though the diverse social, religious and caste groups have their own distinct customs, they share certain common values. Respect for elders is deeply ingrained, so it is important to treat older people with special courtesy. Indians are extremely hospitable and helpful to visitors – sometimes to an almost embarassing degree. It is a good idea to respond to this by bringing your hosts flowers, or a small gift, even though this is not an Indian custom. If you find yourself facing delays and inefficient services, or grappling with bureaucracy, it is far more effective to be firm and polite than to lose your temper.

Eating off banana leaves at a ceremonial temple feast

Greeting People

The traditional greeting in India is the *namaskar* or *namaste* (pronounced "namastay") when meeting or parting. The palms are pressed together, raised towards the face, and the head is bent slightly forward. Greetings and gestures vary somewhat according to religion or regional group. Muslims raise their right hand towards the forehead with the words *adaab* or *salaam aleikum* (to which you reply *walekum salaam*). The Western handshake is also widely used, though more conservative women still prefer to greet visitors with a *namaskar*.

The suffix "*ji*" after someone's name is a mark of respect. Using first names only can be taken as overly familiar, so it's best to address new acquaintances as Mr, Miss or Mrs, or simply "*ji*".

Older people, particularly grandparents, are treated with great respect, and younger relatives often greet them by touching their feet. Your host will not expect you to do the same, but a courteous greeting in any form is important.

Indians will think nothing of asking you apparently very personal questions within minutes of first meeting you, so don't take offence if a

relative stranger asks you how much you earn or whether you are married. Such questions are seen as nothing more than taking a normal friendly interest in a new acquaintance.

Body Language

The feet are considered to be the lowliest part of the body, and shoes are treated as unclean. People will usually take their shoes off before entering a house. Putting your feet up on the furniture is considered bad manners, as is touching someone inadvertently with your feet. If you are sitting on the floor, as is often the case, try to keep your feet tucked underneath rather than stretched out, and avoid stepping over people.

Namaskar, the traditional greeting

The head, on the other hand, is thought to be a person's spiritual centre. An older person may bless someone younger by touching his or her head.

Living in close quarters with family and neighbours gives Indians a different sense of "personal space" than many Westerners are used to. If you find yourself crowded or jostled, particularly while travelling, be as tolerant as you can, since space is often at a premium.

You should also be aware that public displays of affection between couples are frowned upon in Indian society.

Suitable Dress

Indians tend to dress conservatively and keep the body well covered. In small towns, most women wear saris or *salwar-kameez (see p34)*. In cities, jeans, skirts, and t-shirts are common, particularly among the younger generation. However, men do tend to stare at skimpily-clad women, so try to avoid short skirts, halter-neck tops, or anything that might attract unwanted attention.

It is best to dress formally when visiting Indian homes. In fact, wearing an Indian outfit for the occasion will probably delight your hosts. Inexpensive, ready-made Indian clothes for men and women are widely available.

It is acceptable for men to go shirtless on the beach. Nude sunbathing is never allowed, and women are advised to wear full swimsuits, or sarongs over their bikinis. If you are going out for the evening, remember that most nightclubs have a dress code, and you may not get in if you are wearing shorts or trainers.

Places of Worship

Whether you are visiting a Hindu temple, Buddhist monastery, Islamic mosque or Sikh gurdwara, make sure that you behave and dress appropriately. You should, for example, always ask permission to take photographs. Women should wear dresses that cover the upper arms, and are at least mid- calf length, and take scarves along to cover their heads. It is acceptable for women to wear long trousers. Men should avoid shorts and may be asked to cover their heads with a handkerchief or scarf (rather than a hat).

Jain temples have strict rules, and will not allow leather items, even wallets or watch straps, inside. In some South Indian temples, men are expected to remove their shirts and wear a *dhoti* instead of trousers. These are often provided at the temple entrance. At most places of worship, shoes are taken off at the door, and you should sit with your feet facing away from the main shrine. In a temple or monastery, walk around in a clockwise direction. You may be offered *prasad* (sacred food) in most temples and gurdwaras, which must be taken only in the right hand. The segregation of men and women is common.

In Hindu temples, it is usual for devotees and visitors to offer flowers and incense. Do not sit on or lean against temple walls or shrines. Even those in ruins, as well as simple roadside graves are considered holy. Some Hindu temples, (especially in Kerala and a few in Odisha) are

Sign for removing footwear

out of bounds for non-Hindus. If you are barred from entering, do not take offence. Avoid entering a mosque during Friday prayers, and men should stay away from the women's enclosure.

Bargaining

Bargaining is a way of life in India. Exchanges can be heated, but it is not necessary to be aggressive. Firmly state what you would like to pay and walk away if the shopkeeper does not agree. If you are buying in bulk, you may ask for an extra discount. The prices in larger shops and government emporia are usually fixed *(see p720)*.

Eating Indian Style

Eating with your fingers can take a bit of getting used to, but it is the best way to enjoy traditional Indian food. If in doubt about how to eat a particular dish, don't be embarrassed to ask. It is considered impolite to use your left hand for eating. Sitting on the floor for meals is common and, in the south, banana leaves are often used instead of plates.

Tipping

There are no norms for tipping, or *baksheesh*, as it is called. Porters and doormen at hotels are usually happy with a 20 or 50 rupee tip. In restaurants, check the bill before you decide on the tip, since the larger ones usually include a service charge. If not, ten per cent of the total amount is usually fine. Tipping taxi or auto-rickshaw drivers is optional, and not generally expected. If you hire a car with a driver, however, you are expected to give him a *baksheesh*. The same goes for hairdressers, masseurs or anyone offering you a personal service.

Smoking and Alcohol

In 2008, the Indian government imposed a countrywide ban on smoking in all public places, including restaurants, bars, hotels, offices and flights. Smoking or drinking within the precincts of a temple, gurdwara or mosque is strictly taboo, and in Amritsar, no smoking is permitted within the city limits.

Alcohol is available all over India, though the state of Gujarat is "dry", as are some religious sites and temple towns, such as Haridwar, Rishikesh and Pushkar. In addition, there are certain designated "dry days" all over the country, such as Mahatma Gandhi's birthday (2 October) and Independence Day (15 August). Only some restaurants are licensed to serve alchohol, and you are not allowed to drink alcohol in parks, buses or trains.

Beggars

As a foreign visitor in India, you will get more than your share of harassment from beggars at city traffic lights, markets and outside places of worship. Beggars can be extremely persistent. Although it is very difficult to refuse, visitors who give money to one, will soon find themselves surrounded by a throng. Be especially careful of being pickpocketed in the confusion. The best strategy is to ignore them, and walk on until they leave you alone. If necessary, complain to a nearby policeman. If you do wish to help monetarily, the staff at your hotel will be able to suggest deserving charities to whom donations can be made.

Hindu pilgrims outside a temple in Odisha

Personal Security and Health

Each state in India has its own police force, which is run from local police stations (thanas). If you need to report a crime, such as theft, to the police, try to do so within 24 hours of the incident. Although Indian police are generally helpful, the system itself is extremely bureaucratic and prone to corruption, so it is always best to contact your embassy or consular office for help and advice in the first instance. For a trouble-free visit, a few simple precautions are necessary. Protect your valuables and important documents at all times, stay and eat in places that look clean, and drink only mineral water. If you require medical attention, it is better to opt for a private clinic rather than one of the many government-run hospitals.

Policeman in summer uniform directing traffic in Kolkata

General Precautions

Travelling in India is relatively safe for tourists. Take simple safety measures, such as wearing a money belt under your shirt for cash, traveller's cheques and important documents, such as passports and visas. Protect your camera and avoid wearing jewellery or carrying large amounts of cash in crowded areas. Valuables can be kept in a hotel safe, but do insist on a receipt. While shopping, ensure that shopkeepers make out a bill and process your credit card in front of you. There have been incidents of tourists being drugged and robbed, especially on trains, so it is not advisable to accept food or drink from strangers. Padlock your luggage to your seat during train journeys. It is a good idea to let your hotel know where you are going. Do not stray into deserted areas alone, especially at night, and avoid hitchhiking.

A police jeep

A hospital ambulance

Danger Areas

The border areas are high-security zones, so when trekking or travelling in the Himalayan regions make sure you have an Inner Line Permit (see p734). The state of Jammu and Kashmir has had long-standing militant activity and much of the state is unsafe for visitors (see p158). Before travelling to such areas, it is a good idea to contact the state tourism department in Patna (see p219) for up-to-date information on the law and order situation. In restricted areas always travel in groups rather than on your own.

Communal unrest and even riots are usually confined to the crowded older parts of cities. It is best to avoid these areas if the political situation is uneasy, or during important religious festivals which attract large crowds.

Security

Since the attack on Mumbai on 26 November 2008, security has been tightened throughout India, especially at airports and railway stations. Bag-and body-searches are usual when entering cinemas and public auditoria. Never pick up unattended baggage, and inform the police immediately if you notice anything suspicious.

Narcotics

Since the 1960s, India has been part of the "hippy trail" with marijuana easily available. With the arrival of Ecstasy and other harder drugs in the 1990s, particularly in places such as Goa, the law has tightened considerably. Possession, trafficking and use of narcotics (including marijuana) is now banned by law and punishable by tough jail sentences. Drug convictions lead to a minimum sentence of ten years without parole or remission. Never carry anything for strangers or check in their luggage for them at airports. A Narcotic Drugs and Psychotropic Substances Court has been established specifically to try drug-related offences.

Women Travellers

Women, both Indian and foreign, face a certain amount of unwanted male attention, even though "eve-teasing" is today a punishable offence. When travelling alone, the problems women encounter can range from being stared at to more active harassment such as suggestive comments and body contact in buses and crowded places.

Take your cue from Indian women who continue with their independent lifestyles despite such annoyances. Dress modestly, and avoid wearing clothes that can be thought of as provocative. Ignore men lounging at street corners and, if you find their attention offensive, approach the nearest policeman. Avoid walking about alone in quiet places and in the rougher parts of cities.

When hiring a car or taxi, ask the hotel to book it for you and note the licence plate number. Hitchhiking is not advisable under any circumstances.

When queuing for train or cinema tickets, women are advised to use the "ladies' lines" which are usually much shorter. On many buses and on some trains there are "ladies only" seats or compartments to make the journey that much safer.

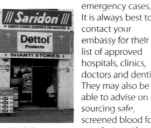
A local pharmacy or chemist shop

Legal Assistance

Legal problems are rare for travellers, but if you do find yourself in a legal tangle, contact your embassy immediately. Always carry your passport and keep a photocopy handy. Do not hand over your travel papers to anyone until your embassy has been informed. Some insurance policies also cover legal costs for emergencies such as accidents.

Public Toilets

Wayside public toilets have poor hygiene and are best avoided. However, although few in number, those known as "Sulabh Shauchalayas" located on city roads are regarded as a great civic invention. Attractively designed, they are easy to spot, extremely clean and charge a nominal fee for use. They are, however, of the Indian "squatting" variety and can be difficult to use if you are not used to them. Some

hotels allow non-residents to use their toilets. It is always a good idea to carry your own toilet paper with you, just in case.

Hospitals and Medical Facilities

Do take out comprehensive medical insurance before arriving in India. **MASTA** (Medical Advisory Service for Travellers Abroad) in the UK can give a health update for travellers to India. The larger cities have reasonably good government and private hospitals and nursing homes, with 24-hour services equipped to handle casualty and emergency cases. It is always best to contact your embassy for their list of approved hospitals, clinics, doctors and dentists. They may also be able to advise on sourcing safe, screened blood for transfusions. If in doubt, the local **Indian Red Cross Society** is one of the safest options for blood transfusion. The best hospitals ensure that staff use disposable syringes.

Pharmacies

Most big markets, in all cities and major towns, have well-stocked pharmacies (or chemist shops, as they are known in India). They stock toiletries, women's sanitary products, baby food and disposable nappies. Pharmacists can also suggest simple and quick remedies.

For special medication, it is advisable to carry a prescription, or show the packaging with the generic name if the brand is unfamiliar, so that the pharmacist can suggest a suitable alternative. Antibiotics are sold only by prescription. Most pharmacies are open between 9am and 7:30pm. Many hospitals also have 24-hour pharmacies.

Heat and Humidity

Northern, central and western India are scorchingly hot *(see pp42–3)* during the summer (Apr–Jun). The east and the south are not as hot but can get oppressively humid during the monsoon.

Take things easy for a few days to get acclimatized. To prevent dehydration, drink plenty of fluids and add an extra pinch of salt to the food. It is wise to stay indoors during the hottest part of the day, and if outdoors, wear a wide-brimmed hat and sunglasses, and use sunscreen to protect your skin. Prolonged exposure to the sun can cause heat stroke, a serious condition with high body temperature, severe headaches and disorientation.

Polyester clothing and covered shoes and socks trap perspiration and can lead to prickly heat and fungal infections, especially in the scalp, between the toes, (athlete's foot), in the groin and other sensitive parts of the body. Prickly heat powder and anti-fungal ointments are available at most pharmacies. The best prevention is to wear light, loose-fitting cotton clothing and open sandals, and to always dry yourself well after washing.

In winter (Oct–Feb), cities have a lot of smog, as the pollution in the air tends to settle. This aggravates chest infections, and asthmatic travellers should always carry their own medication, although inhalers, such as Asthaline, are readily available on prescription.

First Aid Kit

A basic first aid kit for travelling in India should include all personal medication, aspirin or painkillers for fevers and minor aches and pains, tablets for nausea, antiseptic and calamine lotion for cuts and bites, an anti-fungal ointment, plaster and crêpe bandages, a pair of scissors, insect repellent and tweezers. Your first aid kit should also have anti-histamines for allergies, anti-diarrhoea tablets, water purification tablets, disposable syringes and a hermometer. Note that most of these items are also available at Indian pharmacies. They stock effective herbal remedies as well; only buy brands that have been recommended by a reliable practitioner or pharmacist.

Hand fan

Stomach Upsets and Diarrhoea

Diarrhoea, usually caused by a change of diet, water and climate, is common among visitors. Spicy Indian food often leads to digestive disorders, in which case it is best to eat plain, boiled food until the attack subsides. Most importantly, drink plenty of liquids to keep well hydrated. Avoid raw salad, cut fruit, cold cuts, fresh juice and yogurt. Instead of tap water, opt for bottles of sealed mineral water of well-known brands, such as Evian or Himalayan, if available. Most international brands of carbonated drinks are widely available, and fresh coconut water is also safe. Although street food often looks tempting, it is safer to avoid it unless it is hot and freshly cooked right in front of you.

A good pharmacist can suggest standard diarrhoea medication, though if the attack is severe, it is best to consult a doctor. Also, take a course of oral rehydrating salts (ORS), commercially available under the popular Indian brand names of Electral or Electrobion. An effective home-made remedy is half a teaspoon of salt and three teaspoons of sugar mixed in boiled water.

Food and Water-borne Diseases

Visitors to India must guard against dysentery. Bacillary dysentery lasts about a week and is accompanied by severe stomach pains, vomiting and fever, while amoebic dysentery has similar symptoms but takes longer to manifest. If left untreated, this can become chronic. The same is true of giardiasis, a type of diarrhoea caused by contaminated water. Vaccination against hepatitis A is advisable before travelling to India. The symptoms of this unpleasant disease include fever, fatigue, severe chills and jaundice. The only treatment is rest and a strictly controlled diet. Other waterborne diseases such as cholera (prevalent in flood-hit areas) and typhoid can also be prevented with vaccines.

Intestinal worms, common in most tropical areas, include tapeworms, which are found in under-cooked meats and green leafy vegetables. Others, such as hookworms, can be contracted by walking barefoot on contaminated soil. Ensure that all food is well cooked and always wear sturdy shoes in remote or waterlogged areas. A course of medication can be taken for worm infestation, which normally does not recur.

Sexually Transmitted and Other Infectious Diseases

Awareness of sexually transmitted diseases such as HIV, which causes Acquired

Green coconut-water, good for soothing an upset stomach

Immune Deficiency Syndrome (AIDS), is high in India. However, screening at blood banks is still unreliable, and for blood transfusions it is best to contact the **Indian Red Cross Society** *(see p741)*. Hepatitis B is also transmitted through infected blood, sexual contact, unsterilized needles, tattoos and shaves from roadside barbers. However, it can be prevented with a vaccine. Using a condom is essential for protection against all sexually transmitted diseases.

General precautions to follow are: before an inoculation, buy a disposable syringe, or insist that a new syringe and needle is unwrapped in front of you. Never have shaves from roadside barbers and stay away from seedy-looking beauty parlours, as you can pick up infections during manicures and pedicures. Any procedure using needles, such as tattooing and ear-piercing, is best avoided in places where hygiene is dubious.

Vaccination against tetanus is essential when travelling. Tuberculosis (TB), though common in India, is not a great risk for visitors. Meningitis, spread through droplet infection, is a more real threat – it needs immediate medical attention. Symptoms include fever, stiff neck and headache.

Rabies

Animal bites, especially from dogs and monkeys, can cause rabies. Clean the bite with an antiseptic solution and seek medical help at once, as treatment involves a course of injections, even if you have been bitten by a pet dog. There is a vaccination that partially protects against rabies, but this is only advised if you are going to high-risk areas. You should only take this vaccine if your doctor advises it.

Insect-borne Diseases

Malaria is prevalent in most parts of India during the summer and monsoon (Jul–Sep). The parasite is carried by mosquitoes, and symptoms include shivering followed by high fever and sweating. Seek medical help immediately. You should take a preventive course of anti-malarial drugs before, during and after your trip. For information on medication, call a travel clinic or MASTA *(see p741)*.

Another serious mosquito-borne disease is dengue fever, with symptoms similar to malaria, including severe pain in the joints and muscles, and rashes. Seek medical treatment if you think you might be infected.

To guard against mosquito bites, use mosquito-repellent devices and a net over the bed while sleeping. If outdoors in the evenings, wear shoes and clothes that cover the arms and legs, and rub mosquito-repellent cream on exposed skin. As a rule, carry mosquito-repellent cream with you at all times.

Mosquito repellent coil and cream

Cuts and Bites

Insect bites are common, especially in areas prone to heavy rainfall, such as the coasts, the Nilgiri Hills, parts of Kerala and the northeastern states. To avoid insect and ant bites, it is best not to sleep on the ground. Ticks, lice and mites are another problem, since they are carriers of typhus and Lyme's disease. Use insect repellents, avoid staying in places with poor hygiene and, if bitten, apply antiseptic cream. An antihistamine is the best antidote if you get stung by a wasp or bee. Rainforests are usually infested with blood-sucking leeches that attach themselves to the skin. Never try and pull them off since their heads remain embedded in the skin. A very effective way of getting them to drop off is to sprinkle them with salt, or touch them with a lighted cigarette. Clean the bite and apply an antiseptic.

Snake bites are rare, but if bitten, tie a tight crêpe bandage or tourniquet above the bite to prevent the blood flowing. Keep the limb immobile, note the time of the bite, and seek immediate medical help. Scorpion stings can also be serious, and the victim can sometimes go into shock. The treatment is similar to that of snake bite. If you are stung by a jellyfish while swimming, vinegar or lemon juice, calamine lotion and antihistamines help reduce the pain and swelling. Clean the area with an antiseptic lotion.

Swine Flu

Swine flu is an infection caused by any one of several types of swine influenza virus, the most common one being H1N1. The virus is highly contagious. If there is an outbreak of swine flu, and you have flu-like symptoms, you may wish to consult a doctor.

Altitude Sickness

A lack of sufficient oxygen at altitudes higher than 2,500 m (8,202 ft) can cause Acute Mountain Sickness (AMS); symptoms are dizziness, severe headaches and loss of appetite. These often subside within a day or two, but if they persist, seek medical attention at once. Though some doctors recommend Acetaolamide (Diamox) and dexamethasone, they are controversial drugs and should not be used.

A few tips to avoid AMS are: ascend slowly; once above 3,000 m (9,842 ft), do not increase camping altitude by more than 300 m (984 ft) a day; drink plenty of fluids; and avoid alcohol and sedatives.

Banking and Currency

India provides a range of accessible banking facilities and money exchange services, with English speaking staff at the counters. These facilities are available in all the larger cities, at international airports, major banks and hotels, travel agencies and registered moneychangers. Touts might offer enticing exchange rates, but they are illegal operators and should be avoided. Traveller's cheques are the safest way to carry money, but always keep some cash for telephones, tips, transport and purchases, especially when travelling in smaller towns or off the beaten track, where credit cards and traveller's cheques are not always accepted.

Banks and Banking Hours

Most international banks now have branches in all the cities across the country. The Indian bank with the largest distribution network is the **State Bank of India**, though there are other major banks with a national presence. The services they offer include international money transfers.

Banking hours are between 9:30/10am–2pm (Mon–Fri), and 9:30/10am–noon (Sat). Arrive early to avoid the long queues. Banks are closed on regional and national holidays (see p39) and occasionally they shut down without any notice at all in response to public protests or strikes.

Changing Money

In India, banks offer the best exchange rates, though most good hotels also change money for resident guests. **VKC Credit & Forex Services Pvt Ltd** is a reliable foreign exchange broker, and there are numerous other brokers who also change money at the official rates for major international currencies. Rates of exchange are subject to fluctuation, so check any national daily newspaper for the current rate. The "blackmarket" in India, operating through literally thousands of touts, offers much better rates than the official ones, but it is safer to go to authorized dealers.

Traveller's Cheques

Traveller's cheques are convenient, safer to carry than large amounts of cash, and give better exchange rates than currency. All major brands of traveller's cheques are accepted in India, with **American Express** and **Thomas Cook** being the most widely used, and US dollars and pounds sterling the most widely exchanged currencies. Banks have the lowest surcharge and give the best value. They charge a small fee per cheque so using large denomination cheques is more economical. Traveller's cheques can be encashed easily in large cities and towns. Smaller towns, though not all of them, also have registered dealers. Keep a record of the serial numbers of cheques, as well as the proof of purchase slips, in case of loss or theft.

Also, be sure to keep records of encashment, as you will need these should you wish to reconvert rupees to other currencies when leaving the country.

DIRECTORY

State Bank of India

Chennai
Aparna Complex,
16 College Lane,
Nungambakkam.
Tel (044) 2825 7404.

Delhi
11 Sansad Marg.
Tel (011) 2340 7777.

Kolkata
Middleton Row.
Tel (033) 2229 5811.

Mumbai
State Bank Bhavan,
Madame Cama Rd.
Tel (022) 2202 2426.

ICICI Bank

Chennai
New No 298, Anna Salai.
Tel (044) 3366 7777.

Delhi
1st Floor, 9-A, Phelps Bldg,
Connaught Pl, New Delhi.
Tel (011) 4171 8000.

Kolkata
Rishikesh, 1/1, Ashutosh
Chowdhury Avenue,
Ballygunge.
Tel (033) 2283 0313.

Mumbai
9th Floor, South Towers,
ICICI Towers, Bandra Kurla
Complex, Bandra (E).
Tel (022) 2653 7753.

HSBC

Chennai
30 Rajaji Salai.
Tel (044) 2526 9696.

Delhi
25, Birla Towers, Kasturba
Gandhi Marg.
Tel (011) 5101 2619.

Kolkata
31 Shakespeare Sarani.
Tel (033) 2289 3333.

Mumbai
Mahatma Gandhi Rd, Fort.
Tel (022) 2268 5555.

Bureaux de Changes

American Express
Barakhamba Rd, Delhi.
Tel (011) 4151 1905.
Oriental Bldg, 364 Dadabhai
Naoroji Rd, Mumbai.
Tel (022) 2285 0016. BBD
Bagh, Kolkata G.P.O, Kolkata.
Tel (033) 2248 5426.
187 Anna Salai, Chennai.
Tel (044) 2841 6387.

Thomas Cook
C–33 Connaught Pl, New
Delhi. Tel (011) 6627 1923.
Dr Dadabhai Naoroji Rd,
Fort, Mumbai.

Tel (022) 6160 3333.
19B Shakespeare Sarani,
1st Floor, Kolkata.
Tel (033) 6652 6231.
G-4, Eldorado Bldg
No 112, Nungambakkam
High Road, Chennai.
Tel (044) 6454 9212.

VKC Credit & Forex Services Pvt Ltd
Flat No. 309, 3rd Floor,
Mercantile House, No. 15,
Kasturba Gandhi Marg,
Delhi. Tel (011) 3240 7691.
No. 2, First Floor, Rahimtoola
House, 7 Homji St, Mumbai.
Tel (022) 6514 5350.
Landmark, 228A, AIC Bose
Road, 2nd floor, Room No.
28, Minto Park, Kolkata.
Tel (033) 2282 4377.
Jeyamkonder Apts, Unit
No. 3A, 2nd floor, No.
40/12, Murray's Gate Rd,
Alwarpet, Chennai.
Tel (044) 4314 4106.

Debit and Credit Cards

Debit and Credit cards are now widely accepted in most big hotels, restaurants and department stores. The most common are VISA, MasterCard, Diner's Club and American Express. Air and rail tickets can also be paid for by debit and credit card, and cash advances can be made at the parent bank. For example, ICICI account holders can directly access their account with their ICICI card. However, many smaller establishments, even in the bigger cities, only accept cash. Debit and Credit card-related fraud is on the increase, so keep your cards safe, and insist that receipt vouchers are made out in front of you. If your debit or credit card gets stolen or lost, contact your bank to cancel the card.

ATM Services

Most foreign, and many Indian, banks in large cities have 24-hour ATMs (automatic teller machines). Instructions are displayed in English, and cash is dispensed in rupees. Check with your bank at home which Indian banks will accept your ATM card, as not all machines are compatible. Some ATMs will dispense cash against credit cards. Cards with a PLUS or CIRRUS symbol are accepted at the following ATMs: Citibank, Standard Chartered, and Hong Kong and Shanghai Bank (HSBC).

Currency

The Indian rupee (₹) is divided into 100 paisas. The most commonly used coins are 50 paisa, 1, 2, and 5 rupee coins. Currency notes are available in denominations of ₹5, 10, 20, 50, 100, 500 and 1,000. Be careful not to mix up the 100 and 500 rupee notes as they look very similar. Beware of accepting torn or damaged notes, as shops and even banks are often reluctant to accept or exchange them. Banks often give notes stapled together in large packs. Ask them to remove the staples for you as you will find it difficult to do it yourself without tearing the notes. Foreign nationals are not permitted to bring or take Indian currency into or out of the country.

Bank Notes
All currency is minted by the Reserve Bank of India. The notes have either Mahatma Gandhi or the Ashoka lion symbol on one side.

10-rupee note

20-rupee note

50-rupee note

100-rupee note

500-rupee note

1,000-rupee note

Coins
Visitors should always keep some loose change handy. Some older variations of these silver coins are still in circulation.

1 rupee   ₹2   ₹5   ₹10

Communications

The Indian postal system is fairly efficient, with a wide variety of options, from registered post to reliable courier services, offered by post offices countrywide. Telecommunications systems are sophisticated even in smaller towns: all main hotels have business centres, and most markets have shops or booths from where international calls can be made, e-mails sent and the Internet accessed. A range of English-language newspapers and magazines are available, and foreign newspapers and magazines are sold in bookshops, particularly in the main cities.

Postage stamps in 5-rupee denomination

International and Local Telephone Calls

All major hotels offer subscriber trunk dialling (STD) for calls within India, and international subscriber dialling (ISD) for international calls. Trunk calls can also be booked from private telephones. Calls made from STD/ISD booths, identified by their yellow signage, are much cheaper than at hotels. Rates are fixed for international calls, but STD rates depend on the distance of the city called and the time of day when the call is made. Calls are cheapest between 11pm and 6am. Medium rate is between 8pm and 11pm. Local calls made from public booths take 1 rupee coins for every three minutes.

Bharat Sanchar Nigam Ltd (BSNL) offers a pre-paid card for local, STD and ISD calls. It can be used from all BSNL landlines and mobile phones. India Telephone cards are available from BSNL customer service centres and franchises throughout the country. They come in denominations of ₹50, ₹100, ₹200, ₹500, ₹1,000, ₹2,000 and ₹5,000.

Mobile Phone Rentals

Mobile phones can easily be bought from service counters at international airports, as well as at registered offices located in most large cities. In Delhi and Mumbai, Airtel and Vodafone are the main service networks, while in Kolkata, the networks are

provided by BSNL, Airtel, Idea and Vodafone. Chennai has RPG Cellular and Skycell. Hire charges range between ₹100 and ₹300 per day inclusive of a SIM card (rates are higher for roaming cards) and a handset. If hiring a handset, you will pay a fairly sizeable deposit, which is refundable.

Fax, E-mail and Internet Facilities

Fax and telegraph services are available at main post offices and also at local STD/ISD booths which, though often more accessible, have higher charges. The business centres of all large hotels also have centralized telecommunication services, which only residents can use.

The Internet is widely used in India. Most large hotels offer net access to guests in their business centres, while privately operated Internet cafés with the latest facilities can be found in markets and shopping areas in most large cities. Even smaller towns usually have enterprising hole-in-the-wall Internet outlets. Some main post offices and

Internet café, Bengaluru

many STD/ISD phone booths also offer Internet facilities. All outlets have fixed hourly or half-hourly rates.

Postal Services

There are many different services offered by India Post – general or registered mail, parcel post, poste restante, and a special courier service known as EMS-Speed Post.

Letterboxes are colour coded: local letters, green; metropolitan and other cities, as well as international mail, red; and Quick Mail Service (QMS) yellow. Post offices are open Monday to Friday between 10am and 5pm, and on Saturdays until noon. Some services, such as registered mail, close earlier.

Letters sent poste restante are held at the **General Post Office** for up to one month, and you will need some form of identification – preferably your passport – to retrieve your mail. The same service is also provided by **Foreign Post Offices** in the four main cities, as well as American Express in most major cities. Envelopes should be addressed with the surname underlined and in capitals, c/o Poste Restante, followed by the name and address of the post office. Parcels sent overseas cannot exceed 20 kg (44 pounds). Check the details at the post office. Book Post is a cheaper option for documents, books and printed material. The maximum weight is 5 kg (11 pounds). Some hotels sell stamps and may offer to post letters and parcels. Always be sure to stick stamps and post postcards and letters yourself.

Addresses

In India, addresses always begin with the house number, followed by the name of the street, and finally the city and its pin code. The newer residential localities are divided into blocks, and the block number usually appears with the house number. Therefore, B4/88 Safdarjung Enclave would be: house number 88 in the B4 block of Safdarjung Enclave Colony. Each state and city has its own variations, which can be confusing and hard to decipher, especially if trying to locate a house number. Often there may not even be a road sign. If you are lost, a passerby will always help, but the best bet is to get directions from a taxi or rickshaw driver.

Courier Services

Courier services are available across the country, but even in rural and remote areas. While it is better to ship larger items such as furniture by regular land, sea or air cargo, letters, documents or smaller parcels are best sent through a courier agency, even though

it may be more expensive. **United Parcel Service (UPS)**, **Federal Express TNT** and **DHL Worldwide Express** are international courier agencies, with a widespread network all over India and the world. Shops offer to send purchases by courier, but except for the government emporia and well-known establishments, you will be doing so at your own risk.

Newspapers and Magazines

India's leading national English language newspapers include *The Times of India*, *Hindustan Times*, *The Indian Express*, *The Hindu* and *The Asian Age*. In the east, *The Statesman* and *The Telegraph* are widely read. There are other regional news-papers as well that provide local news. Many international newspapers, such as the *International Herald Tribune* and the *Financial Times,* are available alongside Indian weekly news magazines, such as *India Today* and *Outlook*. *Time* and *Newsweek* are available in large cities. For local news and cultural events, the city sections of the newspapers give reasonable coverage.

A typical post box

Television and Radio

The introduction of Direct to Home (DTH) in India has made television watching a whole new experience, with a plethora of channels. The prime DTH operators are Tata

Sky, Dish TV and Big TV. Cable TV is also available everywhere, for international channels, such as the BBC World Service, Discovery, CNN, National Geographic and the Hong Kong-based Star network. Star Sports and ESPN are exclusive sports channels, and Channel V and MTV are the main music channels. Most Indian TV channels show popular Hindi films or song-and-dance sequences; there are many regional Indian-language channels as well.

India also has a wide radio network, with programmes in English and local languages. It is still the best form of communication, especially in the rural areas. Radio and TV listings and reviews can be found in all major daily newspapers.

Useful Dialling Codes and Numbers

- To make an inter-city call, dial the STD code of that city and the local number. For Delhi, dial 011; Mumbai, 022; Kolkata, 033; Chennai, 044.
- To make an international call (ISD), dial 00, the country code, area code and the local number.

- Country codes: UK 44; France 33; USA & Canada 1; Australia 61; Ireland 353; New Zealand 64; South Africa 27; Japan 81.
- Dial 180 to book a trunk call in the country, and 186 to book an international call.
- Dial 197 to obtain a phone number in Delhi, Mumbai, Kolkata and Chennai.

TRAVEL INFORMATION

Most international visitors to India arrive by air, though road and ferry links also connect India and her neighbours, such as Pakistan, Bangladesh, Nepal and Sri Lanka. Travelling within the country is possible by air, train, road and, in some places, either ferry or boat. Even remote regions are accessible. However, whatever your mode of transport, you should be prepared for delays and unexpected detours that may test your patience. The state-run Indian Airlines has the widest network of air routes. Private airlines, such as Kingfisher, Indigo and Jet Airways, also cover a number of cities and offer excellent services. Indian Railways is one of the world's largest networks, and travelling first class is a good way to see the country. The long- distance air-conditioned luxury coach is another option.

Arriving by Air

All major international airlines fly to India, usually as stop-overs on air routes between the East and West. Air India is India's international carrier. North American and European airlines such as British Airways, Lufthansa, KLM/Northwest, Air France and Swiss have regular flights to either some or all of India's four major cities – Delhi, Mumbai, Chennai and Kolkata. There are also numerous connections to the Far East and Australia, offered by Thai Airways, Singapore Airlines, Malaysian Airlines, Japan Airlines, and Cathay Pacific. Flights to destinations in the Gulf and Central Asia are offered by Emirates, Air Lanka and Gulf Air.

Virgin Atlantic currently flies to Delhi and Mumbai, though it plans to introduce flights to other Indian cities soon. Delta, South African Airways and Kenya Airlines fly only to Mumbai. Lufthansa flies to Bengaluru, Mumbai, Delhi and other destinations, while Emirates flies to Hyderabad, Mumbai, Delhi and Kolkata, among others; and Malaysian Airlines serves Hyderabad and Bengaluru. In addition, Air Lanka flies to Tiruchirapalli and Thiruvanathapuram.

International Flights and Airports

India's four main international airports are at Delhi, Mumbai, Kolkata and Chennai. Other international airports offering flights to select destinations are at Hyderabad (Kuwait, Muscat, Sharjah and Kuala Lumpur), Bengaluru (Muscat, Sharjah, Singapore, Kuala Lumpur, London, Frankfurt and a few flights via Mumbai to Paris, the Gulf and New York), Goa (UK and Germany), Ahmedabad (UK and the US), Kochi and Thiruvananthapuram (the Gulf, Singapore, Sri Lanka and the Maldives). A limited number of international flights also operate from Kozhikode, Amritsar, Varanasi, Lucknow, Guwahati, Tiruchirapalli, Jaipur and Agra. These are designated "customs airports" and permit landing of charter planes as well as certain international flights.

Air Fares

Air fares vary according to the airline and the season. It is best to book tickets well in advance of the peak season (Oct–Mar). At this time of year, flights to India are overbooked, as Indian families settled abroad and students at universities abroad make their annual visit home.

On Arrival

Before landing, visitors must fill in a disembarkation form that has to be submitted along with their passport at the immigration counter.

International airports offer a range of facilities that include currency exchange counters, left-luggage services, air-conditioned visitors' lounges, duty-free shops, restaurants, business centres and rest rooms with access for the disabled. In addition, there are counters for pre-paid taxis, car rentals and mobile phone rentals. Travel agencies located within the arrival area can help with tour itineraries, hotel reservations and onward bookings. There is also a Tourism Department information counter.

Customs

The green channel is for those who do not have dutiable goods as listed in the Immigration Certificate. The Red Channel is for passengers with any goods that are liable to customs duty, including money in excess of US$2,500.

Terminal 3 at Indira Gandhi International Airport, Delhi

Getting from the Airport

Coaches connect the airport with the city for a fee. Pre-paid taxis with fixed rates can be booked from counters both inside and outside the arrivals area. Metered auto-rickshaws are also available. Make sure you agree on the fare before taking one, and ask an airport policeman to note down its licence plate number. If you have booked accommodation, check if your hotel offers a free pick-up service.

Airport Transfers

Visitors who are travelling onwards to other Indian cities will need to transfer to domestic terminals. Be sure to allow enough time to get between the two terminals. At all major aiports there is a free transit service from one terminal to the other. Delhi's Indira Gandhi (IG) International Airport has three terminals: Terminal 1 for domestic flights, Terminal 2 for international flights and Terminal 3 for both domestic and international flights. In Mumbai, the international terminal at Chhatrapati Shivaji is 4 km (2.5 miles) from the domestic terminal. Kolkata's Netaji Subhash Chandra Bose

DL1Y 5732

Yellow licence plate of a taxi

International Airport has both the international and domestic terminals in the same building. Chennai's Aringar Anna International Airport is next door to the Kamaraj Domestic Airport. In Thiruvananthapuram, both domestic and international flights operate from the same building.

Check-in

For international flights, check-in is usually three hours ahead of departure. Tele-check-in is allowed by some airlines for business and first-class passengers. Most airlines allow an economy-class passenger 15 kg (33 pounds) in the hold and one item of hand baggage. Make sure that your luggage is within the weight limit set by your airline, as excess baggage charges can be very high.

Departure Tax

A foreign travel tax of ₹500–750 (US$10–15) is charged when leaving India, unless already included in your ticket. Only ₹150 (US$3) needs to be paid if travelling to neighbouring countries, such as Nepal, Pakistan or Sri Lanka.

DIRECTORY

Airline Offices

Air France
Tel (0124) 272 0272, Gurgaon, Delhi.

Air India
Tel (011) 2462 2220, Delhi.
Tel (022) 2831 8056, Mumbai.
Tel (033) 2211 0730, Kolkata.
Tel (044) 2345 3366, Chennai.

British Airways
Tel (124) 2540543, Gurgaon.
Tel (044) 2256 0952, Chennai.
W britishairways.com

Cathay Pacific
Tel (011) 4354 4777, Delhi.
Tel (022) 6685 9016, Mumbai.
Tel (044) 4298 8400, Chennai.
W cathaypacific.com

KLM/Northwest Airline
Tel (0124) 272 0273, Gurgaon, Delhi.

Lufthansa
Tel (0124) 488 8999, Gurgaon, Delhi.
Tel 1800 102 5838, Mumbai.
Tel (044) 2256 9393, Chennai.
Tel (080) 6678 4050, Bengaluru.

Thai Airways
Tel (011) 4149 7777, Delhi.
Tel (033) 2283 8865, Kolkata.
Tel (022) 6637 3777, Mumbai.
Tel (044) 4206 3311, Chennai.
W thaiairways.com

Virgin Atlantic
Tel 1800 102 3000.
Tel (011) 2565 5747, Delhi.
W virgin-atlantic.com

Airport	Information	Distance to City Centre	Average Journey Time
Delhi: IG International (Terminal II)	(0124) 337 6000	20 km (12 miles)	Road: 45–60 minutes
Mumbai: Chhatrapati Shivaji International Airport	(022) 6685 1010	30 km (19 miles)	Road: 50 minutes
Kolkata: Netaji Subhash Chandra Bose International	(033) 2511 8787	20 km (12 miles)	Road: 30–60 minutes
Chennai: Aringar Anna International	(044) 2256 0551	16 km (10 miles)	Road: 30 minutes
Thiruvananthapuram: International Airport	(0471) 250 1591	6 km (4 miles)	Road: 20 minutes
Bengaluru: International Airport	(080) 6678 2425	40 km (25 miles)	Road: 45–60 minutes
Goa: Dabolim International Airport	(0832) 540 806	29 km (18 miles)	Road: 50 minutes
Kochi: Kochi International Airport	(0484) 261 0115	30 km (19 miles)	Road: 45–60 minutes

Domestic Air Travel

Although more expensive than travelling by train, air travel in India is the most comfortable and convenient mode of travel, especially considering the huge distances between the major cities. There are as many as 115 domestic airports in India, many of which offer good services in terms of both technology and customer facilities. The main cities of Chennai, Delhi, Kolkata and Mumbai are very well connected to all domestic airports within the country. The national carrier is the government-run Air India, offers the widest choice of routes and the most frequent services. If you have booked internal flights before leaving for India, it is highly recommended to reconfirm on arrival. Erratic flight timetables, flight cancellations and delays due to bad weather conditions in winter (Dec–Jan) are common, so remember to reconfirm not just your ticket but the flight timing as well.

Domestic Airlines

The national carrier **Indian Airlines** offers the largest number of routes and the most frequent connections across the country. Three major private airlines – **Jet Airways**, **Indigo** and **Spicejet Airlines** – also connect a number of cities. Indigo offers domestic flights on the Delhi–Mumbai, Delhi–Kolkata, Mumbai–Kolkata and Mumbai–Chennai routes. A few regional airlines such asJagson Airlines and Gujarat Airways with limited operations within India, fly short feeder routes. Baggage allowance is 15 kg (33 pounds) for business class and 20 kg (44 pounds) for economy class.

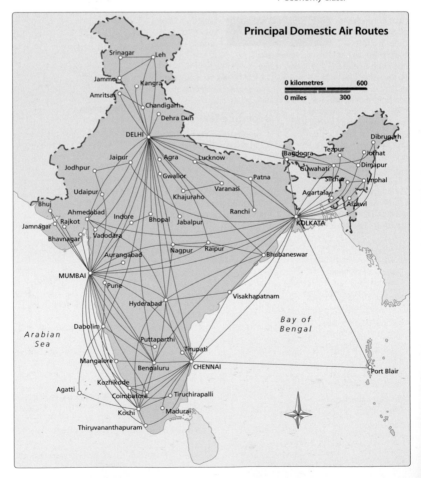

Principal Domestic Air Routes

0 kilometres 600
0 miles 300

Srinagar
Leh
Jammu
Kangra
Amritsar
Chandigarh
Dehra Dun
DELHI
Dibrugarh
Jaipur
Agra
Lucknow
Bagdogra
Tezpur
Jorhat
Jodhpur
Dimapur
Gwalior
Suwahati
Patna
Silchar
Imphal
Udaipur
Varanasi
Agartala
Khajuraho
Aizawl
Bhuj
Ahmedabad
Indore
Bhopal
Jabalpur
Ranchi
KOLKATA
Jamnagar
Rajkot
Vadodara
Bhavnagar
Aurangabad
Nagpur
Raipur
Bhubaneswar
MUMBAI
Pune
Hyderabad
Visakhapatnam
Dabolim
Bay of Bengal
Arabian Sea
Puttaparthi
Mangalore
Tirupati
Bengaluru
CHENNAI
Port Blair
Agatti
Kozhikode
Coimbatore
Tiruchirapalli
Kochi
Madurai
Thiruvananthapuram

Domestic Airports

Airports at the four main cities – Delhi, Mumbai, Kolkata and Chennai – and cities such as Agra, Bhubaneswar, Kochi, Hyderabad, and Bengaluru have modern terminal buildings with up-to-date facilities. However, smaller towns, such as Dehra Dun, have tiny airports with almost no facilities.

Getting to and from the Airport

The distance from airports to city centres varies, so it is useful to check the travel time beforehand. Also always allow time for unforeseen delays en route. Airport coaches run regularly for a fee. Pre-paid taxis with fixed rates can usually be booked from counters both inside and outside the arrivals area. Metered auto-rickshaws are also available. Make sure the meter is working, or agree on a fixed amount before taking one. If you are booking accommodation, check if your hotel offers a free pick-up service.

Check-in

For most domestic flights, the check-in time is normally 2 hours before departure. If travelling to politically sensitive places such as Kashmir, Jammu, Leh and some of the northeastern states, security checks are more stringent and can require up to an extra half hour. Make sure all bags are tagged, and do not carry batteries, lighters or any sharp objects, not even scissors, nail files or tweezers. As part of the security measures on some routes, you may be asked to identify your baggage on the tarmac, before boarding the flight.

Reservations

All domestic airlines have their own booking offices in the city, as well as a reservation counter at the airport (usually only in larger towns and cities). Tickets can also be booked through travel agents *(see p735)*. However, the easiest way to book tickets is online at travel websites such as www.makemytrip.com and www.yatra.com. All airlines have computerized booking and flight information facilities all over the country, even in smaller towns. Tickets can be paid for in US dollars or sterling, as well as in rupees. Payment can also be made by credit card. There are special fares for infants and children, and students carrying an international student ID card get a 25 per cent discount; Indian nationals aged 65 and above get a 50 per cent senior citizens discount, subject to identity and age proof. All ticket cancellations must be done at least two hours before your flight. Some airlines will waive a cancellation charge if given sufficient notice. If you fail to do so, you may lose the full value of the ticket. If flights are cancelled or delayed, you can claim a refund.

The Maharaja, mascot of Air India

Travel Packages

Air India offers two travel packages if the payment is in US dollars. The "Discover India Fare" for 15 or 21 days is about US$500–750, and allows unlimited travel with certain route restrictions. The "India Wonder Fare" for about US$300 is for seven days of travel in one region. This package does not include the Andaman Islands. Private airlines, such as Jet Airways, Indigo and Spicejet, also offer special packages for foreign nationals. The "Visit India" offer by Jet Airways ranges from US$550–800 for economy class travel over a period of 15–20 days. Airlines have started offering discounts on tickets, and value add-ons such as free stays and gourmet dining to beat the competition. It is therefore worth doing a little research before purchasing your ticket.

Aircraft lined up at Indira Gandhi International Airport

Travelling by Train

For most visitors, train journeys add a fascinating new dimension to their experience of India – there are few better ways of getting to know the people and see the countryside. The Indian Railways network is the fourth largest in the world, with tracks running over 63,940 km (39,730 miles) and connecting 7,150 stations. Over 14,000 trains run daily, transporting an average of 13 million people. Trains are always crowded, so try to book your tickets in advance. There are computerized ticket counters at railway stations, and most travel agents can also get tickets for you.

The Railway Network

The Indian rail network, established in 1853, runs the length and breadth of the country. The network is divided by region, and there are 16 zonal divisions. Delhi is served by Northern Railways, Mumbai by both Central and Western Railways, Kolkata by Eastern Railways and Chennai by Southern Railways. All four cities have either two or three main train stations, so it is important to confirm from which station your train is leaving. Indian Railways employ over 1.6 million people, making them the world's largest single employer.

Trains and Timetables

Of the three kinds of trains (passenger, express and mail), it is best to take the air-conditioned express trains, as they have fewer stops and offer better facilities and services. They provide fast and punctual connections to some of India's most important cities. The Rajdhani Express links the capital, Delhi, to most of the large cities such as Mumbai, Kolkata, Chennai, Thiruvan-anthapuram and others. The superfast inter-city train, the Shatabdi Express, connects main cities with many well-known tourist destinations, with connections such as Chennai–Bengaluru, Delhi– Dehra Dun and Delhi–Agra. The Konkan Railway *(see p441)*, on the western coast, offers speedy connections to Maharashtra, Goa, Karnataka and Kerala.

Each train is known by its name and number. When consulting the information board, do check both, since there may be more than one "Shatabdi" for example. Trains have first and second class chair-cars, and two- and three-tiered sleeper coaches. If these are air conditioned, the fares increase. Sleeper coaches have berths that fold back during the daytime to provide seating. Fares for express trains such as the Shatabdi or Rajdhani include meals and mineral water, and the Rajdhani also provides its overnight passengers with bedding. Food items, such as biscuits, and reading material are sold by vendors en route. Toilets are of the Indian and Western style. Carry your own toilet paper, soap and towel.

Train times are subject to change. The printed timetable is available in most station bookshops, or check the very useful official websites: www.indianrail.gov.in and www.irctc.co.in

Train Tickets, Fares and Reservations

It is important to make train bookings well in advance for a confirmed reservation. Railway stations now have computerized ticket counters, otherwise the hotel travel counter or a travel agent can arrange them for a fee. Never buy tickets from touts, as this is both illegal and unreliable.

Tickets can be booked up to six months in advance, and reservation fees are nominal. You will be asked for your age and gender and these details will appear on your ticket, along with the coach and seat number. Once at the station, find your coach and check for your name and seat number, which are usually posted on a list outside the coach. If wait listed, arrive at the station early to take advantage of any last-minute cancellations. The station-master will help.

If reserved tickets are unavailable, you can get an RAC (Reservation Against Cancellation) ticket. This allows you to board the train and get seating space. You may eventually be given a berth, but there is no guarantee. Reserved tickets can be cancelled, for a fee. If cancellation is more than a day in advance, a nominal fee is charged. Up to 4 hours before train departure, the charge is 25 per cent of the fare, and less than that, you forfeit 50 per cent of the fare.

Stations at Delhi, Mumbai, Kolkata and Chennai as well as other major cities have special booking counters for foreigners, called "Tourist Bureaus", within

Churchgate Station, Mumbai, during rush hour

the main booking offices. These provide information regarding reservations, itinerary and other inquiries. Payments may be made in US dollars or pounds sterling, or the rupee equivalent, and you must show your passport. You get priority reservation and are exempted from reservation fees. At New Delhi Railway Station, the International Tourist Bureau is located on the first floor of the main hall.

Indrail Pass

To travel extensively around India, the Indrail Pass is a convenient option. It offers unlimited travel across the country, and is available for second or first class and for different periods (half-day, 2 days, 4 days and anywhere between 7 and 90 days). It can be bought in India or abroad, but must be paid for in foreign currency. Indrail Passes are available from sales agents abroad, as well as overseas offices of Indian Airlines and Air India. They are also available at tourist counters and Tourist Bureaus at major railway stations, and from travel agents in Delhi, Mumbai, Kolkata and Chennai. Unless you do a lot of travelling, the pass may work out more expensive than buying individual tickets. Even with a pass you will still need to reserve your seat.

Services

At the station, look for the licensed porters or coolies who wear a red shirt and an armband with a metal tag bearing a licence number on it. Porters are always well-informed about delays and platform changes which may not be announced on the board. Note your porter's number because you could lose sight of him in the crowds. His tariff varies according to weight, although ₹40–50 per item is acceptable. Indian stations are crowded and confusing. Keep your cool and keep an eye out for pickpockets who take advantage of the chaos. Railway waiting rooms (especially first class ones) are good places to spend the night if you are stranded. You need a valid ticket or Indrail Pass to use this facility. There are also waiting rooms only for women travellers. Left luggage facilities, called cloakrooms, are offered at most stations. Station canteens are reasonably clean and provide mineral water and hygienically packed meals.

Official porter in red jacket

DIRECTORY

Railway Enquiries

w indianrail.gov.in
w irctc.co.in
Chennai
Tel (044) 139 or
(044) 253 000 000.
Delhi
Tel (011) 139 or (011) 3934 0000.
Kolkata
Tel (033) 139.
Mumbai
Tel (022) 139.

Booking Centres for Special Trains

Blue Mountain Railway
Chennai Central Railway,
Chennai. Tel (044) 2535 3816.
Darjeeling Himalayan Railway
West Bengal Tourist Centre,
Baba Kharak Singh Marg, Delhi.
Tel (011) 2374 2840.
Fairy Queen
Rail Museum, Delhi.
Tel (011) 2688 1816.
Kalka–Shimla Railways
Divisional Railway, Ambala.
Matheran Hill Railway
Govt of India Tourist Office,
123 M Karve Rd, Mumbai.
Tel (022) 2203 3144.
Palace On Wheels
Bikaner House, Delhi.
Tel (011) 2338 1884
Royal Rajasthan on Wheels
Tel (011) 2338 3037.
w rtdc.in

Special Trains

You can travel in style on board some of India's luxury trains, particularly the **Palace on Wheels** and the **Royal Rajasthan on Wheels**. Both operate week-long tours from September to April. The former covers mainly Rajasthan, and includes Jaipur, Udaipur, Jaisalmer and Agra. The latter goes through Rajasthan to Ahmedabad in Gujarat. The **Fairy Queen**, a 150-year-old restored steam engine, is the oldest in the world, featuring in the *Guinness Book of Records*. It runs from Delhi to Alwar between October and February. India's quaint "toy trains", connecting numerous hill stations with tracks laid across precariously steep slopes, include the World Heritage **Darjeeling Himalayan Railway** *(see p298)*, which goes from New Jalpaiguri to Darjeeling. The Kangra Valley Railway connects Pathankot and Jogindernagar *(see p124)*, while another toy train, the **Matheran Hill Railway**, runs from Neral Junction to Matheran *(see p476)*. The luxurious **Blue Mountain Railway**, built in 1898, offers spectacular views of the Nilgiri Hills, up to Ooty *(see p609)*, and **Kalka–Shimla Railways** runs trips on three deluxe rail motor cars.

Royal service in the Palace on Wheels

Travel by Road

India has an extensive network of major and minor roads, as well as a number of well-maintained national highways, linking all the major cities. Driving is on the left, with right-hand drive cars. Indian traffic, particularly in the cities, is very chaotic, so visitors are strongly advised to hire a driver along with a car, rather than trying to negotiate the roads themselves. A number of international car rental companies, hotels and taxi stands provide excellent car rental services. In case of breakdowns, the remarkably ingenious roadside mechanics can solve most problems.

Driving Licences

It is necessary to have an international driving licence to drive in India. If not, the **Automobile Association of India (AAI)** has several branches across the country that will issue a temporary license, provided you have a passport and an ordinary driving licence. This may take a day or two. You must be over 25 years old, and there is a refundable insurance deposit of ₹10,000. Note that you may be asked to take a driving test.

Roads

India has a network of over 3,000,000 km (1,860,000 miles) of roads. The primary arterial roads, the national highways, cover 79,243 km (49,239 miles) and carry 45 per cent of the country's total traffic. State highways run a total length of 1,31,899 km (81, 958 miles). The National Highway Authority of India is in the process of improving links between the country's four major cities: Delhi, Mumbai, Chennai and Kolkata.

The countryside is crisscrossed with numerous major and minor roads of very variable quality. Some village roads are little more than dirt tracks riddled with potholes, so be prepared for a dusty, bumpy ride.

Most highways and major roads are well-equipped with tourist facilities such as motels, petrol pumps and STD/ISD telephone booths. Midway refreshment points and *dhabas* (see p183) are well-marked with hoardings, and provide clean food as well as toilets.

Car Rentals

Several reputed car rental companies – such as **Avis**, **Budget** and **Autoriders International Limited** – operate in India. They offer both chauffeur-driven and self-driven cars, which can be hired at travel desks in larger hotels, tourist offices, travel agencies or directly from the companies themselves. Most of them operate through collaborations with local companies. Avis is in partnership with the Oberoi Group while Budget operates through Sapna Travel Agency. Autoriders International Limited, a reliable Indian company, was earlier a partner of Hertz. Local hire services and private taxis are also available in cities from taxi stands and agencies. These can usually be arranged by your hotel or through a reliable local travel agent (see p735).

A car-rental booth operated by Budget in Delhi

Hiring a Chauffeur-Driven Car

Indian road and traffic conditions can be a trial for anyone unused to these conditions. Hiring a driver is much the safest option, and not all that expensive. All taxis as well as agency-hired cars are distinguished by their yellow number plates with black lettering. Most taxi stands also have private cars for hire, which are usually white with yellow number plates. All car rental companies with "All India Tourist Permits" have licenses for interstate travel.

All drivers are familiar with Indian traffic rules, but insist on getting a driver who knows the area that you plan to visit. Also, do test both the driver and the car before embarking on a long journey.

Chauffeur-driven cars for long-distance travel usually charge per kilometre, with a minimum of 250 km (155 miles) per day, plus additional charges per extra kilometre. If you are travelling only one way, additional charges will be levied for the return journey on the assumption that the car will return empty. Costs are also dependent on the car model and the region of hire, with air-conditioned cars being the most expensive. For travelling outside the state or city boundaries, extra charges as well as interstate taxes are added. If the driver has to stay overnight, you will have to pay for his board and lodging, so it is best to negotiate a flat rate in advance. Car hire is more expensive in hill regions.

In certain areas, shared taxis are available for long journeys, which are cheaper. Certain companies require foreign nationals to pay in foreign currency, though most accept payment in rupees as well.

Fuel

Highways and main roads have well-maintained filling stations (or petrol pumps as they are called) at regular intervals, usually closer to towns. Many

A typical petrol station on the side of a Delhi highway

pumps in cities as well as on highways are open 24 hours, and carry both leaded and unleaded petrol, as well as diesel, which is cheaper. Most cars run on petrol, though some of the newer models also use diesel, as do most taxis. Unleaded petrol is not available everywhere, especially in remote areas, so ensure that your fuel tank is full when visiting these areas. Many petrol pumps in the main cities are now equipped with utility stores where mineral water, soft drinks, magazines and snacks are sold. Often they also have telephone booths and toilets.

Since 2001, most taxis, auto-rickshaws and buses in Delhi and Mumbai are being run on CNG (Compressed Natural Gas), in an effort to tackle the severe air pollution caused by vehicular emissions.

Maps and Road Signs

The Automobile Association of India, the Survey of India and the State Tourism offices provide good maps, brochures and information on all cities and regions in India. However, the placement of road signs is often erratic, and at times they are in the regional language rather than English. It is fine to stop and ask for directions, repeatedly if necessary – people are always happy to help.

Rules of the Road

If you plan to drive in India, you need to ensure that you are well accustomed to the chaotic traffic conditions. Though there are established traffic rules, such as lane driving and discreet use of high-beam lights, more often than not these are not followed. Vehicles drive on the left-hand side of the road, but often, you will find a stray car – or cow, for that matter – coming at you on the wrong side of the road.

On the highways, beware of trucks, who often use muscle power to force you off the road while overtaking. As a rule, stay clear of buses and trucks.

Few drivers adhere to the rules for overtaking, which is meant to be from the right. Many vehicles often overtake from the left, with no prior warning. Avoid night driving on highways unless absolutely necessary, as a lot of heavy traffic (especially trucks) use them then. Also, never offer lifts to strangers, as this could prove to be very dangerous. It is wise to make liberal use of your horn. If you are unlucky enough to be caught speeding, or jumping a red light, a fine is payable on the spot.

In cities, ensure that your car is parked only in an authorized parking area, otherwise it may be towed away to the nearest police station, and released only on the payment of a heavy fine. Parking attendants should hand you a parking slip, with the parking charges printed on it. Charges are usually between ₹20 and ₹50.

Travelling by Bus, Coach and Ferry

India has an extensive bus and coach network, offering excellent connect- ions to most cities as well as to the remotest parts of the country. Buses refer to the ordinary transport corporation-run vehicles, which are cheaper and ply interstate or within cities. Coaches are usually much more comfortable, with air conditioning. These are often hired out for guided tours and also ply between cities. The advantage of travelling by bus or coach rather than by train is that you have a wider choice of timings, stops and itineraries. A busy network of passenger ferries serve places along India's east and west coasts, and luxury cruises link the mainland to the Lakshadweep Islands as well as to the Andamans.

State Transport Corporation-run Buses

The various state transport departments in India run extensive interstate bus services. The Interstate Bus Terminus (ISBT) in Delhi is the main point of departure for Punjab, Haryana, Himachal Pradesh, Uttar Pradesh and Rajasthan. Buses for Agra leave from Sarai Kale Khan, near Nizamuddin railway station. Mumbai's Central Bus Stand provides information on the Maharashtra Road Transport Corporation that runs services to all major cities within the state, as well as to Goa, Ahmedabad, Vadodara, Mangalore, Indore and Hyderabad. Kolkata too has an extensive network throughout West Bengal and the neighbouring states of Bihar, Odisha and Sikkim. Guwahati is the main entrance point for visitors to the northeastern states. The Assam State Transport Corporation runs buses within the city and to the neighbouring states. The Paltan Bazaar Bus Stand provides the best information on these services.

Computerized advance bookings can be made at the **Government of India Tourism Offices** in the four metropolitan cities.

Most interstate bus terminals are chaotic places, so do arrive early to book tickets. Then check at the enquiry counter to find the stand from where your bus will depart. Finally, be prepared for a lot of jostling as passengers tend to push to get the best seats.

State Tourism-run Coaches and Package Tours

Some of the best guided tours, both within cities and to neighbouring towns, are offered by the Government of India Tourism Department and the various state tourism departments *(see p737)*. The Government of India Tourist Offices in most cities offer the latest information on schedules, routes and pick-up points. It is a good idea to buy tickets in advance though they can also be bought on the spot. Coach operators can also customize itineraries keeping in mind the size of the group and the destination.

Coaches run by the tourism departments are, by and large, clean, uncrowded and comfortable. Coach tours organized by them tend to include a guide, so you are also less likely to be surrounded by "freelance" guides or touts when you reach your destination.

Private Operators and Package Tours

Private tour operators and travel agencies also offer a wide variety of coach trips for visitors. These are good value for money, especially if you have a tight budget and limited time.

Agencies usually use either 18 seater or 35 seater super deluxe air-conditioned coaches with pushback seats. Tariffs depend on the quality of service and the itinerary. The ticket price will often include a guide as well as an overnight stay at a hotel as part of the package. Most travel agents have a partnership with luxury coach companies who pick up tourists from designated hotels. Reservations can be made either through the hotel's reception desk or from one of their recommended local agencies.

Bus and Coach Tickets and Fares

Bus or coach fares are cheaper than train fares and depend on the kind of transport you opt for. Travel by "ordinary" bus is not advisable for tourists. Deluxe buses are somewhat better, but, if you are travelling in summer, the best option are the deluxe air-conditioned (a/c) coaches. Many deluxe coaches, known as "video coaches" blast loud music and Hindi movies through the night. If you have an option, it is better to take a

A luxury coach, run by Rajasthan Tourism

Passenger ferry near the Gateway of India, Mumbai

deluxe coach that is not a "video coach". If opting for a deluxe or a/c deluxe bus, you can book your ticket in advance and also reserve your seat.

The charges for bus and coach package tours often include airport transfers, road taxes, overnight stays, guides and any monument or museum entry fees en route.

Logo of
the Rajasthan
Transport Corporation

Ferries and Boats

Ferry connections link some of India's more exotic island destinations, as well as cities along the coasts. They are available from Kolkata to Chennai and Mumbai to Goa. There is also a catamaran service between Mumbai and Goa, although it is suspended during the monsoon season from July to September. Passenger liners also operate from both Chennai and Kolkata to the Andaman Islands, as well as from Kochi to Lakshadweep. Many luxury cruise fares include meals on board, ferrying charges between the ship and islands, sightseeing, lagoon cruising and land accommodation. These are very popular, so it is advisable to book at least two months in advance.

Five passenger liners, the *MV Nancowry, MV Nicobar, MV Swarajdweep, MV Harshavardhana* and *MV Akbar,* run by the **Shipping Corporation of India** (SCI), operate between Chennai and Port Blair in the Andaman Islands, once every ten days, and another SCI ship sails to Port Blair once a month from Visakhapatnam. Within the Andamans, there are four passenger-cum-cargo ferries for transport from Port Blair to the other islands.

Ships also ply between Kochi and Lakshadweep. **S.P.O.R.T.S.,** the Society for Promotion of Nature Tourism and Sports, the official tourist agency of the Lakshadweep Islands, operates four ships, the *MV Bharat Seema, MV Amindivi, MV Minicoy* and the *MV Tipu Sultan,* between Kochi and Lakshadweep. The Goa Tourism Development Corporation (see p737) operates river cruises within the state, whereas in Kerala, half- or full-day backwater cruises are organized by the Kollam (Quilon) District Tourism Promotion Council (see p638–9). The Kerala Tourism Development Corporation in Kochi (see p737) also organizes cruises through the state's beautiful backwaters, on vessels ranging from luxury houseboats in traditional *kettuvallams* (rice boats) to modern 12-seater safari boats.

In Goa and Kerala, travelling by boat is often quicker than going by car. Ferries connect the mainland to nearby islands, such as Ernakulam to Willingdon Island. In Lakshadweep and the Andamans, they offer the only link for people travelling between the islands. In the northeastern states, ferry rides on the River Brahmaputra are available at Guwahati. In Varanasi, boats can be hired at the ghats on the River Ganges. Mumbai has taxi boats plying between the Gateway of India and Elephanta Island.

DIRECTORY

Government of India Tourism Offices

Chennai
154 Anna Salai.
Tel (044) 2846 1459.

Delhi
88 Janpath. **Tel** (011) 2332 0005.

Kolkata
4 Shakespeare Sarani.
Tel (033) 2282 1475.

Mumbai
123 M Karve Rd.
Tel (022) 2203 3144.

Bus Stations

APSRTC
Tel (044) 2479 2233.

Chennai
Metropolitan Transport Corporation Tel (044) 2461 5989.
State Express Bus Stand Parry's Circle. **State Express Transport Corporation Tel** (044) 2536 4656.

Delhi
ISBT, Ring Rd.
Tel (011) 2386 8836.

Kolkata
Esplanade Terminus, Calcutta State Transport Corporation Tel (033) 2248 6259.
North Bengal State Transport Corporation Tel (033) 2243 0736.

Mumbai
MTDC, Madame Cama Rd.
Tel (022) 2204 4040.

Sarai Kale Khan
Tel (011) 2435 8092.

Ship/boat Tours

Shipping Corporation of India
No. 245, Madame Cama Road, Mumbai. **Tel** (022) 2202 6666.

Shipping Corporation of India
Tel (044) 2523 1401.

Sports

Lakshadweep Tourism, Indira Gandhi Rd, Willingdon Island, Kochi. **Tel** (0484) 266 8387.

Local Transport in Cities

Transport options vary from city to city. Most large cities have reliable bus, taxi and auto-rickshaw services. The main cities also have suburban trains that provide speedy connections to areas within city limits. There is also a wide variety of other transport available, especially in the smaller towns and in the old quarters of cities where it is better to opt for a small, light vehicle to cut through narrow congested lanes. Cycle-rickshaws, auto-rickshaws, vikrams (larger versions of auto-rickshaws), tempos and jeeps can be found in most cities, and in some areas horse-drawn carriages *(tongas)* and camel carts are still in use.

Taxis and Auto-Rickshaws

Yellow-topped black taxis operate in most cities except Kolkata, where they are completely yellow, and Bengaluru, where they are totally black. These metered taxis can be hailed in the street or hired from the local taxi stand. They are available for point-to-point service or for a fixed rate for half a day, which is four hours or 40 km (28 miles); or a full day, which is eight hours or 80 km (50 miles). The Ambassador is the favourite model, though Maruti vans are becoming increasingly popular.

Private cabs (some of which are air conditioned), are usually white in colour, and are also available at some of the regular taxi stands. In some cities, there are no yellow-topped taxis, but private taxis can be hired from agencies or hotels. Radio cabs have been introduced in some cities such as Delhi and Mumbai. These are more expensive than ordinary cabs, because they are air conditioned.

The ubiquitous auto-rickshaws (popularly called autos, scooters, or *phat-phats*) are the most common mode of transport in most places. Autos are more economical than taxis, but be prepared for some hair-raising drives – they love squeezing between buses. In Delhi and Mumbai, the anti-pollution drive has seen the

introduction of vehicles run on Compressed Natural Gas (CNG). Taxis and autos that have converted to CNG usage have a green band across the usual yellow and black body. All new autos run on CNG and are painted yellow and green, instead of yellow and black.

An auto-rickshaw, cheap, fast and sometimes hair-raising

Fares and Meters

All taxis and autos have meters, though fares fluctuate according to the price of fuel. Often, meters are not updated and drivers are required by law to carry a rate (tariff) chart listing both the old and current fare, based on the rate per kilometre. Night charges are higher than day fares and payment is extra for luggage. Drivers are notorious for over-charging passengers. The most common argument is that the

meter is not working. It is best to firmly negotiate in advance, and insist on seeing the tariff chart. You can also negotiate a flat rate before getting in. Carry some small change, as drivers often claim not to have return change. They are also prone to taking you via a long route so, if possible, try to find out the best route to take.

Buses

Though city bus networks are very extensive, travelling by these buses is not a pleasant experience. Unable to cope with the large numbers of commuters, buses are overcrowded, and you will have to battle your way to even buy your ticket from the conductor. Buses that are full rarely stop at bus stops, which are usually seen full of waiting commuters. Drivers are known for their reckless driving. Even the so-called luxury buses drive at break-neck speed. Unless absolutely necessary, it is best to use some other form of transport.

Suburban Trains and Metro Rails

Mumbai has the best suburban train network in India, providing efficient and affordable connections. However, it is extremely overcrowded and the rush hour is best avoided. Women should use the "ladies only" compartments. There are three main lines, the most popular of which leaves from Churchgate and goes past

Modern, air-conditioned buses on the busy streets of Delhi

Motorcycle taxis, a convenient way of getting around in Goa

Mumbai Central and Andheri. The others begin at Victoria Terminus (VT). The first phase was between Chembur in the eastern suburbs of the Mumbai Metropolitan Region (MMR) and Wadala, on the outskirts of the island city of Mumbai. The work on the second phase, stretching till Jacob Circle, near Byculla in south Mumbai, is scheduled to be completed by 2015.

In Chennai, the surburban trains offer fast connections from Egmore to Central Station or George Town, and to Guindy or the airport.

India's first underground metro railway is in Kolkata. Limited routes in the northern and southern sectors are open, and the lines are still being extended. The network consists of one operational line (Line 1) and one under construction (Line 2), with four further lines in various stages of planning. The service is clean and efficient, and trains run between 7am and 10pm every day. The main stations are situated opposite the Oberoi Grand and near Dr M Ishaque Road. Certain sections of Chennai's local above-ground trains, the Mass Rapid Transit System (MRTS), are operational, while Delhi's metro has three lines running through the city to neighbouring centres like Gurgaon and Noida. The third and fourth phase of the Delhi Metro will introduce the Magenta Line and the Brown Line and several extensions that should be operational in 2016 and 2021 respectively.

Motorcycles and Bicycles

Often the best way to explore smaller towns and cities and their environs is by motorcycle or bicycle. In Goa, motorcycle taxis are distinguished by their yellow mudguards and white number plates, and are available everywhere. If you prefer to travel independently, motorcycles are also available for hire on a daily basis. Towns such as Puducherry, Hampi, Belur and Halebid, can be explored by bicycle, available for rent at reasonable rates.

Other Modes of Transport

Other transport options include minibuses, cycle- rickshaws and horse-drawn carriages. Cycle-rickshaws are a popular and practical means of transport to traverse the congested pockets of the old quarters of cities. They are more plentiful in smaller towns, where they can easily manoeuvre through narrow bylanes and *galis*. It is best to negotiate rates in advance, though some of them may have a flat rate for fixed routes. Tempos are battery-powered wagon-like vehicles, equipped with seats in the rear half. Uncomfortable and overcrowded,

they charge flat rates for fixed routes. Horse-drawn carriages (*tongas* or *ikkas*) are also very common in small towns and around railway stations, and offer leisurely rides. In Rajasthan, camel carts are also available – they offer a novel, if jerky, journey.

Jeeps and vans can be hired from cities (*see p755*), for short trips to explore the environs and neighbouring towns. They are also the main form of transport in Ladakh. Jeeps are also the best way of exploring the hills. Many areas have shared jeep taxis, which work out cheaper than private jeeps. A flat rate is usually charged, which includes any tolls en route. Private cars are often not allowed in hill towns, where the easiest options are to hire cycle-rickshaws or to explore the area on foot.

Road Names

In most cities, especially in the four main cities, many roads which were named after Raj-era figures, have been renamed after well-known Indian and international figures. This might cause some confusion, as maps often carry the newer names, while locals usually refer to the road by the old name. When in doubt, it is best to ask two or three people, and cross-check the directions that you are given.

Hand-pulled rickshaws in Kolkata, a practical means of transport especially during the monsoons

General Index

Acknowledgments

Dorling Kindersley would like to thank the following people whose contributions and assistance have made this book possible.

Main Contributors
Roshen Dalal has a PhD in Ancient Indian History from the Jawaharlal Nehru University, Delhi, and is the author of *A History of India for Children*.
Partho Datta teaches Indian History at a college in Delhi University.
Divya Gandhi, an environmentalist and geographer, is pursuing a doctorate at the University of Michigan.
Premola Ghose has travelled extensively, especially in Madhya Pradesh and Maharashtra. She is the Programme Officer at the India International Centre, Delhi.
Ashok Koshy is a senior civil servant who has spent many years in Gujarat and Kerala.
Abha Narain Lambah is an architectural conservationist, who is the Director of Bombay Collaborative, a pioneering firm in the field of urban design and conservation in Mumbai.
Annabel Lopez is a practising architect as well as an architectural historian who has co-authored the book *Houses of Goa*.
Sumita Mehta is a journalist and travel writer based in Delhi, who has worked on conservation projects in Rajasthan.
Rudrangshu Mukherji is a leading columnist, journalist and author based in Kolkata
Meenu Nageshwaran runs a travel agency, Incent Tours, in Delhi.
Rushad R Nanavatty is a keen mountaineer who has trekked extensively in northern, central and eastern India.
Ira Pande is the editor of *IIC Quarterly* in Delhi.
Usha Raman is a freelance writer and editor based in Hyderabad.
Janet Rizvi, a PhD from Cambridge, is a leading authority on Ladakh and author of two books, *Ladakh, Crossroads of High Asia* and *Trans-Himalayan Caravans: Merchant Princes and Peasant Traders in Ladakh*.
Ranee Sahaney is a well-known travel writer, and regular contributor to *outlooktraveller.com*.
Deepak Sanan is a senior civil servant who has spent many years working in Himachal Pradesh. He has written extensively on the region.
Darsana Selvakumar has a post-graduate degree in Ancient Indian History and archaeology.
Sankarshan Thakur is a senior journalist and author of a book on Bihar.
Shikha Trivedi is an authority on traditional crafts. She is presently working with India's leading television news channel.
Lakshmi Viswanathan is a Bharat Natyam dancer based in Chennai. She also sits on the governing body of the Music Academy Madras, one of South India's leading cultural organizations.

Consultant
George Michell is an architectural and cultural historian specializing in India. Among his many publications are books on Hindu temples, royal palaces, the Vijayanagar Empire and Deccani art and architecture.

Additional Contributors
John Abraham, Anvar Alikhan, Usha Balakrishnan, Manini Chatterjee, Anuradha Chaturvedi, Rta Kapur Chishti, Anna Dallapiccola, Dharmendar Kanwar, Ranjana Sengupta.

Additional Illustrations
Naveed Ahmed Vali, Ampersand.

Additional Photography
Ashwin Raju Adimari Idris Ahmed, Akhil Bakshi, Andy Crawford Geoff Dann (Ashmolean Museum, Oxford) Neha Dhingra Urmila Dongre DN Dube Gables Ellen Howdon (Glasgow Museum, Glasgow Benu Joshi, Aditya Katyal Dave King Mathew Kurien Ian O'Leary, Aditya Patankar, Ram Rahman.

Proof Reader and Indexer
Anita Roy, Ranjana Saklani.

Fact Check
Ranee Sahaney.

Revision & Relaunch Team
Ashwin Raju Adimari, Emma Anacootee, Saumya Ancheri, Brigitte Arora, Raja Bhasin, Vamsi Chaitanya, Divya Chowfin, Jo Cowen, Aparup Das, Neha Dhingra, Fay Franklin, Nasreen Habib, Emily Hatchwell, Jason Little, Snehal Kanodia, Juliet Kenny, Carly Madden, Sonal Modha, Casper Morris, Sushmita Malaviya, Souvik Mukherjee, Rina Mukherji, Anil Mulchandani, Alka Pande, Dave Pugh, Marisa Renzullo, Lakshmi Sharath, Preeti Singh, Beverly Smart, Azeem Siddiqui, Sands Publishing Solutions, Vivien Stone, Julie Thompson, Janis Utton, Dora Whitaker.

Publishing Manager
Anna Streiffert.

Art Director
Gillian Allan.

Publisher
Douglas Amrine.

Special Assistance
Arundhti Bhanot; Mahesh Buch; Tarun Chhabria; Manosh De; Sharada Dwivedi; Asit Gopal; Sandhya Iyer; GM Kakpori; Vijayan Kannampilly; Kurt Kessler Dias; Sumita Khatwani; Meenal Kshirsagar; Aparajita Kumar; Ritu Kumar; Anna Madhavan; Aditi Mehta; Milan Moudgill; Sunil Philip; Nihar Rao; Anita Roy; KJ Ravinder; Samit Roychoudhury; Shweta Sachdeva; Saba Shaikh; Lalit Sharma; Parvati Sharma; Tara Sharma; Yuthika Sharma; Luiyo Shimray; Dr A Jaya Thilak; Maharao Brijraj Singh of Kotah; Maharaja Gaj Singh II of Jodhpur; Vijay Singh. American Institute of Indian Studies. Archaeological Survey of India, New Delhi. Architecture Autonomous, Goa: Gerard da Cunha and Amit Modi. Architectural Conservation Cell of the Associated Cement Companies Ltd. Aurobindo Ashram. Central Cottage Industries.

Department of Culture, Government of India: Kasturi Gupta Menon, Joint Secretary., Department of Tourism, New Delhi:, Rekha Khosla, Director; Ashwini Lohani, Director. Indian Institute of Public Administration. Indian Museum, Kolkata: Dr SK Chakravarty, Director; Chanda Mukherjee. Indian National Trust for Art and Cultural Heritage: Martand Singh., Maharana Mewar Historical Publications Trust, Mewar: Shriji Arvind Singhji, Chairman and Managing Trustee. Mehrangarh Museum Trust, Jodhpur: Trustees; Mahendra Singh, CEO, Sangath: BV Doshi., Tibet House, New Delhi, Tibetan Institute of Performing Arts, Dharamsala. Wildlife Trust of India: Vivek Menon., World Wide Fund: Krishna Kumar.

Special Assistance in Photography
Archaeological Survey of India, New Delhi: Komal Anand, Director General; Dr KM Poonacha, Director (Monuments); Dr RC Aggarwal, Director (Museums); Mr Bakshi, Assistant Director (Monuments).
Crafts Museum, New Delhi: Dr Jyotindra Jain. Government Museum, Chennai: R Kannan. Khuda Baksh Oriental Library, Patna: HR Chigani. Mathura Museum, Mathura: Jitendra Kumar. Maharaja Fatehsingh Museum Trust, Baroda. National Museum, New Delhi. RD Chowdhourie; U Dass; JC Grover; Dr Daljeet Kaur. Prince of Wales Museum of Western India, Mumbai: Dr Kalpana Desai, Director.
Rampur Raza Library, Rampur: WH Siddiqi. Sarabhai Foundation, Calico Museum of Textiles, Ahmedabad: DS Mehta, Secretary; A Sen Gupta. Sanskriti Museum, New Delhi: OP Jain. State Museum, Patna: Naseena Akhtar.

Dorling Kindersley would like to thank all regional and local tourist offices throughout India for their valuable help. Particular thanks to Ravi Babu; Chandana Khan, Secretary, Tourism & Culture Department, Hyderabad; Victoria Memorial, Kolkata: CR Panda; Indian Museum, Kolkata: Shyamalkanti Chakravarti; The Asiatic Society, Kolkata: Ms Sarkar; Kunjo Tashi; Rajiv Mehrotra; Tenzin Geyche Tethong, Secretary to His Holiness, the Dalai Lama, Dharamsala; Chief PRO, Central Railways, Mumbai: Mukul Marwah; Quila House, Patna: BM Jalan; Secretary, Department of Cultural Affairs, Thiruvananthapuram: Prof HV Pradhan; INTACH (Pune): RK Saini.

Photography Permissions
Dorling Kindersley would like to thank all those at temples, forts, palaces, museums, restaurants, shops and other sights, for their cooperation and contribution to this publication. The Publisher would also like to thank the following for their assistance and kind permission to photograph at their establishments: Brindavan, New Delhi; Crafts Museum, New Delhi; Good Earth, New Delhi; Annie Kumar, Regalia, India Tea House, New Delhi; Ramji Bharany, Bharany's, New Delhi. Particular thanks also to Urmila Dongre and Vivek Narang for their kind permission to photograph their products.

Picture Credits
t = top; tl = top left; tlc = top left centre; tc = top centre; tr = top right; cla = centre left above; ca = centre above; cra = centre right above; cl = centre left; c = centre; cr = centre right; clb = centre left below; cb = centre below; crb = centre right below; bl = bottom left; b = bottom; bc =

bottom centre; bcl = bottom centre left; br = bottom right; bra = bottom right above; d = detail.

The publishers are grateful to the following individuals, picture libraries and companies, for permission to reproduce their photographs:

Idris Ahmed: 136-137,373crb.
Alamy Images: Adams Picture Library t/a apl/Dhanwant Plahay 5cl, 352cl; China Span/Keren Su 71c,269tl; City Image 498-499; Ellen Clark 13br, Dinodia Photos 318-319, 560, Michele Falzone 71tl; Chris Fredriksson 12b Tim Gainey 559c; Blaine Harrington III 13tl, ImageBROKER 691tl, Indiascapes 16tr, John Warburton-Lee Photography 17tc, Huw Jones 558cl; Michael Juno 169tl; David Pearson 15bl, 709tr, 714tr, PhotosIndia.com LLC 14tr, Photo Provider Network 268cl; Tanya_R 640-641 Simon Reddy 17br,444cl,445tl,662; Robert Harding Picture Library Ltd/Jeremy Bright 168cl, 269c; Travelib Asia 326, Ravi Verma 70cl; Andrew H Williams 445c, ZUMA Press, Inc. 464bl

AMR Vastra Kosh Trust, New Delhi 321crb/bl/c.
Arya, Aditya 218c, 221c, 229cr, 237t/c/b, 243cr, 246bl/br, 250l, 256t, 265c, 342c, 461b, 463t, 753b
Pallava Bagla: 22cr, 28-29c, 32tr, 69bl, 166cl, 197b, 225cl, 254b, 375c, 381cb, 645b.
Manu Bahuguna: 38br, 79br, 89cr, 434tr, 449cr, 458tr, 475bl, 525b, 547br, 563c, 574t, 576t, 622b, 623t, 650c, 726b,728t, 729t.
Akhil Bakshi: 32b/br, 33bl, 190b, 223br, 395b, 440c.
M Balan: 22crb, 34br, 373b, 524b, 554c, 630b, 631t, 632cl/tr, 633bl, 634tr, 635tl, 637c/bl, 638-639c, 639tl/br, 644tl/clb, 645tl/cr, 650br, 651t/c/br, 652c, 653t/c, 654cl, 656b, 658t/c, 660t/c, 661cr/c, 692b, 705br.
Kakoli Barkakoti: 328c, 329br, 337t.
Pablo Bartholomew/Mediaweb India: 266cl, 266-267c.
Benoy Behl: 46tr, 51tr, 140t/c, 141b, 142tr/cl/cr/br, 143tl/cl/b, 144b, 145bl/bc/br, 14/cl/clb, 148tr/br/b, 149cr/crb/br, 150c/b, 151cl/b, 155c/b, 480tr/clb, 481t/c, 482t, 483t/b, 484t/cl/c/cr/clb/crb/bl/b/br, 485cr/bl/br, 569b, 570c.
Subhash Bhargava: 27clb, 60bl, 183c, 350br, 362c/bl, 368b, 371cla/cr, 377t, 381cl/bc/b, 382t, 383t, 385b, 394b, 402tr, 405clb, 406t/b, 407t, 408t, 411t, 727t.
Big Screen Entertainment Pvt.Ltd.: 37tr, 37cra. **Bihar School of Yoga Ganga Darshan, Munger**: 221t. **Dean Brown K**: 82b.
Ashish Chandola: 66ca, 372b.
Chettinadu Mansion: 702tl
Tarun Chhabra: 611cl. **Rta Kapur Chishti**: 213cr/clb/crb/bl/br (a, b, c, d), 587c/cb/crb, 677cr (a, b, c, d, e, f).
Chokelao Restaurant: 713tr
RS Chundawat: 68cla, 140b, 144t, 146c, 147t, 157b, 190t, 196cl/cb, 198b, 259crb, 299b, 325c, 375b, 427br, 524crb.
Claridges: 694bl
Cochrane Place: 698tr;
Costumes & Textiles of Royal India: Ritu Kumar 34cl.
Corbis: Dinodia 428-429,Blaine Harrington III 353tl; Jon Hicks 12br Eric Meola 468, Calle Montes 9cr, Douglas Pearson 8clb,; Steve Raymer 746bc; Robert Harding World Imagery/Leplat Véronique 169c

Crafts Museum: 84cl/clb, 85ca/crb, 256c.
Gilles Crampes: 127cl. **Tanmoy Das**: 322bl.
Vivek Das: 266bl/br. **Prosenjit Dasgupta**: 320tl.
Deen Dayal Trust: 669clb.
Dharma Productions: 37tl **Ashok Dilwali**: 116t, 117c/br, 118b, 119tr, 120c, 121cr, 122cr/b, 124t/c/b, 125t/c, 126t, 127tr, 128c, 129c/b, 130t/c, 131bl, 132c/bl, 133t/c/b, 134cra, 135br, 162cl, 167cl, 174t, 191t, 193b, 195b, 263b, 303crb, 304cla, 305b, 306b, 622t/c, 623ca, 624clb, 625b, 627t/c/b. Thomas Dix: 240tr/c, 241b, 350-351c, , 375cr, 398t, 401tr/bl, 418tr/cl/cr, 419cl/b, 422/tr/c, 423cra/cr, 426t, 480b, 481b, 482b, 485t/cl/crb, 683br.
Dhole's Den: 693tr;

Dreamstime.com: Anyacola 688-689, Rafał Cichawa 216, Cyberjade 62-63, Rene Drouyer 11tc, Jorg Hackemann 2-3, 10bl, Javarman 16b, Mattyc1965 230, Aliaksandr Mazurkevich 170, Merzzie 628, Luciano Mortula 102, Amith Nag 593bl, Noppasinw 532-533, Marina Pissarova 550-551, Rodrigolab 160-161, Dmitry Rukhlenko 72, 344-345, Saiko3p 514, 580, Samrat35 308, Sergeychernov 11br, 354, Nickolay Stanev 620, Aleksandar Todorovic 436-437

Fotomedia Picture Library: 59tr, 146t, 156b, 200b, 290b, 475cl; Jyoti M Banerjee 197t, 338c; Francois Gautier 400cl, 445br, 730t; Nihal Mathur 410tr; Sanjiv Mishra 41br; Sundeep Nayak 372c; Christine Pemberton 26cl, 162b, 199t, 310tr, 312b, 447b, 448cl, 458c, 477cr, 704b; Otto Pfister 134bl, 372t/clb, 373tl/cr; Sanjay Saxena 189cl, 307c, 359bl; Mathew Titus 59tl; Henry Wilson 207br.

RK Gaur: 65br, 262cl, 330b, 337b, 340cl.
Getty Images: AFP/Emmanuel Dunand 432br/Prakash Singh 730br; AFP/Prakash Singh 758br;Aurora/PatitucciPhoto 559tl; Dinodia Photos 488, Miles Ertman 204-205, Michele Falzone 396-397 Amar Grover 332-333 National Geographic/James L. Stanfield 657b; Hindustan Times 36c , Francesco Pavanetto 412, Robert Harding World Imagery / Gavin Hellier 73b, Robert Nickelsberg 720cr; Dmitry Rukhlenko 112, Sankar Salvady 606-607, Sapna Reddy Photography 152-153, The India Today Group/Mail Today 711br.
Premola Ghose: 225crb.
Ashim Ghosh: 52bc, 187br.
Joanna van Gruisen: 22clb/bl/cla, 23tr, 69tr, 131c, 142clb, 146bl/br, 197crb, 228c, 258t, 292tr, 323t/c/b, 330c,394c, 410cl, 524cr, 644bl,

Harbour Restaurant: 718tl
House of Mangaldas Girdhardas: 699br

Fawzan Husain: 440b. **Hyatt Regenc**y: 725b.
Image Bank, London: 68-69c.
India Picture: Hemant Mehta 35cr.
India Today Magazine: 451b, 669cl.
Prakash Israni: 22tr, 40c, 67t, 105bl, 187bl, 313c, 471b, 476c/b. **Ravi Kaimal**: 128t.
ITC Grand: 717tr
Prem Kapoor: 46c, 60br,132t, 199bl, 636t, 643c, 724b.
Kanika Kapoor: 34-35c.
Sudhir Kasliwal: 364b, 365clb/bl/b, 722bl.
Dinesh Khanna: 34bl, 35bl, 109b, 167cla, 183b, 206cl/c/cr/b,

207cl/crb/bl, 210cl, 211cr/bl, 317tr/br, 349t, 381c, 384tr, 425c, 441c, 442br, 443tl/tc/bc/br, 510b, 555t, 667tl, 669bl, 722cr.
BN Khazanchi: 38cl, 40br, 41c, 331tr.
Ashish Khokar: 32cl, 257br.
Rupinder Khullar: 34tr,107b, 108b, 225cb, 229b, 316b, 322br, 325t/br, 462t, 463b.
Bobby Kohli: 267tl.
Krishna Kumar: 624t/cl/cr/crb, .
Karoki Lewis: 208cra, 211tl/cl.
Lakkhotaa Lodge: 691br
Lonely Planet Images: Dallas Stribley 353c.

Mehrangarh Fort, Jodhpur: 386b,
Nakli Dhaba: 712bl
Dalip Mehta: 381clb, 303cr/c/clb.
Vishwanath Mishra: 443bl.
V Muthuraman: 6 & 7, 26br, 28cl, 29cr/br, 40tl, 42bl, 49clb, 51tl/bl/br, 58br, 208bl/br, 209tl/tr, 210bl, 211tr, 212cl/b, 214t, 224t/b, 225b, 226c/br, 241c, 242c, 271b, 273t, 275crb, 278tr/b, 279t, 285c, 328t, 338b, 339t/c, 520b, 521t/br, 522b, 523tl/cra, 528cr/crb/b, 539cla/cl/clb, 552t/c, 555c/b, 564t/b, 569t, 570bl/br, 573t/c/b, 575br, 582t, 586t/b, 587cl/ cr/clb/b, 588t/bl/br, 589t/c/b, 590tr, 591tl/cr/crb, 592c, 593br, 594b, 595br, 596c, 597t/c/b, 598t/c/b, 599bl/br, 600t/c/b, 601cl, 602b, 603t/c, 604t/c, 605t/c/b, 608t/b, 609c/crb/br, 610t/bl/ br, 611c/cr/crb/bl/br, 612c/b, 613t, 614cl/b, 615t/c/b, 616cl/ cr/clb/crb/bl/br, 617t/b, 618t/b, 619t/b, 632b, 637cb, 654clb, 656t, 657t, 658b, 659t/c/b, 660b, 661cl/bl/br, 729b, 738t.

Aman Nath: 49br, 54br.
Ashok Nath: 331tl, 336b,
National Museum, New Delhi: 30cla, 44, 45bl, 47c/br/bc, 52br, 53t, 54c/clb, 55c/cr, 57bl, 80tr/c/clb/bl/br, 81t, 145cl, 253b, 409cr/bl, 669br;
RC Dutta Gupta 33tl, 46bc, 48bc, 56t;. P Roy 365crb (a) & (b)
National School of Drama, New Delhi: 30crb.
Nehru Memorial Library, Teen Murti, New Delhi: 61tl.

Atithi Parinay: 700br
Amit Pasricha: 22cr, 35br, 42tl, 43ca, 48c, 59bl, 64cl,144c, 166br, 340bl/b, 341tl, 342t/b,389cla/cr/bl, 404tr, 430b, 431t/b, 591b.
Avinash Pasricha: 32c/cr, 33cl/cr/bc/br, 106t, 317bl, 518t, 554b, 561b, 599cl/c/cr/crb/cra/
Aditya Patankar: 32tl, 232tl/c/b, 233t/cl/cr/b, 350clb/bl, 351cr, 360tr, 376t/c, 394t, 407b,
K Prabhakar: 667tr/c/b, 671c, 673t/cr.
Prince of Wales Museum of Western India, Mumbai: 454tr/c/b, 455c/b.
Press Information Bureau: 60tl.
Ram Rahman: 76bl.
VK Rajamani: 29tr, 50tr/clb/cb, 50-51c, 556c/bl, 557tl/bl, 565b, 568c, 569c, 723cb.
Bharath Ramamrutham: 519cl/c/ca/bl/cb/br.
CR Rao: Anantha Padmanabha 656c.
E Rao: Hanumantha 23bl,411crb/b, 654cr.
Reshi Maryam: 39tl, 67br, 158t/c, 159t/c, 434c, 435c.
Reuters: Sherwin Crasto 36bl; Kieran Doherty 36clb; Lucas Jackson 37bl.
Rex Features: Courtesy Everett Collection 14bl, Everett

Collection 36-37c

Janet Rizvi: 151t/cr.

Roli Books: 31cl, 35tl, 392b; "Tradition & Beyond: Handcrafted Indian Textiles", 2001 by Rta Kapur Chishti & Rahul Jain 321cl/cr (a) & (b)/br.

Kamal Sahai: 47bl.

Sanjeev Saith: 64clb, 104bc, 107t, 158b, 166tr, 167cb, 191b, 192c, 194t/c/b, 195t, 201c, 211crb, 213cl, 220c, 228t/b, 264c, 292c, 304crb, 415c, 728b

Deepak Sanan: 122cl, 123t/c, 331b, 336c, 337c, 341cl.

Sanctuary Features & Photo Library: 442cb, 443tr; Parvish Pandya 626c; Shailendra Yashwant 471cl.

Sanghvi, Hemen 27tr/cl/cr/crb/bl, 265b, 328b, 329t, 338t, 340tl, 341tr/b, 343t/c/b.

Sangla Camp & Retreat: 695tr

R Sankaran: 623b.

Saran Shalini: 39br, 52cl, 54bl, 55tl/bl, 56br, 81cb, 95bc, 99tl, 164c,174b, 175b,188b, 198t/c, 203br, 211br, 225cra, 244tr, 246c, 248tr/c/cb, 249t, 252b, 255br, 409crb, 433t, 435tl/tr/bc

Sarabhai Foundation, Calico Museum of Textiles, Ahmedabad: 416tr/cl/bl, 417t/c/b.

TS Satyan: 23br, 31cr, 33tr, 169br (a, b), 521bl, 522tr/c, 539bl/br, 594t, 639cra, 738cb.

Pepita Seth: 220b, 653b.

Ajay & Mugdha Sethi: 105t, 168br, 169bl, 178ca/crb, 179cl/bl, 207t, 209b, 210br, 285b, 295br, 736t, 745clb.

Siddharth: 267b.

Toby Sinclair: 22cl/crb; 23tl/clb/crb/b,29bl, 35tr, 117bl, 128h, 143tr, 159b,163b, 165b, 167tr, 191c, 196t/b, 197cr, 215t/b, 241t, 242t/b, 243cl/clb/crb/b, 258cl/clb/b, 259t, 265t, 292b, 293t/c/b, 295t, 296t, 302t/c, 303cl, 311c, 313t, 325bl,329cl, 330t, 334tr/c/b, 335t/cb, 339b, 340tr, 383c, 385t, 388b, 400b, 401cr, 405cra, 408b, 410c/b, 411c, 420t, 427bl, 433c/b, 443crb,582b, 584tr, 625c, 635cr, 638cl/br, 644c,649c, 650bl, 651bl, 654crb, 674c/b, 683bc,736b, 757t

NP Singh: 358bl, Dhruv Singh: 398b,

Hashmat Singh: 66b, 68clb,118c, 119tl/b, 120tl, 123b, 127clh/bl, 129t, 130b, 131br, 134tr/c/br, 135tl/cl/bl, 143cr, 147cr, 154t, 155t, 156c/cb, 157t, 193t, 266tr/clb, 298t, 300t, 301t/c/b, 302b, 305t, 306c, 307t/b, 349b, 385c, 399b, 401tl/crb, 692tr.

Siolim House: 701tr

SuperStock: Age Fotostock 732-733, Hemis.fr 234-235

Dalip Singh Thakur: 23bc, 69cr/crb/br, 116c, 190c, 195c, 299c, 303bl, 335c, 486b, 524cl/clb.

Stock Transparency Services: 470t/c, 475c, 486t, 487t.

Amar Talwar: 61bc 69cra, 117t, 121br, 131t, 165t, 167cra, 186b, 192b, 229t, 252cb, 257cl, 432t, 434br, 435bl.

Taj Hotels: 690bl, 696bl, 703bl, 707tr, 708bl, 715bl, 716br

The Bodhi Tree: 697tr

The Oberoi Grand: Baan Thai 710tl

The Statesman: R De 41tr.

UTV Motion Pictures: 37br.

V & A Museum, London (Courtesy of the Board of Trustees): 54tr, 57bc.

Ritu Varuni: 340cr/br, 341cr.

Verma Bimla: 27tl, 30tr, 31crb, 106c, 127crb/br, 166cr, 221b, 225cr, 257cr/cb/clb, 299t, 313b, 316c, 324t, 402c, 435br, 474c, 679t/bl:

BPS Walia: 105c/cr, 107c, 108t/c, 109t/c, 110tr/cl/cr/b, 111t/b, 125b, 127tl/cr (a) & (b), 145c, 203bl, 247c, 248b,251t/c, 252tr/cl, 253tl/tr, 259cr, 310b, 312cb, 314cl, 400tr, 401br, 427t, 462b, 528cl.

Wedding Affair Magazine: 35c.

Rom Whitaker: 625t.

World Wildlife Fund: 334clb, 335b.

Yash Raj Flims: 36tr,

Works of art have been reproduced with the permission of the following copyright holders © Courtesy Shriji Arvind Singhji Mewar, Chairman and Managing Trustee, Maharana Mewar Historical Publications Trust 409cl; Ramachandra Maharana, Puri, Orissa 317cl; Mundrika Devi, Madhubani, Bihar 31tl;

FEP: Left: Corbis: Eric Meola (cb). Dorling Kindersley: Mathew Kurien (tl). Dreamstime.com: Merzzie (bc); Luciano Mortula (tc); Dmitry Rukhlenko (tr); Sergeychernov (cl); Saiko3p (crb). Getty Images: Dinodia Photos (bl); Francesco Pavanetto (clb)

FEP: Right Alamy Images: Simon Reddy (crb); Travelib Asia (tr). Dreamstime.com: Rafał Cichawa (tc); Aliaksandr Mazurkevich (tl); Mattyc1965 (clb); Samrat35 (cb); Saiko3p (bl); Nickolay Stanev (bc). Getty Images: Dmitry Rukhlenko (ftl)

Jacket:

Front: 4Corners SIME / Luigi Vaccarella c; Corbis: Atlantide Phototravel bl;

Spine: 4Corners SIME / Luigi Vaccarella t.

All other images © Dorling Kindersley. For further information see: www.dkimages.com

---

Further Reading

History

A Discovery of India Jawaharlal Nehru, Oxford University Press, New Delhi, 1997.
A History of India (Vol 1) Romila Thapar, Penguin, New Delhi, 1990.
A History of India (Vol 2) Percival Spear, Penguin, New Delhi, 1990.
A History of South India KA Nilakanta Sastri, Oxford University Press, New Delhi, 1999.
A History of the Sikhs Khushwant Singh, Oxford University Press, New Delhi, 1991.
Alberuni's India Edward C Sachau, Routledge & Kegan Paul, London, 1988.
A New History of India Stanley Wolpert, Oxford University Press, New York, 1990.
Annals and Antiquities of Rajasthan Col James Tod, South Asia Books, Columbia, 1987.
Babur Nama: Memoirs of Babur (trans) Wheeler M Thackston, Oxford University Press, London, 1996.
Delhi Between Two Empires Narayani Gupta, Oxford University Press, New Delhi, 1981.
Freedom at Midnight Dominique Lapierre and Larry Collins, Avon Books, New York, 1955.
India: A History John Keay, HarperCollins, New Delhi, 2000.
India Britannica Geoffrey Moor-house, Harvill, London, 1983.
India's Struggle for Independence Bipan Chandra et al, Penguin, New Delhi, 1989.
Ladakh: Crossroads of High Asia Janet Rizvi, Oxford University Press, New Delhi, 1996.
Liberty or Death Patrick French, HarperCollins, London, 1997.
Lives of the Indian Princes Charles Allen & Sharada Dwivedi, Century, London, 1985.
Plain Tales from the Raj Charles Allen, Andre Deutsch, London, 1975.
The Great Moghuls Bamber Gascoigne, Dorset Press, London, 1971.
The Last Mughal: The Fall of a Dynasty, Delhi, 1857 William Dalrymple, Bloomsbury, London, 2007.
The Idea that was India Sunil Khilnani, Farrar Strauss Giroux, New York, 1997.
The Wonder that was India AL Basham,

Rupa, New Delhi, 1967.
The Wonder that was India Part II, SAA Rizvi, Sidgwick & Jackson, London, 1987. *Tuzuk-i-Jahangiri: Memoirs of Jahangir* (trans) Alexander Rogers and Henry Beveridge, London, 1909–14.
Xuanzang: A Buddhist Pilgrim on the Silk Road Sally H Wriggins, Boulder Press, Colorado, 1996.

Religion and Philosophy
Buddhism Christmas Humphreys, Penguin, London, 1951.
Hinduism Kshiti Mohan Sen, Penguin, London, 1961.
Hindu Myths Wendy O'Flaherty, Penguin, London, 1974.
Manifestations of Shiva (exhibition catalogue), Stella Kramrisch, Philadelphia Museum of Art, Philadelphia, 1981.
The Bhagwadgita Robert Charles Zaehner, Oxford University Press, London, 1969.
The Ramayana and the Mahabharata Chakravarti Rajagopalachari, Bharati Vidya Bhavan, Mumbai, 1951.

Culture and Society
A Taste of India Madhur Jaffrey, Atheneum Publishers, New York, 1986.
Banaras, City of Light Diana L Eck, Alfred A Knopf, New York, 1982.
Bombay: City of Gold Gillian Tindall, Penguin, London, 1992.
Bombay: The Cities Within Sharada Dwivedi & Rahul Mehrotra, India Book House, Bombay, 1995.
Butter Chicken in Ludhiana Pankaj Mishra, Penguin, New Delhi, 1995.
Calcutta, The City Revealed Geoffrey Moorhouse, Weidenfeld & Nicolson, 1971.
Dance of the Peacock: Jewellery Traditions of India Usha R Bala Krishnan & Meera S Kumar, India Book House, Mumbai, 1999.
Desert Places Robyn Davidson, Viking, London, 1996.
Eyewitness India, Manini Chatterjee & Anita Roy, Dorling Kindersley, London, 2002.
Garden of Life: An Introduction to the Healing Plants of India Naveen Patnaik, Doubleday, New York, 1993.
Hanklyn-Janklin Nigel B Hankin, Banyan Books, New Delhi, 1992.
Historical Dictionary of Indian Food KT Achaya, Oxford University Press, New Delhi, 1998.
India: A Million Mutinies Now VS

Naipaul, Heinemann, Oxford, 1990.
India: A Wounded Civilization VS Naipaul, Vintage Books, New York, 1977.
Indian Cinema, Past and Present Feroze Rangoonwala, Clarion Books, New Delhi, 1983.
Madras Rediscovered S Muthiah, EastWest Books, Chennai, 1999.
May You Be the Mother of a Hundred Sons Elizabeth Bumiller, Random House Inc, New York, 1990.
No Fullstops in India Mark Tully, Viking, London, 1991.
The Great Indian Middle Class Pavan K Varma, Penguin, New Delhi, 1998.
The Muslim Community of the Indo-Pakistan Subcontinent Dr Ishtiaq Hussain Qureshi, Oxford University Press, New Delhi, 1977.
The Remembered Village MN Srinivas, Oxford University Press, New Delhi, 1996.

Architecture
Forts Walks: Around Bombay's Fort Areas Sharda Dwivedi & Rahul Mehrotra, Eminence Designs, Bombay, 1999.
Indian Architecture Percy Brown, (2 vols), DB Taraporevala Sons and Co, Bombay, 1964
Mughal Architecture Ebba Koch, PRESTEL-Verlag, Munich, 1991.
Stones of Empire Jan Morris, Oxford University Press, Oxford, 1983.
The Moonlight Garden Elizabeth B Moynihan, Smithsonian Institution, Washington DC, 2000.
The Forts of India Virginia Fass, Collins, London, 1986.
The Hindu Temple George Michell, University of Chicago Press, Chicago, 1988.
The History of Architecture in India Christopher Tadgell, Phaidon, London, 1990.
The Palaces of India Virginia Fass and Maharaja of Baroda, Collins, London, 1980.
The Penguin Guide to the Monuments of India (2 vols) George Michell and Phillip Davies, Viking, London, 1989.
Rajput Palaces GHR Tillotson, Oxford University Press, New Delhi, 1987.
Traditional Buildings of India Ilay Cooper & Barry Dawson, Thames & Hudson, New York, 1998.

Arts and Crafts
Art of the Imperial Cholas Vidya Dehejia, Columbia University Press, New York, 1990.
A Second Paradise Naveen Patnaik,

Further Reading

Sidgwick & Jackson, London, 1985.
Company Paintings: Indian Paintings of the British Period Mildred Archer, Victoria and Albert Museum, London in association with Mapin Publishing, Ahmedabad, 1992.
Costumes and Textiles of Royal India Ritu Kumar, Christie's Books, London, 1999.
Himalayan Art Madanjeet Singh, Macmillan, New York, 1963.
India: Art and Culture 1300–1900 (exhibition catalogue), Stuart Cary Welch, The Metropolitan Museum of Art, New York, 1985.
Indian Art Vidya Dehejia, Phaidon, London, 1997.
Indian Interiors Sunil Sethi, Taschen, Cologne, 2000.
Indian Painting MS Randhawa, and John Kenneth Galbraith, Vakils, Feffer and Simon, Mumbai, 1982.
Kalighat Paintings: Images from a Changing World Jyotindra Jain, Mapin Publishing, Ahmedabad, 1999.
Masterpieces from the National Museum Collection SP Gupta, New Delhi, 1985.
Paradise as a Garden Elizabeth B Moynihan, George Braziller Inc, New York, 1979.
Penguin Dictionary of Indian Classical Music Raghava Menon, Penguin, New Delhi, 1995.
South Indian Bronzes C Sivaramamurti, Lalit Kala Akademi, New Delhi, 1963.
The Art of India: Traditions of Indian Sculpture, Painting and Architecture Stella Kramrisch, Phaidon, New York, 1954.
The Essence of Indian Art (exhibition catalogue), Asian Art Museum of San Francisco, 1986.
The New Cambridge History of India: Architecture and Art of the Deccan Sultanates George Michell and Mark Zebrowski, Cambridge University Press, Cambridge, 1999.
The New Cambridge History of India: Mughal and Rajput Painting Milo C Beach, Cambridge University Press, Cambridge, 1992.
Tradition & Beyond: Handcrafted Indian Textiles Rta Kapur Chishti and Rahul Jain, Roli Books, New Delhi, 2000.
Traditions of Indian Classical Dance Mohan Khokar, Clarion Books, New Delhi, 1979.

Nature and Wildlife

Collins Handguide to Birds of the Indian Subcontinent Martin, Williams Woodcock, Collins Sons & Co, London, 1980.

Encyclopaedia of Indian Natural History RE Hawkins (ed), Oxford University Press, Bombay, 1986.
Flowers of the Himalaya Oleg Polunin and Adam Stainton, Oxford University Press, New Delhi, 1984.
Handbook of Birds of India and Pakistan, 2nd edition, Salim Ali and S Dillon Ripley, Oxford University Press, London, 1995.
In Danger Paola Manfredi (ed), Ranthambhore Foundation, New Delhi, 1997.
Indian Wildlife S Israel and T Sinclair (eds), APA Publications, Hong Kong, 1987.
India's Wildlife History: An Introduction Mahesh Rangarajan, Permanent Black, New Delhi, 2001.
Land of the Tiger Valmik Thapar, BBC Consumer Publishing, London, 1997.
Trees of India Pallava Bagla, Timeless, New Delhi, 2000.

Literature

A Passage to India EM Forster, Harcourt, Brace & World, New York, 1924.
A Suitable Boy Vikram Seth, Viking-Penguin, New Delhi, 1993.
Gitanjali Rabindranath Tagore, Chiswick Press, London, 1912.
Heat and Dust Ruth P Jhabvala, John Murray, London, 1975.
In Custody Anita Desai, Heinemann, Oxford, 1984.
Kim Rudyard Kipling, Tuttle Publishing, Boston, 1994.
Malgudi Days RK Narayan, Viking, New York, 1982.
Midnight's Children Salman Rushdie, Penguin, London, 1991.
Such a Long Journey Rohinton Mistry, Faber & Faber, London, 1991.
Sunlight on a Broken Column Attiya Hussain, Virago Press, London, 1988.
The Far Pavilions MM Kaye, St Martin's Press, New York, 1978.
The Glass Palace Amitav Ghosh, Ravi Dayal, New Delhi, 2000.
The God of Small Things Arundhati Roy, Indialnk, New Delhi, 1999.
The House of Blue Mangoes David Davidar, Viking in association with Weidenfeld & Nicolson, New Delhi, 2002.
The Jungle Books Rudyard Kipling, Lancer Books, New York, 1968.
The Raj Quartet Paul Scott, William Morrow and Company, New York, 1976.
The Shadow Lines Amitav Ghosh, Ravi Dayal, New Delhi, 1988.
Those Days Sunil Gangopadhyaya, Penguin, New Delhi, 1997.

Three Plays: Nagamandala, Hayavadana and Tughlaq, Girish Karnad, Oxford University Press, New Delhi, 1997.
Train to Pakistan Khushwant Singh, Ravi Dayal, New Delhi, 1988.

Memoirs/Biography

A Princess Remembers Gayatri Devi, Rupa, New Delhi, 1995.
India's Bandit Queen: The True Story of Phoolan Devi Mala Sen, Harvill, London, 1991.
Indira Gandhi Katherine Frank, HarperCollins, New Delhi, 2001.
My Experiments with Truth Mohandas Karamchand Gandhi, Navjivan, Ahmedabad, 1927.
The Hill of Devi EM Forster, Harcourt Brace, New York, 1953.
The Life of Mahatma Gandhi Louis Fischer, Harper & Row, New York, 1950.
The Tribal World of Verrier Elwin Ramachandra Guha, Oxford University Press, New Delhi, 1999.

Travelogues

Branch Line to Eternity Bill Aitken, Penguin India, New Delhi 2001.
Chasing the Monsoon Alexander Frater, Alfred Knopf Inc, New York, 1992.
City of Djinns William Dalrymple, Flamingo, London, 1994.
Elsewhere: Unusual Takes on India Kai Friese (ed), Penguin India, New Delhi, 2001.
India By Rail Royston Ellis, Bradt Publications, UK, 1991.
In the Court of the Fish-Eyed Goddess William Dalrymple, HarperCollins, New Delhi, 1998.
Sikkim: A Traveller's Guide Sujoy Das, Permanent Black, New Delhi, 2001.
Slowly Down the Ganges Eric Newby, Lonely Planet Publications, Hawthorn, 1998.
The Goddess in the Stones Norman Lewis, TransAtlantic Publications Inc, Philadelphia, 1995.
The Great Railway Bazaar Paul Theroux, Viking, London, 1995.
Travels on my Elephant Mark Shand, Penguin India, New Delhi, 1993.
Travels through Sacred India Roger Thorsons Housden, HarperCollins, London, 1996.
Travels with a Tangerine: A Journey in the Footnotes of Ibn Battuta Tim Mackintosh Smith, John Murray, London, 2001.

Glossary

Architecture
amalaka circular ribbed stone atop a Hindu temple tower
apsara celestial maiden (p240)
bagh garden
bangaldar roof curved roof, like those on thatched huts in Bengal (p294)
baoli stone-clad stepwell, with galleries on its sides (see vav)
baradari 12-pillared pavilion
bhavan house or abode
bhulbhulaiya labyrinth
chaitya rock-cut Buddhist shrine
chaitya griha prayer hall in a rock-cut Buddhist shrine (p24)
charbagh formal Mughal garden, divided into four quarters (p25)
chhatri, cenotaph small ornamental pavilion or kiosk, topped by a cupola; also pavilion with a canopy, built at the site of a royal cremation
chorten Mahayana Buddhist reliquary shrine or memorial stupa
chowk courtyard in a palace or fort; also main square in a city
dargah shrine of a Muslim saint
darwaza door or gateway
Diwan-i-Aam Hall of Public Audience
Diwan-i-Khas Hall of Private Audience
dukhang assembly hall in a Mahayana Buddhist monastery
dvarapala guardian deities near Hindu temple doorways; literally, doorkeeper (p28)
garbhagriha womb chamber or inner sanctum in a Hindu temple
garh fort
ghat steps on river bank; also a hilly range
gompa Mahayana Buddhist monastery in Himachal Pradesh, Ladakh and Arunachal Pradesh
gonkhang temple of the guardian deities in a gompa
gopura towering pyramidal gateway in a South Indian Hindu temple complex (p614)
gurdwara Sikh temple (p25)
hamam traditional steam bath of the Turkish type
haveli large traditional town house or mansion, with inner courtyards (p391)
jali ornamental pierced or latticed stone screen (p179)
jharokha decorative projecting balcony (p391)
kalasha pot-like finial crowning a Hindu temple spire (p25)
khirkee window
kund tank or lake

lhakhang Mahayana Buddhist temple in Ladakh and Himachal Pradesh
mahal palace
mandapa pillared hall leading to a Hindu temple sanctuary
mandir Hindu temple
mani stones/mani walls stones carved with sacred Mahayana Buddhist chants
masjid mosque
mihrab arched niche in a mosque that faces west towards Mecca
pol fortified gateway
prakara wall enclosing South Indian Hindu temple compound
qila fort
salabhanjika tree nymph (p249)
shikhara spire of a North Indian Hindu temple (p24)
tharavad ancestral home in Kerala; also matrilineal clan
torana ceremonial gateway, usually leading to a religious site
tshog-khang/jokhang secondary assembly hall in a Buddhist monastery in Ladakh or Himachal Pradesh
vav stepwell in Gujarat (p418)
vihara Buddhist monastery
vimana multi-staged pyramidal spire above the inner sanctum of a South Indian Hindu temple
yakshi female attendant
yali fierce mythical leonine creature
yogini attendant, or manifestation, of Devi, a form of Parvati
zenana area of a palace or house where women live in seclusion

Crafts and Culture
asanas physical postures in Yoga
Ayurveda ancient Indian system of medicine, largely based on plants (p633)
Baramasa series of paintings or verses depicting the seasons; literally 12 months
dhurrie woven cotton rug
ganjifa cards painted, circular playing cards (p30)
gharana school of classical music or dance (p32)
ikat textile pattern where the yarn is resist-dyed or tie-dyed before being woven (p323)
jauhar mass suicide by immolation practised by Rajput women, to escape dishonour at the hands of their captors
-ji honorific suffix added to a person's name
kundankari inlay work with gems (p365)
kushti Indian style of wrestling

meenakari enamel work (p365)
mela fair, fête
Natya Shastra ancient Sanskrit treatise on dance
nautanki vaudeville
pandit learned Sanskrit scholar, wise elder or priest
pattachitra religious paintings from Odisha (p317)
phad long painted cloth scroll from Rajasthan (p385)
pichhwai a vibrant form of painting on cloth from Rajasthan, depicting 27 scenes from the Krishna legend (p403)
qawwals Sufi musicians
raga melodic structure with a fixed sequence of musical notes
rasa mood or emotion; also essence
sati the custom of a widow immolating herself on her husband's funeral pyre
satyagraha a form of non-violent, moral protest started by Mahatma Gandhi
Shilpa Shastra ancient Sanskrit treatise on sculpture
shishya disciple
tala rhythm/rhythmic cycle in classical Indian music
thangka scroll painting framed in silk, depicting Mahayana Buddhist deities (p127)
thumri light classical music, sung in North India

Dress
bindi circular dot on forehead
chappal handcrafted leather slippers; sandals
chikankari finely embroidered cotton textile from Lucknow
choli tight-fitting blouse
ghaghara/lehenga women's gathered skirt
juttis traditional leather shoes with pointed or upturned toes
kurta long stitched shirt (p35)
mukut crown
odhni/dupatta women's veil or long scarf (p34)
pallav end-piece of a sari (p34)
safa/pagri turban (p34)
salwar loose pantaloons, tapered at the ankle (p34)
sarpech jewelled turban ornament (p669)
sherwani long formal coat for men (p35)
topi cap (p35)
zardozi elaborate gold thread embroidery (p175)
zari gold thread

Religion

aarti Hindu prayer ritual with oil or butter lamps

ahimsa doctrine of non-violence

alams ceremonial standards used by Shia Muslims during Muharram (p673)

amrit divine nectar of immortality

ashram Hindu spiritual centre or religious retreat

avatar incarnation of a Hindu deity (p683)

bhajans Hindu devotional songs

bhakti cult of intense personal devotion to God, without going through priests

Bodhisattvas highly enlightened Mahayana Buddhist beings who refuse nirvana so that they can devote themselves to the service of others

chador ceremonial cloth to cover Muslim saint's grave; literally, a sheet

chakra discus or wheel; also Buddhist symbol of eight-spoked wheel, representing the Eightfold Path of Righteousness

darshan an auspicious sighting of a Hindu deity, religious person, temple or holy river, also formal audience given by a ruler or holy man

devadasi Hindu temple dancer

dharamshala rest house for pilgrims

dorje thunderbolt symbol in Mahayana Buddhism

dukka ablution tank in a mosque complex

Gangajal holy water from the Ganges river

gopis Lord Krishna's milkmaid companions

Hinayana "Small Vehicle" school of Buddhism practised in parts of India, Sri Lanka and Thailand, which emphasizes the importance of an ascetic, monastic way of life

imam Muslim religious leader

imambara shrine of a Shia Muslim holy man; ceremonial halls used by Shia Muslims during Muharram (p201)

Jataka Tales stories based on legends of the Buddha's previous lives (p484)

jyotirlinga linga symbolizing Shiva's energy, believed to have miraculously materialized out of light; found in the 12 most sacred sites linked to Shiva

kumbh cosmic pot holding the nectar of immortality (amrit)

linga phallic emblem representing the Hindu god Shiva

madrasa Islamic theological school

Mahayana "Greater Vehicle" school of Buddhism which emphasizes the importance of Bodhisattvas

mandala circular diagram symbolizing the universe, used as an aid to meditation by Buddhists

mantra meditational Hindu or Buddhist chant

matha Hindu or Jain religious centre

maya Hindu concept of illusion

moksha Hindu term for salvation

mudra symbolic hand gestures

namaaz Muslim daily prayers

navaratri nine-day fasting period preceding the Hindu festivals of Ramnavami and Dussehra

Om sacred Buddhist and Hindu syllable, invoking the divine

parikrama clockwise circumambulation of a Hindu or Buddhist holy site

prasad specially consecrated food from a Hindu or Sikh temple

puja Hindu prayer ritual

ratha temple chariot

samadhi memorial platform at Hindu cremation site

sangam holy confluence of rivers

Shaivite devotee of Lord Shiva

Shia a sect of Islam that reveres the Prophet Mohammed's cousin Ali and his successors as the true imams

Sufi mystical Islamic philosophy

Sunni a sect of Islam to which the majority of Indian Muslims belong; Sunnis follow traditional Islamic law, believed to be based on the words and acts of the Prophet Mohammed

takhts principal seats of Sikhism

tandava nritya Shiva's cosmic dance of destruction (p594)

tazia ornately decorated tower of wood, metal and paper carried by Shia Muslims at Muharram

thiru/tiru holy

tirtha Hindu holy place, usually near sacred river or tank

tirthankaras the 24 religious teachers worshipped by Jains

trishul trident carried by Hindu god, Lord Shiva

tuk fortified cluster of Jain temples

tulsi the sacred basil plant

Urs festival commemorating a Muslim saint

vahanas vehicles of Hindu gods

Vaishnavite devotee of Hindu god, Lord Vishnu

Vedas the oldest known Indian texts, written in Sanskrit, codifying Aryan beliefs and principles

vibhuti sacred ash

yagna Hindu ritual sacrifice

yatra Hindu pilgrimage

Miscellaneous

adivasi tribal person

akash sky

attar/ittar perfume, usually distilled from flowers

badal cloud

bagh tiger

basti settlement or slum; also Jain temple complex

chaugan ancient Persian form of polo, played with a curved stick

diya oil or butter lamp

dhaba roadside eatery (p183)

durbar royal court or royal gathering; audience held by a ruler

dzo cross between yak and cow

gali lane or narrow alleyway

ghee clarified butter

gulal coloured powder used during the Holi festival (p39)

haat open-air market, usually held once a week

howdah ceremonial seat on an elephant's back

kettuvallam Kerala rice boat (p637)

kheda elephant corral

machaan raised observation platform in a forest

mahout elephant trainer

marg major road

mayil/mayur peacock

nava ratna nine principle jewels

nawab Muslim prince

paan betel leaf, a digestive (p169)

pandal marquee or decorated stage made of cloth and bamboo

padma lotus

prithvi earth

purnima full moon

pushpa flower

pyav drinking water fountain

rumal handkerchief or square cloth

sagar large lake or reservoir; also ocean or sea

shikar hunting expedition

shila stone

tal lake

taluka sub-district

thakur Hindu chieftain

thali platter

thuggees highway bandits

vayu air

zamindar landowner

Phrase Book

India has 18 major regional languages, many with their own scripts. While Hindi, spoken by 30 per cent of the people and widely understood throughout India, is the official national language, other languages enjoy predominance in their respective regions. Our phrase book covers five languages, four of them spoken in India's four largest cities and their surrounding regions: Hindi (spoken in Delhi); Bengali (spoken in Kolkata); Marathi (spoken in Mumbai); and Tamil (spoken in Chennai). The fifth language, Malayalam, is spoken in Kerala. While Hindi, Bengali and Marathi are Indo-European languages, descended from Sanskrit, Tamil and Malayalam are Dravidian languages, unrelated to the Indo-European group, though influenced by Sanskrit over the centuries. English is widely spoken and understood throughout the country and serves as a link language between the different regions. One can get by with English almost anywhere in India, but most Indians are delighted and warmly appreciative if a visitor makes an attempt to speak their language.

Hindi

In an Emergency

Help!	Bachao!
Stop!	Roko!
Call a doctor!	Doctor ko bulao!
Where is the nearest telephone?	Yahan phone kahan hai?

Communication Essentials

Yes	Haan
No	Na/Naheen
Thank you	Dhanyavad/Shukria
Please	Kripaya/Meharbani sé
Excuse me/Sorry	Kshama karen/ Maaf karen
Hello/Goodbye	Namasté
Stop	Rook jao
Let's go	Chalo
Straight ahead	Seedha
Big/Small	Bara/Chhota
This/That	Yeh/Voh
Near/Far	Paas/Door
Way	Raasta
Road	Sarak
Yesterday	Beeta hua kal
Today	Aaj
Tomorrow	Aane wala kal
Here	Yahaan
There	Wahaan
What?	Kya?
Where?	Kahaan?
When?	Kab?
Why?	Kyon?
How?	Kaisé?
Up	Upar
Down	Neeché
More	Aur zyada
A little	Thora
Before	Pehlé
Opposite/ Facing	Saamné
Very	Bahut
Less	Kam
Louder/Harder	Zor sé
Softly/Gently	Dheeré sé
Go	Jao
Come	Aao

Useful Phrases

How are you?	Aap kaisé hain?
What is your name?	Aapka naam kya hai?
My name is ...	Mera naam ... hai
Do you speak English?	Angrezi ati hai?
I understand	Samajh gaya (male)/ gayi (female)
I don't understand	Nahin samjha (m)/ samjhi (f)
What is the time?	Kya baja hai?
Where is ...?	... Kahaan hai?
What is this?	Yeh kya hai?
Hurry up	Jaldi karo

How far is ...?	... Kitni door hai?
I don't know	Pata nahin
All right	Achha/Theek hai
Now/Instantly	Abhi/Isi waqt
Well done!	Shabash!
See you	Phir milengé
Go away!	Hat jao/Hato
I don't want it	Mujhe nahin chahiye
Not now	Abhi nahin

Useful Words

Which?	Kaun sa?
Who?	Kaun?
Hot	Garam
Cold	Thanda
Good	Achha
Bad	Kharaab
Enough	Bus/Kafi hai
Open	Khula
Closed	Bundh
Left	Baayan
Right	Daayan
Straight on	Seedha
Near	Paas/Nazdeek
Quickly	Jaldi
Late	Der sé
Later	Baad mein
Entrance	Pravesh
Exit	Nikas
Behind	Peechhé
Full	Bhara
Empty	Khali
Toilet	Shauchaalaya
Free/No charge	Nih shulka/Muft
Direction	Disha
Book	Kitaab
Newspaper	Akhbaar

Shopping

How much does this cost?	Iska kya daam hai?
I would like...	Mujhe ... chahiye
Do you have...?	Kya aap ké paas ... hai?
I am just looking	Abhi dekh rahen hain
Does it come in other colours?	Yeh dooserey rangon main bhi aata hai kya?
This one	Yeh wala
That one	Voh wala
Black	Kaala
Blue	Neela
White	Safed
Red	Lal
Yellow	Peela
Green	Hara
Brown	Bhura
Cheap	Sasta
Expensive	Mehanga
Tailor	Darzi

Bargaining

How much is this?	Yeh kitne ka hai?
How much will you take?	Kya logé?
That's a little	Yeh to mehanga

expensive	hai
Could you lower the price a bit?	Daam thoda kam kariyé
How about xx rupees?	xx rupeye laingé?
I'll settle for xx rupees	xx rupeye mein dena hai to dijiyé

Staying in a Hotel

Do you have any vacant rooms?	Aapke hotel mein khali kamre hain kya?
What is the charge per night?	Ek raat ka kiraya kya hai?
Can I see the room first?	Kya mein pehle kamra dekh sakta hoon?
Key	Chaabhi
Soap	Sabun
Towel	Tauliya
Hot/Cold water	Garam/Thanda pani

Eating Out

Breakfast	Nashta
Food	Khaana
Water	Pani
Ice	Baraf
Tea	Chai
Coffee	Kaufi
Sugar	Cheeni
Salt	Namak
Milk	Doodh
Yoghurt	Dahi
Egg	Anda
Fruit	Phal
Vegetable	Sabzi
Rice	Chaawal
Pulses (lentil, split peas etc)	Dal
Fixed price menu	Ek daam menu
Is it spicy?	Mirch-masala tez hai kya?
Make it less spicy please	Mirch-masala kam, theek hai?
Knife	Chhuri
Fork	Kanta
Spoon	Chammach
Finished	Khatam

Numbers

1	Ek
2	Do
3	Teen
4	Char
5	Panch
6	Chhé
7	Saat
8	Aath
9	Nau
10	Dus
11	Gyarah
12	Barah
13	Terah
14	Chaudah

15	Pandrah	100	Sau	A day	Ek din
16	Solah	1,000	Hazar	A week	Ek haftah
17	Satrah	100,000	Lakh	Monday	Somwar
18	Atharah	10,000,000	Karod (crore)	Tuesday	Mangalwar
19	Unnees			Wednesday	Budhwar
20	Bees			Thursday	Veerwar
30	Tees			Friday	Shukrawar
40	Chalees			Saturday	Shaniwar
50	Pachaas			Sunday	Raviwar
60	Saath			Morning	Subah
70	Sattar			Afternoon	Dopahar
80	Assi			Evening	Shaam
90	Nabbé			Night	Raat

Time

One minute	Ek minit
One hour	Ek ghanta
Half an hour	Aadha ghanta
Quarter hour	Pauna ghanta
Half past one	Derh
Half past two	Dhai

Bengali

In an Emergency

Help!	Shahaajjo korun!
Stop!	Thamun!
Call a doctor!	Daktar dakun!
Where is the nearest telephone?	Ekhanay phone kothai?

Communication Essentials

Yes	Haen
No	Na
Thank you	Dhonnobad
Please	Doya koray
Excuse me/Sorry	Maap korben
Hello/Goodbye	Nomoshkar
Stop	Thamun
Let's go	Cholun
Straight ahead	Shoja
Big/Small	Boro/Chhoto
This/That	Eta/Ota
Near/Far	Kaachhé/Dooré
Way	Raasta
Road	Raasta
Yesterday	Goto kaal
Today	Aaj
Tomorrow	Kaal
Here	Ekhaané
There	Okhaané
What?	KI?
Where?	Kothayé?
When?	Kokhon?
Why?	Kaeno?
How?	Ki koray?
Up	Opor
Down	Neeche
More	Aaro
A little	Ektu
Before	Aagey
Opposite/Facing	Shaamney
Very	Khoob
Less	Kom
Louder/Harder	Jorey
Softly/Gently	Aastey
Go	Jao
Come	Esho

Useful Phrases

How are you?	Kaemon aachhen?
What is your name?	Aapnaar naam ki?
My name is ...	Aamaar naam ...
Do you speak English?	Ingriji bolen?
I understand	Bujhi
I don't understand	Bujhi na
What is the time?	Kota bajé?
Where is ...?	... Kothhai?
What is this?	Eta ki?
Hurry up	Taarataari
How far is ...?	... Koto door?
I don't know	Jaani na
All right	Theek achhey

Now/Instantly	Ekkhuni
Well done!	Bah!
See you	Aashi
Go away!	Jao
I don't want it	Chai na
Not now	Ekhon na

Useful Words

Which?	Konta?
Who?	Kay?
Hot	Gorom
Cold	Thanda
Good	Bhalo
Bad	Khaaraap
Enough	Bus
Open	Khola
Closed	Bondho
Left	Baayen
Right	Daayiné
Straight on	Shojaa
Near	Kaachhey
Quickly	Taarataari
Late	Deri
Later	Porey
Entrance	Probesh
Exit	Prosthaan
Behind	Pechhoney
Full	Bhora
Empty	Khaali
Toilet	Shauchaalaya
Free/No charge	Bina poisha
Direction	Disha
Book	Boi
Magazine	Potrika
Newspaper	Khoborer kagoj

Shopping

How much does this cost?	Koto?
I would like...	Aami chaai
Do you have...?	Aapnaar kaachhe aachhe?
I am just looking	Shudhu dekchhi
Does it come in other colours?	Aaro rong aachhey?
This one	Eta
That one	Ota
Black	Kaalo
Blue	Neel
White	Shaadaa
Red	Laal
Yellow	Holud
Green	Shobuj
Brown	Khoiri
Cheap	Shostaa
Expensive	Daami
Tailor	Dorji

Bargaining

How much is this?	Eta koto?
How much will you take?	Koto neben?
That's a little expensive	Beshi daam
Could you lower the price a bit?	Ektu komaan
How about xx rupees?	xx taka cholbé?
I'll settle for xx rupees	xx takar beshi debo na

Staying in a Hotel

Do you have any vacant rooms?	Ghor khaali aachhey?
What is the charge per night?	Ek raater bhaara koto?
Can I see the room first?	Aagey ghor dekhte paari?
Key	Chaabi
Soap	Shaabaan
Towel	Towaaley
Hot/Cold water	Gorom/Thanda jol

Eating Out

Breakfast	Jolkhaabaar
Food	Khaabaar
Water	Jol
Ice	Borof
Tea	Chaa
Coffee	Koffee
Sugar	Cheeni
Salt	Noon
Milk	Doodh
Yoghurt	Dohi
Egg	Deem
Fruit	Phol
Vegetable	Shobji
Rice	Bhaat
Pulses (lentils, split peas etc)	Daal
Fixed price menu	Ek daam menu
Is it spicy?	Jhaal ki?
Make it less spicy	Beshi jhaal chaai na
Knife	Chhuri
Fork	Kanta
Spoon	Chaamoch
Finished	Shesh

Numbers

1	Ek
2	Dooi
3	Teen
4	Chaar
5	Paanch
6	Chhoy
7	Shaat
8	Aath
9	Noy
10	Dosh
11	Egaro
12	Baaro
13	Tero
14	Chaudoh
15	Ponero
16	Sholo
17	Shotero
18	Aathero
19	Unneesh
20	Kuri/Beesh
30	Tirish
40	Cholleesh
50	Ponchaash
60	Shaat
70	Shottor
80	Aashi

90	**Nobboi**	One hour	**Ek ghonta**	Wednesday	**Budhbar**		
100	**Eksho**	Half an hour	**Aadh ghonta**	Thursday	**Bishuttbar**		
1,000	**Haajaar**	Quarter hour	**Pauney ghonta**	Friday	**Shukkurbar**		
100,000	**Lakh**	Half past one	**Derh**	Saturday	**Shonibar**		
10,000,000	**Koti**	Half past two	**Aadhai**	Sunday	**Robibar**		
		A day	**Ek din**	Morning	**Shokaal**		
Time		A week	**Ek shopta**	Afternoon	**Duphur**		
		Monday	**Shombar**	Evening	**Bikel**		
One minute	**Ek minit**	Tuesday	**Mongolbar**	Night	**Raat**		

Marathi

In an Emergency

Help!	**Vachva!**
Stop!	**Thamba!**
Call a doctor!	**Doctorana bolwaa!**
Where is the nearest telephone?	**Ithé jawal phone kuthé aáhé?**

Communication Essentials

Yes	**Ho**
No	**Nahi**
Thank you	**Dhanyavad**
Please	**krupaya**
Excuse me/ Sorry	**Kshama pahijé**
Hello/ Goodbye	**Namaskar**
Stop	**Thamba**
Let's go	**Chala**
Straight ahead	**Saral**
Big/Small	**Mota/Lahan**
This/That	**Hé/Thé**
Near/Far	**Zawal/Laamb**
Way	**Marga**
Road	**Rastha**
Yesterday	**Kaal**
Today	**Aaj**
Tomorrow	**Udya**
Here	**Ithé**
There	**Tithé**
What?	**Kay?**
Where?	**Kuthé?**
When?	**Kenhvah?**
Why?	**Ka?**
How?	**Kasè?**
Up	**Varti**
Down	**Khali**
More	**Aankhi**
A little	**Thodé**
Before	**Aadhi**
Opposite/ Facing	**Samor**
Very	**Khoop**
Less	**Kami**
Louder/Harder	**Mothyané/ Zorané**
Softly/Gently	**Haloo**
Go	**Za**
Come	**Ya**

Useful Phrases

How are you?	**Kasa Kain?**
What is your name?	**Apla nao?**
My name is ...	**Maajhe nao ...**
Do you speak English?	**Inglish yeté ka?**
I understand	**Samazté**
I don't understand	**Kalale nahin**
What is the time?	**Kiti vajlé?**
Where is ...?	**Kuthé aáhé?**
What is this?	**Hé kay aáhé?**
Hurry up	**Aatpa lavkar**
How far is ...?	**Kiti laamb aáhé?**
I don't know	**Mahiti nahin**
All right	**Theek aáhé**
Now/Instantly	**Aathach**
Well done!	**Chhan!**
See you	**Bhétuya**
Go away!	**Chalta ho**
I don't want it	**Nakoy malaa**
Not now	**Aatha naahin**

Useful Words

Which?	**Konté?**
Who?	**Kon?**
Hot	**Garam**
Cold	**Thanda**
Good	**Changla**
Bad	**Vait**
Enough	**Puré**
Open	**Ughadé**
Closed	**Banda**
Left	**Davikadé**
Right	**Uzavikadé**
Straight on	**Saral**
Near	**Zawal**
Quickly	**Lavkar**
Late	**Ushira**
Later	**Nanthar**
Entrance	**Pravesh**
Exit	**Baaher**
Behind	**Maagé**
Full	**Bharalelé**
Empty	**Rikamé**
Toilet	**Shauchaalaya**
Free/No charge	**Mophat**
Direction	**Disha**
Book	**Pusthak**
Magazine	**Maasik**
Newspaper	**Vartaman patra**

Shopping

How much does this cost?	**Hé kevdyala?**
I would like...	**Mala... hava hotha**
Do you have...?	**Tumechyakadé ... aáhé ka?**
I am just looking	**Ajun bagté/Aáhé bagto**
Does it come? in other colours	**Aankhi ranga aahetka?**
This one	**Hé**
That one	**Té**
Black	**Kaala**
Blue	**Neelé**
White	**Pandhra**
Red	**Lal**
Yellow	**Piwala**
Green	**Hirvva**
Brown	**Chocoleti**
Cheap	**Svastha**
Expensive	**Mahaag**
Tailor	**Shimpi**

Bargaining

How much is this?	**He kevdhyala?**
How much will you take?	**Kithi dyayché?**
That's a little expensive	**Zara mahaag aahe**
Could you lower the price a bit?	**Zara kami karana ka?**
How about? xx rupees	**Xx rupyé thik aáhé?**
I'll settle for xx rupees	**Xx barobar aáhé**

Staying in a Hotel

Do you have any vacant rooms?	**Tumchya hotel madhé jagaa aáhé ka?**
What is the charge per night?	**Eka ratri ché kiti?**
Can I see the room first?	**Mee aadhi kholi baghoon ka?**
Key	**Killi**

Soap	**Saban**
Towel	**Towel**
Hot/Cold water	**Garam/Thanda pani**

Eating Out

Breakfast	**Nasta**
Food	**Jewan**
Water	**Pani**
Ice	**Barpha**
Tea	**Chaha**
Coffee	**Kofi**
Sugar	**Saakhar**
Salt	**Mith**
Milk	**Doodh**
Yoghurt	**Dahi**
Egg	**Andé**
Fruit	**Phal**
Vegetable	**Bhaji**
Rice	**Bhath**
Pulses (lentils, split peas etc)	**Dal**
Fixed price menu	**Ekach bhav**
Is it spicy?	**Tikhat aáhé ka?**
Make it less spicy please	**Har tikhat nakon bara ka?**
Knife	**Suri**
Fork	**Kata**
Spoon	**Chammcha**
Finished	**Samplé**

Numbers

1	**Ek**
2	**Don**
3	**Teen**
4	**Char**
5	**Pach**
6	**Saha**
7	**Sath**
8	**Aath**
9	**Nou**
10	**Daha**
11	**Akara**
12	**Barah**
13	**Terah**
14	**Chawda**
15	**Pandhra**
16	**Solah**
17	**Satara**
18	**Atharah**
19	**Ekonees**
20	**Vees**
30	**Tees**
40	**Chalees**
50	**Pannas**
60	**Saath**
70	**Sattar**
80	**Aishi**
90	**Nauwad**
100	**Shambhar**
1,000	**Hazaar**
100,000	**Lakh**
10,000,000	**Koti**

Time

One minute	**Ek minit**
One hour	**Ek taas**
Half an hour	**Ardha taas**
Quarter hour	**Pandhra minit**
Half past one	**Deed**
Half past two	**Adhich**
A day	**Ek divas**
A week	**Ek athavda**
Monday	**Somwar**
Tuesday	**Mangalwar**
Wednesday	**Budhwar**

Thursday	Guruwar
Friday	Shukrawar
Saturday	Shaniwar

Sunday	Raviwar
Morning	Sakali
Afternoon	Dupari

Evening	Sandhyakali
Night	Ratri

Tamil

In an Emergency

Help!	Udhaivi véndum!
Stop!	Nillu!
Call a doctor!	Doctor koopiddunga!
Where is the nearest phone?	Pakkatatillé phone engu irrukku?

Communication Essentials

Yes	Aama/Seri
No	Illai/Véndaam
Thank you	Nanri
Please	Daivusaidhu
Excuse me/Sorry	Mannikavum
Hello/Goodbye	Vannakkam/Paankalaam
Stop	Nillu
Let's go	Pohalaam
Straight ahead	Néré
Big/Small	Perisu/Chinannadu
This/That	Idhu/Adhu
Near/Far	Pakkatilai/Duoram
Way	Vazhi
Road	Theruvu
Yesterday	Nétru/Néthiku
Today	Inru/Innikki
Tomorrow	Naallai/Naallaiku
Here	Ingé
There	Angé
What?	Ennai?
Where?	Engé?
When?	Eppo?
Why?	Ain?
How?	Eppiddi?
Up	Mélai
Down	Kizhai
More	Unnum konjam
A little	Konjam
Before	Minaalai
Opposite/Facing	Edhirai
Very	Romba
Less	Kammi
Louder/Harder	Perisa/Unnum ongi
Softly/Gently	Molla
Go	Pongo/Po
Come	Vaango/Vaa

Useful Phrases

How are you?	Neenga eppudi irukénga?
What is your name?	Onge peyar enna?
My name is ...	Enodia peyar ...
Do you speak English?	English pése theriyuma?
I understand	Ennakku puriyum
I don't understand	Ennakku puriyadu
What is the time?	Ippo ena mani?
Where is ...?	... Enga irrukku?
What is this?	Idhu ennadhu?
Hurry up	Seekrama vaango
How far is ...?	... Evallavu dooram?
I don't know	Ennaku theriyadu
All right	Seri
Now/Instantly	Ippovai
Well done!	Shabash!
See you	Apram parkalaam
Go away!	Poividu!
I don't want it	Ennaku véndaam
Not now	Ippo illai

Useful Words

Which?	Edhu?
Who?	Yaaru?
Hot	Soodu
Cold	Kulluru
Good	Nalladhu
Bad	Kettadhu

Enough	Porum
Open	Thirandurikku
Closed	Moodirukku
Left	Edudhu
Right	Valadhu
Straight on	Nérai
Near	Pakkatillai
Quickly	Seekrama
Late	Nerama
Later	Apram
Entrance	Varuvu
Exit	Velivaasal
Behind	Pinalai
Full	Rombiruku
Empty	Kaali
Toilet	Kaizhupu arai
Free/No charge	Ilevasaasam
Direction	Disai/Pakkam
Book	Pustagam
Magazine	Patrigai
Newspaper	Samachara patrigai

Shopping

How much does this cost?	Idhodiya vilai ennai?
I would like...	Ennakku idhu venum ...
Do you have...?	... onga kitta irrukku?
I am just looking	Naan summa paakaren
Does it come? in other colours	Idh vera colouril kidaikuma?
This one	Idhu
That one	Adhu
Black	Karuppu
Blue	Neelam
White	Vellai
Red	Seguppu
Yellow	Manjhal
Green	Pachchai
Brown	Kappi niram
Cheap	Maluvu
Expensive	Vilai jasti
Tailor	Theyalkaran

Bargaining

How much is this?	Idhu enna vilai?
How much will you take?	Neengu evalave edithipél?
That's a little expensive	Adhu konjam vilai jasti
Could you lower the price a bit?	Vilai konjam kurrakkai mudduyuma?
How about xx rupees?	xx rubaai seria?
I'll settle for xx rupees	xx rubaai tharuven

Staying in a Hotel

Do you have any vacant rooms?	Kaali arai irruka?
What is the charge per night?	Oru raatriku evaluvu caasu?
Can I see the room first?	Naan mudulai araiya parrakalama?
Key	Chaavi
Soap	Soapu
Towel	Thundu
Hot/Cold water	Soodu/Jillu thanni

Eating Out

Breakfast	Kaalai chittrundi
Food	Saapadu
Water	Thanni/Jalam
Ice	Ice
Tea	Chai
Coffee	Coffee
Sugar	Shakarai
Salt	Uppu

Milk	Paal
Yoghurt	Thairu
Egg	Muttai
Fruit	Pazham
Vegetable	Kayagiri
Rice	Arusi
Pulses (lentils,etc)	Paruppu
Fixed price menu	Ore vilai menu
Is it spicy?	Naraya masala irukka?
Make it less spicy please	Masala seriya irukka?
Knife	Kaththi
Fork	Fork
Spoon	Spoon/Theikarandi
Finished	Mudivu

Numbers

1	Onru/Onu
2	Erundu
3	Moonru
4	Naanqu/Naalu
5	Anju/Aindhu
6	Aaru
7	Yezhu
8	Ettu
9	Ombodhu
10	Pathu
11	Pathinonru
12	Panandu
13	Pathimoonru
14	Pathinaalu
15	Pathinainthu
16	Pathnaaru
17	Pathinezhu
18	Pathinettu
19	Pathombadhu
20	Iravadhu
30	Mupaddu
40	Napadhu
50	Aimbadhu
60	Aravadhu
70	Yezhuvadu
80	Yenbadhu
90	Thonnuru
100	Nooru
1,000	Aayiram
100,00	Latcham
10,000,000	Kodi

Time

One minute	Oru nimisham
One hour	Oru manéram
Half an hour	Ara manéram
Quarter hour	Kaal manéram
Half past one	Onre mani
Half past two	Erendarai mani
A day	Oru naal
A week	Oru vaaram
Monday	Thingakazhamai
Tuesday	Sevvaikazhami
Wednesday	Budhankazhami
Thursday	Viyaikazhami
Friday	Vellikazhami
Saturday	Nyayatrikazhami
Morning	Kaalai
Afternoon	Madhyanam
Evening	Sayankaalam
Night	Raatri

Malayalam

In an Emergency

Help!	Sahayikoo!
Stop!	Nilku/Nirthu!
Call a doctor!	Doctore viliku!
Where is the nearest phone?	Evide annu aduth phone?

Communication Essentials

Yes	Athe/Seri
No	Illa/Alla/Véndaa
Thank you	Nanni
Please	Dayavuchaidu
Excuse me/Sorry	Kshamikkanam
Hello/Goodbye	Namaskaram/ Veendum kanaam
Stop	Nilku
Let's go	Namuku pokaam
Straight ahead	Néré povuu
Big/Small	Valudu/Cherudu
This/That	Idhe/Adhe
Near/Far	Aduthu/Akalé
Way	Vazhi
Road	Patha/Road
Yesterday	Innalé
Today	Innu
Tomorrow	Naallé
Here	Evidé
There	Avidé
What?	Entha?
Where?	Evidé?
When?	Eppol?
Why?	Entha/Enthukonda?
How?	Engané?
Up	Mukalil
Down	Kizhé/Thazhé
More	Eniyum kooduthal
A little	Kurachu/Alpam
Before	Munpé/Munnll
Opposite/Facing	Edhirvasam/Edhirai
Very	Valaré
Less	Kurachu/Kuravu
Louder/Harder	Uchchathil/Urakké
Softly/Gently	Pathiyé/Swaram thazhthi
Go	Pokoo/Po
Come	Varoo/Vaa

Useful Phrases

How are you?	Sukhamano?
What is your name?	Ningaludé peru entha?
My name is …	Ente peru …
Do you speak English?	Ningal English samsarikumo?
I understand	Enikku manasilayi
I don't understand	Enikku manasilakilla
What is the time?	Samayam enthai?
Where is …?	Evideyanu …?
What is this?	Idhu enthanu?
Hurry up	Vegamakatté
How far is …?	Ethra dooramundu…?
I don't know	Enikku ariyilla
All right	Seri
Now/Instantly	Ippol thanné
Well done!	Kémamai!/Nannai!
See you	Pinne kanaam
Go away!	Dooré po!
I don't want it	Enikku véndaa
Not now	Ippo illa/Véndaa

Useful Words

Which?	Edhu?
Who?	Aaré?
Hot	Choodé
Cold	Thanuppé/Kulluré
Good	Nalladhé
Bad	Cheetha/Mosam
Enough	Madhi
Open	Thurannu
Closed	Adachu
Left	Edadhu
Right	Valadhu
Straight on	Néré
Near	Aduthu
Quickly	Végum
Late	Vaiki
Later	Pinné/Pinneedu
Entrance	Munvasam/ Parvésana vathil
Exit	Purathékkulla vazhi
Behind	Pinnalé/Pinnil
Full	Nirayé
Empty	Kaali
Toilet	Moothrappura
Free/no charge	Saujanyam
Direction	Dikku
Book	Pustakam
Magazine	Masika/Varika
Newspaper	Newspaper

Shopping

How much does this cost?	Idhinu enthu vila?
I would like…	Enikku idhu venum …
Do you have…?	… Ningaludé pakkal ondo?
I am just looking	Naan veruthé nokukayanu
Does it come in other colours?	Idhu vereyum colouril kittumo?
This one	Idhu
That one	Adhu
Black	Karuppé
Blue	Neela
White	Vella
Red	Chuvappé
Yellow	Manja
Green	Pachcha
Brown	Kappi niram
Cheap	Vilakuravu
Expensive	Vilakuduthal
Tailor	Thayalkaran

Bargaining

How much is this?	Idhinu enthu vila?
How much will you take?	Idhu enthu vilaku tharum?
That's a little expensive	Vila kurachu kooduthalanu
Could you lower the price a bit?	Vila kurachu kuraikumo?
How about? xx rupees	xx rupaku tharumo?
I'll settle for xx rupees	Njyan xx rupaku edukkam

Staying in a Hotel

Do you have any vacant rooms?	Muri (room) ozhivundo?
What is the charge per night?	Oru raatriku entha vaadaka?
Can I see the room first?	Eniku aadyam muri kaanan sadhikumo?
Key	Thakol
Soap	Soap
Towel	Thorthé/Towel
Hot/Cold water	Choodu/Thanutha véllam

Eating Out

Breakfast	Prathal
Food	Aaharam/ Bhakshanam
Water	Véllam
Ice	Ice katta
Tea	Chaya
Coffee	Kaapi
Sugar	Panchasaara
Salt	Uppé
Milk	Paal
Yoghurt	Thairé
Egg	Mutta
Fruit	Pazham
Vegetable	Pachchakari
Rice	Ari/Chorué
Pulses (lentils, split peas etc)	Parippé
Fixed price menu	Otta vila menu/ Krithya vila menu
Is it spicy?	Ithu frivullathano?
Make it less spicy please	Erivu kooduthal vendaa?
Knife	Kaththi
Fork	Mullé/Fork
Spoon	Spoon
Finished	Kazhinju/Theernu

Numbers

1	Onné/Oru
2	Randé
3	Moonné
4	Naalé
5	Anché
6	Aaré
7	Yezhé
8	Etté
9	Onpadhé
10	Paththé
11	Pathinonné
12	Panthrandé
13	Pathimoonné
14	Pathinaalé
15	Pathinanché
16	Pathinaaré
17	Pathinezhé
18	Pathinetté
19	Pathompadhé
20	Irupadhé
30	Muppaddé
40	Nappadhé
50	Ambadhé
60	Arupadhé
70	Yezhupadé
80	Yenpadhé
90	Thonnuré
100	Nooré
1,000	Aayiram
100,000	Lakshaṃ
10,000,000	Kodi

Time

One minute	Oru nimisham/ wMinute
One hour	Oru manikoor
Half an hour	Ara manikoor
Quarter hour	Kaal manikoor
Half past one	Onnara mani
Half past two	Randara mani
A day	Oru divasam
A week	Oru aazhcha
Monday	Thingal
Tuesday	Chovva
Wednesday	Budhan
Thursday	Vyazham
Friday	Velli
Saturday	Sani
Morning	Raavilé
Afternoon	Uchcha
Evening	Vaikunneram
Night	Raatri

Railway Map of India

The external boundaries of India as shown on this map are neither correct nor authentic.

SEE INSET

INDIA